Oxford
Spanish
Minidictionary

THIRD EDITION

Spanish–English
English–Spanish

UNIVERSITY PRESS

OXFORD
UNIVERSITY PRESS

Great Clarendon Street, Oxford OX2 6DP

Oxford University Press is a department of the University of Oxford.
It furthers the University's objective of excellence in research, scholarship,
and education by publishing worldwide in

Oxford New York

Auckland Cape Town Dar es Salaam Hong Kong Karachi Kuala Lumpur
Madrid Melbourne Mexico City Nairobi New Delhi Shanghai Taipei
Toronto

With offices in
Argentina Austria Brazil Chile Czech Republic France Greece
Guatemala Hungary Italy Japan South Korea Poland Portugal
Singapore Switzerland Thailand Turkey Ukraine Vietnam

Oxford is a registered trade mark of Oxford University Press
in the UK and in certain other countries

Published in the United States
by Oxford University Press Inc., New York

© Oxford University Press 1993, 1999, 2005

British Library Cataloguing in Publication Data
Data available

Library of Congress Cataloging in Publication Data
Data available

ISBN 0-19-861043-2
ISBN 978-0-19-861043-4
ISBN 0-19-861046-7 (Spanish cover edition)
ISBN 978-0-19-861046-5

10 9 8 7 6 5 4 3 2 1

Typeset by Interactive Sciences Ltd, Gloucester
Printed and bound in Italy by
Legoprint S.p.A.

Oxford Spanish Minidictionary
Diccionario Oxford Mini

Spanish–English • English–Spanish
español-inglés • inglés-español

Diccionario Oxford Mini

TERCERA EDICIÓN

español–inglés
inglés–español

OXFORD
UNIVERSITY PRESS

Contents/Índice

Proprietary terms

This dictionary includes some words which have, or are asserted to have, proprietary status as trademarks. Their inclusion does not imply that they have acquired for legal purposes a non-proprietary or general significance, nor any other judgement concerning their legal status. In cases where the editorial staff have some evidence that a word has proprietary status this is indicated in the entry for that word by the symbol ®, but no judgement concerning the legal status of such words is made or implied thereby.

Marcas registradas

Este diccionario incluye algunas palabras que son o pretenden ser marcas registradas. Cuando al editor le consta que una palabra es una marca registrada, esto se indica por medio del símbolo ®. No debe atribuirse ningún valor jurídico ni a la presencia ni a la ausencia de tal designación.

Contributors/Colaboradores

Third Edition/Tercera edición

Nicholas Rollin
Carol Styles Carvajal

Second Edition/Segunda edición

Editors/Editores
Carol Styles Carvajal
Michael Britton
Jane Horwood

Phrasefinder/Índice temático de frases
Idoia Noble
Neil and Roswitha Morris

Data input/Entrada de datos
Susan Wilkin

First Edition/Primera edición

Editor/Editora
Christine Lea

Introduction

This new edition of the *Oxford Spanish Minidictionary* is designed as an effective and practical reference tool for the student, adult learner, traveller, and business professional.

The wordlist has been revised and updated to reflect recent additions to both languages. The *Phrasefinder* section has been expanded. It aims to provide the user with the confidence to communicate in the most commonly encountered social situations such as travel, shopping, eating out, and organizing leisure activities.

Another valuable feature of the dictionary is the special status given to more complex grammatical words which provide the basic structure of both languages. Boxed entries in the text for these *function words* provide extended treatment, including notes to warn of possible pitfalls.

The dictionary has an easy-to-use, streamlined layout. Bullets separate each new part of speech within an entry. Nuances of sense or usage are pinpointed by indicators or by typical collocates with which the word frequently occurs. Extra help is given in the form of symbols to mark the register of words and phrases. An exclamation mark 🗓 indicates colloquial language, and a cross 🗷 indicates slang.

Each English headword is followed by its phonetic transcription between slashes. The symbols used are those of the International Phonetic Alphabet. Pronunciation is also shown for derivatives and compounds where it is not easily deduced from that of a headword. The rules for the pronunciation of Spanish are given on pages xii–xiii.

The swung dash (∼) is used to represent a headword or that part of a headword preceding the vertical bar (|).

In both English and Spanish only irregular plurals are given. Normally Spanish nouns and adjectives ending in an unstressed vowel form the plural by adding s (e.g. *libro*, *libros*). Nouns and adjectives ending in a stressed vowel or a consonant add es (e.g. *rubí*, *rubíes*, *pared*, *paredes*). An accent on the final syllable is not required when es is added (e.g. *nación*, *naciones*). Final *z* becomes *ces* (e.g. *vez*, *veces*).

Spanish nouns and adjectives ending in o form the feminine by changing the final o to a (e.g. *hermano*, *hermana*). Most Spanish nouns and adjectives ending in anything other than final o do not have a separate feminine form, with the exception of those denoting nationality etc.; these add a to the masculine singular form (e.g. *español*, *española*). An accent on the penultimate syllable is then not required (e.g. *inglés*, *inglesa*). Adjectives ending in *án*, *ón*, or *or* behave like those denoting nationality, with the following exceptions: *inferior*, *mayor*, *mejor*, *menor*, *peor*, *superior*, where the feminine has the same form as the masculine. Spanish verb tables will be found at the end of the book.

The Spanish alphabet

In Spanish *ñ* is considered a separate letter and in the Spanish–English section, therefore, is alphabetized after *ny*.

Introducción

Esta nueva edición del *Minidiccionario de Oxford* ha sido concebida a fin de proporcionar una herramienta de referencia práctica y eficaz al estudiante, joven y adulto, al viajero y a la persona de negocios.

Se ha revisado la lista de palabras con el objeto de incorporar nuevos términos en ambos idiomas. La sección central contiene una *Lista temática de frases*, que se ha ampliado, destinada a que el usuario adquiera la confianza necesaria para comunicarse en las situaciones más normales de la vida diaria, como las que se encuentran al viajar, hacer compras, comer fuera y organizar actividades recreativas.

Otro valioso aspecto del diccionario es la importancia especial que se da a palabras con una función más compleja dentro de la gramática y que proveen la estructura básica de ambos idiomas. Estos *vocablos clave* están contenidos en recuadros dentro del texto, donde se les da un tratamiento amplio y se incluyen notas para advertir sobre posibles escollos.

El diccionario tiene una presentación clara y es fácil de usar. Símbolos distintivos separan las diferentes categorías gramaticales dentro de cada entrada. Los matices de sentido y de uso se muestran con precisión mediante indicadores o por colocaciones típicas con las que la palabra se usa frecuentemente. Se encuentra ayuda adicional en los signos que indican el registro idiomático de las palabras y frases. Un signo de exclamación 🔣 señala el uso coloquial y una cruz 🔣 el uso argot.

Cada palabra cabeza de artículo en inglés va seguida de su transcripción fonética entre barras oblicuas. Los símbolos que se usan son los del Alfabeto Fonético Internacional. También aparece la pronunciación de derivados y nombres compuestos cuando no es posible deducirla de la palabra cabeza de artículo. Las reglas sobre pronunciación inglesa se encuentran en la página xiv.

La tilde (∼) se emplea para sustituir la palabra cabeza de artículo o aquella parte de tal palabra que precede a la barra vertical (|).

Tanto en inglés como en español se dan los plurales solamente si son irregulares. Para formar el plural regular en inglés se añade la letra s al sustantivo singular, pero se añade es cuando se trata de una palabra que termina en *ch*, *sh*, *s*, *ss*, *us*, *x*, *o*, *z* (p.ej. *sash*, *sashes*). En el caso de una palabra que termine en *y* precedida por una consonante, la *y* se transforma en *ies* (p.ej. *baby*, *babies*). Para formar el tiempo pasado y el participio pasado se añade *ed* al infinitivo de los verbos regulares ingleses (p.ej. *last*, *lasted*). En el caso de los verbos ingleses que terminan en *e* muda se añade sólo la *d* (p.ej. *move*, *moved*). En el caso de los verbos ingleses que terminan en *y*, se debe cambiar la *y* por *ied* (p.ej. *carry*, *carried*). Los verbos irregulares se encuentran en el diccionario por orden alfabético remitidos al infinitivo, y también en la lista que aparece en las últimas páginas del diccionario.

Pronunciation of Spanish

Vowels

a   between pronunciation of *a* in English *cat* and *arm*

e   like *e* in English *bed*

i   like *ee* in English *see* but a little shorter

o   like *o* in English *hot* but a little longer

u   like *oo* in English *too*

y   when a vowel is as Spanish **i**

Consonants

b   (1) in initial position or after a nasal consonant is like English *b*
    (2) in other positions is between English *b* and English *v*

c   (1) before **e** or **i** is like *th* in English *thin*. In Latin American Spanish is like English *s*.
    (2) in other positions is like *c* in English *cat*

ch like *ch* in English *chip*

d   (1) in initial position, after nasal consonants and after **l** is like English *d*
    (2) in other positions is like *th* in English *this*

f   like English *f*

g   (1) before **e** or **i** is like *ch* in Scottish *loch*
    (2) in initial position is like *g* in English *get*
    (3) in other positions is like (2) but a little softer

h	silent in Spanish but see also **ch**
j	like *ch* in Scottish *loch*
k	like English *k*
l	like English *l* but see also **ll**
ll	like *ll/j* in English *million*
m	like English *m*
n	like English *n*
ñ	like *ni* in English *opinion*
p	like English *p*
q	like English *k*
r	rolled or trilled
s	like *s* in English *sit*
t	like English *t*
v	(1) in initial position or after a nasal consonant is like English b
	(2) in other positions is between English b and English v
w	like Spanish **b** or **v**
x	like English *x*
y	like English *y*
z	like *th* in English *thin*

Pronunciación inglesa

Símbolos fonéticos

Vocales y diptongos

iː	see	ɔː	saw	eɪ	page	ɔɪ	join
ɪ	sit	ʊ	put	əʊ	home	ɪə	near
e	ten	uː	too	aɪ	five	eə	hair
æ	hat	ʌ	cup	aɪə	fire	ʊə	poor
ɑː	arm	ɜː	fur	aʊ	now		
ɒ	got	ə	ago	aʊə	flour		

Consonantes

p	pen	tʃ	chin	s	so	n	no
b	bad	dʒ	June	z	zoo	ŋ	sing
t	tea	f	fall	ʃ	she	l	leg
d	dip	v	voice	ʒ	measure	r	red
k	cat	θ	thin	h	how	j	yes
g	got	ð	then	m	man	w	wet

El símbolo ' precede a la sílaba sobre la cual recae el acento tónico.

Aa

a *preposición*

Note that **a** followed by **el** becomes **al**, e.g. **vamos al cine**

···▸ (*dirección*) to. **fui a México** I went to Mexico. **muévete a la derecha** move to the right

···▸ (*posición*) **se sentaron a la mesa** they sat at the table. **al lado del banco** next to the bank. **a orillas del río** on the banks of the river

···▸ (*distancia*) **queda a 5 km** it's 5 km away. **a pocos metros de aquí** a few meters from here

···▸ (*fecha*) **hoy estamos a 5** today is the 5th. **¿a cuánto estamos?**, (*LAm*) **¿a cómo estamos?** what's the date?

···▸ (*hora, momento*) at. **a las 2** at 2 o'clock. **a fin de mes** at the end of the month. **a los 21 años** at the age of 21; (*después de*) after 21 years

···▸ (*precio*) **¿a cómo están las peras?** how much are the pears? **están a 3 euros el kilo** they're 3 euros a kilo. **salen a 15 euros cada uno** they work out at 15 euros each.

···▸ (*medio, modo*) **fuimos a pie** we went on foot. **hecho a mano** hand made. **pollo al horno** (*LAm*) roast chicken

···▸ (*cuando precede al objeto*

directo de persona) *no se traduce.* **conocí a Juan** I met Juan. **quieren mucho a sus hijos** they love their children very much

···▸ (*con objeto indirecto*) to. **se lo di a Juan** I gave it to Juan. **le vendí el coche a mi amigo** I sold my friend the car, I sold the car to my friend. **se lo compré a mi madre** I bought it from my mother; (*para*) I bought it for my mother

➡ Cuando la preposición **a** se emplea precedida de ciertos verbos como **empezar, faltar, ir, llegar** etc., ver bajo el respectivo verbo

ábaco *m* abacus

abadejo *m* pollack

abadía *f* abbey

abajo *adv* (*down*) below; (*dirección*) down(wards); (*en casa*) downstairs. ● *int* down with. **~ de** (*LAm*) under(neath). **calle ~** down the street. **el ~ firmante** the undersigned. **escaleras ~** down the stairs. **la parte de ~** the bottom (part). **más ~** further down

abalanzarse ⑩ *vpr* rush (**hacia** towards)

abanderado *m* standard-bearer; (*Mex, en fútbol*) linesman

abandon|ado *adj* abandoned; (*descuidado*) neglected; (*persona*) untidy. **~ar** *vt* leave (*un lugar*); abandon (*persona, cosa*). ● *vi* give

a

up. **~arse** vpr give in; (*descuidarse*) let o.s. go. **~o** m abandonment; (*estado*) neglect

abani|car 7 vt fan. **~co** m fan

abaratar vt reduce

abarcar 7 vt put one's arms around, embrace; (*comprender*) embrace

abarrotar vt overfill, pack full

abarrotes mpl (*LAm*) groceries; (*tienda*) grocer's shop

abast|ecer 11 vt supply. **~ecimiento** m supply; (*acción*) supplying. **~o** m supply. **no dar ~o** be unable to cope (**con**)

abati|do adj depressed. **~miento** m depression

abdicar 7 vt give up. ● vi abdicate

abdom|en m abdomen. **~inal** adj abdominal

abec|é m 1 alphabet, ABC. **~edario** m alphabet

abedul m birch (tree)

abej|a f bee. **~orro** m bumblebee

aberración f aberration

abertura f opening

abeto m fir (tree)

abierto pp véase **ABRIR**. ● adj open

abism|al adj abysmal; (*profundo*) deep. **~ar** vt throw into an abyss; (*fig, abatir*) humble. **~arse** vpr be absorbed (**en**), be lost (**en**). **~o** m abyss; (*fig, diferencia*) world of difference

ablandar vt soften. **~se** vpr soften

abnega|ción f self-sacrifice. **~do** adj self-sacrificing

abochornar vt embarrass. **~se** vpr feel embarrassed

abofetear vt slap

aboga|cía f law. **~do** m lawyer, solicitor; (*ante tribunal superior*) barrister (*Brit*), attorney (*Amer*).

abolengo m ancestry

aboli|ción f abolition. **~cionismo** m abolitionism. **~cionista** m & f abolitionist. **~r** 24 vt abolish

abolla|dura f dent. **~r** vt dent

abolsado adj baggy

abomba|do adj convex; (*LAm, atontado*) dopey. **~r** vt make convex. **~rse** vpr (*LAm, descomponerse*) go bad

abominable adj abominable

abona|ble adj payable. **~do** adj paid. ●m subscriber. **~r** vt pay; (*en agricultura*) fertilize. **~rse** vpr subscribe.

abono m payment; (*estiércol*) fertilizer; (*a un periódico*) subscription

aborda|ble adj reasonable; (*persona*) approachable. **~je** m boarding. **~r** vt tackle (*un asunto*); approach (*una persona*); (*Naut*) come alongside; (*Mex, Aviac*) board

aborigen adj & m native

aborrec|er 11 vt loathe. **~ible** adj loathsome. **~ido** adj loathed. **~imiento** m loathing

abort|ar vi have a miscarriage. **~ivo** adj abortive. **~o** m miscarriage; (*voluntario*) abortion. **hacerse un ~o** have an abortion

abotonar vt button (up). **~se** vpr button (up)

abovedado adj vaulted

abrasa|dor adj burning. **~r** vt burn. **~rse** vpr burn

abraz|ar vt 10 embrace. **~arse** vpr embrace. **~o** m hug. **un fuerte ~o de** (*en una carta*) with best wishes from

abre|botellas m invar bottle-opener. **~cartas** m invar paper-knife. **~latas** m invar tin opener (Brit), can opener

abrevia|ción f abbreviation; (texto abreviado) abridged text. **~do** adj brief; (texto) abridged. **~r** vt abbreviate; abridge (texto); cut short (viaje etc). ● vi be brief. **~tura** f abbreviation

abrig|ado adj (lugar) sheltered; (persona) well wrapped up. **~ador** adj (Mex, ropa) warm. **~ar** 12 vt shelter; cherish (esperanza); harbour (duda, sospecha). **~arse** vpr (take) shelter; (con ropa) wrap up. **~o** m (over)coat; (lugar) shelter

abril m April. **~eño** adj April

abrillantar vt polish

abrir (pp **abierto**) vt/i open. **~se** vpr open; (extenderse) open out; (el tiempo) clear

abrochar vt do up; (con botones) button up

abruma|dor adj overwhelming. **~r** vt overwhelm

abrupto adj steep; (áspero) harsh

abrutado adj brutish

absentismo m absenteeism

absolución f (Relig) absolution; (Jurid) acquittal

absolut|amente adv absolutely, completely. **~o** adj absolute. **en ~o** (not) at all. **~orio** adj of acquittal

absolver 2 (pp **absuelto**) vt (Relig) absolve; (Jurid) acquit

absor|bente adj absorbent; (fig, interesante) absorbing. **~ber** vt absorb. **~ción** f absorption. **~to** adj absorbed

abstemio adj teetotal. ● m teetotaller

absten|ción f abstention. **~erse** 40 vpr abstain, refrain (de from)

abstinencia f abstinence

abstra|cción f abstraction. **~cto** adj abstract. **~er** 41 vt abstract. **~erse** vpr be lost in thought. **~ído** adj absent-minded

absuelto adj (Relig) absolved; (Jurid) acquitted

absurdo adj absurd. ● m absurd thing

abuche|ar vt boo. **~o** m booing

abuel|a f grandmother. **~o** m grandfather. **~os** mpl grandparents

ab|ulia f apathy. **~úlico** adj apathetic

abulta|do adj bulky. **~r** vt (fig, exagerar) exaggerate. ● vi be bulky

abunda|ncia f abundance. **nadar en la ~ncia** be rolling in money. **~nte** adj abundant, plentiful. **~r** vi be plentiful

aburguesarse vpr become middle-class

aburri|do adj (con estar) bored; (con ser) boring. **~dor** adj (LAm) boring. **~miento** m boredom; (cosa pesada) bore. **~r** vt bore. **~rse** vpr get bored

abus|ar vi take advantage. **~ar de la bebida** drink too much. **~ivo** adj excessive. **~o** m abuse

acá adv here. **~ y allá** here and there. **de ~ para allá** to and fro. **de ayer ~** since yesterday. **más ~** nearer

acaba|do adj finished; (perfecto) perfect. ● m finish. **~r** vt/i finish. **~rse** vpr finish; (agotarse) run out; (morirse) die. **~r con** put an end to. **~r de** (+ infinitivo) have just (+ pp). **~ de llegar** he has just arrived. **~r por** (+ infinitivo) end up (+ gerundio). **¡se acabó!** that's it!

acabóse m. **ser el ~** be the end, be the limit

acad|emia f academy. **~émico** adj academic

acallar vt silence

acalora|do adj heated; (persona) hot. **~rse** vpr get hot; (fig, excitarse) get excited

acampar vi camp

acantilado m cliff

acapara|r vt hoard; (monopolizar) monopolize. **~miento** m hoarding; (monopolio) monopolizing

acariciar vt caress; (animal) stroke; (idea) nurture

ácaro m mite

acarre|ar vt transport; (desgracias etc) cause. **~o** m transport

acartona|do adj (piel) wizened. **~rse** vpr (ponerse rígido) go stiff; (piel) become wizened

acaso adv maybe, perhaps. ● m chance. **~ llueva mañana** perhaps it will rain tomorrow. **por si ~** (just) in case

acata|miento m compliance (**de** with). **~r** vt comply with

acatarrarse vpr catch a cold, get a cold

acaudalado adj well off

acceder vi agree; (tener acceso) have access

acces|ible adj accessible; (persona) approachable. **~o** m access, entry; (Med, ataque) attack

accesorio adj & m accessory

accident|ado adj (terreno) uneven; (agitado) troubled; (persona) injured. **~al** adj accidental. **~arse** vpr have an accident. **~e** m accident

acci|ón f (incl Jurid) action; (hecho) deed; (Com) share. **~onar** vt work. ● vi gesticulate. **~onista** m & f shareholder

acebo m holly (tree)

acech|ar vt lie in wait for. **~o** m spying. **al ~o** on the look-out

aceit|ar vt oil; (Culin) add oil to. **~e** m oil. **~e de oliva** olive oil. **~te de ricino** castor oil. **~era** f cruet; (para engrasar) oilcan. **~ero** adj oil. **~oso** adj oily

aceitun|a f olive. **~ado** adj olive. **~o** m olive tree

acelera|dor m accelerator. **~r** vt accelerate; (fig) speed up, quicken

acelga f chard

acent|o m accent; (énfasis) stress. **~uación** f accentuation. **~uar** 21 vt stress; (fig) emphasize. **~uarse** vpr become noticeable

acepción f meaning, sense

acepta|ble adj acceptable. **~ción** f acceptance; (éxito) success. **~r** vt accept

acequia f irrigation channel

acera f pavement (Brit), sidewalk (Amer)

acerca de prep about

acerca|miento m approach; (fig) reconciliation. **~r** 7 vt bring near. **~rse** vpr approach

acero m steel. **~ inoxidable** stainless steel

acérrimo adj (fig) staunch

acert|ado adj right, correct; (apropiado) appropriate. **~ar** 1 vt (adivinar) get right, guess. ● vi get right; (en el blanco) hit. **~ar a** happen to. **~ar con** hit on. **~ijo** m riddle

achacar 7 vt attribute

achacoso adj sickly

achaque m ailment

achatar vt flatten

achicar 7 vt make smaller; (fig, fam, empequeñecer) belittle; (Naut) bale out. **~rse** vpr become smaller; (humillarse) be intimidated

achicharra|r vt burn; (fig) pester. **~rse** vpr burn

achichincle m & f (Mex) hanger-on

achicopalado adj (Mex) depressed

achicoria f chicory

achiote m (LAm) annatto

achispa|do adj tipsy. **~rse** vpr get tipsy

achulado adj cocky

acicala|do adj dressed up. **~r** vt dress up. **~rse** vpr get dressed up

acicate m spur

acidez f acidity; (Med) heartburn

ácido adj sour. ● m acid

acierto m success; (idea) good idea; (habilidad) skill

aclama|ción f acclaim; (aplausos) applause. **~r** vt acclaim; (aplaudir) applaud

aclara|ción f explanation. **~r** vt lighten (colores); (explicar) clarify; (enjuagar) rinse. ● vi (el tiempo) brighten up. **~rse** vpr become clear. **~torio** adj explanatory

aclimata|ción f acclimatization, acclimation (Amer). **~r** vt acclimatize, acclimate (Amer). **~rse** vpr become acclimatized, become acclimated (Amer)

acné m acne

acobardar vt intimidate. **~se** vpr lose one's nerve

acocil m (Mex) freshwater shrimp

acog|edor adj welcoming; (ambiente) friendly. **~er** 14 vt welcome; (proteger) shelter; (recibir) receive. **~erse** vpr take refuge. **~ida** f welcome; (refugio) refuge

acolcha|do adj quilted. **~r** vt quilt, pad

acomedido adj (Mex) obliging

acomet|er vt attack; (emprender) undertake. **~ida** f attack

acomod|ado adj well off. **~ador** m usher. **~adora** f usherette. **~ar** vt arrange; (adaptar) adjust. ● vi be suitable. **~arse** vpr settle down; (adaptarse) conform

acompaña|miento m accompaniment. **~nte** m & f companion; (Mus) accompanist. **~r** vt go with; (hacer compañía) keep company; (adjuntar) enclose

acondicionar vt fit out; (preparar) prepare

aconseja|ble adj advisable. **~do** adj advised. **~r** vt advise. **~rse** vpr. **~rse con** consult

acontec|er 11 vi happen. **~imiento** m event

acopla|miento m coupling; (Elec) connection. **~r** vt fit; (Elec) connect; (Rail) couple

acorazado adj armour-plated. ● m battleship

acord|ar 2 vt agree (upon); (decidir) decide; (recordar) remind. **~arse** vpr remember. **~e** adj in agreement; (Mus) harmonious. ● m chord

acorde|ón m accordion. **~onista** m & f accordionist

acordona|do adj (lugar) cordoned off; (zapatos) lace-up. **~r** vt lace (up); (rodear) cordon off

acorralar vt round up (animales); corner (personas)

acortar vt shorten; cut short (permanencia). **~se** vpr get shorter

acos|ar vt hound; (fig) pester. **~o** m pursuit; (fig) pestering

acostar 2 vt put to bed; (Naut) bring alongside. ● vi (Naut) reach land. **~se** *vpr* go to bed; (*echarse*) lie down. **~se con** (*fig*) sleep with

acostumbra|do *adj* (*habitual*) usual. **~do a** used to. **~r** get used. **me ha ~do a levantarme por la noche** he's got me used to getting up at night. ● *vi.* **~r** be accustomed to. **acostumbra a comer a la una** I usually have lunch at one o'clock. **~rse** *vpr* become accustomed, get used

acota|ción *f* (*nota*) margin note (*en el teatro*) stage direction; (*cota*) elevation mark. **~miento** *m* (*Mex*) hard shoulder

acrecentar ① *vt* increase. **~se** *vpr* increase

acredita|do *adj* reputable; (*Pol*) accredited. **~r** *vt* prove; accredit (*diplomático*); (*garantizar*) guarantee; (*autorizar*) authorize. **~rse** *vpr* make one's name

acreedor *adj* worthy (**de** of). ● *m* creditor

acribillar *vt* (*a balazos*) riddle (a with); (*a picotazos*) cover (a with); (*fig, a preguntas etc*) bombard (a with)

acr|obacia *f* acrobatics. **~obacias aéreas** aerobatics. **~óbata** *m & f* acrobat. **~obático** *adj* acrobatic

acta *f* minutes; (*certificado*) certificate

actitud *f* posture, position; (*fig*) attitude, position

activ|ar *vt* activate; (*acelerar*) speed up. **~idad** *f* activity. **~o** *adj* active. ● *m* assets

acto *m* act; (*ceremonia*) ceremony. **en el ~** immediately

act|or *m* actor. **~riz** *f* actress

actuación *f* action; (*conducta*) behaviour; (*Theat*) performance

actual *adj* present; (*asunto*) top-

ical. **~idad** *f* present; (*de asunto*) topicality. **en la ~idad** (*en el momento*) currently; (*hoy en día*) nowadays. **~idades** *fpl* current affairs. **~ización** *f* modernization. **~izar** ⑩ *vt* modernize. **~mente** *adv* now, at the present time

actuar ㉑ *vi* act. **~ de** act as

acuarel|a *f* watercolour. **~ista** *m & f* watercolourist

acuario *m* aquarium. A**~** Aquarius

acuartelar *vt* quarter, billet; (*mantener en cuartel*) confine to barracks

acuático *adj* aquatic

acuchillar *vt* slash; stab (*persona*)

acuci|ante *adj* urgent. **~ar** *vt* urge on; (*dar prisa a*) hasten. **~oso** *adj* keen

acudir *vi.* **~ a** go to; (*asistir*) attend; turn up for (*a una cita*); (*en auxilio*) go to help

acueducto *m* aqueduct

acuerdo *m* agreement. ● *vb véase* ACORDAR. **¡de ~!** OK! **de ~ con** in accordance with. **estar de ~** agree. **ponerse de ~** agree

acuesto *vb véase* ACOSTAR

acumula|dor *m* accumulator. **~r** *vt* accumulate. **~rse** *vpr* accumulate

acunar *vt* rock

acuñar *vt* mint, coin

acupuntura *f* acupuncture

acurrucarse ⑦ *vpr* curl up

acusa|do *adj* accused; (*destacado*) marked. ● *m* accused. **~r** *vt* accuse; (*mostrar*) show; (*denunciar*) denounce; acknowledge (*recibo*)

acuse *m.* **~ de recibo** acknowledgement of receipt

acus|ica *m & f* ① telltale. **~ón** *m*

① telltale

acústic|a *f* acoustics. **~o** *adj* acoustic

adapta|ble *adj* adaptable. **~ción** *f* adaptation. **~dor** *m* adapter. **~r** *vt* adapt; (*ajustar*) fit. **~rse** *vpr* adapt o.s.

adecua|do *adj* suitable. **~r** *vt* adapt, make suitable

adelant|ado *adj* advanced; (*niño*) precocious; (*reloj*) fast. **por ~ado** in advance.. **~amiento** *m* advance(ment); (*Auto*) overtaking. **~ar** *vt* advance, move forward; (*acelerar*) speed up; put forward (*reloj*); (*Auto*) overtake. ● *vi* advance, go forward; (*reloj*) gain, be fast. **~arse** *vpr* advance, move forward; (*reloj*) gain; (*Auto*) overtake. **~e** *adv* forward. ● *int* come in!; (*¡siga!*) carry on! **más ~e** (*lugar*) further on; (*tiempo*) later on. **~o** *m* advance; (*progreso*) progress

adelgaza|miento *m* slimming. **~r** ⑩ *vt* make thin; lose (kilos). ● *vi* lose weight; (*adrede*) slim. **~rse** *vpr* lose weight; (*adrede*) slim

ademán *m* gesture. **en ~ de** as if to. **ademanes** *mpl* (*modales*) manners.

además *adv* besides; (*también*) also; (*lo que es más*) what's more. **~ de** besides

adentr|arse *vpr.* **~arse en** penetrate into; study thoroughly (tema etc). **~o** *adv* in(side). **~o de** (*LAm*) in(side). **mar ~o** out at sea. **tierra ~o** inland

adepto *m* supporter

aderez|ar ⑩ *vt* flavour (bebidas); (*condimentar*) season; dress (ensalada). **~o** *m* flavouring; (*con condimentos*) seasoning; (*para ensalada*) dressing

adeud|ar *vt* owe. **~o** *m* debit

adhe|rir ④ *vt/i* stick. **~rirse** *vpr* stick; (*fig*) follow. **~sión** *f* adhesion; (*fig*) support. **~sivo** *adj & m* adhesive

adici|ón *f* addition. **~onal** *adj* additional. **~onar** *vt* add

adicto *adj* addicted. ● *m* addict; (*seguidor*) follower

adiestra|do *adj* trained. **~miento** *m* training. **~r** *vt* train. **~rse** *vpr* practise

adinerado *adj* wealthy

adiós *int* goodbye!; (*al cruzarse con alguien*) hello!

adit|amento *m* addition; (*accesorio*) accessory. **~ivo** *m* additive

adivin|anza *f* riddle. **~ar** *vt* foretell; (*acertar*) guess. **~o** *m* fortune-teller

adjetivo *adj* adjectival. ● *m* adjective

adjudica|ción *f* award. **~r** ⑦ *vt* award. **~rse** *vpr* appropriate. **~tario** *m* winner of an award

adjunt|ar *vt* enclose. **~o** *adj* enclosed; (*auxiliar*) assistant. ● *m* assistant

administra|ción *f* administration; (*gestión*) management. **~dor** *m* administrator; (*gerente*) manager. **~dora** *f* administrator; manageress. **~r** *vt* administer. **~tivo** *adj* administrative

admira|ble *adj* admirable. **~ción** *f* admiration. **~dor** *m* admirer. **~r** *vt* admire; (*sorprender*) amaze. **~rse** *vpr* be amazed

admi|sibilidad *f* admissibility. **~sible** *adj* acceptable. **~sión** *f* admission; (*aceptación*) acceptance. **~tir** *vt* admit; (*aceptar*) accept

adobar *vt* (*Culin*) pickle; (*condimentar*) marinade

adobe *m* sun-dried brick

adobo *m* pickle; (*condimento*) marinade

adoctrinar *vt* indoctrinate

adolecer 🔢 *vi*. ~ **de** suffer from

adolescen|cia *f* adolescence. ~**te** *adj* adolescent. ● *m & f* teenager, adolescent

adonde *adv* where

adónde *adv* where?

adop|ción *f* adoption. ~**tar** *vt* adopt. ~**tivo** *adj* adoptive; (*hijo*) adopted; (*patria*) of adoption

adoquín *m* paving stone; (*imbécil*) idiot. ~**inado** *m* paving. ~**inar** *vt* pave

adora|ción *f* adoration. ~**r** *vt* adore

adormec|er 🔢 *vt* send to sleep; (*fig, calmar*) calm, soothe. ~**erse** *vpr* fall asleep; (*un miembro*) go to sleep. ~**ido** *adj* sleepy; (*un miembro*) numb

adormilarse *vpr* doze

adorn|ar *vt* adorn (**con, de** with). ~**o** *m* decoration

adosar *vt* lean (**a** against); (*Mex, adjuntar*) to enclose

adqui|rir 🔢 *vt* acquire; (*comprar*) purchase. ~**sición** *f* acquisition; (*compra*) purchase. ~**sitivo** *adj* purchasing

adrede *adv* on purpose

adrenalina *f* adrenalin

aduan|a *f* customs. ~**ero** *adj* customs. ● *m* customs officer

aducir 🔢 *vt* allege

adueñarse *vpr* take possession

adul|ación *f* flattery. ~**ador** *adj* flattering. ● *m* flatterer. ~**ar** *vt* flatter

ad|ulterar *vt* adulterate. ~**ulterio** *m* adultery

adulto *adj & m* adult, grown-up

advenedizo *adj & m* upstart

advenimiento *m* advent, arrival; (*subida al trono*) accession

adverbio *m* adverb

advers|ario *m* adversary. ~**idad** *f* adversity. ~**o** *adj* adverse, unfavourable

advert|encia *f* warning. ~**ir** 🔢 *vt* warn; (*notar*) notice

adviento *m* Advent

adyacente *adj* adjacent

aéreo *adj* air; (*foto*) aerial; (*ferrocarril*) overhead

aeróbico *adj* aerobic

aerodeslizador *m* hovercraft

aero|ligero *m* microlight. ~**lito** *m* meteorite. ~**moza** *f* (*LAm*) flight attendant. ~**puerto** *m* airport. ~**sol** *m* aerosol

afab|ilidad *f* affability. ~**le** *adj* affable

afamado *adj* famous

af|án *m* hard work; (*deseo*) desire. ~**anador** *m* (*Mex*) cleaner. ~**anar** *vt* ▣ pinch 🔢. ~**anarse** *vpr* strive (**en, por** to)

afear *vt* disfigure, make ugly; (*censurar*) censure

afecta|ción *f* affectation. ~**do** *adj* affected. ~**r** *vt* affect

afect|ivo *adj* sensitive. ~**o** *m* (*cariño*) affection. ● *a.* ~**o a** attached to. ~**uoso** *adj* affectionate. **con un** ~**uoso saludo** (*en cartas*) with kind regards. **suyo** ~**ísimo** (*en cartas*) yours sincerely

afeita|do *m* shave. ~**dora** *f* electric razor. ~**r** *vt* shave. ~**rse** *vpr* shave, have a shave

afeminado *adj* effeminate. ● *m* effeminate person

aferrar *vt* grasp. ~**se** *vpr* to

cling (**a** to)

afianza|miento *m* (*refuerzo*) strengthening; (*garantía*) guarantee. **~rse 10** *vpr* become established

afiche *m* (*LAm*) poster

afici|ón *f* liking; (*conjunto de aficionados*) fans. **por ~ón** as a hobby. **~onado** *adj* keen (**a** on), fond (**a** of). ● *m* fan. **~onar** *vt* make fond. **~onarse** *vpr* take a liking to

afila|do *adj* sharp. **~dor** *m* knife-grinder. **~r** *vt* sharpen

afilia|ción *f* affiliation. **~do** *adj* affiliated. **~rse** *vpr* become a member (**a** of)

afín *adj* similar; (*contiguo*) adjacent; (*personas*) related

afina|ción *f* (*Auto, Mus*) tuning. **~do** *adj* (*Mus*) in tune. **~dor** *m* tuner. **~r** *vt* (*afilar*) sharpen; (*Auto, Mus*) tune. **~rse** *vpr* become thinner

afincarse 7 *vpr* settle

afinidad *f* affinity; (*parentesco*) relationship by marriage

afirma|ción *f* affirmation. **~r** *vt* make firm; (*asentir*) affirm. **~rse** *vpr* steady o.s. **~tivo** *adj* affirmative

aflicción *f* affliction

afligi|do *adj* distressed. **~r 14** *vt* distress. **~rse** *vpr* distress o.s.

aflojar *vt* loosen; (*relajar*) ease. ● *vi* let up. **~se** *vpr* loosen

aflu|encia *f* flow. **~ente** *adj* flowing. ● *m* tributary. **~ir 17** *vi* flow (**a** into)

afónico *adj* hoarse

aforismo *m* aphorism

aforo *m* capacity

afortunado *adj* fortunate, lucky

afrancesado *adj* Frenchified

afrenta *f* insult; (*vergüenza*) disgrace

África *f* Africa. **~ del Sur** South Africa

africano *adj & m* African

afrodisíaco *adj & m* aphrodisiac

afrontar *vt* bring face to face; (*enfrentar*) face, confront

afuera *adv* out(side) **¡~!** out of the way! **~ de** (*LAm*) outside. **~s** *fpl* outskirts

agachar *vt* lower. **~se** *vpr* bend over

agalla *f* (*de los peces*) gill. **~s** *fpl* (*fig*) guts

agarradera *f* (*LAm*) handle

agarr|ado *adj* (*fig, fam*) mean. **~ar** *vt* grasp; (*esp LAm*) take; (*LAm, pillar*) catch. **~arse** *vpr* hold on; (*fam, reñirse*) have a fight. **~ón** *m* tug; (*LAm, riña*) row

agarrotar *vt* tie tightly; (*el frío*) stiffen; garotte (*un reo*). **~se** *vpr* go stiff; (*Auto*) seize up

agasajar *m* guest of honour. **~ar** *vt* look after well. **~o** *m* good treatment

agazaparse *vpr* crouch

agencia *f* agency. **~ de viajes** travel agency. **~ inmobiliaria** estate agency (*Brit*), real estate agency (*Amer*). **~rse** *vpr* find (out) for o.s.

agenda *f* diary (*Brit*), appointment book (*Amer*); (*programa*) agenda

agente *m* agent; (*de policía*) policeman. ● *f* agent; (*de policía*) policewoman. **~ de aduanas** customs officer. **~ de bolsa** stockbroker

ágil *adj* agile

agili|dad *f* agility. **~zación** *f* speeding up. **~zar** *vt* speed up

agita|ción *f* waving; (*de un lí-*

quido) stirring; (*intranquilidad*) agitation. **~do** *adj* (el mar) rough; (*fig*) agitated. **~dor** *m* (Pol) agitator

agitar *vt* wave; shake (botellas etc); stir (líquidos); (*fig*) stir up. **~se** *vpr* wave; (el mar) get rough; (*fig*) get excited

aglomera|ción *f* agglomeration; (*de tráfico*) traffic jam. **~r** *vt* amass. **~rse** *vpr* form a crowd

agnóstico *adj* & *m* agnostic

agobi|ante *adj* (*trabajo*) exhausting; (calor) oppressive. **~ar** *vt* weigh down; (*fig, abrumar*) overwhelm. **~o** *m* weight; (*cansancio*) exhaustion; (*opresión*) oppression

agolparse *vpr* crowd together

agon|ía *f* death throes; (*fig*) agony. **~izante** *adj* dying; (luz) failing. **~izar** ⑩ *vi* be dying

agosto *m* August. **hacer su ~** feather one's nest

agota|do *adj* exhausted; (todo vendido) sold out; (libro) out of print. **~dor** *adj* exhausting. **~miento** *m* exhaustion. **~r** *vt* exhaust. **~rse** *vpr* be exhausted; (existencias) sell out; (libro) go out of print

agracia|do *adj* attractive; (*que tiene suerte*) lucky. **~r** *vt* make attractive

agrada|ble *adj* pleasant, nice. **~r** *vt/i* please. **esto me ~** I like this

agradec|er ⑪ *vt* thank (persona); be grateful for (cosa). **~ido** *adj* grateful. **¡muy ~ido!** thanks a lot! **~imiento** *m* gratitude

agrado *m* pleasure; (*amabilidad*) friendliness

agrandar *vt* enlarge; (*fig*) exaggerate. **~se** *vpr* get bigger

agrario *adj* agrarian, land; (*polí-*

tica) agricultural

agrava|nte *adj* aggravating. ● *f* additional problem. **~r** *vt* aggravate; (*aumentar el peso*) make heavier. **~rse** *vpr* get worse

agravi|ar *vt* offend; (*perjudicar*) wrong. **~o** *m* offence

agredir ㉔ *vt* attack. **~ de palabra** insult

agrega|do *m* aggregate; (*diplomático*) attaché. **~r** ⑫ *vt* add; appoint (persona). **~rse** *vpr* to join

agres|ión *f* aggression; (*ataque*) attack. **~ividad** *f* aggressiveness. **~ivo** *adj* aggressive. **~or** *m* aggressor

agreste *adj* country; (*terreno*) rough

agriar regular, o raramente ㉔ *vt* sour. **~se** *vpr* turn sour; (*fig*) become embittered

agr|ícola *adj* agricultural. **~icultor** *m* farmer. **~icultura** *f* agriculture, farming

agridulce *adj* bitter-sweet; (Culin) sweet-and-sour

agrietar *vt* crack. **~se** *vpr* crack; (piel) chap

agrio *adj* sour. **~s** *mpl* citrus fruits

agro|nomía *f* agronomy. **~pecuario** *adj* farming

agrupa|ción *f* group; (acción) grouping. **~r** *vt* group. **~rse** *vpr* form a group

agruras *fpl* (Mex) heartburn

agua *f* water; (*lluvia*) rain; (*marea*) tide; (*vertiente del tejado*) slope. **~ abajo** downstream. **~ arriba** upstream. **~ bendita** holy water. **~ corriente** running water. **~ de colonia** eau de cologne. **~ dulce** fresh water. **~ mineral con gas** fizzy mineral water. **~ mineral sin gas** still mineral water. **~ potable**

11

aguacate | ahuyentaraguacate | ahuyentar

drinking water. ∼ **salada** salt water. **hacer** ∼ (*Naut*) leak. **se me hizo** ∼ **la boca** (*LAm*) my mouth watered

aguacate *m* avocado pear; (*árbol*) avocado pear tree

aguacero *m* downpour, heavy shower

aguado *adj* watery; (*Mex, aburrido*) boring

agua|fiestas *m & f invar* spoilsport, wet blanket. ∼**mala** *f* (*Mex*), ∼**mar** *m* jellyfish. ∼**marina** *f* aquamarine

aguant|ar *vt* put up with, bear; (*sostener*) support. ● *vi* hold out. ∼**arse** *vpr* restrain o.s. ∼**e** *m* patience; (*resistencia*) endurance

aguar [15] *vt* water down

aguardar *vt* wait for. ● *vi* wait

agua|rdiente *m* (cheap) brandy. ∼**rrás** *m* turpentine, turps [1]

agud|eza *f* sharpness; (*fig, perspicacia*) insight; (*fig, ingenio*) wit. ∼**izar** [10] *vt* sharpen. ∼**izarse** *vpr* (*enfermedad*) get worse. ∼**o** *adj* sharp; (*ángulo, enfermedad*) acute; (*voz*) high-pitched

agüero *m* omen. **ser de mal** ∼ be a bad omen

aguijón *m* sting; (*vara*) goad

águila *f* eagle; (*persona perspicaz*) astute person; (*Mex, de moneda*) heads. **¿**∼ **o sol?** heads or tails?

aguileño *adj* aquiline

aguinaldo *m* Christmas box; (*LAm, paga*) Christmas bonus

aguja *f* needle; (*del reloj*) hand; (*de torre*) steeple. ∼**s** *fpl* (*Rail*) points

agujer|ear *vt* make holes in. ∼**o** *m* hole

agujetas *fpl* stiffness; (*Mex, de zapatos*) shoe laces. **tener** ∼ be stiff

aguzado *adj* sharp

ah *int* ah!, oh!

ahí *adv* there. ∼ **nomás** (*LAm*) right there. **de** ∼ **que** that is why. **por** ∼ that way; (*aproximadamente*) thereabouts

ahija|da *f* god-daughter, godchild. ∼**do** *m* godson, godchild. ∼**dos** *mpl* godchildren

ahínco *m* enthusiasm; (*empeño*) insistence

ahog|ado *adj* (en el agua) drowned; (*asfixiado*) suffocated. ∼**ar** [12] *vt* (en el agua) drown; (*asfixiar*) suffocate; put out (*fuego*). ∼**arse** *vpr* (en el agua) drown; (*asfixiarse*) suffocate. ∼**o** *m* breathlessness; (*fig, angustia*) distress

ahondar *vt* deepen. ● *vi* go deep. ∼ **en** (*fig*) examine in depth. ∼**se** *vpr* get deeper

ahora *adv* now; (*hace muy poco*) just now; (*dentro de poco*) very soon. ∼ **bien** however. ∼ **mismo** right now. **de** ∼ **en adelante** from now on, in future. **por** ∼ for the time being

ahorcar [7] *vt* hang. ∼**se** *vpr* hang o.s.

ahorita *adv* (*esp LAm fam*) now. ∼ **mismo** right now

ahorr|ador *adj* thrifty. ∼**ar** *vt* save. ∼**arse** *vpr* save o.s. ∼**o** *m* saving. ∼**os** *mpl* savings

ahuecar [7] *vt* hollow; fluff up (colchón); deepen (la voz)

ahuizote *m* (*Mex*) scourge

ahuma|do *adj* (*Culin*) smoked; (*de colores*) smoky. ∼**r** *vt* (*Culin*) smoke; (*llenar de humo*) fill with smoke. ● *vi* smoke. ∼**rse** *vpr* become smoky; (*comida*) acquire a smoky taste

ahuyentar *vt* drive away; banish (pensamientos etc)

aimará adj & m Aymara. ● m & f Aymara indian

airado adj annoyed

aire m air; (viento) breeze; (corriente) draught; (aspecto) appearance; (Mus) tune, air. ~ acondicionado air-conditioning. al ~ libre outdoors. darse ~s give o.s. airs. ~ar vt air; (ventilar) ventilate; (fig, publicar) make public. ~arse vpr. salir para ~arse go out for some fresh air

airoso adj graceful; (exitoso) successful

aisla|do adj isolated; (Elec) insulated. ~dor adj (Elec) insulating. ~nte adj insulating. ~r **23** vt isolate; (Elec) insulate

ajar vt crumple; (estropear) spoil

ajedre|cista m & f chess-player. ~z m chess

ajeno adj (de otro) someone else's; (de otros) other people's; (extraño) alien

ajetre|ado adj hectic, busy. ~o m bustle

ají m (LAm) chilli; (salsa) chilli sauce

aj|illo m garlic. al ~illo cooked with garlic. ~o m garlic. ~onjolí m sesame

ajuar m furnishings; (de novia) trousseau; (de bebé) layette

ajust|ado adj right; (vestido) tight. ~ar vt fit; (adaptar) adapt; (acordar) agree; settle (una cuenta); (apretar) tighten. ● vi fit. ~arse vpr fit; (adaptarse) adapt o.s.; (acordarse) come to an agreement. ~e m fitting; (adaptación) adjustment; (acuerdo) agreement; (de una cuenta) settlement

al = a + el

ala f wing; (de sombrero) brim. ● m & f (deportes) winger

alaba|nza f praise. ~r vt praise

alacena f cupboard (Brit), closet (Amer)

alacrán m scorpion

alambr|ada f wire fence. ~ado m (LAm) wire fence. ~e m wire. ~e de púas barbed wire

alameda f avenue; (plantío de álamos) poplar grove

álamo m poplar. ~ temblón aspen

alarde m show. hacer ~ de boast of

alarga|do adj long. ~dor m extension. ~r **12** vt lengthen; stretch out (mano etc); (dar) give, pass. ~rse vpr get longer

alarido m shriek

alarm|a f alarm. ~ante adj alarming. ~ar vt alarm, frighten. ~arse vpr be alarmed. ~ista m & f alarmist

alba f dawn

albacea m & f executor

albahaca f basil

albanés adj & m Albanian

Albania f Albania

albañil m builder; (que coloca ladrillos) bricklayer

albarán m delivery note

albaricoque m apricot. ~ro m apricot tree

albedrío m will. libre ~ free will

alberca f tank, reservoir; (Mex, piscina) swimming pool

alberg|ar **12** vt (alojar) put up; (vivienda) house; (dar refugio) shelter. ~ar vpr stay; (refugiarse) shelter. ~ue m accommodation; (refugio) shelter. ~ue de juventud youth hostel

albino adj & m albino

albóndiga f meatball, rissole

albornoz *m* bathrobe

alborot|ado *adj* excited; *(aturdido)* hasty. **~ador** *adj* rowdy. ● *m* trouble-maker. **~ar** *vt* disturb, upset. ● *vi* make a racket. **~arse** *vpr* get excited; (el mar) get rough. **~o** *m* row, uproar

álbum *m* (*pl* **~es** o **~s**) album

alcachofa *f* artichoke

alcald|e *m* mayor. **~esa** *f* mayoress. **~ía** *f* mayoralty; *(oficina)* mayor's office

alcance *m* reach; *(de arma, telescopio etc)* range; *(déficit)* deficit

alcancía *f* money-box; *(LAm, de niño)* piggy bank

alcantarilla *f* sewer; *(boca)* drain

alcanzar 🔟 *vt* (*llegar a*) catch up; *(coger)* reach; catch (un autobús); *(bala etc)* strike, hit. ● *vi* reach; *(ser suficiente)* be enough. **~ a** manage

alcaparra *f* caper

alcázar *m* fortress

alcoba *f* bedroom

alcohol *m* alcohol. **~ol desnaturalizado** methylated spirits, meths. **~ólico** *adj & m* alcoholic. **~olímetro** *m* Breathalyser . **~olismo** *m* alcoholism

alcornoque *m* cork-oak; *(persona torpe)* idiot

aldaba *f* door-knocker

aldea *f* village. **~no** *adj* village. ● *m* villager

alea|ción *f* alloy. **~r** *vt* alloy

aleatorio *adj* uncertain

aleccionar *vt* instruct

aledaños *mpl* outskirts

alega|ción *f* allegation; *(LAm, disputa)* argument. **~r** 🔢 *vt* claim; *(Jurid)* plead. ● *vi* (*LAm*) argue. **~ta** *f* (*Mex*) argument. **~to** *m* plea

alegoría *f* allegory

alegr|ar *vt* make happy; *(avivar)* brighten up. **~arse** *vpr* be happy; *(emborracharse)* get merry. **~e** *adj* happy; *(achispado)* merry, tight. **~ía** *f* happiness

aleja|do *adj* distant. **~miento** *m* removal; *(entre personas)* estrangement; *(distancia)* distance. **~r** *vt* remove; *(ahuyentar)* get rid of, *(fig, apartar)* separate. **~rse** *vpr* move away

alemán *adj & m* German

Alemania *f* Germany. **~ Occidental** *(historia)* West Germany. **~ Oriental** *(historia)* East Germany

alenta|dor *adj* encouraging. **~r** 🔢 *vt* encourage. ● *vi* breathe

alerce *m* larch

al|ergia *f* allergy. **~érgico** *adj* allergic

alero *m* (*del tejado*) eaves

alerta *adj* alert. ¡**~**! look out! **estar ~** be alert; *(en guardia)* be on the alert. **~r** *vt* alert

aleta *f* wing; *(de pez)* fin

aletarga|do *adj* lethargic. **~r** 🔢 *vt* make lethargic. **~rse** *vpr* become lethargic

alet|azo *m* (*de un ave*) flap of the wings; *(de un pez)* flick of the fin. **~ear** *vi* flap its wings, flutter

alevosía *f* treachery

alfab|ético *adj* alphabetical. **~etizar** 🔟 *vt* alphabetize; teach to read and write. **~eto** *m* alphabet. **~eto Morse** Morse code

alfalfa *f* alfalfa

alfar|ería *m* pottery. **~ero** *m* potter

alféizar *m* (window)sill

alférez *m* second lieutenant

alfil *m* (*en ajedrez*) bishop

a alfile|r m pin. **∼tero** m pincushion; (estuche) pin-case

alfombr|a f (grande) carpet; (pequeña) rug, mat. **∼ado** adj (LAm) carpeted. **∼ar** vt carpet. **∼illa** f rug, mat; (Med) type of measles

alforja f saddle-bag

algarabía f hubbub

algas fpl seaweed

álgebra f algebra

álgido adj (fig) decisive

algo pron something; (en frases interrogativas, condicionales) anything. ● adv rather. **¿∼ más?** anything else? **¿quieres tomar ∼?** would you like a drink?; (de comer) would you like something to eat?

algod|ón m cotton. **∼ón de azúcar** candy floss (Brit), cotton candy (Amer). **∼ón hidrófilo** cotton wool. **∼onero** adj cotton. ● m cotton plant

alguacil m bailiff

alguien pron someone, somebody; (en frases interrogativas, condicionales) anyone, anybody

algún véase ALGUNO

alguno adj (delante de nombres masculinos en singular **algún**) some; (en frases interrogativas, condicionales) any; (pospuesto al nombre en frases negativas) at all. **no tiene idea alguna** he hasn't any idea at all. **alguna que otra vez** from time to time. **algunas veces, alguna vez** sometimes. ● pron one; (en plural) some; (alguien) someone

alhaja f piece of jewellery; (fig) treasure. **∼s** fpl jewellery

alharaca f fuss

alhelí m wallflower

alia|do adj allied. ● m ally. **∼nza** f alliance; (anillo) wedding ring. **∼r**

20 vt combine. **∼rse** vpr be combined; (formar una alianza) form an alliance

alias adv & m alias

alicaído adj (fig, débil) weak; (fig, abatido) depressed

alicates mpl pliers

aliciente m incentive; (de un lugar) attraction

alienado adj mentally ill

aliento m breath; (ánimo) courage

aligerar vt make lighter; (aliviar) alleviate, ease; (apresurar) quicken

alijo m (de contrabando) consignment

alimaña f pest. **∼s** fpl vermin

aliment|ación f diet; (acción) feeding. **∼ar** vt feed; (nutrir) nourish. ● vi be nourishing. **∼arse** vpr feed (**con, de** on). **∼icio** adj nourishing. **productos** mpl **∼icios** foodstuffs. **∼o** m food. **∼os** mpl (Jurid) alimony

alinea|ción f alignment; (en deportes) line-up. **∼r** vt align, line up

aliñ|ar vt (Culin) season; dress (ensalada). **∼o** m seasoning; (para ensalada) dressing

alioli m garlic mayonnaise

alisar vt smooth

alistar vt put on a list; (Mil) enlist. **∼se** vpr enrol; (Mil) enlist; (LAm, prepararse) get ready

alivi|ar vt lighten; relieve (dolor, etc); (arg, hurtar) steal, pinch 🅟. **∼arse** vpr (dolor) diminish; (persona) get better. **∼o** m relief

aljibe m tank

allá adv (over) there. **¡∼ él!** that's his business! **∼ fuera** out there. **∼ por 1970** back in 1970. **el más ∼** the beyond. **más ∼** further on. **más ∼ de** beyond. **por ∼** that way

allana|miento *m.* **~miento (de morada)** breaking and entering; (*LAm, por la autoridad*) raid. **~r** *vt* level; remove (*obstáculos*); (*fig*) iron out (*dificultades etc*); break into (*una casa*); (*LAm, por la autoridad*) raid

allega|do *adj* close. • *m* close friend; (*pariente*) close relative. **~r** **12** *vt* collect

allí *adv* there; (*tiempo*) then. **~ fuera** out there. **por ~** that way

alma *f* soul; (*habitante*) inhabitant

almac|én *m* warehouse; (*LAm, tienda*) grocer's shop; (*de un arma*) magazine. **~enes** *mpl* department store. **~enaje** *m* storage; (*derechos*) storage charges. **~enar** *vt* store; stock up with (*provisiones*)

almanaque *m* almanac

almeja *f* clam

almendr|a *f* almond. **~ado** *adj* almond-shaped. **~o** *m* almond tree

alm|íbar *m* syrup. **~ibarar** *vt* cover in syrup

almid|ón *m* starch. **~onado** *adj* starched; (*fig, estirado*) starchy

almirante *m* admiral

almizcle *m* musk. **~ra** *f* muskrat

almohad|a *f* pillow. **consultar con la ~a** sleep on it. **~illa** *f* small cushion. **~ón** *m* large pillow, bolster

almorranas *fpl* haemorrhoids, piles

alm|orzar **2** & **10** *vt* (*a mediodía*) have for lunch; (*desayunar*) have for breakfast. • *vi* (*a mediodía*) have lunch; (*desayunar*) have breakfast. **~uerzo** *m* (*a mediodía*) lunch; (*desayuno*) breakfast

alocado *adj* scatter-brained

aloja|miento *m* accommoda-

tion. **~r** *vt* put up. **~rse** *vpr* stay

alondra *f* lark

alpaca *f* alpaca

alpargata *f* canvas shoe, espadrille

alpin|ismo *m* mountaineering, climbing. **~ista** *m & f* mountaineer, climber. **~o** *adj* Alpine

alpiste *m* birdseed

alquil|ar *vt* (*tomar en alquiler*) hire (*vehículo*), rent (*piso, casa*); (*dar en alquiler*) hire (out) (*vehículo*), rent (out) (*piso, casa*). **se alquila** to let (*Brit*), for rent (*Amer*). **~er** *m* (*acción — de alquilar un piso etc*) renting; (*— de alquilar un vehículo*) hiring; (*precio — por el que se alquila un piso etc*) rent; (*— por el que se alquila un vehículo*) hire charge. **de ~er** for hire

alquimi|a *f* alchemy. **~sta** *m* alchemist

alquitrán *m* tar

alrededor *adv* around. **~ de** around; (*con números*) about. **~es** *mpl* surroundings; (*de una ciudad*) outskirts

alta *f* discharge

altaner|ía *f* (*arrogancia*) arrogance. **~o** *adj* arrogant, haughty

altar *m* altar

altavoz *m* loudspeaker

altera|ble *adj* changeable. **~ción** *f* change, alteration. **~r** *vt* change, alter; (*perturbar*) disturb; (*enfadar*) anger, irritate. **~rse** *vpr* change, alter; (*agitarse*) get upset; (*enfadarse*) get angry; (*comida*) go off

altercado *m* argument

altern|ar *vt/i* alternate. **~arse** *vpr* take turns. **~ativa** *f* alternative. **~ativo** *adj* alternating. **~o** *adj* alternate; (*Elec*) alternating

Alteza *f* (*título*) Highness

a **altibajos** *mpl* (de terreno) unevenness; (fig) ups and downs
altiplanicie *f,* **altiplano** *m* high
plateau
altisonante *adj* pompous
altitud *f* altitude
altiv|ez *f* arrogance. ∼**o** *adj* arro-
gant
alto *adj* high; (persona, edificio)
tall; (voz) loud; (fig, elevado) lofty;
(Mus) (nota) high(-pitched); (Mus)
(voz, instrumento) alto; (horas)
early. ● *adv* high; (de sonidos)
loud(ly). ● *m* height; (de un edificio) top floor; (viola) viola; (voz)
alto; (parada) stop. ● *int* halt!,
stop! **en lo** ∼ **de** on the top of.
tiene 3 metros de ∼ it is 3
metres high
altoparlante *m* (esp LAm) loudspeaker
altruis|mo *m* altruism. ∼**ta** *adj*
altruistic. ● *m & f* altruist
altura *f* height; (Aviac, Geog) altitude; (de agua) depth; (fig, cielo)
sky. **a estas** ∼ at this stage.
tiene 3 metros de ∼ it is 3
metres high
alubia *f* (haricot) bean
alucinación *f* hallucination
alud *m* avalanche
aludi|do *adj* in question. **darse**
por ∼**do** take it personally. **no**
darse por ∼**do** turn a deaf ear.
∼**r** *vi* mention
alumbra|do *adj* lit. ● *m* lighting.
∼**miento** *m* lighting; (parto) child-
birth. ∼**r** *vt* light
aluminio *m* aluminium (Brit), aluminum (Amer)
alumno *m* pupil; (Univ) student
aluniza|je *m* landing on the
moon. ∼**r** **10** *vi* land on the moon
alusi|ón *f* allusion. ∼**vo** *adj*

allusive
alza *f* rise. ∼**da** *f* (de caballo)
height; (Jurid) appeal. ∼**do** *adj*
raised; (Mex, soberbio) vain; (precio) fixed. ∼**miento** *m* (Pol) upris-
ing. ∼**r** **10** *vt* raise, lift (up); raise
(precios). ∼**rse** *vpr* (Pol) rise up
ama *f* lady of the house. ∼ **de**
casa housewife. ∼ **de cría** wet-
nurse. ∼ **de llaves** housekeeper
amab|ilidad *f* kindness. ∼**le** *adj*
kind; (simpático) nice
amaestra|do *adj* trained. ∼**r** *vt*
train
amag|ar **12** *vt* (mostrar intención
de) make as if to; (Mex, amenazar)
threaten. ● *vi* threaten; (algo
bueno) be in the offing. ∼**o** *m*
threat; (señal) sign; (Med) symptom
amainar *vi* let up
amalgama *f* amalgam. ∼**r** *vt*
amalgamate
amamantar *vt/i* breast-feed;
(animal) to suckle
amanecer *m* dawn. ● *vi* dawn;
(persona) wake up. **al** ∼ at dawn,
at daybreak. ∼**se** *vpr* (Mex) stay up
all night
amanera|do *adj* affected. ∼**rse**
vpr become affected
amansar *vt* tame; break in (un
caballo); soothe (dolor etc). ∼**se**
vpr calm down
amante *adj* fond. ● *m & f* lover
amapola *f* poppy
amar *vt* love
amara|je *m* landing on water; (de
astronave) splash-down. ∼**r** *vi* land
on water; (astronave) splash down
amarg|ado *adj* embittered. ∼**ar**
12 *vt* make bitter; embitter (persona). ∼**arse** *vpr* become bitter.
∼**o** *adj* bitter. ∼**ura** *f* bitterness
amariconado *adj* **1** effe-

minate

amarill|ento adj yellowish; (tez) sallow. **~o** adj & m yellow

amarra|s fpl. soltar las **~s** cast off. **~do** adj (LAm) mean. **~r** vt moor; (esp LAm, atar) tie. **~rse** vpr LAm tie up

amas|ar vt knead; (acumular) to amass. **~ijo** m dough; (acción) kneading; (fig, fam, mezcla) hotch-potch

amate m (Mex) fig tree

amateur adj & m f amateur

amazona f Amazon; (jinete) horsewoman

ámbar m amber

ambici|ón f ambition. **~onar** vt aspire to. **~onar ser** have an ambition to be. **~oso** adj ambitious. ● m ambitious person

ambidextro adj ambidextrous. ● m ambidextrous person

ambient|ar vt give an atmosphere to. **~arse** vpr adapt o.s. **~e** m atmosphere; (entorno) environment

ambig|üedad f ambiguity. **~uo** adj ambiguous

ámbito m sphere; (alcance) scope

ambos adj & pron both

ambulancia f ambulance

ambulante adj travelling

ambulatorio m out-patients' department

amedrentar vt frighten, scare. **~se** vpr be frightened

amén m amen. ● int amen! **en un decir ~** in an instant

amenaza f threat. **~r** 10 vt threaten

amen|idad f pleasantness. **~izar** 10 vt brighten up. **~o** adj pleasant

América f America. **~ Central**

Central America. **~ del Norte** North America. **~ del Sur** South America. **~ Latina** Latin America

american|a f jacket. **~ismo** m Americanism. **~o** adj American

amerita|do adj (LAm) meritorious. **~r** vt (LAm) deserve

amerizaje m véase AMARAJE

ametralla|dora f machine-gun. **~r** vt machine-gun

amianto m asbestos

amig|a f friend; (novia) girl-friend; (amante) lover. **~able** adj friendly. **~ablemente** adv amicably

amigo adj friendly. ● m friend; (novio) boyfriend; (amante) lover. ser **~ de** be fond of. ser muy **~s** be close friends

amilanar vt daunt. **~se** vpr be daunted

aminorar vt lessen; reduce (velocidad)

amist|ad f friendship. **~ades** fpl friends. **~oso** adj friendly

amn|esia f amnesia. **~ésico** adj amnesiac

amnist|ía f amnesty. **~iar** 20 vt grant an amnesty to

amo m master; (dueño) owner

amodorrarse vpr feel sleepy

amoldar vt mould; (adaptar) adapt; (acomodar) fit. **~se** vpr adapt

amonestar vt rebuke, reprimand; (anunciar la boda) publish the banns

amoniaco, amoníaco m ammonia

amontonar vt pile up; (fig, acumular) accumulate. **~se** vpr pile up; (gente) crowd together

amor m love. **~es** mpl (relaciones amorosas) love affairs. **~ propio** pride. **con mil ~es, de mil ~es** with (the greatest of) pleasure. **hacer el ~** make love. **por (el) ~ de Dios** for God's sake

amoratado adj purple; (de frío) blue

amordazar 10 vt gag; (fig) silence

amorfo adj amorphous, shapeless

amor|ío m affair. **~oso** adj loving; (cartas) love; (LAm), encantador) cute

amortajar vt shroud

amortigua|dor adj deadening. ● m (Auto) shock absorber. **~r** 15 vt deaden (ruido); dim (luz); cushion (golpe); tone down (color)

amortiza|ble adj redeemable. **~ción** f (de una deuda) repayment; (de bono etc) redemption. **~r** 10 vt repay (una deuda)

amotinar vt incite to riot. **~se** vpr rebel; (Mil) mutiny

ampar|ar vt help; (proteger) protect. **~arse** vpr seek protection; (de la lluvia) shelter. **~o** m protection; (de la lluvia) shelter. **al ~o de** under the protection of

amperio m ampere, amp 🔟

amplia|ción f extension; (photo) enlargement. **~r** 20 vt enlarge, extend; (photo) enlarge

amplifica|ción f amplification. **~dor** m amplifier. **~r** 7 amplify

ampli|o adj wide; (espacioso) spacious; (ropa) loose-fitting. **~tud** f extent; (espaciosidad) spaciousness; (espacio) space

ampolla f (Med) blister; (de medicamento) ampoule, phial

ampuloso adj pompous

amputar vt amputate; (fig) delete

amueblar vt furnish

amuleto m charm, amulet

amuralla|do adj walled. **~r** vt build a wall around

anacr|ónico adj anachronistic. **~onismo** m anachronism

anales mpl annals

analfabet|ismo m illiteracy. **~o** adj & m illiterate

analgésico adj analgesic. ● m painkiller

an|álisis m invar analysis. **~álisis de sangre** blood test. **~alista** m & f analyst. **~alítico** adj analytical. **~alizar** 10 vt analyze

an|alogía f analogy. **~álogo** adj analogous

anaranjado adj orangey

an|arquía f anarchy. **~árquico** adj anarchic. **~arquismo** m anarchism. **~arquista** adj anarchistic. ● m & f anarchist

anat|omía f anatomy. **~ómico** adj anatomical

anca f haunch; (parte superior) rump; (fam, nalgas) bottom. **en ~s** (LAm) on the crupper

ancestro m ancestor

ancho adj wide; (ropa) loose-fitting; (fig) relieved; (demasiado grande) too big; (ufano) smug. ● m width; (Rail) gauge. **~ de banda** bandwidth. **tiene 3 metros de ~** it is 3 metres wide

anchoa f anchovy

anchura f width; (medida) measurement

ancian|o adj elderly, old. ● m elderly man, old man. **~a** f elderly woman, old woman. **los ~os** old people

ancla f anchor. **echar ~s** drop anchor. **levar ~s** weigh anchor. **~r** vi anchor

andad|eras *fpl* (*Mex*) baby-walker. **~or** *m* baby-walker

Andalucía *f* Andalusia

andaluz *adj* & *m* Andalusian

andamio *m* platform. **~s** *mpl* scaffolding

and|anzas *fpl* adventures. **~ar** [25] *vt* (*recorrer*) cover, go. ● *vi* walk; (*máquina*) go, work; (*estar*) be; (*moverse*) move. **~ar a caballo** (*LAm*) ride a horse. **~ar en bicicleta** (*LAm*) ride a bicycle. ¡**anda**! go on!, come on! **~ar por** be about. **~arse** *vpr* (*LAm, en imperativo*) ¡**andate**! go away! ● *m* walk. **~ariego** *adj* fond of walking

andén *m* platform

Andes *mpl*. **los ~** the Andes

andin|o *adj* Andean. **~ismo** *m* (*LAm*) mountaineering, climbing. **~ista** *m* & *f* (*LAm*) mountaineer, climber

andrajo *m* rag. **~so** *adj* ragged

anduve *vb* véase **ANDAR**

anécdota *f* anecdote

anecdótico *adj* anecdotal

anegar [12] *vt* flood. **~se** *vpr* be flooded, flood

anejo *adj* véase **ANEXO**

an|emia *f* anaemia. **~émico** *adj* anaemic

anest|esia *f* anaesthesia; (*droga*) anaesthetic. **~esiar** *vt* anaesthetize. **~ésico** *adj* & *m* anaesthetic. **~esista** *m* & *f* anaesthetist

anex|ar *vt* annex. **~o** *adj* attached. ● *m* annexe

anfibio *adj* amphibious. ● *m* amphibian

anfiteatro *m* amphitheatre; (*en un teatro*) upper circle

anfitri|ón *m* host. **~ona** *f* hostess

ángel *m* angel; (*encanto*) charm

angelical *adj*, **angélico** *adj* angelic

angina *f*. **~ de pecho** angina (pectoris). **tener ~s** have tonsillitis

anglicano *adj* & *m* Anglican

angl|icismo *m* Anglicism. **~ófilo** *adj* & *m* Anglophile. **~ohispánico** *adj* Anglo-Spanish. **~osajón** *adj* & *m* Anglo-Saxon

angosto *adj* narrow

angu|ila *f* eel. **~la** *f* elver, baby eel

ángulo *m* angle; (*rincón, esquina*) corner; (*curva*) bend

angusti|a *f* anguish. **~ar** *vt* distress; (*inquietar*) worry. **~arse** *vpr* get distressed; (*inquietarse*) get worried. **~oso** *adj* anguished; (*que causa angustia*) distressing

anhel|ar *vt* (+ *nombre*) long for; (+ *verbo*) long to. **~o** *m* (*fig*) yearning

anidar *vi* nest

anill|a *f* ring. **~o** *m* ring. **~o de boda** wedding ring

ánima *f* soul

anima|ción *f* (*de personas*) life; (*de cosas*) liveliness; (*bullicio*) bustle; (*en el cine*) animation. **~do** *adj* lively; (*sitio etc*) busy. **~dor** *m* host. **~dora** *f* hostess; (*de un equipo*) cheerleader

animadversión *f* ill will

animal *adj* animal; (*fig, fam, torpe*) stupid. ● *m* animal; (*fig, fam, idiota*) idiot; (*fig, fam, bruto*) brute

animar *vt* give life to; (*dar ánimo*) encourage; (*dar vivacidad*) liven up. **~se** *vpr* (*decidirse*) decide; (*ponerse alegre*) cheer up. ¿**te animas a ir al cine**? do you feel like going to the cinema?

ánimo *m* soul; (*mente*) mind; (*valor*) courage; (*intención*) inten-

a tion. ¡~! come on!, cheer up! **dar ~s** encourage

animos|idad *f* animosity. **~o** *adj* brave; *(resuelto)* determined

aniquilar *vt* annihilate; *(acabar con)* ruin

anís *m* aniseed; *(licor)* anisette

aniversario *m* anniversary

anoche *adv* last night, yesterday evening

anochecer 🔟 *vi* get dark. **anochecí en Madrid** I was in Madrid at dusk. ● *m* nightfall, dusk. **al ~** at nightfall

anodino *adj* bland

an|omalía *f* anomaly. **~ómalo** *adj* anomalous

an|onimato *m* anonymity. **~ónimo** *adj* anonymous; *(sociedad)* limited. ● *m (carta)* anonymous letter

anormal *adj* abnormal. ● *m & f* 🔟 idiot. **~idad** *f* abnormality

anota|ción *f (nota)* note; *(acción de poner notas)* annotation. **~r** *vt (poner nota)* annotate; *(apuntar)* make a note of; *(LAm)* score *(un gol)*

anquilosa|miento *m (fig)* paralysis. **~rse** *vpr* become paralyzed

ansi|a *f* anxiety, worry; *(anhelo)* yearning. **~ar** 🟤 *vt* long for. **~edad** *f* anxiety. **~oso** *adj* anxious; *(deseoso)* eager

antag|ónico *adj* antagonistic. **~onismo** *m* antagonism. **~onista** *m & f* antagonist

antaño *adv* in days gone by

antártico *adj & m* Antarctic

ante *prep* in front of, before; *(frente a)* in the face of; *(en vista de)* in view of. ● *m* elk; *(piel)* suede. **~anoche** *adv* the night before last. **~ayer** *adv* the day before

yesterday. **~brazo** *m* forearm

antece|dente *adj* previous. ● *m* antecedent. **~dentes** *mpl* history, background. **~dentes penales** criminal record. **~der** *vt* precede. **~sor** *m* predecessor; *(antepasado)* ancestor

antelación *f (advance)* notice. **con ~** in advance

antemano *adv*. **de ~** beforehand

antena *f* antenna; *(radio, TV)* aerial

antenoche *adv (LAm)* the night before last

anteojeras *fpl* blinkers. **~o** *m* telescope. **~os** *mpl* binoculars; *(LAm, gafas)* glasses, spectacles. **~os de sol** sunglasses

ante|pasados *mpl* forebears, ancestors. **~poner** 🟤 *vt* put in front *(a* of*)*; *(fig)* put before, prefer. **~proyecto** *m* preliminary sketch; *(fig)* blueprint

anterior *adj* previous; *(delantero)* front. **~idad** *f*. **con ~idad** previously. **con ~idad a** prior to

antes *adv* before; *(antiguamente)* in the past; *(mejor)* rather; *(primero)* first. **~ de** before. **~ de ayer** the day before yesterday. **~ de que** + *subjuntivo* before. **~ de que llegue** before he arrives. **cuanto ~, lo ~ posible** as soon as possible

anti|aéreo *adj* anti-aircraft. **~biótico** *adj & m* antibiotic. **~ciclón** *m* anticyclone

anticip|ación *f*. **con ~ación** in advance. **con media hora de ~ación** half an hour early. **~ado** *adj* advance. **por ~ado** in advance. **~ar** *vt* bring forward; advance *(dinero)*. **~arse** *vpr* be early. **~o** *m (dinero)* advance; *(fig)* foretaste

anti|conceptivo *adj & m* contraceptive. ∼ **de emergencia** morning-after pill. ∼**congelante** *m* antifreeze

anticua|do *adj* old-fashioned. ∼**rio** *m* antique dealer

anticuerpo *m* antibody

antídoto *m* antidote

anti|estético *adj* ugly. ∼**faz** *m* mask

antig|ualla *f* old relic. ∼**uamente** *adv* formerly; (*hace mucho tiempo*) long ago. ∼**uedad** *f* antiquity; (*objeto*) antique; (*en un empleo*) length of service. ∼**uo** *adj* old; (*ruinas*) ancient; (*mueble*) antique

Antillas *fpl.* **las** ∼ the West Indies

antílope *m* antelope

antinatural *adj* unnatural

antip|atía *f* dislike; (*cualidad de antipático*) unpleasantness. ∼**ático** *adj* unpleasant, unfriendly

anti|semita *m & f* anti-Semite. ∼**séptico** *adj & m* antiseptic. ∼**social** *adj* antisocial

antítesis *f invar* antithesis

antoj|adizo *adj* capricious. ∼**arse** *vpr* fancy. **se le** ∼**a un caramelo** he fancies a sweet. ∼**itos** *mpl* (*Mex*) snacks bought at street stands. ∼**o** *m* whim; (*de embarazada*) craving

antología *f* anthology

antorcha *f* torch

ántrax *m* anthrax

antro *m* (*fig*) dump, hole. ∼ **de perversión** den of iniquity

antrop|ología *f* anthropology. ∼**ólogo** *m* anthropologist

anua|l *adj* annual. ∼**lidad** *f* annuity. ∼**lmente** *adv* yearly. ∼**rio** *m* yearbook

anudar *vt* tie, knot. ∼**se** *vpr* tie

anula|ción *f* annulment, cancellation. ∼**r** *vt* annul, cancel. ● *adj* (*dedo*) ring. ● *m* ring finger

anunci|ante *m & f* advertiser. ∼**ar** *vt* announce; advertise (*producto comercial*); (*presagiar*) be a sign of. ∼**o** *m* announcement; (*para vender algo*) advertisement, advert **1**; (*cartel*) poster

anzuelo *m* (fish)hook; (*fig*) bait. **tragar el** ∼ swallow the bait

añadi|dura *f* addition. **por** ∼**dura** in addition. ∼**r** *vt* add

añejo *adj* (*vino*) mature

añicos *mpl.* **hacer(se)** ∼ smash to pieces

año *m* year. ∼ **bisiesto** leap year. ∼ **nuevo** new year. **al** ∼ per year, a year. **¿cuántos** ∼**s tiene?** how old is he? **tiene 5** ∼**s** he's 5 (years old). **el** ∼ **pasado** last year. **el** ∼ **que viene** next year. **entrado en** ∼**s** elderly. **los** ∼**s 60** the sixties

añora|nza *f* nostalgia. ∼**r** *vt* miss

apabulla|nte *adj* overwhelming. ∼**r** *vt* overwhelm

apacible *adj* gentle; (*clima*) mild

apacigua|r 18 *vt* pacify; (*calmar*) calm; relieve (*dolor etc*). ∼**rse** *vpr* calm down

apadrinar *vt* sponsor; be godfather to (*a un niño*)

apag|ado *adj* extinguished; (*color*) dull; (*aparato eléctrico, luz*) off; (*persona*) lifeless; (*sonido*) muffled. ∼**ar 12** *vt* put out (*fuego, incendio*); turn off, switch off (*aparato eléctrico, luz*); quench (*sed*); muffle (*sonido*). ∼**arse** *vpr* (*fuego, luz*) go out; (*sonido*) die away. ∼**ón** *m* blackout

apalabrar *vt* make a verbal agreement; (*contratar*) engage

apalear *vt* winnow (*grano*); beat

(alfombra, frutos, persona)

apantallar vt (Mex) impress

apañar vt (arreglar) fix; (remendar) mend; (agarrar) grasp, take hold of. ~**se** vpr get along, manage

apapachar vt (Mex) cuddle

aparador m sideboard; (Mex, de tienda) shop window

aparato m apparatus; (máquina) machine; (doméstico) appliance; (teléfono) telephone; (radio, TV) set; (ostentación) show, pomp. ~**so** adj showy, ostentatious; (caída) spectacular

aparca|miento m car park (Brit), parking lot (Amer). ~**r** 🗗 vt/i park

aparear vt mate (animales). ~**se** vpr mate

aparecer 🗓 vi appear. ~**se** vpr appear

aparej|ado adj. llevar ~**ado**, traer ~**ado** mean, entail. ~**o** m (avíos) equipment; (de caballo) tack; (de pesca) tackle

aparent|ar vt (afectar) feign; (parecer) look. ● vi show off. ~**a** 20 años she looks like she's 20. ~**e** adj apparent

apari|ción f appearance; (visión) apparition. ~**encia** f appearance; (fig) show. guardar las ~**encias** keep up appearances

apartado adj (aislado) isolated. ● m (de un texto) section. ~ (de correos) post-office box, PO box

apartamento m apartment, flat (Brit)

apart|ar vt separate; (alejar) move away; (quitar) remove; (guardar) set aside. ~**arse** vpr leave; (quitarse de en medio) get out of the way; (aislarse) cut o.s. off. ~**e** adv apart; (por separado) separately; (además)

besides. ● m aside; (párrafo) new paragraph. ~**e de** apart from. dejar ~**e** leave aside. eso ~**e** apart from that

apasiona|do adj passionate; (entusiasta) enthusiastic; (falto de objetividad) biased. ● m. ~**do de** lover. ~**miento** m passion. ~**r** vt excite. ~**rse** vpr be mad (por about); (ser parcial) become biased

apatía f apathy. ~**ático** adj apathetic

apea|dero m (Rail) halt. ~**rse** vpr get off

apechugar 🗗 vi. 🗓 ~ **con** put up with

apedrear vt stone

apeg|ado adj attached (a to). ~**o** m 🗓 attachment. tener ~**o a** be fond of

apela|ción f appeal. ~**r** vi appeal; (recurrir) resort (a to). ● vt (apodar) call. ~**tivo** m (nick)name

apellid|ar vt call. ~**arse** vpr be called. ¿cómo te apellidas? what's your surname? ~**o** m surname

apelmazarse vpr (lana) get matted

apenar vt sadden; (LAm, avergonzar) embarrass. ~**se** vpr be sad; (LAm, avergonzarse) be embarrassed

apenas adv hardly, scarcely; (Mex, sólo) only. ● conj (esp LAm, en cuanto) as soon as. ~ si 🗓 hardly

ap|éndice m appendix. ~**endicitis** f appendicitis

apergaminado adj (piel) wrinkled

aperitivo m (bebida) aperitif; (comida) appetizer

aperos mpl implements; (de labranza) agricultural equipment; (LAm, de un caballo) tack

apertura *f* opening

apesadumbrar *vt* upset. **~se** *vpr* sadden

apestar *vt* infect. ● *vi* stink (**a** of)

apet|ecer 🔢 *vi.* ¿te **~ece una copa?** do you fancy a drink? do you feel like a drink?. **no me ~ece** I don't feel like it. **~ecible** *adj* attractive. **~ito** *m* appetite; (*fig*) desire. **~itoso** *adj* appetizing

apiadarse *vpr* feel sorry (**de** for)

ápice *m* (*nada, en frases negativas*) anything. **no ceder un ~** not give an inch

apilar *vt* pile up

apiñar *vt* pack in. **~se** *vpr* (*personas*) crowd together; (*cosas*) be packed tight

apio *m* celery

aplacar 🔢 *vt* placate; soothe (*dolor*)

aplanar *vt* level. **~ calles** (*LAm fam*) loaf around

aplasta|nte *adj* overwhelming. **~r** *vt* crush. **~rse** *vpr* flatten o.s.

aplau|dir *vt* clap, applaud; (*fig*) applaud. **~so** *m* applause; (*fig*) praise

aplaza|miento *m* postponement. **~r** 🔟 *vt* postpone; defer (*pago*)

aplica|ble *adj* applicable. **~ción** *f* application. **~do** *adj* (*persona*) diligent. **~r** 🔢 *vt* apply. ● *vi* (*LAm, a un puesto*) apply (for). **~rse** *vpr* apply o.s.

aplom|ado *adj* composed. **~o** *m* composure

apocado *adj* timid

apocar 🔢 *vt* belittle (*persona*). **~se** *vpr* feel small

apodar *vt* nickname

apodera|do *m* representative.

~rse *vpr* seize

apodo *m* nickname

apogeo *m* (*fig*) height

apolilla|do *adj* moth-eaten. **~rse** *vpr* get moth-eaten

apolítico *adj* non-political

apología *f* defence

apoltronarse *vpr* settle o.s. down

apoplejía *f* stroke

aporrear *vt* hit, thump; beat up (*persona*)

aport|ación *f* contribution. **~ar** *vt* contribute. **~e** *m* (*LAm*) contribution

aposta *adv* on purpose

apostar¹ 🔢 *vt/i* bet

apostar² *vt* station. **~se** *vpr* station o.s.

apóstol *m* apostle

apóstrofo *m* apostrophe

apoy|ar *vt* lean (**en** against); (*descansar*) rest; (*asentar*) base; (*reforzar*) support. **~arse** *vpr* lean, rest. **~o** *m* support

apreci|able *adj* appreciable; (*digno de estima*) worthy. **~ación** *f* appreciation; (*valoración*) appraisal. **~ar** *vt* value; (*estimar*) appreciate. **~o** *m* appraisal; (*fig*) esteem

apremi|ante *adj* urgent, pressing. **~ar** *vt* urge; (*obligar*) compel; (*dar prisa a*) hurry up. ● *vi* be urgent. **~o** *m* urgency; (*obligación*) obligation

aprender *vt/i* learn. **~se** *vpr* learn

aprendiz *m* apprentice. **~aje** *m* learning; (*período*) apprenticeship

aprensi|ón *f* apprehension; (*miedo*) fear. **~vo** *adj* apprehensive, fearful

apresar *vt* seize; (*capturar*) capture

aprestar vt prepare. **~se** vpr prepare

apresura|do adj in a hurry; (hecho con prisa) hurried. **~r** vt hurry. **~rse** vpr hurry up

apret|ado adj tight; (difícil) difficult; (tacaño) stingy, mean. **~ar 1** vt tighten; press (botón); squeeze (persona); (comprimir) press down. ● vi be too tight. **~arse** vpr crowd together. **~ón** m squeeze. **~ón de manos** handshake

aprieto m difficulty. **verse en un ~** be in a tight spot

aprisa adv quickly

aprisionar vt trap

aproba|ción f approval. **~r 2** vt approve (of); pass (examen). ● vi pass

apropia|ción f appropriation. **~do** adj appropriate. **~rse** vpr. **~rse de** be appropriate, take

aprovecha|ble adj usable. **~do** adj (aplicado) diligent; (ingenioso) resourceful; (oportunista) opportunist. **bien ~do** well spent. **~miento** m advantage; (uso) use. **~r** vt take advantage of; (utilizar) make use of. ● vi make the most of it. **¡que aproveche!** enjoy your meal! **~rse** vpr. **~rse de** take advantage of

aprovisionar vt provision (con, de with). **~se** vpr stock up

aproxima|ción f approximation; (proximidad) closeness; (en la lotería) consolation prize. **~damente** adv roughly, approximately. **~do** adj approximate, rough. **~r** vt bring near; (fig) bring together (personas). **~rse** vpr come closer, approach

apt|itud f suitability; (capacidad) ability. **~o** adj (capaz) capable;

(adecuado) suitable

apuesta f bet

apuesto m handsome. ● vb véase **APOSTAR** [1]

apuntalar vt shore up

apunt|ar vt aim (arma); (señalar) point at; (anotar) make a note of, note down; (inscribir) enrol; (en el teatro) prompt. ● vi (con un arma) to aim (**a** at). **~arse** vpr put one's name down; score (triunfo, tanto etc). **~e** m note; (bosquejo) sketch. **tomar ~s** take notes

apuñalar vt stab

apur|ado adj difficult; (sin dinero) hard up; (LAm, con prisa) in a hurry. **~ar** vt (acabar) finish; drain (vaso etc); (causar vergüenza) embarrass; (LAm, apresurar) hurry. **~arse** vpr worry; (LAm, apresurarse) hurry up. **~o** m tight spot, difficult situation; (vergüenza) embarrassment; (estrechez) hardship, want; (LAm, prisa) hurry

aquejar vt afflict

aquel adj (f **aquella**, mpl **aquellos**, fpl **aquellas**) that; (en plural) those

aquél pron (f **aquélla**, mpl **aquéllos**, fpl **aquéllas**) that one; (en plural) those

aquello pron that; (asunto) that business

aquí adv here. **de ~** from here. **de ~ a 15 días** in a fortnight's time. **~ mismo** right here. **de ~ para allá** to and fro. **de ~ que** that is why. **hasta ~** until now. **por ~** around here

aquietar vt calm (down)

árabe adj & m & f Arab; (lengua) Arabic

Arabia f Arabia. **~ Saudita**, **~ Saudí** Saudi Arabia

arado m plough. **~r** m ploughman

arancel m tariff; (*impuesto*) duty. **~ario** adj tariff

arándano m blueberry

arandela f washer

araña f spider; (*lámpara*) chandelier. **~r** vt scratch

arar vt plough

arbitra|je m arbitration; (*en deportes*) refereeing. **~r** vt/i arbitrate; (*en fútbol etc*) referee; (*en tenis etc*) umpire

arbitr|ariedad f arbitrariness. **~ario** adj arbitrary. **~io** m (*free*) will

árbitro m arbitrator; (*en fútbol etc*) referee; (*en tenis etc*) umpire

árbol m tree; (*eje*) axle; (*palo*) mast. **~ genealógico** family tree. **~ de Navidad** Christmas tree

arbol|ado m trees. **~eda** f wood

arbusto m bush

arca f (*caja*) chest. **~ de Noé** Noah's ark

arcada f arcade; (*de un puente*) arch; (*náuseas*) retching

arcaico adj archaic

arce m maple (tree)

arcén m (*de autopista*) hard shoulder; (*de carretera*) verge

archipiélago m archipelago

archiv|ador m filing cabinet. **~ar** vt file (away). **~o** m file; (*de documentos históricos*) archives

arcilla f clay

arco m (*Elec, Mat*) arc; (*Mus, arma*) bow; (*LAm, en fútbol*) goal. **~ iris** rainbow

arder vi burn; (*LAm, escocer*) sting; (*fig, de ira*) seethe. **estar que arde** be very tense

ardid m trick, scheme

ardiente adj burning

ardilla f squirrel

ardor m heat; (*fig*) ardour; (*LAm, escozor*) smarting. **~ de estómago** heartburn

arduo adj arduous

área f area

arena f sand; (*en deportes*) arena; (*en los toros*) (bull)ring. **~ movediza** quicksand

arenoso adj sandy

arenque m herring. **~ ahumado** kipper

arete m (*Mex*) earring

Argel m Algiers. **~ia** f Algeria

Argentina f Argentina

argentino adj Argentinian, Argentine. ● m Argentinian

argolla f ring. **~ de matrimonio** (*LAm*) wedding ring

arg|ot m slang. **~ótico** adj slang

argucia f cunning argument

argüir 19 vt (*probar*) prove, show; (*argumentar*) argue. ● vi argue

argument|ación f argument. **~ar** vt/i argue. **~o** m argument; (*de libro, película etc*) story, plot

aria f aria

aridez f aridity, dryness

árido adj arid, dry. **~s** mpl dry goods

Aries m Aries

arisco adj unfriendly

arist|ocracia f aristocracy. **~ócrata** m & f aristocrat. **~ocrático** adj aristocratic

aritmética f arithmetic

arma f arm, weapon; (*sección*) section. **~ de fuego** firearm, **~s de destrucción masiva** weapons of mass destruction. **~da** f navy; (*flota*) fleet. **~do** adj armed (**de** with). **~dura** f armour; (*de gafas etc*) frame; (*Tec*) framework. **~mentismo** m build up of arms.

∼mento m arms, armaments; (*acción de armar*) armament. **∼r** vt arm (**de** with); (*montar*) put together. **∼r un lío** kick up a fuss

armario m cupboard; (*para ropa*) wardrobe (*Brit*), closet (*Amer*)

armatoste m huge great thing

armazón m & f frame(work)

armiño m ermine

armisticio m armistice

armonía f harmony

armónica f harmonica, mouth organ

armoni|oso *adj* harmonious. **∼zar** [10] vt harmonize. ● vi harmonize; (*personas*) get on well (**con** with); (*colores*) go well (**con** with)

arn|és m armour. **∼eses** mpl harness

aro m ring, hoop

arom|a m aroma; (*de flores*) scent; (*de vino*) bouquet. **∼ático** *adj* aromatic

arpa f harp

arpía f harpy; (*fig*) hag

arpillera f sackcloth, sacking

arpón m harpoon

arquear vt arch, bend. **∼se** vpr arch, bend

arque|ología f archaeology. **∼ológico** *adj* archaeological. **∼ólogo** m archaeologist

arquero m archer; (*LAm, en fútbol*) goalkeeper

arquitect|o m architect. **∼ónico** *adj* architectural. **∼ura** f architecture

arrabal m suburb; (*barrio pobre*) poor area. **∼es** mpl outskirts. **∼ero** *adj* suburban; (*de modales groseros*) common

arraiga|do *adj* deeply rooted. **∼r** [12] vi take root. **∼rse** vpr take root; (*fig*) settle

arran|car [7] vt pull up (*planta*); pull out (*diente*); (*arrebatar*) snatch; (*Auto*) start. ● vi start. **∼carse** vpr pull out. **∼que** m sudden start; (*Auto*) start; (*fig*) outburst

arras fpl security; (*en boda*) coins

arrasar vt level, smooth; raze to the ground (*edificio etc*); (*llenar*) fill to the brim. ● vi (*en deportes*) sweep to victory; (*en política*) win a landslide victory

arrastr|ar vt pull; (*por el suelo*) drag (along); give rise to (*consecuencias*). ● vi trail on the ground. **∼arse** vpr crawl; (*humillarse*) grovel. **∼e** m dragging; (*transporte*) haulage. **estar para el ∼e** [1] be done in

arre int gee up! **∼ar** vt urge on

arrebat|ado *adj* (*irreflexivo*) impetuous. **∼ar** vt snatch (away); (*fig*) win (over); captivate (*corazón etc*). **∼arse** vpr get carried away. **∼o** m (*de cólera etc*) fit; (*éxtasis*) ecstasy

arrech|ar vt (*LAm fam, enfurecer*) to infuriate. **∼arse** vpr get furious. **∼o** *adj* furious

arrecife m reef

arregl|ado *adj* neat; (*bien vestido*) well-dressed; (*LAm, amañado*) fixed. **∼ar** vt arrange; (*poner en orden*) tidy up; sort out (*asunto, problema etc*); (*reparar*) mend. **∼arse** vpr (*solucionarse*) get sorted out; (*prepararse*) get ready; (*apañarse*) manage, make do; (*ponerse de acuerdo*) come to an agreement. **∼árselas** manage, get by. **∼o** m (*incl Mus*) arrangement; (*acción de reparar*) repair; (*acuerdo*) agreement; (*solución*) solution. **con**

~o a according to.

arrellanarse *vpr* settle o.s. (**en** into)

arremangar 🔢 *vt* roll up (mangas); tuck up (falda). ● ~**se** *vpr* roll up one's sleeves

arremeter *vi* charge (**contra** at); (*atacar*) attack

arremolinarse *vpr* mill about; (el agua) to swirl

arrenda|dor *m* landlord. ~**dora** *f* landlady. ~**miento** *m* renting; (*contrato*) lease; (*precio*) rent. ● ~**r** 🔢 *vt* (*dar casa en alquiler*) let; (*dar cosa en alquiler*) hire out; (*tomar en alquiler*) rent. ~**tario** *m* tenant

arreos *mpl* tack

arrepenti|miento *m* repentance, regret. ~**rse** 🔢 *vpr* (*retractarse*) to change one's mind; (*lamentarse*) be sorry. ~**rse de** regret; repent of (*pecados*)

arrest|ar *vt* arrest, detain; (*encarcelar*) imprison. ~**o** *m* arrest; (*encarcelamiento*) imprisonment

arriar 🔢 *vt* lower (bandera, vela)

arriba *adv* up; (*dirección*) up(wards); (*en una casa*) upstairs. ● *int* up with; (*¡levántate!*) up you get!; (*¡ánimo!*) come on! **¡~ España!** long live Spain! ~ **de** (*LAm*) on top of. ~ **mencionado** aforementioned. **calle** ~ up the street. **de** ~ **abajo** from top to bottom. **de 10 euros para** ~ over 10 euros. **escaleras** ~ upstairs. **la parte de** ~ the top part. **los de** ~ those at the top. **más** ~ higher up

arrib|ar *vi* (barco) reach port; (*esp LAm, llegar*) arrive. ~**ista** *m* & *f* social climber. ~**o** *m* (*esp LAm*) arrival

arriero *m* muleteer

arriesga|do *adj* risky; (person) daring. ~**r** 🔢 *vt* risk; (*aventurar*)

venture. ~**rse** *vpr* take a risk

arrim|ar *vt* bring close(r). ~**arse** *vpr* come closer, approach

arrincona|do *adj* forgotten; (*acorralado*) cornered. ~**r** *vt* put in a corner; (*perseguir*) corner (*arrumbar*) put aside. ~**rse** *vpr* become a recluse

arroba *f* (*Internet*) at (@); measure of weight

arrocero *adj* rice

arrodillarse *vpr* kneel (down)

arrogan|cia *f* arrogance; (*orgullo*) pride. ~**te** *adj* arrogant; (*orgulloso*) proud

arroj|ar *vt* throw; (*emitir*) give off, throw out; (*producir*) produce. ● *vi* (*esp LAm, vomitar*) throw up. ~**arse** *vpr* throw o.s. ~**o** *m* courage

arrollar *vt* roll (up); (*atropellar*) run over; (*vencer*) crush

arropar *vt* wrap up; (*en la cama*) tuck up. ~**se** *vpr* wrap (o.s.) up

arroy|o *m* stream; (*de una calle*) gutter. ~**uelo** *m* small stream

arroz *m* rice. ~ **con leche** rice pudding. ~**al** *m* rice field

arruga *f* (*en la piel*) wrinkle, line; (*en tela*) crease. ~**r** 🔢 *vt* wrinkle; crumple (papel); crease (tela). ~**rse** *vpr* (la piel) become wrinkled; (tela) crease, get creased

arruinar *vt* ruin; (*destruir*) destroy. ~**se** *vpr* (persona) be ruined

arrullar *vt* lull to sleep. ● *vi* (palomas) coo

arrumbar *vt* put aside

arsenal *m* (*astillero*) shipyard; (*de armas*) arsenal; (*fig*) mine

arsénico *m* arsenic

arte *m* (*f en plural*) art; (*habilidad*) skill; (*astucia*) cunning. **bellas ~s** fine arts. **con ~** skilfully. **malas**

a ~s trickery. **por amor al** ~ for the fun of it

artefacto *m* device

arteria *f* artery; (*fig, calle*) main road

artesan|al *adj* craft. ~**ía** *f* handicrafts. **objeto** *m* **de** ~**ía** traditional craft object. ~**o** *m* artisan, craftsman

ártico *adj* Arctic. **Á**~ *m.* **el Á**~ the Arctic

articula|ción *f* joint; (*pronunciación*) articulation. ~**do** *adj* articulated; (lenguaje) articulate. ~**r** *vt* articulate

artículo *m* article. ~**s** *mpl* (*géneros*) goods. ~ **de exportación** export product. ~ **de fondo** editorial, leader

artífice *m & f* artist; (creador) architect

artificial *adj* artificial. ~**o** *m* (habilidad) skill; (dispositivo) device; (engaño) trick

artiller|ía *f* artillery. ~**o** *m* artilleryman, gunner

artilugio *m* gadget

artimaña *f* trick

art|ista *m & f* artist. ~**ístico** *adj* artistic

artritis *f* arthritis

arveja *f* (LAm) pea

arzobispo *m* archbishop

as *m* ace

asa *f* handle

asado *adj* roast(ed) ● *m* roast (meat), joint; (LAm, reunión) barbecue. ~**o a la parrilla** grilled meat; (LAm) barbecued meat

asalariado *adj* salaried. ● *m* employee

asalt|ante *m* attacker; (de un banco) robber. ~**ar** *vt* storm (fortaleza); attack (persona); raid (banco etc); (*fig*) (duda) assail; (*fig*) (idea etc) cross one's mind. ~**o** *m* attack; (robo) robbery; (en boxeo) round

asamblea *f* assembly; (reunión) meeting

asar *vt* roast. ~**se** *vpr* be very hot. ~ **a la parrilla** grill; (LAm) barbecue. ~ **al horno** (sin grasa) bake; (con grasa) roast

asbesto *m* asbestos

ascend|encia *f* descent; (LAm, influencia) influence. ~**ente** *adj* ascending. ~**er** 🔟 *vt* promote. ● *vi* go up, ascend; (cuenta etc) come to, amount to; (ser ascendido) be promoted. ~**iente** *m & f* ancestor; (influencia) influence

ascens|ión *f* ascent; (de grado) promotion. **día** *m* **de la A~ión** Ascension Day. ~**o** *m* ascent; (de grado) promotion

ascensor *m* lift (Brit), elevator (Amer). ~**ista** *m & f* lift attendant (Brit), elevator operator (Amer)

asco *m* disgust. **dar** ~ be disgusting; (*fig, causar enfado*) be infuriating. **estar hecho un** ~ be disgusting. **me da** ~ it makes me feel sick. **¡qué** ~**!** how disgusting! **ser un** ~ be disgusting

ascua *f* ember. **estar en** ~**s** be on tenterhooks

asea|do *adj* clean; (arreglado) neat. ~**r** *vt* (lavar) wash; (limpiar) clean; (arreglar) tidy up

asedi|ar *vt* besiege; (*fig*) pester. ~**o** *m* siege

asegura|do *adj & m* insured. ~**dor** *m* insurer. ~**r** *vt* secure, make safe; (decir) assure; (concertar un seguro) insure; (preservar) safeguard. ~**rse** *vpr* make sure

asemejarse *vpr* be alike

asenta|do *adj* situated; (*arraigado*) established. **~r** ❶ *vt* place; (*asegurar*) settle; (*anotar*) note down; (*Mex, afirmar*) state. **~rse** *vpr* settle; (*estar situado*) be situated; (*esp LAm, sentar cabeza*) settle down

asentir ❹ *vi* agree (a to). **~ con la cabeza** nod

aseo *m* cleanliness. **~s** *mpl* toilets

asequible *adj* obtainable; (*precio*) reasonable; (*persona*) approachable

asesin|ar *vt* murder; (*Pol*) assassinate. **~ato** *m* murder; (*Pol*) assassination. **~o** *m* murderer; (*Pol*) assassin

asesor *m* adviser, consultant. **~ar** *vt* advise. **~arse** *vpr*. **~arse con** consult. **~ía** *f* consultancy; (*oficina*) consultant's office

asfalt|ado *adj* asphalt. **~ar** *vt* asphalt. **~o** *m* asphalt

asfixia *f* suffocation. **~nte** *adj* suffocating. ● **~r** *vt* suffocate. **~rse** *vpr* suffocate

así *adv* (*de esta manera*) like this, like that. ● *adj* such. **~ ~** so-so. **como** just as. **~ como** ~, (*LAm*) **~ nomás** just like that. **~ ...** **como** both ... and. **~ pues** so. **~ que** so; (*en cuanto*) as soon as. **~ sea** so be it. **~ y todo** even so. **aun ~** even so. **¿no es ~?** isn't that right? **si es ~** if that is the case. **y ~** (*sucesivamente*) and so on

Asia *f* Asia

asiático *adj* & *m* Asian

asidero *m* handle; (*fig, pretexto*) excuse

asidu|amente *adv* regularly. **~o** *adj* & *m* regular

asiento *m* seat; (*en contabilidad*) entry. **~ delantero** front seat. **~ trasero** back seat

asignar *vt* assign; allot (*porción, tiempo etc*)

asignatura *f* subject. **~ pendiente** (*en enseñanza*) failed subject; (*fig*) matter still to be resolved

asil|ado *m* inmate; (*Pol*) refugee. **~o** *m* asylum; (*ayuda*) shelter; (*de ancianos etc*) home. **pedir ~o político** ask for political asylum

asimétrico *adj* asymmetrical

asimila|ción *f* assimilation. **~r** *vt* assimilate

asimismo *adv* also; (*igualmente*) in the same way, likewise

asir ❺ *vt* grasp

asist|encia *f* attendance; (*gente*) people (present); (*en un teatro etc*) audience; (*ayuda*) assistance. **~encia médica** medical care. **~enta** *f* (*mujer de la limpieza*) charwoman. **~ente** *m* & *f* assistant. **~ente social** social worker. **~ido** *adj* assisted. **~ir** *vt* assist, help. ● *vi*. **~ir a** attend, be present at

asm|a *f* asthma. **~ático** *adj* & *m* asthmatic

asno *m* donkey; (*fig*) ass

asocia|ción *f* association; (*Com*) partnership. **~do** *adj* associated; (*socio*) associate. ● *m* associate. **~r** *vt* associate; (*Com*) take into partnership. **~rse** *vpr* associate; (*Com*) become a partner

asolar ❶ *vt* devastate

asomar *vt* show. ● *vi* appear, show. **~se** *vpr* (*persona*) lean out (a, por of); (*cosa*) appear

asombr|ar *vt* (*pasmar*) amaze; (*sorprender*) surprise. **~arse** *vpr* be amazed; (*sorprenderse*) be surprised. **~o** *m* amazement, surprise.

~oso adj amazing, astonishing

asomo m sign. **ni por ~** by no means

aspa f cross, X-shape; (de molino) (windmill) sail. **en ~** X-shaped

aspaviento m show, fuss. **~s** mpl gestures. **hacer ~s** make a big fuss

aspecto m look, appearance; (fig) aspect

aspereza f roughness; (de sabor etc) sourness

áspero adj rough; (sabor etc) bitter

aspersión f sprinkling

aspiración f breath; (deseo) ambition

aspirador m, **aspiradora** f vacuum cleaner

aspira|nte m & f candidate. **~r** vt breathe in; (máquina) suck up. ● vi breathe in; (máquina) suck. **~r a** aspire to

aspirina f aspirin

asquear vt sicken. ● vi be sickening. **~se** vpr be disgusted

asqueroso adj disgusting

asta f spear; (de la bandera) flagpole; (cuerno) horn. **a media ~** at half-mast. **~bandera** f (Mex) flagpole

asterisco m asterisk

astilla f splinter. **~s** fpl firewood

astillero m shipyard

astringente adj & m astringent

astr|o m star. **~ología** f astrology. **~ólogo** m astrologer. **~onauta** m & f astronaut. **~onave** f spaceship. **~onomía** f astronomy. **~ónomo** m astronomer

astu|cia f cleverness; (ardid) cunning trick. **~to** adj astute; (taimado) cunning

asumir vt assume

asunción f assumption. **la A~** the Assumption

asunto m (cuestión) matter; (de una novela) plot; (negocio) business. **~s** mpl **exteriores** foreign affairs. **el ~ es que** the fact is that

asusta|dizo adj easily frightened. **~r** vt frighten. **~rse** vpr be frightened

ataca|nte m & f attacker. **~r 7** vt attack

atad|o adj tied. ● m bundle. **~ura** f tie

atajar vi take a short cut; (Mex, en tenis) pick up the balls. ● vt (LAm, agarrar) catch. **~o** m short cut

atañer 22 vt concern

ataque m attack; (Med) fit, attack. **~ al corazón** heart attack. **~ de nervios** fit of hysterics

atar vt tie. **~se** vpr tie up

atarantar vt (LAm) fluster. **~se** vpr (LAm) get flustered

atardecer 11 vi get dark. ● m dusk. **al ~** at dusk

atareado adj busy

atasc|ar 7 vt block; (fig) hinder. **~arse** vpr get stuck; (tubo etc) block. **~o** m blockage; (Auto) traffic jam

ataúd m coffin

atav|iar 20 vt dress up. **~iarse** vpr dress up, get dressed up. **~ío** m dress, attire

atemorizar 10 vt frighten. **~se** vpr be frightened

atención f attention; (cortesía) courtesy, kindness; (interés) interest. **¡~!** look out!. **llamar la ~** attract attention, catch the eye; **prestar ~** pay attention

atender 1 vt attend to; (cuidar) look after. ● vi pay attention

atenerse 49 *vpr* abide (**a** by)

atentado *m* (*ataque*) attack; (*afrenta*) affront (**contra** to). ~ **contra la vida de uno** attempt on s.o.'s life

atentamente *adv* attentively; (*con cortesía*) politely; (*con amabilidad*) kindly. **lo saluda** ~ (*en cartas*) yours faithfully

atentar *vi.* ~ **contra** threaten. ~ **contra la vida de uno** make an attempt on s.o.'s life

atento *adj* attentive; (*cortés*) polite; (*amable*) kind

atenua|nte *adj* extenuating. ● *f* extenuating circumstance. ~**r** 21 *vt* attenuate; (*hacer menor*) diminish, lessen

ateo *adj* atheistic. ● *m* atheist

aterciopelado *adj* velvety

aterra|dor *adj* terrifying. ~**r** *vt* terrify

aterriza|je *m* landing. ~**je forzoso** emergency landing. ~**r** 10 *vt* land

aterrorizar 10 *vt* terrify

atesorar *vt* hoard; amass (*fortuna*)

atesta|do *adj* packed, full up. ● *m* sworn statement. ~**r** *vt* fill up, pack; (*Jurid*) testify

atestiguar 15 *vt* testify to; (*fig*) prove

atiborrar *vt* fill, stuff. ~**se** *vpr* stuff o.s.

ático *m* attic

atina|do *adj* right; (*juicioso*) wise, sensible. ~**r** *vt/i* hit upon; (*acertar*) guess right

atizar 10 *vt* poke; (*fig*) stir up

atlántico *adj* Atlantic. **el (océano) A~** the Atlantic (Ocean)

atlas *m* atlas

atl|eta *m & f* athlete. ~**ético** *adj* athletic. ~**etismo** *m* athletics

atmósfera *f* atmosphere

atole *m* (*LAm*) boiled maize drink

atolladero *m* bog; (*fig*) tight corner

atolondra|do *adj* scatterbrained; (*aturdido*) stunned. ~**r** *vt* fluster; (*pasmar*) stun. ~**rse** *vpr* get flustered

at|ómico *adj* atomic. ~**omizador** *m* spray, atomizer

átomo *m* atom

atónito *m* amazed

atonta|do *adj* stunned; (*tonto*) stupid. ~**r** *vt* stun. ~**rse** *vpr* get confused

atorar *vt* (*esp LAm*) to block; (*Mex*, *sujetar*) secure. ~**rse** *vpr* (*esp LAm*, *atragantarse*) choke; (*atascarse*) get blocked; (*puerta*) get jammed

atormentar *vt* torture. ~**se** *vpr* worry, torment o.s.

atornillar *vt* screw on

atosigar 12 *vt* pester

atraca|dor *m* mugger; (*de banco*) bank robber. ~**r** 7 *vt* dock; (*arrimar*) bring alongside; hold up (*banco*); mug (*persona*). ● *vi* (*barco*) dock

atracci|ón *f* attraction. ~**ones** *fpl* entertainment, amusements

atrac|o *m* hold-up, robbery. ~**ón** *m.* **darse un** ~**ón** stuff o.s. (**de** with)

atractivo *adj* attractive. ● *m* attraction; (*encanto*) charm

atraer 41 *vt* attract

atragantarse *vpr* choke (**con** on). **la historia se me atraganta** I can't stand history

atrancar 7 *vt* bolt (*puerta*). ~**se**

a *vpr* get stuck

atrapar *vt* catch; (*encerrar*) trap

atrás *adv* back; (*tiempo*) previously, before. **años** ~ years ago. ~ **de** (*LAm*) behind. **dar un paso** ~ step backwards. **hacia** ~, **para** ~ backwards

atras|ado *adj* behind; (*reloj*) slow; (*con deudas*) in arrears; (*país*) backward. **llegar** ~**ado** (*esp LAm*) arrive late. ~**ar** *vt* put back (*reloj*); (*demorar*) delay, postpone. ● *vi* (*reloj*) be slow. ~**arse** *vpr* be late; (*reloj*) be slow; (*quedarse atrás*) fall behind. ~**o** *m* delay; (*de un reloj*) slowness; (*de un país*) backwardness. ~**os** *mpl* (*Com*) arrears

atravesa|do *adj* lying across. ~**r 1** *vt* cross; (*traspasar*) go through (*poner transversalmente*) lay across. ~**rse** *vpr* lie across; (*en la garganta*) get stuck, stick

atrayente *adj* attractive

atrev|erse *vpr* dare. ~**erse con** tackle. ~**ido** *adj* daring; (*insolente*) insolent. ~**imiento** *m* daring; (*descaro*) insolence

atribu|ción *f* attribution. ~**ciones** *fpl* authority. ~**uir 17** *vt* attribute; confer (*función*). ~**irse** *vpr* claim

atribulado *adj* afflicted

atributo *m* attribute

atril *m* lectern; (*Mus*) music stand

atrocidad *f* atrocity. ¡**qué** ~! how awful!

atrofiarse *vpr* atrophy

atropell|ado *adj* hasty. ~**ar** *vt* knock down; (*por encima*) run over; (*empujar*) push aside; (*fig*) outrage, insult. ~**arse** *vpr* rush. ~**o** *m* (*Auto*) accident; (*fig*) outrage

atroz *adj* appalling; (*fig*) atrocious

atuendo *m* dress, attire

atún *m* tuna (fish)

aturdi|do *adj* bewildered; (*por golpe*) stunned. ~**r** *vt* bewilder; (*golpe*) stun; (*ruido*) deafen

auda|cia *f* boldness, audacity. ~**z** *adj* bold

audi|ble *adj* audible. ~**ción** *f* hearing; (*prueba*) audition.~**encia** *f* audience; (*tribunal*) court; (*sesión*) hearing

auditor *m* auditor. ~**io** *m* audience; (*sala*) auditorium

auge *m* peak; (*Com*) boom

augur|ar *vt* predict; (*cosas*) augur. ~**io** *m* prediction. **con nuestros mejores** ~**ios para** with our best wishes for. **mal** ~ bad omen

aula *f* class-room; (*Univ*) lecture room

aull|ar 23 *vi* howl. ~**ido** *m* howl

aument|ar *vt* increase; magnify (*imagen*). ● *vi* increase. ~**o** *m* increase; (*de sueldo*) rise

aun *adv* even. ~ **así** even so. ~ **cuando** although. **más** ~ even more. **ni** ~ not even

aún *adv* still, yet. ~ **no ha llegado** it still hasn't arrived, it hasn't arrived yet

aunar 23 *vt* join. ~**se** *vpr* join together

aunque *conj* although, (even) though

aúpa *int* up! **de** ~ wonderful

aureola *f* halo

auricular *m* (*de teléfono*) receiver. ~**es** *mpl* headphones

aurora *f* dawn

ausen|cia *f* absence. **en** ~**cia de** in the absence of. ~**tarse** *vpr* leave. ~**te** *adj* absent. ● *m & f* absentee; (*Jurid*) missing person. **∼tismo** *m* (*LAm*) absenteeism

auspici|ador *m* sponsor. **∼ar** *vt* sponsor. **∼o** *m* sponsorship; (*signo*) omen. **bajo los ∼s de** sponsored by

auster|idad *f* austerity. **∼o** *adj* austere

austral *adj* southern

Australia *m* Australia

australiano *adj* & *m* Australian

Austria *f* Austria

austriaco, austríaco *adj* & *m* Austrian

aut|enticar 🔢 authenticate. **∼enticidad** *f* authenticity. **∼éntico** *adj* authentic

auto *m* (*Jurid*) decision; (*orden*) order; (*Auto, fam*) car. **∼s** *mpl* proceedings

auto|abastecimiento *m* self-sufficiency. **∼biografía** *f* autobiography

autobús *m* bus. **en ∼** by bus

autocar *m* (long-distance) bus, coach (*Brit*)

autocontrol *m* self-control

autóctono *adj* indigenous

auto|determinación *f* self-determination. **∼didacta** *adj* self-taught. **●** *m* & *f* self-taught person. **∼escuela** *f* driving school. **∼financiamiento** *m* self-financing

autógrafo *m* autograph

autómata *m* robot

autom|ático *adj* automatic. **●** *m* press-stud. **∼atización** *f* automation

automotor *m* diesel train

autom|óvil *adj* motor. **●** *m* car. **∼ovilismo** *m* motoring. **∼ovilista** *m* & *f* driver, motorist

aut|onomía *f* autonomy. **∼onómico** *adj*, **∼ónomo** *adj* autonomous

autopista *f* motorway (*Brit*), freeway (*Amer*)

autopsia *f* autopsy

autor *m* author. **∼a** *f* author(ess)

autori|dad *f* authority. **∼tario** *adj* authoritarian

autoriza|ción *f* authorization. **∼do** *adj* authorized, official; (opinión etc) authoritative. **∼r** 🔟 *vt* authorize

auto|rretrato *m* self-portrait. **∼servicio** *m* self-service restaurant. **∼stop** *m* hitch-hiking. **hacer ∼stop** hitch-hike

autosuficiente *adj* self-sufficient

autovía *f* dual carriageway

auxili|ar *adj* auxiliary; (profesor) assistant. **●** *m* & *f* assistant. **●** *vt* help. **∼o** *m* help. **¡∼o!** help! **en ∼o de** in aid of. **pedir ∼o** shout for help. **primeros ∼os** first aid

Av. *abrev* (**Avenida**) Ave

aval *m* guarantee

avalancha *f* avalanche

avalar *vt* guarantee

aval|uar *vt* 🔢 (*LAm*) value. **∼úo** *m* valuation

avance *m* advance; (en el cine) trailer. **avances** *mpl* (*Mex*) trailer

avanzar 🔟 *vt* move forward. **∼ la pantalla** scroll up. **●** *vi* advance

avar|icia *f* avarice. **∼icioso** *adj*, **∼iento** *adj* greedy; (*tacaño*) miserly. **∼o** *adj* miserly. **●** *m* miser

avasallar *vt* dominate

Avda. *abrev* (**Avenida**) Ave

ave *f* bird. **∼ de paso** (incl fig) of passage. **∼ de rapiña** bird of prey

AVE - Alta Velocidad Española A high-speed train service linking Madrid, Seville and Huelva via Cadiz, established in 1992 in time for the international exhibition, Expo 92 in Seville. Lines under construction include: Madrid-Barcelona, with an extension to France, and Barcelona-Valencia. An Ave service linking Madrid and Galicia is planned.

avecinarse vpr approach

avejentar vt age

avellana f hazelnut. **~o** m hazel (tree)

avemaría f Hail Mary

avena f oats

avenida f (calle) avenue

avenir 53 vt reconcile. **~se** vpr come to an agreement; (entenderse) get on well (con with)

aventaja|do adj outstanding. **~r** vt be ahead of; (superar) surpass

avent|ar 1 vt fan; winnow (grano etc); (Mex, lanzar) throw; (Mex, empujar) push. **~arse** vpr (Mex) throw o.s.; (atreverse) dare. **~ón** m (Mex) ride, lift (Brit)

aventur|a f adventure. **~a amorosa** love affair. **~ado** adj risky. **~ero** adj adventurous. ● m adventurer

avergonzar 10 & 16 vt shame; (abochornar) embarrass. **~se** vpr be ashamed; (abochornarse) be embarrassed

aver|ía f (Auto) breakdown; (en máquina) failure. **~iado** adj broken down. **~iarse** 20 vpr break down

averigua|ción f inquiry; (Mex, disputa) argument. **~r** 15 vt find out. ● vi (Mex) argue

aversión f aversion (a, hacia,

por to)

avestruz m ostrich

avia|ción f aviation; (Mil) air force. **~dor** m (piloto) pilot

av|ícola adj poultry. **~icultura** f poultry farming

avidez f eagerness, greed

ávido adj eager, greedy

avinagra|do adj sour. **~rse** vpr go sour; (fig) become embittered

avi|ón m aeroplane (Brit), airplane (Amer); (Mex, juego) hopscotch. **~onazo** m (Mex) plane crash

avis|ar vt warn; (informar) notify, inform; call (médico etc). **~o** m warning; (comunicación) notice; (LAm, anuncio, cartel) advertisement; (en televisión) commercial. **estar sobre ~o** be on the alert. **sin previo ~o** without prior warning

avisp|a f wasp. **~ado** adj sharp. **~ero** m wasps' nest; (fig) mess. **~ón** m hornet

avistar vt catch sight of

avivar vt stoke up (fuego); brighten up (color); arouse (interés, pasión); intensify (dolor). **~se** vpr revive; (animarse) cheer up; (LAm, despabilarse) wise up

axila f armpit, axilla

axioma m axiom

ay int (de dolor) ouch!; (de susto) oh!; (de pena) oh dear! **¡~ de ti!** poor you!

aya f governess, child's nurse

ayer adv yesterday. ● m past. **antes de ~** the day before yesterday. **~ por la mañana**, (LAm) **en la mañana** yesterday morning

ayuda f help, aid. **~ de cámara** valet. **~nta** f, **~nte** m assistant; (Mil) adjutant. **~r** vt help

ayun|ar vi fast. **~as** fpl. **estar en**

~as have had nothing to eat or drink; (*fig, fam*) be in the dark. **~o** *m* fasting

ayuntamiento *m* town council, city council; (*edificio*) town hall

azabache *m* jet

azad|a *f* hoe. **~ón** *m* (large) hoe

azafata *f* air hostess

azafate *m* (*LAm*) tray

azafrán *m* saffron

azahar *m* orange blossom; (*del limonero*) lemon blossom

azar *m* chance; (*desgracia*) misfortune. **al ~** at random. **por ~** by chance. **~es** *mpl* ups and downs

azaros|amente *adv* hazardously. **~o** *adj* hazardous, risky; (*vida*) eventful

azorar *vt* embarrass. **~rse** *vpr* be embarrassed

Azores *fpl* **las ~** the Azores

azotador *m* (*Mex*) caterpillar

azot|ar *vt* whip, beat; (*Mex, puerta*) slam. **~e** *m* whip; (*golpe*) smack; (*fig, calamidad*) calamity

azotea *f* flat roof

azteca *adj* & *m* & *f* Aztec

> **Aztecas** A Náhuatl-speaking people who in the fourteenth century established a brilliant and tyrannical civilization in central and southern Mexico. Its capital was Tenochtitlán, built on reclaimed marshland, and which became Mexico City. The Aztec empire collapsed in 1521 after defeat by the Spaniards led by Hernán Cortés.

az|úcar *m* & *f* sugar. **~ucarado** *adj* sweet, sugary. **~ucarar** *vt* sweeten. **~ucarero** *m* sugar bowl

azucena *f* (white) lily

azufre *m* sulphur

azul *adj* & *m* blue. **~ado** *adj* bluish. **~ marino** navy blue

azulejo *m* tile

azuzar 🔟 *vt* urge on, incite

> **Año Nuevo** See ▷**NOCHEVIEJA** *i*

Bb

bab|a *f* spittle. **~ear** *vi* drool, slobber; (*niño*) dribble. **caérsele la ~a a uno** be delighted. **~eo** *m* drooling; (*de un niño*) dribbling. **~ero** *m* bib

babor *m* port. **a ~** to port, on the port side

babosa *f* slug

babosada *f* (*Mex*) drivel

babos|ear *vt* slobber over; (*niño*) dribble over. ● *vi* (*Mex*) day dream. **~o** *adj* slimy; (*LAm, tonto*) silly

babucha *f* slipper

baca *f* luggage rack

bacalao *m* cod

bache *m* pothole; (*fig*) bad patch

bachillerato *m* school-leaving examination

bacteria *f* bacterium

bagaje *m.* **~ cultural** cultural knowledge; (*de un pueblo*) cultural heritage

bahía *f* bay

bail|able *adj* dance. **~aor** *m* Flamenco dancer. **~ar** *vt/i* dance. **ir a ~ar** go dancing. **~arín** *m* dancer.

~arina f dancer; (de ballet) ballerina. **~e** m dance; (actividad) dancing. **~e de etiqueta** ball

baja f drop, fall; (Mil) casualty. **~ por maternidad** maternity leave. **darse de ~** take sick leave. **~da** f slope; (acto de bajar) descent; (camino) way down. **~r** vt lower; (llevar abajo) get down; go down (escalera); bow (la cabeza). ● vi go down; (temperatura, precio) fall. **~rse** vpr pull down (pantalones). **~r(se) de** get out of (coche); get off (autobús, caballo, tren, bicicleta)

bajeza f vile deed

bajío m shallows; (de arena) sandbank; (LAm, terreno bajo) low-lying area

bajo adj low; (de estatura) short, small; (cabeza, ojos) lowered; (humilde) humble, low; (vil) vile; (voz) low; (Mus) deep. ● m lowland; (Mus) bass. ● adv quietly; (volar) low. ● prep under. **~ cero** below zero. **~ la lluvia** in the rain. **los ~s** (LAm) ground floor (Brit), first floor (Amer); **los ~s fondos** the underworld

bajón m sharp drop; (de salud) sudden decline

bala f bullet; (de algodón etc) bale. (LAm, en atletismo) shot. **como una ~** like a shot. **lanzamiento de ~** (LAm) shot put

balada f ballad

balan|ce m balance; (documento) balance sheet; (resultado) outcome. **~cear** vt balance. **~cearse** vpr swing. **~ceo** m swinging. **~cín** m rocking chair; (de niños) seesaw. **~za** f scales; (Com) balance

balar vi bleat

balazo m (disparo) shot; (herida) bullet wound

balboa f (unidad monetaria panameña) balboa

balbuc|ear vt/i stammer; (niño) babble. **~eo** m stammering; (de niño) babbling. **~ir 24** vt/i stammer; (niño) babble

balcón m balcony

balda f shelf

balde m bucket. **de ~** free (of charge). **en ~** in vain

baldío adj (terreno) waste

baldosa f (floor) tile; (losa) flagstone

bale|ar adj Balearic. ● **las (Islas) B~ares** the Balearics, the Balearic Islands. ● vt (LAm) to shoot. **~o** m (LAm, tiroteo) shooting

balero m (Mex) cup and ball toy; (rodamiento) bearing

balido m bleat; (varios sonidos) bleating

balística f ballistics

baliza f (Naut) buoy; (Aviac) beacon

ballena f whale

ballet /ba'le/ (pl ~s) m ballet

balneario m spa; (con playa) seaside resort

balompié m soccer, football (Brit)

bal|ón m ball. **~oncesto** m basketball. **~onmano** m handball. **~onvolea** m volleyball

balotaje m (LAm) voting

balsa f (de agua) pool; (plataforma flotante) raft

bálsamo m balsam; (fig) balm

---

balseros The name given to illegal Cuban immigrants who try to enter a country in small boats or on rafts. It applies particularly to Cubans who try to enter the US by sailing to

Florida and to immigrants attempting to enter Spain by crossing the Straits of Gibraltar.

baluarte m (incl fig) bastion

bambalina f drop curtain. **entre ∼s** behind the scenes

bambole|ar vi sway; (mesa etc) wobble; (barco) rock. **∼o** m swaying; (de mesa etc) wobbling; (de barco) rocking

bambú m (pl ∼es) bamboo

banal adj banal. **∼idad** f banality

banan|a f (esp LAm) banana. **∼ero** adj banana. **∼o** m (LAm) banana tree

banc|a f banking; (conjunto de bancos) banks; (en juegos) bank; (LAm, asiento) bench. **∼ario** adj bank, banking. **∼arrota** f bankruptcy. **hacer ∼arrota, ir a la ∼arrota** go bankrupt. **∼o** m (asiento) bench; (Com) bank; (bajío) sandbank; (de peces) shoal

banda f (incl Mus, Radio) band; (Mex, para el pelo) hair band; (raya ancha) stripe; (cinta ancha) sash; (grupo) gang, group. **∼ sonora** sound-track. **∼da** f (de pájaros) flock; (de peces) shoal

bandeja f tray

bandejón m (Mex) central reservation (Brit), median strip (Amer)

bander|a f flag. **∼illa** f banderilla. **∼ear** vt stick the banderillas in. **∼ero** m banderillero. **∼ín** m pennant, small flag

bandido m bandit

bando m edict, proclamation; (facción) camp, side. **∼s** mpl banns. **pasarse al otro ∼** go over to the other side

bandolero m bandit

bandoneón m large accordion

banjo m banjo

banquero m banker

banquete m banquet; (de boda) wedding reception

banquillo m bench; (Jurid) dock; (taburete) footstool

bañ|ador m (de mujer) swimming costume; (de hombre) swimming trunks. **∼ar** vt bath (niño); (Culin, recubrir) coat. **∼arse** vpr go swimming, have a swim; (en casa) have a bath. **∼era** f bath (tub). **∼ista** m & f bather. **∼o** m bath; (en piscina, mar etc) swim; (cuarto) bathroom; (LAm, wáter) toilet; (bañera) bath(tub); (capa) coat(ing)

baqueano (LAm), **baquiano** m guide

bar m bar

baraja f pack of cards. **∼r** vt shuffle; juggle (cifras etc); consider (posibilidades); (Mex, explicar) explain

baranda, barandilla f rail; (de escalera) banisters

barat|a f (Mex) sale. **∼ija** f trinket. **∼illo** m junk shop; (géneros) cheap goods. **∼o** adj cheap. ● adv cheap(ly)

barba f chin; (pelo) beard

barbacoa f barbecue; (carne) barbecued meat

barbari|dad f atrocity; (fam, mucho) awful lot 🔢. **¡qué ∼dad!** how awful! **∼e** f barbarity; (fig) ignorance. **∼smo** m barbarism

bárbaro adj barbaric, cruel; (bruto) uncouth; (fam, estupendo) terrific 🔢. ● m barbarian. **¡qué ∼!** how marvellous!

barbear vt (Mex, lisonjear) suck up to

barbecho m. **en ∼** fallow

barber|ía f barber's (shop). **∼o** m

barber; (*Mex, adulador*) creep

barbilla *f* chin

barbitúrico *m* barbiturate

barbudo *adj* bearded

barca *f* (small) boat. ~ **de pasaje** ferry. ~**za** *f* barge

barcelonés *adj* of Barcelona, from Barcelona. ● *m* native of Barcelona

barco *m* boat; (*navío*) ship. ~ **cisterna** tanker. ~ **de vapor** steamer. ~ **de vela** sailing boat. **ir en** ~ go by boat

barda *f* (*Mex*) wall; (*de madera*) fence

barítono *adj & m* baritone

barman *m* (*pl* ~**s**) barman

barniz *m* varnish; (*para loza etc*) glaze; (*fig*) veneer. ~**ar** **[10]** *vt* varnish; glaze (*loza etc*)

barómetro *m* barometer

bar|ón *m* baron. ~**onesa** *f* baroness

barquero *m* boatman

barquillo *m* wafer; (*Mex, de helado*) ice-cream cone

barra *f* bar; (*pan*) loaf of French bread; (*palanca*) lever; (*de arena*) sandbank; (*LAm, de hinchas*) supporters. ~ **de labios** lipstick

barrabasada *f* mischief, prank

barraca *f* hut; (*vivienda pobre*) shack, shanty

barranco *m* ravine, gully; (*despeñadero*) cliff, precipice

barrer *vt* sweep; thrash (*rival*)

barrera *f* barrier. ~ **del sonido** sound barrier

barriada *f* district; (*LAm, barrio marginal*) slum

barrial *m* (*LAm*) quagmire

barrida *f* sweep; (*LAm, redada*) police raid

barrig|a *f* belly. ~**ón** *adj*, ~**udo** *adj* pot-bellied

barril *m* barrel

barrio *m* district, area. ~**s bajos** poor quarter, poor area. **el otro** ~ (*fig, fam*) the other world. ~**bajero** *adj* vulgar, common

barro *m* mud; (*arcilla*) clay; (*arcilla cocida*) earthenware

barroco *adj* Baroque. ● *m* Baroque style

barrote *m* bar

bartola *f*. **tirarse a la** ~ take it easy

bártulos *mpl* things. **liar los** ~ pack one's bags

barullo *m* racket; (*confusión*) confusion. **a** ~ galore

basar *vt* base. ~**se** *vpr.* ~**se en** be based on

báscula *f* scales

base *f* base; (*fig*) basis, foundation. **a** ~ **de** thanks to; (*mediante*) by means of; (*en una receta*) mainly consisting of. ~ **de datos** database. **partiendo de la** ~ **de, to-mando como** ~ on the basis of

básico *adj* basic

basílica *f* basilica

básquetbol, basquetbol *m* (*LAm*) basketball

---

bastante

● *adjetivo/pronombre*

····▸ (*suficiente*) enough. **¿hay** ~**s sillas?** are there enough chairs? **ya tengo** ~ I have enough already

····▸ (*mucho*) quite a lot. **vino** ~ **gente** quite a lot of people came. **tiene** ~**s amigos** he has quite a lot of friends **¿te gusta?- sí,** ~ do you like it?

— yes, quite a lot
● **adverbio**
····▸ (*suficientemente*) enough. **no has estudiado** ~ you haven't studied enough. **no es lo** ~ **inteligente** he's not clever enough (**como para** to)
····▸ **bastante** + *adjetivo/adverbio* (*modificando la intensidad*) quite, fairly. **parece** ~ **simpático** he looks quite friendly. **es** ~ **fácil de hacer** it's quite easy to do. **canta** ~ **bien** he sings quite well
····▸ **bastante** *con verbo* (*considerablemente*) quite a lot. **el lugar ha cambiado** ~ the place has changed quite a lot

bastar *vi* be enough. **¡basta!** that's enough! **basta con decir que** suffice it to say that. **basta y sobra** that's more than enough

bastardilla *f* italics

bastardo *adj* & *m* bastard

bastidor *m* frame; (*Auto*) chassis. ~**es** *mpl* (*en el teatro*) wings. **entre** ~**es** behind the scenes

basto *adj* coarse. ~**s** *mpl* (*naipes*) clubs

bast|ón *m* walking stick; (*de esquí*) ski pole. ~**onazo** *m* blow with a stick; (*de mando*) staff of office

basur|a *f* rubbish, garbage (*Amer*); (*en la calle*) litter. ~**al** *m* (*LAm, lugar*) rubbish dump. ~**ero** *m* dustman (*Brit*), garbage collector (*Amer*); (*sitio*) rubbish dump; (*Mex, recipiente*) dustbin (*Brit*), garbage can (*Amer*)

bata *f* dressing-gown; (*de médico etc*) white coat; (*esp LAm, de baño*) bathrobe

batahola *f* (*LAm*) pandemonium

batall|a *f* battle. ~**a campal** pitched battle. **de** ~**a** everyday. ~**ador** *adj* fighting. ● *m* fighter. ~**ar** *vi* battle, fight. ~**ón** *m* battalion.

batata *f* sweet potato

bate *m* bat. ~**ador** *m* batter; (*cricket*) batsman. ~**ar** *vi* bat

batería *f* battery; (*Mus*) drums. ● *m* & *f* drummer. ~ **de cocina** kitchen utensils, pots and pans

baterista *m* & *f* drummer

batido *adj* beaten; (*nata*) whipped. ● *m* batter; (*bebida*) milk shake. ~**ra** *f* (*food*) mixer

batir *vt* beat; break (*récord*); whip (*nata*). ~ **palmas** clap. ~**se** *vpr* fight

batuta *f* baton. **llevar la** ~ be in command, be the boss

baúl *m* trunk

bauti|smal *adj* baptismal. ~**smo** *m* baptism, christening. ~**zar** [10] *vt* baptize, christen. ~**zo** *m* christening

baya *f* berry

bayeta *f* cloth

bayoneta *f* bayonet

baza *f* (*naipes*) trick; (*fig*) advantage. **meter** ~ interfere

bazar *m* bazaar

bazofia *f* revolting food; (*fig*) rubbish

beato *adj* blessed; (*piadoso*) devout; (*pey*) overpious

bebé *m* baby

beb|edero *m* drinking trough; (*sitio*) watering place. ~**edizo** *m* potion; (*veneno*) poison. ~**edor** *m* heavy drinker. ~**er** *vt/i* drink. ~**ida** *f* drink. ~**ido** *adj* drunk

beca *f* grant, scholarship. ~**do** *m* (*LAm*) scholarship holder, scholar.

~r **7** vt give a scholarship to. **~rio** m scholarship holder, scholar

beige /beis, beʒ/ adj & m beige

béisbol m, (Mex) **beisbol** m baseball

belén m crib, nativity scene

belga adj & m & f Belgian

Bélgica f Belgium

bélico adj, **belicoso** adj warlike

bell|eza f beauty. **~o** adj beautiful. **~as artes** fpl fine arts

bellota f acorn

bemol m flat. **tener (muchos) ~es** be difficult

bend|ecir **46** (pero imperativo **bendice**, futuro, condicional y pp regulares) vt bless. **~ición** f blessing. **~ito** adj blessed; (que tiene suerte) lucky; (feliz) happy

benefactor m benefactor

benefic|encia f charity. **de ~encia** charitable. **~iar** vt benefit. **~iarse** vpr benefit. **~iario** m beneficiary; (de un cheque etc) payee. **~io** m benefit; (ventaja) advantage; (ganancia) profit, gain. **~ioso** adj beneficial

benéfico adj beneficial; (de beneficencia) charitable

ben|evolencia f benevolence. **~évolo** adj benevolent

bengala f flare. **luz** f **de ~** flare

benigno adj kind; (moderado) gentle, mild; (tumor) benign

berberecho m cockle

berenjena f aubergine (Brit), eggplant (Amer)

berr|ear vi (animales) bellow; (niño) bawl. **~ido** m bellow; (de niño) bawling

berrinche m temper; (de un niño) tantrum

berro m watercress

besamel(a) f white sauce

bes|ar vt kiss. **~arse** vpr kiss (each other). **~o** m kiss

bestia f beast; (bruto) brute; (idiota) idiot. **~ de carga** beast of burden. **~l** adj bestial, animal; (fig, fam) terrific. **~lidad** f (acción brutal) horrid thing; (insensatez) stupidity

besugo m red bream

besuquear vt cover with kisses

betabel f (Mex) beetroot

betún m (para el calzado) shoe polish

biberón m feeding-bottle

Biblia f Bible

bibliografía f bibliography

bibliotec|a f library; (mueble) bookcase. **~ de consulta** reference library. **~rio** m librarian

bicarbonato m bicarbonate

bicho m insect, bug; (animal) small animal, creature. **~ raro** odd sort

bici f **1** bike. **~cleta** f bicycle. **ir en ~cleta** cycle. **~moto** (LAm) moped

bidé, bidet /biˈðei/ m bidet

bidón m drum, can

bien adv well; (muy) very, quite; (correctamente) right; (de buena gana) willingly. ● m good; (efectos) property. **¡~!** fine!, OK!, good! **~... (o)** either... or. **¡está ~!** fine!, alright!; (basta) that is enough!. **más ~** rather. **¡muy ~!** good! **no ~** as soon as. **¡qué ~!** marvellous!, great! **1. si ~** although

bienal adj biennial

bien|aventurado adj fortunate. **~estar** m well-being. **~hablado** adj well-spoken. **~hechor** m benefactor. **~intencionado** adj wellmeaning

bienio m two year-period

bienvenid|a f welcome. **dar la ~a a uno** welcome s.o. **~o** adj welcome. **¡~o!** welcome!

bifurca|ción f junction. **~rse** 7 vpr fork; (rail) branch off

b|igamia f bigamy. **~ígamo** adj bigamous. ● m bigamist

bigot|e m moustache. **~ón** (Mex), **~udo** adj with a big moustache

bikini m bikini

bilingüe adj bilingual

billar m billiards

billete m ticket; (de banco) (bank) note (Brit), bill (Amer). **~ de ida y vuelta** return ticket (Brit), round-trip ticket (Amer). **~ sencillo** single ticket (Brit), one-way ticket (Amer). **~ra** f, **~ro** m wallet, billfold (Amer)

billón m billion (Brit), trillion (Amer)

bi|mensual adj fortnightly, twice-monthly. **~mestral** adj two-monthly. **~mestre** two-month period. **~motor** adj twin-engined. ● m twin-engined plane

binoculares mpl binoculars

bi|ografía f biography. **~ográfico** adj biographical

bi|ología f biology. **~ológico** adj biological. **~ólogo** m biologist

biombo m folding screen

biopsia f biopsy

bioterrorismo m bioterrorism

biplaza m two-seater

biquini m bikini

birlar vt 1 steal, pinch 1

bis m encore. **¡~!** encore! **vivo en el 3 ~** I live at 3A

bisabuel|a f great-grandmother. **~o** m great-grandfather. **~os** mpl great-grandparents

bisagra f hinge

bisiesto adj. **año m ~** leap year

bisniet|a f great-granddaughter. **~o** m great-grandson. **~os** mpl great-grandchildren

bisonte m bison

bisoño adj inexperienced

bisté, bistec m steak

bisturí m scalpel

bisutería f imitation jewellery, costume jewellery

bitácora f binnacle

bizco adj cross-eyed

bizcocho m sponge (cake)

bizquear vi squint

blanc|a f white woman; (Mus) minim. **~o** adj white; (tez) fair. ● m white; (persona) white man; (espacio) blank; (objetivo) target. **dar en el ~o** hit the mark. **dejar en ~o** leave blank. **pasar la noche en ~o** have a sleepless night. **~ura** f whiteness

blandir 24 vt brandish

bland|o adj soft; (carácter) weak; (cobarde) cowardly; (carne) tender. **~ura** f softness; (de la carne) tenderness

blanque|ar vt whiten; whitewash (paredes); bleach (tela); launder (dinero). ● vi turn white. **~o** m whitening; (de dinero) laundering

blasón m coat of arms

bledo m. **no me importa un ~** I couldn't care less

blinda|je m armour (plating). **~r** vt armour(-plate)

bloc m (pl **~s**) pad

bloque m block; (Pol) bloc. **en ~** en bloc. **~ar** vt block; (Mil) blockade; (Com) freeze. **~o** m blockade; (Com) freezing

blusa f blouse

bob|ada f silly thing. **decir ~adas** talk nonsense. **~ería** f silly thing

bobina f reel; (*Elec*) coil

bobo adj silly, stupid. ● m idiot, fool

boca f mouth; (fig, entrada) entrance; (de buzón) slot; (de cañón) muzzle. **~ abajo** face down. **~ arriba** face up

bocacalle f junction. **la primera ~ a la derecha** the first turning on the right

bocad|illo m (filled) roll; (fam, comida ligera) snack. **~o** m mouthful; (mordisco) bite; (de caballo) bit

boca|jarro. a ~jarro point-blank. **~manga** f cuff

bocanada f puff; (de vino etc) mouthful; (ráfaga) gust

bocata f sandwich

bocatería f sandwich bar

bocaza m & f invar big-mouth

boceto m sketch; (de proyecto) outline

bochinche m row; (alboroto) racket. **~ro** adj (LAm) rowdy

bochorno m sultry weather; (fig, vergüenza) embarrassment. **¡qué ~!** how embarrassing!. **~so** adj oppressive; (fig) embarrassing

bocina f horn; (Mex, auricular) receiver. **tocar la ~** (LAm) sound one's horn. **~zo** m toot

boda f wedding

bodega f cellar; (de vino) wine cellar; (LAm, almacén) warehouse; (de un barco) hold. **~ón** m cheap restaurant; (pintura) still life

bodoque m & f (fam, tonto) thickhead; (Mex, niño) kid

bofes mpl lights. **echar los ~** slog away

bofet|ada f slap; (fig) blow. **~ón** m punch

boga f (moda) fashion. **estar en ~** be in fashion, be in vogue. **~r** 12 vt row. **~vante** m (crustáceo) lobster

Bogotá f Bogotá

bogotano adj from Bogotá. ● m native of Bogotá

bohemio adj & m Bohemian

bohío m (LAm) hut

boicot m (pl ~s) boycott. **~ear** vt boycott. **~eo** m boycott. **hacer un ~** boycott

boina f beret

bola f ball; (canica) marble; (mentira) fib; (Mex, reunión desordenada) rowdy party; (Mex, montón). **una ~ de** a bunch of; (Mex, revolución) revolution; (Mex, brillo) shine

boleadoras (LAm) fpl bolas

bolear vt (Mex) polish, shine

bolera f bowling alley

bolero m (baile, chaquetilla) bolero; (fig, fam, mentiroso) liar; (Mex, limpiabotas) bootblack

bole|ta f (LAm, de rifa) ticket; (Mex, de notas) (school) report; (Mex, electoral) ballot paper. **~taje** m (Mex) tickets. **~tería** f (LAm) ticket office; (de teatro, cine) box office. **~tero** m (LAm) ticket-seller

boletín m bulletin; (publicación periódica) journal; (de notas) report

boleto m (esp LAm) ticket; (Mex, de avión) (air) ticket. **~ de ida y vuelta**, (Mex) **~ redondo** return ticket (Brit), round-trip ticket (Amer). **~ sencillo** single ticket (Brit), one-way ticket (Amer)

boli m 1 Biro (P), ball-point pen

boliche m (juego) bowls; (bolera) bowling alley

bolígrafo m Biro (P), ball-point pen

bolillo m bobbin; (Mex, pan) roll (bread) roll

bolívar m (unidad monetaria venezolana) bolívar

Bolivia f Bolivia

boliviano adj Bolivian. ● m Bolivian; (unidad monetaria de Bolivia) boliviano

boll|ería f baker's shop. ~o m roll; (con azúcar) bun

bolo m skittle; (Mex, en bautizo) coins. ~s mpl (juego) bowling

bols|a f bag; (Mex, bolsillo) pocket; (Mex, de mujer) handbag; (Com) stock exchange; (cavidad) cavity. ~a de agua caliente hot-water bottle. ~illo m pocket. de ~illo pocket. ~o m (de mujer) handbag. ~o de mano, ~o de viaje (overnight) bag

bomba f bomb; (máquina) pump; (noticia) bombshell. ~ de aceite (Auto) oil pump. ~ de agua (Auto) water pump. pasarlo ~ have a marvellous time

bombachos mpl baggy trousers, baggy pants (Amer)

bombarde|ar vt bombard; (desde avión) bomb. ~o m bombardment; (desde avión) bombing. ~ro m (avión) bomber

bombazo m explosion

bombear vt pump

bombero m fireman. cuerpo m de ~s fire brigade (Brit), fire department (Amer)

bombilla f (light) bulb; (LAm, para mate) pipe for drinking maté

bombín m pump; (fam, sombrero) bowler (hat) (Brit), derby (Amer)

bombo m (tambor) bass drum. a ~ y platillos with a lot of fuss

bomb|ón m chocolate; (Mex, malvavisco) marshmallow. ~ona f gas

cylinder

bonachón adj easygoing; (bueno) good-natured

bonaerense adj from Buenos Aires. ● m native of Buenos Aires

bondad f goodness; (amabilidad) kindness; (del clima) mildness. tenga la ~ de would you be kind enough to. ~oso adj kind

boniato m sweet potato

bonito adj nice; (mono) pretty. ¡muy ~!, ¡qué ~! that's nice!, very nice!. ● m bonito

bono m voucher; (título) bond. ~ del Tesoro government bond

boñiga f dung

boquea|da f gasp. dar la última ~ be dying

boquerón m anchovy

boquete m hole; (brecha) breach

boquiabierto adj openmouthed; (fig) amazed, dumbfounded. quedarse ~ be amazed

boquilla f mouthpiece; (para cigarrillos) cigarette-holder; (filtro de cigarrillo) tip

borbotón m. hablar a borbotones gabble. salir a borbotones gush out

borda|do adj embroidered. ● m embroidery. ~r vt embroider

borde m edge; (de carretera) side; (de plato etc) rim; (de un vestido) hem. al ~e de on the edge of; (fig) on the brink of. ● adj (Esp fam) stroppy. ~ear vt go round; (fig) border on. ~illo m kerb (Brit), curb (esp Amer)

bordo. a ~ on board

borla f tassel

borrach|era f drunkenness. pegarse una ~era get drunk. ~ín m drunk; (habitual) drunkard. ~o adj drunk. ● m drunkard. estar ~o be drunk. **ser ~o** be a drunkard

borrador m rough draft; (de contrato) draft; (para la pizarra) (black)board rubber; (goma) eraser

borrar vt rub out; (tachar) cross out; delete (información)

borrasc|a f depression; (tormenta) storm. **~oso** adj stormy

borrego m year-old lamb; (Mex, noticia falsa) canard

borrico m donkey; (fig, fam) ass

borrón m smudge; (de tinta) inkblot. **~ y cuenta nueva** let's forget about it!

borroso adj blurred; (fig) vague

bos|coso adj wooded. **~que** m wood, forest

bosquejar vt sketch; outline (plan). **~o** m sketch; (de plan) outline

bosta f dung

bostez|ar 10 vi yawn. **~o** m yawn

bota f boot; (recipiente) wineskin

botana f (Mex) snack, appetizer

botánic|a f botany. **~o** adj botanical. ● m botanist

botar vt launch; bounce (pelota); (esp LAm, tirar) throw away. ● vi bounce

botarate m irresponsible person; (esp LAm, derrochador) spendthrift

bote m boat; (de una pelota) bounce; (lata) tin, can; (vasija) jar. **~ de la basura** (Mex) rubbish bin (Brit), trash can (Amer). **~ salvavidas** lifeboat. **de ~ en ~** packed

botella f bottle

botica f chemist's (shop) (Brit), drugstore (Amer). **~rio** m chemist (Brit), druggist (Amer)

botijo m earthenware jug

botín m half boot; (de guerra) booty; (de ladrones) haul

botiquín m medicine chest; (de primeros auxilios) first aid kit

bot|ón m button; (yema) bud; (LAm, insignia) badge. **~ones** m invar bellboy (Brit), bellhop (Amer)

bóveda f vault

boxe|ador m boxer. **~ar** vi box. **~o** m boxing

boya f buoy; (corcho) float. **~nte** adj buoyant

bozal m (de perro etc) muzzle; (de caballo) halter

bracear vi wave one's arms; (nadar) swim, crawl

bracero m seasonal farm labourer

braga(s) f(pl) panties, knickers (Brit)

bragueta f flies

bram|ar vi bellow. **~ido** m bellowing

branquia f gill

bras|a f ember. **a la ~a** grilled. **~ero** m brazier

brasier m (Mex) bra

Brasil m. (el) ~ Brazil

brasile|ño adj & m Brazilian. **~ro** adj & m (LAm) Brazilian

bravío adj wild

brav|o adj fierce; (valeroso) brave; (mar) rough. **¡~!** int well done! bravo! **~ura** f ferocity; (valor) bravery

braz|a f fathom. **nadar a ~a** swim breast-stroke. **~ada** f (en natación) stroke. **~alete** m bracelet; (brazal) arm-band. **~o** m arm; (de caballo) foreleg; (rama) branch. **~o derecho** right-hand man. **del ~o** arm in arm

brea f tar, pitch

brebaje m potion; (pej) concoction

brecha f opening; (Mil) breach; (Med) gash. **~ generacional** generation gap. **estar en la ~** be in the thick of it

brega f struggle. **andar a la ~** work hard

breva f early fig

breve adj short. **en ~** soon, shortly. **en ~s momentos** soon. **~dad** f shortness

brib|ón m rogue, rascal. **~onada** f dirty trick

brida f bridle

brigad|a f squad; (Mil) brigade. **~ier** m brigadier (Brit), brigadier-general (Amer)

brill|ante adj bright; (lustroso) shiny; (persona) brilliant. ● m diamond. **~ar** vi shine; (centellear) sparkle. **~o** m shine; (brillantez) brilliance; (centelleo) sparkle. **sacar ~o** polish. **~oso** adj (LAm) shiny

brinc|ar **7** vi jump up and down. **~o** m jump. **dar un ~o, pegar un ~o** jump

brind|ar vt offer. ● vi. **~ por** toast, drink a toast to. **~is** m toast

br|ío m energy; (decisión) determination. **~ioso** adj spirited; (garboso) elegant

brisa f breeze

británico adj British. ● m Briton, British person

brocha f paintbrush; (para afeitarse) shaving-brush

broche m clasp, fastener; (joya) brooch; (Mex, para el pelo) hairslide (Brit), barrete (Amer)

brocheta f skewer; (plato) kebab

brócoli m broccoli

brom|a f joke. **~a pesada** practical joke. **en ~a** in fun. **ni de ~a** no way. **~ear** vi joke. **~ista** adj

fond of joking. ● m & f joker

bronca f row; (reprensión) telling-off; (LAm, rabia) foul mood. **dar ~ a uno** bug s.o.

bronce m bronze; (LAm) brass. **~ado** adj bronze; (por el sol) tanned. **~ar** vt tan (piel). **~arse** vpr get a suntan

bronquitis f bronchitis

brot|ar vi (plantas) sprout; (Med) break out; (líquido) gush forth; (lágrimas) well up. **~e** m shoot; (Med) outbreak

bruces: de ~ face down(wards). **caer de ~** fall flat on one's face

bruj|a f witch. **~ería** f witchcraft. **~o** m wizard, magician. ● adj (Mex) broke

brújula f compass

brum|a f mist; (fig) confusion. **~oso** adj misty, foggy

brusco adj (repentino) sudden; (persona) brusque

Bruselas f Brussels

brusquedad f roughness; (de movimiento) abruptness

brut|al adj brutal. **~alidad** f brutality; (estupidez) stupidity. **~o** adj ignorant; (tosco) rough; (peso, sueldo) gross

bucal adj oral; (lesión) mouth

buce|ar vi dive; (nadar) swim under water. **~o** m diving; (natación) underwater swimming

bucle m ringlet

budín m pudding

budi|smo m Buddhism. **~ta** m & f Buddhist

buen véase **BUENO**

buenaventura f good luck; (adivinación) fortune

bueno adj (delante de nombre masculino en singular **buen**) good; (agradable) nice; (tiempo) fine. ● *int* well!; (de acuerdo) OK!, very well! **¡buena la has hecho!** you've gone and done it now! **¡buenas noches!** good night! **¡buenas tardes!** (antes del atardecer) good afternoon!; (después del atardecer) good evening! **¡~s días!** good morning! **estar de buenas** be in a good mood. **por las buenas** willingly. **¡qué bueno!** (LAm) great!

Buenos Aires *m* Buenos Aires

buey *m* ox

búfalo *m* buffalo

bufanda *f* scarf

bufar *vi* snort

bufete *m* (mesa) writing-desk; (despacho) lawyer's office

buf|o *adj* comic. **~ón** *adj* comical. ● *m* buffoon; (Historia) jester

buhardilla *f* attic; (ventana) dormer window

búho *m* owl

buhonero *m* pedlar

buitre *m* vulture

bujía *f* (Auto) spark plug

bulbo *m* bulb

bulevar *m* avenue, boulevard

Bulgaria *f* Bulgaria

búlgaro *adj & m* Bulgarian

bull|a *f* noise. **~icio** *m* hubbub; (movimiento) bustle. **~icioso** *adj* bustling; (ruidoso) noisy

bullir **22** *vi* boil; (burbujear) bubble; (fig) bustle

bulto *m* (volumen) bulk; (forma) shape; (paquete) package; (maleta etc) piece of luggage; (protuberancia) lump

buñuelo *m* fritter

BUP *abrev* (**Bachillerato Unificado**

Polivalente) secondary school education

buque *m* ship, boat

burbuj|a *f* bubble. **~ear** *vi* bubble; (vino) sparkle

burdel *m* brothel

burdo *adj* rough, coarse; (excusa) clumsy

burgu|és *adj* middle-class, bourgeois. ● *m* middle-class person. **~esía** *f* middle class, bourgeoisie

burla *f* taunt; (broma) joke; (engaño) trick. **~r** *vt* evade. **~rse** *vpr*. **~rse de** mock, make fun of

burlesco *adj* (en literatura) burlesque

burlón *adj* mocking

bur|ocracia *f* bureaucracy; (Mex, funcionariado) civil service. **~ócrata** *m & f* bureaucrat; (Mex, funcionario) civil servant. **~ocrático** *adj* bureaucratic; (Mex) (empleado) government

burro *adj* stupid; (obstinado) pig-headed. ● *m* donkey; (fig) ass

bursátil *adj* stock-exchange

bus *m* bus

busca *f* search. **a la ~ de** in search of. ● *m* beeper

buscador *m* search engine

buscapleitos *m & f invar* (LAm) trouble-maker

buscar **7** *vt* look for. ● *vi* look. **buscársela** ask for it; **ir a ~ a uno** fetch s.o.

búsqueda *f* search

busto *m* bust

butaca *f* armchair; (en el teatro etc) seat

buzo *m* diver

buzón *m* postbox (Brit), mailbox (Amer)

Cc

C/ abrev (**Calle**) St, Rd
cabal adj exact; (completo) complete. **no estar en sus ~es** not be in one's right mind
cabalga|dura f mount, horse. **~r** 12 vt ride. ● vi ride, go riding. **~ta** f ride; (desfile) procession
caballa f mackerel
caballerango m (Mex) groom
caballeresco adj gentlemanly. **literatura** f caballeresca books of chivalry
caballer|ía f mount, horse. **~iza** f stable. **~izo** m groom
caballero m gentleman; (de orden de caballería) knight; (tratamiento) sir. **~so** adj gentlemanly
caballete m (del tejado) ridge; (para mesa) trestle; (de pintor) easel
caballito m pony. **~ del diablo** dragonfly. **~ de mar** sea-horse. **~s** mpl (carrusel) merry-go-round
caballo m horse; (del ajedrez) knight; (de la baraja española) queen. **~ de fuerza** horsepower. **a ~** on horseback
cabaña f hut
cabaret /kaba're/ m (pl **~s**) night-club
cabecear vi nod off; (en fútbol) head the ball; (caballo) toss its head
cabecera f (de la cama) headboard; (de la mesa) head; (en un impreso) heading
cabecilla m ringleader
cabello m hair. **~s** mpl hair

caber 28 vi fit (en into). **no cabe duda** there's no doubt
cabestr|illo m sling. **~o** m halter
cabeza f head; (fig, inteligencia) intelligence. **andar de ~** have a lot to do. **~da** f nod. **dar una ~da** nod off. **~zo** m butt; (en fútbol) header
cabida f capacity; (extensión) area; (espacio) room. **dar ~ a** have room for, accommodate
cabina f (de pasajeros) cabin; (de pilotos) cockpit; (electoral) booth; (de camión) cab. **~ telefónica** telephone box (Brit), telephone booth (Amer)
cabizbajo adj crestfallen
cable m cable
cabo m end; (trozo) bit; (Mil) corporal; (mango) handle; (en geografía) cape; (Naut) rope. **al ~ de** after. **de ~ a rabo** from beginning to end. **llevar a ~** carry out
cabr|a f goat. **~iola** f jump, skip. **~itilla** f kid. **~ito** m kid
cábula f (Mex) crook
cacahuate m, (Mex) **cacahuete** m peanut
cacalote m (Mex) crow
cacao m (planta y semillas) cacao; (polvo) cocoa; (fig) confusion
cacarear vt boast about. ● vi (gallo) crow; (gallina) cluck
cacería f hunt. **ir de ~** go hunting
cacerola f saucepan, casserole
cacharro m (earthenware) pot; (coche estropeado) wreck; (cosa inútil) piece of junk; (chisme) thing. **~s** mpl pots and pans
cachear vt frisk
cachemir m, **cachemira** f cashmere

cacheo m frisking

cachetada f (LAm) slap

cache|te m slap; (esp LAm, mejilla) cheek. **~tear** vt (LAm) slap. **~tón** adj (LAm) chubby-cheeked

cachimba f pipe

cachiporra f club, truncheon

cachivache m piece of junk. **~s** mpl junk

cacho m bit, piece; (LAm, cuerno) horn

cachondeo m ① joking, joke

cachorro m (perrito) puppy; (de león, tigre) cub

cachucha f (Mex) cup

caciqu|e m cacique, chief; (Pol) local political boss; (hombre poderoso) tyrant. **~il** adj despotic. **~ismo** m despotism

caco m thief

cacofonía f cacophony

cacto m, **cactus** m invar cactus

cada adj invar each, every. **~ uno** each one, everyone. **uno de ~ cinco** one in five. **~ vez más** more and more

cadáver m corpse

cadena f chain; (TV) channel. **~ de fabricación** production line. **~ de montañas** mountain range. **~ perpetua** life imprisonment

cadera f hip

cadete m cadet

caduc|ar ⁷ vi expire. **~idad** f. **fecha** f **de ~idad** sell-by date. **~o** adj outdated

cae|r ²⁹ vi fall. **dejar ~** drop. **este vestido no me ~ bien** this dress doesn't suit me. **hacer ~r** knock over. **Juan me ~ bien** I like Juan. **su cumpleaños cayó en martes** his birthday fell on a Tuesday. **~rse** vpr fall (over). **se le**

cayó he dropped it

café m coffee; (cafetería) café; (Mex, marrón) brown. ● adj. **color ~** coffee-coloured. **~ con leche** white coffee. **~ cortado** coffee with a little milk. **~ negro** (LAm) expresso. **~ solo** black coffee

cafe|ína f caffeine. **~tal** m coffee plantation. **~tera** f coffee-pot. **~tería** f café. **~tero** adj coffee

caíd|a f fall; (disminución) drop; (pendiente) slope. **~o** adj fallen

---

> **cafetería** In Spain, a place *i*
> to have a coffee or other
> drinks, pastries and cakes.
> *Cafeterías* are frequently com-
> bined with *bares* and are very
> similar. However, *cafeterías* are
> usually smarter, and serve a
> wider variety of dishes.

---

caigo vb véase CAER

caimán m cayman, alligator

caj|a f box; (de botellas) case; (ataúd) coffin; (en tienda) cash desk; (en supermercado) check-out; (en banco) cashier's desk. **~a de ahorros** savings bank. **~a de cambios** gearbox. **~a de caudales**, **~a fuerte** safe. **~a negra** black box. **~a registradora** till. **~ero** m cashier. **~ero automático** cash dispenser. **~etilla** f packet. **~ita** f small box. **~ón** m (de mueble) drawer; (caja grande) crate; (LAm, ataúd) coffin; (Mex, en estacionamiento) parking space. **ser de ~ón** be obvious. **~uela** f (Mex) boot (Brit), trunk (Amer)

cal m lime

cala f cove

calaba|cín m, **~cita** f (Mex) courgette (Brit), zucchini (Amer). **~za** f pumpkin; (fig, fam, idiota) idiot.

dar ~zas a uno give s.o. the brush-off

calabozo m prison; (*celda*) cell

calado adj soaked. **estar ~ hasta los huesos** be soaked to the skin. ● m (*Naut*) draught

calamar m squid

calambre m cramp

calami|dad f calamity, disaster. **~toso** adj calamitous

calaña f sort

calar vt soak; (*penetrar*) pierce; (*fig, penetrar*) see through; rumble (*persona*); sample (*fruta*). **~se** vpr get soaked; (*zapatos*) leak; (*Auto*) stall

calavera f skull; (*Mex, Auto*) tail light

calcar 🔢 vt trace; (*fig*) copy

calcet|a f. **hacer ~** knit. **~ín** m sock

calcetín m sock

calcinar vt burn

calcio m calcium

calcomanía f transfer

calcula|dor adj calculating. **~dora** f calculator. **~r** vt calculate; (*suponer*) reckon, think; (*imaginar*) imagine

cálculo m calculation; (*Med*) stone

caldear vt heat, warm. **~se** vpr get hot

caldera f boiler

calderilla f small change

caldo m stock; (*sopa*) clear soup, broth

calefacción f heating. **~ central** central heating

caleidoscopio m kaleidoscope

calendario m calendar; (*programa*) schedule

calent|ador m heater. **~amiento** m warming; (*en depor-*

tes) warm-up. **~ar** 🔢 vt heat; (*templar*) warm. **~arse** vpr get hot; (*templarse*) warm up; (*LAm, enojarse*) get mad. **~ura** f fever, (high) temperature. **~uriento** adj feverish

calibr|ar vt calibrate; (*fig*) weigh up. **~e** m calibre; (*diámetro*) diameter; (*fig*) importance

calidad f quality; (*condición*) capacity. **en ~ de** as

calidez f (*LAm*) warmth

cálido adj warm

caliente adj hot; (*habitación, ropa*) warm; (*LAm, enojado*) angry

califica|ción f qualification; (*evaluación*) assessment; (*nota*) mark. **~do** adj (*esp LAm*) qualified; (*mano de obra*) skilled. **~r** 🔢 vt qualify; (*evaluar*) assess; mark (*examen* etc). **~r de** describe as, label

cáliz m chalice; (*en botánica*) calyx

caliz|a f limestone. **~o** adj lime

calla|do adj quiet. **~r** vt silence; keep (*secreto*); hush up (*asunto*). ● vi be quiet, keep quiet, shut up 🔢. **~rse** vpr be quiet, keep quiet, shut up 🔢 **¡cállate!** be quiet!, shut up! 🔢

calle f street, road; (*en deportes, autopista*) lane. **~ de dirección única** one-way street. **~ mayor** high street, main street. **de ~** everyday. **~ja** f narrow street. **~jear** vi hang out on the streets. **~jero** adj street. ● m street plan. **~jón** m alley. **~jón sin salida** dead end. **~juela** f back street, side street

call|ista m & f chiropodist. **~o** m corn, callus. **~os** mpl tripe. **~osidad** f callus

calma f calm. **¡~a!** calm down!. **en ~a** calm. **perder la ~a** lose

calor | camisa

50

one's composure. **~ante** m tranquilizer; (*para el dolor*) painkiller. **~ar** vt calm; (*aliviar*) soothe. ● vi (viento) abate. **~arse** vpr calm down; (viento) abate. **~o** adj calm. **~oso** adj calm; (*fam, flemático*) slow

calor m heat; (*afecto*) warmth. **hace ~** it's hot. **tener ~** be hot. **~ía** f calorie. **~ífero** adj heat-producing. **~ífico** adj calorific

calumni|a f calumny; (*oral*) slander; (*escrita*) libel. **~ar** vt slander; (*por escrito*) libel. **~oso** adj slanderous; (*cosa escrita*) libellous

caluroso adj warm; (*clima*) hot

calv|a f bald head; (*parte sin pelo*) bald patch. **~icie** f baldness. **~o** adj bald

calza f wedge

calzada f road; (*en autopista*) carriageway

calza|do adj wearing shoes. ● m footwear, shoe. **~dor** m shoehorn. **~r 10** vt put shoes on; (*llevar*) wear. **¿qué número calza Vd?** what size shoe do you take? ● vi wear shoes. **~rse** vpr put on

calz|ón m shorts. **~ones** mpl shorts; (*LAm, ropa interior*) panties. **~oncillos** mpl underpants

cama f bed. **~ de matrimonio** double bed. **~ individual** single bed. **guardar ~** stay in bed

camada f litter

camafeo m cameo

camaleón m chameleon

cámara f (*aposento*) chamber; (*fotográfica*) camera. **~ fotográfica** camera. **a ~ lenta** in slow motion

camarad|a m & f colleague; (*de colegio*) schoolfriend; (*Pol*) comrade. **~ería** f camaraderie

camarer|a f chambermaid; (*de*

restaurante etc) waitress. **~o** m waiter

camarógrafo m cameraman

camarón m shrimp

camarote m cabin

cambi|able adj changeable; (*Com* etc) exchangeable. **~ante** adj variable; (persona) moody. **~ar** vt change; (*trocar*) exchange. ● vi change. **~ar de idea** change one's mind. **~arse** vpr change. **~o** m change; (*Com*) exchange rate; (*moneda menuda*) (small) change; (*Auto*) gear. **en ~o** on the other hand

camello m camel

camellón m (*Mex*) traffic island

camerino m dressing room

camilla f stretcher

camin|ante m traveller. **~ar** vt/i walk. **~ata** f long walk. **~o** m road; (sendero) path, track; (*dirección, ruta*) way. **~o de** towards, on the way to. **abrir ~o** make way. **a medio ~o, a la mitad del ~o** half-way. **de ~o** on the way

cami|ón m truck, lorry; (Mex, autobús) bus. **~onero** m lorry-driver; (*Mex, de autobús*) bus driver. **~oneta** f van; (*LAm, coche familiar*) estate car

> ### Camino de Santiago A
> pilgrimage route since the Middle Ages across north-western Spain to Santiago de Compostela in Galicia. The city was founded at a place where a shepherd is said to have discovered the tomb of St James the Apostle, and its cathedral reputedly houses the saint's relics.

camis|a f shirt. **~a de fuerza** strait-jacket. **~ería** f shirtmaker's.

~eta f T-shirt; (*ropa interior*) vest. **~ón** m nightdress

camorra f ⚄ row. **buscar ~** look for a fight

camote m (*LAm*) sweet potato

campamento m camp. **de ~** adj camping

campana f bell. **~ada** f stroke. **~ario** m bell tower, belfry. **~illa** f bell

campaña f campaign

campe|ón adj & m champion. **~onato** m championship

campes|ino adj country. ● m peasant. **~tre** adj country

camping /'kampin/ m (*pl* **~s**) camping; (*lugar*) campsite. **hacer ~** go camping

camp|iña f countryside. **~o** m country; (*agricultura, fig*) field; (*de fútbol*) pitch; (*de golf*) course. **~osanto** m cemetery

camufla|je m camouflage. **~r** vt camouflage

cana f grey hair, white hair. **peinar ~s** be getting old

Canadá m. **el ~** Canada

canadiense adj & m & f Canadian

canal m (*incl TV*) channel; (*artificial*) canal; (*del tejado*) gutter. **~ de la Mancha** English Channel. **~ de Panamá** Panama Canal. **~ón** m (*horizontal*) gutter; (*vertical*) drainpipe

canalla f rabble. ● m (*fig, fam*) swine. **~da** f dirty trick

canapé m sofa, couch; (*Culin*) canapé

Canarias fpl. **las (islas) ~** the Canary Islands, the Canaries

canario adj of the Canary Islands. ● m native of the Canary Islands; (*pájaro*) canary

canast|a f (*large*) basket **~illa** f small basket; (*para un bebé*) layette. **~illo** m small basket. **~o** m (*large*) basket

cancela|ción f cancellation. **~r** vt cancel; write off (deuda)

cáncer m cancer. **C~** Cancer

cancha f court; (*LAm, de fútbol, rugby*) pitch, ground

canciller m chancellor; (*LAm, ministro*) Minister of Foreign Affairs

canci|ón f song. **~ón de cuna** lullaby. **~onero** m song-book

candado m padlock

candel|a f candle. **~abro** m candelabra. **~ero** m candlestick

candente adj (*rojo*) red-hot; (*fig*) burning

candidato m candidate

candidez f innocence; (*ingenuidad*) naivety

cándido adj naive

candil m oil lamp. **~ejas** fpl footlights

candor m innocence; (*ingenuidad*) naivety

canela f cinnamon

cangrejo m crab. **~ de río** crayfish

canguro m kangaroo. ● m & f (*persona*) baby-sitter

caníbal adj & m & f cannibal

canica f marble

canijo adj weak; (*Mex, terco*) stubborn; (*Mex, intenso*) incredible

canilla f (*LAm*) shinbone

canino adj canine. ● m canine (tooth)

canje m exchange. **~ar** vt exchange

cano adj grey. **de pelo ~** greyhaired

canoa f canoe

52

can|ónigo m canon. **~onizar** 🔟 vt canonize

canoso adj grey-haired

cansa|do adj tired; (que cansa) tiring. **~dor** (LAm) tiring. **~ncio** m tiredness. **~r** vt tire; (aburrir) bore. ● vi be tiring; (aburrir) get boring. **~rse** vpr get tired

canta|nte adj singing. ● m & f singer. **~or** m Flamenco singer. **~r** vt/i sing. **~rlas claras** speak frankly. ● m singing; (poema) poem

cántaro m pitcher. **llover a ~s** pour down

cante m folk song. **~ flamenco**, **~ jondo** Flamenco singing

cantera f quarry

cantidad f quantity; (número) number; (de dinero) sum. **una ~ de** lots of

cantimplora f water-bottle

cantina f canteen; (Rail) buffet; (LAm, bar) bar

cant|inela f song. **~o** m singing; (canción) chant; (borde) edge; (de un cuchillo) blunt edge. **~o rodado** boulder; (guijarro) pebble. **de ~o** on edge

canturre|ar vt/i hum. **~o** m humming

canuto m tube

caña f (planta) reed; (del trigo) stalk; (del bambú) cane; (de pescar) rod; (de la bota) leg; (vaso) glass. **~ de azúcar** sugar-cane. **~da** f ravine; (camino) track; (LAm, arroyo) stream

cáñamo m hemp. **~ indio** cannabis

cañ|ería f pipe; (tubería) piping. **~o** m pipe, tube; (de fuente) jet. **~ón** m (de pluma) quill; (de artillería) cannon; (de arma de fuego)

barrel; (desfiladero) canyon. **~onera** f gunboat

caoba f mahogany

ca|os m chaos. **~ótico** adj chaotic

capa f layer; (de pintura) coat; (Culin) coating; (prenda) cloak; (más corta) cape; (en geología) stratum

capaci|dad f capacity; (fig) ability. **~tar** vt qualify, enable; (instruir) train

caparazón m shell

capataz m foreman

capaz adj capable, able

capcioso adj sly, insidious

capellán m chaplain

caperuza f hood; (de bolígrafo) cap

capilla f chapel

capital adj capital, very important. ● m (dinero) capital. ● f (ciudad) capital. **~ de provincia** county town. **~ino** adj (LAm) of/from the capital. **~ismo** m capitalism. **~ista** adj & m & f capitalist. **~izar** 🔟 vt capitalize

capit|án m captain; (de pesquero) skipper. **~anear** vt lead, command; skipper (pesquero); captain (un equipo)

capitel m (de columna) capital

capitulaci|ón f surrender. **~ones** fpl marriage contract

capítulo m chapter; (de serie) episode

capó m bonnet (Brit), hood (Amer)

capón m (pollo) capon

caporal m (Mex) foreman

capot|a f (de mujer) bonnet; (Auto) folding top; (de cochecito) hood. **~e** m (Mex, de coche) bonnet (Brit), hood (Amer)

capricho m whim. **~so** adj capricious, whimsical

Capricornio m Capricorn

cápsula f capsule

captar vt harness (agua); grasp (sentido); capture (atención); win (confianza); (radio) pick up

captura f capture. ~r vt capture

capucha f hood

capullo m bud; (de insecto) cocoon

caqui m khaki

cara f face; (de una moneda) heads; (de un objeto) side; (aspecto) look, appearance; (descaro) cheek. ~ a facing. ~ a ~ face to face. ~ dura véase CARADURA. ~ o cruz heads or tails. dar la ~ a face up to. hacer ~ a face. tener mala ~ look ill. volver la ~ look the other way

carabela f caravel

carabina f carbine; (fig, fam, señora) chaperone

caracol m snail; (de mar) winkle; (LAm, concha) conch; (de pelo) curl. ¡~es! Good Heavens!. ~a f conch

carácter m (pl caracteres) character; (índole) nature. con ~ de as

característic|a f characteristic. ~o adj characteristic, typical

caracteriza|do adj characterized; (prestigioso) distinguished. ~r 10 vt characterize

caradura f cheek, nerve. ● m & f cheeky person

caramba int good heavens!

carambola f (en billar) cannon; (Mex, choque múltiple) pile-up. de ~ by pure chance

caramelo m sweet (Brit), candy (Amer); (azúcar fundido) caramel

caraqueño adj from Caracas

carátula f (de disco) sleeve (Brit), jacket (Amer); (de vídeo) case; (de

libro) cover; (Mex, del reloj) face

caravana f caravan; (de vehículos) convoy; (Auto) long line, traffic jam; (remolque) caravan (Brit), trailer (Amer); (Mex, reverencia) bow

caray int 🔟 good heavens!

carb|ón m coal; (para dibujar) charcoal. ~ de leña charcoal. ~oncillo m charcoal. ~onero adj coal. ● m coal-merchant. ~onizar 10 vt (fig) burn (a cinder). ~ono m carbon

carbura|dor m carburettor. ~nte m fuel

carcajada f guffaw. reírse a ~s roar with laughter. soltar una ~ burst out laughing

cárcel f prison, jail

carcelero m jailer

carcom|er vt eat away; (fig) undermine. ~erse vpr be eaten away; (fig) waste away

cardenal m cardinal; (contusión) bruise

cardiaco, cardíaco adj cardiac, heart

cardinal adj cardinal

cardo m thistle

carear vt bring face to face (personas); compare (cosas)

care|cer 11 vi. ~cer de lack. ~cer de sentido not to make sense. ~ncia f lack. ~nte adj lacking

care|ro adj pricey. ~stía f (elevado) high cost

careta f mask

carey m tortoiseshell

carga f load; (fig) burden; (acción) loading; (de barco, avión) cargo; (de tren) freight; (de arma) charge; (Elec, ataque) charge; (obligación) obligation. llevar la ~ de algo be responsible for sth. ~da f (Mex,

cargo *Pol*) supporters. **~do** *adj* loaded; (*fig*) burdened; (atmósfera) heavy; (café) strong; (pila) charged. **~mento** *m* load; (acción) loading; (de un barco) cargo. **~r** 🔟 *vt* load; (*fig*) burden; (*Elec, atacar*) charge; fill (pluma etc). ● *vi* load. **~r con** carry. **~rse** *vpr* (pila) charge. **~rse de** to load s.o. down with

cargo *m* (*puesto*) post; (*acusación*) charge. **a ~ de** in the charge of. **hacerse ~ de** take responsibility for. **tener a su ~** be in charge of

carguero *m* (*Naut*) cargo ship

caria|do *adj* decayed. **~rse** *vpr* decay

caribeño *adj* Caribbean

caricatura *f* caricature

caricia *f* caress; (*a animal*) stroke

caridad *f* charity. **¡por ~!** for goodness sake!

caries *f invar* tooth decay; (*lesión*) cavity

cariño *m* affection; (*caricia*) caress. **~ mío** my darling. **con ~** (*en carta*) with love from. **tener ~ a** be fond of. **tomar ~ a** become fond of. **~so** *adj* affectionate

carisma *m* charisma

caritativo *adj* charitable

cariz *m* look

carmesí *adj & m* crimson

carmín *m* (*de labios*) lipstick; (*color*) red

carnal *adj* carnal. **primo ~** first cousin

carnaval *m* carnival. **~esco** *adj* carnival

carne *f* meat; (*Anat, de frutos, pescado*) flesh. **~ de cerdo** pork. **~ de cordero** lamb. **~ de gallina** goose pimples. **~ molida** (*LAm*), **~ picada** mince (*Brit*), ground beef (*Amer*). **~ de ternera** veal. **~ de**

vaca beef. **me pone la ~ de gallina** it gives me the creeps. **ser de ~ y hueso** be only human

carné, carnet *m* card. **~ de conducir** driving licence (*Brit*), driver's license (*Amer*) **~ de identidad** identity card. **~ de manejar** (*LAm*) driving licence (*Brit*), driver's license (*Amer*). **~ de socio** membership card

carnero *m* ram

carnicer|ía *f* butcher's (shop); (*fig*) massacre. **~o** *adj* carnivorous. ● *m* butcher

carnívoro *adj* carnivorous. ● *m* carnivore

carnoso *adj* fleshy; (*pollo*) meaty

caro *adj* expensive. ● *adv* dear, dearly. **costar ~ a uno** cost s.o. dear.

carpa *f* carp; (*LAm, tienda*) tent

carpeta *f* folder, file. **~zo** *m. dar ~zo a** shelve

carpinter|ía *f* carpentry. **~o** *m* carpenter, joiner

carraspe|ar *vi* clear one's throat. **~ra** *f.* **tener ~ra** have a frog in one's throat

carrera *f* run; (*prisa*) rush; (*concurso*) race; (*estudios*) degree course; (*profesión*) career; (*de taxi*) journey

carreta *f* cart. **~da** *f* cartload

carrete *m* reel; (*película*) film

carretear *vi* (*LAm*) taxi

carretera *f* road. **~ de circunvalación** bypass, ring road. **~ nacional** A road (*Brit*), highway (*Amer*)

carretilla *f* wheelbarrow

carril *m* lane; (*Rail*) rail

carrito *m* (*en supermercado, para equipaje*) trolley (*Brit*), cart (*Amer*)

carro *m* cart; (*LAm, coche*) car;

(*Mex, vagón*) coach. **~ de combate** tank. **~cería** f (*Auto*) bodywork

carroña f carrion

carroza f coach, carriage; (*en desfile de fiesta*) float

carruaje m carriage

carrusel m merry-go-round

cart|a f letter; (*lista de platos*) menu; (*lista de vinos*) list; (*mapa*) map; (*naipe*) card. **~ blanca** free hand. **~ de crédito** letter of credit. **~ verde** green card. **~earse** vpr correspond

cartel m poster; (*letrero*) sign. **~era** f hoarding; (*en periódico*) listings; (*LAm en escuela, oficina*) notice board (*Brit*); bulletin board (*Amer*). **de ~** celebrated

carter|a f wallet; (*de colegial*) satchel; (*para documentos*) briefcase; (*LAm, de mujer*) handbag (*Brit*), purse (*Amer*). **~ista** m & f pickpocket

cartero m postman, mailman (*Amer*)

cartílago m cartilage

cartilla f first reading book. **~ de ahorros** savings book. **leerle la ~ a uno** tell s.o. off

cartón m cardboard

cartucho m cartridge

cartulina f card

casa f house; (*hogar*) home; (*empresa*) firm. **~ de huéspedes** boarding-house. **~ de socorro** first aid post. **ir a ~** go home. **salir de ~** go out

casaca f jacket

casado adj married. **los recién ~s** the newly-weds

casa|mentero m matchmaker. **~miento** m marriage; (*ceremonia*) wedding. **~r** vt marry. **~rse** vpr get married

cascabel m small bell; (*de serpiente*) rattle

cascada f waterfall

casca|nueces m invar nutcrackers. **~r** ⁊ vt crack (*nuez, huevo*); (*pegar*) beat. **~rse** vpr crack

cáscara f (*de huevo, nuez*) shell; (*de naranja*) peel; (*de plátano*) skin

cascarrabias adj invar grumpy

casco m helmet; (*de cerámica etc*) piece, fragment; (*cabeza*) scalp; (*de barco*) hull; (*envase*) empty bottle; (*de caballo*) hoof; (*de una ciudad*) part, area

cascote m piece of rubble. **~s** mpl rubble

caserío m country house; (*poblado*) hamlet

casero adj home-made; (*doméstico*) domestic; (*amante del hogar*) home-loving; (*reunión*) family. ● m owner; (*vigilante*) caretaker

caseta f hut; (*puesto*) stand. **~ de baño** bathing hut

casete m & f cassette

casi adv almost, nearly; (*en frases negativas*) hardly. **~ ~** very nearly. **~ nada** hardly any. **¡~ nada!** is that all? **~ nunca** hardly ever

casill|a f hut; (*en ajedrez etc*) square; (*en formulario*) box; (*compartimiento*) pigeonhole; **~ electrónica** e-mail address. **~ero** m pigeonholes; (*compartimiento*) pigeonhole

casino m casino; (*club social*) club

caso m case. **el ~ es que** the fact is that. **en ~ de** in the event of. **en cualquier ~** in any case, whatever happens. **en ese ~** in that case. **en todo ~** in any case. **en último ~** as a last resort. **hacer ~ de** take notice of. **poner por ~** suppose

caspa f dandruff

casquivana f flirt

cassette m & f cassette

casta f (de animal) breed; (de persona) descent; (grupo social) caste

castaña f chestnut

castañetear vi (dientes) chatter

castaño adj chestnut; (ojos) brown. ● m chestnut (tree)

castañuela f castanet

castellano adj Castilian. ● m (persona) Castilian; (lengua) Castilian, Spanish. ~**parlante** adj Castilian-speaking, Spanish-speaking. ¿habla Vd ~? do you speak Spanish?

> **castellano** In Spain the term *castellano*, rather than *español*, refers to the Spanish language as opposed to Catalan, Basque etc. The choice of word has political overtones; *castellano* has separatist connotations and *español* is considered neutral. In Latin America *castellano* is another term for Spanish.

castidad f chastity

castig|ar 12 vt punish; (en deportes) penalize. ~**o** m punishment; (en deportes) penalty

castillo m castle

cast|izo adj traditional; (puro) pure. ~**o** adj chaste

castor m beaver

castrar vt castrate

castrense m military

casual adj chance, accidental. ~**idad** f chance, coincidence. **dar la ~idad** happen. **de ~idad, por ~idad** by chance. **¡qué ~idad!** what a coincidence!. ~**mente** adv by chance; (precisamente) actually

cataclismo m cataclysm

catador m taster

catalán adj & m Catalan

catalizador m catalyst

cat|alogar 12 vt catalogue; (fig) classify. ~**álogo** m catalogue

Cataluña f Catalonia

catamarán m catamaran

catapulta f catapult

catar vt taste, try

catarata f waterfall, falls; (Med) cataract

catarro m cold

cat|ástrofe m catastrophe. ~**astrófico** adj catastrophic

catecismo m catechism

cátedra f (en universidad) professorship, chair; (en colegio) post of head of department

catedral f cathedral

catedrático m professor; (de colegio) teacher, head of department

categ|oría f category; (clase) class. **de ~oría** important. **de primera ~oría** first-class. ~**órico** adj categorical

cat|olicismo m catholicism. ~**ólico** adj (Roman) Catholic ● m (Roman) Catholic

catorce adj & m fourteen

cauce m river bed; (fig, artificial) channel

caucho m rubber

caudal m (de río) volume of flow; (riqueza) wealth. ~**oso** adj (río) large

caudillo m leader

causa f cause; (motivo) reason; (Jurid) trial. **a ~ de, por ~ de** because of. ~**r** vt cause

cautel|a f caution. ~**oso** adj cautious, wary

cauterizar 10 vt cauterize

cautiv|ar vt capture; (fig, fascinar) captivate. **~erio** m, **~idad** f captivity. **~o** adj & m captive

cauto adj cautious

cavar vt/i dig

caverna f cave, cavern

caviar m caviare

cavidad f cavity

caza f hunting; (con fusil) shooting; (animales) game. ● m fighter. andar a (la) ~ de be in search of. ~ mayor game hunting. dar ~ chase, go after. ir de ~ go hunting/shooting. **~dor** m hunter. **~dora** f jacket. **~r** vt 🔟 vt hunt; (con fusil) shoot; (fig) track down; (obtener) catch, get

caz|o m saucepan; (cucharón) ladle. **~oleta** f (small) saucepan. **~uela** f casserole

cebada f barley

ceb|ar vt fatten (up); bait (anzuelo); prime (arma de fuego). **~o** m bait; (de arma de fuego) charge

cebolla f onion. **~eta** f spring onion (Brit), scallion (Amer). **~ino** m chive

cebra f zebra

cece|ar vi lisp. **~o** m lisp

cedazo m sieve

ceder vt give up; (transferir) transfer. ● vi give in; (disminuir) ease off; (romperse) give way, collapse. ceda el paso give way (Brit), yield (Amer)

cedro m cedar

cédula f bond. ~ de identidad identity card

CE(E) abrev (**Comunidad Económica Europea**) E(E)C

ceg|ador adj blinding. **~ar** 🔟 & 🔟 vt blind; (tapar) block up. **~arse** vpr be blinded (de by). **~uera** f blindness

ceja f eyebrow

cejar vi give way

celada f ambush; (fig) trap

cela|dor m (de cárcel) prison warder; (de museo etc) security guard. **~r** vt watch

celda f cell

celebra|ción f celebration. **~r** vt celebrate; (alabar) praise. **~rse** vpr take place

célebre adj famous

celebridad f fame; (persona) celebrity

celest|e adj heavenly; (vestido) pale blue. azul **~e** sky-blue. **~ial** adj heavenly

celibato m celibacy

célibe adj celibate

celo m zeal; (de las hembras) heat; (de los machos) rut; (cinta adhesiva) Sellotape (P) (Brit), Scotch (P) tape (Amer). **~s** mpl jealousy. dar **~s** make jealous. tener **~s** be jealous

celofán m cellophane

celoso adj conscientious; (que tiene celos) jealous

celta adj & m (lengua) Celtic. ● m & f Celt

célula f cell

celular adj cellular. ● m (LAm) mobile, cellphone

celulosa f cellulose

cementerio m cemetery

cemento m cement; (hormigón) concrete; (LAm, cola) glue

cena f dinner; (comida ligera) supper

cenag|al m marsh, bog; (fig) tight spot. **~oso** adj boggy

cenar vt have for dinner; (en cena ligera) have for supper. ● vi have dinner; (tomar cena ligera) have supper

cenicero *m* ashtray

ceniza *f* ash

censo *m* census. **~ electoral** electoral roll

censura *f* censure; (*de prensa etc*) censorship. **~r** *vt* censure; **censor** (*prensa etc*)

centavo *adj & m* hundredth; (*moneda*) centavo

centell|a *f* flash; (*chispa*) spark. **~ar**, **~ear** *vi* sparkle

centena *f* hundred. **~r** *m* hundred. **a ~res** by the hundred. **~rio** *adj* centenarian. ● *m* centenary; (*persona*) centenarian

centeno *m* rye

centésim|a *f* hundredth. **~o** *adj* hundredth

cent|ígrado *adj* centigrade, Celsius. ● *m* centigrade. **~ígramo** *m* centigram. **~ilitro** *m* centilitre. **~ímetro** *m* centimetre

céntimo *adj* hundredth. ● *m* cent

centinela *f* sentry

centolla *f*, **centollo** *m* spider crab

central *adj* central. ● *f* head office. **~ de correos** general post office. **~ eléctrica** power station. **~ nuclear** nuclear power station. **~ telefónica** telephone exchange. **~ita** *f* switchboard

centraliza|ción *f* centralization. **~r** 🔟 *vt* centralize

centrar *vt* centre

céntrico *adj* central

centrífugo *adj* centrifugal

centro *m* centre. **~ comercial** shopping centre (*Brit*), shopping mall (*Amer*). **~ de llamadas** call centre

Centroamérica *f* Central America

centroamericano *adj & m* Cen-

tral American

ceñi|do *adj* tight. **~r** 🖪 & 🜺 *vt* take (*corona*); (*vestido*) cling to. **~rse** *vpr* limit o.s. (**a** to)

ceñ|o *m* frown. **fruncir el ~o** frown. **~udo** *adj* frowning

cepill|ar *vt* brush; (*en carpintería*) plane. **~o** *m* brush; (*en carpintería*) plane. **~o de dientes** toothbrush

cera *f* wax

cerámic|a *f* ceramics; (*materia*) pottery; (*objeto*) piece of pottery. **~o** *adj* ceramic

cerca *f* fence; (*de piedra*) wall. ● *adv* near, close. **~ de** *prep* close to, close up, closely

cercan|ía *f* nearness, proximity. **~ías** *fpl* vicinity. **tren ~ de ~ías** local train. **~o** *adj* near, close.

cercar 🛛 *vt* fence in, enclose; (*gente*) surround; (*asediar*) besiege

cerciorar *vt* convince. **~se** *vpr* make sure

cerco *m* (*asedio*) siege; (*círculo*) ring; (*LAm, valla*) fence; (*LAm, seto*) hedge

cerdo *m* pig; (*carne*) pork

cereal *m* cereal

cerebr|al *adj* cerebral. **~o** *m* brain; (*persona*) brains

ceremoni|a *f* ceremony. **~al** *adj* ceremonial. **~oso** *adj* ceremonious

cerez|a *f* cherry. **~o** *m* cherry tree

cerill|a *f* match. **~o** *m* (*Mex*) match

cern|er 🛯 *vt* sieve. **~erse** *vpr* hover. **~idor** *m* sieve

cero *m* nought, zero; (*fútbol*) nil (*Brit*), zero (*Amer*); (*tenis*) love; (*persona*) nonentity

cerquillo *m* (*LAm, flequillo*) fringe (*Brit*), bangs (*Amer*)

cerra|do *adj* shut, closed; (*espa-*

cio) shut in, enclosed; (cielo) overcast; (curva) sharp. **~dura** f lock; (acción de cerrar) shutting, closing. **~jero** m locksmith. **~r 🟥** vt shut, close; (con llave) lock; (cercar) enclose; turn off (grifo); block up (agujero etc). • vi shut, close. **~rse** vpr shut, close; (herida) heal. **~r con llave** lock

cerro m hill

cerrojo m bolt. **echar el ~** bolt

certamen m competition, contest

certero adj accurate

certeza, **certidumbre** f certainty

certifica|do adj (carta etc) registered. • m certificate. **~r 🟥** vt certify

certitud f certainty

cervatillo, **cervato** m fawn

cerve|cería f beerhouse, bar; (fábrica) brewery. **~za** f beer. **~za de barril** draught beer. **~za rubia** lager

cesa|ción f cessation, suspension. **~nte** adj redundant. **~r** vi stop. • vi stop, cease; (dejar un empleo) resign. **sin ~r** incessantly

cesárea f caesarian (section)

cese m cessation; (de un empleo) dismissal. **~ del fuego** (LAm) ceasefire

césped m grass, lawn

cest|a f basket. **~o** m basket. **~o de los papeles** waste-paper basket

chabacano adj common; (chiste etc) vulgar. • m (Mex, albaricoque) apricot

chabola f shack. **~s** fpl shanty town

cháchara f 🔢 chatter; (Mex, objetos sin valor) junk

chacharear vt (Mex) sell. • vi 🔢 chatter

chacra f (LAm) farm

chal m shawl

chalado adj 🔢 crazy

chalé m house (with a garden), villa

chaleco m waistcoat, vest (Amer). **~ salvavidas** life-jacket

chalet m (pl **~s**) house (with a garden), villa

chalote m shallot

chamac|a f (esp Mex) girl. **~o** m (esp Mex) boy

chamarra f sheepskin jacket; (Mex, chaqueta corta) jacket

chamb|a f (Mex, trabajo) work. **por ~a** by fluke. **~ear** vi (Mex, fam) work

champán m, **champaña** m & f champagne

champiñón m mushroom

champú m (pl **~es** o **~s**) shampoo

chamuscar 🟥 vt scorch

chance m (esp LAm) chance

chancho m (LAm) pig

chanchullo m 🔢 swindle, fiddle 🔢

chanclo m clog; (de caucho) rubber overshoe

chándal m (pl **~s**) tracksuit

chantaje m blackmail. **~ar** vt blackmail

chanza f joke

chapa f plate, sheet; (de madera) plywood; (de botella) metal top; (carrocería) bodywork; (LAm cerradura) lock. **~do** adj plated. **~do a la antigua** old-fashioned. **~do en oro** gold-plated

chaparro adj (LAm) short, squat

chaparrón m downpour

chapopote m (Mex) tar

chapotear vi splash

chapucero adj (persona) slap-dash; (trabajo) shoddy

chapulín m (Mex) locust; (saltamontes) grasshopper

chapurrar, **chapurrear** vt have a smattering of, speak a little

chapuza f botched job; (trabajo ocasional) odd job

chaquet|a f jacket. **cambiar de ~a** change sides. **~ón** m three-quarter length coat

charc|a f pond, pool. **~o** m puddle, pool

charcutería f delicatessen

charla f chat; (conferencia) talk. **~dor** adj talkative. **~r** vi 1 chat. **~tán** adj talkative. ● m chatterbox; (vendedor) cunning hawker; (curandero) charlatan

charol m varnish; (cuero) patent leather. **~a** f (Mex) tray

charr|a f (Mex) horsewoman, cowgirl. **~o** m (Mex) horseman, cowboy

chascar 7 vt crack (látigo); click (lengua); snap (dedos). ● vi (madera) creak. **~ con la lengua** click one's tongue

chasco m disappointment

chasis m (Auto) chassis

chasqu|ear vt crack (látigo); click (lengua); snap (dedos). ● vi (madera) creak. **~ con la lengua** click one's tongue. **~ido** m crack; (de la lengua) click; (de los dedos) snap

chatarra f scrap iron; (fig) scrap

chato adj (nariz) snub; (objetos) flat. ● m wine glass

chav|a f (Mex) girl, lass. **~al** m 1 boy, lad. **~o** m (Mex) boy, lad.

checa|da f check; (Mex, Med) checkup. **~r** 7 vt (Mex) check; (vigilar) check up on. **~r tarjeta** clock in

checo adj & m Czech. **~slovaco** adj & m (History) Czechoslovak

chelín m shilling

chelo m cello

cheque m cheque. **~ de viaje** traveller's cheque. **~ar** vt check; (LAm) check in (equipaje). **~o** m check; (Med) checkup. **~ra** f cheque-book

chévere adj (LAm) great

chica f girl; (criada) maid, servant

chicano adj & m Chicano, Mexican-American

> **Chicano** Chicanos are Mexican Americans, descendants of Mexican immigrants living in US. For long looked down by Americans of European descent, Chicanos have found a new pride in their origins and culture. There are numerous Chicano radio stations and many universities and colleges now offer courses in Chicano studies.

chícharo m (Mex) pea

chicharra f cicada; (timbre) buzzer

chichón m bump

chicle m chewing-gum

chico adj 1 small; (esp LAm, de edad) young. ● m boy. **~s** mpl children

chicoria f chicory

chifla|do adj 1 crazy, daft. **~r** vt whistle at, boo. ● vi (LAm) whistle; (1, gustar mucho) **me chifla el chocolate** I'm mad about chocolate. **~rse** vpr be mad (por about)

chilango adj (Mex) from Mexico City

chile m chilli

Chile m Chile

chileno adj & m Chilean

chill|ar vi scream, shriek; (ratón) squeak; (cerdo) squeal. **~ido** m scream, screech. **~ón** adj noisy; (colores) loud; (sonido) shrill

chimenea f chimney; (hogar) fireplace

chimpancé m chimpanzee

china f Chinese (woman)

China f China

chinche m drawing-pin (Brit), thumbtack (Amer); (insecto) bedbug; (fig) nuisance. **~eta** f drawing-pin (Brit), thumbtack (Amer)

chinela f slipper

chino adj Chinese; (Mex rizado) curly. ● m Chinese (man); (Mex, de pelo rizado) curly-haired person

chipriota adj & m & f Cypriot

chiquero m pen; (LAm, pocilga) pigsty (Brit), pigpen (Amer)

chiquillo adj childish. ● m child, kid 🔟

chirimoya f custard apple

chiripa f fluke

chirri|ar 🔟 vi creak; (frenos) screech; (pájaro) chirp. **~do** m creaking; (de frenos) screech; (de pájaros) chirping

chis int sh!, hush!; (fam, para llamar a uno) hey!, psst!

chism|e m gadget, thingumajig 🔟; (chismorreo) piece of gossip. **~es** mpl things, bits and pieces. **~orreo** m gossip. **~oso** adj gossipy.● m gossip

chisp|a f spark; (pizca) drop; (gracia) wit; (fig) sparkle. **estar que echa ~a(s)** be furious. **~eante** adj sparkling. **~ear** vi spark; (lloviznar) drizzle; (fig) sparkle. **~orrotear** vt throw out sparks; (fuego) crackle;

(aceite) spit

chistar vi. **ni chistó** he didn't say a word. **sin ~** without saying a word

chiste m joke, funny story. **tener ~** be funny

chistera f top hat

chistoso adj funny

chiva|rse vpr tip-off; (niño) tell. **~tazo** m tip-off. **~to** m informer; (niño) telltale

chivo m kid; (LAm, macho cabrío) billy goat

choca|nte adj shocking; (Mex desagradable) unpleasant. **~r** 🔽 vt clink (vasos); (LAm) crash (vehículo). **¡chócala!** give me five! ● vi collide, hit. **~r con, ~r contra** crash into

choch|ear vi be gaga. **~o** adj gaga; (fig) soft

choclo m (LAm) corn on the cob

chocolate m chocolate. **tableta** f **de ~** bar of chocolate

chófer, (LAm) **chofer** m chauffeur; (conductor) driver

cholo adj & m (LAm) half-breed

chopo m poplar

choque m collision; (fig) clash; (eléctrico) shock; (Auto, Rail etc) crash, accident; (sacudida) jolt

chorizo m chorizo

chorro m jet, stream; (caudal pequeño) trickle; (fig) stream. **a ~** (avión) jet. **a ~s** (fig) in abundance

chovinista adj chauvinistic. ● m & f chauvinist

choza f hut

chubas|co m shower. **~quero** m raincoat, anorak

chuchería f trinket

chueco adj (LAm) crooked

chufa f tiger nut

chuleta f chop

chulo adj cocky; (bonito) lovely (Brit), neat (Amer); (Mex, atractivo) cute. • m tough guy; (proxeneta) pimp

chup|ada f suck; (al helado) lick; (al cigarro) puff. ~ado adj skinny; (fam, fácil) very easy. ~ar vt suck; puff at (cigarro etc); (absorber) absorb. ~ete m dummy (Brit), pacifier (Amer). ~ón m sucker; (LAm) dummy (Brit), pacifier (Amer); (Mex, del biberón) teat

churrasco m barbecued steak

churro m fritter; 🔲 mess

chut|ar vi shoot. ~e m shot

cianuro m cyanide

cibernética f cybernetics

cicatriz f scar. ~ar 🔟 vt/i heal. ~arse vpr heal

cíclico adj cyclic(al)

ciclis|mo m cycling; (de películas, conciertos) season; (de conferencias) series

ciclomotor m moped

ciclón m cyclone

ciego adj blind. • m blind man, blind person. **a ciegas** in the dark

cielo m sky; (Relig) heaven; (persona) darling. **¡~s!** good heavens!, goodness me!

ciempiés m invar centipede

cien adj a hundred. ~ **por** ~ one hundred per cent

ciénaga f bog, swamp

ciencia f science; (fig) knowledge. ~**s** fpl (Univ etc) science. ~**s empresariales** business studies. **a** ~ **cierta** for certain

cieno m mud

científico adj scientific. • m scientist

ciento adj & m a hundred, one hundred. ~**s de** hundreds of. **por** ~ per cent

cierre m fastener; (acción de cerrar) shutting, closing; (LAm, cremallera) zip, zipper (Amer)

cierto adj certain; (verdad) true. **estar en lo** ~ be right. **lo** ~ **es que** the fact is that. **no es** ~ that's not true. **¿no es** ~**?** isn't that right? **por** ~ by the way. **si bien es** ~ **que** although

ciervo m deer

cifra f figure, number; (cantidad) sum. **en** ~ coded, in code. ~**do** adj coded. ~**r** vt code; place (esperanzas)

cigala f crayfish

cigarra f cicada

cigarr|illera f cigarette box; (de bolsillo) cigarette case. ~**illo** m cigarette. ~**o** m (cigarrillo) cigarette; (puro) cigar

cigüeña f stork

cilantro m coriander

cil|índrico adj cylindrical. ~**indro** m cylinder

cima f top; (fig) summit

cimbr|ear vt shake. ~**earse** vpr sway. ~**onada** f, ~**onazo** m (LAm) jolt; (de explosión) blast

cimentar 🔳 vt lay the foundations of; (fig, reforzar) strengthen

cimientos mpl foundations

cinc m zinc

cincel m chisel. ~**ar** vt chisel

cinco adj & m five; (en fechas) fifth

cincuent|a adj & m fifty; (quincuagésimo) fiftieth. ~**ón** adj in his fifties

cine m cinema; (local) cinema (Brit), movie theater (Amer). ~**asta** m & f film maker (Brit), movie maker (Amer). **~matográfico** adj film (Brit), movie (Amer)

cínico adj cynical. • m cynic

cinismo m cynicism

cinta f ribbon; (película) film (Brit), movie (Amer); (para grabar, en carreras) tape. **~ aislante** insulating tape. **~ métrica** tape measure. **~ virgen** blank tape

cintur|a f waist. **~ón** m belt. **~ón de seguridad** safety belt. **~ón salvavidas** lifebelt

ciprés m cypress (tree)

circo m circus

circuito m circuit; (viaje) tour. **~ cerrado** closed circuit. **corto ~** short circuit

circula|ción f circulation; (vehículos) traffic. **~r** adj circular. • vi circulate; (líquidos) flow; (conducir) drive; (caminar) walk; (autobús) run

círculo m circle. **~ vicioso** vicious circle. **en ~** in a circle

circunci|dar vt circumcise. **~sión** f circumcision

circunferencia f circumference

circunflejo m circumflex

circunscri|bir (pp circunscrito) vt confine. **~birse** vpr confine o.s. (a to). **~pción** f (distrito) district. **~pción electoral** constituency

circunspecto adj circumspect

circunstancia f circumstance

circunv|alar vt bypass. **~olar** vt 2 circle

cirio m candle

ciruela f plum. **~ pasa** prune

ciru|gía f surgery. **~jano** m surgeon

cisne m swan

cisterna f tank, cistern

cita f appointment; (entre chico y chica) date; (referencia) quotation. **~ a ciegas** blind date. **~ flash** speed dating. **~ción** f quotation; (Jurid) summons. **~do** adj aforementioned. **~r** vt make an appointment with; (mencionar) quote; (Jurid) summons. **~rse** vpr arrange to meet

cítara f zither

ciudad f town; (grande) city. **~ balneario** (LAm) coastal resort. **~ perdida** (Mex) shanty town. **~ universitaria** university campus. **~anía** f citizenship; (habitantes) citizens. **~ano** adj civic. • m citizen, inhabitant

cívico adj civic

civil adj civil. • m & f civil guard; (persona no militar) civilian

civiliza|ción f civilization. **~r** 10 vt civilize. **~rse** vpr become civilized

civismo m community spirit

clam|ar vi cry out, clamour. **~or** m clamour; (protesta) outcry. **~oroso** adj noisy; (éxito) resounding

clandestino adj clandestine, secret; (periódico) underground

clara f (de huevo) egg white

claraboya f skylight

clarear vi dawn; (aclarar) brighten up

clarete m rosé

claridad f clarity; (luz) light

clarifica|ción f clarification. **~r** 7 vt clarify

clar|ín m bugle. **~inete** m clarinet. **~inetista** m & f clarinettist

clarividen|cia f clairvoyance; (fig) far-sightedness. **~te** adj clairvoyant; (fig) far-sighted

claro adj clear; (luminoso) bright;

(colores) light; (líquido) thin. ● m (en bosque etc) clearing; (espacio) gap. ● adv clearly. ● int of course! ¡~ que sí! yes, of course! ¡~ que no! of course not!

clase f class; (tipo) kind, sort; (aula) classroom. ~ **media** middle class. ~ **obrera** working class. ~ **social** social class. **dar** ~s teach

clásico adj classical; (típico) classic. ● m classic

clasifica|ción f classification; (deportes) league. ~**r 7** vt classify

claustro m cloister; (Univ) staff

claustrof|obia f claustrophobia. ~**óbico** adj claustrophobic

cláusula f clause

clausura f closure

clava|do adj fixed; (con clavo) nailed. **es** ~**do a su padre** he's the spitting image of his father. ● m (LAm) dive. ~**r** vt knock in (clavo); stick in (cuchillo); (fijar) fix; (juntar) nail together

clave f key; (Mus) clef; (instrumento) harpsichord. ~**cin** m harpsichord

clavel m carnation

clavícula f collarbone, clavicle

clav|ija f peg; (Elec) plug. ~**o** m nail; (Culin) clove

claxon /'klakson/ m (pl ~s) horn

clemencia f clemency, mercy

clementina f tangerine

cleptómano m kleptomaniac

clerical adj clerical

clérigo m priest

clero m clergy

clic m: **hacer** ~ **en** to click on

cliché m cliché; (Foto) negative

cliente m customer; (de médico) patient; (de abogado) client. ~**la** f

clientele, customers; (de médico) patients

clim|a m climate; (ambiente) atmosphere. ~**ático** adj climatic. ~**atizado** adj air-conditioned

clínic|a f clinic. ~**o** adj clinical

cloaca f drain, sewer

clon m clone

cloro m chlorine

club m (pl ~s o ~es) club

coacci|ón f coercion. ~**onar** vt coerce

coagular vt coagulate; clot (sangre); curdle (leche). ~**se** vpr coagulate; (sangre) clot; (leche) curdle

coalición f coalition

coarta|da f alibi. ~**r** vt hinder; restrict (libertad etc)

cobard|e adj cowardly. ● m coward. ~**ía** f cowardice

cobert|izo m shed. ~**ura** f covering; (en radio, TV) coverage

cobij|a f (Mex, manta) blanket. ~**as** fpl (LAm, ropa de cama) bedclothes. ~**ar** vt shelter. ~**arse** vpr (take) shelter. ~**o** m shelter

cobra f cobra

cobra|dor m collector; (de autobús) conductor. ~**r** vt collect; (ganar) earn; charge (precio); cash (cheque); (recuperar) recover. ● vi be paid

cobr|e m copper. ~**izo** adj coppery

cobro m collection; (de cheque) cashing; (pago) payment. **presentar al** ~ cash

coca|ína f cocaine. ~**lero** adj (of) coca farming. ●n coca farmer

cocción f cooking; (Tec) firing

cocer 2 & 9 vt/i cook; (hervir) boil; (Tec) fire. ~**ido** m stew

coche m car, automobile (Amer); (de tren) coach, carriage; (de bebé) pram (Brit), baby carriage (Amer). **~-cama** sleeper. **~ fúnebre** hearse. **~ restaurante** dining-car. **~s de choque** dodgems. **~ra** f garage; (de autobuses) depot

cochin|ada f dirty thing. **~o** adj dirty, filthy. ● m pig

cociente m quotient. **~ intelectual** intelligence quotient, IQ

cocin|a f kitchen; (arte) cookery, cuisine; (aparato) cooker. **~a de gas** gas cooker. **~a eléctrica** electric cooker. **~ar** vt/i cook. **~ero** m cook

coco m coconut; (árbol) coconut palm; (cabeza) head; (que mete miedo) bogeyman. **comerse el ~** think hard

cocoa f (LAm) cocoa

cocodrilo m crocodile

cocotero m coconut palm

cóctel m (pl ~s o ~es) cocktail

cod|azo m nudge (with one's elbow). **~ear** vt/i elbow, nudge. **~earse** vpr rub shoulders (con with)

codicia f greed. **~ado** adj coveted, sought after. **~ar** vt covet. **~oso** adj greedy

código m code. **~ de la circulación** Highway Code

codo m elbow; (dobladura) bend. **~ a ~** side by side. **hablar (hasta) por los ~s** talk too much

codorniz m quail

coeficiente m coefficient. **~ intelectual** intelligence quotient, IQ

coerción f constraint

coetáneo adj & m contemporary

coexist|encia f coexistence. **~ir** vi coexist

cofradía f brotherhood

cofre m chest; (Mex, capó) bonnet (Brit), hood (Amer)

coger 🔢 vt (esp Esp) take; catch (tren, autobús, pelota, catarro); (agarrar) take hold of; (del suelo) pick up; pick (frutos etc); (LAm, vulgar) to screw. **~se** vpr trap, catch; (agarrarse) hold on

cogollo m (de lechuga etc) heart; (brote) bud

cogote m nape; (LAm, cuello) neck

cohech|ar vt bribe. **~o** m bribery

cohe|rente adj coherent. **~sión** f cohesion

cohete m rocket

cohibi|do adj shy; (inhibido) awkward; (incómodo) awkward. **~r** vt inhibit; (incomodar) make s.o. feel embarrassed. **~rse** vpr feel inhibited

coima f (LAm) bribe

coincid|encia f coincidence. **dar la ~encia** happen. **~ir** vi coincide

coje|ar vi limp; (mueble) wobble. **~ra** f lameness

cojín m cushion. **~inete** m small cushion

cojo adj lame; (mueble) wobbly. ● m lame person

col f cabbage. **~es de Bruselas** Brussel sprouts

cola f tail; (fila) queue; (para pegar) glue. **a la ~** at the end. **hacer ~** queue (up) (Brit), line up (Amer)

colabora|ción f collaboration. **~dor** m collaborator. **~r** vi collaborate

colada f washing. **hacer la ~** do the washing

colador m strainer

colapso m collapse; (fig) standstill

colar 2 *vt* strain; pass (moneda falsa etc). ● *vi* (líquido) seep through; (*fig*) be believed. ~**se** *vpr* slip; (*en una cola*) jump the queue; (*en fiesta*) gatecrash

colch|a *f* bedspread. ~**ón** *m* mattress. ~**oneta** *f* air bed; (*en gimnasio*) mat

colear *vi* wag its tail; (*asunto*) not be resolved. **vivito y coleando** alive and kicking

colecci|ón *f* collection. ~**onar** *vt* collect. ~**onista** *m & f* collector

colecta *f* collection

colectivo *adj* collective

colega *m & f* colleague

colegi|al *m* schoolboy. ~**ala** *f* schoolgirl. ~**o** *m* school; (*de ciertas profesiones*) college. ~**o mayor** hall of residence

cólera *m* cholera. ●*f* anger, fury. **montar en** ~ fly into a rage

colérico *adj* furious, irate

colesterol *m* cholesterol

coleta *f* pigtail

colga|nte *adj* hanging. ● *m* pendant. ~**r** 2 & 12 *vt* hang; hang out (ropa lavada); hang up (abrigo etc); put down (teléfono). ●*vi* hang; (*teléfono*) hang up. ~**rse** *vpr* hang o.s. **dejar a uno** ~**do** let s.o. down

colibrí *m* hummingbird

cólico *m* colic

coliflor *f* cauliflower

colilla *f* cigarette end

colina *f* hill

colinda|nte *adj* adjoining. ~**r** *vt* border (**con** on)

colisión *f* collision, crash; (*fig*) clash

collar *m* necklace; (*de perro*) collar

colmar *vt* fill to the brim; try (paciencia); (*fig*) fulfill. ~ **a uno de atenciones** lavish attention on s.o.

colmena *f* beehive, hive

colmillo *m* eye tooth, canine (tooth); (*de elefante*) tusk; (*de carnívoro*) fang

colmo *m* height. **ser el** ~ be the limit, be the last straw

coloca|ción *f* positioning; (*empleo*) job, position. ~**r** 7 *vt* put, place; (*buscar empleo*) find work for. ~**rse** *vpr* find a job

Colombia *f* Colombia

colombiano *adj & m* Colombian

colon *m* colon

colón *m* (*unidad monetaria de Costa Rica y El Salvador*) colon

colon|ia *f* colony; (*comunidad*) community; (*agua de colonia*) cologne; (*Mex, barrio*) residential suburb. ~**ia de verano** holiday camp. ~**iaje** *m* (*LAm*) colonial period. ~**ial** *adj* colonial. ~**ialista** *m & f* colonialist. ~**ización** *f* colonization. ~**izar** 10 colonize. ~**o** *m* colonist, settler; (*labrador*) tenant farmer

coloqui|al *adj* colloquial. ~**o** *m* conversation; (*congreso*) conference

color *m* colour. **de** ~ colour. **en** ~(**es**) (fotos, película) colour. ~**ado** *adj* (rojo) red. ~**ante** *m* colouring. ~**ear** *vt/i* colour. ~**ete** *m* blusher. ~**ido** *m* colour

colosal *adj* colossal; (*fig, fam, magnífico*) terrific

columna *f* column; (*en anatomía*) spine. ~ **vertebral** spinal column; (*fig*) backbone

columpi|ar *vt* swing. ~**arse** *vpr* swing. ~**o** *m* swing

coma *f* comma; (*Mat*) point. ● *m*

(*Med*) coma

comadre *f* (*madrina*) godmother; (*amiga*) friend. **~ar** *vi* gossip

comadreja *f* weasel

comadrona *f* midwife

comal *m* (*Mex*) griddle

command|ancia *f* command. **~ante** *m & f* commander. **~o** *m* command; (*Mil, soldado*) commando; (*de terroristas*) cell

comarca *f* area, region

comba *f* bend; (*juguete*) skipping-rope; (*de viga*) sag. **~r** vi skip. **~rse** *vpr* bend; (*viga*) sag

combat|e *m* combat; (*pelea*) fight. **~iente** *m* fighter. **~ir** *vt/i* fight

combina|ción *f* combination; (*enlace*) connection; (*prenda*) slip. **~r** *vt* combine; put together (*colores*)

combustible *m* fuel

comedia *f* comedy; (*cualquier obra de teatro*) play; (*LAm, telenovela*) soap (opera)

comedi|do *adj* restrained; (*LAm, atento*) obliging. **~rse** 5 *vpr* show restraint

comedor *m* dining-room; (*restaurante*) restaurant

comensal *m* companion at table, fellow diner

comentar *vt* comment on; discuss (*tema*); (*mencionar*) mention. **~io** *m* commentary; (*observación*) comment. **~ios** *mpl* gossip. **~ista** *m & f* commentator

comenzar 1 & 10 *vt/i* begin, start

comer *vt* eat; (*a mediodía*) have for lunch; (*esp LAm, cenar*) have for dinner; (*corroer*) eat away; (*en ajedrez*) take. ● *vi* eat; (*a mediodía*)

have lunch; (*esp LAm, cenar*) have dinner. **dar de ~** a feed. **~se** *vpr* eat (up)

comerci|al *adj* commercial; (*ruta*) trade; (*nombre, trato*) business. ● *m* (*LAm*) commercial, ad. **~ante** *m* trader; (*de tienda*) shopkeeper. **~ar** *vi* trade (**con** with, **en** in); (*con otra persona*) do business. **~o** *m* commerce; (*actividad*) trade; (*tienda*) shop; (*negocios*) business

comestible *adj* edible. **~s** *mpl* food. **tienda de ~s** grocer's (shop) (*Brit*), grocery (*Amer*)

cometa *m* comet. ● *f* kite

comet|er *vt* commit; make (*falta*). **~ido** *m* task

comezón *m* itch

comicios *mpl* elections

cómico *adj* comic; (*gracioso*) funny. ● *m* comic actor; (*humorista*) comedian

comida *f* food; (*a mediodía*) lunch; (*esp LAm, cena*) dinner; (*acto*) meal

comidilla *f*. **ser la ~ del pueblo** be the talk of the town

comienzo *m* beginning, start

comillas *fpl* inverted commas

comil|ón *adj* greedy. **~ona** *f* feast

comino *m* cumin. **(no) me importa un ~** I couldn't care less

comisar|ía *f* police station. **~io** *m* commissioner; (*deportes*) steward

comisión *f* assignment; (*organismo*) commission, committee; (*Com*) commission

comisura *f* corner. **~ de los labios** corner of the mouth

comité *m* committee

como *prep* as; (*comparación*) like. ● *adv* about. ● *conj* as. **~ quieras** as you like. **~ si** as if

cómo *adverbio*

····▸ how. ¿~ se llega? how do you get there? ¿~ es de alto? how tall is it? sé ~ pasó I know how it happened

! Cuando **cómo** va seguido del verbo **llamar** se traduce por *what*, p. ej. ¿~ te llamas? *what's your name?*

····▸ cómo + ser (*sugiriendo descripción*) ¿~ es su marido? what's her husband like? (*físicamente*) what does her husband look like? no sé ~ es la comida I don't know what the food's like

····▸ (*por qué*) why. ¿~ no actuaron antes? why didn't they act sooner?

····▸ (*pidiendo que se repita*) sorry?, pardon? ¿~? no te escuché sorry? I didn't hear you

····▸ (*en exclamaciones*) ¡~ llueve! it's really pouring! ¡~! ¿que no lo sabes? what! you mean you don't know? ¡~ no! of course!

cómoda *f* chest of drawers
comodidad *f* comfort. **a su ~** at your convenience
cómodo *adj* comfortable; (*conveniente*) convenient
comoquiera *conj.* **~ que sea** however it may be
compacto *adj* compact; (*denso*) dense; (*líneas etc*) close
compadecer 11 *vt* feel sorry for. **~se** *vpr.* **~se de** feel sorry for
compadre *m* godfather; (*amigo*) friend
compañ|ero *m* companion; (*de trabajo*) colleague; (*de clase*) class-

mate; (*pareja*) partner. **~ía** *f* company. **en ~ía de** with
compara|ble *adj* comparable. **~ción** *f* comparison. **~r** *vt* compare. **~tivo** *adj & m* comparative
comparecer 11 *vi* appear
comparsa *f* group. ● *m & f* (*en el teatro*) extra
compartim(i)ento *m* compartment
compartir *vt* share
compás *m* (*instrumento*) (pair of) compasses; (*ritmo*) rhythm; (*división*) bar (*Brit*), measure (*Amer*); (*Naut*) compass. **a ~** in time
compasi|ón *f* compassion, pity. **tener ~ón de** feel sorry for. **~vo** *adj* compassionate
compatib|ilidad *f* compatibility. **~le** *adj* compatible
compatriota *m & f* compatriot
compendio *m* summary
compensa|ción *f* compensation. **~ción por despido** redundancy payment. **~r** *vt* compensate
competen|cia *f* competition; (*capacidad*) competence; (*poder*) authority; (*incumbencia*) jurisdiction. **~te** *adj* competent
competi|ción *f* competition. **~dor** *m* competitor. **~r** 5 *vi* compete
compinche *m* accomplice; (*fam, amigo*) friend, mate 11
complac|er 32 *vt* please. **~erse** *vpr* be pleased. **~iente** *adj* obliging; (*marido*) complaisant
complej|idad *f* complexity. **~o** *adj & m* complex
complement|ario *adj* complementary. **~o** *m* complement; (*Gram*) object, complement
complet|ar *vt* complete. **~o** *adj* complete; (*lleno*) full; (*exhaustivo*)

comprehensive

complexión *f* build

complica|ción *f* complication; (*esp AmL, implicación*) involvement. **~r 7** *vt* complicate; involve (persona). **~rse** *vpr* become complicated; (*implicarse*) get involved

cómplice *m & f* accomplice

complot *m* (*pl* **~s**) plot

compon|ente *adj* component. ● *m* component; (*miembro*) member. **~er 34** *vt* make up; (*Mus, Literatura etc*) write, compose; (*esp LAm, reparar*) mend; (*LAm*) set (hueso); settle (estómago). **~erse** *vpr* be made up; (*arreglarse*) get better. **~érselas** manage

comporta|miento *m* behaviour. **~rse** *vpr* behave. **~rse mal** misbehave

composi|ción *f* composition. **~tor** *m* composer

compostura *f* composure; (*LAm, arreglo*) repair

compota *f* stewed fruit

compra *f* purchase. **~ a plazos** hire purchase. **hacer la(s) ~(s)** do the shopping. **ir de ~s** go shopping. **~dor** *m* buyer. **~r** *vt* buy. **~venta** *f* buying and selling; (*Jurid*) sale and purchase contract. **negocio** *m* **de ~venta** second-hand shop

compren|der *vt* understand; (*incluir*) include. **~sión** *f* understanding. **~sivo** *adj* understanding

compresa *f* compress; (*de mujer*) sanitary towel

compr|esión *f* compression. **~imido** *adj* compressed. ● *m* pill, tablet. **~imir** *vt* compress

comproba|nte *m* proof; (*recibo*) receipt. **~r** *vt* check; (*demostrar*) prove

comprom|eter *vt* compromise; (*arriesgar*) jeopardize. **~eterse** *vpr* compromise o.s.; (*obligarse*) agree to; (*novios*) get engaged. **~etido** *adj* (*situación*) awkward, delicate; (*autor*) politically committed; **~iso** *m* obligation; (*apuro*) predicament; (*cita*) appointment; (*acuerdo*) agreement. **sin ~iso** without obligation

compuesto *adj* compound; (*persona*) smart. ● *m* compound

computa|ción *f* (*esp LAm*) computing. **curso** *m* **de ~ción** computer course. **~dor** *m*, **computadora** *f* computer. **~r** *vt* calculate. **~rizar, computerizar 10** *vt* computerize

cómputo *m* calculation

comulgar 12 *vi* take Communion

común *adj* common; (*compartido*) joint. **en ~** in common. **por lo ~** generally. ● *m* **el ~ de** most

comunal *adj* communal

comunica|ción *f* communication. **~do** *m* communiqué. **~do de prensa** press release. **~r 7** *vt* communicate; (*informar*) inform; (*LAm, por teléfono*) put through. **está ~ndo** (*teléfono*) it's engaged. **~rse** *vpr* communicate; (*ponerse en contacto*) get in touch. **~tivo** *adj* communicative

comunidad *f* community. **~ de vecinos** residents' association. **C~ (Económica) Europea** European (Economic) Community. **en ~** together

Comunidad Autónoma
In 1978 Spain was divided into *comunidades autónomas* or *autonomías*, which have far greater powers than the old

regiones. The *comunidades autónomas* are: Andalusia, Aragon, Asturias, Balearic Islands, the Basque Country, Canary Islands, Cantabria, Castilla y León, Castilla-La Mancha, Catalonia, Extremadura, Galicia, Madrid, Murcia, Navarre, La Rioja, Valencia and the North African enclaves of Ceuta and Melilla.

comunión *f* communion; (*Relig*) (Holy) Communion

comunis|mo *m* communism. **~ta** *adj & m & f* communist

con *prep* with; (+ *infinitivo*) by. **~ decir la verdad** by telling the truth. **~ que** so. **~ tal que** as long as

concebir ⑤ *vt/i* conceive

conceder *vt* concede, grant; award (*premio*); (*admitir*) admit

conceja|al *m* councillor. **~ero** *m* (*LAm*) councillor. **~o** *m* council

concentra|ción *f* concentration; (*Pol*) rally. **~r** *vt* concentrate; assemble (*personas*). **~rse** *vpr* concentrate

concep|ción *f* conception. **~to** *m* concept; (*opinión*) opinion. **bajo ningún ~to** in no way

concerniente *adj*. **en lo ~ a** with regard to

concertar ① *vt* arrange; agree (upon) (*plan*)

concesión *f* concession

concha *f* shell; (*carey*) tortoiseshell

conciencia *f* conscience; (*conocimiento*) awareness. **~ limpia** clear conscience. **~ sucia** guilty conscience. **a ~ de que** fully aware that. **en ~** honestly. **tener ~ de** be aware of. **tomar ~ de** become aware of. **~r** *vt* make aware. **~rse**

vpr become aware

concientizar ⑩ *vt* (*esp LAm*) make aware. **~se** *vpr* become aware

concienzudo *adj* conscientious

concierto *m* concert; (*acuerdo*) agreement; (*Mus, composición*) concerto

concilia|ción *f* reconciliation. **~r** *vt* reconcile. **~r el sueño** get to sleep. **~rse** *vpr* gain

concilio *m* council

conciso *adj* concise

conclu|ir ⑰ *vt* finish; (*deducir*) conclude. ● *vi* finish, end. **~sión** *f* conclusion. **~yente** *adj* conclusive

concord|ancia *f* agreement. **~ar** ② *vt* agree. ● *vi* agree. **~e** *adj* in agreement. **~ia** *f* harmony

concret|amente *adv* specifically, to be exact. **~ar** *vt* make specific. **~arse** *vpr* become definite; (*limitarse*) confine o.s. **~o** *adj* concrete; (*determinado*) specific, particular. **en ~o** definite; (*concretamente*) to be exact; (*en resumen*) in short. ● *m* (*LAm, hormigón*) concrete

concurr|encia *f* concurrence; (*reunión*) audience. **~ido** *adj* crowded, busy. **~ir** *vi* meet; ; (*coincidir*) agree. **~ a** (*asistir a*) attend

concurs|ante *m & f* competitor, contestant. **~ar** *vi* compete, take part. **~o** *m* competition; (*ayuda*) help

cond|ado *m* county. **~e** *m* earl, count

condena *f* sentence. **~ción** *f* condemnation. **~do** *m* convicted person. **~r** *vt* condemn; (*Jurid*) convict

condensa|ción *f* condensation.

~**r** vt condense

condesa f countess

condescende|ncia f condescension; (tolerancia) indulgence. ~**r 1** vi agree; (dignarse) condescend

condici|ón f condition. a ~**ón de (que)** on condition that. ~**onal** adj conditional. ~**onar** vt condition

condiment|ar vt season. ~**o** m seasoning

condolencia f condolence

condominio m joint ownership; (LAm, edificio) block of flats (Brit), condominium (esp Amer)

condón m condom

condonar vt (perdonar) reprieve; cancel (deuda)

conducir 47 vt drive (vehículo); carry (electricidad, gas, agua). ● vi drive; (fig, llevar) lead. **¿a qué conduce?** what's the point? ~**se** vpr behave

conducta f behaviour

conducto m pipe, tube; (en anatomía) duct. **por** ~ **de** through. ~**r** m driver; (jefe) leader; (Elec) conductor

conduzco vb véase **CONDUCIR**

conectar vt/i connect

conejo m rabbit

conexión f connection

confabularse vpr plot

confecci|ón f (de trajes) tailoring; (de vestidos) dressmaking. ~**ones** fpl clothing, clothes. **de** ~**ón** ready-to-wear. ~**onar** vt make

confederación f confederation

conferencia f conference; (al teléfono) long-distance call; (Univ) lecture. ~ **en la cima, ~ (en la) cumbre** summit conference. ~**nte** m & f lecturer

conferir 4 vt confer; award (premio)

confes|ar 1 vt/i confess. ~**arse** vpr confess. ~**ión** f confession. ~**ionario** m confessional. ~**or** m confessor

confeti m confetti

confia|do adj trusting; (seguro de sí mismo) confident. ~**nza** f trust; (en sí mismo) confidence; (intimidad) familiarity. ~**r 20** vt entrust. ● vi. ~**r en** trust

confiden|cia f confidence, secret. ~**cial** adj confidential. ~**te** m confidant. ● f confidante

configur|ación f configuration. ~**ar** vt to configure

conf|ín m border. ~**ines** mpl outermost parts. ~**inar** vt confine; (desterrar) banish

confirma|ción f confirmation. ~**r** vt confirm

confiscar 7 vt confiscate

confit|ería f sweet-shop (Brit), candy store (Amer). ~**ura** f jam

conflict|ivo adj difficult; (época) troubled; (polémico) controversial. ~**o** m conflict

confluencia f confluence

conform|ación f conformation, shape. ~**ar** vt (acomodar) adjust. ● vi agree. ~**arse** vpr conform. ~**e** adj in agreement;(contento) happy, satisfied; (según) according (con to). ~**e a** in accordance with, according to. ● conj as. ● int OK!. ~**idad** f agreement; (tolerancia) resignation. ~**ista** m & f conformist

conforta|ble adj comfortable. ~**nte** adj comforting. ~**r** vt comfort

confronta|ción f confrontation. ~**r** vt confront

confu|ndir vt (equivocar) mistake,

confuse; (*mezclar*) mix up, confuse; (*turbar*) embarrass. ∼**ndirse** *vpr* become confused; (*equivocarse*) make a mistake. ∼**sión** *f* confusion; (*vergüenza*) embarrassment. ∼**so** *adj* confused; (*borroso*) blurred

congela|do *adj* frozen. ∼**dor** *m* freezer. ∼**r** *vt* freeze

congeniar *vi* get on

congesti|ón *f* congestion. ∼**onado** *adj* congested. ∼**onarse** *vpr* become congested

congoja *f* distress; (*pena*) grief

congraciarse *vpr* ingratiate o.s.

congratular *vt* congratulate

congrega|ción *f* gathering; (*Relig*) congregation. ∼**rse** 🔢 *vpr* gather, assemble

congres|ista *m & f* delegate, member of a congress. ∼**o** *m* congress, conference. **C**∼**o** Parliament. **C**∼**o de los Diputados** Chamber of Deputies

cónico *adj* conical

conifer|a *f* conifer. ∼**o** *adj* coniferous

conjetura *f* conjecture, guess. ∼**r** *vt* conjecture, guess

conjuga|ción *f* conjugation. ∼**r** 🔢 *vt* conjugate

conjunción *f* conjunction

conjunto *adj* joint. ● *m* collection; (*Mus*) band; (*ropa*) suit, outfit. **en** ∼ altogether

conjurar *vt* exorcise; avert (*peligro*). ● *vi* plot, conspire

conllevar *vt* to entail

conmemora|ción *f* commemoration. ∼**r** *vt* commemorate

conmigo *pron* with me

conmo|ción *f* shock; (*tumulto*) upheaval. ∼ **cerebral** concussion. ∼**cionar** *vt* shock. ∼**ver** 🔢 *vt*

shake; (*emocionar*) move

conmuta|dor *m* switch; (*LAm, de teléfonos*) switchboard. ∼**r** *vt* exchange

connota|ción *f* connotation. ∼**do** *adj* (*LAm, destacado*) distinguished. ∼**r** *vt* connote

cono *m* cone

conoc|edor *adj & m* expert. ∼**er** 🔢 *vt* know; (*por primera vez*) meet; (*reconocer*) recognize, know. **se conoce que** apparently. **dar a** ∼**er** make known. ∼**erse** *vpr* know o.s.; (*dos personas*) know each other; (*notarse*) be obvious. ∼**ido** *adj* well-known. ● *m* acquaintance. ∼**imiento** *m* knowledge; (*sentido*) consciousness. **sin** ∼**imiento** unconscious. **tener** ∼**imiento de** know about

conozco *vb véase* **CONOCER**

conque *conj* so

conquista *f* conquest. ∼**dor** *adj* conquering. ● *m* conqueror; (*de América*) conquistador. ∼**r** *vt* conquer, win

consabido *adj* usual, habitual

> **Conquistadores** The collective term for the succession of explorers, soldiers and adventurers who, from the sixteenth century onward led the settlement and exploitation of Spain's Latin American colonies.

consagra|ción *f* consecration. ∼**r** *vt* consecrate; (*fig*) devote. ∼**rse** *vpr* devote o.s.

consanguíneo *m* blood relation

consciente *adj* conscious

consecuen|cia *f* consequence; (*coherencia*) consistency. **a** ∼**cia de** as a result of. ∼**te** *adj* consistent

consecutivo *adj* consecutive

conseguir 5 & 18 *vt* get, obtain; (*lograr*) manage; achieve (*objetivo*)

consej|ero *m* adviser; (*miembro de consejo*) member. **~o** *m* piece of advice; (*Pol*) council. **~o de ministros** cabinet

consenso *m* assent, consent

consenti|do *adj* (*niño*) spoilt. **~miento** *m* consent. **~r** 4 *vt* allow; spoil (*niño*). ● *vi* consent

conserje *m* porter, caretaker. **~ría** *f* porter's office

conserva *f* (*mermelada*) preserve; (*en lata*) tinned food. **en ~** tinned (*Brit*), canned. **~ción** *f* conservation; (*de alimentos*) preservation

conservador *adj & m* (*Pol*) conservative

conservar *vt* keep; preserve (*alimentos*). **~se** *vpr* keep; (*costumbre*) survive

conservatorio *m* conservatory

considera|ble *adj* considerable. **~ción** *f* consideration; (*respeto*) respect. **de ~ción** serious. **de mi ~ción** (*LAm, en cartas*) Dear Sir. **~do** *adj* considerate; (*respetado*) respected. **~r** *vt* consider; (*respetar*) respect

consigna *f* order; (*para equipaje*) left luggage office (*Brit*), baggage room (*Amer*); (*eslogan*) slogan

consigo *pron* (*él*) with him; (*ella*) with her; (*Ud, Uds*) with you; (*uno mismo*) with o.s.

consiguiente *adj* consequent. **por ~** consequently

consist|encia *f* consistency. **~ente** *adj* consisting (en of); (*firme*) solid; (*LAm, congruente*) consistent. **~ir** *vi.* **~ en** consist of; (*radicar en*) be due to

consola|ción *f* consolation. **~r**

2 *vt* console, comfort. **~rse** *vpr* console o.s.

consolidar *vt* consolidate. **~se** *vpr* consolidate

consomé *m* clear soup, consommé

consonante *adj* consonant. ● *f* consonant

consorcio *m* consortium

conspira|ción *f* conspiracy. **~dor** *m* conspirator. **~r** *vi* conspire

consta|ncia *f* constancy; (*prueba*) proof; (*LAm, documento*) written evidence. **~nte** *adj* constant. **~r** *vi* be clear; (*figurar*) appear, figure; (*componerse*) consist. **hacer ~r** state; (*por escrito*) put on record. **me ~ que** I'm sure that. **que conste que** believe me

constatar *vt* check; (*confirmar*) confirm

constipa|do *m* cold. ● *adj.* **estar ~do** have a cold; (*LAm, estreñido*) be constipated. **~rse** *vpr* catch a cold

constitu|ción *f* constitution; (*establecimiento*) setting up. **~cional** *adj* constitutional. **~ir** 17 *vt* constitute; (*formar*) form; (*crear*) set up, establish. **~irse** *vpr* set o.s. up (en as). **~tivo** *adj*, **~yente** *adj* constituent

constru|cción *f* construction. **~ctor** *m* builder. **~ir** 17 *vt* construct; build (*edificio*)

consuelo *m* consolation

consuetudinario *adj* customary

cónsul *m & f* consul

consulado *m* consulate

consult|a *f* consultation. **horas** *fpl* **de ~a** surgery hours. **obra** *f* **de ~a** reference book. **~ar** *vt* consult. **~orio** *m* surgery

consumar | contraer

consumar vt complete; commit (crimen); carry out (robo); consummate (matrimonio). **~se** vpr
consum|ición f consumption; (bebida) drink; (comida) food. **~ición mínima** minimum charge. **~ido** adj (persona) skinny, wasted. **~idor** m consumer. **~ir** vt consume. **~irse** vpr (persona) waste away; (vela, cigarrillo) burn down; (líquido) dry up. **~ismo** m consumerism. **~o** m consumption; (LAm, en restaurante etc) (bebida) drink; (comida) food. **~o mínimo** minimum charge
contab|ilidad f book-keeping; (profesión) accountancy. **~le** m & f accountant
contacto m contact. **ponerse en ~ con** get in touch with
conta|do adj. **al ~** cash. **~s** adj pl few. **tiene los días ~s** his days are numbered. **~dor** m meter; (LAm, persona) accountant
contagi|ar vt infect (persona); pass on (enfermedad); (fig) contaminate. **~o** m infection; (directo) contagion. **~oso** adj infectious; (por contacto directo) contagious
contamina|ción f contamination, pollution. **~r** vt contaminate, pollute
contante adj. **dinero m ~** cash
contar 2 vt count; tell (relato). **se cuenta que** it's said that. ● vi count. **~ con** rely on, count on. **~se** vpr be included (entre among)
contempla|ción f contemplation. **sin ~ciones** unceremoniously. **~r** vt look at; (fig) contemplate
contemporáneo adj & m contemporary

conten|er 40 vt contain; hold (respiración). **~erse** vpr contain o.s. **~ido** adj contained. ● m contents
content|ar vt please. **~arse** vpr. **~arse con** be satisfied with, be pleased with. **~o** adj (alegre) happy; (satisfecho) pleased
contesta|ción f answer. **~dor** m. **~ automático** answering machine. **~r** vt/i answer; (replicar) answer back
contexto m context
contienda f conflict; (lucha) contest
contigo pron with you
contiguo adj adjacent
continen|tal adj continental. **~te** m continent
continua|ción f continuation. **a ~ación** immediately after. **~ar** 21 vt continue, resume. ● vi continue. **~idad** f continuity. **~o** adj continuous; (frecuente) continual. **corriente f ~a** direct current
contorno m outline; (de árbol) girth; (de caderas) measurement. **~s** mpl surrounding area
contorsión f contortion
contra prep against. **en ~** against. ● m cons. ● f snag. **llevar la ~** contradict
contraata|car 7 vt/i counterattack. **~que** m counter-attack
contrabaj|ista m & f double-bass player. **~o** m double-bass; (persona) double-bass player
contraband|ista m & f smuggler. **~o** m contraband
contracción f contraction
contrad|ecir 46 vt contradict. **~icción** f contradiction. **~ictorio** adj contradictory
contraer 41 vt contract. **~ matri-**

monio marry. ~**se** *vpr* contract

contralto *m* counter tenor. ● *f* contralto

contra|mano. a ~ in the wrong direction. ~**partida** *f* compensation. ~**pelo. a** ~ the wrong way

contrapes|ar *vt* counterweight. ~**o** *m* counterweight

contraproducente *adj* counterproductive

contrari|a *f*. llevar la ~**a** contradict. ~**ado** *adj* upset; (*enojado*) annoyed. ~**ar** 20 *vt* upset; (*enojar*) annoy. ~**edad** *f* setback; (*disgusto*) annoyance. ~**o** *adj* contrary (**a** to); (*dirección*) opposite. **al** ~**o** on the contrary. **al** ~**o de** contrary to. **de lo** ~**o** otherwise. **por el** ~**o** on the contrary. **ser** ~**o a** be opposed to, be against

contrarrestar *vt* counteract

contrasentido *m* contradiction

contraseña *f* (*palabra*) password; (*en cine*) stub

contrast|ar *vt* check, verify. ● *vi* contrast. ~**e** *m* contrast; (*en oro, plata*) hallmark

contratar *vt* contract (*servicio*); hire, take on (*empleados*); sign up (*jugador*)

contratiempo *m* setback; (*accidente*) mishap

contrat|ista *m & f* contractor. ~**o** *m* contract

contraven|ción *f* contravention. ~**ir** 53 *vt* contravene

contraventana *f* shutter

contribu|ción *f* contribution; (*tributo*) tax. ~**ir** 17 *vt/i* contribute. ~**yente** *m & f* contributor; (*que paga impuestos*) taxpayer

contrincante *m* rival, opponent

control *m* control; (*vigilancia*) check; (*lugar*) checkpoint. ~**ar** *vt*

control; (*vigilar*) check. ~**arse** *vpr* control s.o.

controversia *f* controversy

contundente *adj* (*arma*) blunt; (*argumento*) convincing

contusión *f* bruise

convalec|encia *f* convalescence. ~**er** 11 *vi* convalesce. ~**iente** *adj & m & f* convalescent

convalidar *vt* recognize (*título*)

convenc|er 9 *vt* convince. ~**imiento** *m* conviction

convención *f* convention. ~**onal** *adj* conventional

conveni|encia *f* convenience; (*aptitud*) suitability. ~**ente** *adj* suitable; (*aconsejable*) advisable; (*provechoso*) useful. ~**o** *m* agreement. ~**r** 53 *vt* agree. ● *vi* agree (**en** on); (*ser conveniente*) be convenient for, suit; (*ser aconsejable*) be advisable

convento *m* (*de monjes*) monastery; (*de monjas*) convent

conversa|ción *f* conversation. ~**ciones** *fpl* talks. ~**r** *vi* converse, talk

conver|sión *f* conversion. ~**so** *adj* converted. ~**t** *vt* convert. ~**tible** *adj* convertible. ● *m* (*LAm*) convertible. ~**tir** 4 *vt* convert. ~**tirse** *vpr*. ~**tirse en** turn into; (*Relig*) convert

convic|ción *f* conviction. ~**to** *adj* convicted

convida|do *m* guest. ~**r** *vt* invite

convincente *adj* convincing

conviv|encia *f* coexistence; (*de parejas*) life together. ~**ir** *vi* live together; (*coexistir*) coexist

convocar 7 *vt* call (*huelga, elecciones*); convene (*reunión*); summon (*personas*)

convulsión *f* convulsion

conyugal *adj* marital, conjugal; (*vida*) married

cónyuge *m* spouse. **~s** *mpl* married couple

coñac *m* (*pl* **~s**) brandy

coopera|ción *f* cooperation. **~r** *vi* cooperate. **~nte** *m* & *f* voluntary aid worker. **~tiva** *f* cooperative. **~tivo** *adj* cooperative

coordinar *vt* coordinate

copa *f* glass; (*deportes, fig*) cup; (*de árbol*) top. **~s** *fpl* (*naipes*) hearts. **tomar una ~** have a drink

copia *f* copy. **~ en limpio** fair copy. **sacar una ~** make a copy. **~r** *vt* copy

copioso *adj* copious; (lluvia, nevada etc) heavy

copla *f* verse; (*canción*) folksong

copo *m* flake. **~ de nieve** snowflake. **~s de maíz** cornflakes

coquet|a *f* flirt; (*mueble*) dressing-table. **~ear** *vi* flirt. **~o** *adj* flirtatious

coraje *m* courage; (*rabia*) anger

coral *adj* choral. ● *m* coral; (*Mus*) chorale

coraza *f* cuirass; (*Naut*) armour-plating; (*de tortuga*) shell

coraz|ón *m* heart; (*persona*) darling. **sin ~ón** heartless. **tener buen ~ón** be good-hearted. **~onada** *f* hunch; (*impulso*) impulse

corbata *f* tie, necktie (*esp Amer*). **~ de lazo** bow tie

corche|a *f* quaver. **~te** *m* fastener, hook and eye; (*gancho*) hook; (*paréntesis*) square bracket

corcho *m* cork. **~lata** *f* (*Mex*) (crown) cap

corcova *f* hump

cordel *m* cord, string

cordero *m* lamb

cordial *adj* cordial, friendly. ● *m*

tonic. **~idad** *f* cordiality, warmth

cordillera *f* mountain range

córdoba *m* (*unidad monetaria de Nicaragua*) córdoba

cordón *m* string; (*de zapatos*) lace; (*cable*) cord; (*fig*) cordon. **~ umbilical** umbilical cord

coreografía *f* choreography

corista *f* (*bailarina*) chorus girl

cornet|a *f* bugle; (*Mex, de coche*) horn. **~ín** *m* cornet

coro *m* (*Mus*) choir; (*en teatro*) chorus

corona *f* crown; (*de flores*) wreath, garland. **~ción** *f* coronation. **~r** *vt* crown

coronel *m* colonel

coronilla *f* crown. **estar hasta la ~** be fed up

corpora|ción *f* corporation. **~l** *adj* (*castigo*) corporal; (*trabajo*) physical

corpulento *adj* stout

corral *m* farmyard. **aves** *fpl* **de ~** poultry

correa *f* strap; (*de perro*) lead; (*cinturón*) belt

correc|ción *f* correction; (*cortesía*) good manners. **~to** *adj* correct; (*cortés*) polite

corrector ortográfico *m* spell checker

corre|dizo *adj* running. **nudo** *m* **~dizo** slip knot. **puerta** *f* **~diza** sliding door. **~dor** *m* runner; (*pasillo*) corridor; (*agente*) agent, broker. **~dor de coches** racing driver

corregir 5 & 14 *vt* correct

correlación *f* correlation

correo *m* post, mail; (*persona*) courier; (*LAm, oficina*) post office. **~s** *mpl* post office. **~ electrónico**

correr | cosmopolita

e-mail. **echar al ~** post

correr vt run; (mover) move; draw (cortinas). ● vi run; (agua, electricidad etc) flow; (tiempo) pass. **~se** vpr (apartarse) move along; (colores) run

correspond|encia f correspondence. **~er** vi correspond; (ser adecuado) be fitting; (contestar) reply; (pertenecer) belong; (incumbir) fall to. **~erse** vpr (amarse) love one another. **~iente** adj corresponding

corresponsal m correspondent

corrid|a f run. **~a de toros** bullfight. **de ~a** from memory. **~o** adj (continuo) continuous

corriente adj (agua) running; (monedas, publicación, cuenta, año) current; (ordinario) ordinary. ● f current; (de aire) draught; (fig) tendency. ● m current month. **al ~** (al día) up-to-date; (enterado) aware

corr|illo m small group. **~o** m circle

corroborar vt corroborate

corroer [24] & [37] vt corrode; (en geología) erode; (fig) eat away

corromper vt corrupt, rot (materia). **~se** vpr become corrupted; (materia) rot; (alimentos) go bad

corrosi|ón f corrosion. **~vo** adj corrosive

corrupción f corruption; (de materia etc) rot

corsé m corset

corta|do adj cut; (carretera) closed; (leche) curdled; (avergonzado) embarrassed; (confuso) confused. ● m coffee with a little milk. **~dura** f cut. **~nte** adj sharp; (viento) biting; (frío) bitter. **~r** vt cut; (recortar) cut out; (aislar, sepa-

rar, interrumpir) cut off. ● vi cut; (novios) break up. **~rse** vpr cut o.s.; (leche etc) curdle; (fig) be embarrassed. **~rse el pelo** have one's hair cut. **~rse las uñas** cut one's nails. **~uñas** m invar nail-clippers

corte m cut; (de tela) length. **~ de luz** power cut. **~ y confección** dressmaking. ● f court; (LAm, tribunal) Court of Appeal. **hacer la ~** court. **las C~s** the Spanish parliament. **la C~ Suprema** the Supreme Court

cortej|ar vt court. **~o** m (de rey etc) entourage. **~o fúnebre** cortège, funeral procession

cortés adj polite

cortesía f courtesy

corteza f bark; (de queso) rind; (de pan) crust

cortijo m farm; (casa) farmhouse

cortina f curtain

corto adj short; (apocado) shy. **~ de** short of. **~ de alcances** dim, thick. **~ de vista** short-sighted. **a la corta o a la larga** sooner or later. **quedarse ~** fall short; (subestimar) underestimate. **~circuito** m short circuit.

Coruña f. **La ~** Corunna

cosa f thing; (asunto) business; (idea) idea. **como si tal ~** just like that; (como si no hubiera pasado nada) as if nothing had happened. **decirle a uno cuatro ~s** tell s.o. a thing or two

cosecha f harvest; (de vino) vintage. **~r** vt harvest

coser vt sew; sew on (botón); stitch (herida). ● vi sew. **~se** vpr stick to s.o.

cosmético adj & m cosmetic

cósmico adj cosmic

cosmo|polita adj & m & f cosmopolitan. **~s** m cosmos

cosquillas fpl. **dar ~** tickle.
hacer ~ tickle. **tener ~** be tick-
lish

costa f coast. **a ~ de** at the expense of. **a toda ~** at any cost

costado m side

costal m sack

costar 2 vt cost. ● vi cost; (resultar difícil) to be hard. **~ caro** be
expensive. **cueste lo que cueste** at
any cost

costarricense adj & m, **costarriqueño** adj & m Costa Rican

cost|as fpl (Jurid) costs. **~e** m cost.
~ear vt pay for; (Naut) sail along
the coast

costero adj coastal

costilla f rib; (chuleta) chop

costo m cost. **~so** adj expensive

costumbre f custom; (de persona) habit. **de ~** usual; (como
adv) usually

costur|a f sewing; (línea) seam;
(confección) dressmaking. **~era** f
dressmaker. **~ero** m sewing box

cotejar vt compare

cotidiano adj daily

cotille|ar vt gossip. **~o** m gossip

cotiza|ción f quotation, price.
~r 10 vt (en la bolsa) quote. ● vi
pay contributions. **~rse** vpr fetch;
(en la bolsa) stand at; (fig) be valued

coto m enclosure; (de caza) preserve. **~ de caza** game preserve

cotorr|a f parrot; (fig) chatterbox.
~ear vi chatter

coyuntura f joint

coz f kick

cráneo m skull

cráter m crater

crea|ción f creation. **~dor** adj

creative. ● m creator. **~r** vt create

crec|er 11 vi grow; (aumentar) in-
crease; (río) rise. **~ida** f (de río)
flood. **~ido** adj (persona) grown-
up; (número) large, considerable;
(plantas) fully-grown. **~iente** adj
growing; (luna) crescent.
~imiento m growth

credencial f document. ● adj.
cartas fpl ~es credentials

credibilidad f credibility

crédito m credit; (préstamo) loan.
digno de ~ reliable

credo m creed

crédulo adj credulous

cre|encia f belief. **~er** 18 vt/i be-
lieve; (pensar) think. **~o que no** I
don't think so, I think not. **~o que
sí** I think so. **no ~o** I don't think
so. **¡ya lo ~o!** I should think so!.
~erse vpr consider o.s. **no me lo
~o** I don't believe it. **~ible** adj
credible

crema f cream; (Culin) custard;
(LAm, de la leche) cream. **~ batida**
(LAm) whipped cream. **~ broncea-
dora** sun-tan cream

cremallera f zip (Brit), zipper
(Amer)

crematorio m crematorium

crepitar vi crackle

crepúsculo m twilight

crespo adj frizzy; (LAm, rizado)
curly. ● m (LAm) curl

cresta f crest; (de gallo) comb

creyente m believer

cría f breeding; (animal) baby animal. **las ~s** the young

cria|da f maid, servant. **~dero** m
(de pollos etc) farm; (de ostras) bed;
(de plantas) nursery. ● m servant.
~dor m breeder. **~nza** f breeding.
~r 20 vt suckle; grow (plantas);
breed (animales); (educar) bring up

(*Brit*), raise (*esp Amer*). **~rse** *vpr* grow up

criatura *f* creature; (*niño*) baby

crim|en *m* (serious) crime; (*asesinato*) murder; (*fig*) crime. **~inal** *adj* & *m* & *f* criminal

crin *f* mane

crío *m* child

criollo *adj* Creole; (*LAm, música, comida*) traditional. ● *m* Creole; (*LAm, nativo*) Peruvian, Chilean etc

crisantemo *m* chrysanthemum

crisis *f invar* crisis

crispar *vt* twitch; (*fam, irritar*) annoy. **~le los nervios a uno** get on s.o.'s nerves

cristal *m* crystal; (*Esp, vidrio*) glass; (*Esp, de una ventana*) pane of glass. **limpiar los ~es** (*Esp*) clean the windows. **~ino** *adj* crystalline; (*fig*) crystal-clear. **~izar** **10** crystallize. **~izarse** *vpr* crystallize

cristian|dad *f* Christendom. **~ismo** *m* Christianity. **~o** *adj* Christian. **ser ~o** be a Christian. ● *m* Christian

cristo *m* crucifix

Cristo *m* Christ

criterio *m* criterion; (*discernimiento*) judgement; (*opinión*) opinion

cr|ítica *f* criticism; (*reseña*) review. **~iticar** **7** *vt* criticize. **~ítico** *adj* critical. ● *m* critic

croar *vi* croak

crom|ado *adj* chromium-plated. **~o** *m* chromium, chrome

crónic|a *f* chronicle; (*de radio, TV*) report; (*de periódico*) feature. **~a deportiva** sport section. **~o** *adj* chronic

cronista *m* & *f* reporter

crono|grama *m* schedule, timetable. **~logía** *f* chronology

cron|ometrar *vt* time. **~ómetro** *m* (*en deportes*) stop-watch

croqueta *f* croquette

cruce *m* crossing; (*de calles, carreteras*) crossroads; (*de peatones*) (pedestrian) crossing

crucial *adj* crucial

crucifi|car **7** *vt* crucify. **~jo** *m* crucifix

crucigrama *m* crossword (puzzle)

crudo *adj* raw; (*fig*) harsh. ● *m* crude (oil)

cruel *adj* cruel. **~dad** *f* cruelty

cruji|do *m* (*de seda, de hojas secas*) rustle; (*de muebles*) creak. **~r** *vi* (*seda, hojas secas*) rustle; (*muebles*) creak

cruz *f* cross; (*de moneda*) tails. **~ gamada** swastika. **la C~ Roja** the Red Cross

cruza|da *f* crusade. **~r** **10** *vt* cross; exchange (*palabras*). **~rse** *vpr* cross; (*pasar en la calle*) pass each other. **~rse con** pass

cuaderno *m* exercise book; (*para apuntes*) notebook

cuadra *f* (*caballeriza*) stable; (*LAm, distancia*) block

cuadrado *adj* & *m* square

cuadragésimo *adj* fortieth

cuadr|ar *vt* square. ● *vi* suit; (*cuentas*) tally. **~arse** *vpr* (*Mil*) stand to attention; (*fig*) dig one's heels in. **~ilátero** *m* quadrilateral; (*Boxeo*) ring

cuadrilla *f* group; (*pandilla*) gang

cuadro *m* square; (*pintura*) painting; (*Teatro*) scene; (*de números*) table; (*de mando etc*) panel; (*conjunto del personal*) staff. **~ de distribución** switchboard. **a ~s, de ~s** check. **¡qué ~!, ¡vaya un ~!**

what a sight!

cuadrúpedo m quadruped

cuádruple adj & m quadruple

cuajar vt congeal (sangre); curdle (leche); (llenar) fill up. • vi (nieve) settle; (fig, fam) work out. **cuajado de** full of. **~se** vpr coagulate; (sangre) clot; (leche) curdle

cual pron. el ~, la ~ etc (animales y cosas) that, which; (personas, sujeto) who, that; (personas, objeto) whom. • adj (LAm, qué) what. ~ **si** as if. **cada** ~ everyone. **lo** ~ which. **por lo** ~ because of which. **sea** ~ **sea** whatever

cuál pron which; (LAm, qué) what

cualidad f quality

cualquiera adj (delante de nombres cualquier, pl cualesquiera) any. • pron (pl cualesquiera) anyone, anybody; (cosas) whatever, whichever. **un** ~ a nobody. **una** ~ a slut

cuando adv when. • conj when; (si) if. ~ **más** at the most. ~ **menos** at the least. **aun** ~ even if. **de** ~ **en** ~ from time to time

cuándo adv & conj when. **¿de** ~ **acá?, ¿desde** ~? since when? **¡~ no!** (LAm) as usual!, typical!

cuant|ía f quantity; (extensión) extent. **~oso** adj abundant. **~o** adj as much ... as, as many ... as. • pron as much as, as many as. • adv as much as. **~o antes** as soon as possible. **~o más, mejor** the more the merrier. **en ~o** as soon as. **en ~o a** as for. **por ~o** since. **unos ~os** a few, some

cuánto adj (interrogativo) how much?; (interrogativo en plural) how many?; (exclamativo) what a lot of! • pron how much?; (en plural) how many? • adv how much.

¿~ mides? how tall are you? **¿~ tiempo?** how long? **¡~ tiempo sin verte!** it's been a long time! **¿a ~s estamos?** what's the date today? **un Sr. no sé ~s** Mr So-and-So

cuáquero m Quaker

cuarent|a adj & m forty; (cuadragésimo) fortieth. **~ena** f (Med) quarantine. **~ón** adj about forty

cuaresma f Lent

cuarta f (palmo) span

cuartel m (Mil) barracks. ~ **general** headquarters

cuarteto m quartet

cuarto adj fourth. • m quarter; (habitación) room. ~ **de baño** bathroom. ~ **de estar** living room. ~ **de hora** quarter of an hour. **estar sin un** ~ be broke. **y** ~ (a) quarter past

cuarzo m quartz

cuate m (Mex) twin; (amigo) friend; (🇲🇽, tipo) guy

cuatro adj & m four. **~cientos** adj & m four hundred

Cuba f Cuba

cuba|libre m rum and Coke (P). **~no** adj & m Cuban

cúbico adj cubic

cubículo m cubicle

cubiert|a f cover; (neumático) tyre; (Naut) deck. **~o** adj covered; (cielo) overcast. • m place setting, piece of cutlery; (en restaurante) cover charge. **a ~o** under cover

cubilete m bowl; (molde) mould; (para los dados) cup

cubis|mo m cubism. **~ta** adj & m & f cubist

cubo m bucket; (Mat) cube

cubrecama m bedspread

cubrir (pp cubierto) vt cover; fill

(vacante). **~se** *vpr* cover o.s.; (*ponerse el sombrero*) put on one's hat; (*el cielo*) cloud over, become overcast

cucaracha *f* cockroach

cuchar|a *f* spoon. **~ada** *f* spoonful. **~adita** *f* teaspoonful. **~illa**, **~ita** *f* teaspoon. **~ón** *m* ladle

cuchichear *vi* whisper

cuchill|a *f* large knife; (*de carnicero*) cleaver; (*hoja de afeitar*) razor blade. **~ada** *f* stab; (*herida*) knife wound. **~o** *m* knife

cuchitril *m* (*fig*) hovel

cuclillas *en* **~** *adv* squatting

cuco *adj* shrewd; (*mono*) pretty, nice. ● *m* cuckoo

cucurucho *m* cornet

cuello *m* neck; (*de camisa*) collar. **cortar(le) el ~ a uno** cut s.o.'s throat

cuenc|a *f* (*del ojo*) (eye) socket; (*de río*) basin. **~o** *m* hollow; (*vasija*) bowl

cuenta *f* count; (*acción de contar*) counting; (*cálculo*) calculation; (*factura*) bill; (*en banco, relato*) account; (*de collar*) bead. **~ corriente** current account, checking account (*Amer*). **dar ~ de** give an account of. **darse ~ de** realize. **en resumidas ~s** in short. **por mi propia ~** on my own account. **tener en ~** bear in mind

cuentakilómetros *m invar* milometer

cuent|ista *m & f* story-writer; (*de mentiras*) fibber. **~o** *m* story; (*mentira*) fib, tall story. **~ de hadas** fairy tale. ● *vb véase* CONTAR

cuerda *f* rope; (*más fina*) string; (*Mus*) string. **~ floja** tightrope. **dar ~ a** wind up (*un reloj*)

cuerdo *adj* (*persona*) sane; (*ac-*

ción) sensible

cuerno *m* horn

cuero *m* leather; (*piel*) skin; (*del grifo*) washer. **~ cabelludo** scalp. **en ~s** (**vivos**) stark naked

cuerpo *m* body

cuervo *m* crow

cuesta *f* slope, hill. **~ abajo** downhill. **~ arriba** uphill. **a ~s** on one's back

cuestión *f* matter; (*problema*) problem; (*cosa*) thing

cueva *f* cave

cuida|do *m* care; (*preocupación*) worry. **¡~do!** watch out! **tener ~do** be careful. **~doso** *adj* careful. **~r** *vt* look after. ● *vi*. **~r de** look after. **~rse** *vpr* look after o.s. **~rse de** be careful to

culata *f* (*de revólver, fusil*) butt. **~zo** *m* recoil

culebr|a *f* snake. **~ón** *m* soap opera

culinario *adj* culinary

culminar *vi* culminate

culo *m* ⏢ bottom; (*LAm vulg*) arse (*Brit vulg*), ass (*Amer vulg*)

culpa *f* fault. **echar la ~** blame. **por ~ de** because of. **tener la ~** be to blame (**de** for). **~bilidad** *f* guilt. **~ble** *adj* guilty. ● *m & f* culprit. **~r** *vt* blame (**de** for)

cultiv|ar *vt* farm; grow (*plantas*); (*fig*) cultivate. **~o** *m* farming; (*de plantas*) growing

cult|o *adj* (*persona*) educated. ● *m* cult; (*homenaje*) worship. **~ura** *f* culture. **~ural** *adj* cultural

culturismo *m* body-building

cumbre *f* summit

cumpleaños *m invar* birthday

cumplido *adj* perfect; (*cortés*) polite. ● *m* compliment. **de ~** cour-

tesy. **por** ~ out of a sense of duty.
~**r** adj reliable

cumpli|miento m fulfilment; (de ley) observance; (de orden) carrying out. ~**r** vt carry out; observe (ley); serve (condena); reach (años); keep (promesa). **hoy cumple 3 años** he's 3 (years old) today. ● vi do one's duty. **por** ~ **r** as a mere formality. ~**rse** vpr expire; (realizarse) be fulfilled

cuna f cradle; (fig, nacimiento) birthplace

cundir vi spread; (rendir) go a long way

cuneta f ditch

cuña f wedge

cuñad|a f sister-in-law. ~**o** m brother-in-law

cuño m stamp. **de nuevo** ~ new

cuota f quota; (de sociedad etc) membership, fee; (LAm, plazo) instalment; (Mex, peaje) toll

cupe vb véase **CABER**

cupo m cuota; (LAm, capacidad) room; (Mex, plaza) place

cupón m coupon

cúpula f dome

cura f cure; (tratamiento) treatment. ● m priest. ~**ción** f healing. ~**ndero** m faith-healer. ~**r** vt (incl Culin) cure; dress (herida); (tratar) treat; (fig) remedy; tan (pieles). ~**rse** vpr get better

curios|ear vi pry; (mirar) browse. ~**idad** f curiosity. ~**o** adj curious; (raro) odd, unusual ● m onlooker; (fisgón) busybody

curita f (LAm) (sticking) plaster

curriculum (vitae) m curriculum vitae, CV

cursar vt issue; (estudiar) study

cursi adj pretentious, showy

cursillo m short course

cursiva f italics

curso m course; (Univ etc) year. **en** ~ under way; (año etc) current

cursor m cursor

curtir vt tan; (fig) harden. ~**se** vpr become tanned; (fig) become hardened

curv|a f curve; (de carretera) bend. ~**ar** vt bend; bow (estante). ~**arse** vpr bend; (estante) bow; (madera) warp. ~**ilíneo** adj curvilinear; (mujer) curvaceous. ~**o** adj curved

cúspide f top; (fig) pinnacle

custodi|a f safe-keeping; (Jurid) custody. ~**ar** vt guard; (guardar) look after. ~**o** m guardian

cutáneo adj skin

cutis m skin, complexion

cuyo pron (de persona) whose, of whom; (de cosa) whose, of which. **en** ~ **caso** in which case

Dd

dactilógrafo m typist

dado m dice. ● adj given. ~ **que** since, given that

daltónico adj colour-blind

dama f lady. ~ **de honor** bridesmaid. ~**s** fpl draughts (Brit), checkers (Amer)

damasco m damask; (LAm, fruta) apricot

danés adj Danish. ● m Dane; (idioma) Danish

danza f dance; (acción) dancing. ~**r** [10] vt/i dance

dañ|ar vt damage. ~**se** vpr get

dar | debajo

damaged. **~ino** *adj* harmful. **~o** *m* damage; (*a una persona*) harm. **~os y perjuicios** damages. **hacer ~o** a harm, hurt. **hacerse ~o** hurt o.s.

dar 26 *vt* give; bear (frutos); give out (calor); strike (la hora). ● *vi* give. **da igual** it doesn't matter. **¡dale!** go on! **da lo mismo** it doesn't matter. **~ a** (ventana) look on to; (edificio) face. **~ a luz** give birth. **~ con** meet (persona); find (cosa). **¿qué más da?** it doesn't matter! **~se** *vpr* have (baño). **dárselas de** make o.s. out to be. **~se por** consider o.s.

dardo *m* dart

datar *vi*. **~ de** date from

dátil *m* date

dato *m* piece of information. **~s** *mpl* data, information. **~s personales** personal details

de *preposición*

Note that **de** before **el** becomes **del**, e.g. **es del norte**

····▸ (*contenido, material*) of. **un vaso de agua** a glass of water. **es de madera** it's made of wood (*pertenencia*) the **coche de juan** Juan's car. **es de ella** it's hers. **es de María** it's María's. **las llaves del coche** the car keys (*procedencia, origen, época*) from. **soy de Madrid** I'm from Madrid. **una llamada de Lima** a call from Lima. **es del siglo V** it's from the 5th century (*causa, modo*) **se murió de cáncer** he died of cancer. **temblar de miedo** to tremble with fear. **de dos en dos** two by two

····▸ (*parte del día, hora*) **de noche** at night. **de madrugada** early in the morning. **las diez de la mañana** ten (o'clock) in the morning. **de 9 a 12** from 9 to 12

····▸ (*en oraciones pasivas*) by. **rodeado de agua** surrounded by water. **va seguido de coma** is followed by a comma. **es de Mozart** it's by Mozart

····▸ (*al especificar*) **el cajón de arriba** the top drawer. **la clase de inglés** the English lesson. **la chica de verde** the girl in green. **el de debajo** the one underneath

····▸ (*en calidad de*) as. **trabaja de oficinista** he works as a clerk. **vino de chaperón** he came as a chaperon

····▸ (*en comparaciones*) than. **pesa más de un kilo** it weighs more than a kilo

····▸ (*con superlativo*) **el más alto del mundo** the tallest in the world. **el mejor de todos** the best of all

····▸ (*sentido condicional*) if. **de haberlo sabido** if I had known. **de continuar así** if this goes on

➡ Cuando la preposición **de** se emplea como parte de expresiones como **de prisa, de acuerdo** etc., y de nombres compuestos como **hombre de negocios, saco de dormir** etc., ver bajo el respectivo nombre

deambular *vi* roam (**por** about)

debajo *adv* underneath. **~ de** under(neath). **el de ~** the one

underneath. **por ~** underneath.
por ~ de below

debat|e m debate. **~ir** vt debate

deber vt owe. ● verbo auxiliar have
to, must; (en condicional) should.
debo marcharme I must go, I
have to go. ● m duty. **~es** mpl
homework. **~se** vpr. **~se a** be
due to

debido adj due; (correcto) proper.
~ a due to. **como es ~** as is
proper

débil adj weak; (sonido) faint; (luz)
dim

debili|dad f weakness. **~tar** vt
weaken. **~tarse** vpr weaken, get
weak

débito m debit. **~ bancario** (LAm)
direct debit

debut m debut

debutar vi make one's debut

década f decade

deca|dencia f decline. **~dente**
adj decadent. **~er** 29 vi decline;
(debilitarse) weaken. **~ído** adj in
low spirits. **~imiento** m decline,
weakening

decano m dean; (miembro más antiguo) senior member

decapitar vt behead

decena f ten. **una ~ de** about
ten

decencia f decency

decenio m decade

decente adj decent; (decoroso) respectable; (limpio) clean, tidy

decepci|ón f disappointment.
~onar vt disappoint

decidi|do adj decided; (persona)
determined, resolute. **~r** vt decide;
settle (cuestión etc). ● vi decide.
~rse vpr make up one's mind

decimal adj & m decimal

décimo adj & m tenth. ● m (de lotería) tenth part of a lottery ticket

decir 46 vt say; (contar) tell. ● m
saying. **~ que no** say no. **~ que
sí** say yes. **dicho de otro modo** in
other words. **dicho y hecho** no
sooner said than done. **¿dígame?**
can I help you? **¡dígame!** (al teléfono) hello! **digamos** let's say. **es
~** that is to say. **mejor dicho** rather. **¡no me digas!** you don't say!,
really! **por así ~, por ~lo así** so
to speak, as it were. **querer ~**
mean. **se dice que** it is said that,
they say that

decisi|ón f decision. **~vo** adj de-
cisive

declara|ción f declaration; (a au-
toridad, prensa) statement. **~ción
de renta** income tax return. **~r**
vt/i declare. **~rse** vpr declare o.s.;
(epidemia etc) break out

declinar vt turn down; (Gram) decline

declive m slope; (fig) decline. **en
~** sloping

decola|je m (LAm) take-off. **~r** vi
(LAm) take off

decolorarse vpr become discol-
oured, fade

decora|ción f decoration. **~do**
m (en el teatro) set. **~r** vt decorate.
~tivo adj decorative

decoro m decorum. **~so** adj decent, respectable

decrépito adj decrepit

decret|ar vt decree. **~o** m decree

dedal m thimble

dedica|ción f dedication. **~r** 7
vt dedicate; devote (tiempo). **~rse**
vpr. **~rse a** devote o.s. to. **¿a qué
se dedica?** what does he do?
~toria f dedication

dedo m finger; (del pie) toe. **~**

anular ring finger. **~ corazón** middle finger. **~ gordo** thumb; (*del pie*) big toe. **~ índice** index finger. **~ meñique** little finger. **~ pulgar** thumb

deduc|ción *f* deduction. **~ir 47** *vt* deduce; (*descontar*) deduct

defect|o *m* fault, defect. **~uoso** *adj* defective

defen|der 1 *vt* defend. **~sa** *f* defence. **~derse** *vpr* defend o.s. **~sivo** *adj* defensive. **~sor** *m* defender. **abogado** *m* **~sor** defence counsel

defeño *m* (*Mex*) person from the Federal District

deficien|cia *f* deficiency. **~cia mental** mental handicap. **~te** *adj* poor, deficient. ● *m* & *f* **~te mental** mentally handicapped person

déficit *m invar* deficit

defini|ción *f* definition. **~do** *adj* defined. **~r** *vt* define. **~tivo** *adj* definitive. **en ~tiva** all in all

deform|ación *f* deformation; (*de imagen etc*) distortion. **~ar** *vt* deform; distort (imagen, metal). **~arse** *vpr* go out of shape. **~e** *adj* deformed

defraudar *vt* defraud; (*decepcionar*) disappoint

defunción *f* death

degenera|ción *f* degeneration; (*cualidad*) degeneracy. **~do** *adj* degenerate. **~r** *vi* degenerate

degollar 16 *vt* cut s.o.'s throat

degradar *vt* degrade; (*Mil*) demote. **~se** *vpr* demean o.s..

degusta|ción *f* tasting. **~r** *vt* taste

dehesa *f* pasture

deja|dez *f* slovenliness; (*pereza*) laziness. **~do** *adj* slovenly; (*descuidado*) slack, negligent. **~r** *vt* leave;

(*abandonar*) abandon; give up (estudios); (*prestar*) lend; (*permitir*) let. **~r a un lado** leave aside. **~r de** stop

dejo *m* aftertaste; (*tonillo*) slight accent; (*toque*) touch

del = **de + el**

delantal *m* apron

delante *adv* in front. **~ de** in front of. **de ~** front. **~ra** *f* front; (*de teatro etc*) front row; (*ventaja*) lead; (*de equipo*) forward line. **llevar la ~ra** be in the lead. **~ro** *adj* front. ● *m* forward

delat|ar *vt* denounce. **~or** *m* informer

delega|ción *f* delegation; (*oficina*) regional office; (*Mex, comisaría*) police station. **~do** *m* delegate; (*Com*) agent, representative. **~r 12** *vt* delegate

deleit|ar *vt* delight. **~e** *m* delight

deletrear *vt* spell (out)

delfín *m* dolphin

delgad|ez *f* thinness. **~o** *adj* thin; (*esbelto*) slim. **~ucho** *adj* skinny

delibera|ción *f* deliberation. **~do** *adj* deliberate. **~r** *vi* deliberate (**sobre** on)

delicad|eza *f* gentleness; (*fragilidad*) frailty; (*tacto*) tact. **falta de ~eza** tactlessness. **tener la ~** de have the courtesy to. **~o** *adj* delicate; (*refinado*) refined; (*sensible*) sensitive

delici|a *f* delight. **~oso** *adj* delightful; (*sabor etc*) delicious

delimitar *vt* delimit

delincuen|cia *f* delinquency. **~te** *m* & *f* criminal, delinquent

delinquir 8 *vi* commit a criminal offence

delir|ante *adj* delirious. **~ar** *vi* be delirious; (*fig*) talk nonsense. **~io**

m delirium; (*fig*) frenzy

delito *m* crime, offence

demacrado *adj* haggard

demagogo *m* demagogue

demanda *f* demand; (*Jurid*) lawsuit. **~do** *m* defendant. **~nte** *m & f* (*Jurid*) plaintiff. **~r** *vt* (*Jurid*) sue; (*LAm, requerir*) require

demarcación *f* demarcation

demás *adj* rest of the, other. ● *pron* rest, others. **lo ~** the rest. **por ~** extremely. **por lo ~** otherwise

demas|ía *f*. **en ~ía** in excess. **~iado** *adj* too much; (*en plural*) too many. ● *adv* too much; (*con adjetivo*) too

demen|cia *f* madness. **~te** *adj* demented, mad

dem|ocracia *f* democracy. **~ócrata** *m & f* democrat. **~ocrático** *adj* democratic

demol|er 2 *vt* demolish. **~ición** *f* demolition

demonio *m* devil, demon. **¡~s!** hell! **¿cómo ~s?** how the hell? **¡qué ~s!** what the hell!

demora *f* delay. **~r** *vt* delay. ● *vi* stay on. **~rse** *vpr* be too long; (*LAm, cierto tiempo*). **se ~ una hora en llegar** it takes him an hour to get there

demostra|ción *f* demonstration, show. **~r 2** *vt* demonstrate; (*mostrar*) show; (*probar*) prove. **~tivo** *adj* demonstrative

dengue *m* dengue fever

denigrar *vt* denigrate

denominado *adj* named; (*supuesto*) so-called

dens|idad *f* density. **~o** *adj* dense, thick

denta|dura *f* teeth. **~dura postiza** dentures, false teeth. **~l** *adj*

dental

dent|era *f*. **darle ~era a uno** set s.o.'s teeth on edge. **~ífrico** *m* toothpaste. **~ista** *m & f* dentist

dentro *adv* inside; (*de un edificio*) indoors. **~ de** in. **~ de poco** soon. **por ~** inside

denuncia *f* report; (*acusación*) accusation. **~r** *vt* report; (*periódico etc*) denounce

departamento *m* department; (*LAm, apartamento*) flat (*Brit*), apartment (*Amer*)

depend|encia *f* dependence; (*sección*) section; (*oficina*) office. **~encias** *fpl* buildings. **~er** *vi* depend (*de on*). **~ienta** *f* shop assistant. **~iente** *adj* dependent (*de* on). ● *m* shop assistant

depila|r *vt* depilate. **~torio** *adj* depilatory

deplora|ble *adj* deplorable. **~r** *vt* deplore, regret

depone|r 34 *vt* remove from office; depose (*rey*); lay down (*armas*). ● *vi* give evidence

deporta|ción *f* deportation. **~r** *vt* deport

deport|e *m* sport. **hacer ~e** take part in sports. **~ista** *m* sportsman. ● *f* sportswoman. **~ivo** *adj* sports. ● *m* sports car

dep|ositante *m & f* depositor. **~ositar** *vt* deposit; (*poner*) put, place. **~ósito** *m* deposit; (*almacén*) warehouse; (*Mil*) depot; (*de líquidos*) tank

depravado *adj* depraved

deprecia|ción *f* depreciation. **~r** *vt* depreciate. **~rse** *vpr* depreciate

depr|esión *f* depression. **~imido** *adj* depressed. **~imir** *vt* depress. **~imirse** *vpr* get depressed

depura|ción f purification. ∿**do** adj refined. ∿**r** vt purify; (Pol) purge; refine (estilo)

derech|a f (mano) right hand; (lado) right. **a la** ∿**a** on the right; (hacia el lado derecho) to the right. ∿**ista** adj right-wing. ● m & f right-winger. ● **o** adj right; (vertical) upright; (recto) straight. ● adv straight. **todo** ∿**o** straight on. ● m right; (Jurid) law; (lado) right side. ∿**os** mpl dues. ∿**os de autor** royalties

deriva f drift. **a la** ∿ drifting, adrift

deriva|do adj derived. ● m derivative, by-product. ∿**r** vt divert. ● vi. ∿**r de** derive from, be derived from. ∿**rse** vpr. ∿**rse de** be derived from

derram|amiento m spilling. ∿**amiento de sangre** bloodshed. ∿**ar** vt spill; shed (lágrimas). ∿**arse** vpr spill. ∿**e** m spilling; (pérdida) leakage; (Med) discharge; (Med, de sangre) haemorrhage

derretir 5 vt melt

derribar vt knock down; bring down, overthrow (gobierno etc)

derrocar 7 vt bring down, overthrow (gobierno etc)

derroch|ar vt squander. ∿**e** m waste

derrot|a f defeat. ∿**ar** vt defeat. ∿**ado** adj defeated. ∿**ero** m course

derrumba|r vt knock down. ∿**rse** vpr collapse; (persona) go to pieces

desabotonar vt unbutton, undo. ∿**se** vpr come undone; (persona) undo

desabrido adj tasteless; (persona)

surly; (LAm) dull

desabrochar vt undo. ∿**se** vpr come undone; (persona) undo

desacato m defiance; (Jurid) contempt of court

desac|ertado adj ill-advised; (erróneo) wrong. ∿**ierto** m mistake

desacreditar vt discredit

desactivar vt defuse

desacuerdo m disagreement

desafiar 20 vt challenge; (afrontar) defy

desafina|do adj out of tune. ∿**r** vi be out of tune. ∿**rse** vpr go out of tune

desafío m challenge; (a la muerte) defiance; (combate) duel

desafortunada|mente adv unfortunately. ∿**o** adj unfortunate

desagrada|ble adj unpleasant. ∿**r** vt displease. ● vi be unpleasant. **me** ∿ **el sabor** I don't like the taste

desagradecido adj ungrateful

desagrado m displeasure. **con** ∿ unwillingly

desagüe m drain; (acción) drainage. **tubo** m **de** ∿ drain-pipe

desahog|ado adj roomy; (acomodado) comfortable. ∿**ar** 12 vt vent. ∿**arse** vpr let off steam. ∿**o** m comfort; (alivio) relief

desahuci|ar vt declare terminally ill (enfermo); evict (inquilino). ∿**o** m eviction

desair|ar vt snub. ∿**e** m snub

desajuste m maladjustment; (desequilibrio) imbalance

desala|dora f desalination plant. ∿**r** vt to desalinate

desal|entador adj disheartening. ∿**entar** 1 vt discourage. ∿**iento** m discouragement

desaliñado adj slovenly

desalmado adj heartless

desalojar vt (ocupantes) evacuate; (policía) to clear; (LAm) evict (inquilino)

desampar|ado adj helpless; (lugar) unprotected. ~**ar** vt abandon. ~**o** m helplessness; (abandono) lack of protection

desangrar vt bleed. ~**se** vpr bleed

desanima|do adj down-hearted. ~**r** vt discourage. ~**rse** vpr lose heart

desapar|ecer 11 vi disappear; (efecto) wear off. ~**ecido** adj missing. ●m missing person. ~**ición** f disappearance

desapego m indifference

desapercibido adj. pasar ~ go unnoticed

desaprobar 2 vt disapprove of

desarm|able adj collapsible; (estante) easy to dismantle. ~**ar** vt disarm; (desmontar) dismantle; take apart; (LAm) take down (carpa). ~**e** m disarmament

desarraig|ado adj rootless. ~**ar** 12 vt uproot. ~**o** m uprooting

desarregl|ar vt mess up; (alterar) disrupt. ~**o** m disorder

desarroll|ar vt develop. ~**arse** vpr (incl Foto) develop; (suceso) take place. ~**o** m development

desaseado adj dirty; (desordenado) untidy

desasosiego m anxiety; (intranquilidad) restlessness

desastr|ado adj scruffy. ~**e** m disaster. ~**oso** adj disastrous

desatar vt untie; (fig, soltar) unleash. ~**se** vpr come undone; to undo (zapatos)

desatascar 7 vt unblock

desaten|der 1 vt not pay attention to; neglect (deber etc). ~**to** adj inattentive; (descortés) discourteous

desatin|ado adj silly. ~**o** m silliness; (error) mistake

desatornillar vt unscrew

desautorizar 10 vt declare unauthorized; discredit (persona); (desmentir) deny

desavenencia f disagreement

desayun|ar vt have for breakfast. ● vi have breakfast. ~**o** m breakfast

desazón m (fig) unease

desbandarse vpr (Mil) disband; (dispersarse) disperse

desbarajust|ar vt mess up. ~**e** m mess

desbaratar vt spoil; (Mex) mess up (papeles)

desbloquear vt clear; release (mecanismo); unfreeze (cuenta)

desbocado adj (caballo) runaway; (escote) wide

desbordarse vpr overflow; (río) burst its banks

descabellado adj crazy

descafeinado adj decaffeinated. ● m decaffeinated coffee

descalabro m disaster

descalificar 7 vt disqualify; (desacreditar) discredit

descalz|ar 10 vt take off (zapatos). ~**o** adj barefoot

descampado m open ground. **al** ~ (LAm) in the open air

descans|ado adj rested; (trabajo) easy. ~**ar** vt/i rest. ~**illo** m landing. ~**o** m rest; (del trabajo) break; (LAm, rellano) landing; (en deportes) half-time; (en el teatro etc) interval

descapotable adj convertible

descarado *adj* cheeky; (*sin vergüenza*) shameless

descarg|a *f* unloading; (*Mil, Elec*) discharge. **~ar** 12 *vt* unload; (*Mil, Elec*) discharge. (*Informática*) download. **~o** *m* (*recibo*) receipt; (*Jurid*) evidence

descaro *m* cheek, nerve

descarriarse 20 *vpr* go the wrong way; (*res*) stray; (*fig*) go astray

descarrila|miento *m* derailment. **~r** *vi* be derailed. **~rse** *vpr* (*LAm*) be derailed

descartar *vt* rule out

descascararse *vpr* (*pintura*) peel; (*taza*) chip

descen|dencia *f* descent; (*personas*) descendants. **~der** 1 *vt* go down (escalera etc). ● *vi* go down; (*temperatura*) fall, drop; (*provenir*) be descended (**de** from). **~diente** *m & f* descendant. **~so** *m* descent; (*de temperatura, fiebre etc*) fall, drop

descifrar *vt* decipher; decode (*clave*)

descolgar 2 & 12 *vt* take down; pick up (el teléfono). **~se** *vpr* lower o.s.

descolor|ar *vt* discolour, fade. **~ido** *adj* discoloured, faded; (*persona*) pale

descompo|oner 34 *vt* break down; decompose (materia); upset (estómago); (*esp LAm, estropear*) break; (*esp LAm, desarreglar*) mess up. **~onerse** *vpr* decompose; (*esp LAm, estropearse*) break down; (*persona*) feel sick. **~ostura** *f* (*esp LAm, de máquina*) breakdown; (*esp LAm, náuseas*) sickness; (*LAm, diarrea*) diarrhoea; (*LAm, falla*) fault. **~uesto** *adj* decomposed; (*encoleri-*

zado) angry; (*esp LAm, estropeado*) broken. **estar ~uesto** (*del estómago*) have diarrhoea

descomunal *adj* enormous

desconc|ertante *adj* disconcerting. **~ertar** 1 *vt* disconcert; (*dejar perplejo*) puzzle. **~ertarse** *vpr* be put out, be disconcerted

desconectar *vt* disconnect

desconfia|do *adj* distrustful. **~nza** *f* distrust, suspicion. **~r** 20 *vi*. **~r de** mistrust; (*no creer*) doubt

descongelar *vt* defrost; (*Com*) unfreeze

desconoc|er 11 *vt* not know, not recognize. **~ido** *adj* unknown; (*cambiado*) unrecognizable. ● *m* stranger. **~imiento** *m* ignorance

desconsidera|ción *f* lack of consideration. **~do** *adj* inconsiderate

descons|olado *adj* distressed. **~uelo** *m* distress; (*tristeza*) sadness

desconta|do *adj*. **dar por ~do** (**que**) take for granted (that). **~r** 2 *vt* discount; deduct (impuestos etc)

descontento *adj* unhappy (**con** with), dissatisfied (**con** with). ● *m* discontent

descorazonar *vt* discourage. **~se** *vpr* lose heart

descorchar *vt* uncork

descorrer *vt* draw (cortina). **~ el cerrojo** unbolt the door

descort|és *adj* rude, discourteous. **~esía** *f* rudeness

descos|er *vt* unpick. **~erse** *vpr* come undone. **~ido** *adj* unstitched

descrédito *m* disrepute. **ir en ~ de** damage the reputation of

descremado *adj* skimmed

descri|bir (*pp* **descrito**) *vt* describe. **~pción** *f* description

descuartizar [10] *vt* cut up

descubierto *adj* discovered; (*no cubierto*) uncovered; (*vehículo*) open-top; (*piscina*) open-air; (*cielo*) clear; (*cabeza*) bare. ● *m* overdraft. **poner al ~** expose

descubri|miento *m* discovery. **~r** (*pp* **descubierto**) *vt* discover; (*destapar*) uncover; (*revelar*) reveal; unveil (estatua). **~rse** *vpr* (*quitarse el sombrero*) take off one's hat

descuento *m* discount; (*del sueldo*) deduction; (*en deportes*) injury time

descuid|ado *adj* careless; (*aspecto etc*) untidy; (*desprevenido*) unprepared. **~ar** *vt* neglect. ● *vi* not worry. **¡~a!** don't worry!. **~arse** *vpr* be careless. **~o** *m* carelessness; (*negligencia*) negligence

desde *prep* (*lugar etc*) from; (*tiempo*) since, from. **~ ahora** from now on. **~ hace un mes** for a month. **~ luego** of course. **~ Madrid hasta Barcelona** from Madrid to Barcelona. **~ niño** since childhood

desdecirse [46] *vpr.* **~ de** take back (palabras etc); go back on (promesa)

desd|én *m* scorn. **~eñable** *adj* insignificant. **nada ~eñable** significant. **~eñar** *vt* scorn

desdicha *f* misfortune. **por ~** unfortunately. **~do** *adj* unfortunate

desdoblar *vt* (*desplegar*) unfold

desear *vt* want; wish (suerte etc). **le deseo un buen viaje** I hope you have a good journey. **¿qué desea Vd?** can I help you?

desech|able *adj* disposable. **~ar** *vt* throw out; (*rechazar*) reject. **~o** *m* waste

desembalar *vt* unpack

desembarcar [7] *vt* unload. ● *vi* disembark

desemboca|dura *f* (*de río*) mouth; (*de calle*) opening. **~r** [7] *vi*. **~r en** (río) flow into; (*calle*) lead to

desembolso *m* payment

desembragar [12] *vi* declutch

desempaquetar *vt* unwrap

desempat|ar *vi* break a tie. **~e** *m* tie-breaker

desempeñ|ar *vt* redeem; play (papel); hold (cargo); perform, carry out (deber etc). **~arse** *vpr* (*LAm*) perform. **~arse bien** manage well. **~o** *m* redemption; (*de un deber, una función*) discharge; (*LAm, actuación*) performance

desemple|ado *adj* unemployed. ● *m* unemployed person. **los ~ados** the unemployed. **~o** *m* unemployment

desencadenar *vt* unchain (preso); unleash (perro); (*causar*) trigger. **~se** *vpr* be triggered off; (guerra etc) break out

desencajar *vt* dislocate; (*desconectar*) disconnect. **~se** *vpr* become dislocated

desenchufar *vt* unplug

desenfad|ado *adj* uninhibited; (*desenvuelto*) self-assured. **~o** *m* lack of inhibition; (*desenvoltura*) self-assurance

desenfocado *adj* out of focus

desenfren|ado *adj* unrestrained. **~o** *m* licentiousness

desenganchar *vt* unhook; uncouple (vagón)

desengañ|ar *vt* disillusion. **~arse** *vpr* become disillusioned; (*darse cuenta*) realize. **~o** *m* disillusionment, disappointment

desenlace *m* outcome

desenmascarar vt unmask

desenredar vt untangle. ～**se** vpr untangle

desenro|**llar** vt unroll, unwind. ～**scar 7** vt unscrew

desentend|**erse 1** vpr want nothing to do with. ～**ido** m. **hacerse el ～ido** (fingir no oír) pretend not to hear; (fingir ignorancia) pretend not to know

desenterrar 1 vt exhume; (fig) unearth

desentonar vi be out of tune; (colores) clash

desenvoltura f ease; (falta de timidez) confidence

desenvolver 2 (pp **desenvuelto**) vt unwrap; expound (idea etc). ～**se** vpr perform; (manejarse) manage

deseo m wish, desire. ～**so** adj eager. **estar ～so de** be eager to

desequilibr|**ado** adj unbalanced. ～**io** m imbalance

des|**ertar** vt desert; (Pol) defect. ～**értico** adj desert-like. ～**ertor** m (Pol) deserter; (Pol) defector

desespera|**ción** f despair. ～**do** adj desperate. ～**nte** adj infuriating. ～**r** vt drive to despair. ～**rse** vpr despair

desestimar vt (rechazar) reject

desfachat|**ado** adj brazen, shameless. ～**ez** f nerve, cheek

desfallec|**er 11** vt weaken. ● vi become weak; (desmayarse) faint. ～**imiento** m weakness; (desmayo) faint

desfasado adj out of phase; (idea) outdated; (persona) out of touch

desfavorable adj unfavourable

desfil|**adero** m narrow mountain pass; (cañón) narrow gorge. ～**ar** vi

march (past). ～**e** m procession, parade. ～**e de modelos** fashion show

desgana f, (LAm) **desgano** m (falta de apetito) lack of appetite; (Med) weakness, faintness; (fig) unwillingness

desgarr|**ador** adj heart-rending. ～**ar** vt tear; (fig) break (corazón). ～**o** m tear, rip

desgast|**ar** vt wear away; wear out (ropa). ～**arse** vpr wear away; (ropa) be worn out; (persona) wear o.s. out. ～**e** m wear

desgracia f misfortune; (accidente) accident; **por ～** unfortunately. **¡qué ～!** what a shame!. ～**do** adj unlucky; (pobre) poor. ● m unfortunate person, poor devil **1**

desgranar vt shell (habas etc)

desgreñado adj ruffled, dishevelled

deshabitado adj uninhabited; (edificio) unoccupied

deshacer 31 vt undo; strip (cama); unpack (maleta); (desmontar) take to pieces; break (trato); (derretir) melt; (disolver) dissolve. ～**se** vpr come undone; (disolverse) dissolve; (derretirse) melt. ～**se de algo** get rid of sth. ～**se en lágrimas** dissolve into tears. ～**se por hacer algo** go out of one's way to do sth

desheredar vt disinherit

deshidratarse vpr become dehydrated

deshielo m thaw

deshilachado adj frayed

deshincha|**do** adj (neumático) flat. ～**r** vt deflate; (Med) reduce the swelling in. ～**rse** vpr go down

deshollinador m chimney sweep

deshon|esto *adj* dishonest; (*obsceno*) indecent. **~ra** *f* disgrace. **~rar** *vt* dishonour

deshora *f*. a **~** out of hours. comer a **~s** eat between meals

deshuesar *vt* bone (*carne*); stone (*fruta*)

desidia *f* slackness; (*pereza*) laziness

desierto *adj* deserted. ● *m* desert

designar *vt* designate; (*fijar*) fix

desigual *adj* unequal; (*terreno*) uneven; (*distinto*) different. **~dad** *f* inequality

desilusi|ón *f* disappointment; (*pérdida de ilusiones*) disillusionment. **~onar** *vt* disappoint; (*quitar las ilusiones*) disillusion. **~onarse** *vpr* be disappointed; (*perder las ilusiones*) become disillusioned

desinfecta|nte *m* disinfectant. **~r** *vt* disinfect

desinflar *vt* deflate. **~se** *vpr* go down

desinhibido *adj* uninhibited

desintegrar *vt* disintegrate. **~se** *vpr* disintegrate

desinter|és *m* lack of interest; (*generosidad*) unselfishness. **~esado** *adj* uninterested; (*liberal*) unselfish

desistir *vi*. **~ de** give up

desleal *adj* disloyal. **~tad** *f* disloyalty

desligar 12 *vt* untie; (*separar*) separate; (*fig, librar*) free. **~se** *vpr* break away; (*de un compromiso*) free o.s. (de from)

desliza|dor *m* (*Mex*) hang glider. **~r** 10 *vt* slide, slip. **~se** *vpr* slide, slip; (*patinador*) glide; (*tiempo*) slip by, pass; (*fluir*) flow

deslucido *adj* tarnished; (*gastado*) worn out; (*fig*) undistinguished

deslumbrar *vt* dazzle

desmadr|arse *vpr* get out of control. **~e** *m* excess

desmán *m* outrage

desmanchar *vt* (*LAm*) remove the stains from

desmantelar *vt* dismantle; (*despojar*) strip

desmaquillador *m* make-up remover

desmay|ado *adj* unconscious. **~arse** *vpr* faint. **~o** *m* faint

desmedido *adj* excessive

desmemoriado *adj* forgetful

desmenti|do *m* denial. **~r** 4 *vt* deny; (*contradecir*) contradict

desmenuzar 10 *vt* crumble; shred (carne etc)

desmerecer 11 *vi*. no **~ de** compare favourably with

desmesurado *adj* excessive; (*enorme*) enormous

desmonta|ble *adj* collapsible; (*armario*) easy to dismantle; (*separable*) removable. **~r** *vt* (*quitar*) remove; (*desarmar*) dismantle, take apart. ● *vi* dismount

desmoralizar 10 *vt* demoralize

desmoronarse *vpr* crumble; (*edificio*) collapse

desnatado *adj* skimmed

desnivel *m* unevenness; (*fig*) difference, inequality

desnud|ar *vt* strip; undress, strip (persona). **~arse** *vpr* undress. **~ez** *f* nudity. **~o** *adj* naked; (*fig*) bare. ● *m* nude

desnutri|ción *f* malnutrition. **~do** *adj* undernourished

desobed|ecer 11 *vt* disobey. **~iencia** *f* disobedience

desocupa|do *adj* (*asiento etc*) vacant, free; (*sin trabajo*) unemployed; (*ocioso*) idle. **~r** vt vacate; (*vaciar*) empty; (*desalojar*) clear

desodorante m deodorant

desolado adj desolate; (*persona*) sorry, sad

desorbitante adj excessive

desorden m disorder, untidiness; (*confusión*) confusion. **~ado** adj untidy. **~ar** vt disarrange, make a mess of

desorganizar 10 vt disorganize; (*trastornar*) disturb

desorienta|do adj confused. **~r** vt disorientate. **~rse** vpr lose one's bearings

despabila|do adj wide awake; (*listo*) quick. **~r** vt (*despertar*) wake up; (*avivar*) wise up. **~rse** vpr wake up; (*avivarse*) wise up

despach|ar vt finish; (*tratar con*) deal with; (*atender*) serve; (*vender*) sell; (*enviar*) send; (*despedir*) fire. **~o** m dispatch; (*oficina*) office; (*venta*) sale; (*de localidades*) box office

despacio adv slowly

despampanante adj stunning

desparpajo m confidence; (*descaro*) impudence

desparramar vt scatter; spill (*líquidos*)

despavorido adj terrified

despecho m spite. **a ~ de** in spite of. **por ~** out of spite

despectivo adj contemptuous; (*sentido etc*) pejorative

despedazar 10 vt tear to pieces

despedi|da f goodbye, farewell. **~da de soltero** stag-party. **~r 5** vt say goodbye to, see off; dismiss (*empleado*); evict (*inquilino*); (*arrojar*) throw; give off (*olor* etc). **~rse** vpr say goodbye (**de** to)

despeg|ar 12 vt unstick. ● vi (*avión*) take off. **~ue** m take-off

despeinar vt ruffle the hair of

despeja|do adj clear; (*persona*) wide awake. **~r** vt clear; (*aclarar*) clarify. ● vi clear. **~rse** vpr (*aclararse*) become clear; (*tiempo*) clear up

despellejar vt skin

despenalizar vt decriminalize

despensa f pantry, larder

despeñadero m cliff

desperdici|ar vt waste. **~o** m waste. **~os** mpl rubbish

desperta|dor m alarm clock. **~r 1** vt wake (up); (*fig*) awaken. **~rse** vpr wake up

despiadado adj merciless

despido m dismissal

despierto adj awake; (*listo*) bright

despilfarr|ar vt waste. **~o** m squandering

despintarse vpr (*Mex*) run

despista|do adj (*con estar*) confused; (*con ser*) absent-minded. **~r** vt throw off the scent; (*fig*) mislead. **~rse** vpr (*fig*) get confused

despiste m mistake; (*confusión*) muddle

desplaza|miento m displacement; (*de opinión etc*) swing, shift. **~r 10** vt displace. **~rse** vpr travel

desplegar 1 & 12 vt open out; spread (*alas*); (*fig*) show

desplomarse vpr collapse

despoblado m deserted area

despoj|ar vt deprive (*persona*); strip (*cosa*). **~os** mpl remains; (*de res*) offal; (*de ave*) giblets

depreci|able adj despicable; (*cantidad*) negligible. **~ar** vt despise; (*rechazar*) scorn. **~o** m contempt; (*desaire*) snub

desprender vt remove; give off

(olor). **~se** vpr fall off; (fig) part with; (deducirse) follow

despreocupa|do adj unconcerned; (descuidado) careless. **~rse** vpr not worry

desprestigiar vt discredit

desprevenido adj unprepared. pillar a uno ~ catch s.o. unawares

desproporcionado adj disproportionate

desprovisto adj. ~ de lacking in, without

después adv after, afterwards; (más tarde) later; (a continuación) then. ~ de after. ~ de comer after eating. ~ de todo after all. ~ (de) que after. poco ~ soon after

desquitar|se vpr get even (de with). **~e** m revenge

destaca|do adj outstanding. **~r** **7** vt emphasize. ● vi stand out. **~rse** vpr stand out. **~rse en** excel at

destajo m. trabajar a ~ do piece-work

destap|ar vt uncover; open (botella). **~arse** vpr reveal one's true self. **~e** m (fig) permissiveness

destartalado adj (coche) clapped-out; (casa) ramshackle

destello m sparkle; (de estrella) twinkle; (fig) glimmer

destemplado adj discordant; (nervios) frayed

desteñir **5** & **22** vt fade. ● vi fade; (color) run. **~se** vpr fade; (color) run

desterra|do m exile. **~r** **1** vt banish

destetar vt wean

destiempo m. a ~ at the wrong moment; (Mus) out of time

destierro m exile

destil|ar vt distil. **~ería** f distillery

destin|ar vt destine; (nombrar) post. **~atario** m addressee. **~o** m (uso) use, function; (lugar) destination; (suerte) destiny. con ~o a (going) to

destituir **17** vt dismiss

destornilla|dor m screwdriver. **~r** vt unscrew

destreza f skill

destroz|ar **10** vt destroy; (fig) shatter. **~os** mpl destruction, damage

destru|cción f destruction. **~ir** **17** vt destroy

desus|ado adj old-fashioned; (insólito) unusual. **~o** m disuse. caer en ~o fall into disuse

desvalido adj needy, destitute

desvalijar vt rob; ransack (casa)

desvalorizar **10** vt devalue

desván m loft

desvanec|er **11** vt make disappear; (borrar) blur; (fig) dispel. **~erse** vpr disappear; (desmayarse) faint. **~imiento** m (Med) faint

desvariar **20** vi be delirious; (fig) talk nonsense

desvel|ar vt keep awake. **~arse** vpr stay awake, have a sleepless night. **~o** m sleeplessness

desvencijado adj (mueble) rickety

desventaja f disadvantage

desventura f misfortune. **~do** adj unfortunate

desvergÜonzado adj impudent, cheeky. **~Üenza** f impudence, cheek

desvestirse **5** vpr undress

desv|iación f deviation; (Auto) diversion. **~iar** **20** vt divert; deflect (pelota). **~iarse** vpr (carretera) branch off; (*del camino*) make a detour; (*del tema*) stray. **~ío** *m* diversion

desvivirse *vpr.* **~se por** be completely devoted to; (*esforzarse*) go out of one's way to

detall|ar *vt* relate in detail. **~e** *m* detail; (*fig*) gesture. **al ~e** retail. **entrar en ~es** go into detail. **¡qué ~e!** how thoughtful! **~ista** *m & f* retailer

detect|ar *vt* detect. **~ive** *m* detective

deten|ción *f* stopping; (*Jurid*) arrest; (*en la cárcel*) detention. **~er 40** *vt* stop; (*Jurid*) arrest; (*encarcelar*) detain; (*retrasar*) delay. **~erse** *vpr* stop; (*entretenerse*) spend a lot of time. **~idamente** *adv* at length. **~ido** *adj* (*Jurid*) under arrest. ● *m* prisoner

detergente *adj & m* detergent

deterior|ar *vt* damage, spoil. **~arse** *vpr* deteriorate. **~o** *m* deterioration

determina|ción *f* determination; (*decisión*) decison. **~nte** *adj* decisive. **~r** *vt* determine; (*decidir*) decide

detestar *vt* detest

detrás *adv* behind; (*en la parte posterior*) on the back. **~ de** behind. **por ~** at the back; (*por la espalda*) from behind

detrimento *m* detriment. **en ~ de** to the detriment of

deud|a *f* debt. **~or** *m* debtor

devalua|ción *f* devaluation. **~r 21** *vt* devalue. **~se** *vpr* depreciate

devastador *adj* devastating

devoción *f* devotion

devol|ución *f* return; (*Com*) repayment, refund. **~ver 5** (*pp devuelto*) *vt* return; (*Com*) repay, re-

fund. ● *vi* be sick

devorar *vt* devour

devoto *adj* devout; (*amigo etc*) devoted. ● *m* admirer

di *vb véase* **DAR, DECIR**

día *m* day. **~ de fiesta** (public) holiday. **~ del santo** saint's day. **~ feriado** (*LAm*), **~ festivo** (public) holiday. **al ~** up to date. **al ~ siguiente** (on) the following day. **¡buenos ~s!** good morning! **de ~** by day. **el ~ de hoy** today. **el ~ de mañana** tomorrow. **un ~ sí y otro no** every other day. **vivir al ~** live from hand to mouth

Día de la raza In Latin America, the anniversary of Columbus's discovery of America, October 12. In Spain it is known as *Día de la Hispanidad*. It is a celebration of the cultural ties shared by Spanish-speaking countries.

diab|etes *f* diabetes. **~ético** *adj* diabetic

diab|lo *m* devil. **~lura** *f* mischief. **~ólico** *adj* diabolical

diadema *f* diadem

diáfano *adj* diaphanous; (*cielo*) clear

diafragma *m* diaphragm

diagn|osis *f* diagnosis. **~osticar 7** *vt* diagnose. **~óstico** *m* diagnosis

diagonal *adj & f* diagonal

diagrama *m* diagram

dialecto *m* dialect

dia|logar 12 *vi* talk. **~álogo** *m* dialogue; (*Pol*) talks

diamante *m* diamond

diámetro *m* diameter

diana *f* reveille; (*blanco*) bull's-eye

diapositiva f slide, transparency

diario adj daily. ● m newspaper; (libro) diary. **a** ~**o** daily. **de** ~**o** everyday, ordinary

diarrea f diarrhoea

dibuj|ante m draughtsman. ●f draughtswoman. ~**ar** vt draw. ~**o** m drawing. ~**os animados** cartoons

diccionario m dictionary

dich|a f happiness. **por** ~**a** fortunately. ~**o** adj said; (tal) such. ● m saying. ~**o y hecho** no sooner said than done. **mejor** ~**o** rather. **propiamente** ~**o** strictly speaking. ~**oso** adj happy; (afortunado) fortunate

diciembre m December

dicta|do m dictation. ~**dor** m dictator. ~**dura** f dictatorship. ~**men** m opinion; (informe) report. ~**r** vt dictate; pronounce (sentencia etc); (LAm) give (clase)

didáctico adj didactic

dieci|nueve adj & m nineteen. ~**ocho** adj & m eighteen. ~**séis** adj & m sixteen. ~**siete** adj & m seventeen

diente m tooth; (de tenedor) prong; (de ajo) clove. ~ **de león** dandelion. **hablar entre** ~**s** mumble

diestro adj right-handed; (hábil) skillful

dieta f diet

diez adj & m ten

diezmar vt decimate

difamación f (con palabras) slander; (por escrito) libel

diferen|cia f difference; (desacuerdo) disagreement. ~**ciar** vt differentiate between. ~**ciarse** vpr differ. ~**te** adj different; (diversos) various

diferido adj (TV etc) **en** ~ recorded

dif|ícil adj difficult; (poco probable) unlikely. ~**icultad** f difficulty. ~**icultar** vt make difficult

difteria f diphtheria

difundir vt spread; (TV etc) broadcast

difunto adj late, deceased. ● m deceased

difusión f spreading

dige|rir 4 vt digest. ~**stión** f digestion. ~**stivo** adj digestive

digital adj digital; (de los dedos) finger

dign|arse vpr deign to. ~**atario** m dignitary. ~**idad** f dignity. ~**o** adj honourable; (decoroso) decent; (merecedor) worthy (**de** of). ~ **de elogio** praiseworthy

digo vb véase **DECIR**

dije vb véase **DECIR**

dilatar vt expand; (Med) dilate; (prolongar) prolong. ~**se** vpr expand; (Med) dilate; (extenderse) extend; (Mex, demorarse) be late

dilema m dilemma

diligen|cia f diligence; (gestión) job; (carruaje) stagecoach. ~**te** adj diligent

dilucidar vt clarify; solve (misterio)

diluir 17 vt dilute

diluvio m flood

dimensión f dimension; (tamaño) size

diminut|ivo adj & m diminutive. ~**o** adj minute

dimitir vt/i resign

Dinamarca f Denmark

dinamarqués adj Danish. ● m Dane

dinámic|a f dynamics. ~**o** adj

dynamic

dinamita f dynamite

dínamo m dynamo

dinastía f dynasty

dineral m fortune. **~o** m money. **~o efectivo** cash. **~o suelto** change

dinosaurio m dinosaur

dios m god. **~a** f goddess. ¡**D~ mío!** good heavens! ¡**gracias a D~**! thank God!

diplomla f diploma. **~acia** f diplomacy. **~ado** adj qualified. **~arse** vpr (LAm) graduate. **~ático** adj diplomatic. ● m diplomat

diptongo m diphthong

diputalción f delegation. **~ción provincial** county council. **~do** m deputy; (Pol, en España) member of the Cortes; (Pol, en Inglaterra) Member of Parliament; (Pol, en Estados Unidos) congressman

dique m dike

direclción f direction; (señas) address; (los que dirigen) management; (Pol) leadership; (Auto) steering. **~ción prohibida** no entry. **~ción única** one-way. **~ta** f (Auto) top gear. **~tiva** f board; (Pol) executive committee. **~tivas** fpl guidelines. **~to** adj direct; (línea) straight; (tren) through. **en ~to** (TV etc) live. **~tor** m director; (Mus) conductor; (de escuela) headmaster; (de periódico) editor; (gerente) manager. **~tora** f (de escuela etc) headmistress. **~torio** m board of directors; (LAm, de teléfonos) telephone directory

diriglente adj ruling. ● m & f leader; (de empresa) manager. **~ir 14** vt direct; (Mus) conduct; run (empresa etc); address (carta etc). **~irse** vpr make one's way; (hablar)

address

disciplina f discipline. **~r** vt discipline. **~rio** adj disciplinary

discípulo m disciple; (alumno) pupil

disco m disc; (Mus) record; (deportes) discus; (de teléfono) dial; (de tráfico) sign; (Rail) signal. **~ duro** hard disk. **~ flexible** floppy disk

disconforme adj not in agreement

discordle adj discordant. **~ia** f discord

discoteca f discothèque, disco 1; (colección de discos) record collection

discreción f discretion

discrepalncia f discrepancy; (desacuerdo) disagreement. **~r** vi differ

discreto adj discreet; (moderado) moderate

discriminalción f discrimination. **~r** vt (distinguir) discriminate between; (tratar injustamente) discriminate against

disculpa f apology; (excusa) excuse. **pedir ~s** apologize. **~r** vt excuse, forgive. **~rse** vpr apologize

discurslar vi speak (**sobre** about). **~o** m speech

discusión f discussion; (riña) argument

discutilble adj debatable. **~r** vt discuss; (contradecir) contradict. ● vi argue (**por** about)

disecar 7 vt stuff; (cortar) dissect

diseminar vt disseminate, spread

disentir 4 vi disagree (**de** with, **en** on)

diseñlador m designer. **~ar** vt design. **~o** m design; (fig) sketch

disertación f dissertation

disfraz *m* fancy dress; (*para engañar*) disguise. **~ar** 🔟 *vt* dress up; (*para engañar*) disguise. **~arse** *vpr.* **~arse de** dress up as; (*para engañar*) disguise o.s. as.

disfrutar *vt* enjoy. ● *vi* enjoy o.s. **~ de** enjoy

disgust|ar *vt* displease; (*molestar*) annoy. **~arse** *vpr* get annoyed, get upset; (*dos personas*) fall out. **~o** *m* annoyance; (*problema*) trouble; (*riña*) quarrel; (*dolor*) sorrow, grief

disidente *adj & m & f* dissident

disimular *vt* conceal. ● *vi* pretend

disipar *vt* dissipate; (*derrochar*) squander

dislocarse 🖊 *vpr* dislocate

disminu|ción *f* decrease. **~ir** 🔟 *vi* diminish

disolver 🟦 (*pp* **disuelto**) *vt* dissolve. **~se** *vpr* dissolve

dispar *adj* different

disparar *vt* fire; (*Mex, pagar*) buy. ● *vi* shoot (**contra** at)

disparate *m* silly thing; (*error*) mistake. **decir ~s** talk nonsense. **¡qué ~!** how ridiculous!

disparidad *f* disparity

disparo *m* (*acción*) firing; (*tiro*) shot

dispensar *vt* give; (*eximir*) exempt. ● *vi.* **¡Vd dispense!** forgive me

dispers|ar *vt* scatter, disperse. **~arse** *vpr* scatter, disperse. **~ión** *f* dispersion. **~o** *adj* scattered

dispon|er 🟥 *vt* arrange; (*Jurid*) order. ● *vi.* **~er de** have; (*vender etc*) dispose of. **~erse** *vpr* prepare (**a** to). **~ibilidad** *f* availability. **~ible** *adj* available

disposición *f* arrangement; (*aptitud*) talent; (*disponibilidad*) dis-

posal; (*Jurid*) order, decree. **~ de ánimo** frame of mind. **a la ~ de** at the disposal of. **a su ~** at your service

dispositivo *m* device

dispuesto *adj* ready; (*persona*) disposed (**a** to); (*servicial*) helpful

disputa *f* dispute; (*pelea*) argument

disquete *m* diskette, floppy disk

dista|ncia *f* distance. **a ~ncia** from a distance. **guardar las ~ncias** keep one's distance. **~nciar** *vt* space out; distance (*amigos*). **~nciarse** *vpr* (*dos personas*) fall out. **~nte** *adj* distant. **~r** *vi* be away; (*fig*) be far. **~ 5 kilómetros** it's 5 kilometres away

distin|ción *f* distinction; (*honor*) award. **~guido** *adj* distinguished. **~guir** 🔞 *vt/i* distinguish. **~guirse** *vpr* distinguish o.s.; (*diferenciarse*) differ. **~tivo** *adj* distinctive. ● *m* badge. **~to** *adj* different, distinct

distra|cción *f* amusement; (*descuido*) absent-mindedness, inattention. **~er** 🔟 *vt* distract; (*divertir*) amuse. **~erse** *vpr* amuse o.s.; (*descuidarse*) not pay attention. **~ído** *adj* (*desatento*) absent-minded

distribu|ción *f* distribution. **~idor** *m* distributor. **~ir** 🔟 *vt* distribute

distrito *m* district

disturbio *m* disturbance

disuadir *vt* deter, dissuade

diurno *adj* daytime

divagar 🟥 *vi* digress; (*hablar sin sentido*) ramble

diván *m* settee, sofa

diversi|dad *f* diversity. **~ficar** 🖊 *vt* diversify

diversión *f* amusement, entertainment; (*pasatiempo*) pastime

diverso *adj* different

diverti|do *adj* amusing; *(que tiene gracia)* funny. **~r** 4 *vt* amuse, entertain. **~rse** *vpr* enjoy o.s.

dividir *vt* divide; *(repartir)* share out

divino *adj* divine

divisa *f* emblem. **~s** *fpl* currency

divisar *vt* make out

división *f* division

divorci|ado *adj* divorced. ● *m* divorcee. **~ar** *vt* divorce. **~arse** *vpr* get divorced. **~o** *m* divorce

divulgar 12 *vt* spread; divulge *(secreto)*

dizque *adv* (LAm) apparently; *(supuestamente)* supposedly

do *m* C; *(solfa)* doh

dobl|adillo *m* hem; *(de pantalón)* turn-up (Brit), cuff (Amer). **~ar** *vt* double; *(plegar)* fold; *(torcer)* bend; turn *(esquina)*; dub *(película)*. ● *vi* turn; *(campana)* toll. **~arse** *vpr* double; *(curvarse)* bend. **~e** *adj* double. ● *m* double. **el ~e** twice as much (**de**, **que** as). **~egar** 12 *vt* *(fig)* force to give in. **~egarse** *vpr* give in

doce *adj* & *m* twelve. **~na** *f* dozen

docente *adj* teaching. ● *m* & *f* teacher

dócil *adj* obedient

doctor *m* doctor. **~ado** *m* doctorate

doctrina *f* doctrine

document|ación *f* documentation, papers. **~al** *adj* & *m* documentary. **~o** *m* document. **D~o Nacional de Identidad** identity

card

documento de identidad An identity card that all residents over a certain age in Spain and Latin America must carry at all times. Holders must quote their identity card number on most official forms. The card is also known as *carné de identidad*, and in Spain as the **DNI** (*Documento Nacional de Identidad*).

dólar *m* dollar

dolarizar *vt* dollarize

dol|er 2 *vi* hurt, ache; *(fig)* grieve. **me duele la cabeza** I have a headache. **le duele el estómago** he has (a) stomach-ache. **~or** *m* pain; *(sordo)* ache; *(fig)* sorrow. **~or de cabeza** headache. **~or de muelas** toothache. **~oroso** *adj* painful

domar *vt* tame; break in *(caballo)*

dom|esticar 7 *vt* domesticate. **~éstico** *adj* domestic

domicili|ar *vt*. **~ar los pagos** pay by direct debit. **~o** *m* address. **~o particular** home address. **reparto a ~** home delivery service

domina|nte *adj* dominant; *(persona)* domineering. **~r** *vt* dominate; *(contener)* control; *(conocer)* have a good command of. ● *vi* dominate. **~rse** *vpr* control o.s.

domingo *m* Sunday

dominio *m* authority; *(territorio)* domain; *(fig)* command

dominó *m* (*pl* **~s**) dominoes; *(ficha)* domino

don *m* talent, gift; *(en un sobre)* Mr. **~ Pedro** Pedro

donación *f* donation

donaire *m* grace, charm

dona|nte m& f (de sangre) donor. ~r vt donate

doncella f maiden; (criada) maid

donde adv where

dónde adv where?; (LAm, cómo) how; ¿hasta ~? how far? ¿por ~? whereabouts?; (por qué camino?) which way? ¿a ~ vas? where are you going? ¿de ~ eres? where are you from?

dondequiera adv. ~ que wherever. por ~ everywhere

doña f (en un sobre) Mrs. ~ María María

dora|do adj golden; (cubierto de oro) gilt. ~r vt gilt; (Culin) brown

dormi|do adj asleep. **quedarse** ~**do** fall asleep; (no despertar) oversleep. ~**r** 6 vt send to sleep. • vi sleep. ~**rse** vpr fall asleep. ~**r la siesta** have an afternoon nap, have a siesta. ~**tar** vi doze. ~**torio** m bedroom

dors|al adj back. • m (en deportes) number. ~**o** m back. **nadar de** ~ (Mex) do (the) backstroke

dos adj & m two. **de** ~ **en** ~ in twos, in pairs. **los** ~, **las** ~ both (of them). ~**cientos** adj & m two hundred

dosi|ficar 7 vt dose; (fig) measure out. ~**s** f invar dose

dot|ado adj gifted. ~**ar** vt give a dowry; (proveer) provide (**de** with). ~**e** m dowry

doy vb véase DAR

dragar 12 vt dredge

drama m drama; (obra de teatro) play. ~**turgo** m playwright

drástico adj drastic

droga f drug. ~**dicto** m drug addict. ~**do** m drug addict. ~**r** 12 vt drug. ~**rse** vpr take drugs

droguería f hardware store

ducha f shower. ~**rse** vpr have a shower

dud|a f doubt. **poner en** ~**a** question. **sin** ~**a** (**alguna**) without a doubt. ~**ar** vt/i doubt. ~**oso** adj doubtful; (sospechoso) dubious

duelo m duel; (luto) mourning

duende m imp

dueñ|a f owner, proprietress; (de una pensión) landlady. ~**o** m owner, proprietor; (de una pensión) landlord

duermo vb véase DORMIR

dul|ce adj sweet; (agua) fresh; (suave) soft, gentle. • m (LAm) sweet. ~**zura** f sweetness; (fig) gentleness

duna f dune

dúo m duet, duo

duplica|do adj duplicated. **por** ~ in duplicate. • m duplicate. ~**r** 7 vt duplicate. ~**rse** vpr double

duque m duke. ~**sa** f duchess

dura|ción f duration, length. ~**dero** adj lasting. ~**nte** prep during; (medida de tiempo) for. ~ **todo el año** all year round. ~**r** vi last

durazno m (LAm, fruta) peach

dureza f hardness; (Culin) toughness; (fig) harshness

duro adj hard; (Culin) tough; (fig) harsh. • adv (esp LAm) hard

DVD m (Disco Versátil Digital) DVD. ~**teca** f DVD library

Ee

e *conj* and
Ébola *m* ebola
ebrio *adj* drunk
ebullición *f* boiling
eccema *m* eczema
echar *vt* throw; post (carta); give off (olor); pour (líquido); (*expulsar*) expel; (*de recinto*) throw out; fire (empleado); (*poner*) put on; get (gasolina); put out (raíces); show (película). ~ **a** start. ~ **a perder** spoil. ~ **de menos** miss. ~**se atrás** (*fig*) back down. **echárselas de** feign. ~**se** *vpr* throw o.s.; (*tumbarse*) lie down
eclesiástico *adj* ecclesiastical
eclipse *m* eclipse
eco *m* echo. **hacerse** ~ **de** echo
ecolog|ía *f* ecology. ~**ista** *m & f* ecologist
economato *m* cooperative store
econ|omía *f* economy; (*ciencia*) economics. ~**ómico** *adj* economic; (*no caro*) inexpensive. ~**omista** *m & f* economist. ~**omizar** 10 *vt/i* economize
ecoturismo *m* ecotourism
ecuación *f* equation
ecuador *m* equator. **el E**~ the Equator. **E**~ (*país*) Ecuador
ecuánime *adj* level-headed; (*imparcial*) impartial
ecuatoriano *adj & m* Ecuadorian
ecuestre *adj* equestrian
edad *f* age. ~ **avanzada** old age. **E**~ **de Piedra** Stone Age. **E**~ **Media** Middle Ages. **¿qué** ~ **tiene?** how old is he?

edición *f* edition; (*publicación*) publication
edicto *m* edict
edific|ación *f* building. ~**ante** *adj* edifying. ~**ar** 7 *vt* build; (*fig*) edify. ~**io** *m* building; (*fig*) structure
edit|ar *vt* edit; (*publicar*) publish. ~**or** *adj* publishing. ● *m* editor; (*que publica*) publisher. ~**orial** *adj* editorial. ● *m* leading article. ● *f* publishing house
edredón *m* duvet
educa|ción *f* upbringing; (*modales*) (good) manners; (*enseñanza*) education. **falta de** ~**ción** rudeness, bad manners. ~**do** *adj* polite. **bien** ~**do** polite. **mal** ~**do** rude. ~**r** 7 *vt* bring up; (*enseñar*) educate. ~**tivo** *adj* educational
edulcorante *m* sweetener
EE.UU. *abrev* (**Estados Unidos**) USA
efect|ivamente *adv* really; (*por supuesto*) indeed. ~**ivo** *adj* effective; (*auténtico*) real. ● *m* cash. ~**o** *m* effect; (*impresión*) impression. **en** ~**o** really; (*como respuesta*) indeed. ~**os** *mpl* belongings; (*Com*) goods. ~**uar** 21 *vt* carry out; make (viaje, compras etc)
efervescente *adj* effervescent; (*bebidas*) fizzy
efica|cia *f* effectiveness; (*de persona*) efficiency. ~**z** *adj* effective; (*persona*) efficient
eficien|cia *f* efficiency. ~**te** *adj* efficient
efímero *adj* ephemeral
efusi|vidad *f* effusiveness. ~**vo** *adj* effusive; (*persona*) demonstrative
egipcio *adj & m* Egyptian
Egipto *m* Egypt

ego|ísmo m selfishness, egotism. **∼ista** adj selfish

egresar vi (LAm) graduate; (de colegio) leave school, graduate (Amer)

eje m axis; (Tec) axle

ejecu|ción f execution; (Mus) performance. **∼tar** vt carry out; (Mus) perform; (matar) execute. **∼tivo** m executive

ejempl|ar adj exemplary; (ideal) model. ● m specimen; (libro) copy; (revista) issue, number. **∼ificar 7** vt exemplify. **∼o** m example. **dar (el) ∼o** set an example. **por ∼o** for example

ejerc|er 9 vt exercise; practise (profesión); exert (influencia). ● vi practise. **∼icio** m exercise; (de profesión) practice. **hacer ∼icios** take exercise. **∼itar** vt exercise

ejército m army

ejido m (Mex) cooperative

ejote m (Mex) green bean

---

el artículo definido masculino (pl **los**)

The masculine article **el** is also used before feminine nouns which begin with stressed **a** or **ha**, e.g. **el ala derecha**, **el hada madrina**. Also, **de** followed by **el** becomes **del** and **el** preceded by **a** becomes **al**

····▸ the. **el tren de las seis** the six o'clock train. **el vecino de al lado** the next-door neighbour. **cerca del hospital** near the hospital

····▸ No se traduce en los siguientes casos: (con nombre abstracto, genérico) **el tiempo vuela** time flies. **odio el queso** I

---

hate cheese. **el hilo es muy durable** linen is very durable

····▸ (con colores, días de la semana) **el rojo está de moda** red is in fashion. **el lunes es fiesta** Monday is a holiday

····▸ (con algunas instituciones) **termino el colegio mañana** I finish school tomorrow. **lo ingresaron en el hospital** he was admitted to hospital

····▸ (con nombres propios) **el Sr. Díaz** Mr Díaz. **el doctor Lara** Doctor Lara

····▸ (antes de infinitivo) **es muy cuidadosa en el vestir** she takes great care in the way she dresses. **me di cuenta al verlo** I realized when I saw him

····▸ (con partes del cuerpo, articulos personales) se traduce por un posesivo. **apretó el puño** he clenched his fist. **tienes el zapato desatado** your shoe is undone

····▸ **el + de**. es el de Pedro it's Pedro's. **el del sombrero** the one with the hat

····▸ **el + que** (persona) **el que me atendió** the one who served me. (cosa) **el que se rompió** the one that broke.

····▸ **el + que** + subjunctive (quienquiera) whoever. **el que gane la lotería** whoever wins the lottery. (cualquiera) whichever. **compra el que sea más barato** buy whichever is cheaper

él pron (persona) he; (persona con prep) him; (cosa) it. **es de ∼** it's his

elabora|ción f elaboration; (fabricación) manufacture. **∼r** vt elaborate; manufacture (producto);

(*producir*) produce

el|asticidad *f* elasticity. **~ástico** *adj & m* elastic

elec|ción *f* choice; (*de político etc*) election. **~ciones** *fpl* (*Pol*) election. **~tor** *m* voter. **~torado** *m* electorate. **~toral** *adj* electoral; (*campaña*) election

electrici|dad *f* electricity. **~sta** *m & f* electrician

eléctrico *adj* electric; (*aparato*) electrical

electri|ficar ⁊ *vt* electrify. **~zar** ⑩ *vt* electrify

electrocutar *vt* electrocute. **~se** *vpr* be electrocuted

electrodoméstico *adj* electrical appliance

electrónic|a *f* electronics. **~o** *adj* electronic

elefante *m* elephant

elegan|cia *f* elegance. **~te** *adj* elegant

elegía *f* elegy

elegi|ble *adj* eligible. **~do** *adj* chosen. **~r** ⑤ & ⑭ *vt* choose; (*por votación*) elect

element|al *adj* elementary; (*esencial*) fundamental. **~o** *m* element; (*persona*) person, bloke (*Brit, fam*). **~os** *mpl* (*nociones*) basic principles

elenco *m* (*en el teatro*) cast

eleva|ción *f* elevation; (*de precios*) rise, increase; (*acción*) raising. **~dor** *m* (*Mex*) lift (*Brit*), elevator (*Amer*). **~r** *vt* raise; (*promover*) promote

elimina|ción *f* elimination. **~r** *vt* eliminate; (*Informática*) delete. **~toria** *f* preliminary heat

élite /e'lit, e'lite/ *f* elite

ella *pron* (*persona*) she; (*persona con prep*) her; (*cosa*) it. **es de ~s** it's theirs. **~s** *pron pl* they; (*con*

prep) them. **es de ~** it's hers

ello *pron* it

ellos *pron pl* they; (*con prep*) them. **es de ~** it's theirs

elocuen|cia *f* eloquence. **~te** *adj* eloquent

elogi|ar *vt* praise. **~o** *m* praise

elote *m* (*Mex*) corncob; (*Culin*) corn on the cob

eludir *vt* avoid, elude

emanar *vi* emanate (*de* from); (*originarse*) originate (*de* from, in)

emancipa|ción *f* emancipation. **~r** *vt* emancipate. **~rse** *vpr* become emancipated

embadurnar *vt* smear

embajad|a *f* embassy. **~or** *m* ambassador

embalar *vt* pack

embaldosar *vt* tile

embalsamar *vt* embalm

embalse *m* reservoir

embaraz|ada *adj* pregnant. ● *f* pregnant woman. **~ar** ⑩ *vt* get pregnant. **~o** *m* pregnancy; (*apuro*) embarrassment; (*estorbo*) hindrance. **~oso** *adj* awkward, embarrassing

embar|cación *f* vessel. **~cadero** *m* jetty, pier. **~car** ⁊ *vt* load (*mercancías etc*). **~carse** *vpr* board. **~carse en** (*fig*) embark upon

embargo *m* embargo; (*Jurid*) seizure. **sin ~** however

embarque *m* loading; (*de pasajeros*) boarding

embaucar ⁊ *vt* trick

embelesar *vt* captivate

embellecer ⑪ *vt* make beautiful

embesti|da *f* charge. **~r** ⑤ *vt/i* charge

emblema *m* emblem

embolsarse vpr pocket

embonar vt (Mex) fit

emborrachar vt get drunk. **~se** vpr get drunk

emboscada f ambush

embotar vt dull

embotella|miento m (de vehículos) traffic jam. **~r** vt bottle

embrague m clutch

embriag|arse 12 vpr get drunk. **~uez** f drunkenness

embrión m embryo

embroll|ar vt mix up; involve (persona). **~arse** vpr get into a muddle; (en un asunto) get involved. **~o** m tangle; (fig) muddle

embruj|ado adj bewitched; (casa) haunted. **~ar** vt bewitch. **~o** m spell

embrutecer 11 vt brutalize

embudo m funnel

embuste m lie. **~ro** adj deceitful. ● m liar

embuti|do m (Culin) sausage. **~r** vt stuff

emergencia f emergency

emerger 14 vi appear, emerge

emigra|ción f emigration. **~nte** adj m & f emigrant. **~r** vi emigrate

eminen|cia f eminence. **~te** adj eminent

emisario m emissary

emi|sión f emission; (de dinero) issue; (TV etc) broadcast. **~sor** adj issuing; (TV etc) broadcasting. **~sora** f radio station. **~tir** vt emit, give out; (TV etc) broadcast; cast (voto); (poner en circulación) issue

emoci|ón f emotion; (excitación) excitement. **¡qué ~ón!** how exciting!. **~onado** adj moved.

~onante adj exciting; (conmovedor) moving. **~onar** vt move. **~onarse** vpr get excited; (conmoverse) be moved

emotivo adj emotional; (conmovedor) moving

empacar 7 vt (LAm) pack

empacho m indigestion

empadronar vt register. **~se** vpr register

empalagoso adj sickly; (persona) cloying

empalizada f fence

empalm|ar vt connect, join. ● vi meet. **~e** m junction; (de trenes) connection

empan|ada f (savoury) pie; (LAm, individual) pasty. **~adilla** f pasty

empantanarse vpr become swamped; (coche) get bogged down

empañar vt steam up; (fig) tarnish. **~se** vpr steam up

empapar vt soak. **~se** vpr get soaked

empapela|do m wallpaper. **~r** vt wallpaper

empaquetar vt package

emparedado m sandwich

emparentado adj related

empast|ar vt fill (muela). **~e** m filling

empat|ar vi draw. **~e** m draw

empedernido adj confirmed; (bebedor) inveterate

empedrar 11 vt pave

empeine m instep

empeñ|ado adj in debt; (decidido) determined (en to). **~ar** vt pawn; pledge (palabra). **~arse** vpr get into debt; (estar decidido a) be determined (en to). **~o** m pledge; (resolución) determination. **casa** f de ~s pawnshop. ~oso adj (LAm) hardworking

empeorar vt make worse. ● vi get worse. ~se vpr get worse

empequeñecer 🔟 vt become smaller; (fig) belittle

empera|dor m emperor. ~triz f empress

empezar 🔟 & 🔟 vt/i start, begin. para ~ to begin with

empina|do adj (cuesta) steep. ~r vt raise. ~rse vpr (persona) stand on tiptoe

empírico adj empirical

emplasto m plaster

emplaza|miento m (Jurid) summons; (lugar) site. ~r 🔟 vt summon; (situar) site

emple|ada f employee; (doméstica) maid. ~ado m employee. ~ar vt use; employ (persona); spend (tiempo). ~arse vpr get a job. ~o m use; (trabajo) employment; (puesto) job

empobrecer 🔟 vt impoverish. ~se vpr become poor

empoll|ar vt incubate (huevos); (arg, estudiar) cram 🔟. ● vi (ave) sit; (estudiante) 🄴 cram. ~ón m 🄴 swot (Brit, fam), grind (Amer, fam)

empolvarse vpr powder

empotra|do adj built-in, fitted. ~r vt fit

emprende|dor adj enterprising. ~r vt undertake; set out on (viaje). ~rla con uno pick a fight with s.o.

empresa f undertaking; (Com) company, firm. ~ puntocom dotcom company. ~rio m businessman; (patrón) employer; (de teatro etc) impresario

empuj|ar vt push. ~e m (fig) drive. ~ón m push, shove

empuña|dura f handle

emular vt emulate

en prep in; (sobre) on; (dentro) inside, in; (medio de transporte) by. ~ casa at home. ~ coche by car. ~ 10 días in 10 days. de pueblo ~ pueblo from town to town

enagua f petticoat

enajena|ción f alienation. ~ción mental insanity. ~r vt alienate; (volver loco) derange

enamora|do adj in love. ● m lover. ~r vt win the love of. ~rse vpr fall in love (de with)

enano adj & m dwarf

enardecer 🔟 vt inflame. ~se vpr get excited (por about)

encabeza|do m (Mex) headline. ~miento m heading; (de periódico) headline. ~r 🔟 vt head; lead (revolución etc)

encabritarse vpr rear up

encadenar vt chain; (fig) tie down

encaj|ar vt fit; fit together (varias piezas). ● vi fit; (cuadrar) tally. ~arse vpr put on. ~e m lace; (Com) reserve

encaminar vt direct. ~se vpr make one's way

encandilar vt dazzle; (estimular) stimulate

encant|ado adj enchanted; (persona) delighted. ¡~ado! pleased to meet you! ~ador adj charming. ~amiento m spell. ~ar vt bewitch; (fig) charm, delight. me ~a la leche I love milk. ~o m spell; (fig) delight

encapricharse vpr. ~ con take a fancy to

encarar vt face; (LAm) stand up to (persona). ~se vpr. ~se con stand up to

encarcelar vt imprison

encarecer 🔟 vt put up the price of. • **~se** vpr become more expensive

encarg|ado adj in charge. • m manager, person in charge. **~ar** 🔟 vt entrust; (pedir) order. **~arse** vpr take charge (**de** of). **~o** m job; (Com) order; (recado) errand. **hecho de ~o** made to measure

encariñarse vpr. **~ con** take to, become fond of

encarna|ción f incarnation. **~do** adj incarnate; (rojo) red; (uña) ingrowing. • m red

encarnizado adj bitter

encarpetar vt file; (LAm, dar carpetazo) shelve

encarrilar vt put back on the rails; (fig) direct, put on the right track

encasillar vt classify; (fig) pigeonhole

encauzar 🔟 vt channel

enceguecer vt 🔟 (LAm) blind

encend|edor m lighter. **~er** 🔟 vt light; switch on, turn on (aparato eléctrico); start (motor); (fig) arouse. **~erse** vpr light; (aparato eléctrico) come on; (excitarse) get excited; (ruborizarse) blush. **~ido** adj lit; (aparato eléctrico) on; (rojo) bright red. • m (Auto) ignition

encera|do adj waxed. • m (pizarra) blackboard. **~r** vt wax

encerr|ar 🔟 vt shut in; (con llave) lock up; (fig, contener) contain. **~ona** f trap

enchilar vt (Mex) add chili to

enchinar vt (Mex) perm

enchuf|ado adj switched on. **~ar** vt plug in; fit together (tubos etc). **~e** m socket; (clavija) plug; (de tubos etc) joint; (fam, influen-

cia) contact. **tener ~e** have friends in the right places

encía f gum

enciclopedia f encyclopaedia

encierro m confinement; (cárcel) prison

encim|a adv on top; (arriba) above. **~ de** on, on top of; (sobre) over; (además de) besides, as well as. **por ~** on top; (adj la ligera) superficially. **por ~ de todo** above all. **~ar** vt (Mex) stack up. **~era** f worktop

encina f holm oak

encinta adj pregnant

enclenque adj weak; (enfermizo) sickly

encoger 🔟 vt shrink; (contraer) contract. **~se** vpr shrink. **~erse de hombros** shrug one's shoulders

encolar vt glue; (pegar) stick

encolerizar 🔟 vt make angry. **~se** vpr get furious

encomendar 🔟 vt entrust

encomi|ar vt praise. **~o** m praise. **~oso** adj (LAm) complimentary

encono m bitterness, ill will

encontra|do adj contrary, conflicting. **~r** 🔟 vt find; (tropezar con) meet. **~rse** vpr meet; (hallarse) be. **no ~rse** feel uncomfortable

encorvar vt hunch. **~se** vpr stoop

encrespa|do adj (pelo) curly; (mar) rough. **~r** vt curl (pelo); make rough (mar)

encrucijada f crossroads

encuaderna|ción f binding. **~dor** m bookbinder. **~r** vt bind

encub|ierto adj hidden. **~rir** (pp encubierto) vt hide, conceal; cover up (delito); shelter (delincuente)

encuentro m meeting; (en depor-

tes) match; (*Mil*) encounter

encuesta *f* survey; (*investigación*) inquiry

encumbrado *adj* eminent; (*alto*) high

encurtidos *mpl* pickles

endeble *adj* weak

endemoniado *adj* possessed; (*muy malo*) wretched

enderezar 10 *vt* straighten out; (*poner vertical*) put upright; (*fig, arreglar*) put right, sort out; (*dirigir*) direct. ~se *vpr* straighten out

endeudarse *vpr* get into debt

endiablado *adj* possessed; (*malo*) terrible; (*difícil*) difficult

endosar *vt* endorse (cheque)

endulzar 10 *vt* sweeten; (*fig*) soften

endurecer 11 *vt* harden. ~se *vpr* harden

enemi|go *adj* enemy. ● *m* enemy. ~stad *f* enmity. ~star *vt* make an enemy of. ~starse *vpr* fall out (**con** with)

en|ergía *f* energy. ~érgico *adj* (*persona*) lively; (*decisión*) forceful

energúmeno *m* madman

enero *m* January

enésimo *adj* nth, umpteenth 1

enfad|ado *adj* angry; (*molesto*) annoyed. ~ar *vt* make cross, anger; (*molestar*) annoy. ~arse *vpr* get angry; (*molestarse*) get annoyed. ~o *m* anger; (*molestia*) annoyance

énfasis *m invar* emphasis, stress. **poner** ~ stress, emphasize

enfático *adj* emphatic

enferm|ar *vi* fall ill. ~arse *vpr* (*LAm*) fall ill. ~edad *f* illness. ~era *f* nurse. ~ería *f* sick bay; (*carrera*) nursing. ~ero *m* (male) nurse

~**izo** *adj* sickly. ~**o** *adj* ill. ● *m* patient

enflaquecer 11 *vt* make thin. ● *vi* lose weight

enfo|car 7 *vt* shine on; focus (lente); (*fig*) approach. ~**que** *m* focus; (*fig*) approach

enfrentar *vt* face, confront; (*poner frente a frente*) bring face to face. ~se *vpr*. ~se **con** confront; (*en deportes*) meet

enfrente *adv* opposite. ~ **de** opposite. **de** ~ opposite

enfria|miento *m* cooling; (*catarro*) cold. ~**r** 20 *vt* cool (down); (*fig*) cool down. ~**rse** *vpr* go cold; (*fig*) cool off

enfurecer 11 *vt* infuriate. ~se *vpr* get furious

engalanar *vt* adorn. ~se *vpr* dress up

enganchar *vt* hook; hang up (ropa). ~se *vpr* get caught; (*Mil*) enlist

engañ|ar *vt* deceive, trick; (*ser infiel*) be unfaithful. ~arse *vpr* be wrong, be mistaken; (*no admitir la verdad*) deceive o.s. ~**o** *m* deceit, trickery; (*error*) mistake. ~**oso** *adj* deceptive; (*persona*) deceitful

engarzar 10 *vt* string (cuentas); set (joyas)

engatusar *vt* 1 coax

engendr|ar *vt* father; (*fig*) breed. ~**o** *m* (*monstruo*) monster; (*fig*) brainchild

englobar *vt* include

engomar *vt* glue

engordar *vt* fatten, gain (kilo). ● *vi* get fat, put on weight

engorro *m* nuisance

engranaje *m* (*Auto*) gear

engrandecer 11 *vt* (*enaltecer*) exalt, raise

engrasar vt grease; (con aceite) oil; (ensuciar) get grease on

engreído adj arrogant

engullir 22 vt gulp down

enhebrar vt thread

enhorabuena f congratulations. dar la ~ congratulate

enigm|a m enigma. ~ático adj enigmatic

enjabonar vt soap. ~se vpr to soap o.s.

enjambre m swarm

enjaular vt put in a cage

enjuag|ar 12 vt rinse. ~ue m rinsing; (para la boca) mouthwash

enjugar 12 vt wipe (away)

enjuiciar vt pass judgement on

enjuto adj (persona) skinny

enlace m connection; (matrimonial) wedding

enlatar vt tin, can

enlazar 10 vt link; tie together (cintas); (Mex, casar) marry

enlodar vt, **enlodazar** 10 vt cover in mud

enloquecer 11 vt drive mad. • vi go mad. ~se vpr go mad

enlosar vt (con losas) pave; (con baldosas) tile

enmarañar vt tangle (up), entangle; (confundir) confuse. ~se vpr get into a tangle; (confundirse) get confused

enmarcar 7 vt frame

enm|endar vt correct. ~endarse vpr mend one's way. ~ienda f correction; (de ley etc) amendment

enmohecerse 11 vpr (con óxido) go rusty; (con hongos) go mouldy

enmudecer 11 vi be dumbstruck; (callar) fall silent

ennegrecer 11 vt blacken

ennoblecer 11 vt ennoble; (fig) add style to

enoj|adizo adj irritable. ~ado adj angry; (molesto) annoyed. ~ar vt anger; (molestar) annoy. ~arse vpr get angry; (molestarse) get annoyed. ~o m anger; (molestia) annoyance. ~oso adj annoying

enorgullecerse 11 vpr be proud

enorm|e adj huge, enormous. ~emente adv enormously. ~idad f immensity; (de crimen) enormity

enraizado adj deeply rooted

enrarecido adj rarefied

enred|adera f creeper. ~ar vt tangle (up), entangle; (confundir) confuse; (involucrar) involve. ~arse vpr get tangled; (confundirse) get confused; (persona) get involved (con with). ~o m tangle; (fig) muddle, mess

enrejado m bars

enriquecer 11 vt make rich; (fig) enrich. ~se vpr get rich

enrojecerse 11 vpr (persona) go red, blush

enrolar vt enlist

enrollar vt roll (up), wind (hilo etc)

enroscar 7 vt coil; (atornillar) screw in

ensalad|a f salad. armar una ~a make a mess. ~era f salad bowl. ~illa f Russian salad

ensalzar 10 vt praise; (enaltecer) exalt

ensambla|dura f, **ensamblaje** m (acción) assembling; (efecto) joint. ~r vt join

ensanch|ar vt widen; (agrandar) enlarge. ~arse vpr get wider. ~e m widening

ensangrentar 1 vt stain with blood

ensañarse *vpr.* ~ **con** treat cruelly

ensartar *vt* string (cuentas etc)

ensay|ar *vt* test; rehearse (obra de teatro etc). ~**o** *m* test, trial; (*composición literaria*) essay

enseguida *adv* at once, immediately

ensenada *f* inlet, cove

enseña|nza *f* education; (*acción de enseñar*) teaching. ~**nza media** secondary education. ~**r** *vt* teach; (*mostrar*) show

enseres *mpl* equipment

ensillar *vt* saddle

ensimismarse *vpr* be lost in thought

ensombrecer 11 *vt* darken

ensordecer 11 *vt* deafen. ● *vi* go deaf

ensuciar *vt* dirty. ~**se** *vpr* get dirty

ensueño *m* dream

entablar *vt* (*empezar*) start

entablillar *vt* put in a splint

entallar *vt* tailor (un vestido). ● *vi* fit

entarimado *m* parquet; (*plataforma*) platform

ente *m* entity, being; (*fam, persona rara*) weirdo; (*Com*) firm, company

entend|er 1 *vt* understand; (*opinar*) believe, think. ● *vi* understand. ~**er de** know about. **a mi ~er** in my opinion. **dar a ~er** hint. **darse a ~er** (*LAm*) make o.s. understood ~**erse** *vpr* make o.s. understood; (*comprenderse*) be understood. ~**erse con** get on with. ~**ido** *adj* understood; (*enterado*) well-informed. **no darse por ~ido** pretend not to understand. ● *interj* agreed!, OK! 11. ~**imiento** *m* understanding

entera|do *adj* well-informed; (*que sabe*) aware. **darse por ~do** take the hint. ~**r** *vt* inform (**de** of). ~**rse** *vpr.* ~**rse de** find out about, hear of. **¡entérate!** listen! **¿te ~s?** do you understand?

entereza *f* (*carácter*) strength of character

enternecer 11 *vt* (*fig*) move, touch. ~**se** *vpr* be moved, be touched

entero *adj* entire, whole. **por ~** entirely, completely

enterra|dor *m* gravedigger. ~**r** 11 *vt* bury

entibiar *vt* (*enfriar*) cool; (*calentar*) warm (up). ~**se** *vpr* (*enfriarse*) cool down; (*fig*) cool; (*calentarse*) get warm

entidad *f* entity; (*organización*) organization; (*Com*) company; (*importancia*) significance

entierro *m* burial; (*ceremonia*) funeral

entona|ción *f* intonation. ~**r** *vt* intone; sing (nota). ● *vi* (*Mus*) be in tune; (*colores*) match. ~**rse** *vpr* (*emborracharse*) get tipsy

entonces *adv* then. **en aquel ~** at that time, then

entorn|ado *adj* (puerta) ajar; (ventana) slightly open. ~**o** *m* environment; (*en literatura*) setting

entorpecer 11 *vt* dull; slow down (tráfico); (*dificultar*) hinder

entra|da *f* entrance; (*incorporación*) admission, entry; (*para cine* etc) ticket; (de datos, Tec) input; (de una comida) starter. **de ~da** right away. ~**do** *adj.* ~**do en años** elderly. **ya ~da la noche** late at night. ~**nte** *adj* next, coming

entraña *f* (*fig*) heart. ~**s** *fpl* entrails; (*fig*) heart. ~**ble** *adj* (cariño) deep; (amigo) close. **~r** vt involve

entrar vt (traer) bring in; (llevar) take in. ● vi go in, enter; (venir) come in, enter; (empezar) start, begin; (incorporarse) join. **~ en**, (LAm) **~ a** go into

entre prep (dos personas o cosas) between; (más de dos) among(st)

entre|abierto adj half-open. **~abrir** (pp entreabierto) vt half open. **~acto** m interval. **~cejo** m forehead. **fruncir el ~cejo** frown. **~cerrar** 1 vt (LAm) half close. **~cortado** adj (voz) faltering; (respiración) laboured. **~cruzar** 10 vt intertwine

entrega f handing over; (de mercancías etc) delivery; (de novela etc) instalment; (dedicación) commitment. **~r** 12 vt deliver; (dar) give; hand in (deberes); hand over (poder). **~rse** vpr surrender, give o.s. up; (dedicarse) devote o.s. (a to)

entre|lazar 10 vt intertwine. **~més** m hors-d'oeuvre; (en el teatro) short comedy. **~mezclar** vt intermingle

entrena|dor m trainer. **~miento** m training. **~r** vt train. **~rse** vpr train

entre|pierna f crotch; medida inside leg measurement. **~piso** m (LAm) mezzanine. **~sacar** 7 vt pick out; (peluquería) thin out **~suelo** m mezzanine; (de cine) dress circle **~tanto** adv meanwhile, in the meantime **~tejer** vt weave; (entrelazar) interweave

entreten|ción f (LAm) entertainment. **~er** 40 vt entertain, amuse; (detener) delay, keep. **~erse** vpr amuse o.s.; (tardar) delay, linger. **~ido** adj (con ser) entertaining;

(con estar) busy. **~imiento** m entertainment

entrever 43 vt make out, glimpse

entrevista f interview; (reunión) meeting. **~rse** vpr have an interview

entristecer 11 vt sadden, make sad. **~se** vpr grow sad

entromet|erse vpr interfere. **~ido** adj interfering

entumec|erse 11 vpr go numb. **~ido** adj numb

enturbiar vt cloud

entusi|asmar vt fill with enthusiasm; (gustar mucho) delight. **~asmarse** vpr **~asmarse con** get enthusiastic about. **~asmo** m enthusiasm. **~asta** adj enthusiastic. ● m & f enthusiast

enumerar vt enumerate

envalentonar vt encourage. **~se** vpr become bolder

envas|ado m packaging; (en latas) canning; (en botellas) bottling. **~ar** vt package; (en latas) tin, can; (en botellas) bottle. **~e** m packaging; (lata) tin, can; (botella) bottle

envejec|er 11 vt make (look) older. ● vi age, grow old. **~erse** vpr age, grow old

envenenar vt poison

envergadura f importance

envia|do m envoy; (de la prensa) correspondent. **~r** 20 vt send

enviciarse vpr become addicted (con to)

envidi|a f envy; (celos) jealousy. **~ar** vt envy, be envious of. **~oso** adj envious; (celoso) jealous. **tener ~a a** envy

envío m sending, dispatch; (de

mercancías) consignment; (*de dinero*) remittance. ~ **contra reembolso** cash on delivery. **gastos** *mpl* **de** ~ postage and packing (costs)

enviudar *vi* be widowed

env|oltura *f* wrapping. ~**olver** ❷ (*pp* **envuelto**) *vt* wrap; (*cubrir*) cover; (*rodear*) surround; (*fig, enredar*) involve. ~**uelto** *adj* wrapped (up)

enyesar *vt* plaster; (*Med*) put in plaster

épica *f* epic

épico *adj* epic

epid|emia *f* epidemic. ~**émico** *adj* epidemic

epil|epsia *f* epilepsy. ~**éptico** *adj* epileptic

epílogo *m* epilogue

episodio *m* episode

epístola *f* epistle

epitafio *m* epitaph

época *f* age; (*período*) period. **hacer** ~ make history, be epoch-making

equidad *f* equity

equilibr|ado *adj* (well-)balanced. ~**ar** *vt* balance. ~**io** *m* balance; (*de balanza*) equilibrium. ~**ista** *m & f* tightrope walker

equinoccio *m* equinox

equipaje *m* luggage (*esp Brit*), baggage (*esp Amer*)

equipar *vt* equip; (*de ropa*) fit out

equiparar *vt* make equal; (*comparar*) compare

equipo *m* equipment; (*de personas*) team

equitación *f* riding

equivale|nte *adj* equivalent. ~**r** ❷ *vi* be equivalent; (*significar*) mean

equivoca|ción *f* mistake, error.

~**do** *adj* wrong. ~**rse** *vpr* make a mistake; (*estar en error*) be wrong, be mistaken. ~**rse de** be wrong about. ~**rse de número** dial the wrong number. **si no me equivoco** if I'm not mistaken

equívoco *adj* equivocal; (*sospechoso*) suspicious ● *m* misunderstanding; (*error*) mistake

era *f* era. ● *vb véase* **SER**

erario *m* treasury

erección *f* erection

eres *vb véase* **SER**

erguir ❹ *vt* raise. ~**se** *vpr* raise

erigir ❹ *vt* erect. ~**se** *vpr*. ~**se en** set o.s. up as; (*llegar a ser*) become

eriza|do *adj* prickly. ~**rse** ❿ *vpr* stand on end; (*LAm*) (*persona*) get goose pimples

erizo *m* hedgehog; (*de mar*) sea urchin. ~ **de mar** sea urchin

ermita *f* hermitage. ~**ño** *m* hermit

erosi|ón *f* erosion. ~**onar** *vt* erode

er|ótico *adj* erotic. ~**otismo** *m* eroticism

err|ar ❶ (*la* **i** *inicial pasa a ser* **y**) *vt* miss. ● *vi* wander; (*equivocarse*) make a mistake, be wrong. ~**ata** *f* misprint. ~**óneo** *adj* erroneous, wrong. ~**or** *m* error, mistake. **estar en un** ~**or** be wrong, be mistaken

eruct|ar *vi* belch. ~**o** *m* belch

erudi|ción *f* learning, erudition. ~**to** *adj* learned; (*palabra*) erudite

erupción *f* eruption; (*Med*) rash

es *vb véase* **SER**

esa *adj véase* **ESE**

ésa *pron véase* **ÉSE**

esbelto *adj* slender, slim

esboz|ar ❿ *vt* sketch, outline. ~**o**

_m_ sketch, outline

escabeche _m_ brine. **en ~** pickled

escabroso _adj_ (terreno) rough; (asunto) difficult; (atrevido) crude

escabullirse 22 _vpr_ slip away

escafandra _f_ diving-suit

escala _f_ scale; (escalera de mano) ladder; (Aviac) stopover. **hacer ~ en** stop at. **vuelo sin ~s** non-stop flight. **~da** _f_ climbing; (Pol) escalation. **~r** _vt_ climb; break into (una casa). ● _vi_ climb, go climbing

escaldar _vt_ scald

escalera _f_ staircase, stairs; (de mano) ladder. **~ de caracol** spiral staircase. **~ de incendios** fire escape. **~ de tijera** step-ladder. **~ mecánica** escalator

escalfa|do _adj_ poached. **~r** _vt_ poach

escalinata _f_ flight of steps

escalofrío _m_ shiver. **tener ~s** be shivering

escalón _m_ step, stair; (de escala) rung

escalope _m_ escalope

escam|a _f_ scale; (de jabón, de la piel) flake. **~oso** _adj_ scaly; (piel) flaky

escamotear _vt_ make disappear; (robar) steal, pinch

escampar _vt_ stop raining

escandalizar 10 _vt_ scandalize, shock. **~andalizarse** _vpr_ be shocked. **~ándalo** _m_ scandal; (alboroto) commotion, racket. **armar un ~** make a scene. **~andaloso** _adj_ scandalous; (alborotador) noisy

escandinavo _adj_ & _m_ Scandinavian

escaño _m_ bench; (Pol) seat

escapa|da _f_ escape; (visita) flying visit. **~r** _vi_ escape. **dejar ~r** let

out **~rse** _vpr_ escape; (líquido, gas) leak

escaparate _m_ (shop) window

escap|atoria _f_ (fig) way out. **~e** _m_ (de gas, de líquido) leak; (fuga) escape; (Auto) exhaust

escarabajo _m_ beetle

escaramuza _f_ skirmish

escarbar _vt_ scratch; pick (dientes, herida); (fig, escudriñar) pry (en into). **~se** _vpr_ pick

escarcha _f_ frost. **~do** _adj_ (fruta) crystallized

escarlat|a _adj invar_ scarlet. **~ina** _f_ scarlet fever

escarm|entar 1 _vt_ teach a lesson to. ● _vi_ learn one's lesson. **~iento** _m_ punishment; (lección) lesson

escarola _f_ endive

escarpado _adj_ steep

escas|ear _vi_ be scarce. **~ez** _f_ scarcity, shortage; (pobreza) poverty. **~o** _adj_ scarce; (poco) little; (muy justo) barely. **~o de** short of

escatimar _vt_ be sparing with

escayola _f_ plaster

esc|ena _f_ scene; (escenario) stage. **~enario** _m_ stage; (fig) scene. **~énico** _adj_ stage. **~enografía** _f_ set design

esc|epticismo _m_ scepticism. **~éptico** _adj_ sceptical. ● _m_ sceptic

esclarecer 11 _vt_ (fig) throw light on, clarify

esclav|itud _f_ slavery. **~izar** 10 _vt_ enslave. **~o** _m_ slave

esclusa _f_ lock; (de presa) floodgate

escoba _f_ broom

escocer 2 & 9 _vi_ sting

escocés _adj_ Scottish. ● _m_ Scot

Escocia _f_ Scotland

escog|er ⓘ *vt* choose. **~ido** *adj* chosen; (mercancía) choice; (clientela) select

escolar *adj* school. ● *m* schoolboy. ● *f* schoolgirl

escolta *f* escort

escombros *mpl* rubble

escond|er *vt* hide. **~erse** *vpr* hide. **~idas** *fpl* (LAm, juego) hide-and-seek. **a ~idas** secretly. **~ite** *m* hiding place; (juego) hide-and-seek. **~rijo** *m* hiding place

escopeta *f* shotgun

escoria *f* slag; (fig) dregs

escorpión *m* scorpion

Escorpión *m* Scorpio

escot|ado *adj* low-cut. **~e** *m* low neckline. **pagar a ~e** share the expenses

escozor *m* stinging

escri|bano *m* clerk. **~bir** (pp escrito) *vt/i* write. **~bir a máquina** type. **¿cómo se escribe...?** how do you spell...? **~birse** *vpr* write to each other. **~to** *adj* written. **por ~to** in writing. ● *m* document. **~tor** *m* writer. **~torio** *m* desk; (oficina) office; (LAm, en una casa) study. **~tura** *f* (hand)writing; (Jurid) deed

escrú|pulo *m* scruple. **~puloso** *adj* scrupulous

escrut|ar *vt* scrutinize; count (votos). **~inio** *m* count

escuadr|a *f* (instrumento) square; (Mil) squad; (Naut) fleet. **~ón** *m* squadron

escuálido *adj* skinny

escuchar *vt* listen to; (esp LAm, oír) hear. ● *vi* listen

escudo *m* shield. **~ de armas** coat of arms

escudriñar *vt* examine

escuela *f* school. **~ normal** teachers' training college

escueto *adj* simple

escuincle *m* (Mex fam) kid ⓘ

escul|pir *vt* sculpture. **~tor** *m* sculptor. **~tora** *f* sculptress. **~tura** *f* sculpture

escupir *vt/i* spit

escurr|eplatos *m invar* plate rack. **~idizo** *adj* slippery. **~ir** *vt* drain; wring out (ropa). ● *vi* drain; (ropa) drip. **~irse** *vpr* slip

ese *adj* (f esa) that; (mpl esos, fpl esas) those

ése *pron* (f ésa) that one; (mpl ésos, fpl ésas) those; (primero de dos) the former

esencia *f* essence. **~l** *adj* essential. **lo ~l** the main thing

esf|era *f* sphere; (de reloj) face. **~érico** *adj* spherical

esf|orzarse ② & ⑩ *vpr* make an effort. **~uerzo** *m* effort

esfumarse *vpr* fade away; (persona) vanish

esgrim|a *f* fencing. **~ir** *vt* brandish; (fig) use

esguince *m* sprain

eslabón *m* link

eslavo *adj* Slavic, Slavonic

eslogan *m* slogan

esmalt|ar *vt* enamel. **~e** *m* enamel. **~e de uñas** nail polish

esmerado *adj* careful; (persona) painstaking

esmeralda *f* emerald

esmer|arse *vpr* take care (en over).

esmero *m* care

esmoquin (pl esmóquines) *m* dinner jacket, tuxedo (Amer)

esnob *adj invar* snobbish. ● *m & f* (pl ~s) snob. **~ismo** *m* snobbery

esnórkel *m* snorkel

eso *pron* that. ¡~ es! that's it! ~ mismo exactly. a ~ de about. en ~ at that moment. ¿no es ~? isn't that right? por ~ that's why. y ~ que even though

esos *adj pl véase* ESE

ésos *pron pl véase* ÉSE

espabila|do *adj* bright; (*despierto*) awake. ~r *vt* (*avivar*) brighten up; (*despertar*) wake up. ~rse *vpr* wake up; (*avivarse*) wise up; (*apresurarse*) hurry up

espaci|al *adj* space. ~ar *vt* space out. ~o *m* space. ~oso *adj* spacious

espada *f* sword. ~s *fpl* (*en naipes*) spades

espaguetis *mpl* spaghetti

espald|a *f* back. a ~as de uno behind s.o.'s back. volver la(s) ~a(s) a uno give s.o. the cold shoulder. ~ mojada wetback. ~illa *f* shoulder-blade

espant|ajo *m*, ~apájaros *m invar* scarecrow. ~ar *vt* frighten; (*ahuyentar*) frighten away. ~arse *vpr* be frightened; (*ahuyentarse*) be frightened away. ~o *m* terror; (*horror*) horror. ¡qué ~o! how awful! ~oso *adj* horrific; (*terrible*) terrible

España *f* Spain

español *adj* Spanish. ● *m* (*persona*) Spaniard; (*lengua*) Spanish. los ~es the Spanish

esparadrapo *m* (sticking) plaster

esparcir 9 *vt* scatter; (*difundir*) spread. ~rse *vpr* be scattered; (*difundirse*) spread; (*divertirse*) enjoy o.s.

espárrago *m* asparagus

espasm|o *m* spasm. ~ódico *adj* spasmodic

espátula *f* spatula; (*en pintura*)

palette knife

especia *f* spice

especial *adj* special. en ~ especially. ~idad *f* speciality (*Brit*), specialty (*Amer*). ~ista *adj* & *m* & *f* specialist. ~ización *f* specialization. ~izarse 10 *vpr* specialize. ~mente *adv* especially

especie *f* kind, sort; (*en biología*) species. en ~ in kind

especifica|ción *f* specification. ~r 7 *vt* specify

específico *adj* specific

espect|áculo *m* sight; (*de circo etc*) show. ~acular *adj* spectacular. ~ador *m* & *f* spectator

espectro *m* spectre; (*en física*) spectrum

especula|dor *m* speculator. ~r *vi* speculate

espejismo *m* mirage. ~o *m* mirror. ~o retrovisor (*Auto*) rear-view mirror

espeluznante *adj* horrifying

espera *f* wait. a la ~ waiting (de for). ~nza *f* hope. ~r *vt* hope; (*aguardar*) wait for; expect (vista, carta, bebé). espero que no I hope not. espero que sí I hope so. ● *vi* (*aguardar*) wait. ~rse *vpr* hang on; (*prever*) expect

esperma *f* sperm

esperpento *m* fright

espes|ar *vt/i* thicken. ~arse *vpr* thicken. ~o *adj* thick. ~or *m* thickness

espetón *m* spit

esp|ía *f* spy. ~iar 20 *vt* spy on. ● *vi* spy

espiga *f* (*de trigo etc*) ear

espina *f* thorn; (*de pez*) bone; (*en anatomía*) spine. ~ dorsal spine

espinaca *f* spinach

espinazo m spine

espinilla f shin; (Med) blackhead; (LAm, grano) spot

espino m hawthorn. **~so** adj thorny; (fig) difficult

espionaje m espionage

espiral adj & f spiral

esp|iritista m & f spiritualist. **~iritu** m spirit; (mente) mind. **~iritual** adj spiritual

espl|éndido adj splendid; (persona) generous. **~endor** m splendour

espolear vt spur (on)

espolvorear vt sprinkle

esponj|a f sponge. **~oso** adj spongy

espont|aneidad f spontaneity. **~áneo** adj spontaneous

esporádico adj sporadic

espos|a f wife. **~as** fpl handcuffs. **~ar** vt handcuff. **~o** m husband

espuela f spur; (fig) incentive

espum|a f foam; (en bebidas) froth; (de jabón) lather; (de las olas) surf. **echar ~a** foam, froth. **~oso** adj (vino) sparkling

esqueleto m skeleton; (estructura) framework

esquema m outline

esqu|í m (pl **~is**, **~íes**) ski; (deporte) skiing. **~iar** 20 vi ski

esquilar vt shear

esquimal adj & m Eskimo

esquina f corner

esquiv|ar vt avoid; dodge (golpe). **~o** adj elusive

esquizofrénico adj & m schizophrenic

esta adj véase **ESTE**

ésta pron véase **ÉSTE**

estab|ilidad f stability. **~le** adj stable

establec|er 11 vt establish. **~erse** vpr settle; (Com) set up. **~imiento** m establishment

establo m cattleshed

estaca f stake

estación f station; (del año) season. **~ de invierno** winter (sports) resort. **~ de servicio** service station

estaciona|miento m parking; (LAm, lugar) car park (Brit), parking lot (Amer). **~r** vt station; (Auto) park. **~rio** adj stationary

estadía f (LAm) stay

estadio m stadium; (fase) stage

estadista m statesman. • f stateswoman

estadístic|a f statistics; (cifra) statistic. **~o** adj statistical

estado m state; (Med) condition. **~ civil** marital status. **~ de ánimo** frame of mind. **~ de cuenta** bank statement. **~ mayor** (Mil) staff. **en buen ~** in good condition

Estados Unidos mpl United States

estadounidense adj American, United States. • m & f American

estafa f swindle. **~r** vt swindle

estafeta f (oficina de correos) (sub-)post office

estala|ctita f stalactite. **~gmita** f stalagmite

estall|ar vi explode; (olas) break; (guerra etc) break out; (fig) burst. **~ar en llanto** burst into tears. **~ar de risa** burst out laughing. **~ido** m explosion; (de guerra etc) outbreak

estamp|a f print; (aspecto) appearance. **~ado** adj printed. • m printing; (motivo) pattern; (tela) cotton print. **~ar** vt stamp;

(*imprimir*) print

estampido *m* bang

estampilla *f* (*LAm, de correos*) (postage) stamp

estanca|do *adj* stagnant. ~**r** 🔢 *vt* stem. ~**rse** *vpr* stagnate

estancia *f* stay; (*cuarto*) large room

estanco *adj* watertight. ● *m* tobacconist's (shop)

> **estanco** In Spain, an establishment selling tobacco, stamps, bus and metro passes and other products whose sale is restricted. Cigarettes etc are sold in bars and cafés but at higher prices. *Estancos* also sell stationery and sometimes papers.

---

estandarte *m* standard, banner

estanque *m* pond; (*depósito de agua*) (water) tank

estanquero *m* tobacconist

estante *m* shelf. ~**ría** *f* shelves; (*para libros*) bookcase

estaño *m* tin

---

estar 🔢

● *verbo intransitivo*

····▸ to be ¿**cómo estás?** how are you? **estoy enfermo** I'm ill. **está muy cerca** it's very near. ¿**está Pedro?** is Pedro in? ¿**cómo está el tiempo?** what's the weather like? **ya estamos en invierno** it's winter already

····▸ (*quedarse*) to stay. **sólo** ~**é una semana** I'll only be staying for a week. **estoy en un hotel** I'm staying in a hotel

····▸ (*con fecha*) ¿**a cuánto estamos?** what's the date today?

estamos a 8 de mayo it's the 8th of May.

····▸ (*en locuciones*) ¿**estamos?** all right? **¡ahí está!** that's it! ~ **por** (*apoyar a*) to support; (*LAm, encontrarse a punto de*) to be about to; (*quedar por*) **eso está por verse** that remains to be seen. **son cuentas que están por pagar** they're bills still to be paid

● *verbo auxiliar*

····▸ (*con gerundio*) **estaba estudiando** I was studying

····▸ (*con participio*) **está condenado a muerte** he's been sentenced to death. **está mal traducido** it's wrongly translated. **estarse** *verbo pronominal* to stay. **no se está quieto** he won't stay still

---

> ➡ Cuando el verbo **estar** forma parte de expresiones como estar de acuerdo, estar a la vista, estar constipado, etc., ver bajo el respectivo nombre o adjetivo

---

estatal *adj* state

estático *adj* static

estatua *f* statue

estatura *f* height

estatuto *m* statute; (*norma*) rule

este *adj* (*región*) eastern; (*viento, lado*) east. ● *m* east. ● *adj* (*f* **esta**) this; (*mpl* **estos**, *fpl* **estas**) these. ● *int* (*LAm*) well, er

éste *pron* (*f* **ésta**) this one; (*mpl* **éstos**, *fpl* **éstas**) these; (*segundo de dos*) the latter

estela *f* wake; (*de avión*) trail; (*lápida*) carved stone

estera *f* mat; (*tejido*) matting

est|éreo adj stereo. **~ereofónico** adj stereo, stereophonic

estereotipo m stereotype

estéril adj sterile; (terreno) barren

esterilla f mat

esterlina adj. **libra f ~** pound sterling

estético adj aesthetic

estiércol m dung; (abono) manure

estigma m stigma. **~s** mpl (Relig) stigmata

estil|arse vpr be used. **~o** m style; (en natación) stroke. **~ mariposa** butterfly. **~ pecho** (LAm) breaststroke. **por el ~o** of that sort

estilográfica f fountain pen

estima f esteem. **~do** adj (amigo, colega) valued. **~do señor** (en cartas) Dear Sir. **~r** vt esteem; have great respect for (persona); (valorar) value; (juzgar) consider

estimulante adj stimulating. ● m stimulant. **~imular** vt stimulate; (incitar) incite. **~ímulo** m stimulus

estir|ado adj stretched; (persona) haughty. **~ar** vt stretch; (fig) stretch out. **~ón** m pull, tug; (crecimiento) sudden growth

estirpe m stock

esto pron neutro this; (este asunto) this business. **en ~** at this point. **en ~ de** in this business of. **por ~** therefore

estofa|do adj stewed. ● m stew. **~r** vt stew

estómago m stomach. **dolor** m **de ~** stomach ache

estorb|ar vt obstruct; (molestar) bother. ● vi be in the way. **~o** m hindrance; (molestia) nuisance

estornud|ar vi sneeze. **~o** m sneeze

estos adj mpl véase **ESTE**

éstos pron mpl véase **ÉSTE**

estoy vb véase **ESTAR**

estrabismo m squint

estrado m stage; (Mus) bandstand

estrafalario adj eccentric; (ropa) outlandish

estrago m devastation. **hacer ~os** devastate

estragón m tarragon

estrambótico adj eccentric; (ropa) outlandish

estrangula|dor m strangler; (Auto) choke. **~r** vt strangle

estratagema f stratagem

estrat|ega m & f strategist. **~egia** f strategy. **~égico** adj strategic

estrato m stratum

estrech|ar vt make narrower; take in (vestido); embrace (persona). **~ar la mano a uno** shake hands with s.o. **~arse** vpr become narrower; (abrazarse) embrace. **~ez** f narrowness. **~eces** fpl financial difficulties. **~o** adj narrow; (vestido etc) tight; (fig, íntimo) close. **~o de miras** narrow-minded. ● m strait(s)

estrella f star. **~ de mar** starfish. **~ado** adj starry

estrellar vt smash; crash (coche). **~se** vpr crash (contra into)

estremec|er 🚹 vt shake; **~erse** vpr shake; (de emoción etc) tremble (de with). **~imiento** m shaking

estren|ar vt wear for the first time (vestido etc); show for the first time (película). **~arse** vpr make one's début. **~o** m (de película) première; (de obra de teatro) first night; (de persona) debut

estreñi|do adj constipated. **~miento** m constipation

estrés m stress

estría f groove; (de la piel) stretch mark

estribillo m (incl Mus) refrain

estribo m stirrup; (de coche) step. **perder los ~s** lose one's temper

estribor m starboard

estricto adj strict

estridente adj strident, raucous

estrofa f stanza, verse

estropajo m scourer

estropear vt damage; (plan) spoil; ruin (ropa). **~se** vpr be damaged; (averiarse) break down; (ropa) get ruined; (fruta etc) go bad; (fracasar) fail

estructura f structure. **~l** adj structural

estruendo m roar; (de mucha gente) uproar

estrujar vt squeeze; wring (out) (ropa); (fig) drain

estuario m estuary

estuche m case

estudi|ante m & f student. **~antil** adj student. **~ar** vt study. **~o** m study; (de artista) studio. **~oso** adj studious

estufa f heater; (Mex, cocina) cooker

estupefac|iente m narcotic. **~to** adj astonished

estupendo adj marvellous; (persona) fantastic; **¡~!** that's great!

est|upidez f stupidity; (acto) stupid thing. **~úpido** adj stupid

estupor m amazement

estuve vb véase ESTAR

etapa f stage. **por ~s** in stages

etéreo adj ethereal

etern|idad f eternity. **~o** adj eternal

étic|a f ethics. **~o** adj ethical

etimología f etymology

etiqueta f ticket, tag; (ceremonial) etiquette. **de ~** formal

étnico adj ethnic

eucalipto m eucalyptus

eufemismo m euphemism

euforia f euphoria

euro m euro. **~escéptico** adj & m Eurosceptic

Europa f Europe

euro|peo adj & m European. **~zona** f eurozone

eutanasia f euthanasia

evacua|ción f evacuation. **~r** 21 vt evacuate

evadir vt avoid; evade (impuestos). **~se** vpr escape

evalua|ción f evaluation. **~r** 21 vt assess; evaluate (datos)

evangeli|o m gospel. **~sta** m & f evangelist; (Mex, escribiente) scribe

evapora|ción f evaporation. **~rse** vpr evaporate; (fig) disappear

evasi|ón f evasion; (fuga) escape. **~vo** adj evasive

evento m event; (caso) case

eventual adj possible. **~idad** f eventuality

eviden|cia f evidence. **poner en ~cia a uno** show s.o. up. **~ciar** vt show. **~ciarse** vpr be obvious. **~te** adj obvious. **~temente** adv obviously

evitar vt avoid; (ahorrar) spare; (prevenir) prevent

evocar 7 vt evoke

evoluci|ón f evolution. **~onar** vi evolve; (Mil) manoeuvre

ex prefijo ex-, former

exacerbar vt exacerbate

exact|amente adv exactly. **~itud** f exactness. **~o** adj exact; (preciso) accurate; (puntual) punctual. ¡~! exactly!

exagera|ción f exaggeration. ~**do** adj exaggerated. ~**r** vt/i exaggerate

exalta|do adj exalted; (excitado) (over)excited; (fanático) hot-headed. ~**r** vt exalt. ~**rse** vpr get excited

exam|en m exam, examination. ~**inar** vt examine. ~**inarse** vpr take an exam

exasperar vt exasperate. ~**se** vpr get exasperated

excarcela|ción f release (from prison). ~**r** vt release

excava|ción f excavation. ~**dora** f digger. ~**r** vt excavate

excede|ncia f leave of absence. ~**nte** adj & m surplus. ~**r** vi exceed. ~**rse** vpr go too far

excelen|cia f excellence; (tratamiento) Excellency. ~**te** adj excellent

exc|entricidad f eccentricity. ~**éntrico** adj & m eccentric

excepci|ón f exception. ~**onal** adj exceptional. a ~**ón de**, con ~**ón de** except (for)

except|o prep except (for). ~**uar** 21 vt except

exces|ivo adj excessive. ~**o** m excess. ~**o de equipaje** excess luggage (esp Brit), excess baggage (esp Amer)

excita|ción f excitement. ~**r** vt excite; (incitar) incite. ~**rse** vpr get excited

exclama|ción f exclamation. ~**r** vi exclaim

exclu|ir 17 vt exclude. ~**sión** f exclusion. ~**siva** f sole right; (reportaje) exclusive (story). ~**sivo** adj exclusive

excomu|lgar 12 vt excommuni-

exageración | expandir

cate. ~**nión** f excommunication

excremento m excrement

excursi|ón f excursion, outing. ~**onista** m & f day-tripper

excusa f excuse; (disculpa) apology. **presentar sus ~s** apologize. ~**r** vt excuse

exento adj exempt; (libre) free

exhalar vt exhale, breath out; give off (olor etc)

exhaust|ivo adj exhaustive. ~**o** adj exhausted

exhibi|ción f exhibition; (demostración) display. ~**cionista** m & f exhibitionist. ~**r** vt exhibit ~**rse** vpr show o.s.; (hacerse notar) draw attention to o.s.

exhumar vt exhume; (fig) dig up

exig|encia f demand. ~**ente** adj demanding. ~**ir** 14 vt demand

exiguo adj meagre

exil|(i)ado adj exiled. ● m exile. ~**(i)arse** vpr go into exile. ~**io** m exile

exim|ente m reason for exemption; (Jurid) grounds for acquittal. ~**ir** vt exempt

existencia f existence. ~**s** fpl stock. ~**lismo** m existentialism

exist|ente adj existing. ~**ir** vi exist

éxito m success. **no tener ~** fail. **tener ~** be successful

exitoso adj successful

éxodo m exodus

exonerar vt exonerate

exorbitante adj exorbitant

exorci|smo m exorcism. ~**zar** 10 vt exorcise

exótico adj exotic

expan|dir vt expand; (fig) spread. ~**dirse** vpr expand. ~**sión** f expansion. **~sivo** adj expansive

expatria|do adj & m expatriate.
~rse vpr emigrate; (exiliarse) go
into exile

expectativa f prospect; (esperanza) expectation. **estar a la ~**
be waiting

expedi|ción f expedition; (de documento) issue; (de mercancías) dispatch. **~ente** m record, file; (Jurid)
proceedings. **~r** 5 vt issue; (enviar) dispatch, send. **~to** adj clear;
(LAm, fácil) easy

expeler vt expel

expend|edor m dealer. **~edor
automático** vending machine. **~io**
m (LAm) shop; (venta) sale

expensas fpl (Jurid) costs. **a ~ de**
at the expense of. **a mis ~** at my
expense

experiencia f experience

experiment|al adj experimental.
~ar vt test, experiment with; (sentir) experience. **~o** m experiment

experto adj & m expert

expiar 20 vt atone for

expirar vi expire

explanada f levelled area;
(paseo) esplanade

explayarse vpr speak at length;
(desahogarse) unburden o.s. (**con**
a)

explica|ción f explanation. **~r**
7 vt explain. **~rse** vpr understand;
(hacerse comprender) explain o.s.
no me lo explico I can't understand it

explícito adj explicit

explora|ción f exploration.
~dor m explorer; (muchacho) boy
scout. **~r** vt explore

explosi|ón f explosion; (fig) outburst. **~onar** vt blow up. **~vo**
adj & m explosive

explota|ción f working; (abuso)
exploitation. **~r** vt work (mina);
farm (tierra); (abusar) exploit. ● vi
explode

expone|nte m exponent. **~r** 34
vt expose; display (mercancías);
present (tema); set out (hechos);
exhibit (cuadros etc); (arriesgar)
risk. ● vi exhibit. **~rse** vpr. **~se a
que** run the risk of

exporta|ción f export. **~dor** m
exporter. **~r** vt export

exposición f exposure; (de cuadros etc) exhibition; (de hechos) exposition

expres|ar vt express. **~arse** vpr
express o.s. **~ión** f expression.
~ivo adj expressive; (cariñoso) affectionate

expreso adj express. ● m express;
(café) expresso

exprimi|dor m squeezer. **~r** vt
squeeze

expropiar vt expropriate

expuesto adj on display; (lugar
etc) exposed; (peligroso) dangerous. **estar ~ a** be exposed to

expuls|ar vt expel; throw out
(persona); send off (jugador).
~ión f expulsion

exquisito adj exquisite; (de sabor)
delicious

éxtasis m invar ecstasy

extend|er 1 vt spread (out);
(ampliar) extend; issue (documento). **~erse** vpr spread; (paisaje
etc) extend, stretch. **~ido** adj
spread out; (generalizado) widespread; (brazos) outstretched

extens|amente adv widely; (detalladamente) in full. **~ión** f extension; (área) expanse; (largo) length.

~o adj extensive

extenuar 21 vt exhaust

exterior adj external, exterior; (del extranjero) foreign; (aspecto etc) outward. ● m outside, exterior; (países extranjeros) abroad

extermin|ación f extermination. **~ar** vt exterminate. **~io** m extermination

externo adj external; (signo etc) outward. ● m day pupil

extin|ción f extinction. **~guidor** m (LAm) fire extinguisher. **~guir** 13 vt extinguish. **~guirse** vpr die out; (fuego) go out. **~to** adj (raza etc) extinct. **~tor** m fire extinguisher

extirpar vt eradicate; remove (tumor)

extorsión f extortion

extra adj invar extra; (de buena calidad) good-quality; (huevos) large. **paga** f ~ bonus

extracto m extract

extradición f extradition

extraer 41 vt extract

extranjer|ía f (Esp) la ley de ~ immigration law. **~o** adj foreign. ● m foreigner; (países) foreign countries. del ~ from abroad. en el ~, por el ~ abroad

extrañ|ar vt surprise; (encontrar extraño) find strange; (LAm, echar de menos) miss. **~arse** vpr be surprised (de at). **~eza** f strangeness; (asombro) surprise. **~o** adj strange. ● m stranger

extraoficial adj unofficial

extraordinario adj extraordinary

extrarradio m outlying districts

extraterrestre adj extraterrestrial. ● m alien

extravagan|cia f oddness, ec-

centricity. **~te** adj odd, eccentric

extrav|iado adj lost. **~iar** 20 vt lose. **~iarse** vpr get lost; (objetos) go missing. **~ío** m loss

extremar vt take extra (precauciones); tighten up (vigilancia). **~se** vpr make every effort

extremeño adj from Extremadura

extrem|idad f end. **~idades** fpl extremities. **~ista** adj & m & f extremist. **~o** adj extreme. ● m end; (colmo) extreme. en ~o extremely. en último ~o as a last resort

extrovertido adj & m extrovert

exuberan|cia f exuberance. **~te** adj exuberant

eyacular vt/i ejaculate

- -

Ff

- -

fa m F; (solfa) fah

fabada f bean and pork stew

fábrica f factory. **marca** f **de ~** trade mark

fabrica|ción f manufacture. **~ción en serie** mass production. **~nte** m & f manufacturer. **~r** 7 vt manufacture

fábula f fable; (mentira) fabrication

fabuloso adj fabulous

facci|ón f faction. **~ones** fpl (de la cara) features

faceta f facet

facha f (fam, aspecto) look. **~da** f façade

fácil adj easy; (probable) likely

facili|dad f ease; (*disposición*) aptitude. **~dades** fpl facilities. **~tar** vt facilitate; (*proporcionar*) provide

factible adj feasible

factor m factor

factura f bill, invoice. **~r** vt (*hacer la factura*) invoice; (*al embarcar*) check in

faculta|d f faculty; (*capacidad*) ability; (*poder*) power. **~tivo** adj optional

faena f job. **~s domésticas** housework

faisán m pheasant

faja f (*de tierra*) strip; (*corsé*) corset; (*Mil etc*) sash

fajo m bundle; (*de billetes*) wad

falda f skirt; (*de montaña*) side

falla f fault; (*defecto*) flaw. **~ humana** (*LAm*) human error. **~r** vi fail. **me falló** he let me down. **sin ~r** without fail. ● vt (*error*) miss

fallec|er 🔢 vi die. **~ido** m deceased

fallido adj vain; (*fracasado*) unsuccessful

fallo m (*defecto*) fault; (*error*) mistake. **~ humano** human error; (*en certamen*) decision; (*Jurid*) ruling

falluca f (*Mex*) smuggled goods

fals|ear vt falsify, distort. **~ificación** f forgery. **~ificador** m forger. **~ificar** 🔢 vt forge. **~o** adj false; (*falsificado*) forged; (*joya*) fake

falt|a f lack; (*ausencia*) absence; (*escasez*) shortage; (*defecto*) fault, defect; (*culpa*) fault; (*error*) mistake; (*en fútbol etc*) foul; (*en tenis*) fault. **a ~ de** for lack of. **echar en ~a** miss. **hacer ~a** be necessary. **me hace ~** I need. **sacar ~as** find fault. **~o** adj lacking (**de** in)

❗ cuando el verbo **faltar** va
❗ precedido del complemento indirecto **le** (o **les, nos** etc) el sujeto en español pasa a ser el objeto en inglés p.ej: **les falta experiencia** *they lack experience*

••••➤ (*no estar*) to be missing **¿quién falta?** who's missing? **falta una de las chicas** one of the girls is missing. **al abrigo le faltan 3 botones** the coat has three buttons missing. **~ a algo** (*no asistir*) to be absent from sth; (*no acudir*) to miss sth

••••➤ (*no haber suficiente*) **va a ~ leche** there won't be enough milk. **nos faltó tiempo** we didn't have enough time

••••➤ (*no tener*) **le falta cariño** he lacks affection

••••➤ (*hacer falta*) **le falta sal** it needs more salt. **¡es lo que nos faltaba!** that's all we needed!

••••➤ (*quedar*) **¿te falta mucho?** are you going to be much longer? **falta poco para Navidad** it's not long until Christmas. **aún falta mucho** (*distancia*) there's a long way to go yet **¡no faltaba más!** of course!

fama f fame; (*reputación*) reputation

famélico adj starving

familia f family; (*hijos*) children. **~ numerosa** large family. **~r** adj familiar; (*de la familia*) family; (*sin ceremonia*) informal; (*lenguaje*) colloquial. ● m & f relative. **~ridad** f familiarity. **~rizarse** 🔟 vpr be-

famoso | feo

come familiar (**con** with)

famoso adj famous

fanático adj fanatical. ● m fanatic

fanfarr|ón adj boastful. ● m braggart. **∼onear** vi show off

fango m mud. **∼so** adj muddy

fantasía f fantasy. **de ∼** fancy; (joya) imitation

fantasma m ghost

fantástico adj fantastic

fardo m bundle

faringe f pharynx

farmac|éutico adj chemist (Brit), pharmacist, druggist (Amer). **∼ia** f (ciencia) pharmacy; (tienda) chemist's (shop) (Brit), pharmacy

faro m lighthouse; (Aviac) beacon; (Auto) headlight

farol m lantern; (de la calle) street lamp. **∼a** f street lamp

farr|a f partying. **∼ear** vi (LAm) go out partying

farsa f farce. **∼nte** m & f fraud

fascículo m instalment

fascinar vt fascinate

fascis|mo m fascism

fase f phase

fastidi|ar vt annoy; (estropear) spoil. **∼arse** vpr (máquina) break down; hurt (pierna); (LAm, molestarse) get annoyed. **¡para que te ∼es!** so there!. **∼o** m nuisance; (aburrimiento) boredom. **∼oso** adj annoying

fatal adj fateful; (mortal) fatal; (fam, pésimo) terrible. **∼idad** f fate; (desgracia) misfortune

fatig|a f fatigue. **∼ar** [12] vt tire. **∼arse** vpr get tired. **∼oso** adj tiring

fauna f fauna

favor m favour. **a ∼ de, en ∼ de** in favour of. **haga el ∼ de** would

you be so kind as to, please. **por ∼** please

favorec|er [11] vt favour; (vestido, peinado etc) suit. **∼ido** adj favoured

favorito adj & m favourite

fax m fax

faxear vt fax

faz f face

fe f faith. **dar ∼ de** certify. **de buena ∼** in good faith

febrero m February

febril adj feverish

fecha f date. **a estas ∼s** now; (todavía) still. **hasta la ∼** so far. **poner la ∼** date. **∼r** vt date

fecund|ación f fertilization. **∼ación artificial** artificial insemination. **∼ar** vt fertilize. **∼o** adj fertile; (fig) prolific

federa|ción f federation. **∼l** adj federal

felici|dad f happiness. **∼dades** fpl best wishes; (congratulaciones) congratulations. **∼tación** f letter of congratulation. **¡∼taciones!** (LAm) congratulations! **∼tar** vt congratulate

feligrés m parishioner

feliz adj happy; (afortunado) lucky. **¡Felices Pascuas!** Happy Christmas! **¡F∼ Año Nuevo!** Happy New Year!

felpudo m doormat

femen|il adj (Mex) women's. **∼ino** adj feminine; (equipo) women's; (en biología) female. ● m feminine. **∼inista** adj & m & f feminist.

fen|omenal adj phenomenal. **∼ómeno** m phenomenon; (monstruo) freak

feo adj ugly; (desagradable) nasty. ● adv (LAm) (mal) bad

feria f fair; (*verbena*) carnival; (*Mex, cambio*) small change. **~do** m (*LAm*) public holiday

ferment|ar vt/i ferment. **~o** m ferment

fero|cidad f ferocity. **~z** adj fierce

férreo adj iron; (*disciplina*) strict

ferreter|ía f hardware store, ironmonger's (*Brit*). **~o** m hardware dealer, ironmonger (*Brit*)

ferro|carril m railway (*Brit*), railroad (*Amer*). **~viario** adj rail. **●** m railwayman (*Brit*), railroader (*Amer*)

fértil adj fertile

fertili|dad f fertility. **~zante** m fertilizer. **~zar** [10] vt fertilize

ferv|iente adj fervent. **~or** m fervour

festej|ar vt celebrate; entertain (*persona*). **~o** m celebration

festiv|al m festival. **~idad** f festivity. **~o** adj festive. **●** m public holiday

fétido adj stinking

feto m foetus

fiable adj reliable

fiado m. **al ~** on credit. **~r** m (*Jurid*) guarantor

fiambre m cold meat. **~ría** f (*LAm*) delicatessen

fianza f (*dinero*) deposit; (*objeto*) surety. **bajo ~** on bail

fiar [20] vt (*vender*) sell on credit; (*confiar*) confide. **●** vi give credit. **~se** vpr. **~se de** trust

fibra f fibre. **~ de vidrio** fibreglass

ficción f fiction

fich|a f token; (*tarjeta*) index card; (*en juegos*) counter. **~ar** vt open a file on. **estar ~ado** have a (police) record. **~ero** m card index; (*en informática*) file

fidedigno adj reliable

fidelidad f faithfulness

fideos mpl noodles

fiebre f fever. **~ aftosa** foot-and-mouth disease. **~ del heno** hay fever. **~ porcina** swine fever. **tener ~** have a temperature

fiel adj faithful; (*memoria, relato etc*) reliable. **●** m believer

fieltro m felt

fier|a f wild animal. **~o** adj fierce

fierro m (*LAm*) metal bar; (*hierro*) iron

fiesta f party; (*día festivo*) holiday. **~s** fpl celebrations

---

i

fiestas A *fiesta* in Spain can be a day of local celebrations, a larger event for a town or city, or a national holiday to commemorate a saint's day or a historical event. Famous Spanish *fiestas* include The *Fallas* in Valencia, the *Sanfermines* in Pamplona, and the *Feria de Sevilla*. In Latin America *fiestas patrias* are a period of one or more days when each country celebrates its independence. There are usually military parades, firework displays, and cultural events typical of the country.

---

figura f figure; (*forma*) shape. **~r** vi appear; (*destacar*) show off. **~rse** vpr imagine. **¡figúrate!** just imagine!

fij|ación f fixing; (*obsesión*) fixation. **~ar** vt fix; establish (*residencia*). **~arse** vpr (*poner atención*) pay attention; (*percatarse*) notice. **¡fíjate!** just imagine! **~o** adj fixed; (*firme*) stable; (*permanente*) permanent. **●** adv. **mirar ~o** stare

fila f line; (*de soldados etc*) file; (*en el teatro, cine etc*) row; (*cola*) queue. **ponerse en** ~ line up

filántropo *m* philanthropist

filat|elia *f* stamp collecting, philately. **~élico** *adj* philatelic. ● *m* stamp collector, philatelist

filete *m* fillet

filial *adj* filial. ● *f* subsidiary

Filipinas *fpl*. **las (islas)** ~ the Philippines

filipino *adj* Philippine, Filipino

filmar *vt* film; shoot (película)

filo *m* edge; (*de hoja*) cutting edge. **al** ~ **de las doce** at exactly twelve o'clock. **sacar** ~ **a** sharpen

filología *f* philology

filón *m* vein; (*fig*) gold-mine

fil|osofía *f* philosophy. **~ósofo** *m* philosopher

filtr|ar *vt* filter. **~arse** *vpr* filter; (*dinero*) disappear; (*noticia*) leak. **~o** *m* filter; (*bebida*) philtre. **~ solar** sunscreen

fin *m* end; (*objetivo*) aim. ~ **de semana** weekend. **a** ~ **de** in order to. **a** ~ **de cuentas** at the end of the day. **a** ~ **de que** in order that. **a** ~**es de** at the end of. **al** ~ finally. **al** ~ **y al cabo** after all. **dar** ~ **a** end. **en** ~ in short. **por** ~ finally. **sin** ~ endless

final *adj* final. ● *m* end. ● *f* final. **~idad** *f* aim. **~ista** *m & f* finalist. **~izar** 10 *vt* finish. ● *vi* end

financi|ación *f* financing; (*fondos*) funds; (*facilidades*) credit facilities. **~ar** *vt* finance. **~ero** *adj* financial. ● *m* financier

finca *f* property; (*tierras*) estate; (*rural*) farm; (*de recreo*) country house

fingir 14 *vt* feign; (*simular*) simulate. ● *vi* pretend. **~se** *vpr* pretend to be

finlandés *adj* Finnish. ● *m* (*per-*

sona) Finn; (*lengua*) Finnish

Finlandia *f* Finland

fino *adj* fine; (*delgado*) thin; (*oído*) acute; (*de modales*) refined; (*sutil*) subtle

firma *f* signature; (*acto*) signing; (*empresa*) firm

firmar *vt/i* sign

firme *adj* firm; (*estable*) stable, steady; (*color*) fast. ● *m* (*pavimento*) (road) surface. ● *adv* hard. **~za** *f* firmness

fiscal *adj* fiscal, tax. ● *m & f* public prosecutor. **~o** *m* treasury

fisg|ar 12 *vi* snoop (around). **~ón** *adj* nosy. ● *m* snooper

físic|a *f* physics. **~o** *adj* physical. ● *m* physique; (*persona*) physicist

fisonomista *m & f.* **ser buen** ~ be good at remembering faces

fístol *m* (*Mex*) tiepin

flaco *adj* thin, skinny; (*débil*) weak

flagelo *m* scourge

flagrante *adj* flagrant. **en** ~ red-handed

flama *f* (*Mex*) flame

flamante *adj* splendid; (*nuevo*) brand-new

flamear *vi* flame; (*bandera etc*) flap

flamenco *adj* flamenco; (*de Flandes*) Flemish. ● *m* (*ave*) flamingo; (*música etc*) flamenco; (*idioma*) Flemish

---

flamenco Flamenco is *i* performed in three forms: guitar, singing and dancing. Originally a gypsy art form, it also has Arabic and North African influences. Modern flamenco blends traditional forms with rock, jazz and salsa. In its pure form the music and lyrics are improvised, but tourists are more likely to see rehearsed performances.

flan m crème caramel

flaqueza f thinness; (*debilidad*) weakness

flauta f flute

flecha f arrow. **~zo** m love at first sight

fleco m fringe; (*Mex, en el pelo*) fringe (*Brit*), bangs (*Amer*)

flem|a f phlegm. **~ático** adj phlegmatic

flequillo m fringe (*Brit*), bangs (*Amer*)

fletar vt charter; (*LAm, transportar*) transport

flexible adj flexible

flirte|ar vi flirt. **~o** m flirting

floj|ear vi flag; (*holgazanear*) laze around. **~o** adj loose; (*poco fuerte*) weak; (*perezoso*) lazy

flor f flower. la **~ y nata** the cream. **~a** f flora. **~ecer 11** vi flower, bloom; (*fig*) flourish. **~eciente** adj (*fig*) flourishing. **~ero** m flower vase. **~ista** m & f florist

flot|a f fleet. **~ador** m float; (*de niño*) rubber band. **~ar** vi float. **~e. a ~e** afloat

fluctua|ción f fluctuation. **~r 21** vi fluctuate

flu|idez f fluidity; (*fig*) fluency. **~ido** adj fluid; (*fig*) fluent. ● m fluid. **~ir 17** vi flow

fluoruro m fluoride

fluvial adj river

fobia f phobia

foca f seal

foco m focus; (*lámpara*) floodlight;

(*LAm, de coche*) (head)light; (*Mex, bombilla*) light bulb

fogón m cooker; (*LAm, fogata*) bonfire

folio m sheet

folklórico adj folk

follaje m foliage

follet|ín m newspaper serial. **~o** m pamphlet

follón m ① mess; (*alboroto*) row; (*problema*) trouble

fomentar vt promote; boost (*ahorro*); stir up (*odio*)

fonda f (*pensión*) boarding-house; (*LAm, restaurant*) cheap restaurant

fondo m bottom; (*de calle, pasillo*) end; (*de sala etc*) back; (*de escenario, pintura etc*) background. **~ de reptiles** slush fund. **~s** mpl funds, money. **a ~** thoroughly

fonétic|a f phonetics. **~o** adj phonetic

fontanero m plumber

footing /ˈfutin/ m jogging

forastero m stranger

forcejear vi struggle

forense adj forensic. ● m & f forensic scientist

forjar vt forge. **~se** vpr forge; build up (*ilusiones*)

forma f form; (*contorno*) shape; (*modo*) way; (*Mex, formulario*) form. **~s** fpl conventions. **de todas ~s** anyway. **estar en ~** be in good form. **~ción** f formation; (*educación*) training. **~l** adj formal; (*de fiar*) reliable; (*serio*) serious. **~lidad** f formality; (*fiabilidad*) reliability; (*seriedad*) seriousness. **~r** vt form; (*componer*) make up; (*enseñar*) train. **~rse** vpr form; (*desarrollarse*) develop; (*educarse*) to be educated. **~to m** format

formidable adj formidable; (*muy*

grande) enormous

fórmula f formula; (*sistema*) way. ~ **de cortesía** polite expression

formular vt formulate; make (queja etc). **~io** m form

fornido adj well-built

forr|ar vt (en el interior) line; (en el exterior) cover. **~o** m lining; (cubierta) cover

fortale|cer 🔢 vt strengthen. **~za** f strength; (Mil) fortress; (fuerza moral) fortitude

fortuito adj fortuitous; (encuentro) chance

fortuna f fortune; (suerte) luck

forz|ar 🔢 & 🔢 vt force; strain (vista). **~osamente** adv necessarily. **~oso** adj necessary

fosa f ditch; (tumba) grave. **~s nasales** nostrils

fósforo m phosphorus; (cerilla) match

fósil adj & m fossil

foso m ditch; (en castillo) moat; (de teatro) pit

foto f photo. **sacar ~s** take photos

fotocopia f photocopy. **~dora** f photocopier. **~r** vt photocopy

fotogénico adj photogenic

fot|ografía f photography; (Foto) photograph. **~ografiar** 🔢 vt photograph. **~ógrafo** m photographer

foul /faʊl/ m (pl ~s) (LAm) foul

frac m (pl ~s o **fraques**) tails

fracas|ar vi fail. **~o** m failure

fracción f fraction; (Pol) faction

fractura f fracture. **~r** vt fracture. **~rse** vpr fracture

fragan|cia f fragrance. **~te** adj fragrant

frágil adj fragile

fragmento m fragment; (de canción etc) extract

fragua f forge. **~r** 🔢 vt forge; (fig) concoct. ● vi set

fraile m friar; (monje) monk

frambuesa f raspberry

franc|és adj French. ● m (persona) Frenchman; (lengua) French. **~esa** f Frenchwoman

Francia f France

franco adj frank; (evidente) marked; (Com) free. ● m (moneda) franc

francotirador m sniper

franela f flannel

franja f border; (banda) stripe; (de terreno) strip

franque|ar vt clear; (atravesar) cross; pay the postage on (carta). **~o** m postage

franqueza f frankness

frasco m bottle; (de mermelada etc) jar

frase f phrase; (oración) sentence. **~ hecha** set phrase

fratern|al adj fraternal. **~idad** f fraternity

fraud|e m fraud. **~ulento** adj fraudulent

fray m brother, friar

frecuen|cia f frequency. **con ~cia** frequently. **~tar** vt frequent. **~te** adj frequent

frega|dero m sink. **~r** 🔢 & 🔢 vt scrub; wash (los platos); mop (el suelo); (LAm, fam, molestar) annoy

freír 🔢 (pp **frito**) vt fry. **~se** vpr fry; (persona) roast

frenar vt brake; (fig) check

frenético adj frenzied; (furioso) furious

freno m (de caballería) bit; (Au

brake; (*fig*) check

frente *m* front. ∼ a opposite. ∼ a ∼ face to face. al ∼ at the head; (*hacia delante*) forward. chocar de ∼ crash head on. de ∼ a (*LAm*) facing. hacer ∼ a face (*cosa*); stand up to (*persona*). ∼f forehead. arrugar la ∼ frown

fresa *f* strawberry

fresc|o *adj* (*frío*) cool; (*reciente*) fresh; (*descarado*) cheeky. ● *m* fresh air; (*frescor*) coolness; (*mural*) fresco; (*persona*) impudent person. al ∼o in the open air. hacer ∼o be cool. tomar el ∼o get some fresh air. ∼or *m* coolness. ∼ura *f* freshness; (*frío*) coolness; (*descaro*) cheek

frialdad *f* coldness; (*fig*) indifference

fricci|ón *f* rubbing; (*fig, Tec*) friction; (*masaje*) massage. ∼onar *vt* rub

frigidez *f* frigidity

frígido *adj* frigid

frigorífico *m* fridge, refrigerator

frijol *m* (*LAm*) bean. ∼es refritos (*Mex*) fried purée of beans

frío *adj* & *m* cold. tomar ∼ catch cold. hacer ∼ be cold. tener ∼ be cold

frito *adj* fried; (🔲, *harto*) fed up. me tiene ∼ I'm sick of him

fr|ivolidad *f* frivolity. ∼ívolo *adj* frivolous

fronter|a *f* border, frontier. ∼izo *adj* border; (*país*) bordering

frontón *m* pelota court; (*pared*) fronton

frotar *vt* rub; strike (*cerilla*)

fructífero *adj* fruitful

fruncir 🔟 *vt* gather (*tela*). ∼ el ceño frown

frustra|ción *f* frustration. ∼r *vt* frustrate. ∼rse *vpr* (*fracasar*) fail. quedar ∼do be disappointed

frut|a *f* fruit. ∼al *adj* fruit. ∼ería *f* fruit shop. ∼ero *m* fruit seller; (*recipiente*) fruit bowl. ∼icultura *f* fruit-growing. ∼o *m* fruit

fucsia *f* fuchsia. ● *m* fuchsia

fuego *m* fire. ∼s artificiales fireworks. a ∼ lento on a low heat. tener ∼ have a light

fuente *f* fountain; (*manantial*) spring; (*plato*) serving dish; (*fig*) source

fuera *adv* out; (*al exterior*) outside; (*en otra parte*) away; (*en el extranjero*) abroad. ∼ de outside; (*excepto*) except for, besides. por ∼ on the outside. ● *vb véase* IR y SER

fuerte *adj* strong; (*color*) bright; (*sonido*) loud; (*dolor*) severe; (*duro*) hard; (*grande*) large; (*lluvia, nevada*) heavy. ● *m* fort; (*fig*) strong point. ● *adv* hard; (*con hablar etc*) loudly; (*llover*) heavily; (*mucho*) a lot

fuerza *f* strength; (*poder*) power; (*en física*) force; (*Mil*) forces. ∼ de voluntad will-power. a ∼ de by (*dint of*). a la ∼ by necessity. por ∼ by force; (*por necesidad*) by necessity. tener ∼s para have the strength to

fuese *vb véase* IR y SER

fug|a *f* flight, escape; (*de gas etc*) leak; (*Mus*) fugue. ∼arse 🔢 *vpr* flee, escape. ∼az *adj* fleeting. ∼itivo *adj* & *m* fugitive

fui *vb véase* IR, SER

fulano *m* so-and-so. ∼, mengano y zutano every Tom, Dick and Harry

fulminar *vt* (*fig, con mirada*) look daggers at

fuma|dor *adj* smoking. • *m* smoker. **~r** *vt/i* smoke. **~r en pipa** smoke a pipe. **~rse** *vpr* smoke. **~rada** *f* puff of smoke

funci|ón *f* function; (*de un cargo etc*) duty; (*de teatro*) show, performance. **~onal** *adj* functional. **~onar** *vi* work, function. **no ~ona** out of order. **~onario** *m* civil servant

funda *f* cover. **~ de almohada** pillowcase

funda|ción *f* foundation. **~mental** *adj* fundamental. **~mentar** *vt* base (en on). **~mento** *m* foundation. **~r** *vt* found; (*fig*) base. **~rse** *vpr* be based

fundi|ción *f* melting; (*de metales*) smelting; (*taller*) foundry. **~r** *vt* melt; smelt (metales); cast (objeto); blend (colores); (*fusionar*) merge; (*Elec*) blow; (*LAm*) seize up (motor). **~rse** *vpr* melt; (*unirse*) merge

fúnebre *adj* funeral; (*sombrío*) gloomy

funeral *adj* funeral. • *m* funeral. **~es** *mpl* funeral

funicular *adj & m* funicular

furgón *m* van. **~oneta** *f* van

fur|ia *f* fury; (*violencia*) violence. **~ibundo** *adj* furious. **~ioso** *adj* furious. **~or** *m* fury

furtivo *adj* furtive. **cazador ~** poacher

furúnculo *m* boil

fusible *m* fuse

fusil *m* rifle. **~ar** *vt* shoot

fusión *f* melting; (*unión*) fusion; (*Com*) merger

fútbol *m*, (*Mex*) **futbol** *m* football

futbolista *m & f* footballer

futur|ista *adj* futuristic. • *m & f*
futurist. **~o** *adj & m* future

Gg

gabardina *f* raincoat

gabinete *m* (*Pol*) cabinet; (*en museo etc*) room; (*de dentista, médico etc*) consulting room

gaceta *f* gazette

gafa *f* hook. **~s** *fpl* glasses, spectacles. **~s de sol** sunglasses

gaf|ar *vt* 🄴 bring bad luck to. **~e** *m* jinx

gaita *f* bagpipes

gajo *m* segment

gala *f* gala. **~s** *fpl* finery, best clothes. **estar de ~** be dressed up. **hacer ~ de** show off

galán *m* (*en el teatro*) (*romantic*) hero; (*enamorado*) lover

galante *adj* gallant. **~ar** *vt* court. **~ría** *f* gallantry

galápago *m* turtle

galardón *m* award

galaxia *f* galaxy

galera *f* galley

galer|ía *f* gallery. **~ía comercial** (*shopping*) arcade. **~ón** *m* (*Mex*) hall

Gales *m* Wales. **país de ~** Wales

gal|és *adj* Welsh. • *m* Welshman; (*lengua*) Welsh. **~esa** *f* Welshwoman

galgo *m* greyhound

Galicia *f* Galicia

galimatías *m invar* gibberish

gallard|ía *f* elegance. **~o** *adj* elegant

gallego adj & m Galician

galleta f biscuit (Brit), cookie (Amer)

gall|ina f hen, chicken; (fig, fam) coward. ~o m cock

galón m gallon; (cinta) braid; (Mil) stripe

galop|ar vi gallop. ~e m gallop

gama f scale; (fig) range

gamba f prawn (Brit), shrimp (Amer)

gamberro m hooligan

gamuza f (piel) chamois leather; (de otro animal) suede

gana f wish, desire; (apetito) appetite. **de buena** ~ willingly. **de mala** ~ reluctantly. **no me da la** ~ I don't feel like it. **tener** ~s **de** (+ infinitivo) feel like (+ gerundio)

ganad|ería f cattle raising; (ganado) livestock. ~o m livestock. ~o lanar sheep. ~o porcino pigs. ~o vacuno cattle

gana|dor adj winning. ● m winner. ~ncia f gain; (Com) profit. ~r vt earn; (en concurso, juego etc) win; (alcanzar) reach. ● vi (vencer) win; (mejorar) improve. ~rle a uno beat s.o. ~rse la vida earn a living. **salir** ~ndo come out better off

ganch|illo m crochet. **hacer** ~illo crochet. ~o m hook; (LAm, colgador) hanger. **tener** ~o be very attractive

ganga f bargain

ganso m goose

garabat|ear vt/i scribble. ~o m scribble

garaje m garage

garant|e m & f guarantor. ~ía f guarantee. ~izar [10] vt guarantee

garapiña f (Mex) pineapple

squash. ~do adj. **almendras** fpl ~das sugared almonds

garbanzo m chick-pea

garbo m poise; (de escrito) style. ~so adj elegant

garganta f throat; (valle) gorge

gárgaras fpl. **hacer** ~ gargle

garita f hut; (de centinela) sentry box

garra f (de animal) claw; (de ave) talon

garrafa f carafe

garrafal adj huge

garrapata f tick

garrapat|ear vi scribble. ~o m scribble

garrote m club, cudgel; (tormento) garrotte

gar|úa f (LAm) drizzle. ~uar vi [21] (LAm) drizzle

garza f heron

gas m gas. **con** ~ fizzy. **sin** ~ still

gasa f gauze

gaseosa f fizzy drink

gas|óleo m diesel. ~olina f petrol (Brit), gasoline (Amer), gas (Amer). ~olinera f petrol station (Brit), gas station (Amer)

gast|ado adj spent; (vestido etc) worn out. ~ador m spendthrift. ~ar vt spend; (consumir) use; (malgastar) waste; (desgastar) wear out; wear (vestido etc); crack (broma). ~arse vpr wear out. ~o m expense; (acción de gastar) spending

gastronomía f gastronomy

gat|a f cat. **a** ~as on all fours. ~ear vi crawl

gatillo m trigger

gat|ito m kitten. ~o m cat. **dar** ~o **por liebre** take s.o. in

gaucho m Gaucho

i **gaucho** A peasant of the pampas of Argentina, Uruguay and Brazil. Modern gauchos work as foremen on farms and ranches and take part in rodeos. Traditionally, a gaucho's outfit was characterized by its baggy trousers, leather chaps, and *chiripá*, a waist-high garment. They also used *boleadoras* for catching cattle.

gaveta *f* drawer

gaviota *f* seagull

gazpacho *m* gazpacho

gelatina *f* gelatine; (*jalea*) jelly

gema *f* gem

gemelo *f* twin. **~s** *mpl* (*anteojos*) binoculars; (*de camisa*) cuff-links

gemido *m* groan

Géminis *m* Gemini

gemir 5 *vi* moan; (*animal*) whine, howl

gen *m*, **gene** *m* gene

genealogía *f* genealogy. **~ógico** *adj* genealogical. **árbol** *m* **~ógico** family tree

generación *f* generation. **~onal** *adj* generation

general *adj* general. **en ~** in general. **por lo ~** generally. ● *m* general. **~izar** 10 *vt/i* generalize. **~mente** *adv* generally

generar *vt* generate

género *m* type, sort; (*en biología*) genus; (*Gram*) gender; (*en literatura etc*) genre; (*producto*) product; (*tela*) material. **~s de punto** knitwear. **~ humano** mankind

generosidad *f* generosity. **~o** *adj* generous

genética *f* genetics. **~o** *adj* genetic

genial *adj* brilliant; (*divertido*) funny. **~o** *m* temper; (*carácter*) nature; (*talento, persona*) genius

genital *adj* genital. **~es** *mpl* genitals

genoma *m* genome

gente *f* people; (*nación*) nation; (*fam, familia*) family, folks; (*Mex, persona*) person. ● *adj* (*LAm*) respectable; (*amable*) kind

gentil *adj* charming. **~eza** *f* kindness. **tener la ~eza de** be kind enough to

gentío *m* crowd

genuflexión *f* genuflection

genuino *adj* genuine

geografía *f* geography. **~ográfico** *adj* geographical.

geología *f* geology. **~ólogo** *m* geologist

geometría *f* geometry. **~étrico** *adj* geometrical

geranio *m* geranium

gerencia *f* management. **~ciar** *vt* (*LAm*) manage. **~te** *m & f* manager

germen *m* germ

germinar *vi* germinate

gestación *f* gestation

gesticulación *f* gesticulation. **~r** *vi* gesticulate

gestión *f* step; (*administración*) management. **~onar** *vt* take steps to arrange; (*dirigir*) manage

gesto *m* expression; (*ademán*) gesture; (*mueca*) grimace

gibraltareño *adj & m* Gibraltarian

gigante *adj* gigantic. ● *m* giant. **~sco** *adj* gigantic

gimnasia *f* gymnastics. **~asio** *m* gymnasium, gym 🔟. **~asta** *m & f* gymnast. **~ástic** *adj* gymnastic

gimotear *vi* whine

ginebra f gin

ginec|ólogo m gynaecologist

gira f tour. ~r vt spin; draw (cheque); transfer (dinero). ● vi rotate, go round; (en camino) turn

girasol m sunflower

gir|atorio adj revolving. ~o m turn; (Com) draft; (locución) expression. ~o postal money order

gitano adj & m gypsy

glacia|l adj icy. ~r m glacier

glándula f gland

glasear vt glaze; (Culin) ice

glob|al adj global; (fig) overall. ~o m globe; (aerostato, juguete) balloon

glóbulo m globule

gloria f glory; (placer) delight. ~rse vpr boast (de about)

glorieta f square; (Auto) roundabout (Brit), (traffic) circle (Amer)

glorificar 7 vt glorify

glorioso adj glorious

glotón adj gluttonous. ● m glutton

gnomo /'nomo/ m gnome

gob|ernación f government. Ministerio m de la G~ernación Home Office (Brit), Department of the Interior (Amer). ~ernador adj governing. ● m governor. ~ernante adj governing. ● m & f leader. ~ernar 1 vt govern. ~ierno m government

goce m enjoyment

gol m goal

golf m golf

golfo m gulf; (niño) urchin; (holgazán) layabout

golondrina f swallow

golos|ina f titbit; (dulce) sweet. ~o adj fond of sweets

golpe m blow; (puñetazo) punch; (choque) bump; (de emoción) shock; (arg, atraco) job 1; (en golf, en tenis, de remo) stroke. ~ de estado coup d'etat. ~ de fortuna stroke of luck. ~ de vista glance. ~ militar military coup. de ~ suddenly. de un ~ in one go. ~ar vt hit; (dar varios golpes) beat; (con mucho ruido) bang; (con el puño) punch. ● vi knock

goma f rubber; (para pegar) glue; (banda) rubber band; (de borrar) eraser. ~ de mascar chewing gum. ~ espuma foam rubber

googlear ® vt/i 1 to google

gord|a f (Mex) small thick tortilla. ~o adj (persona) fat; (con ser) big; (carne) have put on weight; (carne) fatty; (grueso) thick; (grande) large, big. ● m first prize. ~ura f fatness; (grasa) fat

gorila f gorilla

gorje|ar vi chirp. ~o m chirping

gorra f cap. ~ de baño (LAm) bathing cap

gorrión m sparrow

gorro m cap; (de niño) bonnet. ~ de baño bathing cap

got|a f drop; (Med) gout. ni ~a nothing. ~ear vi drip. ~era f leak

gozar 10 vt enjoy. ● vi. ~ de enjoy

gozne m hinge

gozo m pleasure; (alegría) joy. ~so adj delighted

graba|ción f recording. ~do m engraving, print; (en libro) illustration. ~dora f tape-recorder. ~r vt engrave; record (discos etc)

graci|a f grace; (favor) favour; (humor) wit. ~as fpl thanks. ¡~as! thank you!, thanks! dar las ~as thank. hacer ~a amuse; (gustar) please. ¡muchas ~as! thank you very much! **tener** ~a be funny. ~**oso** adj funny. ● m fool, comic character

grad|a f step. ~**as** fpl stand(s). ~**ación** f gradation. ~**o** m degree; (en enseñanza) year (Brit), grade (Amer). **de buen** ~ willingly

gradua|ción f graduation; (de alcohol) proof. ~**do** m graduate. ~**l** adj gradual. ~**r** 21 vt graduate; (regular) adjust. ~**rse** vpr graduate

gráfic|a f graph. ~**o** adj graphic. ● m graph

gram|ática f grammar. ~**atical** adj grammatical

gramo m gram, gramme (Brit)

gran adj véase **GRANDE**

grana f (color) deep red

granada f pomegranate; (Mil) grenade

granate m (color) maroon

Gran Bretaña f Great Britain

grande adj (delante de nombre en singular **gran**) big, large; (alto) tall; (fig) great; (LAm, de edad) grown up. ~**za** f greatness

grandioso adj magnificent

granel m. **a** ~ in bulk; (suelto) loose; (fig) in abundance

granero m barn

granito m granite; (grano) small grain

graniz|ado m iced drink. ~**ar** 10 vi hail. ~**o** m hail

granj|a f farm. ~**ero** m farmer

grano m grain; (semilla) seed; (de café) bean; (Med) spot. ~**s** mpl cereals

granuja m & f rogue

grapa f staple. ~**r** vt staple

gras|a f grease; (Culin) fat. ~**iento** adj greasy

gratifica|ción f (de sueldo)

bonus (recompensa) reward. ~**r** 7 vt reward

grat|is adv free. ~**itud** f gratitude. ~**o** adj pleasant ~**uito** adj free; (fig) uncalled for

grava|men m tax; (carga) burden; (sobre inmueble) encumbrance. ~**r** vt tax; (cargar) burden

grave adj serious; (voz) deep; (sonido) low; (acento) grave. ~**dad** f gravity

gravilla f gravel

gravitar vi gravitate; (apoyarse) rest (**sobre** on); (peligro) hang (**sobre** over)

gravoso adj costly

graznar vi (cuervo) caw; (pato) quack; honk (ganso)

Grecia f Greece

gremio m union

greña f mop of hair

gresca f rumpus; (riña) quarrel

griego adj & m Greek

grieta f crack

grifo m tap, faucet (Amer)

grilletes mpl shackles

grillo m cricket. ~**s** mpl shackles

gringo m (LAm) foreigner; (norteamericano) Yankee [T]

gripe f flu

gris adj grey. ● m grey; (fam, policía) policeman

grit|ar vi shout. ~**ería** f, ~**erío** m uproar. ~**o** m shout; (de dolor, sorpresa) cry; (chillido) scream. **dar** ~**s** shout

grosella f redcurrant. ~ **negra** blackcurrant

groser|ía f rudeness; (ordinariez) coarseness; (comentario etc) coarse remark; (palabra) swearword. ~**o** adj coarse; (descortés) rude

grosor m thickness

grotesco adj grotesque

grúa f crane

grueso adj thick; (persona) fat, stout. ● m thickness; (fig) main body

grumo m lump

gruñi|do m grunt; (de perro) growl. ~r **22** vi grunt; (perro) growl

grupa f hindquarters

grupo m group

gruta f grotto

guacamole m guacamole

guadaña f scythe

guaje m (Mex) gourd

guajolote m (Mex) turkey

guante m glove

guapo adj good-looking; (chica) pretty; (elegante) smart

guarda m & f guard; (de parque etc) keeper. ~barros m invar mudguard. ~bosque m gamekeeper. ~costas m invar coastguard vessel. ~espaldas m invar bodyguard. ~meta m goalkeeper. ~r vt keep; (proteger) protect; (en un lugar) put away; (reservar) save, keep. ~rse vpr. ~rse de (+ infinitivo) avoid (+ gerundio). ~rropa m wardrobe; (en local público) cloakroom. ~vallas m invar (LAm) goalkeeper

guardería f nursery

guardia f guard; (policía) policewoman; (de médico) shift. G~ Civil Civil Guard. ~ municipal police. estar de ~ be on duty. estar en ~ be on one's guard. montar la ~ mount guard. ● m policeman. ~ de tráfico m traffic policeman. ● f traffic policewoman

guardián m guardian; (de parque etc) keeper; (de edificio) security guard

guar|ecer **11** vt (albergar) give shelter to. ~ecerse vpr take shelter. ~ida f den, lair; (de personas) hideout

guarn|ecer **11** vt (adornar) adorn; (Culin) garnish. ~ición f adornment; (de caballo) harness; (Culin) garnish; (Mil) garrison; (de piedra preciosa) setting

guas|a f joke. ~ón adj humorous. ● m joker

Guatemala f Guatemala

guatemalteco adj & m Guatemalan

guateque m party, bash

guayab|a f guava; (dulce) guava jelly. ~era f lightweight jacket

gubernatura f (Mex) government

güero adj (Mex) fair

guerr|a f war; (método) warfare. dar ~a annoy. ~ero adj warlike; (belicoso) fighting. ● m warrior. ~illa f band of guerrillas. ~illero m guerrilla

guía m & f guide. ● f guidebook; (de teléfonos) directory

guiar **20** vt guide; (llevar) lead; (Auto) drive. ~se vpr be guided (por by)

guijarro m pebble

guillotina f guillotine

guind|a f morello cherry. ~illa f chilli

guiñapo m rag; (fig, persona) wreck

guiñar vt/i wink. ~o m wink. hacer ~os wink

guión m hyphen, dash; (de película etc) script. ~ista m & f scriptwriter

guirnalda f garland

guisado m stew

guisante m pea. **~ de olor** sweet pea

guis|ar vt/i cook. **~o** m stew

guitarr|a f guitar. **~ista** m & f guitarist

gula f gluttony

gusano m worm; (*larva de mosca*) maggot

---

gustar

● verbo intransitivo

! Cuando el verbo **gustar** va precedido del complemento indirecto le (o **les, nos** etc), el sujeto en español pasa a ser el objeto en inglés. **me gusta mucho la música** I like music very much. **le gustan los helados** he likes ice cream. **a Juan no le gusta** Juan doesn't like it (or her etc)

····▶ gustar + *infinitivo*. **les gusta ver televisión** they like watching television

····▶ gustar que + *subjuntivo*. **me ~ía que vinieras** I'd like you to come. **no le gusta que lo corrijan** he doesn't like being corrected. **¿te ~ía que te lo comprara?** would you like me to buy it for you?

····▶ gustar de algo to like sth. **gustan de las fiestas** they like parties

····▶ (*tener acogida*) to go down well. **ese tipo de cosas que siempre gusta** those sort of things always go down well. **el libro no gustó** the book didn't go down well

····▶ (*en frases de cortesía*) to wish. **como guste** as you

wish. **cuando gustes** whenever you wish

● verbo transitivo

····▶ (LAm, querer) **¿gusta un café?** would you like a coffee? **¿gustan pasar?** would you like to come in? **gustarse** verbo pronominal to like each other

gusto m taste; (*placer*) pleasure. **a ~** comfortable. **a mi ~** to my liking. **buen ~** good taste. **con mucho ~** with pleasure. **dar ~** please. **mucho ~** pleased to meet you. **~so** adj tasty; (*de buen grado*) willingly

gutural adj guttural

Hh

ha vb véase **HABER**

haba f broad bean

Habana f **La ~** Havana

habano m (*puro*) Havana

haber verbo auxiliar **30** have. ● v impersonal (presente s & pl **hay**, imperfecto s & pl **había**, pretérito s & pl **hubo**). **hay una carta para ti** there's a letter for you. **hay 5 bancos en la plaza** there are 5 banks in the square. **hay que hacerlo** it must be done, you have to do it. **he aquí** here is, here are. **no hay de qué** don't mention it, not at all. **¿qué hay?** (*¿qué pasa?*) what's the matter?; (*¿qué tal?*) how are you?

habichuela f bean

hábil adj skilful; (*listo*) clever; (*día*) working; (*Jurid*) competent

habili|dad f skill; (*astucia*) clever-

ness; (*Jurid*) competence. **~tar** *vt*
qualify

habita|ción *f* room; (*dormitorio*)
bedroom; (*en biología*) habitat.
~ción de matrimonio, **~ción
doble** double room. **~ción individual**, **~ción sencilla** single room.
~do *adj* inhabited. **~nte** *m* inhabitant. **~r** *vt* live in. ● *vi* live

hábito *m* habit

habitua|l *adj* usual, habitual;
(*cliente*) regular. **~r** 21 *vt* accustom. **~rse** *vpr*. **~rse a** get used to

habla *f* speech; (*idioma*) language;
(*dialecto*) dialect. **al ~** (*al teléfono*)
speaking. **ponerse al ~ con** get in
touch with. **~dor** *adj* talkative. ● *m*
chatterbox. **~duría** *f* rumour.
~durías *fpl* gossip. **~nte** *adj*
speaking. ● *m & f* speaker. **~r** *vt*
speak. ● *vi* speak, talk (**con** to);
(*Mex, por teléfono*) call. **¡ni ~r!** out
of the question! **se ~ español**
Spanish spoken

hacend|ado *m* landowner; (*LAm*)
farmer. **~oso** *adj* hard-working

hacer 31

● *verbo transitivo*

••••▶ to do. **¿qué haces?** what are
you doing? **~ los deberes** to
do one's homework. **no sé qué
~** I don't know what to do.
hazme un favor can you do
me a favour?

••••▶ (*fabricar, preparar, producir*)
to make. **me hizo un vestido**
she made me a dress. **~ un
café** to make a (cup of) coffee.
no hagas tanto ruido don't
make so much noise

••••▶ (*construir*) to build (casa,
puente)

••••▶ **hacer que uno haga algo** to

make s.o. do sth. **haz que se
vaya** make him leave. **hizo
que se equivocara** he made
her go wrong

••••▶ **hacer hacer algo** to have
sth done. **hizo arreglar el
techo** he had the roof repaired

➡ Cuando el verbo **hacer**
se emplea en expresiones
como **hacer una pregunta**,
hacer trampa etc., ver bajo el
respectivo nombre

● *verbo intransitivo*

••••▶ (*actuar, obrar*) to do. **hiciste bien en llamar** you did
the right thing to call **¿cómo
haces para parecer tan
joven?** what do you do to
look so young?

••••▶ (*fingir, simular*) hacer
como que to pretend. **hizo
como que no me conocía** he
pretended not to know me.
haz como que estás dormido
pretend you're asleep

••••▶ **hacer de** (*en teatro*) to play
the part of; (*ejercer la función
de*) to act as

••••▶ (*LAm, sentar*) **tanta sal
hace mal** so much salt is not
good for you. **dormir le hizo
bien** the sleep did him good.
el pepino me hace mal cucumber doesn't agree with me
verbo impersonal

••••▶ (*hablando del tiempo atmosférico*) to be. **hace sol** it's
sunny. **hace 3 grados** it's 3
degrees

••••▶ (*con expresiones temporales*)
hace una hora que espero
I've been waiting for an hour.

llegó hace 3 días he arrived 3 days ago. **hace mucho tiempo** a long time ago. **hasta hace poco** until recently

● **hacerse** *verbo pronominal*

····▶ (*para sí*) to make o.s. (*falda, café*)

····▶ (*hacer que otro haga*) **se hizo la permanente** she had her hair permed. **me hice una piscina** I had a pool built

····▶ (*convertirse en*) to become. **se hicieron amigos** they became friends

····▶ (*acostumbrarse*) **~se a algo** to get used to sth

····▶ (*fingirse*) to pretend. **~se el enfermo** to pretend to be ill

····▶ (*moverse*) to move. **hazte para atrás** move back

····▶ **hacerse de** (*LAm*) to make (*amigo, dinero*)

hacha *f* axe; (*antorcha*) torch
hacia *prep* towards; (*cerca de*) near; (*con tiempo*) at about. **~ abajo** downwards. **~ arriba** upwards. **~ atrás** backwards. **~ las dos** (at) about two o'clock
hacienda *f* country estate; (*en LAm*) ranch; **la ~ pública** the Treasury. **Ministerio** *m* **de H~** Ministry of Finance; (*en Gran Bretaña*) Exchequer; (*en Estados Unidos*) Treasury
hada *f* fairy. **el ~ madrina** the fairy godmother
hago *vb véase* HACER
Haití *m* Haiti
halag|ar 🕛 *vt* flatter. **~üeño** *adj* flattering; (*esperanzador*) promising
halcón *m* falcon
halla|r *vt* find; (*descubrir*) discover.

~rse *vpr* be. **~zgo** *m* discovery
hamaca *f* hammock; (*asiento*) deck-chair
hambr|e *f* hunger; (*de muchos*) famine. **tener ~e** be hungry. **~iento** *adj* starving
hamburguesa *f* hamburger
harag|án *adj* lazy, idle. ● *m* layabout. **~anear** *vi* laze around
harap|iento *adj* in rags. **~o** *m* rag
harina *f* flour
hart|ar *vt* (*fastidiar*) annoy. **me estás ~ando** you're annoying me. **~arse** *vpr* (*llenarse*) gorge o.s. (*de* on); (*cansarse*) get fed up (*de* with). **~o** *adj* full; (*cansado*) tired; (*fastidiado*) fed up (*de* with). ● *adv* (*LAm*) (*muy*) very; (*mucho*) a lot
hasta *prep* as far as; (*en el tiempo*) until, till; (*Mex*) not until. ● *adv* even. **~ la vista!** goodbye!, see you! 🔲 **¡~ luego!** see you later! **¡~ mañana!** see you tomorrow! **¡~ pronto!** see you soon!
hast|iar 🔢 *vt* (*cansar*) weary, tire; (*aburrir*) bore. **~iarse** *vpr* get fed up (*de* with). **~ío** *m* weariness; (*aburrimiento*) boredom
haya *f* beech (tree). ● *vb véase* HABER
hazaña *f* exploit
hazmerreír *m* laughing stock
he *vb véase* HABER
hebilla *f* buckle
hebra *f* thread; (*fibra*) fibre
hebreo *adj & m* Hebrew
hechi|cera *f* witch. **~cería** *f* witchcraft. **~cero** *m* wizard. **~zar** 🔟 *vt* cast a spell on; (*fig*) captivate. **~zo** *m* spell; (*fig*) charm
hech|o *pp de* hacer. ● *adj* (*manufacturado*) made; (*terminado*) done; (*vestidos etc*) ready-made; (*Culin*)

done. ● m fact; (acto) deed; (cuestión) matter; (suceso) event. **de ~o** in fact. **~ura** f making; (forma) form; (del cuerpo) build; (calidad de fabricación) workmanship

hed|er **1** vi stink. **~iondez** f stench. **~iondo** adj stinking, smelly. **~or** m stench

hela|da f frost. **~dera** f (LAm) fridge, refrigerator. **~dería** f ice-cream shop. **~do** adj freezing; (congelado) frozen; (LAm, bebida) chilled. ● m ice-cream. **~r** **1** vt/i freeze. **anoche heló** there was a frost last night. **~rse** vpr freeze

helecho m fern

hélice f propeller

helicóptero m helicopter

hembra f female; (mujer) woman

hemorr|agia f haemorrhage. **~oides** fpl haemorrhoids

hendidura f crack, split; (en geología) fissure

heno m hay

heráldica f heraldry

hered|ar vt/i inherit. **~era** f heiress. **~ero** m heir. **~itario** adj hereditary

hereje m heretic. **~ía** f heresy

herencia f inheritance; (fig) heritage

heri|da f injury; (con arma) wound. **~do** adj injured; (con arma) wounded; (fig) hurt. ● m injured person. **~r** **4** vt injure; (con arma) wound; (fig) hurt. **~rse** vpr hurt o.s.

herman|a f sister. **~a política** sister-in-law. **~astra** f stepsister. **~astro** m stepbrother. **~o** m brother. **~o político** brother-in-law. **~os** mpl brothers; (chicos y chicas) brothers and sisters. **~os gemelos** twins

hermético adj hermetic; (fig) watertight

hermos|o adj beautiful; (espléndido) splendid. **~ura** f beauty

héroe m hero

hero|ico adj heroic. **~ína** f heroine; (droga) heroin. **~ismo** m heroism

herr|adura f horseshoe. **~amienta** f tool. **~ero** m blacksmith

herv|idero m (fig) hotbed; (multitud) throng. **~ir** **4** vt/i boil. **~or** m (fig) ardour. **romper el ~** come to the boil

hiberna|ción f hibernation. **~r** vi hibernate

híbrido adj & m hybrid

hice vb véase **HACER**

hidalgo m nobleman

hidrata|nte adj moisturizing. **~r** vt hydrate; (crema etc) moisturize

hidráulico adj hydraulic

hidr|oavión m seaplane. **~oeléctrico** adj hydroelectric. **~ofobia** f rabies. **~ófobo** adj rabid. **~ógeno** m hydrogen

hiedra f ivy

hielo m ice

hiena f hyena

hierba f grass; (Culin, Med) herb. **mala ~** weed. **~buena** f mint.

hierro m iron

hígado m liver

higi|ene f hygiene. **~énico** adj hygienic

hig|o m fig. **~uera** f fig tree

hij|a f daughter. **~astra** f stepdaughter. **~astro** m stepson. **~o** m son. **~os** mpl sons; (chicos y chicas) children

hilar vt spin. **~ delgado** split hairs

hilera f row; (Mil) file

hilo *m* thread; (*Elec*) wire; (*de líquido*) trickle; (*lino*) linen

hilv|án *m* tacking. **~anar** *vt* tack; (*fig*) put together

himno *m* hymn. **~ nacional** anthem

hincapié *m*. **hacer ~ en** stress, insist on

hincar **7** *vt* drive (estaca) (en into). **~se** *vpr*. **~se de rodillas** kneel down

hincha *f* **1** grudge. ● *m & f* (*fam, aficionado*) fan

hincha|do *adj* inflated; (*Med*) swollen. **~r** *vt* inflate, blow up. **~rse** *vpr* swell up; (*fig, fam, comer mucho*) gorge o.s. **~zón** *f* swelling

hinojo *m* fennel

hiper|mercado *m* hypermarket. **~sensible** *adj* hypersensitive. **~tensión** *f* high blood pressure

hípic|a *f* horse racing. **~o** *adj* horse

hipn|osis *f* hypnosis. **~otismo** *m* hypnotism. **~otizar** **10** *vt* hypnotize

hipo *m* hiccup. **tener ~** have hiccups

hipo|alérgeno *adj* hypoallergenic. **~condríaco** *adj & m* hypochondriac

hip|ocresía *f* hypocrisy. **~ócrita** *adj* hypocritical. ● *m & f* hypocrite

hipódromo *m* racecourse

hipopótamo *m* hippopotamus

hipoteca *f* mortgage. **~r** **7** *vt* mortgage

hip|ótesis *f invar* hypothesis. **~otético** *adj* hypothetical

hiriente *adj* offensive, wounding

hirsuto *adj* (*barba*) bristly; (*pelo*) wiry

hispánico *adj* Hispanic

Hispanoamérica *f* Spanish America

hispano|americano *adj* Spanish American. **~hablante** *adj* Spanish-speaking

hist|eria *f* hysteria. **~érico** *adj* hysterical

hist|oria *f* history; (*relato*) story; (*excusa*) tale, excuse. **pasar a la ~oria** go down in history. **~oriador** *m* historian. **~órico** *adj* historical. **~orieta** *f* tale; (*con dibujos*) strip cartoon

hito *m* milestone

hizo *vb* *véase* **HACER**

hocico *m* snout

hockey /'(x)oki/ *m* hockey. **~ sobre hielo** ice hockey

hogar *m* home; (*chimenea*) hearth. **~eño** *adj* domestic; (*persona*) home-loving

hoguera *f* bonfire

hoja *f* leaf; (*de papel, metal etc*) sheet; (*de cuchillo, espada etc*) blade. **~ de afeitar** razor blade. **~lata** *f* tin

hojaldre *m* puff pastry

hojear *vt* leaf through

hola *int* hello!

Holanda *f* Holland

holand|és *adj* Dutch. ● *m* Dutchman; (*lengua*) Dutch. **~esa** *f* Dutchwoman. **los ~eses** the Dutch

holg|ado *adj* loose; (*fig*) comfortable. **~ar** **2** & **12** *vi*. **huelga decir que** needless to say. **~azán** *adj* lazy. ● *m* idler. **~ura** *f* looseness; (*fig*) comfort

hollín *m* soot

hombre m man; (*especie humana*) man(kind). ● *int* Good Heavens!; (*de duda*) well. ~ **de negocios** businessman. ~ **rana** frogman

hombr|era f shoulder pad. ~**o** m shoulder

homenaje m homage, tribute. **rendir** ~ **a** pay tribute to

home|ópata m homoeopath. ~**opatía** f homoeopathy. ~**opático** adj homoeopathic

homicid|a adj murderous. ● m & f murderer. ~**io** m murder

homosexual adj & m & f homosexual. ~**idad** f homosexuality

hond|o adj deep. ~**onada** f hollow

Honduras f Honduras

hondureño adj & m Honduran

honest|idad f honesty. ~**o** adj honest

hongo m fungus; (*LAm, Culin*) mushroom; (*venenoso*) toadstool

hon|or m honour. ~**orable** adj honourable. ~**orario** adj honorary. ~**orarios** mpl fees. ~**ra** f honour; (*buena fama*) good name. ~**radez** f honesty. ~**rado** adj honest. ~**rar** vt honour

hora f hour; (*momento puntual*) time; (*cita*) appointment. ~ **pico**, ~ **punta** rush hour. ~**s** fpl **de trabajo** working hours. ~**s** fpl **extraordinarias** overtime. ~**s** fpl **libres** free time. **a estas** ~**s** now. ¿**a qué** ~? (at) what time? **a última** ~ at the last moment. **de última** ~ last-minute. **en buena** ~ at the right time. **media** ~ half an hour. **pedir** ~ to make an appointment. ¿**qué** ~ **es?** what time is it?

horario adj hourly. ● m timetable. ~ **de trabajo** working hours

horca f gallows

horcajadas fpl. **a** ~ astride

horchata f tiger-nut milk

horizont|al adj & f horizontal. ~**e** m horizon

horma f mould; (*para fabricar calzado*) last; (*para conservar su forma*) shoe-tree. **de** ~ **ancha** broad-fitting

hormiga f ant

hormigón m concrete

hormigue|ar vi tingle; (*bullir*) swarm. **me** ~**a la mano** I've got pins and needles in my hand. ~**o** m tingling; (*fig*) anxiety

hormiguero m anthill; (*de gente*) swarm

hormona f hormone

horn|ada f batch. ~**illa** f (*LAm*) burner. ~**illo** m burner; (*cocina portátil*) portable electric cooker. ~**o** m oven; (*para cerámica etc*) kiln; (*Tec*) furnace

horóscopo m horoscope

horquilla f pitchfork; (*para el pelo*) hairpin

horr|endo adj awful. ~**ible** adj horrible. ~**ipilante** adj terrifying. ~**or** m horror; (*atrocidad*) atrocity. ¡**qué** ~**or!** how awful. ~**orizar** [10] vt horrify. ~**orizarse** vpr be horrified. ~**oroso** adj horrifying

hort|aliza f vegetable. ~**elano** m market gardener

hosco adj surly

hospeda|je m accommodation. ~**r** vt put up. ~**rse** vpr stay

hospital m hospital. ~**ario** adj hospitable. ~**idad** f hospitality

hostal m boarding-house

hostería f inn

hostia f (*Relig*) host

hostigar [12] vt whip; (*fig, molestar*) pester

...ility
● m

141 ...w
...ent
h...m
...

...ático adj
...rasy
...iot.

...lize

huipil m (Mex) traditional embroidered smock

> ℹ️
>
> **huipil** A traditional garment worn by Indian and mestizo women in Mexico and Central America. Huipiles are generally made of richly embroidered cotton. They are very wide and low-cut, and are either waist- or thigh-length.

...(palabras)
...esonant; (persona)
... ● m hollow; (espacio)
...(vacío) gap

...elg|a f strike. **~a de brazos caídos** sit-down strike. **~a de hambre** hunger strike. **declararse en ~a** come out on strike. **~uista** m & f striker

huella f footprint; (de animal, vehículo etc) track. **~ digital** fingerprint

huelo vb véase **OLER**

huérfano adj orphaned. ● m orphan. **~ de** without

huert|a f market garden (Brit), truck farm (Amer); (terreno de regadío) irrigated plain. **~o** m vegetable garden; (de árboles frutales) orchard

hueso m bone; (de fruta) stone

huésped m guest; (que paga) lodger

huesudo adj bony

huev|a f roe. **~o** m egg. **~o duro** hard-boiled egg. **~o escalfado** poached egg. **~o estrellado**, **~o frito** fried egg. **~o pasado por agua** boiled egg. **~os revueltos** scrambled eggs. **~o tibio** (Mex) boiled egg

hui|da f flight, escape. **~dizo** adj (tímido) shy; (esquivo) elusive

huir vi 🔟 flee, run away; (evitar). **~ de** avoid. **me huye** he avoids me

huitlacoche m (Mex) edible black fungus

hule m oilcloth; (Mex, goma) rubber

human|idad f mankind; (fig) humanity. **~itario** adj humanitarian. **~o** adj human; (benévolo) humane

humareda f cloud of smoke

humed|ad f dampness; (en meteorología) humidity; (gotitas de agua) moisture. **~ecer** 🔟 vt moisten. **~ecerse** vpr become moist

húmedo adj damp; (clima) humid; (labios) moist; (mojado) wet

humil|dad f humility. **~de** adj humble. **~llación** f humiliation. **~llar** vt humiliate. **~llarse** vpr lower o.s.

humo m smoke; (vapor) steam; (gas nocivo) fumes. **~s** mpl airs

humor m mood, temper; (gracia) humour. **estar de mal ~** be in a bad mood. **~ista** m & f humorist. **~ístico** adj humorous

hundi|miento m sinking. **~r** vt sink; destroy (persona). **~rse** vpr sink; (edificio) collapse

húngaro adj & m Hungarian

Hungría f Hungary

huracán m hurricane

h

huraño adj unsociable

hurgar [12] vi rummage (**en** through). ~**se** vpr. ~**se la nariz** pick one's nose

hurra int hurray!

hurtadillas fpl. **a** ~ stealthily

hurt|ar vt steal. ● **o** m theft; (*cosa robada*) stolen object

husmear vt sniff out; (*fig*) pry into

huyo vb véase HUIR

i

iba véase IR

ibérico adj Iberian

iberoamericano adj & m Latin American

iceberg /iθ'ber/ m (pl ~s) iceberg

icteria f jaundice

ida f outward journey; (*partida*) departure. **de** ~ **y vuelta** (billete) return (Brit), round-trip (Amer); (viaje) round

idea f idea; (*opinión*) opinion. **cambiar de** ~ change one's mind. **no tener la más remota** ~, **no tener la menor** ~ not have the slightest idea, not have a clue [1]

ideal adj & m ideal. ~**ista** m & f idealist. ~**izar** [10] vt idealize

idear vt think up, conceive; (*inventar*) invent

ídem pron & adv the same

idéntico adj identical

identi|dad f identity. ~**ficación** f identification. ~**ficar** [7] vt identify. ~**ficarse** vpr identify o.s. ~**ficarse con** identify with

ideo|logía f ideology. ~**lógico** adj ideological

idílico adj idyllic

idilio m idyll

idioma m language. ~**tico** adj idiomatic

idiosincrasia f idiosyncrasy.

idiot|a adj idiotic. ● m & f. ~**ez** f stupidity

idolatrar vt worship; (*fig*) idolize

ídolo m idol

idóneo adj suitable (**para** for)

iglesia f church

iglú m igloo

ignora|ncia f ignorance. ~**nte** adj ignorant. ● m ignoramus. ~**r** vt not know, be unaware of; (*no hacer caso de*) ignore

igual adj equal; (*mismo*) the same; (*similar*) like; (*llano*) even; (*liso*) smooth. ● adv the same. ● m equal. ~ **que** (the same) as. **al** ~ **que** the same as. **da** ~, **es** ~ it doesn't matter. **sin** ~ unequalled

igual|ar vt make equal; equal (*éxito, récord*); (*allanar*) level. ~**arse** vpr be equal. ~**dad** f equality. ~**mente** adv equally; (*también*) also, likewise; (*respuesta de cortesía*) the same to you

ilegal adj illegal

ilegible adj illegible

ilegítimo adj illegitimate

ileso adj unhurt

ilícito adj illicit

ilimitado adj unlimited

ilógico adj illogical

ilumina|ción f illumination; (*alumbrado*) lighting. ~**r** vt light (up). ~**rse** vpr light up

ilusi|ón f illusion; (*sueño*) dream; (*alegría*) joy. **hacerse** ~**ones** build up one's hopes. **me hace** ~**ón** I'm

...unforeseen
... (pp impr...
...illidad f
...nlikely, im...
...te adj inadmissible:
...roper; (despido) un-
...sult unproductive
...per ~s mpl
...provisation.
...ar vt im-
...nexpect-
...ce.
...~rio adj
...imaginative
...pid. ● m & f idiot
...te adj indelible; (re-
...cc) unforgettable
...ción f imitation. ~r vt imi-

mpacien|cia f impatience.
~tarse vpr lose one's patience.
~te adj impatient
impacto m impact; (huella) mark.
~ de bala bullet hole
impar adj odd
imparcial adj impartial. **~idad** f
impartiality
impartir vt impart, give
impasible adj impassive
impávido adj fearless; (impasible)
impassive
impecable adj impeccable
impedi|do adj disabled. **~mento**
m impediment. **~r** 5 vt prevent;
(obstruir) hinder
impenetrable adj impenetrable

impensa|ble adj unthin...
~do adj unexpected
impera|r vi prevail. **~t**...
...perative; (necesidad) ur...
imperceptible adj im...
...perdible m safety...
...perdonable adj u...
...perfec|ción f imp...
...o adj imperfect
...peri|al adj imperial
...mperialism. ~o m...
...oder) rule. ~oso ad...
...mpermeable adj...
m raincoat
impersonal adj im...
impertinen|cia f impertinence.
~te adj impertinent
imperturbable adj imperturbable
impetu m impetus; (impulso) impulse; (violencia) force
impetuos|idad f impetuosity.
~o adj impetuous
implacable adj implacable
implantar vt introduce
implementación f implementation
implica|ción f implication. **~r**
7 vt implicate; (significar) imply
implícito adj implicit
implorar vt implore
impon|ente adj imposing; 11 ter-
rific. **~er** 34 vt impose; (requerir)
demand; deposit (dinero). **~erse**
vpr (hacerse obedecer) assert o.s.;
(hacerse respetar) command respect; (prevalecer) prevail. **~ible**
adj taxable
importa|ción f importation; (ar-
tículo) import. **~clones** fpl im-
ports. **~dor** adj importing. ● m
importer
importa|ncia f importance.

~nte adj important; (en cantidad) considerable. **~r** vt import; (ascender a) amount to. ● vi be important, matter. **¿le ~ría...?** would you mind...? **no ~** it doesn't matter

importe m price; (total) amount

importun|ar vt bother. **~o** adj troublesome; (inoportuno) inopportune

imposib|ilidad f impossibility. **~le** adj impossible. **hacer lo ~le para** do all one can to

imposición f imposition; (impuesto) tax

impostor m impostor

impoten|cia f impotence. **~te** adj impotent

impracticable adj impracticable; (intransitable) unpassable

imprecis|ión f vagueness; (error) inaccuracy. **~o** adj imprecise

impregnar vt impregnate; (empapar) soak

imprenta f printing; (taller) printing house, printer's

imprescindible adj indispensable, essential

impresión f impression; (acción de imprimir) printing; (tirada) edition; (huella) imprint. **~onable** adj impressionable. **~onante** adj impressive; (espantoso) frightening. **~onar** vt impress; (negativamente) shock; (conmover) move; (Foto) expose. **~onarse** vpr be impressed; (negativamente) be shocked; (conmover) be moved

impresionis|mo m impressionism. **~ta** adj & m & f impressionist

impreso adj printed. ● m form. **~s** mpl printed matter. **~ra** f printer

imprevis|ible adj unforeseeable.

~to adj unforeseen

imprim|ir (pp **impreso**) vt print (libro etc)

improbab|ilidad f improbability. **~le** adj improbable, unlikely

improceden|te adj inadmissible; (conducta) improper; (despido) unfair

improductivo adj unproductive

improperio m insult. **~s** mpl abuse

impropio adj improper

improvis|ación f improvisation. **~ado** adj improvised. **~ar** vt improvise. **~o** adj. **de ~o** unexpectedly

impruden|cia f imprudence. **~te** adj imprudent

imp|udicia f indecency; (desvergüenza) shamelessness. **~údico** adj indecent; (desvergonzado) shameless. **~udor** m indecency; (desvergüenza) shamelessness

impuesto adj imposed. ● m tax. **~ a la renta** income tax. **~ sobre el valor agregado** (LAm), **~ sobre el valor añadido** VAT, value added tax

impuls|ar vt propel; drive (persona); boost (producción etc). **~ividad** f impulsiveness. **~ivo** adj impulsive. **~o** m impulse

impun|e adj unpunished. **~idad** f impunity

impur|eza f impurity. **~o** adj impure

imputa|ción f charge. **~r** vt attribute; (acusar) charge

inaccesible adj inaccessible

inaceptable adj unacceptable

inactiv|idad f inactivity. **~o** adj inactive

inadaptado adj maladjusted

hostil adj hostile. ∼**idad** f hostility

hotel m hotel. ∼**ero** adj hotel. • m hotelier

hoy adv today. ∼ **(en) día** nowadays. ∼ **por** ∼ at the present time. **de** ∼ **en adelante** from now on

hoy|o m hole. ∼**uelo** m dimple

hoz f sickle

hube vb véase **HABER**

hucha f money box

hueco adj hollow; (palabras) empty; (voz) resonant; (persona) superficial. • m hollow; (espacio) space; (vacío) gap

huelg|a f strike. ∼**a de brazos caídos** sit-down strike. ∼**a de hambre** hunger strike. **declararse en** ∼ **a** come out on strike. ∼**uista** m & f striker

huella f footprint; (de animal, vehículo etc) track. ∼ **digital** fingerprint

huelo vb véase **OLER**

huérfano adj orphaned. • m orphan. ∼ **de** without

huert|a f market garden (Brit), truck farm (Amer); (terreno de regadío) irrigated plain. ∼**o** m vegetable garden; (de árboles frutales) orchard

hueso m bone; (de fruta) stone

huésped m guest; (que paga) lodger

huesudo adj bony

huev|a f roe. ∼**o** m egg. ∼**o duro** hard-boiled egg. ∼**o escalfado** poached egg. ∼**o estrellado**, ∼**o frito** fried egg. ∼**o pasado por agua** boiled egg. ∼**os revueltos** scrambled eggs. ∼**o tibio** (Mex) boiled egg

hui|da f flight, escape. ∼**dizo** adj (tímido) shy; (esquivo) elusive

huipil m (Mex) traditional embroidered smock

huipil A traditional garment worn by Indian and mestizo women in Mexico and Central America. Huipiles are generally made of richly embroidered cotton. They are very wide and low-cut, and are either waist- or thigh-length.

huir vi [17] flee, run away; (evitar). ∼ **de** avoid. **me huye** he avoids me

huitlacoche m (Mex) edible black fungus

hule m oilcloth; (Mex, goma) rubber

human|idad f (mankind); (fig) humanity. ∼**itario** adj humanitarian. ∼**o** adj human; (benévolo) humane

humareda f cloud of smoke

humed|ad f dampness; (en meteorología) humidity; (gotitas de agua) moisture. ∼**ecer** [11] vt moisten. ∼**ecerse** vpr become moist

húmedo adj damp; (clima) humid; (labios) moist; (mojado) wet

humi|ldad f humility. ∼**lde** adj humble. ∼**llación** f humiliation. ∼**llar** vt humiliate. ∼**llarse** vpr lower o.s.

humo m smoke; (vapor) steam; (gas nocivo) fumes. ∼**s** mpl airs

humor m mood, temper; (gracia) humour. **estar de mal** ∼ be in a bad mood. ∼**ista** m & f humorist. ∼**ístico** adj humorous

hundi|miento m sinking. ∼**r** vt sink; destroy (persona). ∼**rse** vpr sink; (edificio) collapse

húngaro adj & m Hungarian

Hungría f Hungary

huracán m hurricane

huraño adj unsociable

hurgar 🔢 vi rummage (**en through**). **~se** vpr. **~se la nariz** pick one's nose

hurra int hurray!

hurtadillas fpl. **a ~** stealthily

hurt|ar vt steal. **~o** m theft; (cosa robada) stolen object

husmear vt sniff out; (fig) pry into

huyo vb véase **HUIR**

I i

iba véase **IR**

ibérico adj Iberian

iberoamericano adj & m Latin American

iceberg /iθ'ber/ m (pl **~s**) iceberg

ictericia f jaundice

ida f outward journey; (partida) departure. **de ~ y vuelta** (billete) return (Brit), round-trip (Amer); (viaje) round

idea f idea; (opinión) opinion. **cambiar de ~** change one's mind. **no tener la más remota ~**, **no tener la menor ~** not have the slightest idea, not have a clue 🔢

ideal adj & m ideal. **~ista** m & f idealist. **~izar** 🔟 vt idealize

idear vt think up, conceive; (inventar) invent

ídem pron & adv the same

idéntico adj identical

identi|dad f identity. **~ficación** f identification. **~ficar** 🔢 vt identify. **~ficarse** vpr identify o.s. **~ficarse con** identify with

ideol|ogía f ideology. **~ógico** adj ideological

idílico adj idyllic

idilio m idyll

idioma m language. **~ático** adj idiomatic

idiosincrasia f idiosyncrasy

idiot|a adj idiotic. ● m & f idiot. **~ez** f stupidity

idolatrar vt worship; (fig) idolize

ídolo m idol

idóneo adj suitable (**para** for)

iglesia f church

iglú m igloo

ignora|ncia f ignorance. **~nte** adj ignorant. ● m ignoramus. **~r** vt not know, be unaware of; (no hacer caso de) ignore

igual adj equal; (mismo) the same; (similar) like; (llano) even; (liso) smooth. ● adv the same. ● m equal. **~ que** (the same) as. **al ~ que** the same as. **da ~**, **es ~** it doesn't matter. **sin ~** unequalled

igual|ar vt make equal; equal (éxito, récord); (allanar) level. **~arse** vpr be equal. **~dad** f equality. **~mente** adv equally; (también) also, likewise; (respuesta de cortesía) the same to you

ilegal adj illegal

ilegible adj illegible

ilegítimo adj illegitimate

ileso adj unhurt

ilícito adj illicit

ilimitado adj unlimited

ilógico adj illogical

ilumina|ción f illumination; (alumbrado) lighting. **~r** vt light (up). **~rse** vpr light up

ilusi|ón f illusion; (sueño) dream; (alegría) joy. **hacerse ~ones** build up one's hopes. **me hace ~ón** I'm thrilled; I'm looking forward to (algo en el futuro). **~onado** adj excited. **~onar** vt give false hope. **~onarse** vpr have false hopes

ilusionis|mo m conjuring. **~ta** m & f conjurer

iluso adj naive. ● m dreamer. **~rio** adj illusory

ilustra|ción f learning; (dibujo) illustration. **~do** adj learned; (con dibujos) illustrated. **~r** vt explain; (instruir) instruct; (añadir dibujos etc) illustrate. **~rse** vpr acquire knowledge. **~tivo** adj illustrative

ilustre adj illustrious

imagen f image; (TV etc) picture

imagina|ble adj imaginable. **~ción** f imagination. **~r** vt imagine. **~rse** vpr imagine. **~rio** m imaginary. **~tivo** adj imaginative

imán m magnet

imbécil adj stupid. ● m & f idiot

imborrable adj indelible; (recuerdo etc) unforgettable

imita|ción f imitation. **~r** vt imitate

impacien|cia f impatience. **~tarse** vpr lose one's patience. **~te** adj impatient

impacto m impact; (huella) mark. **~ de bala** bullet hole

impar adj odd

imparcial adj impartial. **~idad** f impartiality

impartir vt impart, give

impasible adj impassive

impávido adj fearless; (impasible) impassive

impecable adj impeccable

impedi|do adj disabled. **~mento** m impediment. **~r** ☁ vt prevent; (obstruir) hinder

impenetrable adj impenetrable

impensa|ble adj unthinkable. **~do** adj unexpected

impera|r vi prevail. **~tivo** adj imperative; (necesidad) urgent

imperceptible adj imperceptible

imperdible m safety pin

imperdonable adj unforgivable

imperfec|ción f imperfection. **~to** adj imperfect

imperi|al adj imperial. **~alismo** m imperialism. **~o** m empire; (poder) rule. **~oso** adj imperious

impermeable adj waterproof. ● m raincoat

impersonal adj impersonal

impertinen|cia f impertinence. **~te** adj impertinent

imperturbable adj imperturbable

ímpetu m impetus; (impulso) impulse; (violencia) force

impetuos|idad f impetuosity. **~o** adj impetuous

implacable adj implacable

implantar vt introduce

implementación f implementation

implica|ción f implication. **~r** ☁ vt implicate; (significar) imply

implícito adj implicit

implorar vt implore

impon|ente adj imposing; ☁ terrific. **~er** ☁ vt impose; (requerir) demand; deposit (dinero). **~erse** vpr (hacerse obedecer) assert o.s.; (hacerse respetar) command respect; (prevalecer) prevail. **~ible** adj taxable

importa|ción f importation; (artículo) import. **~ciones** fpl imports. **~dor** adj importing. ● m importer

importa|ncia f importance.

~**nte** adj important; (en cantidad) considerable. ~**r** vt import; (ascender a) amount to. • vi be important, matter. ¿**le ~ría...?** would you mind...? **no ~** it doesn't matter

importe m price; (total) amount

importun|ar vt bother. ~**o** adj troublesome; (inoportuno) inopportune

imposib|ilidad f impossibility. ~**le** adj impossible. **hacer lo ~le para** do all one can to

imposición f imposition; (impuesto) tax

impostor m impostor

impoten|cia f impotence. ~**te** adj impotent

impracticable adj impracticable; (intransitable) unpassable

imprecis|ión f vagueness; (error) inaccuracy. ~**o** adj imprecise

impregnar vt impregnate; (empapar) soak

imprenta f printing; (taller) printing house, printer's

imprescindible adj indispensable, essential

impresión f impression; (acción de imprimir) printing; (tirada) edition; (huella) imprint. ~**onable** adj impressionable. ~**onante** adj impressive; (espantoso) frightening. ~**onar** vt impress; (negativamente) shock; (conmover) move; (Foto) expose. ~**onarse** vpr be impressed; (negativamente) be shocked; (conmover) be moved

impresionis|mo m impressionism. ~**ta** adj & m & f impressionist

impreso adj printed. • m form. ~**s** mpl printed matter. ~**ra** f printer

imprevis|ible adj unforeseeable.

~**to** adj unforeseen

imprimir (pp impreso) vt print (libro etc)

improbab|ilidad f improbability. ~**le** adj unlikely, improbable

improcedente adj inadmissible; (conducta) improper; (despido) unfair

improductivo adj unproductive

improperio m insult. ~**s** mpl abuse

impropio adj improper

improvis|ación f improvisation. ~**ado** adj improvised. ~**ar** vt improvise. ~**o** adj. **de ~o** unexpectedly

impruden|cia f imprudence. ~**te** adj imprudent

imp|udicia f indecency; (desvergüenza) shamelessness. ~**údico** adj indecent; (desvergonzado) shameless. ~**udor** m indecency; (desvergüenza) shamelessness

impuesto adj imposed. • m tax. ~ **a la renta** income tax. ~ **sobre el valor agregado** (LAm), ~ **sobre el valor añadido** VAT, value added tax

impuls|ar vt propel; drive (persona); boost (producción etc). ~**ividad** f impulsiveness. ~**ivo** adj impulsive. ~**o** m impulse

impun|e adj unpunished. ~**idad** f impunity

impur|eza f impurity. ~**o** adj impure

imputa|ción f charge. ~**r** vt attribute; (acusar) charge

inaccesible adj inaccessible

inaceptable adj unacceptable

inactiv|idad f inactivity. ~**o** adj inactive

inadaptado adj maladjusted

inadecuado *adj* inadequate; (*inapropiado*) unsuitable

inadmisible *adj* inadmissible; (*inaceptable*) unacceptable

inadvertido *adj* distracted. **pasar ~** go unnoticed

inagotable *adj* inexhaustible

inaguantable *adj* unbearable

inaltera|ble *adj* impassive; (*color*) fast; (*convicción*) unalterable. **~do** *adj* unchanged

inapreciable *adj* invaluable; (*imperceptible*) imperceptible

inapropiado *adj* inappropriate

inasequible *adj* out of reach

inaudito *adj* unprecedented

inaugura|ción *f* inauguration. **~l** *adj* inaugural. **~r** *vt* inaugurate

inca *adj & m & f* Inca. **~ico** *adj* Inca

Incas Founded in the *i* twelfth century, the Andean empire of the Quechua-speaking Incas grew and extended from southern Colombia to Argentina and central Chile. Its capital was Cuzco. The Incas built an extensive road network and impressive buildings, including Machu Picchu. The empire collapsed in 1533 after defeat by the Spaniards led by Francisco Pizarro.

---

incalculable *adj* incalculable

incandescente *adj* incandescent

incansable *adj* tireless

incapa|cidad *f* incapacity; (*física*) disability. **~citado** *adj* disabled. **~citar** *vt* incapacitate. **~z** *adj* incapable

incauto *adj* unwary; (*fácil de engañar*) gullible

incendi|ar *vt* set fire to. **~arse**

vpr catch fire. **~ario** *adj* incendiary. ● *m* arsonist. **~o** *m* fire

incentivo *m* incentive

incertidumbre *f* uncertainty

incesante *adj* incessant

incest|o *m* incest. **~uoso** *adj* incestuous

inciden|cia *f* incidence; (*efecto*) impact; (*incidente*) incident. **~tal** *adj* incidental. **~te** *m* incident

incidir *vi* fall (**en** into); (*influir*) influence

incienso *m* incense

incierto *adj* uncertain

incinera|dor *m* incinerator. **~r** *vt* incinerate; cremate (*cadáver*)

incipiente *adj* incipient

incisi|ón *f* incision. **~vo** *adj* incisive. ● *m* incisor

incitar *vt* incite

inclemen|cia *f* harshness. **~te** *adj* harsh

inclina|ción *f* slope; (*de la cabeza*) nod; (*fig*) inclination. **~r** *vt* tilt; (*inducir*) incline. **~rse** *vpr* lean; (*en saludo*) bow; (*tender*) be inclined (**a** to)

inclu|ido *adj* included; (*precio*) inclusive. **~ir** [17] *vt* include; (*en cartas*) enclose. **~sión** *f* inclusion. **~sive** *adv* inclusive. **hasta el lunes ~sive** up to and including Monday. **~so** *adv* even

incógnito *adj* unknown. **de ~** incognito

incoheren|cia *f* incoherence. **~te** *adj* incoherent

incoloro *adj* colourless

incomestible *adj*, **incomible** *adj* uneatable, inedible

incomodar *vt* inconvenience; (*causar vergüenza*) make feel uncomfortable. **~se** *vpr* feel uncomfortable; (*enojarse*) get angry

incómodo *adj* uncomfortable; (*inconveniente*) inconvenient

incomparable *adj* incomparable

incompatib|ilidad *f* incompatibility. ~**le** *adj* incompatible

incompeten|cia *f* incompetence. ~**te** *adj & m & f* incompetent

incompleto *adj* incomplete

incompren|dido *adj* misunderstood. ~**sible** *adj* incomprehensible. ~**sión** *f* incomprehension

incomunicado *adj* cut off; (*preso*) in solitary confinement

inconcebible *adj* inconceivable

inconcluso *adj* unfinished

incondicional *adj* unconditional

inconfundible *adj* unmistakable

incongruente *adj* incoherent; (*contradictorio*) inconsistent

inconmensurable *adj* immeasurable

inconscien|cia *f* unconsciousness; (*irreflexión*) recklessness. ~**te** *adj* unconscious; (*irreflexivo*) reckless

inconsecuente *adj* inconsistent

inconsistente *adj* flimsy

inconsolable *adj* unconsolable

inconstan|cia *f* lack of perseverance. ~**te** *adj* changeable; (*persona*) lacking in perseverance; (*voluble*) fickle

incontable *adj* countless

incontenible *adj* irrepressible

incontinen|cia *f* incontinence. ~**te** *adj* incontinent

inconvenien|cia *f* inconvenience. ~**te** *adj* inconvenient; (*inapropiado*) inappropriate; (*incorrecto*) improper. ● *m* problem; (*desventaja*) drawback

incorpora|ción *f* incorporation.

~**r** *vt* incorporate; (*Culin*) add. ~**rse** *vpr* sit up; join (sociedad, regimiento etc)

incorrecto *adj* incorrect; (*descortés*) discourteous

incorregible *adj* incorrigible

incorruptible *adj* incorruptible

incrédulo *adj* sceptical; (*mirada, gesto*) incredulous

increíble *adj* incredible

increment|ar *vt* increase. ~**o** *m* increase

incriminar *vt* incriminate

incrustar *vt* encrust

incuba|ción *f* incubation. ~**dora** *f* incubator. ~**r** *vt* incubate; (*fig*) hatch

incuestionable *adj* unquestionable

inculcar 🔢 *vt* inculcate

inculpar *vt* accuse

inculto *adj* uneducated

incumplimiento *m* non-fulfilment; (*de un contrato*) breach

incurable *adj* incurable

incurrir *vi*. ~ **en** incur (gasto); fall into (error); commit (crimen)

incursión *f* raid

indagar 🔢 *vt* investigate

indebido *adj* unjust; (*uso*) improper

indecen|cia *f* indecency. ~**te** *adj* indecent

indecible *adj* indescribable

indecis|ión *f* indecision. ~**o** *adj* (*con ser*) indecisive; (*con estar*) undecided

indefenso *adj* defenceless

indefini|ble *adj* indefinable. ~**do** *adj* indefinite; (*impreciso*) undefined

indemnizar 🔢 *vt* compensate

independ|encia *f* independ-

ence. **~iente** *adj* independent.
~izarse 🔟 *vpr* become independent

indes|cifrable *adj* indecipherable. **~criptible** *adj* indescribable

indeseable *adj* undesirable

indestructible *adj* indestructible

indetermina|ble *adj* indeterminable. **~do** *adj* indeterminate; (*tiempo*) indefinite

India *f*. la ~ India

indica|ción *f* indication; (*señal*) signal. **~ciones** *fpl* directions. **~dor** *m* indicator; (*Tec*) gauge. **~r** 🔟 *vt* show, indicate; (*apuntar*) point at; (*hacer saber*) point out; (*aconsejar*) advise. **~tivo** *adj* indicative. ● *m* indicative; (*al teléfono*) dialling code

índice *m* index; (*dedo*) index finger; (*catálogo*) catalogue; (*indicación*) indication; (*aguja*) pointer

indicio *m* indication, sign; (*vestigio*) trace

indiferen|cia *f* indifference. **~te** *adj* indifferent. **me es ~te** it's all the same to me

indígena *adj* indigenous. ● *m & f* native

indigen|cia *f* poverty. **~te** *adj* needy

indigest|ión *f* indigestion. **~o** *adj* indigestible

indign|ación *f* indignation. **~ado** *adj* indignant. **~ar** *vt* make indignant. **~arse** *vpr* become indignant. **~o** *adj* unworthy; (*despreciable*) contemptible

indio *adj* & *m* Indian

indirect|a *f* hint. **~o** *adj* indirect

indisciplinado *adj* undisciplined

indiscre|ción *f* indiscretion. **~to** *adj* indiscreet

indiscutible *adj* unquestionable

indisoluble *adj* indissoluble

indispensable *adj* indispensable

indisp|oner 🔢 *vt* (*enemistar*) set against. **~onerse** *vpr* fall out; (*ponerse enfermo*) fall ill. **~osición** *f* indisposition. **~uesto** *adj* indisposed

individu|al *adj* individual; (*cama*) single. ● *m* (*en tenis etc*) singles. **~alidad** *f* individuality. **~alista** *m & f* individualist. **~alizar** 🔟 *vt* individualize. **~o** *m* individual

indocumentado *m* person without identity papers; (*inmigrante*) illegal immigrant

índole *f* nature; (*clase*) type

indolen|cia *f* indolence. **~te** *adj* indolent

indoloro *adj* painless

indomable *adj* untamable

inducir 🔢 *vt* induce. **~ a error** be misleading

indudable *adj* undoubted

indulgen|cia *f* indulgence. **~te** *adj* indulgent

indult|ar *vt* pardon. **~o** *m* pardon

industria *f* industry. **~l** *adj* industrial. ● *m & f* industrialist. **~lización** *f* industrialization. **~lizar** 🔟 *vt* industrialize

inédito *adj* unpublished; (*fig*) unknown

inefable *adj* indescribable

ineficaz *adj* ineffective; (*sistema etc*) inefficient

ineficiente *adj* inefficient

ineludible *adj* inescapable, unavoidable

inept|itud *f* ineptitude. **~o** *adj* inept

inequívoco *adj* unequivocal

inercia *f* inertia

inerte *adj* inert; (*sin vida*) lifeless

inesperado adj unexpected

inestable adj unstable

inestimable adj inestimable

inevitable adj inevitable

inexistente adj non-existent

inexorable adj inexorable

inexper|iencia f inexperience.
~**to** adj inexperienced

inexplicable adj inexplicable

infalible adj infallible

infam|ar vt defame. ~**atorio** adj
defamatory. ~**e** adj infamous; (fig,
fam, muy malo) awful. ~**ia** f in-
famy

infancia f infancy

infant|a f infanta, princess. ~**e** m
infante, prince. ~**ería** f infantry.
~**il** adj children's; (población) child;
(actitud etc) childish, infantile

infarto m heart attack

infec|ción f infection. ~**cioso** adj
infectious. ~**tar** vt infect. ~**tarse**
vpr become infected. ~**to** adj infected; 🅣 disgusting

infeli|cidad f unhappiness. ~**z**
adj unhappy

inferior adj inferior. ● m & f inferior. ~**idad** f inferiority

infernal adj infernal, hellish

infestar vt infest; (fig) inundate

infi|delidad f unfaithfulness. ~**el**
adj unfaithful

infierno m hell

infiltra|ción f infiltration. ~**rse**
vpr infiltrate

ínfimo adj lowest; (calidad) very
poor

infini|dad f infinity. ~**tivo** m in-
finitive. ~**to** adj infinite. ● m. **el**
~**to** the infinite; (en matemáticas)
infinity. ~**dad de** countless

inflación f inflation

inflama|ble adj (in)flammable.

~**ción** f inflammation. ~**r** vt set
on fire; (fig, Med) inflame. ~**rse**
vpr catch fire; (Med) become in-
flamed

inflar vt inflate; blow up (globo);
(fig, exagerar) exaggerate

inflexi|ble adj inflexible. ~**ón** f
inflexion

influ|encia f influence (en on).
~**ir** 🔟 vt influence. ● vi. ~ **en** influence. ~**jo** m influence. ~**yente**
adj influential

informa|ción f information; (no-
ticias) news; (en aeropuerto etc)
information desk; (de teléfonos) directory enquiries. ~**dor** m inform-
ant

informal adj informal; (persona)
unreliable

inform|ante m & f informant.
~**ar** vt/i inform. ~**arse** vpr find
out. ~**ática** f information technol-
ogy, computing. ~**ativo** adj in-
formative; (programa) news. ~**atizar** 🔟 vt computerize

informe adj shapeless. ● m report. ~**s** fpl references, information

infracción f infringement. ~ **de**
tráfico traffic offence

infraestructura f infrastructure

infranqueable adj impassable;
(fig) insuperable

infrarrojo adj infrared

infringir 🔢 vt infringe

infructuoso adj fruitless

ínfulas fpl. darse ~ give o.s. airs.
tener ~ de fancy o.s. as

infundado adj unfounded

infu|ndir vt instil. ~**sión** f infu-
sion

ingeni|ar vt invent. ~**árselas
para** find a way to

ingenier|ía f engineering. ~**o** m
engineer

ingenio m ingenuity; (*agudeza*) wit; (*LAm, de azúcar*) refinery. **~so** adj ingenious

ingenu|idad f naivety. **~o** adj naive

Inglaterra f England

ingl|és adj English. ● m Englishman; (*lengua*) English. **~esa** f Englishwoman. **los ~eses** the English

ingrat|itud f ingratitude. **~o** adj ungrateful; (*desagradable*) thankless

ingrediente m ingredient

ingres|ar vt deposit. ● vi. **~ar en** come in, enter; join (sociedad). **~o** m entrance; (*de dinero*) deposit; (*en sociedad, hospital*) admission. **~os** mpl income

inh|ábil adj unskilful; (*no apto*) unfit. **~abilidad** f unskilfulness; (*para cargo*) ineligibility

inhabitable adj uninhabitable

inhala|dor m inhaler. **~r** vt inhale

inherente adj inherent

inhibi|ción f inhibition. **~r** vt inhibit

inhóspito adj inhospitable

inhumano adj inhuman

inici|ación f beginning. **~al** adj & f initial. **~ar** vt initiate; (*comenzar*) begin, start. **~ativa** f initiative. **~o** m beginning

inigualado adj unequalled

ininterrumpido adj uninterrupted

injert|ar vt graft. **~to** m graft

injuri|a f insult. **~ar** vt insult. **~oso** adj insulting

injust|icia f injustice. **~o** adj unjust, unfair

inmaculado adj immaculate

inmaduro adj unripe; (*persona*) immature

inmediaciones fpl. **las ~** the vicinity, the surrounding area

inmediat|amente adv immediately. **~o** adj immediate; (*contiguo*) next. **de ~o** immediately

inmejorable adj excellent

inmemorable adj immemorial

inmens|idad f immensity. **~o** adj immense

inmersión f immersion

inmigra|ción f immigration. **~nte** adj & m & f immigrant. **~r** vt immigrate

inminen|cia f imminence. **~te** adj imminent

inmiscuirse 17 vpr interfere

inmobiliario adj property

inmolar vt sacrifice

inmoral adj immoral. **~idad** f immorality

inmortal adj immortal. **~izar** 10 vt immortalize

inmóvil adj immobile

inmovilizador m immobilizer

inmueble adj. **bienes ~s** property

inmund|icia f filth. **~o** adj filthy

inmun|e adj immune. **~idad** f immunity. **~ización** f immunization. **~izar** 10 vt immunize

inmuta|ble adj unchangeable. **~rse** vpr be perturbed. **sin ~rse** unperturbed

innato adj innate

innecesario adj unnecessary

innegable adj undeniable

innova|ción f innovation. **~r** vi innovate. ● vt make innovations in

innumerable adj innumerable

inocen|cia f innocence. **~tada** f practical joke. **~te** adj innocent. **~tón** adj naive

inocuo adj innocuous

inodoro adj odourless. • m toilet

inofensivo adj inoffensive

inolvidable adj unforgettable

inoperable adj inoperable

inoportuno adj untimely; (comentario) ill-timed

inoxidable adj stainless

inquiet|ar vt worry. ~**arse** vpr get worried. ~**o** adj worried; (agitado) restless. ~**ud** f anxiety

inquilino m tenant

inquirir 4 vt enquire into, investigate

insaciable adj insatiable

insalubre adj unhealthy

insatisfecho adj unsatisfied; (descontento) dissatisfied

inscri|bir (pp inscrito) vt (en registro) register; (en curso) enrol; (grabar) inscribe. ~**birse** vpr register. ~**pción** f inscription; (registro) registration

insect|icida m insecticide. ~**o** m insect

insegur|idad f insecurity. ~**o** adj insecure; (ciudad) unsafe, dangerous

insemina|ción f insemination. ~**r** vt inseminate

insensato adj foolish

insensible adj insensitive

inseparable adj inseparable

insertar vt insert

insidi|a f malice. ~**oso** adj insidious

insigne adj famous

insignia f badge; (bandera) flag

insignificante adj insignificant

insinua|ción f insinuation. ~**ante** adj insinuating. ~**ar** 21 vt imply; insinuate (algo ofensivo). ~**arse** vpr. ~**árse** a make a pass at

insípido adj insipid

insist|encia f insistence. ~**ente** adj insistent. ~**ir** vi insist; (hacer hincapié) stress

insolación f sunstroke

insolen|cia f rudeness, insolence. ~**te** adj rude, insolent

insólito adj unusual

insolven|cia f insolvency. ~**te** adj & m & f insolvent

insomn|e adj sleepless. • m & f insomniac. ~**io** m insomnia

insondable adj unfathomable

insoportable adj unbearable

insospechado adj unexpected

insostenible adj untenable

inspec|ción f inspection. ~**cionar** vt inspect. ~**tor** m inspector

inspira|ción f inspiration. ~**r** vt inspire. ~**rse** vpr be inspired

instala|ción f installation. ~**r** vt install. ~**rse** vpr settle

instancia f request. **en última ~** as a last resort

instant|ánea f snapshot. ~**áneo** adj instantaneous; (café etc) instant. ~**e** m instant. **a cada ~e** constantly. **al ~e** immediately

instaura|ción f establishment. ~**r** vt establish

instiga|ción f instigation. ~**dor** m instigator. ~**r** 12 vt instigate; (incitar) incite

instint|ivo adj instinctive. ~**o** m instinct

institu|ción f institution. ~**cional** adj institutional. ~**ir** 17 vt establish. ~**to** m institute; (en enseñanza) (secondary) school. ~**triz** f governess

instru|cción f education; (Mil) training. ~**cciones** fpl instruction. ~**ctivo** adj instructive; (película etc) educational. ~**ctor** m instructor. ~**ir 17** vt instruct, teach; (Mil) train

instrument|ación f instrumentation. ~**al** adj instrumental. ~**o** m instrument; (herramienta) tool

insubordina|ción f insubordination. ~**r** vt stir up. ~**rse** vpr rebel

insuficien|cia f insufficiency; (inadecuación) inadequacy. ~**te** adj insufficient

insufrible adj insufferable

insular adj insular

insulina f insulin

insulso adj tasteless; (fig) insipid

insult|ar vt insult. ~**o** m insult

insuperable adj insuperable; (inmejorable) unbeatable

insurgente adj insurgent

insurrec|ción f insurrection. ~**to** adj insurgent

intachable adj irreproachable

intacto adj intact

intangible adj intangible

integra|ción f integration. ~**l** adj integral; (completo) complete; (incorporado) built-in; (pan) wholemeal (Brit), wholewheat (Amer). ~**r** vt make up

integridad f integrity; (entereza) wholeness

íntegro adj complete; (fig) upright

intelect|o m intellect. ~**ual** adj & m & f intellectual

inteligen|cia f intelligence. ~**te** adj intelligent

inteligible adj intelligible

intemperie f. **a la** ~ in the open

intempestivo adj untimely

intenci|ón f intention. **con doble** ~**ón** implying sth else. ~**onado** adj deliberate. **bien** ~**onado** wellmeaning. **mal** ~**onado** malicious.

~**onal** adj intentional

intens|idad f intensity. ~**ificar 7** vt intensify. ~**ivo** adj intensive. ~**o** adj intense

intent|ar vt try. ~**o** m attempt; (Mex, propósito) intention

inter|calar vt insert. ~**cambio** m exchange. ~**ceder** vt intercede

interceptar vt intercept

interdicto m ban

inter|és m interest; (egoísmo) selfinterest. ~**esado** adj interested; (parcial) biassed; (egoísta) selfish. ~**esante** adj interesting. ~**esar** vt interest; (afectar) concern. ● vi be of interest. ~**esarse** vpr take an interest (por in)

interfaz m & f interface

interfer|encia f interference. ~**ir 4** vi interfere

interfono m intercom

interino adj temporary; (persona) acting. ● m stand-in

interior adj interior; (comercio etc) domestic. ● m inside. **Ministerio del I**~ Interior Ministry

interjección f interjection

inter|locutor m speaker. ~**mediario** adj & m intermediary. ~**medio** adj intermediate. ● m interval

interminable adj interminable

intermitente adj intermittent. ● m indicator

internacional adj international

intern|ado m (Escol) boardingschool. ~**ar** vt (en manicomio) commit; (en hospital) admit. ~**arse** vpr penetrate

internauta m & f netsurfer

Internet m Internet

interno adj internal; (en enseñanza) boarding. ● m boarder

interponer 🟥 vt interpose. ~se vpr intervene

int|erpretación f interpretation. ~erpretar vt interpret; (Mús etc) play. ~érprete m interpreter; (Mus) performer

interroga|ción f interrogation; (signo) question mark. ~r 🟦 vt question. ~tivo adj interrogative

interru|mpir vt interrupt; cut off (suministro); cut short (viaje etc); block (tráfico). ~pción f interruption. ~ptor m switch

inter|sección f intersection. ~urbano adj inter-city; (llamada) long-distance

intervalo m interval; (espacio) space. a ~s at intervals

interven|ir 🟦 vt control; (Med) operate on. ● vi intervene; (participar) take part. ~tor m inspector; (Com) auditor

intestino m intestine

intim|ar vi become friendly. ~idad f intimacy

intimidar vt intimidate

íntimo adj intimate; (amigo) close. ● m close friend

intolera|ble adj intolerable. ~nte adj intolerant

intoxicar 🟥 vt poison

intranquilo adj worried

intransigente adj intransigent

intransitable adj impassable

intransitivo adj intransitive

intratable adj impossible

intrépido adj intrepid

intriga f intrigue. ~nte adj intriguing. ~r 🟦 vt intrigue

intrincado adj intricate

intrínseco adj intrinsic

introduc|ción f introduction. ~ir 🟦 vt introduce; (meter) insert.

~irse vpr get into

intromisión f interference

introvertido adj introverted. ● m introvert

intruso m intruder

intui|ción f intuition. ~r 🟦 vt sense. ~tivo adj intuitive

inunda|ción f flooding. ~r vt flood

inusitado adj unusual

in|útil adj useless; (vano) futile. ~utilidad f uselessness

invadir vt invade

inv|alidez f invalidity; (Med) disability. ~álido adj & m invalid

invariable adj invariable

invas|ión f invasion. ~or adj invading. ● m invader

invencible adj invincible

inven|ción f invention. ~tar vt invent

inventario m inventory

invent|iva f inventiveness. ~ivo adj inventive. ~or m inventor

invernadero m greenhouse

invernal adj winter

inverosímil adj implausible

inver|sión f inversion; (Com) investment. ~sionista m & f investor

inverso adj inverse; (contrario) opposite. **a la inversa** the other way round. **a la inversa de** contrary to

inversor m investor

invertir 🟦 vt reverse; (Com) invest; put in (tiempo)

investidura f investiture

investiga|ción f investigation; (Univ) research. ~dor m investigator; (Univ) researcher. ~r 🟦 vt investigate; (Univ) research

investir 🟦 vt invest

invicto adj unbeaten

invierno *m* winter

inviolable *adj* inviolate

invisible *adj* invisible

invita|ción *f* invitation. **~do** *m* guest. **~r** *vt* invite. **te invito a una copa** I'll buy you a drink

invocar 7 *vt* invoke

involuntario *adj* involuntary

invulnerable *adj* invulnerable

inyec|ción *f* injection. **~tar** *vt* inject

ir 49

● *verbo intransitivo*

····▸ to go. **fui a verla** I went to see her. **ir a pie** to go on foot. **ir en coche** to go by car. **vamos a casa** let's go home. **fue (a) por el pan** he went to get some bread

❗ Cuando la acción del verbo **ir** significa trasladarse hacia o con el interlocutor la traducción es *to come*, p.ej: **¡ya voy!** I'm coming! **yo voy contigo** I'll come with you

····▸ (*estar*) to be. **iba con su novio** she was with her boyfriend. **¿cómo te va?** how are you?

····▸ (*sentar*) to suit. **ese color no le va** that colour doesn't suit her. **no me va ni me viene** I don't mind at all

····▸ (*Méx*, *apoyar*) **irle a** to support. **le va al equipo local** he supports the local team

····▸ (*en exclamaciones*) **¡vamos!** come on! **¡vaya!** what a surprise! (*contrariedad*) oh, dear! **¡vaya noche!** what a night!

¡qué va! nonsense!

➡ Cuando el verbo intransitivo se emplea con expresiones como **ir de paseo, ir de compras, ir tirando** etc., ver bajo el respectivo nombre, verbo etc.

● *verbo auxiliar*

····▸ **ir a** + *infinitivo* (*para expresar futuro, propósito*) to be going to + *infinitive*; (*al prevenir*) **no te vayas a caer** be careful you don't fall. **no vaya a ser que llueva** in case it rains; (*en sugerencias*) **vamos a dormir** let's go to sleep. **vamos a ver** let's see

····▸ **ir** + *gerundio*. **ve arreglándote** start getting ready. **el tiempo va mejorando** the weather is gradually getting better.

● **irse** *verbo pronominal*

····▸ to go. **se ha ido a casa** he's gone home

····▸ (*marcharse*) to leave. **se fue sin despedirse** he left without saying goodbye. **se fue de casa** she left home

ira *f* anger. **~cundo** *adj* irascible

Irak *m* Iraq

Irán *m* Iran

iraní *adj* & *m* & *f* Iranian

iraquí *adj* & *m* & *f* Iraqi

iris *m* (*del ojo*) iris

Irlanda *f* Ireland

irland|és *adj* Irish. ● *m* Irishman; (*lengua*) Irish. **~esa** *f* Irishwoman. **los ~eses** the Irish

ir|onía *f* irony. **~ónico** *adj* ironic

irracional *adj* irrational

irradiar vt radiate

irreal adj unreal. **~idad** f unreality

irrealizable adj unattainable

irreconciliable adj irreconcilable

irreconocible adj unrecognizable

irrecuperable adj irretrievable

irreflexión f impetuosity

irregular adj irregular. **~idad** f irregularity

irreparable adj irreparable

irreprimible adj irrepressible

irreprochable adj irreproachable

irresistible adj irresistible

irrespetuoso adj disrespectful

irresponsable adj irresponsible

irriga|ción f irrigation. **~r** vt irrigate

irrisorio adj derisory

irrita|ble adj irritable. **~ción** f irritation. **~r** vt irritate. **~rse** vpr get annoyed

irrumpir vi burst (**en** in)

isla f island. **las l~s Británicas** the British Isles

islámico adj Islamic

islandés adj Icelandic. ● m Icelander; (lengua) Icelandic

Islandia f Iceland

isleño adj island. ● m islander

Israel m Israel

israelí adj & m Israeli

Italia f Italy

italiano adj & m Italian

itinerario adj itinerary

IVA abrev (**Impuesto sobre el valor agregado** (LAm), **impuesto sobre el valor añadido**) VAT

izar vt hoist

izquierd|a f. la **~a** the left hand; (Pol) left. **a la ~a** on the left; (con movimiento) to the left. **de ~a**

left-wing. **~ista** m & f leftist. **~o** adj left

Jj

ja int ha!

jabalí m (pl **~es**) wild boar

jabalina f javelin

jab|ón m soap. **~onar** vt soap. **~onoso** adj soapy

jaca f pony

jacinto m hyacinth

jactarse vpr boast

jadea|nte adj panting. **~r** vi pant

jaguar m jaguar

jaiba f (LAm) crab

jalar vt (LAm) pull

jalea f jelly

jaleo m row, uproar. **armar un ~** kick up a fuss

jalón m (LAm, tirón) pull; (Mex fam, trago) drink; (Mex, tramo) stretch

jamás adv never. **nunca ~** never ever

jamelgo m nag

jamón m ham. **~ de York** boiled ham. **~ serrano** cured ham

Japón m. **el ~** Japan

japonés adj & m Japanese

jaque m check. **~ mate** checkmate

jaqueca f migraine

jarabe m syrup

jardín m garden. **~ de la infancia**, (Mex) **~ de niños** kindergarten, nursery school

jardiner|ía f gardening. **~o** m gardener

jarr|a f jug. **en ~as** with hands on hips. **~o** m jug. **caer como un ~o de agua fría** come as a shock. **~ón** m vase

jaula f cage

jauría f pack of hounds

jazmín m jasmine

jef|a f boss. **~atura** f leadership; (*sede*) headquarters. **~e** m boss; (*Pol etc*) leader. **~e de camareros** head waiter. **~e de estación** station-master. **~e de ventas** sales manager

jengibre m ginger

jer|arquía f hierarchy. **~árquico** adj hierarchical

jerez m sherry. **al ~** with sherry

> *i* **Jerez** Sherry is produced in an area around Jerez de la Frontera near Cádiz. Sherries are drunk worldwide as an aperitif, and in Spain as an accompaniment to tapas. The main types are: the pale *fino* and *manzanilla* and the darker *oloroso* and *amontillado*. It is from *Jerez* that sherry takes its English name.

jerga f coarse cloth; (*argot*) jargon

jerigonza f jargon; (*galimatías*) gibberish

jeringa f syringe; (*LAm fam, molestia*) nuisance. **~r** 12 vt (*fig, fam, molestar*) annoy

jeroglífico m hieroglyph(ic)

jersey m (pl **~s**) jersey

Jesucristo m Jesus Christ. **antes de ~** BC, before Christ

jesuita adj & m Jesuit

Jesús m Jesus. ● *int* good heavens!; (*al estornudar*) bless you!

jícara f (Mex) gourd

jilguero m goldfinch

jinete m & f rider

jipijapa m panama hat

jirafa f giraffe

jirón m shred, tatter

jitomate m (Mex) tomato

jorna|da f working day; (*viaje*) journey; (*etapa*) stage. **~l** m day's wage. **~lero** m day labourer

joroba f hump. **~do** adj hunchbacked. ● m hunchback. **~r** vt 1 annoy

jota f letter J; (*danza*) jota, popular dance. **ni ~** nothing

joven (pl **jóvenes**) adj young. ● m young man. ● f young woman

jovial adj jovial

joy|a f jewel. **~as** fpl jewellery. **~ería** f jeweller's (shop). **~ero** m jeweller; (*estuche*) jewellery box

juanete m bunion

jubil|ación f retirement. **~ado** adj retired. **~ar** vt pension off. **~arse** vpr retire. **~eo** m jubilee

júbilo m joy

judaísmo m Judaism

judía f Jewish woman; (*alubia*) bean. **~ blanca** haricot bean. **~ escarlata** runner bean. **~ verde** French bean

judicial adj judicial

judío adj Jewish. ● m Jewish man

judo m judo

juego m play; (*de mesa, niños*) game; (*de azar*) gambling; (*conjunto*) set. **estar en ~** be at stake. **estar fuera de ~** be offside. **hacer ~** match. **~s** mpl malabares juggling. **J~s** mpl Olímpicos Olympic Games. ● *vb véase* **JUGAR**

juerga f spree

jueves m invar Thursday

juez m judge. **~ de instrucción** examining magistrate. **~ de línea**

linesman

juga|dor *m* player; *(habitual, por dinero)* gambler. **~r** 🔢 *vt* play. ● *vi* play; *(apostar fuerte)* gamble. **~rse** *vpr* risk. **~r al fútbol**, *(LAm)* **~r fútbol** play football

juglar *m* minstrel

jugo *m* juice; *(de carne)* gravy; *(fig)* substance. **~so** *adj* juicy; *(fig)* substantial

juguet|e *m* toy. **~ear** *vi* play. **~ón** *adj* playful

juicio *m* judgement; *(opinión)* opinion; *(razón)* reason. **a mi ~** in my opinion. **~so** *adj* wise

juliana *f* vegetable soup

julio *m* July

junco *m* rush, reed

jungla *f* jungle

junio *m* June

junt|a *f* meeting; *(consejo)* board, committee; *(Pol)* junta; *(Tec)* joint. **~ar** *vt* join; *(reunir)* collect. **~arse** *vpr* join; *(gente)* meet. **~o** *adj* joined; *(en plural)* together. **~o a** next to. **~ura** *f* joint

jura|do *adj* sworn. ● *m* jury; *(miembro de jurado)* juror. **~mento** *m* oath. **prestar ~mento** take an oath. **~r** *vt/i* swear. **~r en falso** commit perjury. **jurárselas a uno** have it in for s.o.

jurel *m* (type of) mackerel

jurídico *adj* legal

juris|dicción *f* jurisdiction. **~prudencia** *f* jurisprudence

justamente *adj* exactly; *(con justicia)* fairly

justicia *f* justice

justifica|ción *f* justification. **~r** 🔢 *vt* justify

justo *adj* fair, just; *(exacto)* exact;

(ropa) tight. ● *adv* just. **~ a tiempo** just in time

juven|il *adj* youthful. **~tud** *f* youth; *(gente joven)* young people

juzga|do *m* *(tribunal)* court. **~r** 🔢 *vt* judge. **a ~r por** judging by

Kk

kilo *m*, **kilogramo** *m* kilo, kilogram

kil|ometraje *m* distance in kilometres, mileage. **~ométrico** *adj* 🔢 endless. **~ómetro** *m* kilometre. **~ómetro cuadrado** square kilometre

kilovatio *m* kilowatt

kiosco *m* kiosk

Ll

la *articulo definido femenino (pl* **las)**

••••➤ the. **la flor azul** the blue flower. **la casa de al lado** the house next door. **cerca de la iglesia** near the church *No se traduce en los siguientes casos:*

••••➤ *(con nombre abstracto, genérico)* **la paciencia es una virtud** patience is a virtue. **odio la leche** I hate milk. **la madera es muy versátil** wood is very versatile

••••➤ *(con algunas instituciones)*

termino la universidad mañana I finish university tomorrow. **no va nunca a la iglesia** he never goes to church. **está en la cárcel** he's in jail

····▶ (*con nombres propios*) **la Sra. Díaz** Mrs Díaz. **la doctora Lara** doctor Lara

····▶ (*con partes del cuerpo, artículos personales*) *se traduce por un posesivo.* **apretó la mano** he clenched his fist. **tienes la camisa desabrochada** your shirt is undone

····▶ **la + de. es la de Ana** it's Ana's. **la del sombrero** the one with the hat

····▶ **la + que** (*persona*) **la que me atendió** the one who served me. (*cosa*) **la que se rompió** the one that broke

····▶ **la + que** + *subjuntivo* (*quienquiera*) whoever. **la que gane pasará a la final** whoever wins will go to the final. (*cualquiera*) whichever. **compra la que sea más barata** buy whichever is cheaper

laberinto *m* labyrinth, maze
labia *f* gift of the gab
labio *m* lip
labor *f* work. **~es de aguja** needlework. **~es de ganchillo** crochet. **~es de punto** knitting. **~es domésticas** housework. **~able** *adj* working. **~ar** *vi* work
laboratorio *m* laboratory
laborioso *adj* laborious
laborista *adj* Labour. ● *m & f* member of the Labour Party
labra|do *adj* worked; (*madera*) carved; (*metal*) wrought; (*tierra*)

ploughed. **~dor** *m* farmer; (*obrero*) farm labourer. **~nza** *f* farming. **~r** *vt* work; carve (*madera*); cut (*piedra*); till (*la tierra*). **~rse** *vpr*. **~rse un porvenir** carve out a future for o.s.
labriego *m* peasant
laca *f* lacquer
lacayo *m* lackey
lacio *adj* straight; (*flojo*) limp
lacón *m* shoulder of pork
lacónico *adj* laconic
lacr|ar *vt* seal. **~e** *m* sealing wax
lactante *adj* (*niño*) still on milk
lácteo *adj* milky. **productos** *mpl* **~s** dairy products
ladear *vt* tilt. **~se** *vpr* lean
ladera *f* slope
ladino *adj* astute
lado *m* side. **al ~** near. **al ~ de** next to, beside. **de ~** sideways. **en todos ~s** everywhere. **los de al ~** the next door neighbours. **por otro ~** on the other hand. **por todos ~s** everywhere. **por un ~** on the one hand
ladr|ar *vi* bark. **~ido** *m* bark
ladrillo *m* brick
ladrón *m* thief, robber; (*de casas*) burglar
lagart|ija *f* (small) lizard. **~o** *m* lizard
lago *m* lake
lágrima *f* tear
lagrimoso *adj* tearful
laguna *f* small lake; (*fig, omisión*) gap
laico *adj* lay
lament|able *adj* deplorable; (*que da pena*) pitiful; (*pérdida*) sad. **~ar** *vt* be sorry about. **~arse** *vpr* lament; (*quejarse*) complain. **~o** *m* moan

lamer vt lick

lámina f sheet; (*ilustración*) plate; (*estampa*) picture card

lamina|do adj laminated. **~r** vt laminate

lámpara f lamp. **~ de pie** standard lamp

lamparón m stain

lampiño adj beardless; (*cuerpo*) hairless

lana f wool. **de ~** wool(len)

lanceta f lancet

lancha f boat. **~ motora** motor boat. **~ salvavidas** lifeboat

langost|a f (*de mar*) lobster; (*insecto*) locust. **~ino** m king prawn

languide|cer 🔢 vi languish. **~z** f languor

lánguido adj languid; (*decaído*) listless

lanilla f nap; (*tela fina*) flannel

lanudo adj woolly; (*perro*) shaggy

lanza f lance, spear

lanza|llamas m invar flamethrower. **~miento** m throw; (*acción de lanzar*) throwing; (*de proyectil, de producto*) launch. **~miento de peso**, (*LAm*) **~miento de bala** shot put. **~r** 🔟 vt throw; (*de un avión*) drop; launch (*proyectil, producto*). **~rse** vpr throw o.s.

lapicero m (*propelling*) pencil

lápida f tombstone; (*placa conmemorativa*) memorial tablet

lapidar vt stone

lápiz m pencil. **~ de labios** lipstick. **a ~** in pencil

lapso m lapse

laptop m laptop

larg|a f. **a la ~a** in the long run. **dar ~as** put off. **~ar** 🔢 vt (*Naut*) let out; (*fam, dar*) give; 🔟 deal

it 🔟. **~o** adj long. ● m length. **¡~o!** go away! **a lo ~o** lengthwise. **a lo ~o de** along. **tener 100 metros de ~o** be 100 metres long

laring|e f larynx. **~itis** f laryngitis

larva f larva

las *artículo definido fpl* the. *véase tb* **LA.** ● *pron* them. **~ de** those, the ones. **~ de Vd** your ones, yours. **~ que** whoever, the ones

láser m laser

lástima f pity; (*queja*) complaint. **da ~ verlo así** it's sad to see him like that. **ella me da ~** I feel sorry for her. **¡qué ~!** what a pity!

lastim|ado adj hurt. **~ar** vt hurt. **~arse** vpr hurt o.s. **~ero** adj doleful. **~oso** adj pitiful

lastre m ballast; (*fig*) burden

lata f tinplate; (*envase*) tin (*esp Brit*) can; (*fam, molestia*) nuisance. **dar la ~** be a nuisance. **¡qué ~!** what a nuisance!

latente adj latent

lateral adj side, lateral

latido m beating; (*cada golpe*) beat

latifundio m large estate

latigazo m (*golpe*) lash; (*chasquido*) crack

látigo m whip

latín m Latin. **saber ~** 🔟 know what's what 🔟

latino adj Latin. **L~américa** f Latin America. **~americano** adj & m Latin American

latir vi beat; (*herida*) throb

latitud f latitude

latón m brass

latoso adj annoying; (*pesado*) boring

laúd *m* lute

laureado *adj* honoured; (*premiado*) prize-winning

laurel *m* laurel; (*Culin*) bay

lava *f* lava

lava|ble *adj* washable. **∼bo** *m* wash-basin; (*retrete*) toilet. **∼do** *m* sink. **∼do** *m* washing. **∼do de cerebro** brainwashing. **∼do en seco** dry-cleaning. **∼dora** *f* washing machine. **∼ndería** *f* laundry. **∼ndería automática** launderette, laundromat (*esp Amer*). **∼platos** *m & f invar* dishwasher; (*Mex, fregadero*) sink. **∼r** *vt* wash. **∼r en seco** dry-clean. **∼rse** *vpr* have a wash. **∼rse las manos** (*incl fig*) wash one's hands. **∼tiva** *f* enema. **∼vajillas** *m invar* dishwasher; (*detergente*) washing-up liquid (*Brit*), dishwashing liquid (*Amer*)

laxante *adj & m* laxative

lazada *f* bow

lazarillo *m* guide for a blind person

lazo *m* knot; (*lazada*) bow; (*fig, vínculo*) tie; (*con nudo corredizo*) lasso; (*Mex, cuerda*) rope

le *pron* (*acusativo, él*) him; (*acusativo, Vd*) you; (*dativo, él*) (to) him; (*dativo, ella*) (to) her; (*dativo, cosa*) (to) it; (*dativo, Vd*) (to) you

leal *adj* loyal; (*fiel*) faithful. **∼tad** *f* loyalty; (*fidelidad*) faithfulness

lección *f* lesson

leche *f* milk; (*golpe*) bash. **∼ condensada** condensed milk. **∼ desnatada** skimmed milk. **∼ en polvo** powdered milk. **∼ sin desnatar** whole milk. **tener mala ∼** be spiteful. **∼ra** *f* (*vasija*) milk jug. **∼ría** *f* dairy. **∼ro** *adj* milk, dairy. ● *m* milkman

lecho *m* (*en literatura*) bed. **∼ de**

río river bed

lechoso *adj* milky

lechuga *f* lettuce

lechuza *f* owl

lect|or *m* reader; (*Univ*) language assistant. **∼ura** *f* reading

leer 18 *vt/i* read

legación *f* legation

legado *m* legacy; (*enviado*) legate

legajo *m* bundle, file

legal *adj* legal. **∼idad** *f* legality. **∼izar** 10 *vt* legalize; (*certificar*) authenticate. **∼mente** *adv* legally

legar 12 *vt* bequeath

legible *adj* legible

legi|ón *f* legion. **∼onario** *m* legionary. **∼onella** *f* legionnaire's disease

legisla|ción *f* legislation. **∼dor** *m* legislator. **∼r** *vi* legislate. **∼tura** *f* term (of office); (*año parlamentario*) session; (*LAm, cuerpo*) legislature

legit|imidad *f* legitimacy. **∼ítimo** *adj* legitimate; (*verdadero*) real

lego *adj* lay; (*ignorante*) ignorant. ● *m* layman

legua *f* league

legumbre *f* vegetable

lejanía *f* distance. **∼o** *adj* distant

lejía *f* bleach

lejos *adv* far. **∼ de** far from. **a lo ∼** in the distance. **desde ∼** from a distance, from afar

lema *m* motto

lencería *f* linen; (*de mujer*) lingerie

lengua *f* tongue; (*idioma*) language. **irse de la ∼** talk too much. **morderse la ∼** hold one's tongue *i*

lenguas cooficiales The regional languages of Spain, *catalán*, *euskera* and *gallego*, which now have equal status with Castilian in the regions where they are spoken. Banned under Franco, they continued to be spoken privately. They are now widely used in public life, education, the media, cinema and literature.

lenguado *m* sole

lenguaje *m* language

lengüeta *f* (*de zapato*) tongue. **~da** *f*, **~zo** *m* lick

lente *f* lens. **~s** *mpl* glasses. **~s de contacto** contact lenses

lenteja *f* lentil. **~uela** *f* sequin

lentilla *f* contact lens

lent|itud *f* slowness. **~o** *adj* slow

leña *f* firewood. **~ador** *m* woodcutter. **~o** *m* log

Leo *m* Leo

le|ón *m* lion. **~ona** *f* lioness

leopardo *m* leopard

leotardo *m* thick tights

lepra *f* leprosy. **~oso** *m* leper

lerdo *adj* dim; (*torpe*) clumsy

les *pron* (*acusativo*) them; (*acusativo, Vds*) you; (*dativo*) (to) them; (*dativo, Vds*) (to) you

lesbiana *f* lesbian

lesi|ón *f* wound. **~onado** *adj* injured. **~onar** *vt* injure; (*dañar*) damage

letal *adj* lethal

let|árgico *adj* lethargic. **~argo** *m* lethargy

letr|a *f* letter; (*escritura*) handwriting; (*de una canción*) words, lyrics. **~a de cambio** bill of exchange. **~a de imprenta** print. **~ado** *adj* learned. **~ero** *m* notice; (*cartel*) poster

letrina *f* latrine

leucemia *f* leukaemia

levadura *f* yeast. **~ en polvo** baking powder

levanta|miento *m* lifting; (*sublevación*) uprising. **~r** *vt* raise, lift; (*construir*) build; (*recoger*) pick up. **~rse** *vpr* get up; (*ponerse de pie*) stand up; (*erguirse, sublevarse*) rise up

levante *m* east; (*viento*) east wind

levar *vt.* **~ anclas** weigh anchor

leve *adj* light; (*enfermedad*) mild; (*de poca importancia*) trivial. **~dad** *f* lightness; (*fig*) slightness

léxico *m* vocabulary

lexicografía *f* lexicography

ley *f* law; (*parlamentaria*) act

leyenda *f* legend

liar 20 *vt* tie; (*envolver*) wrap up; roll (*cigarrillo*); (*fig, confundir*) confuse; (*fig, enredar*) involve. **~se** *vpr* get involved

libanés *adj & m* Lebanese

libelo *m* (*escrito*) libellous article; (*Jurid*) petition

libélula *f* dragonfly

libera|ción *f* liberation. **~dor** *adj* liberating. ● *m* liberator

liberal *adj & m & f* liberal. **~idad** *f* liberality

liber|ar *vt* free. **~tad** *f* freedom. **~tad de cultos** freedom of worship. **~tad de imprenta** freedom of the press. **~tad provisional** bail. **~tad** *vt* free. **~tador** *m* liberator. **~tar** *vt* free

libertino *m* libertine

libido *f* libido

libio *adj & m* Libyan

libra f pound. ~ **esterlina** pound sterling

Libra m Libra

libra|dor m (Com) drawer. ~**r** vt free; (de un peligro) save. ~**rse** vpr free o.s. ~**rse de** get rid of

libre adj free. **estilo** ~ (en natación) freestyle. ~ **de impuestos** tax-free

librea f livery

libr|ería f bookshop (Brit), bookstore (Amer); (mueble) bookcase. ~**ero** m bookseller; (Mex, mueble) bookcase. ~**eta** f notebook. ~**o** m book. ~**o de bolsillo** paperback. ~**o de ejercicios** exercise book. ~**o de reclamaciones** complaints book

licencia f permission; (documento) licence. ~**do** m graduate; (Mex, abogado) lawyer. ~ **para manejar** (Mex) driving licence. ~**r** vt (Mil) discharge; (echar) dismiss. ~**tura** f degree

licencioso adj licentious

licitar vt bid for

lícito adj legal; (permisible) permissible

licor m liquor; (dulce) liqueur

licua|dora f blender. ~**r** 21 liquefy; (Culin) blend

lid f fight. **en buena** ~ by fair means. ~**es** fpl matters

líder m leader

liderato m, **liderazgo** m leadership

lidia f bullfighting; (lucha) fight. ~**r** vt/i fight

liebre f hare

lienzo m linen; (del pintor) canvas; (muro, pared) wall

liga f garter; (alianza) league; (LAm, gomita) rubber band. ~**dura** f bond; (Mus) slur; (Med) ligature.

~**mento** m ligament. ~**r** 12 vt bind; (atar) tie; (Mus) slur. ● vi mix. ~**r con** (fig) pick up. ~**rse** vpr (fig) commit o.s.

liger|eza f lightness; (agilidad) agility; (rapidez) swiftness; (de carácter) fickleness. ~**o** adj light; (rápido) quick; (ágil) agile; (superficial) superficial; (de poca importancia) slight. ● adv quickly. **a la** ~**a** lightly, superficially

liguero m suspender belt

lija f dogfish; (papel de lija) sandpaper. ~**r** vt sand

lila f lilac. ● m (color) lilac

lima f file; (fruta) lime. ~**duras** fpl filings. ~**r** vt file (down)

limita|ción f limitation. ~**do** adj limited. ~**r** vt limit. ~**r con** border on. ~**tivo** adj limiting

límite m limit. ~ **de velocidad** speed limit

limítrofe adj bordering

lim|ón m lemon; (Mex) lime. ~**onada** f lemonade

limosn|a f alms. **pedir** ~**a** beg. ~**ear** vi beg

limpia|botas m invar bootblack. ~**parabrisas** m invar windscreen wiper (Brit), windshield wiper (Amer). ~**pipas** m invar pipe-cleaner. ~**r** vt clean; (enjugar) wipe. ~**vidrios** m invar (LAm) window cleaner

limpi|eza f cleanliness; (acción de limpiar) cleaning. ~**eza en seco** dry-cleaning. ~**o** adj clean; (cielo) clear; (fig, honrado) honest; (neto) net. **pasar a** ~**o**, (LAm) **pasar en** ~**o** make a fair copy. ● adv fairly. **jugar** ~**o** play fair

linaje m lineage; (fig, clase) kind

lince m lynx

linchar vt lynch

lind|ar vi border (con on). ~**e** f

lindo | llegada

boundary. **~ero** m border

lindo adj pretty, lovely. **de lo ~** 🇪 a lot

línea f line. **en ~s generales** broadly speaking. **guardar la ~** watch one's figure

lingote m ingot

lingüista m & f linguist. **~ística** f linguistics. **~ístico** adj linguistic

lino m flax; (tela) linen

linterna f lantern; (de bolsillo) torch, flashlight (Amer)

lío m bundle; (jaleo) fuss; (embrollo) muddle; (amorío) affair

liquida|ción f liquidation; (venta especial) sale. **~r** vt liquify; (Com) liquidate; settle (cuenta)

líquido adj (Com) net. • m liquid; (Com) cash

lira f lyre; (moneda italiana) lira

liric|a f lyric poetry. **~o** adj lyric(al)

lirio m iris

lirón m dormouse; (fig) sleepyhead. **dormir como un ~** sleep like a log

lisiado adj crippled

liso adj smooth; (pelo) straight; (tierra) flat; (sencillo) plain

lisonj|a f flattery. **~eador** adj flattering. • m flatterer. **~ear** vt flatter. **~ero** adj flattering

lista f stripe; (enumeración) list. **~ de correos** poste restante. **a ~s** striped. **pasar ~** take the register. **~do** adj striped

listo adj clever; (preparado) ready

listón m strip; (en saltos) bar; (Mex, cinta) ribbon

litera f (en barco, tren) berth; (en habitación) bunk bed

literal adj literal

litera|rio adj literary. **~tura** f literature

litig|ar 🔢 vi dispute; (Jurid) litigate. **~io** m dispute; (Jurid) litigation

litografía f (arte) lithography; (cuadro) lithograph

litoral adj coastal. • m coast

litro m litre

lituano adj & m Lithuanian

liturgia f liturgy

liviano adj fickle; (LAm, de poco peso) light

lívido adj livid

llaga f wound; (úlcera) ulcer

llama f flame; (animal) llama

llamada f call

llama|do adj called. • m (LAm) call. **~miento** m call. **~r** vt call; (por teléfono) phone. • vi call; (golpear en la puerta) knock; (tocar el timbre) ring. **~r por teléfono** phone, telephone. **~rse** vpr be called. **¿cómo te ~s?** what's your name?

llamarada f sudden blaze; (fig, de pasión etc) outburst

llamativo adj flashy; (color) loud; (persona) striking

llamear vi blaze

llano adj flat, level; (persona) natural; (sencillo) plain. • m plain

llanta f (Auto) (wheel) rim; (LAm, neumático) tyre

llanto m crying

llanura f plain

llave f key; (para tuercas) spanner; (LAm, del baño etc) tap (Brit), faucet (Amer); (Elec) switch. **~ inglesa** monkey wrench. **cerrar con ~** lock. **echar la ~** lock up. **~ro** m key-ring

llega|da f arrival. **~r** 🔢 vi arrive, come; (alcanzar) reach; (bastar) be enough. **~r a** (conseguir) manage to. ~**r a saber** find out. ~**r a ser** become. ~**r hasta** go as far as

llen|ar *vt* fill (up); (*rellenar*) fill in; (*cubrir*) cover (de with). ~**o** *adj* full. ● *m* (*en el teatro etc*) full house. **de** ~ entirely

lleva|dero *adj* tolerable. ~**r** *vt* carry; (*inducir, conducir*) lead; (*acompañar*) take; wear (ropa). **¿cuánto tiempo ~s aquí?** how long have you been here? **llevo 3 años estudiando inglés** I've been studying English for 3 years. ~**rse** *vpr* take away; win (premio etc); (*comprar*) take. ~**rse bien** get on well together

llor|ar *vi* cry; (ojos) water. ~**iquear** *vi* whine. ~**iqueo** *m* whining. ~**o** *m* crying. ~**ón** *adj* whining. ● *m* cry-baby. ~**oso** *adj* tearful

llov|er 2 *vi* rain. ~**izna** *f* drizzle. ~**iznar** *vi* drizzle

llueve *vb* véase **LLOVER**

lluvi|a *f* rain; (*fig*) shower. ~**oso** *adj* rainy; (clima) wet

lo *artículo definido neutro*. ~ **importante** what is important, the important thing. ● *pron* (él) him; (cosa) it. ~ **que** what, that which

loa *f* praise. ~**ble** *adj* praiseworthy. ~**r** *vt* praise

lobo *m* wolf

lóbrego *adj* gloomy

lóbulo *m* lobe

local *adj* local. ● *m* premises. ~**idad** *f* locality; (*de un espectáculo*) seat; (*entrada*) ticket. ~**izador** *m* pager; (*de reserva*) booking reference. ~**izar** 10 *vt* find, locate

loción *f* lotion

loco *adj* mad, crazy. ● *m* lunatic. ~ **de alegría** mad with joy. **estar** ~ **por** be crazy about. **volverse** ~

go mad

locomo|ción *f* locomotion. ~**tora** *f* locomotive

locuaz *adj* talkative

locución *f* expression

locura *f* madness; (*acto*) crazy thing. **con** ~ madly

locutor *m* broadcaster

lod|azal *m* quagmire. ~**o** *m* mud

lógic|a *f* logic. ~**o** *adj* logical

logr|ar *vt* get; win (premio). ~ **hacer** manage to do. ~**o** *m* achievement; (*de premio*) winning; (*éxito*) success

loma *f* small hill

lombriz *f* worm

lomo *m* back; (*de libro*) spine. ~ **de cerdo** loin of pork

lona *f* canvas

loncha *f* slice; (*de tocino*) rasher

londinense *adj* from London. ● *m* Londoner

Londres *m* London

loneta *f* thin canvas

longaniza *f* sausage

longev|idad *f* longevity. ~**o** *adj* long-lived

longitud *f* length; (*en geografía*) longitude

lonja *f* slice; (*de tocino*) rasher; (*Com*) market

loro *m* parrot

los *artículo definido mpl* the. *véase tb* **EL**. ● *pron* them. ~ **de Antonio** Antonio's. ~ **que** whoever, the ones

losa *f* (*baldosa*) flagstone. ~ **sepulcral** tombstone

lote *m* share; (*de productos*) batch; (*terreno*) plot (Brit), lot (Amer)

lotería *f* lottery

loto *m* lotus

loza f crockery; (*fina*) china

lozano adj fresh; (*vegetación*) lush; (*persona*) healthy-looking

lubina f sea bass

lubrica|nte adj lubricating. • m lubricant. **~r 7** vt lubricate

lucero m bright star. **~ del alba** morning star

lucha f fight; (*fig*) struggle. **~dor** m fighter. **~r** vi fight; (*fig*) struggle

lucidez f lucidity. **~o** adj splendid

lúcido adj lucid

luciérnaga f glow-worm

lucimiento m brilliance

lucio m pike

lucir 11 vt (*fig*) show off. • vi shine; (*joya*) sparkle; (*LAm, mostrarse*) look. **~se** vpr (*fig*) shine, excel; (*presumir*) show off

lucr|ativo adj lucrative. **~o** m gain

luego adv then; (*más tarde*) later (on); (*Mex, pronto*) soon. • conj therefore. **~ que** as soon as. **desde ~** of course

lugar m place; (*espacio libre*) room. **~ común** cliché. **dar ~ a** give rise to. **en ~ de** instead of. **en primer ~** first. **hacer ~** make room. **tener ~** take place. **~eño** adj local, village

lugarteniente m deputy

lúgubre adj gloomy

lujo m luxury. **~so** adj luxurious. **de ~** luxury

lumbago m lumbago

lumbre f fire; (*luz*) light

luminoso adj luminous; (*fig*) bright; (*letrero*) illuminated

luna f moon; (*espejo*) mirror. **~ de miel** honeymoon. **claro de ~** moonlight. **estar en la ~** be miles away. **~r** adj lunar. • m mole;

(*en tela*) spot

lunes m invar Monday

lupa f magnifying glass

lustr|abotas m invar (*LAm*) bootblack. **~ar** vt shine, polish. **~e** m shine; (*fig, esplendor*) splendour. **dar ~e a**, **sacar ~e a** polish. **~oso** adj shining

luto m mourning. **estar de ~** be in mourning

luz f light; (*electricidad*) electricity. **luces altas** (*LAm*) headlights on full beam. **luces bajas** (*LAm*), **luces cortas** dipped headlights. **luces antiniebla** fog light. **luces largas** headlights on full beam. **a la ~ de** in the light of. **a todas luces** obviously. **dar a ~** give birth. **hacer la ~ sobre** shed light on. **sacar a la ~** bring to light

Mm

macabro adj macabre

macaco m macaque (monkey)

macanudo adj 1 great 1

macarrones mpl macaroni

macerar vt macerate (*fruta*); marinade (*carne* etc)

maceta f mallet; (*tiesto*) flowerpot

machacar 7 vt crush. • vi go on (*sobre about*)

machamartillo. a ~ adj ardent; (*como adv*) firmly

machet|azo m blow with a machete; (*herida*) wound from a machete. **~e** m machete

mach|ista m male chauvinist. **~o** adj male; (*varonil*) macho

machu|car `7` vt bruise; (*aplastar*) crush. ~**cón** m (*LAm*) bruise

macizo adj solid. ● m mass; (*de plantas*) bed

madeja f skein

madera m (*vino*) Madeira. ● f wood; (*naturaleza*) nature. ~**ble** adj yielding timber. ~**men** m woodwork

madero m log; (*de construcción*) timber

madona f Madonna

madr|astra f stepmother. ~**e** f mother. ~**eperla** f mother-of-pearl. ~**eselva** f honeysuckle

madrigal m madrigal

madriguera f den; (*de conejo*) burrow

madrileño adj of Madrid. ● m person from Madrid

madrina f godmother; (*en una boda*) matron of honour

madrug|ada f dawn. **de** ~**ada** at dawn. ~**ador** adj who gets up early. ● m early riser. ~**ar** `12` vi get up early

madur|ación f maturing; (*de fruta*) ripening. ~**ar** vt/i mature; (*fruta*) ripen. ~**ez** f maturity; (*de fruta*) ripeness. ~**o** adj mature; (*fruta*) ripe

maestr|ía f skill; (*Univ*) master's degree. ~**o** m master; (*de escuela*) schoolteacher

mafia f mafia

magdalena f fairy cake (*Brit*), cup cake (*Amer*)

magia f magic

mágico adj magic; (*maravilloso*) magical

magist|erio m teaching (profession); (*conjunto de maestros*) teachers. ~**rado** m magistrate; (*juez*) judge. ~**ral** adj teaching; (*bien* *hecho*) masterly. ~**ratura** f magistracy

magn|animidad f magnanimity. ~**ánimo** adj magnanimous. ~**ate** m magnate, tycoon

magnavoz m (*Mex*) megaphone

magnético adj magnetic

magneti|smo m magnetism. ~**zar** `10` vt magnetize

magn|ificar vt extol; (*LAm*) magnify (*objeto*). ~**ificencia** f magnificence. ~**ífico** adj magnificent. ~**itud** f magnitude

magnolia f magnolia

mago m magician; (*en cuentos*) wizard

magro adj lean; (*tierra*) poor

magulla|dura f bruise. ~**r** vt bruise. ~**rse** vpr bruise

mahometano adj Islamic

maíz m maize, corn (*Amer*)

majada f sheepfold; (*estiércol*) manure; (*LAm*) flock of sheep

majader|ía f silly thing. ~**o** m idiot. ● adj stupid

majest|ad f majesty. ~**uoso** adj majestic

majo adj nice

mal adv badly; (*poco*) poorly; (*difícilmente*) hardly; (*equivocadamente*) wrongly; (*desagradablemente*) bad. ● adj. **estar** ~ be ill; (*anímicamente*) be in a bad way; (*incorrecto*) be wrong. **estar** ~ **de** (*escaso de*) be short of. *véase tb* **MALO**. ● m evil; (*daño*) harm; (*enfermedad*) illness. ~ **que bien** somehow (or other). **de** ~ **en peor** from bad to worse. **hacer** ~ en be wrong to. **¡menos** ~**!** thank goodness!

malabaris|mo m juggling. ~**ta** m & f juggler

mala|consejado adj ill-advised.

~costumbrado adj spoilt.
~crianza (LAm) rudeness. ~gradecido adj ungrateful

malagueño adj of Málaga. • m person from Málaga

malaria f malaria

Malasia f Malaysia

malavenido adj incompatible

malaventura adj unfortunate

malayo adj Malay(an)

malbaratar vt sell off cheap; (malgastar) squander

malcarado adj nasty looking

malcriado adj (niño) spoilt

maldad f evil; (acción) wicked thing

maldecir 46 (pero imperativo maldice, futuro y condicional regulares, pp maldecido o maldito) vt curse. vi curse; speak ill (de of)

maldi|ciente adj backbiting; (que blasfema) foul-mouthed. ~ción f curse. ~to adj damned. ¡~to sea! damn (it)!

maleab|ilidad f malleability. ~le adj malleable

malea|nte m criminal. ~r vt damage; (pervertir) corrupt. ~rse vpr be spoilt; (pervertirse) be corrupted

malecón m breakwater; (embarcadero) jetty; (Rail) embankment; (LAm, paseo marítimo) seafront

maledicencia f slander

mal|eficio m curse. ~éfico adj evil

malestar m discomfort; (fig) uneasiness

malet|a f (suit)case. hacer la ~a pack (one's case). ~ero m porter; (Auto) boot, trunk (Amer). ~ín m small case; (para documentos) briefcase

malevolencia f malevolence. ~évolo adj malevolent

maleza f weeds; (matorral) undergrowth

mal|gastar vt waste. ~hablado adj foul-mouthed. ~hechor m criminal. ~humorado adj bad-tempered

malici|a f malice; (picardía) mischief. ~arse vpr suspect. ~oso adj malicious; (pícaro) mischievous

maligno adj malignant; (persona) evil

malintencionado adj malicious

malla f mesh; (de armadura) mail; (de gimnasia) leotard

Mallorca f Majorca

mallorquín adj & m Majorcan

malmirado adj (con estar) frowned upon

malo adj (delante de nombre masculino en singular **mal**) bad; (enfermo) ill. ~ de difficult to. **estar de malas** (malhumorado) be in a bad mood; (LAm, con mala suerte) be out of luck. **lo ~ es que** the trouble is that. **por las malas** by force

malogr|ar vt waste; (estropear) spoil. ~arse vpr fall through

maloliente adj smelly

malpensado adj nasty, malicious

malsano adj unhealthy

malsonante adj ill-sounding; (grosero) offensive

malt|a f malt. ~eada f (LAm) milk shake. ~ear vt malt

maltr|atar vt ill-treat; (pegar) batter; mistreat (juguete etc). ~echo adj battered

malucho adj 🔢 under the weather

malva f mallow. **(color de)** ~ adj invar mauve

malvado adj wicked

malvavisco m marshmallow

malversa|ción f embezzlement. **~dor** adj embezzling. ● m embezzler. **~r** vt embezzle

Malvinas fpl. **las (islas)** ~ the Falklands, the Falkland Islands

mama f mammary gland; (de mujer) breast

mamá f mum; (usado por niños) mummy

mama|da f sucking. **~r** vt suck; (fig) grow up with. ● vi (bebé) feed; (animal) suckle. **dar de** ~ breastfeed

mamario adj mammary

mamarracho m clown; (cosa ridícula) (ridiculous) sight; (cosa mal hecha) botch; (cosa fea) mess. **ir hecho un** ~ look a sight

mameluco m (LAm) overalls; (de niño) rompers

mamífero adj.mammalian. ● m mammal

mamila f (Mex) feeding bottle

mamotreto m (libro) hefty volume; (armatoste) huge thing

mampara f screen

mampostería f masonry

mamut m mammoth

manada f herd; (de lobos) pack; (de leones) pride. **en** ~ in crowds

mana|ntial m spring; (fig) source. **~r** vi flow; (fig) abound. ● vt drip with

manaza f big hand

mancha f stain; (en la piel) blotch. **~do** adj stained; (sucio) dirty; (animal) spotted. **~r** vt stain; (ensuciar) dirty. **~rse** vpr get stained; (ensuciarse) get dirty

manchego adj of la Mancha. ● m person from la Mancha

manchón m large stain

mancilla f blemish. **~r** vt stain

manco adj (de una mano) one-handed; (de las dos manos) handless; (de un brazo) one-armed; (de los dos brazos) armless

mancomun|adamente adv jointly. **~ar** vt unite; (Jurid) make jointly liable. **~arse** vpr unite. **~idad** f union

manda f (Mex) religious offering

manda|dero m messenger. **~do** m (LAm) shopping; (diligencia) errand. **hacer los ~dos** (LAm) do the shopping. **~miento** m order; (Relig) commandment. **~r** vt order; (enviar) send; (gobernar) rule. ● vi be in command. **¿mande?** (Mex) pardon?

mandarin|a f (naranja) mandarin (orange). **~o** m mandarin tree

mandat|ario m attorney; (Pol) head of state. **~o** m mandate; (Pol) term of office

mandíbula f jaw

mando m command. ~ **a distancia** remote control. **al** ~ **de** in charge of. **altos ~s** mpl high-ranking officers

mandolina f mandolin

mandón adj bossy

manducar [7] vt [1] stuff oneself with

manecilla f hand

manej|able adj manageable. **~ar** vt use; handle (asunto etc); (fig) manage; (LAm, conducir) drive. **~arse** vpr get by. **~o** m handling. **~os** mpl scheming

manera f way. ~ **de alguna** ~ somehow. **de** ~ **que** so (that). **de ninguna** ~ by no means. **de otra** ~ otherwise. **de todas ~s** anyway

manga f sleeve; (tubo de goma) hose; (red) net; (para colar) filter; (LAm, de langostas) swarm

mango m handle; (fruta) mango. **~near** vt boss about. • vi (entrometerse) interfere

manguera f hose(pipe)

manguito m muff

maní m (pl ~es) (LAm) peanut

manía f mania; (antipatía) dislike. **tener la ~ de** have an obsession with

maniaco adj, **maníaco** adj maniac(al). • m maniac

maniatar vt tie s.o.'s hands

maniático adj maniac(al); (obsesivo) obsessive; (loco) crazy; (delicado) finicky

manicomio m lunatic asylum

manicura f manicure; (mujer) manicurist

manido adj stale

manifesta|ción f manifestation, sign; (Pol) demonstration. **~nte** m demonstrator. **~r** **1** vt show; (Pol) state. **~rse** vpr show; (Pol) demonstrate

manifiesto adj clear; (error) obvious; (verdad) manifest. • m manifiesto

manilargo adj light-fingered

manilla f (de cajón etc) handle; (de reloj) hand. **~r** m handlebar(s)

maniobra f manoeuvre. **~r** vt operate; (Rail) shunt. • vt/i manoeuvre. **~s** fpl (Mil) manoeuvres

manipula|ción f manipulation. **~r** vt manipulate

maniquí m dummy. • m & f model

mani|rroto adj & m spendthrift. **~ta** f, (LAm) **~to** m little hand

manivela f crank

manjar m delicacy

mano f hand; (de animales) front foot; (de perros, gatos) front paw. **~ de obra** work force. **¡~s arriba!** hands up! **a ~** by hand; (próximo) handy. **a ~ derecha** on the right. **de segunda ~** second hand. **echar una ~** lend a hand. **tener buena ~ para** be good at. • m (LAm, fam) mate (Brit), buddy (Amer)

manojo m bunch

manose|ar vt handle. **~o** m handling

manota f, **manotazo** m slap

manote|ar vi gesticulate. **~o** m gesticulation

mansalva: a ~ adv without risk

mansarda f attic

mansión f mansion. **~ señorial** stately home

manso adj gentle; (animal) tame

manta f blanket

manteca f fat. **~oso** adj greasy

mantel m tablecloth; (del altar) altar cloth. **~ería** f table linen

manten|er **40** vt support; (conservar) keep; (sostener) maintain. **~erse** vpr support o.s.; (permanecer) remain. **~se de/con** live off. **~imiento** m maintenance

mantequ|era f butter churn. **~illa** f butter

mant|illa f mantilla. **~o** m cloak. **~ón** m shawl

manual adj & m manual

manubrio m crank; (LAm, de bicicleta) handlebars

manufactura f manufacture. **~r** vt manufacture, make

manuscrito adj handwritten. • m manuscript

manutención f maintenance

manzana f apple; (de edificios)

block. **~r** m (apple) orchard. **~ de Adán** (LAm) Adam's apple

manzan|illa f camomile tea. ●m manzanilla, pale dry sherry. **~o** m apple tree

maña f skill. **~s** fpl cunning

mañan|a f morning. **~a por la ~a** tomorrow morning. **pasado ~a** the day after tomorrow. **en la ~a** (LAm), **por la ~a** in the morning. ● m future. ● adv tomorrow. **~ero** adj who gets up early. ● m early riser

mañoso adj clever; (astuto) crafty; (LAm, caprichoso) difficult

mapa m map

mapache m racoon

maqueta f scale model

maquiladora f (Mex) cross-border assembly plant

maquilla|je m make-up. **~r** vt make up. **~rse** vpr make up

máquina f machine; (Rail) engine. **~ de afeitar** shaver. **~ de escribir** typewriter. **~ fotográfica** camera

maquin|ación f machination. **~al** adj mechanical. **~aria** f machinery. **~ista** m & f operator; (Rail) engine driver

mar m & f sea. **alta ~** high seas. **~ de** 🔟 lots of

maraña f thicket; (enredo) tangle; (embrollo) muddle

maratón m & f marathon

maravill|a f wonder. **a las mil ~as**, **de ~as** marvellously. **contar/decir ~as de** speak wonderfully of. **hacer ~as** work wonders. **~ar** vt astonish. **~arse** vpr be astonished (**de** at). **~oso** adj marvellous, wonderful

marca f mark; (de coches etc) make; (de alimentos, cosméticos)

brand; (Deportes) record. **~ de fábrica** trade mark. **de ~** brand name; (fig) excellent. **de ~ mayor** 🔟 absolute. **~do** adj marked. **~dor** m marker; (Deportes) scoreboard. **~r** 🔽 vt mark; (señalar) show; score (un gol); dial (número de teléfono). ● vi score

marcha f (incl Mus) march; (Auto) gear; (desarrollo) course; (partida) departure. **a toda ~** at full speed. **dar/hacer ~ atrás** put into reverse. **poner en ~** start; (fig) set in motion

marchante m (f marchanta) art dealer; (Mex, en mercado) stall holder

marchar vi go; (funcionar) work, go; (Mil) march. **~se** vpr leave

marchit|ar vt wither. **~arse** vpr wither. **~o** adj withered

marcial adj martial

marciano adj & m Martian

marco m frame; (moneda alemana) mark; (deportes) goal-posts

marea f tide. **~do** adj sick; (en el mar) seasick; (aturdido) dizzy; (borracho) drunk. **~r** vt make feel sick; (aturdir) make feel dizzy; (confundir) confuse. **~rse** vpr feel sick; (en un barco) get seasick; (estar aturdido) feel dizzy; (irse la cabeza) feel faint; (emborracharse) get slightly drunk; (confundirse) get confused

marejada f swell; (fig) wave

mareo m sickness; (en el mar) seasickness; (aturdimiento) dizziness; (confusión) muddle

marfil m ivory

margarina f margarine

margarita f daisy; (cóctel) margarita

marg|en m margin; (de un ca-

mino) side. ● *f* (*de un río*) bank.
~**inado** *adj* excluded. ● *m* outcast.
al ~**en** (*fig*) outside. ~**inal** *adj*
marginal. ~**inar** *vt* (*excluir*) exclude; (*fijar márgenes*) set margins
mariachi *m* (*Mex*) (*música popular de Jalisco*) Mariachi music; (*conjunto*) Mariachi band; (*músico*)
Mariachi musician

---

mariachi The word can mean the traditional Mexican musical ensemble, the musicians and the lively mestizo music they play. *Mariachis* wearing costumes based on those worn by *charros* can be seen in the Plaza Garibaldi, in Mexico City, where they are hired for parties, or to sing *mañanitas* or serenades.

---

maric|a *m* 🔲 sissy 🔲. ~**ón** *m* 🔲
homosexual, queer 🔲; (*LAm, cobarde*) wimp
marido *m* husband
mariguana *f*, **marihuana** *f* marijuana
marimacho *f* mannish woman
marimba *f* (*type of*) drum (*LAm, especie de xilofón*) marimba
marin|a *f* navy; (*barcos*) fleet;
(*cuadro*) seascape. ~**a de guerra**
navy. ~**a mercante** merchant
navy. ~**ería** *f* seamanship; (*marineros*) sailors. ~**ero** *adj* marine;
(*barco*) seaworthy. ● *m* sailor. **a la**
~**era** in tomato and garlic sauce.
~**o** *adj* marine
marioneta *f* puppet. ~**s** *fpl* puppet show
maripos|a *f* butterfly. ~**a nocturna** moth. ~**ear** *vi* be fickle;
(*galantear*) flirt. ~**ón** *m* flirt
mariquita *f* ladybird (*Brit*), ladybug (*Amer*). ● *m* 🔲 sissy 🔲

mariscador *m* shell-fisher
mariscal *m* marshal
maris|car *vt* fish for shellfish.
~**co** *m* seafood, shellfish. ~**quero**
m (*pescador de mariscos*) seafood fisherman; (*vendedor de mariscos*)
seafood seller
marital *adj* marital; (*vida*) married
marítimo *adj* maritime; (*ciudad etc*) coastal, seaside
marmita *f* cooking pot
mármol *m* marble
marmota *f* marmot
maroma *f* rope; (*Mex, voltereta*)
somersault
marqu|és *m* marquess. ~**esa** *f*
marchioness. ~**esina** *f* glass canopy; (*en estadio*) roof
marran|a *f* sow. ~**ada** *f* filthy
thing; (*cochinada*) dirty trick. ~**o**
adj filthy. ● *m* hog
marrón *adj & m* brown
marroqu|í *adj & m & f* Moroccan.
● *m* (*leather*) morocco. ~**inería** *f*
leather goods
Marruecos *m* Morocco
marsopa *f* porpoise
marsupial *adj & m* marsupial
marta *f* marten
martajar *vt* (*Mex*) crush (*maíz*)
Marte *m* Mars
martes *m invar* Tuesday. ~ **de carnaval** Shrove Tuesday
martill|ar *vt* hammer. ~**azo** *m*
blow with a hammer. ~**ear** *vt*
hammer. ~**eo** *m* hammering. ~**o**
m hammer
martín *m* **pescador** kingfisher
martinete *m* (*del piano*) hammer;
(*ave*) heron
martingala *f* (*ardid*) trick
mártir *m & f* martyr
martir|io *m* martyrdom; (*fig*) tor-

marxismo | maternal

ment. **~izar** 10 vt martyr; (fig) torment, torture

marxis|mo m Marxism. **~ta** adj &
m & f Marxist

marzo m March

más adv & adj (comparativo) more;
(superlativo) most. **~ caro** dearer.
~ doloroso more painful. **el ~
caro** the dearest; (de dos) the
dearer. **el ~ curioso** the most
curious; (de dos) the more curious.
● prep plus. ● m plus (sign). **~ bien**
rather. **~ de** (cantidad indetermi-
nada) more than. **~ o menos**
more or less. **~ que** more than.
~ y ~ more and more. **a lo ~** at
(the) most. **dos ~ dos** two plus
two. **de ~** too many. **es ~** moreover. **nadie ~** nobody else. **no ~**
no more

masa f mass; (Culin) dough. **en ~**
en masse

masacre f massacre

masaj|e m massage. **~ear** vt mas-
sage. **~ista** m masseur. ● f mas-
seuse

mascada f (Mex) scarf

mascar 7 vt chew

máscara f mask

mascar|ada f masquerade. **~illa**
f mask. **~ón** m (Naut) figurehead

mascota f mascot

masculin|idad f masculinity.
~o adj masculine; (sexo) male. ●
m masculine

mascullar 3 vt mumble

masilla f putty

masivo adj massive, large-scale

mas|ón m Freemason. **~onería** f
Freemasonry. **~ónico** adj Masonic

masoquis|mo m masochism.
~ta adj masochistic. ● m & f maso-
chist

mastica|ción f chewing. **~r** 7

vt chew

mástil m (Naut) mast; (de bandera)
flagpole; (de guitarra, violín) neck

mastín m mastiff

mastodonte m mastodon; (fig)
giant

masturba|ción f masturbation.
~rse vpr masturbate

mata f (arbusto) bush; (LAm,
planta) plant

matad|ero m slaughterhouse.
~or adj killing. ● m (torero) mata-
dor

matamoscas m invar fly swatter

mata|nza f killing. **~r** vt kill (per-
sonas); slaughter (reses). **~rife** m
butcher. **~rse** vpr kill o.s.; (en un
accidente) be killed; (Mex, para un
examen) cram. **~rse trabajando**
work like mad

mata|polillas m invar moth killer.
~rratas m invar rat poison

matasanos m invar quack

matasellos m invar postmark

mate adj matt. ● m (ajedrez)
(check)mate (LAm, bebida) maté

matemátic|as fpl mathematics,
maths (Brit), math (Amer). **~o** adj
mathematical. ● m mathematician

materia f matter; (material) material; (LAm, asignatura) subject. **~
prima** raw material. **en ~ de** on
the question of

material adj & m material. **~idad**
f material nature. **~ismo** m materi-
alism. **~ista** adj materialistic. ●
& f materialist; (Mex, constructor)
building contractor. **~izar** 10 vt
materialize. **~izarse** vpr materialize. **~mente** adv materially; (absolutamente) absolutely

matern|al adj maternal; (amor)
motherly. **~idad** f motherhood;
(hospital) maternity hospital; (sala)

maternity ward. **~o** adj motherly; (lengua) mother

matin|al adj morning. **~ée** m matinée

matiz m shade; (fig) nuance.
~ación f combination of colours.
~ar [10] vt blend (colores); (introducir variedad) vary; (teñir) tinge (**de** with)

mat|ón m bully; (de barrio) thug.
~onismo m bullying; (de barrio) thuggery

matorral m scrub; (conjunto de matas) thicket

matraca f rattle. **dar ~** pester

matraz m flask

matriarca f matriarch. **~do** m matriarchy. **~l** adj matriarchal

matr|ícula f (lista) register, list; (inscripción) registration; (Auto) registration number; (placa) licence plate. **~icular** vt register. **~icularse** vpr enrol, register

matrimoni|al adj matrimonial.
~o m marriage; (pareja) married couple

matriz f matrix; (molde) mould; (útero) womb, uterus

matrona f matron; (partera) midwife

matutino adj morning

maull|ar vi miaow. **~ido** m miaow

mausoleo m mausoleum

maxilar adj maxillary. ● m jaw(bone)

máxim|a f maxim. **~e** adv especially. **~o** adj maximum; (punto) highest. ● m maximum

maya f daisy. ● adj Mayan. ● m & f (persona) Maya

mayo m May

mayonesa f mayonnaise

mayor adj (más grande, comparativo) bigger; (más grande, superlativo) biggest; (de edad, comparativo) older; (de edad, superlativo) oldest; (adulto) grown-up; (principal) main, major; (Mus) major. ● m & f (adulto) adult. **al por ~** wholesale. **~al** m foreman. **~azgo** m entailed estate

mayordomo m butler

mayor|ía f majority. **~ista** m & f wholesaler. **~itario** adj majority; (socio) principal. **~mente** adv especially

mayúscul|a f capital (letter). **~o** adj capital; (fig, grande) big

mazacote m hard mass

mazapán m marzipan

mazmorra f dungeon

mazo m mallet; (manojo) bunch; (LAm, de naipes) pack (Brit), deck (Amer)

mazorca f cob. **~ de maíz** corncob

me pron (acusativo) me; (dativo) (to) me; (reflexivo) (to) myself

mecánic|a f mechanics. **~o** adj mechanical. ● m mechanic

mecani|smo m mechanism.
~zación f mechanization. **~zar** [10] vt mechanize

mecanograf|ía f typing. **~iado** adj typed, typewritten. **~iar** [20] vt type

mecanógrafo m typist

mecate m (Mex) string; (más grueso) rope

mecedora f rocking chair

mecenas m & f invar patron

mecer [9] vt rock; swing (columpio). **~se** vpr rock; (en un columpio) swing

mecha f (de vela) wick; (de explosivo) fuse. **~s** fpl highlights

mechar vt stuff, lard

mechero m (cigarette) lighter

mechón m (de pelo) lock

medall|a f medal. **~ón** m medallion; (relicario) locket

media f stocking; (promedio) average. a **~s** half each

mediación f mediation

mediado adj half full; (a mitad de) halfway through. **~s** mpl. a **~s de marzo** in mid-March

mediador m mediator

medialuna f (pl **medialunas**) croissant

median|amente adv fairly. **~a** f (Auto) central reservation (Brit), median strip (Amer). **~era** f party wall. **~ero** adj (muro) party. **~o** adj medium; (mediocre) average, mediocre

medianoche f (pl **medianoches**) midnight; (Culin) type of roll

mediante prep through, by means of

mediar vi mediate; (llegar a la mitad) be halfway through; (interceder) intercede (**por** for)

medic|ación f medication. **~amento** m medicine. **~ina** f medicine. **~inal** adj medicinal

medición f measurement

médico adj medical. ● m doctor. **~ de cabecera** GP, general practitioner

medid|a f measurement; (unidad) measure; (disposición) measure, step; (prudencia) moderation. a la **~a** made to measure. a **~a que** as. **en cierta ~a** to a certain extent. **~or** m (LAm) meter

medieval adj medieval. **~ista** m & f medievalist

medio adj half (a); (mediano) average. **dos horas y media** two and a

half hours. **~ litro** half a litre. **las dos y media** half past two. ● m middle; (Math) half; (manera) means; (en deportes) half(-back). **en ~** in the middle (**de** of). **por ~ de** through. **~ ambiente** m environment

medioambiental adj environmental

mediocr|e adj mediocre. **~idad** f mediocrity

mediodía m midday, noon; (sur) south

medioevo m Middle Ages

Medio Oriente m Middle East

medir 5 vt measure; weigh up (palabras etc). ● vi measure, be. **¿cuánto mide de alto?** how tall is it? **~se** vpr (moderarse) measure o.s.; (Mex, probarse) try on

medita|bundo adj thoughtful. **~ción** f meditation. **~r** vt think about. ● vi meditate

mediterráneo adj Mediterranean

Mediterráneo m Mediterranean

médium m & f medium

médula f marrow

medusa f jellyfish

megáfono m megaphone

megalómano m megalomaniac

mejicano adj & m Mexican

Méjico m Mexico

mejilla f cheek

mejillón m mussel

mejor adj & adv (comparativo) better; (superlativo) best. **~ dicho** rather. **a lo ~** perhaps. **tanto ~** so much the better. a **~** f improvement. **~able** adj improvable. **~amiento** m improvement

mejorana f marjoram

mejorar vt improve, better. ● vi

get better. **~se** vpr get better

mejunje m mixture

melancolía f melancholy. **~ólico** adj melancholic

melaza f molasses

melen|a f long hair; (de león) mane. **~udo** adj long-haired

melindr|es mpl affectation. hacer **~es con la comida** be picky about food. **~oso** adj affected

mellizo adj & m twin

melocot|ón m peach. **~onero** m peach tree

mel|odía f melody. **~ódico** adj melodic. **~odioso** adj melodious

melodrama m melodrama. **~ático** adj melodramatic

melómano m music lover

melón m melon

meloso adj sickly-sweet; (canción) slushy

membran|a f membrane. **~oso** adj membranous

membrete m letterhead

membrill|ero m quince tree. **~o** m quince

memo adj stupid. ● m idiot

memorable adj memorable

memorando m, **memorándum** m notebook; (nota) memorandum, memo

memori|a f memory; (informe) report; (tesis) thesis. **~as** fpl (autobiografía) memoirs. **de ~a** by heart; (citar) from memory. **~al** m memorial. **~ón** m good memory. **~zación** f memorizing. **~zar** 10 vt memorize

menaje m household goods. **~ de cocina** kitchenware

menci|ón f mention. **~onado** adj aforementioned. **~onar** vt mention

mendi|cidad f begging. **~gar** 12 vt beg for. ● vi beg. **~go** m beggar

mendrugo m piece of stale bread

mene|ar vt wag (rabo); shake (cabeza); wiggle (caderas). **~arse** vpr move; (con inquietud) fidget; (balancearse) swing. **~o** m movement; (sacudida) shake

menester m occupation. ser **~** be necessary. **~oso** adj needy

menestra f vegetable stew

mengano m so-and-so

mengua f decrease; (falta) lack. **~do** adj diminished. **~nte** adj (luna) waning; (marea) ebb. **~r** 15 vt/i decrease, diminish

meningitis f meningitis

menjurje m mixture

menopausia f menopause

menor (adj (más pequeño, comparativo) smaller; (más pequeño, superlativo) smallest; (más joven, comparativo) younger; (más joven, superlativo) youngest; (Mus) minor. ● m & f (menor de edad) minor. **al por ~** retail

menos adj (comparativo) less; (comparativo, con plural) fewer; (superlativo) least; (superlativo, con plural) fewest. ● adv (comparativo) less; (superlativo) least. ● prep except. **al ~** at least. **a ~ que** unless. **las dos ~ diez** ten to two. **ni mucho ~** far from it. **por lo ~** at least. **~cabar** vt lessen; (fig, estropear) damage. **~cabo** m lessening. **~preciable** adj contemptible. **~preciar** vt despise. **~precio** m contempt

mensaje m message. **~ro** m messenger

menso adj (LAm, fam) stupid

menstru|ación f menstruation. **~al** adj menstrual. **~ar** [21] vi menstruate

mensual adj monthly. **~idad** f monthly pay; (cuota) monthly payment

mensurable adj measurable

menta f mint

mental adj mental. **~idad** f mentality. **~mente** adv mentally

mentar [1] vt mention, name

mente f mind

mentecato adj stupid. • m idiot

mentir [4] vi lie. **~a** f lie. **~ijillas** fpl. **de ~ijillas** for a joke. **~oso** adj lying. • m liar

mentís m invar denial

mentor m mentor

menú m menu

menud|ear vi happen frequently; (Mex, Com) sell retail. **~encia** f trifle. **~encias** fpl (LAm) giblets. **~eo** m (Mex) retail trade. **~illos** mpl giblets. **~o** adj small; (lluvia) fine. **a ~o** often. **~os** mpl giblets

meñique adj (dedo) little. • m little finger

meollo m (médula) marrow; (de tema etc) heart

merca|chifle m hawker; (fig) profiteer. **~der** m merchant. **~dería** f (LAm) merchandise. **~do** m market. **M~do Común** Common Market. **~do negro** black market

mercan|cía(s) f(pl) goods, merchandise. **~te** adj merchant. • m merchant ship. **~til** adj mercantile, commercial. **~tilismo** m mercantilism

merced f favour. **su/vuestra ~** your honour

mercenario adj & m mercenary

---

mercer|ía f haberdashery (Brit), notions (Amer).

mercurial adj mercurial

mercurio m mercury

merec|edor adj worthy (de of). **~er** [11] vt deserve. **~erse** vpr deserve. **~idamente** adv deservedly. **~ido** adj well deserved. **~imiento** m (mérito) merit

merend|ar [1] vt have as an afternoon snack. • vi have an afternoon snack. **~ero** m snack bar; (lugar) picnic area

merengue m meringue

meridi|ano adj midday; (fig) dazzling. • m meridian. **~onal** adj southern. • m southerner

merienda f afternoon snack

merino adj merino

mérito m merit; (valor) worth

meritorio adj praiseworthy. • m unpaid trainee

merluza f hake

merma f decrease. **~r** vt/i decrease, reduce

mermelada f jam

mero adj mere; (Mex, verdadero) real. • adv (Mex, precisamente) exactly; (Mex, casi) nearly. • m grouper

merode|ador m prowler. **~ar** vi prowl

mes m month

mesa f table; (para escribir o estudiar) desk. **poner la ~** lay the table

mesarse vpr tear at one's hair

meser|a f (LAm) waitress. **~o** m (LAm) waiter

meseta f plateau; (descansillo) landing

Mesías m Messiah

mesilla f, **mesita** f small table. **~**

de noche bedside table

mesón m inn

mesoner|a f landlady. ~o m landlord

mestiz|aje m crossbreeding. ~o adj (persona) half-caste; (animal) cross-bred. ● m (persona) half-caste; (animal) cross-breed

mesura f moderation. ~do adj moderate

meta f goal; (de una carrera) finish

metabolismo m metabolism

metafisic|a f metaphysics. ~o adj metaphysical

met|áfora f metaphor. ~afórico adj metaphorical

met|al m metal; (de la voz) timbre. ~ales mpl (instrumentos de latón) brass. ~álico adj (objeto) metal; (sonido) metallic

metal|urgia f metallurgy. ~úrgico adj metallurgical

metamorfosis f invar metamorphosis

metedura de pata f blunder

mete|órico adj meteoric. ~orito m meteorite. ~oro m meteor. ~orología f meteorology. ~orológico adj meteorological. ~oró logo m meteorologist

meter vt put; score (un gol); (enredar) involve; (causar) make. ~se vpr get involved (en in); (entrometerse) meddle. ~se con uno pick a quarrel with s.o.

meticulos|idad f meticulousness. ~o adj meticulous

metida de pata f (LAm) blunder

metido m reprimand. ● adj. ~ en años getting on. estar ~ en algo be involved in sth. estar muy ~ con uno be well in with s.o.

metódico adj methodical

metodis|mo m Methodism. ~ta adj & m & f Methodist

método m method

metodología f methodology

metraje m length. de largo ~ (película) feature

metrall|a f shrapnel. ~eta f submachine gun

métric|a f metrics. ~o adj metric; (verso) metrical

metro m metre; (tren) underground (Brit), subway (Amer). ~ cuadrado square metre

metrónomo m metronome

metr|ópoli f metropolis. ~opolitano adj metropolitan. ● m metropolitan; (tren) underground (Brit), subway (Amer)

mexicano adj & m Mexican

México m Mexico. ~ D. F. Mexico City

mezcal m (Mex) mescal

mezc|la f (acción) mixing; (substancia) mixture; (argamasa) mortar. ~lador m mixer. ~lar vt mix; shuffle (los naipes). ~larse vpr mix; (intervenir) interfere. ~olanza f mixture

mezquin|dad f meanness. ~o adj mean; (escaso) meagre. ● m mean person

mezquita f mosque

mi adj my. ● m (Mus) E; (solfa) mi

mí pron me

miau m miaow

mica f (silicato) mica

mico m (long-tailed) monkey

micro|bio m microbe. ~biología f microbiology. ~cosmos m invar microcosm. ~film(e) m microfilm

micrófono m microphone

microonda f microwave. ~s m invar microwave oven

microordenador *m* microcomputer

micros|cópico *adj* microscopic. **~copio** *m* microscope. **~urco** *m* long-playing record

miedo *m* fear (**a** for). **dar ~** frighten. **morirse de ~** be scared to death. **tener ~** be frightened. **~so** *adj* fearful

miel *f* honey

miembro *m* limb; (*persona*) member

mientras *conj* while. ● *adv* meanwhile. **~ que** whereas. **~ tanto** in the meantime

miércoles *m invar* Wednesday. **~ de ceniza** Ash Wednesday

mierda *f* (🔲) shit

mies *f* ripe, grain

miga *f* crumb; (*fig, meollo*) essence. **~jas** *fpl* crumbs; (*sobras*) scraps. **~r** 🔢 *vt* crumble

migra|ción *f* migration. **~torio** *adj* migratory

mijo *m* millet

mil *adj & m* a/one thousand. **~es de** thousands of. **~ novecientos noventa y nueve** nineteen ninety-nine. **~ euros** a thousand euros

milagro *m* miracle. **~so** *adj* miraculous

milen|ario *adj* millenial. **~io** *m* millennium

milésimo *adj & m* thousandth

mili *f* (🔲) military service. **~cia** *f* soldiering; (*gente armada*) militia

mili|gramo *m* milligram. **~litro** *m* millilitre

milímetro *m* millimetre

militante *adj & m & f* activist

militar *adj* military. ● *m* soldier. **~ismo** *m* militarism. **~ista** *adj* militaristic. ● *m & f* militarist.

~izar 🔟 *vt* militarize

milla *f* mile

millar *m* thousand. **a ~es** by the thousand

mill|ón *m* million. **un ~ón de libros** a million books. **~onada** *f* fortune. **~onario** *m* millionaire. **~onésimo** *adj & m* millionth

milonga *f* popular dance and music from the River Plate region

milpa *f* (*Mex*) maize field, cornfield (*Amer*)

milpiés *m invar* woodlouse

mimar *vt* spoil

mimbre *m & f* wicker. **~arse** *vpr* sway. **~ra** *f* osier. **~ral** *m* osierbed

mimetismo *m* mimicry

mímic|a *f* mime. **~o** *adj* mimic

mimo *m* mime; (*adj un niño*) spoiling; (*caricia*) cuddle

mimosa *f* mimosa

mina *f* mine. **~r** *vt* mine; (*fig*) undermine

minarete *m* minaret

mineral *m* mineral; (*mena*) ore. **~ogía** *f* mineralogy. **~ogista** *m & f* mineralogist

miner|ía *f* mining. **~o** *adj* mining. ● *m* miner

miniatura *f* miniature

minifundio *m* smallholding

minimizar 🔟 *vt* minimize

mínim|o *adj & m* minimum. **como ~** at least. **~um** *m* minimum

minino *m* (🔲) cat, puss (🔲)

minist|erial *adj* ministerial; (*reunión*) cabinet. **~erio** *m* ministry. **~ro** *m* minister

minor|ia *f* minority. **~idad** *f* minority. **~ista** *m & f* retailer

minuci|a *f* trifle. **~osidad** *f* thoroughness. **~oso** *adj* thorough; (*de-*

tallado) detailed

minúscul|a *f* lower case letter. **~o** *adj* tiny

minuta *f* draft copy; (*de abogado*) bill

minut|ero *m* minute hand. **~o** *m* minute

mío *adj & pron* mine. **un amigo ~** a friend of mine

miop|e *adj* short-sighted. ● *m & f* short-sighted person. **~ía** *f* short-sightedness

mira *f* sight; (*fig, intención*) aim. **a la ~** on the lookout. **con ~s a** with a view to. **~da** *f* look. **echar una ~da** a glance at. **~do** *adj* careful with money; (*comedido*) considerate. **bien ~do** highly regarded. **no estar bien ~do** be frowned upon. **~dor** *m* viewpoint. **~miento** *m* consideration. **~r** *vt* look at; (*observar*) watch; (*considerar*) consider. **~r fijamente a** stare at. ● *vi* look (edificio etc). **~r hacia** face. **~rse** *vpr* (personas) look at each other

mirilla *f* peephole

miriñaque *m* crinoline

mirlo *m* blackbird

mirón *adj* nosey. ● *m* nosey-parker; (*espectador*) onlooker

mirto *m* myrtle

misa *f* mass. **~l** *m* missal

misántropo *m* misanthropist

miscelánea *f* miscellany; (*Mex, tienda*) corner shop (*Brit*), small general store (*Amer*)

miser|able *adj* very poor; (*lastimoso*) miserable; (*tacaño*) mean. **~ia** *f* extreme poverty; (*suciedad*) squalor

misericordi|a *f* pity; (*piedad*) mercy. **~oso** *adj* merciful

mísero *adj* miserable; (*tacaño*)

mean; (*malvado*) wicked

misil *m* missile

misi|ón *f* mission. **~onero** *m* missionary

misiva *f* missive

mism|ísimo *adj* very same. **~o** *adj* same; (*después de pronombre personal*) myself, yourself, himself, herself, itself, ourselves, yourselves, themselves; (*enfático*) very. ● *adv*. **ahora ~** right now. **aquí ~** right here. **lo ~** the same

misterio *m* mystery. **~so** *adj* mysterious

místic|a *f* mysticism. **~o** *adj* mystical. ● *m* mystic

mistifica|ción *f* mystification. **~r 7** *vt* mystify

mitad *f* half; (*centro*) middle. **cortar algo por la ~** cut sth in half

mitigar 12 *vt* mitigate; quench (sed); relieve (dolor etc)

mitin, mítin *m* meeting

mito *m* myth. **~logía** *f* mythology. **~lógico** *adj* mythological

mitón *m* mitten

mitote *m* (*Mex*) Aztec dance

mixt|o *adj* mixed. **educación mixta** coeducation

mobbing *m* harassment

mobiliario *m* furniture

moce|dad *f* youth. **~río** *m* young people. **~tón** *m* strapping lad. **~tona** *f* strapping girl

mochales *adj invar*. **estar ~** be round the bend

mochila *f* rucksack

mocho *adj* blunt. ● *m* butt end

mochuelo *m* little owl

moción *f* motion

moco *m* mucus. **limpiarse los ~s** blow one's nose

moda *f* fashion. **estar de ~** be in

fashion. ~l *adj* modal. ~les *mpl* manners. ~lidad *f* kind

model|ado *m* modelling. ~ador *m* modeller. ~ar *vt* model; (*fig*, *configurar*) form. ~o *m & f* model

módem *m* modem

modera|ción *f* moderation. ~do *adj* moderate. ~r *vt* moderate; reduce (velocidad). ~rse *vpr* control oneself

modern|idad *f* modernity. ~ismo *m* modernism. ~ista *m & f* modernist. ~izar 🔟 *vt* modernize. ~o *adj* modern; (a la moda) fashionable

modest|ia *f* modesty. ~o *adj* modest

módico *adj* moderate

modifica|ción *f* modification. ~r 🔽 *vt* modify

modismo *m* idiom

modist|a *f* dressmaker. ~o *m* designer

modo *m* manner, way; (*Gram*) mood; (*Mus*) mode. ~ de ser character. de ~ que so that. de ningún ~ certainly not. de todos ~s anyhow. ni ~ (*LAm*) no way

modorra *f* drowsiness

modula|ción *f* modulation. ~dor *m* modulator. ~r *vt* modulate

módulo *m* module

mofa *f* mockery. ~rse *vpr*. ~rse de make fun of

mofeta *f* skunk

moflet|e *m* chubby cheek. ~udo *adj* with chubby cheeks

mohín *m* grimace. hacer un ~ pull a face

moho *m* mould; (*óxido*) rust. ~so *adj* mouldy; (*metales*) rusty

moisés *m* Moses basket

mojado *adj* wet

mojar *vt* wet; (*empapar*) soak; (*humedecer*) moisten, dampen

mojigat|ería *f* prudishness. ~o *m* prude. ● *adj* prudish

mojón *m* boundary post; (*señal*) signpost

molar *m* molar

mold|e *m* mould; (*aguja*) knitting needle. ~ear *vt* mould, shape; (*fig*) form. ~ura *f* moulding

mole *f* mass, bulk. ● *m* (*Mex, salsa*) chili sauce with chocolate and sesame

mol|écula *f* molecule. ~ecular *adj* molecular

mole|dor *adj* grinding. ● *m* grinder. ~r 🔟 *vt* grind

molest|ar *vt* annoy; (*incomodar*) bother. ¿le ~a que fume? do you mind if I smoke? ● *vi* be a nuisance. no ~ar do not disturb. ~arse *vpr* bother; (*ofenderse*) take offence. ~ia *f* bother, nuisance; (*inconveniente*) inconvenience; (*incomodidad*) discomfort. ~o *adj* annoying; (*inconveniente*) inconvenient; (*ofendido*) offended

molicie *f* softness; (*excesiva comodidad*) easy life

molido *adj* ground; (*fig*, *muy cansado*) worn out

molienda *f* grinding

molin|ero *m* miller. ~ete *m* toy windmill. ~illo *m* mill; (*juguete*) toy windmill. ~o *m* mill. ~ de agua watermill. ~o de viento windmill

molleja *f* gizzard

mollera *f* (*de la cabeza*) crown; (*fig, sesera*) brains

molusco *m* mollusc

moment|áneamente *adv* momentarily. ~áneo *adj* (*breve*) mo-

mentary; (*pasajero*) temporary. **~o**
m moment; (*ocasión*) time. **al ~o**
at once. **de ~o** for the moment

momia *f* mummy. **~ficar 7** *vt*
mummify. **~ficarse** *vpr* become
mummified

monacal *adj* monastic

monada *f* beautiful thing; (*niño
bonito*) cute kid; (*acción tonta*) silliness

monaguillo *m* altar boy

monarca *m & f* monarch. **~arquía** *f* monarchy. **~árquico** *adj* monarchical

monasterio *m* monastery

monda *f* peeling; (*piel*) peel.
~adientes *m invar* toothpick.
~adura *f* peeling; (*piel*) peel. **~ar** *vt* peel (fruta etc). **~o** *adj* (*sin pelo*) bald

mondongo *m* innards

moneda *f* coin; (*de un país*) currency. **~ero** *m* purse (*Brit*), change purse (*Amer*)

monetario *adj* monetary

mongolismo *m* Down's syndrome

monigote *m* weak character;
(*muñeco*) rag doll; (*dibujo*) doodle

monitor *m* monitor

monja *f* nun. **~e** *m* monk. **~il** *adj* nun's; (*como de monja*) like a nun

mono *m* monkey; (*sobretodo*) overalls. ● *adj* pretty

monocromo *adj & m* monochrome

monogamia *f* monogamy.
~ógamo *adj* monogamous

monografía *f* monograph.
~ma *m* monogram

monologar 12 *vi* soliloquize.
~ólogo *m* monologue

monoplano *m* monoplane

monopoli|o *m* monopoly. **~zar
10** *vt* monopolize

monos|ilábico *adj* monosyllabic.
~ílabo *m* monosyllable

monoteís|mo *m* monotheism.
~ta *adj* monotheistic. ● *m & f* monotheist

monotonía *f* monotony.
~ótono *adj* monotonous

monseñor *m* monsignor

monstruo *m* monster. **~sidad** *f* monstrosity; (*atrocidad*) atrocity.
~so *adj* monstrous

monta *f* mounting; (*valor*) total value

montacargas *m invar* service lift
(*Brit*), service elevator (*Amer*)

monta|dor *m* fitter. **~je** *m* assembly; (*Cine*) montage; (*teatro*) staging, production

montaña *f* mountain. **~a rusa** roller coaster. **~ero** *adj* mountaineer. **~és** *adj* mountain. ● *m* highlander. **~ismo** *m* mountaineering.
~oso *adj* mountainous

montaplatos *m invar* dumb waiter

montar *vt* ride; (*subirse a*) get on;
(*ensamblar*) assemble; cock (arma);
set up (una casa, un negocio). ● *vi* ride; (*subirse*) mount. **~ a caballo** ride a horse

monte *m* (*montaña*) mountain;
(*terreno inculto*) scrub; (*bosque*) woodland. **~ de piedad** pawnshop

montepío *m* charitable fund for dependents

montés *adj* wild

montevideano *adj & m* Montevidean

montículo *m* hillock

montón *m* heap, pile. **a montones** in abundance. **un ~ de**

ombligo *m* navel

omi|sión *f* omission. **~tir** *vt* omit

ómnibus *adj* omnibus

omnipotente *adj* omnipotent

omóplato *m* shoulder blade

once *adj* & *m* eleven

ond|a *f* wave. **~a corta** short wave. **~a larga** long wave. **longitud** *f* **de ~a** wavelength. **~ear** *vi* wave; (agua) ripple. **~ulación** *f* undulation; (del pelo) wave. **~ular** *vi* wave

onomásti|co *adj* (índice) of names. ● *m* (*LAm*) saint's day

onomástica See **▷SANTO**

ONU *abrev* (**Organización de las Naciones Unidas**) UN

OPA *f* take-over bid

opac|ar **7** (*LAm*) make opaque; (deslucir) mar; (anular) overshadow. **~o** *adj* opaque; (*fig*) dull

opci|ón *f* option. **~onal** *adj* optional

open-jaw *m* open jaws ticket

ópera *f* opera

opera|ción *f* operation; (*Com*) transaction; **~ retorno** (*Esp*) return to work (after the holidays). **~dor** *m* operator; (*TV*) cameraman, (*Mex, obrero*) machinist. **~r** *vt* operate on; work (milagro etc); (*Mex*) operate (máquina). ● *vi* operate; (*Com*) deal. **~rio** *m* machinist. **~rse** *vpr* take place; (*Med*) have an operation. **~torio** *adj* operative

opereta *f* operetta

opin|ar *vi* express one's opinion. ● *vt* think. **~ que** think that. **¿qué opinas?** what do you think? **~ión** *f* opinion. **la ~ión pública** public opinion

opio *m* opium

opone|nte *adj* opposing. ● *m & f* opponent. **~r** *vt* oppose; offer (resistencia); raise (objeción). **~rse** *vpr* be opposed; (dos personas) oppose each other

oporto *m* port (wine)

oportun|idad *f* opportunity; (cualidad de oportuno) timeliness; (*LAm, ocasión*) occasion. **~ista** *m & f* opportunist. **~o** *adj* opportune; (apropiado) suitable

oposi|ción *f* opposition. **~ciones** *fpl* public examination. **~tor** *m* candidate; (*Pol*) opponent

opres|ión *f* oppression; (ahogo) difficulty in breathing. **~ivo** *adj* oppressive. **~or** *m* oppressor

oprimir *vt* squeeze; press (botón etc); (ropa) be too tight for; (*fig*) oppress

optar *vi* choose. **~ por** opt for

óptic|a *f* optics; (tienda) optician's (shop). **~o** *adj* optic(al). ● *m* optician

optimis|mo *m* optimism. **~ta** *adj* optimistic. ● *m & f* optimist

óptimo *adj* ideal; (condiciones) perfect

opuesto *adj* opposite; (opiniones) conflicting

opulen|cia *f* opulence. **~to** *adj* opulent

oración *f* prayer; (*Gram*) sentence

ora|dor *m* speaker. **~l** *adj* oral

órale *int* (*Mex*) come on!; (de acuerdo) OK!

orar *vi* pray (**por** for)

órbita *f* orbit

orden *f* order. **~ del día** agenda. **órdenes** *fpl* sagradas Holy Orders. **a sus órdenes** (*esp Mex*) can I help you? **~ de arresto** arrest warrant. **en ~** in order. **por ~** in turn.

~ado adj tidy

ordenador m computer

ordena|nza f ordinance. ● m (Mil) orderly. **~r** vt put in order; (mandar) order; (Relig) ordain; (LAm, en restaurante) order

ordeñar vt milk

ordinario adj ordinary; (grosero) common; (de mala calidad) poor-quality

orear vt air

orégano m oregano

oreja f ear

orfanato m orphanage

orfebre m goldsmith, silversmith

orfeón m choral society

orgánico adj organic

organillo m barrel-organ

organismo m organism

organista m & f organist

organiza|ción f organization. **~dor** m organizer. **~r 10** vt organize. **~rse** vpr get organized

órgano m organ

orgasmo m orgasm

orgía f orgy

orgullo m pride. **~so** adj proud

orientación f orientation; (guía) guidance; (Archit) aspect

oriental adj m & f oriental

orientar vt position; advise (persona). **~se** vpr point; (persona) find one's bearings

oriente m east

orificio m hole

orig|en m origin. dar **~en a** give rise to. (excéntrico) odd. **~inalidad** f originality. **~inar** vt give rise to. **~inario** adj original; (nativo) native. ser **~inario de** come from. **~inarse** vpr originate; (incendio) start

orilla f (del mar) shore; (de río) bank; (borde) edge. a **~s del mar** by the sea

orina f urine. **~l** m chamber-pot. **~r** vi urinate

oriundo adj native. ser **~ de** (persona) come from; (especie etc) native to

ornamental adj ornamental

ornitología f ornithology

oro m gold. **~s** mpl Spanish card suit. **~ de ley** 9 carat gold. hacerse de **~** make a fortune. prometer el **~ y el moro** promise the moon

orquesta f orchestra. **~l** adj orchestral. **~r** vt orchestrate

orquídea f orchid

ortiga f nettle

ortodoxo adj orthodox

ortografía f spelling

ortopédico adj orthopaedic

oruga f caterpillar

orzuelo m sty

os pron (acusativo) you; (dativo) (to) you; (reflexivo) (to) yourselves; (recíproco) (to) each other

osad|ía f boldness. **~o** adj bold

oscila|ción f swinging; (de precios) fluctuation; (Tec) oscillation. **~r** vi swing; (precio) fluctuate; (Tec) oscillate

oscur|ecer 11 vi get dark. ● vt darken; (fig) obscure. **~ecerse** vpr grow dark; (nublarse) cloud over. **~idad** f darkness; (fig) obscurity. **~o** adj dark; (fig) obscure. a **~as** in the dark

óseo adj bone

oso m bear. **~ de felpa**, **~ de peluche** teddy bear

ostensible adj obvious

ostent|ación f ostentation. **~ar**

vt show off; (*mostrar*) show. **~oso** *adj* ostentatious

osteópata *m & f* osteopath

ostión *m* (*esp Mex*) oyster

ostra *f* oyster

ostracismo *m* ostracism

Otan *abrev* (**Organización del Tratado del Atlántico Norte**) NATO, North Atlantic Treaty Organization

otitis *f* inflammation of the ear

otoño *m* autumn (*Brit*), fall (*Amer*)

otorga|miento *m* granting. **~r** 🔢 *vt* give; grant (*préstamo*); (*Jurid*) draw up (*testamento*)

otorrinolaringólogo *m* ear, nose and throat specialist

otro, otra

● *adjetivo*

····▸ another; (*con artículo, posesivo*) other. **come ~ pedazo** have another piece. **el ~ día** the other day. **mi ~ coche** my other car. **otra cosa** something else. **otra persona** somebody else. **otra vez** again

····▸ (*en plural*) other; (*con numeral*) another. **en otras ocasiones** on other occasions. **~s 3 vasos** another 3 glasses

····▸ (*siguiente*) next. **al ~ día** the next day. **me bajo en la otra estación** I get off at the next station

● *pronombre*

····▸ (*cosa*) another one. **lo cambié por ~** I changed it for another one

····▸ (*persona*) someone else. **invitó a ~** she invited someone else

····▸ (*en plural*) (some) others. **tengo ~s en casa** I have

(some) others at home. **~s piensan lo contrario** others think the opposite

····▸ (*con artículo*) **el ~** the other one. **los ~s** the others. **uno detrás del ~** one after the other. **los ~s no vinieron** the others didn't come. **esta semana no, la otra** not this week, next week. **de un día para el ~** from one day to the next

➡️ Para usos complementarios ver **uno**, **tanto**

ovación *f* ovation

oval *adj*, **ovalado** *adj* oval

óvalo *m* oval

ovario *m* ovary

oveja *f* sheep; (*hembra*) ewe

overol *m* (*LAm*) overalls

ovillo *m* ball. **hacerse un ~** curl up

OVNI *abrev* (**objeto volante no identificado**) UFO

ovulación *f* ovulation

oxida|ción *f* rusting. **~r** *vi* rust. **~rse** *vpr* go rusty

óxido *m* rust; (*en química*) oxide

oxígeno *m* oxygen

oye *vb véase* **OÍR**

oyente *adj* listening. ● *m & f* listener; (*Univ*) occasional student

ozono *m* ozone

Pp

pabellón m pavilion; (en jardín) summerhouse; (en hospital) block; (de instrumento) bell; (bandera) flag

pacer [11] vi graze

pachucho adj (fruta) overripe; (persona) poorly

pacien|cia f patience. **perder la ~cia** lose patience. **~te** adj & m & f patient

pacificar [7] vt pacify. **~se** vpr calm down

pacífico adj peaceful. **el (Océano) P~** the Pacific (Ocean)

pacifis|mo m pacifism. **~ta** adj & m & f pacifist

pact|ar vi agree, make a pact. **~o** m pact, agreement

padec|er [11] vt/i suffer (de from); (soportar) bear. **~er del corazón** have heart trouble. **~imiento** m suffering

padrastro m stepfather

padre adj [1] terrible; (Mex, estupendo) great. ● m father. **~s** mpl parents

padrino m godfather; (en boda) man who gives away the bride

padrón m register. **~ electoral** (LAm) electoral roll

paella f paella

paga f payment; (sueldo) pay. **~dero** adj payable

pagano adj & m pagan

pagar [12] vt pay; pay for (compras). ● vi pay. **~é** m IOU

página f page

pago m payment

país m country; (ciudadanos) na-

tion. **~ natal** native land. **el P~ Vasco** the Basque Country. **los P~es Bajos** the Low Countries

paisaje m landscape, scenery

paisano m compatriot

paja f straw; (en texto) padding

pájaro m bird. **~ carpintero** woodpecker

paje m page

pala f shovel; (para cavar) spade; (para basura) dustpan; (de pimpón) bat

palabr|a f word; (habla) speech. **pedir la ~a** ask to speak. **tomar la ~a** take the floor. **~ota** f swear-word. **decir ~otas** swear

palacio m palace

paladar m palate

palanca f lever; (fig) influence. **~ de cambio (de velocidades)** gear lever (Brit), gear shift (Amer)

palangana f washbasin (Brit), washbowl (Amer)

palco m (en el teatro) box

palestino adj & m Palestinian

paleta f (de pintor) palette; (de albañil) trowel

paleto m yokel

paliativo adj & m palliative

palide|cer [11] vi turn pale. **~z** f paleness

pálido adj pale. **ponerse ~** turn pale

palillo m (de dientes) toothpick; (para comer) chopstick

paliza f beating

palma f (de la mano) palm; (árbol) palm (tree); (de dátiles) date palm. **dar ~s** clap. **~da** f pat; (LAm) slap. **~das** fpl applause

palmera f palm tree

palmo m span; (fig) few inches. **~ a ~** inch by inch

palmote|ar vi clap. **~o** m clapping, applause

palo m stick; (de valla) post; (de golf) club; (golpe) blow; (de naipes) suit; (mástil) mast

paloma f pigeon; (blanca, símbolo) dove

palomitas fpl popcorn

palpar vt feel

palpita|ción f palpitation. **~nte** adj throbbing. **~r** vi beat; (latir con fuerza) pound; (vena, sien) throb

palta f (LAm) avocado (pear)

paludismo m malaria

pamela f (woman's) broad-brimmed dress hat

pamp|a f pampas. **~ero** adj of the pampas

pan m bread; (barra) loaf. **~ integral** wholewheat bread, wholemeal bread (Brit). **~ tostado** toast. **~ rallado** breadcrumbs. **ganarse el ~ pan** earn one's living

pana f corduroy

panader|ía f bakery; (tienda) baker's (shop). **~o** m baker

panal m honeycomb

panameño adj & m Panamanian

pancarta f banner, placard

panda m panda

pander|eta f (small) tambourine **~o** m tambourine

pandilla f gang

panecillo m (bread) roll

panel m panel

panfleto m pamphlet

pánico m panic. **tener ~** be terrified (a of)

panor|ama m panorama. **~ámico** adj panoramic

panque m (Mex) sponge cake

pantaletas fpl (Mex) panties, knickers (Brit)

pantalla f screen; (de lámpara) (lamp)shade

pantalón m, **pantalones** mpl trousers. **~ a la cadera** bumsters

pantano m marsh; (embalse) reservoir. **~so** adj marshy

pantera f panther

panti m, (Mex) **pantimedias** fpl tights (Brit), pantyhose (Amer)

pantomima f pantomime

pantorrilla f calf

pantufla f slipper

panz|a f belly. **~udo** adj pot-bellied

pañal m nappy (Brit), diaper (Amer)

paño m material; (de lana) woollen cloth; (trapo) cloth. **~ de cocina** dishcloth; (para secar) tea towel. **~ higiénico** sanitary towel. **en ~s menores** in one's underclothes

pañuelo m handkerchief; (de cabeza) scarf

papa m pope. ●f (LAm) potato. **~s fritas** (LAm) chips (Brit), French fries (Amer); (de paquete) crisps (Brit), chips (Amer)

papá m dad(dy). **~s** mpl parents. **P~ Noel** Father Christmas

papada f (de persona) double chin

papagayo m parrot

papalote m (Mex) kite

papanatas m invar simpleton

paparrucha f (tontería) silly thing

papaya f papaya, pawpaw

papel m paper; (en el teatro etc) role. **~ carbón** carbon paper. **~ de calcar** tracing paper. **~ de envolver** wrapping paper. **~ de plata** silver paper. **~ higiénico** toi-

let paper. **~ pintado** wallpaper. **~
secante** blotting paper. **~eo** *m*
paperwork. **~era** *f* waste-paper
basket. **~ería** *f* stationer's (shop).
~eta *f* (*para votar*) (ballot) paper

paperas *fpl* mumps

paquete *m* packet; (*bulto*) parcel;
(*LAm, de papas fritas*) bag; (*Mex,
problema*) headache. **~ postal** parcel

Paquistán *m* Pakistan

paquistaní *adj & m* Pakistani

par *adj* (*número*) even. ● *m* couple;
(*dos cosas iguales*) pair. **a ~es** two
by two. **de ~ en ~** wide open.
~es y nones odds and evens. **sin
~** without equal. ● *f* par. **a la ~**
(*Com*) at par. **a la ~ que** at the
same time

para *preposición*

····▸ for. **es ~ ti** it's for you. **~
siempre** for ever. **¿~ qué?**
what for? **~ mi cumpleaños**
for my birthday

····▸ (*con infinitivo*) to. **es muy
tarde ~ llamar** it's too late to
call. **salió ~ divertirse** he went
out to have fun. **lo hago ~
ahorrar** I do it (in order) to
save money

····▸ (*dirección*) **iba ~ la oficina**
he was going to the office. **em-
pújalo ~ atrás** push it back.
¿vas ~ casa? are you going
home?

····▸ (*tiempo*) by. **debe estar listo
~ el 5** it must be ready by the
5th. **~ entonces** by then

····▸ (*LAm, hora*) to. **son 5 ~ la
una** it's 5 to one

····▸ **~ que** so (that). **grité ~
que me oyera** I shouted so

(that) he could hear me.

Note that **para que** is always
followed by a verb in the subjunctive

---

parabienes *mpl* congratulations

parábola *f* (*narración*) parable

parabólica *f* satellite dish

para|brisas *m invar* windscreen
(*Brit*), windshield (*Amer*). **~caidas** *m
invar* parachute. **~caidista** *m & f*
parachutist; (*Mil*) paratrooper.
~choques *m invar* bumper (*Brit*),
fender (*Amer*) (*Rail*) buffer

parad|a *f* (*acción*) stop; (*lugar*) bus
stop; (*de taxis*) rank; (*Mil*) parade.
~ero *m* whereabouts; (*LAm, lugar*)
bus stop. **~o** *adj* stationary; (*desempleado*) unemployed. **estar ~**
(*LAm, de pie*) be standing

paradoja *f* paradox

parador *m* state-owned hotel

**parador (nacional de
turismo)** *i* A national chain
of hotels in Spain. They are often
converted castles, palaces and
monasteries. They provide a high
standard of accommodation but
are relatively inexpensive and
often act as showcases for local
craftsmanship and cooking.

---

parafina *f* paraffin

paraguas *m invar* umbrella

Paraguay *m* Paraguay

paraguayo *adj & m* Paraguayan

paraíso *m* paradise; (*en el teatro*)
gallery

paralel|a *f* parallel (line). **~as** *fpl*
parallel bars. **~o** *adj & m* parallel

par|álisis *f invar* paralysis. **~alí-
tico** *adj* paralytic. **~alizar** [10] *vt*

paralyse

parámetro *m* parameter

paramilitar *adj* paramilitary

páramo *m* bleak upland

parangón *m* comparison.

paraninfo *m* main hall

paranoi|a *f* paranoia. ~**co** *adj* paranoiac

parar *vt/i* stop. **sin** ~ continuously. ~**se** *vpr* stop; (*LAm, ponerse de pie*) stand

pararrayos *m invar* lightning conductor

parásito *adj* parasitic. ● *m* parasite

parcela *f* plot. ~**r** *vt* divide into plots

parche *m* patch

parcial *adj* partial. **a tiempo** ~ part-time. ~**idad** *f* prejudice

parco *adj* laconic; (*sobrio*) sparing, frugal

parear *vt* put into pairs

parec|er *m* opinion. **al** ~**er** apparently. **a mi** ~**er** in my opinion. ● *vi* 🔟 seem; (*asemejarse*) look like; (*tener aspecto de*) look. **me** ~**e** I think. ~**e fácil** it looks easy. **¿qué te** ~**e?** what do you think? **según** ~**e** apparently. ~**erse** *vpr* resemble, look like. ~**ido** *adj* similar. **bien** ~**ido** good-looking. ● *m* similarity

pared *f* wall. ~ **por medio** next door. ~**ón** *m* (*de fusilamiento*) wall. **llevar al** ~**ón** shoot

parej|a *f* pair; (*hombre y mujer*) couple; (*compañero*) partner. ~**o** *adj* the same; (*LAm, sin desniveles*) even; (*LAm, liso*) smooth; (*Mex, equitativo*) equal. ● *adv* (*LAm*) evenly

parente|la *f* relations. ~**sco** *m* relationship

paréntesis *m invar* parenthesis, bracket (*Brit*); (*intervalo*) break. **entre** ~ in brackets (*Brit*), in parenthesis: (*fig*) by the way

paria *m & f* outcast

paridad *f* equality; (*Com*) parity

pariente *m & f* relation, relative

parir *vt* give birth to. ● *vi* give birth

parisiense *adj & m & f*, **parisino** *adj & m* Parisian

parking /'parkin/ *m* car park (*Brit*), parking lot (*Amer*)

parlament|ar *vi* talk. ~**ario** *adj* parliamentary. ● *m* member of parliament (*Brit*), congressman (*Amer*). ~**o** *m* parliament

parlanchín *adj* talkative. ● *m* chatterbox

parlante *m* (*LAm*) loudspeaker

paro *m* stoppage; (*desempleo*) unemployment; (*subsidio*) unemployment benefit; (*LAm, huelga*) strike. ~ **cardíaco** cardiac arrest

parodia *f* parody

parpadear *vi* blink; (*luz*) flicker

párpado *m* eyelid

parque *m* park. ~ **de atracciones** funfair. ~ **eólico** wind farm. ~ **infantil** playground. ~ **zoológico** zoo, zoological gardens

parquímetro *m* parking meter

parra *f* grapevine

párrafo *m* paragraph

parrilla *f* grill; (*LAm, Auto*) luggage rack. **a la** ~ grilled. ~**da** *f* grill

párroco *m* parish priest

parroquia *f* parish; (*iglesia*) parish church. ~**no** *m* parishioner

parte *m* (*informe*) report. **dar** ~ report. **de mi** ~ for me ●*f* part; (*porción*) share; (*Jurid*) party; (*Mex,*

repuesto spare (part). **de ~ de from.** **¿de ~ de quién?** (al teléfono) who's speaking? **en cualquier ~** anywhere. **en gran ~** largely. **en ~** partly. **en todas ~s** everywhere. **la mayor ~** the majority. **la ~ superior** the top. **ninguna ~** nowhere. **por otra ~** on the other hand. **por todas ~s** everywhere

partera f midwife

partición f division; (Pol) partition

participa|ción f participation; (noticia) announcement; (de lotería) share. **~nte** adj participating. • m & f participant. **~r** vt announce. • vi take part

participio m participle

particular adj particular; (clase) private. **nada de ~** nothing special. • m private individual

partida f departure; (en registro) entry; (documento) certificate; (de mercancías) consignment; (juego) game; (de gente) group

partidario adj & m partisan. **~ de** in favour of

parti|do m (Pol) party; (encuentro) match, game; (de ajedrez) game. **~r** vt cut; (romper) break; crack (nueces). • vi leave. **a ~r de** from. **~se de** start from. **~rse** vpr (romperse) break; (dividirse) split

partitura f (Mus) score

parto m labour. **estar de ~** be in labour

parvulario m kindergarten, nursery school (Brit)

pasa f raisin. **~ de Corinto** currant

pasa|da f passing; (de puntos) row. **de ~da** in passing. **~dero** adj passable. **~dizo** m passage.

~do adj past; (día, mes etc) last; (anticuado) old-fashioned; (comida) bad, off. **~do mañana** the day after tomorrow. **~dos tres días** after three days. **~dor** m bolt; (de pelo) hair-slide

pasaje m passage; (pasajeros) passengers; (LAm, de avión etc) ticket. **~ro** adj passing. • m passenger

pasamano(s) m handrail; (barandilla de escalera) banister(s)

pasamontañas m invar balaclava

pasaporte m passport

pasar vt pass; (atravesar) go through; (filtrar) strain; spend (tiempo); show (película); (tolerar) tolerate; give (mensaje, enfermedad). • vi pass; (suceder) happen; (ir) go; (venir) come; (tiempo) go by. **~ de** have no interest in. **~lo bien** have a good time. **~ frío** be cold. **~ la aspiradora** vacuum. **~ por alto** leave out. **lo que pasa es que** the fact is that. **pase lo que pase** whatever happens. **¡pase Vd!** come in!, go in! **¡que lo pases bien!** have a good time! **¿qué pasa?** what's the matter?, what's happening? **~se** vpr pass; (dolor) go away; (flores) wither; (comida) go bad; spend (tiempo); (excederse) go too far

pasarela f footbridge; (Naut) gangway

pasatiempo m hobby, pastime

Pascua f (fiesta de los hebreos) Passover; (de Resurrección) Easter; (Navidad) Christmas. **~s** fpl Christmas

pase m pass

pase|ante m & f passer-by. **~ar** vt walk (perro); (exhibir) show off. • vi walk. **ir a ~ar, salir a ~ar** walk. **~arse** vpr walk. **~o** m walk; (en coche etc) ride; (calle) avenue. **~o**

marítimo promenade. **dar un ~o**, **ir de ~** go for a walk. **¡vete a ~o!** 🆇 get lost! 🆇

pasillo m corridor; (de cine, avión) aisle

pasión f passion

pasivo adj passive

pasm|ar vt astonish. **~arse** vpr be astonished

paso m step; (acción de pasar) passing; (camino) way; (entre montañas) pass; (estrecho) strait(s). **~ a nivel** level crossing (Brit), grade crossing (Amer). **~ de cebra** zebra crossing. **~ de peatones** pedestrian crossing. **~ elevado** flyover (Brit), overpass (Amer). **a cada ~** at every turn. **a dos ~s** very near. **de ~** in passing. **de ~ por** just passing through. **oír ~s** hear footsteps. **prohibido el ~** no entry

pasota m & f drop-out

pasta f paste; (masa) dough; (sl, dinero) dough 🆇. **~s** fpl pasta; (pasteles) pastries. **~ de dientes**, **~ dentífrica** toothpaste

pastel m cake; (empanada) pie; (lápiz) pastel. **~ería** f cake shop

pasteurizado adj pasteurized

pastilla f pastille; (de jabón) bar; (de chocolate) piece

pasto m pasture; (hierba) grass; (LAm, césped) lawn. **~r** m shepherd; (Relig) minister. **~ra** f shepherdess

pata f leg; (pie de perro, gato) paw; (de ave) foot. **~s arriba** upside down. **a cuatro ~s** on all fours. **meter la ~** put one's foot in it. **tener mala ~da** f kick. **~ear** vi stamp one's feet; (niño) kick

patata f potato. **~s fritas** chips (Brit), French fries (Amer); (de bolsa)

(potato) crisps (Brit), (potato) chips (Amer)

patente adj obvious. ● f licence

patern|al adj paternal; (cariño etc) fatherly. **~idad** f paternity. **~o** adj paternal; (cariño etc) fatherly

patético adj moving

patillas fpl sideburns

patín m skate; (con ruedas) roller skate. **patines en línea** Rollerblades (P)

patina|dor m skater. **~je** m skating. **~r** vi skate; (resbalar) slide; (coche) skid

patio m patio. **~ de butacas** stalls (Brit), orchestra (Amer)

pato m duck

patológico adj pathological

patoso adj clumsy

patraña f hoax

patria f homeland

patriarca m patriarch

patrimonio m patrimony; (fig) heritage

patri|ota adj patriotic. ● m & f patriot. **~otismo** m patriotism

patrocin|ar vt sponsor. **~io** m sponsorship

patrón m (jefe) boss; (de pensión etc) landlord; (en costura) pattern

patrulla f patrol; (fig, cuadrilla) group. **~r** vt/i patrol

pausa f pause. **~do** adj slow

pauta f guideline

paviment|ar vt pave. **~o** m pavement

pavo m turkey. **~ real** peacock

pavor m terror

payas|ada f buffoonery. **~o** m clown

paz f peace

P

peaje m toll

peatón m pedestrian

peca f freckle

peca|do m sin; (defecto) fault. **~dor** m sinner. **~minoso** adj sinful. **~r** [7] vi sin

pech|o m chest; (de mujer) breast; (fig, corazón) heart. **dar el ~o a un niño** breast-feed a child. **tomar a ~o** take to heart. **~uga** f breast

pecoso adj freckled

peculiar adj peculiar, particular. **~idad** f peculiarity

pedal m pedal. **~ear** vi pedal

pedante adj pedantic

pedazo m piece, bit. **a ~s** in pieces. **hacer(se) ~s** smash

pediatra m & f paediatrician

pedicuro m chiropodist

pedi|do m order; (LAm, solicitud) request. **~r** [5] vt ask for; (Com, en restaurante) order. ● vi ask. **~r prestado** borrow

pega|dizo adj catchy. **~joso** adj sticky

pega|mento m glue. **~r** [12] vt stick (on); (coser) sew on; give (enfermedad etc); (juntar) join; (golpear) hit; (dar) give. **~r fuego a** set fire to ● vi stick. **~rse** vpr stick; (pelearse) hit each other. **~tina** f sticker

pein|ado m hairstyle. **~ar** vt comb. **~arse** vpr comb one's hair. **~e** m comb. **~eta** f ornamental comb

p.ej. abrev (por ejemplo) e.g.

pelado adj (fruta) peeled; (cabeza) bald; (terreno) bare

pela|je m (de animal) fur; (fig, aspecto) appearance. **~mbre** m (de animal) fur; (de persona) thick hair

pelar vt peel; shell (habas); skin (tomates); pluck (ave)

peldaño m step; (de escalera de mano) rung

pelea f fight; (discusión) quarrel. **~r** vi fight; (discutir) quarrel. **~rse** vpr fight; (discutir) quarrel

peletería f fur shop

peliagudo adj difficult, tricky

pelícano m pelican

película f film (esp Brit), movie (esp Amer). **~ de dibujos animados** cartoon (film)

peligro m danger; (riesgo) hazard, risk. **poner en ~** endanger. **~so** adj dangerous

pelirrojo adj red-haired

pellejo m skin

pellizc|ar [7] vt pinch. **~o** m pinch

pelma m & f, **pelmazo** m bore, nuisance

pelo m hair. **no tener ~s en la lengua** be outspoken. **tomar el ~ a uno** pull s.o.'s leg

pelota f ball. **~ vasca** pelota. **hacer la ~ a uno** suck up to s.o.

pelotera f squabble

peluca f wig

peludo adj hairy

peluquer|ía f hairdresser's. **~o** m hairdresser

pelusa f down

pena f sadness; (lástima) pity; (LAm, vergüenza) embarrassment; (Jurid) sentence. **~ de muerte** death penalty. **a duras ~s** with difficulty. **da ~ que** it's a pity that. **me da ~** it makes me sad. **merecer la ~** be worthwhile. **pasar ~s** suffer hardship. **¡qué ~!** what a pity! **valer la ~** be worthwhile

penal adj penal; (derecho) criminal. ● m prison; (LAm, penalty)

penalty. ~**idad** f suffering; (Jurid) penalty. ~**ty** m penalty

pendiente adj hanging; (cuenta) outstanding; (asunto etc) pending. ● m earring. ● f slope

péndulo m pendulum

pene m penis

penetra|nte adj penetrating; (sonido) piercing; (viento) bitter. ~**r** vt penetrate; (fig) pierce. ● vi. ~**r en** penetrate; (entrar) go into

penicilina f penicillin

pen|ínsula f peninsula. ~**insular** adj peninsular

penique m penny

penitencia f penitence; (castigo) penance

penoso adj painful; (difícil) difficult; (LAm, tímido) shy; (LAm, embarazoso) embarrassing

pensa|do adj. **bien** ~**do** all things considered. **menos** ~**do** least expected. ~**dor** m thinker. ~**miento** m thought. ~**r** **1** vt think; (considerar) consider. **cuando menos se piensa** when least expected. **¡ni** ~**rlo!** no way! **pienso que sí** I think so. ● vi think. ~**r en** think about. ~**tivo** adj thoughtful

pensi|ón f pension; (casa de huéspedes) guest-house. ~**ón completa** full board. ~**onista** m & f pensioner; (huésped) lodger

penúltimo adj & m penultimate, last but one

penumbra f half-light

penuria f shortage. **pasar** ~**s** suffer hardship

peña f rock; (de amigos) group; (LAm, club) folk club. ~**m** m rock. **el P**~**ón de Gibraltar** The Rock (of Gibraltar)

peón m labourer; (en ajedrez)

pawn; (en damas) piece

peonza f (spinning) top

peor adj (comparativo) worse; (superlativo) worst. ● adv worse. **de mal en** ~ from bad to worse. **lo** ~ the worst thing. **tanto** ~ so much the worse

pepin|illo m gherkin. ~**o** m cucumber. **(no) me importa un** ~**o** I couldn't care less

pepita f pip; (de oro) nugget

pequeñ|ez f smallness; (minucia) trifle. ~**o** adj small, little; (de edad) young; (menor) younger. ● m little one. **es el** ~**o** he's the youngest

pera f (fruta) pear. ~**l** m pear (tree)

percance m mishap

percatarse vpr. ~ **de** notice

perc|epción f perception. ~**ibir** vt perceive; earn (dinero)

percha f hanger; (de aves) perch

percusión f percussion

perde|dor adj losing. ● m loser. ~**r** **1** vt lose; (malgastar) waste; miss (tren etc). ● vi lose. ~**rse** vpr get lost; (desaparecer) disappear; (desperdiciarse) be wasted; (estropearse) be spoilt. **echar(se) a** ~**r** spoil

pérdida f loss; (de líquido) leak; (de tiempo) waste

perdido adj lost

perdiz f partridge

perd|ón m pardon, forgiveness. **pedir** ~**ón** apologize. ● int sorry! ~**onar** vt excuse, forgive; (Jurid) pardon. **¡** ~**one (Vd)!** sorry!

perdura|ble adj lasting. ~**r** vi last

perece|dero adj perishable. ~**r** **11** vi perish

peregrin|ación f pilgrimage.

~o adj strange. ● m pilgrim

perejil m parsley

perengano m so-and-so

perenne adj everlasting; (planta) perennial

perez|a f laziness. ~oso adj lazy

perfec|ción f perfection. a la ~ción perfectly, to perfection. ~cionar vt perfect; (mejorar) improve. ~cionista m & f perfectionist. ~to adj perfect; (completo) complete

perfil m profile; (contorno) outline. ~ado adj well-shaped

perfora|ción f perforation. ~dora f punch. ~r vt pierce, perforate; punch (papel, tarjeta etc)

perfum|ar vt perfume. ~arse vpr put perfume on. ~e m perfume, scent. ~ería f perfumery

pericia f skill

perif|eria f (de ciudad) outskirts. ~érico adj (barrio) outlying. ● m (Mex, carretera) ring road

perilla f (barba) goatee

perímetro m perimeter

periódico adj periodic(al). ● m newspaper

periodis|mo m journalism. ~ta m & f journalist

período m, **periodo** m period

periquito m budgerigar

periscopio m periscope

perito adj & m expert

perju|dicar 7 vt damage; (desfavorecer) not suit. ~dicial adj damaging. ~icio m damage. en ~icio de to the detriment of

perla f pearl. de ~s adv very well

perman|ecer 11 vi remain. ~encia f permanence; (estancia) stay. ~nte adj permanent. ● f perm. ● m (Mex) perm

permi|sivo adj permissive. ~so m permission; (documento) licence; (Mil etc) leave. ~so de conducir driving licence (Brit), driver's license (Amer). con ~so excuse me. ~tir vt allow, permit. ¿me ~te? may I? ~tirse vpr allow s.o.

pernicioso adj pernicious; (persona) wicked

perno m bolt

pero conj but. ● m fault; (objeción) objection

perogrullada f platitude

perpendicular adj & f perpendicular

perpetrar vt perpetrate

perpetu|ar 21 vt perpetuate. ~o adj perpetual

perplejo adj perplexed

perr|a f (animal) bitch; (moneda) coin, penny (Brit), cent (Amer); (rabieta) tantrum. estar sin una ~a be broke. ~era f dog pound; (vehículo) dog catcher's van. ~o adj awful. ● m dog. ~o galgo greyhound. de ~os awful

persa adj & m & f Persian

perse|cución f pursuit; (política etc) persecution. ~guir 5 & 13 vt pursue; (por ideología etc) persecute

persevera|nte adj persevering. ~r vi persevere

persiana f blind; (LAm, contraventana) shutter

persignarse vpr cross o.s.

persist|ente adj persistent. ~ir vi persist

person|a f person. ~as fpl people. ~aje m (persona importante) important figure; (de obra literaria) character. ~al adj personal. ● m staff. ~alidad f personality. ~arse vpr appear in person. ~ifi-

203

perspectiva | picaflor

car **7** vt personify
perspectiva f perspective
perspica|cia f shrewdness; (de vista) keen eyesight. **~z** adj shrewd; (vista) keen
persua|dir vt persuade. **~sión** f persuasion. **~sivo** adj persuasive
pertenecer 🔟 vi belong
pértiga f pole. salto m con **~** pole vault
pertinente adj relevant
perturba|ción f disturbance. **~ción del orden público** breach of the peace. **~r** vt disturb; disrupt (orden)
Perú m. el **~** Peru
peruano adj & m Peruvian
perver|so adj evil. ● m evil person. **~tir** 🔟 vt pervert
pesa f weight. **~dez** f weight; (de cabeza etc) heaviness; (lentitud) sluggishness; (cualidad de fastidioso) tediousness; (cosa fastidiosa) bore, nuisance
pesadilla f nightmare
pesado adj heavy; (sueño) deep; (viaje) tiring; (duro) hard; (aburrido) boring, tedious
pésame m sympathy, condolences
pesar vt weigh. ● vi be heavy. ● m sorrow; (remordimiento) regret. a **~ de (que)** in spite of. pese a **(que)** in spite of
pesca f fishing; (peces) fish; (pescado) catch. ir de **~** go fishing. **~da** f hake. **~dería** f fish shop. **~dilla** f whiting. **~do** m fish. **~dor** adj fishing. ● m fisherman. **~r** 🔟 vt catch. ● vi fish
pescuezo m neck
pesebre m manger
pesero m (Mex) minibus
peseta f peseta

pesimista adj pessimistic. ● m & f pessimist
pésimo adj very bad, awful
peso m weight; (moneda) peso. **~ bruto** gross weight. **~ neto** net weight. al **~** by weight. de **~** influential
pesquero adj fishing
pestaña f eyelash. **~ear** vi blink
pest|e f plague; (hedor) stench. **~icida** m pesticide
pestillo m bolt; (de cerradura) latch
petaca f cigarette case; (Mex, maleta) suitcase
pétalo m petal
petardo m firecracker
petición f request; (escrito) petition
petirrojo m robin
petrificar 🔟 vt petrify
petr|óleo m oil. **~olero** adj oil. ● m oil tanker
petulante adj smug
peyorativo adj pejorative
pez f fish; (substancia negruzca) pitch. **~ espada** swordfish
pezón m nipple
pezuña f hoof
piadoso adj compassionate; (devoto) devout
pian|ista m & f pianist. **~o** m piano. **~o de cola** grand piano
piar 🔟 vi chirp
picad|a f. caer en **~a** (LAm) nosedive. **~o** adj perforated; (carne) minced (Brit), ground (Amer); (ofendido) offended; (mar) choppy; (diente) bad. ● m. caer en **~o** nosedive. **~ura** f bite, sting; (de polilla) moth hole
picaflor m (LAm) hummingbird

picante adj hot; (chiste etc) risqué

picaporte m door-handle; (aldaba) knocker

picar 7 vt (ave) peck; (insecto, pez) bite; (abeja, avispa) sting; (comer poco) pick at; mince (Brit), grind (Amer) (carne); chop (up) (cebolla etc); (Mex, pinchar) prick. • vi itch; (ave) peck; (insecto, pez) bite; (sol) scorch; (comida) be hot

picardía f craftiness; (travesura) naughty thing

pícaro adj crafty; (niño) mischievous. • m rogue

picazón f itch

pichón m pigeon; (Mex, novato) beginner

pico m beak; (punta) corner; (herramienta) pickaxe; (cima) peak. y ~ (con tiempo) a little after; (con cantidad) a little more than. ~**tear** vt peck; (fam, comer) pick at

picudo adj pointed

pido vb véase PEDIR

pie m foot; (Bot, de vaso) stem. ~ cuadrado square foot. a cuatro ~s on all fours. al ~ de la letra literally. a ~ on foot. a ~(s) juntillas (fig) firmly. buscarle tres ~s al gato split hairs. de ~ standing (up). de ~s a cabeza from head to toe. en ~ standing (up). ponerse de ~ stand up

piedad f pity; (Relig) piety

piedra f stone; (de mechero) flint

piel f skin; (cuero) leather

pienso vb véase PENSAR

pierdo vb véase PERDER

pierna f leg

pieza f piece; (parte) part; (obra teatral) play; (moneda) coin; (habitación) room. ~ de recambio spare part

pijama m pyjamas

pila f (montón) pile; (recipiente) basin; (eléctrica) battery. ~ bautismal font. ~r m pillar

píldora f pill

pilla|je m pillage. ~r vt catch

pillo adj wicked. • m rogue

pilot|ar vt pilot. ~o m pilot

pim|entero m (vasija) pepperpot. ~entón m paprika; (LAm, fruto) pepper. ~ienta f pepper. grano m de ~ienta peppercorn. ~iento m pepper

pináculo m pinnacle

pinar m pine forest

pincel m paintbrush. ~ada f brush-stroke. la última ~ada (fig) the finishing touch

pinch|ar vt pierce, prick; puncture (neumático); (fig, incitar) push; (Med, fam) give an injection to. ~azo m prick; (en neumático) puncture. ~itos mpl kebab(s); (tapas) savoury snacks. ~o m point

ping-pong m table tennis, ping-pong

pingüino m penguin

pino m pine (tree)

pint|a f spot; (fig, aspecto) appearance. tener ~a de look like. ~ada f graffiti. ~ar vt paint. no ~a nada (fig) it doesn't count. ~arse vpr put on make-up. ~or m painter. ~oresco adj picturesque. ~ura f painting; (material) paint

pinza f (clothes-)peg (Brit), clothespin (Amer); (de cangrejo etc) claw. ~s fpl tweezers

piña|a f pine cone; (fruta) pineapple. ~ón m (en semilla) pine nut

pío adj pious. • m chirp. no decir ni ~ not say a word

piojo m louse

pionero m pioneer

pipa f pipe; (semilla) seed; (de girasol) sunflower seed

pique m resentment; (rivalidad) rivalry. **irse a** ~ sink

piquete m picket; (Mex, herida) prick; (Mex, de insecto) sting

piragua f canoe

pirámide f pyramid

pirata adj invar pirate. ● m & f pirate

Pirineos mpl. los ~the Pyrenees

piropo m flattering comment

pirueta f pirouette

pirulí m lollipop

pisa|da f footstep; (huella) footprint. ~**papeles** m invar paperweight. ~**r** vt tread on. ● vi tread

piscina f swimming pool

Piscis m Pisces

piso m floor; (vivienda) flat (Brit), apartment (Amer); (de autobús) deck

pisotear vt trample (on)

pista f track; (fig, indicio) clue. ~ **de aterrizaje** runway. ~ **de baile** dance floor. ~ **de carreras** racing track. ~ **de hielo** ice-rink. ~ **de tenis** tennis court

pistol|a f pistol. ~**era** f holster. ~**ero** m gunman

pistón m piston

pit|ar, (LAm) ~**ear** vt whistle at; (conductor) hoot at; award (falta). ● vi blow a whistle; (Auto) sound one's horn. ~**ido** m whistle

pitill|era f cigarette case. ~**o** m cigarette

pito m whistle; (Auto) horn

pitón m python

pitorre|arse vpr. ~**arse de** make fun of. ~**o** m teasing

pitorro m spout

piyama m (LAm) pyjamas

pizarr|a f slate; (en aula) blackboard. ~**ón** m (LAm) blackboard

pizca f ① tiny piece; (de sal) pinch. **ni** ~ not at all

placa f plate; (con inscripción) plaque; (distintivo) badge. ~ **de matrícula** number plate

place|ntero adj pleasant. ~**r** 32 vi. **haz lo que te plazca** do as you please. **me** ~ **hacerlo** I'm pleased to do it. ● m pleasure

plácido adj placid

plaga f (also fig) plague. ~**do** adj. ~**do de** filled with

plagio m plagiarism

plan m plan. **en** ~ **de** as

plana f page. **en primera** ~ on the front page

plancha f iron; (lámina) sheet. **a la** ~ grilled. **tirarse una** ~ put one's foot in it. ~**do** m ironing. ~**r** vt iron. ● vi do the ironing

planeador m glider

planear vt plan. ● vi glide

planeta m planet

planicie f plain

planifica|ción f planning. ~**r** 7 vt plan

planilla f (LAm) payroll; (personal) staff

plano adj flat. ● m plane; (de edificio) plan; (de ciudad) street plan. **primer** ~ foreground; (Foto) close-up

planta f (del pie) sole; (en botánica, fábrica) plant; (piso) floor. ~ **baja** ground floor (Brit), first floor (Amer)

planta|ción f plantation. ~**r** vt plant; deal (golpe). ~**r en la calle** throw out. ~**rse** vpr stand; (fig) stand firm

plantear vt (exponer) expound; (causar) create; raise (cuestión)

plantilla f insole; (nómina) payroll; (personal) personnel

plaqué m plating. **de ~** plated

plástico adj & m plastic

plata f silver; (fig, fam, dinero) money. **~ de ley** hallmarked silver

plataforma f platform

plátano m plane (tree); (fruta) banana. **platanero** m banana tree

platea f stalls (Brit), orchestra (Amer)

plateado adj silver-plated; (color de plata) silver

pl|ática f talk. **~aticar** 🔢 vi (Mex) talk. ● vt (Mex) tell

platija f plaice

platillo m saucer; (Mus) cymbal. **~ volador** (LAm), **~ volante** flying saucer

platino m platinum. **~s** mpl (Auto) points

plato m plate; (comida) dish; (parte de una comida) course

platónico adj platonic

playa f beach; (fig) seaside

plaza f square; (mercado) market (place); (sitio) place; (empleo) job. **~ de toros** bullring

plazco vb véase PLACER

plazo m period; (pago) instalment; (fecha) date. **comprar a ~s** buy on hire purchase (Brit), buy on the installment plan (Amer)

plazuela f little square

pleamar f high tide

pleb|e f common people. **~eyo** adj & m plebeian. **~iscito** m plebiscite

plega|ble adj pliable; (silla) folding. **~r** 🔢 & 🔢 vt fold. **~rse** vpr

bend; (fig) yield

pleito m (court) case; (fig) dispute

plenilunio m full moon

plen|itud f fullness; (fig) height. **~o** adj full. **en ~o día** in broad daylight. **en ~o verano** at the height of the summer

plieg|o m sheet. **~ue** m fold; (en ropa) pleat

plisar vt pleat

plom|ero m (LAm) plumber. **~o** m lead; (Elec) fuse. **con ~o** leaded. **sin ~o** unleaded

pluma f feather; (para escribir) pen. **~ atómica** (Mex) ballpoint pen. **~ estilográfica** fountain pen. **~je** m plumage

plum|ero m feather duster; (para plumas, lápices etc) pencil-case. **~ón** m down; (edredón) downfilled quilt

plural adj & m plural. **en ~** in the plural

pluri|empleo m having more than one job. **~partidismo** m multi-party system. **~étnico** adj multiethnic

plus m bonus

pluscuamperfecto m pluperfect

plusvalía f capital gain

pluvial adj rain

pobla|ción f population; (ciudad) city, town; (pueblo) village. **~do** adj populated. ● m village. **~r** 🔢 vt populate; (habitar) inhabit. **~rse** vpr get crowded

pobre adj poor. ● m & f poor person; (fig) poor thing. **¡~cito!** poor (little) thing! **¡~ de mí!** poor (old) me! **~za** f poverty

pocilga f pigsty

poción f potion

poco

● *adjetivo/pronombre*

••••▸ **poco, poca** little, not much. **tiene poca paciencia** he has little patience. **¿cuánta leche queda?** - **poca** how much milk is there left? - not much

••••▸ **pocos, pocas** few. **muy ~s días** very few days. **unos ~s dólares** a few dollars. **compré unos ~s** I bought a few. **aceptaron a muy ~s** very few (people) were accepted

••••▸ **a ~ de llegar** soon after he arrived. **¡a ~!** (*Mex*) really? **dentro de ~** soon. **~ a ~,** (*LAm*) **de a ~** gradually, little by little. **hace ~** recently, not long ago. **por ~** nearly. **un ~** (*cantidad*) a little; (*tiempo*) a while. **un ~ de** a (little) bit of, a little, some

● *adverbio*

••••▸ (*con verbo*) not much. **lee muy ~** he doesn't read very much

••••▸ (*con adjetivo*) **un lugar ~ conocido** a little known place. **es ~ inteligente** he's not very intelligent

❗ Cuando **poco** modifica a un adjetivo, muchas veces el inglés prefiere el uso del prefijo *un-*, p. ej. **poco amistoso** *unfriendly*. **poco agradecido** *ungrateful*

podar *vt* prune
poder 🔢 *verbo auxiliar* be able to. **no voy a ~ terminar** I won't be able to finish. **no pudo venir** he couldn't come. **¿puedo hacer algo?** can I do anything? **¿puedo pasar?** may I come in? **no ~ con** not be able to cope with; (*no aguantar*) not be able to stand. **no ~ más** be exhausted; (*estar harto de algo*) not be able to manage any more. **no ~ menos que** have no alternative but. **puede que** it is possible that. **puede ser** it is possible. **¿se puede ...?** may I...? ● *m* power. **en el ~** in power. **~es públicos** authorities. **~oso** *adj* powerful

podrido *adj* rotten
po|ema *m* poem. **~esía** *f* poetry; (*poema*) poem. **~eta** *m & f* poet. **~ético** *adj* poetic
polaco *adj* Polish. ● *m* Pole; (*lengua*) Polish
polar *adj* polar. **estrella ~** polestar
polea *f* pulley
pol|émica *f* controversy. **~emizar** 🔟 *vi* argue
polen *m* pollen
policía *f* police (force); (*persona*) policewoman. ● *m* policeman. **~co** *adj* police; (*novela etc*) detective
policromo *adj*, **polícromo** *adj* polychrome
polideportivo *m* sports centre
polietileno *m* polythene
poligamia *f* polygamy
polígono *m* polygon
polilla *f* moth
polio(mielitis) *f* polio(myelitis)
polític|a *f* politics; (*postura*) policy; (*mujer*) politician. **~ interior** domestic policy. **~o** *adj* political. **familia ~a** in-laws. ● *m* politician
póliza *f* (*de seguros*) policy
poll|o *m* chicken; (*gallo joven*) chick. **~uelo** *m* chick
polo *m* pole; (*helado*) ice lolly (*Brit*),

Popsicle (P) (*Amer*); (*juego*) polo.
P~ norte North Pole
Polonia *f* Poland
poltrona *f* armchair
polución *f* pollution
polv|areda *f* dust cloud; (*fig, escándalo*) uproar. **~era** *f* compact. **~o** *m* powder; (*suciedad*) dust. **~os** *mpl* powder. **en ~o** powdered. **estar hecho ~o** be exhausted. **quitar el ~o** dust
pólvora *f* gunpowder; (*fuegos artificiales*) fireworks
polvoriento *adj* dusty
pomada *f* ointment
pomelo *m* grapefruit
pómez *adj*. **piedra** *f* ~ pumice stone
pomp|a *f* bubble; (*esplendor*) pomp. **~as fúnebres** funeral. **~oso** *adj* pompous; (*espléndido*) splendid
pómulo *m* cheekbone
ponchar *vt* (*Mex*) puncture
ponche *m* punch
poncho *m* poncho
ponderar *vt* (*alabar*) speak highly of
poner 34 *vt* put; put on (ropa, obra de teatro, TV etc); lay (la mesa, un huevo); set (examen, deberes); (*contribuir*) contribute; give (nombre); make (nervioso); pay (atención); show (película, interés); open (una tienda); equip (una casa). **~ con** (*al teléfono*) put through to. **~ por escrito** put into writing. **~ una multa** fine. **pongamos** let's suppose. ● *vi* lay. **~se** *vpr* put o.s.; (*volverse*) get; put on (ropa); (sol) set. **~se a** start to. **~se mal con uno** fall out with s.o.
pongo *vb véase* PONER

poniente *m* west; (*viento*) west wind
pont|ificar 7 *vi* pontificate. **~ífice** *m* pontiff
popa *f* stern
popote *m* (*Mex*) (drinking) straw
popul|acho *m* masses. **~ar** *adj* popular; (*costumbre*) traditional; (lenguaje) colloquial. **~aridad** *f* popularity. **~arizar** 10 *vt* popularize.
póquer *m* poker
poquito *m*. **un ~ a** a little bit. ● *adv* a little

por *preposición*

····▸ for. **es ~ tu bien** it's for your own good. **lo compró por 5 dólares** he bought it for 5 dollars. **si no fuera por ti** if it weren't for you. **vino por una semana** he came for a week

➡️ Para expresiones como **por la mañana, por la noche** etc., ver bajo el respectivo nombre

····▸ (*causa*) because of. **se retrasó ~ la lluvia** he was late because of the rain. **no hay trenes ~ la huelga** there aren't any trains because of the strike

····▸ (*medio, agente*) by. **lo envié ~ correo** I sent it by post. **fue destruida ~ las bombas** it was destroyed by the bombs

····▸ (*a través de*) through. **entró ~ la ventana** he got in through the window. **me enteré ~ un amigo** I found out through a friend. **~ todo el**

país throughout the country
┈┈▶ (a lo largo de) along. **caminar ~ la playa** to walk along the beach. **cortar ~ la línea de puntos** cut along the dotted line
┈┈▶ (proporción) per. **cobra 30 dólares ~ hora** he charges 30 dollars per hour. **uno ~ persona** one per person. **10 ~ ciento** 10 per cent
┈┈▶ (Mat) times. **dos ~ dos (son) cuatro** two times two is four
┈┈▶ (modo) in. **~ escrito** in writing. **pagar ~ adelantado** to pay in advance

➡ Para expresiones como **por dentro, por fuera** etc., ver bajo el respectivo adverbio

┈┈▶ (en locuciones) **~ más que** no matter how much. **¿~ qué?** why? **~ si** in case. **~ supuesto** of course

porcelana f china
porcentaje m percentage
porcino adj pig
porción f portion; (de chocolate) piece
pordiosero m beggar
porfia|do adj stubborn. **~r 20** vi insist
pormenor m detail
pornogr|afía f pornography. **~áfico** adj pornographic
poro m pore; (Mex, puerro) leek. **~so** adj porous
porque conj because; (para que) so that
porqué m reason

porquería f filth; (basura) rubbish; (grosería) dirty trick
porra f club
porrón m wine jug (with a long spout)
portaaviones m invar aircraft carrier
portada f (de libro) title page; (de revista) cover
portadocumentos m invar (LAm) briefcase
portador m bearer
portaequipaje(s) m invar boot (Brit), trunk (Amer); (encima del coche) roof-rack
portal m hall; (puerta principal) main entrance. **~es** mpl arcade
porta|ligas m invar suspender belt. **~monedas** m invar purse
portarse vpr behave
portátil adj portable. ● m portable computer, laptop
portavoz m spokesman. ● f spokeswoman
portazo m bang. **dar un ~** slam the door
porte m transport; (precio) carriage; (LAm, tamaño) size. **~ador** m carrier
portento m marvel
porteño adj from Buenos Aires
porter|ía f porter's lodge; (en deportes) goal. **~o** m caretaker, porter; (en deportes) goalkeeper. **~o automático** entryphone
pórtico m portico
portorriqueño adj & m Puerto Rican
Portugal m Portugal
portugués adj & m Portuguese
porvenir m future
posada f inn. **dar ~** give shelter
posar vt put. ● vi pose. **~se** vpr

P

(pájaro) perch; (avión) land

posdata f postscript

pose|edor m owner; (de récord, billete, etc) holder. **~er** 18 vt own; hold (récord); have (conocimientos). **~sión** f possession. **~sionarse** vpr. **~sionarse de** take possession of. **~sivo** adj possessive

posgraduado adj & m postgraduate

posguerra f post-war years

posib|ilidad f possibility. **~le** adj possible. **de ser ~le** if possible. **en lo ~le** as far as possible. **si es ~le** if possible

posición f position; (en sociedad) social standing

positivo adj positive

poso m sediment

posponer 34 vt put after; (diferir) postpone

posta f **a ~** on purpose

postal adj postal. ● f postcard

poste m pole; (de valla) post

póster m (pl ~s) poster

postergar 12 vt pass over; (diferir) postpone

posteri|dad f posterity. **~or** adj back; (años) later; (capítulos) subsequent. **~ormente** adv later

postigo m door; (contraventana) shutter

postizo adj false, artificial. ● m hairpiece

postrarse vpr prostrate o.s.

postre m dessert, pudding (Brit)

postular vt postulate; (LAm) nominate (candidato)

póstumo adj posthumous

postura f position, stance

potable adj drinkable; (agua) drinking

potaje m vegetable stew

potasio m potassium

pote m pot

poten|cia f power. **~cial** adj & m potential. **~te** adj powerful

potro m colt; (en gimnasia) horse

pozo m well; (hoyo seco) pit; (de mina) shaft; (fondo común) pool

práctica f practice. **en la ~** in practice

practica|nte m & f nurse. **~r** 7 vt practise; play (deportes); (ejecutar) carry out

práctico adj practical; (conveniente, útil) handy. ● m practitioner

prad|era f meadow; (terreno grande) prairie. **~o** m meadow

pragmático adj pragmatic

preámbulo m preamble

precario adj precarious; (medios) scarce

precaución f precaution; (cautela) caution. **con ~** cautiously

precaverse vpr take precautions

prece|ncia f precedence; (prioridad) priority. **~nte** adj preceding. ● m precedent. **~r** vt/i precede

precepto m precept. **~r** m tutor

precia|do adj valued; (don) valuable. **~rse** vpr. **~rse de** pride o.s. on

precio m price. **~ de venta al público** retail price. **al ~ de** at the cost of. **no tener ~** be priceless. **¿qué ~ tiene?** how much is it?

precios|idad f (cosa preciosa) beautiful thing. **¡es una ~idad!** it's beautiful! **~o** adj precious; (bonito) beautiful

precipicio m precipice

precipita|ción f precipitation; (prisa) rush. **~damente** adv hastily. **~do** adj hasty. **~r** vt (apre-

surar) hasten; (*arrojar*) hurl. ~**se**
vpr throw o.s.; (*correr*) rush; (*actuar sin reflexionar*) act rashly

precis|amente *adv* exactly. ~**ar**
vt require; (*determinar*) determine.
~**ión** *f* precision. ~**o** *adj* precise;
(*necesario*) necessary. **si es** ~**o** if
necessary

preconcebido *adj* preconceived

precoz *adj* early; (*niño*) precocious

precursor *m* forerunner

predecesor *m* predecessor

predecir 46, (*pero imperativo* **pre-
dice**, *futuro y condicional regulares*) *vt*
foretell

predestinado *adj* predestined

prédica *f* sermon

predicar 7 *vt/i* preach

predicción *f* prediction; (*del
tiempo*) forecast

predilec|ción *f* predilection.
~**to** *adj* favourite

predisponer 34 *vt* predispose

predomin|ante *adj* predomin-
ant. ~**ar** *vi* predominate. ~**io** *m*
predominance

preeminente *adj* pre-eminent

prefabricado *adj* prefabricated

prefacio *m* preface

prefer|encia *f* preference; (*Auto*)
right of way. **de** ~**encia** prefer-
ably. ~**ente** *adj* preferential. ~**ible**
adj preferable. ~**ido** *adj* favourite.
~**ir 4** *vt* prefer

prefijo *m* prefix; (*telefónico*) dialling code

pregonar *vt* announce

pregunta *f* question. **hacer una
~** ask a question. ~**r** *vt/i* ask (**por**
about). ~**rse** *vpr* wonder

prehistórico *adj* prehistoric

preju|icio *m* prejudice. ~**zgar 12**
vt prejudge

preliminar *adj* & *m* preliminary

preludio *m* prelude

premarital *adj*, **prematrimonial**
adj premarital

prematuro *adj* premature

premedita|ción *f* premedita-
tion. ~**r** *vt* premeditate

premi|ar *vt* give a prize to; (*re-
compensar*) reward. ~**o** *m* prize;
(*recompensa*) reward. ~**o gordo**
jackpot

premonición *f* premonition

prenatal *adj* antenatal

prenda *f* garment; (*garantía*)
surety; (*en juegos*) forfeit. **en** ~ **de**
as a token of. ~**r** *vt* captivate.
~**rse** *vpr* fall in love (**de** with)

prende|dor *m* brooch. ~**r** *vt*
capture; (*sujetar*) fasten; light (*cigarrillo*); (*LAm*) turn on (gas, radio,
etc). ● *vi* catch; (*arraigar*) take
root. ~**rse** *vpr* (*encenderse*) catch
fire

prensa *f* press. ~**r** *vt* press

preñado *adj* pregnant; (*fig*) full

preocupa|ción *f* worry. ~**do** *adj*
worried. ~**r** *vt* worry. ~**rse** *vpr*
worry. ~**rse de** look after

prepara|ción *f* preparation.
~**do** *adj* prepared. ● *m* prepar-
ation. ~**r** *vt* prepare. ~**rse** *vpr* get
ready. ~**tivos** *mpl* preparations.
~**torio** *adj* preparatory

preposición *f* preposition

prepotente *adj* arrogant; (*actitud*) high-handed

prerrogativa *f* prerogative

presa *f* (*cosa*) prey; (*embalse*) dam

presagi|ar *vt* presage. ~**o** *m*
omen

presb|iteriano *adj* & *m* Presby-
terian. ~**ítero** *m* priest

prescindir *vi*. ~ **de** do without;

(deshacerse de) dispense with

prescri|bir *(pp prescrito) vt* prescribe. **~pción** *f* prescription

presencia *f* presence; *(aspecto)* appearance. **en ~ de** in the presence of. **~r** *vt* be present at; *(ver)* witness

presenta|ble *adj* presentable. **~ción** *f* presentation; *(de una persona a otra)* introduction. **~dor** *m* presenter. **~r** *vt* present; *(ofrecer)* offer; *(entregar)* hand in; *(hacer conocer)* introduce; show *(película)*. **~rse** *vpr* present o.s.; *(hacerse conocer)* introduce o.s.; *(aparecer)* turn up

presente *adj* present; *(actual)* this. ● *m* present. **los ~s** those present. **tener ~** remember

presenti|miento *m* premonition. **~r** **4** *vt* have a feeling *(que* that)

preserva|r *vt* preserve. **~tivo** *m* condom

presiden|cia *f* presidency; *(de asamblea)* chairmanship. **~cial** *adj* presidential. **~ta** *f* (woman) president. **~te** *m* president; *(de asamblea)* chairman. **~te del gobierno** prime minister

presidi|ario *m* convict. **~o** *m* prison

presidir *vt* be president of; preside over *(tribunal)*; chair *(reunión, comité)*

presi|ón *f* pressure. **a ~ón** under pressure. **hacer ~ón** press. **~onar** *vt* press; *(fig)* put pressure on

preso *adj.* **estar ~** be in prison. **llevarse a uno ~** take s.o. away under arrest. ● *m* prisoner

presta|do *adj (de uno)* lent; *(a uno)* borrowed. **pedir ~do** bor-

row. **~mista** *m & f* moneylender

préstamo *m* loan; *(acción de pedir prestado)* borrowing; *(acción de prestar)* lending

prestar *vt* lend; give *(ayuda etc)*; pay *(atención)*. **~se** *vpr.* **~se a** be open to; *(ser apto)* be suitable *(para* for)

prestidigita|ción *f* conjuring. **~dor** *m* conjurer

prestigio *m* prestige. **~so** *adj* prestigious

presu|mido *adj* conceited. **~mir** *vi* show off; boast *(de* about). **~nción** *f* conceit; *(suposición)* presumption. **~nto** *adj* alleged. **~ntuoso** *adj* conceited

presup|oner **34** *vt* presuppose. **~uesto** *m* budget; *(precio estimado)* estimate

preten|cioso *adj* pretentious. **~der** *vt* try to; *(afirmar)* claim; *(solicitar)* apply for; *(cortejar)* court. **~diente** *m* pretender; *(a una mujer)* suitor. **~sión** *f* pretension; *(aspiración)* aspiration

pretérito *m* preterite, past

pretexto *m* pretext. **con el ~ de** on the pretext of

prevalecer **11** *vi* prevail *(sobre* over)

preven|ción *f* prevention; *(prejuicio)* prejudice. **~ido** *adj* ready; *(precavido)* cautious. **~ir** **53** *vt* prevent; *(advertir)* warn. **~tiva** *f (Mex)* amber light. **~tivo** *adj* preventive

prever **43** *vt* foresee; *(planear)* plan

previo *adj* previous

previs|ible *adj* predictable. **~ión** *f* forecast; *(prudencia)* precaution

prima *f (pariente)* cousin; *(cantidad)* bonus

primario *adj* primary

primavera f spring. **∼l** adj spring

primer adj véase **PRIMERO. ∼a** f (Auto) first (gear); (en tren etc) first class. **∼o** adj (delante de nombre masculino en singular **primer**) first; (mejor) best; (principal) leading. **la ∼a fila** the front row. **lo ∼o es** the most important thing is. **∼a enseñanza** primary education. **a ∼os de** at the beginning of. **de ∼a** first-class. ● n (the) first. ● adv first

primitivo adj primitive

primo m cousin; 🄵 fool. **hacer el ∼** be taken for a ride

primogénito adj & m first-born, eldest

primor m delicacy; (cosa) beautiful thing

primordial adj fundamental; (interés) paramount

princesa f princess

principal adj main. **lo ∼ es que** the main thing is that

príncipe m prince

principi|ante m & f beginner. **∼o** m beginning; (moral, idea) principle; (origen) origin. **al ∼o** at first. **a ∼o(s) de** at the beginning of. **desde el ∼o** from the start. **en ∼o** in principle. **∼os** mpl (nociones) rudiments

prión m prion

prioridad f priority

prisa f hurry, haste. **darse ∼** hurry (up). **de ∼** quickly. **tener ∼** be in a hurry

prisi|ón f prison; (encarcelamiento) imprisonment. **∼onero** m prisoner

prismáticos mpl binoculars

priva|ción f deprivation. **∼da** f (Mex) private road. **∼do** adj (particular) private. **∼r** vt deprive (**de** of). **∼tivo** adj exclusive (**de** to)

privilegi|ado adj privileged; (muy bueno) exceptional. **∼o** m privilege

pro prep. **en ∼ de** for, in favour of. ● m advantage. **los ∼s y los contras** the pros and cons

proa f bow

probab|ilidad f probability. **∼le** adj probable, likely. **∼lemente** adv probably

proba|dor m fitting-room. **∼r** 🄾 vt try; try on (ropa); (demostrar) prove. ● vi try. **∼rse** vpr try on

probeta f test-tube

problema m problem. **hacerse ∼as** (LAm) worry

procaz adj indecent

proced|encia f origin. **∼ente** adj (razonable) reasonable. **∼ente de** (coming) from. **∼er** m conduct. ● vi proceed. **∼er contra** start legal proceedings against. **∼er de** come from. **∼imiento** m procedure; (sistema) process; (Jurid) proceedings

proces|ador m. **∼ de textos** word processor. **∼al** adj procedural. **costas ∼ales** legal costs. **∼amiento** m processing; (Jurid) prosecution. **∼amiento de textos** word-processing.. **∼ar** vt process; (Jurid) prosecute

procesión f procession

proceso m process; (Jurid) trial; (transcurso) course

proclamar vt proclaim

procrea|ción f procreation. **∼r** vt procreate

procura|dor m attorney, solicitor; (asistente) clerk (Brit), paralegal (Amer). **∼r** vt try; (obtener) obtain

prodigar 🄵 vt lavish

prodigio m prodigy; (maravilla) wonder; (milagro) miracle. **∼so** adj prodigious

pródigo | propaganda

214

pródigo *adj* prodigal

produc|ción *f* production. ~**ir**
47 *vt* produce; (*causar*) cause.
~**irse** *vpr* (*suceder*) happen. ~**tivo**
adj productive. ~**to** *m* product.
~**tos agrícolas** farm produce.
~**tos alimenticios** foodstuffs.
~**tos de belleza** cosmetics. ~**tos**
de consumo consumer goods.
~**tor** *m* producer.

proeza *f* exploit

profan|ación *f* desecration. ~**ar**
vt desecrate. ~**o** *adj* profane

profecía *f* prophecy

proferir **4** *vt* utter; hurl (*insultos*
etc)

profes|ión *f* profession. ~**ional**
adj professional. ~**or** *m* teacher;
(*en universidad*) lecturer. ~**orado**
m teaching profession; (*conjunto de
profesores*) staff

prof|eta *m* prophet. ~**etizar** **10**
vt/i prophesize

prófugo *adj & m* fugitive

profund|idad *f* depth. ~**o** *adj*
deep; (*fig*) profound. **poco** ~**o**
shallow

progenitor *m* ancestor

programa *m* programme; (*de estudios*) syllabus. ~ **concurso** quiz
show. ~ **de entrevistas** chat
show. ~**ción** *f* programming; (*TV
etc*) programmes; (*en periódico*) TV
guide. ~**r** *vt* programme. ~**dor** *m*
computer programmer

progres|ar *vi* (make) progress.
~**ión** *f* progression. ~**ista** *adj* progressive. ~**ivo** *adj* progressive. ~**o**
m progress. **hacer** ~**os** make progress

prohibi|ción *f* prohibition. ~**do**
adj forbidden. **prohibido fumar** no
smoking. ~**r** *vt* forbid. ~**tivo** *adj*
prohibitive

prójimo *m* fellow man

prole *f* offspring

proletari|ado *m* proletariat. ~**o**
adj & m proletarian

prol|iferación *f* proliferation.
~**iferar** *vi* proliferate. ~**ífico** *adj*
prolific

prolijo *adj* long-winded

prólogo *m* prologue

prolongar **12** *vt* prolong; (*alargar*) lengthen. ~**se** *vpr* go on

promedio *m* average. **como** ~
on average

prome|sa *f* promise. ~**ter** *vt*
promise. ● *vi* show promise.
~**terse** *vpr* (*novios*) get engaged.
~**tida** *f* fiancée. ~**tido** *adj* prom-
ised; (*novios*) engaged. ● *m* fiancé

prominente *f* prominence

promiscu|idad *f* promiscuity.
~**o** *adj* promiscuous

promo|ción *f* promotion. ~**tor**
m promoter. ~**ver** **2** *vt* promote;
(*causar*) cause

promulgar **12** *vt* promulgate

pronombre *m* pronoun

pron|osticar **7** *vt* predict; fore-
cast (*tiempo*). ~**óstico** *m* prediction; (*del tiempo*) forecast; (*Med*)
prognosis

pront|itud *f* promptness. ~**o** *adj*
quick. ● *adv* quickly; (*dentro de
poco*) soon; (*temprano*) early. **de**
~**o** suddenly. **por lo** ~**o** for the
time being. **tan** ~**o como** as
soon as

pronuncia|ción *f* pronunciation.
~**miento** *m* revolt. ~**r** *vt* pro-
nounce; deliver (*discurso*). ~**rse**
vpr (*declararse*) declare o.s.; (*sublevarse*) rise up

propagación *f* propagation

propaganda *f* propaganda;

(*anuncios*) advertising

propagar 12 *vt/i* propagate. **~se** *vpr* spread

propasarse *vpr* go too far

propens|ión *f* inclination. **~o** *adj* inclined

propici|ar *vt* favour; (*provocar*) bring about. **~o** *adj* favourable

propie|dad *f* property. **~tario** *m* owner

propina *f* tip

propio *adj* own; (*característico*) typical; (*natural*) natural; (*apropiado*) proper. **el ~ médico** the doctor himself

proponer 34 *vt* propose; put forward (*persona*). **~se** *vpr*. **~se hacer** intend to do

proporci|ón *f* proportion. **~onado** *adj* proportioned. **~onal** *adj* proportional. **~onar** *vt* provide

proposición *f* proposition

propósito *m* intention. **a ~** (*adrede*) on purpose; (*de paso*) by the way. **a ~ de** with regard to

propuesta *f* proposal

propuls|ar *vt* propel; (*fig*) promote. **~ión** *f* propulsion. **~ión a chorro** jet propulsion

prórroga *f* extension

prorrogar 12 *vt* extend

prosa *f* prose. **~ico** *adj* prosaic

proscri|bir (*pp* proscrito) *vt* exile; (*prohibir*) ban. **~to** *adj* banned. ● *m* exile; (*bandido*) outlaw

proseguir 5 & 13 *vt/i* continue

prospecto *m* prospectus; (*de fármaco*) directions for use

prosper|ar *vi* prosper; (*persona*) do well. **~idad** *f* prosperity

próspero *adj* prosperous. **¡P~**

Año Nuevo! Happy New Year!

prostit|ución *f* prostitution. **~uta** *f* prostitute

protagonista *m & f* protagonist

prote|cción *f* protection. **~ctor** *adj* protective. ● *m* protector; (*benefactor*) patron. **~ger** 14 *vt* protect. **~gida** *f* protegée. **~gido** *adj* protected. ● *m* protegé

proteína *f* protein

protesta *f* protest; (*manifestación*) demonstration; (*Mex, promesa*) promise; (*Mex, juramento*) oath

protestante *adj & m & f* Protestant

protestar *vt/i* protest

protocolo *m* protocol

provecho *m* benefit. **¡buen ~!** enjoy your meal! **de ~** useful. **en ~ de** to the benefit of. **sacar ~ de** benefit from

proveer 18 (*pp* proveído y provisto) *vt* supply, provide

provenir 53 *vi* come (**de** from)

proverbi|al *adj* proverbial. **~o** *m* proverb

provincia *f* province. **~l** *adj*, **~no** *adj* provincial

provisional *adj* provisional

provisto *adj* provided (**de** with)

provoca|ción *f* provocation. **~r** 7 *vt* provoke; (*causar*) cause. **~tivo** *adj* provocative

proximidad *f* proximity

próximo *adj* next; (*cerca*) near

proyec|ción *f* projection. **~tar** *vt* hurl; cast (*luz*); show (*película*). **~til** *m* missile. **~to** *m* plan. **~to de ley** bill. **en ~to** planned. **~tor** *m* projector

pruden|cia *f* prudence; (*cuidado*) caution. **~te** *adj* prudent, sensible

prueba f proof; (examen) test; (de ropa) fitting. **a ~** on trial. **a ~ de** proof against. **a ~ de agua** waterproof. **a ~ de** water test

pruebo vb véase **PROBAR**

psicoan|álisis f psychoanalysis. **~alista** m & f psychoanalyst. **~alizar** ⑩ vt psychoanalyse

psic|ología f psychology. **~ológico** adj psychological. **~ólogo** m psychologist. **~ópata** m & f psychopath. **~osis** f invar psychosis

psiqu|e f psyche. **~iatra** m & f psychiatrist. **~iátrico** adj psychiatric

psíquico adj psychic

ptas, pts abrev (**pesetas**) pesetas

púa f sharp point; (espina) thorn; (de erizo) quill; (de peine) tooth; (Mus) plectrum

pubertad f puberty

publica|ción f publication. **~r** ⑦ vt publish

publici|dad f publicity; (Com) advertising. **~tario** adj advertising

público adj public. ● m public; (de espectáculo etc) audience

puchero m cooking pot; (guisado) stew. **hacer ~s** (fig, fam) pout

pude vb véase **PODER**

pudor m modesty. **~oso** adj modest

pudrir (pp podrido) vt rot; (fig, molestar) annoy. **~se** vpr rot

puebl|ecito m small village. **~erino** m country bumpkin. **~o** m town; (aldea) village; (nación) nation, people

puedo vb véase **PODER**

puente m bridge; (fig, fam) long weekend. **~ colgante** suspension bridge. **~ levadizo** drawbridge. **hacer ~** ❶ have a long weekend

puente Puentes are very important in Spain and Latin America. Hacer Puente means that when a working day falls between two public holidays, it too is taken as a holiday.

puerco adj filthy; (grosero) coarse. ● m pig. **~ espín** porcupine

puerro m leek

puerta f door; (en deportes) goal; (de ciudad, en jardín) gate. **~ principal** main entrance. **a ~ cerrada** behind closed doors

puerto m port; (fig, refugio) refuge; (entre montañas) pass. **~ franco** free port

puertorriqueño adj & m Puerto Rican

pues adv (entonces) then; (bueno) well. ● conj since

puest|a f setting; (en juegos) bet. **~a de sol** sunset. **~a en escena** staging. **~a en marcha** starting. **~o** adj (vestido) dressed. ● m place; (empleo) position, job; (en mercado etc) stall. ● conj. **~o que** since

pugna f struggle. **~r** vi. **~r por** strive to

puja f struggle (**por** to); (en subasta) bid. **~r** vt struggle; (en subasta) bid

pulcro adj neat

pulga f flea. **tener malas ~s** be bad-tempered

pulga|da f inch. **~r** m thumb; (del pie) big toe

puli|do adj polished; (modales) refined. **~r** vt polish; (suavizar) smooth

pulla f gibe

pulm|ón m lung. **~onar** adj pulmonary. **~onía** f pneumonia

pulpa f pulp

pulpería f (LAm) grocer's shop (Brit), grocery store (Amer)

púlpito m pulpit

pulpo m octopus

pulque m (Mex) pulque, alcoholic Mexican drink. **~ría** f bar

pulsa|ción f pulsation. **~dor** m button. **~r** vt press; (Mus) pluck

pulsera f bracelet

pulso m pulse; (firmeza) steady hand. **echar un ~** arm wrestle. **tomar el ~ a uno** take s.o.'s pulse

pulular vi teem with

puma m puma

puna f puna, high plateau

punitivo adj punitive

punta f point; (extremo) tip. **estar de ~** be in a bad mood. **ponerse de ~ con uno** fall out with s.o. **sacar ~ a** sharpen

puntada f stitch

puntaje m (LAm) score

puntal m prop, support

puntapié m kick

puntear vt mark; (Mus) pluck; (LAm, en deportes) lead

puntería f aim; (destreza) markmanship

puntiagudo adj pointed; (afilado) sharp

puntilla f (encaje) lace. **en ~s** (LAm), **de ~s** on tiptoe

punto m point; (señal, trazo) dot; (de examen) mark; (lugar) spot, place; (de taxis) stand; (momento) moment; (punto final) full stop (Brit), period (Amer); (puntada) stitch. **~ de vista** point of view. **~ com** dot-com. **~ final** full stop (Brit), period (Amer). **~ muerto** (Auto) neutral (gear). **~ y aparte** full stop, new paragraph (Brit),

period, new paragraph (Amer). **~ y coma** semicolon. **a ~** on time; (listo) ready. **a ~ de** on the point of. **de ~** knitted. **dos ~s** colon. **en ~** exactly. **hacer ~** knit. **hasta cierto ~** to a certain extent

puntuación f punctuation; (en deportes, acción) scoring; (en deportes, número de puntos) score

puntual adj punctual; (exacto) accurate. **~idad** f punctuality; (exactitud) accuracy

puntuar 21 vt punctuate; mark (Brit), grade (Amer) (examen). ● vi score (points)

punza|da f sharp pain; (fig) pang. **~nte** adj sharp. **~r** 10 vt prick

puñado m handful. **a ~s** by the handful

puñal m dagger. **~ada** f stab

puñ|etazo m punch. **~o** m fist; (de ropa) cuff; (mango) handle. **de su ~o (y letra)** in his own handwriting

pupa f (fam, en los labios) cold sore

pupila f pupil

pupitre m desk

puré m purée; (sopa) thick soup. **~ de papas** (LAm), **~ de patatas** mashed potatoes

pureza f purity

purga f purge. **~torio** m purgatory

puri|ficación f purification. **~ificar** 7 vt purify. **~sta** m & f purist. **~tano** adj puritanical. ● m puritan

puro adj pure; (cielo) clear. **de pura casualidad** by sheer chance. **de ~ tonto** out of sheer stupidity. ● m cigar

púrpura f purple

pus m pus

puse vb véase PONER

p

pusilánime adj fainthearted
puta f (vulg) whore

Qq

que pron rel (personas, sujeto) who; (personas, complemento) whom; (cosas) which, that. ● conj that. ¡~ tengan Vds buen viaje! have a good journey! ¡~ venga! let him come! ~ venga o no venga whether he comes or not. creo ~ tiene razón I think (that) he is right. más ~ more than. lo ~ what. yo ~ tú if I were you

qué adj (con sustantivo) what; (con a o adv) how. ● pron what. ¡~ bonito! how nice! ¿en ~ piensas? what are you thinking about?

quebra|da f gorge; (paso) pass. ~dizo adj fragile. ~do adj broken; (Com) bankrupt. ● m (Math) fraction. ~ntar vt break; disturb (paz). ~nto m (pérdida) loss; (daño) damage. ~r **1** vt break. ● vi break; (Com) go bankrupt. ~rse vpr break

quechua adj Quechua. ● m & f Quechua. ● m (lengua) Quechua

quedar vi stay, remain; (estar) be; (haber todavía) be left. ~ bien come off well. ~se vpr stay. ~ con arrange to meet. ~ en agree to. ~ en nada come to nothing. ~ por (+ infinitivo) remain to be (+ pp)

quehacer m work. ~es domésticos household chores

queja f complaint; (de dolor) moan. ~rse vpr complain (de about); (gemir) moan. ~ido m moan

quema|do adj burnt; (LAm, bronceado) tanned; (fig) annoyed. ~dor m burner. ~dura f burn. ~r vt/i burn. ~rse vpr burn o.s.; (consumirse) burn up; (con el sol) get sunburnt. ~rropa adv. a ~rropa point-blank

quena f Indian flute

quepo vb véase CABER

querella f (riña) quarrel, dispute; (Jurid) criminal action

quer|er 35 vt want; (amar) love; (necesitar) need. ~er decir mean. ● m love; (amante) lover. como quiera que however. cuando quiera que whenever. donde quiera wherever. ¿quieres darme ese libro? would you pass me that book? ¿quieres un helado? would you like an ice-cream? quisiera ir a la playa I'd like to go to the beach. sin ~er without meaning to. ~ido adj dear; (amado) loved

querosén m, **queroseno** m kerosene

querubín m cherub

quesadilla f (Mex) tortilla filled with cheese. ~o m cheese

quetzal m (unidad monetaria ecuatoriana) quetzal

quicio m frame. sacar de ~ a uno infuriate s.o.

quiebra f (Com) bankruptcy

quien pron rel (sujeto) who; (complemento) whom

quién pron interrogativo (sujeto) who; (tras preposición) ¿con ~? who with?, to whom? ¿de ~ son estos libros? whose are these books?

quienquiera pron whoever

quiero vb véase QUERER

Rr

quiet|o adj still; (inmóvil) motionless; (carácter etc) calm. **~ud** f stillness

quijada f jaw

quilate m carat

quilla f keel

quimera f (fig) illusion

químic|a f chemistry. **~o** adj chemical. ● m chemist

quince adj & m fifteen. **~ días** a fortnight. **~na** f fortnight. **~nal** adj fortnightly

quincuagésimo adj fiftieth

quiniela f pools coupon. **~s** fpl (football) pools

quinientos adj & m five hundred

quinquenio m (period of) five years

quinta f (casa) villa

quintal m a hundred kilograms

quinteto m quintet

quinto adj & m fifth

quiosco m kiosk; (en jardín) summerhouse; (en parque etc) bandstand

quirúrgico adj surgical

quise vb véase QUERER

quisquill|a f trifle; (camarón) shrimp. **~oso** adj irritable; (exigente) fussy

quita|esmalte m nail polish remover. **~manchas** m invar stain remover. **~nieves** m invar snow plough. **~r** vt remove, take away; take off (ropa); (robar) steal. **~ndo** (fam, a excepción de) apart from. **~rse** vpr get rid of (dolor); take off (ropa). **~rse de** (no hacerlo más) stop. **~rse de en medio** get out of the way. **~sol** m sunshade

quizá(s) adv perhaps

quórum m quorum

rábano m radish. **~ picante** horseradish. **me importa un ~** I couldn't care less

rabi|a f rabies; (fig) rage. **~ar** vi (de dolor) be in great pain; (estar enfadado) be furious. **dar ~a** infuriate. **~eta** f tantrum

rabino m rabbi

rabioso adj rabid; (furioso) furious

rabo m tail

racha f gust of wind; (fig) spate. **pasar por una mala ~** go through a bad patch

racial adj racial

racimo m bunch

ración f share, ration; (de comida) portion

raciona|l adj rational. **~lizar** 🔟 vt rationalize. **~r** vt (limitar) ration; (repartir) ration out

racis|mo m racism. **~ta** adj racist

radar m radar

radiación f radiation

radiactiv|idad f radioactivity. **~o** adj radioactive

radiador m radiator

radiante adj radiant; (brillante) brilliant

radical adj & m & f radical

radicar 🔟 vi lie (en in). **~se** vpr settle

radio m radius; (de rueda) spoke; (LAm) radio. ● f radio. **~actividad** f radioactivity. **~activo** adj radioactive. **~difusión** f broadcasting. **~emisora** f radio station. **~escucha** m & f listener. **~grafía** f radiography

radi|ólogo m radiologist. **~ote-rapia** f radiotherapy

radioyente m & f listener

raer 36 vt scrape; (quitar) scrape off

ráfaga f (de viento) gust; (de ametralladora) burst

rafia f raffia

raído adj threadbare

raíz f root. a ~ de as a result of. echar raíces (fig) settle

raja f split; (Culin) slice. **~r** vt split. **~rse** vpr split; (fig) back out

rajatabla. a ~ rigorously

ralea f sort

ralla|dor m grater. **~r** vt grate

ralo adj (pelo) thin

rama f branch. **~je** m branches. **~l** m branch

rambla f watercourse; (avenida) avenue

ramera f prostitute

ramifica|ción f ramification. **~rse** 7 vpr branch out

ram|illete m bunch. **~o** m branch; (de flores) bunch, bouquet

rampa f ramp, slope

rana f frog

ranch|era f (Mex) folk song. **~ero** m cook; (Mex, hacendado) rancher. **~o** m (LAm, choza) hut; (LAm, casucha) shanty; (Mex, hacienda) ranch

rancio adj rancid; (vino) old; (fig) ancient

rango m rank

ranúnculo m buttercup

ranura f groove; (para moneda) slot

rapar vt shave; crop (pelo)

rapaz adj rapacious; (ave) of prey

rape m monkfish

rapidez f speed

rápido adj fast, quick. ● adv quickly. ● m (tren) express. **~s** mpl rapids

rapiña f robbery. ave f de ~ bird of prey

rapsodia f rhapsody

rapt|ar vt kidnap. **~o** m kidnapping; (de ira etc) fit

raqueta f racquet

rar|eza f rarity; (cosa rara) oddity. **~o** adj rare; (extraño) odd. es **~o** que it is strange that. **¡qué ~o!** how strange!

ras. a ~ de level with

rasca|cielos m invar skyscraper. **~r** 7 vt scratch; (raspar) scrape

rasgar 12 vt tear

rasgo m characteristic; (gesto) gesture; (de pincel) stroke. **~s** mpl (facciones) features

rasguear vt strum

rasguñ|ar vt scratch. **~o** m scratch

raso adj (cucharada etc) level; (vuelo etc) low. al ~ in the open air. ● m satin

raspa|dura f scratch; (acción) scratching. **~r** vt scratch; (rozar) scrape

rastr|a. a **~as** dragging. **~ear** vt track. **~ero** adj creeping. **~illar** vt rake. **~illo** m rake. **~o** m track; (señal) sign. **ni ~o** not a trace

rata f rat

ratero m petty thief

ratifica|ción f ratification. **~r** 7 vt ratify

rato m moment, short time. **~s libres** spare time. a **~s** at times. a cada ~ (LAm) always. hace un ~ a moment ago. pasar un mal ~ have a rough time

rat|ón m mouse. **~onera** f

mousetrap; (*madriguera*) mouse hole

raudal *m* torrent. **a ~les** in abundance

raya *f* line; (*lista*) stripe; (*de pelo*) parting. **a ~s** striped. **pasarse de la ~** go too far. **~r** *vt* scratch. **~r en** border on

rayo *m* ray; (*descarga eléctrica*) lightning. **~ de luna** moonbeam. **~ láser** laser beam. **~s X** X-rays

raza *f* race; (*de animal*) breed. **de ~** (*caballo*) thoroughbred; (*perro*) pedigree

razón *f* reason. **a ~ón de** at the rate of. **tener ~ón** be right. **~onable** *adj* reasonable. **~onar** *vt* reason out. ● *vi* reason

RDSI *abrev* (**Red Digital de Servicios Integrados**) ISDN

re *m* D; (*solfa*) re

reac|ción *f* reaction; (*LAm, Pol*) right wing. **~ción en cadena** chain reaction. **~cionario** *adj & m* reactionary. **~tor** *m* reactor; (*avión*) jet

real *adj* real; (*de rey etc*) royal; (*hecho*) true. ● *m* real, old Spanish coin

realidad *f* reality; (*verdad*) truth. **en ~** in fact. **hacerse ~** come true

realis|mo *m* realism. **~ta** *adj* realistic. ● *m & f* realist

realiza|ción *f* fulfilment. **~r** 🔟 *vt* carry out; make (*viaje*); fulfil (*ilusión*); (*vender*) sell. **~rse** *vpr* (*sueño, predicción etc*) come true; (*persona*) fulfil o.s.

realzar 🔟 *vt* (*fig*) enhance

reanimar *vt* revive. **~se** *vpr* revive

reanudar *vt* resume; renew (*amistad*)

reavivar *vt* revive

rebaja *f* reduction. **en ~s** in the sale. **~do** *adj* (*precio*) reduced. **~r** *vt* lower; lose (*peso*)

rebanada *f* slice

rebaño *m* herd; (*de ovejas*) flock

rebasar *vt* exceed; (*dejar atrás*) leave behind; (*Mex, Auto*) overtake

rebatir *vt* refute

rebel|arse *vpr* rebel. **~de** *adj* rebellious; (*grupo*) rebel. ● *m* rebel. **~día** *f* rebelliousness. **~ión** *f* rebellion

rebosa|nte *adj* brimming (**de** with). **~r** *vi* overflow; (*abundar*) abound

rebot|ar *vt* bounce; (*rechazar*) repel. ● *vi* bounce; (*bala*) ricochet. **~e** *m* bounce, rebound. **de ~e** on the rebound

reboz|ar 🔟 *vt* wrap up; (*Culin*) coat in batter. **~o** *m* (*LAm*) shawl

rebusca|do *adj* affected; (*complicado*) over-elaborate. **~r** 🥇 *vt* search through

rebuznar *vi* bray

recado *m* errand; (*mensaje*) message

reca|er 🮄 *vi* fall back; (*Med*) relapse; (*fig*) fall. **~ída** *f* relapse

recalcar 🥇 *vt* stress

recalcitrante *adj* recalcitrant

recalentar 🬋 *vt* reheat; (*demasiado*) overheat

recámara *f* small room; (*de arma de fuego*) chamber; (*Mex, dormitorio*) bedroom

recambio *m* (*Mec*) spare (part); (*de pluma etc*) refill. **de ~** spare

recapitular *vt* sum up

recarg|ar 🬋 *vt* overload; (*aumentar*) increase; recharge (*batería*). **~o** *m* increase

recat|ado adj modest. **~o** m prudence; (*modestia*) modesty. **sin ~o** openly

recauda|ción f (*cantidad*) takings. **~dor** m tax collector. **~r** vt collect

recel|ar vt suspect. ● vi be suspicious (**de** of). **~o** m distrust; (*temor*) fear. **~oso** adj suspicious

recepci|ón f reception. **~onista** m & f receptionist

receptáculo m receptacle

receptor m receiver

recesión f recession

receta f recipe; (*Med*) prescription

rechaz|ar vt reject; defeat (*moción*); repel (*ataque*); (*no aceptar*) turn down. **~o** m rejection

rechifla f booing

rechinar vi squeak. **le rechinan los dientes** he grinds his teeth

rechoncho adj stout

recib|imiento m (*acogida*) welcome. **~ir** vt receive; (*acoger*) welcome ● vi entertain. **~irse** vpr graduate. **~o** m receipt. **acusar ~o** acknowledge receipt

reci|én adv recently; (*LAm, hace poco*) just. **~ casado** newly married. **~ nacido** newborn. **~ente** adj recent; (*Culin*) fresh

recinto m enclosure; (*local*) premises

recio adj strong; (*voz*) loud. ● adv hard; (*en voz alta*) loudly

recipiente m receptacle. ● m & f recipient

recíproco adj reciprocal; (*sentimiento*) mutual

recita|l m recital; (*de poesías*) reading. **~r** vt recite

reclama|ción f claim; (*queja*) complaint. **~r** vt claim. ● vi appeal

réclame m (*LAm*) advertisement

reclamo m (*LAm*) complaint

reclinar vi lean. **~se** vpr lean

reclus|ión f imprisonment. **~o** m prisoner

recluta m & f recruit. **~miento** m recruitment. **~r** vt recruit

recobrar vt recover. **~se** vpr recover

recodo m bend

recog|er **14** vt collect; pick up (*cosa caída*); (*cosechar*) harvest. **~erse** vpr withdraw; (*ir a casa*) go home; (*acostarse*) go to bed. **~ida** f collection; (*cosecha*) harvest

recomenda|ción f recommendation. **~r** **1** vt recommend; (*encomendar*) entrust

recomenzar **1** & **10** vt/i start again

recompensa f reward. **~r** vt reward

reconcilia|ción f reconciliation. **~r** vt reconcile. **~rse** vpr be reconciled

reconoc|er **11** vt recognize; (*admitir*) acknowledge; (*examinar*) examine. **~imiento** m recognition; (*admisión*) acknowledgement; (*agradecimiento*) gratitude; (*examen*) examination

reconozco vb véase **RECONOCER**

reconquista f reconquest. **~r** vt reconquer; (*fig*) win back

---

Reconquista The period in Spain's history during which the Christian kingdoms slowly recovered the territories occupied by the Moslem Moors of North Africa. The Moorish invasion began in 711 AD and was halted in 718. The expulsion of

223

the last Moorish ruler of Granada in 1492 completed the *Reconquista*.

reconsiderar vt reconsider

reconstruir 🔟 vt reconstruct

récord /'rekor/ m (pl ~s) record

recordar 🔁 vt remember; (*hacer acordar*) remind. ● vi remember. **que yo recuerde** as far as I remember. **si mal no recuerdo** if I remember rightly

recorr|er vt tour (país); go round (zona, museo); cover (distancia). ~ **mundo** travel all around the world. ~**ido** m journey; (*trayecto*) route

recort|ar vt cut (out). ~**e** m cutting (out); (*de periódico etc*) cutting

recostar 🔁 vt lean. ~**se** vpr lie down

recoveco m bend; (*rincón*) nook

recre|ación f recreation. ~**ar** vt recreate; (*divertir*) entertain. ~**arse** vpr amuse o.s. ~**ativo** adj recreational. ~**o** m recreation; (*en escuela*) break

recrudecer 🔟 vi intensify

recta f straight line. ~ **final** home stretch

rect|angular adj rectangular. ~**ángulo** adj rectangular; (*triángulo*) right-angled. ● m rectangle

rectifica|ción f rectification. ~**r** 🔟 vt rectify

rect|itud f straightness; (*fig*) honesty. ~**o** adj straight; (*fig, justo*) fair; (*fig, honrado*) honest. **todo** ~**o** straight on. ● m rectum

rector adj governing. ● m rector

recubrir (*pp recubierto*) vt cover (con, de with)

recuerdo m memory; (*regalo*) souvenir. ~**s** mpl (*saludos*) regards.
● vb véase **RECORDAR**

recupera|ción f recovery. ~**r** vt recover. ~**r el tiempo perdido** make up for lost time. ~**rse** vpr recover

recur|rir vi. ~**rir a** resort to (cosa); turn to (persona). ~**so** m resort; (*medio*) recourse; (*Jurid*) appeal. ~**sos** mpl resources

red f network; (*malla*) net; (*para equipaje*) luggage rack; (*Com*) chain; (*Elec, gas*) mains. **la R~** the Net

redac|ción f writing; (*lenguaje*) wording; (*conjunto de redactores*) editorial staff; (*oficina*) editorial office; (*Escol, Univ*) essay. ~**tar** vt write. ~**tor** m writer; (*de periódico*) editor

redada f catch; (*de policía*) raid

redecilla f small net; (*para el pelo*) hairnet

redentor adj redeeming

redimir vt redeem

redoblar vt redouble; step up (vigilancia)

redomado adj utter

redond|a f (*de imprenta*) roman (type); (*Mus*) semibreve (*Brit*), whole note (*Amer*). **a la** ~**a** around. ~**ear** vt round off. ~**el** m circle; (*de plaza de toros*) arena. ~**o** adj round; (*completo*) complete; (*Mex, boleto*) return, round-trip (*Amer*). **en** ~**o** round; (*categóricamente*) flatly

reduc|ción f reduction. ~**ido** adj reduced; (*limitado*) limited; (*pequeño*) small; (*precio*) low. ~**ir** 🔢 vt reduce. ~**irse** vpr be reduced to; (*fig*) amount

reduje vb véase **REDUCIR**

redundan|cia f redundancy. ~**te** adj redundant

reduzco vb véase **REDUCIR**

reconsiderar | reduzco

reembols|ar *vt* reimburse. **~o** *m* repayment. **contra ~o** cash on delivery

reemplaz|ar 🔟 *vt* replace. **~o** *m* replacement

refacci|ón *f* (*LAm*) refurbishment; (*Mex, Mec*) spare part. **~onar** *vt* (*LAm*) refurbish. **~onaria** *f* (*Mex*) repair shop

referencia *f* reference; (*información*) report. **con ~ a** with reference to. **hacer ~ a** refer to

referéndum *m* (*pl* **~s**) referendum

referir 🔠 *vt* tell; (*remitir*) refer. **~se** *vpr* refer. **por lo que se refiere a** as regards

refiero *vb véase* **REFERIR**

refilón. de ~ obliquely

refin|amiento *m* refinement. **~ar** *vt* refine. **~ería** *f* refinery

reflector *m* reflector; (*proyector*) searchlight

reflej|ar *vt* reflect. **~o** *adj* reflex. ● *m* reflection; (*Med*) reflex; (*en el pelo*) highlights

reflexi|ón *f* reflection. **sin ~ón** without thinking. **~onar** *vi* reflect. **~vo** *adj* (*persona*) thoughtful; (*Gram*) reflexive

reforma *f* reform. **~s** *fpl* (*reparaciones*) repairs. **~r** *vt* reform. **~rse** *vpr* reform

reforzar 🔢 & 🔟 *vt* reinforce

refrac|ción *f* refraction. **~tario** *adj* heat-resistant

refrán *m* saying

refregar 🔝 & 🔢 *vt* scrub

refresc|ar 🔽 *vt* refresh; (*enfriar*) cool. ● *vi* get cooler. **~arse** *vpr* refresh o.s. **~o** *m* cold drink. **~os** *mpl* refreshments

refrigera|ción *f* refrigeration; (*aire acondicionado*) air-

conditioning; (*de motor*) cooling. **~r** *vt* refrigerate; air-condition (*lugar*); cool (*motor*). **~dor** *m* refrigerator

refuerzo *m* reinforcement

refugi|ado *m* refugee. **~arse** *vpr* take refuge. **~o** *m* refuge, shelter

refunfuñar *vi* grumble

refutar *vt* refute

regadera *f* watering-can; (*Mex, ducha*) shower

regala|do *adj* as a present, free; (*cómodo*) comfortable. **~r** *vt* give

regalo *m* present, gift

regañ|adientes. a ~adientes reluctantly. **~ar** *vt* scold. ● *vi* moan; (*dos personas*) quarrel. **~o** *m* (*represión*) scolding

regar 🔝 & 🔢 *vt* water

regata *f* boat race; (*serie*) regatta

regate|ar *vt* haggle over; (*economizar*) economize on. ● *vi* haggle; (*en deportes*) dribble. **~o** *m* haggling; (*en deportes*) dribbling

regazo *m* lap

regenerar *vt* regenerate

régimen *m* (*pl* **regímenes**) regime; (*Med*) diet; (*de lluvias*) pattern

regimiento *m* regiment

regi|ón *f* region. **~onal** *adj* regional

regir 🔢 & 🔢 *vt* govern. ● *vi* apply, be in force

registr|ado *adj* registered. **~ar** *vt* register; (*Mex*) check in (*equipaje*); (*grabar*) record; (*examinar*) search. **~arse** *vpr* register; (*darse*) be reported. **~o** *m* (*acción de registrar*) registration; (*libro*) register; (*cosa anotada*) entry; (*inspección*) search. **~o civil** (*oficina*) registry office

regla *f* ruler; (*norma*) rule; (*mens-*

loads of

montura f mount; (*silla*) saddle

monument|al *adj* monumental; (*fig, muy grande*) enormous. **~o** m monument

monzón m & f monsoon

moñ|a f ribbon. **~o** m bun; (*LAm, lazo*) bow

moque|o m runny nose. **~ro** m 🔟 handkerchief

moqueta f fitted carpet

moquillo m distemper

mora f mulberry; (*de zarzamora*) blackberry; (*Jurid*) default

morada f dwelling

morado *adj* purple

morador m inhabitant

moral m mulberry tree. ● f morals. ● *adj* moral. **~eja** f moral. **~idad** f morality. **~ista** m & f moralist. **~izador** *adj* moralizing. ● m moralist. **~izar** 🔟 vt moralize

morar vi live

moratoria f moratorium

mórbido *adj* soft; (*malsano*) morbid

morbo m illness. **~sidad** f morbidity. **~so** *adj* unhealthy

morcilla f black pudding

morda|cidad f sharpness. **~z** *adj* scathing

mordaza f gag

morde|dura f bite. **~r** 🔁 vt bite; (*Mex, exigir soborno a*) extract a bribe from. ● vi bite. **~rse** *vpr* bite o.s. **~rse las uñas** bite one's nails

mordi|da f (*Mex*) bribe. **~sco** m bite. **~squear** vt nibble (at)

moreno *adj* (*con ser*) dark; (*de pelo obscuro*) dark-haired; (*de raza negra*) dark-skinned; (*con estar*) brown, tanned

morera f white mulberry tree

moretón m bruise

morfema m morpheme

morfin|a f morphine. **~ómano** m morphine addict

morfol|ogía f morphology. **~ógico** *adj* morphological

moribundo *adj* dying

morir 🔟 (*pp* **muerto**) vi die; (*fig, extinguirse*) die away; (*fig, terminar*) end. **~ ahogado** drown. **~se** *vpr* die. **~se de hambre** starve to death; (*fig*) be starving. **se muere por una flauta** she's dying to have a flute

morisco *adj* Moorish. ● m Moor

morm|ón m Mormon. **~ónico** *adj* Mormon. **~onismo** m Mormonism

moro *adj* Moorish. ● m Moor

morral m (*mochila*) rucksack; (*de cazador*) gamebag; (*para caballos*) nosebag

morrillo m nape of the neck

morriña f homesickness

morro m snout

morrocotudo *adj* (🔟, *tremendo*) terrible; (*estupendo*) terrific 🔟

morsa f walrus

mortaja f shroud

mortal *adj* & m & f mortal. **~idad** f mortality. **~mente** *adv* mortally

mortandad f loss of life; (*Mil*) carnage

mortecino *adj* failing; (*color*) pale

mortero m mortar

mortífero *adj* deadly

mortifica|ción f mortification. **~r** 🔟 vt (*atormentar*) torment. **~rse** *vpr* distress o.s.

mortuorio *adj* death

mosaico m mosaic; (*Mex, baldosa*) floor tile

mosca f fly. **~rda** f blowfly. **~rdón** m botfly; (*de cuerpo azul*) bluebottle

moscatel adj muscatel

moscón m botfly; (mosca de cuerpo azul) bluebottle

moscovita adj & m & f Muscovite

mosque|arse vpr get cross. **~o** m resentment

mosquete m musket. **~ro** m musketeer

mosquit|ero m mosquito net. **~o** m mosquito

mostacho m moustache

mostaza f mustard

mosto m must, grape juice

mostrador m counter

mostrar ☒ vt show. **~se** vpr (show oneself to) be. **se mostró muy amable** he was very kind

mota f spot, speck

mote. m nickname

motea|do adj speckled. **~r** vt speckle

motejar vt call

motel m motel

motete m motet

motín m riot; (de tropas, tripulación) mutiny

motiv|ación f motivation. **~ar** vt motivate. **~o** m reason. **con ~o de** because of

motocicl|eta f motor cycle, motor bike ☒. **~ista** m & f motorcyclist

motoneta f (LAm) (motor) scooter

motor adj motor. ● m motor, engine. **~ de arranque** starter motor. **~a** f motor boat. **~ismo** m motorcycling. **~ista** m & f motorist; (de una moto) motorcyclist. **~izar** ☒ vt motorize

motriz adj motor

move|dizo adj movable; (poco firme) unstable; (persona) fickle. **~r** ☒ vt move; shake (la cabeza); (provocar) cause. **~rse** vpr move; (darse prisa) hurry up

movi|ble adj movable. **~do** adj moved; (Foto) blurred

móvil adj mobile; (Esp, teléfono) mobile phone, cellphone. ● m motive

movili|dad f mobility. **~zación** f mobilization. **~zar** ☒ vt mobilize

movimiento m movement, motion; (agitación) bustle

moza f young girl. **~lbete** m lad

mozárabe adj Mozarabic. ● m & f Mozarab

moz|o m young boy. **~uela** f young girl. **~uelo** m young boy/ lad

mucam|a f (LAm) servant. **~o** m (LAm) servant

muchach|a f girl; (sirvienta) servant, maid. **~o** m boy, lad

muchedumbre f crowd

mucho adj a lot of; (en negativas, preguntas) much, a lot of. **~s** a lot of; (en negativas, preguntas) many, a lot of. ● pron a lot; (personas) many (people). **como ~** at the most. **ni ~ menos** by no means. **por ~ que** however much. ● adv a lot, very much; (tiempo) long, a long time

mucos|idad f mucus. **~o** adj mucous

muda f change of clothing; (de animales) shedding. **~ble** adj changeable; (personas) fickle. **~nza** f move, removal (Brit). **~r** vt change; shed (piel). **~rse** vpr (de ropa) change one's clothes; (de casa) move (house)

mudéjar adj & m & f Mudejar

mud|ez f dumbness. **~o** adj

dumb; (*callado*) silent

mueble *adj* movable. ● *m* piece of furniture. **~s** *mpl* furniture

mueca *f* grimace, face. **hacer una ~** pull a face

muela *f* back tooth, molar; (*piedra de afilar*) grindstone; (*piedra de molino*) millstone. **~ del juicio** wisdom tooth

muelle *adj* soft. ● *m* spring; (*Naut*) wharf; (*malecón*) jetty

muérdago *m* mistletoe

muero *vb véase* MORIR

muert|e *f* death; (*homicidio*) murder. **~o** *adj* dead. ● *m* dead person

muesca *f* nick; (*ranura*) slot

muestra *f* sample; (*prueba*) proof; (*modelo*) model; (*señal*) sign. **~rio** *m* collection of samples

muestro *vb véase* MOSTRAR

muevo *vb véase* MOVER

mugi|do *m* moo. **~r 14** *vi* moo

mugr|e *m* dirt. **~iento** *adj* dirty, filthy

mugrón *m* sucker

mujer *f* woman; (*esposa*) wife. ● *int* my dear! **~iego** *adj* fond of the women. **~zuela** *f* prostitute

mula *f* mule. **~da** *f* drove of mules

mulato *adj* of mixed race (*black and white*). ● *m* person of mixed race

mulero *m* muleteer

muleta *f* crutch; (*toreo*) stick with a red flag

mulli|do *adj* soft. **~r 22** *vt* soften

mulo *m* mule

multa *f* fine. **~r** *vt* fine

multi|color *adj* multicoloured. **~copista** *m* duplicator. **~cultural** *adj* multicultural. **~forme** *adj*

multiform. **~lateral** *adj* multilateral. **~lingüe** *adj* multilingual. **~millonario** *m* multimillionaire

múltiple *adj* multiple

multiplic|ación *f* multiplication. **~ar 7** *vt* multiply. **~arse** *vpr* multiply. **~idad** *f* multiplicity

múltiplo *m* multiple

multitud *f* multitude, crowd. **~inario** *adj* mass; (*concierto*) with mass audience

mund|ano *adj* wordly; (*de la sociedad elegante*) society. **~ial** *adj* world-wide. **la segunda guerra ~ial** the Second World War. **~illo** *m* world, circles. **~o** *m* world. **todo el ~o** everybody

munición *f* ammunition; (*provisiones*) supplies

municip|al *adj* municipal. **~alidad** *f* municipality. **~io** *m* municipality; (*ayuntamiento*) town council

muñe|ca *f* (*en anatomía*) wrist; (*juguete*) doll; (*maniquí*) dummy. **~co** *m* doll. **~quera** *f* wristband

muñón *m* stump

mura|l *adj* mural, wall. ● *m* mural. **~lla** *f* (*city*) wall. **~r** *vt* wall

murciélago *m* bat

murga *f* street band

murmullo *m* (*incl fig*) murmur

murmura|ción *f* gossip. **~dor** *adj* gossiping. ● *m* gossip. **~r** *vi* murmur; (*criticar*) gossip

muro *m* wall

murria *f* depression

mus *m* card game

musa *f* muse

musaraña *f* shrew

muscula|r *adj* muscular. **~tura** *f* muscles

músculo *m* muscle

musculoso *adj* muscular

muselina f muslin

museo m museum. ~ **de arte** art gallery

musgo m moss. ~**so** adj mossy

música f music

musical adj & m musical

músico adj musical. ● m musician

music|ología f musicology. ~**ólogo** m musicologist

muslo m thigh

mustio adj (plantas) withered; (cosas) faded; (personas) gloomy; (Mex, hipócrita) two-faced

musulmán adj & m Muslim

muta|bilidad f mutability. ~**ción** f mutation

mutila|ción f mutilation. ~**do** adj crippled. ● m cripple. ~**r** vt mutilate; maim (persona)

mutis (en el teatro) exit. ~**mo** m silence

mutu|alidad f mutuality; (asociación) friendly society. ~**amente** adv mutually. ~**o** adj mutual

muy adv very; (demasiado) too

. . . .

Nn

. . . .

nabo m turnip

nácar m mother-of-pearl

nac|er 11 vi be born; (pollito) hatch out; (planta) sprout. ~**ido** adj born. **recien** ~**ido** newborn. ~**iente** adj (sol) rising. ~**imiento** m birth; (de río) source; (belén) crib. **lugar** m **de** ~**imiento** place of birth

naci|ón f nation. ~**onal** adj national. ~**onalidad** f nationality.

~onalismo m nationalism. ~**onalista** m & f nationalist. ~**onalizar** 10 vt nationalize. ~**onalizarse** vpr become naturalized

nada pron nothing, not anything. ● adv not at all. ¡~ **de eso!** nothing of the sort! **antes que** ~ first of all. ¡**de** ~! (después de 'gracias') don't mention it! **para** ~ (not) at all. **por** ~ **del mundo** not for anything in the world

nada|dor m swimmer. ~**r** vi swim. ~**r de espalda(s)** do (the) backstroke

nadería f trifle

nadie pron no one, nobody

nado m (Mex) swimming. ● adv **a** ~ swimming

naipe m (playing) card. **juegos** mpl **de** ~**s** card games

nalga f buttock. ~**s** fpl bottom. ~**da** f (Mex) smack on the bottom

nana f lullaby

naranj|a f orange. ~**ada** f orangeade. ~**al** m orange grove. ~**ero** m orange tree

narcótico adj & m narcotic

nariz f nose. ¡**narices!** rubbish!

narra|ción f narration. ~**dor** m narrator. ~**r** vt tell. ~**tivo** adj narrative

nasal adj nasal

nata f cream

natación f swimming

natal adj native; (pueblo etc) home. ~**idad** f birth rate

natillas fpl custard

nativo adj & m native

nato adj born

natural adj natural. ● m native. ~**eza** f nature. ~**eza muerta** still life. ~**idad** f naturalness. ~**ista** m & f naturalist. ~**izar** 10 vt naturalize. **~izarse** vpr become naturalized. **~mente** adv naturally. ● int of course!

naufrag|ar 12 vi (barco) sink; (persona) be shipwrecked; (fig) fail. **~io** m shipwreck

náufrago adj shipwrecked. ● m shipwrecked person

náuseas fpl nausea. **dar ~s a uno** make s.o. feel sick. **sentir ~s** feel sick

náutico adj nautical

navaja f penknife; (de afeitar) razor. **~zo** m slash

naval adj naval

nave f ship; (de iglesia) nave. **~ espacial** spaceship. **quemar las ~s** burn one's boats

navega|ble adj navigable; (barco) seaworthy. **~ción** f navigation; (tráfico) shipping. **~dor** m (Informática) browser. **~nte** m & f navigator. **~r** 12 vi (Informática) browse

Navid|ad f Christmas. **~eño** adj Christmas. **en ~ades** at Christmas. **¡feliz ~ad!** Happy Christmas! **por ~ad** at Christmas

nazi adj & m & f Nazi. **~smo** m Nazism

neblina f mist

nebuloso adj misty; (fig) vague

necedad f foolishness. **decir ~es** talk nonsense. **hacer una ~** do sth stupid

necesari|amente adv necessarily. **~o** adj necessary

necesi|dad f need; (cosa esencial) necessity; (pobreza) poverty. **~dades** fpl hardships. **no hay ~dad** there's no need. **por ~dad** (out) of necessity. **~tado** adj in need (**de** of). **~tar** vt need. ● vi. **~tar de** need

necio adj silly. ● m idiot

néctar m nectar

nectarina f nectarine

nefasto adj unfortunate; (consecuencia) disastrous; (influencia) harmful

nega|ción f denial; (Gram) negative. **~do** adj useless. **~r** 1 & 12 vt deny; (rehusar) refuse. **~rse** vpr refuse (**a** to). **~tiva** f (acción) denial; (acción de rehusar) refusal. **~tivo** adj & m negative

negligen|cia f negligence. **~te** adj negligent

negoci|able adj negotiable. **~ación** f negotiation. **~ante** m & f dealer. **~ar** vt/i negotiate. **~ar en** trade in. **~o** m business; (Com, trato) deal. **~os** mpl business. **hombre de ~os** businessman

negr|a f black woman; (Mus) crotchet. **~o** adj black; (ojos) dark. ● m (color) black; (persona) black man. **~ura** f blackness. **~uzco** adj blackish

nen|a f little girl. **~o** m little boy

nenúfar m water lily

neocelandés adj from New Zealand. ● m New Zealander

neón m neon

nepotismo m nepotism

nervio m nerve; (tendón) sinew; (en botánica) vein. **~sidad** f, **~sismo** m nervousness; (impaciencia) impatience. **~so** adj nervous; (de temperamento) highly-strung. **ponerse ~so** get nervous

neto adj clear; (verdad) simple; (Com) net

neumático adj pneumatic. ● m tyre

neumonía f pneumonia

neur|algia f neuralgia. **~ología** f neurology. **~ólogo** m neurologist. **~osis** f neurosis. **~ótico** adj neurotic

neutr|al adj neutral. **~alidad** f neutrality. **~alizar** 10 vt neutralize. **~o** adj neutral; (Gram) neuter

neva|da f snowfall. **~r** 1 vi snow. **~sca** f blizzard

nevera f refrigerator, fridge (Brit)

nevisca f light snowfall

nexo m link

ni conj. **~...~** neither... nor. **~ aunque** not even if. **~ siquiera** not even. **sin...~ ...** without ... or...

Nicaragua f Nicaragua

nicaragüense adj & m & f Nicaraguan

nicho m niche

nicotina f nicotine

nido m nest; (de ladrones) den

niebla f fog. **hay ~** it's foggy. **un día de ~** a foggy day

niet|a f granddaughter. **~o** m grandson. **~os** mpl grandchildren

nieve f snow; (Mex, helado) sorbet

niki m polo shirt

nimi|edad f triviality. **~o** adj insignificant

ninfa f nymph

ningún véase NINGUNO

ninguno adj (delante de nombre masculino en singular **ningún**) no; (con otro negativo) any. **de ninguna manera, de ningún modo** by no means. **en ninguna parte** nowhere. **sin ningún amigo** without any friends. ● pron (de dos) neither; (de más de dos) none; (nadie) no-one, nobody

niñ|a f (little) girl. **~era** f nanny. **~ería** f childish thing. **~ez** f childhood. **~o** adj childish. ● m (little) boy **de ~o** as a child. **desde ~o** from childhood

níquel m nickel

níspero m medlar

nitidez f clarity; (de foto, imagen) sharpness

nítido adj clear; (foto, imagen) sharp

nitrógeno m nitrogen

nivel m level; (fig) standard. **~ de vida** standard of living. **~ar** vt level. **~arse** vpr become level

no adv not; (como respuesta) no. **¿~?** isn't it? **¡a que ~!** I bet you don't! **¡cómo ~!** of course! **Felipe ~ tiene hijos** Felipe has no children. **¡que ~!** certainly not!

nob|iliario adj noble. **~le** adj m & f noble. **~leza** f nobility

noche f night. **~ vieja** New Year's Eve. **de ~** at night. **hacerse de ~** get dark. **hacer ~** spend the night. **media ~** midnight. **en la ~** (LAm), **por la ~** at night

---

Nochevieja In Spain and other Spanish-speaking countries, where it is known as Año Nuevo, it is customary to see the New Year in by eating twelve grapes for good luck, one on each chime of the clock at midnight.

Nochebuena f Christmas Eve

noción f notion. **nociones** fpl rudiments

nocivo adj harmful

nocturno adj nocturnal; (clase) evening; (tren etc) night. ● m nocturne

nodriza f wet nurse

nogal m walnut tree; (madera) walnut

nómada adj nomadic. ● m & f nomad

nombr|ado adj famous; (*susodicho*) aforementioned. **∼amiento** m appointment. **∼ar** vt appoint; (*citar*) mention. **∼e** m name; (*Gram*) noun; (*fama*) renown. **∼e de pila** Christian name. **en ∼e de** in the name of. **no tener ∼e** be unspeakable. **poner de ∼e** call

nomeolvides m invar forget-me-not

nómina f payroll

nomina|l adj nominal. **∼tivo** adj & m nominative. **∼tivo a** (*cheque etc*) made out to

non adj odd. ● m odd number. **pares y ∼es** odds and evens

nono adj ninth

nordeste adj (*región*) north-eastern; (*viento*) north-easterly. ● m northeast

nórdico adj Nordic. ● m Northern European

noria f water-wheel; (*en una feria*) big wheel (*Brit*), Ferris wheel (*Amer*)

norma f rule

normal adj normal. ● f teachers' training college. **∼idad** f normality (*Brit*), normalcy (*Amer*). **∼izar** 10 vt normalize. **∼mente** adv normally, usually

noroeste adj (*región*) north-western; (*viento*) north-westerly. ● m northwest

norte adj (*región*) northern; (*viento, lado*) north. ● m north; (*fig, meta*) aim

Norteamérica f (North) America

norteamericano adj & m (North) American

norteño adj northern. ● m northerner

Noruega f Norway

noruego adj & m Norwegian

nos pron (*acusativo*) us; (*dativo*) (to) us; (*reflexivo*) (to) ourselves; (*recíproco*) (to) each other

nosotros pron we; (*con prep*) us

nost|algia f nostalgia; (*de casa, de patria*) homesickness. **∼álgico** adj nostalgic

nota f note; (*de examen etc*) mark. **de ∼** famous. **de mala ∼** notorious. **digno de ∼** notable. **∼ble** adj notable. **∼ción** f notation. **∼r** vt notice. **es de ∼r** it should be noted. **hacerse ∼r** stand out

notario m notary

notici|a f (piece of) news. **∼as** fpl news. **atrasado de ∼as** behind with the news. **tener ∼as de** hear from. **∼ario**, (*LAm*) **∼ero** m news

notifica|ción f notification. **∼r** 7 vt notify

notori|edad f notoriety. **∼o** adj well-known; (*evidente*) obvious; (*notable*) marked

novato adj inexperienced. ● m novice

novecientos adj & m nine hundred

noved|ad f newness; (*cosa nueva*) innovation; (*cambio*) change; (*moda*) latest fashion. **llegar sin ∼ad** arrive safely. **∼oso** adj novel

novel|a f novel. **∼ista** m & f novelist

noveno adj ninth

noventa adj & m ninety; (*nonagésimo*) ninetieth

novia f girlfriend; (*prometida*) fiancée; (*en boda*) bride. **llegar a ∼a** go out together. **∼zgo** m engagement

novicio m novice

noviembre m November

novill|a f heifer. **∼o** m bullock. **hacer ∼os** play truant

189

objeción | ocupación

obje|ción f objection. **~tar** vt/i object

objetivo adj objective. ● m objective; (foto etc) lens

objeto m object. **~r** m objector. **~ de conciencia** conscientious objector

oblicuo adj oblique

obliga|ción f obligation; (Com) bond. **~do** adj obliged; (forzoso) obligatory; **~r** 12 vt force, oblige. **~rse** vpr. **~rse a** undertake to. **~torio** adj obligatory

oboe m oboe. ● m & f (músico) oboist

obra f work; (acción) deed; (de teatro) play; (construcción) building work. **~ maestra** masterpiece. **en ~s** under construction. **por ~ de** thanks to. **~r** vt do

obrero adj labour; (clase) working. ● m workman; (de fábrica, construcción) worker

obscen|idad f obscenity. **~o** adj obscene

obscu... véase **oscu...**

obsequi|ar vt lavish attention on. **~ar con** give, present with. **~o** m gift, present; (agasajo) attention. **~oso** adj obliging

observa|ción f observation. **hacer una ~ción** make a remark. **~dor** m observer. **~ncia** f observance. **~r** vt observe; (notar) notice. **~torio** m observatory

obses|ión f obsession. **~ionar** vt obsess. **~ivo** adj obsessive. **~o** adj obsessed

obst|aculizar 10 vt hinder; hold up (tráfico). **~áculo** m obstacle

obstante: **no ~** adv however, nevertheless; (como prep) in spite of

obstar vi. **eso no obsta para que vaya** that should not prevent him

from going

obstina|do adj obstinate. **~rse** vpr. **~rse en** (+ infinitivo) insist on (+ gerundio)

obstru|cción f obstruction. **~ir** 17 vt obstruct

obtener 40 vt get, obtain

obtura|dor m (Foto) shutter. **~r** vt plug; fill (muela etc)

obvio adj obvious

oca f goose

ocasi|ón f occasion; (oportunidad) opportunity. **aprovechar la ~ón** take the opportunity. **con ~ón de** on the occasion of. **de ~ón** bargain; (usado) second-hand. **en ~ones** sometimes. **perder una ~ón** miss a chance. **~onal** adj chance. **~onar** vt cause

ocaso m sunset; (fig) decline

occident|al adj western. ● m & f westerner. **~e** m west

océano m ocean

ochenta adj & m eighty

ocho adj & m eight. **~cientos** adj & m eight hundred

ocio m idleness; (tiempo libre) leisure time. **~sidad** f idleness. **~so** adj idle; (inútil) pointless

oct|agonal adj octagonal. **~ágono** m octagon

octano m octane

octav|a f octave. **~o** adj & m eighth

octogenario adj & m octogenarian

octubre m October

ocular adj eye

oculista m & f ophthalmologist, ophthalmic optician

ocult|ar vt hide. **~arse** vpr hide. **~o** adj hidden; (secreto) secret

ocupa|ción f occupation. **~do**

adj occupied; (persona) busy. **estar ~do** (asiento) be taken; (línea telefónica) be engaged (Brit), be busy (Amer). **~nte** *m & f* occupant. **~r** *vt* occupy, take up (espacio). **~rse** *vpr* look after

ocurr|encia *f* occurrence, event; (idea) idea; (que tiene gracia) witty remark. **~ir** *vi* happen. **¿qué ~e?** what's the matter? **~irse** *vpr* occur. **se me ~e que** it occurs to me that

oda *f* ode

odi|ar *vt* hate. **~o** *m* hatred. **~oso** *adj* hateful; (persona) horrible

oeste *adj* (región) western; (viento, lado) west. ● *m* west

ofen|der *vt* offend; (insultar) insult. **~derse** *vpr* take offence. **~sa** *f* offence. **~siva** *f* offensive. **~sivo** *adj* offensive

oferta *f* offer; (en subasta) bid. **~s de empleo** situations vacant. **en ~** on (special) offer

oficial *adj* official. ● *m* skilled worker; (Mil) officer

oficin|a *f* office. **~a de colocación** employment office. **horas de ~a** business hours. **~ista** *m & f* office worker

oficio *m* trade. **~so** *adj* (no oficial) unofficial

ofrec|er 11 *vt* offer; give (fiesta, banquete etc); (prometer) promise. **~erse** *vpr* (persona) volunteer. **~imiento** *m* offer

ofrenda *f* offering. **~r** *vt* offer

ofuscar 7 *vt* blind; (confundir) confuse. **~se** *vpr* get worked up

oí|ble *adj* audible. **~do** *m* ear; (sentido) hearing. **al ~do** in one's ear. **de ~das** by hearsay. **conocer**

de ~das have heard of. **de ~do** by ear. **duro de ~do** hard of hearing

oigo *vb véase* **oír**

oír 50 *vt* hear. **¡oiga!** listen!; (al teléfono) hello!

ojal *m* buttonhole

ojalá *int* I hope so! ● *conj* if only

ojea|da *f* glance. **dar una ~da a, echar una ~da a** have a quick glance at. **~r** *vt* have a look at

ojeras *fpl* rings under one's eyes

ojeriza *f* ill will. **tener ~ a** have a grudge against

ojo *m* eye; (de cerradura) keyhole; (de un puente) span. **¡~!** careful!

ola *f* wave

olé *int* bravo!

olea|da *f* wave. **~je** *m* swell

óleo *m* oil; (cuadro) oil painting

oleoducto *m* oil pipeline

oler 2 (las formas que empiecen por ue se escriben hue) *vt* smell. ● *vi* smell (a of). **me huele mal** (fig) it sounds fishy to me

olfat|ear *vt* sniff; scent (rastro). **~o** *m* (sense of) smell; (fig) intuition

olimpiada *f*, **olimpíada** *f* Olympic games, Olympics

olímpico *adj* Olympic; (fig, fam) total

oliv|a *f* olive. **~ar** *m* olive grove. **~o** *m* olive tree

olla *f* pot, casserole. **~ a/de presión, ~ exprés** pressure cooker

olmo *m* elm (tree)

olor *m* smell. **~oso** *adj* sweet-smelling

olvida|dizo *adj* forgetful. **~r** *vt* forget. **~rse** *vpr* forget. **~rse de** forget. **se me ~ó** I forgot. **~o** *m* oblivion; (acto) omission truación) period. **en** ~ in order. **por** ~ **general** as a rule. ~**mentación** f regulation. ~**mentar** vt regulate. ~**mentario** adj regulation; (horario) set. ~**mento** m regulations

regocij|arse vpr be delighted. ~**o** m delight

regode|arse vpr (+ gerundio) delight in (+ gerund). ~**o** m delight

regordete adj chubby

regres|ar vi return; (LAm) send back (persona). ~**ar** vpr (LAm) return. ~**ivo** adj backward. ~**o** m return

regula|ble adj adjustable. ~**dor** m control. ~**r** adj regular; (mediano) average; (no bueno) so-so. ● vt regulate; adjust (volumen etc). ~**ridad** f regularity. **con** ~**ridad** regularly

rehabilita|ción f rehabilitation; (en empleo etc) reinstatement. ~**r** vt rehabilitate; (en cargo) reinstate

rehacer 31 vt redo; (repetir) repeat; rebuild (vida). ~**se** vpr recover

rehén m hostage

rehogar 12 vt sauté

rehuir 17 vt avoid

rehusar vt/i refuse

reimpr|esión f reprinting. ~**imir** (pp reimpreso) vt reprint

reina f queen. ~**do** m reign. ~**nte** adj ruling; (fig) prevailing. ~**r** vi reign; (fig) prevail

reincidir vi (Jurid) reoffend

reino m kingdom. **R~ Unido** United Kingdom

reintegr|ar vt reinstate (persona); refund (cantidad). ~**arse** vpr return. ~**o** m refund

reír 51 vi laugh. ~**se** vpr laugh. ~**se de** laugh at. **echarse a** ~

burst out laughing

reivindica|ción f claim. ~**r** 7 vt claim; (rehabilitar) restore

rej|a f grille; (verja) railing. **entre** ~**as** behind bars. ~**illa** f grille, grating; (red) luggage rack

rejuvenecer 11 vt/i rejuvenate. ~**se** vpr be rejuvenated

relaci|ón f connection; (trato) relation(ship); (relato) account; (lista) list. **con** ~**ón a, en** ~**ón a** in relation to. ~**onado** adj related. **bien** ~**onado** well-connected. ~**onar** vt relate (con to). ~**onarse** vpr be connected; (tratar) mix (con with)

relamerse vpr lick one's lips

relámpago m (flash of) lightning

relatar vt tell, relate

relativ|idad f relativity. ~**o** adj relative

relato m tale; (relación) account

relegar 12 vt relegate. ~ **al olvido** consign to oblivion

relev|ante adj outstanding. ~**ar** vt relieve; (substituir) replace. ~**o** m relief. **carrera** f **de** ~**os** relay race

relieve m relief; (fig) importance. **de** ~ important. **poner de** ~ emphasise

religi|ón f religion. ~**osa** f nun. ~**oso** adj religious. ● m monk

relinch|ar vi neigh. ~**o** m neigh

reliquia f relic

rellano m landing

rellen|ar vt refill; (Culin) stuff; fill in (formulario). ~**o** adj full up; (Culin) stuffed. ● m filling; (Culin) stuffing

reloj m clock; (de bolsillo o pulsera)

r

reluciente | renegar

watch. **~ de caja** grandfather clock. **~ de pulsera** wrist-watch. **~ de sol** sundial. **~ despertador** alarm clock. **~ería** f watchmaker's (shop). **~ero** m watchmaker

reluci|ente adj shining. **~r 11** vi shine; (destellar) sparkle

relumbrar vi shine

remach|ar vt rivet. **~e** m rivet

remangar 12 vt roll up

remar vi row

remat|ado adj (total) complete. **~ar** vt finish off; (agotar) use up; (Com) sell off cheap; (LAm, subasta) auction; (en tenis) smash. **~e** m end; (fig) finishing touch; (LAm, subastar) auction; (en tenis) smash. **de ~e** completely

remedar vt imitate

remedi|ar 2 vt remedy; repair (daño); (fig, resolver) solve. **no lo pude ~ar** I couldn't help it. **~o** m remedy; (fig) solution; (LAm, medicamento) medicine. **como último ~o** as a last resort. **no hay más ~o** there's no other way. **no tener más ~o** have no choice

remedo m poor imitation

rem|endar 1 vt repair. **~iendo** m patch

remilg|ado adj fussy; (afectado) affected. **~o** m fussiness; (afectación) affectation. **~oso** adj (Mex) fussy

reminiscencia f reminiscence

remisión f remission; (envío) sending; (referencia) reference

remit|e m sender's name and address. **~ente** m sender. **~ir** vt send; (referir) refer ● vi diminish

remo m oar

remoj|ar vt soak; (fig, fam) celebrate. **~o** m soaking. **poner a ~o** soak

remolacha f beetroot. **~ azucarera** sugar beet

remolcar 7 vt tow

remolino m swirl; (de aire etc) whirl

remolque m towing; (cabo) towrope; (vehículo) trailer. **a ~** on tow. **dar ~ a** tow

remontar vt overcome. **~ el vuelo** soar up; (avión) gain height. **~se** vpr soar up; (en el tiempo) go back to

remord|er 2 vi. **eso le remuerde** he feels guilty for it. **me remuerde la conciencia** I have a guilty conscience. **~imiento** m remorse. **tener ~imientos** feel remorse

remoto adj remote; (época) distant

remover 2 vt stir (líquido); turn over (tierra); (quitar) remove; (fig, activar) revive

remunera|ción f remuneration. **~r** vt remunerate

renac|er 11 vi be reborn; (fig) revive. **~imiento** m rebirth. **R~imiento** Renaissance

renacuajo m tadpole; (fig) tiddler

rencilla f quarrel

rencor m bitterness. **guardar ~ a** have a grudge against. **~oso** adj resentful

rendi|ción f surrender. **~do** adj submissive; (agotado) exhausted

rendija f crack

rendi|miento m performance; (Com) yield. **~r 5** vt yield; (agotar) exhaust; pay (homenaje); present (informe). ● vi pay; (producir) produce. **~rse** vpr surrender

renegar 1 & 12 vt deny. ● vi grumble. **~ de** renounce (fe etc); disown (personas)

renglón m line; (Com) item. **a ~ seguido** straight away

reno m reindeer

renombr|ado adj renowned. **~e** m renown

renova|ción f renewal; (de edificio) renovation; (de mobiliario) complete change. **~r** vt renew; renovate (edificio); change (mobiliario)

rent|a f income; (Mex, alquiler) rent. **~a vitalicia** (life) annuity. **~able** adj profitable. **~ar** vt yield; (Mex, alquiler) rent, hire. **~ista** m & f person of independent means

renuncia f renunciation; (dimisión) resignation. **~r** vi. **~r a** renounce, give up; (dimitir) resign

reñi|do adj hard-fought. **estar ~do con** be incompatible with (cosa); be on bad terms with (persona). **~r** **5** & **22** vt scold. ● vi quarrel

reo m & f (Jurid) accused; (condenado) convicted offender; (pez) sea trout

reojo. mirar de ~ look out of the corner of one's eye at

reorganizar **10** vt reorganize

repar|ación f repair; (acción) repairing (fig, compensación) reparation. **~ar** vt repair; (fig) make amends for; (notar) notice. ● vi. **~ar en** notice; (hacer caso de) pay attention to. **~o** m fault; (objeción) objection. **poner ~os** raise objections

repart|ición f distribution. **~idor** m delivery man. **~imiento** m distribution. **~ir** vt distribute, share out; deliver (cartas, leche etc); hand out (folleto, premio). **~o** m distribution; (de cartas, leche etc) delivery; (actores) cast

repas|ar vt go over; check (cuenta); revise (texto); (leer a la ligera) glance through; (coser) mend. ● vi revise. **~o** m revision; (de ropa) mending. **dar un ~o** look through

repatria|ción f repatriation. **~r** vt repatriate

repele|nte adj repulsive. ● m insect repellent. **~r** vt repel

repent|e. de ~ suddenly. **~ino** adj sudden

repercu|sión f repercussion. **~tir** vi reverberate; (fig) have repercussions (**en** on)

repertorio m repertoire

repeti|ción f repetition; (de programa) repeat. **~damente** adv repeatedly. **~r** **5** vt repeat; have a second helping of (plato); (imitar) copy. ● vi have a second helping of

repi|car **7** vt ring (campanas). **~que** m peal

repisa f shelf. **~ de chimenea** mantlepiece

repito vb véase **REPETIR**

replegarse **1** & **12** vpr withdraw

repleto adj full up. **~ de gente** packed with people

réplica adj reply; (copia) replica

replicar **7** vi reply

repollo m cabbage

reponer **34** vt replace; revive (obra de teatro); (contestar) reply. **~se** vpr recover

report|aje m report; (LAm, entrevista) interview. **~ar** vt yield; (LAm, denunciar) report. **~e** m (Mex, informe) report; (Mex, queja) complaint. **~ero** m reporter

repos|ado adj quiet; (sin prisa) unhurried. **~ar** vi rest; (líquido) settle. **~o** m rest

repost|ar vt replenish. ● vi (avión)

refuel; (Auto) fill up. **~ería** f pastrymaking

reprender vt reprimand

represalia f reprisal. **tomar ~s** retaliate

representa|ción f representation; (en el teatro) performance. **en ~ción de** representing. **~nte** m representative. **~r** vt represent; perform (obra de teatro); play (papel); (aparentar) look. **~rse** vpr imagine. **~tivo** adj representative

represi|ón f repression. **~vo** adj repressive

reprimenda f reprimand

reprimir vt supress. **~se** vpr control o.s.

reprobar 2 vt condemn; (LAm, Univ, etc) fail

reproch|ar vt reproach. **~e** m reproach

reproduc|ción f reproduction. **~ir** 47 vt reproduce. **~tor** adj reproductive; (animal) breeding

reptil m reptile

rep|ública f republic. **~ublicano** adj & m republican

repudiar vt condemn; (Jurid) repudiate

repuesto m (Mec) spare (part). **de ~** spare

repugna|ncia f disgust. **~nte** adj repugnant; (olor) disgusting. **~r** vt disgust

repuls|a f rebuff. **~ión** f repulsion. **~ivo** adj repulsive

reputa|ción f reputation. **~do** adj reputable. **~r** vt consider

requeri|miento m request; (necesidad) requirement. **~r** 4 vt require; summons (persona)

requesón m curd cheese

requete... prefijo (fam) extremely

requis|a f requisition; (confiscación) seizure; (inspección) inspection; (Mil) requisition. **~ar** vt requisition; (confiscar) seize; (inspeccionar) inspect. **~ito** m requirement

res f animal. **~ lanar** sheep. **~ vacuna** (vaca) cow; (toro) bull; (buey) ox. **carne de ~** (Mex) beef

resabido adj well-known; (persona) pedantic

resaca f undercurrent; (después de beber) hangover

resaltar vi stand out. **hacer ~** emphasize

resarcir 9 vt repay; (compensar) compensate. **~se** vpr make up for

resbal|adilla f (Mex) slide. **~adizo** adj slippery. **~ar** vi slip; (Auto) skid; (líquido) trickle. **~arse** vpr slip; (Auto) skid; (líquido) trickle. **~ón** m slip; (de vehículo) skid. **~oso** adj (LAm) slippery

rescat|ar vt rescue; (fig) recover. **~e** m ransom; (recuperación) recovery; (salvamento) rescue

rescoldo m embers

resecar 7 vt dry up. **~se** vpr dry up

resenti|do adj resentful. **~miento** m resentment. **~rse** vpr feel the effects; (debilitarse) be weakened; (ofenderse) take offence (**de** at)

reseña f summary; (de persona) description; (en periódico) report, review. **~r** vt describe; (en periódico) report on, review

reserva f reservation; (provisión) reserve(s). **de ~** in reserve. **~ción** f (LAm) reservation. **~do** adj reserved. **~r** vt reserve; (guardar) keep, save. **~rse** vpr save o.s.

resfria|do m cold. **~rse** vpr catch

229

resguardar | resultado

a cold

resguard|ar vt protect. **~arse** vpr protect o.s.; (fig) take care. **~o** m protection; (garantía) guarantee; (recibo) receipt

resid|encia f residence; (Univ) hall of residence (Brit), dormitory (Amer); (de ancianos etc) home. **~encial** adj residential. **~ente** adj & m & f resident. **~ir** vi reside; (fig) lie (**en** in)

residu|al adj residual. **~o** m residue. **~os** mpl waste

resigna|ción f resignation. **~rse** vpr resign o.s. (**a** to)

resist|encia f resistance. **~ente** adj resistent. **~ir** vt resist; (soportar) bear. ● vi resist. **ya no resisto más** I can't take it any more

resol|ución f resolution; (solución) solution; (decisión) decision. **~ver 2** (pp **resuelto**) resolve; solve (problema etc). **~verse** vpr resolve itself; (resultar bien) work out; (decidir) decide

resona|ncia f resonance. **tener ~ncia** cause a stir. **~nte** adj resonant; (fig) resounding. **~r 2** vi resound

resorte m spring; (Mex, elástico) elastic. **tocar (todos los) ~s** (fig) pull strings

respald|ar vt back; (escribir) endorse. **~arse** vpr lean back. **~o** m backing; (de asiento) back

respect|ar vi. **en lo que ~a a** with regard to. **en lo que a mí ~a** as far as I'm concerned. **~ivo** adj respective. **~o** m respect. **al ~o** on this matter. **(con) ~o a** with regard to

respet|able adj respectable. ● m audience. **~ar** vt respect. **~o** m respect. **faltar al ~o a** be disres-

pectful to. **~uoso** adj respectful

respir|ación f breathing; (ventilación) ventilation. **~ar** vi breathe; (fig) breathe a sigh of relief. **~o** m breathing; (fig) rest

respland|ecer 11 vi shine. **~eciente** adj shining. **~or** m brilliance; (de llamas) glow

responder vi answer; (replicar) answer back; (reaccionar) respond. **~ de** be responsible for. **~ por uno** vouch for s.o.

responsab|ilidad f responsibility. **~le** adj responsible

respuesta f reply, answer

resquebrajar vt crack. **~se** vpr crack

resquemor m (fig) uneasiness

resquicio m crack; (fig) possibility

resta f subtraction

restablecer 11 vt restore. **~se** vpr recover

rest|ante adj remaining. **lo ~nte** the rest. **~ar** vt take away; (substraer) subtract. ● vi be left

restaura|ción f restoration. **~nte** m restaurant. **~r** vt restore

restitu|ción f restitution. **~ir 17** vt return; (restaurar) restore

resto m rest, remainder; (en matemática) remainder. **~s** mpl remains; (de comida) leftovers

restorán m restaurant

restregar 1 & 12 vt rub

restri|cción f restriction. **~ngir 14** vt restrict, limit

resucitar vt resuscitate; (fig) revive. ● vi return to life

resuello m breath; (respiración) heavy breathing

resuelto adj resolute

resulta|do m result (**en** in). **~r** vi result; (salir) turn out; (dar resul-

tado) work; (*ser*) be; (*costar*) come to

resum|en *m* summary. **en ~en** in short. **~ir** *vt* summarize; (*recapitular*) sum up

resur|gir 14 *vi* reemerge; (*fig*) revive. **~gimiento** *m* resurgence. **~rección** *f* resurrection

retaguardia *f* (*Mil*) rearguard

retahíla *f* string

retar *vt* challenge

retardar *vt* slow down; (*demorar*) delay

retazo *m* remnant; (*fig*) piece, bit

reten|ción *f* retention. **~er** 40 *vt* keep; (*en la memoria*) retain; (*no dar*) withhold

reticencia *f* insinuation; (*reserva*) reluctance

retina *f* retina

retir|ada *f* withdrawal. **~ado** *adj* remote; (*vida*) secluded; (*jubilado*) retired. **~ar** *vt* move away; (*quitar*) remove; withdraw (*dinero*); (*jubilar*) pension off. **~arse** *vpr* draw back; (*Mil*) withdraw; (*jubilarse*) retire; (*acostarse*) go to bed. **~o** *m* retirement; (*pensión*) pension; (*lugar apartado*) retreat; (*LAm*, *de apoyo*, *fondos*) withdrawal

reto *m* challenge 7

retocar 7 *vt* retouch

retoño *m* shoot; (*fig*) kid

retoque *m* (*acción*) retouching; (*efecto*) finishing touch

retorc|er 2 & 9 *vt* twist; wring (*ropa*). **~erse** *vpr* get twisted up; (*de dolor*) writhe. **~ijón** *m* (*LAm*) stomach cramp

retóric|a *f* rhetoric; (*grandilocuencia*) grandiloquence. **~o** *m* rhetorical

retorn|ar *vt/i* return. **~o** *m* return

retortijón *m* twist; (*de tripas*) stomach cramp

retractarse *vpr* retract. **~ de lo dicho** withdraw what one said

retransmitir *vt* repeat; (*radio*, *TV*) broadcast. **~ en directo** broadcast live

retras|ado *adj* (*con ser*) mentally handicapped; (*con estar*) behind; (*reloj*) slow; (*poco desarrollado*) backward; (*anticuado*) old-fashioned. **~ar** *vt* delay; put back (*reloj*); (*retardar*) slow down; (*posponer*) postpone. ● *vi* (*reloj*) be slow. **~arse** *vpr* be late; (*reloj*) be slow. **~o** *m* delay; (*poco desarrollo*) backwardness; (*de reloj*) slowness. **traer ~o** be late. **~os** *mpl* arrears

retrato *m* portrait; (*fig*, *descripción*) description. **ser el vivo ~ de** be the living image of

retrete *m* toilet

retribu|ción *f* payment; (*recompensa*) reward. **~ir** 17 *vt* pay; (*recompensar*) reward; (*LAm*) return (*favor*)

retroce|der *vi* move back; (*fig*) back down. **~so** *m* backward movement; (*de arma de fuego*) recoil; (*Med*) relapse

retrógrado *adj* & *m* (*Pol*) reactionary

retrospectivo *adj* retrospective

retrovisor *m* rear-view mirror

retumbar *vt* echo; (*trueno etc*) boom

reum|a *m*, **reúma** *m* rheumatism. **~ático** *adj* rheumatic. **~atismo** *m* rheumatism

reuni|ón *f* meeting; (*entre amigos*) reunion. **~r** 23 *vt* join together; (*recoger*) gather (together); raise (*fondos*). **~rse** *vpr* meet; (*amigos etc*) get together

revalidar vt confirm; (Mex, estudios) validate

revalorizar 10 vt, (LAm) **revaluar** 21 vt revalue; increase (pensiones). **~se** vpr appreciate

revancha f revenge; (en deportes) return match. **tomar la ~** get one's own back

revela|ción f revelation. **~do** m developing. **~dor** adj revealing. **~r** vt reveal; (Foto) develop

revent|ar 1 vi burst; (tener ganas) be dying to. **~arse** vpr burst. **~ón** m burst; (Auto) blow out; (Mex, fiesta) party

reveren|cia f reverence; (de hombre, niño) bow; (de mujer) curtsy. **~ciar** vt revere. **~do** adj (Relig) reverend. **~te** adj reverent

revers|ible adj reversible. **~o** m reverse; (de papel) back

revertir 4 vi revert (a to)

revés m wrong side; (de prenda) inside; (contratiempo) setback; (en deportes) backhand. **al ~** the other way round; (con lo de arriba abajo) upside down; (con lo de dentro fuera) inside out

revesti|miento m coating. **~r** 5 vt cover

revis|ar vt check; overhaul (mecanismo); service (coche etc); (LAm, equipaje) search. **~ión** f check(ing); (Med) checkup; (de coche etc) service; (LAm, de equipaje) inspection. **~or** m inspector

revista f magazine; (inspección) inspection; (artículo) review; (espectáculo) revue. **pasar ~ a** inspect

revivir vi revive

revolcar 2 & 7 vt knock over. **~se** vpr roll around

revolotear vi flutter

revoltijo m, **revoltillo** m mess

revoltoso adj rebellious; (niño) naughty

revoluci|ón f revolution. **~onar** vt revolutionize. **~onario** adj & m revolutionary

revolver 2 (pp revuelto) vt mix; stir (líquido); (desordenar) mess up

revólver m revolver

revuelo m fluttering; (fig) stir

revuelt|a f revolt; (conmoción) disturbance. **~o** adj mixed up; (líquido) cloudy; (mar) rough; (tiempo) unsettled; (huevos) scrambled

rey m king. **los ~es** the king and queen. **los R~es Magos** the Three Wise Men

reyerta f brawl

rezagarse 12 vpr fall behind

rez|ar 10 vt say. ● vi pray; (decir) say. **~o** m praying; (oración) prayer

rezongar 12 vi grumble

ría f estuary

riachuelo m stream

riada f flood

ribera f bank

ribete m border; (fig) embellishment

rico adj rich; (Culin, fam) good, nice. ● m rich person

ridículo adj ridiculous. **~iculizar** 10 vt ridicule

riego m watering; (irrigación) irrigation

riel m rail

rienda f rein

riesgo m risk. **correr (el) ~ de** run the risk of

rifa f raffle. **~r** vt raffle

rifle m rifle

rigidez f rigidity; (fig) inflexibility

rígido adj rigid; (fig) inflexible

rig|or m strictness; (*exactitud*) exactness; (*de clima*) severity. **de ~or** compulsory. **en ~or** strictly speaking. **~uroso** adj rigorous

rima f rhyme. **~r** vt/i rhyme

rimbombante adj resounding; (*lenguaje*) pompous; (*fig, ostentoso*) showy

rímel m mascara

rin m (*Mex*) rim

rincón m corner

rinoceronte m rhinoceros

riña f quarrel; (*pelea*) fight

riñón m kidney

río m river; (*fig*) stream. **~ abajo** downstream. **~ arriba** upstream.
● vb véase REÍR

riqueza f wealth; (*fig*) richness. **~s** fpl riches

ris|a f laugh. **desternillarse de ~a** split one's sides laughing. **la ~a** laughter. **~otada** f guffaw. **~ueño** adj smiling; (*fig*) cheerful

rítmico adj rhythmic(al)

ritmo m rhythm; (*fig*) rate

rit|o m rite; (*fig*) ritual. **~ual** adj & m ritual

rival adj & m & f rival. **~idad** f rivalry. **~izar** 10 vi vie

riz|ado adj curly. **~ar** 10 vt curl; ripple (agua). **~o** m curl; (*en agua*) ripple

róbalo m bass

robar vt steal (cosa); rob (banco); (*raptar*) kidnap

roble m oak (tree)

robo m theft; (*de banco, museo*) robbery; (*en vivienda*) burglary

robusto adj robust

roca f rock

roce m rubbing; (*señal*) mark; (*fig, entre personas*) regular contact; (*Pol*) friction. **tener un ~ con uno** have a brush with s.o.

rociar 20 vt spray

rocín m nag

rocío m dew

rodaballo m turbot

rodaja f slice. **en ~s** sliced

roda|je m (*de película*) shooting; (*de coche*) running in. **~r** 2 vt shoot (película); run in (coche). ● vi roll; (coche) run; (*hacer una película*) shoot

rode|ar vt surround; (*LAm*) round up (ganado). **~arse** vpr surround o.s. (**de** with). **~o** m detour; (*de ganado*) round-up. **andar con ~os** beat about the bush. **sin ~os** plainly

rodill|a f knee. **ponerse de ~as** kneel down. **~era** f knee-pad

rodillo m roller; (*Culin*) rolling-pin

roe|dor m rodent. **~r** 37 vt gnaw

rogar 2 & 12 vt/i beg; (*Relig*) pray; **se ruega a los Sres. pasajeros...** passengers are requested.... **se ruega no fumar** please do not smoke

roj|izo adj reddish. **~o** adj & m red. **ponerse ~o** blush

roll|izo adj plump; (bebé) chubby. **~o** m roll; (*de cuerda*) coil; (*Culin*, rodillo) rolling-pin; (*fig, fam, pesadez*) bore

romance adj Romance. ● m (*idilio*) romance; (*poema*) ballad

roman|o adj & m Roman. **a la ~a** (*Culin*) (deep-)fried in batter

rom|anticismo m romanticism. **~ántico** adj romantic

romería f pilgrimage; (*LAm, multitud*) mass

romero m rosemary

romo adj blunt; (nariz) snub

rompe|cabezas m invar puzzle;

(de piezas) jigsaw (puzzle). ~**olas**
m invar breakwater

romp|er (pp **roto**) vt break; tear
(hoja, camisa etc); break off (relaciones etc). ● vi break; (novios)
break up. ~**er a** a burst out. ~**erse**
vpr break

ron m rum

ronc|ar 7 vi snore. ~**o** adj hoarse

roncha f lump; (por alergia) rash

ronda f round; (patrulla) patrol;
(serenata) serenade. ~**r** vt patrol.
● vi be on patrol; (merodear) hang
around

ronqu|era f hoarseness. ~**ido** m
snore

ronronear vi purr

roñ|a f (suciedad) grime. ~**oso** adj
dirty; (oxidado) rusty; (tacaño)
mean

rop|a f clothes, clothing. ~**a
blanca** linen, underwear. ~**a de
cama** bedclothes. ~**a interior**
underwear. ~**aje** m robes; (excesivo) heavy clothing. ~**ero** m
wardrobe

ros|a adj invar pink. ● f rose. ● m
pink. ~**áceo** adj pinkish. ~**ado** adj
pink; (mejillas) rosy. ● m (vino)
rosé. ~**al** m rose-bush

rosario m rosary; (fig) series

ros|ca f (de tornillo) thread; (de
pan) roll; (bollo) type of doughnut.
~**co** m roll. ~**quilla** f type of
doughnut

rostro m face

rota|ción f rotation. ~**r** vt/i ro-
tate. ~**rse** vpr take turns. ~**tivo**
adj rotary

roto adj broken

rótula f kneecap

rotulador m felt-tip pen

rótulo m sign; (etiqueta) label; (lo-
gotipo) logo

rotundo adj categorical

rotura f tear; (grieta) crack

rozadura f scratch

rozagante adj (LAm) healthy

rozar 10 vt rub against; (ligeramente) brush against; (raspar)
graze. ~**se** vpr rub; (con otras personas) mix

Rte. abrev (**Remite(nte)**) sender

rubéola f German measles

rubí m ruby

rubicundo adj ruddy

rubio adj (pelo) fair; (persona) fair-
haired; (tabaco) Virginia

rubor m blush; (Mex, cosmético)
blusher. ~**izarse 10** vpr blush

rúbrica f (de firma) flourish;
(firma) signature; (título) heading

rudeza f roughness

rudiment|ario adj rudimentary.
~**os** mpl rudiments

rueca f distaff

rueda f wheel; (de mueble) castor;
(de personas) ring; (Culin) slice. ~
de prensa press conference

ruedo m edge; (redondel) bullring

ruego m request; (súplica) entreaty. ● vb véase **ROGAR**

rufián m pimp; (granuja) rogue

rugby m rugby

rugi|do m roar. ~**r 14** vi roar

ruibarbo m rhubarb

ruido m noise. ~**so** adj noisy; (fig)
sensational

ruin adj despicable; (tacaño) mean

ruin|a f ruin; (colapso) collapse.
~**oso** adj ruinous

ruiseñor m nightingale

ruleta f roulette

rulo m curler

rumano adj & m Romanian

rumbo m direction; (fig) course;

(fig, esplendidez) lavishness. **con ~** a in the direction of. **~so** adj lavish

rumia|nte adj & m ruminant. **~r** vt chew; (fig) brood over. ● vi ruminate

rumor m rumour; (ruido) murmur. **~earse** vpr se **~ea que** rumour has it that. **~oso** adj murmuring

runrún m (de voces) murmur; (de motor) whirr

ruptura f breakup; (de relaciones etc) breaking off; (de contrato) breach

rural adj rural

ruso adj & m Russian

rústico adj rural; (de carácter) coarse. **en rústica** paperback

ruta f route; (fig) course

rutina f routine. **~rio** adj routine; (trabajo) monotonous

Ss

S.A. abrev (**Sociedad Anónima**) Ltd, plc, Inc (Amer)

sábado m Saturday

sábana f sheet

sabañón m chilblain

sabático adj sabbatical

sab|elotodo m & f invar know-all **1**. **~er 38** vt know; (ser capaz de) be able to, know how to; (enterarse de) find out. ● vi know. **~er a** taste of. **hacer ~er** let know. **¡qué sé yo!** how should I know? **que yo sepa** as far as I know. **¿~es nadar?** can you swim? **un no sé qué** a certain sth. **¡yo qué sé!** how should I know? **¡vete a ~er!** who

knows? **~er** m knowledge. **~ido** adj well-known. **~iduría** f wisdom; (conocimientos) knowledge

sabi|endas. a ~ knowingly; (a propósito) on purpose. **~hondo** m know-all. **~o** adj learned; (prudente) wise

sabor m taste, flavour; (fig) flavour. **~ear** vt taste; (fig) savour

sabot|aje m sabotage. **~eador** m saboteur. **~ear** vt sabotage

sabroso adj tasty; (chisme) juicy; (LAm, agradable) pleasant

sabueso m (perro) bloodhound; (fig, detective) detective

saca|corchos m invar corkscrew. **~puntas** m invar pencil-sharpener

sacar 7 vt take out; put out (parte del cuerpo); (quitar) remove; take (foto); win (premio); get (billete, entrada); withdraw (dinero); reach (solución); draw (conclusión); make (copia). **~ adelante** bring up (niño); carry on (negocio)

sacarina f saccharin

sacerdo|cio m priesthood. **~te** m priest

saciar vt satisfy; quench (sed)

saco m sack; (LAm, chaqueta) jacket. **~ de dormir** sleeping-bag

sacramento m sacrament

sacrific|ar 7 vt sacrifice; slaughter (res); put to sleep (perro, gato). **~arse** vpr sacrifice o.s. **~io** m sacrifice; (de res) slaughter

sacr|ilegio m sacrilege. **~ílego** adj sacrilegious

sacudi|da f shake; (movimiento brusco) jolt, jerk; (fig) shock. **~da eléctrica** electric shock. **~r** vt shake; (golpear) beat. **~rse** vpr shake off; (fig) get rid of

sádico adj sadistic. ● m sadist

sadismo m sadism

safari m safari

sagaz adj shrewd

Sagitario m Sagittarius

sagrado adj (lugar) holy, sacred; (altar, escrituras) holy; (fig) sacred

sal f salt. • vb véase **SALIR**

sala f room; (en casa) living room; (en hospital) ward; (para reuniones etc) hall; (en teatro) house; (Jurid) courtroom. ~ **de embarque** departure lounge. ~ **de espera** waiting room. ~ **de estar** living room. ~ **de fiestas** nightclub

salado adj salty; (agua del mar) salt; (no dulce) savoury; (fig) witty

salario m wage

salchich|a f (pork) sausage. ~**ón** m salami

sald|ar vt settle (cuenta); (vender) sell off. ~**o** m balance. ~**os** mpl sales. **venta de** ~**os** clearance sale

salero m salt-cellar

salgo vb véase **SALIR**

sali|da f departure; (puerta) exit, way out; (de gas, de líquido) leak; (de astro) rising; (Com, venta) sale; (chiste) witty remark; (fig) way out; ~**da de emergencia** emergency exit. ~**ente** adj (Archit) projecting; (pómulo etc) prominent. ~**r** 52 vi leave; (ir afuera) go out; (Informática) exit; (revista etc) be published; (resultar) turn out; (astro) rise; (aparecer) appear. ~**r adelante** get by. ~**rse** vpr leave; (recipiente, líquido etc) leak. ~**rse con la suya** get one's own way

saliva f saliva

salmo m psalm

salm|ón m salmon. ~**onete** m red mullet

salón m living-room, lounge. ~ **de**

actos assembly hall. ~ **de clases** classroom. ~ **de fiestas** dancehall

salpica|dera f (Mex) mudguard. ~**dero** m (Auto) dashboard. ~**dura** f splash; (acción) splashing. ~**r** 7 vt splash; (fig) sprinkle

salsa f sauce; (para carne asada) gravy; (Mus) salsa. ~**a verde** parsley sauce. ~**era** f sauce-boat

salt|amontes m invar grasshopper. ~**ar** vt jump (over); (fig) miss out. • vi jump; (romperse) break; (líquido) spurt out; (desprenderse) come off; (pelota) bounce; (estallar) explode. ~**eador** m highwayman. ~**ear** vt (Culin) sauté

salt|o m jump; (al agua) dive. ~**o de agua** waterfall. ~ **mortal** somersault. **de un** ~**o** with one jump. ~**ón** adj (ojos) bulging

salud f health. • int cheers!; (LAm, al estornudar) bless you! ~**able** adj healthy

salud|ar vt greet, say hello to; (Mil) salute. **lo** ~**a atentamente** (en cartas) yours faithfully. ~ **con la mano** wave. ~**o** m greeting; (Mil) salute. ~**os** mpl best wishes

salva f salvo. **una** ~ **de aplausos** a burst of applause

salvación f salvation

salvado m bran

salvaguardia f safeguard

salvaje adj (planta, animal) wild; (primitivo) savage. • m & f savage

salva|mento m rescue. ~**r** vt save, rescue; (atravesar) cross (recorrer); travel (distancia); (fig) overcome. ~**rse** vpr save o.s. ~**vidas** m & f invar lifeguard. • m lifebelt. **chaleco** m ~**vidas** life-jacket

salvo adj safe. • adv & prep except (for). **a** ~ out of danger. **poner a** ~ put in a safe place. ~ **que** unless. **~conducto** *m* safe-conduct.

San *adj* Saint, St. **~ Miguel** St Michael

sana|r *vt* cure. ● *vi* recover; heal (herida). **~torio** *m* sanatorium

sanci|ón *f* sanction. **~onar** *vt* sanction

sandalia *f* sandal

sandía *f* watermelon

sándwich /'sangwitʃ/ *m* (*pl* **~s**, **~es**) sandwich

sangr|ante *adj* bleeding; (*fig*) flagrant. **~ar** *vt/i* bleed. **~e** *f* blood. **a ~e fría** in cold blood

sangría *f* (*bebida*) sangria

sangriento *adj* bloody

sangu|ijuela *f* leech. **~íneo** *adj* blood

san|idad *f* health. **~itario** *adj* sanitary. ● *m* (*Mex*) toilet. **~o** *adj* healthy; (*mente*) sound. **~o y salvo** safe and sound. **cortar por lo ~o** settle things once and for all

santiamén *m*. **en un ~** in an instant

sant|idad *f* sanctity. **~ificar** 🔢 *vt* sanctify. **~iguarse** 🔢 *vpr* cross o.s. **~o** *adj* holy; (*delante de nombre*) Saint, St ● *m* saint; (*día*) saint's day, name day. **~uario** *m* sanctuary. **~urrón** *adj* sanctimonious

santo Most first names in Spanish-speaking countries are those of saints. A person's *santo* (also known as *onomástico* in Latin America and *onomástica* in Spain) is the saint's day of the saint they are named after. As well as celebrating their calendar birthday many people also celebrate their *santo*.

saña *f* viciousness. **con ~** viciously

sapo *m* toad

saque *m* (*en tenis*) service; (*inicial en fútbol*) kick-off. **~ de banda** throw-in; (*en rugby*) line-out. **~ de esquina** corner (kick)

saque|ar *vt* loot. **~o** *m* looting

sarampión *m* measles

sarape *m* (*Mex*) colourful blanket

sarc|asmo *m* sarcasm. **~ástico** *adj* sarcastic

sardina *f* sardine

sargento *m* sergeant

sarpullido *m* rash

sartén *f* or *m* frying-pan (*Brit*), frypan (*Amer*)

sastre *m* tailor. **~ría** *f* tailoring; (*tienda*) tailor's (shop)

Sat|anás *m* Satan. **~ánico** *adj* satanic

satélite *m* satellite

satinado *adj* shiny

sátira *f* satire

satírico *adj* satirical. ● *m* satirist

satisf|acción *f* satisfaction. **~acer** 🔢 *vt* satisfy; (*pagar*) pay; (*gustar*) please; meet (*gastos, requisitos*). **~acerse** *vpr* satisfy o.s.; (*vengarse*) take revenge. **~actorio** *adj* satisfactory. **~echo** *adj* satisfied. **~echo de sí mismo** smug

satura|ción *f* saturation. **~r** *vt* saturate

Saturno *m* Saturn

sauce *m* willow. **~ llorón** weeping willow

sauna *f*, (*LAm*) **sauna** *m* sauna

saxofón *m*, **saxófono** *m* saxophone

sazona|do *adj* ripe; (*Culin*) seasoned. **~r** *vt* ripen; (*Culin*) season

se *pronombre*

● (*en lugar de le, les*) **se lo di** (*a él*) I gave it to him; (*a ella*) I gave it to her; (*a usted, ustedes*) I gave it to you; (*a ellos, ellas*) I gave it to them. **se lo compré** I bought it for him (*or her etc*). **se lo quité** I took it away from him (*or her etc*). **se lo dije** I told him (*or her etc*)

····▶ (*reflexivo*) **se secó** (*él*) he dried himself; (*ella*) she dried herself; (*usted*) you dried yourself. (*sujeto no humano*) it dried itself. **se secaron** (*ellos, ellas*) they dried themselves. (*ustedes*) you dried yourselves. (*con partes del cuerpo*) **se lavó la cara** (*él*) he washed his face; (*con efectos personales*) **se limpian los zapatos** they clean their shoes

····▶ (*recíproco*) each other, one another. **se ayudan mucho** they help each other a lot. **no se hablan** they don't speak to each other

····▶ (*cuando otro hace la acción*) **va a operarse** she's going to have an operation. **se cortó el pelo** he had his hair cut

····▶ (*enfático*) **se bebió el café** he drank his coffee. **se subió al tren** he got on the train

➡ se also forms part of certain pronominal verbs such as **equivocarse, arrepentirse, caerse** etc., which are treated under the respective entries

····▶ (*voz pasiva*) **se construyeron muchas casas** many houses were built. **se vendió**

rápidamente it was sold very quickly

····▶ (*impersonal*) **antes se escuchaba más radio** people used to listen to the radio more in the past. **no se puede entrar** you can't get in. **se está bien aquí** it's very nice here

····▶ (*en instrucciones*) **sírvase frío** serve cold

sé *vb véase* **SABER** *y* **SER**

sea *vb véase* **SER**

seca|dor *m* drier; (*de pelo*) hairdrier. **∼nte** *adj* drying. ● *m* blotting-paper. **∼r 7** *vt* dry. **∼rse** *vpr* (*río etc*) dry up; (*persona*) dry o.s.

sección *f* section

seco *adj* dry; (*frutos, flores*) dried; (*flaco*) thin; (*respuesta*) curt. **a secas** just. **en ∼** (*bruscamente*) suddenly. **lavar en ∼** dry-clean

secretar|ía *f* secretariat; (*Mex, ministerio*) ministry. **∼io** *m* secretary; (*Mex, Pol*) minister

secreto *adj & m* secret

secta *f* sect. **∼rio** *adj* sectarian

sector *m* sector

secuela *f* consequence

secuencia *f* sequence

secuestr|ar *vt* confiscate; kidnap (*persona*); hijack (*avión*). **∼o** *m* seizure; (*de persona*) kidnapping; (*de avión*) hijack(ing)

secundar *vt* second, help. **∼io** *adj* secondary

sed *f* thirst. ● *vb véase* **SER**. **tener ∼** be thirsty. **tener ∼ de** (*fig*) be hungry for

seda *f* silk. **∼ dental** dental floss

sedante *adj & m* sedative

sede *f* seat; (*Relig*) see; (*de organismo*) headquarters; (*de congreso*, *juegos etc*) venue

sedentario *adj* sedentary

sedici|ón *f* sedition. **~oso** *adj* seditious

sediento *adj* thirsty

seduc|ción *f* seduction. **~ir** 47 *vt* seduce; (*atraer*) attract. **~tor** *adj* seductive. ● *m* seducer

seglar *adj* secular. ● *m* layman

segrega|ción *f* segregation. **~r** 12 *vt* segregate

segui|da *f*. en **~da** immediately. **~do** *adj* continuous; (*en plural*) consecutive. **~de** followed by. ● *adv* straight; (*LAm, a menudo*) often. **todo ~do** straight ahead. **~dor** *m* follower; (*en deportes*) supporter. **~r** 5 & 13 *vt* follow. ● *vi* (*continuar*) continue; (*por un camino*) go on. **~r adelante** carry on

según *prep* according to. ● *adv* it depends; (*a medida que*) as

segund|a *f* (*Auto*) second gear; (*en tren, avión etc*) second class. **~o** *adj* & *m* second

segur|amente *adv* certainly; (*muy probablemente*) surely. **~idad** *f* security; (*ausencia de peligro*) safety; (*certeza*) certainty; (*aplomo*) confidence. **~idad en sí mismo** self-confidence. **~idad social** social security. **~o** *adj* safe; (*cierto*) certain, sure; (*estable*) secure; (*de fiar*) reliable. ● *adv* for certain. ● *m* insurance; (*dispositivo de seguridad*) safety device. **~o de sí mismo** self-confident. **~o contra terceros** third-party insurance

seis *adj* & *m* six. **~cientos** *adj* & *m* six hundred

seísmo *m* earthquake

selec|ción *f* selection. **~cionar** *vt* select, choose. **~tivo** *adj* selective.

~to *adj* selected; (*fig*) choice

sell|ar *vt* stamp; (*cerrar*) seal. **~o** *m* stamp; (*precinto*) seal; (*fig, distintivo*) hallmark; (*LAm, en moneda*) reverse

selva *f* forest; (*jungla*) jungle

semáforo *m* (*Auto*) traffic lights; (*Rail*) signal; (*Naut*) semaphore

semana *f* week. **S~ Santa** Holy Week. **~l** *adj* weekly. **~rio** *adj* & *m* weekly

---

Semana Santa The most famous Holy Week celebrations in the Spanish-speaking world are held in Sevilla between Palm Sunday and Easter Sunday. Lay brotherhoods, *cofradías*, process through the city in huge parades. During the processions they sing *saetas*, flamenco verses mourning Christ's passion. *i*

---

semántic|a *f* semantics. **~o** *adj* semantic

semblante *m* face; (*fig*) look

sembrar 1 *vt* sow; (*fig*) scatter

semejan|te *adj* similar; (*tal*) such. ● *m* fellow man. **~za** *f* similarity. **a ~za de** like. **~r** *vi*. **~r a** resemble

semen *m* semen. **~tal** *adj* stud. ● *m* stud animal

semestr|al *adj* half-yearly. **~e** *m* six months

semi|circular *adj* semicircular. **~círculo** *m* semicircle. **~final** *f* semifinal

semill|a *f* seed. **~ero** *m* seedbed; (*fig*) hotbed

seminario *m* (*Univ*) seminar; (*Relig*) seminary

sémola *f* semolina

senado *m* senate. **~r** *m* senator

sencill|ez f simplicity. **~o** adj simple; (para viajar) single ticket; (disco) single; (LAm, dinero suelto) change

senda f, **sendero** m path

sendos adj pl each

seno m bosom. **~ materno** womb

sensaci|ón f sensation; (percepción, impresión) feeling. **~onal** adj sensational

sensat|ez f good sense. **~o** adj sensible

sensi|bilidad f sensibility. **~ble** adj sensitive; (notable) notable; (lamentable) lamentable. **~tivo** adj (órgano) sense

sensual adj sensual. **~idad** f sensuality

senta|do adj sitting (down); **dar algo por ~do** take something for granted. **~dor** adj (LAm) flattering. **~r ① vt** sit; (establecer) establish. ● vi suit; (de medidas) fit; (comida) agree with. **~rse** vpr sit (down)

sentencia f (Jurid) sentence. **~r** vt sentence (**a** to)

sentido adj heartfelt; (sensible) sensitive. ● m sense; (dirección) direction; (conocimiento) consciousness. **~ común** common sense. **~ del humor** sense of humour. **~ único** one-way. **doble ~** double meaning. **no tener ~** not make sense. **perder el ~** faint. **sin ~** senseless

sentim|ental adj sentimental. **~iento** m feeling; (sentido) sense; (pesar) regret

sentir ④ vt feel; (oír) hear; (lamentar) be sorry for. **lo siento mucho** I'm really sorry. ● m (opinión) opinion. **~se** vpr feel; (Mex, ofenderse) be offended

seña f sign. **~s** fpl (dirección) address; (descripción) description. **dar ~s de** show signs of

señal f signal; (letrero, aviso) sign; (telefónica) tone; (Com) deposit. **dar ~es de** show signs of. **en ~ de** as a token of. **~ado** adj (hora, día) appointed. **~ar** vt signal; (poner señales en) mark; (apuntar) point out; (manecilla, aguja) point to; (determinar) fix. **~arse** vpr stand out

señor m man, gentleman; (delante de nombre propio) Mr; (tratamiento directo) sir. **~a** f lady, woman; (delante de nombre propio) Mrs; (esposa) wife; (tratamiento directo) madam. **el ~ Mr. muy ~ mío** Dear Sir. **¡no ~!** certainly not!. **~ial** adj (casa) stately. **~ita** f young lady; (delante de nombre propio) Miss; (tratamiento directo) miss. **~ito** m young gentleman

señuelo m lure

sepa vb véase **SABER**

separa|ción f separation. **~do** adj separate. **por ~do** separately. **~r** vt separate; (de empleo) dismiss. **~rse** vpr separate; (amigos) part. **~tista** adj & m & f separatist

septentrional adj north(ern)

septiembre m September

séptimo adj seventh

sepulcro m sepulchre

sepult|ar vt bury. **~ura** f burial; (tumba) grave. **~urero** m gravedigger

sequ|edad f dryness. **~ía** f drought

séquito m entourage; (fig) train

---

ser ㊟

● verbo intransitivo

····➤ to be. **es bajo** he's short. **es abogado** he's a lawyer.

ábreme, soy yo open up, it's me. **¿como es?** (*como persona*) what's he like?; (*físicamente*) what does he look like? **era invierno** it was winter

⋯▸ **ser de** (*indicando composición*) to be made of. **es de hierro** it's made of iron. (*provenir de*) to be from. **es de México** he's from Mexico. (*pertenecer a*) to belong to. **el coche es de Juan** the car belongs to Juan, it's Juan's car

⋯▸ (*sumar*) **¿cuánto es todo?** how much is that altogether? **son 40 dólares** that's 40 dollars. **somos 10** there are 10 of us

⋯▸ (*con la hora*) **son las 3** it's 3 o'clock. **~ía la una** it must have been one o'clock

⋯▸ (*tener lugar*) to be held. **~á en la iglesia** it will be held in the church

⋯▸ (*ocurrir*) to happen **¿dónde fue el accidente?** where did the accident happen? **me contó cómo fue** he told me how it happened

⋯▸ (*en locuciones*) **a no ~ que** unless. **como sea** no matter what. **cuando sea** whenever. **donde sea** wherever. **¡eso es!** that's it! **es que** the thing is. **lo que sea** anything. **no sea que, no vaya a ~ que** in case. o **sea** in other words. **sea ... sea ...** either ... or ... **sea como sea** at all costs

● *nombre masculino* being; (*persona*) person. **el ~ humano** the human being. **un ~ amargado**

a bitter person. **los ~es queridos** the loved ones

seren|ar *vt* calm down. **~arse** *vpr* calm down. **~ata** *f* serenade. **~idad** *f* serenity. **~o** *adj* serene; (*cielo*) clear; (*mar*) calm

seri|al *m* serial. **~e** *f* series. **fuera de ~e** (*fig*) out of this world. **producción** *f* **en ~e** mass production

seri|edad *f* seriousness. **~o** *adj* serious; (*confiable*) reliable; **en ~o** seriously. **poco ~o** frivolous

sermón *m* sermon; (*fig*) lecture

serp|enteante *adj* winding. **~entear** *vi* wind. **~iente** *f* snake. **~iente de cascabel** rattlesnake

serr|ar 🔟 *vt* saw. **~ín** *m* sawdust. **~uchar** *vt* (*LAm*) saw. **~ucho** *m* (hand)saw

servi|cial *adj* helpful. **~cio** *m* service; (*conjunto*) set; (*aseo*) toilet; **~cio a domicilio** delivery service. **~dor** *m* servant. **su (seguro) ~dor** (*en cartas*) yours faithfully. **~dumbre** *f* servitude; (*criados*) servants, staff. **~l** *adj* servile

servidor *m* server; (*criado*) servant

servilleta *f* napkin, serviette

servir 🔟 *vt* serve; (*en restaurante*) wait on. ● *vi* serve; (*ser útil*) be of use. **~e** *vpr* help o.s.. **~se de** use. **no ~ de nada** be useless. **para ~le** at your service. **sírvase sentarse** please sit down

sesent|a *adj* & *m* sixty. **~ón** *adj* & *m* sixty-year-old

seseo *m* pronunciation of the Spanish *c* as an *s*

sesión *f* session; (*en el cine, teatro*) performance

seso *m* brain

seta *f* mushroom

sete|cientos adj & m seven hundred. **~nta** adj & m seventy. **~ntón** adj & m seventy-year-old

setiembre m September

seto m fence; (de plantas) hedge. **~ vivo** hedge

seudónimo m pseudonym

sever|idad f severity; (de profesor etc) strictness. **~o** adj severe; (profesor etc) strict

sevillan|as fpl popular dance from Seville. **~o** m person from Seville

sexo m sex

sext|eto m sextet. **~o** adj sixth

sexual adj sexual. **~idad** f sexuality

si m (Mus) B; (solfa) te. ● conj if; (dubitativo) whether; **~ no** otherwise. **por ~ (acaso)** in case

si[1] pron reflexivo (él) himself; (ella) herself; (de cosa) itself; (uno) oneself; (Vd) yourself; (ellos, ellas) themselves; (Vds) yourselves; (recíproco) each other

sí[2] adv yes. ● m consent

sida m Aids

sidra f cider

siembra f sowing; (época) sowing time

siempre adv always; (LAm, todavía) still; (Mex, por fin) after all. **~ que** if; (cada vez) whenever. **como ~** as usual. **de ~** (acostumbrado) usual. **lo de ~** the usual thing. **para ~** for ever

sien f temple

siento vb véase SENTAR y SENTIR

sierra f saw; (cordillera) mountain range

siesta f nap, siesta

siete adj & m seven

sífilis f syphilis

sifón m U-bend; (de soda) syphon

sigilo m stealth; (fig) secrecy

sigla f abbreviation

siglo m century; (época) age. **hace ~s que no escribe** he hasn't written for ages

significa|ción f significance. **~do** adj (conocido) well-known. ● m meaning; (importancia) significance. **~r** [7] vt mean; (expresar) express. **~tivo** adj meaningful; (importante) significant

signo m sign. **~ de admiración** exclamation mark. **~ de interrogación** question mark

sigo vb véase SEGUIR

siguiente adj following, next. **lo ~** the following

sílaba f syllable

silb|ar vt/i whistle. **~ato** m, **~ido** m whistle

silenci|ador m silencer. **~ar** vt hush up. **~o** m silence. **~oso** adj silent

sill|a f chair; (de montar) saddle (Relig) see **~a de ruedas** wheelchair. **~ín** m saddle. **~ón** m armchair

silueta f silhouette; (dibujo) outline

silvestre adj wild

simb|ólico adj symbolic(al). **~olismo** m symbolism. **~olizar** [10] vt symbolize

símbolo m symbol

sim|etría f symmetry. **~étrico** adj symmetric(al)

similar adj similar (a to)

simp|atía f friendliness; (cariño) affection. **~ático** adj nice, likeable; (ambiente) pleasant. **~atizante** m & f sympathizer. **~atizar** [10] vi get on (well together)

s

simpl|e adj simple; (*mero*) mere. **~eza** f simplicity; (*tontería*) stupid thing; (*insignificancia*) trifle. **~icidad** f simplicity. **~ificar** **7** vt simplify. **~ista** adj simplistic. **~ón** m simpleton

simula|ción f simulation. **~r** vt simulate; (*fingir*) feign

simultáneo adj simultaneous

sin prep without. **~** saber without knowing. **~** querer accidentally

sinagoga f synagogue

sincer|idad f sincerity. **~o** adj sincere

sincronizar **10** vt synchronize

sindica|l adj (trade-)union. **~lista** m & f trade-unionist. **~to** m trade union

síndrome m syndrome

sinfín m endless number (de of)

sinfonía f symphony

singular adj singular; (*excepcional*) exceptional. **~izarse** vpr stand out

siniestro adj sinister. ● m disaster; (*accidente*) accident

sinnúmero m endless number (de of)

sino m fate. ● conj but

sinónimo adj synonymous. ● m synonym (de for)

sintaxis f syntax

síntesis f invar synthesis; (*resumen*) summary

sint|ético adj synthetic. **~etizar** **10** vt synthesize; (*resumir*) summarize

síntoma m symptom

sintomático adj symptomatic

sinton|ía f tuning; (*Mus*) signature tune. **~izar** **10** vt (*con la radio*) tune (in) to

sinvergüenza m & f crook

siquiera conj even if. ● adv at

least. **ni ~** not even

sirena f siren; (*en cuentos*) mermaid

sirio adj & m Syrian

sirvient|a f maid. **~e** m servant

sirvo vb véase **SERVIR**

sísmico adj seismic

sismo m earthquake

sistema m system. **por ~a** as a rule. **~ático** adj systematic

sitiar vt besiege; (*fig*) surround

sitio m place; (*espacio*) space; (*Mil*) siege; (*Mex*, *parada de taxi*) taxi rank. **en cualquier ~** anywhere. **~ web** website

situa|ción f situation; (*estado*, *condición*) position. **~r** **21** vt place, put; locate (*edificio*). **~rse** vpr be successful, establish o.s.

slip /es'lip/ m (pl ~s) underpants, briefs

smoking /es'mokin/ m (pl ~s) dinner jacket (*Brit*), tuxedo (*Amer*)

sobaco m armpit

sobar vt handle; knead (*masa*)

soberan|ía f sovereignty. **~o** adj sovereign; (*fig*) supreme. ● m sovereign

soberbi|a f pride; (*altanería*) arrogance. **~o** adj proud; (*altivo*) arrogant

soborn|ar vt bribe. **~o** m bribe

sobra f surplus. **de ~** more than enough. **~s** fpl leftovers. **~do** adj more than enough. **~nte** adj surplus. **~r** vi be left over; (*estorbar*) be in the way

sobre prep on; (*encima de*) on top of; (*más o menos*) about; (*por encima de*) above; (*sin tocar*) over. **~ todo** above all, especially. ● m envelope. **~cargar** **12** vt overload. **~coger** **14** vt startle; (*conmover*) move. **~cubierta** f dustcover. **~dosis** f invar overdose. **~entender 1** vt understand, infer. **~girar** vt (LAm) overdraw. **~giro** m (LAm) overdraft. **~humano** adj superhuman. **~llevar** vt bear. **~mesa** f. **de ~mesa** after-dinner. **~natural** adj supernatural. **~nombre** m nickname. **~pasar** vt exceed. **~peso** m (LAm) excess baggage. **~poner 34** vt superimpose. **~ponerse** vpr overcome. **~saliente** adj (fig) outstanding. ● m excellent mark. **~salir 52** vi stick out; (fig) stand out. **~saltar** vt startle. **~salto** m fright. **~sueldo** m bonus. **~todo** m overcoat. **~venir 53** vi happen. **~viviente** adj surviving. ● m & f survivor. **~vivir** vi survive. **~volar** vt fly over

sobriedad f moderation; (de estilo) simplicity

sobrin|a f niece. **~o** m nephew. **~os** (varones) nephews; (varones y mujeres) nieces and nephews

sobrio adj moderate, sober

socavar vt undermine

soci|able adj sociable. **~al** adj social. **~aldemócrata** m & f social democrat. **~alismo** m socialism. **~alista** adj & m & f socialist. **~edad** f society; (Com) company. **~edad anónima** limited company. **~o** m member; (Com) partner. **~ología** f sociology. **~ólogo** m sociologist

socorr|er vt help. **~o** m help

soda f (bebida) soda (water)

sodio m sodium

sofá m sofa, settee

sofistica|ción f sophistication. **~do** adj sophisticated

sofo|cante adj suffocating; (fig) stifling. **~car 7** vt smother

(fuego); (fig) stifle. **~carse** vpr get upset

soga f rope

soja f soya (bean)

sojuzgar 12 vt subdue

sol m sun; (luz) sunlight; (Mus) G; (solfa) soh. **al ~** in the sun. **día m de ~** sunny day. **hace ~, hay ~** it is sunny. **tomar el ~** sunbathe

solamente adv only

solapa f lapel; (de bolsillo etc) flap. **~do** adj sly

solar adj solar. ● m plot

solariego adj (casa) ancestral

soldado m soldier. **~ raso** private

solda|dor m welder; (utensilio) soldering iron. **~r 2** vt weld, solder

soleado adj sunny

soledad f solitude; (aislamiento) loneliness

solemn|e adj solemn. **~idad** f solemnity

soler 2 vi be in the habit of. **suele despertarse a las 6** he usually wakes up at 6 o'clock

sol|icitante m applicant. **~ de asilo** asylum seeker. **~icitar** vt request, ask for; apply for (empleo). **~ícito** adj solicitous. **~icitud** f request; (para un puesto) application; (formulario) application form; (preocupación) concern

solidaridad f solidarity

solid|ez f solidity; (de argumento etc) soundness. **~ificarse 7** vpr solidify

sólido adj solid; (argumento etc) sound. ● m solid

soliloquio m soliloquy

solista m & f soloist

solitario adj solitary; (aislado) lonely. ● m loner; (juego, diamante) solitaire

solloz|ar 10 vi sob. **~o** m sob

solo adj (sin compañía) alone; (aislado) lonely; (sin ayuda) by oneself; (único) only; (Mus) solo; (café) black. ● m solo; (juego) solitaire. **a solas** alone

sólo adv only. **~ que** except that. **no ~... sino también** not only... but also.... **tan ~** only

solomillo m sirloin

soltar 2 vt let go of; (dejar ir) release; (dejar caer) drop; (dejar salir, decir) let out; give (golpe etc). **~se** vpr come undone; (librarse) break loose

solter|a f single woman. **~o** adj single. ● m bachelor

soltura f looseness; (fig) ease, fluency

solu|ble adj soluble. **~ción** f solution. **~cionar** vt solve; settle (huelga, asunto)

solvente adj & m solvent

sombr|a f shadow; (lugar sin sol) shade. **a la ~a** in the shade. **~eado** adj shady

sombrero m hat. **~ hongo** bowler hat

sombrío adj sombre

somero adj superficial

someter vt subdue; subject (persona); (presentar) submit. **~se** vpr give in

somn|oliento adj sleepy. **~ífero** m sleeping-pill

somos vb véase SER

son m sound. ● vb véase SER

sonámbulo m sleepwalker. **ser ~** walk in one's sleep

sonar 2 vt blow; ring (timbre). ● vi sound; (timbre, teléfono etc) ring; (despertador) go off; (Mus) play; (fig, ser conocido) be familiar. **~ a** sound like. **~se** vpr blow

one's nose

sonde|ar vt sound out; explore (espacio); (Naut) sound. **~o** m poll; (Naut) sounding

soneto m sonnet

sonido m sound

sonoro adj sonorous; (ruidoso) loud

sonr|eír 51 vi smile. **~eírse** vpr smile. **~isa** f smile

sonroj|arse vpr blush. **~o** m blush

sonrosado adj rosy, pink

sonsacar 7 vt wheedle out

soñ|ado adj dream. **~ador** m dreamer. **~ar** 2 vi dream (con of). **¡ni ~arlo!** not likely!

sopa f soup

sopesar vt (fig) weigh up

sopl|ar vt blow; blow out (vela); blow off (polvo); (inflar) blow up. ● vi blow. **~ete** m blowlamp. **~o** m puff

soport|al m porch. **~ales** mpl arcade. **~ar** vt support; (fig) bear, put up with. **~e** m support

soprano f soprano

sor f sister

sorb|er vt sip; (con ruido) slurp; (absorber) absorb. **~ por la nariz** sniff. **~ete** m sorbet, water-ice. **~o** m (pequeña cantidad) sip; (trago grande) gulp

sordera f deafness

sórdido adj squalid; (asunto) sordid

sordo adj deaf; (ruido etc) dull. ● m deaf person. **hacerse el ~** turn a deaf ear. **~mudo** adj deaf and dumb

soroche m (LAm) mountain sickness

sorpre|ndente adj surprising.

~nder vt surprise. ~nderse vpr be surprised. ~sa f surprise

sorte|ar vt draw lots for; (fig) avoid. ~o m draw. por ~o by drawing lots

sortija f ring; (de pelo) ringlet

sortilegio m sorcery; (embrujo) spell

sos|egar **1** & **12** vt calm. ~iego m calmness

soslayo. de ~ sideways

soso adj tasteless; (fig) dull

sospech|a f suspicion. ~ar vt suspect. • vi. ~ de suspect. ~oso adj suspicious. • m suspect

sost|én m support; (prenda femenina) bra **1**, brassière. ~ener **40** vt support; bear (peso); (sujetar) hold; (sustentar) maintain; (alimentar) sustain. ~enerse vpr support o.s.; (continuar) remain. ~enido adj sustained; (Mus) sharp. • m (Mus) sharp

sota f (de naipes) jack

sótano m basement

soviético adj (Historia) Soviet

soy vb véase SER

Sr. abrev (Señor) Mr. ~a. abrev (Señora) Mrs. ~ta. abrev (Señorita) Miss

su adj (de él) his; (de ella) her; (de animal, objeto) its; (de uno) one's; (de Vd) your; (de ellos, de ellas) their; (de Vds) your

suav|e adj smooth; (fig) gentle; (color, sonido) soft; (tabaco, sedante) mild. ~idad f smoothness, softness. ~izante m conditioner; (para ropa) softener. ~izar **10** vt smooth, soften

subalimentado adj underfed

subarrendar **1** vt sublet

subasta f auction. ~r vt auction

sub|campeón m runner-up. ~consciencia f subconscious. ~consciente adj & m subconscious. ~continente m subcontinent. ~desarrollado adj underdeveloped. ~director m assistant manager

súbdito m subject

sub|dividir vt subdivide. ~estimar vt underestimate

subi|da f rise; (a una montaña) ascent; (pendiente) slope. ~do adj (color) intense. ~r vt go up; climb (montaña); (llevar) take up; (aumentar) raise; turn up (radio, calefacción). • vi go up. ~r a get into (coche); get on (autobús, avión, barco, tren); (aumentar) rise. ~ a pie walk up. ~r por climb up. ~rse a get on (tren etc)

súbito adj sudden. de ~ suddenly

subjetivo adj subjective

subjuntivo adj & m subjunctive

subleva|ción f uprising. ~rse vpr rebel

sublim|ar vt sublimate. ~e adj sublime

submarino adj underwater. • m submarine

subordinado adj & m subordinate

subrayar vt underline

subsanar vt rectify; overcome (dificultad); make up for (carencia)

subscri|bir vt (pp subscrito) sign. ~birse vpr subscribe (a to). ~pción f subscription

subsidi|ario adj subsidiary. ~o m subsidy. ~o de desempleo, ~ de paro unemployment benefit

subsiguiente adj subsequent

subsist|encia f subsistence. ~ir vi subsist; (perdurar) survive

substraer **41** vt take away

subterráneo adj underground

subtítulo m subtitle

suburb|ano adj suburban. **~io** m suburb; (barrio pobre) depressed area

subvenci|ón f subsidy. **~onar** vt subsidize

subver|sión f subversion. **~sivo** adj subversive. **~tir** [4] vt subvert

succi|ón f suction. **~onar** vt suck

suce|der vi happen; (seguir) **~ a** follow. ● vt (sustituir) succeed. **lo que ~de es que** the trouble is that. **¿qué ~de?** what's the matter? **~sión** f succession. **~sivo** adj successive; (consecutivo) consecutive. **en lo ~sivo** in future. **~so** m event; (incidente) incident. **~sor** m successor

suciedad f dirt; (estado) dirtiness

sucinto adj concise; (prenda) scanty

sucio adj dirty; (conciencia) guilty. **en ~** in rough

sucre m (unidad monetaria del Ecuador) sucre

suculento adj succulent

sucumbir vi succumb (a to)

sucursal f branch (office)

Sudáfrica f South Africa

sudafricano adj & m South African

Sudamérica f South America

sudamericano adj & m South American

sudar vi sweat

sud|este m south-east. **~oeste** m south-west

sudor m sweat

Suecia f Sweden

sueco adj Swedish. ● m (persona) Swede; (lengua) Swedish. **hacerse el ~** pretend not to hear

suegr|a f mother-in-law. **~o** m father-in-law. **mis ~os** my in-laws

suela f sole

sueldo m salary

suelo m ground; (dentro de edificio) floor; (territorio) soil; (en la calle etc) road surface. ● vb véase **SOLER**

suelto adj loose; (cordones) undone; (sin pareja) odd; (lenguaje) fluent. **con el pelo ~** with one's hair down. **~** m change

sueño m sleep; (lo soñado, ilusión) dream. **tener ~** be sleepy

suerte f luck; (destino) fate; (azar) chance. **de otra ~** otherwise. **de ~ que** so. **echar ~s** draw lots. **por ~** fortunately. **tener ~** be lucky

suéter m sweater, jersey

suficien|cia f (aptitud) aptitude; (presunción) smugness. **~te** adj enough, sufficient; (presumido) smug. **~temente** adv sufficiently

sufijo m suffix

sufragio m (voto) vote

sufri|miento m suffering. **~r** vt suffer; undergo (cambio); have (accident). ● vi suffer

suge|rencia f suggestion. **~rir** [4] vt suggest. **~stión** f (en psicología) suggestion. **es pura ~stión** it's all in one's mind. **~stionable** adj impressionable. **~stionar** vt influence. **~stivo** adj (estimulante) stimulating; (atractivo) sexy

suicid|a adj suicidal. ● m & f suicide victim; (fig) maniac. **~arse** vpr commit suicide. **~io** m suicide

Suiza f Switzerland

suizo adj & m Swiss

suje|ción f subjection. **con ~ a** in accordance with. **~tador** m bra [1], brassière. **~tapapeles** m invar paper-clip. **~tar** vt fasten; (agarrar) hold. **~tarse** *vpr.* **~se** a hold on to; (*someterse*) abide by. **~to** *adj* fastened; (*susceptible*) subject (**a** to). ● *m* individual; (*Gram*) subject.

suma *f* sum; (*Math*) addition; (*combinación*) combination. **en ~** in short. **~mente** *adv* extremely. **~r** *vt* add (up); (*totalizar*) add up to. ● *vi* add up. **~rse** *vpr.* **~rse a** join in

sumario *adj* brief; (*Jurid*) summary. ● *m* table of contents; (*Jurid*) pre-trial proceedings

sumergi|ble *adj* submersible. **~r** 🔟 *vt* submerge

suministr|ar *vt* supply. **~o** *m* supply; (*acción*) supplying

sumir *vt* sink; (*fig*) plunge

sumis|ión *f* submission. **~o** *adj* submissive

sumo *adj* great; (*supremo*) supreme. **a lo ~** at the most

suntuoso *adj* sumptuous

supe *vb véase* **SABER**

superar *vt* surpass; (*vencer*) overcome; beat (marca); (*dejar atrás*) get over. **~se** *vpr* better o.s.

superchería *f* swindle

superfici|al *adj* superficial. **~e** *f* surface; (*extensión*) area. **de ~e** surface

superfluo *adj* superfluous

superior *adj* superior; (*más alto*) higher; (*mejor*) better; (*piso*) upper. ● *m* superior. **~idad** *f* superiority

superlativo *adj* & *m* superlative

supermercado *m* supermarket

superstici|ón *f* superstition. **~oso** *adj* superstitious

supervis|ar *vt* supervise. **~ión** *f* supervision. **~or** *m* supervisor

supervivencia *f* survival. ● *m* & *f*

survivor

suplantar *vt* supplant

suplement|ario *adj* supplementary. **~o** *m* supplement

suplente *adj* & *m* & *f* substitute

súplica *f* entreaty; (*Jurid*) request

suplicar 🛛 *vt* beg

suplicio *m* torture

suplir *vt* make up for; (*reemplazar*) replace

supo|ner 🔢 *vt* suppose; (*significar*) mean; involve (gasto, trabajo). **~sición** *f* supposition

suprem|acía *f* supremacy. **~o** *adj* supreme

supr|esión *f* suppression; (*de impuesto*) abolition; (*de restricción*) lifting. **~imir** *vt* suppress; abolish (impuesto); lift (restricción); delete (párrafo)

supuesto *adj* supposed; (*falso*) false; (*denominado*) so-called. ● *m* assumption. **¡por ~!** of course!

sur *m* south; (*viento*) south wind

surc|ar 🛛 *vt* plough; cut through (agua). **~o** *m* furrow; (*de rueda*) rut

surfear *vi* (*Informática*) surf

surgir 🔟 *vi* spring up; (*elevarse*) loom up; (*aparecer*) appear; (*dificultad, oportunidad*) arise

surrealis|mo *m* surrealism. **~ta** *adj* & *m* & *f* surrealist

surti|do *adj* well-stocked; (*variado*) assorted. ● *m* assortment, selection. **~dor** *m* (*de gasolina*) petrol pump (*Brit*), gas pump (*Amer*). **~r** *vt* supply; have (efecto). **~rse** *vpr* provide o.s. (**de** with)

susceptib|ilidad *f* sensitivity. **~le** *adj* susceptible; (*sensible*) sensitive

suscitar *vt* provoke; arouse

(curiosidad, interés)

suscr... véase **SUBSCR...**

susodicho adj aforementioned

suspen|der vt suspend; stop (tratamiento); call off (viaje); (en examen) fail; (colgar) hang (de from). **~se** m suspense. **novela de ~se** thriller. **~sión** f suspension. **~so** m fail; (LAm, en libro, película) suspense. **en ~so** suspended

suspir|ar vi sigh. **~o** m sigh

sust... véase **SUBST...**

sustanci|a f substance. **~al** adj substantial. **~oso** adj substantial

sustantivo m noun

sustent|ación f support. **~ar** vt support; (alimentar) sustain; (mantener) maintain. **~o** m support; (alimento) sustenance

substitu|ción f substitution; (permanente) replacement. **~ir** 17 vt substitute, replace. **~to** m substitute; (permanente) replacement

susto m fright

susurr|ar vi (persona) whisper; (agua) murmur; (hojas) rustle

sutil adj fine; (fig) subtle. **~eza** f subtlety

suyo adj & pron (de él) his; (de ella) hers; (de animal) its; (de Vd) yours; (de ellos, de ellas) theirs; (de Vds) yours. **un amigo ~** a friend of his, a friend of theirs, etc

Tt

tabac|alera f (state) tobacco monopoly. **~o** m tobacco; (cigarrillos) cigarettes

tabern|a f bar. **~ero** m barman; (dueño) landlord

tabique m partition wall; (Mex, ladrillo) brick

tabl|a f plank; (del suelo) floorboard; (de vestido) pleat; (índice) index; (gráfico, en matemática etc) table. **hacer ~as** (en ajedrez) draw. **~a de surf** surfboard. **~ado** m platform; (en el teatro) stage. **~ao** m place where flamenco shows are held. **~ero** m board. **~ero de mandos** dashboard

tableta f tablet; (de chocolate) bar

tabl|illa f splint; (Mex, de chocolate) bar. **~ón** m plank. **~ón de anuncios** notice board (esp Brit), bulletin board (Amer)

tabú m (pl **~es**, **~s**) taboo

tabular vt tabulate

taburete m stool

tacaño adj mean

tacha f stain, blemish. **sin ~** unblemished; (conducta) irreproachable. **~r** vt (con raya) cross out; (Jurid) impeach. **~ de** accuse of

tácito adj tacit

taciturno adj taciturn; (triste) glum

taco m plug; (LAm, tacón) heel; (de billar) cue; (de billetes) book; (fig, fam, lío) mess; (palabrota) swearword; (Mex, Culin) taco, filled tortilla

tacón m heel

táctic|a f tactics. **~o** adj tactical

táctil *adj* tactile

tacto *m* touch; (*fig*) tact

tahúr *m* card-sharp

tailandés *adj & m* Thai

Tailandia *f* Thailand

taimado *adj* sly

taj|ada *f* slice. **sacar ∼ada** profit. **∼ante** *adj* categorical; (*tono*) sharp. **∼ear** *vt* (*LAm*) slash. **∼o** *m* cut; (*en mina*) face

tal *adj* such. **de ∼ manera** in such a way. **un ∼** someone called. ●*pron.* **como ∼** as such. **y ∼ and** things like that. ●*adv.* **con ∼ de que** as long as. **∼ como** the way. **∼ para cual** ① two of a kind. **∼ vez** maybe. **¿qué ∼?** how are you? **¿qué ∼ es ella?** what's she like?

taladr|ar *vt* drill. **∼o** *m* drill

talante *m* mood. **de buen ∼** (*estar*) in a good mood; (*ayudar*) willingly

talar *vt* fell

talco *m* talcum powder

talega *f*, **talego** *m* sack

talento *m* talent; (*fig*) talented person

talismán *m* talisman

talla *f* carving; (*de diamante etc*) cutting; (*estatura*) height; (*tamaño*) size. **∼do** *m* carving; (*de diamante etc*) cutting. **∼dor** *m* carver; (*cortador*) cutter; (*LAm, de naipes*) dealer. **∼r** *vt* carve; sculpt (*escultura*); cut (*diamante*); (*Mex, restregar*) scrub. **∼rse** *vpr* (*Mex*) rub o.s.

tallarín *m* noodle

talle *m* waist; (*figura*) figure

taller *m* workshop; (*de pintor etc*) studio; (*Auto*) garage

tallo *m* stem, stalk

tal|ón *m* heel; (*recibo*) counterfoil;

(*cheque*) cheque. **∼onario** *m* receipt book; (*de cheques*) cheque book

tamal *m* (*LAm*) tamale

tamaño *adj* such a. ● *m* size. **de ∼ natural** life-size

tambalearse *vpr* (*persona*) stagger; (*cosa*) wobble

también *adv* also, too

tambor *m* drum. **∼ del freno** brake drum. **∼ilear** *vi* drum

tamiz *m* sieve. **∼ar** ⑩ *vt* sieve

tampoco *adv* neither, nor, not either. **yo ∼ fui** I didn't go either

tampón *m* tampon; (*para entintar*) ink-pad

tan *adv* so. **∼... como** as... as. **¿qué ∼...?** (*LAm*) how...?

tanda *f* group; (*de obreros*) shift

tang|ente *adj & f* tangent. **∼ible** *adj* tangible

tango *m* tango

tanque *m* tank

tante|ar *vt* estimate; sound up (*persona*); (*ensayar*) test; (*fig*) weigh up; (*LAm, palpar*) feel. ● *vi* (*LAm*) feel one's way. **∼o** *m* estimate; (*prueba*) test; (*en deportes*) score

tanto *adj* (*en singular*) so much; (*en plural*) so many; (*comparación en singular*) as much; (*comparación en plural*) as many. ● *pron* so much; (*en plural*) so many. ● *adv* so; (*con verbo*) so much. **hace ∼ tiempo** it's been so long. **∼... como** both ...and. **¿qué ∼...?** (*LAm*) how much...? **∼ como** as well as; (*cantidad*) as much as. **∼ más... cuanto que** all the more ... because. **∼ si... como si** whether ... or. **a ∼s de** sometime in. **en ∼, entre ∼** meanwhile. **en ∼ que** while. **entre ∼** meanwhile. **hasta**

t

$\sim$ **que** until. **no es para $\sim$** it's not as bad as all that. **otro $\sim$** the same; (*el doble*) as much again. **por (lo) $\sim$** therefore. ● *m* certain amount; (*punto*) point; (*gol*) goal. **estar al $\sim$ de** be up to date with

tañer 22 *vi* peal

tapa *f* lid; (*de botella*) top; (*de libro*) cover. $\sim$**s** *fpl* savoury snacks. $\sim$**dera** *f* cover, lid; (*fig*) cover. $\sim$**r** *vt* cover; (*abrigar*) wrap up; (*obturar*) plug. $\sim$**rrabo(s)** *m invar* loincloth

> **tapas** In Spain these are small portions of food served in bars and cafés with a drink. There is a wide variety, including Spanish omelette, seafood, different kinds of cooked potatoes, cheese, ham, chorizo etc. The practice of going out for a drink and *tapas* is known as *tapeo*.

tapete *m* (*de mesa*) table cover; (*Mex, alfombra*) rug

tapia *f* wall. $\sim$**r** *vt* enclose

tapi|cería *f* tapestry; (*de muebles*) upholstery. $\sim$**z** *m* tapestry. $\sim$**zar** 10 *vt* upholster (*muebles*)

tapón *m* stopper; (*Tec*) plug

taqu|igrafía *f* shorthand. $\sim$**ígrafo** *m* shorthand writer

taquill|a *f* ticket office; (*fig, dinero*) takings. $\sim$**ero** *adj* box-office

tara *f* (*peso*) tare; (*defecto*) defect

tarántula *f* tarantula

tararear *vt/i* hum

tarda|nza *f* delay. $\sim$**r** *vt* take. ● *vi* (*retrasarse*) be late; (*emplear mucho tiempo*) take a long time. **a más $\sim$r** at the latest. **sin $\sim$r** without delay

tard|e *adv* late. ● *f* (*antes del atardecer*) afternoon; (*después del atardecer*) evening. **en la $\sim$e** (*LAm*), **por la $\sim$e** in the afternoon. $\sim$**ío** *adj* late

tarea *f* task, job

tarifa *f* rate; (*en transporte*) fare; (*lista de precios*) tariff

tarima *f* dais

tarjeta *f* card. $\sim$ **de crédito** credit card. $\sim$ **de fidelidad** loyalty card. $\sim$ **postal** postcard. $\sim$ **telefónica** telephone card

tarro *m* jar; (*Mex, taza*) mug

tarta *f* cake; (*con base de masa*) tart. $\sim$ **helada** ice-cream gateau

tartamud|ear *vi* stammer. $\sim$**o** *adj*. **es $\sim$o** he stammers

tasa *f* valuation; (*impuesto*) tax; (*índice*) rate. $\sim$**r** *vt* value; (*limitar*) ration

tasca *f* bar

tatarabuel|a *f* great-great-grandmother. $\sim$**o** *m* great-great-grandfather. $\sim$**os** *mpl* great-great-grandparents

tatua|je *m* (*acción*) tattooing; (*dibujo*) tattoo. $\sim$**r** 21 *vt* tattoo

taurino *adj* bullfighting

Tauro *m* Taurus

tauromaquia *f* bullfighting

taxi *m* taxi. $\sim$**ista** *m & f* taxi-driver

taz|a *f* cup. $\sim$**ón** *m* bowl

te *pron* (*acusativo*) you; (*dativo*) to you; (*reflexivo*) (to) yourself

té *m* tea; (*LAm, reunión*) tea party

teatr|al *adj* theatre; (*exagerado*) theatrical. $\sim$**o** *m* theatre; (*literatura*) drama

tebeo *m* comic

tech|ado *m* roof. $\sim$**ar** *vt* roof. $\sim$**o** *m* (*interior*) ceiling; (*LAm, tejado*) roof. $\sim$**umbre** *f* roof

tecl|a f key. **~ado** m keyboard. **~ear** vt key in

técnica f technique

tecnicismo m technical nature; (*palabra*) technical term

técnico adj technical. ● m technician; (*en deportes*) trainer

tecnol|ogía f technology. **~ógico** adj technological

tecolote m (*Mex*) owl

teja f tile. **~s de pizarra** slates. **~do** m roof. **a toca ~** cash

teje|dor m weaver. **~r** vt weave; (*hacer punto*) knit

tejemaneje m 🔢 intrigue. **~s** mpl scheming

tejido m material; (*Anat, fig*) tissue. **~s** mpl textiles

tejón m badger

tela f material, fabric; (*de araña*) web; (*en líquido*) skin

telar m loom. **~es** mpl textile mill

telaraña f spider's web, cobweb

tele f 🔢 TV, telly

tele|banca f telephone banking. **~comunicación** f telecommunication. **~diario** m television news. **~dirigido** adj remote-controlled; (*misil*) guided. **~férico** m cable-car

tel|efonear vt/i telephone. **~efónico** adj telephone. **~efonista** m & f telephonist.

teléfono m telephone. **~ celular** (*LAm*) mobile phone, cellular phone. **~ móvil** (*Esp*) mobile phone, cellular phone. **~ satélite** satphone

tel|egrafía f telegraphy. **~égrafo** m telegraph. **~egrama** m telegram

telenovela f television soap opera

teleobjetivo m telephoto lens

telep|atía f telepathy. **~ático** adj telepathic

telesc|ópico adj telescopic. **~opio** m telescope

telesilla m & f chair-lift

telespectador m viewer

telesquí m ski-lift

televi|dente m & f viewer. **~sar** vt televise. **~sión** f television. **~sor** m television (set)

télex m invar telex

telón m curtain

tema m subject; (*Mus*) theme

tembl|ar 🔢 vi shake; (*de miedo*) tremble; (*de frío*) shiver. **~or** m shaking; (*de miedo*) trembling; (*de frío*) shivering. **~or de tierra** earth tremor. **~oroso** adj trembling

tem|er vt be afraid (of). ● vi be afraid. **~erse** vpr be afraid. **~erario** adj reckless. **~eroso** adj frightened. **~ible** adj fearsome. **~or** m fear

témpano m floe

temperamento m temperament

temperatura f temperature

tempest|ad f storm. **~uoso** adj stormy

templ|ado adj (*tibio*) warm; (*clima, tiempo*) mild; (*valiente*) courageous. **~anza** f mildness. **~ar** vt temper; (*calentar*) warm up. **~e** m tempering; (*coraje*) courage; (*humor*) mood

templo m temple

tempora|da f season. **~l** adj temporary. ● m storm

tempran|ero adj (*frutos*) early. **ser ~ero** be an early riser. **~o** adj & adv early

tenacidad f tenacity

tenacillas fpl tongs

tenaz *adj* tenacious

tenaza *f*, **tenazas** *fpl* pliers; *(de chimenea, Culin)* tongs; *(de cangrejo)* pincer

tende|ncia *f* tendency. **~nte** *m*. **~nte** *a* aimed at. **~r** **1** *vt* spread (out); (ropa a secar); (colocar) lay. • *vi* tend (a to). **~rse** *vpr* lie down

tender|ete *m* stall. **~o** *m* shopkeeper

tendido *adj* spread out; (ropa) hung out; (persona) lying down. • *m* (en plaza de toros) front rows

tendón *m* tendon

tenebroso *adj* gloomy; (asunto) sinister

tenedor *m* fork; (poseedor) holder

tener 40

● *verbo transitivo*

! El presente del verbo **tener** admite dos traducciones: to have y to have got, este último de uso más extendido en el inglés británico

····▶ to have. ¿tienen hijos? do you have any children?, have you got any children? no tenemos coche we don't have a car, we haven't got a car. tiene gripe he has (the) flu, he's got (the) flu

····▶ to be. (dimensiones, edad) tiene 1 metro de largo it's 1 meter long. tengo 20 años I'm 20 (years old)

····▶ (sentir) tener + nombre to be + adjective. **~** celos to be jealous. **~** frío to be cold

····▶ (sujetar, sostener) to hold. tenme la escalera hold the

ladder for me

····▶ (indicando estado) tiene las manos sucias his hands are dirty. me tiene preocupada I'm worried about him. me tuvo esperando he kept me waiting

····▶ (llevar puesto) to be wearing, to have on. ¡qué zapatos más elegantes tienes! those are very smart shoes you're wearing! tienes el suéter al revés you have your sweater on inside out

····▶ (considerar) **~** a uno por algo to think s.o. is sth. lo tenía por tímido I thought he was shy

● *verbo auxiliar*

····▶ **~** que hacer algo to have to do sth. tengo que irme I have to go

····▶ tener + participio pasado. tengo pensado comprarlo I'm thinking of buying it. tenía entendido otra cosa I understood something else

····▶ (LAm, con expresiones temporales) tienen 2 años de estar aquí they've been here for 2 months. tiene mucho tiempo sin verlo she hasn't seen him for a long time

····▶ (en locuciones) aquí tiene here you are. ¿qué tienes? what's the matter with you? ¿y eso qué tiene? (LAm) and what's wrong with that?

● **tenerse** *verbo pronominal*

····▶ (sostenerse) no podía **~**se en pie (de cansancio) he was dead on his feet; (de borracho) he could hardly stand

····➤ *(considerarse)* to consider o.s. **se tiene por afortunado** he considers himself lucky

tengo *vb véase* **TENER**

teniente *m* lieutenant

tenis *m* tennis. ~ **de mesa** table tennis. ~**ta** *m & f* tennis player

tenor *m* sense; *(Mus)* tenor. **a** ~ **de** according to

tens|ión *f* tension; *(arterial)* blood pressure; *(Elec)* voltage; *(estrés)* strain. ~**o** *adj* tense

tentación *f* temptation

tentáculo *m* tentacle

tenta|dor *adj* tempting. ~**r** 🛙 *vt* tempt; *(palpar)* feel

tentativa *f* attempt

tenue *adj* thin; *(luz, voz)* faint; *(color)* subdued

teñi|r 🖥 & 🏿 *vt* dye; *(fig)* tinge *(de* with). ~**rse** *vpr* dye one's hair

teología *f* theology

te|oría *f* theory. ~**órico** *adj* theoretical

tequila *f* tequila

terap|euta *m & f* therapist. ~**éutico** *adj* therapeutic. ~**ia** *f* therapy

terc|er *adj véase* **TERCERO**. ~**era** *f (Auto)* third (gear). ~**ero** *adj (delante de nombre masculino en singular* **tercer**) third. ● *m* third party. ~**io** *m* third

terciopelo *m* velvet

terco *adj* obstinate

tergiversar *vt* distort

termal *adj* thermal

térmico *adj* thermal

termina|ción *f* ending; *(conclusión)* conclusion. ~**l** *adj & m* terminal. ~**nte** *adj* categorical. ~**r** *vt* finish, end. ~**r por** end up. ~**rse** *vpr* come to an end

término *m* end; *(palabra)* term;

(plazo) period. ~ **medio** average. **dar** **a** ~ finish off. **en primer** ~ first of all. **en último** ~ as a last resort. **estar en buenos** ~**s con** be on good terms with. **llevar a** ~ carry out

terminología *f* terminology

termita *f* termite

termo *m* Thermos (P) flask, flask

termómetro *m* thermometer

termo|nuclear *adj* thermonuclear. ~**stato** *m* thermostat

terner|a *f (carne)* veal. ~**o** *m* calf

ternura *f* tenderness

terquedad *f* stubbornness

terrado *m* flat roof

terraplén *m* embankment

terrateniente *m & f* landowner

terraza *f* terrace; *(balcón)* balcony; *(terrado)* flat roof

terremoto *m* earthquake

terre|no *adj* earthly. ● *m* land; *(solar)* plot *(fig)* field. ~**stre** *adj* land; *(Mil)* ground

terrible *adj* terrible. ~**mente** *adv* awfully

territori|al *adj* territorial. ~**o** *m* territory

terrón *m (de tierra)* clod; *(Culin)* lump

terror *m* terror. ~**ífico** *adj* terrifying. ~**ismo** *m* terrorism. ~**ista** *m & f* terrorist

terso *adj* smooth

tertulia *f* gathering

tesina *f* dissertation

tesón *m* tenacity

tesor|ería *f* treasury. ~**ero** *m* treasurer. ~**o** *m* treasure; *(tesorería)* treasury; *(libro)* thesaurus

testaferro *m* figurehead

testa|mento *m* will. T~**mento** *(Relig)* Testament. ~**r** *vi* make a will

t

testarudo adj stubborn

testículo m testicle

testi|ficar 7 vt/i testify. ~go m witness. ~go ocular, ~go presencial eyewitness. ser ~go de witness. ~monio m testimony

teta f tit (fam o vulg); (de biberón) teat

tétanos m tetanus

tetera f (para el té) teapot

tetilla f nipple; (de biberón) teat

tétrico adj gloomy

textil adj & m textile

text|o m text. ~ual adj textual; (traducción) literal; (palabras) exact

textura f texture

tez f complexion

ti pron you

tía f aunt; 1 woman

tiara f tiara

tibio adj lukewarm

tiburón m shark

tiempo m time; (atmosférico) weather; (Mus) tempo; (Gram) tense; (en partido) half. **a su** ~ in due course. **a** ~ in time. **¿cuánto** ~? how long? **hace buen** ~ the weather is fine. **hace** ~ some time ago. **mucho** ~ a long time. **perder el** ~ waste time

tienda f shop (esp Brit), store (esp Amer); (de campaña) tent. ~ **de comestibles**, ~ **de ultramarinos** grocer's (shop) (Brit), grocery store (Amer)

tiene vb véase TENER

tienta. andar a ~s feel one's way

tierno adj tender; (joven) young

tierra f land; (planeta, Elec) earth; (suelo) ground; (en geología) soil, earth; (LAm, polvo) dust. **por** ~ overland, by land

tieso adj stiff; (engreído) conceited

tiesto m flowerpot

tifón m typhoon

tifus m typhus; (fiebre tifoidea) typhoid (fever)

tigre m tiger. ~**sa** f tigress

tijera f, **tijeras** fpl scissors; (de jardín) shears

tijeretear vt snip

tila f (infusión) lime tea

tild|ar vt. ~**ar de** (fig) brand as. ~**e** f tilde

tilo m lime(-tree)

timar vt swindle

timbal m kettledrum; (Culin) timbale, meat pie. ~**es** mpl (Mus) timpani

timbr|ar vt stamp. ~**e** m (sello) fiscal stamp; (Mex) postage stamp; (Elec) bell; (sonido) timbre

timidez f shyness

tímido adj shy

timo m swindle

timón m rudder; (rueda) wheel; (fig) helm

tímpano m eardrum

tina f tub. ~**co** m (Mex) water tank. ~**ja** f large earthenware jar

tinglado m mess; (asunto) racket

tinieblas fpl darkness; (fig) confusion

tino f good sense; (tacto) tact

tint|a f ink. **de buena** ~**a** on good authority. ~**e** m dyeing; (color) dye; (fig) tinge. ~**ero** m ink-well

tintinear vi tinkle; (vasos) chink, clink

tinto adj (vino) red

tintorería f dry cleaner's

tintura f dyeing; (color) dye

tío m uncle; 1 man. ~**s** mpl uncle and aunt

tiovivo m merry-go-round

típico adj typical

tipo m type; (fam, persona) person; (figura de mujer) figure; (figura de hombre) build; (Com) rate

tip|ografía f typography. **~ográfico** adj typographic(al)

tira f strip. **la ~** de lots of

tirabuzón m corkscrew; (de pelo) ringlet

tirad|a f distance; (serie) series; (de periódico etc) print-run. **de una ~a** in one go. **~o** adj (barato) very cheap; (fam, fácil) very easy. **~or** m (asa) handle

tiran|ía f tyranny. **~izar** [10] vt tyrannize. **~o** adj tyrannical. ● m tyrant

tirante adj tight; (fig) tense; (relaciones) strained. ● m strap. **~s** mpl braces (esp Brit), suspenders (Amer)

tirar vt throw; (desechar) throw away; (derribar) knock over; drop (bomba); fire (cohete); (imprimir) print. ● vi (disparar) shoot. **~** a tend to (be); (parecerse a) resemble. **~ abajo** knock down. **~ de** pull. **a todo ~** at the most. **ir tirando** get by. **~se** vpr throw o.s.; (tumbarse) lie down

tirita f (sticking) plaster

tiritar vi shiver (de with)

tiro m throw; (disparo) shot. **~ libre** free kick. **a ~** within range. **errar el ~** miss. **pegarse un ~** shoot o.s.

tiroides m thyroid (gland)

tirón m tug. **de un ~** in one go

tirote|ar vt shoot at. **~o** m shooting

tisana f herb tea

tisú m (pl ~s, ~es) tissue

títere m puppet. **~s** mpl puppet show

titilar vi (estrella) twinkle

titiritero m puppeteer; (acróbata) acrobat

titube|ante adj faltering; (fig) hesitant. **~ar** vi falter. **~o** m hesitation

titula|do adj (libro) entitled; (persona) qualified. **~r** m headline; (persona) holder. ● vt call. **~rse** vpr be called; (persona) graduate

título m title; (académico) qualification; (Univ) degree. **a ~ de** as, by way of

tiza f chalk

tiz|nar vt dirty. **~ne** m soot

toall|a f towel. **~ero** m towel-rail

tobillo m ankle

tobogán m slide; (para la nieve) toboggan

tocadiscos m invar record-player

toca|do adj touched [1]. ● m headdress. **~dor** m dressing-table. **~nte** adj. **en lo ~nte a** with regard to. **~r** [7] vt touch; (palpar) feel; (Mus) play; ring (timbre); (mencionar) touch on; (barco) stop at. ● vi ring; (corresponder a uno). **te ~ a ti** it's your turn. **en lo que ~ a** as for. **~rse** vpr touch; (personas) touch each other

tocayo m namesake

tocino m bacon

tocólogo m obstetrician

todavía adv still; (con negativos) yet. **~ no** not yet

---

todo, **toda**

● adjetivo

····▶ (la totalidad) all. ~ **el vino** all the wine. ~**s los edificios** all the buildings. ~ **ese dinero** all that money. ~ **el mundo** everyone. (como adv) **está toda sucia** it's all dirty

····▸ (entero) whole. **~ el día** the whole day, all day. **toda su familia** his whole family. **el tiempo** the whole time, all the time

····▸ (cada, cualquiera) every. **~ tipo de coche** every type of car. **~s los días** every day

····▸ (enfático) **a toda velocidad** at top speed. **es ~ un caballero** he's a real gentleman

····▸ (en locuciones) **ante ~** above all. **a ~ esto** meanwhile. **con ~ even so. **del ~** totally. **~ lo contrario** quite the opposite

➡ Para expresiones como **todo recto, todo seguido** etc., ver bajo el respectivo adjetivo

● pronombre

····▸ all; (todas las cosas) everything. **eso es ~** that's all. **lo perdieron ~** they lost everything. **quiere comprar ~** he wants to buy everything

····▸ **todos, todas** all; (todo el mundo) everyone. **los compró ~s** he bought them all, he bought all of them. **~s queríamos ir** we all wanted to go. **vinieron ~s** everyone came

● nombre masculino **el/un ~** the/a whole

toldo m awning

tolera|ncia f tolerance. **~nte** adj tolerant. **~r** vt tolerate

toma f taking; (de universidad etc) occupation; (Med) dose; (de agua) intake; (Elec) socket; (LAm, acequia) irrigation channel. ● int well!, fancy

that! **~ de corriente** power point. **~dura** f. **~dura de pelo** hoax. **~r** vt take; catch (autobús, tren); occupy (universidad etc); (beber) drink, have; (comer) eat, have. ● vi take; (esp LAm, beber) drink; (LAm, dirigirse) go. **~r a bien** take well. **~r a mal** take badly. **~r en serio** take seriously. **~rla con uno** pick on s.o. **~r por** take for. **~ y daca** give and take. **¿qué va a ~r?** what would you like? **~rse** vpr take; (beber) drink, have; (comer) eat, have

tomate m tomato

tomillo m thyme

tomo m volume

ton: sin ~ ni son without rhyme or reason

tonad|a f tune; (canción) popular song; (LAm, acento) accent. **~illa** f tune

tonel m barrel. **~ada** f ton. **~aje** m tonnage

tónic|a f trend; (bebida) tonic water. **~o** adj tonic; (sílaba) stressed. ● m tonic

tonificar [7] vt invigorate

tono m tone; (Mus, modo) key; (color) shade

tont|ería f silliness; (cosa) silly thing; (dicho) silly remark. **dejarse de ~erías** stop fooling around. **~o** adj silly. ● m fool, idiot; (payaso) clown. **hacer el ~o** act the fool. **hacerse el ~o** act dumb

topacio m topaz

topar vi. **~ con** run into

tope adj maximum. ● m end; (de tren) buffer; (Mex, Auto) speed bump. **hasta los ~s** crammed full. **ir a ~** go flat out

tópico adj trite. **de uso ~** (Med) for external use only. ● m cliché

topo m mole

topogr|afía f topography. **~áfico** adj topographical

toque m touch; (sonido) sound; (de campana) peal; (de reloj) stroke. **~ de queda** curfew. **dar los últimos ~s** put the finishing touches. **~tear** vt fiddle with

toquilla f shawl

tórax m invar thorax

torcer 2 & 9 vt twist; (doblar) bend; wring out (ropa). ● vi turn. **~se** vpr twist

tordo adj dapple grey. ● m thrush

tore|ar vt fight; (evitar) dodge. ● vi fight (bulls). **~o** m bullfighting. **~ro** m bullfighter

torment|a f storm. **~o** m torture. **~oso** adj stormy

tornado m tornado

tornasolado adj irridescent

torneo m tournament

tornillo m screw

torniquete m (Med) tourniquet; (entrada) turnstile

torno m lathe; (de alfarero) wheel. **en ~ a** around

toro m bull. **~s** mpl bullfighting. **ir a los ~s** go to a bullfight

---

> ### (la fiesta de) los toros   i
>
> Bullfighting is popular in Spain and some Latin American countries. The season runs from March to October in Spain, from November to March in Latin America. The bullfighters who take part in a corrida gather in cuadrillas. The principal bullfighter or matador is assisted by peones.

---

toronja f (LAm) grapefruit

torpe adj clumsy; (estúpido) stupid

torpedo m torpedo

torpeza f clumsiness; (de inteligencia) slowness. **una ~** a blunder

torre f tower; (en ajedrez) castle, rook; (Elec) pylon; (edificio) tower block (Brit), apartment block (Amer)

torren|cial adj torrential. **~te** m torrent; (circulatorio) bloodstream; (fig) flood

tórrido adj torrid

torsión f twisting

torso m torso

torta f tart; (LAm, de verduras) pie; (golpe) slap, punch; (Mex, bocadillo) filled roll. **no entender ni ~** not understand a thing. **~zo** m slap, punch. **pegarse un ~zo** have a bad accident

tortícolis f stiff neck

tortilla f omelette; (Mex, de maíz) tortilla. **~ española** potato omelette. **~ francesa** plain omelette

tórtola f turtle-dove

tortuoso adj winding; (fig) devious

tortura f torture. **~r** vt torture

tos f cough. **~ ferina** whooping cough

tosco adj crude; (persona) coarse

toser vi cough

tost|ada f piece of toast. **~adas** fpl toast; (Mex, de tortilla) fried tortillas. **~ado** adj (pan) toasted; (café) roasted; (persona, color) tanned. **~ar** vt toast (pan); roast (café); tan (piel)

total adj total. ● adv after all. **~ que** so, to cut a long story short. ● m total; (totalidad) whole. **~idad** f whole. **~itario** adj totalitarian. **~izar** 10 vt total

tóxico adj toxic

toxi|cómano m drug addict. **~na** f toxin

t

tozudo adj stubborn

traba f catch; (fig, obstáculo) obstacle. **poner ~s a** hinder

trabaj|ador adj hard-working. • m worker. **~ar** vt work; knead (masa). • vi work (**de** as); (actor) act. **¿en qué ~as?** what do you do? **~o** m work. **costar ~o** be difficult. **~oso** adj hard

trabalenguas m invar tongue-twister

traba|r vt (sujetar) fasten; (unir) join; (entablar) strike up. **~rse** vpr get stuck. **trabársele la lengua** get tongue-tied

trácala m (Mex) cheat. • f (Mex) trick

tracción f traction

tractor m tractor

tradici|ón f tradition. **~onal** adj traditional

traduc|ción f translation. **~ir** [47] vt translate (**a** into). **~tor** m translator

traer [41] vt bring; (llevar) carry; (causar) cause. **traérselas** be difficult

trafica|nte m & f dealer. **~r** [7] vi deal

tráfico m traffic; (Com) trade

traga|luz m skylight. **~perras** f invar slot-machine. **~r** [12] vt swallow; (comer mucho) devour; (soportar) put up with. **no lo trago** I can't stand him. **~rse** vpr swallow up; (fig) swallow up

tragedia f tragedy

trágico adj tragic. • m tragedian

trag|o m swallow, gulp; (pequeña porción) sip; (fig, disgusto) blow; (LAm, bebida alcohólica) drink. **echar(se) un ~o** have a drink. **~ón** adj greedy. • m glutton

trai|ción f treachery; (Pol) trea-son. **~cionar** vt betray. **~cionero** adj treacherous. **~dor** adj treacherous. • m traitor

traigo vb véase **TRAER**

traje m dress; (de hombre) suit. **~ de baño** swimming-costume. **~ de etiqueta**, **~ de noche** evening dress. • vb véase **TRAER**.

traj|ín m coming and going; (ajetreo) hustle and bustle. **~inar** vi bustle about

trama f weft; (fig, argumento) plot. **~r** vt weave; (fig) plot

tramitar vt negotiate

trámite m step. **~s** mpl procedure

tramo m (parte) section; (de escalera) flight

tramp|a f trap; (fig) trick. **hacer ~a** cheat. **~illa** f trapdoor

trampolín m trampoline; (de piscina) springboard; (rígido) diving board

tramposo adj cheating. • m cheat

tranca f bar. **~r** vt bar

trance m moment; (hipnótico etc) trance

tranco m stride

tranquil|idad f peace; (de espíritu) peace of mind. **con ~** calmly. **~izar** [10] vt calm down; (reconfortar) reassure. **~o** adj calm; (lugar) quiet; (conciencia) clear. **estáte ~o** don't worry

transa|cción f transaction; (acuerdo) settlement. **~r** vi (LAm) compromise

transatlántico adj transatlantic. • m (ocean) liner

transbord|ador m ferry. **~ar** vt transfer. **~o** m transfer. **hacer ~o** change (**en** at)

transcri|bir (pp transcrito) vt transcribe. **~pción** f transcription

transcur|rir vi pass. ~**so** m course

transeúnte m & f passer-by

transfer|encia f transfer. ~**ir** ④ vt transfer

transforma|ción f transformation. ~**dor** m transformer. ~**r** vt transform

transfusión f transfusion

transgre|dir vt transgress. ~**sión** f transgression

transición f transition

transigir ⑭ vi give in, compromise

transistor m transistor

transita|ble adj passable. ~**r** vi go

transitivo adj transitive

tránsito m transit; (tráfico) traffic

transitorio adj transitory

transmi|sión f transmission; (radio, TV) broadcast. ~**sor** m transmitter. ~**sora** f broadcasting station. ~**tir** vt transmit; (radio, TV) broadcast; (fig) pass on

transparen|cia f transparency. ~**tar** vt show. ~**te** adj transparent

transpira|ción f perspiration. ~**r** vi transpire; (sudar) sweat

transport|ar vt transport. ~**e** m transport. **empresa** f **de** ~**es** removals company

transversal adj transverse. **una calle** ~ **a la Gran Vía** a street which crosses the Gran Vía

tranvía m tram

trapear vt (LAm) mop

trapecio m trapeze; (Math) trapezium

trapo m cloth. ~**s** mpl rags; (▣, ropa) clothes **a todo** ~ out of control

tráquea f windpipe, trachea

traquete|ar vt bang, rattle; (persona) rush around. ~**o** m banging, rattle

tras prep after; (detrás) behind

trascende|ncia f significance; (alcance) implication. ~**ntal** adj transcendental; (importante) important. ~**r** ❶ vi (saberse) become known; (extenderse) spread

trasero adj back, rear. ● m (de persona) bottom

trasfondo m background

traslad|ar vt move; transfer (empleado etc); (aplazar) postpone. ~**o** m transfer; (copia) copy. (mudanza) removal. **dar** ~**o** notify

trasl|úcido adj translucent. ~**ucirse** ⑪ vpr be translucent; (dejarse ver) show through; (fig, revelarse) be revealed. ~**uz** m. **al** ~**uz** against the light

trasmano. a ~ out of the way

trasnochar vt (acostarse tarde) go to bed late; (no acostarse) stay up all night; (no dormir) be unable to sleep

traspas|ar vt go through; (transferir) transfer; go beyond (límite). **se** ~**a** for sale. ~**o** m transfer

traspié m trip; (fig) slip. **dar un** ~ stumble; (fig) slip up

trasplant|ar vt transplant. ~**e** m transplant

trastada f prank; (jugada) dirty trick

traste m fret. **dar al** ~ **con** ruin. **ir al** ~ fall through. ~**s** mpl (Mex) junk

trastero m storeroom

trasto m piece of junk. ● ~**s** mpl junk

trastorn|ado adj mad. ~**ar** vt upset; (volver loco) drive mad; (fig, fam, gustar mucho) delight. ~**arse**

vpr get upset; (*volverse loco*) go mad. **~o** *m* (*incl Med*) upset; (*Pol*) disturbance; (*fig*) confusion

trat|able *adj* friendly; (*Med*) treatable. **~ado** *m* treatise; (*acuerdo*) treaty. **~amiento** *m* treatment; (*título*) title. **~ante** *m & f* dealer. **~ar** *vt* (*incl Med*) treat; deal with (*asunto etc*); (*manejar*) handle; (*de tú, de Vd*) address (de as). ● *vi* deal (with). **~ar con** have to do with; (*Com*) deal in. **~ar de** be about; (*intentar*) try. **¿de qué se ~a?** what's it about? **~o** *m* treatment; (*acuerdo*) agreement; (*título*) title; (*relación*) relationship. **¡~o hecho!** agreed! **~os** *mpl* dealings

traum|a *m* trauma. **~ático** *adj* traumatic

través: a ~ de through; (*de lado a lado*) crossways

travesaño *m* crossbeam; (*de portería*) crossbar

travesía *f* crossing; (*calle*) side-street

trav|esura *f* prank. **~ieso** *adj* (*niño*) mischievous, naughty

trayecto *m* (*tramo*) stretch; (*ruta*) route; (*viaje*) journey. **~ria** *f* trajectory; (*fig*) course

traz|a *f* (*aspecto*) appearance. **~as** *fpl* signs. **~ado** *m* plan. **~ar** 10 *vt* draw; (*bosquejar*) sketch. **~o** *m* stroke; (*línea*) line

trébol *m* clover. **~es** *mpl* (*en naipes*) clubs

trece *adj & m* thirteen

trecho *m* stretch; (*distancia*) distance; (*tiempo*) while. **a ~s** here and there. **de ~ en ~** at intervals

tregua *f* truce; (*fig*) respite

treinta *adj & m* thirty

tremendo *adj* terrible; (*extraordinario*) terrific

tren *m* train. **~ de aterrizaje** landing gear. **~ de vida** lifestyle

tren|cilla *f* braid. **~za** *f* braid; (*de pelo*) plait. **~zar** 10 *vt* plait

trepa|dor *adj* climbing. **~dora** *f* climber. **~r** *vt/i* climb. **~rse** *vpr*. **~rse a** climb (*árbol*); climb onto (*silla etc*)

tres *adj & m* three. **~cientos** *adj & m* three hundred. **~illo** *m* three-piece suite; (*Mus*) triplet

treta *f* trick

tri|angular *adj* triangular. **~ángulo** *m* triangle

trib|al *adj* tribal. **~u** *f* tribe

tribuna *f* platform; (*de espectadores*) stand. **~l** *m* court; (*de examen etc*) board; (*fig*) tribunal

tribut|ar *vt* pay. **~o** *m* tribute; (*impuesto*) tax

triciclo *m* tricycle

tricolor *adj* three-coloured

tricotar *vt/i* knit

tridimensional *adj* three-dimensional

trig|al *m* wheat field. **~o** *m* wheat

trigésimo *adj* thirtieth

trigueño *adj* olive-skinned; (*pelo*) dark blonde

trilla|do *adj* (*fig, manoseado*) trite; (*fig, conocido*) well-known. **~r** *vt* thresh

trilogía *f* trilogy

trimestr|al *adj* quarterly. **~e** *m* quarter; (*en enseñanza*) term

trin|ar *vi* warble. **estar que trina** be furious

trinchar *vt* carve

trinchera *f* ditch; (*Mil*) trench; (*abrigo*) trench coat

trineo *m* sledge

trinidad *f* trinity

trino *m* warble

trío m trio

tripa f intestine; (fig, vientre) tummy, belly. **~s** fpl (de máquina etc) parts, workings. **revolver las ~s** turn one's stomach

tripl|e adj triple. ● m. **el ~e (de)** three times as much (as). **~icado** adj. **por ~icado** in triplicate. **~icar 7** vt treble

tripula|ción f crew. **~nte** m & f member of the crew. **~r** vt man

tris m. **estar en un ~** be on the point of

triste adj sad; (paisaje, tiempo etc) gloomy; (fig, insignificante) miserable. **~za** f sadness

triturar vt crush

triunf|al adj triumphal. **~ante** adj triumphant. **~ar** vi triumph (**de, sobre** over). **~o** m triumph

trivial adj trivial. **~idad** f triviality

trizas. hacer algo ~ smash sth to pieces. **hacerse ~** smash

trocear vt cut up, chop

trocha f narrow path; (LAm, rail) gauge

trofeo m trophy

tromba f whirlwind; (marina) waterspout. **~ de agua** heavy downpour

trombón m trombone

trombosis f invar thrombosis

trompa f horn; (de orquesta) French horn; (de elefante) trunk; (hocico) snout; (en anatomía) tube. **coger una ~** 1 get drunk. **~zo** m bump

trompet|a f trumpet; (músico) trumpet player; (Mil) trumpeter. **~illa** f ear-trumpet

trompo m (juguete) (spinning) top

tronar vt (Mex) shoot. ● vi thunder

tronchar vt bring down; (fig) cut short. **~se de risa** laugh a lot

tronco m trunk. **dormir como un ~** sleep like a log

trono m throne

trop|a f troops. **~el** m mob

tropez|ar 1 & 10 vi trip; (fig) slip up. **~ar con** run into. **~ón** m stumble; (fig) slip

tropical adj tropical

trópico adj tropical. ● m tropic

tropiezo m slip; (desgracia) hitch

trot|ar vi trot. **~e** m trot; (fig) toing and froing. **al ~e** at a trot; (de prisa) in a rush. **de mucho ~e** hard-wearing

trozo m piece, bit. **a ~s** in bits

trucha f trout

truco m trick. **coger el ~** get the knack

trueno m thunder; (estampido) bang

trueque m exchange; (Com) barter

trufa f truffle

truhán m rogue

truncar 7 vt truncate; (fig) cut short

tu adj your

tú pron you

tuba f tuba

tubérculo m tuber

tuberculosis f tuberculosis

tub|ería f pipes; (oleoducto etc) pipeline. **~o** m tube. **~o de ensayo** test tube. **~o de escape** (Auto) exhaust (pipe). **~ular** adj tubular

tuerca f nut

tuerto adj one-eyed, blind in one eye. ● m one-eyed person

tuétano m marrow; (fig) heart. **hasta los ~s** completely

tufo *m* stench

tugurio *m* hovel

tul *m* tulle

tulipán *m* tulip

tulli|do *adj* paralysed. **~r** 22 *vt* cripple

tumba *f* grave, tomb

tumb|ar *vt* knock over, knock down (estructura); (fig, fam, en examen) fail. **~arse** *vpr* lie down. **~o** *m* jolt. **dar un ~o** tumble. **~ona** *f* sun lounger

tumor *m* tumour

tumulto *m* turmoil; (Pol) riot

tuna *f* prickly pear; (de estudiantes) student band

tunante *m & f* rogue

túnel *m* tunnel

túnica *f* tunic

tupé *m* toupee; (fig) nerve

tupido *adj* thick

turba *f* peat; (muchedumbre) mob

turbado *adj* upset

turbante *m* turban

turbar *vt* upset; (molestar) disturb. **~se** *vpr* be upset

turbina *f* turbine

turbi|o *adj* cloudy; (vista) blurred; (asunto etc) shady. **~ón** *m* squall

turbulen|cia *f* turbulence; (disturbio) disturbance. **~te** *adj* turbulent

turco *adj* Turkish. ● *m* Turk; (lengua) Turkish

tur|ismo *m* tourism; (coche) car. **hacer ~** travel around. **~ cultural** heritage tourism. **~ patrimonial** (LAm) heritage tourism. **~ista** *m & f* tourist. **~ístico** *adj* tourist

turn|arse *vpr* take turns (para to). **~o** *m* turn; (de trabajo) shift. **de ~** on duty

turquesa *f* turquoise

Turquía *f* Turkey

turrón *m* nougat

tutear *vt* address as tú. **~se** *vpr* be on familiar terms

tutela *f* (Jurid) guardianship; (fig) protection

tutor *m* guardian; (en enseñanza) form master

tuve *vb* véase TENER

tuyo *adj & pron* yours. **un amigo ~** a friend of yours

Uu

u *conj* or

ubic|ar *vt* (LAm) place; (localizar) find. **~arse** *vpr* (LAm) be situated; (orientarse) find one's way around

ubre *f* udder

Ud. *abrev* (Usted) you

UE *abrev* (Unión Europea) EU

uf *int* phew!; (de repugnancia) ugh!

ufan|arse *vpr* be proud (con, de of); (jactarse) boast (con, de about). **~o** *adj* proud

úlcera *f* ulcer

últimamente *adv* (recientemente) recently; (finalmente) finally

ultim|ar *vt* complete; (LAm, matar) kill. **~átum** *m* ultimatum

último *adj* last; (más reciente) latest; (más lejano) furthest; (más alto) top; (más bajo) bottom; (definitivo) final. ● *m* last one. **estar en las últimas** be on one's last legs; (sin dinero) be down to one's last penny. **por ~** finally. **vestido a la última** dressed in the latest fashion

ultra *adj* ultra, extreme

ultraj|ante *adj* offensive. **~e** *m* insult, outrage

ultramar *m*. **de ~** overseas; (productos) foreign. **~inos** *mpl* groceries. **tienda de ~s** grocer's (shop) (Brit), grocery store (Amer)

ultranza. **a ~** (con decisión) decisively; (extremo) all-out-out

ultravioleta *adj invar* ultraviolet

umbilical *adj* umbilical

umbral *m* threshold

---

un , **una** *artículo indefinido*

! The masculine article **un** is also used before feminine nouns which begin with stressed **a** or **ha**, e.g. **un alma piadosa**, **un hada madrina**

····▸ (en sing) a; (antes de sonido vocálico) an. **un perro** a dog. **una hora** an hour

····▸ **unos**, **unas** (cantidad incierta) some. **compré ~os libros** I bought some books. (cantidad cierta) **tiene ~os ojos preciosos** she has beautiful eyes. **tiene ~os hijos muy buenos** her children are very good. (en aproximaciones) about. **en ~as 3 horas** in about 3 hours

  ➤ For further information see **uno**

un|ánime *adj* unanimous. **~animidad** *f* unanimity

undécimo *adj* eleventh

ungüento *m* ointment

únic|amente *adv* only. **~o** *adj* only; (fig, incomparable) unique

unicornio *m* unicorn

---

unid|ad *f* unit; (cualidad) unity. **~ad de disco** disk drive. **~o** *adj* united

unifica|ción *f* unification. **~r 7** *vt* unite, unify

uniform|ar *vt* standardize. **~e** *adj* & *m* uniform. **~idad** *f* uniformity

unilateral *adj* unilateral

uni|ón *f* union; (cualidad) unity; (Tec) joint. **~r** *vt* join; mix (líquidos). **~rse** *vpr* join together; (caminos) converge; (compañías) merge

unísono *m* unison. **al ~** in unison

univers|al *adj* universal. **~idad** *f* university. **~itario** *adj* university. **~o** *m* universe

---

uno , **una**
● *adjetivo*

Note that **uno** becomes **un** before masculine nouns

one. **una peseta** one peseta. **un dólar** one dollar. **ni una persona** not one person, not a single person. **treinta y un años** thirty one years

● *pronombre*

····▸ one. **~ es mío** one (of them) is mine. **es la una** it's one o'clock. **se ayudan el ~ al otro** they help one another, they help each other. **lo que sienten el ~ por el otro** what they feel for each other

····▸ (fam, alguien) someone. **le pregunté a ~** I asked someone

····▸ **unos**, **unas** some. **no tenía vasos así es que le presté ~s** she didn't have any glasses so I lent her some. **a ~s les**

  u

gusta, a otros no some like it, others don't. **los ~s a los otros** one another, each other
⋯▸ (*impersonal*) you. **~ no sabe qué decir** you don't know what to say

untar *vt* grease; (*cubrir*) spread; (*fig, fam, sobornar*) bribe

uña *f* nail; (*de animal*) claw; (*casco*) hoof

uranio *m* uranium

Urano *m* Uranus

urban|idad *f* politeness. **~ismo** *m* town planning. **~ización** *f* development. **~izar** 🔟 *vt* develop. **~o** *adj* urban

urbe *f* big city

urdir *vt* (*fig*) plot

urg|encia *f* urgency; (*emergencia*) emergency. **~encias** A & E, (*Amer*) emergency room. **~ente** *adj* urgent; (*carta*) express. **~ir** 🔢 *vi* be urgent.

urinario *m* urinal

urna *f* urn; (*Pol*) ballot box

urraca *f* magpie

URSS *abrev* (*History*) USSR

Uruguay *m*. **el ~** Uruguay

uruguayo *adj & m* Uruguayan

us|ado *adj* (*con estar*) used; (*ropa* etc) worn; (*con ser*) secondhand. **~ar** *vt* use; (*llevar*) wear. **~arse** *vpr* (*LAm*) be in fashion. **~o** *m* use; (*costumbre*) custom. **al ~o de** in the style of

usted *pron* you. **~es** you

usual *adj* usual

usuario *adj* user

usur|a *f* usury. **~ero** *m* usurer

usurpar *vt* usurp

utensilio *m* utensil; (*herramienta*) tool

útero *m* womb, uterus

útil *adj* useful. **~es** *mpl* implements; (*equipo*) equipment

utili|dad *f* usefulness. **~dades** *fpl* (*LAm*) profits. **~zación** *f* use, utilization. **~zar** 🔟 *vt* use, utilize

utopía *f* Utopia

uva *f* grape. **~ pasa** raisin. **mala ~** bad mood

Vv

vaca *f* cow. **carne de ~** beef

vacaciones *fpl* holiday(s), vacation(s) (*Amer*). **de ~** on holiday, on vacation (*Amer*)

vacante *adj* vacant. ● *f* vacancy

vaciar 🔃 *vt* empty; (*ahuecar*) hollow out; (*en molde*) cast

vacila|ción *f* hesitation. **~nte** *adj* unsteady; (*fig*) hesitant. **~r** *vi* hesitate (🔢, *bromear*) tease; (*LAm*, *divertirse*) have fun

vacío *adj* empty; (*frívolo*) frivolous. ● *m* empty space; (*estado*) emptiness; (*en física*) vacuum; (*fig*) void

vacuna *f* vaccine. **~ción** *f* vaccination. **~r** *vt* vaccinate

vacuno *adj* bovine

vad|ear *vt* ford. **~o** *m* ford

vaga|bundear *vi* wander. **~bundo** *adj* vagrant; (*perro*) stray. **niño ~** street urchin. ● *m* tramp, vagrant. **~ncia** *f* vagrancy; (*fig*) laziness. **~r** 🔢 *vi* wander (about)

vagina *f* vagina

vago *adj* vague; (*holgazán*) lazy. ● *m* layabout

vag|ón *m* coach, carriage; (*de mer-*

cancías) wagon. **~ón restaurante** dining-car. **~oneta** f small freight wagon; (Mex, para pasajeros) van

vaho m breath; (vapor) steam. **~s** mpl inhalation

vain|a f sheath; (de semillas) pod. **~illa** f vanilla

vaivén m swinging; (de tren etc) rocking. **~enes** mpl (fig, de suerte) swings

vajilla f dishes, crockery

vale m voucher; (pagaré) IOU. **~dero** adj valid

valenciano adj from Valencia

valentía f bravery, courage

valer ▣ vt be worth; (costar) cost; (fig, significar) mean. ● vi be worth; (costar) cost; (servir) be of use; (ser valedero) be valid; (estar permitido) be allowed. **~ la pena** be worthwhile, be worth it. **¿cuánto vale?** how much is it? **no ~ para nada** be useless. **eso no me vale** (Mex, fam) I don't give a damn about that. **¡vale!** all right!, OK! ▣

valeroso adj courageous

valgo vb véase **VALER**

valía f worth

validez f validity. **dar ~ a** validate

válido adj valid

valiente adj brave; (en sentido irónico) fine. ● m brave person

valija f suitcase. **~ diplomática** diplomatic bag

valioso adj valuable

valla f fence; (en atletismo) hurdle

valle m valley

val|or m value, worth; (coraje) courage. **objetos** mpl **de ~or** valuables. **sin ~or** worthless. **~ores** mpl securities. **~oración** f valu-

ation. **~orar** vt value

vals m invar waltz

válvula f valve

vampiro m vampire

vanagloriarse vpr boast

vandalismo m vandalism

vándalo m & f vandal

vanguardia f vanguard. **de ~** (en arte, música etc) avant-garde

van|idad f vanity. **~idoso** adj vain. **~o** adj vain; (inútil) futile; (palabras) empty. **en ~** in vain

vapor m steam, vapour; (Naut) steamer. **al ~** (Culin) steamed. **~izador** m vaporizer. **~izar** ▣ vaporize

vaquer|o m cowherd, cowboy. **~os** mpl jeans

vara f stick; (de autoridad) staff (medida) yard

varar vi run aground

varia|ble adj & f variable. **~ción** f variation. **~do** adj varied. **~nte** f variant; (Auto) by-pass. **~ntes** fpl hors d'oeuvres. **~r** ▣ vt change; (dar variedad a) vary. ● vi vary; (cambiar) change

varicela f chickenpox

variedad f variety

varilla f stick; (de metal) rod

varios adj several

varita f wand

variz f (pl varices, (LAm) várices) varicose vein

var|ón adj male. ● m man; (niño) boy. **~onil** adj manly

vasco adj & m Basque

vaselina f Vaseline (P), petroleum jelly

vasija f vessel, pot

vaso m glass; (en anatomía) vessel

vástago m shoot; (descendiente) descendant

vasto adj vast

vaticin|ar vt forecast. ~**io** m prediction, forecast

vatio m watt

vaya vb véase IR

Vd. abrev (**Usted**) you

vecin|al adj local. ~**dad** f neighbourhood; (vecinos) residents; (Mex, edificio) tenement house. ~**dario** m neighbourhood; (vecinos) residents. ~**o** adj neighbouring. ● m neighbour; (de barrio, edificio) resident

ve|da f close season. ~**do** m reserve. ~**do de caza** game reserve. ~**r** vt prohibit

vega f fertile plain

vegeta|ción f vegetation. ~**l** adj & m plant, vegetable. ~**r** vi grow; (persona) vegetate. ~**riano** adj & m vegetarian

vehemente adj vehement

vehículo m vehicle

veinte adj & m twenty

veinti|cinco adj & m twenty-five. ~**cuatro** adj & m twenty-four. ~**dós** adj & m twenty-two. ~**nueve** adj & m twenty-nine. ~**ocho** adj & m twenty-eight. ~**séis** adj & m twenty-six. ~**siete** adj & m twenty-seven. ~**trés** adj & m twenty-three. ~**uno** adj & m (delante de nombre masculino **veintiún**) twenty-one

vejación f humiliation

vejar vt ill-treat

veje|storio m old crock; (LAm, cosa) old relic. ~**z** f old age

vejiga f bladder

vela f (Naut) sail; (de cera) candle; (vigilia) vigil. **pasar la noche en** ~ have a sleepless night

velada f evening

vela|do adj veiled; (Foto) exposed.

~**r** vt watch over; hold a wake over (difunto); (encubrir) veil; (Foto) expose. ● vi stay awake. ~**r por** look after. ~**rse** vpr (Foto) get exposed

velero m sailing-ship

veleta f weather vane

vell|o m hair; (pelusa) down. ~**ón** m fleece

velo m veil

veloc|idad f speed; (Auto, Mec) gear. **a toda** ~**idad** at full speed. ~**ímetro** m speedometer. ~**ista** m & f sprinter

velódromo m cycle-track

veloz adj fast, quick

vena f vein; (en madera) grain. **estar de/en** ~ be in the mood

venado m deer; (Culin) venison

vencedor adj winning. ● m winner

venc|er 🗓 vt defeat; (superar) overcome. ● vi win; (pasaporte) expire. ~**erse** vpr collapse; (LAm, pasaporte) expire. ~**ido** adj beaten; (pasaporte) expired; (Com, atrasado) in arrears. **darse por** ~**ido** give up. ~**imiento** m due date; (de pasaporte) expiry date

venda f bandage. ~**je** m dressing. ~**r** vt bandage

vendaval m gale

vende|dor adj selling. ● m seller; (en tienda) salesperson. ~**dor ambulante** pedlar. ~**r** vt sell. **se** ~ for sale. ~**rse** vpr (persona) sell out

vendimia f grape harvest

veneciano adj Venetian

veneno m poison; (malevolencia) venom. ~**so** adj poisonous

venera|ble adj venerable. ~**ción** f reverence. ~**r** vt revere

venéreo adj venereal

venezolano *adj & m* Venezuelan

Venezuela *f* Venezuela

venga\|nza *f* revenge. **~r** 🔢 *vt* avenge. **~rse** *vpr* take revenge (**de, por** for) (**en** on). **~tivo** *adj* vindictive

vengo *vb véase* VENIR

venia *f* (*permiso*) permission. **~l** *adj* venial

veni\|da *f* arrival; (*vuelta*) return. **~dero** *adj* coming. **~r** 🔢 *vi* come. **~r bien** suit. **la semana que viene** next week. **¡venga!** come on!

venta *f* sale; (*posada*) inn. **en ~** for sale

ventaj\|a *f* advantage. **~oso** *adj* advantageous

ventan\|a *f* (*inc informática*) window; (*de la nariz*) nostril. **~illa** *f* window

ventarrón *m* 🔢 strong wind

ventila\|ción *f* ventilation. **~dor** *m* fan. **~r** *vt* air

vent\|isca *f* blizzard. **~olera** *f* gust of wind. **~osa** *f* sucker. **~osidad** *f* wind, flatulence. **~oso** *adj* windy

ventrílocuo *m* ventriloquist

ventur\|a *f* happiness; (*suerte*) luck. **a la ~a** with no fixed plan. **echar la buena ~a a** uno tell s.o.'s fortune. **por ~a** fortunately; (*acaso*) perhaps. **~oso** *adj* happy, lucky

Venus *m* Venus

ver 🔢 *vt* see; watch (televisión). ● *vi* see. **a mi modo de ~** in my view. **a ~** let's see. **dejarse ~** show. **no lo puedo ~** I can't stand him. **no tener nada que ~ con** have nothing to do with. **vamos a ~** let's see. **ya lo veo** that's obvious. **ya ~emos** we'll see. **~se** *vpr*

see o.s.; (*encontrarse*) find o.s.; (*dos personas*) meet; (*LAm, parecer*) look

veran\|eante *m & f* holidaymaker, vacationer (*Amer*). **~ear** *vi* spend one's summer holiday. **~eo** *m.* **ir de ~eo** spend one's summer holiday. **lugar m de ~eo** summer resort. **~iego** *adj* summer. **~o** *m* summer

vera\|s. **de ~** really; (*verdadero*) real. **~z** *adj* truthful

verbal *adj* verbal

verbena *f* (*fiesta*) fair; (*baile*) dance

verbo *m* verb. **~so** *adj* verbose

verdad *f* truth. **¿~?** isn't it?, aren't they?, won't it? etc. **a decir ~** to tell the truth. **de ~** really. **~eramente** *adv* really. **~ero** *adj* true; (*fig*) real

verd\|e *adj* green; (*fruta*) unripe; (*chiste*) dirty. ● *m* green; (*hierba*) grass. **~or** *m* greenness

verdugo *m* executioner; (*fig*) tyrant

verdu\|lería *f* greengrocer's (shop). **~lero** *m* greengrocer

vereda *f* path; (*LAm, acera*) pavement (*Brit*), sidewalk (*Amer*)

veredicto *m* verdict

verg\|onzoso *adj* shameful; (*tímido*) shy. **~üenza** *f* shame; (*bochorno*) embarrassment. **¡es una ~üenza!** it's a disgrace! **me da ~üenza** I'm ashamed/ embarrassed. **tener ~üenza** be ashamed/embarrassed

verídico *adj* true

verifica\|ción *f* verification. **~r** 🔢 *vt* check. **~rse** *vpr* take place; (*resultar verdad*) come true

verja *f* (*cerca*) railings; (*puerta*) iron gate

v

vermú *m*, **vermut** *m* vermouth

verosímil *adj* likely; (relato) credible

verruga *f* wart

versa|do *adj* versed. **~r** *vi*. **~ sobre** deal with

versátil *adj* versatile; (*fig*) fickle

versión *f* version; (*traducción*) translation

verso *m* verse; (*poema*) poem

vértebra *f* vertebra

verte|dero *m* dump; (*desagüe*) drain **~r** **1** *vt* pour; (*derramar*) spill ● *vi* flow

vertical *adj & f* vertical

vértice *f* vertex

vertiente *f* slope

vertiginoso *adj* dizzy

vértigo *m* (*Med*) vertigo. **dar ~** make dizzy

vesícula *f* vesicle. **~ biliar** gall bladder

vespertino *adj* evening

vestíbulo *m* hall; (*de hotel, teatro*) foyer

vestido *m* dress

vestigio *m* trace. **~s** *mpl* remains

vest|imenta *f* clothes. **~ir** **5** *vt* (*llevar*) wear; dress (niño etc). ● *vi* dress. **~ir de** wear. **~irse** *vpr* get dressed. **~irse de** wear; (*disfrazarse*) dress up as. **~uario** *m* wardrobe; (*en gimnasio etc*) changing room (*Brit*), locker room (*Amer*)

vetar *vt* veto

veterano *adj* veteran

veterinari|a *f* veterinary science. **~o** *adj* veterinary. ● *m* vet **1**, veterinary surgeon (*Brit*), veterinarian (*Amer*)

veto *m* veto

vez *f* time; (*turno*) turn. **a la ~** at the same time. **alguna ~** some-

times; (*en preguntas*) ever. **algunas veces** sometimes. **a su ~** in turn. **a veces** sometimes. **cada ~** each time. **cada ~ más** more and more. **de una ~** in one go. **de una ~ para siempre** once and for all. **de ~ en cuando** from time to time. **dos veces** twice. **en ~ de** instead of. **érase una ~, había una ~** once upon a time there was. **otra ~** again. **pocas veces, rara ~** seldom. **una ~ (que)** once

vía *f* road; (*Rail*) line; (*en anatomía*) tract; (*fig*) way. **~ férrea** railway (*Brit*), railroad (*Amer*). **~ rápida** fast lane. **estar en ~s de** be in the process of. ● *prep* via. **~ aérea** by air. **~ de comunicación** means of communication.

viab|ilidad *f* viability. **~le** *adj* viable

viaducto *m* viaduct

viaj|ante *m & f* commercial traveller. **~ar** *vi* travel. **~e** *m* journey; (*corto*) trip. **~e de novios** honeymoon. **¡buen ~e!** have a good journey!. **estar de ~** be away. **salir de ~** go on a trip. **~ero** *m* traveller; (*pasajero*) passenger

víbora *f* viper

vibra|ción *f* vibration. **~nte** *adj* vibrant. **~r** *vt/i* vibrate

vicario *m* vicar

viceversa *adv* vice versa

vici|ado *adj* (*texto*) corrupt; (*aire*) stale. **~ar** *vt* corrupt; (*estropear*) spoil. **~o** *m* vice; (*mala costumbre*) bad habit. **~oso** *adj* dissolute; (*círculo*) vicious

víctima *f* victim; (*de un accidente*) casualty

victori|a *f* victory. **~oso** *adj* victorious

vid *f* vine

vida f life; (*duración*) lifetime. **¡~ mía!** my darling! **de por ~** for life. **en mi ~** never (in my life). **estar con ~** be still alive

vídeo m, (*LAm*) **video** m video; (*cinta*) videotape; (*aparato*) video recorder

videojuego m video game

vidri|era f stained glass window; (*puerta*) glass door; (*LAm, escaparate*) shop window. **~ería** f glass works. **~ero** m glass worker. **~o** m glass; (*LAm, en ventana*) window pane. **limpiar los ~os** clean the windows. **~oso** adj glassy

vieira f scallop

viejo adj old. ● m old person

viene vb véase VENIR

viento m wind. **hacer ~** be windy

vientre m stomach; (*cavidad*) abdomen; (*matriz*) womb; (*intestino*) bowels; (*de vasija etc*) belly

viernes m invar Friday. **V~ Santo** Good Friday

viga f beam; (*de metal*) girder

vigen|cia f validity. **~te** adj valid; (*ley*) in force. **entrar en ~cia** come into force

vigésimo adj twentieth

vigía f watch-tower. ● m & f (*persona*) lookout

vigil|ancia f vigilance. **~ante** adj vigilant. ● m & f security guard; (*nocturno*) watchman. **~ar** vt keep an eye on. ● vi be vigilant; (*vigía*) keep watch. **~ia** f vigil; (*Relig*) fasting

vigor m vigour; (*vigencia*) force. **entrar en ~** come into force. **~oso** adj vigorous

vil adj vile. **~eza** f vileness; (*acción*) vile deed

villa f (*casa*) villa; (*Historia*) town. **la V~** Madrid

villancico m (Christmas) carol

villano adj villanous; (*Historia*) peasant

vilo. en ~ in the air

vinagre m vinegar. **~ra** f vinegar bottle. **~ras** fpl cruet. **~ta** f vinaigrette

vincular vt bind

vínculo m tie, bond

vindicar 7 vt (*rehabilitar*) vindicate

vine vb véase VENIR

vinicult|or m wine-grower. **~ura** f wine growing

vino m wine. **~ de la casa** house wine. **~ de mesa** table wine. **~ tinto** red wine

viñ|a f vineyard. **~atero** m (*LAm*) wine-grower. **~edo** m vineyard

viola f viola

viola|ción f violation; (*de una mujer*) rape. **~r** vt violate; break (*ley*); rape (*mujer*)

violen|cia f violence; (*fuerza*) force. **~tarse** vpr get embarrassed. **~to** adj violent; (*fig*) awkward

violeta adj invar & f violet

viol|ín m violin. ● m & f (*músico*) violinist. **~inista** m & f violinist. **~ón** m double bass. **~onc(h)elista** m & f cellist. **~onc(h)elo** m cello

vira|je m turn. **~r** vt turn. ● vi turn; (*fig*) change direction. **~r bruscamente** swerve

virg|en adj. **ser ~en** be a virgin. ● f virgin. **~inal** adj virginal. **~inidad** f virginity

Virgo m Virgo

viril adj virile. **~idad** f virility

virtu|al adj virtual. **~d** f virtue; (*capacidad*) power. **en ~ de** by virtue of. **~oso** adj virtuous. ● m virtuoso

viruela f smallpox

virulento adj virulent

virus m invar virus

visa f (LAm) visa. **~ado** m visa. **~r** vt endorse

vísceras fpl entrails

viscoso adj viscous

visera f visor; (de gorra) peak

visib|ilidad f visibility. **~le** adj visible

visillo m (cortina) net curtain

visi|ón f vision; (vista) sight. **~onario** adj & m visionary

visita f visit; (visitante) visitor; (invitado) guest; (Internet) hit. **~nte** m & f visitor. **~r** vt visit

vislumbrar vt glimpse

viso m sheen; (aspecto) appearance

visón m mink

visor m viewfinder

víspera f day before, eve

vista f sight, vision; (aspecto, mirada) look; (panorama) view. **apartar la ~** look away. **a primera ~, a simple ~** at first sight. **con ~s a** with a view to. **en ~ de** in view of. **estar a la ~** be obvious. **hacer la ~ gorda** turn a blind eye. **perder la ~** lose one's sight. **tener a la ~** have in front of one. **volver la ~ atrás** look back. **~zo** m glance. **dar/echar un ~zo a** glance at

visto adj seen; (poco original) common (considerado) considered. **~ que** since. **bien ~** acceptable. **está ~ que** it's obvious that. **mal ~** unacceptable. **por lo ~** apparently. ● vb véase VESTIR. **~ bueno** m approval. **~so** adj colourful, bright

visual adj visual. **campo ~** field of

vision

vital adj vital. **~icio** adj life; (cargo) held for life. **~idad** f vitality

vitamina f vitamin

viticult|or m wine-grower. **~ura** f wine growing

vitorear vt cheer

vítreo adj vitreous

vitrina f showcase; (en casa) glass cabinet; (LAm, escaparate) shop window

viud|a f widow. **~ez** f widowhood. **~o** adj widowed. ● m widower

viva m cheer. **~cidad** f liveliness. **~mente** adv vividly. **~z** adj lively

víveres mpl supplies

vivero m nursery; (de peces) hatchery; (de moluscos) bed

viveza f vividness; (de inteligencia) sharpness; (de carácter) liveliness

vívido adj vivid

vividor m pleasure seeker

vivienda f housing; (casa) house; (piso) flat (Brit), apartment (esp Amer). **sin ~** homeless

viviente adj living

vivificar 7 vt vivisection

vivir vt live through. ● vi live; (estar vivo) be alive. ¡viva! hurray! ¡viva el rey! long live the king! ● m life. **~ de** live on. **de mal ~** dissolute

vivisección f vivisection

vivo adj alive; (viviente) living; (color) bright; (listo) clever, (fig) lively. ● m,sharp operator

vocab|lo m word. **~ulario** m vocabulary

vocación f vocation

vocal adj vocal. ● f vowel. ● m & f member. **~ista** m & f vocalist

voce|ar vt call (mercancías); (fig)

proclaim; (*Mex*) page (persona). •
vi shout. **~rio** *m* shouting. **~ro**
(*LAm*) spokeperson

vociferar *vi* shout

vola|dor *adj* flying. • *m* rocket.
~ndas. en ~ndas in the air.
~nte *adj* flying. • *m* (*Auto*)
steering-wheel; (*nota*) note; (*rehi-lete*) shuttlecock. **~r 2** *vt* blow up.
• *vi* fly; (*fam, desaparecer*) disap-pear

volátil *adj* volatile

volcán *m* volcano. **~ico** *adj* vol-canic

volcar 2 & **7** *vt* knock over; (*va-ciar*) empty out; turn over (*molde*).
• *vi* overturn. **~se** *vpr* fall over; (*ve-hículo*) overturn; (*fig*) do one's ut-most. **~se en** throw o.s. into

vóleibol *m*, (*Mex*) **volibol** *m* vol-leyball

voltaje *m* voltage

volte|ar *vt* turn over; (*en el aire*)
toss; ring (*campanas*); (*LAm*) turn
over (*colchón etc*). **~arse** *vpr* (*LAm*)
turn around; (*carro*) overturn.
~reta *f* somersault

voltio *m* volt

voluble *adj* (*fig*) fickle

volum|en *m* volume. **~inoso** *adj*
voluminous

voluntad *f* will; (*fuerza de volun-tad*) willpower; (*deseo*) wish; (*inten-ción*) intention. **buena ~** goodwill.
mala ~ ill will

voluntario *adj* voluntary. • *m*
volunteer

voluptuoso *adj* voluptuous

volver 2 (*pp* **vuelto**) *vt* turn; (*de
arriba a abajo*) turn over; (*devolver*)
restore. • *vi* return; (*fig*) revert. **~
a hacer algo** do sth again. **~ en
sí** come round. **~se** *vpr* turn

round; (*hacerse*) become

vomit|ar *vt* bring up. • *vi* be sick,
vomit. **~ivo** *adj* disgusting

vómito *m* vomit; (*acción*) vomit-ing

voraz *adj* voracious

vos *pron* (*LAm*) you. **~otros** *pron*
you; (*reflexivo*) yourselves

vot|ación *f* voting; (*voto*) vote.
~ante *m* & *f* voter. **~ar** *vt* vote for.
• *vi* vote (**por** for). **~o** *m* vote;
(*Relig*) vow

voy *vb* *véase* **IR**

voz *f* voice; (*rumor*) rumour; (*pala-bra*) word. **~ pública** public opin-ion. **a media ~** softly. **a una ~**
unanimously. **dar voces** shout. **en
~ alta** loudly

vuelco *m* upset. **el corazón me
dio un ~** my heart missed a beat

vuelo *m* flight; (*acción*) flying; (*de
ropa*) flare. **al ~** in flight; (*fig*) in
passing

vuelta *f* turn; (*curva*) bend;
(*paseo*) walk; (*revolución*) revolu-tion; (*regreso*) return; (*dinero*)
change. **a la ~** on one's return. **a
la ~ de la esquina** round the cor-ner. **dar la ~ al mundo** go round
the world. **dar una ~** go for a
walk. **estar de ~** be back

vuelvo *vb* *véase* **VOLVER**

vuestro *adj* your. • *pron* yours. **un
amigo ~** a friend of yours

vulg|ar *adj* vulgar; (*persona*) com-mon. **~aridad** *f* vulgarity. **~ari-zar 10** *vt* popularize. **~o** *m* com-mon people

vulnerable *adj* vulnerable

Ww

wáter /'(g)water/ m toilet
Web m /'(g)web/. **el ~** the Web
whisky /'(g)wiski/ m whisky

Xx

xenofobia f xenophobia
xilófono m xylophone

Yy

y conj and
ya adv already; (ahora) now; (con negativos) any more; (para afirmar) yes, sure; (en seguida) immediately; (pronto) soon. **~ mismo** (LAm) right away. ● int of course! **~ no** no longer. **~ que** since. **¡~, ~!** oh sure!
yacaré m (LAm) alligator
yac|er 44 vi lie. **~imiento** m deposit; (de petróleo) oilfield
yanqui m & f American, Yank(ee)
yate m yacht
yegua f mare
yelmo m helmet
yema f (en botánica) bud; (de huevo) yolk; (golosina) sweet. **~ del dedo** fingertip

yerba f (LAm) grass; (Med) herb
yergo vb véase **ERGUIR**
yermo adj uninhabited; (no cultivable) barren. ● m wasteland
yerno m son-in-law
yerro m mistake. ● vb véase **ERRAR**
yeso m plaster; (mineral) gypsum
yo pron I. **~ mismo** myself. **¿quién, ~?** who, me? **soy ~** it's me
yodo m iodine
yoga m yoga
yogur m yog(h)urt
yuca f yucca
yugo m yoke
Yugoslavia f Yugoslavia
yugoslavo adj & m Yugoslav
yunque m anvil
yunta f yoke

Zz

zafarrancho m (confusión) mess; (riña) quarrel
zafarse vpr escape; get out of (obligación etc); (Mex, dislocarse) dislocate
zafiro m sapphire
zaga f rear; (en deportes) defence. **a la ~** behind
zaguán m hall
zaherir 4 vt hurt
zahorí m dowser
zaino adj (caballo) chestnut; (vaca) black
zalamer|ía f flattery. **~o** adj flattering. ● m flatterer
zamarra f (piel) sheepskin; (prenda) sheepskin jacket

zamarrear vt shake

zamba f South American dance

zambulli|da f dive; (baño) dip. ~**rse** vpr dive

zamparse vpr gobble up

zanahoria f carrot

zancad|a f stride. ~**illa** f trip. **hacer una** ~**illa a uno** trip s.o. up

zanc|o m stilt. ~**udo** adj long-legged; (ave) wading. ● m (LAm) mosquito

zanganear vi idle

zángano m drone. ● m & f (persona) idler

zangolotear vt shake. ● vi rattle; (persona) fidget

zanja f ditch; (para tuberías etc) trench. ~**r** vt (fig) settle

zapat|ear vi tap with one's feet. ~**ería** f shoe shop; (arte) shoe-making. ~**ero** m shoemaker; (el que remienda zapatos) cobbler. ~**illa** f slipper; (de deportes) trainer. ~**illa de ballet** ballet shoe. ~**o** m shoe

zarand|a f sieve. ~**ear** vt (sacudir) shake

zarcillo m earring

zarpa f paw

zarpar vi set sail, weigh anchor

zarza f bramble. ~**mora** f blackberry

zarzuela f Spanish operetta

zarzuela A musical drama 𝒊 consisting of alternating passages of dialogue, songs, choruses, and dancing that originated in Spain in the seventeenth century. Also popular in Latin America, its name derives from the Palacio de la Zarzuela, the Madrid palace where the Royal family now lives.

zigzag m zigzag. ~**uear** vi zigzag

zinc m zinc

zócalo m skirting-board; (pedestal) plinth; (Mex, plaza) main square

zodiaco m, **zodíaco** m zodiac

zona f zone; (área) area

zoo m zoo. ~**logía** f zoology. ~**lógico** adj zoological

zoólogo m zoologist

zopenco adj stupid. ● m idiot

zoquete m blockhead

zorr|a f vixen ~**illo** m (LAm) skunk.. ~**o** m fox

zorzal m thrush

zozobra f (fig) anxiety. ~**r** vi founder

zueco m clog

zumb|ar vt 🔢 give (golpe etc). ● vi buzz. ~**ido** m buzzing

zumo m juice

zurci|do m darning. ~**r** 🔢 vt darn

zurdo adj left-handed; (mano) left

zurrar vt (fig, fam, dar golpes) beat (up)

zutano m so-and-so

Phrasefinder

Useful phrases

yes, please/no, thank you
sorry
excuse me
I'm sorry, I don't understand

Meeting people
hello/goodbye
how are you?
nice to meet you

Asking questions
do you speak English/Spanish?
what's your name?
where are you from?
how much is it?
where is...?
can I have...?
would you like...?

Statements about yourself
my name is...
I'm American/I'm Mexican
I don't speak Spanish/English
I live near Seville/Chester
I'm a student
I work in an office

Emergencies
can you help me, please?
I'm lost
I'm ill
call an ambulance

Reading signs
no entry
no smoking
fire exit
for sale

Expresiones útiles

sí, por favor/no, gracias
perdone
disculpe
perdone, pero no le entiendo

Saludos
hola/adiós
¿cómo está usted?
mucho gusto

Preguntas
¿habla usted inglés/español?
¿cómo se llama?
¿de dónde es?
¿cuánto es?
¿dónde está...?
¿me da...?
¿quiere usted...?

Información personal
me llamo...
soy americano/-a mexicano/-a
no hablo español/inglés
vivo cerca de Sevilla/Chester
soy estudiante
trabajo en una oficina

Emergencias
¿me ayuda, por favor?
me he perdido
no me encuentro bien
llamen a una ambulancia

Carteles y señales
prohibido el paso
prohibido fumar
salida de emergencia
en venta

❶ Going Places

On the road

| where's the nearest garage/ petrol station, (*Amer*) gas station |
| what's the best way to get there? |
| I've got a puncture |
| I'd like to hire a bike/car |
| there's been an accident |
| my car's broken down |
| the car won't start |

Por carretera

¿dónde está el taller más cercano/ la gasolinera más cercana?

¿cuál es la mejor forma de llegar allí?

he pinchado, (*Mex*) se nos ponchó una llanta

quisiera alquilar, (*Mex*) rentar una bicicleta/un coche

ha habido un accidente

se me ha estropeado el coche, (*LAm*) se me descompuso el carro

el coche no arranca

By rail

where can I buy a ticket?

what time is the next train to Barcelona/York?

do I have to change?

can I take my bike on the train?

which platform for the train to San Sebastian/Bath?

there's a train to London at 10 o'clock

a single/return to Leeds/Valencia, please

I'd like an all-day ticket

I'd like to reserve a seat

En tren

¿dónde se sacan los billetes, (*LAm*) boletos?

¿a qué hora sale el próximo tren para Barcelona/York?

¿tengo que hacer algún transbordo?

¿puedo llevar la bicicleta en el tren?

¿de qué andén sale el tren para San Sebastián/Bath?

hay un tren que sale para Londres a las 10

un billete, (*LAm*) boleto de ida/ida y vuelta para Leeds/Valencia, por favor

quiero un billete, (*LAm*) boleto que valga para todo el día

quisiera reservar una plaza

At the airport	**En el aeropuerto**
when's the next flight to Paris/Rome?	¿cuándo sale el próximo vuelo para París/Roma?
where do I check in?	¿dónde puedo facturar, (LAm) chequear, (Mex) registrar el equipaje?
I'd like to confirm my flight	quisiera confirmar mi vuelo
I'd like a window seat/an aisle seat	quisiera un asiento de ventanilla/pasillo
I want to change/cancel my reservation	quiero cambiar/cancelar mi reserva

---

Getting there	**Cómo llegar a los sitios**
could you tell me the way to the castle?	¿me podría decir cómo se llega al castillo?
how long will it take to get there?	¿cuánto tiempo se tarda en llegar?
how far is it from here?	¿a qué distancia está?
which bus do I take for the cathedral?	¿qué autobús debo tomar para ir a la catedral?
can you tell me where to get off?	¿podría decirme dónde me tengo que bajar?
what time is the last bus?	¿a qué hora sale el último autobús?
how do I get to the airport?	¿cómo se llega al aeropuerto?
where's the nearest underground station, (Amer) subway station?	¿dónde está la estación de metro más cercana?
can you call me a taxi?	¿me puede pedir un taxi?
take the first turning on the right	gire por la primera (calle) a la derecha
turn left at the traffic lights/just past the church	al llegar al semáforo/después de pasar la iglesia, gire a la izquierda
I'll take a taxi	tomaré un taxi

❷ Keeping in touch

On the phone	Por teléfono
where can I buy a phone card?	¿dónde puedo comprar una tarjeta para el teléfono?
may I use your phone?	¿puedo llamar por teléfono?
do you have a mobile, (Amer) cell phone?	¿tiene usted un móvil, (LAm) un celular?
what is the code for Alava/Cardiff?	¿cuál es el prefijo de Álava/Cardiff?
I want to make a phone call	quiero hacer una llamada
I'd like to reverse the charges, (Amer) call collect	quisiera hacer una llamada a cobro revertido, (LAm) una llamada por cobrar
the line's engaged/busy	está comunicando, (esp LAm) está ocupado
there's no answer	no contestan
hello, this is Natalia	hola, soy, (esp LAm) habla Natalia
is Juan there, please?	¿está Juan, por favor?
who's calling?	¿de parte de quién?
sorry, wrong number	perdone, se ha confundido
just a moment, please	un momento, por favor
would you like to hold?	¿quiere esperar?
please tell him/her I called	dígale que lo/la he llamado, por favor
I'd like to leave a message for him/her	quisiera dejarle un mensaje
...I'll try again later	lo/la volveré a llamar más tarde
please tell him/her that Maria called	dígale que lo/la ha llamado María, por favor
can he/she ring me back?	¿le puede decir que me llame?
my home number is...	mi número (de teléfono) es el...
my business number is...	el número del trabajo es el...
my fax number is...	mi número de fax es el...
we were cut off	se ha cortado

Cómo mantenerse en contacto ❷

Writing

what's your address?

where is the nearest post office?

could I have a stamp for Argentina/Italy, please?

I'd like to send a parcel/a telegram

Por carta

¿cuál es su dirección?

¿dónde está la oficina de correos más cercana?, (*LAm*) ¿dónde está el correo más cercano?

¿me da un sello, (*LAm*) una estampilla, (*Mex*) un timbre para Argentina/Italia, por favor?

quisiera mandar un paquete/telegrama

On line

are you on the Internet?

what's your e-mail address?

we could send it by e-mail

I'll e-mail it to you on Tuesday

I looked it up on the Internet

the information is on their website

En línea

¿está conectado/-a a Internet?

¿cuál es su dirección de correo electrónico?

lo podríamos mandar por correo electrónico

se lo mandaré por correo electrónico el martes

lo he mirado en Internet

la información está en su página web

Meeting up

what shall we do this evening?

where shall we meet?

I'll see you outside the café at 6 o'clock

see you later

I can't today, I'm busy

Citas, encuentros

¿qué hacemos esta tarde?

¿dónde podemos encontrarnos?

nos vemos a las 6 en la puerta de la cafetería

hasta luego

hoy no puedo, estoy ocupado/-a

❸ Food and Drink

Booking a restaurant

can you recommend a good restaurant?

I'd like to reserve a table for four

a reservation for tomorrow evening at eight o'clock

Reservar mesa en un restaurante

¿me puede recomendar un buen restaurante?

quisiera reservar una mesa para cuatro

una reserva para mañana a las ocho de la tarde

Ordering

could we see the menu/wine list, please?

do you have a vegetarian/children's menu?

as a starter... and to follow

could we have some more bread/rice?

what would you recommend?

I'd like a
...white coffee
...black coffee
...a decaffeinated coffee
...a liqueur

could I have the bill, (*Amer*) check

Pedir la comida

¿nos enseña el menú/la carta de vinos, por favor?

¿tienen un menú especial para vegetarianos/niños?

de primero... y de segundo...

¿nos puede traer más pan/arroz?

¿qué recomienda?

Quisiera
...un café con leche
...café solo, (*LAm*) café negro
...un café descafeinado
...un licor

¿me trae la cuenta, por favor?

You will hear

¿Ya han decidido lo que van a pedir?

¿Quieren un aperitivo?

¿Quieren entrada?

¿Qué van a pedir de segundo plato?

¿Quieren postre?

¿Quieren café?/licores?

¿Algo más?

¡Buen provecho!

El servicio (no) está incluido.

Oirás

Are you ready to order?

Would you like an aperitif?

Would you like a starter?

What will you have for the main course?

Would you like a dessert?

Would you like coffee?/liqueurs?

Anything else?

Enjoy your meal!

Service is (not) included.

Comer y beber ❸

The menu

starters/entradas, (Esp) entrantes
hors d'oeuvres	entremeses, (Mex) botanas
omelette	omelette, tortilla
soup	sopa

fish/pescado
bass	lubina
cod	bacalao
eel	anguila
hake	merluza
herring	arenque
monk fish	rapé
mullet	mújol, (LAm) lisa
mussels	mejillones
oyster	ostra
prawns	gambas
salmon	salmón
sardines	sardinas
shrimps	gambas
sole	lenguado
squid	calamares
trout	trucha
tuna	atún
turbot	rodaballo

meat/carne
beef	carne de vaca
chicken	pollo
duck	pato
goose	ganso
hare	liebre
ham	jamón
kidneys	riñones
lamb	cordero
liver	hígado
pork	cerdo
rabbit	conejo
steak	bistec, filete

La carta/El menú

entradas, (Esp) entrantes/starters
entremeses, botanas (Mex)	hors d'oeuvres
omelette, tortilla	omelette
sopa	soup

pescado/fish
anguila	eel
arenque	herring
atún	tuna
bacalao	cod
calamares	squid
camarones (LAm)	prawns, shrimps
gambas	prawns,
lenguado	sole
lisa (LAm)	mullet
lubina	bass
mejillones	mussels
merluza	hake
mújol	mullet
ostra, (Mex) ostión	oyster
rapé	monk fish
róbalo	bass
rodaballo	turbot
trucha	trout

carne/meat
bistec, filete	steak
carne de vaca, de res (Mex)	beef
cerdo	pork
conejo	rabbit
cordero	lamb
ganso	goose
hígado	liver
jamón	ham
liebre	hare
pato	duck
pollo	chicken

❸ Food and Drink

tenderloin	lomo	puerco (*Mex*)	pork
turkey	pavo	riñones	kidneys
veal	ternera	solomillo (*Esp*)	sirloin steak
venison	venado	ternera	veal
white meat	carne blanca	venado	venison

vegetables/verduras

artichoke	alcachofa
asparagus	ésparragos
aubergine	berenjena
beans	frijoles
carrots	zanahorias
cabbage	col, repollo
celery	apio
endive	endivia
lettuce	lechuga
mushrooms	champiñones
peas	guisantes, (*LAm*) arvejas
pepper	pimiento
potatoes	patatas, (*LAm*) papas
runner bean	habichuela
tomato	tomate, (*Mex*) jitomate
sweet potato	batata, camote (*LAm*)
zucchini	calabacines

verduras/vegetables

alcachofa	artichoke
arvejas (*LAm*)	peas
apio	celery
batata	sweet potato
berenjena	aubergine
camote (*LAm*)	sweet potato
cebollas	onions
champiñones	mushrooms
chícharos (*Mex*)	peas
col, repollo	cabbage
coliflor	cauliflower
ésparragos	asparagus
frijoles	beans
guisantes	peas
haba	broad bean
jitomate (*Mex*)	tomato
papas	potatoes
patatas	potatoes
pimiento	pepper
zanahorias	carrots

the way it's cooked/cómo se prepara

boiled	cocido –da
roast	asado –da
fried	frito –ta
pureed	puré de
grilled	a la parilla
griddled	a la plancha
stewed	estofado –da, guisado –da
rare	poco hecho
well done	bien hecho

cómo se prepara/the way it's cooked

a la parilla	grilled
a la plancha	griddled
asado –da	roast
bien cocido	well done
bien hecho	well done
cocido –da	boiled
estofado –da	stewed
guisado –da	stewed
frito –ta	fried
poco hecho	rare

deserts/postres

ice cream	helados
fruits	fruta
pie	tarta, (LAm) pay
tart	tarta

postres/deserts

fruta	fruit
helados	ice cream
pastel, (LAm) pay	pie
tarta	tart

other

bread	pan
butter	mantequilla
cheese	queso
cheeseboard	tabla de quesos
garlic	ajo
mayonnaise	mayonesa
mustard	mostaza
olive oil	aceite de oliva
pepper	pimienta
rice	arroz
salt	sal
sauce	salsa
seasoning	condimento
vinegar	vinagre

otros

aceite de oliva	olive oil
ajo	garlic
arroz	rice
condimento	seasoning
mantequilla	butter
mayonesa	mayonnaise
mostaza	mustard
pan	bread
pimienta	pepper
queso	cheese
sal	salt
salsa	sauce
tabla de quesos	cheeseboard
vinagre	vinegar

drinks/bebidas

beer	cerveza
bottle	botella
carbonated	con gas
half-bottle	media botella
liqueur	licor
mineral water	agua mineral
red wine	vino tinto
rosé	vino rosado
soft drink	bebida no alcohólica
still	sin gas
house wine	vino de la casa
table wine	vino de mesa
white wine	vino blanco
wine	vino

bebidas/drinks

agua mineral	mineral water
bebida no alcohólica	soft drink
botella	bottle
cerveza	beer
con gas	carbonated
licor	liqueur
media botella	half-bottle
sin gas	still
vino	wine
vino blanco	white wine
vino de la casa	house wine
vino de mesa	table wine
vino rosado	rosé
vino tinto	red wine

Camping

can we pitch our tent here?	¿podemos montar la tienda (de campaña) aquí?
can we park our caravan here?	¿podemos aparcar la caravana aquí?, (LAm) ¿podemos estacionar el tráiler aquí?
what are the facilities like?	¿cómo son las instalaciones?
how much is it per night?	¿cuánto cobran por (pasar la) noche?
where do we park the car?	¿dónde podemos aparcar, (esp LAm) estacionar?
we're looking for a campsite	estamos buscando un camping
this is a list of local campsites	ésta es una lista de los campings de la zona
we go on a camping holiday every year	todos los años pasamos las vacaciones en un camping

Campings

At the hotel

I'd like a double/single room with bath	quisiera una habitación individual/doble con baño
we have a reservation in the name of Morris	tenemos una reserva a nombre de Morris
we'll be staying three nights, from Friday to Sunday	nos quedaremos tres noches, de viernes a domingo
how much does the room cost?	¿cuánto cuesta la habitación?
I'd like to see the room	quisiera ver la habitación
what time is breakfast?	¿a qué hora se sirve el desayuno?
can I leave this in your safe?	¿puedo dejar esto en la caja fuerte?
bed and breakfast	(lugar donde dan) alojamiento y desayuno
we'd like to stay another night	nos gustaría quedarnos una noche más
please call me at 7:30	¿me podría despertar a las 7:30, por favor?
are there any messages for me?	¿hay algún mensaje para mí?

Hoteles

Hostels | Albergues

could you tell me where the youth hostel is?
: ¿me podría indicar dónde está el albergue?

what time does the hostel close?
: ¿a qué hora cierra el albergue?

I'll be staying in a hostel
: me alojaré en un albergue

the hostel we're staying in is great value
: el albergue donde nos alojamos ofrece una buena relación calidad-precio

I know a really good hostel in Dublin
: conozco un albergue estupendo en Dublín

I'd like to go backpacking in Australia
: me gustaría irme a Australia con la mochila al hombro

Rooms to rent | Alquiler de habitaciones

I'm looking for a room with a reasonable rent
: quiero alquilar, (Mex) rentar una habitación que tenga un precio razonable

I'd like to rent an apartment for a few weeks
: me gustaría alquilar, (Mex) rentar un apartamento para unas cuantas semanas

where do I find out about rooms to rent?
: ¿dónde me puedo informar sobre alquileres, (Mex) rentas de habitaciones?

what's the weekly rent?
: ¿cuánto cuesta el alquiler, (Mex) la renta semanal?

I'm staying with friends at the moment
: en este momento estoy alojado en casa de unos amigos

I rent an apartment on the outskirts of town
: vivo en un apartamento alquilado, (Mex) rentado en las afueras

the room's fine — I'll take it
: la habitación está muy bien, me quedo

the deposit is one month's rent in advance
: como depósito, se paga un mes de alquiler, (Mex) renta por adelantado

❺ Shopping and money

At the bank | En el banco

I'd like to change some money	quisiera cambiar dinero
I want to change some dollars into euros	quisiera cambiar dólares a euros
do you take Eurocheques?	¿acepan Eurocheques?
what's the exchange rate today?	¿a cuánto está hoy el cambio?
I prefer traveller's cheques, (Amer) traveler's checks to cash	prefiero cheques de viaje que dinero en metálico, (esp LAm) en efectivo
I'd like to transfer some money from my account	quisiera hacer una transferencia desde mi cuenta corriente
I'll get some money from the cash machine	sacaré dinero del cajero (automático)
I usually pay by direct debit, (Amer) direct billing	suelo domiciliar los pagos en mi cuenta, (LAm) acostumbro a pagar por débito bancario
I'm with another bank	no soy cliente/-a de este banco

Finding the right shop | Dar con la tienda adecuada

where's the main shopping district?	¿dónde está la zona de tiendas?
where can I buy batteries/postcards?	¿dónde puedo comprar unas pilas/postales?
where's the nearest pharmacy/bookshop?	¿dónde está la farmacia/librería más cercana?
is there a good food shop around here?	¿hay una buena tienda de comestibles por aquí?
what time do the shops open/close?	¿a qué hora abren/cierran las tiendas?
where did you get those?	¿dónde los/las ha comprado?
I'm looking for presents for my family	estoy buscando regalos para mi familia
we'll do our shopping on Saturday	(nosotros) haremos las compras el sábado
I love shopping	me encanta ir de compras

Las compras y el dinero ❺

Are you being served?

how much does that cost?

can I try it on?

could you wrap it for me, please?

can I pay by credit card/cheque, (Amer) check?

do you have this in another colour, (Amer) color?

could I have a bag, please?

I'm just looking

I'll think about it

I'd like a receipt, please

I need a bigger/smaller size

I take a size 10/a medium

it doesn't suit me

I'm sorry, I don't have any change/anything smaller

that's all, thank you

¿Lo/La atienden?

¿cuánto cuesta?

¿me lo puedo probar?

¿me lo envuelve, por favor?

¿puedo pagar con tarjeta/cheque?

¿tiene éste/-a en otro color?

¿me da una bolsa, por favor?

sólo estoy mirando

me lo voy a pensar

¿me da el recibo, por favor?

necesito una talla más grande/más pequeña

uso la talla 38/mediana

no me queda bien

perdone, pero no tengo cambio/billetes más pequeños

nada más, gracias

Changing things

can I have a refund?

can you mend it for me?

can I speak to the manager?

it doesn't work

I'd like to change it, please

I bought this here yesterday

Devoluciones

¿me podría devolver el dinero?

¿me lo/la podrían arreglar?

quisiera hablar con el encargado/la encargada

no funciona

quisiera cambiarlo/-a, por favor

compré esto ayer

❻ Sport and leisure

Keeping fit

where can we play football/squash?

where is the local sports centre, (Amer) center?

what's the charge per day?

is there a reduction for children/ a student discount?

I'm looking for a swimming pool/ tennis court

you have to be a member

I play tennis on Mondays

I would like to go fishing/riding

I want to do aerobics

I love swimming/rollerblading

we want to hire skis/snowboards

Mantenerse en forma

¿dónde se puede jugar al fútbol/ squash, (LAm) jugar fútbol/squash?

¿dónde está el polideportivo?

¿cuánto cobran (al día)?

¿hacen descuentos a niños/ estudiantes?

estoy buscando una piscina, (Mex) alberca/un club de tenis

(para entrar) hace falta ser socio

los lunes juego al tenis, (LAm) juego tenis

me gustaría ir a pescar/montar a caballo

quiero hacer aerobic

me encanta nadar/patinar con patines en línea

queremos alquilar unos esquís/ unas tablas de nieve

Watching sport

is there a football match on Saturday?

which teams are playing?

where can I get tickets?

I'd like to see a rugby/football match

my favourite, (Amer) favorite team is...

let's watch the match on TV

Ver espectáculos deportivos

¿hay algún partido de fútbol el sábado?

¿qué equipos juegan?

¿dónde se compran las entradas?

me gustaría ver un partido de rugby/fútbol

mi equipo favorito es el...

veamos el partido en la tele

Going to the cinema/theatre/club

what's on?

when does the box office open/close?

what time does the concert/ performance start?

when does it finish?

are there any seats left for tonight?

how much are the tickets?

where can I get a programme, (Amer) program?

I want to book tickets for tonight's performance

I'll book seats in the circle

I'd rather have seats in the stalls

somewhere in the middle, but not too far back

four, please

for Saturday

we'd like to go to a club

I go clubbing every weekend

Cine/Teatro/Discotecas

¿qué ponen, (esp LAm) dan (en el cine/teatro)?

¿a qué hora abren/cierran la taquilla, (LAm) boletería?

¿a qué hora empieza el concierto/ la representación?

¿a qué hora termina?

¿quedan entradas para esta noche?

¿cuánto cuestan las entradas?

¿dónde puedo conseguir un programa?

quiero reservar entradas para esta noche

reservaré entradas de platea

prefiero el patio de butacas

que sean centrales, pero no demasiado atrás

cuatro, por favor

para el sábado

nos gustaría ir a una discoteca

voy a la discoteca todos los fines de semana

Hobbies

what do you do at the weekend?

I like yoga/listening to music

I spend a lot of time surfing the Net

I read a lot

I collect musical instruments

Aficiones y hobbies

¿qué hace los fines de semana?

me gusta el yoga/escuchar música

me paso mucho tiempo navegando por la Red

leo mucho

colecciono instrumentos musicales

❼ Good timing

Telling the time

what time is it?

it's 2 o'clock

at about 8 o'clock

from 10 o'clock onwards

at 5 o'clock in the morning/afternoon

it's five past/quarter past/half past one

it's twenty-five to/quarter to one

a quarter/three quarters of an hour

La hora

¿qué hora es?

son las 2

hacia 8

a partir de las 10

a las cinco de la mañana/tarde

es la una y cinco/y cuarto/y media

es la una menos veinticinco/menos cuarto/(LAm) son veinticinco/un cuarto para la una

un cuarto/tres cuartos de hora

Days and dates

Sunday*, Monday, Tuesday, Wednesday, Thursday, Friday, Saturday

January, February, March, April, May, June, July, August, September, October, November, December

what's the date?

it's the second of June

we meet up every Monday

we're going away in August

on November 8th

Días y fechas

domingo, lunes, martes, miércoles, jueves, viernes, sábado

enero, febrero, marzo, abril, mayo, junio, julio, agosto, septiembre, octubre, noviembre, diciembre

¿qué fecha es hoy?

(es el) dos de junio

nos vemos todos los lunes

nos vamos fuera en agosto

el 8 de noviembre

---

* Para los anglosajones la semana empieza un domingo y acaba el sábado siguiente, meintras que los latinos solemos empezar la semana el lunes.

Public holidays and special days	Fiestas y celebraciones especiales
Bank holiday	día festivo en el Reino Unido
Bank holiday Monday	lunes de puente
New Year's Day (Jan 1)	Año Nuevo (1 de enero)
Epiphany (Jan 6)	Reyes (6 de enero)
St Valentine's Day (Feb 14)	San Valentín (14 de febrero)
Shrove Tuesday/Pancake Day	Martes de Carnaval (este día es tradicional merendar crêpes con azúcar y zumo de limón)
Ash Wednesday	Miércoles de Ceniza
Independence Day	4 de julio, fiesta de la independencia de los EEUU
Maundy Thursday	Jueves Santo
Good Friday	Viernes Santo
May Day (May 1)	1 de mayo, día del trabajador
Thanksgiving	día de Acción de Gracias, fiesta típica de EEUU y Canadá
Halloween (Oct 31)	Halloween (fiesta de fantasmas y brujas que se celebra la víspera de Todos los Santos)
All Saints' Day	Todos los Santos
Guy Fawkes Day/Bonfire Night (Nov 5)	fiesta de Guy Fawkes (5 de noviembre: se celebra que el católico Guy Fawkes fracasó en su intento de incendiar el parlamento)
Remembrance Sunday	fiesta en recuerdo a los caídos en las dos guerras mundiales
St Nicholas' Day (Dec 6)	San Nicolás (6 de diciembre)
Christmas Eve (Dec 24)	Nochebuena (24 de diciembre)
Christmas Day (Dec 25)	Navidad (25 de diciembre)
Boxing Day (Dec 26)	día de fiesta que sigue al día de Navidad
New Year's Eve (Dec 31)	Nochevieja (31 de diciembre)

❽ Weights & measures/Pesos y medidas

Length/Longitud

inches/pulgadas	0.39	3.9	7.8	11.7	15.6	19.7	39
cm/centímetros	1	10	20	30	40	50	100

Distance/Distancia

miles/millas	0.62	6.2	12.4	18.6	24.9	31	62
km/km	1	10	20	30	40	50	100

Weight/Peso

pounds/libras	2.2	22	44	66	88	110	220
kg/kilos	1	10	20	30	40	50	100

Capacity/Capacidad

gallons/galones	0.22	2.2	4.4	6.6	8.8	11	22
litres/litros	1	10	20	30	40	50	100

Temperature/Temperatura

°C	0	5	10	15	20	25	30	37	38	40
°F	32	41	50	59	68	77	86	98.4	100	104

Clothing and shoe sizes/Tallas de ropa y calzado

Women's clothing sizes/Ropa de señora

UK	8	10	12	14	16	18
US	6	8	10	12	14	16
Continent	36	38	40	42	44	46

Men's clothing sizes/Ropa de caballero

UK/US	36	38	40	42	44	46
Continent	46	48	50	52	54	56

Men's and women's shoes/Calzado de señora y caballero

UK women	4	5	6	7	7.5	8			
UK men				6	7	8	9	10	11
US	6.5	7.5	8.5	9.5	10.5	11.5	12.5	13.5	14.5
Continent	37	38	39	40	41	42	43	44	45

Aa

a /ə/, stressed form /eɪ/

before vowel sound or silent 'h' **an**

indefinite article

····➤ un (m), una (f). **a problem** un problema. **an apple** una manzana. **have you got a pencil?** ¿tienes un lápiz?

❗ Feminine singular nouns beginning with stressed or accented *a* or *ha* take the article *un* instead of *una*, e.g. *un águila, un hada*

····➤ (*when talking about prices and quantities*) por. **30 miles an hour** 30 millas por hora. **twice a week** dos veces por semana, dos veces a la semana

❗ There are many cases in which **a** is not translated, such as when talking about people's professions, in exclamations, etc: **she's a lawyer** *es abogada.* **what a beautiful day!** *¡qué día más precioso!.* **have you got a car?** ¿tienes coche? **half a cup** media taza

A & E /eɪənd'iː/ n urgencias *fpl*

aback /ə'bæk/ *adv.* **be taken ~** quedar desconcertado

abandon /ə'bændən/ *vt* abandonar. ● n abandono m, desenfado m. **~ed** a abandonado

abashed /ə'bæʃt/ *adj* confuso

abate /ə'beɪt/ *vi* disminuir; (*storm etc*) calmarse

abattoir /'æbətwɑː(r)/ n matadero m

abbess /'æbɪs/ n abadesa f

abbey /'æbɪ/ n abadía f

abbot /'æbət/ n abad m

abbreviat|e /ə'briːvɪeɪt/ *vt* abreviar. **~ion** /-'eɪʃn/ n abreviatura f; (*act*) abreviación f

abdicat|e /'æbdɪkeɪt/ *vt/i* abdicar. **~ion** /-'eɪʃn/ n abdicación f

abdom|en /'æbdəmən/ n abdomen m. **~inal** /-'dɒmɪnl/ *adj* abdominal

abduct /æb'dʌkt/ *vt* secuestrar. **~ion** /-ʃn/ n secuestro m

abhor /əb'hɔː(r)/ *vt* (*pt* abhorred) aborrecer. **~rence** /-'hɒrəns/ n aborrecimiento m. **~rent** /-'hɒrənt/ *adj* aborrecible

abide /ə'baɪd/ *vt* (*pt* abided) soportar. ● *vi* (*old use*, *pt* abode) morar. □ **~ by** *vt* atenerse a; cumplir (promise)

ability /ə'bɪlətɪ/ n capacidad f; (*cleverness*) habilidad f

abject /'æbdʒekt/ *adj* (*wretched*) miserable

ablaze /ə'bleɪz/ *adj* en llamas

able /'eɪbl/ *adj* (**-er, -est**) capaz. **be ~** poder; (*know how to*) saber. **~-bodied** /-'bɒdɪd/ *adj* sano, no discapacitado

ably /'eɪblɪ/ *adv* hábilmente

abnormal /æb'nɔːml/ *adj* anormal. **~ity** /-'mælətɪ/ n anormalidad f

aboard /ə'bɔːd/ adv a bordo. ● prep a bordo de

abode /ə'bəʊd/ see ABIDE. ● n (old use) domicilio m

aboli|sh /ə'bɒlɪʃ/ vt abolir. ~tion /æbə'lɪʃn/ n abolición f

abominable /ə'bɒmɪnəbl/ adj abominable

aborigin|al /æbə'rɪdʒənl/ adj & n aborigen (m & f), indígena (m & f). ~es /-iːz/ npl aborígenes mpl

abort /ə'bɔːt/ vt hacer abortar. ~ion /-ʃn/ n aborto m provocado; (fig) aborto m. have an ~ion hacerse un aborto. ~ive adj fracasado

abound /ə'baʊnd/ vi abundar (in en)

about /ə'baʊt/ adv (approximately) alrededor de; (here and there) por todas partes; (in existence) por aquí. ~ here por aquí. be ~ to estar a punto de. ● prep sobre; (around) alrededor de; (somewhere in) en. talk ~ hablar de. ~-face, ~-turn n (fig) cambio m rotundo

above /ə'bʌv/ adv arriba. ● prep encima de; (more than) más de. ~ all sobre todo. ~ board adj legítimo. ● adv abiertamente. ~-mentioned adj susodicho

abrasi|on /ə'breɪʒn/ n abrasión f. ~ve /-sɪv/ adj abrasivo

abreast /ə'brest/ adv. march four ~ marchar en columna de cuatro en fondo. keep ~ of mantenerse al corriente de

abroad /ə'brɔːd/ adv (be) en el extranjero; (go) al extranjero; (far and wide) por todas partes

abrupt /ə'brʌpt/ adj brusco. ~ly adv (suddenly) repentinamente; (curtly) bruscamente

abscess /'æbsɪs/ n absceso m

abscond /əb'skɒnd/ vi fugarse

absen|ce /'æbsəns/ n ausencia f; (lack) falta f. ~t /'æbsənt/ adj ausente. ~t-minded /-'maɪndɪd/ adj distraído. ~t-mindedness n distracción f, despiste m. ~tee /-'tiː/ n ausente m & f. ~teeism n absentismo m, ausentismo m (LAm)

absolute /'æbsəluːt/ adj absoluto. ~ly adv absolutamente

absolve /əb'zɒlv/ vt (from sin) absolver; (from obligation) liberar

absor|b /əb'zɔːb/ vt absorber. ~bent /-bent/ adj absorbente. ~bent cotton (Amer) algodón m hidrófilo. ~ption /əb'zɔːpʃən/ n absorción f

abstain /əb'steɪn/ vi abstenerse (from de)

abstemious /əb'stiːmɪəs/ adj abstemio

abstention /əb'stenʃn/ n abstención f

abstract /'æbstrækt/ adj abstracto. ● n (summary) resumen m; (painting) cuadro m abstracto. ● /əb'strækt/ vt extraer; (summarize) resumir. ~ion /-ʃn/ n abstracción f

absurd /əb'sɜːd/ adj absurdo. ~ity n absurdo m, disparate m

abundan|ce /ə'bʌndəns/ n abundancia f. ~t adj abundante

abus|e /ə'bjuːz/ vt (misuse) abusar de; (ill-treat) maltratar; (insult) insultar. ● /ə'bjuːs/ n abuso m; (insults) insultos mpl. ~ive /ə'bjuːsɪv/ adj injurioso

abysmal /ə'bɪzməl/ adj 🔟 pésimo

abyss /ə'bɪs/ n abismo m

academic /ækə'demɪk/ adj académico; (pej) teórico. ● n universitario m, catedrático m

academy /ə'kædəmɪ/ n academia f.

accelerat|e /ək'seləreɪt/ vt acelerar. ● vi acelerar; (Auto) apretar el acelerador. ~**ion** /-'reɪʃn/ n aceleración f. ~**or** n acelerador m

accent /'æksənt/ n acento m

accept /ək'sept/ vt aceptar. ~**able** adj aceptable. ~**ance** n aceptación f; (approval) aprobación f

access /'ækses/ n acceso m. ~**ible** /ək'sesəbl/ adj accesible; (person) tratable

accession /ək'seʃn/ n (to power, throne etc) ascenso m; (thing added) adquisición f

accessory /ək'sesərɪ/ adj accesorio. ● n accesorio m, complemento m; (Jurid) cómplice m & f

accident /'æksɪdənt/ n accidente m; (chance) casualidad f. **by** ~ sin querer; (by chance) por casualidad. ~**al** /-'dentl/ adj accidental, fortuito. ~**ally** /-'dentəlɪ/ adv sin querer; (by chance) por casualidad. ~**prone** adj propenso a los accidentes

acclaim /ə'kleɪm/ vt aclamar. ● n aclamación f

accolade /'ækəleɪd/ n (praise) encomio m

accommodat|e /ə'kɒmədeɪt/ vt (give hospitality to) alojar; (adapt) acomodar; (oblige) complacer. ~**ing** adj complaciente. ~**ion** /-'deɪʃn/ n, ~**ions** npl (Amer) alojamiento m

accompan|iment n a'kʌmpənɪmənt/ n acompañamiento m. ~**ist** n acompañante m & f. ~**y** /ə'kʌmpənɪ/ vt acompañar

accomplice /ə'kʌmplɪs/ n cómplice m & f

accomplish /ə'kʌmplɪʃ/ vt (complete) acabar; (achieve) realizar; (carry out) llevar a cabo. ~**ed** adj consumado. ~**ment** n realización f; (ability) talento m; (thing achieved) triunfo m, logro m

accord /ə'kɔːd/ vi concordar. ● vt conceder. ● n acuerdo m; (harmony) armonía f. **of one's own** ~ espontáneamente. ~**ance** n. **in** ~**ance with** de acuerdo con. ~**ing** adv. ~**ing to** según. ~**ingly** adv en conformidad; (therefore) por consiguiente

accordion /ə'kɔːdɪən/ n acordeón m

accost /ə'kɒst/ vt abordar

account /ə'kaʊnt/ n cuenta f; (description) relato m. ~**s** npl (in business) contabilidad f. **on** ~ **of** a causa de. **on no** ~ de ninguna manera. **on this** ~ por eso. **take into** ~ tener en cuenta. ● vt considerar. □ ~ **for** vt dar cuenta de, explicar

accountan|cy /ə'kaʊntənsɪ/ n contabilidad f. ~**t** n contable m & f, contador m (LAm)

accumulat|e /ə'kjuːmjʊleɪt/ vt acumular. ● vi acumularse. ~**ion** /-'leɪʃn/ n acumulación f

accura|cy /'ækjʊrəsɪ/ n exactitud f, precisión f. ~**te** /-ət/ adj exacto, preciso

accus|ation /ækjuː'zeɪʃn/ n acusación f. ~**e** /ə'kjuːz/ vt acusar

accustom /ə'kʌstəm/ vt acostumbrar. ~**ed** adj. **be** ~**ed (to)** estar acostumbrado (a). **get** ~**ed (to)** acostumbrarse (a)

ace /eɪs/ n as m

ache /eɪk/ n dolor m. ● vi doler. **my leg** ~**s** me duele la pierna

achieve /ə'tʃiːv/ vt realizar; lograr

a

(success). **~ment** n realización f; (feat) proeza f; (thing achieved) logro m

acid /'æsɪd/ adj & n ácido (m). **~ic** adj /ə'sɪdɪk/ adj ácido. **~ rain** n lluvia f ácida

acknowledge /ək'nɒlɪdʒ/ vt reconocer. **~ receipt of** acusar recibo de. **~ment** n reconocimiento m; (Com) acuse m de recibo

acne /'æknɪ/ n acné m

acorn /'eɪkɔːn/ n bellota f

acoustic /ə'kuːstɪk/ adj acústico. **~s** npl acústica f

acquaint /ə'kweɪnt/ vt. **~ s.o. with** poner a uno al corriente de. **be ~ed with** conocer (person); saber (fact). **~ance** n conocimiento m; (person) conocido m

acquiesce /ækwɪ'es/ vi consentir (in en). **~nce** n aquiescencia f, consentimiento m

acqui|re /ə'kwaɪə(r)/ vt adquirir; aprender (language). **~re a taste for** tomar gusto a. **~sition** /ækwɪ'zɪʃn/ n adquisición f. **~sitive** /ə'kwɪzətɪv/ adj codicioso

acquit /ə'kwɪt/ vt (pt acquitted) absolver. **~tal** n absolución f

acre /'eɪkə(r)/ n acre m

acrid /'ækrɪd/ adj acre

acrimonious /ækrɪ'məʊnɪəs/ adj cáustico, mordaz

acrobat /'ækrəbæt/ n acróbata m & f. **~ic** /-'bætɪk/ adj acrobático. **~ics** npl acrobacia f

acronym /'ækrənɪm/ n acrónimo m, siglas fpl

across /ə'krɒs/ adv & prep (side to side) de un lado al otro; (on other side) al otro lado de; (crosswise) a través. **it is 20 metres ~** tiene 20 metros de ancho. **go** or **walk ~** atravesar, cruzar

act /ækt/ n acto m; (action) acción f; (in variety show) número m; (decree) decreto m. ● vt hacer (part, role). ● vi actuar; (pretend) fingir. **~ as** actuar de; (object) servir de. **~ for** representar. **~ing** adj interino. ● n (of play) representación f; (by actor) interpretación f; (profession) profesión f de actor

action /'ækʃn/ n acción f; (Jurid) demanda f; (plot) argumento m. **out of ~** (on sign) no funciona. **put out of ~** inutilizar. **take ~** tomar medidas. **~ replay** n repetición f de la jugada

activate /'æktɪveɪt/ vt activar

activ|e /'æktɪv/ adj activo; (energetic) lleno de energía; (volcano) en actividad. **~ist** n activista m & f. **~ity** /-'tɪvətɪ/ n actividad f

act|or /'æktə(r)/ n actor m. **~ress** /-trɪs/ n actriz f

actual /'æktʃʊəl/ adj verdadero. **~ly** adv en realidad, efectivamente; (even) incluso

ad /æd/ n 🔢 anuncio m, aviso m (LAm)

AD /eɪ'diː/ abbr (= **Anno Domini**) d. de J.C.

Adam's apple /ædəmz'æpl/ n nuez f (de Adán)

adapt /ə'dæpt/ vt adaptar. ● vi adaptarse. **~ability** /-ə'bɪlətɪ/ n adaptabilidad f. **~able** /-əbl/ adj adaptable. **~ation** n adaptación f; (of book etc) versión f. **~or** /ə'dæptə(r)/ n (Elec, with several sockets) enchufe m múltiple; (Elec, for different sockets) adaptador m

add /æd/ vt añadir. ● vi sumar. □ **~ up** vt sumar; (fig) tener sentido. **~**

up to equivaler a

adder /'ædə/n víbora f

addict /'ædıkt/n adicto m; (*fig*) entusiasta m & f. ~**ed** /ə'dıktıd/ adj. ~**ed to** adicto a; (*fig*) fanático de. ~**ion** /ə'dıkʃn/n (*Med*) dependencia f; (*fig*) afición f. ~**ive** /ə'dıktıv/ adj que crea adicción; (*fig*) que crea hábito

addition /ə'dıʃn/n suma f. **in** ~ además. ~**al** adj suplementario

address /ə'dres/n dirección f; (*on form*) domicilio m; (*speech*) discurso m. • vt poner la dirección en; (*speak to*) dirigirse a. ~ **book** n libreta f de direcciones. ~**ee** /ædre'si:/n destinatario m

adept /'ædept/ adj & n experto (m)

adequa|cy /'ædıkwəsı/n suficiencia f. ~**te** /-ət/ adj suficiente, adecuado. ~**tely** adv suficientemente, adecuadamente

adhere /əd'hıə(r)/vi adherirse (**to** a); observar (rule). ~**nce** /-rəns/n adhesión f; (*to rules*) observancia f

adhes|ion /əd'hi:ʒn/n adherencia f. ~**ive** /-sıv/ adj & n adhesivo (m)

adjacent /ə'dʒeısnt/ adj contiguo

adjective /'ædʒıktıv/n adjetivo m

adjourn /ə'dʒɜ:n/ vt aplazar; (*suspend*) suspender (meeting etc). • vi suspenderse

adjust /ə'dʒʌst/ vt ajustar (machine); (*arrange*) arreglar. • vi. ~ (**to**) adaptarse (a). ~**able** adj ajustable. ~**ment** n adaptación f; (*Tec*) ajuste m

administer /əd'mınıstə(r)/ vt administrar

administrat|ion /ədmını'streıʃn/n administración f. ~**ive** /əd'mınıstrətıv/ adj administrativo. ~**or** /əd'mınıstreıtə(r)/ n administrador m

admirable /'ædmərəbl/ adj admirable

admiral /'ædmərəl/ n almirante m

admir|ation /ædmə'reıʃn/ n admiración f. ~**e** /əd'maıə(r)/ vt admirar. ~**er** /əd'maıərə(r)/ n admirador m

admission /əd'mıʃn/ n admisión f; (*entry*) entrada f

admit /əd'mıt/ vt (*pt* **admitted**) dejar entrar; (*acknowledge*) admitir, reconocer. ~ **to** confesar. be ~**ted** (**to** hospital etc) ingresar. ~**tance** n entrada f. ~**tedly** adv es verdad que

admonish /əd'mɒnıʃ/ vt reprender; (*advise*) aconsejar

ado /ə'du:/n alboroto m; (*trouble*) dificultad f. **without more** or **further** ~ en seguida, sin más

adolescen|ce /ædə'lesns/ n adolescencia f. ~**t** adj & n adolescente (m & f)

adopt /ə'dɒpt/ vt adoptar. ~**ed** adj (child) adoptivo. ~**ion** /-ʃn/ n adopción f

ador|able /ə'dɔ:rəbl/ adj adorable. ~**ation** /ædə'reıʃn/ n adoración f. ~**e** /ə'dɔ:(r)/ vt adorar

adorn /ə'dɔ:n/ vt adornar. ~**ment** n adorno m

adrift /ə'drıft/ adj & adv a la deriva

adult /'ædʌlt/ adj & n adulto (m)

adulter|er /ə'dʌltərə(r)/ n adúltero m. ~**ess** /-ıs/ n adúltera f. ~**y** n adulterio m

advance /əd'vɑ:ns/ vt adelantar. • vi adelantarse. • n adelanto m. **in** ~ con anticipación, por adelantado. ~**d** adj avanzado; (studies) superior

advantage /əd'vɑ:ntıdʒ/ n ventaja f. **take** ~ **of** aprovecharse de; abusar de (person). ~**ous** /ædvən 'teɪdʒəs/ *adj* ventajoso

advent /'ædvənt/ *n* venida *f*. **A~** *n* adviento *m*

adventur|e /əd'ventʃə(r)/ *n* aventura *f*. **~er** *n* aventurero *m*. **~ous** *adj* (person) aventurero; (thing) arriesgado; (*fig, bold*) audaz

adverb /'ædvɜːb/ *n* adverbio *m*

adversary /'ædvəsərɪ/ *n* adversario *m*

advers|e /'ædvɜːs/ *adj* adverso, contrario, desfavorable. **~ity** /əd'vɜːsətɪ/ *n* infortunio *m*

advert /'ædvɜːt/ *n* ▣ anuncio *m*, aviso *m* (LAm). **~ise** /'ædvətaɪz/ *vt* anunciar. ● *vi* hacer publicidad; (*seek, sell*) poner un anuncio. **~isement** /əd'vɜːtɪsmənt/ *n* anuncio *m*, aviso *m* (LAm). **~iser** /'ædvətaɪzə(r)/ *n* anunciante *m & f*

advice /əd'vaɪs/ *n* consejo *m*; (*report*) informe *m*

advis|able /əd'vaɪzəbl/ *adj* aconsejable. **~e** /əd'vaɪz/ *vt* aconsejar; (*inform*) avisar. **~e against** aconsejar en contra de. **~er** *n* consejero *m*; (*consultant*) asesor *m*. **~ory** *adj* consultivo

advocate /'ædvəkət/ *n* defensor *m*; (*Jurid*) abogado *m*. ● /'ædvəkeɪt/ *vt* recomendar

aerial /'eərɪəl/ *adj* aéreo. ● *n* antena *f*

aerobics /eə'rəʊbɪks/ *npl* aeróbica *f*

aerodrome /'eərədrəʊm/ *n* aeródromo *m*

aerodynamic /eərəʊdə'næmɪk/ *adj* aerodinámico

aeroplane /'eərəpleɪn/ *n* avión *m*

aerosol /'eərəsɒl/ *n* aerosol *m*

aesthetic /iːs'θetɪk/ *adj* estético

afar /ə'fɑː(r)/ *adv* lejos

affable /'æfəbl/ *adj* afable

affair /ə'feə(r)/ *n* asunto *m*. (love) **~** aventura *f*, amorío *m*. **~s** *npl* (business) negocios *mpl*

affect /ə'fekt/ *vt* afectar; (*pretend*) fingir. **~ation** /æfek'teɪʃn/ *n* afectación *f*. **~ed** *adj* afectado, amanerado

affection /ə'fekʃn/ *n* cariño *m*. **~ate** /-ət/ *adj* cariñoso

affiliate /ə'fɪlɪeɪt/ *vt* afiliar

affirm /ə'fɜːm/ *vt* afirmar. **~ative** /-ətɪv/ *adj* afirmativo. ● *n* respuesta *f* afirmativa

afflict /ə'flɪkt/ *vt* afligir. **~ion** /-ʃn/ *n* aflicción *f*, pena *f*

affluen|ce /'æfluəns/ *n* riqueza *f*. **~t** *adj* rico.

afford /ə'fɔːd/ *vt* permitirse; (*provide*) dar. **he can't ~ a car** no le alcanza el dinero para comprar un coche

affront /ə'frʌnt/ *n* afrenta *f*, ofensa *f*. ● *vt* afrentar, ofender

afield /ə'fiːld/ *adv*. **far ~** muy lejos

afloat /ə'fləʊt/ *adv* a flote

afraid /ə'freɪd/ *adj*. **be ~** tener miedo (**of** a); (*be sorry*) sentir, lamentar

afresh /ə'freʃ/ *adv* de nuevo

Africa /'æfrɪkə/ *n* África *f*. **~n** *adj & n* africano (*m*). **~n-American** *adj & n* norteamericano (*m*) de origen africano

after /'ɑːftə(r)/ *adv* después; (*behind*) detrás. ● *prep* después de; (*behind*) detrás de. **it's twenty ~ four** (Amer) son las cuatro y veinte. **be ~** (*seek*) andar en busca de. ● *conj* después de que. ● *adj* posterior. **~effect** *n* consecuencia *f*, efecto *m* secundario. **~math** /'ɑːftəmæθ/ *n* secuelas *fpl*. **~noon** /-'nuːn/ *n* tarde *f*. **~shave** *n* loción *f* para después de afeitarse. **~thought** *n* ocurrencia *f* tardía. **~wards** /-wədz/ *adv* después

again /ə'gen/ *adv* otra vez; (*besides*) además. **do ~** volver a hacer, hacer otra vez. **~ and ~** una y otra vez

against /ə'genst/ *prep* contra; (*in opposition to*) en contra de, contra

age /eɪdʒ/ *n* edad *f*. **at four years of ~** a los cuatro años. **under ~** menor de edad. **~s** *npl* [I] siglos *mpl*. ● *vt/i* (*pres p* **ageing**) envejecer. **~d** /eɪdʒd/ *adj* de ... años. **~d 10** de 10 años. **~d** /'eɪdʒɪd/ *adj* viejo, anciano

agency /'eɪdʒənsɪ/ *n* agencia *f*; (*department*) organismo *m*

agenda /ə'dʒendə/ *n* orden *m* del día

agent /'eɪdʒənt/ *n* agente *m & f*; (*representative*) representante *m & f*

aggravat|e /'ægrəveɪt/ *vt* agravar; (*fam*, *irritate*) irritar. **~ion** /-'veɪʃn/ *n* agravación *f*; (*fam*, *irritation*) irritación *f*

aggress|ion /ə'greʃn/ *n* agresión *f*. **~ive** *adj* agresivo. **~iveness** *n* agresividad *f*. **~or** *n* agresor *m*

aggrieved /ə'griːvd/ *adj* apenado, ofendido

aghast /ə'ɡɑːst/ *adj* horrorizado

agil|e /'ædʒaɪl/ *adj* ágil. **~ity** /ə'dʒɪlətɪ/ *n* agilidad *f*

aging /'eɪdʒɪŋ/ *adj* envejecido. ● *n* envejecimiento *m*

agitat|e /'ædʒɪteɪt/ *vt* agitar. **~ed** *adj* nervioso. **~ion** /-'teɪʃn/ *n* agitación *f*, excitación *f*. **~or** *n* agitador *m*

ago /ə'ɡəʊ/ *adv*. **a long time ~** hace mucho tiempo. **3 days ~** hace 3 días

agon|ize /'ægənaɪz/ *vi* atormen-

tarse. **~izing** *adj* (*pain*) atroz; (*experience*) angustioso. **~y** *n* dolor *m* (*agudo*); (*mental*) angustia *f*

agree /ə'griː/ *vi* estar de acuerdo; (*of figures*) concordar; (*get on*) entenderse. ● *vt* acordar. □ **~ with** *vt* (*of food etc*) sentarle bien a. **~able** /ə'griːəbl/ *adj* agradable. **be ~able** (*willing*) estar de acuerdo. **~d** *adj* (*time, place*) convenido. **~ment** /-mənt/ *n* acuerdo *m*. **in ~ment** de acuerdo

agricultur|al /ægrɪ'kʌltʃərəl/ *adj* agrícola. **~e** /'ægrɪkʌltʃə(r)/ *n* agricultura *f*

aground /ə'ɡraʊnd/ *adv*. **run ~** (*of ship*) varar, encallar

ahead /ə'hed/ *adv* delante; (*in time*) antes de. **be ~** ir delante

aid /eɪd/ *vt* ayudar. ● *n* ayuda *f*. **in ~ of** a beneficio de

AIDS /eɪdz/ *n* sida *m*

ailment /'eɪlmənt/ *n* enfermedad *f*

aim /eɪm/ *vt* apuntar; (*fig*) dirigir. ● *vi* apuntar; (*fig*) pretender. ● *n* puntería *f*; (*fig*) objetivo *m*. **~less** *adj*, **~lessly** *adv* sin objeto, sin rumbo

air /eə(r)/ *n* aire *m*. **be on the ~** (*Radio, TV*) estar en el aire. **put on ~s** darse aires. ● *vt* airear. **~ bag** *n* (*Auto*) bolsa *f* de aire. **~ base** *n* base *f* aérea. **~borne** *adj* en el aire; (*Mil*) aerotransportado. **~-conditioned** *adj* climatizado, con aire acondicionado. **~ conditioning** *n* aire *m* acondicionado. **~craft** *n* (*pl invar*) avión *m*. **~craft carrier** *n* portaaviones *m*. **~crome** *n* aeródromo *m*. **A~ Force** *n* fuerzas *fpl* aéreas. **~ freshener** *n* ambientador *m*. **~gun** *n* escopeta *f* de aire comprimido. **~ hostess** *n* aza-

fata f, aeromoza f (LAm). ~line n
línea f aérea. ~mail n correo m
aéreo. ~plane n (Amer) avión m.
~port n aeropuerto m. ~sick adj
mareado (en un avión). ~tight
adj hermético. ~ traffic controller
n controlador m aéreo. ~y adj (-ier,
-iest) aireado; (manner) desenfa-
dado

aisle /aɪl/ n nave f lateral; (gangway) pasillo m

ajar /ə'dʒɑː(r)/ adj entreabierto

alarm /ə'lɑːm/ n alarma f. • vt
asustar. ~clock n despertador m.
~ist n alarmista m & f

Albania /æl'beɪnɪə/ n Albania f.
~n adj & n albanés (m)

albatross /'ælbətrɒs/ n alba-
tros m

album /'ælbəm/ n álbum m

alcohol /'ælkəhɒl/ n alcohol m.
~ic /-'hɒlɪk/ adj & n alcohólico (m)

alcove /'ælkəʊv/ n nicho m

ale /eɪl/ n cerveza f

alert /ə'lɜːt/ adj vivo; (watchful) vigilante. • n alerta f. on the ~
alerta. • vt avisar

algebra /'ældʒɪbrə/ n álgebra f

Algeria /æl'dʒɪərɪə/ n Argelia f.
~n adj & n argelino (m)

alias /'eɪlɪəs/ n (pl -ases) alias m.
• adv alias

alibi /'ælɪbaɪ/ n (pl -is) coartada f

alien /'eɪlɪən/ n extranjero m. • adj
ajeno. ~ate /-eɪt/ vt enajenar.
~ation /-'neɪʃn/ n enajenación f

alienat|e /'eɪlɪəneɪt/ vt enajenar.
~ion /-'neɪʃn/ n enajenación f

alight /ə'laɪt/ adj ardiendo; (light)
encendido

align /ə'laɪn/ vt alinear. ~ment n
alineación f

alike /ə'laɪk/ adj parecido, seme-

jante. **look** or **be** ~ parecerse.
• adv de la misma manera

alive /ə'laɪv/ adj vivo. ~ **with**
lleno de

alkali /'ælkəlaɪ/ n (pl -is) álcali m.
~ne adj alcalino

• adjective todo, -da; (pl) todos,
-das. ~ **day** todo el día. **the
windows** todas las ventanas. ~
four of us went fuimos los
cuatro

• pronoun

····▸ (everything) todo. **that's** ~
eso es todo. **I did** — **I could to
persuade her** hice todo lo que
pude para convencerla

····▸ (after pronoun) todo, -da;
(pl) todos, -das. **he helped us**
~ nos ayudó a todos

····▸ **all of** todo, -da, (pl) todos,
-das. ~ **of the paintings** todos
los cuadros. ~ **of the milk**
toda la leche

····▸ (in phrases) **all in all** en general. **not at all** (in no way) de
ninguna manera; (after thanks)
de nada, no hay de qué. **it's
not at** ~ **bad** no está nada
mal. **I don't like it at** ~ no me
gusta nada

• adverb

····▸ (completely) completamente.
she was ~ **alone** estaba completamente sola. **I got** ~ **dirty**
me ensucié todo/toda. **I don't
know him** ~ **that well** no lo
conozco tan bien

····▸ (in scores) **the score was
one** ~ iban empatados uno a
uno

····▸ (in phrases) **to be all for sth**

estar completamente a favor de algo. **to be all in** 🄘 estar rendido

all-around /ɔːləˈraʊnd/ adj (Amer) completo

allay /əˈleɪ/ vt aliviar (pain); aquietar (fears etc)

all-clear /ɔːlˈklɪə(r)/ n fin m de (la) alarma; (permission) visto m bueno

alleg|ation /ælɪˈgeɪʃn/ n alegato m. ~**e** /əˈledʒ/ vt alegar. ~**ed** adj presunto. ~**edly** /-ɪdlɪ/ adv según se dice, supuestamente

allegiance /əˈliːdʒəns/ n lealtad f

allegory /ˈælɪgərɪ/ n alegoría f

allerg|ic /əˈlɜːdʒɪk/ adj alérgico (**to** a). ~**y** /ˈælədʒɪ/ n alergia f

alleviate /əˈliːvɪeɪt/ vt aliviar

alley /ˈælɪ/ (pl -**eys**) n callejuela f

alliance /əˈlaɪəns/ n alianza f

alligator /ˈælɪgeɪtə(r)/ n caimán m

allocat|e /ˈæləkeɪt/ vt asignar; (share out) repartir. ~**ion** /-ˈkeɪʃn/ n asignación f; (distribution) reparto m

allot /əˈlɒt/ vt (pt allotted) asignar. ~**ment** n asignación f; (land) parcela f

allow /əˈlaʊ/ vt permitir; (grant) conceder; (reckon on) prever; (agree) admitir. □ ~ **for** vt tener en cuenta. ~**ance** /əˈlaʊəns/ n concesión f; (pension) pensión f; (Com) rebaja f. **make** ~**ances for** ser indulgente con (person); (take into account) tener en cuenta

alloy /ˈælɔɪ/ n aleación f

all: ~ **right** adj & adv bien. ● int ¡vale!, ¡okey! (esp LAm), ¡órale! (Mex). ~-**round** adj completo

allusion /əˈluːʒn/ n alusión f

ally /ˈælaɪ/ n aliado m. ● /əˈlaɪ/ vt. ~ **o.s.** aliarse (**with** con)

almighty /ɔːlˈmaɪtɪ/ adj todopoderoso

almond /ˈɑːmənd/ n almendra f

almost /ˈɔːlməʊst/ adv casi

alone /əˈləʊn/ adj solo. ● adv sólo, solamente

along /əˈlɒŋ/ prep por, a lo largo de. ● adv. ~ **with** junto con. **all** ~ todo el tiempo. **come** ~ venga. ~**side** /-ˈsaɪd/ adv (Naut) al costado. ● prep al lado de

aloof /əˈluːf/ adv apartado. ● adj reservado

aloud /əˈlaʊd/ adv en voz alta

alphabet /ˈælfəbet/ n alfabeto m. ~**ical** /-ˈbetɪkl/ adj alfabético

Alps /ælps/ npl. **the** ~ los Alpes

already /ɔːlˈredɪ/ adv ya

Alsatian /ælˈseɪʃn/ n pastor m alemán

also /ˈɔːlsəʊ/ adv también; (moreover) además

altar /ˈɔːltə(r)/ n altar m

alter /ˈɔːltə(r)/ vt cambiar. ● vi cambiarse. ~**ation** /-ˈreɪʃn/ n modificación f; (to garment) arreglo m

alternate /ɔːlˈtɜːnət/ adj alterno; (Amer) see **ALTERNATIVE**. ● /ˈɔːltəneɪt/ vt/i alternar. ~**ly** /ɔːlˈtɜːnətlɪ/ adv alternativamente

alternative /ɔːlˈtɜːnətɪv/ adj alternativo. ● n alternativa f. ~**ly** adv en cambio, por otra parte

although /ɔːlˈðəʊ/ conj aunque

altitude /ˈæltɪtjuːd/ n altitud f

altogether /ɔːltəˈgeðə(r)/ adv completamente; (on the whole) en total

aluminium /æljʊˈmɪnɪəm/, **aluminum** /əˈluːmɪnəm/ (Amer) n aluminio m

always /ˈɔːlweɪz/ adv siempre

am /æm/ see BE

a.m. abbr (= ante meridiem) de la mañana

amalgamate /əˈmælɡəmeɪt/ vt amalgamar. ● vi amalgamarse

amass /əˈmæs/ vt acumular

amateur /ˈæmətə(r)/ adj & n amateur (m & f). ~ish adj (pej) torpe, chapucero

amaze /əˈmeɪz/ vt asombrar. ~ed adj asombrado, estupefacto. be ~ed at quedarse asombrado de, asombrarse de. ~ement n asombro m. ~ing adj increíble

ambassador /æmˈbæsədə(r)/ n embajador m

ambiguity /æmbɪˈɡjuːəti/ n ambigüedad f. ~ous /æmˈbɪɡjʊəs/ adj ambiguo

ambition /æmˈbɪʃn/ n ambición f. ~ous /-ʃəs/ adj ambicioso

ambivalent /æmˈbɪvələnt/ adj ambivalente

amble /ˈæmbl/ vi andar despacio, andar sin prisa

ambulance /ˈæmbjʊləns/ n ambulancia f

ambush /ˈæmbʊʃ/ n emboscada f. ● vt tender una emboscada a

amen /ɑːˈmen/ int amén

amend /əˈmend/ vt enmendar. ~ment n enmienda f. ~s npl. make ~s reparar

amenities /əˈmiːnətɪz/ npl servicios mpl; (of hotel, club) instalaciones fpl

America /əˈmerɪkə/ n (continent) América; (North America) Estados mpl Unidos, Norteamérica f. ~n adj & n americano (m); (North American) estadounidense (m & f), norteamericano (m). ~nism n americanismo m

American dream El sueño americano se basa en la idea de que cualquier persona en los Estados Unidos puede prosperar mediante el trabajo duro. Para los inmigrantes y las minorías, el concepto abarca la libertad y la igualdad de derechos.

amiable /ˈeɪmɪəbl/ adj simpático

amicable /ˈæmɪkəbl/ adj amistoso

amid(st) /əˈmɪd(st)/ prep entre, en medio de

ammonia /əˈməʊnɪə/ n amoníaco m, amoniaco m

ammunition /æmjʊˈnɪʃn/ n municiones fpl

amnesty /ˈæmnəsti/ n amnistía f

amok /əˈmɒk/ adv. run ~ volverse loco

among(st) /əˈmʌŋ(st)/ prep entre

amount /əˈmaʊnt/ n cantidad f; (total) total m, suma f. □ ~ to vt sumar; (fig) equivaler a, significar

amp(ere) /ˈæmp(eə(r))/ n amperio m

amphibian /æmˈfɪbɪən/ n anfibio m. ~ous /-əs/ adj anfibio

amphitheatre /ˈæmfɪθɪətə(r)/ n anfiteatro m

ample /ˈæmpl/ adj (-er, -est) amplio; (enough) suficiente; (plentiful) abundante. ~y adv ampliamente, bastante

amplifier /ˈæmplɪfaɪə(r)/ n amplificador m. ~y /ˈæmplɪfaɪ/ vt amplificar

amputate /ˈæmpjʊteɪt/ vt amputar. ~ion n amputación f

amuse /əˈmjuːz/ vt divertir. ~ed adj (expression) divertido. keep s.o. ~ed entretener a uno. ~ement n diversión f. ~ing adj divertido

an /an, æn/ *see* **A**

anaemia /əˈniːmɪə/ *n* anemia *f*. **~c** *adj* anémico

anaesthe|tic /ænɪsˈθetɪk/ *n* anestésico *m*. **~tist** /əˈniːsθɪtɪst/ *n* anestesista *f*

anagram /ˈænəgræm/ *n* anagrama *m*

analogy /əˈnælədʒɪ/ *n* analogía *f*

analy|se /ˈænəlaɪz/ *vt* analizar. **~sis** /əˈnæləsɪs/ *n* (*pl* **-ses** /-siːz/) análisis *m*. **~st** /ˈænəlɪst/ *n* analista *m* & *f*. **~tic(al)** /ænəˈlɪtɪk(əl)/ *adj* analítico

anarch|ist /ˈænəkɪst/ *n* anarquista *m* & *f*. **~y** *n* anarquía *f*

anatom|ical /ænəˈtɒmɪkl/ *adj* anatómico. **~y** /əˈnætəmɪ/ *n* anatomía *f*

ancest|or /ˈænsestə(r)/ *n* antepasado *m*. **~ral** /-ˈsestrəl/ *adj* ancestral. **~ry** /ˈænsestrɪ/ *n* ascendencia *f*

anchor /ˈæŋkə(r)/ *n* ancla *f*. ● *vt* anclar; (*fig*) sujetar. ● *vi* anclar. **~man** *n* (*on* TV) presentador *m*. **~woman** *n* (*on* TV) presentadora *f*.

ancient /ˈeɪnʃənt/ *adj* antiguo, viejo

ancillary /ænˈsɪlərɪ/ *adj* auxiliar

and /ənd, ænd/ *conj* y; (*before* i- *and* hi-) e. bread **~** butter pan *m* con mantequilla. go **~** see him ve a verlo. more **~** more cada vez más. try **~** come trata de venir

anecdot|al /ænɪkˈdəʊtl/ *adj* anecdótico. **~e** /ˈænɪkdəʊt/ *n* anécdota *f*

anew /əˈnjuː/ *adv* de nuevo

angel /ˈeɪndʒl/ *n* ángel *m*. **~ic** /ænˈdʒelɪk/ *adj* angélico

anger /ˈæŋgə(r)/ *n* ira *f*. ● *vt* enfa-

dar, (*esp* LAm) enojar

angle /ˈæŋgl/ *n* ángulo *m*; (*fig*) punto de vista. **~r** /ˈæŋglə(r)/ *n* pescador *m*

Anglican /ˈæŋglɪkən/ *adj* & *n* anglicano (*m*)

angr|ily /ˈæŋgrɪlɪ/ *adv* con enfado, (*esp* LAm) con enojo. **~y** /ˈæŋgrɪ/ *adj* (**-ier**, **-iest**) enfadado, (*esp* LAm) enojado. get **~y** enfadarse, enojarse (*esp* LAm)

anguish /ˈæŋgwɪʃ/ *n* angustia *f*

animal /ˈænɪml/ *adj* & *n* animal (*m*)

animat|e /ˈænɪmeɪt/ *vt* animar. **~ion** /-ˈmeɪʃn/ *n* animación *f*

animosity /ænɪˈmɒsətɪ/ *n* animosidad *f*

ankle /ˈæŋkl/ *n* tobillo *m*. **~ boot** botín *m*. **~ sock** calcetín *m* corto

annexe /ˈæneks/ *n* anexo *m*

annihilat|e /əˈnaɪəleɪt/ *vt* aniquilar. **~ion** /-ˈleɪʃn/ *n* aniquilación *f*

anniversary /ænɪˈvɜːsərɪ/ *n* aniversario *m*

announce /əˈnaʊns/ *vt* anunciar, comunicar. **~ment** *n* anuncio *m*; (*official*) comunicado *m*. **~r** *n* (*Radio*, TV) locutor *m*

annoy /əˈnɔɪ/ *vt* molestar. **~ance** *n* molestia *f*. **~ed** *adj* enfadado, enojado (LAm). **~ing** *adj* molesto

annual /ˈænjʊəl/ *adj* anual. ● *n* anuario *m*. **~ly** *adv* cada año

annul /əˈnʌl/ *vt* (*pt* **annulled**) anular. **~ment** *n* anulación *f*

anonymous /əˈnɒnɪməs/ *adj* anónimo

anorak /ˈænəræk/ *n* anorac *m*

another /əˈnʌðə(r)/ *adj* & *pron* otro. **~** 10 minutes 10 minutos más. in **~** way de otra manera. one **~** el uno al otro; (*pl*) unos a otros

a

answer /'ɑːnsə(r)/ n respuesta f; (solution) solución f. ● vt contestar; escuchar, oír (prayer). ~ **the door** abrir la puerta. ~ **back** vi contestar. □ ~ **for** vt ser responsable de. ~**able** adj responsable. ~**ing machine** n contestador m automático

ant /ænt/ n hormiga f

antagoni|sm /æn'tægənɪzəm/ n antagonismo m. ~**stic** /-'nɪstɪk/ adj antagónico, opuesto. ~**ze** /æn 'tægənaɪz/ vt provocar la enemistad de

Antarctic /æn'tɑːktɪk/ adj antártico. ● the ~ la región antártica

antelope /'æntɪləʊp/ n antílope m

antenatal /'æntɪneɪtl/ adj prenatal

antenna /æn'tenə/ (pl -**nae** /-niː/) (of insect etc) n antena f; (pl -**nas**) (of radio, TV) antena f

anthem /'ænθəm/ n himno m

anthology /æn'θɒlədʒɪ/ n antología f

anthrax /'ænθræks/ n ántrax m

anthropolog|ist /ænθrə 'pɒlədʒɪst/ n antropólogo m. ~**y** n antropología f

anti-... /ænti/ pref anti... ~**aircraft** /-'eəkrɑːft/ adj antiaéreo

antibiotic /æntɪbaɪ'ɒtɪk/ adj & n antibiótico (m)

anticipat|e /æn'tɪsɪpeɪt/ vt anticiparse a; (foresee) prever; (forestall) prevenir. ~**ion** /-'peɪʃn/ n (foresight) previsión f; (expectation) expectativa f

anti: ~climax /-'klaɪmæks/ n decepción f. ~**clockwise** /-'klɒkwaɪz/ adv & adj en sentido contrario a las agujas del reloj

antidote /'æntɪdəʊt/ m antídoto m

antifreeze /'æntɪfriːz/ n anticongelante m

antiperspirant /ænti 'pɜːspɪrənt/ n antitranspirante m

antiquated /'æntɪkweɪtɪd/ adj anticuado

antique /æn'tiːk/ adj antiguo. ● n antigüedad f. ~ **dealer** anticuario m. ~ **shop** tienda f de antigüedades

antiquity /æn'tɪkwətɪ/ n antigüedad f

anti: ~septic /-'septɪk/ adj & n antiséptico (m). ~**social** /-'səʊʃl/ adj antisocial

antlers /'æntləz/ npl cornamenta f

anus /'eɪnəs/ n ano m

anvil /'ænvɪl/ n yunque m

anxi|ety /æŋ'zaɪətɪ/ n ansiedad f; (worry) inquietud f; (eagerness) anhelo m. ~**ous** /'æŋkʃəs/ adj inquieto; (eager) deseoso. ~**ously** adv con inquietud; (eagerly) con impaciencia

any /'enɪ/ adj algún; (negative) ningún m; (whatever) cualquier; (every) todo. at ~ moment en cualquier momento. have you ~ wine? ¿tienes vino? ● pron alguno; (negative) ninguno. have we ~? ¿tenemos algunos? not ~ ninguno. ● adv (a little) un poco, algo. is it ~ better? ¿está algo mejor?

anybody /'enɪbɒdɪ/ pron alguien; (after negative) nadie. ~ **can do it** cualquiera puede hacerlo

anyhow /'enɪhaʊ/ adv de todas formas; (in spite of all) a pesar de todo; (badly) de cualquier manera

anyone /'enɪwʌn/ pron see **ANYBODY**

anything /'enɪθɪŋ/ pron algo; (whatever) cualquier cosa; (after negative) nada. ~ **but** todo menos

anyway /'enɪweɪ/ adv de todas formas

anywhere /'enɪweə(r)/ adv en cualquier parte; (after negative) en ningún sitio. ~ **else** en cualquier otro lugar. ~ **you go** dondequiera que vayas

apart /ə'pɑːt/ adv aparte; (separated) separado. ~ **from** aparte de. **come** ~ romperse. **take** ~ desmontar

apartheid /ə'pɑːtheɪt/ n apartheid m

apartment /ə'pɑːtmənt/ n (Amer) apartamento m, piso m. ~ **building** n (Amer) edificio m de apartamentos, casa f de pisos

apath|etic /æpə'θetɪk/ adj apático. ~**y** /'æpəθɪ/ n apatía f

ape /eɪp/ n mono m. • vt imitar

aperitif /ə'perətɪf/ n aperitivo m

aperture /'æpətʃuə(r)/ n abertura f

apex /'eɪpeks/ n ápice m

aphrodisiac /æfrə'dɪzɪæk/ adj & n afrodisíaco (m), afrodisiaco (m)

apolog|etic /əpɒlə'dʒetɪk/ adj lleno de disculpas. **be** ~**etic** disculparse. ~**ize** /ə'pɒlədʒaɪz/ vi disculparse (**for** de). ~**y** /ə'pɒlədʒɪ/ n disculpa f

apostle /ə'pɒsl/ n apóstol m

apostrophe /ə'pɒstrəfɪ/ n apóstrofo m

appal /ə'pɔːl/ vt (pt **appalled**) horrorizar. ~**ling** adj espantoso

apparatus /æpə'reɪtəs/ n aparato m

apparel /ə'pærəl/ n (Amer) ropa f

apparent /ə'pærənt/ adj aparente; (clear) evidente. ~**ly** adv por lo visto

apparition /æpə'rɪʃn/ n aparición f

appeal /ə'piːl/ vi apelar; (attract) atraer. • n llamamiento m; (attraction) atractivo m; (Jurid) apelación f. ~**ing** adj atrayente

appear /ə'pɪə(r)/ vi aparecer; (seem) parecer; (in court) comparecer. ~**ance** n aparición f; (aspect) aspecto m; (in court) comparecencia f

appease /ə'piːz/ vt aplacar; (pacify) apaciguar

append /ə'pend/ vt adjuntar

appendicitis /əpendɪ'saɪtɪs/ n apendicitis f

appendix /ə'pendɪks/ n (pl **-ices** /-ɪsiːz/) (of book) apéndice m. (pl **-ixes**) (organ) apéndice m

appetite /'æpɪtaɪt/ n apetito m

applau|d /ə'plɔːd/ vt/i aplaudir. ~**se** /ə'plɔːz/ n aplausos mpl. **round of** ~**se** aplauso m

apple /'æpl/ n manzana f. ~ **tree** n manzano m

appliance /ə'plaɪəns/ n aparato m. **electrical** ~ electrodoméstico m

applic|able /'æplɪkəbl/ adj aplicable; (relevant) pertinente. ~**ant** /'æplɪkənt/ n candidato m, solicitante m & f. ~**ation** /æplɪ'keɪʃn/ n aplicación f; (request) solicitud f. ~**ation form** formulario m (de solicitud)

appl|ied /ə'plaɪd/ adj aplicado. ~**y** /ə'plaɪ/ vt aplicar. • vi aplicarse; (ask) presentar una solicitud. ~**y for** solicitar (job etc)

appoint /ə'pɔɪnt/ vt nombrar; (fix) señalar. ~**ment** n cita f

apprais|al /ə'preɪzl/ n evaluación f. ~**e** /ə'preɪz/ vt evaluar

appreciable /ə'priːʃəbl/ adj (considerable) considerable

appreciat|e /ə'priːʃɪeɪt/ vt (value)

apreciar; (*understand*) comprender; (*be grateful for*) agradecer. **~ion** /-'etʃn/ n aprecio m; (*gratitude*) agradecimiento m. **~ive** /ə 'priːʃɪətɪv/ adj agradecido

apprehen|sion /ˌæprɪ'henʃn/ n (*fear*) recelo f. **~sive** adj aprensivo

apprentice /ə'prentɪs/ n aprendiz m. ● vt. **be ~d to s.o.** estar de aprendiz con uno. **~ship** n aprendizaje m

approach /ə'prəʊtʃ/ vt acercarse a. ● vi acercarse. ● n acercamiento m; (*to problem*) enfoque m; (*access*) acceso m

appropriate /ə'prəʊprɪət/ adj apropiado. ● /ə'prəʊprɪeɪt/ vt apropiarse de. **~ly** /-ətlɪ/ adv apropiadamente

approv|al /ə'pruːvl/ n aprobación f. **on ~al** a prueba. **~e** /ə'pruːv/ vt/i aprobar. **~ingly** adv con aprobación

approximat|e /ə'prɒksɪmət/ adj aproximado. ● /ə'prɒksɪmeɪt/ vt aproximarse a. **~ely** /-ətlɪ/ adv aproximadamente. **~ion** /-'meɪʃn/ n aproximación f

apricot /'eɪprɪkɒt/ n albaricoque m, chabacano m (*Mex*)

April /'eɪprəl/ n abril m. **~ fool!** ¡inocentón!

apron /'eɪprən/ n delantal m

apt /æpt/ adj apropiado. **be ~ to** tener tendencia a. **~itude** /'æptɪtjuːd/ n aptitud f. **~ly** adv acertadamente

aquarium /ə'kweərɪəm/ n (*pl* -ums) acuario m

Aquarius /ə'kweərɪəs/ n Acuario m

aquatic /ə'kwætɪk/ adj acuático

aqueduct /'ækwɪdʌkt/ n acueducto m

Arab /'ærəb/ adj & n árabe (m & f). **~ian** /ə'reɪbɪən/ adj árabe. **~ic** /'ærəbɪk/ adj & n árabe (m). **~ic numerals** números mpl arábigos

arable /'ærəbl/ adj cultivable

arbitrary /'ɑːbɪtrərɪ/ adj arbitrario

arbitrat|e /'ɑːbɪtreɪt/ vi arbitrar. **~ion** /-'treɪʃn/ n arbitraje m. **~or** n árbitro m

arc /ɑːk/ n arco m

arcade /ɑː'keɪd/ n arcada f; (*around square*) soportales mpl; (*shops*) galería f

arch /ɑːtʃ/ n arco m. ● vt arquear. ● vi arquearse

archaeolog|ical /ˌɑːkɪə'lɒdʒɪkl/ adj arqueológico. **~ist** /ɑːkɪ 'ɒlədʒɪst/ n arqueólogo m. **~y** /ɑːkɪ'ɒlədʒɪ/ n arqueología f

archaic /ɑː'keɪɪk/ adj arcaico

archbishop /ɑːtʃ'bɪʃəp/ n arzobispo m

archer /'ɑːtʃə(r)/ n arquero m. **~y** n tiro m con arco

architect /'ɑːkɪtekt/ n arquitecto m. **~ure** /-tʃə(r)/ n arquitectura f. **~ural** /-'tektʃərəl/ adj arquitectónico

archives /'ɑːkaɪvz/ npl archivo m. **~ist** /-vɪst/ n archivero m

archway /'ɑːtʃweɪ/ n arco m

Arctic /'ɑːktɪk/ adj ártico. ● n. **the ~** el Ártico

ard|ent /'ɑːdənt/ adj fervoroso; (*supporter, lover*) apasionado. **~our** /'ɑːdə(r)/ n fervor m; (*love*) pasión f

arduous /'ɑːdjʊəs/ adj arduo

are /ɑː(r)/ *see* BE

area /'eərɪə/ n (*Math*) superficie f; (*of country*) zona f; (*of city*) barrio m

arena /ə'riːnə/ n arena f; (*scene of activity*) ruedo m

aren't /ɑːnt/ = **are not**

Argentin|a /ɑ:dʒən'ti:nə/ n Argentina f. **~ian** /-'tɪnɪən/ adj & n argentino (m)

argu|able /'ɑ:gjʊəbl/ adj discutible. **~e** /'ɑ:gju:/ vi discutir; (reason) razonar. **~ment** /'ɑ:gjʊmənt/ n disputa f; (reasoning) argumento m. **~mentative** /ɑ:gjʊ'mentətɪv/ adj discutidor

arid /'ærɪd/ adj árido

Aries /'eərɪ:z/ n Aries m

arise /ə'raɪz/ vi (pt arose, pp arisen) surgir (from de)

aristocra|cy /ærɪ'stɒkrəsɪ/ n aristocracia f. **~t** /'ærɪstəkræt/ n aristócrata m & f. **~tic** /-'krætɪk/ adj aristocrático

arithmetic /ə'rɪθmətɪk/ n aritmética f

ark /ɑ:k/ n (Relig) arca f

arm /ɑ:m/ n brazo m; (of garment) manga f. **~s** npl armas fpl. ● vt armar

armament /'ɑ:məmənt/ n armamento m

· **arm:** **~band** n brazalete m. **~chair** n sillón m

armed /ɑ:md/ adj armado. **~ robbery** n robo m a mano armada

armful /'ɑ:mfʊl/ n brazada f

armour /'ɑ:mə(r)/ n armadura f. **~ed** /ɑ:məd/ adj blindado. **~y** /'ɑ:mərɪ/ n arsenal m

armpit /'ɑ:mpɪt/ n sobaco m, axila f

army /'ɑ:mɪ/ n ejército m

aroma /ə'rəʊmə/ n aroma m

arose /ə'rəʊz/ see ARISE

around /ə'raʊnd/ adv alrededor; (near) cerca. **all ~** por todas partes. ● prep alrededor de; (with time) a eso de

arouse /ə'raʊz/ vt despertar

arrange /ə'reɪndʒ/ vt arreglar;

(fix) fijar. **~ment** n arreglo m; (agreement) acuerdo m. **~ments** npl (plans) preparativos mpl

arrears /ə'rɪəz/ npl atrasos mpl. **in ~** atrasado en el pago (with de)

arrest /ə'rest/ vt detener. ● n detención f. **under ~** detenido

arriv|al /ə'raɪvl/ n llegada f. **new ~al** recién llegado m. **~e** /ə'raɪv/ vi llegar

arrogan|ce /'ærəgəns/ n arrogancia f. **~t** adj arrogante. **~tly** adv con arrogancia

arrow /'ærəʊ/ n flecha f

arse /ɑ:s/ n (vulgar) culo m

arsenal /'ɑ:sənl/ n arsenal m

arsenic /'ɑ:snɪk/ n arsénico m

arson /'ɑ:sn/ n incendio m provocado. **~ist** n incendiario m

art¹ /ɑ:t/ n arte m. **A~s** npl (Univ) Filosofía y Letras fpl. **fine ~s** bellas artes fpl

art² /ɑ:t/ (old use, with thou) see ARE

artery /'ɑ:tərɪ/ n arteria f

art gallery n museo m de arte, pinacoteca f; (commercial) galería f de arte

arthritis /ɑ:'θraɪtɪs/ n artritis f

article /'ɑ:tɪkl/ n artículo m. **~ of clothing** prenda f de vestir

articulat|e /ɑ:'tɪkjʊlət/ adj (utterance) articulado; (person) que sabe expresarse. ● /ɑ:'tɪkjʊleɪt/ vt/i articular. **~ed lorry** n camión m articulado. **~ion** /-'leɪʃn/ n articulación f

artificial /ɑ:tɪ'fɪʃl/ adj artificial. **~ respiration** respiración f artificial

artillery /ɑ:'tɪlərɪ/ n artillería f

artist /'ɑ:tɪst/ n artista m & f. **~tic** /ɑ:'tɪstɪk/ adj artístico. **~ry** /'ɑ:tɪstrɪ/ n arte m, habilidad f

as /æz, əz/ adv & conj como; (since) ya que; (while) mientras. **~ big**

a

tan grande como. ~ **far** ~ (*distance*) hasta; (*qualitative*) en cuanto a. ~ **far** ~ **I know** que yo sepa. ~ **if** como si. ~ **long** ~ mientras. ~ **much** ~ tanto como. ~ **soon** ~ tan pronto como. ~ **well** también

asbestos /æz'bestɒs/ n amianto m, asbesto m

ascend /ə'send/ vt/i subir. **A~sion** /ə'senʃn/ n. **the A~sion** la Ascensión. ~ /ə'sent/ n subida f

ascertain /æsə'teɪn/ vt averiguar

ash /æʃ/ n ceniza f. ● n. ~ **(tree)** fresno m

ashamed /ə'ʃeɪmd/ adj avergonzado (**of** de). **be** ~ **of** s.o. avergonzarse de uno

ashore /ə'ʃɔː(r)/ adv a tierra. **go** ~ desembarcar

ash: ~**tray** n cenicero m. **A~ Wednesday** n Miércoles m de Ceniza

Asia /'eɪʃə/ n Asia f. ~**n** adj & n asiático (m). ~**tic** /-ɪ'ætɪk/ adj asiático

aside /ə'saɪd/ adv a un lado. ● n (*theatre*) aparte m

ask /ɑːsk/ vt pedir; hacer (*question*); (*invite*) invitar. ~ **about** enterarse de. ~ **s.o. to do something** pedirle a uno que haga algo. □ ~ **after** vt preguntar por. □ ~ **for** vt. ~ **for help** pedir ayuda. ~ **for trouble** buscarse problemas. □ ~ **in** vt. ~ **s.o. in** invitar a uno a pasar

askew /ə'skjuː/ adv & adj torcido

asleep /ə'sliːp/ adv & adj dormido. **fall** ~ dormirse

asparagus /ə'spærəgəs/ n espárrago m

aspect /'æspekt/ n aspecto m

asphalt /'æsfælt/ n asfalto m. ● vt

asfaltar

aspiration /æspə'reɪʃn/ n aspiración f. ~**e** /əs'paɪə(r)/ vi aspirar

aspirin /'æsprɪn/ n aspirina f

ass /æs/ n asno m; (*fig, fam*) imbécil m; (*Amer vulgar*) culo m

assassin /ə'sæsɪn/ n asesino m. ~**ate** /-eɪt/ vt asesinar. ~**ation** /-'eɪʃn/ n asesinato m

assault /ə'sɔːlt/ n (*Mil*) ataque m; (*Jurid*) atentado m. ● vt asaltar

assemble /ə'sembl/ vt reunir; (*Mec*) montar. ● vi reunirse. ~**y** n reunión f; (*Pol etc*) asamblea f. ~**y line** n línea f de montaje

assent /ə'sent/ n asentimiento m. ● vi asentir

assert /ə'sɜːt/ vt afirmar; hacer valer (*one's rights*). ~**ion** /-ʃn/ n afirmación f. ~**ive** adj positivo, firme

assess /ə'ses/ vt evaluar; (*determine*) determinar; fijar (*tax etc*). ~**ment** n evaluación f

asset /'æset/ n (*advantage*) ventaja f. ~**s** npl (*Com*) bienes mpl

assign /ə'saɪn/ vt asignar; (*appoint*) nombrar. ~**ment** n asignación f; (*mission*) misión f; (*task*) función f. (*for school*) trabajo m

assimilate /ə'sɪmɪleɪt/ vt asimilar. ● vi asimilarse

assist /ə'sɪst/ vt/i ayudar. ~**ance** n ayuda f. ~**ant** n ayudante m & f; (*shop*) dependienta f, dependiente m. ● adj auxiliar, adjunto

associate /ə'səʊʃɪeɪt/ vt asociar. ● vi asociarse. ~ /ə'səʊʃɪət/ adj asociado. ● n colega m & f; (*Com*) socio m. ~**ion** /-'eɪʃn/ n asociación f.

assorted /ə'sɔːtɪd/ adj surtido. ~**ment** n surtido m

assume /ə'sjuːm/ vt suponer; tomar (*power, attitude*); asumir (role, burden). **~ption** /əˈsʌmpʃn/ n suposición f

assur|ance /əˈʃʊərəns/ n seguridad f; (insurance) seguro m. **~e** /ə'ʃʊə(r)/ vt asegurar. **~ed** adj seguro

asterisk /ˈæstərɪsk/ n asterisco m

asthma /ˈæsmə/ n asma f. **~tic** /-ˈmætɪk/ adj & n asmático (m)

astonish /əˈstɒnɪʃ/ vt asombrar. **~ed** adj asombrado. **~ing** adj asombroso. **~ment** n asombro m

astound /əˈstaʊnd/ vt asombrar. **~ed** adj atónito. **~ing** adj increíble

astray /əˈstreɪ/ adv. **go ~** extraviarse. **lead ~** llevar por mal camino

astrology /əˈstrɒlədʒɪ/ n astrología f

astronaut /ˈæstrənɔːt/ n astronauta m & f

astronom|er /əˈstrɒnəmə(r)/ n astrónomo m. **~ical** /æstrə'nɒmɪkl/ adj astronómico. **~y** /ə'strɒnəmɪ/ n astronomía f

astute /əˈstjuːt/ adj astuto

asylum /əˈsaɪləm/ n asilo m. **lunatic ~** manicomio m. **~ seeker** n solicitante m & f de asilo

---

at | /æt/ preposition

••••▸ (location) en. **she's at the office** está en la oficina. **at home** en casa. **call me at the office** llámame a la oficina

➡️ For translations of phrases such as **at the top**, **at the front of**, **at the back of** see entries for **top**, **front** etc

••••▸ (at the house of) en casa

de. **I'll be at Rachel's** estaré en casa de Rachel

••••▸ (Comput: @) arroba f

••••▸ (talking about time) **at night** por la noche, de noche, en la noche (LAm). **at Christmas** en Navidad

••••▸ (talking about age) a. **at six (years of age)** a los seis años

••••▸ (with measurements, numbers etc) a. **at 60 miles an hour** a 60 millas por hora. **at a depth of** a una profundidad de. **three at a time** de tres en tres

➡️ For translations of phrasal verbs with **at**, such as **look at**, see entries for those verbs

---

ate /et/ see EAT

atheis|m /ˈeɪθɪɪzəm/ n ateísmo m. **~t** n ateo m

athlet|e /ˈæθliːt/ n atleta m & f. **~ic** /-ˈletɪk/ adj atlético. **~ics** npl atletismo m; (Amer, Sport) deportes mpl

Atlantic /ətˈlæntɪk/ adj atlántico. ●n. the ~ **(Ocean)** el (Océano) Atlántico

atlas /ˈætləs/ n atlas m

ATM abbr (= **automated teller machine**) cajero m automático

atmospher|e /ˈætməsfɪə(r)/ n atmósfera f; (fig) ambiente m. **~ic** /-ˈferɪk/ adj atmosférico

atom /ˈætəm/ n átomo m. **~ic** /ə'tɒmɪk/ adj atómico

atroci|ous /əˈtrəʊʃəs/ adj atroz. **~ty** /əˈtrɒsətɪ/ n atrocidad f

attach /əˈtætʃ/ vt sujetar; adjuntar (document etc). **be ~ed to** (be fond of) tener cariño a. **~ment** n (affection) cariño m; (tool) accesorio m

attack /ə'tæk/ n ataque m. ● vt/i atacar. **~er** n agresor m

attain /ə'tem/ vt conseguir. **~able** adj alcanzable

attempt /ə'tempt/ vt intentar. ● n tentativa f; (attack) atentado m

attend /ə'tend/ vt asistir a; (escort) acompañar. ● vi prestar atención. □ **~ to** vt (look after) ocuparse de. **~ance** n asistencia f; (people present) concurrencia f.

atten|tion /ə'tenʃn/ n atención f. **~tion!** (Mil) ¡firmes! **pay ~tion** prestar atención. **~tive** adj atento

attic /'ætɪk/ n desván m

attire /ə'taɪə(r)/ n atavío m. ● vt ataviar

attitude /'ætɪtjuːd/ n postura f

attorney /ə'tɜːnɪ/ n (pl -eys) (Amer) abogado m

attract /ə'trækt/ vt atraer. **~ion** /-ʃn/ n atracción f; (charm) atractivo m. **~ive** adj atractivo; (interesting) atrayente

attribute /ə'trɪbjuːt/ vt atribuir. ● /'ætrɪbjuːt/ n atributo m

aubergine /'əʊbəʒiːn/ n berenjena f

auction /'ɔːkʃn/ n subasta f. ● vt subastar. **~eer** /-ə'nɪə(r)/ n subastador m

audaci|ous /ɔː'deɪʃəs/ adj audaz. **~ty** /ɔː'dæsətɪ/ n audacia f

audible /'ɔːdəbl/ adj audible

audience /'ɔːdɪəns/ n (at play, film) público m; (TV) audiencia f; (interview) audiencia f

audiovisual /ɔːdɪəʊ'vɪʒʊəl/ adj audiovisual

audit /'ɔːdɪt/ n revisión f de cuentas. ● vt revisar

audition /ɔː'dɪʃn/ n audición f.

● vt hacerle una audición a. ● vi dar una audición (for para)

auditor /'ɔːdɪtə(r)/ n interventor m de cuentas

auditorium /ɔːdɪ'tɔːrɪəm/ (pl -riums or -ria /-rɪə/) n sala f, auditorio m

augment /ɔːg'ment/ vt aumentar

augur /'ɔːɡə(r)/ vt augurar. **it ~s well** es de buen agüero

August /'ɔːgəst/ n agosto m

aunt /ɑːnt/ n tía f

au pair /əʊ'peə(r)/ n chica f au pair

aura /'ɔːrə/ n aura f, halo m

auster|e /ɔː'stɪə(r)/ adj austero. **~ity** /ɔː'sterətɪ/ n austeridad f

Australia /ɒ'streɪlɪə/ n Australia f. **~n** adj & n australiano (m)

Austria /'ɒstrɪə/ n Austria f. **~n** adj & n austríaco (m)

authentic /ɔː'θentɪk/ adj auténtico. **~ate** /-keɪt/ vt autenticar. **~ity** /-ən'tɪsətɪ/ n autenticidad f

author /'ɔːθə(r)/ n autor m. **~ess** /-ɪs/ n autora f

authoritative /ɔː'θɒrɪtətɪv/ adj autorizado; (manner) autoritario

authority /ɔː'θɒrətɪ/ n autoridad f; (permission) autorización f

authoriz|ation /ɔːθəraɪ'zeɪʃn/ n autorización f. **~e** /'ɔːθəraɪz/ vt autorizar

autobiography /ɔːtəʊbaɪ'ɒɡrəfɪ/ n autobiografía f

autograph /'ɔːtəɡrɑːf/ n autógrafo m. ● vt firmar, autografiar

automat|e /'ɔːtəmeɪt/ vt automatizar. **~ic** /-'mætɪk/ adj automático. **~ion** /-'meɪʃn/ n automatización f. **~on** /ɔː'tɒmətən/ n (pl -tons or -ta /-tə/) autómata m

automobile /'ɔːtəməbiːl/ n

293

(*Amer*) coche *m*, carro *m* (*LAm*), automóvil *m*

autonom|ous /ɔːˈtɒnəməs/ *adj* autónomo. ~**y** *n* autonomía *f*

autopsy /ˈɔːtɒpsɪ/ *n* autopsia *f*

autumn /ˈɔːtəm/ *n* otoño *m*. ~**al** /ɔːˈtʌmnəl/ *adj* otoñal

auxiliary /ɔːgˈzɪlɪərɪ/ *adj & n* auxiliar (*m & f*)

avail /əˈveɪl/ *n*. to no ~ inútil

availab|ility /əveɪləˈbɪlɪtɪ/ *n* disponibilidad *f*. ~**le** /əˈveɪləbl/ *adj* disponible

avalanche /ˈævəlɑːnʃ/ *n* avalancha *f*

avaric|e /ˈævərɪs/ *n* avaricia *f*. ~**ious** /-ˈrɪʃəs/ *adj* avaro

avenue /ˈævənjuː/ *n* avenida *f*; (*fig*) vía *f*

average /ˈævərɪdʒ/ *n* promedio *m*. **on** ~ por término medio. ● *adj* medio

avers|e /əˈvɜːs/ *adj*. **be** ~**e to** ser reacio a. ~**ion** /-ʃn/ *n* repugnancia *f*

avert /əˈvɜːt/ *vt* (*turn away*) apartar; (*ward off*) desviar

aviation /eɪvɪˈeɪʃn/ *n* aviación *f*

avid /ˈævɪd/ *adj* ávido

avocado /ævəˈkɑːdəʊ/ *n* (*pl -os*) aguacate *m*

avoid /əˈvɔɪd/ *vt* evitar. ~**able** *adj* evitable. ~**ance** *n* el evitar

await /əˈweɪt/ *vt* esperar

awake /əˈweɪk/ *vt/i* (*pt* **awoke**, *pp* **awoken**) despertar. ● *adj* despierto. **wide** ~ completamente despierto; (*fig*) despabilado. ~**n** /əˈweɪkən/ *vt/i* despertar. ~**ning** *n* el despertar

award /əˈwɔːd/ *vt* otorgar; (*Jurid*) adjudicar. ● *n* premio *m*; (*Jurid*) adjudicación *f*; (*scholarship*) beca *f*

aware /əˈweə(r)/ *adj*. **be** ~ **of sth** ser consciente de algo, darse cuenta de algo. ~**ness** *n* conciencia *f*

awash /əˈwɒʃ/ *adj* inundado

away /əˈweɪ/ *adv* (*absent*) fuera. **far** ~ muy lejos. ● *adj* ~ **match** partido *m* fuera de casa

awe /ɔː/ *n* temor *m*. ~**-inspiring** *adj* impresionante. ~**some** /-səm/ *adj* imponente

awful /ˈɔːfʊl/ *adj* terrible, malísimo. **feel** ~ sentirse muy mal

awkward /ˈɔːkwəd/ *adj* difícil; (*inconvenient*) inoportuno; (*clumsy*) desmañado; (*embarrassed*) incómodo. ~**ness** *n* dificultad *f*; (*discomfort*) molestia *f*; (*clumsiness*) torpeza *f*

awning /ˈɔːnɪŋ/ *n* toldo *m*

awoke /əˈwəʊk/, **awoken** /əˈwəʊkən/ *see* **AWAKE**

axe /æks/ *n* hacha *f*. ● *vt* (*pres p* **axing**) cortar con hacha; (*fig*) recortar

axis /ˈæksɪs/ *n* (*pl* **axes** /-iːz/) eje *m*

axle /ˈæksl/ *n* eje *m*

Bb

BA /biːˈeɪ/ *abbr see* **BACHELOR**

babble /ˈbæbl/ *vi* balbucir; (*chatter*) parlotear; (*stream*) murmurar.

baboon /bəˈbuːn/ *n* mandril *m*

baby /ˈbeɪbɪ/ *n* niño *m*, bebé *m*. ~ **buggy**, ~ **carriage** *n* (*Amer*) cochecito *m*. ~**ish** *adj* /ˈbeɪbɪʃ/ infantil. ~**-sit** *vi* cuidar a los niños, hacer de canguro. ~**-sitter** *n* baby sitter m & f, canguro m & f

bachelor /'bætʃələ(r)/ n soltero m. B~ of Arts (BA) licenciado m en filosofía y letras. B~ of Science (BSc) licenciado m en ciencias

back /bæk/ n espalda f; (of car) parte f trasera; (of chair) respaldo m; (of cloth) revés m; (of house) parte f de atrás; (of page, book) lomo m; (of hand, document) dorso m; (football) defensa m & f. in the ~ of beyond en el quinto infierno. ● adj trasero. the ~ door la puerta trasera. ● adv atrás; (returned) de vuelta. ● vt apoyar; (betting) apostar a; dar marcha atrás a (car). ● vi retroceder; (car) dar marcha atrás. □ ~ **down** vi volverse atrás. □ ~ **out** vi retirarse. □ ~ **up** vt apoyar; (Comp) hacer una copia de seguridad de. ~**ache** n dolor m de espalda. ~**bone** n columna f vertebral; (fig) pilar m. ~**date** /-'deɪt/ vt antedatar. ~**er** n partidario m; (Com) financiador m. ~**fire** /-'faɪə(r)/ vi (Auto) petardear; (fig) fallar. his plan ~**fired** on him le salió el tiro por la culata. ~**ground** n fondo m; (environment) antecedentes mpl. ~**hand** n (Sport) revés m. ~**ing** n apoyo m. ~**lash** n reacción f. ~**log** n atrasos mpl. ~**side** /-'saɪd/ n 🔟 trasero m. ~**stage** /-'steɪdʒ/ adj de bastidores. ● adv entre bastidores. ~**stroke** n (tennis etc) revés m; (swimming) estilo m espalda, estilo m dorso (Mex). ~**up** n apoyo m; (Comp) copia f de seguridad. ~**ward** /-wəd/ adj (step etc) hacia atrás; (retarded) retrasado; (undeveloped) atrasado. ● adv (Amer) see BACKWARDS. ~**wards** adv hacia atrás; (fall) de espaldas; (back to front) al revés. **go** ~**wards and forwards** ir de acá para allá. ~**water** n agua f estan-

cada; (fig) lugar m apartado

bacon /'beɪkən/ n tocino m

bacteria /bæk'tɪərɪə/ npl bacterias fpl

bad /bæd/ adj (worse, worst) malo, (before masculine singular noun) mal; (serious) grave; (harmful) nocivo; (language) indecente. feel ~ sentirse mal

bade /beɪd/ see **BID**

badge /bædʒ/ n distintivo m, chapa f

badger /'bædʒə(r)/ n tejón m. ● vt acosar

bad: ~**ly** adv mal. **want** ~**ly** desear muchísimo. ~**ly injured** gravemente herido. ~**ly off** mal de dinero. ~**-mannered** /-'mænəd/ adj mal educado

badminton /'bædmɪntən/ n bádminton m

bad-tempered /bæd'tempəd/ adj (always) de mal carácter; (temporarily) de mal humor

baffle /'bæfl/ vt desconcertar. ~**d** adj perplejo

bag /bæg/ n bolsa f; (handbag) bolso m. ● vt (pt **bagged**) ensacar; (take) coger (esp Spain), agarrar (LAm). ~**s** npl (luggage) equipaje m

baggage /'bægɪdʒ/ n equipaje m. ~ **room** n (Amer) consigna f

baggy /'bægɪ/ adj (clothes) holgado

bagpipes /'bægpaɪps/ npl gaita f

baguette /bæ'get/ n baguette f

bail¹ /beɪl/ n fianza f. ● vt poner en libertad bajo fianza. ~ **s.o. out** pagar la fianza a uno

bail² vt. ~ **out** (Naut) achicar

bait /beɪt/ n cebo m

bak|e /beɪk/ vt cocer al horno. ● vi cocerse. ~**er** n panadero m. ~**ery**

balance /'bæləns/ n equilibrio m; (Com) balance m; (sum) saldo m; (scales) balanza f; (remainder) resto m. ● vt equilibrar (load); mantener en equilibrio (object); nivelar (budget). ● vi equilibrarse; (Com) cuadrar. ~d adj equilibrado

balcony /'bælkənɪ/ n balcón m

bald /bɔːld/ adj (-er, -est) calvo, pelón (Mex)

bale /beɪl/ n bala f, fardo m. ● vi. ~ **out** lanzarse en paracaídas

Balearic /bælɪˈærɪk/ adj. the ~ Islands las Islas fpl Baleares

ball /bɔːl/ n bola f; (tennis etc) pelota f; (football etc) balón m, pelota f (esp LAm); (of yarn) ovillo m; (dance) baile m

ballad /'bæləd/ n balada f

ballast /'bæləst/ n lastre m

ball bearing n cojinete m de bolas

ballerina /bæləˈriːnə/ f bailarina f

ballet /'bæleɪ/ n ballet m. ~ **dancer** n bailarín m de ballet, bailarina f de ballet

balloon /bəˈluːn/ n globo m

ballot /'bælət/ n votación f. ~ **box** n urna f. ~ **paper** n papeleta f

ball: ~**point** n. ~**point (pen)** bolígrafo m, pluma f atómica (Mex). ~**room** n salón m de baile

bamboo /bæmˈbuː/ n bambú m

ban /bæn/ vt (pt banned) prohibir. ~ **s.o. from sth** prohibir algo a uno. ● n prohibición f

banal /bəˈnɑːl/ adj banal. ~**ity** /bəˈnælətɪ/ n banalidad f

banana /bəˈnɑːnə/ n plátano m

band /bænd/ n (strip) banda f. ● n (Mus) orquesta f; (military, brass)

banda f. ● ~ **together** vi juntarse

bandage /'bændɪdʒ/ n venda f. ● vt vendar

Band-Aid /'bændeɪd/ n (Amer, ®) tirita f, curita f (LAm)

B & B /'biːənbiː/ abbr (= bed and breakfast) cama f y desayuno; (place) pensión f

bandit /'bændɪt/ n bandido m

band: ~**stand** n quiosco m de música. ~**wagon** n. **jump on the** ~**wagon** (fig) subirse al carro

bandy /'bændɪ/ adj (-ier, -iest) patizambo

bang /bæŋ/ n (noise) ruido m; (blow) golpe m; (of gun) estampido m; (of door) golpe m. ● vt (strike) golpear. ~ **the door** dar un portazo. ● adv exactamente. ● int ¡pum! ~**s** npl (Amer) flequillo m, cerquillo m (LAm), fleco m (Mex)

banger /'bæŋə(r)/ n petardo m; (🚗, Culin) salchicha f

bangle /'bæŋgl/ n brazalete m

banish /'bænɪʃ/ vt desterrar

banisters /'bænɪstəz/ npl pasamanos m

banjo /'bændʒəʊ/ n (pl -os) banjo m

bank /bæŋk/ n (Com) banco m; (of river) orilla f. ● vt depositar. ● vi (in flying) ladearse. □ ~ **on** vt contar con. □ ~ **with** vi tener una cuenta con. ~ **card** n tarjeta f bancaria; (Amer) tarjeta f de crédito (expedida por un banco). ~**er** n banquero m. ~ **holiday** n día m festivo, día m feriado (LAm). ~**ing** n (Com) banca f. ~**note** n billete m de banco

bankrupt /'bæŋkrʌpt/ adj & n quebrado (m). **go** ~ quebrar. ● vt hacer quebrar. ~**cy** /-rʌpsɪ/ n bancarrota f, quiebra f

bank statement n estado m

de cuenta

banner /'bænə(r)/ n bandera f; (in demonstration) pancarta f

banquet /'bæŋkwɪt/ n banquete m

banter /'bæntə(r)/ n chanza f

bap /bæp/ n panecillo m blando

baptism /'bæptɪzəm/ n bautismo m; (act) bautizo m

Baptist /'bæptɪst/ n bautista m & f

baptize /bæp'taɪz/ vt bautizar

bar /ba:(r)/ n barra f; (on window) reja f; (of chocolate) tableta f; (of soap) pastilla f; (pub) bar m; (Mus) compás f; (Jurid) abogacía f; (fig) obstáculo m. • vt (pt **barred**) atrancar (door); (exclude) excluir; (prohibit) prohibir. • prep excepto

barbar|ian /ba:'beərɪən/ adj & n bárbaro (m). ~**ic** /ba:'bærɪk/ adj bárbaro

barbecue /'ba:bɪkju:/ n barbacoa f. • vt asar a la parilla

barbed wire /ba:bd 'waɪə(r)/ n alambre m de púas

barber /'ba:bə(r)/ n peluquero m, barbero m

barbwire /'ba:b'waɪə(r)/ n (Amer) see **BARBED WIRE**

bare /beə(r)/ adj (**-er, -est**) desnudo; (room) con pocos muebles; (mere) simple; (empty) vacío. • vt desnudar; (uncover) descubrir. ~ **one's teeth** mostrar los dientes. ~**back** adv a pelo. ~**faced** adj descarado. ~**foot** adj descalzo. ~**headed** /-'hedɪd/ adj descubierto. ~**ly** adv apenas

bargain /'ba:gɪn/ n (agreement) pacto m; (good buy) ganga f. • vi negociar; (haggle) regatear. □ ~ **for** vt esperar, contar con

barge /ba:dʒ/ n barcaza f. • vi. ~ **in** irrumpir

baritone /'bærɪtəʊn/ n barítono m

bark /ba:k/ n (of dog) ladrido m; (of tree) corteza f. • vi ladrar

barley /'ba:lɪ/ n cebada f

bar: ~**maid** n camarera f. ~**man** /-mən/ n camarero m, barman m

barmy /'ba:mɪ/ adj chiflado

barn /ba:n/ n granero m

barometer /bə'rɒmɪtə(r)/ n barómetro m

baron /'bærən/ n barón m. ~**ess** /-ɪs/ n baronesa f

barracks /'bærəks/ npl cuartel m

barrage /'bæra:ʒ/ n (Mil) barrera f; (dam) presa f. **a** ~ **of questions** un aluvión de preguntas

barrel /'bærəl/ n barril m; (of gun) cañón m

barren /'bærən/ adj estéril

barrette /bə'ret/ n (Amer) pasador m

barricade /bærɪ'keɪd/ n barricada f. • vt cerrar con barricadas

barrier /'bærɪə(r)/ n barrera f

barrister /'bærɪstə(r)/ n abogado m

bartender /'ba:tendə(r)/ n (Amer) (male) camarero m, barman m; (female) camarera f

barter /'ba:tə(r)/ n trueque m. • vt trocar

base /beɪs/ n base f. • vt basar. ~**ball** n béisbol m, beisbol m (Mex)

basement /'beɪsmənt/ n sótano m

bash /bæʃ/ vt golpear. • n golpe m. **have a** ~ 🄣 probar

bashful /'bæʃfl/ adj tímido

basic /'beɪsɪk/ adj básico, fundamental. ~**ally** adv fundamentalmente

basin /'beɪsn/ n (for washing) palangana f; (for food) cuenco m; (of river) cuenca f

basis /'beɪsɪs/ n (pl bases/-si:z/) base f

bask /bɑːsk/ vi asolearse; (fig) gozar (**in** de)

basket /'bɑːskɪt/ n cesta f; (big) cesto m. **~ball** n baloncesto m, básquetbol m (LAm)

bass[1] /beɪs/ adj bajo. ● n (Mus) bajo m

bass[2] /bæs/ n (fish) lubina f

bassoon /bə'suːn/ n fagot m

bastard /'bɑːstəd/ n bastardo m. **~ you ...!** (vulgar) ¡cabrón! (vulgar)

bat /bæt/ n (for baseball, cricket) bate m; (for table tennis) raqueta f; (mammal) murciélago m. **off one's own ~** por sí solo. ● vt (pt batted) golpear. **without ~ting an eyelid** sin pestañear. ● vi batear

batch /bætʃ/ n (of people) grupo m; (of papers) pila f; (of goods) remesa f; (of bread) hornada f; (Comp) lote m

bated /'beɪtɪd/ adj. **with ~ breath** con aliento entrecortado

bath /bɑːθ/ n (pl -s /bɑːðz/) baño m; (tub) bañera f, tina f (LAm). **~s** npl (swimming pool) piscina f, alberca f (Mex). **have a ~**, **take a ~** (Amer) bañarse. ● vt bañar. ● vi bañarse

bathe /beɪð/ vt bañar. ● vi bañarse. ● n baño m. **~r** n bañista m & f

bathing /'beɪðɪŋ/ n baños mpl. **~ costume**, **~ suit** n traje m de baño

bathroom /'bɑːθrʊm/ n cuarto m de baño; (Amer, toilet) servicio m, baño m (LAm)

batsman /'bætsmən/ n (pl -men) bateador m

battalion /bə'tælɪən/ n batallón m

batter /'bætə(r)/ vt (beat) apalear; (cover with batter) rebozar. ● n batido m para rebozar; (Amer, for cake) masa f. **~ed** /'bætəd/ adj (car etc) estropeado; (wife etc) maltratado

battery /'bætərɪ/ n (Mil, Auto) batería f; (of torch, radio) pila f

battle /'bætl/ n batalla f; (fig) lucha f. ● vi luchar. **~field** n campo m de batalla. **~ship** n acorazado m

bawl /bɔːl/ vt/i gritar

bay /beɪ/ n (on coast) bahía f. **keep at ~** mantener a raya

bayonet /'beɪənet/ n bayoneta f

bay window /beɪ 'wɪndəʊ/ n ventana f saladiza

bazaar /bə'zɑː(r)/ n bazar m

BC abbr (= **before Christ**) a. de C., antes de Cristo

---

be /biː/

present **am, are, is;** past **was, were;** past participle **been**

● intransitive verb

! Spanish has two verbs meaning **be**, *ser* and *estar*. See those entries for further information about the differences between them.

••••➤ (position, changed condition or state) estar. **where is the library?** ¿dónde está la biblioteca? **she's tired** está cansada. **how are you?** ¿cómo estás?

••••➤ (identity, nature or permanent characteristics) ser. **she's tall** es alta. **he's Scottish** es escocés. **I'm a journalist** soy periodista. **he's very kind** es muy bondadoso

···▶ *(feel)* **to be** + *adjective* tener + *sustantivo.* **to be cold/hot** tener frío/calor. **he's hungry/thirsty** tiene hambre/sed

···▶ *(age)* **he's thirty** tiene treinta años

···▶ *(weather)* **it's cold/hot** hace frío/calor. **it was 40 degrees** hacía 40 grados

● *auxiliary verb*

···▶ *(in tenses)* estar. **I'm working** estoy trabajando. **they were singing** estaban cantando, cantaban

···▶ *(in tag questions)* **it's a beautiful house, isn't it?** es una casa preciosa, ¿verdad? or ¿no? or ¿no es cierto?

···▶ *(in short answers)* **are you disappointed? - yes, I am** ¿estás desilusionado? - sí ¡(lo estoy). **I'm surprised, aren't you?** estoy sorprendido, ¿tú no?

···▶ *(in passive sentences)* **it was built in 1834** fue construido en 1834, se construyó en 1834. **she was told that ...** le dijeron que..., se le dijo que ...

! Note that passive sentences in English are often translated using the pronoun *se* or using the third person plural.

beach /biːtʃ/ n playa f

beacon /ˈbiːkən/ n faro m

bead /biːd/ n cuenta f; *(of glass)* abalorio m

beak /biːk/ n pico m

beaker /ˈbiːkə(r)/ n taza f *(alta y*

sin asa)

beam /biːm/ n *(of wood)* viga f; *(of light)* rayo m; *(Naut)* bao m. ● vt emitir. ● vi irradiar; *(smile)* sonreír

bean /biːn/ n alubia f, frijol m *(LAm)*; *(broad bean)* haba f; *(of coffee)* grano m

bear /beə(r)/ vt *(pt* **bore**, *pp* **borne)** llevar; parir (niño); *(endure)* soportar. **~ right** torcer a la derecha. **~ in mind** tener en cuenta. **□~ with** vt tener paciencia con. ● n oso m. **~able** adj soportable

beard /bɪəd/ n barba f. **~ed** adj barbudo

bearer /ˈbeərə(r)/ n portador m; *(of passport)* titular m & f

bearing /ˈbeərɪŋ/ n comportamiento m; *(relevance)* relación f; *(Mec)* cojinete m. **get one's ~s** orientarse. **lose one's ~s** desorientarse

beast /biːst/ n bestia f; *(person)* bruto m. **~ly** adj *(-ier, -iest)* bestial; 🔢 horrible

beat /biːt/ vt *(pt* **beat**, *pp* **beaten)** *(hit)* pegar; *(Culin)* batir; *(defeat)* derrotar; *(better)* sobrepasar; batir *(record)*; *(baffle)* dejar perplejo. **~ it** 🔢 largarse. ● vi *(heart)* latir. ● n latido m; *(Mus)* ritmo m; *(of policeman)* ronda f. **□~ up** vt darle una paliza a; *(Culin)* batir. **~ up on** *(Amer, fam)* darle una paliza a. **~er** n batidor m. **~ing** n paliza f

beautician /bjuːˈtɪʃn/ n esteticista m & f

beautiful /ˈbjuːtɪfl/ adj hermoso. **~ly** adv maravillosamente

beauty /ˈbjuːtɪ/ n belleza f. **~ salon, ~ shop** *(Amer)* n salón m de belleza. **~ spot** n *(on face)* lunar m; *(site)* lugar m pintoresco

beaver /ˈbiːvə(r)/ n castor m

became | being

became /bɪ'keɪm/ *see* BECOME

because /bɪ'kɒz/ *conj* porque.
● *adv.* ~ **of** por, a causa de

beckon /'bekən/ *vt/i.* ~ **(to)** hacer señas (a)

become /bɪ'kʌm/ *vi* (*pt* **became**, *pp* **become**) hacerse, llegar a ser, volverse, convertirse en. **what has** ~ **of her?** ¿qué es de ella?

bed /bed/ *n* cama *f*; (*layer*) estrato *m*; (*of sea, river*) fondo *m*; (*of flowers*) macizo *m*. **go to** ~ acostarse. ● *vi* (*pt* **bedded**) ~ **and breakfast** (B & B) cama y desayuno; (*place*) pensión *f*. ~**bug** *n* chinche *f*. ~**clothes** *npl*, ~**ding** *n* ropa *f* de cama, cobijas *fpl* (LAm)

> **Bed and breakfast** Los *i*
> bed & breakfast o B&B
> son casas privadas o pequeños
> hoteles que ofrecen alojamiento y
> desayuno a precios generalmente
> módicos.

bed: ~**room** *n* dormitorio *m*, cuarto *m*, habitación *f*, recámara *f* (Mex). ~**sitter** /-'sɪtə(r)/ *n* habitación *f* con cama y uso de cocina y baño compartidos, estudio *m*. ~**spread** *n* colcha *f*. ~**time** *n* hora *f* de acostarse

bee /biː/ *n* abeja *f*; (Amer, *social gathering*) círculo *m*

beech /biːtʃ/ *n* haya *f*

beef /biːf/ *n* carne *f* de vaca, carne *f* de res (Mex). ● *vi* 🗵 quejarse. ~**burger** *n* hamburguesa *f*. ~**y** *adj* (**-ier, -iest**) musculoso

bee: ~**hive** *n* colmena *f*. ~**line** *n*. **make a** ~**line for** ir en línea recta hacia

been /biːn/ *see* BE

beer /bɪə(r)/ *n* cerveza *f*

beet /biːt/ *n* (Amer) remolacha *f*,

betabel *f* (Mex)

beetle /'biːtl/ *n* escarabajo *m*

beetroot /'biːtruːt/ *n invar* remolacha *f*, betabel *f* (Mex)

befall /bɪ'fɔːl/ *vt* (*pt* **befell**, *pp* **befallen**) ocurrirle a. ● *vi* ocurrir

before /bɪ'fɔː(r)/ *prep* (*time*) antes de; (*place*) delante de. ~ **leaving** antes de marcharse. ● *adv* (*place*) delante; (*time*) antes. **a week** ~ una semana antes. **the week** ~ la semana anterior. ● *conj* (*time*) antes de que. ~ **he leaves** antes de que se vaya. ~**hand** *adv* de antemano

befriend /bɪ'frend/ *vt* hacerse amigo de

beg /beg/ *vt/i* (*pt* **begged**) mendigar; (*entreat*) suplicar; (*ask*) pedir. ~ **s.o.'s pardon** pedir perdón a uno. **I** ~ **your pardon!** ¡perdone Vd! **I** ~ **your pardon?** ¿cómo?

began /bɪ'gæn/ *see* BEGIN

beggar /'begə(r)/ *n* mendigo *m*

begin /bɪ'gɪn/ *vt/i* (*pt* **began**, *pp* **begun**, *pres p* **beginning**) comenzar, empezar. ~**ner** *n* principiante *m* & *f*. ~**ning** *n* principio *m*

begrudge /bɪ'grʌdʒ/ *vt* envidiar; (*give*) dar de mala gana

begun /bɪ'gʌn/ *see* BEGIN

behalf /bɪ'hɑːf/ *n*. **on** ~ **of, in** ~ **of** (Amer) de parte de, en nombre de

behav|e /bɪ'heɪv/ *vi* comportarse, portarse. ~**e (o.s.)** portarse bien. ~**iour** /bɪ'heɪvjə(r)/ *n* comportamiento *m*

behead /bɪ'hed/ *vt* decapitar

behind /bɪ'haɪnd/ *prep* detrás de, atrás de (LAm). ● *adv* detrás; (*late*) atrasado. ● *n* 🗓 trasero *m*

beige /beɪʒ/ *adj* & *n* beige (*m*)

being /'biːɪŋ/ *n* ser *m*. **come into** ~ nacer

belated /bɪ'leɪtɪd/ adj tardío

belch /beltʃ/ vi eructar. □ **~ out** vt arrojar (smoke)

belfry /'belfrɪ/ n campanario m

Belgi|an /'beldʒən/ adj & n belga (m & f). **~um** /'beldʒəm/ n Bélgica f

belie|f /bɪ'li:f/ n (trust) fe f; (opinion) creencia f. **~ve** /bɪ'li:v/ vt/i creer. **~ve in** creer en. **make ~ve** fingir

belittle /bɪ'lɪtl/ vt menospreciar (achievements); denigrar (person)

bell /bel/ n campana f; (on door, bicycle) timbre m

belligerent /bɪ'lɪdʒərənt/ adj beligerante

bellow /'beləʊ/ vt gritar. ● vi bramar. **~s** npl fuelle m

bell pepper n (Amer) pimiento m

belly /'belɪ/ n barriga f

belong /bɪ'lɒŋ/ vi pertenecer (**to** a); (club) ser socio (**to** de); (have as usual place) ir. **~ings** /bɪ'lɒŋɪŋz/ npl pertenencias fpl. **personal ~ings** efectos mpl personales

beloved /bɪ'lʌvɪd/ adj querido

below /bɪ'ləʊ/ prep debajo de, abajo de (LAm); (fig) inferior a. ● adv abajo

belt /belt/ n cinturón m; (area) zona f. ● vt (fig) rodear; ⊠ darle una paliza a. **~way** n (Amer) carretera f de circunvalación

bench /bentʃ/ n banco m

bend /bend/ n curva f. ● vt (pt & pp bent) doblar; torcer (arm, leg). ● vi doblarse; (road) torcerse. □ **~ down** vi inclinarse □ **~ over** vi agacharse

beneath /bɪ'ni:θ/ prep debajo de; (fig) inferior a. ● adv abajo

beneficial /benɪ'fɪʃl/ adj provechoso

beneficiary /benɪ'fɪʃərɪ/ n beneficiario m

benefit /'benɪfɪt/ n provecho m, ventaja f; (allowance) prestación f; (for unemployed) subsidio m; (perk) beneficio m. ● vt (pt benefited, pres p benefiting) beneficiar. ● vi beneficiarse

benevolent /bə'nevələnt/ adj benévolo

benign /bɪ'naɪn/ adj benigno

bent /bent/ see BEND. ● n inclinación f. ● adj torcido; (⊠, corrupt) corrompido

bereave|d /bɪ'ri:vd/ n. **the ~d** la familia del difunto. **~ment** n pérdida f; (mourning) luto m

beret /'bereɪ/ n boina f

berry /'berɪ/ n baya f

berserk /bə'sɜ:k/ adj. **go ~** volverse loco

berth /bɜ:θ/ n litera f; (anchorage) amarradero m. **give a wide ~ to** evitar. ● vt/i atracar

beside /bɪ'saɪd/ prep al lado de. **be ~ o.s.** estar fuera de sí

besides /bɪ'saɪdz/ prep además de; (except) excepto. ● adv además

besiege /bɪ'si:dʒ/ vt sitiar, asediar; (fig) acosar

best /best/ adj (el) mejor. **the ~ thing is to...** lo mejor es... ● adv mejor. **like ~** preferir. ● n lo mejor; (person) el mejor. **at ~** a lo más. **do one's ~** hacer todo lo posible. **make the ~ of** contentarse con. **~ man** n padrino m (de boda)

bestow /bɪ'stəʊ/ vt conceder

bestseller /best'selə(r)/ n éxito m de librería, bestseller m

bet /bet/ n apuesta f. ● vt/i (pt bet or betted) apostar

betray /bɪ'treɪ/ vt traicionar. **~al** n traición f

better /'betə(r)/ adj & adv mejor. ~ **off** en mejores condiciones; (richer) más rico. **get** ~ mejorar. **all the** ~ tanto mejor. **I'd** ~ **be off** me tengo que ir. **the** ~ **part** of la mayor parte de. ● vt mejorar; (beat) sobrepasar. ~ **o.s.** superarse. ● n superior m. **get the** ~ **of** vencer a. **my** ~**s** mis superiores mpl

between /bɪ'twiːn/ prep entre. ● adv en medio

beverage /'bevərɪdʒ/ n bebida f

beware /bɪ'weə(r)/ vi tener cuidado. ● int ¡cuidado!

bewilder /bɪ'wɪldə(r)/ vt desconcertar. ~**ment** n aturdimiento m

bewitch /bɪ'wɪtʃ/ vt hechizar; (delight) cautivar

beyond /bɪ'jɒnd/ prep más allá de; (fig) fuera de. ~ **doubt** sin lugar a duda. ● adv más allá

bias /'baɪəs/ n tendencia f; (prejudice) prejuicio m. ● vt (pt biased) influir en. ~**ed** adj parcial

bib /bɪb/ n babero m

Bible /'baɪbl/ n Biblia f

biblical /'bɪblɪkl/ adj bíblico

bibliography /bɪblɪ'ɒgrəfɪ/ n bibliografía f

biceps /'baɪseps/ n invar bíceps m

bicker /'bɪkə(r)/ vi altercar

bicycle /'baɪsɪkl/ n bicicleta f

bid /bɪd/ n (offer) oferta f; (attempt) tentativa f. ● vi hacer una oferta. ● vt (pt & pp bid, pres p **bidding**) ofrecer; (pt bid, pp bidden, pres p bidding) mandar; dar (welcome, good day etc). ~**der** n postor m. ~**ding** n (at auction) ofertas fpl; (order) mandato m

bide /baɪd/ vt. ~ **one's time** esperar el momento oportuno

bifocals /baɪ'fəʊklz/ npl gafas fpl

bifocales, anteojos mpl bifocales (LAm)

big /bɪg/ adj (bigger, biggest) grande, (before singular noun) gran. ● adv. **talk** ~ fanfarronear

bigam|ist /'bɪgəmɪst/ n bígamo m. ~**ous** /'bɪgəməs/ adj bígamo. ~**y** n bigamia f

big-headed /-'hedɪd/ adj engreído

bigot /'bɪgət/ n fanático m. ~**ed** adj fanático

bike /baɪk/ n 🔲 bici f 🔲

bikini /bɪ'kiːnɪ/ n (pl -is) bikini m

bile /baɪl/ n bilis f

bilingual /baɪ'lɪŋgwəl/ adj bilingüe

bill /bɪl/ n cuenta f; (invoice) factura f; (notice) cartel m; (Amer, banknote) billete m; (Pol) proyecto m de ley; (of bird) pico m

billet /'bɪlɪt/ n (Mil) alojamiento m. ● vt alojar

billfold /'bɪlfəʊld/ n (Amer) cartera f, billetera f

billiards /'bɪlɪədz/ n billar m

billion /'bɪlɪən/ n billón m; (Amer) mil millones mpl

bin /bɪn/ n recipiente m; (for rubbish) cubo m de basura, bote m de basura (Mex); (for waste paper) papelera f

bind /baɪnd/ vt (pt bound) atar; encuadernar (book); (Jurid) obligar. ● n 🔲 lata f. ~**ing** n (of books) encuadernación f; (braid) ribete m

binge /bɪndʒ/ n 🔲, (of food) comilona f; (of drink) borrachera f. **go on a** ~ ir de juerga

bingo /'bɪŋgəʊ/ n bingo m

binoculars /bɪ'nɒkjʊləz/ npl gemelos mpl

biograph|er /baɪ'ɒgrəfə(r)/ n

biógrafo m. **~y** n biografía f

biolog|ical /baɪə'lɒdʒɪkl/ adj biológico. **~ist** /baɪ'ɒlədʒɪst/ n biólogo m. **~y** /baɪ'ɒlədʒɪ/ n biología f

bioterrorism /baɪəʊ'terərɪzm/ n bioterrorismo m

birch /bɜːtʃ/ n (tree) abedul m

bird /bɜːd/ n ave f; (small) pájaro m; (sl, girl) chica f

Biro /'baɪərəʊ/ n (pl -os) (®) bolígrafo m

birth /bɜːθ/ n nacimiento m. **give ~** dar a luz. **~ certificate** n partida f de nacimiento. **~ control** n control m de la natalidad. **~day** n cumpleaños m. **~mark** n marca f de nacimiento. **~place** n lugar m de nacimiento. **~ rate** n natalidad f

biscuit /'bɪskɪt/ n galleta f

bisect /baɪ'sekt/ vt bisecar

bishop /'bɪʃəp/ n obispo m; (Chess) alfil m

bit /bɪt/ see **BITE**. ●n trozo m; (quantity) poco m; (of horse) bocado m; (Mec) broca f; (Comp) bit m

bitch /bɪtʃ/ n perra f; (fam, woman) bruja f 🔢

bit|e /baɪt/ vt/i (pt bit, pp bitten) morder; (insect) picar. **~e one's nails** morderse las uñas. ●n mordisco m; (mouthful) bocado m; (of insect etc) picadura f. **~ing** /'baɪtɪŋ/ adj mordaz

bitter /'bɪtə(r)/ adj amargo; (of weather) glacial. ●n cerveza f amarga. **~ly** adv amargamente. **it's ~ly cold** hace un frío glacial. **~ness** n amargor m; (resentment) amargura f

bizarre /bɪ'zɑː(r)/ adj extraño

black /blæk/ adj (-er, -est) negro. **~ and blue** amoratado. ●n negro m; (coffee) solo, negro (LAm). ●vt

ennegrecer; limpiar (shoes). **~ out** vi desmayarse. **~ and white** n blanco y negro m. **~-and-white** adj en blanco y negro. **~berry** /-bərɪ/ n zarzamora f. **~bird** n mirlo m. **~board** n pizarra f. **~currant** /-'kʌrənt/ n grosella f negra. **~en** vt ennegrecer. **~ eye** n ojo m morado. **~list** vt poner en la lista negra. **~mail** n chantaje m. ●vt chantajear. **~mailer** n chantajista m & f. **~out** n apagón m; (Med) desmayo m; (of news) censura f. **~smith** n herrero m

bladder /'blædə(r)/ n vejiga f

blade /bleɪd/ n (of knife, sword) hoja f. **~ of grass** brizna f de hierba

blame /bleɪm/ vt echar la culpa a. **be to ~** tener la culpa. ●n culpa f. **~less** adj inocente

bland /blænd/ adj (-er, -est) suave

blank /blæŋk/ adj (page, space) en blanco; (cassette) virgen; (cartridge) sin bala; (fig) vacío. ●n blanco m

blanket /'blæŋkɪt/ n manta f, cobija f (LAm), frazada f (LAm); (fig) capa f. ●vt (pt blanketed) (fig) cubrir (in, with de)

blare /bleə(r)/ vi sonar muy fuerte. ●n estrépito m

blasphem|e /blæs'fiːm/ vt/i blasfemar. **~ous** /'blæsfəməs/ adj blasfemo. **~y** /'blæsfəmɪ/ n blasfemia f

blast /blɑːst/ n explosión f; (gust) ráfaga f; (sound) toque m. ●vt volar. **~ed** adj maldito. **~-off** n despegue m

blatant /'bleɪtnt/ adj patente; (shameless) descarado

blaze /bleɪz/ n llamarada f; (of light) resplandor m; (fig) arranque m. ●vi arder en llamas; (fig) brillar

blazer /'bleɪzə(r)/ n chaqueta f

bleach /bliːtʃ/ n lejía f, cloro m (LAm), blanqueador m (LAm). ● vt blanquear; decolorar (hair).

bleak /bliːk/ adj (-er, -est) desolado; (fig) sombrío

bleat /bliːt/ n balido m. ● vi balar

bleed /bliːd/ vt/i (pt bled /bled/) sangrar

bleep /bliːp/ n pitido m

blemish /'blemɪʃ/ n mancha f

blend /blend/ n mezcla f. ● vt mezclar. ● vi combinarse. **~er** n licuadora f

bless /bles/ vt bendecir. **~ you!** (on sneezing) ¡Jesús!, ¡salud! (Mex). **~ed** /'blesɪd/ adj bendito. **~ing** n bendición f; (advantage) ventaja f

blew /bluː/ see BLOW

blight /blaɪt/ n añublo m, tizón m; (fig) plaga f. ● vt añublar, atizonar; (fig) destrozar

blind /blaɪnd/ adj ciego. **~ alley** callejón m sin salida. ● n persiana f; (fig) pretexto m. ● vt dejar ciego; (dazzle) deslumbrar. **~fold** adj & adv con los ojos vendados. ● n venda f. ● vt vendar los ojos a. **~ly** adv a ciegas. **~ness** n ceguera f

blink /blɪŋk/ vi parpadear; (light) centellear. **~ers** npl (on horse) anteojeras fpl

bliss /blɪs/ n felicidad f. **~ful** adj feliz

blister /'blɪstə(r)/ n ampolla f

blizzard /'blɪzəd/ n ventisca f

bloated /'bləʊtɪd/ adj hinchado (with de)

blob /blɒb/ n (drip) gota f; (stain) mancha f

bloc /blɒk/ n (Pol) bloque m

block /blɒk/ n bloque m; (of wood) zoquete m; (of buildings)

manzana f, cuadra f (LAm). **in ~ letters** en letra de imprenta. **~ of flats** edificio m de apartamentos, casa f de pisos. ● vt bloquear. **~ade** /blɒ'keɪd/ n bloqueo m. ● vt bloquear. **~age** /-ɪdʒ/ n obstrucción f. **~head** n 🛈 zopenco m

bloke /bləʊk/ n 🛈 tipo m, tío m 🛈

blond /blɒnd/ adj & n rubio m, güero (m) (Mex fam). **~e** adj & n rubia (f), güera (f) (Mex fam)

blood /blʌd/ n sangre f. **~bath** n masacre m. **~-curdling** /-kɜːdlɪŋ/adj horripilante. **~hound** n sabueso m. **~ pressure** n tensión f arterial. **high ~ pressure** hipertensión f. **~shed** n derramamiento m de sangre. **~shot** adj sanguinolento; (eye) inyectado de sangre. **~stream** n torrente m sanguíneo. **~thirsty** adj sanguinario. **~y** adj (-ier, -iest) sangriento; (stained) ensangrentado; 🅧 maldito

bloom /bluːm/ n flor f. ● vi florecer

blossom /'blɒsəm/ n flor f. ● vi florecer. **~ (out) into** (fig) llegar a ser

blot /blɒt/ n borrón m. ● vt (pt blotted) manchar; (dry) secar. □ **~ out** vt oscurecer

blotch /blɒtʃ/ n mancha f. **~y** adj lleno de manchas

blotting-paper /'blɒtɪŋ/ n papel m secante

blouse /blaʊz/ n blusa f

blow /bləʊ/ vt (pt blew, pp blown) soplar; fundir (fuse); tocar (trumpet). ● vi soplar; (fuse) fundirse; (sound) sonar. ● n golpe m. □ **~ down** vt derribar. □ **~ out** vt apagar (candle). □ **~ over** vi pasar. □ **~ up** vt inflar; (explode) volar;

(*Photo*) ampliar. ● *vi* (*explode*) estallar; (*burst*) reventar. ~**dry** *vt* secar con secador. ~**lamp** *n* soplete *m*. ~**out** *n* (*of tyre*) reventón *m*. ~ **torch** *n* soplete *m*

blue /blu:/ *adj* (-**er**, -**est**) azul; (*joke*) verde. ● *n* azul *m*. **out of the** ~ totalmente inesperado. ~**s** *npl*. **have the** ~**s** tener tristeza. ~**bell** *n* campanilla *f*. ~**berry** *n* arándano *m*. ~**bottle** *n* moscarda *f*. ~**print** *n* plano *m*; (*fig*, *plan*) programa *m*

bluff /blʌf/ *n* (*poker*) farol *m*, bluff *m* (*LAm*), blof *m* (*Mex*). ● *adj* (*person*) directo, abrupto. ● *vi* tirarse un farol, hacer un bluf (*LAm*), blofear (*Mex*)

blunder /ˈblʌndə(r)/ *vi* cometer un error. ● *n* metedura *f* de pata

blunt /blʌnt/ *adj* desafilado; (*person*) directo, abrupto. ● *vt* desafilar. ~**ly** *adv* francamente

blur /blɜ:(r)/ *n* impresión *f* indistinta. ● *vt* (*pt* **blurred**) hacer borroso

blurb /blɜ:b/ *n* resumen *m* publicitario

blurt /blɜ:t/ *vt*. ~ **out** dejar escapar

blush /blʌʃ/ *vi* ruborizarse. ● *n* rubor *m*

boar /bɔ:(r)/ *n* verraco *m*. **wild** ~ jabalí *m*

board /bɔ:d/ *n* tabla *f*, tablero *m*; (*for notices*) tablón *m* de anuncios, tablero *m* de anuncios (*LAm*); (*blackboard*) pizarra *f*; (*food*) pensión *f*; (*of company*) junta *f*. **full** ~ **and lodging** casa *y* comida. **full** ~ pensión *f* completa. **go by the** ~ ser abandonado. ● *vt* alojar; ~ **a ship** embarcarse. ● *vi* alojarse (**with** en casa de); (*at school*) ser interno. ~**er** *n* huésped *m* & *f*; (*school*) interno *m*. ~**ing card** *n* tarjeta *f* de embarque. ~**ing**

house *n* casa *f* de huéspedes, pensión *f*. ~**ing pass** *n* see ~**ing CARD**. ~**ing school** *n* internado *m*

boast /bəʊst/ *vt* enorgullecerse de. ● *vi* jactarse. ● *n* jactancia *f*. ~**ful** *adj* jactancioso

boat /bəʊt/ *n* barco *m*; (*small*) bote *m*, barca *f*

bob /bɒb/ *vi* (*pt* **bobbed**) menearse, subir y bajar. □ ~ **up** *vi* presentarse súbitamente

bobbin /ˈbɒbɪn/ *n* carrete *m* (*in sewing machine*) canilla *f*, bobina *f*

bobby pin /ˈbɒbɪ/ *n* (*Amer*) horquilla *f*, pasador *m* (*Mex*). ~ **sox** /sɒks/ *npl* (*Amer*) calcetines *mpl* cortos

bobsleigh /ˈbɒbsleɪ/ *n* bob (sleigh) *m*

bode /bəʊd/ *vi*. ~ **well**/**ill** ser de buen/mal agüero

bodice /ˈbɒdɪs/ *n* corpiño *m*

bodily /ˈbɒdɪlɪ/ *adj* físico, corporal. ● *adv* físicamente

body /ˈbɒdɪ/ *n* cuerpo *m*; (*dead*) cadáver *m*. ~**guard** *n* guardaespaldas *m*. ~ **part** *n* pedazo *m* de cuerpo. ~**work** *n* carrocería *f*

bog /bɒg/ *n* ciénaga *f*. □ ~ **down** *vt* (*pt* **bogged**). **get** ~**ged down** empantanarse

boggle /ˈbɒgl/ *vi* sobresaltarse. **the mind** ~**s** uno se queda atónito

bogus /ˈbəʊgəs/ *adj* falso

boil /bɔɪl/ *vt*/*i* hervir. **be** ~**ing hot** estar ardiendo; (*weather*) hacer mucho calor. ● *n* furúnculo *m*. □ ~ **away** *vi* evaporarse. □ ~ **down to** *vt* reducirse a. □ ~ **over** *vi* rebosar. ~**ed** *adj* hervido; (*egg*) pasado por agua. ● *n* **caldera** *f*. ~**er suit** *n* mono *m*, overol *m* (*LAm*)

boisterous /ˈbɔɪstərəs/ *adj* rui-

bold | boss

doso, bullicioso

bold /bəʊld/ adj (**-er, -est**) audaz. **~ly** adv con audacia, audazmente

Bolivia /bə'lɪvɪə/ n Bolivia f. **~n** adj & n boliviano (m)

bolster /'bəʊlstə(r)/ □ **~ up** vt sostener

bolt /bəʊlt/ n (on door) cerrojo m; (for nut) perno m; (lightning) rayo m; (leap) fuga f. ● vt echar el cerrojo a (a door); engullir (food). ● vi fugarse. ● adv. **~ upright** rígido

bomb /bɒm/ n bomba f. ● vt bombardear. **~ard** /bɒm'bɑːd/ vt bombardear **~er** /'bɒmə(r)/ n (plane) bombardero m; (terrorist) terrorista m & f. **~ing** /'bɒmɪŋ/ n bombardeo m. **~shell** n bomba f

bond /bɒnd/ n (agreement) obligación f; (link) lazo m; (Com) bono m. ● vi (stick) adherirse. **~age** /-ɪdʒ/ n esclavitud f

bone /bəʊn/ n hueso m; (of fish) espina f. ● vt deshuesar; quitar las espinas a (fish). **~ idle** adj completamente seco. **~ idle** adj holgazán

bonfire /'bɒnfaɪə(r)/ n hoguera f, fogata f

bonnet /'bɒnɪt/ n gorra f; (Auto) capó m, capote m (Mex)

bonus /'bəʊnəs/ n (payment) bonificación f; (fig) ventaja f

bony /'bəʊnɪ/ adj (**-ier, -iest**) huesudo; (fish) lleno de espinas

boo /buː/ int ¡bu! ● vt/i abuchear

boob /buːb/ n (fam, mistake) metedura f de pata. ● vi 🅱 meter la pata

book /bʊk/ n libro m; (of cheques etc) talonario m, chequera f; (notebook) libreta f; (exercise book) cuaderno m. **~s** (mpl) (Com) cuentas fpl. ● vt (enter) registrar; (reserve) reservar. ● vi reservar. **~case** n bi-

blioteca f, librería f, librero m (Mex). **~ing** n reserva f, reservación f (LAm). **~ing office** n (in theatre) taquilla f, boletería f (LAm). **~keeping** n contabilidad f. **~let** /'bʊklɪt/ n folleto m. **~maker** n corredor m de apuestas. **~mark** n señal f. **~seller** n librero m. **~shop**, (Amer) **~store** n librería f. **~worm** n (fig) ratón m de biblioteca

boom /buːm/ vi retumbar; (fig) prosperar. ● n estampido m, (Com) boom m

boost /buːst/ vt estimular; reforzar (morale). ● n empuje m. **~er** n (Med) revacunación f. **~er cable** n (Amer) cable m de arranque

boot /buːt/ n bota f; (Auto) maletero m, cajuela f (Mex). □ **~ up** vt (Comp) cargar

booth /buːð/ n cabina f; (at fair) puesto m

booze /buːz/ vi 🅱 beber mucho. ● n 🅱 alcohol m

border /'bɔːdə(r)/ n borde m; (frontier) frontera f; (in garden) arriate m. □ **~ on** vt lindar con. **~line** n línea f divisoria. **~line case** n caso m dudoso

bor|e /bɔː(r)/ see BEAR. ● vt (annoy) aburrir; (Tec) taladrar. ● vi taladrar. ● n (person) pelmazo m; (thing) lata f. **~ed** adj aburrido. be **~ed** estar aburrido. get **~ed** aburrirse. **~edom** /'bɔːdəm/ n aburrimiento m. **~ing** adj aburrido, pesado

born /bɔːn/ adj nato. be **~** nacer

borne /bɔːn/ see BEAR

borough /'bʌrə/ n municipio m

borrow /'bɒrəʊ/ vt pedir prestado

boss /bɒs/ n 🅱 jefe m. ● vt. **~ (about)** 🅱 dar órdenes a. **~y** adj mandón

botan|ical /bəˈtænɪkl/ adj botánico. **~ist** /ˈbɒtənɪst/ n botánico m. **~y** /ˈbɒtənɪ/ n botánica f

both /bəʊθ/ adj & pron ambos (mpl), los dos (mpl). ● adv al mismo tiempo, a la vez. **~ Ann and Brian came** tanto Ann como Bob vinieron.

bother /ˈbɒðə(r)/ vt (inconvenience) molestar; (worry) preocupar. **~ it!** ¡caramba! ● vi molestarse. **~ about** preocuparse de. **~ doing** tomarse la molestia de hacer. ● n molestia f

bottle /ˈbɒtl/ n botella, mamila f (Mex); (for baby) biberón m. ● vt embotellar. □ **~ up** vt (fig) reprimir. **~neck** n (traffic jam) embotellamiento m. **~ opener** n abrebotellas m, destapador m (LAm)

bottom /ˈbɒtəm/ n fondo m; (of hill) pie m; (buttocks) trasero m. ● adj de más abajo; (price) más bajo; (lip, edge) inferior. **~less** adj sin fondo

bough /baʊ/ n rama f

bought /bɔːt/ see BUY

boulder /ˈbəʊldə(r)/ n canto m

bounce /baʊns/ vt hacer rebotar. ● vi rebotar; (person) saltar; ⊞ (cheque) ser rechazado. ● n rebote m

bound /baʊnd/ see BIND. ● vi saltar. ● n (jump) salto m. **~s** npl (limits) límites mpl. **out of ~s** zona f prohibida. ● adj. **be ~ for** dirigirse a. **~ to** obligado a; (certain) seguro de

boundary /ˈbaʊndərɪ/ n límite m

bouquet /bʊˈkeɪ/ n ramo m; (of wine) buqué m, aroma m

bout /baʊt/ n período m; (Med) ataque m; (Sport) encuentro m

bow¹ /baʊ/ n (weapon, Mus) arco

m; (knot) lazo m, moño m (LAm)

bow² /baʊ/ n reverencia f; (Naut) proa f. ● vi inclinarse. ● vt inclinar

bowels /ˈbaʊəlz/ npl intestinos mpl; (fig) entrañas fpl

bowl /bəʊl/ n (container) cuenco m; (for washing) palangana f; (ball) bola f. ● vt (cricket) arrojar. ● vi (cricket) arrojar la pelota. □ **~ over** vt derribar

bowl: **~er** n (cricket) lanzador m. **~er (hat)** sombrero m de hongo, bombín m. **~ing** n bolos mpl. **~ing alley** n bolera f

bow tie /bəʊ ˈtaɪ/ n corbata f de lazo, pajarita f

box /bɒks/ n caja f; (for jewels etc) estuche m; (in theatre) palco m. ● vt boxear contra. **~ s.o.'s ears** dar una manotada a uno. ● vi boxear. **~er** n boxeador m. **~ing** n boxeo m. **B~ing Day** n el 26 de diciembre. **~ office** n taquilla f, boletería f (LAm). **~ room** n trastero m

boy /bɔɪ/ n chico m, muchacho m; (young) niño m

boy: **~ band** n grupo m pop de chicos. **~friend** n novio m. **~hood** n niñez f. **~ish** adj de muchacho; (childish) infantil

boycott /ˈbɔɪkɒt/ vt boicotear. ● n boicoteo m

bra /brɑː/ n sostén m, sujetador m, brasier m (Mex)

brace /breɪs/ n abrazadera f. ● vt asegurar. **~ o.s.** prepararse. **~s** npl tirantes mpl; (Amer, dental) aparato(s) m(pl)

bracelet /ˈbreɪslɪt/ n pulsera f

bracken /ˈbrækən/ n helecho m

bracket /ˈbrækɪt/ n soporte m; (group) categoría f; (parenthesis) paréntesis m. **square ~s** corchetes mpl. ● vt poner entre paréntesis;

(*join together*) agrupar

brag /bræg/ vi (pt **bragged**) jactarse (**about** de)

braid /breɪd/ n galón m; (Amer, in hair) trenza f

brain /breɪn/ n cerebro m. ● vt romper la cabeza a. **~child** invento m. **~ drain** n 🄸 fuga f de cerebros. **~storm** n ataque m de locura; (Amer, brainwave) idea f genial. **~wash** vt lavar el cerebro. **~wave** n idea f genial. **~y** adj (**-ier**, **-iest**) inteligente

brake /breɪk/ n freno m. ● vt/i frenar. **~ fluid** n líquido m de freno. **~ lights** npl luces fpl de freno

bramble /ˈbræmbl/ n zarza f

bran /bræn/ n salvado m

branch /brɑːntʃ/ n rama f; (of road) bifurcación f; (Com) sucursal m; (fig) ramo m. **~ off** vi bifurcarse. □**~ out** vi ramificarse

brand /brænd/ n marca f. ● vt marcar; (label) tildar de

brandish /ˈbrændɪʃ/ vt blandir

brand: ~ name n marca f. **~-new** /-ˈnjuː/ adj flamante

brandy /ˈbrændɪ/ n coñac m

brash /bræʃ/ adj descarado

brass /brɑːs/ n latón m. **get down to ~ tacks** (fig) ir al grano. **~ band** n banda f de música

brassière /ˈbræsjeə(r)/ n see BRA

brat /bræt/ n (pej) mocoso m

bravado /brəˈvɑːdəʊ/ n bravata f

brave /breɪv/ adj (**-er, -est**) valiente. ● n (North American Indian) guerrero m indio. **the ~** npl los valientes. ● vt afrontar. **~ry** /-ərɪ/ n valentía f, valor m

brawl /brɔːl/ n alboroto m. ● vi pelearse

brazen /ˈbreɪzn/ adj descarado

Brazil /brəˈzɪl/ n Brasil m. **~ian** /-jən/ adj & n brasileño (m)

breach /briːtʃ/ n infracción f, violación f; (of contract) incumplimiento m; (gap) brecha f. **~ of the peace** alteración f del orden público. ● vt abrir una brecha en

bread /bred/ n pan m. **a loaf of ~** un pan. **~crumbs** npl migajas fpl; (Culin) pan m rallado, pan m molido (Mex)

breadth /bredθ/ n anchura f

breadwinner /ˈbredwɪnə(r)/ n sostén m de la familia

break /breɪk/ vt (pt **broke**, pp **broken**) romper; infringir, violar (law); batir (record); comunicar (news); interrumpir (journey). ● vi romperse; (news) divulgarse. ● n ruptura f; (interval) intervalo m; (fam, chance) oportunidad f; (in weather) cambio m. □**~ away** vi escapar. □**~ down** vt derribar; analizar (figures). vi estropearse, descomponerse (LAm); (Auto) averiarse; (cry) deshacerse en lágrimas. □**~ in** (intruder) entrar (para robar). □**~ into** vt entrar en (para robar) (house etc); (start doing) ponerse a. □**~ off** vi interrumpirse. □**~ out** vi (war, disease) estallar; (run away) escaparse. □**~ up** vi romperse; (band, lovers) separarse; (schools) terminar. **~able** adj frágil. **~age** /-ɪdʒ/ n rotura f. **~down** n (Tec) falla f; (Med) colapso m, crisis f nerviosa; (of figures) análisis f. **~er** n (wave) ola f grande

breakfast /ˈbrekfəst/ n desayuno m. **have ~** vt desayunar

break: ~through n adelanto m. **~water** n rompeolas m

breast /brest/ n pecho m; (of chicken etc) pechuga f. (estilo m)

~**stroke** n braza f, (estilo m) pecho m (LAm)

breath /breθ/ n aliento m, respiración f. **be out of** ~ estar sin aliento. **hold one's** ~ aguantar la respiración. **under one's** ~ a media voz

breath|e /briːð/ vt/i respirar. ~**er** n descanso m, pausa f. ~**ing** n respiración f

breathtaking /ˈbreθteɪkɪŋ/ adj impresionante

bred /bred/ see **BREED**

breed /briːd/ vt (pt **bred**) criar; (fig) engendrar. ● vi reproducirse. ● n raza f

breez|e /briːz/ n brisa f. ~**y** adj de mucho viento

brew /bruː/ vt hacer (beer); preparar (tea). ● vi hacer cerveza; (tea) reposar; (fig) prepararse. ● n infusión f. ~**er** n cervecero m. ~**ery** n cervecería f, fábrica f de cerveza

bribe /braɪb/ n soborno m. ● vt sobornar. ~**ry** /braɪbərɪ/ n soborno m

brick /brɪk/ n ladrillo m. ~**layer** n albañil m

bridal /braɪdl/ adj nupcial

bride /braɪd/ n novia f. ~**groom** n novio m. ~**smaid** /ˈbraɪdzmeɪd/ n dama f de honor

bridge /brɪdʒ/ n puente m; (of nose) caballete m; (Cards) bridge m. ● vt tender un puente sobre. ~ **a gap** llenar un vacío

bridle /braɪdl/ n brida f. ~ **path** n camino m de herradura

brief /briːf/ adj (-er, -est) breve. ● n (Jurid) escrito m. ● vt dar instrucciones a. ~**case** n maletín m, portafolio(s) m (LAm). ~**ly** adv brevemente. ~**s** npl (man's) calzoncillos mpl; (woman's) bragas fpl, calzo-

nes mpl (LAm), pantaletas fpl (Mex)

brigade /brɪˈɡeɪd/ n brigada f

bright /braɪt/ adj (-er, -est) brillante, claro; (clever) listo; (cheerful) alegre. ~**en** vt aclarar; hacer más alegre (house etc). ● vi (weather) aclararse; (face) illuminarse

brillian|ce /ˈbrɪljəns/ n brillantez f, brillo m. ~**t** adj brillante

brim /brɪm/ n borde m; (of hat) ala f. ▫~ **over** vi (pt **brimmed**) desbordarse

brine /braɪn/ n salmuera f

bring /brɪŋ/ vt (pt **brought**) traer; (lead) llevar. ▫~ **about** vt causar. ▫~ **back** vt devolver. ▫~ **down** vt derribar. ▫~ **off** vt lograr. ▫~ **on** vt causar. ▫~ **out** vt sacar; lanzar (product); publicar (book). ▫~ **round/to** vt hacer volver en sí. ▫~ **up** vt (Med) vomitar; educar (children); plantear (question)

brink /brɪŋk/ n borde m

brisk /brɪsk/ adj (-er, -est) enérgico, vivo

bristle /ˈbrɪsl/ n cerda f. ● vi erizarse

Brit|ain /ˈbrɪtən/ n Gran Bretaña f. ~**ish** /ˈbrɪtɪʃ/ adj británico. ● npl **the** ~ los británicos. ~**on** /ˈbrɪtən/ n británico m

Brittany /ˈbrɪtənɪ/ n Bretaña f

brittle /ˈbrɪtl/ adj frágil, quebradizo

broach /brəʊtʃ/ vt abordar

broad /brɔːd/ adj (-er, -est) ancho. **in** ~ **daylight** a plena luz del día. ~ **bean** n haba f. ~**cast** n emisión f. ● vt/i (pt **broadcast**) emitir. ● vi hablar por la radio. ~**caster** n locutor m. ~**casting** n radio-difusión f. ~**en** vt ensanchar. ● vi ensancharse. ~**ly** adv en general. ~**-minded** /-ˈmaɪndɪd/ adj de miras amplias, tolerante

broccoli /'brɒkəlɪ/ n invar brécol m

brochure /'brəʊʃə(r)/ n folleto m

broil /brɔɪl/ vt (Amer) asar a la parrilla. ~**er** n (Amer) parrilla f

broke /brəʊk/ see BREAK. ● adj 🗊 sin blanca, en la ruina

broken /'brəʊkən/ see BREAK. ● adj roto

broker /'brəʊkə(r)/ n corredor m

brolly /'brɒlɪ/ n 🗊 paraguas m

bronchitis /brɒŋ'kaɪtɪs/ n bronquitis f

bronze /brɒnz/ n bronce m. ● adj de bronce

brooch /brəʊtʃ/ n broche m

brood /bruːd/ n cría f; (humorous) prole m. ● vi empollar; (fig) meditar

brook /brʊk/ n arroyo m. ● vt soportar

broom /bruːm/ n escoba f. ~**stick** n palo m de escoba

broth /brɒθ/ n caldo m

brothel /'brɒθl/ n burdel m

brother /'brʌðə(r)/ n hermano m. ~**hood** n fraternidad f. ~**-in-law** (pl ~**s-in-law**) n cuñado m. ~**ly** adj fraternal

brought /brɔːt/ see BRING

brow /braʊ/ n frente f; (of hill) cima f. ~**beat** vt (pt **-beaten**, pp **-beat**) intimidar

brown /braʊn/ adj (**-er**, **-est**) marrón, café (Mex); (hair) castaño; (skin) moreno; (tanned) bronceado. ● n marrón m, café m (Mex). ● vt poner moreno; (Culin) dorar. ~ **bread** n pan m integral. ~ **sugar** n azúcar m moreno, azúcar f morena

browse /braʊz/ vi (in a shop) curiosear; (animal) pacer; (Comp) navegar. ~**r** (Comp) browser m

navegador m

bruise /bruːz/ n magulladura f. ● vt magullar; machucar (fruit)

brunch /brʌntʃ/ n 🗊 desayuno m tardío

brunette /bruː'net/ n morena f

brunt /brʌnt/ n. **bear** o **take the** ~ **of sth** sufrir algo

brush /brʌʃ/ n cepillo m; (large) escoba; (for decorating) brocha f; (artist's) pincel; (skirmish) escaramuza f. ● vt cepillar. □ ~ **against** vt rozar. □ ~ **aside** vt rechazar. □ ~ **off** vt (rebuff) desairar. □ ~ **up (on)** vt refrescar

brusque /bruːsk/ adj brusco. ~**ly** adv bruscamente

Brussels /'brʌslz/ n Bruselas f. ~ **sprout** n col f de Bruselas

brutal /'bruːtl/ adj brutal. ~**ity** /-'tælətɪ/ n brutalidad f. ~**ly** adv brutalmente

brute /bruːt/ n bestia f. ~ **force** n fuerza f bruta

BSc abbr see BACHELOR

BSE abbr (**bovine spongiform encephalopathy**) EBE f

bubble /'bʌbl/ n burbuja f. ● vi burbujear. □ ~ **over** vi desbordarse. ~**ly** adj burbujeante

buck /bʌk/ adj macho. ● n (deer) ciervo m; (Amer fam) dólar m. **pass the** ~ pasar la pelota

bucket /'bʌkɪt/ n balde m, cubo m, cubeta f (Mex)

buckle /'bʌkl/ n hebilla f. ● vt abrochar. ● vi torcerse

bud /bʌd/ n brote m. ● vi (pt **budded**) brotar

Buddhism /'bʊdɪzəm/ n budismo m. ~**t** adj & n budista (m & f)

budding /'bʌdɪŋ/ adj (fig) en ciernes

buddy /'bʌdɪ/ n 🔲 amigo m, cuate m (Mex)

b **budge** /bʌdʒ/ vt mover. ● vi moverse

budgerigar /'bʌdʒərɪgɑː(r)/ n periquito m

budget /'bʌdʒɪt/ n presupuesto m

buffalo /'bʌfələʊ/ n (pl -oes or -o) búfalo m

buffer /'bʌfə(r)/ n parachoques m

buffet[1] /'bʊfeɪ/ n (meal) buffet m; (in train) bar m

buffet[2] /'bʌfɪt/ n golpe m

bug /bʌg/ n bicho m; 🔲 (germ) microbio m; (fam, device) micrófono m oculto. ● vt (pt bugged) 🔲 ocultar un micrófono en; (bother) molestar

buggy /'bʌgɪ/ n. **baby** ~ sillita f de paseo (plegable); (Amer) cochecito m

bugle /'bjuːgl/ n corneta f

build /bɪld/ vt/i (pt built) construir. ● n (of person) figura f, tipo m. □ ~ **up** vt/i fortalecer; (increase) aumentar. ~**er** n (contractor) contratista m & f; (labourer) albañil m. ~**ing** n edificio m; (construction) construcción f. ~**up** n aumento m; (of gas etc) acumulación f

built /bɪlt/ see BUILD. ~-**in** adj empotrado. ~-**up area** n zona f urbanizada

bulb /bʌlb/ n bulbo m; (Elec) bombilla f, foco m (Mex)

Bulgaria /bʌl'geərɪə/ n Bulgaria f. ~**n** adj & n búlgaro (m)

bulge /bʌldʒ/ n protuberancia f. ● vi pandearse. ~**ing** adj abultado; (eyes) saltón

bulk /bʌlk/ n bulto m, volumen m. **in** ~ a granel; (loose) suelto. **the** ~ **of** la mayor parte de. ~**y** adj voluminoso

bull /bʊl/ n toro m. ~**dog** n bulldog m. ~**dozer** /-dəʊzə(r)/ n bulldozer m

bullet /'bʊlɪt/ n bala f

bulletin /'bʊlətɪn/ n anuncio m; (journal) boletín m. ~ **board** n (Amer) tablón m de anuncios, tablero m de anuncios (LAm)

bulletproof /'bʊlɪtpruːf/ adj a prueba de balas

bullfight /'bʊlfaɪt/ n corrida f (de toros). ~**er** n torero m. ~**ing** n (deporte m de) los toros

bull: ~**ring** n plaza f de toros. ~**'s-eye** n diana f. ~**shit** n (vulgar) sandeces fpl 🔲, gillipolleces fpl ✖

bully /'bʊlɪ/ n matón m. ● vt intimidar. ~**ing** n intimidación f

bum /bʌm/ n (fam, backside) trasero m; (Amer fam, tramp) holgazán m

bumblebee /'bʌmblbiː/ n abejorro m

bump /bʌmp/ vt chocar contra. ● vi dar sacudidas. ● n (blow) golpe m; (jolt) sacudida f. □ ~ **into** vt chocar contra; (meet) encontrar

bumper /'bʌmpə(r)/ n parachoques m. adj récord. ~ **edition** n edición f especial

bun /bʌn/ n bollo m; (bread roll) panecillo m, bolillo m (Mex); (hair) moño m, chongo m (Mex)

bunch /bʌntʃ/ n (of people) grupo m; (of bananas, grapes) racimo m; (of flowers) ramo m

bundle /'bʌndl/ n bulto m; (of papers) legajo m. □ ~ **up** vt atar

bungalow /'bʌŋgələʊ/ n casa f de un solo piso

bungle /'bʌŋgl/ vt echar a perder

bunk /bʌŋk/ n litera f

bunker /'bʌŋkə(r)/ n carbonera f;

(*Golf, Mil*) búnker *m*

bunny /'bʌnɪ/ *n* conejito *m*

buoy /bɔɪ/ *n* boya *f*. ◻ **~ up** *vt* hacer flotar; (*fig*) animar

buoyant /'bɔɪənt/ *adj* flotante; (*fig*) optimista

burden /'bɜːdn/ *n* carga *f*. ● *vt* cargar (**with** de)

bureau /'bjʊərəʊ/ *n* (*pl* **-eaux** /-əʊz/) agencia *f*; (*desk*) escritorio *m*; (*Amer, chest of drawers*) cómoda *f*

bureaucra|cy /bjʊə'rɒkrəsɪ/ *n* burocracia *f*. **~t** /'bjʊərəkræt/ *n* burócrata *m & f*. **~tic** /-'krætɪk/ *adj* burocrático

burger /'bɜːɡə(r)/ *n* 🅣 hamburguesa *f*

burgl|ar /'bɜːɡlə(r)/ *n* ladrón *m*. **~ar alarm** *n* alarma *f* antirrobo. **~ary** *n* robo *m* (en casa o edificio). **~e** /'bɜːɡl/ *vt* entrar a robar en. **we were ~ed** nos entraron a robar

burial /'berɪəl/ *n* entierro *m*

burly /'bɜːlɪ/ *adj* (**-ier, -iest**) corpulento

burn /bɜːn/ *vt* (*pt* **burned** or **burnt**) quemar. ● *vi* quemarse. ● *n* quemadura *f*. **~er** *n* quemador *m*. ◻ **~ down** *vt* incendiar. *vi* incendiarse

burnt /bɜːnt/ *see* **BURN**

burp /bɜːp/ *n* 🅣 eructo *m*. ● *vi* 🅣 eructar

burrow /'bʌrəʊ/ *n* madriguera *f*. ● *vt* excavar

burst /bɜːst/ *vt* (*pt* **burst**) reventar. ● *vi* reventarse. **~ into tears** echarse a llorar. **~ out laughing** echarse a reír. ● *n* (*Mil*) ráfaga *f*; (*of activity*) arrebato *m*; (*of applause*) salva *f*

bury /'berɪ/ *vt* enterrar; (*hide*) ocultar

bus /bʌs/ *n* (*pl* **buses**) autobús *m*, camión *m* (*Mex*)

bush /bʊʃ/ *n* arbusto *m*; (*land*) monte *m*. **~y** *adj* espeso

business /'bɪznɪs/ *n* negocio *m*; (*Com*) negocios *mpl*; (*profession*) ocupación *f*; (*fig*) asunto *m*. **mind one's own ~** ocuparse de sus propios asuntos. **~like** *adj* práctico, serio. **~man** /-mən/ *n* hombre de negocios. **~woman** *n* mujer *f* de negocios

busker /'bʌskə(r)/ *n* músico *m* ambulante

bus stop *n* parada *f* de autobús, paradero *m* de autobús (*LAm*)

bust /bʌst/ *n* busto *m*; (*chest*) pecho *m*. ● *vt* (*pt* **busted** or **bust**) 🅣 romper. ● *vi* romperse. ● *adj* roto. **go ~** 🅣 quebrar

bust-up /'bʌstʌp/ *n* 🅣 riña *f*

busy /'bɪzɪ/ *adj* (**-ier, -iest**) ocupado; (*street*) concurrido. **be ~** (*Amer*) (*phone*) estar comunicando, estar ocupado (*LAm*). ● *v.t.* **~ o.s. with** ocuparse de algo. **~body** *n* entrometido *m*

but /bʌt/ *conj* pero; (*after negative*) sino. ● *prep* menos. **~ for** si no fuera por. **last ~ one** penúltimo

butcher /'bʊtʃə(r)/ *n* carnicero *m*. ● *vt* matar; (*fig*) hacer una carnicería con

butler /'bʌtlə(r)/ *n* mayordomo *m*

butt /bʌt/ *n* (*of gun*) culata *f*; (*of cigarette*) colilla *f*; (*target*) blanco *m*; (*Amer fam, backside*) trasero *m*. ● *vi* topar. ◻ **~ in** *vi* interrumpir

butter /'bʌtə(r)/ *n* mantequilla *f*. ● *vt* untar con mantequilla. **~cup** *n* ranúnculo *m*. **~fingers** *n* manazas *m*, torpe *m*. **~fly** *n* mariposa *f*; (*swimming*) estilo *m* mariposa

buttock /'bʌtək/ *n* nalga *f*

button /'bʌtn/ n botón m. • vt
abotonar. • vi abotonarse. ~**hole** n
ojal m. • vt (fig) detener
buy /baɪ/ vt/i (pt **bought**) comprar.
• n compra f. ~**er** n comprador m
buzz /bʌz/ n zumbido m. • vi zumbar. □ ~ **off** vi ☒ largarse. ~**er** n
timbre m
by /baɪ/ prep por; (near) cerca de;
(before) antes de; (according to)
según. ~ **and large** en conjunto,
en general. ~ **car** en coche. ~
oneself por sí solo
bye /baɪ/, **bye-bye** /'baɪbaɪ/ int ①
¡adiós!
by: ~**election** n elección f parcial. ~**law** n reglamento m
(local). ~**pass** n carretera f de circunvalación. • vt eludir; (road) cir-
cunvalar. ~**product** n subpro-
ducto m. ~**stander** /-stændə(r)/
n espectador m
byte /baɪt/ n (Comp) byte m, oc-
teto m

Cc

cab /kæb/ n taxi m; (of lorry, train)
cabina f
cabaret /'kæbəreɪ/ n cabaret m
cabbage /'kæbɪdʒ/ n col f, repollo m
cabin /'kæbɪn/ n (house) cabaña f;
(in ship) camarote m; (in plane) cabina f
cabinet /'kæbɪnɪt/ n (cupboard)
armario m; (for display) vitrina f.
C~ (Pol) gabinete m
cable /'keɪbl/ n cable m. ~ **car** n
teleférico m. ~ **TV** n televisión f

por cable, cablevisión f (LAm)
cackle /'kækl/ n (of hen) cacareo
m; (laugh) risotada f. • vi cacarear;
(laugh) reírse a carcajadas
cactus /'kæktəs/ n (pl -**ti** /-taɪ/ or
-**tuses**) cacto m
caddie, caddy /'kædɪ/ n (golf)
portador m de palos
cadet /kə'det/ n cadete m
cadge /kædʒ/ vt/i gorronear
café /'kæfeɪ/ n cafetería f
cafeteria /kæfɪ'tɪərɪə/ n restaurante m autoservicio
caffeine /'kæfiːn/ n cafeína f
cage /keɪdʒ/ n jaula f. • vt enjaular
cake /keɪk/ n pastel m, tarta f;
(sponge) bizcocho m. ~ **of soap**
pastilla f de jabón
calamity /kə'læmətɪ/ n calami-
dad f
calcium /'kælsɪəm/ n calcio m
calculat|e /'kælkjʊleɪt/ vt/i calcu-
lar. ~**ion** /-'leɪʃn/ n cálculo m. ~**or**
n calculadora f
calculus /'kælkjʊləs/ n (Math) cálculo m
calendar /'kælɪndə(r)/ n calendario m
calf /kɑːf/ n (pl **calves**) (animal)
ternero m; (of leg) pantorrilla f
calibre /'kælɪbə(r)/ n calibre m
call /kɔːl/ vt/i llamar. • n llamada f;
(shout) grito m; (visit) visita f. **be
on** ~ estar de guardia. **long-
distance** ~ llamada f de larga distancia, conferencia f. □ ~ **back** vt
hacer volver; (on phone) volver a
llamar. vi volver; (on phone) volver
a llamar. □ ~ **for** vt pedir; (fetch) ir
a buscar. □ ~ **off** vt suspender.
□ ~ **on** vt pasar a visitar. □ ~ **out**
vi dar voces. □ ~ **together** vt convocar. □ ~ **up** vt (Mil) llamar al servicio militar; (phone) llamar. ~

box n cabina f telefónica. **~ centre** n centro m de llamadas. **~er** n visita f; (*phone*) persona que llama m. **~ing** n vocación f

callous /'kæləs/ adj insensible, cruel

calm /kɑːm/ adj (-er, -est) tranquilo; (sea) en calma. ● n tranquilidad f, calma f. ● vt calmar. ● vi calmarse. **~ down** vi tranquilizarse. vt calmar. **~ly** adv con calma

calorie /'kælərɪ/ n caloría f

calves /kɑːvz/ npl see **CALF**

camcorder /'kæmkɔːdə(r)/ n videocámara f, camcórder m

came /keɪm/ see **COME**

camel /'kæml/ n camello m

camera /'kæmərə/ n cámara f, máquina f fotográfica **~man** /-mən/ n camarógrafo m, cámara m

camouflage /'kæməflɑːʒ/ n camuflaje m. ● vt camuflar

camp /kæmp/ n campamento m. ● vi acampar. **go ~ing** hacer camping

campaign /kæm'peɪn/ n campaña f. ● vi hacer campaña

camp: **~bed** n catre m de tijera. **~er** n campista m & f; (vehicle) cámper m. **~ground** n (Amer) see **~SITE**. **~ing** n camping m. **~site** n camping m

campus /'kæmpəs/ n (pl -puses) campus m, ciudad f universitaria

can¹ /kæn/kən/

negative **can't, cannot** (formal); past **could**

auxiliary verb

····▸ (be able to) poder. I **~'t lift it** no lo puedo levantar. **she**

says she **~ come** dice que puede venir

····▸ (be allowed to) poder. **~ I smoke?** ¿puedo fumar?

····▸ (know how to) saber. **~ you swim?** ¿sabes nadar?

····▸ (with verbs of perception) not translated. I **~'t see you** no te veo. I **~ hear you better now** ahora te oigo mejor

····▸ (in requests) **~ I have a glass of water, please?** ¿me trae un vaso de agua, por favor?. **~ I have a kilo of cheese, please?** ¿me da un kilo de queso, por favor?

····▸ (in offers) **~ I help you?** (in shop) ¿lo/la atienden?

can² /kæn/ n lata f, bote m. ● vt (pt canned) enlatar. **~ned music** música f grabada

Canada /'kænədə/ n (el) Canadá m. **~ian** /kə'neɪdɪən/ adj & n canadiense (m & f)

canal /kə'næl/ n canal m

Canaries /kə'neərɪz/ npl = **CANARY ISLANDS**

canary /kə'neərɪ/ n canario m. **C~ Islands** npl. the **C~ Islands** las Islas Canarias

cancel /'kænsl/ vt (pt cancelled) cancelar; anular (command, cheque); (delete) tachar. **~lation** /-'leɪʃn/ n cancelación f

cancer /'kænsə(r)/ n cáncer m. **C~** n (in astrology) Cáncer m. **~ous** adj canceroso

candid /'kændɪd/ adj franco

candidate /'kændɪdeɪt/ n candidato m

candle /'kændl/ n vela f. **~stick** n candelero m

candour /'kændə(r)/ n franqueza f

candy /'kændɪ/ n (Amer) caramelo m, dulce f (LAm). **~floss** /-flɒs/ n algodón m de azúcar

cane /keɪn/ n caña f; (for baskets) mimbre m; (stick) bastón m; (for punishment) palmeta f. ● vt castigar con palmeta

canister /'kænɪstə(r)/ n bote m

cannabis /'kænəbɪs/ n cáñamo m índico, hachís m, cannabis m

cannibal /'kænɪbl/ n caníbal m. **~ism** n canibalismo m

cannon /'kænən/ n invar cañón m. **~ ball** n bala f de cañón

cannot /'kænɒt/ see CAN¹

canoe /kə'nuː/ n canoa f, piragua f. ● vi ir en canoa

canon /'kænən/ n canon m; (person) canónigo m. **~ize** vt canonizar

can opener n abrelatas m

canopy /'kænəpɪ/ n dosel m

can't /kɑːnt/ see CAN¹

cantankerous /kæn'tæŋkərəs/ adj mal humorado

canteen /kæn'tiːn/ n cantina f; (of cutlery) juego m de cubiertos

canter /'kæntə(r)/ n medio galope m. ● vi ir a medio galope

canvas /'kænvəs/ n lona f; (artist's) lienzo m

canvass /'kænvəs/ vi hacer campaña, solicitar votos. **~ing** n solicitación f (de votos)

canyon /'kænjən/ n cañón m

cap /kæp/ n gorra f; (lid) tapa f; (of cartridge) cápsula f; (of pen) capuchón m. ● vt (pt capped) tapar, poner cápsula a; (outdo) superar

capab|ility /keɪpə'bɪlətɪ/ n capacidad f. **~le** /'keɪpəbl/ adj capaz

capacity /kə'pæsətɪ/ n capacidad

f; (function) calidad f

cape /keɪp/ n (cloak) capa f; (headland) cabo m

capital /'kæpɪtl/ adj capital. **~ letter** mayúscula f. ● n (town) capital f; (money) capital m. **~ism** n capitalismo m. **~ist** adj & n capitalista (m & f.) **~ize** vt capitalizar; escribir con mayúsculas (word). ● vi. **~ize on** aprovechar

capitulat|e /kə'pɪtʃʊleɪt/ vi capitular. **~ion** /-'leɪʃn/ n capitulación f

---

> **Capitol** El Capitolio o sede del Congreso (Congress) de EE.UU., en Washington DC. Situado en Capitol Hill, a menudo la prensa emplea este nombre para hacer referencia al Congreso de EE.UU.   *i*

Capricorn /'kæprɪkɔːn/ n Capricornio m

capsize /kæp'saɪz/ vt hacer volcar. ● vi volcarse

capsule /'kæpsjuːl/ n cápsula f

captain /'kæptɪn/ n capitán m; (of plane) comandante m & f. ● vt capitanear

caption /'kæpʃn/ n (heading) título m; (of cartoon etc) leyenda f

captivate /'kæptɪveɪt/ vt encantar

captiv|e /'kæptɪv/ adj & n cautivo (m). **~ity** /-'tɪvətɪ/ n cautiverio m, cautividad f

capture /'kæptʃə(r)/ vt capturar; atraer (attention); (Mil) tomar. ● n apresamiento m; (Mil) toma f

car /kɑː(r)/ n coche m, carro m (LAm); (Amer, of train) vagón m

caramel /'kærəmel/ n azúcar m quemado; (sweet) caramelo m, dulce m (LAm)

caravan /'kærəvæn/ n caravana f

carbohydrate /kɑ:bəʊ'haɪdreɪt/ n hidrato m de carbono

carbon /'kɑ:bən/ n carbono m; (paper) carbón m. ~ **copy** n copia f al carbón. ~ **dioxide** /daɪ'ɒksaɪd/ n anhídrido m carbónico. ~ **monoxide** /mə'nɒksaɪd/ n monóxido de carbono

carburettor /kɑ:bju'retə(r)/ n carburador m

carcass /'kɑ:kəs/ n cuerpo m de animal muerto; (for meat) res f muerta

card /kɑ:d/ n tarjeta f; (for games) carta f; (membership) carnet m; (records) ficha f. ~**board** n cartón m

cardigan /'kɑ:dɪgən/ n chaqueta f de punto, rebeca f

cardinal /'kɑ:dɪnəl/ adj cardinal. ● n cardenal m

care /keə(r)/ n cuidado m; (worry) preocupación f; (protection) cargo m. ~ **of** a cuidado de, en casa de. take ~ tener cuidado. take ~ of cuidar de (person); ocuparse de (matter). ● vi interesarse. I don't ~ me da igual. □ ~ **about** vt preocuparse por. □ ~ **for** vt cuidar de; (like) querer

career /kə'rɪə(r)/ n carrera f. ● vi correr a toda velocidad

care:: ~**free** adj despreocupado. ~**ful** adj cuidadoso; (cautious) prudente. be ~**ful** tener cuidado. ~**fully** adv con cuidado. ~**less** adj negligente; (not worried) indiferente. ~**lessly** adv descuidadamente. ~**lessness** n descuido m. ~**r** n persona que cuida de un discapacitado

caress /kə'res/ n caricia f. ● vt acariciar

caretaker /'keəteɪkə(r)/ n vigilante m; (of flats etc) portero m

car ferry n transbordador m de coches

cargo /'kɑ:gəʊ/ n (pl -oes) carga f

Caribbean /kærɪ'bi:ən/ adj caribeño. **the** ~ **(Sea)** n el mar Caribe

caricature /'kærɪkətʃʊə(r)/ n caricatura f. ● vt caricaturizar

carnage /'kɑ:nɪdʒ/ n carnicería f, matanza f

carnation /kɑ:'neɪʃn/ n clavel m

carnival /'kɑ:nɪvl/ n carnaval m

carol /'kærəl/ n villancico m

carousel /kærə'sel/ n tiovivo m, carrusel m (LAm); (for baggage) cinta f transportadora

carp /kɑ:p/ n invar carpa f. □ ~ **at** vi quejarse de

car park n aparcamiento m, estacionamiento m

carpent|er /'kɑ:pɪntə(r)/ n carpintero m. ~**ry** /-trɪ/ n carpintería f

carpet /'kɑ:pɪt/ n alfombra f. ~ **sweeper** n cepillo m mecánico

carriage /'kærɪdʒ/ n coche m; (Mec) carro m; (transport) transporte m; (cost, bearing) porte m; (of train) vagón m. ~**way** n calzada f, carretera f

carrier /'kærɪə(r)/ n transportista m & f; (company) empresa f de transportes; (Med) portador m. ~ **bag** n bolsa f

carrot /'kærət/ n zanahoria f

carry /'kærɪ/ vt llevar; transportar (goods); (involve) llevar consigo, implicar. ● vi (sounds) llegar, oírse. □ ~ **off** vt llevarse. □ ~ **on** vi seguir, continuar. □ ~ **out** vt realizar; cumplir (promise, threat). ~ **cot** n cuna f portátil

carsick /'kɑ:sɪk/ adj mareado (por viajar en coche)

cart /kɑːt/ n carro m; (Amer, in supermarket, market) carrito m. • vt acarrear; (fam, carry) llevar

carton /ˈkɑːtən/ n caja f de cartón

cartoon /kɑːˈtuːn/ n caricatura f, chiste m; (strip) historieta f; (film) dibujos mpl animados

cartridge /ˈkɑːtrɪdʒ/ n cartucho m

carve /kɑːv/ vt tallar; trinchar (meat)

cascade /kæsˈkeɪd/ n cascada f. • vi caer en cascadas

case /keɪs/ n caso m; (Jurid) proceso m; (crate) cajón m; (box) caja f; (suitcase) maleta f, petaca f (Mex). in any ~ en todo caso. in ~ he comes por si viene. in ~ of en caso de

cash /kæʃ/ n dinero m efectivo. pay (in) ~ pagar al contado. • vt cobrar. ~ in (on) aprovecharse de. ~ desk n caja f. ~ dispenser n cajero m automático

cashier /kæˈʃɪə(r)/ n cajero m

cashpoint /ˈkæʃpɔɪnt/ n cajero m automático

casino /kəˈsiːnəʊ/ n (pl -os) casino m

cask /kɑːsk/ n barril m

casket /ˈkɑːskɪt/ n cajita f; (Amer) ataúd m, cajón m (LAm)

casserole /ˈkæsərəʊl/ n cacerola f; (stew) guiso m, guisado m (Mex)

cassette /kæˈset/ n cassette m & f

cast /kɑːst/ vt (pt cast) arrojar; fundir (metal); emitir (vote). • n lanzamiento m; (in play) reparto m; (mould) molde m

castanets /kæstəˈnets/ npl castañuelas fpl

castaway /ˈkɑːstəweɪ/ n náufrago m

caster /ˈkɑːstə(r)/ n ruedecita f. ~

sugar n azúcar m extrafino

Castille /kæˈstiːl/ n Castilla f. ~ian /kæˈstɪlɪən/ adj & n castellano (m)

cast: ~ **iron** n hierro m fundido. ~-**iron** adj (fig) sólido

castle /ˈkɑːsl/ n castillo m; (Chess) torre f

cast-offs /ˈkɑːstɒfs/ npl desechos mpl

castrat|e /kæˈstreɪt/ vt castrar. ~ion /-ʃn/ n castración f

casual /ˈkæʒʊəl/ adj casual; (meeting) fortuito; (work) ocasional; (attitude) despreocupado; (clothes) informal, de sport. ~ly adv de paso

casualt|y /ˈkæʒʊəltɪ/ n (injured) herido m; (dead) víctima f; (in hospital) urgencias fpl. ~ies fpl (Mil) bajas fpl

cat /kæt/ n gato m

Catalan /ˈkætəlæn/ adj & n catalán (m)

catalogue /ˈkætəlɒg/ n catálogo m. • vt catalogar

Catalonia /kætəˈləʊnɪə/ n Cataluña f

catalyst /ˈkætəlɪst/ n catalizador m

catamaran /kætəməˈræn/ n catamarán m

catapult /ˈkætəpʌlt/ n catapulta f; (child's) tirachinas f, resortera f (Mex)

catarrh /kəˈtɑː(r)/ n catarro m

catastroph|e /kəˈtæstrəfi/ n catástrofe m. ~ic /kætəˈstrɒfɪk/ adj catastrófico

catch /kætʃ/ vt (pt caught) coger (esp Spain), agarrar; tomar (train, bus); (unawares) sorprender, pillar; (understand) entender; contagiarse de (disease). ~ **a cold** resfriarse.

~ sight of avistar. ● *vi* (*get stuck*) engancharse; (*fire*) prenderse. ● *n* (*by goalkeeper*) parada *f*; (*of fish*) pesca *f*; (*on door*) pestillo *m*; (*on window*) cerradura *f*. □ **~ on** *vi* 𝐈 hacerse popular. □ **~ up** *vi* poner al día. **~ up with** alcanzar; ponerse al corriente de (*news* etc.). **~ing** *adj* contagioso. **~phrase** *n* eslogan *m*. **~y** *adj* pegadizo

categor|ical /'kætɪ'gɒrɪkl/ *adj* categórico. **~y** /'kætɪgərɪ/ *n* categoría *f*

cater /'keɪtə(r)/ *vi* encargarse del servicio de comida. **~ for** proveer a (*needs*). **~er** *n* proveedor *m*

caterpillar /'kætəpɪlə(r)/ *n* oruga *f*, azotador *m* (*Mex*)

cathedral /kə'θiːdrəl/ *n* catedral *f*

catholic /'kæθəlɪk/ *adj* universal. **C~** *adj* & *n* católico (*m*). **C~ism** /kə'θɒlɪsɪzəm/ *n* catolicismo *m*

cat: **~nap** *n* sueñecito *m*. **C~seyes** *npl* (®) catafaros *mpl*

cattle /'kætl/ *npl* ganado *m*

catwalk *n* pasarela *f*

Caucasian /kɔː'keɪʒən/ *n*. **a male ~** (*Amer*) un hombre de raza blanca

caught /kɔːt/ *see* CATCH

cauliflower /'kɒlɪflaʊə/ *n* coliflor *f*

cause /kɔːz/ *n* causa *f*, motivo *m*. ● *vt* causar

cautio|n /'kɔːʃn/ *n* cautela *f*; (*warning*) advertencia *f*. ● *vt* advertir; (*Jurid*) amonestar. **~us** /-ʃəs/ *adj* cauteloso, prudente

cavalry /'kævəlrɪ/ *n* caballería *f*

cave /keɪv/ *n* cueva *f*. □ **~ in** *vi* hundirse. **~man** *n* troglodita *m*

cavern /'kævən/ *n* caverna *f*

caviare /'kævɪɑː(r)/ *n* caviar *m*

cavity /'kævətɪ/ *n* cavidad *f*; (*in*

tooth) caries *f*

CCTV *abbr* (**closed circuit television**) CCTV *n*

CD *abbr* (= **compact disc**) CD *m*. **~ player** (reproductor *m* de) compact-disc *m*. **~-ROM** *n* CD-ROM *m*

cease /siːs/ *vt/i* cesar. **~-fire** *n* alto *m* el fuego

cedar /'siːdə(r)/ *n* cedro *m*

ceiling /'siːlɪŋ/ *n* techo *m*

celebrat|e /'selɪbreɪt/ *vt* celebrar. ● *vi* divertirse. **~ed** *adj* célebre. **~ion** /-'breɪ̃n/ *n* celebración *f*; (*party*) fiesta *f*

celebrity /sɪ'lebrətɪ/ *n* celebridad *f*

celery /'selərɪ/ *n* apio *m*

cell /sel/ *n* celda *f*; (*in plants, electricity*) célula *f*

cellar /'selə(r)/ *n* sótano *m*; (*for wine*) bodega *f*

cello /'tʃeləʊ/ *n* (*pl* **-os**) violonc(h)elo *m*, chelo *m*

Cellophane /'seləfeɪn/ *n* (®) celofán *m* (®)

cellphone /'selfəʊn/ *n* celular *m* (*LAm*), móvil *m* (*Esp*)

cellul|ar /'seljʊlə(r)/ *adj* celular. **~phone** *n* teléfono celular *m* (*LAm*), teléfono móvil *m* (*Esp*). **~oid** *n* celuloide *m*

Celsius /'selsɪəs/ *adj*. **20 degrees ~** 20 grados centígrados or Celsio(s)

cement /sɪ'ment/ *n* cemento *m*. ● *vt* cementar

cemetery /'semɪtrɪ/ *n* cementerio *m*

cens|or /'sensə(r)/ *n* censor *m*. ● *vt* censurar. **~ship** *n* censura *f*. **~ure** /'senʃə(r)/ *vt* censurar

census /'sensəs/ *n* censo *m*

cent /sent/ n ($) centavo m; (€) céntimo m

centenary /sen'tiːnərɪ/ n centenario m

centigrade /'sentɪɡreɪd/ adj centígrado. **~litre** n centilitro m. **~metre** n centímetro m. **~pede** /-piːd/ n ciempiés m

central /'sentrəl/ adj central; (of town) céntrico. **~ heating** n calefacción f central. **~ize** vt centralizar

centre /'sentə(r)/ n centro m. ● vt (pt **centred**) centrar. ● vi centrarse (on en)

century /'sentʃərɪ/ n siglo m

cereal /'sɪərɪəl/ n cereal m

ceremonial /serɪ'məʊnɪəl/ adj & n ceremonial (m). **~y** /'serɪmənɪ/ n ceremonia f

certain /'sɜːtn/ adj cierto. for **~** seguro. make **~** of asegurarse de. **~ly** adv desde luego

certificate /sə'tɪfɪkət/ n certificado m; (of birth, death etc) partida f

certify /'sɜːtɪfaɪ/ vt certificar

chafe /tʃeɪf/ vt rozar. ● vi rozarse

chaffinch /'tʃæfɪntʃ/ n pinzón m

chagrin /'ʃæɡrɪn/ n disgusto m

chain /tʃeɪn/ n cadena f. ● vt encadenar. **~ reaction** n reacción f en cadena. **~-smoker** n fumador m que siempre tiene un cigarrillo encendido. **~ store** n tienda f de una cadena

chair /tʃeə(r)/ n silla f; (Univ) cátedra f. ● vt presidir. **~-lift** n telesquí m, telesilla m (LAm). **~man** /-mən/ n presidente m

chalet /'ʃæleɪ/ n chalé m

chalk /tʃɔːk/ n (in geology) creta f; (stick) tiza f, gis m (Mex)

challenge /'tʃælɪndʒ/ n desafío

m; (fig) reto m. ● vt desafiar; (question) poner en duda. **~ing** adj estimulante

chamber /'tʃeɪmbə(r)/ n (old use) cámara f. **~maid** n camarera f. **~ pot** n orinal m

champagne /ʃæm'peɪn/ n champaña m, champán m

champion /'tʃæmpɪən/ n campeón m. ● vt defender. **~ship** n campeonato m

chance /tʃɑːns/ n casualidad f; (likelihood) posibilidad f; (opportunity) oportunidad f; (risk) riesgo m. by **~** por casualidad. ● adj fortuito

chancellor /'tʃɑːnsələ(r)/ n canciller m; (Univ) rector m. C**~ of the Exchequer** Ministro m de Hacienda

chandelier /ʃændə'lɪə(r)/ n araña f (de luces)

change /tʃeɪndʒ/ vt cambiar; (substitute) reemplazar. **~ one's mind** cambiar de idea. ● vi cambiarse. ● n cambio m; (coins) cambio m, sencillo m (LAm), feria f (Mex); (money returned) cambio m, vuelta f, vuelto m (LAm). **~able** adj cambiable; (weather) variable. **~ing room** n (Sport) vestuario m, vestidor m (Mex); (in shop) probador m

channel /'tʃænl/ n canal m; (fig) medio m. ● vt (pt **channelled**) acanalar; (fig) encauzar. **the (English) C~** el Canal de la Mancha. C**~ Islands** npl. las islas Anglonormandas. C**~ Tunnel** n. the C**~ Tunnel** el Eurotúnel

chant /tʃɑːnt/ n canto m. ● vt/i cantar

chaos /'keɪɒs/ n caos m. **~tic** /-'ɒtɪk/ adj caótico

chap /tʃæp/ n 🔢 tipo m, tío m 🔢. ● vt (pt **chapped**) agrietar. ● vi agrietarse

chapel /'tʃæpl/ n capilla f

chaperon /'ʃæpərəʊn/ n acompañante f

chapter /'tʃæptə(r)/ n capítulo m

char /tʃɑː(r)/ vt (pt charred) carbonizar

character /'kærəktə(r)/ n carácter m; (in book, play) personaje m. **in ~** característico. **~istic** /-'rɪstɪk/ adj típico. ● n característica f. **~ize** vt caracterizar

charade /ʃə'rɑːd/ n farsa f. **~s** npl (game) charada f

charcoal /'tʃɑːkəʊl/ n carbón m vegetal; (for drawing) carboncillo m

charge /tʃɑːdʒ/ n precio m; (Elec, Mil) carga f; (Jurid) acusación f; (task, custody) encargo m; (responsibility) responsabilidad f. **in ~ of** responsable de, encargado de. **the person in ~** la persona responsable. **take ~ of** encargarse de. ● vt pedir; (Elec, Mil) cargar; (Jurid) acusar. ● vi cargar; (animal) embestir (at contra)

charit|able /'tʃærɪtəbl/ adj caritativo. **~y** /'tʃærɪtɪ/ n caridad f; (society) institución f benéfica

charm /tʃɑːm/ n encanto m; (spell) hechizo m; (on bracelet) dije m, amuleto m. ● vt encantar. **~ing** adj encantador

chart /tʃɑːt/ n (for navigation) carta f de navegación; (table) tabla f

charter /'tʃɑːtə(r)/ n carta f. ● vt alquilar (bus, train); fletar (plane, ship). **~ flight** n vuelo m chárter

chase /tʃeɪs/ vt perseguir. ● vi correr (after tras). ● n persecución f. **□ ~ away, ~ off** vt ahuyentar

chassis /'ʃæsɪ/ n chasis m

chastise /tʃæs'taɪz/ vt castigar

chastity /'tʃæstɪtɪ/ n castidad f

chat /tʃæt/ n charla f, conversación f (LAm), plática f (Mex). ● vi (pt chatted) charlar, conversar (LAm), platicar (Mex)

chatter /'tʃætə(r)/ n charla f. ● vi charlar. **his teeth are ~ing** le castañetean los dientes. **~box** n parlanchín m

chauffeur /'ʃəʊfə(r)/ n chófer m

chauvinis|m /'ʃəʊvɪnɪzəm/ n patriotería f; (male) machismo m. **~t** n patriotero m; (male) machista m

cheap /tʃiːp/ adj (-er, -est) barato; (poor quality) de baja calidad; (rate) económico. **~(ly)** adv barato, a bajo precio

cheat /tʃiːt/ vt defraudar; (deceive) engañar. ● vi (at cards) hacer trampas. ● n trampa f; (person) tramposo m

check /tʃek/ vt comprobar; (examine) inspeccionar; (curb) frenar. ● vi comprobar. n comprobación f; (of tickets) control m; (curb) freno m; (Chess) jaque m; (pattern) cuadro m; (Amer, bill) cuenta f; (Amer, cheque) cheque m. **□ ~ in** vi registrarse; (at airport) facturar el equipaje, chequear el equipaje (LAm), registrar el equipaje (Mex). **□ ~ out** vi pagar la cuenta y marcharse. **□ ~ up** vi confirmar. **□ ~ up on** vt investigar. **~book** n (Amer) see CHEQUEBOOK. **~ered** /'tʃekəd/ adj (Amer) see CHEQUERED

checkers /'tʃekəz/ n (Amer) damas fpl

check: **~mate** n jaque m mate. ● vt dar mate a. **~out** n caja f. **~point** control m. **~up** n chequeo m, revisión f

cheek /tʃiːk/ n mejilla f; (fig) descaro m. **~bone** n pómulo m. **~y** adj descarado

cheep /tʃiːp/ vi piar

cheer /tʃɪə(r)/ n alegría f; (applause) viva m. **~s!** ¡salud!• vt alegrar; (applause) aplaudir. • vi alegrarse; (applause) aplaudir. **~ up!** ¡anímate! **~ful** adj alegre

cheerio /tʃɪərɪˈəʊ/ int ¡adiós!, ¡hasta luego!

cheerless /ˈtʃɪəlɪs/ adj triste

cheese /tʃiːz/ n queso m

cheetah /ˈtʃiːtə/ n guepardo m

chef /ʃef/ n jefe m de cocina

chemical /ˈkemɪkl/ adj químico. • n producto m químico

chemist /ˈkemɪst/ n farmacéutico m; (scientist) químico m. **~ry** n química f. **~'s (shop)** n farmacia f

cheque /tʃek/ n cheque m, talón m. **~book** n chequera f, talonario m

cherish /ˈtʃerɪʃ/ vt cuidar; (love) querer; abrigar (hope)

cherry /ˈtʃerɪ/ n cereza f. **~ tree** n cerezo m

chess /tʃes/ n ajedrez m. **~board** n tablero m de ajedrez

chest /tʃest/ n pecho m; (box) cofre m, cajón m

chestnut /ˈtʃesnʌt/ n castaña f. • adj castaño. **~ tree** n castaño m

chest of drawers n cómoda f

chew /tʃuː/ vt masticar. **~ing gum** n chicle m

chic /ʃiːk/ adj elegante

chick /tʃɪk/ n polluelo m. **~en** /ˈtʃɪkɪn/ n pollo m. • adj 🔲 cobarde. □ **~en out** vi 🔲 acobardarse. **~enpox** /ˈtʃɪkɪnpɒks/ n varicela f. **~pea** n garbanzo m

chicory /ˈtʃɪkərɪ/ n (in coffee) achicoria f; (in salad) escarola f

chief /tʃiːf/ n jefe m. • adj principal. **~ly** adv principalmente

chilblain /ˈtʃɪlbleɪn/ n sabañón m

child /tʃaɪld/ n (pl children /ˈtʃɪldrən/) niño m; (offspring) hijo m. **~birth** n parto m. **~hood** n niñez f. **~ish** adj infantil. **~less** adj sin hijos. **~like** adj ingenuo, de niño

Chile /ˈtʃɪlɪ/ n Chile m. **~an** adj & n chileno (m)

chill /tʃɪl/ n frío m; (illness) resfriado m. • adj frío. • vt enfriar; refrigerar (food)

chilli /ˈtʃɪlɪ/ n (pl -ies) chile m

chilly /ˈtʃɪlɪ/ adj frío

chime /tʃaɪm/ n carillón m. • vt tocar (bells); dar (hours). • vi repicar

chimney /ˈtʃɪmnɪ/ n (pl -eys) chimenea f. **~ sweep** n deshollinador m

chimpanzee /tʃɪmpænˈziː/ n chimpancé m

chin /tʃɪn/ n barbilla f

china /ˈtʃaɪnə/ n porcelana f

Chin|a /ˈtʃaɪnə/ n China f. **~ese** /-ˈniːz/ adj & n chino (m)

chink /tʃɪŋk/ n (crack) grieta f; (sound) tintín m. • vi tintinear

chip /tʃɪp/ n pedacito m; (splinter) astilla f; (Culin) patata f frita, papa f frita (LAm); (in gambling) ficha f; (Comp) chip m. **have a ~ on one's shoulder** guardar rencor. • vt (pt chipped) desportillar. □ **~ in** vi 🔲 interrumpir; (with money) contribuir

chiropodist /kɪˈrɒpədɪst/ n callista m & f, pedicuro m

chirp /tʃɜːp/ n pío m. • vi piar. **~y** adj alegre

chisel /ˈtʃɪzl/ n formón m. • vt (pt chiselled) cincelar

chivalr|ous /ˈʃɪvəlrəs/ adj caballeroso. **~y** /-rɪ/ n caballerosidad f

chlorine /ˈklɔːriːn/ n cloro m

chock /tʃɒk/ n cuña f. ~**-block** adj, ~**-full** adj atestado

chocolate /'tʃɒklət/ n chocolate m; (individual sweet) bombón m, chocolate m (LAm)

choice /tʃɔɪs/ n elección f; (preference) preferencia f. • adj escogido

choir /'kwaɪə(r)/ n coro m

choke /tʃəʊk/ vt sofocar. • vi sofocarse. • n (Auto) choke m, estárter m, ahogador m (Mex)

cholera /'kɒlərə/ n cólera m

cholesterol /kə'lestərɒl/ n colesterol m

choose /tʃuːz/ vt/i (pt chose, pp chosen) elegir, escoger. ~**y** adj 🅘 exigente

chop /tʃɒp/ vt (pt chopped) cortar. • n (Culin) chuleta f. □ ~ **down** vt talar. □ ~ **off** vt cortar. ~**per** n hacha f; (butcher's) cuchilla f. ~**py** adj picado

chord /kɔːd/ n (Mus) acorde m

chore /tʃɔː(r)/ n tarea f, faena f. **household** ~**s** npl quehaceres mpl domésticos

chorus /'kɔːrəs/ n coro m; (of song) estribillo m

chose/tʃəʊz/, **chosen** /'tʃəʊzn/ see CHOOSE

Christ /kraɪst/ n Cristo m

christen /'krɪsn/ vt bautizar. ~**ing** n bautizo m

Christian /'krɪstjən/ adj & n cristiano (m). ~**ity** /krɪstɪ'ænətɪ/ n cristianismo m. ~ **name** n nombre m de pila

Christmas /'krɪsməs/ n Navidad f. Merry ~**!** ¡Feliz Navidad!, ¡Felices Pascuas! **Father** ~ n Papá m Noel. • adj de Navidad, navideño. ~ **card** n tarjeta f de Navidad f. ~ **day** n día m de Navidad. ~ **Eve** n Nochebuena f. ~ **tree** n árbol m de Navidad

chrome /krəʊm/ n cromo m. ~**ium** /'krəʊmɪəm/ n cromo m

chromosome /'krəʊməsəʊm/ n cromosoma m

chronic /'krɒnɪk/ adj crónico; (fam, bad) terrible

chronicle /'krɒnɪkl/ n crónica f. • vt historiar

chronological /krɒnə'lɒdʒɪkl/ adj cronológico

chubby /'tʃʌbɪ/ adj (-ier, -iest) regordete; (person) gordinflón 🅘

chuck /tʃʌk/ vt tirar. □ ~ **out** vt tirar

chuckle /'tʃʌkl/ n risa f ahogada. • vi reírse entre dientes

chug /tʃʌg/ vi (pt chugged) (of motor) traquetear

chum /tʃʌm/ n amigo m, compinche m, cuate m (Mex)

chunk /tʃʌŋk/ n trozo m grueso. ~**y** adj macizo

church /tʃɜːtʃ/ n iglesia f. ~**yard** n cementerio m

churn /tʃɜːn/ n (for milk) lechera f, cántara f; (for making butter) mantequera f. • vt agitar. □ ~ **out** vt producir en profusión

chute /ʃuːt/ n tobogán m

cider /'saɪdə(r)/ n sidra f

cigar /sɪ'gɑː(r)/ n puro m

cigarette /sɪgə'ret/ n cigarrillo m. ~ **end** n colilla f. ~ **holder** n boquilla f. ~ **lighter** n mechero m, encendedor m

cinecamera /'sɪnɪkæmərə/ n tomavistas m, filmadora f (LAm)

cinema /'sɪnəmə/ n cine m

cipher /'saɪfə(r)/ n (Math, fig) cero m; (code) clave f

circle /'sɜːkl/ n círculo m; (in theatre) anfiteatro m. • vt girar alrededor de. • *vi* dar vueltas

circuit /'sɜːkɪt/ *n* circuito *m*

circular /'sɜːkjʊlə(r)/ *adj & n* circular (*f*)

circulat|e /'sɜːkjʊleɪt/ *vt* hacer circular. • *vi* circular. **~ion** /-'leɪʃn/ *n* circulación *f*; (*number of copies*) tirada *f*

circumcise /'sɜːkəmsaɪz/ *vt* circuncidar

circumference /sə'kʌmfərəns/ *n* circunferencia *f*

circumstance /'sɜːkəmstəns/ *n* circunstancia *f*. **~s** (*means*) *npl* situación *f* económica

circus /'sɜːkəs/ *n* circo *m*

cistern /'sɪstən/ *n* cisterna *f*

cite /saɪt/ *vt* citar

citizen /'sɪtɪzn/ *n* ciudadano *m*; (*inhabitant*) habitante *m & f*

citrus /'sɪtrəs/ *n*. **~ fruits** cítricos *mpl*

city /'sɪtɪ/ *n* ciudad *f*; **the C~** el centro *m* financiero de Londres

City - the Área ubicada dentro de los límites de la antigua ciudad de Londres. Actualmente es el centro financiero de la capital donde tienen sus sedes centrales muchas instituciones financieras. A menudo, cuando se habla de *The City*, se está refiriendo a ésas y no a la zona propiamente dicha.

civic /'sɪvɪk/ *adj* cívico

civil /'sɪvl/ *adj* civil; (*polite*) cortés

civilian /sɪ'vɪlɪən/ *adj & n* civil (*m & f*)

civiliz|ation /sɪvɪlaɪ'zeɪʃn/ *n* civilización *f*. **~ed** /'sɪvəlaɪzd/ *adj* civilizado.

civil: ~ servant *n* funcionario *m*

(del Estado), burócrata *m & f* (Mex). **~ service** *n* administración *f* pública. **~ war** *n* guerra *f* civil

clad /klæd/ *see* CLOTHE

claim /kleɪm/ *vt* reclamar; (*assert*) pretender. • *n* reclamación *f*; (*right*) derecho *m*; (*Jurid*) demanda *f*

clairvoyant /kleə'vɔɪənt/ *n* clarividente *m & f*

clam /klæm/ *n* almeja *f*. • *vi* (*pt* clammed). **~ up** 🄸 ponerse muy poco comunicativo

clamber /'klæmbə(r)/ *vi* trepar a gatas

clammy /'klæmɪ/ *adj* (-ier, -iest) húmedo

clamour /'klæmə(r)/ *n* clamor *m*. • *vi*. **~ for** pedir a gritos

clamp /klæmp/ *n* abrazadera *f*; (*Auto*) cepo *m*. • *vt* sujetar con abrazadera; poner cepo a (car). □ **~ down on** *vt* reprimir

clan /klæn/ *n* clan *m*

clang /klæŋ/ *n* sonido *m* metálico

clap /klæp/ *vt* (*pt* clapped) aplaudir; batir (hands). • *vi* aplaudir. • *n* palmada *f*; (*of thunder*) trueno *m*

clarif|ication /klærɪfɪ'keɪʃn/ *n* aclaración *f*. **~y** /'klærɪfaɪ/ *vt* aclarar. • *vi* aclararse

clarinet /klærɪ'net/ *n* clarinete *m*

clarity /'klærətɪ/ *n* claridad *f*

clash /klæʃ/ *n* choque *m*; (*noise*) estruendo *m*; (*contrast*) contraste *m*; (*fig*) conflicto *m*. • *vt* golpear. • *vi* encontrarse; (colours) desentonar

clasp /klɑːsp/ *n* cierre *m*. • *vt* agarrar; apretar (hand)

class /klɑːs/ *n* clase *f*. **evening ~** *n* clase nocturna. • *vt* clasificar

classic /'klæsɪk/ *adj & n* clásico (*m*). **~al** *adj* clásico. **~s** *npl* estudios *mpl* clásicos

classif|ication /ˌklæsɪfɪˈkeɪʃn/ n clasificación f. **~y** /ˈklæsɪfaɪ/ vt clasificar

class /klɑːs/ **~room** n aula f, clase f. **~y** adj 🔢 elegante

clatter /ˈklætə(r)/ n ruido m; (of train) traqueteo m. ● vi hacer ruido

clause /klɔːz/ n cláusula f; (Gram) oración f

claustrophobia /ˌklɔːstrəˈfəʊbɪə/ n claustrofobia f

claw /klɔː/ n garra f; (of cat) uña f; (of crab) pinza f. ● vt arañar

clay /kleɪ/ n arcilla f

clean /kliːn/ adj (-er, -est) limpio; (stroke) bien definido. ● adv completamente. ● vt limpiar. ● vi limpiar. ◻ **~ up** vt hacer la limpieza. **~er** n persona f que hace la limpieza. **~liness** /ˈklenlɪnɪs/ n limpieza f

cleans|e /klenz/ vt limpiar. **~er** n producto m de limpieza; (for skin) crema f de limpieza. **~ing cream** n crema f de limpieza

clear /klɪə(r)/ adj (-er, -est) claro; (transparent) transparente; (without obstacles) libre; (profit) neto; (sky) despejado. **keep ~ of** evitar. ● adv claramente. ● vt despejar; liquidar (goods); (Jurid) absolver; (jump over) saltar por encima de; quitar, levantar (LAm) (table). ◻ **~ off** vi 🔢, **~ out** vi (🔢, go away) largarse. ◻ **~ up** vt (tidy) ordenar; aclarar (mystery). ● vi (weather) despejarse. **~ance** n (removal of obstructions) despeje m; (authorization) permiso m; (by security) acreditación f. **~ing** n claro m. **~ly** adv evidentemente. **~way** n carretera f en la que no se permite parar

cleavage /ˈkliːvɪdʒ/ n escote m

clef /klef/ n (Mus) clave f

clench /klentʃ/ vt apretar

clergy /ˈklɜːdʒɪ/ n clero m. **~man** /-mən/ n clérigo m

cleric /ˈklerɪk/ n clérigo m. **~al** adj clerical; (of clerks) de oficina

clerk /klɑːk/ n empleado m; (Amer, salesclerk) vendedor m

clever /ˈklevə(r)/ adj (-er, -est) inteligente; (skilful) hábil. **~ly** adv inteligentemente; (with skill) hábilmente. **~ness** n inteligencia f

cliché /ˈkliːʃeɪ/ n lugar m común m, cliché m

click /klɪk/ n golpecito m. ● vi chascar; 🔢 llevarse bien. **~ on sth** hacer clic en algo. ● vt chasquear

client /ˈklaɪənt/ n cliente m

cliff /klɪf/ n acantilado m

climat|e /ˈklaɪmət/ n clima m. **~ic** /-ˈmætɪk/ adj climático

climax /ˈklaɪmæks/ n clímax m; (orgasm) orgasmo m

climb /klaɪm/ vt subir (stairs); trepar (tree); escalar (mountain). ● vi subir. ● n subida f. ◻ **~ down** vi bajar; (fig) ceder. **~er** n (Sport) alpinista m & f, andinista m & f (LAm); (plant) trepadora f

clinch /klɪntʃ/ vt cerrar (deal)

cling /klɪŋ/ vi (pt clung) agarrarse; (stick) pegarse

clinic /ˈklɪnɪk/ n centro m médico; (private hospital) clínica f. **~al** adj clínico

clink /klɪŋk/ n tintineo m. ● vt hacer tintinear. ● vi tintinear

clip /klɪp/ n (fastener) clip m; (for paper) sujetapapeles m; (for hair) horquilla f. ● vt (pt clipped) (cut) cortar; (join) sujetar. **~pers** /ˈklɪpəz/ npl (for hair) maquinilla f para cortar el pelo; (for nails) cortauñas m. ~**ping** n recorte m

cloak /kləuk/ n capa f. ~**room** n guardarropa m; (toilet) lavabo m, baño m (LAm)

clock /klɒk/ n reloj m. ~**wise** a/adv en el sentido de las agujas del reloj. ~**work** n mecanismo m de relojería. like ~**work** con precisión

clog /klɒg/ n zueco m. • vt (pt clogged) atascar

cloister /ˈklɔɪstə(r)/ n claustro m

clone /kləun/ n clon m

close[1] /kləus/ adj (-er, -est) cercano; (together) apretado; (friend) íntimo; (weather) bochornoso; (link etc) estrecho; (game, battle) reñido. have a ~ shave (fig) escaparse de milagro. • adv cerca

close[2] /kləuz/ vt cerrar. • vi cerrarse; (end) terminar. ~ down vt/i cerrar. • n fin m. ~d adj cerrado

closely /ˈkləuslɪ/ adv estrechamente; (at a short distance) de cerca; (with attention) detenidamente; (precisely) rigurosamente

closet /ˈklɒzɪt/ n (Amer) armario m; (for clothes) armario m, closet m (LAm)

close-up /ˈkləusʌp/ n (Cinema etc) primer plano m

closure /ˈkləuʒə(r)/ n cierre m

clot /klɒt/ n (Med) coágulo m; 🇬🇧 tonto m. • vi (pt clotted) cuajarse; (blood) coagularse

cloth /klɒθ/ n tela f; (duster) trapo m; (tablecloth) mantel m

clothe /kləuð/ vt pt **clothed** or **clad**) vestir. ~**es** /kləuðz/ npl ropa. ~**espin**, ~**espeg** (Amer) n pinza f (para tender la ropa). ~**ing** n ropa f

cloud /klaud/ n nube f. • ~ over vi nublarse. ~**y** adj (-ier, -iest) nu-

blado; (liquid) turbio

clout /klaut/ n bofetada f. • vt abofetear

clove /kləuv/ n clavo m. ~ **of garlic** n diente m de ajo

clover /ˈkləuvə(r)/ n trébol m

clown /klaun/ n payaso m. • vi hacer el payaso

club /klʌb/ n club m; (weapon) porra f; (golf club) palo m de golf; (at cards) trébol m. • vt (pt clubbed) aporrear. □ ~ **together** vi contribuir con dinero (to para)

cluck /klʌk/ vi cloquear

clue /klu:/ n pista f; (in crosswords) indicación f. not to have a ~ no tener la menor idea

clump /klʌmp/ n grupo m. • vt agrupar

clums|iness /ˈklʌmzɪnɪs/ n torpeza f. ~**y** /ˈklʌmzɪ/ adj (-ier, -iest) torpe

clung /klʌŋ/ see CLING

cluster /ˈklʌstə(r)/ n grupo m. • vi agruparse

clutch /klʌtʃ/ vt agarrar. • n (Auto) embrague m

clutter /ˈklʌtə(r)/ n desorden m. • vt. ~ (**up**) abarrotar. ~**ed** /ˈklʌtəd/ adj abarrotado de cosas

coach /kəutʃ/ n autocar m, autobús m; (of train) vagón m; (horse-drawn) coche m; (Sport) entrenador m. • vt (Sport) entrenar

coal /kəul/ n carbón m

coalition /kəuəˈlɪʃn/ n coalición f

coarse /kɔ:s/ adj (-er, -est) grueso; (material) basto; (person, language) ordinario

coast /kəust/ n costa f. • vi (with cycle) deslizarse sin pedalear; (with car) ir en punto muerto. ~**al** adj costero. ~**guard** n guardacostas m. ~**line** n litoral m

coat /kəʊt/ n abrigo m; (jacket) chaqueta f; (of animal) pelo m; (of paint) mano f. ● vt cubrir, revestir. **~hanger** n percha f, gancho m (LAm). **~ing** n capa f. **~ of arms** n escudo m de armas

coax /kəʊks/ vt engatusar

cobbler /'kɒblə(r)/ n zapatero m (remendón)

cobblestone /'kɒbəlstəʊn/ n adoquín m

cobweb /'kɒbweb/ n telaraña f

cocaine /kə'keɪn/ n cocaína f

cock /kɒk/ n (cockerel) gallo m; (male bird) macho m. ● vt amartillar (gun); aguzar (ears). **~erel** /'kɒkərəl/ n gallo m. **~-eyed** /-aɪd/ adj 🄵 torcido

cockney /'kɒknɪ/ adj & n (pl -eys) londinense (m & f) (del este de Londres)

cockpit /'kɒkpɪt/ n (in aircraft) cabina f del piloto

cockroach /'kɒkrəʊtʃ/ n cucaracha f

cocktail /'kɒkteɪl/ n cóctel m

cock-up /'kɒkʌp/ n 🄸 lío m

cocky /'kɒkɪ/ adj (-ier, -iest) engreído

cocoa /'kəʊkəʊ/ n cacao m; (drink) chocolate m, cocoa f (LAm)

coconut /'kəʊkənʌt/ n coco m

cocoon /kə'ku:n/ n capullo m

cod /kɒd/ n invar bacalao m

code /kəʊd/ n código m; (secret) clave f; **in ~** en clave

coeducational /kəʊedʒʊ 'keɪʃənl/ adj mixto

coerce /kəʊ'ɜ:s/ vt coaccionar. **~ion** /-ʃn/ n coacción f

coffee /'kɒfɪ/ n café m. **~ bean** n grano m de café. **~ maker** n cafetera f. **~pot** n cafetera f

coffin /'kɒfɪn/ n ataúd m, cajón m (LAm)

cog /kɒg/ n diente m; (fig) pieza f

coherent /kəʊ'hɪərənt/ adj coherente

coil /kɔɪl/ vt enrollar. ● n rollo m; (one ring) vuelta f

coin /kɔɪn/ n moneda f. ● vt acuñar

coincide /kəʊɪn'saɪd/ vi coincidir. **~nce** /kəʊ'ɪnsɪdəns/ n casualidad f. **~ntal** /kəʊɪnsɪ'dentl/ adj casual

coke /kəʊk/ n (coal) coque m. **C~** (®) Coca-Cola f (®)

colander /'kʌləndə(r)/ n colador m

cold /kəʊld/ adj (-er, -est) frío m. be **~** (person) tener frío. **it is ~** (weather) hace frío. ● n frío m; (Med) resfriado m. **have a ~** estar resfriado. **~-blooded** /-'blʌdɪd/ adj (animal) de sangre fría; (murder) a sangre fría. **~-shoulder** /-'ʃəʊldə(r)/ vt tratar con frialdad. **~ sore** n herpes m labial. **~ storage** n conservación f en frigorífico

coleslaw /'kəʊlslɔ:/ n ensalada f de col

collaborat|e /kə'læbəreɪt/ vi colaborar. **~ion** /-'reɪʃn/ n colaboración f. **~or** n colaborador m

collapse /kə'læps/ vi derrumbarse; (Med) sufrir un colapso. ● n derrumbamiento m; (Med) colapso m. **~ible** /-əbl/ adj plegable

collar /'kɒlə(r)/ n cuello m; (for animals) collar m. ● vt 🄸 hurtar. **~bone** n clavícula f

colleague /'kɒli:g/ n colega m & f

collect /kə'lekt/ vt reunir; (hobby) coleccionar, juntar (LAm); (pick up) recoger; cobrar (rent). ● vi (people) reunirse; (things) acumularse. **~ion** /-ʃn/ n colección f; (in church) colecta f; (of post) recogida *f.* ~**or** *n* coleccionista *m & f*

college /'kɒlɪdʒ/ *n* colegio *m*; *(of art, music etc)* escuela *f*; *(Amer)* universidad *f*

colli|de /kə'laɪd/ *vi* chocar. ~**sion** /-'lɪʒn/ *n* choque *m*

colloquial /kə'ləʊkwɪəl/ *adj* coloquial

Colombia /kə'lʌmbɪə/ *n* Colombia *f*. ~**n** *adj & n* colombiano (*m*)

colon /'kəʊlən/ *n* (*Gram*) dos puntos *mpl*; *(Med)* colon *m*

colonel /'kɜːnl/ *n* coronel *m*

colon|ial /kə'ləʊnɪəl/ *adj* colonial. ~**ize** /'kɒlənaɪz/ *vt* colonizar. ~**y** /'kɒlənɪ/ *n* colonia *f*

colossal /kə'lɒsl/ *adj* colosal

colour /'kʌlə(r)/ *n* color *m*. **off** ~ *(fig)* indispuesto. ● *adj* de color(es), en color(es) ● *vt* colorear; *(dye)* teñir. ~**-blind** *adj* daltónico. ~**ed** /'kʌləd/ *adj* de color. ~**ful** *adj* lleno de color; *(fig)* pintoresco. ~**ing** *n* color; *(food colouring)* colorante *m*. ~**less** *adj* incoloro

column /'kɒləm/ *n* columna *f*. ~**ist** *n* columnista *m & f*

coma /'kəʊmə/ *n* coma *m*

comb /kəʊm/ *n* peine *m*. ● *vt (search)* registrar. ~ **one's hair** peinarse

combat /'kɒmbæt/ *n* combate *m*. ● *vt (pt* **combated***)* combatir

combination /kɒmbɪ'neɪʃn/ *n* combinación *f*

combine /kəm'baɪn/ *vt* combinar. ● *vi* combinarse. ● /'kɒmbaɪn/ *n* asociación *f*. ~ **harvester** *n* cosechadora *f*

combustion /kəm'bʌstʃən/ *n* combustión *f*

come /kʌm/ *vi (pt* **came***, pp* **come***)* venir; *(occur)* pasar. ~ **across** *vt* encontrarse con (person); encon-

trar (object). □ ~ **apart** *vi* deshacerse. □ ~ **away** *vi (leave)* salir; *(become detached)* salirse. □ ~ **back** *vi* volver. □ ~ **by** *vt* obtener. □ ~ **down** *vi* bajar. □ ~ **in** *vi* entrar; *(arrive)* llegar. □ ~ **into** *vt* entrar en; heredar (money). □ ~ **off** *vi* desprenderse; *(succeed)* tener éxito. *vt*. ~ **off it!** 🅃 ¡no me vengas con eso! □ ~ **on** *vi (start to work)* encenderse. □ ~ **on**, hurry up! ¡vamos, date prisa! □ ~ **out** *vi* salir. □ ~ **round** *vi (after fainting)* volver en sí; *(be converted)* cambiar de idea; *(visit)* venir. □ ~ **to** *vt* llegar a (decision etc). □ ~ **up** *vi* subir; *(fig)* surgir. □ ~ **up with** *vt* proponer (idea). ~**back** *n* retorno *m*; *(retort)* réplica *f*

comedian /kə'miːdɪən/ *n* cómico *m*

comedy /'kɒmədɪ/ *n* comedia *f*

comet /'kɒmɪt/ *n* cometa *m*

comfort /'kʌmfət/ *n* comodidad *f*; *(consolation)* consuelo *m*. ● *vt* consolar. ~**able** *adj* cómodo. ~**er** *n* (for baby) chupete *m*, chupón *m* (LAm); (Amer, for bed) edredón *m*

comic /'kɒmɪk/ *adj* cómico. ● *n* cómico *m*; *(periodical)* revista *f* de historietas, tebeo *m*. ~**al** *adj* cómico. ~ **strip** *n* tira *f* cómica

coming /'kʌmɪŋ/ *n* llegada *f*. ~**s and goings** idas *fpl* y venidas. ● *adj* próximo; (week, month etc) que viene

comma /'kɒmə/ *n* coma *f*

command /kə'mɑːnd/ *n* orden *f*; *(mastery)* dominio *m*. ● *vt* ordenar; imponer (respect)

commandeer /kɒmən'dɪə(r)/ *vt* requisar

command: ~**er** *n* comandante *m*. ~**ing** *adj* imponente. ~**ment** *n* mandamiento *m*

commando /kəˈmɑːndəʊ/ n (pl -os) comando m

commemorat|e /kəˈmeməreɪt/ vt conmemorar. **~ion** /-ˈreɪʃn/ n conmemoración f. **~ive** /-ətɪv/ adj conmemorativo

commence /kəˈmens/ vt dar comienzo a. ● vi iniciarse

commend /kəˈmend/ vt alabar. **~able** adj loable. **~ation** /kɒmenˈdeɪʃn/ n elogio m

comment /ˈkɒment/ n observación f. ● vi hacer observaciones (**on** sobre)

commentary /ˈkɒməntrɪ/ n comentario m; (Radio, TV) reportaje m

commentat|e /ˈkɒmənteɪt/ vi narrar. **~or** n (Radio, TV) locutor m

commerc|e /ˈkɒmɜːs/ n comercio m. **~ial** /kəˈmɜːʃl/ adj comercial. ● n anuncio m; aviso m (LAm). **~ialize** vt comercializar

commiserat|e /kəˈmɪzəreɪt/ vi compadecerse (**with** de). **~ion** /-ˈreɪʃn/ n conmiseración f

commission /kəˈmɪʃn/ n comisión f. **out of** ~ fuera de servicio. ● vt encargar; (Mil) nombrar oficial

commissionaire /kəmɪʃəˈneə(r)/ n portero m

commit /kəˈmɪt/ vt (pt committed) cometer; (entrust) confiar. ~ **o.s.** comprometerse. **~ment** n compromiso m

committee /kəˈmɪtɪ/ n comité m

commodity /kəˈmɒdətɪ/ n producto m, artículo m

common /ˈkɒmən/ adj (-er, -est) común; (usual) corriente; (vulgar) ordinario. ● n. **in** ~ en común. **~er** n plebeyo m. ~ **law** n derecho m consuetudinario. **~ly** adv comúnmente. **C~ Market** n Mercado m Común. **~place** adj banal.

● n banalidad f. ~ **room** n sala f común, salón m común. **C~s** n. **the (House of) C~s** la Cámara de los Comunes. ~ **sense** n sentido m común. **C~wealth** n. **the C~wealth** la Mancomunidad f Británica

commotion /kəˈməʊʃn/ n confusión f

> **Commonwealth** La Commonwealth es una asociación de las antiguas colonias y territorios que conformaban el Imperio Británico. Cada dos años se celebra una reunión de sus jefes de gobierno. Entre los países miembros existen muchos vínculos culturales, educativos y deportivos. En EE.UU., es el término oficial para referirse a cuatro estados: Kentucky, Massachussets, Pensilvania y Virginia.

commune /ˈkɒmjuːn/ n comuna f

communicat|e /kəˈmjuːnɪkeɪt/ vt comunicar. ● vi comunicarse. **~ion** /-ˈkeɪʃn/ n comunicación f. **~ive** /-ətɪv/ adj comunicativo

communion /kəˈmjuːnɪən/ n comunión f

communis|m /ˈkɒmjʊnɪsəm/ n comunismo m. **~t** n comunista m & f

community /kəˈmjuːnətɪ/ n comunidad f. ~ **centre** n centro m social

commute /kəˈmjuːt/ vi viajar diariamente (entre el lugar de residencia y el trabajo). ● vt (Jurid) conmutar. **~r** n viajero m diario

compact /kəmˈpækt/ adj compacto. ● /ˈkɒmpækt/ n (for powder) polvera f. ~ **disc**, ~ **disk** /ˈkɒmpækt/ n disco m compacto, compact-disc m. ~ disc player n (reproductor m de) compact-disc

companion /kəm'pænɪən/ n compañero m. ~ship n compañía f

company /'kʌmpənɪ/ n compañía f; (guests) visita f; (Com) sociedad f

compar|able /'kɒmpərəbl/ adj comparable. ~ative /kəm'pærətɪv/ adj comparativo; (fig) relativo. ● n (Gram) comparativo m. ~e /kəm'peə(r)/ vt comparar. ~ison /kəm'pærɪsn/ n comparación f

compartment /kəm'pɑːtmənt/ n compartim(i)ento m

compass /'kʌmpəs/ n brújula f. ~es npl compás m

compassion /kəm'pæʃn/ n compasión f. ~ate /-ət/ adj compasivo

compatible /kəm'pætəbl/ adj compatible

compel /kəm'pel/ vt (pt compelled) obligar. ~ling adj irresistible

compensat|e /'kɒmpənseɪt/ vt compensar; (for loss) indemnizar. ● vi. ~e for sth compensar algo. ~ion /-'seɪʃn/ n compensación f; (financial) indemnización f

compère /'kɒmpeə(r)/ n presentador m. ● vt presentar

compete /kəm'piːt/ vi competir

competen|ce /'kɒmpətəns/ n competencia f. ~t adj competente

competit|ion /kɒmpə'tɪʃn/ n (contest) concurso m; (Sport) competición f, competencia f (LAm); (Com) competencia f. ~ive /kəm'petɪtɪv/ adj competidor; (price) competitivo. ~or /kəm'petɪtə(r)/ n competidor m; (in contest) concursante m & f

compile /kəm'paɪl/ vt compilar

complacen|cy /kəm'pleɪsənsɪ/ n autosuficiencia f. ~t adj satisfecho de sí mismo

complain /kəm'pleɪn/ vi. ~ (about) quejarse (de). ● vt. ~ that quejarse de que. ~t n queja f; (Med) enfermedad f

complement /'kɒmplɪmənt/ n complemento m. ● vt complementar. ~ary /-'mentrɪ/ adj complementario

complet|e /kəm'pliːt/ adj completo; (finished) acabado; (downright) total. ● vt acabar; llenar (a form). ~ely adv completamente. ~ion /-ʃn/ n finalización f

complex /'kɒmpleks/ adj complejo. ● n complejo m

complexion /kəm'plekʃn/ n tez f; (fig) aspecto m

complexity /kəm'pleksətɪ/ n complejidad f

complicat|e /'kɒmplɪkeɪt/ vt complicar. ~ed adj complicado. ~ion /-'keɪʃn/ n complicación f

compliment /'kɒmplɪmənt/ n cumplido m; (amorous) piropo m. ● vt felicitar. ~ary /-'mentrɪ/ adj halagador; (given free) de regalo. ~s npl saludos mpl

comply /kəm'plaɪ/ vi. ~ with conformarse con

component /kəm'pəʊnənt/ adj & n componente m

compos|e /kəm'pəʊz/ vt componer. be ~ed of estar compuesto de. ~er n compositor m. ~ition /kɒmpə'zɪʃn/ n composición f

compost /'kɒmpɒst/ n abono m

composure /kəm'pəʊʒə(r)/ n serenidad f

compound /'kɒmpaʊnd/ n compuesto m; (enclosure) recinto m. ● adj compuesto; (fracture) complicado

comprehen|d /ˌkɒmprɪˈhend/ vt comprender. **~sion** /ˌkɒmprɪˈhenʃn/ n comprensión f. **~sive** /ˌkɒmprɪˈhensɪv/ adj extenso; (insurance) contra todo riesgo. **~sive (school)** n instituto m de enseñanza secundaria

compress /ˈkɒmpres/ n (Med) compresa f. ● /kəmˈpres/ vt comprimir. **~ion** /-ˈpreʃn/ n compresión f

comprise /kəmˈpraɪz/ vt comprender

compromis|e /ˈkɒmprəmaɪz/ n acuerdo m, compromiso m, arreglo m. ● vt comprometer. ● vi llegar a un acuerdo. **~ing** adj (situation) comprometido

compuls|ion /kəmˈpʌlʃn/ n (force) coacción f; (obsession) compulsión f. **~ive** /kəmˈpʌlsɪv/ adj compulsivo. **~ory** /kəmˈpʌlsərɪ/ adj obligatorio

comput|e /kəmˈpjuːt/ vb calcular. **comput|er** n ordenador m, computadora f (LAm). **~erize** vt computarizar, computerizar. **~er studies** n, **~ing** n informática f, computación f

comrade /ˈkɒmreɪd/ n camarada m & f

con /kɒn/ vt (pt conned) 🄵 estafar. ● n (fraud) estafa f; (objection) see **PRO**

concave /ˈkɒŋkeɪv/ adj cóncavo

conceal /kənˈsiːl/ vt ocultar

concede /kənˈsiːd/ vt conceder

conceit /kənˈsiːt/ n vanidad f. **~ed** adj engreído

conceiv|able /kənˈsiːvəbl/ adj concebible. **~e** /kənˈsiːv/ vt/i concebir

concentrat|e /ˈkɒnsəntreɪt/ vt

concentrar. ● vi concentrarse (**on** en). **~ion** /-ˈtreɪʃn/ n concentración f

concept /ˈkɒnsept/ n concepto m

conception /kənˈsepʃn/ n concepción f

concern /kənˈsɜːn/ n asunto m; (worry) preocupación f; (Com) empresa f. ● vt tener que ver con; (deal with) tratar de. **as far as I'm ~ed** en cuanto a mí. **be ~ed about** preocuparse por. **~ing** prep acerca de

concert /ˈkɒnsət/ n concierto m. **~ed** /kənˈsɜːtɪd/ adj concertado

concertina /ˌkɒnsəˈtiːnə/ n concertina f

concerto /kənˈtʃɜːtəʊ/ n (pl -os or -ti /-tɪ/) concierto m

concession /kənˈseʃn/ n concesión f

concise /kənˈsaɪs/ adj conciso

conclu|de /kənˈkluːd/ vt/i concluir. **~ding** adj final. **~sion** /-ʃn/ n conclusión f. **~sive** /-sɪv/ adj decisivo. **~sively** adv concluyentemente

concoct /kənˈkɒkt/ vt confeccionar; (fig) inventar. **~ion** /-ʃn/ n mezcla f; (drink) brebaje m

concrete /ˈkɒnkriːt/ n hormigón m, concreto m (LAm). ● adj concreto

concussion /kənˈkʌʃn/ n conmoción f cerebral

condemn /kənˈdem/ vt condenar. **~ation** /ˌkɒndemˈneɪʃn/ n condena f

condens|ation /ˌkɒndenˈseɪʃn/ n condensación f. **~e** /kənˈdens/ vt condensar. ● vi condensarse

condescend /ˌkɒndɪˈsend/ vi dignarse (**to** a). **~ing** adj superior

condition /kənˈdɪʃn/ n condición

f. on ~ that a condición de que.
● *vt* condicionar. **~al** *adj* condicional. **~er** *n* (*for hair*) suavizante *m*,
enjuague *m* (*LAm*)

condo /'kɒndəʊ/ *n* (*pl* **-os**) (*Amer
fam*) see **CONDOMINIUM**

condolences /kən'dəʊlənsɪz/ *npl*
pésame *m*

condom /'kɒndəm/ *n* condón *m*

condominium /kɒndə'mɪnɪəm/
n (*Amer*) apartamento *m*, piso *m* (en
régimen de propiedad horizontal)

condone /kən'dəʊn/ *vt* condonar

conduct /kən'dʌkt/ *vt* llevar a
cabo (business, experiment); conducir (electricity); dirigir (orchestra). ● /'kɒndʌkt/ *n* conducta *f*.
~or /kən'dʌktə(r)/ *n* director *m*;
(*of bus*) cobrador *m*. **~ress** /kən-
'dʌktrɪs/ *n* cobradora *f*

cone /kəʊn/ *n* cono *m*; (*for ice
cream*) cucurucho *m*, barquillo *m*
(*Mex*)

confectionery /kən'fekʃənrɪ/ *n*
productos *mpl* de confitería

confederation /kənfedə'reɪʃn/
n confederación *f*

conference /'kɒnfərəns/ *n* congreso *m*; **an international ~ on** ...
un congreso internacional sobre ...

confess /kən'fes/ *vt* confesar. ● *vi*
confesarse. **~ion** /-ʃn/ *n* confe-
sión *f*

confetti /kən'fetɪ/ *n* confeti *m*

confide /kən'faɪd/ *vt/i* confiar

confiden|ce /'kɒnfɪdəns/ *n* con-
fianza *f*; (*self-confidence*) confianza
en sí mismo; (*secret*) confidencia *f*.
~ce trick *n* estafa *f*, timo *m*. **~t**
/'kɒnfɪdənt/ *adj* seguro de sí
mismo. **be ~t of** confiar en

confidential /kɒnfɪ'denʃl/ *adj*
confidencial. **~ity** /-denʃɪ'ælətɪ/ *n*

confidencialidad *f*

configur|ation /kənfɪgə'reɪʃn/ *n*
configuración *f*. **~e** /kən'fɪgə(r)/ *vt*
configurar

confine /kən'faɪn/ *vt* confinar;
(*limit*) limitar. **~ment** *n* (*imprisonment*) prisión *f*

confirm /kən'fɜːm/ *vt* confirmar.
~ation /kɒnfə'meɪʃn/ *n* confirma-
ción *f*. **~ed** *adj* inveterado

confiscat|e /'kɒnfɪskeɪt/ *vt* confis-
car. **~ion** /-'keɪʃn/ *n* confisca-
ción *f*

conflict /'kɒnflɪkt/ *n* conflicto *m*.
● /kən'flɪkt/ *vi* chocar. **~ing** /kən-
'flɪktɪŋ/ *adj* contradictorio

conform /kən'fɔːm/ *vi* conformarse. **~ist** *n* conformista *m & f*

confound /kən'faʊnd/ *vt* confundir. **~ed** *adj* [T] maldito

confront /kən'frʌnt/ *vt* hacer
frente a; (*face*) enfrentarse con.
~ation /kɒnfrʌn'teɪʃn/ *n* confrontación *f*

confus|e /kən'fjuːz/ *vt* confundir.
~ed *adj* confundido. **get ~ed** confundirse. **~ing** *adj* confuso. **~ion**
/-ʒn/ *n* confusión *f*

congeal /kən'dʒiːl/ *vi* coagularse

congest|ed /kən'dʒestɪd/ *adj* con-
gestionado. **~ion** /-tʃən/ *n* con-
gestión *f*

congratulat|e /kən'grætjʊleɪt/
vt felicitar. **~ions** /-'leɪʃnz/ *npl* enhorabuena *f*, felicitaciones *fpl* (*LAm*)

congregat|e /'kɒŋgrɪgeɪt/ *vi*
congregarse. **~ion** /-'geɪʃn/ *n*
asamblea *f*; (*Relig*) fieles *mpl*, feligre-
ses *mpl*

congress /'kɒŋgres/ *n* congreso
m. **C~** (*Amer*) el Congreso. **~man**
/-mən/ *n* (*Amer*) miembro *m* del
Congreso. **~woman** *n* (*Amer*)
miembro *f* del Congreso.

Congress El Congreso es el organismo legislativo de EE.UU. Se reúne en el Capitolio (*Capitol*) y está compuesto por dos cámaras: El Senado y la Cámara de Representantes. Se renueva cada dos años y su función es elaborar leyes que deben ser aprobadas, primero, por las dos cámaras y posteriormente por el Presidente.

conifer /'kɒnɪfə(r)/ n conífera f

conjugat|e /'kɒndʒʊgeɪt/ vt conjugar. **~ion** /-'geɪʃn/ n conjugación f

conjunction /kən'dʒʌŋkʃn/ n conjunción f

conjur|e /'kʌndʒə(r)/ vi hacer juegos de manos. ● vt. □ **~ e up** vt evocar. **~er, ~or** n prestidigitador m

conk /kɒŋk/ vi. □ **~ out** 🆃 fallar; (person) desmayarse

conker /'kɒŋkə(r)/ n 🆃 castaña f de Indias

conman /'kɒnmæn/ n (pl **-men** 🆃) estafador m, timador m

connect /kə'nekt/ vt conectar; (associate) relacionar. ● vi (be fitted) estar conectado (**to** a). □ **~ with** vt (train) enlazar con. **~ed** adj unido; (related) relacionado. **be ~ed with** tener que ver con, estar emparentado con. **~ion** /-ʃn/ n conexión f; (Rail) enlace m; (fig) relación f. **in ~ion with** a propósito de, con respecto a

connive /kə'naɪv/ vi. **~ e at** ser cómplice en

connoisseur /kɒnə'sɜ:(r)/ n experto m

connotation /kɒnə'teɪʃn/ n connotación f

conquer /'kɒŋkə(r)/ vt conquistar; (fig) vencer. **~or** n conquistador m

conquest /'kɒŋkwest/ n conquista f

conscience /'kɒnʃəns/ n conciencia f

conscientious /kɒnʃɪ'enʃəs/ adj concienzudo

conscious /'kɒnʃəs/ adj consciente; (deliberate) intencional. **~ly** adv a sabiendas. **~ness** n conciencia f; (Med) conocimiento m

conscript /'kɒnskrɪpt/ n recluta m & f, conscripto m (LAm). ● /kən'skrɪpt/ vt reclutar. **~ion** /kən'skrɪpʃn/ n reclutamiento m, conscripción f (LAm)

consecrate /'kɒnsɪkreɪt/ vt consagrar

consecutive /kən'sekjʊtɪv/ adj sucesivo

consensus /kən'sensəs/ n consenso m

consent /kən'sent/ vi consentir. ● n consentimiento m

consequen|ce /'kɒnsɪkwəns/ n consecuencia f. **~t** adj consiguiente. **~tly** adv por consiguiente

conservation /kɒnsə'veɪʃn/ n conservación f, preservación f. **~ist** n conservacionista m & f

conservative /kən'sɜ:vətɪv/ adj conservador; (modest) prudente, moderado. **C~** adj & n conservador (m)

conservatory /kən'sɜ:vətrɪ/ n invernadero m

conserve /kən'sɜ:v/ vt conservar

consider /kən'sɪdə(r)/ vt considerar; (take into account) tomar en cuenta. **~able** adj considerable. **~ably** adv considerablemente

considerat|e /kən'sɪdərət/ adj

considerado. ~ion /-'reɪʃn/ n consideración f. take sth into ~ion tomar algo en cuenta

considering /kən'sɪdərɪŋ/ prep teniendo en cuenta. ● conj. ~ (that) teniendo en cuenta que

consign /kən'saɪn/ vt consignar; (send) enviar. ~ment n envío m

consist /kən'sɪst/ vi. ~ of consistir en. ~ency n consistencia f; (fig) coherencia f. ~ent adj coherente; (unchanging) constante. ~ent with compatible con. ~ently adv constantemente

consolation /kɒnsə'leɪʃn/ n consuelo m

console /kən'səʊl/ vt consolar. ● /'kɒnsəʊl/ n consola f

consolidate /kən'sɒlɪdeɪt/ vt consolidar

consonant /'kɒnsənənt/ n consonante f

conspicuous /kən'spɪkjʊəs/ adj (easily seen) visible; (showy) llamativo; (noteworthy) notable

conspir|acy /kən'spɪrəsɪ/ n conspiración f. ~ator /kən'spɪrətə(r)/ n conspirador m. ~e /kən'spaɪə(r)/ vi conspirar

constable /'kʌnstəbl/ n agente m & f de policía

constant /'kɒnstənt/ adj constante. ~ly adv constantemente

constellation /kɒnstə'leɪʃn/ n constelación f

consternation /kɒnstə'neɪʃn/ n consternación f

constipat|ed /'kɒnstɪpeɪtɪd/ adj estreñido. ~ion /-'peɪʃn/ n estreñimiento m

constituen|cy /kən'stɪtjʊənsɪ/ n distrito m electoral. ~t n (Pol) elector m. ● adj constituyente, constitutivo

constitut|e /'kɒnstɪtjuːt/ vt constituir. ~ion /-'tjuːʃn/ n constitución f. ~ional /-'tjuːʃənl/ adj constitucional. ● n paseo m

constrict /kən'strɪkt/ vt apretar. ~ion /-ʃn/ n constricción f

construct /kən'strʌkt/ vt construir. ~ion /-ʃn/ n construcción f. ~ive adj constructivo

consul /'kɒnsl/ n cónsul m & f. ~ate /'kɒnsjʊlət/ n consulado m

consult /kən'sʌlt/ vt/i consultar. ~ancy n asesoría. ~ant n asesor m; (Med) especialista m & f; (Tec) consejero m técnico. ~ation /kɒnsl'teɪʃn/ n consulta f

consume /kən'sjuːm/ vt consumir. ~r n consumidor m. ● adj de consumo

consummate /'kɒnsəmət/ adj consumado. ● /'kɒnsəmeɪt/ vt consumar

consumption /kən'sʌmpʃn/ n consumo m

contact /'kɒntækt/ n contacto m. ● vt ponerse en contacto con. ~ lens n lentilla f, lente f de contacto (LAm)

contagious /kən'teɪdʒəs/ adj contagioso

contain /kən'teɪn/ vt contener. ~ o.s. contenerse. ~er n recipiente m; (Com) contenedor m

contaminat|e /kən'tæmɪneɪt/ vt contaminar. ~ion /-'neɪʃn/ n contaminación f

contemplate /'kɒntəmpleɪt/ vt contemplar; (consider) considerar

contemporary /kən'tempərərɪ/ adj & n contemporáneo (m)

contempt /kən'tempt/ n desprecio m. ~ible adj despreciable. ~uous /-tjʊəs/ adj desdeñoso

contend /kən'tend/ vi competir.

~er n aspirante m & f **(for a)**

content /kənˈtent/ adj satisfecho. ● /ˈkɒntent/ n contenido m. ● /kənˈtent/ vt contentar. **~ed** /kənˈtentɪd/ adj satisfecho. **~ment** /kənˈtentmənt/ n satisfacción f. **~s** /ˈkɒntents/ n contenido m; (of book) índice m de materias

contest /ˈkɒntest/ n (competition) concurso m; (Sport) competición f, competencia f (LAm). ● /kənˈtest/ vt disputar. **~ant** /kənˈtestənt/ n concursante m & f

context /ˈkɒntekst/ n contexto m

continent /ˈkɒntɪnənt/ n continente m. **the C~** Europa f. **~al** /-ˈnentl/ adj continental. **~al quilt** n edredón m

contingen|cy /kənˈtɪndʒənsɪ/ n contingencia f. **~t** adj & n contingente (m)

continu|al /kənˈtɪnjʊəl/ adj continuo. **~ally** adv continuamente. **~ation** /-ˈeɪʃn/ n continuación f. **~e** /kənˈtɪnjuː/ vt/i continuar, seguir. **~ed** adj continuo. **~ity** /kɒntɪˈnjuːətɪ/ n continuidad f. **~ous** /kənˈtɪnjʊəs/ adj continuo. **~ously** adv continuamente

contort /kənˈtɔːt/ vt retorcer. **~ion** /-ʃn/ n contorsión f. **~ionist** /-ʃənɪst/ n contorsionista m & f

contour /ˈkɒntʊə(r)/ n contorno m

contraband /ˈkɒntrəbænd/ n contrabando m

contraception /kɒntrəˈsepʃn/ n anticoncepción f. **~ve** /-tɪv/ adj & n anticonceptivo (m)

contract /ˈkɒntrækt/ n contrato m. ● /kənˈtrækt/ vt contraer. ● vi contraerse. **~ion** /kənˈtrækʃn/ n contracción f. **~or** /kənˈtræktə(r)/ n contratista m & f

contradict /kɒntrəˈdɪkt/ vt contradecir. **~ion** /-ʃn/ n contradicción f. **~ory** adj contradictorio

contraption /kənˈtræpʃn/ n 🅸 artilugio m

contrary /ˈkɒntrərɪ/ adj contrario. **the ~** lo contrario. **on the ~** al contrario. ● adv. **~ to** contrariamente a. ● /kənˈtreərɪ/ adj (obstinate) terco

contrast /ˈkɒntrɑːst/ n contraste m. ● /kənˈtrɑːst/ vt/i contrastar. **~ing** adj contrastante

contravene /kɒntrəˈviːn/ vt contravenir

contribut|e /kənˈtrɪbjuːt/ vt contribuir con. ● vi contribuir. **~e to** escribir para (newspaper). **~ion** /kɒntrɪˈbjuːʃn/ n contribución f. **~or** n contribuyente m & f; (to newspaper) colaborador m

contrite /ˈkɒntraɪt/ adj arrepentido, pesaroso

contriv|e /kənˈtraɪv/ vt idear. **~e to** conseguir. **~ed** adj artificioso

control /kənˈtrəʊl/ vt (pt controlled) controlar. ● n control m. **~ler** n director m. **~s** npl (Mec) mandos mpl

controvers|ial /kɒntrəˈvɜːʃl/ adj controvertido. **~y** /ˈkɒntrəvɜːsɪ/ n controversia f

conundrum /kəˈnʌndrəm/ n adivinanza f

convalesce /kɒnvəˈles/ vi convalecer. **~nce** n convalecencia f

convector /kənˈvektə(r)/ n estufa f de convección

convene /kənˈviːn/ vt convocar. ● vi reunirse

convenien|ce /kənˈviːnɪəns/ n conveniencia f, comodidad f. **all modern ~ces** todas las comodidades. **at your ~ce** según le convenga. **~ces** npl servicios mpl, baños mpl (LAm). **~t** adj conveniente; (place) bien situado; (time) oportuno. **be ~t** convenir. **~tly** adv convenientemente

convent /'kɒnvənt/ n convento m

convention /kən'venʃn/ n convención f. **~al** adj convencional

converge /kən'vɜːdʒ/ vi converger

conversation /kɒnvə'seɪʃn/ n conversación f. **~al** adj familiar, coloquial.

converse /kən'vɜːs/ vi. ● /'kɒnvɜːs/ adj inverso. ● n lo contrario. **~ly** adv a la inversa

conver|sion /kən'vɜːʃn/ n conversión f. **~t** /kən'vɜːt/ vt convertir. ● /'kɒnvɜːt/ n converso m. **~tible** /kən'vɜːtɪbl/ adj convertible. ● n (Auto) descapotable m, convertible m (LAm)

convex /'kɒnveks/ adj convexo

convey /kən'veɪ/ vt transportar (goods, people); comunicar (idea, feeling). **~or belt** n cinta f transportadora, banda f transportadora (LAm)

convict /kən'vɪkt/ vt condenar. ● /'kɒnvɪkt/ n presidiario m. **~ion** /kən'vɪkʃn/ n condena f; (belief) creencia f

convinc|e /kən'vɪns/ vt convencer. **~ing** adj convincente

convoluted /'kɒnvəluːtɪd/ adj (argument) intrincado

convoy /'kɒnvɔɪ/ n convoy m

convuls|e /kən'vʌls/ vt convulsionar. **be ~ed with laughter** desternillarse de risa. **~ion** /-ʃn/ n convulsión f

coo /kuː/ vi arrullar

cook /kʊk/ vt hacer, preparar. ● vi cocinar; (food) hacerse. ● n coci-

nero m. □ **~ up** vt [T] inventar. **~book** n libro m de cocina. **~er** n cocina f, estufa f (Mex). **~ery** n cocina f

cookie /'kʊkɪ/ n (Amer) galleta f

cool /kuːl/ adj (-er, -est) fresco; (calm) tranquilo; (unfriendly) frío. ● n fresco m; [X] calma f. ● vt enfriar. ● vi enfriarse. □ **~ down** n (person) calmarse. **~ly** adv tranquilamente

coop /kuːp/ n gallinero m. □ **~ up** vt encerrar

co-op /'kəʊp/ n cooperativa f

cooperat|e /kəʊ'ɒpəreɪt/ vi cooperar. **~ion** /-'reɪʃn/ n cooperación f. **~ive** /kəʊ'ɒpərətɪv/ adj cooperativo. ● n cooperativa f

co-opt /kəʊ'ɒpt/ vt cooptar

co-ordinat|e /kəʊ'ɔːdɪneɪt/ vt coordinar. ● /kəʊ'ɔːdɪnət/ n (Math) coordenada f. **~es** npl prendas fpl para combinar. **~ion** /kəʊɔːdɪ'neɪʃn/ n coordinación f

cop /kɒp/ n [T] poli m & f [T], tira m & f (Mex, fam)

cope /kəʊp/ vi arreglárselas. **~ with** hacer frente a

copious /'kəʊpɪəs/ adj abundante

copper /'kɒpə(r)/ n cobre m; (coin) perra f; [T] poli m & f [T], tira m & f (Mex, fam). ● adj de cobre

copy /'kɒpɪ/ n copia f; (of book, newspaper) ejemplar m. ● vt copiar. **~right** n derechos mpl de reproducción

coral /'kɒrəl/ n coral m

cord /kɔːd/ n cuerda f; (fabric) pana f; (Amer, Elec) cordón m, cable m

cordial /'kɔːdɪəl/ adj cordial. ● n refresco m (concentrado)

cordon /'kɔːdn/ n cordón m. □ **~ off** vt acordonar

core /kɔː(r)/ n (of apple) corazón m; (of Earth) centro m; (of problem) meollo m

cork /kɔːk/ n corcho m. **~screw** n sacacorchos m

corn /kɔːn/ n (wheat) trigo m; (Amer) maíz m; (hard skin) callo m

corned beef /kɔːnd 'biːf/ n carne f de vaca en lata

corner /'kɔːnə(r)/ n ángulo m; (inside) rincón m; (outside) esquina f; (football) córner m. ● vt arrinconar; (Com) acaparar

cornet /'kɔːnɪt/ n (Mus) corneta f; (for ice cream) cucurucho m, barquillo m (Mex)

corn: ~flakes npl copos mpl de maíz. **~flour** n maizena f ®

Cornish /'kɔːnɪʃ/ adj de Cornualles

cornstarch /'kɔːnstɑːtʃ/ n (Amer) maizena f ®

corny /'kɔːnɪ/ adj (fam, trite) gastado

coronation /kɒrə'neɪʃn/ n coronación f

coroner /'kɒrənə(r)/ n juez m de primera instancia

corporal /'kɔːpərəl/ n cabo m. ● adj corporal

corporate /'kɔːpərət/ adj corporativo

corporation /kɔːpə'reɪʃn/ n corporación f; (Amer) sociedad f anónima

corps /kɔː(r)/ n (pl corps /kɔːz/) cuerpo m

corpse /kɔːps/ n cadáver m

corpulent /'kɔːpjʊlənt/ adj corpulento

corral /kə'rɑːl/ n (Amer) corral m

correct /kə'rekt/ adj correcto; (time) exacto. ● vt corregir. **~ion** /-ʃn/ n corrección f

correspond /kɒrɪ'spɒnd/ vi corresponder; (write) escribirse. **~ence** n correspondencia f. **~ent** n corresponsal m & f

corridor /'kɒrɪdɔː(r)/ n pasillo m

corro|de /kə'rəʊd/ vt corroer. ● vi corroerse. **~sion** /-ʒn/ n corrosión f. **~sive** /-sɪv/ adj corrosivo

corrugated /'kɒrəgeɪtɪd/ adj ondulado. **~ iron** n chapa f de zinc

corrupt /kə'rʌpt/ adj corrompido. ● vt corromper. **~ion** /-ʃn/ n corrupción f

corset /'kɔːsɪt/ n corsé m

cosmetic /kɒz'metɪk/ adj & n cosmético (m)

cosmic /'kɒzmɪk/ adj cósmico

cosmopolitan /kɒzmə'pɒlɪtən/ adj & n cosmopolita (m & f)

cosmos /'kɒzmɒs/ n cosmos m

cosset /'kɒsɪt/ vt (pt cosseted) mimar

cost /kɒst/ vt (pt cost) costar; (pt costed) calcular el coste de, calcular el costo de (LAm). ● n coste m, costo m (LAm). **at all ~s** cueste lo que cueste. **to one's ~** sus expensas. **~s** npl (Jurid) costas fpl

Costa Rica /kɒstə'riːkə/ n Costa f Rica. **~n** adj & n costarricense (m & f), costarriqueño (m & f)

cost: ~-effective adj rentable. **~ly** adj (-ier, -iest) costoso

costume /'kɒstjuːm/ n traje m; (for party, disguise) disfraz m

cosy /'kəʊzɪ/ adj (-ier, -iest) acogedor. ● n cubreteras m

cot /kɒt/ n cuna f

cottage /'kɒtɪdʒ/ n casita f. **~ cheese** n requesón m. **~ pie** n pastel m de carne cubierta con puré

cotton /'kɒtn/ n algodón m; (thread) hilo m; (Amer) see **~**

wool. □ ~ **on** vi 🔢 comprender. ~ **bud** n bastoncillo m, cotonete m (Mex). ~ **candy** n (Amer) algodón m de azúcar. ~ **swab** n (Amer) see ~ **BUD.** ~ **wool** n algodón m hidrófilo

couch /kautʃ/ n sofá m

cough /kɒf/ vi toser. ● n tos f. □ ~ **up** vt 🔢 pagar. ~ **mixture** n jarabe m para la tos

could /kʊd/ pt of **CAN¹**

couldn't /ˈkʊdnt/ = **could not**

council /ˈkaʊnsl/ n consejo m; (of town) ayuntamiento m. ~ **house** n vivienda f subvencionada. ~**lor** n concejal m

counsel /ˈkaʊnsl/ n consejo m; (pl invar) (Jurid) abogado m. ● vt (pt counselled) aconsejar. ~**ling** n terapia f de apoyo. ~**lor** n consejero m

count /kaʊnt/ n recuento m; (nobleman) conde m. ● vt/i contar. □ ~ **on** vt contar. ~**down** n cuenta f atrás

counter /ˈkaʊntə(r)/ n (in shop) mostrador m; (in bank, post office) ventanilla f; (token) ficha f. ● adv. ~ **to** en contra de. ● adj opuesto. ● vt oponerse a; parar (blow)

counter... /ˈkaʊntə(r)/ pref contra.... ~**act** /-ˈækt/ vt contrarrestar. ~**attack** n contraataque m. ● vt/i contraatacar. ~**balance** n contrapeso m. ● vt/i contrapesar. ~**clockwise** /-ˈklɒkwaɪz/ a/adv (Amer) en sentido contrario a las agujas del reloj

counterfeit /ˈkaʊntəfɪt/ adj falsificado. ● n falsificación f. ● vt falsificar

counterfoil /ˈkaʊntəfɔɪl/ n matriz f, talón m (LAm)

counter-productive /kaʊntəprəˈdʌktɪv/ adj contraproducente

countess /ˈkaʊntɪs/ n condesa f

countless /ˈkaʊntlɪs/ adj innumerable

country /ˈkʌntrɪ/ n (native land) país m; (countryside) campo m; (Mus) (música f) country m. ~**-and-western** /-enˈwestən/ (música f) country m. ~**man** /-mən/ n (of one's own country) compatriota m. ~**side** n campo m; (landscape) paisaje m

county /ˈkaʊntɪ/ n condado m

coup /kuː/ n golpe m

couple /ˈkʌpl/ n (of things) par m; (of people) pareja f; (married) matrimonio m. **a** ~ **of** un par de

coupon /ˈkuːpɒn/ n cupón m

courage /ˈkʌrɪdʒ/ n valor m. ~**ous** /kəˈreɪdʒəs/ adj valiente

courgette /kʊəˈʒet/ n calabacín m

courier /ˈkʊrɪə(r)/ n mensajero m; (for tourists) guía m & f

course /kɔːs/ n curso m; (behaviour) conducta f; (in navigation) rumbo m; (Culin) plato m; (for golf) campo m. **in due** ~ a su debido tiempo. **in the** ~ **of** en el transcurso de, durante. **of** ~ claro, por supuesto. **of** ~ **not** claro que no, por supuesto que no

court /kɔːt/ n corte f; (tennis) pista f; cancha f (LAm); (Jurid) tribunal m. ● vt cortejar; buscar (danger)

courteous /ˈkɜːtɪəs/ adj cortés

courtesy /ˈkɜːtəsɪ/ n cortesía f

courtier /ˈkɔːtɪə(r)/ n (old use) cortesano m

court:: ~ martial n (pl ~**s martial**) consejo m de guerra. **-martial** vt (pt ~**-martialled**) juzgar en consejo de guerra. ~**ship** n cortejo m. ~**yard** n

cousin | crawl

patio m

cousin /'kʌzn/ n primo m. **first** ~ primo carnal. **second** ~ primo segundo

cove /kəʊv/ n ensenada f, cala f

Coventry /'kɒvntrɪ/ n. **send s.o. to** ~ hacer el vacío a uno

cover /'kʌvə(r)/ vt cubrir. ●n cubierta f; (shelter) abrigo m; (lid) tapa f; (for furniture) funda f; (pretext) pretexto m; (of magazine) portada f. □ ~ **up** vt cubrir; (fig) ocultar. ~**age** n cobertura f. ~ **charge** n precio m del cubierto. ~**ing** n cubierta f. ~**ing letter** n carta f adjunta

covet /'kʌvɪt/ vt codiciar

cow /kaʊ/ n vaca f

coward /'kaʊəd/ n cobarde m. ~**ice** /'kaʊədɪs/ n cobardía f. ~**ly** adj cobarde.

cowboy /'kaʊbɔɪ/ n vaquero m

cower /'kaʊə(r)/ vi encogerse, acobardarse

coxswain /'kɒksn/ n timonel m

coy /kɔɪ/ adj (-er, -est) (shy) tímido; (evasive) evasivo

crab /kræb/ n cangrejo m, jaiba f (LAm)

crack /kræk/ n grieta f; (noise) crujido m; (of whip) chasquido m; (drug) crack m. ●adj 🅱 de primera. ●vt agrietar; chasquear (whip, fingers); cascar (nut); gastar (joke); resolver (problem). ●vi agrietarse. **get** ~**ing** 🅱 darse prisa. □ ~ **down on** vt 🅱 tomar medidas enérgicas contra

cracker /'krækə(r)/ n (Culin) cracker f, galleta f (salada); (Christmas cracker) sorpresa f (que estalla al abrirla)

crackle /'krækl/ vi crepitar. ●n crepitación f, crujido m

crackpot /'krækpɒt/ n 🅱 chiflado m

cradle /'kreɪdl/ n cuna f. ●vt acunar

craft /krɑːft/ n destreza f; (technique) arte f; (cunning) astucia f. ●n invar (boat) barco m

craftsman /'krɑːftsmən/ n (pl -men) artesano m. ~**ship** n artesanía f

crafty /'krɑːftɪ/ adj (-ier, -iest) astuto

cram /kræm/ vt (pt crammed) rellenar. ~ **with** llenar de. ●vi (for exams) memorizar, empollar 🇬🇧, zambutir (Mex)

cramp /kræmp/ n calambre m

cramped /kræmpt/ adj apretado

crane /kreɪn/ n grúa f. ●vt estirar (neck)

crank /kræŋk/ n manivela f; (person) excéntrico m. ~**y** adj excéntrico

cranny /'krænɪ/ n grieta f

crash /kræʃ/ n accidente m; (noise) estruendo m; (collision) choque m; (Com) quiebra f. ●vt estrellar. ●vi quebrar con estrépito; (have accident) tener un accidente; (car etc) estrellarse, chocar; (fail) fracasar. ~ **course** n curso m intensivo. ~ **helmet** n casco m protector. ~**land** vi hacer un aterrizaje forzoso

crass /kræs/ adj craso, burdo

crate /kreɪt/ n cajón m. ●vt embalar

crater /'kreɪtə(r)/ n cráter m

crav|e /kreɪv/ vt ansiar. ~**ing** n ansia f

crawl /krɔːl/ vi (baby) gatear; (move slowly) avanzar lentamente; (drag o.s.) arrastrarse. ~ **to** humillarse ante. ~ **with** hervir de. ●n

crayon (*swimming*) crol *m.* **at a ~** a paso lento

crayon /'kreɪən/ *n* lápiz *m* de color; (*made of wax*) lápiz *m* de cera, crayola *f* (®), crayón *m* (*Mex*)

craz|e /kreɪz/ *n* manía *f.* **~y** /'kreɪzɪ/ *adj* (*-ier, -iest*) loco *m.* **be ~y about** estar loco por

creak /kriːk/ *n* crujido *m;* (*of hinge*) chirrido *m.* ● *vi* crujir; (*hinge*) chirriar

cream /kriːm/ *n* crema *f;* (*fresh*) nata *f,* crema *f* (*LAm*). ● *adj* (*colour*) color crema. ● *vt* (*beat*) batir. **~ cheese** *n* queso *m* para untar, queso *m* crema (*LAm*). **~y** *adj* cremoso

crease /kriːs/ *n* raya *f,* pliegue *m* (*Mex*); (*crumple*) arruga *f.* ● *vt* plegar; (*wrinkle*) arrugar. ● *vi* arrugarse

creat|e /kriː'eɪt/ *vt* crear. **~ion** /-ʃn/ *n* creación *f.* **~ive** *adj* creativo. **~or** *n* creador *m*

creature /'kriːtʃə(r)/ *n* criatura *f*

crèche /kreʃ/ *n* guardería *f* (*infantil*)

credib|ility /kredə'bɪlətɪ/ *n* credibilidad *f.* **~le** /'kredəbl/ *adj* creíble

credit /'kredɪt/ *n* crédito *m;* (*honour*) mérito *m.* **take the ~ for** atribuirse el mérito de. ● *vt* (*pt credited*) acreditar; (*believe*) creer. **~ s.o. with** atribuir a uno. **~ card** *n* tarjeta *f* de crédito. **~or** *n* acreedor *m*

creed /kriːd/ *n* credo *m*

creek /kriːk/ *n* ensenada *f.* **up the ~** 🗵 en apuros

creep /kriːp/ *vi* (*pt crept*) arrastrarse; (*plant*) trepar. ● *n* 🗊 adulador. **~s** /kriːps/ *npl.* **give s.o. the ~s** poner los pelos de punta a uno. **~er** *n* enredadera *f*

cremat|e /krɪ'meɪt/ *vt* incinerar. **~ion** /-ʃn/ *n* cremación *f.* **~orium** /kremə'tɔːrɪəm/ *n* (*pl -ia* /-ɪə/) crematorio *m*

crept /krept/ *see* **CREEP**

crescendo /krɪ'ʃendəʊ/ *n* (*pl -os*) crescendo *m*

crescent /'kresnt/ *n* media luna *f;* (*street*) calle *f* en forma de media luna

crest /krest/ *n* cresta *f;* (*on coat of arms*) emblema *m*

crevice /'krevɪs/ *n* grieta *f*

crew /kruː/ *n* tripulación *f;* (*gang*) pandilla *f.* **~ cut** *n* corte *m* al rape

crib /krɪb/ *n* (*Amer*) cuna *f;* (*Relig*) belén *m.* ● *vt/i* (*pt cribbed*) copiar

crick /krɪk/ *n* calambre *m;* (*in neck*) tortícolis *f*

cricket /'krɪkɪt/ *n* (*Sport*) críquet *m;* (*insect*) grillo *m*

crim|e /kraɪm/ *n* delito *m;* (*murder*) crimen *m;* (*acts*) delincuencia *f.* **~inal** /'krɪmɪnl/ *adj & n* criminal (*m & f*)

crimson /'krɪmzn/ *adj & n* carmesí (*m*)

cringe /krɪndʒ/ *vi* encogerse; (*fig*) humillarse

crinkle /'krɪŋkl/ *vt* arrugar. ● *vi* arrugarse. ● *n* arruga *f*

cripple /'krɪpl/ *n* lisiado *m.* ● *vt* lisiar; (*fig*) paralizar

crisis /'kraɪsɪs/ *n* (*pl crises* /-siːz/) crisis *f*

crisp /krɪsp/ *adj* (*-er, -est*) (*Culin*) crujiente; (*air*) vigorizador. **~s** *npl* patatas *fpl* fritas, papas *fpl* fritas (*LAm*) (*de bolsa*)

crisscross /'krɪskrɒs/ *adj* entrecruzado. ● *vt* entrecruzar. ● *vi* entrecruzarse

criterion /kraɪ'tɪərɪən/ *n* (*pl -ia* /-ɪə/) criterio *m*

critic /'krɪtɪk/ n crítico m. **∼al** adj crítico. **∼ally** adv críticamente; (ill) gravemente

critici|sm /'krɪtɪsɪzəm/ n crítica f. **∼ze** /'krɪtɪsaɪz/ vt/i criticar

croak /krəʊk/ n (of person) gruñido m; (of frog) canto m. ● vi gruñir; (frog) croar

Croat /'krəʊæt/ n croata m & f. **∼ia** /krəʊ'eɪʃə/ n Croacia f. **∼ian** adj croata

crochet /'krəʊʃeɪ/ n crochet m, ganchillo m. ● vt tejer a crochet or a ganchillo

crockery /'krɒkərɪ/ n loza f.

crocodile /'krɒkədaɪl/ n cocodrilo m. **∼ tears** npl lágrimas fpl de cocodrilo

crocus /'krəʊkəs/ n (pl **-es**) azafrán m de primavera

crook /krʊk/ n 🅴 sinvergüenza m & f. **∼ed** /'krʊkɪd/ adj torcido, chueco (LAm); (winding) tortuoso; (dishonest) deshonesto

crop /krɒp/ n cosecha f; (haircut) corte m de pelo muy corto. ● vt (pt cropped) cortar. □ **∼ up** vi surgir

croquet /'krəʊkeɪ/ n croquet m

cross /krɒs/ n cruz f; (of animals) cruce m. ● vt cruzar; (oppose) contrariar. **∼ s.o.'s mind** ocurrírsele a uno. ● vi cruzar. **∼ o.s.** santiguarse. ● adj enfadado, enojado (esp LAm). □ **∼ out** vt tachar. **∼bar** n travesaño m. **∼-examine** /-ɪg'zæmɪn/ vt interrogar. **∼-eyed** adj bizco. **∼fire** n fuego m cruzado. **∼ing** n (by boat) travesía f; (on road) cruce m peatonal. **∼ly** adv con enfado, con enojo (esp LAm). **∼-purposes** /-'pɜːpəsɪz/ npl. **talk at ∼-purposes** hablar sin entenderse. **∼-reference** /-'refrəns/ n remisión f. **∼roads** n invar cruce m.

∼-section /-'sekʃn/ n sección f transversal; (fig) muestra f representativa. **∼walk** n (Amer) paso de peatones. **∼word** n **∼word (puzzle)** crucigrama m

crotch /krɒtʃ/ n entrepiernas fpl

crouch /kraʊtʃ/ vi agacharse

crow /krəʊ/ n cuervo m. **as the ∼ flies** en línea recta. ● vi cacarear. **∼bar** n palanca f

crowd /kraʊd/ n muchedumbre f. ● vt amontonar; (fill) llenar. ● vi amontonarse; (gather) reunirse. **∼ed** adj atestado

crown /kraʊn/ n corona f; (of hill) cumbre f; (of head) coronilla f. ● vt coronar

crucial /'kruːʃl/ adj crucial

crucifix /'kruːsɪfɪks/ n crucifijo m. **∼ion** /-'fɪkʃn/ n crucifixión f

crucify /'kruːsɪfaɪ/ vt crucificar

crude /kruːd/ adj (**-er, -est**) (raw) crudo; (rough) tosco; (vulgar) ordinario

cruel /krʊəl/ adj (**crueller, cruellest**) cruel. **∼ty** n crueldad f

cruet /'kruːɪt/ n vinagrera f

cruise /kruːz/ n crucero m. ● vi hacer un crucero; (of car) circular lentamente. **∼r** n crucero m

crumb /krʌm/ n miga f

crumble /'krʌmbl/ vt desmenuzar. ● vi desmenuzarse; (collapse) derrumbarse

crummy /'krʌmɪ/ adj (**-ier, -iest**) 🅴 miserable

crumpet /'krʌmpɪt/ n bollo m blando

crumple /'krʌmpl/ vt arrugar. ● vi arrugarse

crunch /krʌntʃ/ vt hacer crujir; (bite) masticar. **∼y** adj crujiente

crusade /kruː'seɪd/ n cruzada f.

~r n cruzado m

crush /krʌʃ/ vt aplastar; arrugar (clothes). ● n (crowd) aglomeración f. **have a ~ on** 🆃 estar chiflado por

crust /krʌst/ n corteza f. **~y** adj (bread) de corteza dura

crutch /krʌtʃ/ n muleta f; (between legs) entrepiernas fpl

crux /krʌks/ n (pl **cruxes**). **the ~ (of the matter)** el quid (de la cuestión)

cry /kraɪ/ n grito m. **be a far ~ from** (fig) distar mucho de. ● vi llorar; (call out) gritar. □ **~ off** vi echarse atrás, rajarse. **~baby** n llorón m

crypt /krɪpt/ n cripta f

cryptic /'krɪptɪk/ adj enigmático

crystal /'krɪstl/ n cristal m. **~lize** vi cristalizarse

cub /kʌb/ n cachorro m. **C~** (Scout) n lobato m

Cuba /'kjuːbə/ n Cuba f. **~n** adj & n cubano (m)

cubbyhole /'kʌbɪhəʊl/ n cuchitril m

cub|e /kjuːb/ n cubo m. **~ic** adj cúbico

cubicle /'kjuːbɪkl/ n cubículo m; (changing room) probador m

cuckoo /'kʊkuː/ n cuco m, cuclillo m

cucumber /'kjuːkʌmbə(r)/ n pepino m

cuddl|e /'kʌdl/ vt abrazar. ● vi abrazarse. ● n abrazo m. **~y** adj adorable

cue /kjuː/ n (Mus) entrada f; (in theatre) pie m; (in snooker) taco m

cuff /kʌf/ n puño m; (Amer, of trousers) vuelta f, dobladillo m; (blow) bofetada f. **speak off the ~** hablar de improviso. ● vt abofetear. **~link**

n gemelo m, mancuerna f (Mex)

cul-de-sac /'kʌldəsæk/ n callejón m sin salida

culinary /'kʌlɪnərɪ/ adj culinario

cull /kʌl/ vt sacrificar en forma selectiva (animals)

culminat|e /'kʌlmɪneɪt/ vi culminar. **~ion** /-'neɪʃn/ n culminación f

culprit /'kʌlprɪt/ n culpable m & f

cult /kʌlt/ n culto m

cultivat|e /'kʌltɪveɪt/ vt cultivar. **~ion** /-'veɪʃn/ n cultivo m

cultur|al /'kʌltʃərəl/ adj cultural. **~e** /'kʌltʃə(r)/ n cultura f; (Bot etc) cultivo m. **~ed** adj cultivado; (person) culto

cumbersome /'kʌmbəsəm/ adj incómodo; (heavy) pesado

cunning /'kʌnɪŋ/ adj astuto. ● n astucia f

cup /kʌp/ n taza f; (trophy) copa f

cupboard /'kʌbəd/ n armario m

curator /kjʊə'reɪtə(r)/ n (of museum) conservador m

curb /kɜːb/ n freno m; (Amer) bordillo m (de la acera), borde m de la banqueta (Mex). ● vt refrenar

curdle /'kɜːdl/ vt cuajar. ● vi cuajarse; (go bad) cortarse

cure /kjʊə(r)/ vt curar. ● n cura f

curfew /'kɜːfjuː/ n toque m de queda

curio|sity /kjʊərɪ'ɒsətɪ/ n curiosidad f. **~us** /'kjʊərɪəs/ adj curioso

curl /kɜːl/ vt rizar, enchinar (Mex). **~ o.s. up** acurrucarse. ● vi (hair) rizarse, enchinarse (Mex); (paper) ondularse. ● n rizo m, chino m (Mex), rulo m, chino m (Mex). **~y** adj (**-ier**, **-iest**) rizado, chino (Mex)

currant /'kʌrənt/ n pasa f de Corinto

currency /'kʌrənsɪ/ n moneda f

current /'kʌrənt/ adj & n corriente (f); (existing) actual. ~ **affairs** npl sucesos de actualidad. ~**ly** adv actualmente

curriculum /kə'rɪkjʊləm/ n (pl -la) programa m de estudios. ~ **vitae** n currículum m vitae

curry /'kʌrɪ/ n curry m. ● vt preparar al curry

curse /kɜːs/ n maldición f; (oath) palabrota f. ● vt maldecir. ● vi decir palabrotas

cursory /'kɜːsərɪ/ adj superficial

curt /kɜːt/ adj brusco

curtain /'kɜːtn/ n cortina f; (in theatre) telón m

curtsey, curtsy /'kɜːtsɪ/ n reverencia f. ● vi hacer una reverencia

curve /kɜːv/ n curva f. ● vi estar curvado; (road) torcerse

cushion /'kʊʃn/ n cojín m, almohadón m

cushy /'kʊʃɪ/ adj (-ier, -iest) 🄸 fácil

custard /'kʌstəd/ n natillas fpl

custody /'kʌstədɪ/ n custodia f; **be in** ~ Jurid estar detenido

custom /'kʌstəm/ n costumbre f; (Com) clientela f. ~**ary** /-ərɪ/ adj acostumbrado. ~**er** n cliente m. ~**s** npl aduana f. ~**s officer** n aduanero m

cut /kʌt/ vt/i (pt **cut**, pres p **cutting**) cortar; reducir (prices). ● n corte m; (reduction) reducción f. □ ~ **across** vt cortar camino por. □ ~ **back**, ~ **down** vt reducir. □ ~ **in** vi interrumpir. □ ~ **off** vt cortar; (phone) desconectar; (fig) aislar. □ ~ **out** vt recortar; (omit) suprimir. □ ~ **through** vt cortar camino por. □ ~ **up** vt cortar en pedazos

cute /kjuːt/ adj (-er, -est) 🄸

mono, amoroso (LAm); (Amer, attractive) guapo, buen mozo (LAm)

cutlery /'kʌtlərɪ/ n cubiertos mpl

cutlet /'kʌtlɪt/ n chuleta f

cut: ~**-price**, (Amer) ~**-rate** adj a precio reducido. ~**-throat** adj despiadado. ~**ting** adj cortante; (remark) mordaz. ● n (from newspaper) recorte m; (of plant) esqueje m

CV n (= **curriculum vitae**) currículum m vitae

cyberspace /'saɪbəspeɪs/ ciberespacio m

cycl|e /'saɪkl/ n ciclo m; (bicycle) bicicleta f. ● vi ir en bicicleta. ~**ing** n ciclismo m. ~**ist** n ciclista m & f

cylind|er /'sɪlɪndə(r)/ n cilindro m. ~**er head** (Auto) n culata f. ~**rical** /-'lɪndrɪkl/ adj cilíndrico

cymbal /'sɪmbl/ n címbalo m

cynic /'sɪnɪk/ n cínico m. ~**al** adj cínico. ~**ism** /-sɪzəm/ n cinismo m

Czech /tʃek/ adj & n checo (m). ~**oslovakia** /-əslə'vækɪə/ n (History) Checoslovaquia f. ~ **Republic** n the ~ **Republic** n la República Checa

Dd

dab /dæb/ vt (pt **dabbed**) tocar ligeramente. ● n toque m suave. **a** ~ **of** un poquito de

dad /dæd/ n 🄸 papá m. ~**dy** n papi m. ~**dy-long-legs** n invar (cranefly) típula f; (Amer, harvestman) segador m, falangio m

daffodil /'dæfədɪl/ n narciso m

daft /dɑːft/ adj (-er, -est) ⓘ tonto

dagger /'dægə(r)/ n daga f, puñal m

daily /'deɪlɪ/ adj diario. ● adv diariamente, cada día

Dáil Éireann Es el nombre de la cámara baja del Parlamento de la República de Irlanda. Se pronuncia /dɔːl/ y consta de 166 representantes o diputados, comúnmente llamados *TDs*, que representan 41 circunscripciones. Se eligen por medio del sistema de representación proporcional. Según la Constitución debe haber un diputado por cada 20.000 a 30.000 personas.

dainty /'deɪntɪ/ adj (-ier, -iest) delicado

dairy /'deərɪ/ n vaquería f; (shop) lechería f

daisy /'deɪzɪ/ n margarita f

dam /dæm/ n presa f, represa f (LAm)

damage /'dæmɪdʒ/ n daño m; ~s (npl, Jurid) daños mpl y perjuicios mpl. ● vt (fig) dañar, estropear. ~ing adj perjudicial

dame /deɪm/ n (old use) dama f; (Amer, sl) chica f

damn /dæm/ vt condenar; (curse) maldecir. ● int ⓘ ¡caray! ⓘ. ● adj maldito. ● n I don't give a ~ (no) me importa un comino

damp /dæmp/ n humedad f. ● adj (-er, -est) húmedo. ● vt mojar. ~ness n humedad f

danc|e /dɑːns/ vt/i bailar. ● n baile m. ~e hall n salón m de baile. ~er n bailador m; (professional) bailarín m. ~ing n baile m

dandelion /'dændɪlaɪən/ n diente

m de león

dandruff /'dændrʌf/ n caspa f

dandy /'dændɪ/ n petimetre m

Dane /deɪn/ n danés m

danger /'deɪndʒə(r)/ n peligro m; (risk) riesgo m. ~ous adj peligroso

dangle /'dæŋgl/ vt balancear. ● vi suspender, colgar

Danish /'deɪnɪʃ/ adj danés. ● m (language) danés m

dar|e /deə(r)/ vt desafiar. ● vi atreverse a. I ~ say probablemente. ● n desafío m. ~edevil n atrevido m. ~ing adj atrevido

dark /dɑːk/ adj (-er, -est) oscuro; (skin, hair) moreno. ● n oscuridad f; (nightfall) atardecer. in the ~ a oscuras. ~en vt oscurecer. ● vi oscurecerse. ~ness n oscuridad f. ~room n cámara f oscura

darling /'dɑːlɪŋ/ adj querido. ● n cariño m

darn /dɑːn/ vt zurcir

dart /dɑːt/ n dardo m. ● vi lanzarse; (run) precipitarse. ~board n diana f. ~s npl los dardos mpl

dash /dæʃ/ vi precipitarse. ● vt tirar; (break) romper; defraudar (hopes). ● n (small amount) poquito m; (punctuation mark) guión m. ~ off vi marcharse apresuradamente. ~ out vi salir corriendo. ~board n tablero m de mandos

data /'deɪtə/ npl datos mpl. ~base n base f de datos. ~ processing n proceso m de datos

date /deɪt/ n fecha f; (appointment) cita f; (fruit) dátil m. to ~ hasta la fecha. ● vt fechar. ● vi datar; (be old-fashioned) quedar anticuado. ~d adj pasado de moda

daub /dɔːb/ vt embadurnar

daughter /'dɔːtə(r)/ n hija f.
~-in-law n nuera f

dawdle /'dɔːdl/ vi andar despacio;
(waste time) perder el tiempo

dawn /dɔːn/ n amanecer m. ● vi
amanecer; (fig) nacer. **it ~ed on
me that** caí en la cuenta de que

day /deɪ/ n día m; (whole day) jornada f; (period) época f. **~break** n
amanecer m. **~ care center** n
(Amer) guardería f infantil. **~dream**
n ensueño m. ● vi soñar despierto.
~light n luz f del día. **~time** n
día m

daze /deɪz/ vt aturdir. ● n aturdimiento m. **in a ~** aturdido. **~d** adj
aturdido

dazzle /'dæzl/ vt deslumbrar

dead /ded/ adj muerto; (numb)
dormido. ● adv justo; (ℂ, completely) completamente. **~ beat**
rendido. **~ slow** muy lento. **stop
~** parar en seco. **~en** vt amortiguar (sound, blow); calmar (pain).
~ end n callejón m sin salida.
~line n fecha f tope, plazo m de
entrega. **~lock** n punto m muerto.
~ly adj (-ier, -iest) mortal

deaf /def/ adj (-er, -est) sordo.
~en vt ensordecer. **~ness** n sordera f

deal /diːl/ n (agreement) acuerdo
m; (treatment) trato m. **a good ~**
bastante. **a great ~ (of)** muchísimo. ● vt (pt dealt) dar (a blow,
cards). ● vi (cards) dar, repartir.
□ **~ in** vt comerciar en. □ **~ out** vt
repartir, distribuir. □ **~ with** vt tratar con (person); tratar de (subject); ocuparse de (problem). **~er**
n comerciante m. **drug ~er** trafi-
cante m & f de drogas

dean /diːn/ n deán m; (Univ) decano m

dear /dɪə(r)/ adj (-er, -est) querido;

(expensive) caro. ● n querido m.
● adv caro. ● int. **oh ~!** ¡ay por
Dios! **~ me!** ¡Dios mío! **~ly** adv
(pay) caro; (very much) muchísimo

death /deθ/ n muerte f. **~ sentence** n pena f de muerte. **~ trap**
n lugar m peligroso.

debatable /dɪ'beɪtəbl/ adj discutible. **~e** /dɪ'beɪt/ n debate m. ● vt
debatir, discutir

debauchery /dɪ'bɔːtʃərɪ/ vt liber-
tinaje m

debit /'debɪt/ n débito m. ● vt debi-
tar, cargar. **~ card** n tarjeta f de
cobro automático

debris /'debriː/ n escombros mpl

debt /det/ n deuda f. **be in ~**
tener deudas. **~or** n deudor m

debut /'debjuː/ n debut m

decade /'dekeɪd/ n década f

decaden|ce /'dekədəns/ n decaden-
dencia f. **~t** adj decadente

decay /dɪ'keɪ/ vi descomponerse;
(tooth) cariarse. ● n descomposición
f; (of tooth) caries f

deceased /dɪ'siːst/ adj difunto

deceit /dɪ'siːt/ n engaño m. **~ful**
adj falso. **~fully** adv falsamente

deceive /dɪ'siːv/ vt engañar

December /dɪ'sembə(r)/ n diciembre m

decen|cy /'diːsənsɪ/ n decencia f.
~t adj decente; (fam, good)
bueno; (fam, kind) amable. **~tly**
adv decentemente

deception /dɪ'sepʃn/ n engaño
m. **~ve** /-tɪv/ adj engañoso

decibel /'desɪbel/ n decibel(io) m

decide /dɪ'saɪd/ vt/i decidir. **~d**
adj resuelto; (unquestionable) indudable

decimal /'desɪml/ adj & n decimal
(m). **~ point** n coma f (decimal),

punto m decimal

decipher /dɪˈsaɪfə(r)/ vt descifrar

decis|ion /dɪˈsɪʒn/ n decisión f. **~ive** /dɪˈsaɪsɪv/ adj decisivo; (manner) decidido

deck /dek/ n (Naut) cubierta f; (Amer, of cards) baraja f; (of bus) piso m. ● vt adornar. **~chair** n tumbona f, silla f de playa

declar|ation /deklaˈreɪʃn/ n declaración f. **~e** /dɪˈkleə(r)/ vt declarar

decline /dɪˈklaɪn/ vt rehusar; (Gram) declinar. ● vi disminuir; (deteriorate) deteriorarse. ● n decadencia f; (decrease) disminución f

decode /diːˈkəʊd/ vt descifrar

decompose /diːkəmˈpəʊz/ vi descomponerse

décor /ˈdeɪkɔ:(r)/ n decoración f

decorat|e /ˈdekəreɪt/ vt adornar, decorar (LAm); empapelar y pintar (room). **~ion** /-ˈreɪʃn/ n (act) decoración f; (ornament) adorno m. **~ive** /-ətɪv/ adj decorativo. **~or** n pintor m decorador

decoy /ˈdiːkɔɪ/ n señuelo m. ● /dɪˈkɔɪ/ vt atraer con señuelo

decrease /dɪˈkriːs/ vt/i disminuir. ● /ˈdiːkriːs/ n disminución f

decree /dɪˈkriː/ n decreto m. ● vt decretar

decrepit /dɪˈkrepɪt/ adj decrépito

decriminalize /diːˈkrɪmɪnəlaɪz/ vt despenalizar

dedicat|e /ˈdedɪkeɪt/ vt dedicar. **~ion** /-ˈkeɪʃn/ n dedicación f

deduce /dɪˈdjuːs/ vt deducir

deduct /dɪˈdʌkt/ vt deducir. **~ion** /-ʃn/ n deducción f

deed /diːd/ n hecho m; (Jurid) escritura f

deem /diːm/ vt juzgar, considerar

deep /diːp/ adj (-er, -est) adv profundo. ● adv profundamente. **be ~ in thought** estar absorto en sus pensamientos. **~en** vt hacer más profundo. ● vi hacerse más profundo. **~freeze** n congelador m, freezer m (LAm). **~ly** adv profundamente

deer /dɪə/ n invar ciervo m

deface /dɪˈfeɪs/ vt desfigurar

default /dɪˈfɔːlt/ vi faltar. ● n opción por defecto. **by ~** en rebeldía

defeat /dɪˈfiːt/ vt vencer; (frustrate) frustrar. ● n derrota f. **~ism** n derrotismo m. **~ist** n derrotista a & (m & f)

defect /ˈdiːfekt/ n defecto m. ● /dɪˈfekt/ vi desertar. **~ to** pasar a. **~ion** /dɪˈfekʃn/ n (Pol) defección f. **~ive** /dɪˈfektɪv/ adj defectuoso

defence /dɪˈfens/ n defensa f. **~less** adj indefenso

defen|d /dɪˈfend/ vt defender. **~dant** n (Jurid) acusado m. **~sive** /-sɪv/ adj defensivo. ● n defensiva f

defer /dɪˈfɜː(r)/ vt (pt deferred) aplazar. **~ence** /ˈdefərəns/ n deferencia f. **~ential** /defəˈrenʃl/ adj deferente

defian|ce /dɪˈfaɪəns/ n desafío m. **in ~ce of** a despecho de. **~t** adj desafiante. **~tly** adv con actitud desafiante

deficien|cy /dɪˈfɪʃənsɪ/ n falta f. **~t** adj deficiente. **be ~t in** carecer de

deficit /ˈdefɪsɪt/ n déficit m

define /dɪˈfaɪn/ vt definir

definite /ˈdefɪnɪt/ adj (final) definitivo; (certain) seguro; (clear) claro; (firm) firme. **~ly** adv seguramente; (definitively) definitivamente

definition /defɪˈnɪʃn/ n definición f

definitive /dɪˈfɪnətɪv/ adj definitivo

deflate /dɪˈfleɪt/ vt desinflar. • vi desinflarse

deflect /dɪˈflekt/ vt desviar

deform /dɪˈfɔːm/ vt deformar. **~ed** adj deforme. **~ity** n deformidad f

defrost /diːˈfrɒst/ vt descongelar. • vi descongelarse

deft /deft/ adj (-er, -est) hábil. **~ly** adv hábilmente f

defuse /diːˈfjuːz/ vt desactivar (bomb); (fig) calmar

defy /dɪˈfaɪ/ vt desafiar

degenerate /dɪˈdʒenəreɪt/ vi degenerar. • /dɪˈdʒenərət/ adj & n degenerado (m)

degrad|ation /degrəˈdeɪʃn/ n degradación f. **~e** /dɪˈgreɪd/ vt degradar

degree /dɪˈɡriː/ n grado m; (Univ) licenciatura f; (rank) rango m. **to a certain ~** hasta cierto punto

deign /deɪn/ vi. **~ to** dignarse

deity /ˈdiːɪti/ n deidad f

deject|ed /dɪˈdʒektɪd/ adj desanimado. **~ion** /-ʃn/ n abatimiento m

delay /dɪˈleɪ/ vt retrasar, demorar (LAm). • vi tardar, demorar (LAm). • n retraso m, demora f (LAm)

delegat|e /ˈdelɪɡeɪt/ vt/i delegar. • /ˈdelɪɡət/ n delegado m. **~ion** /-ˈɡeɪʃn/ n delegación f

delete /dɪˈliːt/ vt tachar. **~ion** /-ʃn/ n supresión f

deliberat|e /dɪˈlɪbəreɪt/ vt/i deliberar. • /dɪˈlɪbərət/ adj intencionado; (steps etc) pausado. **~ely** adv a propósito. **~ion** /-ˈreɪʃn/ n deliberación f

delica|cy /ˈdelɪkəsi/ n delicadeza f; (food) manjar m. **~te** /ˈdelɪkət/ adj delicado

delicatessen /delɪkəˈtesn/ n charcutería f, salchichonería f (Mex)

delicious /dɪˈlɪʃəs/ adj delicioso

delight /dɪˈlaɪt/ n placer m. • vt encantar. • vi deleitarse. **~ed** adj encantado. **~ful** adj delicioso

deliri|ous /dɪˈlɪriəs/ adj delirante. **~um** /-əm/ n delirio m

deliver /dɪˈlɪvə(r)/ vt entregar; (distribute) repartir; (aim) lanzar; (Med) **he ~ed the baby** la asistió en el parto. **~ance** n liberación f. **~y** n entrega f; (of post) reparto m; (Med) parto m

delta /ˈdeltə/ n (of river) delta m

delude /dɪˈluːd/ vt engañar. **~ o.s.** engañarse

deluge /ˈdeljuːdʒ/ n diluvio m

delusion /dɪˈluːʒn/ n ilusión f

deluxe /dɪˈlʌks/ adj de lujo

delve /delv/ vi hurgar. **~ into** (investigate) ahondar en

demand /dɪˈmɑːnd/ vt exigir. • n petición f, pedido m (LAm); (claim) exigencia f; (Com) demanda f. **in ~** muy popular, muy solicitado. **on ~** a solicitud. **~ing** adj exigente. **~s** npl exigencias fpl

demented /dɪˈmentɪd/ adj demente

demo /ˈdeməʊ/ n (pl -os) 🄳 manifestación f

democra|cy /dɪˈmɒkrəsi/ n democracia f. **~t** /ˈdeməkræt/ n demócrata m & f. **D~t** a & n (in US) demócrata (m & f). **~tic** /demə ˈkrætɪk/ adj democrático

demoli|sh /dɪˈmɒlɪʃ/ vt derribar. **~tion** /deməˈlɪʃn/ n demolición f

demon /ˈdiːmən/ n demonio m

demonstrat|e /ˈdemənstreɪt/ vt demostrar. • vi manifestarse, hacer una manifestación. **~ion** /-ˈstreɪʃn/ n demostración f; (Pol) manifestación f. ~or /'demənstreitə(r)/n (Pol) manifestante m & f; (marketing) demostrador m

demoralize /dɪ'mɒrəlaɪz/ vt desmoralizar

demote /dɪ'məʊt/ vt bajar de categoría

demure /dɪ'mjʊə(r)/ adj recatado

den /den/ n (of animal) guarida f, madriguera f

denial /dɪ'naɪəl/ n denegación f; (statement) desmentimiento m

denim /'denɪm/ n tela f vaquera or de jeans, mezclilla (Mex) f. ~s npl vaqueros mpl, jeans mpl, tejanos mpl, pantalones mpl de mezclilla (Mex)

Denmark /'denmɑːk/ n Dinamarca f

denote /dɪ'nəʊt/ vt denotar

denounce /dɪ'naʊns/ vt denunciar

dens|e /dens/ adj (-er, -est) espeso; (person) torpe. ~ely adv densamente. ~ity n densidad f

dent /dent/ n abolladura f. ● vt abollar

dental /'dentl/ adj dental. ~ floss /flɒs/ n hilo m or seda f dental. ~ surgeon n dentista m & f

dentist /'dentɪst/ n dentista m & f. ~ry n odontología f

dentures /'dentʃəz/ npl dentadura f postiza

deny /dɪ'naɪ/ vt negar; desmentir (rumour); denegar (request)

deodorant /diː'əʊdərənt/ adj & n desodorante (m)

depart /dɪ'pɑːt/ vi partir, salir. ~ from (deviate from) apartarse de

department /dɪ'pɑːtmənt/ n departamento m; (Pol) ministerio m, secretaría f (Mex). ~ store n grandes almacenes mpl, tienda f de departamentos (Mex)

departure /dɪ'pɑːtʃə(r)/ n partida f; (of train etc) salida f

depend /dɪ'pend/ vi depender. ~ on depender de. ~able adj digno de confianza. ~ant n familiar m & f dependiente. ~ence n dependencia f. ~ent adj dependiente. be ~ent on depender de

depict /dɪ'pɪkt/ vt representar; (in words) describir

deplete /dɪ'pliːt/ vt agotar

deplor|able /dɪ'plɔːrəbl/ adj deplorable. ~e /dɪ'plɔː(r)/ vt deplorar

deploy /dɪ'plɔɪ/ vt desplegar

deport /dɪ'pɔːt/ vt deportar. ~ation /-'teɪʃn/ n deportación f

depose /dɪ'pəʊz/ vt deponer

deposit /dɪ'pɒzɪt/ vt (pt deposited) depositar. ● n depósito m

depot /'depəʊ/ n depósito m; (Amer) estación f de autobuses

deprav|ed /dɪ'preɪvd/ adj depravado. ~ity /dɪ'prævətɪ/ n depravación f

depress /dɪ'pres/ vt deprimir; (press down) apretar. ~ed adj deprimido. ~ing adj deprimente. ~ion /-ʃn/ n depresión f

depriv|ation /deprɪ'veɪʃn/ n privación f. ~e /dɪ'praɪv/ vt. ~e of privar de. ~ed adj carenciado

depth /depθ/ n profundidad f. be out of one's ~ perder pie; (fig) meterse en honduras. **in** ~ a fondo

deput|ize /'depjʊtaɪz/ vi. ~ize for sustituir a. ~y /'depjʊtɪ/ n sustituto m. ~y chairman n vicepresidente m

derail /dɪ'reɪl/ vt hacer descarrilar. ~ment n descarrilamiento m

derelict /'derəlɪkt/ adj abandonado y en ruinas

deri|de /dɪ'raɪd/ vt mofarse de.

derivation | detain

~**sion** /dɪˈrɪʒn/ n mofa f. ~**sive** /dɪˈraɪsɪv/ adj burlón. ~**sory** /dɪˈraɪsərɪ/ adj (offer etc) irrisorio

derivation /derɪˈveɪʃn/ n derivación f. ~**ative** /dɪˈrɪvətɪv/ n derivado m. ~**e** /dɪˈraɪv/ vt/i derivar

derogatory /dɪˈrɒɡətrɪ/ adj despectivo

descend /dɪˈsend/ vt/i descender, bajar. ~**dant** n descendiente m & f. ~**t** n descenso m, bajada f; (lineage) ascendencia f

describe /dɪsˈkraɪb/ vt describir. ~**ption** /-ˈkrɪpʃn/ n descripción f. ~**ptive** /-ˈkrɪptɪv/ adj descriptivo

desecrate /ˈdesɪkreɪt/ vt profanar

desert¹ /dɪˈzɜːt/ vt abandonar. ● vi (Mil) desertar. ~**er** /dɪˈzɜːtə(r)/ n desertor m

desert² /ˈdezət/ adj & n desierto (m)

deserts /dɪˈzɜːts/ npl lo merecido. **get one's just** ~ llevarse su merecido

deserve /dɪˈzɜːv/ vt merecer. ~**ing** adj (cause) meritorio

design /dɪˈzaɪn/ n diseño m; (plan) plan m. ~**s** (intentions) propósitos mpl. ● vt diseñar; (plan) planear

designate /ˈdezɪɡneɪt/ vt designar

designer /dɪˈzaɪnə(r)/ n diseñador m; (fashion ~) diseñador de modas. ● adj (clothes) de diseño exclusivo

desirable /dɪˈzaɪərəbl/ adj deseable

desire /dɪˈzaɪə(r)/ n deseo m. ● vt desear

desk /desk/ n escritorio m; (at school) pupitre m; (in hotel) recepción f; (Com) caja f. ~**top publishing** n autoedición f, edición f electrónica

desolate /ˈdesələt/ adj desolado; (uninhabited) deshabitado. ~**ion** /-ˈleɪʃn/ n desolación f

despair /dɪˈspeə(r)/ n desesperación f. **be in** ~ estar desesperado. ● vi. ~ **of** desesperarse de

despatch /dɪˈspætʃ/ vt, n see DISPATCH

desperat|e /ˈdespərət/ adj desesperado. ~**ely** adv desesperadamente. ~**ion** /-ˈreɪʃn/ n desesperación f

despicable /dɪˈspɪkəbl/ adj despreciable

despise /dɪˈspaɪz/ vt despreciar

despite /dɪˈspaɪt/ prep a pesar de

despondent /dɪˈspɒndənt/ adj abatido

despot /ˈdespɒt/ n déspota m

dessert /dɪˈzɜːt/ n postre m. ~**spoon** n cuchara f de postre

destination /destɪˈneɪʃn/ n destino m

destiny /ˈdestɪnɪ/ n destino m

destitute /ˈdestɪtjuːt/ adj indigente

destroy /dɪˈstrɔɪ/ vt destruir. ~**er** n destructor m

destructi|on /dɪˈstrʌkʃn/ n destrucción f. ~**ve** /-ɪv/ adj destructivo

desultory /ˈdesəltrɪ/ adj desganado

detach /dɪˈtætʃ/ vt separar. ~**able** adj separable. ~**ed** adj (aloof) distante; (house) no adosado. ~**ment** n desprendimiento m, (Mil) destacamento m; (aloofness) indiferencia f

detail /ˈdiːteɪl/ n detalle m. **explain sth in** ~ explicar algo detalladamente. ● vt detallar; (Mil) destacar. ~**ed** adj detallado

detain /dɪˈteɪn/ vt detener; (delay) retener. ~**ee** /diːterˈniː/ n detenido m

detect /dɪˈtekt/ vt percibir; (*discover*) descubrir. ~**ive** n (*private*) detective m; (*in police*) agente m & f. ~**or** n detector m

detention /dɪˈtenʃn/ n detención f

deter /dɪˈtɜː(r)/ vt (pt deterred) disuadir; (*prevent*) impedir

detergent /dɪˈtɜːdʒənt/ adj & n detergente (m)

deteriorat|e /dɪˈtɪərɪəreɪt/ vi deteriorarse. ~**ion** /-ˈreɪʃn/ n deterioro m

determin|ation /dɪtɜːmɪˈneɪʃn/ n determinación f. ~**e** /dɪˈtɜːmɪn/ vt determinar; (*decide*) decidir. ~**ed** adj determinado; (*resolute*) decidido

deterrent /dɪˈterənt/ n elemento m de disuasión

detest /dɪˈtest/ vt aborrecer. ~**able** adj odioso

detonat|e /ˈdetəneɪt/ vt hacer detonar. ● vi detonar. ~**ion** /-ˈneɪʃn/ n detonación f. ~**or** n detonador m

detour /ˈdiːtʊə(r)/ n rodeo m; (*Amer, of transport*) desvío m, desviación f. ● vt (*Amer*) desviar

detract /dɪˈtrækt/ vi. ~ from disminuir

detriment /ˈdetrɪmənt/ n. to the ~ of en perjuicio de. ~**al** /-ˈmentl/ adj perjudicial

devalue /diːˈvæljuː/ vt desvalorizar

devastat|e /ˈdevəsteɪt/ vt devastar. ~**ing** adj devastador; (*fig*) arrollador. ~**ion** /-ˈsteɪʃn/ n devastación f

develop /dɪˈveləp/ vt desarrollar; contraer (illness); urbanizar (land). ● vi desarrollarse; (*appear*) surgir. ~**ing** adj (country) en vías de desarrollo. ~**ment** n desarrollo m. (new) ~**ment** novedad f

deviant /ˈdiːvɪənt/ adj desviado

deviat|e /ˈdiːvɪeɪt/ vi desviarse. ~**ion** /-ˈeɪʃn/ n desviación f

device /dɪˈvaɪs/ n dispositivo m; (*scheme*) estratagema f

devil /ˈdevl/ n diablo m

devious /ˈdiːvɪəs/ adj taimado

devise /dɪˈvaɪz/ vt idear

devoid /dɪˈvɔɪd/ adj. be ~ of carecer de

devolution /diːvəˈluːʃn/ n descentralización f; (*of power*) delegación f

devot|e /dɪˈvəʊt/ vt dedicar. ~**ed** adj (couple) unido; (service) leal. ~**ee** /devəˈtiː/ n partidario m. ~**ion** /-ʃn/ n devoción f

devour /dɪˈvaʊə(r)/ vt devorar

devout /dɪˈvaʊt/ adj devoto

dew /djuː/ n rocío m

dexterity /dekˈsterətɪ/ n destreza f

diabet|es /daɪəˈbiːtiːz/ n diabetes f. ~**ic** /-ˈbetɪk/ adj & n diabético (m)

diabolical /daɪəˈbɒlɪkl/ adj diabólico

diagnos|e /ˈdaɪəgnəʊz/ vt diagnosticar. ~**is** /-ˈnəʊsɪs/ n (pl -oses/-siːz/) diagnóstico m

diagonal /daɪˈægənl/ adj & n diagonal (f)

diagram /ˈdaɪəgræm/ n diagrama m

dial /ˈdaɪəl/ n cuadrante m; (on clock, watch) esfera f; (on phone) disco m. ● vt (pt dialled) marcar, discar (LAm)

dialect /ˈdaɪəlekt/ n dialecto m

dialling:. ~ **code** n prefijo m, código m de la zona (LAm). ~ **tone** n tono m de marcar, tono m de discado (LAm)

dialogue /ˈdaɪəlɒg/ n diálogo m

dial tone n (Amer) see DIALLING TONE

diameter /daɪˈæmɪtə(r)/ n diámetro m

diamond /ˈdaɪəmənd/ n diamante m; (shape) rombo m. **~s** npl (Cards) diamantes mpl

diaper /ˈdaɪəpə(r)/ n (Amer) pañal m

diaphragm /ˈdaɪəfræm/ n diafragma m

diarrhoea /daɪəˈrɪə/ n diarrea f

diary /ˈdaɪərɪ/ n diario m; (book) agenda f

dice /daɪs/ n invar dado m. ● vt (Culin) cortar en cubitos

dictat|e /dɪkˈteɪt/ vt/i dictar. **~ion** /dɪkˈteɪʃn/ n dictado m. **~or** n dictador m. **~orship** n dictadura f

dictionary /ˈdɪkʃənərɪ/ n diccionario m

did /dɪd/ see DO

didn't /ˈdɪdnt/ = **did not**

die /daɪ/ vi (pres p dying) morir. be dying to morirse por. □ **~ down** vi irse apagando. □ **~ out** vi extinguirse

diesel /ˈdiːzl/ n (fuel) gasóleo m. **~ engine** n motor m diesel

diet /ˈdaɪət/ n alimentación f; (restricted) régimen m. be on a **~** estar a régimen. ● vi estar a régimen

differ /ˈdɪfə(r)/ vi ser distinto; (disagree) no estar de acuerdo. **~ence** /ˈdɪfrəns/ n diferencia f; (disagreement) desacuerdo m. **~ent** /ˈdɪfrənt/ adj distinto, diferente. **~ently** adv de otra manera

difficult /ˈdɪfɪkəlt/ adj difícil. **~y** n dificultad f

diffus|e /dɪˈfjuːs/ adj difuso. ● /dɪˈfjuːz/ vt difundir. ● vi difundirse. **~ion** /-ʒn/ n difusión f

dig /dɪg/ n (poke) empujón m; (poke with elbow) codazo m; (remark) indirecta f. **~s** npl 🔟 alojamiento m ● vt (pt dug, pres p digging) cavar; (thrust) empujar. ● vi cavar. □ **~ out** vt extraer. □ **~ up** vt desenterrar

digest /ˈdaɪdʒest/ n resumen m. ● /daɪˈdʒest/ vt digerir. **~ion** /-ˈdʒestʃn/ n digestión f. **~ive** /-ˈdʒestɪv/ adj digestivo

digger /ˈdɪgə(r)/ n (Mec) excavadora f

digit /ˈdɪdʒɪt/ n dígito m; (finger) dedo m. **~al** /ˈdɪdʒɪtl/ adj digital

dignified /ˈdɪgnɪfaɪd/ adj solemne

dignitary /ˈdɪgnɪtərɪ/ n dignatario m

dignity /ˈdɪgnətɪ/ n dignidad f

digress /daɪˈgres/ vi divagar. **~ from** apartarse de. **~ion** /-ʃn/ n digresión f

dike /daɪk/ n dique m

dilapidated /dɪˈlæpɪdeɪtɪd/ adj ruinoso

dilate /daɪˈleɪt/ vt dilatar. ● vi dilatarse

dilemma /daɪˈlemə/ n dilema m

diligent /ˈdɪlɪdʒənt/ adj diligente

dilute /daɪˈljuːt/ vt diluir

dim /dɪm/ adj (dimmer, dimmest) (light) débil; (room) oscuro; (fam, stupid) torpe. ● vt (pt dimmed) atenuar. **~ one's headlights** (Amer) poner las (luces) cortas or de cruce, poner las (luces) bajas (LAm). ● vi (light) irse atenuando

dime /daɪm/ n (Amer) moneda de diez centavos

dimension /daɪˈmenʃn/ n dimensión f

diminish /dɪˈmɪnɪʃ/ vt/i disminuir

dimple /ˈdɪmpl/ n hoyuelo m

din /dɪn/ n jaleo m

dine /daɪn/ vi cenar. **~r** n comensal m & f; (*Amer, restaurant*) cafetería f

dinghy /'dɪŋgɪ/ n bote m; (*inflatable*) bote m neumático

dingy /'dɪndʒɪ/ adj (-ier, -iest) miserable, sucio

dinner /'dɪnə(r)/ n cena f, comida f (*LAm*). **have ~** cenar, comer (*LAm*). **~ party** n cena f, comida f (*LAm*)

dinosaur /'daɪnəsɔ:(r)/ n dinosaurio m

dint /dɪnt/ n. **by ~ of** a fuerza de

dip /dɪp/ vt (*pt dipped*) meter; (*in liquid*) mojar. **~ one's headlights** poner (las luces) cortas o de cruce, poner las luces bajas (*LAm*). ● vi bajar. ● n (*slope*) inclinación f; (*in sea*) baño m. □ **~ into** vt hojear (book)

diphthong /'dɪfθɒŋ/ n diptongo m

diploma /dɪ'pləʊmə/ n diploma m

diploma|cy /dɪ'pləʊməsɪ/ n diplomacia f. **~t** /'dɪpləmæt/ n diplomático m. **~tic** /-'mætɪk/ adj diplomático

dipstick /'dɪpstɪk/ n (*Auto*) varilla f del nivel de aceite

dire /daɪə(r)/ adj (-er, -est) terrible; (need, poverty) extremo

direct /dɪ'rekt/ adj directo. ● adv directamente. ● vt dirigir; (show the way) indicar. **~ion** /-ʃn/ n dirección f. **~ions** npl instrucciones fpl. **~ly** adv directamente; (at once) en seguida. ● conj 🇬🇧 en cuanto. **~or** n director m; (of company) directivo m

directory /dɪ'rektərɪ/ n guía f; (*Comp*) directorio m

dirt /dɜ:t/ n suciedad f. **~y** adj

(-ier, -iest) sucio. ● vt ensuciar

disab|ility /dɪsə'bɪlətɪ/ n invalidez f. **~le** /dɪs'eɪbl/ vt incapacitar. **~led** adj minusválido

disadvantage /dɪsəd'vɑ:ntɪdʒ/ n desventaja f. **~d** adj desfavorecido

disagree /dɪsə'gri:/ vi no estar de acuerdo (with con). **~ with** (food, climate) sentarle mal a. **~able** adj desagradable. **~ment** n desacuerdo m; (quarrel) riña f

disappear /dɪsə'pɪə(r)/ vi desaparecer. **~ance** n desaparición f

disappoint /dɪsə'pɔɪnt/ vt decepcionar. **~ing** adj decepcionante. **~ment** n decepción f

disapprov|al /dɪsə'pru:vl/ n desaprobación f. **~e** /dɪsə'pru:v/ vi. **~e of** desaprobar. **~ing** adj de reproche

disarm /dɪs'ɑ:m/ vt desarmar. ● vi desarmarse. **~ament** n desarme m

disarray /dɪsə'reɪ/ n desorden m

disast|er /dɪ'zɑ:stə(r)/ n desastre m. **~rous** /-strəs/ adj catastrófico

disband /dɪs'bænd/ vt disolver. ● vi disolverse

disbelief /dɪsbɪ'li:f/ n incredulidad f

disc /dɪsk/ n disco m

discard /dɪs'kɑ:d/ vt descartar; abandonar (beliefs etc)

discern /dɪ'sɜ:n/ vt percibir. **~ing** adj exigente; (ear, eye) educado

discharge /dɪs'tʃɑ:dʒ/ vt descargar; cumplir (duty); (Mil) licenciar. ● /'dɪstʃɑ:dʒ/ n descarga f; (Med) secreción f; (Mil) licenciamiento m

disciple /dɪ'saɪpl/ n discípulo m

disciplin|ary /dɪsɪ'plɪnərɪ/ adj disciplinario. **~e** /'dɪsɪplɪn/ n disciplina f. ● vt disciplinar; (punish) sancionar

disc jockey /'dɪskdʒɒkɪ/ n pinchadiscos *m* & *f*

disclaim /dɪsˈkleɪm/ *vt* desconocer. **~er** *n* (*Jurid*) descargo *m* de responsabilidad

disclos|e /dɪsˈkləʊz/ *vt* revelar. **~ure** /-ʒə(r)/ *n* revelación *f*

disco /ˈdɪskəʊ/ *n* (*pl* **-os**) 🔟 discoteca *f*

discolour /dɪsˈkʌlə(r)/ *vt* decolorar. ● *vi* decolorarse

discomfort /dɪsˈkʌmfət/ *n* malestar *m*; (*lack of comfort*) incomodidad *f*

disconcert /dɪskənˈsɜ:t/ *vt* desconcertar

disconnect /dɪskəˈnekt/ *vt* separar; (*Elec*) desconectar

disconsolate /dɪsˈkɒnsələt/ *adj* desconsolado

discontent /dɪskənˈtent/ *n* descontento *m*. **~ed** *adj* descontento

discontinue /dɪskənˈtɪnju:/ *vt* interrumpir

discord /ˈdɪskɔ:d/ *n* discordia *f*; (*Mus*) disonancia *f*. **~ant** /-ˈskɔ:dənt/ *adj* discorde; (*Mus*) disonante

discotheque /ˈdɪskətek/ *n* discoteca *f*

discount /ˈdɪskaʊnt/ *n* descuento *m*. ● /dɪsˈkaʊnt/ *vt* hacer caso omiso de; (*Com*) descontar

discourag|e /dɪsˈkʌrɪdʒ/ *vt* desanimar; (*dissuade*) disuadir. **~ing** *adj* desalentador

discourteous /dɪsˈkɜ:tɪəs/ *adj* descortés

discover /dɪsˈkʌvə(r)/ *vt* descubrir. **~y** *n* descubrimiento *m*

discredit /dɪsˈkredɪt/ *vt* (*pt* **discredited**) desacreditar. ● *n* descrédito *m*

discreet /dɪsˈkri:t/ *adj* discreto. **~ly** *adv* discretamente

discrepancy /dɪˈskrepənsɪ/ *n* discrepancia *f*

discretion /dɪˈskreʃn/ *n* discreción *f*

discriminat|e /dɪsˈkrɪmɪneɪt/ *vt* discriminar. **~e between** distinguir entre. **~ing** *adj* perspicaz. **~ion** /-ˈneɪʃn/ *n* discernimiento *m*; (*bias*) discriminación *f*

discus /ˈdɪskəs/ *n* disco *m*

discuss /dɪsˈkʌs/ *vt* discutir. **~ion** /-ʃn/ *n* discusión *f*

disdain /dɪsˈdeɪn/ *n* desdén *m*. **~ful** *adj* desdeñoso

disease /dɪˈzi:z/ *n* enfermedad *f*

disembark /dɪsɪmˈbɑ:k/ *vi* desembarcar

disenchant|ed /dɪsɪnˈtʃɑ:ntɪd/ *adj* desilusionado. **~ment** *n* desencanto *m*

disentangle /dɪsɪnˈtæŋgl/ *vt* desenredar

disfigure /dɪsˈfɪgə(r)/ *vt* desfigurar

disgrace /dɪsˈgreɪs/ *n* vergüenza *f*. ● *vt* deshonrar. **~ful** *adj* vergonzoso

disgruntled /dɪsˈgrʌntld/ *adj* descontento

disguise /dɪsˈgaɪz/ *vt* disfrazar. ● *n* disfraz *m*. **in ~** disfrazado

disgust /dɪsˈgʌst/ *n* repugnancia *f*, asco *m*. ● *vt* dar asco a. **~ed** *adj* indignado; (*stronger*) asqueado. **~ing** *adj* repugnante, asqueroso

dish /dɪʃ/ *n* plato *m*. **wash** or **do the ~es** fregar los platos, lavar los trastes (*Mex*). □ **~ up** *vt/i* servir. **~cloth** *n* bayeta *f*

disheartening /dɪsˈhɑ:tnɪŋ/ *adj* desalentador

dishonest /dɪsˈɒnɪst/ *adj* deshonesto. **~y** *n* falta *f* de honradez

dishonour /dɪsˈɒnə(r)/ *n* deshonra *f*

dish: ~ **soap** n (Amer) lavavajillas m. ~ **towel** n paño m de cocina. ~**washer** n lavaplatos m, lavavajillas m. ~**washing liquid** n (Amer) see ~ **SOAP**

disillusion /dɪsɪ'lu:ʒn/ vt desilusionar. ~**ment** n desilusión f

disinfect /dɪsɪn'fekt/ vt desinfectar. ~**ant** n desinfectante m

disintegrate /dɪs'ɪntɪgreɪt/ vt desintegrar. • vi desintegrarse

disinterested /dɪs'ɪntrəstɪd/ adj desinteresado

disjointed /dɪs'dʒɔɪntɪd/ adj inconexo

disk /dɪsk/ n disco m. ~ **drive** (Comp) unidad f de discos. ~**ette** /dɪs'ket/ n disquete m

dislike /dɪs'laɪk/ n aversión f. • vt. I ~ **dogs** no me gustan los perros

dislocate /'dɪsləkeɪt/ vt dislocar(se) (limb)

dislodge /dɪs'lɒdʒ/ vt sacar

disloyal /dɪs'lɔɪəl/ adj desleal. ~**ty** n deslealtad f

dismal /'dɪzməl/ adj triste; (bad) fatal

dismantle /dɪs'mæntl/ vt desmontar

dismay /dɪs'meɪ/ n consternación f. • vt consternar

dismiss /dɪs'mɪs/ vt despedir; (reject) rechazar. ~**al** n despido m; (of idea) rechazo m

dismount /dɪs'maʊnt/ vi desmontar

disobe|dience /dɪsə'bi:dɪəns/ n desobediencia f. ~**dient** adj desobediente. ~**y** /dɪsə'beɪ/ vt/i desobedecer

disorder /dɪs'ɔ:də(r)/ n desorden m; (ailment) afección f. ~**ly** adj desordenado

disorganized /dɪs'ɔ:gənaɪzd/ adj desorganizado

disorientate /dɪs'ɔ:rɪənteɪt/ vt desorientar

disown /dɪs'əʊn/ vt repudiar

disparaging /dɪs'pærɪdʒɪŋ/ adj despreciativo

dispatch /dɪs'pætʃ/ vt despachar. • n despacho m. ~ **rider** n mensajero m

dispel /dɪs'pel/ vt (pt dispelled) disipar

dispens|able /dɪs'pensəbl/ adj prescindible. ~**e** vt distribuir; (Med) preparar. □ ~ **with** vt prescindir de

dispers|al /dɪ'spɜ:sl/ n dispersión f. ~**e** /dɪ'spɜ:s/ vt dispersar. • vi dispersarse

dispirited /dɪ'spɪrɪtɪd/ adj desanimado

display /dɪs'pleɪ/ vt exponer (goods); demostrar (feelings). • n exposición f; (of feelings) demostración f

displeas|e /dɪs'pli:z/ vt desagradar. **be ~ed with** estar disgustado con. ~**ure** /-'pleʒə(r)/ n desagrado m

dispos|able /dɪs'pəʊzəbl/ adj desechable. ~**al** /dɪs'pəʊzl/ n (of waste) eliminación f. **at s.o.'s ~al** a la disposición de uno. ~**e of** /dɪs'pəʊz/ vt deshacerse de

disproportionate /dɪsprə'pɔ:ʃənət/ adj desproporcionado

disprove /dɪs'pru:v/ vt desmentir (claim); refutar (theory)

dispute /dɪs'pju:t/ vt discutir. • n disputa f. **in ~** disputado

disqualif|ication /dɪskwɒlɪfɪ'keɪʃn/ n descalificación f. ~**y** /dɪs'kwɒlɪfaɪ/ vt incapacitar; (Sport) descalificar

disregard /dɪsrɪ'gɑ:d/ vt no hacer caso de. • n indiferencia f (**for** a)

disreputable /dɪsˈrepjʊtəbl/ adj de mala fama

disrespect /dɪsrɪˈspekt/ n falta f de respeto

disrupt /dɪsˈrʌpt/ vt interrumpir; trastornar (plans). ~ion /-ʃn/ n trastorno m. ~ive adj (influence) perjudicial, negativo

dissatis|faction /dɪsætɪsˈfækʃn/ n descontento m. ~fied /dɪˈsætɪsfaɪd/ adj descontento

dissect /dɪˈsekt/ vt disecar

dissent /dɪˈsent/ vi disentir. ● n disentimiento m

dissertation /dɪsəˈteɪʃn/ n (Univ) tesis f

dissident /ˈdɪsɪdənt/ adj & n disidente (m & f)

dissimilar /dɪˈsɪmɪlə(r)/ adj distinto

dissolute /ˈdɪsəluːt/ adj disoluto

dissolve /dɪˈzɒlv/ vt disolver. ● vi disolverse

dissuade /dɪˈsweɪd/ vt disuadir

distan|ce /ˈdɪstəns/ n distancia f. from a ~ce desde lejos. in the ~ce a lo lejos. ~t adj distante, lejano; (aloof) distante

distaste /dɪsˈteɪst/ n desagrado m. ~ful adj desagradable

distil /dɪsˈtɪl/ vt (pt distilled) destilar. ~lery /dɪsˈtɪləri/ n destilería f

distinct /dɪsˈtɪŋkt/ adj distinto; (clear) claro; (marked) marcado. ~ion /-ʃn/ n distinción f; (in exam) sobresaliente m. ~ive adj distintivo

distinguish /dɪsˈtɪŋgwɪʃ/ vt/i distinguir. ~ed adj distinguido

distort /dɪsˈtɔːt/ vt torcer. ~ion /-ʃn/ n deformación f

distract /dɪsˈtrækt/ vt distraer. ~ed adj distraído. ~ion /-ʃn/ n distracción f; (confusion) aturdimiento m

distraught /dɪsˈtrɔːt/ adj consternado, angustiado

distress /dɪsˈtres/ n angustia f. ● vt afligir. ~ed adj afligido. ~ing adj penoso

distribut|e /dɪsˈtrɪbjuːt/ vt repartir, distribuir. ~ion /-ˈbjuːʃn/ n distribución f. ~or n distribuidor m; (Auto) distribuidor m (del encendido)

district /ˈdɪstrɪkt/ n zona f, región f; (of town) barrio m

distrust /dɪsˈtrʌst/ n desconfianza f. ● vt desconfiar de

disturb /dɪsˈtɜːb/ vt molestar; (perturb) inquietar; (move) desordenar; (interrupt) interrumpir. ~ance n disturbio m; (tumult) alboroto m. ~ed adj trastornado. ~ing adj inquietante

disused /dɪsˈjuːzd/ adj fuera de uso

ditch /dɪtʃ/ n zanja f; (for irrigation) acequia f. ● vt 🔲 abandonar

dither /ˈdɪðə(r)/ vi vacilar

ditto /ˈdɪtəʊ/ adv ídem

divan /dɪˈvæn/ n diván m

dive /daɪv/ vi tirarse (al agua), zambullirse; (rush) meterse (precipitadamente). ● n (into water) zambullida f; (Sport) salto m (de trampolín); (of plane) descenso m en picado, descenso m en picada (LAm); (🔲, place) antro m. ~r n saltador m; (underwater) buzo m

diverge /daɪˈvɜːdʒ/ vi divergir. ~nt adj divergente

divers|e /daɪˈvɜːs/ adj diverso. ~ify vt diversificar. ~ity n diversidad f

diver|sion /daɪˈvɜːʃn/ n desvío m; desviación f; (distraction) diversión f. ~t /daɪˈvɜːt/ vt desviar; (entertain) divertir

divide | dock

354

divide /dɪˈvaɪd/ vt dividir. ● vi dividirse. ~**d highway** n (Amer) autovía f, carretera f de doble pista

dividend /ˈdɪvɪdend/ n dividendo m

divine /dɪˈvaɪn/ adj divino

division /dɪˈvɪʒn/ n división f

divorce /dɪˈvɔːs/ n divorcio m. ● vt divorciarse de. **get** ~**d** divorciarse. ● vi divorciarse. ~**e** /dɪvɔːˈsiː/ n divorciado m

divulge /daɪˈvʌldʒ/ vt divulgar

DIY abbr see **DO-IT-YOURSELF**

dizz|iness /ˈdɪzɪnɪs/ n vértigo m. ~**y** adj (-**ier**, -**iest**) mareado. **be** or **feel** ~**y** marearse

DJ abbr see **DISC JOCKEY**

do /duː/ /dʊ, də/

3rd person singular present **does**; past **did**; past participle **done**

● transitive verb

····▶ hacer. **he does what he wants** hace lo que quiere. **to do one's homework** hacer los deberes. **to do the cooking** preparar la comida, cocinar. **well done!** ¡muy bien!

····▶ (clean) lavar (dishes). limpiar (windows)

····▶ (as job) **what does he do?** ¿en qué trabaja?

····▶ (swindle) estafar. **I've been done!** ¡me han estafado!

····▶ (achieve) **she's done it!** ¡lo ha logrado!

● intransitive verb

····▶ hacer. **do as you're told!** ¡haz lo que se te dice!

····▶ (fare) **how are you doing?**

(with a task) ¿qué tal te va? **how do you do?**, (as greeting) mucho gusto, encantado

····▶ (perform) **she did well/badly** le fue bien/mal

····▶ (be suitable) **will this do?** ¿esto sirve?

····▶ (be enough) ser suficiente, bastar. **one box will do** con una caja basta, con una caja es suficiente

● auxiliary verb

····▶ (to form interrogative and negative) **do you speak Spanish?** ¿hablas español?. **I don't want to** no quiero. **don't shut the door** no cierres la puerta

····▶ (in tag questions) **you eat meat, don't you?** ¿comes carne, ¿verdad? or ¿no? **he lives in London, doesn't he?** vive en Londres, ¿no? or ¿verdad? or ¿no es cierto?

····▶ (in short answers) **do you like it?** - **yes, I do** ¿te gusta? - sí. **who wrote it?** - **I did** ¿quién lo escribió? - yo

····▶ (emphasizing) **do come in!** ¡pase Ud!. **you do exaggerate!** ¡cómo exageras! □ **do away with** vt abolir. □ **do in** vt (sl, kill) eliminar. □ **do up** vt abrochar (coat etc); arreglar (house). □ **do with** vt (need) (with can, could) necesitar; (expressing connection) **it has nothing to do with that** no tiene nada que ver con eso. □ **do without** vt prescindir de

docile /ˈdəʊsaɪl/ adj dócil

dock /dɒk/ n (Naut) dársena f; (wharf, quay) muelle m; (Jurid) banquillo m de los acusados. ~**s** npl (port) puerto m. ● vt cortar (tail);

doctor | DOS

atracar (ship). ● vi (ship) atracar.
~er n estibador m. **~yard** n astillero m

doctor /'dɒktə(r)/ n médico m,
doctor m

doctrine /'dɒktrɪn/ n doctrina f

document /'dɒkjʊmənt/ n documento m. **~ary** /-'mentrɪ/ adj & n
documental (m)

dodg|e /dɒdʒ/ vt esquivar. ● vi esquivarse. ● n treta f. **~ems**
/'dɒdʒəmz/ npl autos mpl de choque. **~y** adj (-ier, -iest) (awkward)
difícil

doe /dəʊ/ n (rabbit) coneja f; (hare)
liebre f hembra; (deer) cierva f

does /dʌz/ see **DO**

doesn't /'dʌznt/ = **does not**

dog /dɒg/ n perro m. ● vt (pt dogged) perseguir

dogged /'dɒgɪd/ adj obstinado

doghouse /'dɒghaʊs/ n (Amer)
casa f del perro. **in the ~** 🗉 en
desgracia

dogma /'dɒgmə/ n dogma m.
~tic /-'mætɪk/ adj dogmático

do|ings npl actividades fpl. **~-it-yourself** /'du:ɪtjɔː'self/ n bricolaje m

dole /dəʊl/ n 🗉 subsidio m de
paro, subsidio m de desempleo. **on
the ~** 🗉 parado, desempleado.
□ **~ out** vt distribuir

doleful /'dəʊlfl/ adj triste

doll /dɒl/ n muñeca f

dollar /'dɒlə(r)/ n dólar m

dollarization /dɒlərai'zeɪʃn/ n
dolarización f

dollop /'dɒləp/ n 🗉 porción f

dolphin /'dɒlfɪn/ n delfín m

domain /dəʊ'meɪn/ n dominio m

dome /dəʊm/ n cúpula f

domestic /də'mestɪk/ adj doméstico; (trade, flights, etc) nacional.

~ated /də'mestɪkeɪtɪd/ adj (animal) domesticado. **~ science** n
economía f doméstica

domin|ance /'dɒmɪnəns/ n dominio m. **~ant** adj dominante.
~ate /-eɪt/ vt/i dominar. **~ation**
/-'neɪʃn/ n dominación f. **~eering**
adj dominante

Dominican Republic /də
'mɪnɪkən/ n República f Dominicana

dominion /də'mɪnjən/ n dominio m

domino /'dɒmɪnəʊ/ n (pl -oes)
ficha f de dominó. **~es** npl (game)
dominó m

donat|e /dəʊ'neɪt/ vt donar. **~ion**
/-ʃn/ n donativo m, donación f

done /dʌn/ see **DO**

donkey /'dɒŋkɪ/ n burro m, asno
m. **~'s years** 🗉 siglos mpl

donor /'dəʊnə(r)/ n donante m & f

don't /dəʊnt/ = **do not**

doodle /'du:dl/ vi/t garrapatear

doom /du:m/ n destino m; (death)
muerte f. ● vt. **be ~ed to** estar
condenado a

door /dɔː(r)/ n puerta f. **~bell** n
timbre m. **~ knob** n pomo m (de
la puerta). **~mat** n felpudo m.
~step n peldaño m. **~way** n entrada f

dope /dəʊp/ n 🗉 droga f; (sl, idiot)
imbécil m. ● vt 🗉 drogar

dormant /'dɔːmənt/ adj aletargado, (volcano) inactivo

dormice /'dɔːmaɪs/ see **DOR-MOUSE**

dormitory /'dɔːmɪtrɪ/ n dormitorio m

dormouse /'dɔːmaʊs/ n (pl
-mice) lirón m

DOS /dɒs/ abbr (= disc-operating
system) DOS m

dos|age /'dəʊsɪdʒ/ n dosis f. **~e** /daʊs/ n dosis f

dot /dɒt/ n punto m. **on the ~** en punto. **~-com** n punto m com. **~-com company** empresa f puntocom

dote /dəʊt/ vi. **~ on** adorar

dotty /'dɒtɪ/ adj (-ier, -iest) 🔲 chiflado

double /'dʌbl/ adj doble. ● adv el doble. ● n doble m; (person) doble m & f. **at the ~** corriendo. ● vt doblar; redoblar (efforts etc). ● vi doblarse. **~ bass** /beɪs/ n contrabajo m. **~ bed** n cama f de matrimonio, cama f de doa plazas (LAm). **~ chin** n papada f. ● **click** /tʃ hacer doble clic en. **~-cross** /-'krɒs/ vt traicionar. **~-decker** /-'dekə(r)/ n autobús m de dos pisos. **~ Dutch** n 🔲 chino m. **~ glazing** /-'gleɪzɪŋ/ n doble ventana f. **~s** npl (tennis) dobles mpl

doubly /'dʌblɪ/ adv doblemente

doubt /daʊt/ n duda f. ● vt dudar; (distrust) dudar de. **~ful** adj dudoso. **~less** adv sin duda

dough /dəʊ/ n masa f; (sl, money) pasta f 🔲, lana f (LAm fam). **~nut** n donut m, dona f (Mex)

dove /dʌv/ n paloma f

down /daʊn/ adv abajo. **~ with** abajo. **come ~** bajar. **go ~** bajar; (sun) ponerse. ● prep abajo. ● adj 🔲 deprimido. ● vt derribar; (fam, drink) beber. **~** n (feathers) plumón m. **~ and out** adj en la miseria. **~cast** adj abatido. **~fall** n perdición f; (of king, dictator) caída f. **~-hearted** /-'hɑːtɪd/ adj abatido. **~hill** /-'hɪl/ adv cuesta abajo. **~load** /-'ləʊd/ vt (Comp) bajar. **~market** /-'mɑːkɪt/ adj (newspaper) popular; (store) barato. **~payment** n depósito m. **~pour** n

aguacero m. **~right** adj completo. ● adv completamente. **~s** npl colinas fpl. **~stairs** /-'steəz/ adv abajo. ● /-steəz/ adj de abajo. **~stream** adv río abajo. **~-to-earth** /-tʊ'ɜːθ/ adj práctico. **~town** /-'taʊn/ n centro m (de la ciudad). ● adv. **go ~town** ir al centro. ● **under** adv en las antípodas; (in Australia) en Australia. **~ward** /-wəd/ adj & adv, **~wards** adv hacia abajo

dowry /'daʊərɪ/ n dote f

Downing Street Es una calle en el barrio londinense de Westminster. El número 10 es la residencia oficial del Primer Ministro y el 11, la del Chancellor of the Exchequer (Ministro de Economía y Hacienda). Los periodistas suelen utilizar las expresiones Downing Street o Number 10 para referirse al Primer Ministro y al Gobierno.

doze /dəʊz/ vi dormitar

dozen /'dʌzn/ n docena f. a **~ eggs** una docena de huevos. **~s of** 🔲 miles de, muchos

Dr /'dɒktə(r)/ abbr (Doctor)

drab /dræb/ adj monótono

draft /drɑːft/ n borrador m; (Com) letra f de cambio; (Amer, Mil) reclutamiento m; (Amer, of air) corriente f de aire. ● vt redactar el borrador de; (Amer, conscript) reclutar

drag /dræg/ vt (pt dragged) arrastrar. ● n 🔲 lata f

dragon /'drægən/ n dragón m. **~fly** n libélula f

drain /dreɪn/ vt vaciar (tank, glass); drenar (land); (fig) agotar. ● vi escurrirse. ● n (pipe) sumidero m, resumidero m (LAm); (plughole) desagüe m. **~board** (Amer), **~ing**

board n escurridero m

drama /'drɑːmə/ n drama m; (art) arte m teatral. ~**tic** /drə'mætɪk/ adj dramático. ~**tist** /'dræmətɪst/ n dramaturgo m. ~**tize** /'dræmətaɪz/ vt adaptar al teatro; (fig) dramatizar

drank /dræŋk/ see **DRINK**

drape /dreɪp/ vt cubrir; (hang) colgar. ~**s** npl (Amer) cortinas fpl

drastic /'dræstɪk/ adj drástico

draught /drɑːft/ n corriente f de aire. ~ **beer** n cerveza f de barril. ~**s** npl (game) juego m de damas fpl. ~**y** adj lleno de corrientes de aire

draw /drɔː/ vt (pt **drew**, pp **drawn**) tirar; (attract) atraer; dibujar (picture); trazar (line). ~ **the line** trazar el límite. ● vi (Art) dibujar; (Sport) empatar; ~ **near** acercarse. ● n (Sport) empate m; (in lottery) sorteo m. □ ~ **in** vi (days) acortarse. □ ~ **out** vt sacar (money). □ ~ **up** vi pararse. vt redactar (document); acercar (chair). ~**back** n desventaja f. ~**bridge** n puente m levadizo

drawer /drɔː(r)/ n cajón m, gaveta f (Mex). ~**s** npl calzones mpl

drawing /'drɔːɪŋ/ n dibujo m. ~ **pin** n tachuela f, chincheta f, chinche f. ~ **room** n salón m

drawl /drɔːl/ n habla f lenta

drawn /drɔːn/ see **DRAW**

dread /dred/ n terror m. ● vt temer. ~**ful** adj terrible. ~**fully** adv terriblemente

dream /driːm/ n sueño m. ● vt/i (pt **dreamed** or **dreamt** /dremt/) soñar. □ ~ **up** vt idear. adj ideal. ~**er** n soñador m

dreary /'drɪərɪ/ adj (-ier, -iest) triste; (boring) monótono

dredge /dredʒ/ n draga f. ● vt dra-

gar. ~**r** n draga f

dregs /dregz/ npl posos mpl, heces fpl; (fig) hez f

drench /drentʃ/ vt empapar

dress /dres/ n vestido m; (clothing) ropa f. ● vt vestir; (decorate) adornar; (Med) vendar. ● vi vestirse. □ ~ **up** vi ponerse elegante. ~ **up as** disfrazarse de. ~ **circle** n primer palco m

dressing /'dresɪŋ/ n (sauce) aliño m; (bandage) vendaje m. ~-**down** /-'daʊn/ n rapapolvo m, reprensión f. ~ **gown** n bata f. ~ **room** n vestidor m; (in theatre) camarín m. ~ **table** n tocador m

dress: ~**maker** n modista m & f. ~**making** n costura f. ~ **rehearsal** n ensayo m general

drew /druː/ see **DRAW**

dribble /'drɪbl/ vi (baby) babear; (in football) driblar, driblear

drie|d /draɪd/ adj (food) seco; (milk) en polvo. ~**r** /'draɪə(r)/ n secador m

drift /drɪft/ vi ir a la deriva; (snow) amontonarse. ● n (movement) dirección f; (of snow) montón m

drill /drɪl/ n (tool) taladro m; (of dentist) torno m; (training) ejercicio m. ● vt taladrar, perforar; (train) entrenar. ● vi entrenarse

drink /drɪŋk/ vt/i (pt **drank**, pp **drunk**) beber, tomar (LAm). ● n bebida f. ~**able** adj bebible; (water) potable. ~**er** n bebedor m. ~**ing water** n agua f potable

drip /drɪp/ vi (pt **dripped**) gotear. ● n gota f; (Med) goteo m intravenoso; (fam, person) soso m. ~-**dry** /-'draɪ/ adj de lava y pon. ~**ping** adj. be ~**ping wet** estar chorreando

drive /draɪv/ vt (pt **drove**, pp

driven) conducir, manejar (*LAm*) (car etc). ~ **s.o. mad** volver loco a uno. ~ **s.o. to do sth** llevar a uno a hacer algo. ● *vi* conducir, manejar (*LAm*). ~ **at** querer decir. ~ **in** (*in car*) entrar en coche. ● *n* paseo *m*; (*road*) calle *f*; (*private road*) camino *m* de entrada; (*fig*) empuje *m*. ~ **r** *n* conductor *m*, chofer *m* (*LAm*). ~ **r's license** *n* (*Amer*) see **DRIVING LICENSE**

drivel /ˈdrɪvl/ *n* tonterías *fpl*

driving /ˈdraɪvɪŋ/ *n* conducción *f*. ~ **licence** *n* permiso *m* de conducir, licencia *f* de conducción (*LAm*), licencia *f* (de manejar) (*Mex*). ~ **test** *n* examen *m* de conducir, examen *m* de manejar (*LAm*)

drizzle /ˈdrɪzl/ *n* llovizna *f*. ● *vi* lloviznar

drone /drəʊn/ *n* zumbido *m*. ● *vi* zumbar

drool /druːl/ *vi* babear

droop /druːp/ *vi* inclinarse; (*flowers*) marchitarse

drop /drɒp/ *n* gota *f*; (*fall*) caída *f*; (*decrease*) descenso *m*. ● *vt* (*pt* **dropped**) dejar caer; (*lower*) bajar. ● *vi* caer. □ ~ **in on** *vt* pasar por casa de. □ ~ **off** *vi* (*sleep*) dormirse. □ ~ **out** *vi* retirarse; (*student*) abandonar los estudios. ~ **out** *n* marginado *m*

drought /draʊt/ *n* sequía *f*

drove /drəʊv/ see **DRIVE**. ● *n* manada *f*

drown /draʊn/ *vt* ahogar. ● *vi* ahogarse

drowsy /ˈdraʊzɪ/ *adj* soñoliento

drudgery /ˈdrʌdʒərɪ/ *n* trabajo *m* pesado

drug /drʌg/ *n* droga *f*; (*Med*) medicamento *m*. ● *vt* (*pt* **drugged**) drogar. ~ **addict** *n* drogadicto *m*.

~ **gist** *n* (*Amer*) farmacéutico *m*. ~ **store** *n* (*Amer*) farmacia *f* (que vende otros artículos también)

drum /drʌm/ *n* tambor *m*; (*for oil*) bidón *m*. ● *vi* (*pt* **drummed**) tocar el tambor. ● *vt*. ~ **sth into s.o.** hacerle aprender algo a uno a fuerza de repetírselo. ~ **mer** *n* tambor *m*; (*in group*) batería *f*. ~ **s** *npl* batería *f*. ~ **stick** *n* baqueta *f*; (*Culin*) muslo *m*

drunk /drʌŋk/ see **DRINK**. ● *adj* borracho. **get** ~ emborracharse. ● *n* borracho *m*. ~ **ard** /-əd/ *n* borracho *m*. ~ **en** *adj* borracho

dry /draɪ/ *adj* (**drier, driest**) seco. ● *vt* secar. ● *vi* secarse. □ ~ **up** *vi* (*stream*) secarse; (*funds*) agotarse. ~ **clean** *vt* limpiar en seco. ~ **cleaner's** tintorería *f*. ~ **er** *n* see **DRIER**

DTD *abbrev* **Document Type Definition** DTD *m*

dual /ˈdjuːəl/ *adj* doble. ~ **carriageway** *n* autovía *f*, carretera *f* de doble pista

dub /dʌb/ *vt* (*pt* **dubbed**) doblar (film)

dubious /ˈdjuːbɪəs/ *adj* dudoso; (*person*) sospechoso

duchess /ˈdʌtʃɪs/ *n* duquesa *f*

duck /dʌk/ *n* pato *m*. ● *vt* sumergir; bajar (head). ● *vi* agacharse. ~ **ling** /ˈdʌklɪŋ/ *n* patito *m*

duct /dʌkt/ *n* conducto *m*

dud /dʌd/ *adj* inútil; (cheque) sin fondos

due /djuː/ *adj* debido; (*expected*) esperado. ~ **to** debido a. ● *adv*. ~ **north** derecho hacia el norte. ~ **s** *npl* derechos *mpl*

duel /ˈdjuːəl/ *n* duelo *m*

duet /djuˈet/ *n* dúo *m*

duffel, duffle /ˈdʌfl/ ~ **bag** *n* bolsa *f* de lona. ~ **coat** *n* trenca *f*

dug /dʌg/ *see* DIG

duke /djuːk/ *n* duque *m*

dull /dʌl/ *adj* (**-er**, **-est**) (weather) gris; (colour) apagado; (person, play, etc) pesado; (sound) sordo

dumb /dʌm/ *adj* (**-er**, **-est**) mudo; ⊞ estúpido. ▫ ~ **down** vt reducir el valor intelectual de. ~**found** /dʌmˈfaʊnd/ vt pasmar

dummy /ˈdʌmɪ/ *n* muñeco *m*; (of tailor) maniquí *m*; (for baby) chupete *m*. ● *adj* falso. ~ **run** prueba *f*

dump /dʌmp/ vt tirar, botar (LAm). ● *n* vertedero *m*; (Mil) depósito *m*; ⊞ lugar *m* desagradable. **be down in the** ~**s** estar deprimido

dumpling /ˈdʌmplɪŋ/ *n* bola *f* de masa hervida

Dumpster /ˈdʌmpstə(r)/ *n* (Amer, ®) contenedor *m* (para escombros)

dumpy /ˈdʌmpɪ/ *adj* (**-ier**, **-iest**) regordete

dunce /dʌns/ *n* burro *m*

dung /dʌŋ/ *n* (manure) estiércol *m*

dungarees /dʌŋɡəˈriːz/ *npl* mono *m*, peto *m*

dungeon /ˈdʌndʒən/ *n* calabozo *m*

dunk /dʌŋk/ vt remojar

dupe /djuːp/ vt engañar. ● *n* inocentón *m*

duplicat|e /ˈdjuːplɪkət/ *adj* & *n* duplicado (*m*). ● /ˈdjuːplɪkeɪt/ vt duplicar; (on machine) reproducir. ~**ing machine**, ~**or** *n* multicopista *f*

durable /ˈdjʊərəbl/ *adj* durable

duration /djʊˈreɪʃn/ *n* duración *f*

duress /djʊˈres/ *n*. **under** ~ bajo coacción

during /ˈdjʊərɪŋ/ *prep* durante

dusk /dʌsk/ *n* anochecer *m*

dust /dʌst/ *n* polvo *m*. ● vt quitar el polvo a; (sprinkle) espolvorear (with con). ~**bin** *n* cubo *m* de la basura, bote *m* de la basura (Mex). ~ **cloth** (Amer), ~**er** *n* trapo *m*. ~**jacket** *n* sobrecubierta *f*. ~**man** /-mən/ *n* basurero *m*. ~**pan** *n* recogedor *m*. ~**y** *adj* (**-ier**, **-iest**) polvoriento

Dutch /dʌtʃ/ *adj* holandés. ● *n* (language) holandés *m*. **the** ~ (people) los holandeses. ~**man** /-mən/ *n* holandés *m*. ~**woman** *n* holandesa *f*

duty /ˈdjuːtɪ/ *n* deber *m*; (tax) derechos *mpl* de aduana. **on** ~ de servicio. ~**-free** /-ˈfriː/ *adj* libre de impuestos

duvet /ˈdjuːveɪ/ *n* edredón *m*

dwarf /dwɔːf/ *n* (*pl* **-s** or **dwarves**) enano *m*

dwell /dwel/ vi (*pt* **dwelt** or **dwelled**) morar.▫ ~ **on** vt detenerse en. ~**ing** *n* morada *f*

dwindle /ˈdwɪndl/ vi disminuir

dye /daɪ/ vt (*pres p* **dyeing**) teñir. ● *n* tinte *m*

dying /ˈdaɪɪŋ/ *see* DIE

dynamic /daɪˈnæmɪk/ *adj* dinámico. ~**s** *npl* dinámica *f*

dynamite /ˈdaɪnəmaɪt/ *n* dinamita *f*. ● vt dinamitar

dynamo /ˈdaɪnəməʊ/ *n* (*pl* **-os**) dinamo *f*, dínamo *f*, dinamo *m* (LAm), dínamo *m* (LAm)

dynasty /ˈdɪnəstɪ/ *n* dinastía *f*

Ee

E abbr (= **East**) E

each /iːtʃ/ adj cada. ● pron cada uno. ~ **one** cada uno. ~ **other** uno a otro, el uno al otro. **they love** ~ **other** se aman

eager /ˈiːgə(r)/ adj impaciente; (enthusiastic) ávido. ~**ness** n impaciencia f; (enthusiasm) entusiasmo m

eagle /ˈiːgl/ n águila f

ear /ɪə(r)/ n oído m; (outer) oreja f. (of corn) espiga f. ~**ache** n dolor m de oído. ~**drum** n tímpano m

earl /ɜːl/ n conde m

early /ˈɜːlɪ/ adj (-ier, -iest) temprano; (before expected time) prematuro. ● adv temprano; (ahead of time) con anticipación

earn /ɜːn/ vt ganar; (deserve) merecer

earnest /ˈɜːnɪst/ adj serio. **in** ~ en serio

earnings /ˈɜːnɪŋz/ npl ingresos mpl; (Com) ganancias fpl

ear: ~**phone** n audífono m. ~**ring** n pendiente m, arete m (LAm). ~**shot** n. **within** ~**shot** al alcance del oído

earth /ɜːθ/ n tierra f. **the E**~ (planet) la Tierra. ● vt (Elec) conectar a tierra. ~**quake** n terremoto m

earwig /ˈɪəwɪg/ n tijereta f

ease /iːz/ n facilidad f; (comfort) tranquilidad f. **at** ~ a gusto; (Mil) en posición de descanso. **ill at** ~ molesto. **with** ~ fácilmente. ● vt calmar; aliviar (pain). ● vi calmarse;

(lessen) disminuir

easel /ˈiːzl/ n caballete m

easily /ˈiːzɪlɪ/ adv fácilmente

east /iːst/ n este m. ● adj este, oriental; (wind) del este. ● adv hacia el este.

Easter /ˈiːstə(r)/ n Semana f Santa; (Relig) Pascua f de Resurrección. ~ **egg** n huevo m de Pascua

east: ~**erly** /-əlɪ/ adj (wind) del este. ~**ern** /-ən/ adj este, oriental. ~**ward** /-wəd/, ~**wards** adv hacia el este

easy /ˈiːzɪ/ adj (-ier, -iest) fácil. ● adv. **go** ~ **on sth** 🅸 no pasarse con algo. **take it** ~ tomarse las cosas con calma. ● int ¡despacio! ~ **chair** n sillón m. ~**going** /-ˈgəʊɪŋ/ adj acomodadizo

eat /iːt/ vt/i (pt **ate**, pp **eaten**) comer. ▫ ~ **into** vt corroer. ~**er** n comedor m

eaves /iːvz/ npl alero m. ~**drop** vi (pt -**dropped**). ~**drop (on)** escuchar a escondidas

ebb /eb/ n reflujo m. ● vi bajar; (fig) decaer

ebola /iːˈbəʊlə/ n Ébola m

ebony /ˈebənɪ/ n ébano m

EC /iːˈsiː/ abbr (= **European Community**) CE f (Comunidad f Europea)

eccentric /ɪkˈsentrɪk/ adj & n excéntrico (m). ~**ity** /eksenˈtrɪsətɪ/ n excentricidad f

echo /ˈekəʊ/ n (pl -**oes**) eco m. ● vi hacer eco

eclipse /ɪˈklɪps/ n eclipse m. ● vt eclipsar

ecolog|ical /iːkəˈlɒdʒɪkl/ adj ecológico. ~**y** n ecología f

e-commerce /ˈiːkɒmɜːs/ n comercio m electrónico

econom|ic /iːkəˈnɒmɪk/ adj eco-

nómico; ~ **refugee** refugiado m económico. ~**ical** adj económico.
~**ics** n economía f. ~**ist** /ɪ'kɒnəmɪst/ n economista m & f.
~**ize** /ɪ'kɒnəmaɪz/ vi economizar.
~**ize on sth** economizar algo. ~**y** /ɪ'kɒnəmɪ/ n economía f

ecsta|sy /'ekstəsɪ/ n éxtasis f.
~**tic** /ɪk'stætɪk/ adj extático

Ecuador /'ekwədɔ:(r)/ n Ecuador m. ~**ean** /ekwə'dɔ:rɪən/ adj & n ecuatoriano (m)

edge /edʒ/ n borde m; (of knife) filo m; (of town) afueras fpl. **have the ~e on** 🔲 llevar la ventaja a. **on ~e** nervioso. ● vt ribetear. ● vi avanzar cautelosamente. ~**eways** adv de lado. ~**y** adj nervioso

edible /'edɪbl/ adj comestible

edit /'edɪt/ vt dirigir (newspaper); preparar una edición de (text); editar (film). ~**ion** /ɪ'dɪʃn/ n edición f. ~**or** n (of newspaper) director m; (of text) redactor m. ~**orial** /edɪ'tɔːrɪəl/ adj editorial. ● n artículo m de fondo

Edinburgh Festival Es el principal acontecimiento cultural británico que, desde 1947, se celebra en agosto, en la capital de Escocia. El festival atrae a un gran número de visitantes y un aspecto muy importante del mismo son los espectáculos que no forman parte del programa oficial, que se conocen como the *Fringe*.

educat|e /'edʒʊkeɪt/ vt educar. ~**ed** adj culto. ~**ion** /-'keɪʃn/ n educación f; (knowledge, culture) cultura f. ~**ional** /-'keɪʃənl/ adj instructivo

EC /iːˈsiː/ abbr (= European Com-

---

mission) CE f (Comisión f Europea)

eel /iːl/ n anguila f

eerie /'ɪərɪ/ adj (-ier, -iest) misterioso

effect /ɪ'fekt/ n efecto m. **in ~** efectivamente. **take ~** entrar en vigor. ~**ive** adj eficaz; (striking) impresionante; (real) efectivo.
~**ively** adv eficazmente. ~**iveness** n eficacia f

effeminate /ɪ'femɪnət/ adj afeminado

efficien|cy /ɪ'fɪʃənsɪ/ n eficiencia f; (Mec) rendimiento m. ~**t** adj eficiente. ~**tly** adv eficientemente

effort /'efət/ n esfuerzo m. ~**less** adj fácil

e.g. /iːˈdʒiː/ abbr = **exempli gratia**) p.ej., por ejemplo

egg /eg/ n huevo m. □ ~ **on** vt 🔲 incitar. ~**cup** n huevera f. ~**plant** n (Amer) berenjena f. ~**shell** n cáscara f de huevo

ego /'iːgəʊ/ n (pl -os) yo m. ~**ism** n egoísmo m. ~**ist** n egoísta m & f. ~**centric** /iːgəʊ'sentrɪk/ adj egocéntrico. ~**tism** n egotismo m. ~**tist** n egotista m & f

eh /eɪ/ int 🔲 ¡eh!

eiderdown /'aɪdədaʊn/ n edredón m

eight /eɪt/ adj & n ocho (m). ~**een** /eɪ'tiːn/ adj & n dieciocho (m).
~**eenth** adj decimoctavo. ● n dieciochavo m. ~**h** /eɪtθ/ adj & n octavo (m) ~**ieth** /'eɪtɪəθ/ adj octogésimo. ● n ochentavo m. ~**y** /'eɪtɪ/ adj & n ochenta (m)

either /'aɪðə(r)/ adj cualquiera de los dos; (negative) ninguno de los dos; (each) cada. ● pron uno u otro; (with negative) ni uno ni otro. ● adv (negative) tampoco. ● conj o. ~

Tuesday or Wednesday o el martes o el miércoles; **(with negative)** ni el martes ni el miércoles

eject /ɪˈdʒekt/ vt expulsar

eke /iːk/ vt. ~ **out** hacer alcanzar (resources). ~ **out a living** ganarse la vida a duras penas

elaborate /ɪˈlæbərət/ adj complicado. ● /ɪˈlæbəreɪt/ vt elaborar. ● /ɪˈlæbəreɪt/ vi explicarse

elapse /ɪˈlæps/ vi transcurrir

elastic /ɪˈlæstɪk/ adj & n elástico (m). ~ **band** n goma f (elástica), liga f (Mex)

elated /ɪˈleɪtɪd/ adj regocijado. ~**ion** /-ʃn/ n regocijo m

elbow /ˈelbəʊ/ n codo m. ● vt dar un codazo a

elder /ˈeldə(r)/ adj mayor. ● n mayor m & f; (tree) saúco m. ~**ly** /ˈeldəlɪ/ adj mayor, anciano

eldest /ˈeldɪst/ adj & n mayor (m & f)

elect /ɪˈlekt/ vt elegir. ~ **to do** decidir hacer. ● adj electo. ~**ion** /-ʃn/ n elección f. ~**or** n elector m. ~**oral** adj electoral. ~**orate** /-ət/ n electorado m

electric /ɪˈlektrɪk/ adj eléctrico. ~**al** adj eléctrico. ~ **blanket** n manta f eléctrica. ~**ian** /ɪlekˈtrɪʃn/ n electricista m & f. ~**ity** /ɪlekˈtrɪsətɪ/ n electricidad f

electrify /ɪˈlektrɪfaɪ/ vt electrificar; (fig) electrizar

electrocute /ɪˈlektrəkjuːt/ vt electrocutar

electrode /ɪˈlektrəʊd/ n electrodo m

electron /ɪˈlektrɒn/ n electrón m

electronic /ɪlekˈtrɒnɪk/ adj electrónico. ~ **mail** n correo m electrónico. ~**s** n electrónica f

elegan|ce /ˈelɪgəns/ n elegancia f.

~**t** adj elegante. ~**tly** adv elegantemente

element /ˈelɪmənt/ n elemento m. ~**ary** /-ˈmentrɪ/ adj elemental. ~**ary school** n (Amer) escuela f primaria

elephant /ˈelɪfənt/ n elefante m

elevat|e /ˈelɪveɪt/ vt elevar. ~**ion** /-ˈveɪʃn/ n elevación f. ~**or** n (Amer) ascensor m

eleven /ɪˈlevn/ adj & n once (m). ~**th** adj undécimo. ● n onceavo m

elf /elf/ n (pl **elves**) duende m

eligible /ˈelɪdʒəbl/ adj elegible. be ~ **for** tener derecho a

eliminat|e /ɪˈlɪmɪneɪt/ vt eliminar. ~**ion** /-ˈneɪʃn/ n eliminación f

élite /eɪˈliːt/ n elite f, élite f

ellip|se /ɪˈlɪps/ n elipse f. ~**tical** adj elíptico

elm /elm/ n olmo m

elope /ɪˈləʊp/ vi fugarse con el amante

eloquen|ce /ˈeləkwəns/ n elocuencia f. ~ **t** adj elocuente

El Salvador /el'sælvədɔː(r)/ n El Salvador

else /els/ adv. **somebody** ~ otra persona. **everybody** ~ todos los demás. **nobody** ~ ningún otro, nadie más. **nothing** ~ nada más. **or** ~ o bien. **somewhere** ~ en otra parte. ~**where** adv en otra parte

elu|de /ɪˈluːd/ vt eludir. ~**sive** /-sɪv/ adj esquivo

elves /elvz/ see ELF

emaciated /ɪˈmeɪʃɪeɪtɪd/ adj consumido

email, e-mail /ˈiːmeɪl/ n correo m electrónico, correo-e m. ● vt mandar por correo electrónico, emailear. ~ **address** n casilla f electrónica, dirección f de correo electrónico

emancipat|e /ɪˈmænsɪpeɪt/ vt emancipar. **~ion** /-ˈpeɪʃn/ n emancipación f

embankment /ɪmˈbæŋkmənt/ n terraplén m; (of river) dique m

embargo /ɪmˈbɑːgəʊ/ n (pl -oes) embargo m

embark /ɪmˈbɑːk/ vi embarcarse. **~ on** (fig) emprender. **~ation** /embɑːˈkeɪʃn/ n embarque m

embarrass /ɪmˈbærəs/ vt avergonzar. **~ed** adj avergonzado. **~ing** adj embarazoso. **~ment** n vergüenza f

embassy /ˈembəsɪ/ n embajada f

embellish /ɪmˈbelɪʃ/ vt adornar. **~ment** n adorno m

embers /ˈembəz/ npl ascuas fpl

embezzle /ɪmˈbezl/ vt desfalcar. **~ment** n desfalco m

emblem /ˈembləm/ n emblema m

embrace /ɪmˈbreɪs/ vt abrazar; (fig) abarcar. ● vi abrazarse. ● n abrazo m

embroider /ɪmˈbrɔɪdə(r)/ vt bordar. **~y** n bordado m

embroil /ɪmˈbrɔɪl/ vt enredar

embryo /ˈembrɪəʊ/ n (pl -os) embrión m. **~nic** /-ˈɒnɪk/ adj embrionario

emend /ɪˈmend/ vt enmendar

emerald /ˈemərəld/ n esmeralda f

emerge /ɪˈmɜːdʒ/ vi salir. **~nce** /-əns/ n aparición f

emergency /ɪˈmɜːdʒənsɪ/ n emergencia f; (Med) urgencia f. **in an ~** en caso de emergencia. **~ exit** n salida f de emergencia. **~ room** n urgencias fpl

emigra|nt /ˈemɪɡrənt/ n emigrante m & f. **~te** /ˈemɪɡreɪt/ vi emigrar. **~tion** /-ˈɡreɪʃn/ n

emigración f

eminen|ce /ˈemɪnəns/ n eminencia f. **~t** adj eminente.

emi|ssion /ɪˈmɪʃn/ n emisión f. **~t** vt (pt emitted) emitir

emot|ion /ɪˈməʊʃn/ n emoción f. **~onal** adj emocional; (person) emotivo; (moving) conmovedor. **~ve** /ɪˈməʊtɪv/ adj emotivo

empathy /ˈempəθɪ/ n empatía f

emperor /ˈempərə(r)/ n emperador m

empha|sis /ˈemfəsɪs/ n (pl ~ses /-siːz/) énfasis m. **~size** /ˈemfəsaɪz/ vt enfatizar. **~tic** /-ˈfætɪk/ adj (gesture) enfático; (assertion) categórico

empire /ˈempaɪə(r)/ n imperio m

empirical /ɪmˈpɪrɪkl/ adj empírico

employ /ɪmˈplɔɪ/ vt emplear. **~ee** /emplɔɪˈiː/ n empleado m. **~er** n patrón m. **~ment** n empleo m. **~ment agency** n agencia f de trabajo

empower /ɪmˈpaʊə(r)/ vt autorizar (to do a hacer)

empress /ˈemprɪs/ n emperatriz f

empty /ˈemptɪ/ adj vacío; (promise) vano. **on an ~y stomach** con el estómago vacío. ● n 🆃 envase m (vacío). ● vt vaciar. ● vi vaciarse

emulate /ˈemjʊleɪt/ vt emular

emulsion /ɪˈmʌlʃn/ n emulsión f

enable /ɪˈneɪbl/ vt. **~ s.o. to do sth** permitir a uno hacer algo

enact /ɪˈnækt/ vt (Jurid) decretar; (in theatre) representar

enamel /ɪˈnæml/ n esmalte m. ● vt (pt enamelled) esmaltar

enchant /ɪnˈtʃɑːnt/ vt encantar. **~ing** adj encantador. **~ment** n encanto m

encircle /ɪnˈsɜːkl/ vt rodear

enclave /'enkleɪv/ n enclave m

enclos|e /ɪn'kləʊz/ vt cercar (land); (Com) adjuntar. **~ed** adj (space) cerrado; (Com) adjunto. **~ure** /ɪn'kləʊʒə(r)/ n cercamiento m

encode /ɪn'kəʊd/ vt codificar, cifrar

encore /'ɒŋkɔː(r)/ int ¡otra! • n bis m, repetición f

encounter /ɪn'kaʊntə(r)/ vt encontrar. • n encuentro m

encourag|e /ɪn'kʌrɪdʒ/ vt animar; (stimulate) fomentar. **~ement** n ánimo m. **~ing** adj alentador

encroach /ɪn'krəʊtʃ/ vi. **~ on** invadir (land); quitar (time)

encyclopaedi|a /ɪnsaɪklə'piːdɪə/ n enciclopedia f. **~c** adj enciclopédico

end /end/ n fin m; (furthest point) extremo m. **in the ~** por fin. **make ~s meet** poder llegar a fin de mes. **put an ~ to** poner fin a. **no ~** of muchísimos. **on ~** de pie; (consecutive) seguido. • vt/i terminar, acabar

endanger /ɪn'deɪndʒə(r)/ vt poner en peligro. **~ed** adj (species) en peligro

endearing /ɪn'dɪərɪŋ/ adj simpático

endeavour /ɪn'devə(r)/ n esfuerzo m, intento m. • vi. **~ to** esforzarse por

ending /'endɪŋ/ n fin m

endless /'endlɪs/ adj interminable

endorse /ɪn'dɔːs/ vt endosar; (fig) aprobar. **~ment** n endoso m; (fig) aprobación f; (Auto) nota f de inhabilitación

endur|ance /ɪn'djʊərəns/ n resistencia f. **~e** /ɪn'djʊə(r)/ vt aguan-

tar. **~ing** adj perdurable

enemy /'enəmɪ/ n & a enemigo (m)

energ|etic /enə'dʒetɪk/ adj enérgico. **~y** /'enədʒɪ/ n energía f

enforce /ɪn'fɔːs/ vt hacer cumplir (law); hacer valer (claim). **~d** adj forzado

engag|e /ɪn'geɪdʒ/ vt emplear (staff); captar (attention); (Mec) hacer engranar. • vi (Mec) engranar. **~e in** dedicarse a. **~ed** adj prometido, comprometido (LAm); (busy) ocupado. **be ~ed** (of phone) estar comunicando, estar ocupado (LAm). **get ~ed** prometerse, comprometerse (LAm). **~ement** n compromiso m

engine /'endʒɪn/ n motor m; (of train) locomotora f. **~ driver** n maquinista f

engineer /endʒɪ'nɪə(r)/ n ingeniero m; (mechanic) mecánico m; (Amer, Rail) maquinista m. • vt (contrive) fraguar. **~ing** n ingeniería f

England /'ɪŋɡlənd/ n Inglaterra f

English /'ɪŋɡlɪʃ/ adj inglés. • n (language) inglés m. • npl. **the ~** los ingleses. **~man** /-mən/ n inglés m. **~woman** n inglesa f

engrav|e /ɪn'greɪv/ vt grabar. **~ing** n grabado m

engrossed /ɪn'grəʊst/ adj absorto

engulf /ɪn'ɡʌlf/ vt envolver

enhance /ɪn'hɑːns/ vt realzar; aumentar (value)

enigma /ɪ'nɪɡmə/ n enigma m. **~tic** /enɪɡ'mætɪk/ adj enigmático

enjoy /ɪn'dʒɔɪ/ vt. **I ~ reading** me gusta la lectura. **~ o.s.** divertirse. **~able** adj agradable. **~ment** n placer m

enlarge /ɪn'lɑːdʒ/ vt agrandar;

(*Photo*) ampliar. ● *vi* agrandarse. ~ **upon** extenderse sobre. ~**ment** *n* (*Photo*) ampliación *f*

enlighten /ɪn'laɪtn/ *vt* ilustrar. ~**ment** *n*. the E~**ment** el siglo de la luces

enlist /ɪn'lɪst/ *vt* alistar; conseguir (support). ● *vi* alistarse

enliven /ɪn'laɪvn/ *vt* animar

enorm|ity /ɪ'nɔːmətɪ/ *n* enormidad *f*. ~**ous** /ɪ'nɔːməs/ *adj* enorme. ~**ously** *adv* enormemente

enough /ɪ'nʌf/ *adj* & *adv* bastante. ● *n* bastante *m*, suficiente *m*. ● *int* ¡basta!

enquir|e /ɪn'kwaɪə(r)/ *vt/i* preguntar. ~**e about** informarse de. ~**y** *n* pregunta *f*; (*investigation*) investigación *f*

enrage /ɪn'reɪdʒ/ *vt* enfurecer

enrol /ɪn'rəʊl/ *vt* (*pt* **enrolled**) inscribir, matricular (student). ● *vi* inscribirse, matricularse

ensue /ɪn'sjuː/ *vi* seguir

ensure /ɪn'ʃʊə(r)/ *vt* asegurar

entail /ɪn'teɪl/ *vt* suponer; acarrear (expense)

entangle /ɪn'tæŋɡl/ *vt* enredar. ~**ment** *n* enredo *m*

enter /'entə(r)/ *vt* entrar en, entrar a (*esp LAm*); presentarse a (competition); inscribirse in (race); (*write*) escribir. ● *vi* entrar

enterpris|e /'entəpraɪz/ *n* empresa *f*; (*fig*) iniciativa *f*. ~**ing** *adj* emprendedor

entertain /entə'teɪn/ *vt* entretener; recibir (guests); abrigar (ideas, hopes); (*consider*) considerar. ~**ing** *adj* entretenido. ~**ment** *n* entretenimiento *m*; (*show*) espectáculo *m*

enthral /ɪn'θrɔːl/ *vt* (*pt* **enthralled**) cautivar

enthuse /ɪn'θjuːz/ *vi*. ~ **over** entusiasmarse por

enthusias|m /ɪn'θjuːzɪæzəm/ *n* entusiasmo *m*. ~**t** *n* entusiasta *m* & *f*. ~**tic** /-'æstɪk/ *adj* entusiasta. ~**tically** *adv* con entusiasmo

entice /ɪn'taɪs/ *vt* atraer

entire /ɪn'taɪə(r)/ *adj* entero. ~**ly** *adv* completamente. ~**ty** /ɪn'taɪərətɪ/ *n*. **in its** ~**ty** en su totalidad

entitle /ɪn'taɪtl/ *vt* titular; (*give a right*) dar derecho a. **be** ~**d to** tener derecho a. ~**ment** *n* derecho *m*

entity /'entətɪ/ *n* entidad *f*

entrails /'entreɪlz/ *npl* entrañas *fpl*

entrance /'entrəns/ *n* entrada *f*. /ɪn'trɑːns/ *vt* encantar

entrant /'entrənt/ *n* participante *m* & *f*; (*in exam*) candidato *m*

entreat /ɪn'triːt/ *vt* suplicar. ~**y** *n* súplica *f*

entrenched /ɪn'trentʃt/ *adj* (position) afianzado

entrust /ɪn'trʌst/ *vt* confiar

entry /'entrɪ/ *n* entrada *f*

entwine /ɪn'twaɪn/ *vt* entrelazar

enumerate /ɪ'njuːməreɪt/ *vt* enumerar

envelop /ɪn'veləp/ *vt* envolver

envelope /'envələʊp/ *n* sobre *m*

enviable /'envɪəbl/ *adj* envidiable

envious /'envɪəs/ *adj* envidioso

environment /ɪn'vaɪərənmənt/ *n* medio *m* ambiente. ~**al** /-'mentl/ *adj* ambiental

envisage /ɪn'vɪzɪdʒ/ *vt* prever; (*imagine*) imaginar

envision /ɪn'vɪʒn/ *vt* (*Amer*) prever

envoy /'envɔɪ/ *n* enviado *m*

envy /'envɪ/ *n* envidia *f*. ● *vt* envidiar

enzyme /'enzaɪm/ *n* enzima *f*

ephemeral /ɪ'femərəl/ *adj*

efímero

epic /'epɪk/ n épica f. ● adj épico

epidemic /epɪ'demɪk/ n epidemia f. ● adj epidémico

epilep|sy /'epɪlepsɪ/ n epilepsia f. **~tic** /-'leptɪk/ adj & n epiléptico (m)

epilogue /'epɪlɒg/ n epílogo m

episode /'episəʊd/ n episodio m

epitaph /'epɪtɑːf/ n epitafio m

epitom|e /ɪ'pɪtəmɪ/ n personificación f, epítome m. **~ize** vt ser la personificación de

epoch /'iːpɒk/ n época f

equal /'iːkwəl/ adj & n igual (m & f). **~ to** (a task) a la altura de. ● vt (pt **equalled**) ser igual a; (Math) ser. **~ity** /ɪ'kwɒlətɪ/ n igualdad f. **~ize** vt igualar. ● vi (Sport) empatar. **~izer** n (Sport) gol m del empate. **~ly** adv igualmente; (share) por igual

equation /ɪ'kweɪʒn/ n ecuación f

equator /ɪ'kweɪtə(r)/ n ecuador m. **~ial** /ekwə'tɔːrɪəl/ adj ecuatorial

equilibrium /iːkwɪ'lɪbrɪəm/ n equilibrio m

equinox /'iːkwɪnɒks/ n equinoccio m

equip /ɪ'kwɪp/ vt (pt **equipped**) equipar. **~ sth with** proveer algo de. **~ment** n equipo m

equivalen|ce /ɪ'kwɪvələns/ n equivalencia f. **~t** adj & n equivalente (m). **be ~t to** equivaler

equivocal /ɪ'kwɪvəkl/ adj equívoco

era /'ɪərə/ n era f

eradicate /ɪ'rædɪkeɪt/ vt erradicar, extirpar

erase /ɪ'reɪz/ vt borrar. **~r** n goma f (de borrar)

erect /ɪ'rekt/ adj erguido. ● vt levantar. **~ion** /-ʃn/ n construcción

f; (physiology) erección f

ero|de /ɪ'rəʊd/ vt erosionar. **~sion** /-ʒn/ n erosión f

erotic /ɪ'rɒtɪk/ adj erótico

err /ɜː(r)/ vi errar; (sin) pecar

errand /'erənd/ n recado m, mandado m (LAm)

erratic /ɪ'rætɪk/ adj desigual; (person) voluble

erroneous /ɪ'rəʊnɪəs/ adj erróneo

error /'erə(r)/ n error m

erudit|e /'eruːdaɪt/ adj erudito. **~ion** /-'dɪʃn/ n erudición f

erupt /ɪ'rʌpt/ vi entrar en erupción; (fig) estallar. **~ion** /-ʃn/ n erupción f

escalat|e /'eskəleɪt/ vt intensificar. ● vi intensificarse. **~ion** /-'leɪʃn/ n intensificación f. **~or** n escalera f mecánica

escapade /eskə'peɪd/ n aventura f

escap|e /ɪ'skeɪp/ vi escaparse. ● vt evitar. ● n fuga f; (of gas, water) escape m. **have a narrow ~e** escapar por un pelo. **~ism** /-ɪzəm/ n escapismo m

escort /'eskɔːt/ n acompañante m; (Mil) escolta f. ● /ɪ'skɔːt/ vt acompañar; (Mil) escoltar

Eskimo /'eskɪməʊ/ n (pl **-os** or invar) esquimal m & f

especial /ɪ'speʃl/ adj especial. **~ly** adv especialmente

espionage /'espɪənɑːʒ/ n espionaje m

Esq. /ɪ'skwaɪə(r)/ abbr (= **Esquire**) (in address) **E. Ashton, ~ Sr. Don E. Ashton**

essay /'eseɪ/ n ensayo m; (at school) composición f

essence /'esns/ n esencia f. **in ~** esencialmente

essential /ɪˈsenʃl/ adj esencial. • n elemento m esencial. **~ly** adv esencialmente

establish /ɪˈstæblɪʃ/ vt establecer. **~ment** n establecimiento m. **the E~ment** los que mandan, el sistema

estate /ɪˈsteɪt/ n finca f; (housing estate) complejo m habitacional, urbanización f, fraccionamiento m (Mex); (possessions) bienes mpl. **~ agent** n agente m inmobiliario. **~ car** n ranchera f, (coche m) familiar m, camioneta f (LAm)

esteem /ɪˈstiːm/ n estima f

estimate /ˈestɪmət/ n cálculo m; (Com) presupuesto m. • /ˈestɪmeɪt/ vt calcular. **~ion** /-ˈmeɪʃn/ n estimación f; (opinion) opinión f

estranged /ɪsˈtreɪndʒd/ adj alejado

estuary /ˈestʃʊərɪ/ n estuario m

etc /etˈsetrə/ abbr (= et cetera) etc., etcétera

etching /ˈetʃɪŋ/ n aguafuerte m

eternal /ɪˈtɜːnl/ adj eterno. **~ity** /-ətɪ/ n eternidad f

ether /ˈiːθə(r)/ n éter m

ethic /ˈeθɪk/ n ética f. **~al** adj ético. **~s** npl ética f

ethnic /ˈeθnɪk/ adj étnico

etiquette /ˈetɪket/ n etiqueta f

etymology /etɪˈmɒlədʒɪ/ n etimología f

EU /iːˈjuː/ abbr (**European Union**) UE (Unión Europea)

euphemism /ˈjuːfəmɪzəm/ n eufemismo m

euphoria /juːˈfɔːrɪə/ n euforia f

euro /ˈjʊərəʊ/ n euro m

Europe /ˈjʊərəp/ n Europa f. **~an** /-ˈpɪən/ adj & n europeo (m). **~an Union** n Unión f Europea

euthanasia /juːθəˈneɪzɪə/ n eutanasia f

evacuate /ɪˈvækjʊeɪt/ vt evacuar; desocupar (building). **~ion** /-ˈeɪʃn/ n evacuación f

evade /ɪˈveɪd/ vt evadir

evaluate /ɪˈvæljʊeɪt/ vt evaluar. **~tion** /-ˈeɪʃn/ vt evaluación f

evangelical /iːvænˈdʒelɪkl/ adj evangélico

evaporate /ɪˈvæpəreɪt/ vi evaporarse. **~ion** /-ˈreɪʃn/ n evaporación f

evasion /ɪˈveɪʒn/ n evasión f. **~ve** /ɪˈveɪsɪv/ adj evasivo

eve /iːv/ n víspera f

even /ˈiːvn/ adj (flat, smooth) plano; (colour) uniforme; (distribution) equitativo; (number) par. **get ~ with** desquitarse con. • vt nivelar. □ **~ up** vt equilibrar. • adv aun, hasta, incluso. **~ if** aunque. **~ so** aun así. **not ~** ni siquiera

evening /ˈiːvnɪŋ/ n tarde f; (after dark) noche f. **~ class** n clase f nocturna

event /ɪˈvent/ n acontecimiento m; (Sport) prueba f. **in the ~ of** en caso de. **~ful** adj lleno de acontecimientos

eventual /ɪˈventʃʊal/ adj final, definitivo. **~ity** /-ˈæləti/ n eventualidad f. **~ly** adv finalmente

ever /ˈevə(r)/ adv (negative) nunca, jamás; (at all times) siempre. **have you ~ been to Greece?** ¿has estado (alguna vez) en Grecia?. **~ after** desde entonces. **~ since** desde entonces. **~ so** 🄴 muy. **for ~** para siempre. **hardly ~** casi nunca. **~green** adj de hoja perenne. • n árbol m de hoja perenne. **~lasting** adj eterno

every /ˈevrɪ/ adj cada, todo. **~**

evict | excursion

evict /ɪ'vɪkt/ vt desahuciar. **~ion** /-ʃn/ n desahucio m

evidence /'evɪdəns/ n evidencia f; (proof) pruebas fpl; (Jurid) testimonio m; **give ~ce** prestar declaración. **~ce of** señales de. in **~ce** visible. **~t** adj evidente. **~tly** adv evidentemente

evil /'iːvl/ adj malvado. ● n mal m

evocative /ɪ'vɒkətɪv/ adj evocador. **~ke** /ɪ'vəʊk/ vt evocar

evolution /iːvə'luːʃn/ n evolución f

evolve /ɪ'vɒlv/ vt desarrollar. ● vi evolucionar

ewe /juː/ n oveja f

exact /ɪg'zækt/ adj exacto. ● vt exigir (from a). **~ing** adj exigente. **~ly** adv exactamente

exaggerat|e /ɪg'zædʒəreɪt/ vt exagerar. **~ion** /-'reɪʃn/ n exageración f

exam /ɪg'zæm/ n examen m. **~ination** /ɪgzæmɪ'neɪʃn/ n examen m. **~ine** /ɪg'zæmɪn/ vt examinar; interrogar (witness). **~iner** n examinador m

example /ɪg'zɑːmpl/ n ejemplo m. **for ~** por ejemplo. **make an ~ of s.o.** darle un castigo ejemplar a uno

exasperat|e /ɪg'zæspəreɪt/ vt exasperar. **~ing** adj exasperante. **~ion** /-'reɪʃn/ n exasperación f

excavat|e /'ekskəveɪt/ vt excavar. **~ion** /-'veɪʃn/ n excavación f

exceed /ɪk'siːd/ vt exceder. **~ingly** adv sumamente

excel /ɪk'sel/ vi (pt excelled) sobresalir. ● vt. **~ o.s.** lucirse. **~lence** /'eksələns/ n excelencia f. **~lent** adj excelente

except /ɪk'sept/ prep menos, excepto. **~ for** si no fuera por. ● vt exceptuar. **~ing** prep con excepción de

exception /ɪk'sepʃn/ n excepción f. **take ~ to** ofenderse por. **~al** adj excepcional. **~ally** adv excepcionalmente

excerpt /'eksɜːpt/ n extracto m

excess /ɪk'ses/ n exceso m. ● /'ekses/ adj excedente. **~ fare** suplemento m. **~ luggage** exceso m de equipaje. **~ive** adj excesivo

exchange /ɪks'tʃeɪndʒ/ vt cambiar. ● n intercambio m; (of money) cambio m. **(telephone) ~** central f telefónica

excise /'eksaɪz/ n impuestos mpl interos. ● /ek'saɪz/ vt quitar

excit|able /ɪk'saɪtəbl/ adj excitable. **~e** /ɪk'saɪt/ vt emocionar; (stimulate) excitar. **~ed** adj entusiasmado. **get ~ed** entusiasmarse. **~ement** n emoción f; (enthusiasm) entusiasmo m. **~ing** adj emocionante

excla|im /ɪk'skleɪm/ vi/t exclamar. **~mation** /ekskləˈmeɪʃn/ n exclamación f. **~mation mark** n signo m de admiración f

exclu|de /ɪk'skluːd/ vt excluir. **~sion** /-ʒən/ n exclusión f. **~sive** /ɪk'skluːsɪv/ adj exclusivo; (club) selecto. **~sive of** excluyendo. **~sively** adv exclusivamente

excruciating /ɪk'skruːʃieɪtɪŋ/ adj atroz, insoportable

excursion /ɪk'skɜːʃn/ n ex-

child todos los niños. **~ one** cada uno. **~ other** day un día sí y otro no. **~body** pron todos, todo el mundo. **~day** adj de todos los días. **~one** todos, todo el mundo. **~thing** pron todo. **~where** adv (be) en todas partes, (go) a todos lados cursión f

excus|able /ɪk'skju:zəbl/ adj perdonable. **~e** /ɪk'skju:z/ vt perdonar. **~e from** dispensar de. **~e me!** ¡perdón! ● /ɪk'skju:s/ n excusa f

ex-directory /eksdɪ'rektərɪ/ adj que no figura en la guía telefónica, privado (Mex)

execut|e /'eksɪkju:t/ vt ejecutar. **~ion** /eksɪ'kju:ʃn/ n ejecución f. **~ioner** n verdugo m

executive /ɪg'zekjʊtɪv/ adj & n ejecutivo (m)

exempt /ɪg'zempt/ adj exento (from de). ● vt dispensar. **~ion** /-ʃn/ n exención f

exercise /'eksəsaɪz/ n ejercicio m. ● vt ejercer. ● vi hacer ejercicio. **~ book** n cuaderno m

exert /ɪg'zɜ:t/ vt ejercer. ~ **o.s.** hacer un gran esfuerzo. **~ion** /-ʃn/ n esfuerzo m

exhale /eks'heɪl/ vt/i exhalar

exhaust /ɪg'zɔ:st/ vt agotar. ● n (Auto) tubo m de escape. **~ed** adj agotado. **~ion** /-stʃən/ n agotamiento m. **~ive** adj exhaustivo

exhibit /ɪg'zɪbɪt/ vt exponer; (fig) mostrar. ● n objeto m expuesto; (Jurid) documento m. **~ion** /eksɪ'bɪʃn/ n exposición. **~ionist** n exhibicionista m & f. **~or** /ɪg'zɪbɪtə(r)/ n expositor f

exhilarat|ing /ɪg'zɪləreɪtɪŋ/ adj excitante. **~ion** /-'reɪʃn/ n regocijo m

exhort /ɪg'zɔ:t/ vt exhortar

exile /'eksaɪl/ n exilio m; (person) exiliado m. ● vt desterrar

exist /ɪg'zɪst/ vi existir. **~ence** n existencia f. **in ~ence** existente

exit /'eksɪt/ n salida f

exorbitant /ɪg'zɔ:bɪtənt/ adj exorbitante

exorcis|e /'eksɔ:saɪz/ vt exorcizar. **~m** /-sɪzəm/ n exorcismo m. **~t** n exorcista m & f

exotic /ɪg'zɒtɪk/ adj exótico

expand /ɪk'spænd/ vt expandir; (develop) desarrollar. ● vi expandirse

expanse /ɪk'spæns/ n extensión f

expansion /ɪk'spænʃn/ n expansión f

expatriate /eks'pætrɪət/ adj & n expatriado (m)

expect /ɪk'spekt/ vt esperar; (suppose) suponer; (demand) contar con. **I ~ so** supongo que sí. **~ancy** n esperanza f. **life ~ancy** esperanza f de vida. **~ant** adj expectante. **~ant mother** n futura madre f

expectation /ekspek'teɪʃn/ n expectativa f

expedient /ɪk'spi:dɪənt/ adj conveniente. ● n expediente m

expedition /ekspɪ'dɪʃn/ n expedición f

expel /ɪk'spel/ vt (pt expelled) expulsar

expend /ɪk'spend/ vt gastar. **~able** adj prescindible. **~iture** /-ɪtʃə(r)/ n gastos mpl

expens|e /ɪk'spens/ n gasto m. **at s.o.'s ~e** a la costa de uno. **~es** npl (Com) gastos mpl. **~ive** adj caro

experience /ɪk'spɪərɪəns/ n experiencia. ● vt experimentar. **~d** adj con experiencia; (driver) experimentado

experiment /ɪk'sperɪmənt/ n experimento m. ● vi experimentar. **~al** /-'mentl/ adj experimental

expert /'ekspɜ:t/ adj & n experto (m). **~ise** /ekspə'ti:z/ n pericia f. **~ly** adv hábilmente

expir|e /ɪkˈspaɪə(r)/ vi (passport, ticket) caducar; (contract) vencer. **~y** n vencimiento m, caducidad f

expla|in /ɪkˈspleɪn/ vt explicar. **~nation** /ekspləˈneɪʃn/ n explicación f. **~natory** /ɪksˈplænətərɪ/ adj explicativo

explicit /ɪkˈsplɪsɪt/ adj explícito

explode /ɪkˈspləʊd/ vt hacer explotar. ● vi estallar

exploit /ˈeksplɔɪt/ n hazaña f. ● /ɪkˈsplɔɪt/ vt explotar. **~ation** /eksplɔɪˈteɪʃn/ n explotación f

explor|ation /ekspləˈreɪʃn/ n exploración f. **~atory** /ɪksˈplɒrətrɪ/ adj exploratorio. **~e** /ɪkˈsplɔː(r)/ vt explorar. **~er** n explorador m

explosi|on /ɪkˈspləʊʒn/ n explosión f. **~ve** /-sɪv/ adj & n explosivo (m)

export /ɪkˈspɔːt/ vt exportar. ● /ˈekspɔːt/ n exportación f; (item) artículo m de exportación. **~er** /ɪksˈpɔːtə(r)/ n exportador m

expos|e /ɪkˈspəʊz/ vt exponer; (reveal) descubrir. **~ure** /-ʒə(r)/ n exposición f. **die of ~ure** morir de frío

express /ɪkˈspres/ vt expresar. ● adj expreso; (letter) urgente. ● adv (by express post) por correo urgente. ● n (train) rápido m, expreso m. **~ion** n expresión f. **~ive** adj expresivo. **~ly** adv expresamente. **~way** n (Amer) autopista f

expulsion /ɪkˈspʌlʃn/ n expulsión f

exquisite /ˈekskwɪzɪt/ adj exquisito

exten|d /ɪkˈstend/ vt extender; (prolong) prolongar; ampliar (house). ● vi extenderse. **~sion** /-ʃn/ n extensión f; (of road, time) prolongación f; (building) anejo m.

~sive /-sɪv/ adj extenso. **~sively** adv extensamente. **~t** n extensión f; (fig) alcance m. **to a certain ~t** hasta cierto punto

exterior /ɪkˈstɪərɪə(r)/ adj & n exterior (m)

exterminat|e /ɪkˈstɜːmɪneɪt/ vt exterminar. **~ion** /-ˈneɪʃn/ n exterminio m

external /ɪkˈstɜːnl/ adj externo

extinct /ɪkˈstɪŋkt/ adj extinto. **~ion** /-ʃn/ n extinción f

extinguish /ɪkˈstɪŋgwɪʃ/ vt extinguir. **~er** n extintor m, extinguidor m (LAm)

extol /ɪkˈstəʊl/ vt (pt extolled) alabar

extort /ɪkˈstɔːt/ vt sacar por la fuerza. **~ion** /-ʃn/ n exacción f. **~ionate** /-ənət/ adj exorbitante

extra /ˈekstrə/ adj de más. ● adv extraordinariamente. ● n suplemento m; (Cinema) extra m & f

extract /ˈekstrækt/ n extracto m. ● /ɪkˈstrækt/ vt extraer. **~ion** /ɪkˈstrækʃn/ n extracción f

extradit|e /ˈekstrədaɪt/ vt extraditar. **~ion** /-dɪʃn/ n extradición f

extra: ~ordinary /ɪkˈstrɔːdnrɪ/ adj extraordinario. **~sensory** /ekstrəˈsensərɪ/ adj extrasensorial

extravagan|ce /ɪkˈstrævəgəns/ n prodigalidad f; (of gestures, dress) extravagancia f. **~t** adj pródigo; (behaviour) extravagante. **~za** n gran espectáculo m

extrem|e /ɪkˈstriːm/ adj & n extremo (m). **~ely** adv extremadamente. **~ist** n extremista m & f

extricate /ˈekstrɪkeɪt/ vt desenredar, librar

extrovert /ˈekstrəvɜːt/ n extrovertido m

exuberan|ce /ɪgˈzjuːbərəns/ n

exuberancia f. **~t** adj exuberante
exude /ɪgˈzjuːd/ vt rezumar
exult /ɪgˈzʌlt/ vi exultar. **~ation** /egzʌlˈteɪʃn/ n exultación f
eye /aɪ/ n ojo m. **keep an ~ on** no perder de vista. **see ~ to ~ with s.o.** estar de acuerdo con uno. ● vt (pt eyed, pres p eyeing) mirar. **~ball** n globo m ocular. **~brow** n ceja f. **~drops** npl colirio m. **~lash** n pestaña f. **~lid** n párpado m. **~opener** n ⓘ revelación f. **~shadow** n sombra f de ojos. **~sight** n vista f. **~sore** n (fig, fam) monstruosidad f, adefesio m. **~witness** n testigo m ocular

Ff

fable /ˈfeɪbl/ n fábula f
fabric /ˈfæbrɪk/ n tejido m, tela f
fabricate /ˈfæbrɪkeɪt/ vt inventar. **~ation** /-ˈkeɪʃn/ n invención f
fabulous /ˈfæbjʊləs/ adj fabuloso
facade /fəˈsɑːd/ n fachada f
face /feɪs/ n cara f, rostro m; (of watch) esfera f, carátula f (Mex); (aspect) aspecto m. **~ down(wards)** boca abajo. **~ up(wards)** boca arriba. **in the ~ of** frente a. **lose ~** quedar mal. **pull ~s** hacer muecas. ● vt mirar hacia; (house) dar a; (confront) enfrentarse con. ● vi volverse. □ **~ up to** vt enfrentarse con. **~ flannel** n paño m (para lavarse la cara). **~less** adj anónimo. **~ lift** n cirugía f estética en la cara
facetious /fəˈsiːʃəs/ adj burlón
facial /ˈfeɪʃl/ adj facial

facile /ˈfæsaɪl/ adj superficial, simplista
facilitate /fəˈsɪlɪteɪt/ vt facilitar
facility /fəˈsɪlɪti/ n facilidad f
fact /fækt/ n hecho m. **as a matter of ~, in ~** en realidad, de hecho
faction /ˈfækʃn/ n facción f
factor /ˈfæktə(r)/ n factor m
factory /ˈfæktəri/ n fábrica f
factual /ˈfæktʃʊəl/ adj basado en hechos, factual
faculty /ˈfækltɪ/ n facultad f
fad /fæd/ n manía f, capricho m
fade /feɪd/ vi (colour) desteñirse; (flowers) marchitarse; (light) apagarse; (memory, sound) desvanecerse
fag /fæg/ n (fam, chore) faena f; (sl, cigarette) cigarrillo m, pitillo m
Fahrenheit /ˈfærənhaɪt/ adj Fahrenheit
fail /feɪl/ vi fracasar; (brakes) fallar; (in an exam) suspender, ser reprobado (LAm). **he ~ed to arrive** no llegó. ● vt suspender, ser reprobado en (LAm) (exam); suspender, reprobar (LAm) (candidate). ● n. **without ~** sin falta. **~ing** n defecto m. ● prep. **~ing that,** si eso no resulta.... **~ure** /ˈfeɪljə(r)/ n fracaso m
faint /feɪnt/ adj (-er, -est) (weak) débil; (indistinct) indistinto. **feel ~** estar mareado. **the ~est idea** la más remota idea. ● vi desmayarse. ● n desmayo m. **~-hearted** /-ˈhɑːtɪd/ adj pusilánime, cobarde. **~ly** adv (weakly) débilmente; (indistinctly) indistintamente; (slightly) ligeramente
fair /feə(r)/ adj (-er, -est) (just) justo; (weather) bueno; (amount) razonable; (hair) rubio, güero (Mex fam); (skin) blanco. ● adv limpio. ● n

feria f. **~-haired** /-'heəd/ adj rubio, güero (Mex fam). **~ly** adv (justly) justamente; (rather) bastante. **~ness** n justicia f. **in all ~ness** sinceramente. **~ play** n juego m limpio

fairy /'feərɪ/ n hada f. **~ story**, **~ tale** n cuento m de hadas

faith /feɪθ/ n (trust) confianza f; (Relig) fe f. **~ful** adj fiel. **~fully** adv fielmente. **yours ~fully** (in letters) (le saluda) atentamente

fake /feɪk/ n falsificación f; (person) farsante m. ● adj falso. ● vt falsificar

falcon /'fɔːlkən/ n halcón m

Falkland Islands /'fɔːklənd/ npl. **the Falkland Islands**, **the Falklands** las (Islas) Malvinas

fall /fɔːl/ vi (pt fell, pp fallen) caer; (decrease) bajar. ● n caída f; (Amer, autumn) otoño m; (in price) bajada f. □ **~ apart** vi deshacerse. □ **~ back on** vt recurrir a. □ **~ down** vi (fall) caerse. □ **~ for** vt 𝟙 enamorarse de (person); dejarse engañar por (trick). □ **~ in** vi (Mil) formar filas. □ **~ off** vi caerse; (diminish) disminuir. □ **~ out** vi (quarrel) reñir (with con); (drop out) caerse; (Mil) romper filas. □ **~ over** vi caerse. vt tropezar con. □ **~ through** vi no salir adelante

fallacy /'fæləsɪ/ n falacia f

fallible /'fælɪbl/ adj falible

fallout /'fɔːlaʊt/ n lluvia f radiactiva. **~ shelter** n refugio m antinuclear

fallow /'fæləʊ/ adj en barbecho

false /fɔːls/ adj falso. **~ alarm** n falsa alarma. **~hood** n mentira f. **~ly** adv falsamente. **~ teeth** npl dentadura f postiza

falsify /'fɔːlsɪfaɪ/ vt falsificar

falter /'fɔːltə(r)/ vi vacilar

fame /feɪm/ n fama f. **~d** adj famoso

familiar /fə'mɪlɪə(r)/ adj familiar. **the name sounds ~** el nombre me suena. **be ~ with** conocer. **~ity** /-'ærətɪ/ n familiaridad f. **~ize** vt familiarizar

family /'fæməlɪ/ n familia f. ● adj de (la) familia, familiar. **~ tree** n árbol m genealógico

famine /'fæmɪn/ n hambre f, hambruna f

famished /'fæmɪʃt/ adj hambriento

famous /'feɪməs/ adj famoso

fan /fæn/ n abanico m; (Mec) ventilador m; (enthusiast) aficionado m; (of group, actor) fan m & f; (of sport, team) hincha m & f. ● vt (pt fanned) abanicar; avivar (interest). □ **~ out** vi desparramarse en forma de abanico

fanatic /fə'nætɪk/ n fanático m. **~al** adj fanático. **~ism** /-sɪzəm/ n fanatismo m

fan belt n correa f de ventilador, banda f del ventilador (Mex)

fanciful /'fænsɪfl/ adj (imaginative) imaginativo; (impractical) extravagante

fancy /'fænsɪ/ n imaginación f; (liking) gusto m. **take a ~ to** tomar cariño a (a person); aficionarse a (a thing). ● adj de lujo. ● vt (imagine) imaginar; (believe) creer; (fam, want) apetecer a. **~ dress** n disfraz m

fanfare /'fænfeə(r)/ n fanfarria f

fang /fæŋ/ n (of animal) colmillo m; (of snake) diente m

fantasize /'fæntəsaɪz/ vi fantasear

fantastic /fæn'tæstɪk/ adj fantástico

fantasy /'fæntəsɪ/ n fantasía f

far /fɑː(r)/ adv lejos; (much) mucho. **as ~ as** hasta. **as ~ as I know** que yo sepa. **by ~** con mucho. ● adj (further, furthest or farther, farthest) lejano. **~ away** lejano

farc|e /fɑːs/ n farsa f. **~ical** adj ridículo

fare /feə(r)/ n (on bus) precio m del billete, precio m del boleto (LAm); (on train, plane) precio m del billete, precio m del pasaje (LAm); (food) comida f

Far East /fɑːr'iːst/ n Extremo or Lejano Oriente m

farewell /feə'wel/ int & n adiós (m)

far-fetched /fɑː'fetʃt/ adj improbable

farm /fɑːm/ n granja f. ● vt cultivar. □ **~ out** vt encargar (a terceros). ● vi ser agricultor. **~er** n agricultor m, granjero m. **~house** n granja f. **~ing** n agricultura f. **~yard** n corral m

far: ~-off adj lejano. **~-reaching** /fɑː'riːtʃɪŋ/ adj trascendental. **~-sighted** /fɑː'saɪtɪd/ adj con visión del futuro; (Med, Amer) hipermétrope

farther, farthest /'fɑːðə(r), 'fɑːðəst/ see FAR

fascinat|e /'fæsɪneɪt/ vt fascinar. **~ed** adj fascinado. **~ing** adj fascinante. **~ion** /-'neɪʃn/ n fascinación f

fasc|ism /'fæʃɪzəm/ n fascismo m. **~t** adj & n fascista (m & f)

fashion /'fæʃn/ n (manner) manera f; (vogue) moda f. **be in/out of ~** estar de moda/estar pasado de moda. **~able** adj de moda

fast /fɑːst/ adj (-er, -est) rápido; (clock) adelantado; (secure) fijo; (colours) sólido. ● adv rápidamente; (securely) firmemente. **~ asleep** profundamente dormido. ● vi ayunar. ● n ayuno m

fasten /'fɑːsn/ vt sujetar; cerrar (case); abrochar (belt etc). ● vi (case) cerrar; (belt etc) cerrarse. **~er, ~ing** n (on box, window) cierre m; (on door) cerrojo m

fat /fæt/ n grasa f. ● adj (fatter, fattest) gordo; (meat) que tiene mucha grasa; (thick) grueso. **get ~** engordar

fatal /'feɪtl/ adj mortal; (fateful) fatídico. **~ity** /fə'tælətɪ/ n muerto m. **~ly** adv mortalmente

fate /feɪt/ n destino m; (one's lot) suerte f. **~d** adj predestinado. **~ful** adj fatídico

father /'fɑːðə(r)/ n padre m. **~hood** n paternidad f. **~-in-law** m (pl **~s-in-law**) n suegro m. **~ly** adj paternal

fathom /'fæðəm/ n braza f. ● vt. **~ (out)** comprender

fatigue /fə'tiːg/ n fatiga f. ● vt fatigar

fat|ten /'fætn/ vt. **~ten (up)** cebar (animal). **~tening** adj que engorda. **~ty** adj graso, grasoso (LAm). ● n 🄵 gordinflón m

fatuous /'fætʃʊəs/ adj fatuo

faucet /'fɔːsɪt/ n (Amer) grifo m, llave f (LAm)

fault /fɔːlt/ n defecto m; (blame) culpa f; (tennis) falta f; (in geology) falla f. **at ~** culpable. ● vt encontrarle defectos a. **~less** adj impecable. **~y** adj defectuoso

favour /'feɪvə(r)/ n favor m. ● vt favorecer; (support) estar a favor de; (prefer) preferir. **~able** adj favorable. **~ably** adv favorablemente. **~ite** adj & n preferido (m). **~itism** n favoritismo m

fawn /fɔːn/ n cervato m. ● adj beige, beis. ● vi. ~ **on** adular

fax /fæks/ n fax m. ● vt faxear

fear /fɪə(r)/ n miedo m. ● vt temer. ~**ful** adj (frightening) espantoso; (frightened) temeroso. ~**less** adj intrépido. ~**some** /-səm/ adj espantoso

feasib|ility /fiːzə'bɪlətɪ/ n viabilidad f. ~**le** /'fiːzəbl/ adj factible; (likely) posible

feast /fiːst/ n (Relig) fiesta f; (meal) banquete m

feat /fiːt/ n hazaña f

feather /'feðə(r)/ n pluma f. ~**weight** n peso m pluma

feature /'fiːtʃə(r)/ n (on face) rasgo m; (characteristic) característica f; (in newspaper) artículo m; ~ (film) película f principal, largometraje m. ● vt presentar; (give prominence to) destacar

February /'februərɪ/ n febrero m

fed /fed/ see FEED

feder|al /'fedərəl/ adj federal. ~**ation** /fedə'reɪʃn/ n federación f

fed up adj 🔢 harto (with de)

fee /fiː/ n (professional) honorarios mpl; (enrolment) derechos mpl; (club) cuota f

feeble /'fiːbl/ adj (-er, -est) débil

feed /fiːd/ vt (pt fed) dar de comer a; (supply) alimentar. ● vi comer. ● n (for animals) pienso m; (for babies) comida f. ~**back** n reacción f

feel /fiːl/ vt (pt felt) sentir; (touch) tocar; (think) considerar. do you ~ it's a good idea? ¿te parece buena idea? ~ **as if** tener la impresión de que. ~ **hot/hungry** tener calor/hambre. ~ **like** (fam, want) tener ganas de. ● n sensación f. **get the** ~ **of sth** acostumbrarse a algo. ~**er** n (of insect) antena f. ~**ing** n

sentimiento m; (physical) sensación f

feet /fiːt/ see FOOT

feign /feɪn/ vt fingir

feint /feɪnt/ n finta f

fell /fel/ see FALL. ● vt derribar; talar (tree)

fellow /'feləʊ/ n 🔢 tipo m; (comrade) compañero m; (of society) socio m. ~ **countryman** n compatriota m. ~ **passenger/traveller** n compañero m de viaje

felony /'feləni/ n delito m grave

felt /felt/ n see FEEL. ● n fieltro m

female /'fiːmeɪl/ adj hembra; (voice, sex etc) femenino. ● n mujer f; (animal) hembra f

femini|ne /'femənɪn/ adj & n femenino; ~**nity** /-'nɪnətɪ/ n feminidad f. ~**st** adj & n feminista f & f

fence /fens/ n cerca f, cerco m (LAm). ● vt. ~**e (in)** encerrar, cercar. ● vi (Sport) practicar la esgrima. ~**er** n esgrimidor m. ~**ing** n (Sport) esgrima f

fend /fend/ vi. ~ **for o.s.** valerse por sí mismo. □ ~ **off** vt defenderse de

fender /'fendə(r)/ n rejilla f; (Amer, Auto) guardabarros m, salpicadera f (Mex)

ferment /fə'ment/ vt/i fermentar. ~**ation** /-'teɪʃn/ n fermentación f

fern /fɜːn/ n helecho m

feroci|ous /fə'rəʊʃəs/ adj feroz. ~**ty** /fə'rɒsətɪ/ n ferocidad f

ferret /'ferɪt/ n hurón m. ● vi (pt ferreted) ~ **about** husmear. ● vt. ~ **out** descubrir

ferry /'ferɪ/ n ferry m. ● vt transportar

fertil|e /'fɜːtaɪl/ adj fértil. ~**ity** /-'tɪlətɪ/ n fertilidad f. ~**ize**

/'fɜːtəlaɪz/ vt fecundar, abonar (soil). ~izer n fertilizante m

ferv|ent /'fɜːvənt/ adj ferviente. ~our /-və(r)/ n fervor m

fester /'festə(r)/ vi enconarse

festival /'festəvl/ n fiesta f; (of arts) festival m

festive /'festɪv/ adj festivo. **the ~e season** n las Navidades. ~ity /fe'stɪvəti/ n festividad f

fetch /fetʃ/ vt (go for) ir a buscar; (bring) traer; (be sold for) venderse en. ~ing adj atractivo

fête /feɪt/ n fiesta f. • vt festejar

fetish /'fetɪʃ/ n fetiche m

fetter /'fetə(r)/ vt encadenar

feud /fjuːd/ n contienda f

feudal /'fjuːdl/ adj feudal. ~ism n feudalismo m

fever /'fiːvə(r)/ n fiebre f. ~ish adj febril

few /fjuː/ adj pocos. **a ~ houses** algunas casas. • n pocos mpl. **a ~** unos (pocos). **a good ~, quite a ~** 🔲 muchos. ~er adj & n menos. ~est adj el menor número de

fiancé /fɪ'ɒnseɪ/ n novio m. ~e /fɪ'ɒnseɪ/ n novia f

fiasco /fɪ'æskəʊ/ n (pl -os) fiasco m

fib /fɪb/ n 🔲 mentirilla f. • vi 🔲 mentir, decir mentirillas

fibre /'faɪbə(r)/ n fibra f. ~glass n fibra f de vidrio

fickle /'fɪkl/ adj inconstante

ficti|on /'fɪkʃn/ n ficción f. **(works of)** ~ novelas fpl. ~onal adj novelesco. ~tious /fɪk'tɪʃəs/ adj ficticio

fiddle /'fɪdl/ n 🔲 violín m; (fam, swindle) trampa f. • vt 🔲 falsificar. ~ with juguetear con

fidget /'fɪdʒɪt/ vi (pt fidgeted) moverse, ponerse nervioso. ~ with

juguetear con. • n persona f inquieta. ~y adj inquieto

field /fiːld/ n campo m. ~ day n. **have a ~ day** hacer su agosto. ~ **glasses** npl gemelos mpl. **F~ Marshal** n mariscal m de campo. ~ **trip** n viaje m de estudio. ~work n investigaciones fpl en el terreno

fiend /fiːnd/ n demonio m. ~ish adj diabólico

fierce /fɪəs/ adj (-er, -est) feroz; (attack) violento. ~ly (growl) con ferocidad; (fight) con fiereza

fiery /'faɪərɪ/ adj (-ier, -iest) ardiente; (temper) exaltado

fifteen /fɪf'tiːn/ adj & n quince (m). ~th adj decimoquinto. • n quinceavo m

fifth /fɪfθ/ adj & n quinto (m)

fift|ieth /'fɪftɪəθ/ adj quincuagésimo. • n cincuentavo m. ~y adj & n cincuenta (m). ~y-~y adv mitad y mitad, a medias. • adj. a ~y-~y **chance** una posibilidad de cada dos

fig /fɪg/ n higo m

fight /faɪt/ vi (pt fought) luchar; (quarrel) disputar. • vt luchar contra. • n pelea m; (struggle) lucha f; (quarrel) disputa f; (Mil) combate m. ~ ~ back v defenderse. ~ **off** vt rechazar (attack); luchar contra (illness). ~er n luchador m; (aircraft) avión m de caza. ~ing n luchas fpl

figment /'fɪgmənt/ n. ~ **of the imagination** producto m de la imaginación

figurative /'fɪgjʊrətɪv/ adj figurado

figure /'fɪgə(r)/ n (number) cifra f; (person) figura f; (shape) forma f; (of woman) tipo m. • vt imaginar

(Amer fam, reckon) calcular. • vi figurar. that ~s (fam) es lógico. □ ~ out vt entender. ~head n testaferro m, mascarón m de proa. ~ of speech n figura f retórica

filch /fɪltʃ/ vt ▣ hurtar

file /faɪl/ n (tool, for nails) lima f; (folder) carpeta f; (set of papers) expediente m; (Comp) archivo m; (row) fila f. in single ~ en fila india. • vt archivar (papers); limar (metal, nails). ~ in vi entrar en fila. ~ past vt desfilar ante

filing cabinet /'faɪlɪŋ/ n archivador m

fill /fɪl/ vt llenar. • vi llenarse. • n. eat one's ~ hartarse de comer. have had one's ~ of estar harto de □ ~ in vt rellenar (form, hole). □ ~ out vt rellenar (form). vi (get fatter) engordar. □ ~ up vt llenar. vi llenarse

fillet /'fɪlɪt/ n filete m. • vt (pt filleted) cortar en filetes (meat); quitar la espina a (fish)

filling /'fɪlɪŋ/ n (in tooth) empaste m, tapadura f (Mex). ~ station n gasolinera f

film /fɪlm/ n película f. • vt filmar. ~ star n estrella f de cine

filter /'fɪltə(r)/ n filtro m. • vt filtrar. • vi filtrarse. ~-tipped adj con filtro

filth /fɪlθ/ n mugre f. ~y adj mugriento

fin /fɪn/ n aleta f

final /'faɪnl/ adj último; (conclusive) decisivo. • n (Sport) final f. ~s npl (Schol) exámenes mpl de fin de curso

finale /fɪ'nɑːlɪ/ n final m

final|list n finalista m & f. ~ize vt ultimar. ~ly adv (lastly) finalmente, por fin

financ|e /'faɪnæns/ n finanzas fpl. • vt financiar. ~ial /faɪ'nænʃl/ adj financiero; (difficulties) económico

find /faɪnd/ vt (pt found) encontrar. ~ out vt descubrir. • vi (learn) enterarse. ~ings npl conclusiones fpl

fine /faɪn/ adj (-er, -est) (delicate) fino; (excellent) excelente. • adv muy bien. • n multa f. • vt multar. ~ arts npl bellas artes fpl. ~ly adv (cut) en trozos pequeños; (adjust) con precisión

finger /'fɪŋgə(r)/ n dedo m. • vt tocar. ~nail n uña f. ~print n huella f digital. ~tip n punta f del dedo

finish /'fɪnɪʃ/ vt/i terminar, acabar. ~ doing terminar de hacer. • n fin m; (of race) llegada f

finite /'faɪnaɪt/ adj finito

Fin|land /'fɪnlənd/ n Finlandia f. ~n n finlandés m. ~nish adj & n finlandés (m)

fiord /fjɔːd/ n fiordo m

fir /fɜː(r)/ n abeto m

fire /faɪə(r)/ n fuego m; (conflagration) incendio m. • vt disparar (gun); (dismiss) despedir; avivar (imagination). • vi disparar. ~ alarm n alarma f contra incendios. ~arm n arma f de fuego. ~ brigade, ~ department (Amer) n cuerpo m de bomberos. ~ engine n coche m de bomberos, carro m de bomberos (Mex). ~escape n escalera f de incendios. ~ extinguisher n extintor m, extinguidor m (LAm). ~fighter n bombero m. ~man /-mən/ n bombero m. ~place n chimenea f. ~side n hogar m. ~ truck n (Amer) see ~ ENGINE. ~wood n leña f. ~work n fuego m artificial

firm /fɜːm/ n empresa f. • adj (-er,

-est) firme. ~ly adv firmemente

first /fɜːst/ adj primero, (before masculine singular noun) primer. **at ~ hand** directamente. ● n primero m. ● adv primero; (first time) por primera vez. ~ **of all** primero. ~ **aid** n primeros auxilios mpl. ~ **aid kit** n botiquín m. ~ **class** /-'klɑːs/ adv (travel) en primera clase. ~-**class** adj de primera clase. ~ **floor** n primer piso m; (Amer) planta f baja. **F~ Lady** n (Amer) Primera Dama f. ~**ly** adv en primer lugar. ~ **name** n nombre m de pila. ~-**rate** /-'reɪt/ adj excelente

fish /fɪʃ/ n (pl pl inv or -es) pez m; (as food) pescado m. ● vi pescar. **go ~ing** ir de pesca. □ ~ **out** vt sacar. ~**erman** n pescador m. ~**ing** n pesca f. ~**ing pole** (Amer), ~**ing rod** n caña f de pesca. ~**monger** n pescadero m. ~ **shop** n pescadería f. ~**y** adj (smell) a pescado; (fam, questionable) sospechoso

fission /'fɪʃn/ n fisión f

fist /fɪst/ n puño m

fit /fɪt/ adj (fitter, fittest) (healthy) en forma; (good enough) adecuado; (able) capaz. ● n (attack) ataque m; (of clothes) corte m. ● vt (pt fitted) (adapt) adaptar; (be the right size for) quedarle bien a; (install) colocar. ● vi encajar; (in certain space) caber; (clothes) quedarle bien a uno. □ ~ **in** vi caber. ~**ful** adj irregular. ~**ness** n salud f; (Sport) (buena) forma f física. ~**ting** adj apropiado. ● n (of clothes) prueba f. ~**ting room** n probador m

five /faɪv/ adj & n cinco (m)

fix /fɪks/ vt fijar; (mend, deal with) arreglar. ● n. **in a** ~ en un aprieto. ~**ed** adj fijo. ~**ture** /'fɪkstʃə(r)/ n

(Sport) partido m.

fizz /fɪz/ vi burbujear. ● n efervescencia f. ~**le** /fɪzl/ vi. ~**le out** fracasar. ~**y** adj efervescente; (water) con gas

fjord /fjɔːd/ n fiordo m

flabbergasted /'flæbəgɑːstɪd/ adj estupefacto

flabby /'flæbɪ/ adj flojo

flag /flæg/ n bandera f. ● vi (pt flagged) (weaken) flaquear; (conversation) languidecer

flagon /'flægən/ n botella f grande, jarro m

flagpole /'flægpəʊl/ n asta f de bandera

flagrant /'fleɪɡrənt/ adj flagrante

flair /fleə(r)/ n don m (for de)

flak|e /fleɪk/ n copo m; (of paint, metal) escama f. ● vi desconcharse. ~**y** adj escamoso

flamboyant /flæm'bɔɪənt/ adj (clothes) vistoso; (manner) extravagante

flame /fleɪm/ n llama f. **go up in** ~**s** incendiarse

flamingo /flə'mɪŋɡəʊ/ n (pl -o(e)s) flamenco m

flammable /'flæməbl/ adj inflamable

flan /flæn/ n tartaleta f

flank /flæŋk/ n (of animal) ijada f; (of person) costado m; (Mil, Sport) flanco m

flannel /'flænl/ n franela f. (for face) toallita m (para lavarse la cara).

flap /flæp/ vi (pt flapped) ondear; (wings) aletear. ● vt batir (wings); agitar (arms). ● n (cover) tapa f; (of pocket) cartera f; (of table) ala f. **get into a** ~ 🔲 ponerse nervioso

flare /fleə(r)/ n llamarada f; (Mil)

flash | float

bengala f; (in skirt) vuelo m. □ ~
up vi llamear; (fighting) estallar;
(person) encolerizarse

flash /flæʃ/ vi destellar. ● vt (aim
torch) dirigir; (flaunt) hacer ostentación de. ~ **past** pasar como un
rayo. ● n destello m; (Photo) flash m.
~**back** n escena f retrospectiva.
~**light** n (Amer, torch) linterna f.
~**y** adj ostentoso

flask /flɑːsk/ n frasco m; (vacuum
flask) termo m

flat /flæt/ adj (**flatter, flattest**)
plano; (tyre) desinflado; (refusal)
categórico; (fare, rate) fijo; (Mus)
bemol. ● adv (Mus) demasiado bajo.
~ **out** (at top speed) a toda velocidad. ● n (rooms) apartamento m,
piso m; 🔲 (Auto,
esp Amer) bemol m. ~**ly** adv cate-
góricamente. ~**ten** vt allanar, aplanar

flatter /flætə(r)/ vt adular. ~**ing**
adj (person) lisonjero; (clothes) fa-
vorecedor. ~**y** n adulación f

flaunt /flɔːnt/ vt hacer ostentación de

flavour /fleɪvə(r)/ n sabor m. ● vt
sazonar. ~**ing** n condimento m

flaw /flɔː/ n defecto m. ~**less** adj
perfecto

flea /fliː/ n pulga f

fleck /flek/ n mancha f, pinta f

fled /fled/ see **FLEE**

flee /fliː/ vi (pt **fled**) huir. ● vt
huir de

fleece /fliːs/ n vellón m. ● vt 🔲
desplumar

fleet /fliːt/ n flota f; (of cars) parque m móvil

fleeting /fliːtɪŋ/ adj fugaz

Flemish /flemɪʃ/ adj & n flamenco
(m)

flesh /fleʃ/ n carne f. **in the** ~ en

persona

flew /fluː/ see **FLY**

flex /fleks/ vt doblar; flexionar
(muscle). ● n (Elec) cable m

flexib|ility /fleksəˈbɪlətɪ/ n flexi-
bilidad f. ~**le** /fleksəbl/ adj flexible

flexitime /fleksɪtaɪm/, (Amer)
flextime /flekstaɪm/ n horario m
flexible

flick /flɪk/ n golpecito m. ● vt dar
un golpecito a. □ ~ **through** vt
hojear

flicker /flɪkə(r)/ vi parpadear. ● n
parpadeo m; (of hope) resquicio m

flies /flaɪz/ npl (on trousers) bragueta f

flight /flaɪt/ n vuelo m; (fleeing)
huida f, fuga f. ~ **of stairs** tramo
m de escalera f. **take (to)** ~ darse
a la fuga. ~ **attendant** n (male)
sobrecargo m, aeromozo m (LAm);
(female) azafata f, aeromoza f
(LAm). ~**-deck** n cubierta f de
vuelo

flimsy /flɪmzɪ/ adj (**-ier, -iest**)
flojo, débil, poco sólido

flinch /flɪntʃ/ vi retroceder (**from**
ante)

fling /flɪŋ/ vt (pt **flung**) arrojar. ● n
(love affair) aventura f; (wild time)
juerga f

flint /flɪnt/ n pedernal m; (for
lighter) piedra f

flip /flɪp/ vt (pt **flipped**) dar un golpecito a. ● n golpecito m. □ ~
through vt hojear

flippant /flɪpənt/ adj poco serio

flipper /flɪpə(r)/ n aleta f

flirt /flɜːt/ vi coquetear. ● n
(woman) coqueta f; (man) co-
queto m

flit /flɪt/ vi (pt **flitted**) revolotear

float /fləʊt/ vi flotar. ● vt hacer flotar; introducir en Bolsa (company).

● *n* flotador *m*; (*cash*) caja *f* chica

flock /flɒk/ *n* (*of birds*) bandada *f*; (*of sheep*) rebaño *m*. ● *vi* congregarse

flog /flɒg/ *vt* (*pt* flogged) (*beat*) azotar; (*fam, sell*) vender

flood /flʌd/ *n* inundación *f*; (*fig*) avalancha *f*. ● *vt* inundar. ● *vi* (*building etc*) inundarse; (*river*) desbordar. **~light** *n* foco *m*. ● *vt* (*pt* **lit**) iluminar (con focos)

floor /flɔ:(r)/ *n* suelo *m*; (*storey*) piso *m*; (*for dancing*) pista *f*. ● *vt* derribar; (*baffle*) confundir

flop /flɒp/ *vi* (*pt* flopped) dejarse caer pesadamente; (*fam, fail*) fracasar. ● *n* □ fracaso *m*. **~py** *adj* flojo. ● *n* see **~PY DISK**. **~py disk** *n* disquete *m*, floppy (disk) *m*

floral /flɔ:rəl/ *adj* floral

florid /flɒrɪd/ *adj* florido

florist /flɒrɪst/ *n* florista *m & f*

flounder /flaʊndə(r)/ *vi* (*in water*) luchar para mantenerse a flote; (*speaker*) quedar sin saber qué decir

flour /flaʊə(r)/ *n* harina *f*

flourish /flʌrɪʃ/ *vi* florecer; (*business*) prosperar. ● *vt* blandir. ● *n* además *m* elegante; (*in handwriting*) rasgo *m*. **~ing** *adj* próspero

flout /flaʊt/ *vt* burlarse de

flow /fləʊ/ *vi* fluir; (*blood*) correr; (*hang loosely*) caer. ● *n* flujo *m*; (*stream*) corriente *f*; (*of traffic, information*) circulación *f*. **~ chart** *n* organigrama *m*

flower /flaʊə(r)/ *n* flor *f*. ● *vi* florecer, florear (*Mex*). **~ bed** *n* macizo *m* de flores. **~y** *adj* florido

flown /fləʊn/ see **FLY**

flu /flu:/ *n* gripe *f*

fluctuat|e /flʌktjʊeɪt/ *vi* fluctuar. **~ion** /-'eɪʃn/ *n* fluctuación *f*

flue /flu:/ *n* tiro *m*

fluen|cy /flu:ənsɪ/ *n* fluidez *f*. **~t** *adj* (*style*) fluido; (*speaker*) elocuente. **be ~t in a language** hablar un idioma con fluidez. **~tly** *adv* con fluidez

fluff /flʌf/ *n* pelusa *f*. **~y** *adj* (**-ier**, **-iest**) velloso

fluid /flu:ɪd/ *adj & n* fluido (*m*)

flung /flʌŋ/ see **FLING**

fluorescent /flʊə'resnt/ *adj* fluorescente

flush /flʌʃ/ *vi* ruborizarse. ● *vt*. **~ the toilet** tirar de la cadena, jalarle a la cadena (*LAm*). ● *n* (*blush*) rubor *m*

fluster /flʌstə(r)/ *vt* poner nervioso

flute /flu:t/ *n* flauta *f*

flutter /flʌtə(r)/ *vi* ondear; (*bird*) revolotear. ● *n* (*of wings*) revoloteo *m*; (*fig*) agitación *f*

flux /flʌks/ *n* flujo *m*. **be in a state of ~** estar siempre cambiando

fly /flaɪ/ *vi* (*pt* **flew**, *pp* **flown**) volar; (*passenger*) ir en avión; (*flag*) flotar; (*rush*) correr. ● *vt* pilotar, pilotear (*LAm*) (*aircraft*); transportar en avión (*passengers*, *goods*); izar (*flag*). ● *n* mosca *f*; (*of trousers*) see **FLIES**. **~ing** *adj* volante. **~ing visit** visita *f* relámpago. ● *n* (*activity*) aviación *f*. **~leaf** *n* guarda *f*. **~over** *n* paso *m* elevado

foal /fəʊl/ *n* potro *m*

foam /fəʊm/ *n* espuma *f*. ● *vi* espumar. **~ rubber** *n* goma *f* espuma, hule *m* espuma (*Mex*)

fob /fɒb/ *vt* (*pt* fobbed). **~ sth off onto s.o.** (*palm off*) encajarle algo a uno

focal /fəʊkl/ *adj* focal

focus /fəʊkəs/ *n* (*pl* **-cuses** *or* **-ci** /-saɪ/) foco *m*; (*fig*) centro *m*. **in ~**

enfocado. **out of ~** desenfocado.
● **vt** (*pt* **focused**) enfocar (*fig*) concentrar. ● **vi** enfocar; (*fig*) concentrarse (**on** en)

fodder /'fɒdə(r)/ n forraje m

foe /fəʊ/ n enemigo m

foetus /'fi:təs/ n (*pl* **-tuses**) feto m

fog /fɒg/ n niebla f

fog|gy adj (**-ier, -iest**) nebuloso. **it is ~gy** hay niebla. **~horn** n sirena f de niebla

foible /'fɔɪbl/ n punto m débil

foil /fɔɪl/ vt (*thwart*) frustrar. ● n papel m de plata

foist /fɔɪst/ vt encajar (**on** a)

fold /fəʊld/ vt doblar; cruzar (arms). ● vi doblarse; (*fail*) fracasar. ● n pliegue m. (*for sheep*) redil m. **~er** n carpeta f. **~ing** adj plegable

foliage /'fəʊlɪɪdʒ/ n follaje m

folk /fəʊk/ n gente f. ● adj popular. **~lore** /-lɔ:(r)/ n folklore m. **~ music** n música f folklórica; (*modern*) música f folk. **~s** npl (*one's relatives*) familia f

follow /'fɒləʊ/ vt/i seguir. □ **~ up** vt seguir. **~er** n seguidor m. **~ing** n partidarios mpl. ● adj siguiente. ● prep después de

folly /'fɒlɪ/ n locura f

fond /fɒnd/ adj (**-er, -est**) (*loving*) cariñoso; (*hope*) vivo. **be ~ of** s.o. tener(le) cariño a uno. **be ~ of** sth ser aficionado a algo

fondle /'fɒndl/ vt acariciar

fondness /'fɒndnɪs/ n cariño m; (*for things*) afición f

font /fɒnt/ n pila f bautismal

food /fu:d/ n comida f. **~ processor** n robot m de cocina

fool /fu:l/ n idiota m & f ● vt engañar. □ **~ about** vi hacer payasadas.

~hardy adj temerario. **~ish** adj tonto. **~ishly** adv tontamente. **~ishness** n tontería f. **~proof** adj infalible

foot /fʊt/ n (*pl* **feet**) pie m; (*measure*) pie m (= 30,48cm); (*of animal, furniture*) pata f. **get under s.o.'s feet** estorbar a uno. **on ~** a pie. **on/to one's feet** de pie. **put one's ~ in it** meter la pata. ● vt pagar (bill). **~age** /-ɪdʒ/ n (*of film*) secuencia f. **~-and-mouth disease** n fiebre f aftosa. **~ball** n (*ball*) balón m; (*game*) fútbol m; (*American ~ball*) fútbol m americano. **~baller** n futbolista m & f. **~bridge** n puente m para peatones. **~hills** npl estribaciones fpl. **~hold** n punto m de apoyo. n pie m. **on an equal ~ing** en igualdad de condiciones. **~lights** npl candilejas fpl. **~man** /-mən/ n lacayo m. **~note** n nota f (al pie de la página). **~path** n (*in country*) senda f; (*in town*) acera f, banqueta f (Mex). **~print** n huella f. **~step** n paso m. **~wear** n calzado m

for /fɔ:(r)/fə(r)/

● preposition

····▸ (*intended for*) para. **it's ~ my mother** es para mi madre. **she works ~ a multinational** trabaja para una multinacional

····▸ (*on behalf of*) por. **I did it ~ you** lo hice por ti

➡ See entries **para** and **por** for further information

····▸ (*expressing purpose*) para. **I use it ~ washing the car** lo uso para limpiar el coche. **what ~?** ¿para qué? **to go out ~ a meal** salir a comer fuera

····▸ (*in favour of*) a favor de. **are you ~ or against the idea?** ¿estás a favor o en contra de la idea?

····▸ (*indicating cost, in exchage for*) por. **I bought it ~ 30 pounds** lo compré por 30 libras. **she left him ~ another man** lo dejó por otro. **thanks ~ everything** gracias por todo. **what's the Spanish ~ toad?** ¿cómo se dice toad' en español?

····▸ (*expressing duration*) **he read ~ two hours** leyó durante dos horas. **how long are you going ~?** ¿por cuánto tiempo vas? **I've been waiting ~ three hours** hace tres horas que estoy esperando, llevo tres horas esperando

····▸ (*in the direction of*) para. **the train ~ Santiago** el tren para Santiago

● *conjunction* (*because*) porque, pues (*literary usage*). **she left at once, ~ it was getting late** se fue en seguida, porque o pues se hacía tarde

forage /ˈfɒrɪdʒ/ *vi* forrajear. ●*n* forraje *m*

forbade /fəˈbæd/ *see* FORBID

forbearance /fɔːˈbeərəns/ *n* paciencia *f*

forbid /fəˈbɪd/ *vt* (*pt* **forbade**, *pp* **forbidden**) prohibir (*s.o. to do a uno hacer*). **~ s.o. sth** prohibir algo a uno. **~ding** *adj* imponente

force /fɔːs/ *n* fuerza *f*. **by ~** a la fuerza. **come into ~** entrar en vigor. **the ~s** las fuerzas *fpl* armadas. ● *vt* forzar; (*compel*) obligar (*s.o. to do sth* a uno a hacer

algo). **~ on** imponer a. **~ open** forzar. **~d** *adj* forzado. **~feed** *vt* alimentar a la fuerza. **~ful** *adj* enérgico

forceps /ˈfɔːseps/ *n* fórceps *m*

forcible /ˈfɔːsəbl/ *adj* a la fuerza. **~y** *adv* a la fuerza

ford /fɔːd/ *n* vado *m* ●*vt* vadear

fore /fɔː(r)/ *adj* anterior. ●*n.* **come to the ~** hacerse evidente

forearm /ˈfɔːrɑːm/ *n* antebrazo *m*

foreboding /fɔːˈbəʊdɪŋ/ *n* presentimiento *m*

forecast /ˈfɔːkɑːst/ *vt* (*pt* **forecast**) pronosticar (weather); prever (result). ●*n* pronóstico *m.* **weather ~** pronóstico *m* del tiempo

forecourt /ˈfɔːkɔːt/ *n* patio *m* delantero

forefinger /ˈfɔːfɪŋgə(r)/ *n* (dedo *m*) índice *m*

forefront /ˈfɔːfrʌnt/ *n* vanguardia *f.* **in the ~** a la vanguardia

forego /fɔːˈgəʊ/ *vt* (*pt* **forewent**, *pp* **foregone**) *see* FORGO

foregone /ˈfɔːgɒn/ *adj.* **~ conclusion** resultado *m* previsto

foreground /ˈfɔːgraʊnd/ *n.* **in the ~** en primer plano

forehead /ˈfɒrɪd/ *n* frente *f*

foreign /ˈfɒrən/ *adj* extranjero; (trade) exterior; (travel) al extranjero, en el extranjero. **~er** *n* extranjero *m*

foreman /ˈfɔːmən/ *n* (*pl* **-men** /-mən/) *n* capataz *m*

foremost /ˈfɔːməʊst/ *adj* primero. ● *adv.* **first and ~** ante todo

forerunner /ˈfɔːrʌnə(r)/ *n* precursor *m*

foresee /fɔːˈsiː/ *vt* (*pt* **-saw**, *pp* **-seen**) prever. **~able** *adj* previsible

foresight /ˈfɔːsaɪt/ *n* previsión *f*

forest /'fɒrist/ n bosque m

forestall /fɔː'stɔːl/ vt (prevent) prevenir; (preempt) anticiparse a

forestry /'fɒristri/ n silvicultura f

foretaste /'fɔːteist/ n anticipo m

foretell /fɔː'tel/ vt (pt foretold) predecir

forever /fə'revə(r)/ adv para siempre; (always) siempre

forewarn /fɔː'wɔːn/ vt advertir

forewent /fɔː'went/ see FOREGO

foreword /'fɔːwɜːd/ n prefacio m

forfeit /'fɔːfit/ n (penalty) pena f; (in game) prenda f. ● vt perder; perder el derecho a (property)

forgave /fə'geiv/ see FORGIVE

forge /fɔːdʒ/ n fragua f. ● vt fraguar; (copy) falsificar. □ ~ **ahead** vi adelantarse rápidamente. ~**r** n falsificador m. ~**ry** n falsificación f

forget /fə'get/ vt (pt forgot, pp forgotten) olvidar, olvidarse de. ● vi olvidarse (about de). **I forgot** se me olvidó. ~**ful** adj olvidadizo

forgive /fə'giv/ vt (pt forgave, pp forgiven) perdonar. ~ **s.o. for sth** perdonar algo a uno. ~**ness** n perdón m

forgo /fɔː'gəʊ/ vt (pt forwent, pp forgone) renunciar a

fork /fɔːk/ n tenedor m; (for digging) horca f; (in road) bifurcación f. ● vi (road) bifurcarse. □ ~ **out** vt Ⓣ desembolsar, aflojar Ⓣ. ~**lift truck** n carretilla f elevadora

forlorn /fə'lɔːn/ adj (hope, attempt) desesperado; (smile) triste

form /fɔːm/ n forma f; (document) formulario m; (Schol) clase f. ● vt formar. ● vi formarse

formal /'fɔːml/ adj formal; (person) formalista; (dress) de etiqueta. ~**ity** /-'mæləti/ n formalidad f. ~**ly** adv oficialmente

format /'fɔːmæt/ n formato m. ● vt (pt formatted) (Comp) formatear

formation /fɔː'meiʃn/ n formación f

former /'fɔːmə(r)/ adj anterior; (first of two) primero. ● n. **the** ~ el primero m, la primera f, los primeros mpl, las primeras fpl. ~**ly** adv antes

formidable /'fɔːmidəbl/ adj formidable

formula /'fɔːmjʊlə/ n (pl -ae /-iː/ or -as) fórmula f. ~**te** -leit/ vt formular

forsake /fə'seik/ vt (pt forsook, pp forsaken) abandonar

fort /fɔːt/ n fuerte m

forth /fɔːθ/ adv. **and so** ~ y así sucesivamente. ~**coming** /-'kʌmɪŋ/ adj próximo, venidero; (sociable) comunicativo. ~**right** adj directo. ~**with** /-'wɪθ/ adv inmediatamente

fortieth /'fɔːtiiθ/ adj cuadragésimo. ● n cuadragésima parte f

fortnight /'fɔːtnait/ n quince días mpl, quincena f. ~**ly** adv bimensual. ● adv cada quince días

fortress /'fɔːtris/ n fortaleza f

fortunate /'fɔːtʃənət/ adj afortunado. **be** ~ tener suerte. ~**ly** adv afortunadamente

fortune /'fɔːtʃuːn/ n fortuna f. ~**-teller** n adivino m

forty /'fɔːti/ adj & n cuarenta (m). ~ **winks** un sueñecito

forum /'fɔːrəm/ n foro m

forward /'fɔːwəd/ adj (movement) hacia adelante; (advanced) precoz; (pert) impertinente. ● n (Sport) delantero m. ● adv adelante. **go** ~ avanzar. ● vt hacer seguir (letter); enviar (goods). ~**s** adv adelante

forwent /fɔː'went/ see FORGO

fossil /'fɒsl/ adj & n fósil (m)

foster | free

foster /'fɒstə(r)/ vt (*promote*) fomentar; criar (*child*). ~ **child** n hijo m adoptivo

fought /fɔːt/ *see* FIGHT

foul /faʊl/ adj (**-er, -est**) (*smell*) nauseabundo; (*weather*) pésimo; (*person*) asqueroso; (*dirty*) sucio; (*language*) obsceno. ● n (*Sport*) falta f. ● vt contaminar; (*entangle*) enredar. ~ **play** (*Sport*) jugada f sucia; (*crime*) delito m

found /faʊnd/ *see* FIND. ● vt fundar.

foundation /faʊn'deɪʃn/ n fundación f; (*basis*) fundamento. (*cosmetic*) base f (de maquillaje). ~**s** npl (*of building*) cimientos mpl

founder /'faʊndə(r)/ n fundador m. ● vi (*ship*) hundirse

fountain /'faʊntɪn/ n fuente f. ~ **pen** n pluma f (estilográfica) f, estilográfica f

four /fɔː(r)/ adj & n cuatro (m). ~**fold** adj cuádruple. ● adv cuatro veces. ~**some** /-səm/ n grupo m de cuatro personas ~**teen** /'fɔːtiːn/ adj & n catorce (m). ~**teenth** adj & n decimocuarto (m). ~**th** /fɔːθ/ adj & n cuarto (m). ~**-wheel drive** n tracción f integral

fowl /faʊl/ n ave f

fox /fɒks/ n zorro m, zorra f ● vt 🔲 confundir

foyer /'fɔɪeɪ/ n (*of theatre*) foyer m; (*of hotel*) vestíbulo m

fraction /'frækʃn/ n fracción f

fracture /'fræktʃə(r)/ n fractura f. ● vt fracturar. ● vi fracturarse

fragile /'frædʒaɪl/ adj frágil

fragment /'frægmənt/ n fragmento m. ~**ary** /-ərɪ/ adj fragmentario

fragran|ce /'freɪgrəns/ n fragan-

cia f. ~**t** adj fragante

frail /freɪl/ adj (**-er, -est**) frágil

frame /freɪm/ n (*of picture, door, window*) marco m; (*of spectacles*) montura f; (*fig, structure*) estructura f. ● vt enmarcar (*picture*); formular (*plan, question*); (*fam, incriminate unjustly*) incriminar falsamente. ~**work** n estructura f; (*context*) marco m

France /frɑːns/ n Francia f

frank /fræŋk/ adj franco. ● vt franquear. ~**ly** adv francamente

frantic /'fræntɪk/ adj frenético. ~ **with** loco de

fratern|al /frə'tɜːnl/ adj fraternal. ~**ity** /-ɪtɪ/ n fraternidad f; (*club*) asociación f. ~**ize** /'frætənaɪz/ vi fraternizar

fraud /frɔːd/ n fraude m; (*person*) impostor m. ~**ulent** /-jʊlənt/ adj fraudulento

fraught /frɔːt/ adj (*tense*) tenso. ~ **with** cargado de

fray /freɪ/ n riña f

freak /friːk/ n fenómeno m; (*monster*) monstruo m. ● adj anormal. ~**ish** adj anormal

freckle /'frekl/ n peca f ~**d** adj pecoso

free /friː/ adj (**freer** /'friːə(r)/, **freest** /'friːɪst/) libre; (*gratis*) gratuito. ~ **of charge** gratis. ● vt (*pt* **freed**) (*set at liberty*) poner en libertad; (*relieve from*) liberar (**from/ of** de); (*untangle*) desenredar. ~**dom** n libertad f. ~**hold** n propiedad f absoluta. ~ **kick** n tiro m libre. ~**lance** adj & adv por cuenta propia. ~**ly** adv libremente. ~**mason** n masón m. ~**-range** adj (*eggs*) de granja. ~ **speech** n libertad f de expresión. ~**style** n estilo m libre. ~**way** n (*Amer*) autopista f

freez|e /friːz/ vt (pt **froze**, pp **frozen**) helar; congelar (food, wages). • vi helarse; (become motionless) quedarse inmóvil. • n (on wages, prices) congelación f. **~er** n congelador m. **~ing** adj glacial. • n. **~ing** (point) punto m de congelación f. **below ~ing** bajo cero

freight /freɪt/ n (goods) mercancías fpl. **~er** n buque m de carga

French /frentʃ/ adj francés. • n (language) francés m. • npl. **the ~** (people) los franceses. **~ fries** npl patatas fpl fritas, papas fpl fritas (LAm). **~man** /-mən/ n francés m. **~ window** n puerta f ventana. **~woman** n francesa f

frenz|ied /frenzɪd/ adj frenético. **~y** n frenesí m

frequency /friːkwənsɪ/ n frecuencia f

frequent /frɪˈkwent/ vt frecuentar. • /friːkwənt/ adj frecuente. **~ly** adv frecuentemente

fresh /freʃ/ adj (-er, -est) fresco; (different, additional) nuevo; (water) dulce. **~en** vi refrescar. □ **~en up** vi (person) refrescarse. **~er** n 🔲 see **~MAN**. **~ly** adv recientemente. **~man** /-mən/ n estudiante m de primer año. **~ness** n frescura f

fret /fret/ vi (pt **fretted**) preocuparse. **~ful** adj (discontented) quejoso; (irritable) irritable

friction /frɪkʃn/ n fricción f

Friday /fraɪdeɪ/ n viernes m

fridge /frɪdʒ/ n 🔲 frigorífico m, nevera f, refrigerador m (LAm)

fried /fraɪd/ see **FRY**. • adj frito

friend /frend/ n amigo m. **~liness** n simpatía f. **~ly** adj (-ier, -iest) simpático. **~ship** n amistad f

fries /fraɪz/ npl see **FRENCH FRIES**

frieze /friːz/ n friso m

frigate /frɪɡət/ n fragata f

fright /fraɪt/ n miedo m; (shock) susto m. **~en** vt asustar. □ **~off** vt ahuyentar. **~ened** adj asustado. **be ~ened** tener miedo (of de.) **~ful** adj espantoso, horrible. **~fully** adv terriblemente

frigid /frɪdʒɪd/ adj frígido

frill /frɪl/ n volante m, olán m (Mex). **~s** npl (fig) adornos mpl. **with no ~s** sencillo

fringe /frɪndʒ/ n (sewing) fleco m; (ornamental border) franja f; (of hair) flequillo m, cerquillo m (LAm), fleco m (Mex); (of area) periferia f; (of society) margen m

fritter /frɪtə(r)/ vt. □ **~ away** vt desperdiciar (time); malgastar (money)

frivol|ity /frɪˈvɒlətɪ/ n frivolidad f. **~ous** /frɪvələs/ adj frívolo

fro /frəʊ/ see **TO AND FRO**

frock /frɒk/ n vestido m

frog /frɒɡ/ n rana f. **have a ~ in one's throat** tener carraspera. **~man** /-mən/ n hombre m rana. **~spawn** n huevos mpl de rana

frolic /frɒlɪk/ vi (pt **frolicked**) retozar

from /frɒm/frəm/ prep de; (indicating starting point) desde; (habit, conviction) por; **~ then on** a partir de ahí

front /frʌnt/ n parte f delantera; (of building) fachada f; (of clothes) delantera f; (Mil, Pol) frente f; (of book) principio m; (fig, appearance) apariencia f; (seafront) paseo m marítimo, malecón m (LAm). **in ~ of** delante de. • adj delantero; (first) primero. **~al** adj frontal; (attack) de frente. **~door** n puerta f principal

frontier /frʌntɪə(r)/ n frontera f

front page n (of newspaper) primera plana f

frost /frɒst/ n (freezing) helada f; (frozen dew) escarcha f. **~bite** n congelación f. **~bitten** adj congelado. **~ed** adj (glass) esmerilado. **~ing** n (Amer) glaseado m. **~y** adj (weather) helado; (night) de helada; (fig) glacial

froth /frɒθ/ n espuma f. • vi espumar. **~y** adj espumoso

frown /fraʊn/ vi fruncir el entrecejo • n ceño m. □ **~ on** vt desaprobar

froze /frəʊz/ see FREEZE. **~n** /'frəʊzn/ see FREEZE. • adj congelado; (region) helado

frugal /'fru:ɡl/ adj frugal

fruit /fru:t/ n (in botany) fruto m; (as food) fruta f. **~ful** /-fʊl/ adj fértil; (fig) fructífero. **~ion** /fru:'ɪʃn/ n. **come to ~ion** realizarse. **~less** adj infructuoso. **~ salad** n macedonia f de frutas. **~y** adj que sabe a fruta

frustrat|e /frʌ'streɪt/ vt frustrar. **~ion** /-ʃn/ n frustración f. **~ed** adj frustrado. **~ing** adj frustrante

fry /fraɪ/ vt (pt fried) freír. • vi freírse. **~ing pan** n sartén f, sartén m (LAm)

fudge /fʌdʒ/ n dulce m de azúcar

fuel /'fju:əl/ n combustible m

fugitive /'fju:dʒɪtɪv/ adj & n fugitivo (m)

fulfil /fʊl'fɪl/ vt (pt fulfilled) cumplir (con) (promise, obligation); satisfacer (condition); hacer realidad (ambition). **~ment** n (of promise, obligation) cumplimiento m; (of conditions) satisfacción f; (of hopes, plans) realización f

full /fʊl/ adj (-er, -est) lleno; (bus, hotel) completo; (account) deta-

llado. **at ~ speed** a máxima velocidad. **be ~ (up)** (with food) no poder más. • n. **in ~** sin quitar nada. **to the ~** completamente. **write in ~** escribir con todas las letras. **~back** n (Sport) defensa m & f. **~-blown** /fʊl'bləʊn/ adj verdadero. **~-fledged** /-'fledʒd/ adj (Amer) see FULLY-FLEDGED. **~ moon** n luna f llena. **~-scale** /-'skeɪl/ adj (drawing) de tamaño natural; (fig) amplio. **~ stop** n punto m. **~-time** adj (employment) de jornada completa. • /-'taɪm/ adv a tiempo completo. **~y** adv completamente. **~-fledged** /fledʒd/ adj (chick) capaz de volar; (lawyer, nurse) hecho y derecho

fulsome /'fʊlsəm/ adj excesivo

fumble /'fʌmbl/ vi buscar (a tientas)

fume /fju:m/ vi despedir gases; (fig, be furious) estar furioso. **~s** npl gases mpl

fumigate /'fju:mɪɡeɪt/ vt fumigar

fun /fʌn/ n (amusement) diversión f; (merriment) alegría f. **for ~** en broma. **have ~** divertirse. **make ~ of** burlarse de

function /'fʌŋkʃn/ n (purpose, duty) función f; (reception) recepción f. • vi funcionar. **~al** adj funcional

fund /fʌnd/ n fondo m. • vt financiar

fundamental /fʌndə'mentl/ adj fundamental. **~ist** adj & n fundamentalista (m & f)

funeral /'fju:nərəl/ n entierro m, funerales mpl. • director n director m de pompas fúnebres

funfair /'fʌnfeə(r)/ n feria f; (permanent) parque m de atracciones, parque m de diversiones (LAm)

fungus /'fʌŋɡəs/ n (pl **-gi** /-ɡaɪ/) hongo m

funnel /'fʌnl/ n (for pouring) embudo m; (of ship) chimenea f

funn|ily /'fʌnɪlɪ/ adv (oddly) curiosamente. **~y** adj (-ier, -iest) divertido, gracioso; (odd) curioso, raro

fur /fɜ:(r)/ n pelo m; (pelt) piel f

furious /'fjʊərɪəs/ adj furioso. **~ly** adv furiosamente

furlough /'fɜ:ləʊ/ n (Amer) permiso m. **on ~** de permiso

furnace /'fɜ:nɪs/ n horno m

furnish /'fɜ:nɪʃ/ vt amueblar, amoblar (LAm); (supply) proveer. **~ings** npl muebles mpl, mobiliario m

furniture /'fɜ:nɪtʃə(r)/ n muebles mpl, mobiliario m. **a piece of ~** un mueble

furrow /'fʌrəʊ/ n surco m

furry /'fɜ:rɪ/ adj peludo

furthe|r /'fɜ:ðə(r)/ adj más lejano; (additional) nuevo. ● adv más lejos; (more) además. ● vt fomentar. **~rmore** adv además. **~st** adj más lejano. ● adv más lejos

furtive /'fɜ:tɪv/ adj furtivo

fury /'fjʊərɪ/ n furia f

fuse /fju:z/ vt (melt) fundir; (fig, unite) fusionar. **~ the lights** fundir los plomos. ● vi fundirse; (fig) fusionarse. ● n fusible m, plomo m; (of bomb) mecha f. **~box** n caja f de fusibles

fuselage /'fju:zəlɑ:ʒ/ n fuselaje m

fusion /'fju:ʒn/ n fusión f

fuss /fʌs/ n (commotion) jaleo m. **kick up a ~** armar un lío, armar una bronca. **make a ~ of** tratar con mucha atención. ● vi preocuparse. **~y** adj (-ier, -iest) (finicky) remilgado; (demanding) exigente

futile /'fju:taɪl/ adj inútil, vano. **~ity** /fju:'tɪlətɪ/ n inutilidad f

futur|e /'fju:tʃə(r)/ adj futuro. ● n futuro m. **in ~** de ahora en adelante. **~istic** /fju:'tʃə'rɪstɪk/ adj futurista

fuzz /fʌz/ n pelusa f. **~y** adj (hair) crespo; (photograph) borroso

Gg

gab /ɡæb/ n. **have the gift of the ~** tener un pico de oro

gabardine /ɡæbə'di:n/ n gabardina f

gabble /'ɡæbl/ vi hablar atropelladamente

gable /'ɡeɪbl/ n aguilón m

gad /ɡæd/ vi (pt gadded). **~ about** callejear

gadget /'ɡædʒɪt/ n chisme m

Gaelic /'ɡeɪlɪk/ adj & n gaélico (m)

gaffe /ɡæf/ n plancha f, metedura f de pata, metida f de pata (LAm)

gag /ɡæɡ/ n mordaza f; (joke) chiste m. ● vt (pt gagged) amordazar. ● vi hacer arcadas

gaiety /'ɡeɪətɪ/ n alegría f

gaily /'ɡeɪlɪ/ adv alegremente

gain /ɡeɪn/ vt ganar; (acquire) adquirir; (obtain) conseguir. ● vi (clock) adelantar. ● n ganancia f; (increase) aumento m

gait /ɡeɪt/ n modo m de andar

gala /'ɡɑ:lə/ n fiesta f. **~ performance** (función f de) gala f

galaxy /'ɡæləksɪ/ n galaxia f

gale /ɡeɪl/ n vendaval m

gall /ɡɔ:l/ n bilis f; (fig) hiel f; (impudence) descaro m

gallant /'ɡælənt/ adj (brave) valiente; (*chivalrous*) galante. **~ry** n valor m

gall bladder /'gɔːlblædə(r)/ n vesícula f biliar

gallery /'ɡælərɪ/ n galería f

galley /'ɡælɪ/ n (*ship*) galera f; (*ship's kitchen*) cocina f. **~ (proof)** n galerada f

gallivant /'ɡælɪvænt/ vi 🔲 callejear

gallon /'ɡælən/ n galón m (*imperial = 4,546l; Amer = 3,785l*)

gallop /'ɡæləp/ n galope m. ●vi (*pt galloped*) galopar

gallows /'ɡæləʊz/ n horca f

galore /ɡə'lɔː(r)/ adj en abundancia

galvanize /'ɡælvənaɪz/ vt galvanizar

gambl|e /'ɡæmbl/ vi jugar. **~e on** contar con. ●vt jugarse. ●n (*venture*) empresa f arriesgada; (*bet*) apuesta f; (*risk*) riesgo m. **~er** n jugador m. **~ing** n juego m

game /ɡeɪm/ n juego m; (*match*) partido m; (*animals, birds*) caza f. ●adj valiente. **~ for** listo para. **~keeper** n guardabosque m. **~s** n (*in school*) deportes mpl

gammon /'ɡæmən/ n jamón m fresco

gamut /'ɡæmət/ n gama f

gander /'ɡændə(r)/ n ganso m

gang /ɡæŋ/ n pandilla f; (*of workmen*) equipo m. **~master** n contratista de mano de obra indocumentada. □ **~ up** vi unirse (**on** contra)

gangling /'ɡæŋɡlɪŋ/ adj larguirucho

gangrene /'ɡæŋɡriːn/ n gangrena f

gangster /'ɡæŋstə(r)/ n bandido m, gángster m & f

gangway /'ɡæŋweɪ/ n pasillo m; (*of ship*) pasarela f

gaol /dʒeɪl/ n cárcel f. **~er** n carcelero m

gap /ɡæp/ n espacio m; (*in fence, hedge*) hueco m; (*in time*) intervalo m; (*in knowledge*) laguna f; (*difference*) diferencia f

> **gap year** En Gran Bretaña, es el periodo, entre el final de los estudios secundarios y el ingreso a la universidad, que muchos estudiantes destinan a obtener experiencia laboral relacionada con sus futuras carreras. Otros emprenden actividades no relacionadas con los estudios y para algunos es la oportunidad para ahorrar dinero o viajar.

gap|e /ɡeɪp/ vi quedarse boquiabierto; (*be wide open*) estar muy abierto. **~ing** adj abierto; (*person*) boquiabierto

garage /'ɡærɑːʒ/ n garaje m, garage m (LAm), cochera f (Mex); (*petrol station*) gasolinera f; (*for repairs, sales*) taller m, garage m (LAm)

garbage /'ɡɑːbɪdʒ/ n basura f. **~ can** n (*Amer*) cubo m de la basura, bote m de la basura (Mex). **~ collector**, **~ man** n (*Amer*) basurero m

garble /'ɡɑːbl/ vt tergiversar, embrollar

garden /'ɡɑːdn/ n (*of flowers*) jardín m; (*of vegetables/fruit*) huerto m. ●vi trabajar en el jardín. **~er** /'ɡɑːdnə(r)/ n jardinero m. **~ing** n jardinería f; (*vegetable growing*) horticultura f

gargle /'ɡɑːɡl/ vi hacer gárgaras

gargoyle /'ɡɑːɡɔɪl/ n gárgola f

garish /'ɡeərɪʃ/ adj chillón

garland /'gɑːlənd/ n guirnalda f

garlic /'gɑːlɪk/ n ajo m

garment /'gɑːmənt/ n prenda f (de vestir)

garnish /'gɑːnɪʃ/ vt adornar, decorar. ● n adorno m

garret /'gærət/ n buhardilla f

garrison /'gærɪsn/ n guarnición f

garrulous /'gærələs/ adj hablador

garter /'gɑːtə(r)/ n liga f

gas /gæs/ n (pl gases) gas m; (anaesthetic) anestésico m; (Amer, petrol) gasolina f ● vt (pt gassed) asfixiar con gas

gash /gæʃ/ n tajo m. ● vt hacer un tajo de

gasket /'gæskɪt/ n junta f

gas: ∼ mask n careta f antigás. **∼ meter** n contador m de gas

gasoline /'gæsəliːn/ n (Amer) gasolina f

gasp /gɑːsp/ vi jadear; (with surprise) dar un grito ahogado. ● n exclamación f, grito m

gas: ∼ ring n hornillo m de gas. **∼ station** n (Amer) gasolinera f

gastric /'gæstrɪk/ adj gástrico

gate /geɪt/ n puerta f; (of metal) verja f; (barrier) barrera f

gate: ∼crash vt colarse en. **∼crasher** n intruso m (que ha entrado sin ser invitado). **∼way** n puerta f

gather /'gæðə(r)/ vt reunir (people, things); (accumulate) acumular; (pick up) recoger; recoger (flowers); (fig, infer) deducir; (sewing) fruncir. ● vi (people) reunirse; (things) acumularse. **∼ing** n reunión f

gaudy /'gɔːdɪ/ adj (-ier, -iest) chillón

gauge /geɪdʒ/ n (measurement) medida f; (Rail) entrevía f; (instrument) indicador m. ● vt medir; (fig) estimar

gaunt /gɔːnt/ adj descarnado; (from illness) demacrado

gauntlet /'gɔːntlɪt/ n. run the ∼ of aguantar el acoso de

gauze /gɔːz/ n gasa f

gave /geɪv/ see GIVE

gawky /'gɔːkɪ/ adj (-ier, -iest) torpe

gawp /gɔːp/ vi. ∼ at mirar como un tonto

gay /geɪ/ adj (-er, -est) (fam, homosexual) homosexual, gay ⒯; (dated, joyful) alegre

gaze /geɪz/ vi. ∼ (at) mirar (fijamente). ● n mirada f (fija)

gazelle /gə'zel/ n (pl invar or -s) gacela f

GB abbr see GREAT BRITAIN

gear /gɪə(r)/ n equipo m; (Tec) engranaje m; (Auto) marcha f, cambio m. **in ∼** engranado. **out of ∼** desengranado. **change ∼s, shift ∼** (Amer) cambiar de marcha. ● vt adaptar. **∼box** n (Auto) caja f de cambios

geese /giːs/ see GOOSE

gel /dʒel/ n gel m

gelatine /'dʒelətiːn/ n gelatina f

gelignite /'dʒelɪgnaɪt/ n gelignita f

gem /dʒem/ n piedra f preciosa

Gemini /'dʒemɪnaɪ/ n Géminis mpl

gender /'dʒendə(r)/ n género m

gene /dʒiːn/ n gen m, gene m

genealogy /dʒiːnɪ'ælədʒɪ/ n genealogía f

general /'dʒenərəl/ adj general. ● n general m. **in ∼** en general. **∼ election** n elecciones fpl generales. **∼ization** /-'zeɪʃn/ n generalización f *f.* ~**ize** *vt/i* generalizar. ~ **knowledge** *n* cultura *f* general. ~**ly** *adv* generalmente. ~ **practitioner** *n* médico *m* de cabecera

generat|e /'dʒenəreɪt/ *vt* generar. ~**ion** /-'reɪʃn/ *n* generación *f*. ~**ion gap** *n* brecha *f* generacional. ~**or** *n* generador *m*

genero|sity /dʒenə'rɒsəti/ *n* generosidad *f*. ~**us** /'dʒenərəs/ *adj* generoso; (*plentiful*) abundante

genetic /dʒɪ'netɪk/ *adj* genético. ~**s** *n* genética *f*

Geneva /dʒɪ'ni:və/ *n* Ginebra *f*

genial /'dʒi:nɪəl/ *adj* simpático, afable

genital /'dʒenɪtl/ *adj* genital. ~**s** *npl* genitales *mpl*

genitive /'dʒenɪtɪv/ *adj & n* genitivo (*m*)

genius /'dʒi:nɪəs/ *n* (*pl* **-uses**) genio *m*

genocide /'dʒenəsaɪd/ *n* genocidio *m*

genome /'dʒi:nəʊm/ *n* genoma *m*

genre /'ʒɒːŋr/ *n* género *m*

gent /dʒent/ *n* 1 señor *m*. ~**s** *n* aseo *m* de caballeros

genteel /dʒen'ti:l/ *adj* distinguido

gentl|e /'dʒentl/ *adj* (-**er**, -**est**) (person) dulce; (murmur, breeze) suave; (hint) discreto. ~**eman** *n* señor *m*; (*well-bred*) caballero *m*. ~**eness** *n* amabilidad *f*

genuine /'dʒenjʊɪn/ *adj* verdadero; (person) sincero

geograph|er /dʒɪ'ɒgrəfə(r)/ *n* geógrafo *m*. ~**ical** /dʒɪə'græfɪkl/ *adj* geográfico. ~**y** /dʒɪ'ɒgrəfɪ/ *n* geografía *f*

geolog|ical /dʒɪə'lɒdʒɪkl/ *adj* geológico. ~**ist** /dʒɪ'ɒlədʒɪst/ *n* geólogo *m*. ~**y** /dʒɪ'ɒlədʒɪ/ *n* geología *f*

geometr|ic(al) /dʒɪə'metrɪk(l)/ *adj* geométrico. ~**y** /dʒɪ'ɒmətrɪ/ *n* geometría *f*

geranium /dʒə'reɪnɪəm/ *n* geranio *m*

geriatric /dʒerɪ'ætrɪk/ *adj* (patient) anciano; (ward) de geriatría. ~**s** *n* geriatría *f*

germ /dʒɜːm/ *n* microbio *m*, germen *m*

German /'dʒɜːmən/ *adj & n* alemán (*m*). ~**ic** /dʒɜː'mænɪk/ *adj* germánico. ~ **measles** *n* rubéola *f*. ~**y** *n* Alemania *f*

germinate /'dʒɜːmɪneɪt/ *vi* germinar

gesticulate /dʒe'stɪkjʊleɪt/ *vi* hacer ademanes, gesticular

gesture /'dʒestʃə(r)/ *n* gesto *m*, ademán *m*; (*fig*) gesto *m*. ● *vi* hacer gestos

---

get /get/

past **got**; past participle **got**, **gotten** (*Amer*); present participle **getting**

● *transitive verb*

····▸ (*obtain*) conseguir, obtener. **did you get the job?** ¿conseguiste el trabajo?

····▸ (*buy*) comprar. **I got it in the sales** lo compré en las rebajas

····▸ (*achieve, win*) sacar. **she got very good marks** sacó muy buenas notas

····▸ (*receive*) recibir. **I got a letter from Alex** recibí una carta de Alex

····▸ (*fetch*) ir a buscar. ~ **your coat** vete a buscar tu abrigo

·····▶ (*experience*) llevarse. **I got a terrible shock** me llevé un shock espantoso

·····▶ (*fam, understand*) entender. **I don't ~ what you mean** no entiendo lo que quieres decir

·····▶ (*ask or persuade*) **to ~ s.o. to do sth** hacer que uno haga algo

Note that *hacer que* is followed by the subjunctive form of the verb

·····▶ (*cause to be done or happen*) **I must ~ this watch fixed** tengo que llevar a arreglar este reloj. **they got the roof mended** hicieron arreglar el techo

● *intransitive verb*

·····▶ (*arrive, reach*) llegar. **I got there late** llegué tarde. **how do you ~ to Paddington?** ¿cómo se llega a Paddington?

·····▶ (*become*) **to ~ tired** cansarse. **she got very angry** se puso furiosa. **it's ~ting late** se está haciendo tarde

➡ For translations of expressions such as **get better, get old** see entries **better, old** etc. See also **got**

·····▶ **to ~ to do sth** (*manage to*) llegar a. **did you get to see him?** ¿llegaste a verlo? □ **get along** vi (*manage*) arreglárselas; (*progress*) hacer progresos. □ **get along with** vt llevarse bien con. □ **get at** vt (*reach*) llegar a; (*imply*) querer decir. □ **get away** vi salir; (*escape*) escaparse. □ **get back** vi

volver. vt (*recover*) recobrar. □ **get by** vi (*manage*) arreglárselas; (*pass*) pasar. □ **get down** vi bajar. vt (*make depressed*) deprimir. □ **get in** vi entrar. □ **get into** vt entrar en; subir a (*car*) □ **get off** vt bajar(se) de (*train etc*). vi (*from train etc*) bajarse; (*Jurid*) salir absuelto. □ **get on** vi (*progress*) hacer progresos; (*succeed*) tener éxito. vt subirse a (*train etc*). □ **get on with** vt (*be on good terms with*) llevarse bien con; (*continue*) seguir con. □ **get out** vi salir. vt (*take out*) sacar. □ **get out of** vt (*fig*) librarse de. □ **get over** vt reponerse de (*illness*). □ **get round** vt soslayar (*difficulty* etc); engatusar (*person*). □ **get through** vi pasar; (*on phone*) comunicarse (**to** con). □ **get together** vi (*meet up*) reunirse. vt (*assemble*) reunir. □ **get up** vi levantarse; (*climb*) subir

geyser /ˈɡiːzə(r)/ n géiser m

ghastly /ˈɡɑːstlɪ/ adj (**-ier, -iest**) horrible

gherkin /ˈɡɜːkɪn/ n pepinillo m

ghetto /ˈɡetəʊ/ n (pl **-os**) gueto m

ghost /ɡəʊst/ n fantasma m. **~ly** adj espectral

giant /ˈdʒaɪənt/ n gigante m. ● adj gigantesco

gibberish /ˈdʒɪbərɪʃ/ n jerigonza f

gibe /dʒaɪb/ n pulla f

giblets /ˈdʒɪblɪts/ npl menudillos mpl

gidd|iness /ˈɡɪdɪnɪs/ n vértigo m. **~y** adj (**-ier, -iest**) mareado. **be/feel ~y** estar/sentirse mareado

gift /ɡɪft/ n regalo m; (*ability*) don

m. **~ed** *adj* dotado de talento. **~-wrap** *vt* envolver para regalo

gigantic /dʒaɪˈɡæntɪk/ *adj* gigantesco

giggle /ˈɡɪɡl/ *vi* reírse tontamente. ● *n* risita *f*

gild /ɡɪld/ *vt* dorar

gills /ɡɪlz/ *npl* agallas *fpl*

gilt /ɡɪlt/ *n* dorado *m.* ● *adj* dorado

gimmick /ˈɡɪmɪk/ *n* truco *m*

gin /dʒɪn/ *n* ginebra *f*

ginger /ˈdʒɪndʒə(r)/ *n* jengibre *m.* ● *adj* rojizo. **he has ~ hair** es pelirrojo. **~bread** *n* pan *m* de jengibre

gipsy /ˈdʒɪpsɪ/ *n* gitano *m*

giraffe /dʒɪˈrɑːf/ *n* jirafa *f*

girder /ˈɡɜːdə(r)/ *n* viga *f*

girdle /ˈɡɜːdl/ *n* (belt) cinturón *m*; (corset) corsé *m*

girl /ɡɜːl/ *n* chica *f*, muchacha *f*; (child) niña *f*. **~ band** *n* grupo *m* pop de chicas. **~friend** *n* amiga *f*; (of boy) novia *f.* **~ish** *adj* de niña; (boy) afeminado. **~ scout** *n* (Amer) exploradora *f*, guía *f*

giro /ˈdʒaɪrəʊ/ *n* (pl -os) giro *m* (bancario)

girth /ɡɜːθ/ *n* circunferencia *f*

gist /dʒɪst/ *n* lo esencial

give /ɡɪv/ *vt* (pt **gave**, pp **given**) dar; (deliver) entregar; regalar (present); prestar (aid, attention). **~ o.s. to** darse a. ● *vi* dar; (yield) ceder; (stretch) dar de sí. ● *n* elasticidad *f.* □ **~ away** *vt* regalar; revelar (secret). □ **~ back** *vt* devolver. □ **~ in** *vi* ceder. □ **~ off** *vt* emitir. □ **~ out** *vt* distribuir. (become used up) agotarse. □ **~ up** *vt* renunciar a; (yield) ceder. **~ up doing sth** dejar de hacer algo. **~ o.s. up** entregarse (to a). *vi* rendirse. **~n** /ˈɡɪvn/ see **GIVE**. ● *adj* dado. **~n name** *n* nombre *m* de pila

glacier /ˈɡlæsɪə(r)/ *n* glaciar *m*

glad /ɡlæd/ *adj* contento. **be ~** alegrarse (about de). **~den** *vt* alegrar

gladly /ˈɡlædlɪ/ *adv* alegremente; (willingly) con mucho gusto

glamo|rous /ˈɡlæmərəs/ *adj* glamoroso. **~ur** /ˈɡlæmə(r)/ *n* glamour *m*

glance /ɡlɑːns/ *n* ojeada *f.* ● *vi.* **~ at** dar un vistazo a

gland /ɡlænd/ *n* glándula *f*

glar|e /ɡleə(r)/ *vi* (light) deslumbrar; (stare angrily) mirar airadamente. ● *n* resplandor *m*; (stare) mirada *f* airada. **~ing** *adj* deslumbrante; (obvious) manifiesto

glass /ɡlɑːs/ *n* (material) cristal *m*, vidrio *m*; (without stem or for wine) vaso *m*; (with stem) copa *f*; (for beer) caña *f*; (mirror) espejo *m.* **~es** *npl* (spectacles) gafas *fpl*, lentes *fpl* (LAm), anteojos *mpl* (LAm). **~y** *adj* vítreo

glaze /ɡleɪz/ *vt* poner cristal(es) or vidrio(s) a (windows, doors); vidriar (pottery). ● *vi.* **~ (over)** (eyes) vidriarse. ● *n* barniz *m*; (for pottery) esmalte *m*

gleam /ɡliːm/ *n* destello *m.* ● *vi* destellar

glean /ɡliːn/ *vt* espigar; recoger (information)

glee /ɡliː/ *n* regocijo *m*

glib /ɡlɪb/ *adj* de mucha labia; (reply) fácil

glid|e /ɡlaɪd/ *vi* deslizarse; (plane) planear. **~er** *n* planeador *m.* **~ing** *n* planeo *m*

glimmer /ˈɡlɪmə(r)/ *n* destello *m.* ● *vi* destellar

glimpse /ɡlɪmps/ *n.* **catch a ~ of** vislumbrar, ver brevemente. ● *vt* vislumbrar

glint /glɪnt/ n destello m. • vi destellar

glisten /'glɪsn/ vi brillar

glitter /'glɪtə(r)/ vi brillar. • n brillo m

gloat /gləʊt/ vi. ~ **on/over** regodearse sobre

glob|al /'gləʊbl/ adj (worldwide) mundial; (all-embracing) global. ~**al warming** n calentamiento m global. ~**e** /gləʊb/ n globo m

gloom /gluːm/ n oscuridad f; (sadness, fig) tristeza f. ~**y** adj (-ier, -iest) triste; (pessimistic) pesimista

glor|ify /'glɔːrɪfaɪ/ vt glorificar. ~**ious** /'glɔːrɪəs/ adj espléndido; (deed, hero etc) glorioso. ~**y** /'glɔːrɪ/ n gloria f

gloss /glɒs/ n lustre m. ~ **(paint)** (pintura f al or de) esmalte m. □ ~ **over** vt (make light of) minimizar; (cover up) encubrir

glossary /'glɒsərɪ/ n glosario m

glossy /'glɒsɪ/ adj brillante

glove /glʌv/ n guante m. ~ **compartment** n (Auto) guantera f, gaveta f

glow /gləʊ/ vi brillar. • n brillo m. ~**ing** /'gləʊɪŋ/ adj incandescente; (account) entusiasta; (complexion) rojo

glucose /'gluːkəʊs/ n glucosa f

glue /gluː/ n cola f, goma f de pegar. • vt (pres p **gluing**) pegar

glum /glʌm/ adj (**glummer**, **glummest**) triste

glutton /'glʌtn/ n glotón m

gnarled /nɑːld/ adj nudoso

gnash /næʃ/ vt. ~ **one's teeth** rechinar los dientes

gnat /næt/ n jején m, mosquito m

gnaw /nɔː/ vt roer. • vi. ~ **at** roer

gnome /nəʊm/ n gnomo m

go /gəʊ/

3rd pers sing present **goes**; past **went**; past participle **gone**

● intransitive verb

····▸ ir. **I'm going to France** voy a Francia. **to go shopping** ir de compras. **to go swimming** ir a nadar

····▸ (leave) irse. **we're going on Friday** nos vamos el viernes

····▸ (work, function) (engine, clock) funcionar

····▸ (become) **to go deaf** quedarse sordo. **to go mad** volverse loco. **his face went red** se puso colorado

····▸ (stop) (headache, pain) irse (+ me/te/le). **the pain's gone** se me ha ido el dolor

····▸ (turn out, progress) ir. **everything's going very well** todo va muy bien. **how did the exam go?** ¿qué tal te fue en el examen?

····▸ (match, suit) combinar. **the jacket and the trousers go well together** la chaqueta y los pantalones combinan bien.

····▸ (cease to function) (bulb, fuse) fundirse. **the brakes have gone** los frenos no funcionan

● auxiliary verb **to be going to** + infinitive ir a + infinitivo. **it's going to rain** va a llover. **she's going to win!** ¡va a ganar!

● noun (pl **goes**)

····▸ (turn) turno m. **you have three goes** tienes tres turnos. **it's your go** te toca a ti

····▸ (attempt) **to have a go at**

doing sth intentar hacer algo. **have another go** inténtalo de nuevo

····▸ (energy, drive) empuje m. **she has a lot of go** tiene mucho empuje

····▸ (in phrases) **I've been on the go all day** no he parado en todo el día. **to make a go of sth** sacar algo adelante o **go across** vt/vi cruzar. □ **go after** vi perseguir. □ **go away** vi irse. □ **go back** vi volver. □ **go back on** vt faltar a (promise etc). □ **go by** vi pasar. □ **go down** vi bajar; (sun) ponerse. □ **go for** vt (fam, attack) atacar. □ **go in** vi entrar. □ **go in for** vt presentarse a (exam); participar en (competition). □ **go off** vi (leave) irse; (go bad) pasarse; (explode) estallar; (lights) apagarse. □ **go on** vi seguir; (happen) pasar; (be switched on) encenderse, prenderse (LAm). □ **go out** vi salir; (fire, light) apagarse. □ **go over** vt (check) revisar; (revise) repasar. □ **go through** vt pasar por; (search) registrar; (check) examinar. □ **go up** vi/vt subir. □ **go without** vt pasar sin

goad /gəʊd/ vt aguijonear

go-ahead /'gəʊəhed/ n luz f verde. ● adj dinámico

goal /gəʊl/ n (Sport) gol m; (objective) meta f. ~**ie** /'gəʊlɪ/ n 🔟, ~**keeper** n portero m, arquero m (LAm). ~**post** n poste m de la portería, poste m del arco (LAm)

goat /gəʊt/ n cabra f

gobble /'gɒbl/ vt engullir

goblin /'gɒblɪn/ n duende m

god /gɒd/ n dios m. **G~** n Dios m.

~**child** n ahijado m. ~**daughter** n ahijada f. ~**dess** /'gɒdes/ n diosa f. ~**father** n padrino m. ~**forsaken** adj olvidado de Dios. ~**mother** n madrina f. ~**send** n beneficio m inesperado. ~**son** n

going /'gəʊɪŋ/ n camino m; (racing) (estado m del) terreno m. **it is slow/hard** ~ es lento/difícil. ● adj (price) actual; (concern) en funcionamiento

gold /gəʊld/ n oro m. ● adj de oro. ~**en** adj de oro; (in colour) dorado; (opportunity) único. ~**en wedding** n bodas fpl de oro. ~**fish** n invar pez m de colores. ~**mine** n mina f de oro; (fig) fuente f de gran riqueza. ~**-plated** /-'pleɪtɪd/ adj chapado en oro. ~**smith** n orfebre m

golf /gɒlf/ n golf m. ~ **ball** n pelota f de golf. ~ **club** n palo m de golf; (place) club m de golf. ~**course** n campo m de golf. ~**er** n jugador m de golf

gondola /'gɒndələ/ n góndola f

gone /gɒn/ see **GO**. ● adj pasado. ~ **six o'clock** después de las seis

gong /gɒŋ/ n gong(o) m

good /gʊd/ adj (better, best) bueno, (before masculine singular noun) buen. ~ **afternoon** buenas tardes. ~ **evening** (before dark) buenas tardes; (after dark) buenas noches. ~ **morning** buenos días. ~ **night** buenas noches. **as** ~ **as** (almost) casi. **feel** ~ sentirse bien. **have a** ~ **time** divertirse. ● n bien m. **for** ~ para siempre. **it is no** ~ **shouting** es inútil gritar etc. ~**bye** /-'baɪ/ int ¡adiós! ● n adiós m. **say** ~**bye to** despedirse de. ~**-for-nothing** /-fənʌθɪŋ/ adj & n inútil (m). **G~ Friday** n Viernes m Santo. ~**-looking**

/-'lʊkɪŋ/ adj guapo, buen mozo m (LAm), buena moza f (LAm). ~ness n bondad f. ~ness!, ~ness gracious!, ~ness me!, my ~ness! ¡Dios mío! ~s npl mercancías fpl. ~will /-'wɪl/ n buena voluntad f. ~y n (Culin, fam) golosina f; (in film) bueno m

gooey /'guːɪ/ adj (**gooier, gooiest**) ① pegajoso; (fig) sentimental

goofy /'guːfɪ/ adj (Amer) necio

google (®) /'guːgl/ vt, vi ① googlear ①

goose /guːs/ n (pl geese) oca f, ganso m. ~berry /'guzbərɪ/ n uva f espina, grosella f espinosa. ~flesh n, ~pimples npl carne f de gallina

gore /gɔː(r)/ n sangre f. • vt cornear

gorge /gɔːdʒ/ n (of river) garganta f. • vt. ~ o.s. hartarse (on de)

gorgeous /'gɔːdʒəs/ adj precioso; (splendid) magnífico

gorilla /gə'rɪlə/ n gorila m

gorse /gɔːs/ n aulaga f

gory /'gɔːrɪ/ adj (-ier, -iest) ① sangriento

gosh /gɒʃ/ int ¡caramba!

go-slow /gəʊ'sləʊ/ n huelga f de celo, huelga f pasiva

gospel /'gɒspl/ n evangelio m

gossip /'gɒsɪp/ n (chatter) chismorreo m; (person) chismoso m. • vi (pt gossiped) (chatter) chismorrear; (repeat scandal) contar chismes

got /gɒt/ see **GET**. **have** ~ tener. **I've** ~ **to do it** tengo que hacerlo.

gotten /'gɒtn/ see **GET**

gouge /gaʊdʒ/ vt abrir (hole). □ ~ **out** vt sacar

gourmet /'gʊəmeɪ/ n gastrónomo m

govern /'gʌvn/ vt/i gobernar.

~ess n institutriz f. ~ment n gobierno m. ~or n gobernador m

gown /gaʊn/ n vestido m; (of judge, teacher) toga f

GP abbr see **GENERAL PRACTITIONER**

GPS abbrev **Global Positioning System** GPS m

grab /græb/ vt (pt **grabbed**) agarrar

grace /greɪs/ n gracia f. ~ful adj elegante

gracious /'greɪʃəs/ adj (kind) amable; (elegant) elegante

grade /greɪd/ n clase f, categoría f; (of goods) clase f, calidad f; (on scale) grado m; (school mark) nota f; (Amer, class) curso m, año m

gradient /'greɪdɪənt/ n pendiente f, gradiente f (LAm)

gradual /'grædʒʊəl/ adj gradual. ~ly adv gradualmente, poco a poco

graduat|e /'grædʒʊət/ n (Univ) licenciado. • /'grædʒʊeɪt/ vi licenciarse. ~ion /-'eɪʃn/ n graduación f

graffiti /grə'fiːtɪ/ npl graffiti mpl, pintadas fpl

graft /grɑːft/ n (Med, Bot) injerto m; (Amer fam, bribery) chanchullos mpl. • vt injertar

grain /greɪn/ n grano m

gram /græm/ n gramo m

gramma|r /'græmə(r)/ n gramática f. ~tical /grə'mætɪkl/ adj gramatical

gramme /græm/ n gramo m

grand /grænd/ adj (-er, -est) magnífico; (fam, excellent) estupendo. ~child n nieto m. ~daughter n nieta f. ~eur /'grændʒə(r)/ n grandiosidad f. ~father n abuelo m. ~father clock n reloj m de caja. ~iose /'grændɪəʊs/ adj grandioso.

~**mother** n abuela f. ~**parents** npl abuelos mpl. ~ **piano** n piano m de cola. ~**son** n nieto m. ~**stand** /ˈgrænstænd/ n tribuna f

granite /ˈgrænɪt/ n granito m

granny /ˈgrænɪ/ n 🄸 abuela f

grant /grɑːnt/ vt conceder; (give) donar; (admit) admitir (that que). **take for** ~**ed** dar por sentado. ● n concesión f; (Univ) beca f

granule /ˈgrænuːl/ n gránulo m

grape /greɪp/ n uva f. ~**fruit** n invar pomelo m, toronja f (LAm)

graph /grɑːf/ n gráfica f

graphic /ˈgræfɪk/ adj gráfico. ~**s** npl diseño m gráfico; (Comp) gráficos mpl

grapple /ˈgræpl/ vi. ~ **with** forcejear con; (mentally) lidiar con

grasp /grɑːsp/ vt agarrar. ● n (hold) agarro m; (fig) comprensión f. ~**ing** adj avaro

grass /grɑːs/ n hierba f. ~**hopper** n saltamontes m. ~ **roots** npl base f popular. ● adj de las bases. ~**y** adj cubierto de hierba

grate /greɪt/ n rejilla f; (fireplace) chimenea f. ● vt rallar. ● vi rechinar; (be irritating) ser crispante

grateful /ˈgreɪtfl/ adj agradecido. ~**ly** adv con gratitud

grater /ˈgreɪtə(r)/ n rallador m

gratif|ied /ˈgrætɪfaɪd/ adj contento. ~**y** /ˈgrætɪfaɪ/ vt satisfacer; (please) agradar a. ~**ying** adj agradable

grating /ˈgreɪtɪŋ/ n reja f.

gratitude /ˈgrætɪtjuːd/ n gratitud f

gratuitous /grəˈtjuːɪtəs/ adj gratuito

gratuity /grəˈtjuːətɪ/ n (tip) propina f

grave /greɪv/ n sepultura f. ● adj (-er, -est) (serious) grave

gravel /ˈgrævl/ n grava f

gravely /ˈgreɪvlɪ/ adv (seriously) seriamente; (solemnly) con gravedad

grave: ~**stone** n lápida f. ~**yard** n cementerio m

gravitate /ˈgrævɪteɪt/ vi gravitar

gravity /ˈgrævətɪ/ n gravedad f

gravy /ˈgreɪvɪ/ n salsa f

gray /greɪ/ adj & n (Amer) see **GREY**

graze /greɪz/ vi (eat) pacer. ● vt (touch) rozar; (scrape) raspar. ● n rasguño m

greas|e /griːs/ n grasa f. ● vt engrasar. ~**eproof paper** n papel m encerado or de cera. ~**y** adj (hands) grasiento; (food) graso; (hair, skin) graso, grasoso (LAm)

great /greɪt/ adj (-er, -est) grande, (before singular noun) gran; (fam, very good) estupendo. **G~ Britain** n Gran Bretaña f. ~**grandfather** /-ˈgrænfɑːðə(r)/ n bisabuelo m. ~**grandmother** /-ˈgrænmʌðə(r)/ n bisabuela f. ~**ly** adv (very) muy; (much) mucho

Greece /griːs/ n Grecia f

greed /griːd/ n avaricia f; (for food) glotonería f. ~**y** adj avaro; (for food) glotón

Greek /griːk/ adj & n griego (m)

green /griːn/ adj (-er, -est) verde. ● n verde m; (grass) césped m. ~**belt** n zona f verde. ~ **card** n (Amer) permiso m de residencia y trabajo. ~**ery** n verdor m. ~**gage** /-geɪdʒ/ n claudia f. ~**grocer** n verdulero m. ~**house** n invernadero m. **the** ~**house effect** el efecto invernadero. ~ **light** n luz f verde. ~**s** npl verduras fpl

greet | ground

Green Card En EE.UU., documento oficial que toda persona que no sea ciudadana norteamericana debe obtener para residir y trabajar en ese país. En el Reino Unido, es el documento que se debe obtener de la compañía de seguros, cuando se lleva un automóvil al extranjero, a fin de que siga vigente la cobertura de la póliza.

greet /griːt/ vt saludar; (receive) recibir. **~ing** n saludo m

gregarious /grɪˈgeərɪəs/ adj gregario; (person) sociable

grenade /grɪˈneɪd/ n granada f

grew /gruː/ see GROW

grey /greɪ/ adj (-er, -est) gris. have ~ hair ser canoso. ●n gris m. **~hound** n galgo m

grid /grɪd/ n reja f; (Elec, network) red f; (on map) cuadriculado m

grief /griːf/ n dolor m. come to ~ (person) acabar mal; (fail) fracasar

grievance /ˈgriːvns/ n queja f formal

grieve /griːv/ vt apenar. ● vi afligirse. ~ for llorar

grievous /ˈgriːvəs/ adj doloroso; (serious) grave. ~ bodily harm (Jurid) lesiones fpl (corporales) graves

grill /grɪl/ n parrilla f. ● vt asar a la parrilla; (🎕, interrogate) interrogar

grille /grɪl/ n rejilla f

grim /grɪm/ adj (grimmer, grimmest) severo

grimace /ˈgrɪməs/ n mueca f. ● vi hacer muecas

grim|e /graɪm/ n mugre f. ~y adj mugriento

grin /grɪn/ vt (pt grinned) sonreír. ●n sonrisa f (abierta)

grind /graɪnd/ vt (pt ground) moler (coffee, corn etc); (pulverize) pulverizar; (sharpen) afilar; (Amer) picar, moler (meat)

grip /grɪp/ vt (pt gripped) agarrar; (interest) captar. ●n (hold) agarro m; (strength of hand) apretón m; (hairgrip) horquilla f, pasador m (Mex). come to ~s with entender (subject)

grisly /ˈgrɪzlɪ/ adj (-ier, -iest) horrible

gristle /ˈgrɪsl/ n cartílago m

grit /grɪt/ n arenilla f; (fig) agallas fpl. ● vt (pt gritted) echar arena en (road). ~ one's teeth (fig) acorazarse

groan /grəʊn/ vi gemir. ●n gemido m

grocer /ˈgrəʊsə(r)/ n tendero m, abarrotero m (Mex). ~ies npl comestibles mpl. ~y n tienda f de comestibles, tienda f de abarrotes (Mex)

groggy /ˈgrɒgɪ/ adj (weak) débil; (unsteady) inseguro; (ill) malucho

groin /grɔɪn/ n ingle f

groom /gruːm/ n mozo m de caballos; (bridegroom) novio m. ● vt almohazar (horses); (fig) preparar

groove /gruːv/ n ranura f; (in record) surco m

grope /grəʊp/ vi (find one's way) moverse a tientas. ~ for buscar a tientas

gross /grəʊs/ adj (-er, -est) (coarse) grosero; (Com) bruto; (fat) grueso; (flagrant) flagrante. ●n invar gruesa f. ~ly adv (very) enormemente

grotesque /grəʊˈtesk/ adj grotesco

ground /graʊnd/ see GRIND. ●n suelo m; (area) terreno m; (reason) razón f; (*Amer, Elec*) toma f de tierra. ●**vt** fundar (theory); retirar del servicio (aircraft). ∼**s** *npl* jardines *mpl*; (*sediment*) poso m. ∼ **beef** n (*Amer*) carne f picada, carne f molida. ∼ **cloth** n (*Amer*) see ∼**SHEET**. ∼ **floor** n planta f baja. ∼**ing** n base f, conocimientos *mpl* (**in** de). ∼**less** adj infundado. ∼**sheet** n suelo m impermeable (de una tienda de campaña). ∼**work** n trabajo m preparatorio

group /gruːp/ n grupo m. ●**vt** agrupar. ●**vi** agruparse

grouse /graʊs/ n *invar* (*bird*) urogallo m. ●**vi** Ⓕ rezongar

grovel /ˈɡrɒvl/ vi (*pt* **grovelled**) postrarse; (*fig*) arrastrarse

grow /ɡrəʊ/ vi (*pt* **grew**, *pp* **grown**) crecer; (*become*) volverse, ponerse. ●**vt** cultivar. ∼ **a beard** dejarse (crecer) la barba. □ ∼ **up** vi hacerse mayor. ∼**ing** adj (*quantity*) cada vez mayor; (*influence*) creciente

growl /graʊl/ vi gruñir. ●n gruñido m

grown /ɡrəʊn/ see GROW. ●adj adulto. ∼**-up** adj & n adulto (m)

growth /ɡrəʊθ/ n crecimiento m; (*increase*) aumento m; (*development*) desarrollo m; (*Med*) bulto m, tumor m

grub /grʌb/ n (*larva*) larva f; (*fam, food*) comida f

grubby /ˈɡrʌbɪ/ adj (**-ier, -iest**) mugriento

grudge /ɡrʌdʒ/ vt see BEGRUDGE. ●n rencilla f. **bear/have a** ∼**e against s.o.** guardarle rencor a uno. ∼**ingly** adv de mala gana

gruelling /ˈɡruːəlɪŋ/ adj agotador

gruesome /ˈɡruːsəm/ adj horrible

gruff /ɡrʌf/ adj (**-er, -est**) (man-

ners) brusco; (*voice*) ronco

grumble /ˈɡrʌmbl/ vi rezongar

grumpy /ˈɡrʌmpɪ/ adj (**-ier, -iest**) malhumorado

grunt /ɡrʌnt/ vi gruñir. ●n gruñido m

guarant|ee /ˌɡærənˈtiː/ n garantía f. ●vt garantizar. ∼**or** n garante m & f

guard /ɡɑːd/ vt proteger; (*watch*) vigilar. ●n (*vigilance, Mil group*) guardia f; (*person*) guardia m; (*on train*) jefe m de tren. □ ∼ **against** vt evitar; protegerse contra (risk). ∼**ed** adj cauteloso. ∼**ian** n guardián m; (*of orphan*) tutor m

Guatemala /ˌɡwɑːtəˈmɑːlə/ n Guatemala f. ∼**n** adj & n guatemalteco (m)

guer(r)illa /ɡəˈrɪlə/ n guerrillero m. ∼ **warfare** n guerrilla f

guess /ɡes/ vt adivinar; (*Amer, suppose*) suponer. ●n conjetura f. ∼**work** n conjeturas fpl

guest /ɡest/ n invitado m; (*in hotel*) huésped m. ∼**house** n casa f de huéspedes

guffaw /ɡʌˈfɔː/ n carcajada f. ●vi reírse a carcajadas

guidance /ˈɡaɪdəns/ n (*advice*) consejos *mpl*; (*information*) información f

guide /ɡaɪd/ n (*person*) guía m & f; (*book*) guía f. **Girl G**∼ exploradora f, guía f. ●vt guiar. ∼**book** n guía f. ∼ **dog** n perro m guía, perro m lazarillo. ∼**d missile** n proyectil m teledirigido. ∼**lines** *npl* pauta f

guild /ɡɪld/ n gremio m

guile /ɡaɪl/ n astucia f

guillotine /ˈɡɪlətiːn/ n guillotina f

guilt /ɡɪlt/ n culpa f; (*Jurid*) culpabilidad f. ∼**y** adj culpable

guinea pig /ˈɡɪnɪ/ n conejillo m

de Indias, cobaya f

guitar /gɪ'tɑː(r)/ n guitarra f. ~**ist** n guitarrista m & f

gulf /gʌlf/ n (part of sea) golfo m; (gap) abismo m

gull /gʌl/ n gaviota f

gullet /'gʌlɪt/ n garganta f, gaznate m 🔊

gullible /'gʌləbl/ adj crédulo

gully /'gʌlɪ/ n (ravine) barranco m

gulp /gʌlp/ vt. □ ~ (**down**) tragarse de prisa. ● vi tragar saliva. ● n trago m

gum /gʌm/ n (in mouth) encía f; (glue) goma f de pegar; (for chewing) chicle m. ● vt (pt **gummed**) engomar

gun /gʌn/ n (pistol) pistola f; (rifle) fusil m, escopeta f; (artillery piece) cañón m. ● vt (pt **gunned**). □ ~ **down** vt abatir a tiros. ~**fire** n tiros mpl

gun: ~**man** /-mən/ n pistolero m, gatillero m (Mex). ~**powder** n pólvora f. ~**shot** n disparo m

gurgle /'gɜːgl/ vi (liquid) gorgotear; (baby) gorjear

gush /gʌʃ/ vi. ~ (**out**) salir a borbotones. ● n (of liquid) chorro m; (fig) torrente m

gusset /'gʌsɪt/ n entretela f

gust /gʌst/ n ráfaga f

gusto /'gʌstəʊ/ n entusiasmo m

gusty /'gʌstɪ/ adj borrascoso

gut /gʌt/ n intestino m. ● vt (pt **gutted**) destripar; (fire) destruir. ~**s** npl tripas fpl; (fam, courage) agallas fpl

gutter /'gʌtə(r)/ n (on roof) canalón m, canaleta f; (in street) cuneta f; (fig, slum) arroyo m

guttural /'gʌtərəl/ adj gutural

guy /gaɪ/ n (fam, man) tipo m 🔊,

tío m 🔊

guzzle /'gʌzl/ vt (drink) chupar 🔊; (eat) tragarse

gym /dʒɪm/ n 🔊 (gymnasium) gimnasio m; (gymnastics) gimnasia f

gymnasium /dʒɪm'neɪzɪəm/ n gimnasio m

gymnast /'dʒɪmnæst/ n gimnasta m & f. ~**ics** /dʒɪm'næstɪks/ npl gimnasia f

gymslip /'dʒɪmslɪp/ n túnica f (de gimnasia)

gynaecolog|ist /gaɪnɪ'kɒlədʒɪst/ n ginecólogo m. ~**y** n ginecología f

gypsy /'dʒɪpsɪ/ n gitano m

gyrate /dʒaɪə'reɪt/ vi girar

Hh

haberdashery /'hæbədæʃərɪ/ n mercería f; (Amer, clothes) ropa f y accesorios mpl para caballeros

habit /'hæbɪt/ n costumbre f; (Relig, costume) hábito m. **be in the ~ of** (+ gerund) tener la costumbre de (+ infinitivo), soler (+ infinitivo). **get into the ~ of** (+ gerund) acostumbrarse a (+ infinitivo)

habitable /'hæbɪtəbl/ adj habitable

habitat /'hæbɪtæt/ n hábitat m

habitation /hæbɪ'teɪʃn/ n habitación f

habitual /hə'bɪtjʊəl/ adj habitual; (liar) inveterado. ~**ly** adv de costumbre

hack /hæk/ n (old horse) jamelgo m

m; (*writer*) escritorzuelo *m*. ● *vt* cortar. ∼**er** *n* (*Comp*) pirata *m* informático

hackneyed /ˈhæknɪd/ *adj* manido

had /hæd/ *see* HAVE

haddock /ˈhædək/ *n invar* eglefino *m*

haemorrhage /ˈhemərɪdʒ/ *n* hemorragia *f*

haemorrhoids /ˈhemərɔɪdz/ *npl* hemorroides *fpl*

hag /hæg/ *n* bruja *f*

haggard /ˈhægəd/ *adj* demacrado

hail /heɪl/ *n* granizo *m*. ● *vi* granizar. ● *vt* (*greet*) saludar; llamar (taxi). □ ∼ **from** *vt* venir de. ∼**stone** *n* grano *m* de granizo

hair /heə(r)/ *n* pelo *m*. ∼**band** *n* cinta *f*, banda *f* (*Mex*). ∼**brush** *n* cepillo *m* (para el pelo). ∼**cut** *n* corte *m* de pelo. **have a** ∼**cut** cortarse el pelo. ∼**do** *n* 🄸 peinado *m*. ∼**dresser** *n* peluquero *m*. ∼**dresser's (shop)** *n* peluquería *f*. ∼**dryer** *n* secador *m*, secadora *f* (*Mex*). ∼**grip** *n* horquilla *f*, pasador *m* (*Mex*). ∼**pin** *n* horquilla *f*. ∼**pin bend** *n* curva *f* cerrada. ∼**raising** *adj* espeluznante. ∼**spray** *n* laca *f*, fijador *m* (para el pelo). ∼**style** *n* peinado *m*. ∼**y** *adj* (**-ier, -iest**) peludo

half /hɑːf/ *n* (*pl* **halves**) mitad *f*. ● *adj* medio. **a** ∼ **dozen** media docena *f*. ∼ **an hour** media hora *f*. ● *adv* medio, a medias. ∼**-hearted** /-ˈhɑːtɪd/ *adj* poco entusiasta. ∼**-mast** /-ˈmɑːst/ *n*. **at** ∼**-mast** a media asta. ∼ **term** *n* vacaciones *fpl* de medio trimestre. ∼**-time** *n* (*Sport*) descanso *m*, medio tiempo *m* (*LAm*). ∼**way** *adj* medio. ● *adv* a medio camino

hall /hɔːl/ *n* (*entrance*) vestíbulo *m*;

(*for public events*) sala *f*, salón *m*. ∼ **of residence** residencia *f* universitaria, colegio *m* mayor. ∼**mark** /-mɑːk/ *n* (*on gold, silver*) contraste *m*; (*fig*) sello *m* (distintivo)

hallo /həˈləʊ/ *int see* HELLO

Hallowe'en /ˈhæləʊiːn/ *n* víspera *f* de Todos los Santos

hallucination /həluːsɪˈneɪʃn/ *n* alucinación *f*

halo /ˈheɪləʊ/ *n* (*pl* **-oes**) aureola *f*

halt /hɔːlt/ *n*. **come to a** ∼ pararse. ● *vt* parar. ● *vi* pararse

halve /hɑːv/ *vt* reducir a la mitad; (*divide into halves*) partir por la mitad

halves /hɑːvz/ *see* HALF

ham /hæm/ *n* jamón *m*

hamburger /ˈhæmbɜːgə(r)/ *n* hamburguesa *f*

hammer /ˈhæmə(r)/ *n* martillo *m*. ● *vt* martill(e)ar

hammock /ˈhæmək/ *n* hamaca *f*

hamper /ˈhæmpə(r)/ *n* cesta *f*. ● *vt* estorbar

hamster /ˈhæmstə(r)/ *n* hámster *m*

hand /hænd/ *n* mano *f*; (*of clock, watch*) manecilla *f*; (*worker*) obrero *m*. **by** ∼ a mano. **lend a** ∼ echar una mano. **on** ∼ a mano. **on the one** ∼ ... **on the other** ∼ por un lado... por otro. **out of** ∼ fuera de control. **to** ∼ a mano. ● *vt* pasar. □ ∼ **down** *vt* pasar. □ ∼ **in** *vt* entregar. □ ∼ **over** *vt* entregar. □ ∼ **out** *vt* distribuir. ∼**bag** *n* bolso *m*, cartera *f* (*LAm*), bolsa *f* (*Mex*). ∼**brake** *n* (*in car*) freno *m* de mano. ∼**cuffs** *npl* esposas *fpl*. ∼**ful** *n* puñado *m*; (*fam, person*) persona *f* difícil

handicap /ˈhændɪkæp/ *n* desventaja *f*; (*Sport*) hándicap *m*. ∼**ped** *adj*

h

minusválido

handicraft /'hændɪkrɑːft/ n artesanía f

handkerchief /'hæŋkətʃɪf/ n (pl **-fs** or **-chieves** /-'tʃiːvz/) pañuelo m

handle /'hændl/ n (of door) picaporte m; (of drawer) tirador m; (of implement) mango m; (of cup, bag, jug) asa f. ● vt manejar; (touch) tocar. **~bars** npl manillar m, manubrio m (LAm).

hand: **~out** n folleto m (of money, food) dádiva f. **~shake** n apretón m de manos

handsome /'hænsəm/ adj (good-looking) guapo, buen mozo, buena moza (LAm); (generous) generoso

handwriting /'hændraɪtɪŋ/ n letra f

handy /'hændɪ/ adj (-ier, -iest) (useful) práctico; (person) diestro; (near) a mano. **come in ~** venir muy bien. **~man** n hombre m habilidoso

hang /hæŋ/ vt (pt **hung**) colgar; (pt **hanged**) (capital punishment) ahorcar. ● vi colgar; (clothing) caer. ● n. **get the ~ of sth** coger el truco de algo. □ **~ about**, **~ around** vi holgazanear. □ **~ on** vi (wait) esperar. □ **~ out** vt tender (washing). □ **~ up** vi (also telephone) colgar

hangar /'hæŋə(r)/ n hangar m

hang: **~er** n (for clothes) percha f. **~glider** n alta f delta, deslizador m (Mex). **~over** n (after drinking) resaca f. **~up** n [[1]] complejo m

hankie, hanky /'hæŋkɪ/ n [[1]] pañuelo m

haphazard /hæp'hæzəd/ adj fortuito. **~ly** adv al azar

happen /'hæpən/ vi pasar, suce-

der, ocurrir. **if he ~s to come** si acaso viene. **~ing** n acontecimiento m

happ|ily /'hæpɪlɪ/ adv alegremente; (fortunately) afortunadamente. **~iness** n felicidad f. **~y** adj (-ier, -iest) feliz; (satisfied) contento

harass /'hærəs/ vt acosar. **~ment** n acoso m

harbour /'hɑːbə(r)/ n puerto m

hard /hɑːd/ adj (-er, -est) duro; (difficult) difícil. ● adv (work) mucho; (pull) con fuerza. **~ done by** tratado injustamente. **~-boiled egg** /-'bɔɪld/ n huevo m duro. **~ disk** n disco m duro. **~en** vt endurecer. ● vi endurecerse. **~-headed** /-'hedɪd/ adj realista

hardly /'hɑːdlɪ/ adv apenas. **~ ever** casi nunca

hard: **~ness** n dureza f. **~ship** n apuro m. **~ shoulder** n arcén m, acotamiento m (Mex). **~ware** /-weə(r)/ ferretería f; (Comp) hardware m. **~ware store** n (Amer) ferretería f. **~-working** /-'wɜːkɪŋ/ adj trabajador

hardy /'hɑːdɪ/ adj (-ier, -iest) fuerte; (plants) resistente

hare /heə(r)/ n liebre f

hark /hɑːk/ vi escuchar. □ **~ back to** vi volver a

harm /hɑːm/ n daño m. **there is no ~ in asking** con preguntar no se pierde nada. ● vt hacer daño a (person); dañar (thing); perjudicar (interests). **~ful** adj perjudicial. **~less** adj inofensivo

harmonica /hɑː'mɒnɪkə/ n armónica f

harmon|ious /hɑː'məʊnɪəs/ adj armonioso. **~y** /'hɑːmənɪ/ n armonía f

harness /'hɑːnɪs/ n arnés m. ● vt poner el arnés a (horse); (fig) aprovechar

harp /hɑːp/ n arpa f. ● vi. ~ **on (about)** machacar (con)

harpoon /hɑː'puːn/ n arpón m

harpsichord /'hɑːpsɪkɔːd/ n clavicémbalo m, clave m

harrowing / 'hærəʊɪŋ/ adj desgarrador

harsh /hɑːʃ/ adj (-er, -est) duro, severo; (light) fuerte; (climate) riguroso. ~**ly** adv severamente. ~**ness** n severidad f

harvest /'hɑːvɪst/ n cosecha f. ● vt cosechar

has /hæz/ see **HAVE**

hassle /'hæsl/ n lío m 🗊, rollo m 🗊. ● vt (harass) fastidiar

haste /heɪst/ n prisa f, apuro m (LAm). **make** ~**e** darse prisa. ~**ily** /'heɪstɪli/ adv de prisa. ~**y** /'heɪsti/ adj (-ier, -iest) rápido; (rash) precipitado

hat /hæt/ n sombrero m

hatch /hætʃ/ n (for food) ventanilla f; (Naut) escotilla f. ● vt empollar (eggs); tramar (plot). ● vi salir del cascarón. ~**back** n coche m con tres/cinco puertas; (door) puerta f trasera

hatchet /'hætʃɪt/ n hacha f

hat|e /heɪt/ n odio m. ● vt odiar. ~**eful** adj odioso. ~**red** /'heɪtrɪd/ n odio m

haughty /'hɔːti/ adj (-ier, -iest) altivo

haul /hɔːl/ vt arrastrar; transportar (goods). ● n (catch) redada f; (stolen goods) botín m; (journey) recorrido m. ~**age** /-ɪdʒ/ n transporte m. ~**er** (Amer), ~**ier** n transportista m & f

haunt /hɔːnt/ vt frecuentar;

(ghost) rondar. ● n sitio m preferido. ~**ed** adj (house) embrujado; (look) angustiado

---

have /hæv/hǝv, ǝv/

3rd person singular present **has**, past **had**

● transitive verb

····▸ tener. I ~ **three sisters** tengo tres hermanas. **do you ~ a credit card?** ¿tiene una tarjeta de crédito?

····▸ (in requests) **can I ~ a kilo of apples, please?** ¿me da un kilo de manzanas, por favor?

····▸ (eat) comer. **I had a pizza** comí una pizza

····▸ (drink) tomar. **come and ~ a drink** ven a tomar una copa

····▸ (smoke) fumar (cigarette)

····▸ (hold, organize) hacer (party, meeting)

····▸ (get, receive) **I had a letter from Tony yesterday** recibí una carta de Tony ayer. **we've had no news of her** no hemos tenido noticias suyas

····▸ (illness) tener (flu, headache). **to ~ a cold** estar resfriado, tener catarro

····▸ **to have sth done: we had it painted** lo hicimos pintar. **I had my haircut** me corté el pelo

····▸ **to have it in for s.o.** tenerle manía a uno

● auxiliary verb

····▸ haber. **I've seen her already** ya la he visto, ya la vi (LAm)

····▸ **to have just done sth** acabar de hacer algo. **I've just**

seen her acabo de verla
····▶ **to have to do sth** tener que hacer algo. **I ∼ to** or **I've got to go to the bank** tengo que ir al banco
····▶ (in tag questions) **you've met her, ∼n't you?** ya la conoces, ¿no? or ¿verdad? or ¿no es cierto?
····▶ (in short answers) **you've forgotten something - have I?** he olvidado algo - ¿sí?

haven /'heɪvn/ n puerto m; (refuge) refugio m

haversack /'hævəsæk/ n mochila f

havoc /'hævək/ n estragos mpl

hawk /hɔːk/ n halcón m

hawthorn /'hɔːθɔːn/ n espino m

hay /heɪ/ n heno m. **∼ fever** n fiebre f del heno. **∼stack** n almiar m. **∼wire** adj. **go ∼wire** (plans) desorganizarse; (machine) estropearse

hazard /'hæzəd/ n riesgo m. **∼ous** adj arriesgado

haze /heɪz/ n neblina f

hazel /'heɪzl/ n avellano m. **∼nut** n avellana f

hazy /'heɪzɪ/ adj (-ier, -iest) nebuloso

he /hiː/ pron él

head /hed/ n cabeza f; (of family, government) jefe m; (of organization) director m; (of beer) espuma f. **∼s or tails** cara o cruz. ● adj principal. ● vt encabezar, cabecear (ball). □ **∼ for** vt dirigirse a. **∼ache** n dolor m de cabeza. **∼er** n (football) cabezazo m. **∼first** /-'fɜːst/ adv de cabeza. **∼ing** n título m, encabezamiento m. **∼lamp** n faro m, foco m (LAm). **∼land** /-lənd/ n promontorio m. **∼line** n

titular m. **the news ∼lines** el resumen informativo. **∼long** adv de cabeza; (precipitately) precipitadamente. **∼master** n director m. **∼mistress** n directora f. **∼-on** /-'ɒn/ adj & adv de frente. **∼phones** npl auriculares mpl, cascos mpl. **∼quarters** /-'kwɔːtəz/ n (of business) oficina f central; (Mil) cuartel m general. **∼strong** adj testarudo. **∼teacher** /-'tiːtʃə(r)/ n director m. **∼y** adj (-ier, -iest) (scent) embriagador

heal /hiːl/ vt curar. ● vi cicatrizarse

health /helθ/ n salud f. **∼y** adj sano

heap /hiːp/ n montón m. ● vt amontonar.

hear /hɪə(r)/ vt/i (pt heard /hɜːd/) oír. **∼, ∼!** ¡bravo! □ **∼ about** oír hablar de. □ **∼ from** recibir noticias de. **∼ing** n oído m; (Jurid) vista f. **∼ing-aid** n audífono m. **∼say** n rumores mpl

hearse /hɜːs/ n coche m fúnebre

heart /hɑːt/ n corazón m. **at ∼** en el fondo. **by ∼** de memoria. **lose ∼** descorazonarse. **∼ache** n congoja f. **∼ attack** n ataque m al corazón, infarto m. **∼break** n congoja f. **∼breaking** adj desgarrador. **∼burn** n ardor m de estómago. **∼felt** adj sincero

hearth /hɑːθ/ n hogar m

heart: ∼ily adv de buena gana. **∼less** adj cruel. **∼y** adj (welcome) caluroso; (meal) abundante

heat /hiːt/ n calor m; (contest) (prueba f) eliminatoria f. ● vt calentar. ● vi calentarse. **∼ed** adj (fig) acalorado. **∼er** n calentador m

heath /hiːθ/ n brezal m, monte m

heathen /'hiːðn/ n & a pagano (m)

heather /'heðə(r)/ n brezo m

heat: ~**ing** n calefacción f.
~**stroke** n insolación f. ~**wave**
n ola f de calor

heave /hiːv/ vt (lift) levantar; exhalar (sigh); (fam, throw) tirar. • vi
(pull) tirar, jalar (LAm); (𝕋, retch)
dar arcadas

heaven /'hevn/ n cielo m. ~**ly** adj
celestial; (astronomy) celeste; (fam,
excellent) divino

heav|ily /'hevɪlɪ/ adv pesadamente; (smoke, drink) mucho. ~**y**
adj (-ier, -iest) pesado; (rain)
fuerte; (traffic) denso. ~**yweight**
n peso m pesado

heckle /'hekl/ vt interrumpir

hectic /'hektɪk/ adj febril

he'd /hiːd/ = **he had, he would**

hedge /hedʒ/ n seto m (vivo). • vi
escaparse por la tangente. ~**hog**
n erizo m

heed /hiːd/ vt hacer caso de. • n.
take ~ tener cuidado

heel /hiːl/ n talón m; (of shoe)
tacón m

hefty /'heftɪ/ adj (-ier, -iest)
(sturdy) fuerte; (heavy) pesado

heifer /'hefə(r)/ n novilla f

height /haɪt/ n altura f; (of person) estatura f; (of fame, glory)
cumbre f. ~**en** vt elevar; (fig) aumentar

heir /eə(r)/ n heredero m. ~**ess** n
heredera f. ~**loom** n reliquia f heredada

held /held/ see HOLD

helicopter /'helɪkɒptə(r)/ n helicóptero m

hell /hel/ n infierno m

he'll /hiːl/ = **he will**

hello /hə'ləʊ/ int ¡hola!; (Telephone,
caller) ¡oiga!, ¡bueno! (Mex); (Telephone, person answering) ¡diga!,
¡bueno! (Mex). **say** ~ to saludar

helm /helm/ n (Naut) timón m

helmet /'helmɪt/ n casco m

help /help/ vt/i ayudar. **he cannot**
~ **laughing** no puede menos de
reír. ~ **o.s.** to servirse. **it cannot**
be ~**ed** no hay más remedio. • n
ayuda f. • int ¡socorro! ~**er** n ayudante m. ~**ful** adj útil; (person)
amable. ~**ing** n porción f. ~**less**
adj (unable to manage) incapaz; (defenceless) indefenso

hem /hem/ n dobladillo m

hemisphere /'hemɪsfɪə(r)/ n hemisferio m

hen /hen/ n (chicken) gallina f; (female bird) hembra f

hence /hens/ adv de aquí. ~**forth**
adv de ahora en adelante

henpecked /'henpekt/ adj dominado por su mujer

her /hɜː(r)/ pron (direct object) la;
(indirect object) le; (after prep) ella. **I**
know ~ la conozco. • adj su, sus pl

herb /hɜːb/ n hierba f. ~**al** adj de
hierbas

herd /hɜːd/ n (of cattle, pigs) manada f; (of goats) rebaño m. • vt
arrear. ~ **together** reunir

here /hɪə(r)/ adv aquí, acá (esp
LAm). ~**!** (take this) ¡tenga!
~**abouts** /-ə'baʊts/ adv por aquí.
~**after** /-ɑːftə(r)/ adv en el futuro.
~**by** /-'baɪ/ adv por este medio

heredit|ary /hɪ'redɪtərɪ/ adj hereditario

here|sy /'herəsɪ/ n herejía f. ~**tic**
n hereje m & f

herewith /hɪə'wɪð/ adv adjunto

heritage /'herɪtɪdʒ/ n herencia f;
(fig) patrimonio m. ~ **tourism** n
turismo m cultural, turismo m patrimonial (LAm)

hermetically /hɜː'metɪklɪ/ adv.
~ **sealed** herméticamente cerrado

h

hermit /'hɜːmɪt/ n ermitaño m, eremita m

hernia /'hɜːnɪə/ n hernia f

hero /'hɪərəʊ/ n (pl -oes) héroe m. **~ic** /hɪ'rəʊɪk/ adj heroico

heroin /'herəʊɪn/ n heroína f

hero: **~ine** /'herəʊɪn/ n heroína f. **~ism** /'herəʊɪzm/ n heroísmo m

heron /'herən/ n garza f (real)

herring /'herɪŋ/ n arenque m

hers /hɜːz/ poss pron (el) suyo m, (la) suya f, (los) suyos mpl, (las) suyas fpl

herself /hɜː'self/ pron ella misma; (reflexive) se; (after prep) sí misma

he's /hiːz/ = **he is**, **he has**

hesit|ate /'hezɪteɪt/ vi vacilante. **~ate** /-teɪt/ vi vacilar. **~ation** /-'teɪʃn/ n vacilación f

heterosexual /hetərəʊ'seksjʊəl/ adj & n heterosexual (m & f)

het up /het'ʌp/ adj 🄳 nervioso

hew /hjuː/ vt (pp **hewed** or **hewn**) cortar; (cut into shape) tallar

hexagon /'heksəgən/ n hexágono m. **~al** /-'ægənl/ adj hexagonal

hey /heɪ/ int ¡eh! ¡hola!; (expressing dismay, protest) ¡oye!

heyday /'heɪdeɪ/ n apogeo m

hi /haɪ/ int 🄳 ¡hola!

hibernat|e /'haɪbəneɪt/ vi hibernar. **~ion** /-'neɪʃn/ n hibernación f

hiccough, hiccup /'hɪkʌp/ n hipo m. **have (the) ~s** tener hipo. ● vi hipar

hide /haɪd/ vt (pt **hid**, pp **hidden**) esconder. ● vi esconderse. ● n piel f; (tanned) cuero m. **~-and-seek** /'haɪdnsiːk/ n. **play ~-and-seek** jugar al escondite, jugar a las escondidas (LAm)

hideous /'hɪdɪəs/ adj (dreadful) horrible; (ugly) feo

hideout /'haɪdaʊt/ n escondrijo m

hiding /'haɪdɪŋ/ n (🄳, thrashing) paliza f. **go into ~** esconderse. **~ place** n escondite m, escondrijo m

hierarchy /'haɪərɑːkɪ/ n jerarquía f

hieroglyphics /haɪərə'glɪfɪks/ n jeroglíficos mpl

hi-fi /'haɪfaɪ/ adj de alta fidelidad. ● n equipo m de alta fidelidad, hi-fi m

high /haɪ/ adj (-er, -est) alto; (ideals) elevado; (wind) fuerte; (fam, drugged) drogado, colocado 🄳; (voice) agudo; (meat) pasado. ● n alto nivel m. **a (new) ~** un récord. ● adv alto. **~er education** n enseñanza f superior. **~-handed** /-'hændɪd/ adj prepotente. **~ heels** npl zapatos mpl de tacón alto. **~lands** /-ləndz/ npl tierras fpl altas. **~-level** adj de alto nivel. **~light** n punto m culminante. ● vt destacar; (Art) realzar. **~ly** adv muy; (paid) muy bien. **~ly strung** adj nervioso. **H~ness** n (title) alteza f. **~-rise** adj (building) alto. **~ school** n (Amer) instituto m, colegio m secundario. **~ street** n calle f principal. **~-strung** adj (Amer) nervioso. **~way** n carretera f

High School En EE.UU., el último ciclo del colegio secundario, generalmente para alumnos de edades comprendidas entre los 14 y los 18 años. En Gran Bretaña, algunos colegios secundarios también reciben el nombre de high schools.

hijack /'haɪdʒæk/ vt secuestrar. ● n secuestro m. **~er** n secuestrador

hike /haɪk/ n caminata f. ● vi ir de

caminata. **~r** n excursionista m & f

hilarious /hɪ'leərɪəs/ adj muy divertido

hill /hɪl/ n colina f; (slope) cuesta f. **~side** n ladera f. **~y** adj accidentado

hilt /hɪlt/ n (of sword) puño m. **to the ~** (fig) totalmente

him /hɪm/ pron (direct object) lo, le (only Spain); (indirect object) le; (after prep) él. **I know ~** lo/le conozco. **~self** pron él mismo; (reflexive) se; (after prep) sí mismo

hind|er /'hɪndə(r)/ vt estorbar. **~rance** /'hɪndrəns/ n obstáculo m

hindsight /'haɪnsaɪt/ n. **with ~** retrospectivamente

Hindu /'hɪndu:/ n & a hindú (m & f). **~ism** n hinduismo m

hinge /hɪndʒ/ n bisagra f

hint /hɪnt/ n indirecta f; (advice) consejo m. ● vi soltar una indirecta. **~ at** dar a entender

hip /hɪp/ n cadera f

hippie /'hɪpɪ/ n hippy m & f

hippopotamus /hɪpə'pɒtəməs/ n (pl -muses or -mi /-maɪ/) hipopótamo m

hire /haɪə(r)/ vt alquilar (thing); contratar (person). ● n alquiler m. **car ~** alquiler m de coches. **~ purchase** n compra f a plazos

his /hɪz/ adj su, sus pl. ● poss pron (el) suyo m, (la) suya f, (los) suyos mpl, (las) suyas fpl

Hispan|ic /hɪ'spænɪk/ adj hispánico. ● n (Amer) hispano m. **~ist** /'hɪspənɪst/ n hispanista m & f

hiss /hɪs/ n silbido. ● vt/i silbar

histor|ian /hɪ'stɔːrɪən/ n historiador m. **~ic(al)** /hɪ'stɒrɪk(l)/ adj histórico. **~y** /'hɪstərɪ/ n historia f

hit /hɪt/ vt (pt hit, pres p hitting) golpear (object); pegarle a (per-

son); (collide with) chocar con; (affect) afectar. ● **it off with** hacer buenas migas con. □ **~ on** vt dar con. ● n (blow) golpe m; (success) éxito m. (Internet) visita f

hitch /hɪtʃ/ vt (fasten) enganchar. ● n (snag) problema m. **a lift**, **a ride** (Amer) see **~HIKE**. **~hike** vi hacer autostop, hacer dedo, ir de aventón (Mex). **~hiker** n autoestopista m & f

hither /'hɪðə(r)/ adv aquí, acá. **~ and thither** acá y allá. **~to** adv hasta ahora

hit-or-miss /hɪtɔ:'mɪs/ adj (approach) poco científico

hive /haɪv/ n colmena f

hoard /hɔːd/ vt acumular. ● n provisión f; (of money) tesoro m

hoarding /'hɔːdɪŋ/ n valla f publicitaria

hoarse /hɔːs/ adj (-er, -est) ronco. **~ly** adv con voz ronca

hoax /həʊks/ n engaño m. ● vt engañar

hob /hɒb/ n (of cooker) hornillos mpl, hornillas fpl (LAm)

hobble /'hɒbl/ vi cojear, renguear (LAm)

hobby /'hɒbɪ/ n pasatiempo m. **~horse** n (toy) caballito m (de niño); (fixation) caballo m de batalla

hockey /'hɒkɪ/ n hockey m; (Amer) hockey m sobre hielo

hoe /həʊ/ n azada f. ● vt (pres p hoeing) azadonar

hog /hɒg/ n (Amer) cerdo m. ● vt (pt hogged) 🔲 acaparar

hoist /hɔɪst/ vt levantar; izar (flag). ● n montacargas m

hold /həʊld/ vt (pt held) tener; (grasp) coger (esp Spain), agarrar; (contain) contener; mantener (interest); (believe) creer. ● vi mantenerse. ● n (influence) influencia f; (Naut, Aviat) bodega f. get ~ of agarrar; (fig, acquire) adquirir. □ ~ back vt (contain) contener. □ ~ on vi (stand firm) resistir; (wait) esperar. □ ~ on to vt (keep) guardar; (cling to) agarrarse a. □ ~ out vt (offer) ofrecer. vi (resist) resistir. □ ~ up vt (raise) levantar; (support) sostener; (delay) retrasar; (rob) atracar. ~all n bolsa f (de viaje). ~er n tenedor m; (of post) titular m; (wallet) funda f. ~up atraco m.

hole /həʊl/ n agujero m; (in ground) hoyo m; (in road) bache m. ● vt agujerear

holiday /ˈhɒlɪdeɪ/ n vacaciones fpl; (public) fiesta f. **go on** ~ ir de vacaciones. ~**maker** n veraneante m & f

holiness /ˈhəʊlɪnɪs/ n santidad f

Holland /ˈhɒlənd/ n Holanda f

hollow /ˈhɒləʊ/ adj & n hueco (m)

holly /ˈhɒlɪ/ n acebo m

holocaust /ˈhɒləkɔːst/ n holocausto m

holster /ˈhəʊlstə(r)/ n pistolera f

holy /ˈhəʊlɪ/ adj (-ier, -iest) santo, sagrado. H~ **Ghost**, H~ **Spirit** Espíritu m Santo. ~ **water** n agua f bendita

homage /ˈhɒmɪdʒ/ n homenaje m. **pay** ~ **to** rendir homenaje a

home /həʊm/ n casa f; (for old people) residencia f de ancianos; (native land) patria f. ● adj (cooking) casero; (address) particular; (background) familiar; (Pol) interior; (match) de casa. ● adv. **(at)** ~ en casa. ~**land** n patria f. ~**land security** seguridad f nacional. ~**less** adj sin hogar. ~**ly** adj (-ier, -iest) casero; (Amer, ugly) feo. ~**-made**

adj hecho en casa. ~ **page** n (Comp) página f frontal. ~**sick** adj. **be** ~**sick** echar de menos a su familia/su país, extrañar a su familia/su país (LAm). ~ **town** n ciudad f natal. ~**work** n deberes mpl

homicide /ˈhɒmɪsaɪd/ n homicidio m

homoeopathic /həʊmɪəʊˈpæθɪk/ adj homeopático

homogeneous /həʊməʊˈdʒiːnɪəs/ adj homogéneo

homosexual /həʊməʊˈseksjʊəl/ adj & n homosexual (m)

honest /ˈɒnɪst/ adj honrado; (frank) sincero. ~**ly** adv honradamente. ~**y** n honradez f

honey /ˈhʌnɪ/ n miel f. ~**comb** n panal m. ~**moon** n luna f de miel. ~**suckle** n madreselva f

honorary /ˈɒnərərɪ/ adj honorario

honour /ˈɒnə(r)/ n honor m. ● vt honrar; cumplir (con) (promise). ~**able** adj honorable

hood /hʊd/ n capucha f; (car roof) capota f; (Amer, car bonnet) capó m, capote m (Mex)

hoodwink /ˈhʊdwɪŋk/ vt engañar

hoof /huːf/ n (pl hoofs or hooves) (of horse) casco m, pezuña f (Mex); (of cow) pezuña f

hook /hʊk/ n gancho m; (on garment) corchete m; (for fishing) anzuelo m. **let s.o. off the** ~ dejar salir a uno del atolladero. **off the** ~ (telephone) descolgado. ● vt. ~**ed on** 🆃 adicto a. □ ~ **up** vt enganchar. ~**ed** adj (tool) en forma de gancho; (nose) aguileño

hookey /ˈhʊkɪ/ n. **play** ~ (Amer fam) faltar a clase, hacer novillos

hooligan /ˈhuːlɪɡən/ n vándalo m, gamberro m

hoop | hound

hoop /huːp/ n aro m

hooray /hʊˈreɪ/ int & n ¡viva! (m)

hoot /huːt/ n (of horn) bocinazo m; (of owl) ululato m. ● vi tocar la bocina; (owl) ulular

Hoover /ˈhuːvə(r)/ n (Ⓟ) aspiradora f. ● vt pasar la aspiradora por, aspirar (LAm)

hooves /huːvz/ see **HOOF**

hop /hɒp/ vi (pt hopped) saltar a la pata coja; (frog, rabbit) brincar, saltar; (bird) dar saltitos. ● n salto m; (flight) etapa f. ~**(s)** (plant) lúpulo m

hope /həʊp/ n esperanza f. ● vt/i esperar. ~ **for** esperar. ~**ful** adj (optimistic) esperanzado; (promising) esperanzador. ~**fully** adv con optimismo; (it is hoped) se espera. ~**less** adj desesperado

horde /hɔːd/ n horda f

horizon /həˈraɪzn/ n horizonte m

horizontal /hɒrɪˈzɒntl/ adj horizontal. ~**ly** adv horizontalmente

hormone /ˈhɔːməʊn/ n hormona f

horn /hɔːn/ n cuerno m, asta f; cacho m (LAm); (of car) bocina f; (Mus) trompa f. ~**ed** adj con cuernos

hornet /ˈhɔːnɪt/ n avispón m

horoscope /ˈhɒrəskəʊp/ n horóscopo m

horrible /ˈhɒrəbl/ adj horrible

horrid /ˈhɒrɪd/ adj horrible

horrific /həˈrɪfɪk/ adj horroroso

horrify /ˈhɒrɪfaɪ/ vt horrorizar

horror /ˈhɒrə(r)/ n horror m

hors-d'oeuvre /ɔːˈdɜːvr/ n (pl **-s** /-ˈdɜːvr/ entremés m, botana f (Mex)

horse /hɔːs/ n caballo m. ~**back** n. **on** ~**back** a caballo. ~**power** n (unit) caballo m (de fuerza). ~**ra-**

cing n carreras fpl de caballos. ~**shoe** n herradura f

horticultural /hɔːtɪˈkʌltʃərəl/ adj hortícola. ~**e** /ˈhɔːtɪkʌltʃə(r)/ n horticultura f

hose /həʊz/ n manguera f, manga f. ● vt. ~ **down** lavar (con manguera). ~**pipe** n manga f

hosiery /ˈhəʊziərɪ/ n calcetería f

hospice /ˈhɒspɪs/ n residencia f para enfermos desahuciados

hospitable /hɒˈspɪtəbl/ adj hospitalario

hospital /ˈhɒspɪtl/ n hospital m

hospitality /hɒspɪˈtælətɪ/ n hospitalidad f

host /həʊst/ n (master of house) anfitrión m; (Radio, TV) presentador m; (multitude) gran cantidad f; (Relig) hostia f

hostage /ˈhɒstɪdʒ/ n rehén m

hostel /ˈhɒstl/ n (for students) residencia f; (for homeless people) hogar m

hostess /ˈhəʊstɪs/ n anfitriona f

hostile /ˈhɒstaɪl/ adj hostil. ~**ity** /-ˈtɪlətɪ/ n hostilidad f

hot /hɒt/ adj (**hotter**, **hottest**) caliente; (weather, day) caluroso; (climate) cálido; (Culin) picante; (news) de última hora. **be/feel** ~ tener calor. **get** ~ calentarse. **it is** ~ hace calor. ~**bed** n (fig) semillero m

hotchpotch /ˈhɒtʃpɒtʃ/ n mezcolanza f

hot dog n perrito m caliente

hotel /həʊˈtel/ n hotel m. ~**ier** /-ɪeɪ/ n hotelero m

hot: ~**house** n invernadero m. ~**plate** n placa f, hornilla f (LAm). ~**-water bottle** /ˈwɔːtə(r)/ n bolsa f de agua caliente

hound /haʊnd/ n perro m de caza.

● *vt* perseguir

hour /aʊə(r)/ *n* hora *f*. ~**ly** *adj* (rate) por hora. ● *adv* (every hour) cada hora; (by the hour) por hora

house /haʊs/ *n* (*pl* -s /'haʊzɪz/) casa *f*; (Pol) cámara *f*. ● /haʊz/ *vt* alojar; (keep) guardar. ~**hold** *n* casa *f*. ~**holder** *n* dueño *m* de una casa. ~**keeper** *n* ama *f* de llaves. ~**maid** *n* criada *f*, mucama *f* (LAm). ~**-proud** *adj* meticuloso. ~**warming** (party) ~ *n* fiesta de inauguración de una casa. ~**wife** *n* ama *f* de casa. ~**work** *n* tareas *fpl* domésticas

housing /'haʊzɪŋ/ *n* alojamiento *m*. ~ **development** (Amer), ~ **estate** *n* complejo *m* habitacional, urbanización *f*

hovel /'hɒvl/ *n* casucha *f*

hover /'hɒvə(r)/ *vi* (bird, threat etc) cernerse; (loiter) rondar. ~**craft** *n* (*pl* invar or -crafts) aerodeslizador *m*

how /haʊ/ *adv* cómo. ~ **about a walk?** ¿qué te parece si damos un paseo? ~ **are you?** ¿cómo está Vd? ~ **do you do?** (in introduction) mucho gusto. ~ **long?** (in time) ¿cuánto tiempo? ~ **long is the room?** ¿cuánto mide de largo el cuarto? ~ **often?** ¿cuántas veces?

however /haʊ'evə(r)/ *adv* (nevertheless) no obstante, sin embargo; (with verb) de cualquier manera que (+ subjunctive); (with adjective or adverb) por... que (+ subjunctive). ~ **much it rains** por mucho que llueva

howl /haʊl/ *n* aullido. ● *vi* aullar

hp *abbr see* **HORSEPOWER**

HP *abbr see* **HIRE-PURCHASE**

hub /hʌb/ *n* (of wheel) cubo *m*;

(fig) centro *m*

hubcap /'hʌbkæp/ *n* tapacubos *m*

huddle /'hʌdl/ *vi* apiñarse

hue /hjuː/ *n* (colour) color *m*

huff /hʌf/ *n*. **be in a** ~ estar enfurruñado

hug /hʌg/ *vt* (*pt* hugged) abrazar. ● *n* abrazo *m*

huge /hjuːdʒ/ *adj* enorme. ~**ly** *adv* enormemente

hulk /hʌlk/ *n* (of ship) barco *m* viejo

hull /hʌl/ *n* (of ship) casco *m*

hullo /hə'ləʊ/ *int see* **HELLO**

hum /hʌm/ *vt/i* (*pt* hummed) (person) canturrear; (insect, engine) zumbar. ● *n* zumbido *m*

human /'hjuːmən/ *adj & n* humano (*m*). ~ **being** *n* ser *m* humano. ~**e** /hjuː'meɪn/ *adj* humano. ~**itarian** /hjuːmænɪ'teərɪən/ *adj* humanitario. ~**ity** /hjuː'mænətɪ/ *n* humanidad *f*

humbl|e /'hʌmbl/ *adj* (-er, -est) humilde. ● *vt* humillar. ~**y** *adv* humildemente

humdrum /'hʌmdrʌm/ *adj* monótono

humid /'hjuːmɪd/ *adj* húmedo. ~**ity** /hjuː'mɪdətɪ/ *n* humedad *f*

humiliat|e /hjuː'mɪlɪeɪt/ *vt* humillar. ~**ion** /-'eɪʃn/ *n* humillación *f*

humility /hjuː'mɪlətɪ/ *n* humildad *f*

humongous /hjuː'mʌŋgəs/ *adj* 🆃 de primera

humo|rist /'hjuːmərɪst/ *n* humorista *m & f*. ~**rous** /-rəs/ *adj* humorístico. ~**rously** *adv* con gracia. ~**ur** /'hjuːmə(r)/ *n* humor *m*. **sense of** ~**ur** sentido *m* del humor

hump /hʌmp/ *n* (of person, camel) joroba *f*; (in ground) montículo *m*

hunch /hʌntʃ/ vt encorvar. ●n presentimiento m; (lump) joroba f. ~**back** n jorobado m

hundred /ˈhʌndrəd/ adj ciento, (before noun) cien. **one** ~ **and ninety-eight** ciento noventa y ocho. **two** ~ doscientos. **three** ~ **pages** trescientas páginas. **four** ~ cuatrocientos. **five** ~ quinientos. ●n ciento m. ~**s of** centenares de. ~**th** adj & n centésimo (m). ~**weight** n 50,8kg; (Amer) 45,36kg

hung /hʌŋ/ see HANG

Hungar|ian /hʌŋˈgeəriən/ adj & n húngaro (m). ~**y** /ˈhʌŋgəri/ n Hungría f

hung|er /ˈhʌŋgə(r)/ n hambre f. ●vi. ~**er for** tener hambre de. ~**rily** /ˈhʌŋgrəli/ adv ávidamente. ~**ry** adj (-ier, -iest) hambriento. **be** ~**ry** tener hambre

hunk /hʌŋk/ n (buen) pedazo m

hunt /hʌnt/ vt cazar. ●vi cazar. ~ **for** buscar. ●n caza f. ~**er** n cazador m. ~**ing** n caza f. **go** ~**ing** ir de caza

hurl /hɜːl/ vt lanzar

hurrah /hʊˈrɑː/, **hurray** /hʊˈreɪ/ int & n ¡vival m.

hurricane /ˈhʌrɪkən/ n huracán m

hurr|ied /ˈhʌrɪd/ adj apresurado. ~**iedly** adv apresuradamente. ~**y** vi darse prisa, apurarse (LAm). ●vt meter prisa a, apurar (LAm). ●n prisa f. **be in a** ~**y** tener prisa, estar apurado (LAm)

hurt /hɜːt/ vt (pt hurt) hacer daño a, lastimar (LAm). ~ **s.o.'s feelings** ofender a uno. ●vi doler. **my head** ~**s** me duele la cabeza. ~**ful** adj hiriente

hurtle /ˈhɜːtl/ vt ir volando. ●vi. ~ **along** mover rápidamente

husband /ˈhʌzbənd/ n marido m, esposo m

hush /hʌʃ/ vt acallar. ●n silencio m. ▫ ~ **up** vt acallar (affair). ~**-hush** adj ① super secreto

husk /hʌsk/ n cáscara f

husky /ˈhʌski/ adj (-ier, -iest) (hoarse) ronco

hustle /ˈhʌsl/ vt (jostle) empujar. ●vi (hurry) darse prisa, apurarse (LAm). ●n empuje m

hut /hʌt/ n cabaña f

hutch /hʌtʃ/ n conejera f

hybrid /ˈhaɪbrɪd/ adj & n híbrido (m)

hydrangea /haɪˈdreɪndʒə/ n hortensia f

hydrant /ˈhaɪdrənt/ n. (fire) ~ n boca f de riego, boca f de incendios (LAm)

hydraulic /haɪˈdrɔːlɪk/ adj hidráulico

hydroelectric /haɪdrəʊˈlektrɪk/ adj hidroeléctrico

hydrofoil /ˈhaɪdrəfɔɪl/ n hidrodeslizador m

hydrogen /ˈhaɪdrədʒən/ n hidrógeno m

hyena /haɪˈiːnə/ n hiena f

hygien|e /ˈhaɪdʒiːn/ n higiene f. ~**ic** /haɪˈdʒiːnɪk/ adj higiénico

hymn /hɪm/ n himno m

hyper... /ˈhaɪpə(r)/ pref hiper...

hyphen /ˈhaɪfn/ n guión m. ~**ate** /-eɪt/ vt escribir con guión

hypno|sis /hɪpˈnəʊsɪs/ n hipnosis f. ~**ic** /-ˈnɒtɪk/ adj hipnótico. ~**tism** /ˈhɪpnətɪzəm/ n hipnotismo m. ~**tist** /ˈhɪpnətɪst/ n hipnotista m & f. ~**tize** /ˈhɪpnətaɪz/ vt hipnotizar

hypochondriac /haɪpəˈkɒndriæk/ n hipocondríaco m

hypocri|sy /hɪˈpɒkrəsɪ/ n hipo-

h

cresia f. **~te** /'hɪpəkrɪt/ n hipócrita m & f. **~tical** /hɪpə'krɪtɪkl/ adj hipócrita

hypodermic /haɪpə'dɜːmɪk/ adj hipodérmico. ● n hipodérmica f.

hypothe|sis /haɪ'pɒθəsɪs/ n (pl -theses/-siːz/) hipótesis f. **~tical** /-ə'θetɪkl/ adj hipotético

hysteri|a /hɪ'stɪərɪə/ n histerismo m. **~cal** /-'terɪkl/ adj histérico. **~cs** /hɪ'sterɪks/ npl histerismo m. have **~cs** ponerse histérico; (laugh) morir de risa

I i

I /aɪ/ pron yo

ice /aɪs/ n hielo m. ● vt helar; glasear (cake). ● vi. **~ (up)** helarse, congelarse. **~berg** /-bɜːg/ n iceberg m. **~ box** n (compartment) congelador; (Amer fam, refrigerator) frigorífico m, refrigerador m (LAm). **~cream** n helado m. **~ cube** n cubito m de hielo

Iceland /'aɪslənd/ n Islandia f

ice: ~ lolly polo m, paleta f helada (LAm). **~ rink** n pista f de hielo. **~ skating** n patinaje m sobre hielo

icicle /'aɪsɪkl/ n carámbano m

icing /'aɪsɪŋ/ n glaseado m

icon /'aɪkɒn/ n icono m

icy /'aɪsɪ/ adj (-ier, -iest) helado; (fig) glacial

I'd /aɪd/ = I had, I would

idea /aɪ'dɪə/ n idea f

ideal /aɪ'dɪəl/ adj & n ideal (m). **~ism** n idealismo m. **~ist** n idea-

lista m & f. **~istic** /-'lɪstɪk/ adj idealista. **~ize** vt idealizar. **~ly** adv idealmente

identical /aɪ'dentɪkl/ adj idéntico. **~ twins** npl gemelos mpl idénticos, gemelos mpl (LAm)

identif|ication /aɪdentɪfɪ'keɪʃn/ n identificación f. **~y** /aɪ'dentɪfaɪ/ vt identificar. ● vi. **~y with** identificarse con

identity /aɪ'dentɪtɪ/ n identidad f. **~ card** n carné m de identidad. **~ theft** n robo m de identidad

ideolog|ical /aɪdɪə'lɒdʒɪkl/ adj ideológico. **~y** /aɪdɪ'ɒlədʒɪ/ n ideología f

idiocy /'ɪdɪəsɪ/ n idiotez f

idiom /'ɪdɪəm/ n locución f. **~atic** /-'mætɪk/ adj idiomático

idiot /'ɪdɪət/ n idiota m & f. **~ic** /-'ɒtɪk/ adj idiota

idle /'aɪdl/ adj (-er, -est) ocioso; (lazy) holgazán; (out of work) desocupado; (machine) parado. ● vi (engine) andar al ralentí. **~ness** n ociosidad f; (laziness) holgazanería f

idol /'aɪdl/ n ídolo m. **~ize** vt idolatrar

idyllic /ɪ'dɪlɪk/ adj idílico

i.e. abbr (= id est) es decir

if /ɪf/ conj si

igloo /'ɪgluː/ n iglú m

ignit|e /ɪg'naɪt/ vt encender. ● vi encenderse. **~ion** /-'nɪʃn/ n ignición f; (Auto) encendido m. **~ion key** n llave f de contacto

ignoramus /ɪgnə'reɪməs/ n (pl -muses) ignorante

ignoran|ce /'ɪgnərəns/ n ignorancia f. **~t** adj ignorante

ignore /ɪg'nɔː(r)/ vt no hacer caso de; hacer caso omiso de (warning)

ill /ɪl/ adj enfermo. ● adv mal. ● n mal m

I'll /aɪl/ = **I will**

ill: **~-advised** /-əd'vaɪzd/ adj imprudente. **~ at ease** /-ət'i:z/ adj incómodo. **~-bred** /-'bred/ adj mal educado

illegal /ɪ'li:gl/ adj ilegal

illegible /ɪ'ledʒəbl/ adj ilegible

illegitima|cy /ɪlɪ'dʒɪtɪməsɪ/ n ilegitimidad f. **~te** /-ət/ adj ilegítimo

illitera|cy /ɪ'lɪtərəsɪ/ n analfabetismo m. **~te** /-ət/ adj analfabeto

illness /'ɪlnɪs/ n enfermedad f

illogical /ɪ'lɒdʒɪkl/ adj ilógico

illuminat|e /ɪ'lu:mɪneɪt/ vt iluminar. **~ion** /-'neɪʃn/ n iluminación f

illus|ion /ɪ'lu:ʒn/ n ilusión f. **~sory** /-sərɪ/ adj ilusorio

illustrat|e /'ɪləstreɪt/ vt ilustrar. **~ion** /-'streɪʃn/ n ilustración f; (example) ejemplo m

illustrious /ɪ'lʌstrɪəs/ adj ilustre

ill will /ɪl'wɪl/ n mala voluntad f

I'm /aɪm/ = **I am**

image /'ɪmɪdʒ/ n imagen f. **~ry** n imágenes fpl

imagin|able /ɪ'mædʒɪnəbl/ adj imaginable. **~ary** /-ərɪ/ adj imaginario. **~ation** /-'neɪʃn/ n imaginación f. **~ative** adj imaginativo. **~e** /ɪ'mædʒɪn/ vt imaginar(se)

imbalance /ɪm'bæləns/ n desequilibrio m

imbecile /'ɪmbəsi:l/ n imbécil m & f

imitat|e /'ɪmɪteɪt/ vt imitar. **~ion** /-'teɪʃn/ n imitación f. ● adj de imitación. **~or** n imitador m

immaculate /ɪ'mækjʊlət/ adj inmaculado

immatur|e /ɪmə'tjʊə(r)/ adj inmaduro. **~ity** n inmadurez f

immediate /ɪ'mi:dɪət/ adj inmediato. **~ly** adv inmediatamente.

● conj en cuanto (+ subjunctive)

immens|e /ɪ'mens/ adj inmenso. **~ely** adv inmensamente; (fam, very much) muchísimo

immers|e /ɪ'mɜ:s/ vt sumergir. **~ion** /-ʃn/ n inmersión f. **~ion heater** n calentador m de inmersión

immigra|nt /'ɪmɪgrənt/ adj & n inmigrante (m & f). **~tion** /-'greɪʃn/ n inmigración f

imminent /'ɪmɪnənt/ adj inminente

immobil|e /ɪ'məʊbaɪl/ adj inmóvil. **~ize** /-bɪlaɪz/ vt inmovilizar. **~izer** /-bɪlaɪzə(r)/ n inmovilizador m

immoderate /ɪ'mɒdərət/ adj inmoderado

immodest /ɪ'mɒdɪst/ adj inmodesto

immoral /ɪ'mɒrəl/ adj inmoral. **~ity** /ɪmə'rælətɪ/ n inmoralidad f

immortal /ɪ'mɔ:tl/ adj inmortal. **~ity** /-'tælətɪ/ n inmortalidad f. **~ize** vt inmortalizar

immun|e /ɪ'mju:n/ adj inmune (to a). **~ity** n inmunidad f. **~ization** /ɪmjʊnaɪ'zeɪʃn/ n inmunización f. **~ize** /'ɪmjʊnaɪz/ vt inmunizar

imp /ɪmp/ n diablillo m

impact /'ɪmpækt/ n impacto m

impair /ɪm'peə(r)/ vt perjudicar

impale /ɪm'peɪl/ vt atravesar (on con)

impart /ɪm'pɑ:t/ vt comunicar (news); impartir (knowledge)

impartial /ɪm'pɑ:ʃl/ adj imparcial. **~ity** /-ɪ'ælətɪ/ n imparcialidad f

impassable /ɪm'pɑ:səbl/ adj (road) intransitable

impassive /ɪm'pæsɪv/ adj impasible

impatience /ɪmˈpeɪʃəns/ n impaciencia f. **~t** adj impaciente. **get ~t** impacientarse. **~tly** adv con impaciencia

impeccable /ɪmˈpekəbl/ adj impecable

impede /ɪmˈpiːd/ vt estorbar

impediment /ɪmˈpedɪmənt/ obstáculo m. **(speech) ~** n defecto m del habla

impending /ɪmˈpendɪŋ/ adj inminente

impenetrable /ɪmˈpenɪtrəbl/ adj impenetrable

imperative /ɪmˈperətɪv/ adj imprescindible. **● n** (Gram) imperativo m

imperceptible /ɪmpəˈseptəbl/ adj imperceptible

imperfect /ɪmˈpɜːfɪkt/ adj imperfecto. **~ion** /ɪmpəˈfekʃn/ n imperfección f

imperial /ɪmˈpɪərɪəl/ adj imperial. **~ism** n imperialismo m

impersonal /ɪmˈpɜːsənl/ adj impersonal

impersonat|e /ɪmˈpɜːsəneɪt/ vt hacerse pasar por; (mimic) imitar. **~ion** /-ˈneɪʃn/ n imitación f. **~or** n imitador m

impertinen|ce /ɪmˈpɜːtɪnəns/ n impertinencia f. **~t** adj impertinente

impervious /ɪmˈpɜːvɪəs/ adj. **~ to** impermeable a

impetuous /ɪmˈpetjʊəs/ adj impetuoso

impetus /ˈɪmpɪtəs/ n ímpetu m

implacable /ɪmˈplækəbl/ adj implacable

implant /ɪmˈplɑːnt/ vt implantar

implement /ˈɪmplɪmənt/ n instrumento m, implemento m (LAm). **●** /ˈɪmplɪment/ vt implementar

implementation /ɪmplɪmen-ˈteɪʃn/ n implementación f

implicat|e /ˈɪmplɪkeɪt/ vt implicar. **~ion** /-ˈkeɪʃn/ n implicación f

implicit /ɪmˈplɪsɪt/ adj (implied) implícito; (unquestioning) absoluto

implore /ɪmˈplɔː(r)/ vt implorar

imply /ɪmˈplaɪ/ vt (involve) implicar; (insinuate) dar a entender, insinuar

impolite /ɪmpəˈlaɪt/ adj mal educado

import /ɪmˈpɔːt/ vt importar. **●** /ˈɪmpɔːt/ n importación f; (item) artículo m de importación; (meaning) significación f

importan|ce /ɪmˈpɔːtəns/ n importancia f. **~t** adj importante

importer /ɪmˈpɔːtə(r)/ n importador m

impos|e /ɪmˈpəʊz/ vt imponer. **● vi. ~e on** abusar de la amabilidad de. **~ing** adj imponente. **~ition** /ɪmpəˈzɪʃn/ n imposición f; (fig) abuso m

impossib|ility /ɪmpɒsəˈbɪlətɪ/ n imposibilidad f. **~le** /ɪmˈpɒsəbl/ adj imposible

impostor /ɪmˈpɒstə(r)/ n impostor m

impoten|ce /ˈɪmpətəns/ n impotencia f. **~t** adj impotente

impound /ɪmˈpaʊnd/ vt confiscar

impoverished /ɪmˈpɒvərɪʃt/ adj empobrecido

impractical /ɪmˈpræktɪkl/ adj poco práctico

impregnable /ɪmˈpregnəbl/ adj inexpugnable

impregnate /ˈɪmpregneɪt/ vt impregnar (with con, de)

impress /ɪmˈpres/ vt impresionar; (make good impression) causar una buena impresión a. **● vi** impresionar

impression /ɪmˈpreʃn/ n impresión f. **~able** adj impresionable. **~ism** n impresionismo m

impressive /ɪmˈpresɪv/ adj impresionante

imprint /ˈɪmprɪnt/ n impresión f. • /ɪmˈprɪnt/ vt imprimir

imprison /ɪmˈprɪzn/ vt encarcelar. **~ment** n encarcelamiento m

improbab|ility /ɪmprɒbəˈbɪlətɪ/ n improbabilidad f. **~le** /ɪmˈprɒbəbl/ adj improbable

impromptu /ɪmˈprɒmptjuː/ adj improvisado. • adv de improviso

improper /ɪmˈprɒpə(r)/ adj impropio; (incorrect) incorrecto

improve /ɪmˈpruːv/ vt mejorar. • vi mejorar. **~ment** n mejora f

improvis|ation /ɪmprəvaɪˈzeɪʃn/ n improvisación f. **~e** /ˈɪmprəvaɪz/ vt/i improvisar

impuden|ce /ˈɪmpjʊdəns/ n insolencia f. **~t** adj insolente

impuls|e /ˈɪmpʌls/ n impulso m. **on ~e** sin reflexionar. **~ive** adj irreflexivo

impur|e /ɪmˈpjʊə(r)/ adj impuro. **~ity** n impureza f

in /ɪn/ prep en; (within) dentro de. **~ a firm manner** de una manera terminante. **~ an hour's (time)** dentro de una hora. **~ doing** al hacer. **~ so far as** en la medida en que. **~ the evening** por la tarde. **~ the rain** bajo la lluvia. **~ the sun** al sol. **one ~ ten** uno de cada diez. **the best ~ the world** el mejor del mundo. • adv (inside) dentro; (at home) en casa. **come ~** entrar. • n. **the ~s and outs of** los detalles de

inability /ɪnəˈbɪlətɪ/ n incapacidad f

inaccessible /ɪnækˈsesəbl/ adj inaccesible

inaccura|cy /ɪnˈækjʊrəsɪ/ n inexactitud f. **~te** /-ət/ adj inexacto

inactiv|e /ɪnˈæktɪv/ adj inactivo. **~ity** /-ˈtɪvətɪ/ n inactividad f

inadequa|cy /ɪnˈædɪkwəsɪ/ adj insuficiencia f. **~te** /-ət/ adj insuficiente

inadvertently /ɪnədˈvɜːtəntlɪ/ adv sin querer

inadvisable /ɪnədˈvaɪzəbl/ adj desaconsejable

inane /ɪˈneɪn/ adj estúpido

inanimate /ɪnˈænɪmət/ adj inanimado

inappropriate /ɪnəˈprəʊprɪət/ adj inoportuno

inarticulate /ɪnɑːˈtɪkjʊlət/ adj incapaz de expresarse claramente

inattentive /ɪnəˈtentɪv/ adj desatento

inaudible /ɪnˈɔːdəbl/ adj inaudible

inaugurate /ɪˈnɔːgjʊreɪt/ vt inaugurar

inborn /ˈɪnbɔːn/ adj innato

inbred /ɪnˈbred/ adj (inborn) innato; (social group) endogámico

Inc /ɪŋk/ abbr (Amer) (= Incorporated). S.A., Sociedad Anónima

incalculable /ɪnˈkælkjʊləbl/ adj incalculable

incapable /ɪnˈkeɪpəbl/ adj incapaz

incapacit|ate /ɪnkəˈpæsɪteɪt/ vt incapacitar. **~y** n incapacidad f

incarcerate /ɪnˈkɑːsəreɪt/ vt encarcelar

incarnat|e /ɪnˈkɑːnət/ adj encarnado. **~ion** /-ˈneɪʃn/ n encarnación f

incendiary /ɪnˈsendɪərɪ/ adj incendiario. **~ bomb** bomba f

incendiaria
incense /'ɪnsens/ n incienso m.
● /ɪn'sens/ vt enfurecer
incentive /ɪn'sentɪv/ n incentivo m
incessant /ɪn'sesnt/ adj incesante.
~**ly** adv sin cesar
incest /'ɪnsest/ n incesto m.
~**uous** /ɪn'sestjʊəs/ adj incestuoso
inch /ɪntʃ/ n pulgada f; (= 2,54cm).
● vi. ~ forward avanzar lentamente
incidence /'ɪnsɪdəns/ n frecuencia f
incident /'ɪnsɪdənt/ n incidente m
incidental /ɪnsɪ'dentl/ adj (effect)
secundario; (minor) incidental. ~**ly**
adv a propósito
incinerat|e /ɪn'sɪnəreɪt/ vt incinerar. ~**or** n incinerador m
incision /ɪn'sɪʒn/ n incisión f
incite /ɪn'saɪt/ vt incitar. ~**ment** n
incitación f
inclination /ɪnklɪ'neɪʃn/ n inclinación f. **have no** ~ **to** no tener deseos de
incline /ɪn'klaɪn/ vt inclinar. **be**
~**d to** tener tendencia a. ● vi inclinarse. /'ɪnklaɪn/ n pendiente f
inclu|de /ɪn'kluːd/ vt incluir.
~**ding** prep incluso. ~**sion** /-ʒn/ n
inclusión f. ~**sive** /-sɪv/ adj inclusivo
incognito /ɪnkɒg'niːtəʊ/ adv de
incógnito
incoherent /ɪnkəʊ'hɪərənt/ adj
incoherente
incom|e /'ɪnkʌm/ n ingresos mpl.
~**e tax** n impuesto m sobre la
renta. ~**ing** adj (tide) ascendente
incomparable /ɪn'kɒmpərəbl/
adj incomparable
incompatible /ɪnkəm'pætəbl/

adj incompatible
incompeten|ce /ɪn'kɒmpɪtəns/
n incompetencia f. ~**t** adj incompetente
incomplete /ɪnkəm'pliːt/ adj incompleto
incomprehensible /ɪnkɒmprɪ'hensəbl/ adj incomprensible
inconceivable /ɪnkən'siːvəbl/
adj inconcebible
inconclusive /ɪnkən'kluːsɪv/ adj
no concluyente
incongruous /ɪn'kɒŋgrʊəs/ adj
incongruente
inconsiderate /ɪnkən'sɪdərət/
adj desconsiderado
inconsisten|cy /ɪnkən'sɪstənsɪ/
n inconsecuencia f. ~**t** adj inconsecuente. **be** ~**t with** no concordar
con
inconspicuous /ɪnkən'spɪkjʊəs/
adj que no llama la atención. ~**ly**
adv sin llamar la atención
incontinent /ɪn'kɒntɪnənt/ adj
incontinente
inconvenien|ce /ɪnkən'viːnɪəns/ adj inconveniencia f;
(drawback) inconveniente m. ~**t** adj
inconveniente
incorporate /ɪn'kɔːpəreɪt/ vt incorporar; (include) incluir; (Com)
constituir (en sociedad)
incorrect /ɪnkə'rekt/ adj incorrecto
increas|e /'ɪnkriːs/ n aumento m
(in de). ● /ɪn'kriːs/ vt/i aumentar.
~**ing** /ɪn'kriːsɪŋ/ adj creciente.
~**ingly** adv cada vez más
incredible /ɪn'kredəbl/ adj increíble
incredulous /ɪn'kredjʊləs/ adj
incrédulo
incriminat|e /ɪn'krɪmɪneɪt/ vt incriminar. ~**ing** adj comprometedor

incubat|e /ˈɪŋkjʊbeɪt/ vt incubar. **~ion** /-ˈbeɪʃn/ n incubación f. **~or** n incubadora f

incur /ɪnˈkɜː/ vt (pt incurred) incurrir en; contraer (debts)

incurable /ɪnˈkjʊərəbl/ adj (disease) incurable; (romantic) empedernido

indebted /ɪnˈdetɪd/ adj. be **~ to s.o.** estar en deuda con uno

indecen|cy /ɪnˈdiːsnsɪ/ n indecencia f. **~t** adj indecente

indecisi|on /ɪndɪˈsɪʒn/ n indecisión f. **~ve** /-ˈsaɪsɪv/ adj indeciso

indeed /ɪnˈdiːd/ adv en efecto; (really?) ¿de veras?

indefinable /ɪndɪˈfaɪnəbl/ adj indefinible

indefinite /ɪnˈdefɪnət/ adj indefinido. **~ly** adv indefinidamente

indelible /ɪnˈdelɪbl/ adj indeleble

indemni|fy /ɪnˈdemnɪfaɪ/ vt (insure) asegurar; (compensate) indemnizar. **~ty** /-ətɪ/ n (insurance) indemnidad f; (payment) indemnización f

indent /ɪnˈdent/ vt sangrar (text). **~ation** /-ˈteɪʃn/ n mella f

independen|ce /ɪndɪˈpendəns/ n independencia f. **~t** adj independiente. **~tly** adv independientemente

in-depth /ɪnˈdepθ/ adj a fondo

indescribable /ɪndɪˈskraɪbəbl/ adj indescriptible

indestructible /ɪndɪˈstrʌktəbl/ adj indestructible

indeterminate /ɪndɪˈtɜːmɪnət/ adj indeterminado

index /ˈɪndeks/ n (pl indexes) (in book) índice m; (pl indexes or indices) (Com, Math) índice m. ● vt poner índice a; (enter in index) poner en un índice. **~ finger** n

(dedo m) índice m. **~-linked** /-ˈlɪŋkt/ adj indexado

India /ˈɪndɪə/ n la India. **~n** adj & n indio (m)

indicat|e /ˈɪndɪkeɪt/ vt indicar. **~ion** /-ˈkeɪʃn/ n indicación f. **~ive** /ɪnˈdɪkətɪv/ adj & n indicativo (m). **~or** /ˈɪndɪkeɪtə(r)/ n indicador m; (Auto) intermitente m

indices /ˈɪndɪsiːz/ see **INDEX**

indict /ɪnˈdaɪt/ vt acusar. **~ment** n acusación f

indifferen|ce /ɪnˈdɪfrəns/ n indiferencia f. **~t** adj indiferente; (not good) mediocre

indigesti|ble /ɪndɪˈdʒestəbl/ adj indigesto. **~on** /-tʃən/ n indigestión f

indigna|nt /ɪnˈdɪgnənt/ adj indignado. **~tion** /-ˈneɪʃn/ n indignación f

indirect /ɪndɪˈrekt/ adj indirecto. **~ly** adv indirectamente

indiscre|et /ɪndɪˈskriːt/ adj indiscreto. **~tion** /-ˈkreʃn/ n indiscreción f

indiscriminate /ɪndɪˈskrɪmɪnət/ adj indistinto. **~ly** adv indistintamente

indispensable /ɪndɪˈspensəbl/ adj indispensable, imprescindible

indisposed /ɪndɪˈspəʊzd/ adj indispuesto

indisputable /ɪndɪˈspjuːtəbl/ adj indiscutible

indistinguishable /ɪndɪˈstɪŋgwɪʃəbl/ adj indistinguible (from de)

individual /ɪndɪˈvɪdjʊəl/ adj individual. ● n individuo m. **~ly** adv individualmente

indoctrinat|e /ɪnˈdɒktrɪneɪt/ vt adoctrinar. **~ion** /-ˈneɪʃn/ n adoctrinamiento m

indolen|ce /ˈɪndələns/ n indolencia f. **~t** adj indolente

indomitable /ɪnˈdɒmɪtəbl/ adj indómito

indoor /ˈɪndɔː(r)/ adj interior; (clothes etc) de casa; (covered) cubierto. **~s** adv dentro, adentro (LAm)

induc|e /ɪnˈdjuːs/ vt inducir. **~ement** n incentivo m

indulge /ɪnˈdʌldʒ/ vt satisfacer (desires); complacer (person). ● vi. **~ in** permitirse. **~nce** /-əns/ n (of desires) satisfacción f; (extravagance) lujo m. **~nt** adj indulgente

industrial /ɪnˈdʌstrɪəl/ adj industrial; (unrest) laboral. **~ist** n industrial m & f. **~ized** adj industrializado

industrious /ɪnˈdʌstrɪəs/ adj trabajador

industry /ˈɪndəstrɪ/ n industria f; (zeal) aplicación f

inebriated /ɪˈniːbrɪeɪtɪd/ adj beodo, ebrio

inedible /ɪnˈedɪbl/ adj incomible

ineffective /ɪnɪˈfektɪv/ adj ineficaz; (person) incompetente

ineffectual /ɪnɪˈfektjʊəl/ adj ineficaz

inefficien|cy /ɪnɪˈfɪʃnsɪ/ n ineficacia f; (of person) incompetencia f. **~t** adj ineficaz; (person) incompetente

ineligible /ɪnˈelɪdʒəbl/ adj inelegible. **be ~ for** no tener derecho a

inept /ɪˈnept/ adj inepto

inequality /ɪnɪˈkwɒlətɪ/ n desigualdad f

inert /ɪˈnɜːt/ adj inerte. **~ia** /ɪˈnɜːʃə/ n inercia f

inescapable /ɪnɪˈskeɪpəbl/ adj ineludible

inevitabl|e /ɪnˈevɪtəbl/ adj inevitable. ● n. **the ~e** lo inevitable. **~y** adv inevitablemente

inexact /ɪnɪgˈzækt/ adj inexacto

inexcusable /ɪnɪkˈskjuːsəbl/ adj imperdonable

inexpensive /ɪnɪkˈspensɪv/ adj económico, barato

inexperience /ɪnɪkˈspɪərɪəns/ n falta f de experiencia. **~d** adj inexperto

inexplicable /ɪnɪkˈsplɪkəbl/ adj inexplicable

infallib|ility /ɪnfæləˈbɪlətɪ/ n infalibilidad f. **~le** /ɪnˈfæləbl/ adj infalible

infam|ous /ˈɪnfəməs/ adj infame. **~y** n infamia f

infan|cy /ˈɪnfənsɪ/ n infancia f. **~t** n niño m. **~tile** /ˈɪnfəntaɪl/ adj infantil

infantry /ˈɪnfəntrɪ/ n infantería f

infatuat|ed /ɪnˈfætjʊeɪtɪd/ adj. **be ~ed with** estar encaprichado con. **~ion** /-ˈeɪʃn/ n encaprichamiento m

infect /ɪnˈfekt/ vt infectar; (fig) contagiar. **~ s.o. with sth** contagiarle algo a uno. **~ion** /-ʃn/ n infección f. **~ious** /-ʃəs/ adj contagioso

infer /ɪnˈfɜː(r)/ vt (pt inferred) deducir

inferior /ɪnˈfɪərɪə(r)/ adj & n inferior (m & f). **~ity** /-ˈɒrətɪ/ n inferioridad f

inferno /ɪnˈfɜːnəʊ/ n (pl -os) infierno m

infertil|e /ɪnˈfɜːtaɪl/ adj estéril. **~ity** /-ˈtɪlətɪ/ n esterilidad f

infest /ɪnˈfest/ vt infestar

infidelity /ɪnfɪˈdelətɪ/ n infidelidad f

infiltrat|e /ˈɪnfɪltreɪt/ vt infiltrarse en. ● vi infiltrarse. **~or** n infiltrado m

infinite /ˈɪnfɪnət/ adj infinito. **~ly**

adv infinitamente

infinitesimal /ɪnfɪnɪ'tesɪml/ adj infinitesimal

infinitive /ɪn'fɪnətɪv/ n infinitivo m

infinity /ɪn'fɪnətɪ/ n (infinite distance) infinito m; (infinite quantity) infinidad f

infirm /ɪn'fɜːm/ adj enfermizo. **~ity** n enfermedad f

inflam|e /ɪn'fleɪm/ vt inflamar. **~mable** /ɪn'flæməbl/ adj inflamable. **~mation** /-ə'meɪʃn/ n inflamación f

inflat|e /ɪn'fleɪt/ vt inflar. **~ion** /-ʃn/ n inflación f. **~ionary** adj inflacionario

inflection /ɪn'flekʃn/ n inflexión f

inflexible /ɪn'fleksəbl/ adj inflexible

inflict /ɪn'flɪkt/ vt infligir (on a)

influen|ce /'ɪnfluəns/ n influencia f. **under the ~ce** (fam, drunk) borracho. ● vt influir (en). **~tial** /-'enʃl/ adj influyente

influenza /ɪnflu'enzə/ n gripe f

influx /'ɪnflʌks/ n afluencia f

inform /ɪn'fɔːm/ vt informar. **keep ~ed** tener al corriente. ● vi. **~ on s.o.** delatar a uno

informal /ɪn'fɔːml/ adj informal; (language) familiar. **~ity** /-'mælətɪ/ n falta f de ceremonia. **~ly** adv (casually) de manera informal; (unofficially) informalmente

inform|ation /ɪnfə'meɪʃn/ n información f. **~ation technology** n informática f. **~ative** adj /ɪn'fɔːmətɪv/ informativo. **~er** /ɪb'fɔːmə(r)/ n informante m

infrared /ɪnfrə'red/ adj infrarrojo

infrequent /ɪn'friːkwənt/ adj poco frecuente. **~ly** adv raramente

infringe /ɪn'frɪndʒ/ vt infringir. **~**

on violar. **~ment** n violación f

infuriat|e /ɪn'fjʊərɪeɪt/ vt enfurecer. **~ing** adj exasperante

ingen|ious /ɪn'dʒiːnɪəs/ adj ingenioso. **~uity** /ɪndʒɪ'njuːətɪ/ n ingeniosidad f

ingot /'ɪŋɡət/ n lingote m

ingrained /ɪn'ɡreɪnd/ adj (belief) arraigado

ingratiate /ɪn'ɡreɪʃɪeɪt/ vt. **~ o.s. with** congraciarse con

ingratitude /ɪn'ɡrætɪtjuːd/ n ingratitud f

ingredient /ɪn'ɡriːdɪənt/ n ingrediente m

ingrowing /'ɪnɡrəʊɪŋ/, **ingrown** /'ɪnɡrəʊn/ adj. **~ nail** n uñero m, uña f encarnada

inhabit /ɪn'hæbɪt/ vt habitar. **~able** adj habitable. **~ant** n habitante m

inhale /ɪn'heɪl/ vt aspirar. ● vi (when smoking) aspirar el humo. **~r** n inhalador m

inherent /ɪn'hɪərənt/ adj inherente. **~ly** adv intrínsecamente

inherit /ɪn'herɪt/ vt heredar. **~ance** /-əns/ n herencia f

inhibit /ɪn'hɪbɪt/ vt inhibir. **~ed** adj inhibido. **~ion** /-'bɪʃn/ n inhibición f

inhospitable /ɪnhə'spɪtəbl/ adj (place) inhóspito; (person) inhospitalario

inhuman /ɪn'hjuːmən/ adj inhumano. **~e** /ɪnhjuː'meɪn/ adj inhumano. **~ity** /ɪnhjuː'mænətɪ/ n inhumanidad f

initial /ɪ'nɪʃl/ n inicial f. ● vt (pt **initialled**) firmar con iniciales. ● adj inicial. **~ly** adv al principio

initiat|e /ɪ'nɪʃɪeɪt/ vt iniciar; promover (scheme etc). **~ion** /-'eɪʃn/ n iniciación f

initiative /ɪˈnɪʃətɪv/ n iniciativa f. **on one's own** ~ por iniciativa propia. **take the** ~ tomar la iniciativa

inject /ɪnˈdʒekt/ vt inyectar. ~**ion** /-ʃn/ n inyección f

injur|e /ˈɪndʒə(r)/ vt herir. ~**y** n herida f

injustice /ɪnˈdʒʌstɪs/ n injusticia f

ink /ɪŋk/ n tinta f. ~**well** n tintero m. ~**y** adj manchado de tinta

inland /ˈɪnlənd/ adj interior. ● /ɪnˈlænd/ adv tierra adentro. **I~ Revenue** /ˈɪnlənd/ n Hacienda f

in-laws /ˈɪnlɔːz/ npl parientes mpl políticos

inlay /ɪnˈleɪ/ vt (pt inlaid) taracear, incrustar. ● /ˈɪnleɪ/ n taracea f, incrustación f

inlet /ˈɪnlet/ n (in coastline) ensenada f; (of river, sea) brazo m

inmate /ˈɪnmeɪt/ n (of asylum) interno m; (of prison) preso m

inn /ɪn/ n posada f

innate /ɪˈneɪt/ adj innato

inner /ˈɪnə(r)/ adj interior; (fig) íntimo. ~**most** adj más íntimo. ~**tube** n cámara f

innocen|ce /ˈɪnəsns/ n inocencia f. ~**t** adj & n inocente (m & f)

innocuous /ɪˈnɒkjuəs/ adj inocuo

innovat|e /ˈɪnəveɪt/ vi innovar. ~**ion** /-ˈveɪʃn/ n innovación f. ~**ive** /ˈɪnəvətɪv/ adj innovador. ~**or** n innovador m

innuendo /ɪnjuːˈendəʊ/ n (pl -oes) insinuación f

innumerable /ɪˈnjuːmərəbl/ adj innumerable

inoculat|e /ɪˈnɒkjʊlet/ vt inocular. ~**ion** /-ˈleɪʃn/ n inoculación f

inoffensive /ɪnəˈfensɪv/ adj inofensivo

inopportune /ɪnˈɒpətjuːn/ adj inoportuno

input /ˈɪnpʊt/ n aportación f, aporte m (LAm); (Comp) entrada f. ● vt (pt input, pres p inputting) entrar (data)

inquest /ˈɪnkwest/ n investigación f judicial

inquir|e /ɪnˈkwaɪə(r)/ vt/i preguntar. ~**e about** informarse de. ~**y** n pregunta f; (investigation) investigación f

inquisition /ɪnkwɪˈzɪʃn/ n inquisición f

inquisitive /ɪnˈkwɪzətɪv/ adj inquisitivo

insan|e /ɪnˈseɪn/ adj loco. ~**ity** /ɪnˈsænəti/ n locura f

insatiable /ɪnˈseɪʃəbl/ adj insaciable

inscri|be /ɪnˈskraɪb/ vt inscribir (letters); grabar (design). ~**ption** /-ɪpʃn/ n inscripción f

inscrutable /ɪnˈskruːtəbl/ adj inescrutable

insect /ˈɪnsekt/ n insecto m. ~**icide** /ɪnˈsektɪsaɪd/ n insecticida f

insecur|e /ɪnsɪˈkjʊə(r)/ adj inseguro. ~**ity** n inseguridad f

insensitive /ɪnˈsensətɪv/ adj insensible

inseparable /ɪnˈsepərəbl/ adj inseparable

insert /ˈɪnsɜːt/ n materia f insertada. ● /ɪnˈsɜːt/ vt insertar. ~**ion** /ɪnˈsɜːʃn/ n inserción f

inside /ɪnˈsaɪd/ n interior m. ~ **out** al revés; (thoroughly) a fondo. ● adj interior. ● adv dentro, adentro (LAm). ● prep dentro de. ~**s** npl tripas fpl

insight /ˈɪnsaɪt/ n perspicacia f. **gain an** ~ **into** llegar a comprender bien

insignificant /ɪnsɪgˈnɪfɪkənt/ adj insignificante

insincer|e /ɪnsɪnˈsɪə(r)/ adj poco sincero. ~ity /-ˈserətɪ/ n falta f de sinceridad

insinuat|e /ɪnˈsɪnjʊeɪt/ vt insinuar. ~ion /-ˈeɪʃn/ n insinuación f

insipid /ɪnˈsɪpɪd/ adj insípido

insist /ɪnˈsɪst/ vt insistir (**that** en que). ● vi insistir. ~ **on** insistir en. ~ence /-əns/ n insistencia f ~ent adj insistente. ~ently adv con insistencia

insolen|ce /ˈɪnsələns/ n insolencia f ~t adj insolente

insoluble /ɪnˈsɒljʊbl/ adj insoluble

insolvent /ɪnˈsɒlvənt/ adj insolvente

insomnia /ɪnˈsɒmnɪə/ n insomnio m. ~c /-ræk/ n insomne m & f

inspect /ɪnˈspekt/ vt (officially) inspeccionar; (look at closely) revisar, examinar. ~ion /-ʃn/ n inspección f. ~or n inspector m; (on train, bus) revisor m, inspector m (LAm)

inspir|ation /ɪnspəˈreɪʃn/ n inspiración f. ~e /ɪnˈspaɪə(r)/ vt inspirar. ~ing adj inspirador

instability /ɪnstəˈbɪlətɪ/ n inestabilidad f

install /ɪnˈstɔːl/ vt instalar. ~ation /-əˈleɪʃn/ n instalación f

instalment /ɪnˈstɔːlmənt/ n (payment) plazo m; (of publication) entrega f; (of radio, TV serial) episodio m

instance /ˈɪnstəns/ n ejemplo m; (case) caso m. **for** ~ por ejemplo. **in the first** ~ en primer lugar

instant /ˈɪnstənt/ adj instantáneo. ● n instante m. ~aneous /ɪnstənˈteɪnɪəs/ adj instantáneo

instead /ɪnˈsted/ adv en cambio.

~ **of** en vez de, en lugar de

instigat|e /ˈɪnstɪgeɪt/ vt instigar. ~ion /-ˈgeɪʃn/ n instigación f

instinct /ˈɪnstɪŋkt/ n instinto m. ~ive adj instintivo

institut|e /ˈɪnstɪtjuːt/ n instituto m. ● vt instituir; iniciar (enquiry etc). ~ion /-ˈtjuːʃn/ n institución f. ~ional adj institucional

instruct /ɪnˈstrʌkt/ vt instruir; (order) mandar. ~ **s.o. in sth** enseñar algo a uno. ~ion f. ~ions npl (for use) modo m de empleo. ~ive adj instructivo. ~or n instructor m

instrument /ˈɪnstrəmənt/ n instrumento m. ~al /ɪnstrəˈmentl/ adj instrumental. **be** ~**al in** jugar un papel decisivo en

insubordinat|e /ɪnsəˈbɔːdɪnət/ adj insubordinado. ~ion /-ˈneɪʃn/ n insubordinación f

insufferable /ɪnˈsʌfərəbl/ adj (person) insufrible; (heat) insoportable

insufficient /ɪnsəˈfɪʃnt/ adj insuficiente

insular /ˈɪnsjʊlə(r)/ adj insular; (narrow-minded) estrecho de miras

insulat|e /ˈɪnsjʊleɪt/ vt aislar. ~ion /-ˈleɪʃn/ n aislamiento m

insulin /ˈɪnsjʊlɪn/ n insulina f

insult /ɪnˈsʌlt/ vt insultar. ● /ˈɪnsʌlt/ n insulto m. ~ing /ɪnˈsʌltɪŋ/ adj insultante

insur|ance /ɪnˈʃʊərəns/ n seguro m. ~e /ɪnˈʃʊə(r)/ vt (Com) asegurar; (Amer) see ENSURE

insurmountable /ɪnsəˈmaʊntəbl/ adj insuperable

intact /ɪnˈtækt/ adj intacto

integral /ˈɪntɪgrəl/ adj integral

integrat|e /ˈɪntɪgreɪt/ vt integrar. ● vi integrarse. ~ion /-ˈgreɪʃn/

integración f

integrity /ɪn'tegrətɪ/ n integridad f

intellect /'ɪntəlekt/ n intelecto m. **~ual** /ɪntə'lektʃʊəl/ adj & n intelectual (m)

intelligen|ce /ɪn'telɪdʒəns/ n inteligencia f. **~t** adj inteligente. **~tly** adv inteligentemente

intelligible /ɪn'telɪdʒəbl/ adj inteligible

intend /ɪn'tend/ vt. **~ to do** pensar hacer

intens|e /ɪn'tens/ adj intenso; (person) apasionado. **~ely** adv intensamente; (very) sumamente. **~ify** /-ɪfaɪ/ vt intensificar. ● vi intensificarse. **~ity** /-ɪtɪ/ n intensidad f

intensive /ɪn'tensɪv/ adj intensivo. **~ care** n cuidados mpl intensivos

intent /ɪn'tent/ n propósito m. ● adj atento. **~ on** absorto en. **~ on** doing resuelto a hacer

intention /ɪn'tenʃn/ n intención f. **~al** adj intencional

intently /ɪn'tentlɪ/ adv atentamente

interact /ɪntər'ækt/ vi relacionarse. **~ion** /-ʃn/ n interacción f

intercept /ɪntə'sept/ vt interceptar. **~ion** /-ʃn/ n interceptación f

interchange /ɪntə'tʃeɪndʒ/ vt intercambiar. ● /'ɪntətʃeɪndʒ/ n intercambio m; (road junction) cruce m. **~able** /-'tʃeɪndʒəbl/ adj intercambiable

intercity /ɪntə'sɪtɪ/ adj rápido interurbano m

intercourse /'ɪntəkɔːs/ n trato m; (sexual) acto m sexual

interest /'ɪntrest/ n interés m. ● vt interesar. **~ed** adj interesado. be

~ed in interesarse por. **~ing** adj interesante

interface /'ɪntəfeɪs/ interfaz m & f; (interaction) interrelación f

interfere /ɪntə'fɪə(r)/ vi entrometerse. **~ in** entrometerse en. **~ with** afectar (a); interferir (radio). **~nce** /-rəns/ n intromisión f; (Radio) interferencia f

interior /ɪn'tɪərɪə(r)/ adj & n interior (m)

interjection /ɪntə'dʒekʃn/ n interjección f

interlude /'ɪntəluːd/ n intervalo m; (theatre, music) interludio m

intermediary /ɪntə'miːdɪərɪ/ adj & n intermediario (m)

interminable /ɪn'tɜːmɪnəbl/ adj interminable

intermittent /ɪntə'mɪtnt/ adj intermitente. **~ly** adv con discontinuidad

intern /ɪn'tɜːn/ vt internar. ● /'ɪntɜːn/ n (Amer, doctor) interno m

internal /ɪn'tɜːnl/ adj interno. **~ly** adv internamente. **I~ Revenue Service** n (Amer) Hacienda f

international /ɪntə'næʃənl/ adj internacional

Internet /'ɪntənet/ n. **the ~** el Internet

interpret /ɪn'tɜːprɪt/ vt/i interpretar. **~ation** /-'teɪʃn/ n interpretación f. **~er** n intérprete m & f

interrogat|e /ɪn'terəgeɪt/ vt interrogar. **~ion** /-'geɪʃn/ n interrogatorio m. **~ive** /-'rɒgətɪv/ adj interrogativo

interrupt /ɪntə'rʌpt/ vt/i interrumpir. **~ion** /-ʃn/ n interrupción f

intersect /ɪntə'sekt/ vt cruzar. ● vi (roads) cruzarse; (geometry) intersecarse. **~ion** /-ʃn/ n (roads) cruce m; (geometry) intersección f

intersperse /ɪntəˈspɜːs/ vt intercalar

interstate (highway) /ˈɪntəsteɪt/ n (Amer) carretera f interestal

intertwine /ɪntəˈtwaɪn/ vt entrelazar. ● vi entrelazarse

interval /ˈɪntəvl/ n intervalo m; (theatre) descanso m. **at ~s** a intervalos

interven|e /ɪntəˈviːn/ vi intervenir. **~tion** /-ˈvenʃn/ n intervención f

interview /ˈɪntəvjuː/ n entrevista f. ● vt entrevistar. **~ee** /-ˈiː/ n entrevistado m. **~er** n entrevistador m

intestine /ɪnˈtestɪn/ n intestino m

intimacy /ˈɪntɪməsɪ/ n intimidad f

intimate /ˈɪntɪmət/ adj íntimo. ● /ˈɪntɪmeɪt/ vt (state) anunciar; (imply) dar a entender. **~ly** /ˈɪntɪmətlɪ/ adv íntimamente

intimidat|e /ɪnˈtɪmɪdeɪt/ vt intimidar. **~ion** /-ˈdeɪʃn/ n intimidación f

into /ˈɪntuː//ˈɪntə/ prep en; (translate) a

intolerable /ɪnˈtɒlərəbl/ adj intolerable

intoleran|ce /ɪnˈtɒlərəns/ n intolerancia f. **~t** adj intolerante

intoxicat|e /ɪnˈtɒksɪkeɪt/ vt embriagar; (Med) intoxicar. **~ed** adj ebrio. **~ing** adj (substance) estupefaciente. **~ion** /-ˈkeɪʃn/ n embriaguez f; (Med) intoxicación f

intransitive /ɪnˈtrænsɪtɪv/ adj intransitivo

intravenous /ɪntrəˈviːnəs/ adj intravenoso

intrepid /ɪnˈtrepɪd/ adj intrépido

intrica|cy /ˈɪntrɪkəsɪ/ n complejidad f. **~te** /-ət/ adj complejo

intrigu|e /ɪnˈtriːg/ vt/i intrigar. ● /ˈɪntriːg/ n intriga f. **~ing** /ɪnˈtriːgɪŋ/ adj intrigante

intrinsic /ɪnˈtrɪnsɪk/ adj intrínseco. **~ally** adj intrínsecamente

introduc|e /ɪntrəˈdjuːs/ vt introducir; presentar (person). **~tion** /-ˈdʌkʃn/ n introducción f; (to person) presentación f. **~tory** /ɪntrəˈdʌktərɪ/ adj preliminar; (course) de introducción

introvert /ˈɪntrəvɜːt/ n introvertido m

intru|de /ɪnˈtruːd/ vi entrometerse; (disturb) importunar. **~der** n intruso m. **~sion** /-ʒn/ n intrusión f. **~sive** /-sɪv/ adj impertinente

intuiti|on /ɪntjuːˈɪʃn/ n intuición f. **~ve** /ɪnˈtjuːɪtɪv/ adj intuitivo

inundat|e /ˈɪnʌndeɪt/ vt inundar. **~ion** /-ˈdeɪʃn/ n inundación f

invade /ɪnˈveɪd/ vt invadir. **~r** n invasor m

invalid /ˈɪnvəlɪd/ n inválido m. ● /ɪnˈvælɪd/ adj inválido. **~ate** /ɪnˈvælɪdeɪt/ vt invalidar

invaluable /ɪnˈvæljʊəbl/ adj inestimable, invalorable (LAm)

invariab|le /ɪnˈveərɪəbl/ adj invariable. **~y** adv invariablemente

invasion /ɪnˈveɪʒn/ n invasión f

invent /ɪnˈvent/ vt inventar. **~ion** /-ˈvenʃn/ n invención f. **~ive** adj inventivo. **~or** n inventor m

inventory /ˈɪnvəntrɪ/ n inventario m

invertebrate /ɪnˈvɜːtɪbrət/ n invertebrado m

inverted commas /ɪnvɜːtɪd ˈkɒməz/npl comillas fpl

invest /ɪnˈvest/ vt invertir. ● vi. **~ in** invertir en

investigat|e /ɪn'vestɪgeɪt/ vt investigar. **~ion** /-'geɪʃn/ n investigación f. **under ~ion** sometido a examen. **~or** n investigador m

investment /ɪn'vestmənt/ n inversión f

investor /ɪn'vestə(r)/ n inversionista m & f

inveterate /ɪn'vetərət/ adj inveterado

invidious /ɪn'vɪdɪəs/ adj (hateful) odioso; (unfair) injusto

invigorating /ɪn'vɪgəreɪtɪŋ/ adj vigorizante; (stimulating) estimulante

invincible /ɪn'vɪnsɪbl/ adj invencible

invisible /ɪn'vɪzəbl/ adj invisible

invit|ation /ɪnvɪ'teɪʃn/ n invitación f. **~e** /ɪn'vaɪt/ vt invitar; (ask for) pedir. ● /'ɪnvaɪt/ n 🄸 invitación f. **~ing** /ɪn'vaɪtɪŋ/ adj atrayente

invoice /'ɪnvɔɪs/ n factura f. ● vt. **~ s.o.** (for sth) pasarle a uno factura (por algo)

involuntary /ɪn'vɒləntərɪ/ adj involuntario

involve /ɪn'vɒlv/ vt (entail) suponer; (implicate) implicar. **~d** in envuelto en. **~d** adj (complex) complicado. **~ment** n participación f; (relationship) enredo m

inward /'ɪnwəd/ adj interior. ● adv hacia adentro. **~s** adv hacia dentro

iodine /'aɪədiːn/ n yodo m

ion /'aɪən/ n ion m

iota /aɪ'əʊtə/ n (amount) pizca f

IOU /aɪəʊ'juː/ abbr (= I owe you) pagaré m

IQ abbr (= intelligence quotient) CI m, cociente m intelectual

Iran /ɪ'rɑːn/ n Irán m. **~ian** /ɪ'reɪnɪən/ adj & n iraní (m)

Iraq /ɪ'rɑːk/ n Irak m. **~i** adj & n iraquí (m & f)

irate /aɪ'reɪt/ adj colérico

Ireland /'aɪələnd/ n Irlanda f

iris /'aɪərɪs/ n (of eye) iris m; (flower) lirio m

Irish /'aɪərɪʃ/ adj irlandés. ● n (language) irlandés m. npl. **the ~** (people) los irlandeses. **~man** /-mən/ n irlandés m. **~woman** n irlandesa f

iron /'aɪən/ n hierro m; (appliance) plancha f. ● adj de hierro. ● vt planchar. □ **~ out** vt allanar

ironic /aɪ'rɒnɪk/ adj irónico. **~ally** adv irónicamente

ironing board /'aɪənɪŋ/ n tabla f de planchar, burro m de planchar (Mex)

iron: ~monger /-mʌŋgə(r)/ n ferretero m. **~monger's** n ferretería f

irony /'aɪərənɪ/ n ironía f

irrational /ɪ'ræʃənl/ adj irracional

irrefutable /ɪrɪ'fjuːtəbl/ adj irrefutable

irregular /ɪ'regjʊlə(r)/ adj irregular. **~ity** /-'lærɪtɪ/ n irregularidad f

irrelevan|ce /ɪ'reləvəns/ n irrelevancia f. **~t** adj irrelevante

irreparable /ɪ'repərəbl/ adj irreparable

irreplaceable /ɪrɪ'pleɪsəbl/ adj irreemplazable

irresistible /ɪrɪ'zɪstəbl/ adj irresistible

irrespective /ɪrɪ'spektɪv/ adj. **~ of** sin tomar en cuenta

irresponsible /ɪrɪ'spɒnsəbl/ adj irresponsable

irretrievable /ɪrɪ'triːvəbl/ adj irrecuperable

irreverent /ɪ'revərənt/ adj irreverente

irrevocable /ɪˈrevəkəbl/ adj irrevocable

irrigat|e /ˈɪrɪgeɪt/ vt regar, irrigar. **∼ion** /-ˈgeɪʃn/ n riego m, irrigación f

irritable /ˈɪrɪtəbl/ adj irritable

irritat|e /ˈɪrɪteɪt/ vt irritar. **∼ed** adj irritado. **∼ing** adj irritante. **∼ion** /-ˈteɪʃn/ n irritación f

IRS abbr (Amer) see **INTERNAL REVENUE SERVICE**

is /ɪz/ see **BE**

ISDN abbr (**Integrated Services Digital Network**) RDSI

Islam /ˈɪzlɑːm/ n el Islam. **∼ic** /ɪzˈlæmɪk/ adj islámico

island /ˈaɪlənd/ n isla f. **∼er** n isleño m

isolat|e /ˈaɪsəleɪt/ vt aislar. **∼ion** /-ˈleɪʃn/ n aislamiento m

Israel /ˈɪzreɪl/ n Israel m. **∼i** /ɪzˈreɪlɪ/ adj & n israelí (m)

issue /ˈɪʃuː/ n tema m, asunto m; (of magazine etc) número m; (of stamps, bank notes) emisión f; (of documents) expedición f. **take ∼ with** discrepar de. ● vt hacer público (statement); expedir (documents); emitir (stamps etc); prestar (library book)

! Note, however, that in some cases él or ella must be used e.g. **he picked up the spoon and hit me with it** agarró la cuchara y me golpeó con ella

it /ɪt/ pronoun

••••▸ (as subject) generally not translated. **it's huge** es enorme. **where is it?** ¿dónde está?. **it's all lies** son todas mentiras

••••▸ (as direct object) **lo** (m), **la** (f). **he read it to me** me lo/la leyó. **give it to me** dámelo/dámela

••••▸ (as indirect object) **le**. **I gave it another coat of paint** le di otra mano de pintura

••••▸ (after a preposition) generally not translated. **there's nothing behind it** no hay nada detrás

••••▸ (at door) **who is it?** ¿quién es?. **it's me** soy yo; (on telephone) **who is it, please?** ¿quién habla, por favor?; (before passing on to sb else) ¿de parte de quién, por favor? **it's Carol** soy Carol (Spain), habla Carol

••••▸ (in impersonal constructions) **it is well known that ...** bien se sabe que ... **it's five o'clock** son las cinco. **so it seems** así parece

••••▸ **that's it** (that's right) eso es; (that's enough, that's finished) ya está

Italian /ɪˈtæljən/ adj & n italiano (m)

italics /ɪˈtælɪks/ npl (letra f) cursiva f

Italy /ˈɪtəlɪ/ n Italia f

itch /ɪtʃ/ n picazón f. ● vi picar. **I'm ∼ing to** estoy que me muero por. **my arm ∼es** me pica el brazo. **∼y** adj que pica. **I've got an ∼y nose** me pica la nariz

it'd /ˈɪtəd/ = **it had**, **it would**

item /ˈaɪtəm/ n artículo m; (on agenda) punto m. **news ∼** n noticia f. **∼ize** vt detallar

itinerary /aɪˈtɪnərərɪ/ n itinerario m

it'll /ˈɪtl/ = **it will**

its /ɪts/ adj su, sus (pl). ● pron (el)

suyo *m*, (la) suya *f*, (los) suyos *mpl*, (las) suyas *fpl*

it's /ɪts/ = **it is, it has**

itself /ɪt'self/ *pron* él mismo, ella misma, ello mismo; (*reflexive*) se; (*after prep*) sí mismo, sí misma

I've /aɪv/ = **I have**

ivory /'aɪvərɪ/ *n* marfil *m*. ~ **tower** *n* torre *f* de marfil

ivy /'aɪvɪ/ *n* hiedra *f*

> **Ivy League - the** El grupo de universidades más antiguas y respetadas de EE.UU. Situadas al noreste del país, son: Harvard, Yale, Columbia, Cornell, Dartmouth College, Brown, Princeton y Pensylvania. El término proviene de la hiedra que crece en los antiguos edificios de estos establecimientos.

Jj

jab /dʒæb/ *vt* (*pt* **jabbed**) pinchar; (*thrust*) hurgonear. ● *n* pinchazo *m*

jack /dʒæk/ *n* (*Mec*) gato *m*; (*socket*) enchufe *m* hembra; (*Cards*) sota *f*. □ ~ **up** *vt* alzar con gato

jackal /'dʒækl/ *n* chacal *m*

jackdaw /'dʒækdɔː/ *n* grajilla *f*

jacket /'dʒækɪt/ *n* chaqueta *f*; (*casual*) americana *f*, saco *m* (*LAm*); (*Amer, of book*) sobrecubierta *f*; (*of record*) funda *f*, carátula *f*

jack: ~ **knife** *vi* (*lorry*) plegarse. ~**pot** *n* premio *m* gordo. **hit the** ~**pot** sacar el premio gordo

jade /dʒeɪd/ *n* (*stone*) jade *m*

jagged /'dʒægɪd/ *adj* (edge, cut) irregular; (rock) recortado

jaguar /'dʒægjʊə(r)/ *n* jaguar *m*

jail /dʒeɪl/ *n* cárcel *m*, prisión *f*. ● *vt* encarcelar. ~**er** *n* carcelero *m*. ~**house** *n* (*Amer*) cárcel *f*

jam /dʒæm/ *vt* (*pt* **jammed**) interferir con (radio); atestar (road). ~ **sth into sth** meter algo a la fuerza en algo. ● *vi* (brakes) bloquearse; (machine) trancarse. ● *n* mermelada *f*; (*fam, situation*) apuro *m*

jangle /'dʒæŋgl/ *n* sonido *m* metálico (y áspero). ● *vi* hacer ruido (metálico)

janitor /'dʒænɪtə(r)/ *n* portero *m*

January /'dʒænjʊərɪ/ *n* enero *m*

Japan /dʒə'pæn/ *n* (el) Japón *m*. ~**ese** /dʒæpə'niːz/ *adj* & *n* invar japonés (*m*)

jar /dʒɑː(r)/ *n* tarro *m*, bote *m*. ● *vi* (*pt* **jarred**) (clash) desentonar. ● *vt* sacudir

jargon /'dʒɑːgən/ *n* jerga *f*

jaundice /'dʒɔːndɪs/ *n* ictericia *f*

jaunt /dʒɔːnt/ *n* excursión *f*

jaunty /'dʒɔːntɪ/ *adj* (**-ier, -iest**) garboso

jaw /dʒɔː/ *n* mandíbula *f*. ~**s** *npl* fauces *fpl*. ~**bone** *n* mandíbula *f*, maxilar *m*; (*of animal*) quijada *f*

jay /dʒeɪ/ *n* arrendajo *m*. ~**walk** *vi* cruzar la calle descuidadamente. ~**walker** *n* peatón *m* imprudente

jazz /dʒæz/ *n* jazz *m*. □ ~ **up** *vt* animar. ~**y** *adj* chillón

jealous /'dʒeləs/ *adj* celoso; (*envious*) envidioso. ~**y** *n* celos *mpl*

jeans /dʒiːnz/ *npl* vaqueros *mpl*, jeans *mpl*, tejanos *mpl*, pantalones *mpl* de mezclilla (*Mex*)

Jeep (*P*), **jeep** /dʒiːp/ *n* jeep *m* (*P*)

jeer /dʒɪə(r)/ *vi*. ~ **at** mofarse de;

(*boo*) abuchear. ● *n* burla *f*; (*boo*) abucheo *m*

Jell-O /'dʒeləʊ/ *n* (P) (*Amer*) gelatina *f* (con sabor a frutas)

jelly /'dʒelɪ/ *n* (*clear jam*) jalea *f*; (*pudding*) see **JELL-O**; (*substance*) gelatina *f*. **~fish** *n* (*pl invar* or **-es**) medusa *f*

jeopardize /'dʒepədaɪz/ *vt* arriesgar

jerk /dʒɜːk/ *n* sacudida *f*; (*sl, fool*) idiota *m* & *f*. ● *vt* sacudir

jersey /'dʒɜːzɪ/ *n* (*pl* **-eys**) jersey *m*, suéter *m*, pulóver *m*

jest /dʒest/ *n* broma *f*. ● *vi* bromear

Jesus /'dʒiːzəs/ *n* Jesús *m*

jet /dʒet/ *n* (*stream*) chorro *m*; (*plane*) avión *m* (con motor a reacción); (*mineral*) azabache *m*. **~-black** /-'blæk/ *adj* azabache negro a *invar*. **~ lag** *n* jet lag *m*, desfase *f* horario. **have ~ lag** estar desfasado. **~-propelled** /-prə 'peld/ *adj* (de propulsión) a reacción

jettison /'dʒetɪsn/ *vt* echar al mar; (*fig, discard*) deshacerse de

jetty /'dʒetɪ/ *n* muelle *m*

Jew /dʒu:/ *n* judío *m*

jewel /'dʒu:əl/ *n* joya *f*. **~ler** *n* joyero *m*. **~lery** *n* joyas *fpl*

Jewish /'dʒu:ɪʃ/ *adj* judío

jiffy /'dʒɪfɪ/ *n* momentito *m*. **do sth in a ~** hacer algo en un santiamén

jig /dʒɪg/ *n* (*dance*) giga *f*

jigsaw /'dʒɪgsɔ:/ *n*. **~ (puzzle)** rompecabezas *m*

jilt /dʒɪlt/ *vt* dejar plantado

jingle /'dʒɪŋgl/ *vt* hacer sonar. ● *vi* tintinear. ● *n* tintineo *m*; (*advert*) jingle *m* (publicitario)

job /dʒɒb/ *n* empleo *m*, trabajo *m*; (*piece of work*) trabajo *m*. **it is a**

good ~ that menos mal que. **~less** *adj* desempleado

jockey /'dʒɒkɪ/ *n* jockey *m*

jocular /'dʒɒkjʊlə(r)/ *adj* jocoso

jog /dʒɒg/ *vt* (*pt* **jogged**) empujar; refrescar (memory). ● *vi* hacer footing, hacer jogging. **~er** *n* persona *f* que hace footing. **~ging** *n* footing *m*, jogging *m*. **go ~ging** salir a hacer footing or jogging

join /dʒɔɪn/ *vt* (*link*) unir; hacerse socio de (club); hacerse miembro de (political group); alistarse en (army); reunirse con (another person). ● *n* juntura. ● *vi*. **~ together** (parts) unirse; (roads etc) empalmar; (rivers) confluir. **~ in** *vi* participar (en). □ **~ up** *vi* (*Mil*) alistarse. **~er** *n* carpintero *m*

joint /dʒɔɪnt/ *adj* conjunto. ● *n* (*join*) unión *f*, junta *f*; (*in limbs*) articulación *f*. (*Culin*) trozo *m* de carne (para asar). **out of ~** descoyuntado. **~ account** *n* cuenta *f* conjunta. **~ly** *adv* conjuntamente. **~ owner** *n* copropietario *m*.

joist /dʒɔɪst/ *n* viga *f*

jok|e /dʒəʊk/ *n* (*story*) chiste *m*; (*practical joke*) broma *f*. ● *vi* bromear. **~er** *n* bromista *m* & *f*; (*Cards*) comodín *m*. **~y** *adj* jocoso

jolly /'dʒɒlɪ/ *adj* (**-ier, -iest**) alegre. ● *adv* 🔲 muy

jolt /dʒɒlt/ *vt* sacudir. ● *vi* (vehicle) dar una sacudida. ● *n* sacudida *f*

jostle /'dʒɒsl/ *vt* empujar. ● *vi* empujarse

jot /dʒɒt/ *n* pizca *f*. ● *vt* (*pt* **jotted**). □ **~ down** *vt* apuntar (rápidamente). **~ter** *n* bloc *m*

journal /'dʒɜ:nl/ *n* (*diary*) diario *m*; (*newspaper*) periódico *m*; (*magazine*) revista *f*. **~ism** *n* periodismo *m*. **~ist** *n* periodista *m* & *f*

journey /'dʒɜːnɪ/ n viaje m. **go on a** ~ hacer un viaje. ● vi viajar

jovial /'dʒəʊvɪəl/ adj jovial

joy /dʒɔɪ/ n alegría f. ~**ful** adj feliz. ~**ous** adj feliz. ~**rider** n joven m que roba un coche para dar una vuelta. ~**stick** n (in aircraft) palanca f de mando; (Comp) mando m, joystick m

jubila|nt /'dʒuːbɪlənt/ adj jubiloso. ~**tion** /-'leɪʃn/ n júbilo m

jubilee /'dʒuːbɪliː/ n aniversario m especial

Judaism /'dʒuːdeɪɪzəm/ n judaísmo m

judge /dʒʌdʒ/ n juez m. ● vt juzgar. ~**ment** n juicio m

judicia|l /dʒuː'dɪʃl/ adj judicial. ~**ry** /-ərɪ/ n judicatura f

judo /'dʒuːdəʊ/ n judo m

jug /dʒʌɡ/ n jarra f

juggernaut /'dʒʌɡənɔːt/ n camión m grande

juggle /'dʒʌɡl/ vi hacer malabarismos. ● vt hacer malabarismos con. ~**r** n malabarista m & f

juic|e /dʒuːs/ n jugo m, zumo m. ~**y** adj jugoso, zumoso; (story etc) ⒤ picante

jukebox /'dʒuːkbɒks/ n máquina f de discos, rocola f (LAm)

July /dʒuː'laɪ/ n julio m

jumble /'dʒʌmbl/ vt. ~ (**up**) mezclar. ● n (muddle) revoltijo m. ~ **sale** n venta f de objetos usados m

jumbo /'dʒʌmbəʊ/ adj gigante. ~ **jet** n jumbo m

jump /dʒʌmp/ vt saltar. ~ **rope** (Amer) saltar a la comba, saltar a la cuerda. ~ **the gun** obrar prematuramente. ~ **the queue** colarse. ● vi saltar; (start) sobresaltarse; (prices) alzarse. ~ **at an opportunity** apresurarse a aprovechar

una oportunidad. ● n salto m; (start) susto m; (increase) aumento m. ~**er** n jersey m, suéter m, pulóver m; (Amer, dress) pichi m, jumper m & f (LAm). ~**er cables** (Amer), ~ **leads** npl cables mpl de arranque. ~ **rope** (Amer) comba f, cuerda f, reata f (Mex). ~**suit** n mono m. ~**y** adj nervioso

junction /'dʒʌŋkʃn/ n (of roads, rails) cruce m; (Elec) empalme m

June /dʒuːn/ n junio m

jungle /'dʒʌŋɡl/ n selva f, jungla f

junior /'dʒuːnɪə(r)/ adj (in age) más joven (**to** sure); (in rank) subalterno. ● n menor m

junk /dʒʌŋk/ n trastos mpl viejos; (worthless stuff) basura f. ● vt ⒤ tirar. ~ **food** n comida f basura, alimento m chatarra (Mex). ~**ie** /'dʒʌŋkɪ/ n ⒤ drogadicto m, yonqui m & f ⒤. ~ **mail** n propaganda f que se recibe por correo. ~ **shop** n tienda f de trastos viejos

junta /'dʒʌntə/ n junta f militar

Jupiter /'dʒuːpɪtə(r)/ n Júpiter m

jurisdiction /dʒʊərɪs'dɪkʃn/ n jurisdicción f

jur|or /'dʒʊərə(r)/ n (miembro m de un) jurado m. ~**y** n jurado m

just /dʒʌst/ adj (fair) justo. ● adv exactamente, justo; (barely) justo; (only) sólo, solamente. ~ **as tall** tan alto (**as** como). ~ **listen!** ¡escucha! **he has** ~ **arrived** acaba de llegar, recién llegó (LAm)

justice /'dʒʌstɪs/ n justicia f. **J**~ **of the Peace** juez m de paz

justif|iable /dʒʌstɪ'faɪəbl/ adj justificable. ~**iably** adv con razón. ~**ication** /dʒʌstɪfɪ'keɪʃn/ n justificación f. ~**y** /'dʒʌstɪfaɪ/ vt justificar

jut /dʒʌt/ vi (pt jutted). ~ (**out**)

sobresalir

juvenile /'dʒuːvənaɪl/ *adj* juvenil; (*childish*) infantil. ●*n* (*Jurid*) menor *m & f*

Kk

kaleidoscope /kə'laɪdəskəʊp/ *n* caleidoscopio *m*

kangaroo /kæŋgə'ruː/ *n* canguro *m*

karate /kə'rɑːtɪ/ *n* kárate *m*, karate *m* (*LAm*)

keel /kiːl/ *n* (*of ship*) quilla *f*. □~ **over** *vi* volcar(se)

keen /kiːn/ *adj* (**-er**, **-est**) (*interest, feeling*) vivo; (*wind, mind, analysis*) penetrante; (*eyesight*) agudo; (*eager*) entusiasta. **I'm ~ on golf** me encanta el golf. **he's ~ on Shostakovich** le gusta Shostakovich. **~ly** *adv* vivamente; (*enthusiastically*) con entusiasmo. **~ness** *n* intensidad *f*; (*enthusiasm*) entusiasmo *m*

keep /kiːp/ *vt* (*pt* **kept**) guardar; cumplir (*promise*); tener (*shop, animals*); mantener (*family*); observar (*rule*); (*celebrate*) celebrar; (*delay*) detener; (*prevent*) impedir. ●*vi* (*food*) conservarse; (*remain*) quedarse; (*continue*) seguir. **~ doing** seguir haciendo. ●*n* subsistencia *f*; (*of castle*) torreón *m*. **for ~s** 🔢 para siempre. □~ **back** *vt* retener. ●*vi* no acercarse. □~ **in** *vt* no dejar salir. □~ **off** *vt* mantenerse alejado de (land). '~ **off the grass**' 'prohibido pisar el césped'. □~ **on** *vi* seguir. □~ **on doing sth**

seguir haciendo. □~ **out** *vt* no dejar entrar. □~ **up** *vt* mantener. □~ **up with** *vt* estar al día en

kennel /'kenl/ *n* casa *f* del perro; (*Amer, for boarding*) residencia *f* canina. **~s** *n invar* residencia *f* canina

kept /kept/ *see* KEEP

kerb /kɜːb/ *n* bordillo *m* (de la acera), borde *m* de la banqueta (*Mex*)

kerosene /'kerəsiːn/ *n* queroseno *m*

ketchup /'ketʃʌp/ *n* salsa *f* de tomate

kettle /'ketl/ *n* pava *f*, tetera *f* (para calentar agua)

key /kiː/ *n* llave *f*; (*of computer, piano*) tecla *f*; (*Mus*) tono *m*. **be off ~** no estar en el tono. ●*adj* clave. □~ **in** *vt* teclear. **~board** *n* teclado *m*. **~hole** *n* ojo *m* de la cerradura. **~ring** *n* llavero *m*

khaki /'kɑːkɪ/ *adj* caqui

kick /kɪk/ *vt* dar una patada a (person); patear (ball). ●*vi* dar patadas; (*horse*) cocear. ●*n* patada *f*; (*of horse*) coz *f*; (*fam, thrill*) placer *m*. □~ **up** *vt* 🔢 echar. □~ **up** *vt* armar (fuss etc). **~off** *n* (*Sport*) saque *m* inicial. □~ **start** *vt* arrancar (con el pedal de arranque) (engine)

kid /kɪd/ *n* (*young goat*) cabrito *m*; (*fam, child*) niño *m*, chaval *m*, escuincle *m* (*Mex*). ●*vt* (*pt* **kidded**) tomar el pelo a. ●*vi* bromear

kidnap /'kɪdnæp/ *vt* (*pt* **kidnapped**) secuestrar. **~per** *n* secuestrador *m*. **~ping** *n* secuestro *m*

kidney /'kɪdnɪ/ *n* riñón *m*

kill /kɪl/ *vt* matar; (*fig*) acabar con. ●*n* matanza *f*. □~ **off** *vt* matar. **~er** *n* asesino *m*. **~ing** *n* matanza *f*; (*murder*) asesinato *m*. **make a**

∼ing (fig) hacer un gran negocio

kiln /kɪln/ n horno m

kilo /'kiːləʊ/ n (pl -os) kilo m. **∼gram(me)** /'kɪləgræm/ n kilogramo m. **∼metre** /'kɪləmiːtə(r), /kɪ'lɒmɪtə(r)/ n kilómetro m. **∼watt** /'kɪləwɒt/ n kilovatio m

kilt /kɪlt/ n falda f escocesa

kin /kɪn/ n familiares mpl

kind /kaɪnd/ n tipo m, clase f. **∼ of** (fam, somewhat) un poco. **in ∼** en especie. **be two of a ∼** ser tal para cual. ● adj amable

kindergarten /'kɪndəgɑːtn/ n jardín m de infancia

kind-hearted /kaɪnd'hɑːtɪd/ adj bondadoso

kindle /'kɪndl/ vt encender

kind|ly adj (-ier, -iest) bondadoso. ● adv amablemente; (please) haga el favor de. **∼ness** n bondad f; (act) favor m

king /kɪŋ/ n rey m. **∼dom** n reino m. **∼fisher** n martín m pescador. **∼-size(d)** adj extragrande

kink /kɪŋk/ n (in rope) vuelta f, curva f; (in hair) onda f. **∼y** adj 🄸 pervertido

kiosk /'kiːɒsk/ n quiosco m

kipper /'kɪpə(r)/ n arenque m ahumado

kiss /kɪs/ n beso m. ● vt besar. ● vi besarse

kit /kɪt/ n avíos mpl. **tool ∼** caja f de herramientas. **□ ∼ out** vt (pt kitted) equipar

kitchen /'kɪtʃɪn/ n cocina f

kite /kaɪt/ n cometa f, papalote m (Mex)

kitten /'kɪtn/ n gatito m

knack /næk/ n truco m

knapsack /'næpsæk/ n mochila f

knead /niːd/ vt amasar

knee /niː/ n rodilla f. **∼cap** n rótula f

kneel /niːl/ vi (pt kneeled or knelt). **∼ (down)** arrodillarse; (be on one's knees) estar arrodillado

knelt /nelt/ see KNEEL

knew /njuː/ see KNOW

knickers /'nɪkəz/ npl bragas fpl, calzones mpl (LAm), pantaletas fpl (Mex)

knife /naɪf/ n (pl knives) cuchillo m. ● vt acuchillar

knight /naɪt/ n caballero m; (Chess) caballo m. ● vt conceder el título de Sir a. **∼hood** n título m de Sir

knit /nɪt/ vt (pt knitted or knit) hacer, tejer (LAm). ● vi tejer, hacer punto. **∼ one's brow** fruncir el ceño. **∼ting** n tejido m, punto m. **∼ting needle** n aguja f de hacer punto, aguja f de tejer

knives /naɪvz/ see KNIFE

knob /nɒb/ n botón m; (of door, drawer etc) tirador m. **∼bly** adj nudoso

knock /nɒk/ vt golpear; (criticize) criticar. ● vi golpear; (at door) llamar, golpear. ● n golpe m. **□ ∼ about** vt maltratar. **□ ∼ down** vt derribar; atropellar (person). **□ ∼ off** vt hacer caer. ● vi (fam, finish work) terminar, salir del trabajo. **□ ∼ out** vt (by blow) dejar sin sentido; (eliminate) eliminar. **□ ∼ over** vt tirar; atropellar (person). **∼er** n aldaba f. **∼-kneed** /-'niːd/ adj patizambo. **∼out** n (Boxing) nocaut m

knot /nɒt/ n nudo m. ● vt (pt knotted) anudar

know /nəʊ/ vt (pt knew) saber; (be acquainted with) conocer. **let s.o. ∼ sth** decirle algo a uno;

(warn) avisarle algo a uno. ● vi saber. ~ **how to do sth** saber hacer algo. ~ **about** entender de (cars etc.). ~ **of** saber de. ● n. **be in the** ~ estar enterado. ~**all** n n sabelotodo m & f. ~**-how** n knowhow m, conocimientos mpl y experiencia. ~**ingly** adv a sabiendas. ~**-it-all** n (Amer) see ~**-ALL**

knowledge /'nɒlɪdʒ/ n saber m; (awareness) conocimiento m; (learning) conocimientos mpl. ~**able** adj informado

known /nəʊn/ see **KNOW**. ● adj conocido

knuckle /'nʌkl/ n nudillo m. □~ **under** vi someterse

Korea /kə'rɪə/ n Corea f. ~**n** adj & n coreano (m)

kudos /'kju:dɒs/ n prestigio m

....

Ll

....

lab /læb/ n 🄴 laboratorio m
label /'leɪbl/ n etiqueta f. ● vt (pt labelled) poner etiqueta a; (fig, describe as) tachar de
laboratory /lə'bɒrətərɪ/ n laboratorio m
laborious /lə'bɔ:rɪəs/ adj penoso
labour /'leɪbə(r)/ n trabajo m; (workers) mano f de obra; (Med) parto m. **in** ~ de parto. ● vi trabajar. ● vt insistir en. **L**~ n el partido m laborista. ● adj laborista. ~**er** n peón m
lace /leɪs/ n encaje m; (of shoe) cordón m, agujeta f (Mex). ● vt (fasten) atar
lacerate /'læsəreɪt/ vt lacerar

lack /læk/ n falta f. **for** ~ **of** por falta de. ● vt faltarle a uno. **he** ~**s confidence** le falta confianza en sí mismo. ~**ing** adj. **be** ~**ing** faltar. **be** ~**ing in** no tener
lad /læd/ n muchacho m
ladder /'lædə(r)/ n escalera f (de mano); (in stocking) carrera f. ● vt hacerse una carrera en. ● vi hacérsele una carrera a
laden /'leɪdn/ adj cargado (**with** de)
ladle /'leɪdl/ n cucharón m
lady /'leɪdɪ/ n señora f. **young** ~ señorita f. ~**bird** n, ~**bug** n (Amer) mariquita f, catarina f (Mex). ~**-in-waiting** n dama f de honor. ~**like** adj fino
lag /læg/ vi (pt lagged). ~ (**behind**) retrasarse. ● vt revestir (pipes). ● n (interval) intervalo m
lager /'lɑ:gə(r)/ n cerveza f (rubia)
lagging /'lægɪŋ/ n revestimiento m
lagoon /lə'gu:n/ n laguna f
laid /leɪd/ see **LAY**
lain /leɪn/ see **LIE**[1]
lair /leə(r)/ n guarida f
lake /leɪk/ n lago m
lamb /læm/ n cordero m
lame /leɪm/ adj (-er, -est) cojo, rengo (LAm); (excuse) pobre, malo
lament /lə'ment/ n lamento m. ● vt lamentar. ~**able** /'læməntəbl/ adj lamentable
lamp /læmp/ n lámpara f
lamp: ~post n farol m. ~**shade** n pantalla f
lance /lɑ:ns/ n lanza f
land /lænd/ n tierra f; (country) país m; (plot) terreno m. ● vt desembarcar; (obtain) conseguir; dar (blow). ● vi (from ship) desembar-

lane | laugh

car; (*aircraft*) aterrizar. □ **~ up** *vi* ir a parar. **~ing** *n* desembarque *m*; (*by aircraft*) aterrizaje *m*; (*top of stairs*) descanso *m*. **~lady** *n* casera *f*; (*of inn*) dueña *f*. **~lord** *n* casero *m*, dueño *m*; (*of inn*) dueño *m*. **~mark** *n* punto *m* destacado. **~scape** /-skeɪp/ *n* paisaje *m*. **~slide** *n* desprendimiento *m* de tierras; (*Pol*) victoria *f* arrolladora

lane /leɪn/ *n* (*path, road*) camino *m*, sendero *m*; (*strip of road*) carril *m*

language /ˈlæŋgwɪdʒ/ *n* idioma *m*; (*speech, style*) lenguaje *m*

lank /læŋk/ *adj* (*hair*) lacio. **~y** *adj* (*-ier, -iest*) larguirucho

lantern /ˈlæntən/ *n* linterna *f*

lap /læp/ *n* (*of body*) rodillas *fpl*; (*Sport*) vuelta *f*. □ **~ up** *vt* (*pt* **lapped**) beber a lengüetazos; (*fig*) aceptar con entusiasmo. ● *vi* (*waves*) chapotear

lapel /ləˈpel/ *n* solapa *f*

lapse /læps/ *vi* (*decline*) degradarse; (*expire*) caducar; (*time*) transcurrir. **~ into silence** callarse. ● *n* error *m*; (*of time*) intervalo *m*

laptop /ˈlæptɒp/ *n*. **~ (computer)** laptop *m*, portátil *m*

lard /lɑːd/ *n* manteca *f* de cerdo

larder /ˈlɑːdə(r)/ *n* despensa *f*

large /lɑːdʒ/ *adj* (*-er, -est*) grande, (*before singular noun*) gran. ● *n*. at **~ en libertad. ~ly** *adv* en gran parte

lark /lɑːk/ *n* (*bird*) alondra *f*; (*joke*) broma *f*; (*bit of fun*) travesura *f*. □ **~ about** *vt* hacer el tonto 🔲

larva /ˈlɑːvə/ *n* (*pl* **-vae** /-viː/) larva *f*

laser /ˈleɪzə(r)/ *n* láser *m*. **~ beam** *n* rayo *m* láser. **~ printer** *n* impresora *f* láser

lash /læʃ/ *vt* azotar. □ **~ out** *vi* atacar. **~ out against** *vt* atacar. ● *n* latigazo *m*; (*eyelash*) pestaña *f*; (*whip*) látigo *m*

lashings /ˈlæʃɪŋz/ *npl*. **~ of** (*fam, cream etc*) montones de

lass /læs/ *n* muchacha *f*

lasso /læˈsuː/ *n* (*pl* **-os**) lazo *m*

last /lɑːst/ *adj* último; (*week etc*) pasado. **~ Monday** el lunes pasado. **~ night** anoche. ● *adv* por último; (*most recently*) la última vez. **he came ~** llegó el último. ● *n* último *m*; (*remainder*) lo que queda. **~ but one** penúltimo. **at (long) ~** por fin. ● *vi/t* durar. □ **~ out** *vi* sobrevivir. **~ing** *adj* duradero. **~ly** *adv* por último

latch /lætʃ/ *n* pestillo *m*

late /leɪt/ *adj* (*-er, -est*) (*not on time*) tarde; (*recent*) reciente; (*former*) antiguo, ex. **be ~** llegar tarde. **in ~ July** a fines de julio. **the ~ Dr Phillips** el difunto Dr. Phillips. ● *adv* tarde. **~ly** *adv* últimamente

latent /ˈleɪtnt/ *adj* latente

later /ˈleɪtə(r)/ *adv* más tarde

lateral /ˈlætərəl/ *adj* lateral

latest /ˈleɪtɪst/ *adj* último. ● *n*. **at the ~** a más tardar

lathe /leɪð/ *n* torno *m*

lather /ˈlɑːðə(r)/ *n* espuma *f*

Latin /ˈlætɪn/ *n* (*language*) latín *m*. ● *adj* latino. **~ America** *n* América *f* Latina, Latinoamérica *f*. **~ American** *adj* & *n* latinoamericano *f*

latitude /ˈlætɪtjuːd/ *n* latitud *m*

latter /ˈlætə(r)/ *adj* último; (*of two*) segundo. ● *n*. **the ~** éste *m*, ésta *f*, éstos *mpl*, éstas *fpl*

laugh /lɑːf/ *vi* reír(se). **~ at** reírse de. ● *n* risa *f*. **~able** *adj* ridículo. **~ing stock** *n* hazmerreír *m*. **~ter**

n risas *fpl*

launch /lɔːntʃ/ *vt* lanzar; botar (new vessel). ● *n* lanzamiento *m*; (of new vessel) botadura *f*; (boat) lancha *f* (a motor). **~ing pad** ~ **pad** *n* plataforma *f* de lanzamiento

laund|er /ˈlɔːndə(r)/ *vt* lavar (y planchar). **~erette** /-et/, **L~romat** /ˈlɔːndrəmæt/ (Amer) (P) *n* lavandería *f* automática. **~ry** *n* (place) lavandería *f*; (dirty clothes) ropa *f* sucia; (clean clothes) ropa *f* limpia

lava /ˈlɑːvə/ *n* lava *f*

lavatory /ˈlævətərɪ/ *n* (cuarto *m* de) baño *m*. **public ~** servicios *mpl*, baños *mpl* (LAm)

lavish /ˈlævɪʃ/ *adj* (lifestyle) de derroche; (meal) espléndido; (production) fastuoso. ● *vt* prodigar (**on** a)

law /lɔː/ *n* ley *f*; (profession, subject of study) derecho *m*. **~ and order** *n* orden *m* público. **~ court** *n* tribunal *m*

lawn /lɔːn/ *n* césped *m*, pasto *m* (LAm). **~mower** *n* cortacésped *f*, cortadora *f* de pasto (LAm)

lawsuit /ˈlɔːsuːt/ *n* juicio *m*

lawyer /ˈlɔːjə(r)/ *n* abogado *m*

lax /læks/ *adj* descuidado; (morals etc) laxo

laxative /ˈlæksətɪv/ *n* laxante *m*

lay /leɪ/ *see* **LIE**. ● *vt* (*pt* **laid**) poner (also table, eggs); tender (trap); formar (plan). **~ hands on** echar mano a. **~ hold of** agarrar. ● *adj* (non-clerical) laico; (opinion etc) profano. □ **~ down** *vt* dejar a un lado; imponer (condition). □ **~ into** *vt* 🙰 dar una paliza a. □ **~ off** *vt* despedir (worker). *vi* 🙰 terminar. □ **~ on** *vt* (provide) proveer. □ **~ out** *vt* (design) disponer; (display) exponer; gastar (money). **~about**

n holgazán. **~by** *n* área *f* de reposo

layer /ˈleɪə(r)/ *n* capa *f*

layette /leɪˈet/ *n* canastilla *f*

layman /ˈleɪmən/ *n* (*pl* **-men**) lego *m*

layout /ˈleɪaʊt/ *n* disposición *f*

laz|e /leɪz/ *vi* holgazanear; (relax) descansar. **~iness** *n* pereza *f*. **~y** *adj* perezoso. **~ybones** *n* holgazán *m*

lead[1] /liːd/ *vt* (*pt* **led**) conducir; dirigir (team); llevar (life); encabezar (parade, attack). **I was led to believe that ...** me dieron a entender que .... ● *vi* (go first) ir delante; (in race) aventajar. ● *n* mando *m*; (clue) pista *f*; (leash) correa *f*; (wire) cable *m*. **be in the ~** llevar la delantera

lead[2] /led/ *n* plomo *m*; (of pencil) mina *f*. **~ed** *adj* (fuel) con plomo

lead: /liːd/ **~er** *n* jefe *m*; (Pol) líder *m* & *f*; (of gang) cabecilla *m*. **~ership** *n* dirección *f*. **~ing** *adj* principal; (in front) delantero

leaf /liːf/ *n* (*pl* **leaves**) hoja *f*. □ **~ through** *vi* hojear. **~let** /ˈliːflɪt/ *n* folleto *m*. **~y** *adj* frondoso

league /liːɡ/ *n* liga *f*. **be in ~ with** estar aliado con

leak /liːk/ *n* (hole) agujero *m*; (of gas, liquid) escape *m*; (of information) filtración *f*; (in roof) gotera *f*; (in boat) vía *f* de agua. ● *vi* gotear; (liquid) salirse; (boat) hacer agua. ● *vt* perder; filtrar (information). **~y** *adj* (receptacle) agujereado; (roof) que tiene goteras

lean /liːn/ *vt* (*pt* **leaned** or **leant** /lent/) apoyar. ● *vi* inclinarse. □ **~ against** *vt* apoyarse en. □ **~ on** *vt* apoyarse en. □ **~ out** *vt* asomarse (**of** a). □ **~ over** *vi* inclinarse ● *adj* (-er, -est) (person) delgado;

(animal) flaco; (meat) magro. **~ing** adj inclinado. **~-to** n colgadizo m

leap /li:p/ vi (pt **leaped** or **leapt** /lept/) saltar. ● n salto m. **~frog** n. **play ~frog** saltar al potro, jugar a la pídola, brincar al burro (Mex). ● vi (pt **-frogged**) saltar. **~ year** n año m bisiesto

learn /lɜ:n/ vt/i (pt **learned** or **learnt**) aprender (**to do** a hacer). **~ed** /-ɪd/ adj culto. **~er** n principiante m & f; (apprentice) aprendiz m. **~ing curve** n. **~ing curve** n curva f del aprendizaje

lease /li:s/ n arriendo m. ● vt arrendar

leash /li:ʃ/ n correa f

least /li:st/ adj (smallest amount of) mínimo; (slightest) menor; (smallest) más pequeño. ● n. **the ~ lo** menos. **at ~** por lo menos. **not in the ~** en absoluto. ● adv menos

leather /'leðə(r)/ n piel f, cuero m

leave /li:v/ vt (pt **left**) dejar; (depart from) salir de. **~ alone** dejar de tocar (thing); dejar en paz (person). ● vi marcharse; (train) salir. ● n permiso m. □ **~ behind** vt dejar. □ **~ out** vt omitir. □ **~ over** vt. **be left over** quedar. **on ~** (Mil) de permiso

leaves /li:vz/ see **LEAF**

lecture /'lektʃə(r)/ n conferencia f; (Univ) clase f; (rebuke) sermón m. ● vi dar clase. ● vt (scold) sermonear. **~r** n conferenciante m & f, conferencista m & f (LAm); (Univ) profesor m universitario

led /led/ see **LEAD**[^1]

ledge /ledʒ/ n cornisa f; (of window) alféizar m

leek /li:k/ n puerro m

leer /'lɪə(r)/ vi. **~ at** mirar impúdicamente. ● n mirada impúdica f

left /left/ see **LEAVE**. adj izquierdo. ● adv a la izquierda. ● n izquierda f. **~-handed** /-'hændɪd/ adj zurdo. **~ luggage** n consigna f. **~overs** npl restos mpl. **~-wing** /-'wɪŋ/ adj izquierdista

leg /leg/ n pierna f; (of animal, furniture) pata f; (of pork) pernil m; (of lamb) pierna f; (of journey) etapa f. **on its last ~s** en las últimas. **pull s.o.'s ~** 🔟 tomarle el pelo a uno

legacy /'legəsɪ/ n herencia f

legal /'li:gl/ adj (permitted by law) lícito; (recognized by law) legítimo; (system etc) jurídico. **~ity** /li:'gælətɪ/ n legalidad f. **~ize** vt legalizar. **~ly** adv legalmente

legend /'ledʒənd/ n leyenda f. **~ary** adj legendario

legible /'ledʒəbl/ adj legible

legislat|e /'ledʒɪsleɪt/ vi legislar. **~ion** /-'leɪʃn/ n legislación f

legitimate /lɪ'dʒɪtɪmət/ adj legítimo

leisure /'leʒə(r)/ n ocio m. **at your ~** cuando le venga bien. **~ly** adj lento, pausado

lemon /'lemən/ n limón m. **~ade** /-'neɪd/ n (fizzy) gaseosa f (de limón); (still) limonada f

lend /lend/ vt (pt **lent**) prestar. **~ing** n préstamo f

length /leŋθ/ n largo m; (of time) duración f; (of cloth) largo m. **at ~** (at last) por fin. **at (great) ~** detalladamente. **~en** /'leŋθən/ vt alargar. ● vi alargarse. **~ways** adv a lo largo. **~y** adj largo

lenient /'li:nɪənt/ adj indulgente

lens /lenz/ n lente f; (of camera) objetivo m. **(contact) ~es** npl (optics) lentillas fpl, lentes mpl de

[^1]: LEAD¹

contacto (LAm)

lent /lent/ see **LEND**

Lent /lent/ n cuaresma f

Leo /'li:əʊ/ n Leo m

leopard /'lepəd/ n leopardo m

leotard /'li:ətɑ:d/ n malla f

lesbian /'lezbiən/ n lesbiana f.
● adj lesbiano

less /les/ adj & n & adv & prep
menos. ~ **than** menos de; (with
numbers) menos de. ~ **and** ~
cada vez menos. none the ~ sin
embargo. ~en vt/i disminuir

lesson /'lesn/ n clase f

lest /lest/ conj no sea que (+ subjunctive)

let /let/ vt (pt **let**, pres p **letting**)
dejar; (lease) alquilar. ~ **me do it**
déjame hacerlo. ● modal verb. ~'s
go! ¡vamos!, ¡vámonos! ~'s **see**
(vamos) a ver. ~'s **talk/drink**
hablemos/bebamos. □ ~ **down** vt
bajar; (deflate) desinflar; (fig) defraudar. □ ~ **go** vt soltar. □ ~ **in** vt
dejar entrar. □ ~ **off** vt disparar
(gun); (cause to explode) hacer explotar; hacer estallar (firework);
(excuse) perdonar. □ ~ **out** vt dejar
salir. □ ~ **through** vt dejar pasar.
□ ~ **up** vi disminuir. ~**down** n
desilusión f

lethal /'li:θl/ adj (dose, wound)
mortal; (weapon) mortífero

letharg|ic /lɪ'θɑːdʒɪk/ adj letár-
gico. ~**y** /'leθədʒi/ n letargo m

letter /'letə(r)/ n (of alphabet)
letra f; (written message) carta f. ~
bomb n carta f bomba. ~**box** n
buzón m. ~**ing** n letras fpl

lettuce /'letɪs/ n lechuga f

let-up /'letʌp/ n interrupción f

leukaemia /lu:'ki:mɪə/ n leucemia f

level /'levl/ adj (flat, even) plano,

parejo (LAm); (spoonful) raso. ~
with (at same height) al nivel de.
● n nivel m. ● vt (pt **levelled**) nivelar; (aim) apuntar. ~ **crossing** n
paso a nivel, crucero m (Mex)

lever /'li:və(r)/ n palanca f. ● vt
apalancar. ~ **open** abrir haciendo
palanca. ~**age** /-ɪdʒ/ n apalanca-
miento m

levy /'levɪ/ vt imponer (tax). ● n
impuesto m

lewd /lu:d/ adj (-er, -est) lascivo

liab|ility /laɪə'bɪlətɪ/ n responsa-
bilidad f; (fam, disadvantage) lastre
m. ~**ilities** npl (debts) deudas fpl.
~**le** /'laɪəbl/ adj. be ~**le to do**
tener tendencia a hacer. ~**le for**
responsable de; ~**le to** susceptible
de; expuesto a (fine)

liais|e /lɪ'eɪz/ vi actuar de enlace
(with con). ~**on** /-ɒn/ n enlace m

liar /'laɪə(r)/ n mentiroso m

libel /'laɪbl/ n difamación f. ● vt (pt
libelled) difamar (por escrito)

liberal /'lɪbərəl/ adj liberal; (generous) generoso. **L~** (Pol) del Partido
Liberal. ● n liberal m & f. ~**ly** adv li-
beralmente; (generously) generosa-
mente

liberat|e /'lɪbəreɪt/ vt liberar.
~**ion** /-'reɪʃn/ n liberación f

liberty /'lɪbətɪ/ n libertad f. **take
liberties** tomarse libertades. **take
the** ~ **of** tomarse la libertad de

Libra /'li:brə/ n Libra f

librar|ian /laɪ'breərɪən/ n biblio-
tecario m. ~**y** /'laɪbrərɪ/ n biblioteca f

> **Library of Congress** La
> biblioteca nacional de
> EEUU, situada en Washington DC.
> Fundada por el Congreso Con-
> gress, alberga más de ochenta

millones de libros en 470 idiomas, y otros objetos.

lice /laɪs/ see LOUSE

licence /'laɪsns/ n licencia f, permiso m

license /'laɪsns/ vt autorizar. ● n (Amer) see LICENCE. **~ number** n (Amer) (número m de) matrícula f. **~ plate** n (Amer) matrícula f, placa f (LAm)

lick /lɪk/ vt lamer; (sl, defeat) dar una paliza a. ● n lametón m

licorice /'lɪkərɪs/ n (Amer) regaliz m

lid /lɪd/ n tapa f; (eyelid) párpado m

lie¹ /laɪ/ vi (pt lay, pp lain, pres p lying) echarse, tenderse; (be in lying position) estar tendido; (be) estar, encontrarse. **~ low** quedarse escondido. □ **~ down** vi echarse, tenderse

lie² /laɪ/ n mentira f. ● vi (pt lied, pres p lying) mentir

lie-in /laɪ'ɪn/ n. **have a ~** quedarse en la cama

lieutenant /lef'tenənt/ n (Mil) teniente m

life /laɪf/ n (pl lives) vida f. **~ belt** n salvavidas m. **~boat** n lancha f de salvamento; (on ship) bote m salvavidas. **~buoy** n boya f salvavidas. **~ coach** n coach m & f personal. **~guard** n salvavidas m & f, socorrista m & f. **~ jacket** n chaleco m salvavidas. **~less** adj sin vida. **~like** adj verosímil. **~line** n cuerda f de salvamento; (fig) tabla f de salvación. **~long** adj de toda la vida. **~ preserver** n (Amer, buoy) see BUOY; (jacket) see JACKET. **~ ring** n (Amer) see BELT. **~saver** n (person) salvavidas m & f; (fig) salvación f. **~-size(d)** adj (de)

tamaño natural. **~time** n vida f. **~ vest** n (Amer) see ~ JACKET

lift /lɪft/ vt levantar. ● vi (fog) disparse. ● n ascensor m. **give a ~** to s.o. llevar a uno en su coche, dar aventón a uno (Mex). □ **~ up** vt levantar. **~-off** n despegue m

light /laɪt/ n luz f; (lamp) lámpara f, luz f; (flame) fuego m. **come to ~** salir a la luz. **have you got a ~?** ¿tienes fuego? **the ~s** npl (traffic signals) el semáforo; (on vehicle) las luces. ● adj (-er, -est) (in colour) claro; (not heavy) ligero. ● vt (pt lit or lighted) encender, prender (LAm); (illuminate) iluminar. ● vi encenderse, prenderse (LAm). □ **~ up** vt iluminar. ● vi iluminarse. **~ bulb** n bombilla f, foco m (Mex). **~en** vt (make less heavy) aligerar, alivianar (LAm); (give light to) iluminar; (make brighter) aclarar. **~er** n (for cigarettes) mechero m, encendedor m. **~-hearted** /-'hɑːtɪd/ adj alegre. **~house** n faro m. **~ly** adv ligeramente

lightning /'laɪtnɪŋ/ n. flash of ~ relámpago m. ● adj relámpago

lightweight adj ligero, liviano (LAm)

like /laɪk/ adj parecido. ● prep como. ● conj 🔲 como. ● vt. I **~ chocolate** me gusta el chocolate. **they ~ swimming** (a ellos) les gusta nadar. **would you ~ a coffee?** ¿quieres un café? **~able** adj simpático.

like|lihood /'laɪklɪhʊd/ n probabilidad f. **~ly** adj (-ier, -iest) probable. **he is ~ly to come** es probable que venga. ● adv probablemente. **not ~ly!** ¡ni hablar! **~n** vt comparar (**to** con, a). **~ness** n parecido m. **be a good ~ness** parecerse mucho. **~wise**

adv (*also*) también; (*the same way*) lo mismo

liking /'laɪkɪŋ/ *n* (*for thing*) afición *f*; (*for person*) simpatía *f*

lilac /'laɪlək/ *adj* lila. ● *n* lila *f*; (*color*) lila *m*

lily /'lɪlɪ/ *n* lirio *m*; (*white*) azucena *f*

limb /lɪm/ *n* miembro *m*. **out on a ~** aislado

lime /laɪm/ *n* (*white substance*) cal *f*; (*fruit*) lima *f*. **~light** *n*. **be in the ~light** ser el centro de atención

limerick /'lɪmərɪk/ *n* quintilla *f* humorística

limit /'lɪmɪt/ *n* límite *m*. ● *vt* limitar. **~ation** /-'teɪʃn/ *n* limitación *f*. **~ed** *adj* limitado. **~ed company** *n* sociedad *f* anónima

limousine /'lɪməziːn/ *n* limusina *f*

limp /lɪmp/ *vi* cojear, renguear (*LAm*). ● *n* cojera *f*, renguera *f* (*LAm*). **have a ~** cojear. ● *adj* (**-er, -est**) flojo

linden /'lɪndn/ *n* (*Amer*) tilo *m*

line /laɪn/ *n* línea *f*; (*track*) vía *f*; (*wrinkle*) arruga *f*; (*row*) fila *f*; (*of poem*) verso *m*; (*rope*) cuerda *f*; (*of goods*) surtido *m*; (*Amer*, *queue*) cola *f*. **stand in ~** (*Amer*) hacer cola. **get in ~** (*Amer*) ponerse en la cola.. **cut in ~** (*Amer*) colarse. **in ~ with** de acuerdo con. ● *vt* forrar (*skirt*, *box*); bordear (*streets* etc). □ **~ up** *vi* alinearse; (*in queue*) hacer cola. *vt* (*form into line*) poner en fila; (*align*) alinear. **~d** /laɪnd/ *adj* (*paper*) con renglones; (*with fabric*) forrado

linen /'lɪnɪn/ *n* (*sheets* etc) ropa *f* blanca; (*material*) lino *m*

liner /'laɪnə(r)/ *n* (*ship*) transatlántico *m*

linger /'lɪŋgə(r)/ *vi* tardar en mar-

charse. **~ (on)** (*smells* etc) persistir. □ **~ over** *vt* dilatarse en

lingerie /'lænʒərɪ/ *n* lencería *f*

linguist /'lɪŋgwɪst/ *n* políglota *m* & *f*; lingüista *m* & *f*. **~ic** /lɪŋ 'gwɪstɪk/ *adj* lingüístico. **~ics** *n* lingüística *f*

lining /'laɪnɪŋ/ *n* forro *m*

link /lɪŋk/ *n* (*of chain*) eslabón *m*; (*connection*) conexión *f*; (*bond*) vínculo *m*; (*transport*, *telecommunications*) conexión *f*, enlace *m*. ● *vt* conectar; relacionar (*facts*, *events*). □ **~ up** *vt/i* conectar

lino /'laɪnəʊ/ *n* (*pl* **-os**) linóleo *m*

lint /lɪnt/ *n* (*Med*) hilas *fpl*

lion /'laɪən/ *n* león *m*. **~ess** /-nɪs/ *n* leona *f*

lip /lɪp/ *n* labio *m*; (*edge*) borde *m*. **~read** *vt* leer los labios. **~salve** *n* crema *f* para los labios. **~ service** *n*. **pay ~ service to** aprobar de boquilla, aprobar de los dientes para afuera (*Mex*). **~stick** *n* lápiz *m* de labios

liqueur /lɪ'kjʊə(r)/ *n* licor *m*

liquid /'lɪkwɪd/ *adj & n* líquido (*m*)

liquidate /'lɪkwɪdeɪt/ *vt* liquidar

liquidize /'lɪkwɪdaɪz/ *vt* licuar. **~r** *n* licuadora *f*

liquor /'lɪkə(r)/ *n* bebidas *fpl* alcohólicas

liquorice /'lɪkərɪs/ *n* regaliz *m*

liquor store *n* (*Amer*) tienda *f* de bebidas alcohólicas

lisp /lɪsp/ *n* ceceo *m*. **speak with a ~** cecear. ● *vi* cecear

list /lɪst/ *n* lista *f*. ● *vt* hacer una lista de; (*enter in a list*) inscribir. ● *vi* (*ship*) escorar

listen /'lɪsn/ *vi* escuchar. **~ in (to)** escuchar. **~ to** escuchar. **~er** *n* oyente *m* & *f*

listless /ˈlɪstlɪs/ adj apático

lit /lɪt/ see **LIGHT**

literacy /ˈlɪtərəsɪ/ n alfabetismo m

literal /ˈlɪtərəl/ adj literal. **~ly** adv literalmente

literary /ˈlɪtərərɪ/ adj literario

literate /ˈlɪtərət/ adj alfabetizado

literature /ˈlɪtərətʃə(r)/ n literatura f; (fig) folletos mpl

lithe /laɪð/ adj ágil

litre /ˈliːtə(r)/ n litro m

litter /ˈlɪtə(r)/ n basura f; (of animals) camada f. • vt ensuciar; (scatter) esparcir. **~ed with** lleno de. **~ bin** n papelera f. **~bug**, **~ lout** n persona f que tira basura en lugares públicos

little /ˈlɪtl/ adj pequeño; (not much) poco. **a ~ water** un poco de agua. • pron poco, poca. **a ~** un poco, poca. **~ by ~** poco a poco. • adv poco. **~ finger** (dedo m) meñique m

live /lɪv/ vt/i vivir. □ **~ down** vt lograr borrar. □ **~ off** vt vivir a costa de (family, friends); (feed on) alimentarse de. □ **~ on** vt (feed o.s. on) vivir de. vi (memory) seguir presente; (tradition) seguir existiendo. □ **~ up** vt. **~ it up** ① darse la gran vida. □ **~ up to** vt vivir de acuerdo con; cumplir (promise). • /laɪv/ adj vivo; (wire) con corriente; (broadcast) en directo

livelihood /ˈlaɪvlɪhʊd/ n sustento m

lively /ˈlaɪvlɪ/ adj (-ier, -iest) vivo

liven up /ˈlaɪvn/ vt animar. • vi animar(se)

liver /ˈlɪvə(r)/ n hígado m

lives /laɪvz/ see **LIFE**

livestock /ˈlaɪvstɒk/ n animales mpl (de cría); (cattle) ganado m

livid /ˈlɪvɪd/ adj lívido; (fam, angry) furioso

living /ˈlɪvɪŋ/ adj vivo. • n vida f. **make a ~** ganarse la vida. **~room** n salón m, sala f (de estar), living m (LAm)

lizard /ˈlɪzəd/ n lagartija f; (big) lagarto m

load /ləʊd/ n (also Elec) carga f; (quantity) cantidad f; (weight, strain) peso m. **~s of** ① montones de. • vt cargar. **~ed** adj cargado

loaf /ləʊf/ n (pl loaves) pan m; (stick of bread) barra f de pan. • vi. **~ (about)** holgazanear

loan /ləʊn/ n préstamo m. **on ~** prestado. • vt prestar

loath|**e** /ləʊð/ vt odiar. **~ing** n odio m (of a). **~esome** /-səm/ adj repugnante

lobby /ˈlɒbɪ/ n vestíbulo m; (Pol) grupo m de presión. • vt ejercer presión sobre. • vi. **~ for sth** ejercer presión para obtener algo

lobe /ləʊb/ n lóbulo m

lobster /ˈlɒbstə(r)/ n langosta f, bogavante m

local /ˈləʊkl/ adj local. **~ (phone) call** llamada f urbana. • n (fam, pub) bar m. **the ~s** los vecinos mpl. **~ government** n administración f municipal. **~ity** /-ˈkælətɪ/ n localidad f. **~ization** n localización f. **~ly** adv (live, work) en la zona

locat|**e** /ləʊˈkeɪt/ vt (situate) situar, ubicar (LAm); (find) localizar, ubicar (LAm). **~ion** /-ʃn/ n situación f, ubicación f (LAm). **on ~ion** fuera del estudio. **to film on ~ion in Andalusia** rodar en Andalucía

lock /lɒk/ n (of door etc) cerradura f; (on canal) esclusa f; (of hair) mechón m. • vt cerrar con llave. • vi cerrarse con llave. □ ~ **in** vt encerrar. □ ~ **out** vt cerrar la puerta a. □ ~ **up** vt encerrar (person); cerrar con llave (building)

locker /'lɒkə(r)/ n armario m, locker m (LAm). ~ **room** n (Amer) vestuario m, vestidor m (Mex)

locket /'lɒkɪt/ n medallón m

lock: ~**out** /'lɒkaʊt/ n cierre m patronal, paro m patronal (LAm). ~**smith** n cerrajero m

locomotive /ləʊkə'məʊtɪv/ n locomotora f

lodge /lɒdʒ/ n (of porter) portería f. ● vt alojar; presentar (complaint). ~**r** n huésped m. ~**ings** n alojamiento m; (room) habitación f alquilada

loft /lɒft/ n desván m, altillo m (LAm)

lofty /'lɒftɪ/ adj (-ier, -iest) elevado; (haughty) altanero

log /lɒg/ n (of wood) tronco m; (as fuel) leño m; (record) diario m. **sleep like a** ~ dormir como un tronco. ● vt (pt logged) registrar. □ ~ **in,** ~ **on** (Comp) entrar (al sistema). □ ~ **off,** ~ **out** (Comp) salir (del sistema)

logarithm /'lɒgərɪðəm/ n logaritmo m

loggerheads /'lɒgəhedz/ npl. **be at** ~ **with** estar a matar con

logic /'lɒdʒɪk/ adj lógica f. ~**al** adj lógico. ~**ally** adv lógicamente

logistics /lə'dʒɪstɪks/ n logística f. ● npl (practicalities) problemas mpl logísticos

logo /'ləʊgəʊ/ n (pl -os) logo m

loin /lɔɪn/ n (Culin) lomo m. ~**s** npl entrañas fpl

loiter /'lɔɪtə(r)/ vi perder el tiempo

loll /lɒl/ vi repantigarse

lollipop /'lɒlɪpɒp/ n pirulí m. ~**y** n polo m, paleta f (helada) (LAm)

London /'lʌndən/ n Londres m.
● adj londinense. ~**er** n londinense m & f

lone /ləʊn/ adj solitario. ~**ly** adj (-ier, -iest) solitario. **feel** ~**ly** sentirse muy solo. ~**r** n solitario m. ~**some** /-səm/ adj solitario

long /lɒŋ/ adj (-er, -est) largo. **a** ~ **time** mucho tiempo. **how** ~ **is it?** ¿cuánto tiene de largo? ● adv largo/mucho tiempo. **as** ~ **as** (while) mientras; (provided that) con tal que (+ subjunctive). **before** ~ dentro de poco. **so** ~**!** ¡hasta luego! **so** ~ **as** (provided that) con tal que (+ subjunctive). ~ **for** vi anhelar. ~ **to do** estar deseando hacer. ~**-distance** /-'dɪstəns/ adj de larga distancia. ~**-distance phone call** llamada f de larga distancia, conferencia f. ~**er** adv. **no** ~**er** ya no. ~**-haul** /-'hɔːl/ adj de larga distancia. ~**ing** n anhelo m, ansia f

longitude /'lɒŋgɪtjuːd/ n longitud f

long: ~ **jump** n salto m de longitud. ~**-playing record** n elepé m. ~**-range** adj de largo alcance. ~**-sighted** /-'saɪtɪd/ adj hipermétrope. ~**-term** adj a largo plazo. ~**-winded** /-'wɪndɪd/ adj prolijo

loo /luː/ n 🔲 váter m, baño m (LAm)

look /lʊk/ vt mirar; representar (age). ● vi mirar; (seem) parecer; (search) buscar. ● n mirada f; (appearance) aspecto m. **good** ~**s** belleza f. □ ~ **after** vt cuidar (person); (be responsible for) encargarse de. □ ~ **at** vt mirar; (consider) considerar. □ ~ **down** vt despreciar. ◻ ~ **for** vt buscar. ◻ ~ **forward to** vt esperar con ansia. ◻ ~ **into** vt investigar. ◻ ~ **like** vt parecerse a. ◻ ~ **on** vi mirar. ◻ ~ **out** vi tener cuidado. ◻ ~ **out for** vt buscar; (*watch*) tener cuidado con. ◻ ~ **round** (visit) ir a ver. ◻ ~ **through** vt hojear. ◻ ~ **up** vt buscar (word); (*visit*) ir a ver. ◻ ~ **up to** vt admirar. **~-alike** n 🆃 doble m & f. **~out** n (Mil, person) vigía m. **be on the ~out for** andar a la caza de. **~s** npl belleza f

loom /luːm/ n telar m. ● vi aparecerse

looney, loony /ˈluːnɪ/ adj & n 🆇 chiflado (m) 🅸, loco (m)

loop /luːp/ n (shape) curva f; (in string) lazada f. ● vt hacer una lazada con. **~hole** n (in rule) escapatoria f

loose /luːs/ adj (-er, -est) suelto; (garment, thread, hair) flojo; (inexact) vago; (not packed) suelto. **be at a ~ end** no tener nada que hacer. **~ly** adv sueltamente; (roughly) aproximadamente. **~n** vt aflojar

loot /luːt/ n botín m. ● vt/i saquear. **~er** n saqueador m

lop /lɒp/ vt (pt lopped). ~ **off** cortar

lop-sided /-ˈsaɪdɪd/ adj ladeado

lord /lɔːd/ n señor m; (British title) lord m. (good) **L~!** ¡Dios mío! the **L~** el Señor. **the (House of) L~s** la Cámara de los Lores

lorry /ˈlɒrɪ/ n camión m. ~ **driver** n camionero m

lose /luːz/ vt/i (pt lost) perder. **~r** n perdedor m

loss /lɒs/ n pérdida f. **be at a ~** estar perplejo. **be at a ~ for words** no encontrar palabras

lost /lɒst/ see **LOSE**. ● adj perdido. **get ~** perderse. ~ **property** n, ~ **and found** (Amer) oficina f de objetos perdidos

lot /lɒt/ n (fate) suerte f; (at auction) lote m; (land) solar m. **a ~ (of)** mucho. **quite a ~ of** 🆃 bastante. **~s (of)** 🆃 muchos. **they ate the ~** se lo comieron todo

lotion /ˈləʊʃn/ n loción f

lottery /ˈlɒtərɪ/ n lotería f

loud /laʊd/ adj (-er, -est) fuerte; (noisy) ruidoso; (gaudy) chillón. **out ~** en voz alta. **~hailer** /-ˈheɪlə(r)/ n megáfono m. **~ly** adv (speak) en voz alta; (shout) fuerte; (complain) a voz en grito. **~speaker** /-ˈspiːkə(r)/ n altavoz m, altoparlante m (LAm)

lounge /laʊndʒ/ vi repantigarse. ● n salón m, sala f (de estar), living m (LAm)

louse /laʊs/ n (pl lice) piojo m. **~y** /ˈlaʊzɪ/ adj (-ier, -iest) (sl, bad) malísimo

lout /laʊt/ n patán m

lov|able /ˈlʌvəbl/ adj adorable. **~e** /lʌv/ n amor m; (tennis) cero m. **be in ~e (with)** estar enamorado (de). **fall in ~e (with)** enamorarse (de). ● vt querer, amar (person). **I ~e milk** me encanta la leche. **~e affair** n aventura f, amorío m

lovely /ˈlʌvlɪ/ adj (-ier, -iest) (appearance) precioso, lindo (LAm); (person) encantador, amoroso (LAm)

lover /ˈlʌvə(r)/ n amante m & f

loving /ˈlʌvɪŋ/ adj cariñoso

low /ləʊ/ adj (-er, -est) bajo. ● vi (cattle) mugir. **~er** vt bajar. **~er o.s.** envilecerse. **~level** adj a bajo nivel. **~ly** adj (-ier, -iest).

humilde

loyal /ˈlɔɪəl/ adj leal, fiel. **~ty** n lealtad f. **~ty card** tarjeta f de fidelidad

lozenge /ˈlɒzɪndʒ/ n (shape) rombo m; (tablet) pastilla f

LP abbr (= **long-playing record**) elepé m

Ltd /ˈlɪmɪtɪd/ abbr (= **Limited**) S.A., Sociedad Anónima

lubricate /ˈluːbrɪkeɪt/ vt lubricar

lucid /ˈluːsɪd/ adj lúcido

luck /lʌk/ n suerte f. **good ~!** ¡(buena) suerte! **~ily** adv por suerte. **~y** adj (-ier, -iest) (person) con suerte. **be ~y** tener suerte. **~y number** número m de la suerte

lucrative /ˈluːkrətɪv/ adj lucrativo

ludicrous /ˈluːdɪkrəs/ adj ridículo

lug /lʌg/ vt (pt lugged) 🄵 arrastrar

luggage /ˈlʌgɪdʒ/ n equipaje m. **~ rack** n rejilla f

lukewarm /ˈluːkwɔːm/ adj tibio; (fig) poco entusiasta

lull /lʌl/ vt (soothe, send to sleep) adormecer; (calm) calmar. ● n periodo m de calma

lullaby /ˈlʌləbaɪ/ n canción f de cuna

lumber /ˈlʌmbə(r)/ n trastos mpl viejos; (wood) maderos mpl. ● vt. ~ **s.o. with sth** 🄵 endilgar algo a uno. **~jack** n leñador m

luminous /ˈluːmɪnəs/ adj luminoso

lump /lʌmp/ n (swelling) bulto m; (as result of knock) chichón m; (in liquid) grumo m; (of sugar) terrón m. ● vt. ~ **together** agrupar. **~ it** 🄵 aguantarse. ~ **sum** n suma f global. **~y** adj (sauce) grumoso; (mattress, cushions) lleno de protuberancias

lunacy /ˈluːnəsɪ/ n locura f

lunar /ˈluːnə(r)/ adj lunar

lunatic /ˈluːnətɪk/ n loco m

lunch /lʌntʃ/ n comida f, almuerzo m. **have ~** comer, almorzar

luncheon /ˈlʌntʃən/ n comida f, almuerzo m. ~ **voucher** n vale m de comida

lung /lʌŋ/ n pulmón m

lunge /lʌndʒ/ n arremetida f. ● vi. ~ **at** arremeter contra

lurch /lɜːtʃ/ vi tambalearse. ● n. **leave in the ~** dejar plantado

lure /ljʊə(r)/ vt atraer

lurid /ˈljʊərɪd/ adj (colour) chillón; (shocking) morboso

lurk /lɜːk/ vi merodear; (in ambush) estar al acecho

luscious /ˈlʌʃəs/ adj delicioso

lush /lʌʃ/ adj exuberante

lust /lʌst/ n lujuria f; (craving) deseo m. ● vi. ~ **after** codiciar

lute /luːt/ n laúd m

Luxembourg, Luxemburg /ˈlʌksəmbɜːg/ n Luxemburgo m

luxuriant /lʌgˈzjʊərɪənt/ adj exuberante

luxur|ious /lʌgˈzjʊərɪəs/ adj lujoso. **~y** /ˈlʌkʃərɪ/ n lujo m. ● adj de lujo

lying /ˈlaɪɪŋ/ see **LIE¹, LIE².** ● n mentiras fpl. ● adj mentiroso

lynch /lɪntʃ/ vt linchar

lyric /ˈlɪrɪk/ adj lírico. **~al** adj lírico. **~s** npl letra f

Mm

MA /em'eɪ/ *abbr see* **MASTER**

mac /mæk/ *n* ⊺ impermeable *m*

macabre /mə'kɑːbrə/ *adj* macabro

macaroni /mækə'rəʊnɪ/ *n* macarrones *mpl*

mace /meɪs/ *n* (*staff*) maza *f*; (*spice*) macis *f*. **M~** (*P*) (*Amer*) gas *m* para defensa personal

machine /mə'ʃiːn/ *n* máquina *f*. **~ gun** *n* ametralladora *f*. **~ry** *n* maquinaria *f*; (*working parts, fig*) mecanismo *m*

mackintosh /'mækɪntɒʃ/ *n* impermeable *m*

macro /'mækrəʊ/ *n* (*pl* **-os**) (*Comp*) macro *m*

macrobiotic /mækrəʊbaɪ'ɒtɪk/ *adj* macrobiótico

mad /mæd/ *adj* (**madder, maddest**) loco; (*fam, angry*) furioso. **be ~ about** estar loco por

madam /'mædəm/ *n* señora *f*

mad: ~cap *adj* atolondrado. **~ cow disease** *n* enfermedad *f* de las vacas locas. **~den** *vt* (*make mad*) enloquecer; (*make angry*) enfurecer

made /meɪd/ *see* **MAKE**. **~-to-measure** hecho a (la) medida

mad: ~house *n* manicomio *m*. **~ly** *adv* (*interested, in love etc*) locamente; (*frantically*) como un loco. **~man** /-mən/ *n* loco *m*. **~ness** *n* locura *f*

Madonna /mə'dɒnə/ *n*. **the ~** (*Relig*) la Virgen

maestro /'maɪstrəʊ/ *n* (*pl* **maes-** tri /-striː/ *or* **-os**) maestro *m*

Mafia /'mæfɪə/ *n* mafia *f*

magazine /mægə'ziːn/ *n* revista *f*; (*of gun*) recámara *f*

magenta /mə'dʒentə/ *adj* magenta, morado

maggot /'mægət/ *n* gusano *m*

magic /'mædʒɪk/ *n* magia *f*. ● *adj* mágico. **~al** *adj* mágico. **~ian** /mə'dʒɪʃn/ *n* mago *m*

magistrate /'mædʒɪstreɪt/ *n* juez *m* que conoce de faltas y asuntos civiles de menor importancia

magnet /'mægnɪt/ *n* imán *m*. **~ic** /-'netɪk/ *adj* magnético; (*fig*) lleno de magnetismo. **~ism** *n* magnetismo *m*. **~ize** *vt* imantar, magnetizar

magnif|ication /mægnɪfɪ'keɪʃn/ *n* aumento *m*. **~y** /'mægnɪfaɪ/ *vt* aumentar. **~ying glass** *n* lupa *f*

magnificen|ce /mæg'nɪfɪsns/ *adj* magnificencia *f*. **~t** *adj* magnífico

magnitude /'mægnɪtjuːd/ *n* magnitud *f*

magpie /'mægpaɪ/ *n* urraca *f*

mahogany /mə'hɒgənɪ/ *n* caoba *f*

maid /meɪd/ *n* (*servant*) criada *f*, sirvienta *f*; (*girl, old use*) doncella *f*. **old ~** solterona *f*

maiden /'meɪdn/ *n* doncella *f*. ● *adj* (*voyage*) inaugural. **~ name** *n* apellido *m* de soltera

mail /meɪl/ *n* correo *m*; (*armour*) (cota *f* de) malla *f*. ● *adj* correo. ● *vt* echar al correo (*letter*); (*send*) enviar por correo. **~box** *n* (*Amer*) buzón *m*. **~ing list** *n* lista *f* de direcciones. **~man** /-mən/ *n* (*Amer*) cartero *m*. **~ order** *n* venta *f* por correo

maim /meɪm/ *vt* mutilar

main /meɪn/ *n*. (**water/gas**) **~** cañería f principal. **in the** ~ en su mayor parte. **the** ~**s** *npl* (*Elec*) la red f de suministro. ● *adj* principal. ~ **course** n plato m principal, plato m fuerte. ~ **frame** n (*Comp*) unidad f central. ~**land** n. **the** ~**land** la masa territorial de un país excluyendo sus islas. ● *adj*. ~**land China** (la) China continental. ~ **land** adv principalmente. ~ **road** n carretera f principal. ~**stream** adj (*culture*) establecido. ~ **street** n calle f principal

maint|ain /meɪnˈteɪn/ vt mantener. ~**enance** /ˈmeɪntənəns/ n mantenimiento m

maisonette /meɪzəˈnet/ n (*small house*) casita f; (*part of house*) dúplex m

maize /meɪz/ n maíz m

majestic /məˈdʒestɪk/ adj majestuoso

majesty /ˈmædʒəstɪ/ n majestad f

major /ˈmeɪdʒə(r)/ adj (*important*) muy importante; (*Mus*) mayor. **a** ~ **road** una calle prioritaria. ● n comandante m & f, mayor m & f (*LAm*). ● vi. ~ **in** (*Amer, Univ*) especializarse en

Majorca /məˈjɔːkə/ n Mallorca f

majority /məˈdʒɒrətɪ/ n mayoría f. ● adj mayoritario

make /meɪk/ vt (pt **made**) hacer; (*manufacture*) fabricar; ganar (*money*); tomar (*decision*); llegar a (*destination*). ~ **s.o. do sth** obligar a uno a hacer algo. **be made of** estar hecho de. **I** ~ **it two o'clock** yo tengo las dos. ~ **believe** fingir. ~ **do** (*manage*) arreglarse. ~ **do with** (*content o.s.*) contentarse con. ~ **it** llegar; (*succeed*) tener éxito. ● n marca f. ~ **for** vt dirigirse a. ~ **good** vt compensar; (*repair*) reparar. □ ~ **off** vi

escaparse (**with** con). □ ~ **out** vt distinguir; (*understand*) entender; (*write out*) hacer; (*assert*) dar a entender. vi (*cope*) arreglárselas. □ ~ **up** vt (*constitute*) formar; (*prepare*) preparar; inventar (*story*); hacer (*become reconciled*) hacer las paces. ~ **up** (**one's face**) maquillarse. □ ~ **up for** vt compensar. ~**believe** adj fingido, simulado. n ficción f. ~**over** n (*Amer*) maquillaje m. ~**r** n fabricante m & f. ~**shift** adj (*temporary*) provisional, provisorio (*LAm*); (*improvised*) improvisado. ~**up** n maquillaje m. **put on** ~**up** maquillarse.

making /ˈmeɪkɪŋ/ n. **he has the** ~**s of** tiene madera de. **in the** ~ en vías de formación

maladjusted /mæləˈdʒʌstɪd/ adj inadaptado

malaria /məˈleərɪə/ n malaria f, paludismo m

Malaysia /məˈleɪzɪə/ n Malasia f. ~**n** adj & n malaisio (m)

male /meɪl/ adj macho; (*voice, attitude*) masculino. ● n macho m; (*man*) varón m

malevolent /məˈlevələnt/ adj malévolo

malfunction /mælˈfʌŋkʃn/ vi fallar, funcionar mal

malic|e /ˈmælɪs/ n mala intención f, maldad f. **bear s.o.** ~**e** guardar rencor a uno. ~**ious** /məˈlɪʃəs/ adj malintencionado. ~**iously** adv con malevolencia

malignant /məˈlɪgnənt/ adj maligno

mallet /ˈmælɪt/ n mazo m

malnutrition /mælnjuːˈtrɪʃn/ n desnutrición f

malpractice /mælˈpræktɪs/ n mala práctica f (en el ejercicio de

m

una profesión)

malt /mɔːlt/ n malta f

Malt|a /ˈmɔːltə/ n Malta f. **~ese** /-ˈtiːz/ adj & n maltés (m)

mammal /ˈmæml/ n mamífero m

mammoth /ˈmæməθ/ n mamut m. ● adj gigantesco

man /mæn/ n (pl **men** /men/) hombre m; (Chess) pieza f. **~ in the street** hombre m de la calle. ● vt (pt **manned**) encargarse de (switchboard); tripular (ship); servir (guns)

manacles /ˈmænəklz/ n (for wrists) esposas fpl; (for legs) grillos mpl

manag|e /ˈmænɪdʒ/ vt dirigir; administrar (land, finances); (handle) manejar. ● vi (Com) dirigir; (cope) arreglárselas. **~e to do** lograr hacer. **~eable** adj (task) posible de alcanzar; (size) razonable. **~ement** n dirección f. **~er** n director m; (of shop) encargado m; (of soccer team) entrenador m, director m técnico (LAm). **~eress** /-ˈres/ n encargada f. **~erial** /-dʒɪərɪəl/ adj directivo, gerencial (LAm). **~ing director** n director m ejecutivo

mandate /ˈmændeɪt/ n mandato m

mandatory /ˈmændətərɪ/ adj obligatorio

mane /meɪn/ n (of horse) crin(es) f(pl); (of lion) melena f

mangle /ˈmæŋgl/ n rodillo m (escurridor). ● vt destrozar

man: ~handle vt mover a pulso; (treat roughly) maltratar. **~hole** n registro m. **~hood** n madurez f; (quality) virilidad f. **~-hour** n hora f hombre. **~-hunt** n persecución f

mania /ˈmeɪnɪə/ n manía f. **~c** /-ræk/ n maníaco m

manicure /ˈmænɪkjʊə(r)/ n manicura f, manicure f (LAm)

manifest /ˈmænɪfest/ adj manifiesto. ● vt manifestar. **~ation** /-ˈsteɪʃn/ n manifestación f

manifesto /mænɪˈfestəʊ/ n (pl **-os**) manifiesto m

manipulat|e /məˈnɪpjʊleɪt/ vt manipular. **~ion** /-ˈleɪʃn/ n manipulación f. **~ive** /-lətɪv/ adj manipulador

man: ~kind n humanidad f. **~ly** adj viril. **~-made** adj artificial

manner /ˈmænə(r)/ n manera f; (demeanour) actitud f; (kind) clase f. **~ed** adj amanerado. **~s** npl modales mpl, educación f. **bad ~s** mala educación

manoeuvre /məˈnuːvə(r)/ n maniobra f. ● vt/i maniobrar

manor /ˈmænə(r)/ n. **~ house** casa f solariega

manpower n mano f de obra

mansion /ˈmænʃn/ n mansión f

man: ~-size(d) adj grande. **~slaughter** n homicidio m sin premeditación

mantelpiece /ˈmæntlpiːs/ n repisa f de la chimenea

manual /ˈmænjʊəl/ adj manual. ● n (handbook) manual m

manufacture /mænjʊ ˈfæktʃə(r)/ vt fabricar. ● n fabricación f. **~r** n fabricante m & f

manure /məˈnjʊə(r)/ n estiércol m

manuscript /ˈmænjʊskrɪpt/ n manuscrito m

many /ˈmenɪ/ adj & pron muchos, muchas. **~ people** mucha gente. **a great ~/good ~** muchísimos. **how ~?** ¿cuántos? **so ~** tantos. **too ~** demasiados

map | mascara

map /mæp/ *n* mapa *m*; *(of streets etc)* plano *m*

mar /mɑː(r)/ *vt (pt* **marred)** estropear

marathon /ˈmærəθən/ *n* maratón *m & f*

marble /ˈmɑːbl/ *n* mármol *m*; *(for game)* canica *f*

march /mɑːtʃ/ *vi (Mil)* marchar. **∼ off** *vi* irse. ● *n* marcha *f*

March /mɑːtʃ/ *n* marzo *m*

march-past /ˈmɑːtʃpɑːst/ *n* desfile *m*

mare /meə(r)/ *n* yegua *f*

margarine /mɑːdʒəˈriːn/ *n* margarina *f*

margin /ˈmɑːdʒɪn/ *n* margen *f*. **∼al** *adj* marginal

marijuana /mærɪˈhwɑːnə/ *n* marihuana *f*

marina /məˈriːnə/ *n* puerto *m* deportivo

marine /məˈriːn/ *adj* marino. ● *n (sailor)* infante *m* de marina

marionette /mærɪəˈnet/ *n* marioneta *f*

marital status /mærɪtl ˈsteɪtəs/ *n* estado *m* civil

mark /mɑːk/ *n* marca *f*; *(stain)* mancha *f*; *(Schol)* nota *f*; *(target)* blanco *m*. ● *vt (indicate)* señalar, marcar; *(stain)* manchar; corregir *(exam)*. **∼ time** marcar el paso. □ **∼ out** *vt (select)* señalar; *(distinguish)* distinguir. **∼ed** *adj* marcado. **∼edly** /-kɪdlɪ/ *adv* marcadamente. **∼er** *n* marcador *m*. **∼er (pen)** *n* rotulador *m*, marcador *m (LAm)*

market /ˈmɑːkɪt/ *n* mercado *m*. **on the ∼** en venta. ● *vt* comercializar. **∼ garden** *n* huerta *f*. **∼ing** *n* marketing *m*

marking /ˈmɑːkɪŋ/ *n* marcas *fpl*; *(on animal, plant)* mancha *f*

marksman /ˈmɑːksmən/ *n (pl* **-men)** tirador *m*. **∼ship** *n* puntería *f*

marmalade /ˈmɑːməleɪd/ *n* mermelada *f* (de cítricos)

maroon /məˈruːn/ *adj & n* granate *(m)*. ● *vt* abandonar (en una isla desierta)

marquee /mɑːˈkiː/ *n* toldo *m*, entoldado *m*; *(Amer, awning)* marquesina *f*

marriage /ˈmærɪdʒ/ *n* matrimonio *m*; *(ceremony)* casamiento *m*

married /ˈmærɪd/ *adj* casado; *(life)* conyugal

marrow /ˈmærəʊ/ *n (of bone)* tuétano *m*; *(vegetable)* calabaza *f* verde alargada. **∼ squash** *n (Amer)* calabaza *f* verde alargada

marry /ˈmærɪ/ *vt* casarse con; *(give or unite in marriage)* casar. ● *vi* casarse. **get married** casarse **(to con)**

Mars /mɑːz/ *n* Marte *m*

marsh /mɑːʃ/ *n* pantano *m*

marshal /ˈmɑːʃl/ *n (Mil)* mariscal *m*; *(Amer, police chief)* jefe *m* de policía. ● *vt (pt* **marshalled)** reunir; poner en orden *(thoughts)*

marsh: ∼mallow /-ˈmæləʊ/ *n* malvavisco *m*, bombón *m (LAm)*. **∼y** *adj* pantanoso

martial /ˈmɑːʃl/ *adj* marcial. **∼ arts** *npl* artes *fpl* marciales. **∼ law** *n* ley *f* marcial

martyr /ˈmɑːtə(r)/ *n* mártir *m & f*

marvel /ˈmɑːvl/ *n* maravilla *f*. ● *vi (pt* **marvelled)** maravillarse **(at** de). **∼lous** *adj* maravilloso

Marxis|m /ˈmɑːksɪzəm/ *n* marxismo *m*. **∼t** *adj* & *n* marxista *(m & f)*

marzipan /ˈmɑːzɪpæn/ *n* mazapán *m*

mascara /mæˈskɑːrə/ *n* rímel® *m*

m

mascot /'mæskɒt/ n mascota f

masculin|e /'mæskjʊlɪn/ adj & n masculino (m). **~ity** /-'lɪnəti/ n masculinidad f

mash /mæʃ/ n (Brit 🔲, potatoes) puré m de patatas, puré m de papas (LAm). ● vt hacer puré de, moler (Mex). **~ed potatoes** n puré m de patatas, puré m de papas (LAm)

mask /mɑːsk/ n máscara f; (Sport) careta f. ● vt ocultar

masochis|m /'mæsəkɪzəm/ n masoquismo m. **~t** n masoquista m & f. **~tic** /-'kɪstɪk/ adj masoquista

mason /'meɪsn/ n (stone ~) mampostero m. **M~** (freemason) masón m. **~ry** /'meɪsnrɪ/ n albañilería f

masquerade /mɑːskə'reɪd/ n mascarada f. ● vi. ~ **as** hacerse pasar por

mass /mæs/ n masa f; (Relig) misa f; (large quantity) montón m. **the ~es** las masas. ● vi concentrarse

massacre /'mæsəkə(r)/ n masacre f, matanza f. ● vt masacrar

mass|age /'mæsɑːʒ/ n masaje m. ● vt masajear. **~eur** /mæ'sɜː(r)/ n masajista m. **~euse** /mæ'sɜːz/ n masajista f

massive /'mæsɪv/ adj masivo; (heavy) macizo; (huge) enorme

mass: ~ **media** n medios mpl de comunicación. **~-produce** /-prə'djuːs/ vt fabricar en serie

mast /mɑːst/ n mástil m; (for radio, TV) antena f repetidora

master /'mɑːstə(r)/ n amo m; (expert) maestro m; (in secondary school) profesor m; (of ship) capitán m; (master copy) original m. **~'s degree** master m, maestría f. **M~ of**

Arts (MA) poseedor m de una maestría en filosofía y letras. **M~ of Science (MSc)** poseedor m de una maestría en ciencias. ● vt llegar a dominar. **~ key** n llave f maestra. **~mind** n cerebro m. ● vt dirigir. **~piece** n obra f maestra. **~stroke** n golpe m de maestro. **~y** n dominio m; (skill) maestría f

masturbat|e /'mæstəbeɪt/ vi masturbarse. **~ion** /-'beɪʃn/ n masturbación f

mat /mæt/ n estera f; (at door) felpudo m. ● adj (Amer) see **MATT**

match /mætʃ/ n (Sport) partido m; (for fire) cerilla f, fósforo m (LAm), cerillo m (Mex); (equal) igual m. ● vt emparejar; (equal) igualar; (clothes, colours) hacer juego con. ● vi hacer juego. **~box** n caja f de cerillas, caja f de fósforos (LAm), caja f de cerillos (Mex). **~ing** adj que hace juego. **~stick** n cerilla f, fósforo m (LAm), cerillo m (Mex)

mate /meɪt/ n (of person) pareja f; (of animals, male) macho m; (of animals, female) hembra f; (assistant) ayudante m; (🔲, friend) amigo m, cuate m (Mex); (Chess) (jaque m) mate m. ● vi aparearse

material /mə'tɪərɪəl/ n material m; (cloth) tela f ● adj material. **~istic** /-'lɪstɪk/ adj materialista. **~ize** vi materializarse. **~s** npl materiales mpl

matern|al /mə'tɜːnl/ adj maternal. **~ity** /-ətɪ/ n maternidad f. ● adj (ward) de obstetricia; (clothes) premamá, de embarazada

math /mæθ/ n (Amer) see **MATHS**

mathematic|ian /mæθəmə'tɪʃn/ n matemático m. **~al** /-'mætɪkl/ adj matemático. **~s** /-'mætɪks/ n matemática(s) f(pl)

maths /mæθs/ n matemática(s) f(pl)

matinée, matinee /'mætɪneɪ/ n (Theatre) función f de tarde; (Cinema) primera sesión f (de la tarde)

matrices /'meɪtrɪsi:z/ see MATRIX

matriculat|e /mə'trɪkjʊleɪt/ vi matricularse. **~ion** /-'leɪʃn/ n matrícula f

matrimon|ial /mætrɪ'məʊnɪəl/ adj matrimonial. **~y** /'mætrɪmənɪ/ n matrimonio m

matrix /'meɪtrɪks/ n (pl **matrices**) matriz f

matron /'meɪtrən/ n (married, elderly) matrona f; (in school) ama f de llaves; (former use, in hospital) enfermera f jefe

matt, matte (Amer) /mæt/ adj mate

matted /'mætɪd/ adj enmarañado y apelmazado

matter /'mætə(r)/ n (substance) materia f; (affair) asunto m; (pus) pus m. **as a ~ of fact** en realidad. **no ~** no importa. **what is the ~?** ¿qué pasa? **to make ~s worse** para colmo (de males). ● vi importar. **it doesn't ~** no importa. **~-of-fact** /-əv'fækt/ adj (person) práctico

mattress /'mætrɪs/ n colchón m

matur|e /mə'tjʊə(r)/ adj maduro. ● vi madurar. **~ity** n madurez f

maudlin /'mɔ:dlɪn/ adj llorón

maul /mɔ:l/ vt atacar (y herir)

mauve /məʊv/ adj n malva (m)

maverick /'mævərɪk/ n inconformista m & f

maxim /'mæksɪm/ n máxima f

maxim|ize /'mæksɪmaɪz/ vt maximizar. **~um** /-əm/ adj & n máximo (m)

may /meɪ/,

past **might**

auxiliary verb

····➤ (expressing possibility) **he ~ come** puede que venga, es posible que venga. **it ~ be true** puede ser verdad. **she ~ not have seen him** es posible que or puede que no lo haya visto

····➤ (asking for or giving permission) **~ I smoke?** ¿puedo fumar?, ¿se puede fumar? **~ I have your name and address, please?** ¿quiere darme su nombre y dirección, por favor?

····➤ (expressing a wish) **~ he be happy** que sea feliz

····➤ (conceding) **he ~ not have much experience, but he's very hardworking** no tendrá mucha experiencia, pero es muy trabajador. **that's as ~ be** puede ser

····➤ **I ~ as well stay** más vale quedarme

May /meɪ/ n mayo m

maybe /'meɪbɪ/ adv quizá(s), tal vez, a lo mejor

May Day n el primero de mayo

mayhem /'meɪhem/ n caos m

mayonnaise /meɪə'neɪz/ n mayonesa f, mahonesa f

mayor /meə(r)/ n alcalde m, alcaldesa f. **~ess** /-ɪs/ n alcaldesa f

maze /meɪz/ n laberinto m

me /mi:/ pron me; (after prep) mí. **he knows ~** me conoce. **it's ~** soy yo

meadow /'medəʊ/ n prado m, pradera f

meagre /'mi:gə(r)/ adj escaso

meal /miːl/ n comida f. **∼time** n hora f de comer

mean /miːn/ vt (pt meant) (intend) tener la intención de, querer; (signify) querer decir, significar. **∼ to do** tener la intención de hacer. **∼ well** tener buenas intenciones. **be meant for** estar destinado a. ● adj (-er, -est) (miserly) tacaño; (unkind) malo; (Math) medio. ● n media f; (average) promedio m

meander /mɪˈændə(r)/ vi (river) serpentear

meaning /ˈmiːnɪŋ/ n sentido m. **∼ful** adj significativo. **∼less** adj sin sentido

meanness /ˈmiːnnɪs/ n (miserliness) tacañería f; (unkindness) maldad f

means /miːnz/ n medio m. **by ∼ of** por medio de, mediante. **by all ∼** por supuesto. **by no ∼** de ninguna manera. ● npl (wealth) medios mpl, recursos mpl. **∼ test** n investigación f de ingresos

meant /ment/ see MEAN

meantime /ˈmiːntaɪm/ adv mientras tanto, entretanto. ● n. **in the ∼** mientras tanto, entretanto

meanwhile /ˈmiːnwaɪl/ adv mientras tanto, entretanto

measles /ˈmiːzlz/ n sarampión m. **∼y** /ˈmiːzlɪ/ adj miserable

measure /ˈmeʒə(r)/ n medida f; (ruler) regla f. ● vt/i medir. □ **∼ up to** vt estar a la altura de. **∼ment** n medida f

meat /miːt/ n carne f. **∼ball** n albóndiga f. **∼y** adj (taste, smell) a carne; (soup, stew) con mucha carne

mechanic /mɪˈkænɪk/ n mecánico m. **∼ical** adj mecánico. **∼ics** n mecánica f. **∼ism** /ˈmekənɪzəm/ n

mecanismo m. **∼ize** /ˈmekənaɪz/ vt mecanizar

medal /ˈmedl/ n medalla f. **∼list** /ˈmedəlɪst/ n medallista m & f. **be a gold ∼list** ganar una medalla de oro

meddle /ˈmedl/ vi meterse, entrometerse (**in** en). **∼ with** (tinker) toquetear

media /ˈmiːdɪə/ see MEDIUM. ● npl. **the ∼** los medios de comunicación

mediate /ˈmiːdɪeɪt/ vi mediar. **∼ion** /-ˈeɪʃn/ n mediación f. **∼or** n mediador m

medical /ˈmedɪkl/ adj médico; (student) de medicina. ● n revisión f médica

medicated /ˈmedɪkeɪtɪd/ adj medicinal. **∼ion** /-ˈkeɪʃn/ n medicación f

medicinal /mɪˈdɪsɪnl/ adj medicinal. **∼e** /ˈmedsɪn/ n medicina f

medieval /medrˈiːvl/ adj medieval

mediocre /miːdrˈəʊkə(r)/ adj mediocre

meditate /ˈmedɪteɪt/ vi meditar. **∼ion** /-ˈteɪʃn/ n meditación f

Mediterranean /meditə ˈreɪnɪən/ adj mediterráneo. ● n. **the ∼** el Mediterráneo

medium /ˈmiːdɪəm/ n (pl media) medio m. **happy ∼** n término m medio. ● adj mediano. **∼-size(d)** /-saɪz(d)/ adj de tamaño mediano

medley /ˈmedlɪ/ n (Mus) popurrí m; (mixture) mezcla f

meek /miːk/ adj (-er, -est) dócil

meet /miːt/ vt (pt met) encontrar; (bump into s.o.) encontrarse con; (fetch) ir a buscar; (get to know, be introduced to) conocer. ● vi encontrarse; (get to know) conocerse; (have meeting) reunirse. **∼ up** vi

encontrarse (**with** con). □ ~ **with**
vt ser recibido con; (*Amer, meet*) encontrarse con. ~**ing** *n* reunión *f*;
(*accidental between two people*) encuentro *m*

megabyte /'megəbaɪt/ *n* (*Comp*)
megabyte *m*, megaocteto *m*

megaphone /'megəfəʊn/ *n* megáfono *m*

melancholic /melən'kɒlɪk/ *adj*
melancólico. ~**y** /'melənkɒlɪ/ *n*
melancolía *f*. ● *adj* melancólico

mellow /'meləʊ/ *adj* (-er, -est)
(fruit) maduro; (sound) dulce;
(colour) tenue; (person) apacible

melodrama /'melədrɑːmə/ *n*
melodrama *m*. ~**tic** /ˌmelədrə-
'mætɪk/ *adj* melodramático

melody /'melədɪ/ *n* melodía *f*

melon /'melən/ *n* melón *m*

melt /melt/ *vt* (*make liquid*) derretir; fundir (metals). ● *vi* (*become liquid*) derretirse; (metals) fundirse.
□ ~ **down** *vt* fundir

member /'membə(r)/ *n* miembro
m & *f*; (of club) socio *m*. ~ **of staff**
empleado *m*. **M~ of Congress** *n*
(*Amer*) miembro *m* & *f* del Congreso.
M~ of Parliament *n* diputado *m*.
~**ship** *n* calidad *f* de socio; (*members*) socios *mpl*, membresía *f* (LAm)

membrane /'membreɪn/ *n* membrana *f*

memento /mɪ'mentəʊ/ *n* (*pl* -os
or -**oes**) recuerdo *m*

memo /'meməʊ/ *n* (*pl* -**os**) memorándum *m*, memo *m*

memoir /'memwɑː(r)/ *n* memoria *f*

memorable /'memərəbl/ *adj* memorable

memorandum /meməˈrændəm/ *n* (*pl* -**ums** *or* -**da** /-də/)
memorándum *m*

memorial /mɪ'mɔːrɪəl/ *n* monumento *m*. ● *adj* conmemorativo

memorize /'meməraɪz/ *vt* aprender de memoria. ~**y** /'memərɪ/ *n*
(*faculty*) memoria *f*; (*thing remembered*) recuerdo *m*. **from** ~**y** de
memoria. **in** ~**y of** a la memoria de

men /men/ *see* **MAN**

menace /'menəs/ *n* amenaza *f*;
(*fam, nuisance*) peligro *m* público.
● *vt* amenazar. ~**ing** *adj* amenazador

mend /mend/ *vt* reparar; arreglar
(garment). ~ **one's ways** enmendarse. ● *n* remiendo *m*. **be on the**
~ ir mejorando

menfolk /'menfəʊk/ *n* hombres
mpl

menial /'miːnɪəl/ *adj* servil

meningitis /menɪn'dʒaɪtɪs/ *n*
meningitis *f*

menopause /'menəpɔːz/ *n* menopausia *f*

menstruate /'menstrʊeɪt/ *vi*
menstruar. ~**ion** /-'eɪʃn/ *n* menstruación *f*

mental /'mentl/ *adj* mental; (hospital) psiquiátrico. ~**ity** /-'tælətɪ/ *n*
mentalidad *f*. ~**ly** *adv* mentalmente. **be** ~**ly ill** ser un enfermo
mental

mention /'menʃn/ *vt* mencionar.
don't ~ **it!** ¡no hay de qué! ● *n*
mención *f*

mentor /'mentɔː(r)/ *n* mentor *m*

menu /'menjuː/ *n* menú *m*

meow /mɪ'aʊ/ *n* & *vi see* **MEW**

mercenary /'mɜːsənərɪ/ *adj* & *n*
mercenario (*m*)

merchandise /'mɜːtʃəndaɪz/ *n*
mercancías *fpl*, mercadería *f* (LAm)

merchant /'mɜːtʃənt/ *n* comerciante *m*. ● *adj* (ship, navy) mercante. ~ **bank** n banco m mercantil

merci|ful /'mɜ:sɪfl/ adj misericordioso. ~**less** adj despiadado

mercury /'mɜ:kjʊrɪ/ n mercurio m. **M~** (planet) Mercurio m

mercy /'mɜ:sɪ/ n compasión f. **at the ~ of** a merced de

mere /mɪə(r)/ adj simple. ~**ly** adv simplemente

merge /mɜ:dʒ/ vt unir; fusionar (companies). ● vi unirse; (companies) fusionarse. ~**r** n fusión f

meridian /mə'rɪdɪən/ n meridiano m

meringue /mə'ræŋ/ n merengue m

merit /'merɪt/ n mérito m. ● vt (pt **merited**) merecer

mermaid /'mɜ:meɪd/ n sirena f

merr|ily /'merəlɪ/ adv alegremente. ~**iment** /'merɪmənt/ n alegría f. ~**y** /'merɪ/ adj (-ier, -iest) alegre. **make ~** divertirse. ~**y-go-round** n tiovivo m, carrusel m (LAm). ~**y-making** n jolgorio m

mesh /meʃ/ n malla f

mesmerize /'mezməraɪz/ vt hipnotizar; (fascinate) cautivar

mess /mes/ n desorden m; (dirt) suciedad f; (Mil) rancho m. **make a ~ of** estropear. □ ~ **up** vt desordenar; (dirty) ensuciar; estropear (plans). □ ~ **about** vi tontear. □ ~ **with** vt (tinker with) manosear

mess|age /'mesɪdʒ/ n mensaje m; (when phoning) recado m. ~**enger** /'mesɪndʒə(r)/ n mensajero m

Messiah /mɪ'saɪə/ n Mesías m

Messrs /'mesəz/ npl. ~ **Smith** los señores Smith, los Sres. Smith

messy /'mesɪ/ adj (-ier, -iest) en desorden; (dirty) sucio

met /met/ see **MEET**

metabolism /mɪ'tæbəlɪzəm/ n metabolismo m

metal /'metl/ n metal. ● adj de metal. ~**lic** /mə'tælɪk/ adj metálico

metaphor /'metəfə(r)/ n metáfora f. ~**ical** /-'fɒrɪkl/ adj metafórico

mete /mi:t/ vt. ~ **out** repartir; dar (punishment)

meteor /'mi:tɪə(r)/ n meteoro m. ~**ic** /-'ɒrɪk/ adj meteórico. ~**ite** /'mi:tɪəraɪt/ n meteorito m

meteorolog|ical /mi:tɪərə'lɒdʒɪkl/ adj meteorológico. ~**ist** /-'rɒlədʒɪst/ n meteorólogo m. ~**y** /-'rɒlədʒɪ/ n meteorología f

meter /'mi:tə(r)/ n contador m, medidor m (LAm); (Amer) see **METRE**

method /'meθəd/ n método m. ~**ical** /mɪ'θɒdɪkl/ adj metódico. **M~ist** /'meθədɪst/ adj & n metodista (m & f)

methylated /'meθɪleɪtɪd/ adj. ~ **spirit(s)** n alcohol m desnaturalizado

meticulous /mɪ'tɪkjʊləs/ adj meticuloso

metre /'mi:tə(r)/ n metro m

metric /'metrɪk/ adj métrico

metropoli|s /mɪ'trɒpəlɪs/ n metrópoli(s) f

mettle /'metl/ n. **be on one's ~** (fig) estar dispuesto a dar lo mejor de sí

mew /mju:/ n maullido m. ● vi maullar

Mexic|an /'meksɪkən/ adj & n mejicano (m), mexicano (m). ~**o** /-kəʊ/ n Méjico m, México m

miaow /mi:'aʊ/ n & vi see **MEW**

mice /maɪs/ see **MOUSE**

mickey /'mɪkɪ/ n. **take the ~ out of** 🆃 tomar el pelo a

micro... /'maɪkrəʊ/ *pref* micro...

microbe /'maɪkrəʊb/ *n* microbio *m*

micro: ~**chip** *n* pastilla *f.*
~**film** *n* microfilme *m.* ~**light** *n* aeroligero *m.* ~**phone** *n* micrófono *m.* ~**processor** /-'prəʊsesə(r)/ *n* microprocesador *m.* ~**scope** *n* microscopio *m.* ~**scopic** /-'skɒpɪk/ *adj* microscópico. ~**wave** *n* microonda *f.* ~**wave oven** *n* horno *m* de microondas

mid- /mɪd/ *pref.* **in** ~ **air** en pleno aire. **in** ~ **March** a mediados de marzo

midday /mɪd'deɪ/ *n* mediodía *m*

middl|e /'mɪdl/ *adj* de en medio. ● *n* medio *m.* **in the** ~**e of** en medio de. ~**e-aged** /-'eɪdʒd/ *adj* de mediana edad. **M~e Ages** *npl* Edad *f* Media. ~**e class** *n* clase *f* media. ~**e-class** *adj* de la clase media. **M~e East** *n* Oriente *m* Medio. ~**eman** *n* intermediario *m.* ~**e name** *n* segundo nombre *m.* ~**ing** *adj* regular

midge /mɪdʒ/ *n* mosquito *m*

midget /'mɪdʒɪt/ *n* enano *m.* ● *adj* minúsculo

Midlands /'mɪdləndz/ *npl* región *f* central de Inglaterra

midnight /'mɪdnaɪt/ *n* medianoche *f*

midriff /'mɪdrɪf/ *n* diafragma *m*

midst /mɪdst/ *n.* **in our** ~ entre nosotros. **in the** ~ **of** en medio de

midsummer /mɪd'sʌmə(r)/ *n* pleno verano *m;* (*solstice*) solsticio *m* de verano

midway /mɪd'weɪ/ *adv* a mitad de camino

Midwest /mɪd'west/ región *f* central de los EE.UU.

midwife /'mɪdwaɪf/ *n* comadrona *f*, partera *f*

midwinter /mɪd'wɪntə(r)/ *n* pleno invierno *m*

might /maɪt/ *see* MAY. ● *n* (*strength*) fuerza *f*; (*power*) poder *m.* ~**y** *adj* (*strong*) fuerte; (*powerful*) poderoso. ● *adv* 🄴 muy

migraine /'miːgreɪn/ *n* jaqueca *f*

migra|nt /'maɪgrənt/ *adj* migratorio. ● *n* (*person*) emigrante *m & f.* ~**te** /maɪ'greɪt/ *vi* emigrar. ~**tion** /-'greɪʃn/ *n* migración *f*

mild /maɪld/ *adj* (-**er**, -**est**) (person) afable; (climate) templado; (slight) ligero; (taste, manner) suave

mildew /'mɪldjuː/ *n* moho *m;* (on plants) mildeu *m*, mildiu *m*

mildly /'maɪldlɪ/ *adv* (gently) suavemente; (slightly) ligeramente

mile /maɪl/ *n* milla *f.* ~**s better** 🄴 mucho mejor. ~**s too big** 🄴 demasiado grande. ~**age** /-ɪdʒ/ *n* (loosely) kilometraje *m.* ~**ometer** /maɪ'lɒmɪtə(r)/ *n* (loosely) cuentakilómetros *m.* ~**stone** *n* mojón *m;* (event, stage, fig) hito *m*

militant /'mɪlɪtənt/ *adj & n* militante (*m & f*)

military /'mɪlɪtərɪ/ *adj* militar

militia /mɪ'lɪʃə/ *n* milicia *f*

milk /mɪlk/ *n* leche *f.* ● *adj* (product) lácteo; (chocolate) con leche. ● *vt* ordeñar (cow). ~**man** /-mən/ *n* lechero *m.* ~**shake** *n* batido *m*, (leche *f*) malteada *f* (LAm), licuado *m* con leche (LAm). ~**y** *adj* lechoso. **M~y Way** *n* Vía *f* Láctea

mill /mɪl/ *n* molino *m;* (for coffee, pepper) molinillo *m;* (factory) fábrica *f* de tejidos de algodón. ● *vt* moler. ▫ ~ **about**, **mill around** *vi* dar vueltas

millennium /mɪˈlenɪəm/ n (pl **-ia** /-ɪə/ or **-iums**) milenio m

miller /ˈmɪlə(r)/ n molinero m

milli... /ˈmɪlɪ/ pref mili...
~**gram(me)** n miligramo m.
~**metre** n milímetro m

milliner /ˈmɪlɪnə(r)/ n sombrerero m

million /ˈmɪljən/ n millón m. **a ~ pounds** un millón de libras. ~**aire** /-ˈeə(r)/ n millonario m

millstone /ˈmɪlstəʊn/ n muela f (de molino). (fig, burden) carga f

mime /maɪm/ n mímica f. ● vt imitar, hacer la mímica de. ● vi hacer la mímica

mimic /ˈmɪmɪk/ vt (pt **mimicked**) imitar. ● n imitador m. ~**ry** n imitación f

mince /mɪns/ vt picar, moler (LAm) (meat). **not to ~ matters/words** no andar(se) con rodeos. ● n carne f picada, carne f molida (LAm). ~ **pie** n pastelito m de Navidad (pastelito relleno de picadillo de frutos secos). ~**r** n máquina f de picar carne, máquina f de moler carne (LAm)

mind /maɪnd/ n mente f; (sanity) juicio m. **to my ~** a mi parecer. **be on one's mind** preocuparle a uno. **make up one's ~** decidirse. ● vt (look after) cuidar (de); atender (shop). ~ **the steps!** ¡cuidado con las escaleras! **never ~ him** no le hagas caso. **I don't ~ the noise** no me molesta el ruido. **would you ~ closing the door?** ¿le importaría cerrar la puerta? ● vi. **never ~** no importa, no te preocupes. **I don't ~** (don't object) me da igual. **do you ~ if I smoke?** ¿le importa si fumo? ~**ful** adj atento (of a). ~**less** adj (activity) mecánico; (violence) ciego

mine¹ /maɪn/ poss pron (sing) mío, mía; (pl) míos, mías. **it is ~** es mío. ~ **are blue** los míos/las mías son azules. **a friend of ~** un amigo mío/una amiga mía

mine² /maɪn/ n mina f; (Mil) mina f. ● vt extraer. ~**field** n campo m de minas. ~**r** n minero m

mineral /ˈmɪnərəl/ adj & n mineral (m). ~ **water** n agua f mineral

mingle /ˈmɪŋgl/ vi mezclarse

mini... /ˈmɪnɪ/ pref mini...

miniature /ˈmɪnɪtʃə(r)/ n miniatura f. ● adj en miniatura

mini: ~**bus** n microbús m. ~**cab** n taxi m (que se pide por teléfono)

minim|al /ˈmɪnɪml/ adj mínimo. ~**ize** vt reducir al mínimo. ~**um** /-məm/ adj & n (pl **-ima** /-mə/) mínimo (m)

mining /ˈmaɪnɪŋ/ n minería f. ● adj minero

miniskirt /ˈmɪnɪskɜːt/ n minifalda f

minist|er /ˈmɪnɪstə(r)/ n ministro m, secretario m (Mex); (Relig) pastor m. ~**erial** /-ˈstɪərɪəl/ adj ministerial. ~**ry** n ministerio m, secretaría f (Mex)

mink /mɪŋk/ n visón m

minor /ˈmaɪnə(r)/ adj (also Mus) menor; (injury) leve; (change) pequeño; (operation) de poca importancia. ● n menor m & f de edad. ~**ity** /maɪˈnɒrətɪ/ n minoría f. ● adj minoritario

minstrel /ˈmɪnstrəl/ n juglar m

mint /mɪnt/ n (plant) menta f; (sweet) pastilla f de menta; (Finance) casa f de la moneda. **in ~ condition** como nuevo. ● vt acuñar

minus /ˈmaɪnəs/ prep menos; (fam, without) sin. ● n (sign) menos *m.* **five ~ three is two** cinco menos tres is igual a dos. **~ sign** *n* (signo *m* de) menos *m*

minute¹ /'mɪnɪt/ *n* minuto *m*. **the ~s** *npl* (*of meeting*) el acta *f*

minute² /maɪ'njuːt/ *adj* diminuto; (*detailed*) minucioso

miracle /'mɪrəkl/ *n* milagro *m*. **~ulous** /mɪ'rækjʊləs/ *adj* milagroso

mirage /'mɪrɑːʒ/ *n* espejismo *m*

mirror /'mɪrə(r)/ *n* espejo *m*; (*driving ~*) (espejo *m*) retrovisor *m*. ● *vt* reflejar

mirth /mɜːθ/ *n* regocijo *m*; (*laughter*) risas *fpl*

misapprehension /mɪsæprɪ'henʃn/ *n* malentendido *m*

misbehave /mɪsbɪ'heɪv/ *vi* portarse mal. **~iour** *n* mala conducta

miscalculate /mɪs'kælkjʊleɪt/ *vt/i* calcular mal. **~ion** /-'leɪʃn/ *n* error *m* de cálculo

miscarriage /'mɪskærɪdʒ/ *n* aborto *m* espontáneo. **~iage of justice** *n* injusticia *f*. **~y** *vi* abortar

miscellaneous /mɪsə'leɪnɪəs/ *adj* heterogéneo

mischief /'mɪstʃɪf/ *n* (*foolish conduct*) travesura *f*; (*harm*) daño *m.* **get into ~f** hacer travesuras. **make ~f** causar daños. **~vous** /'mɪstʃɪvəs/ *adj* travieso; (*grin*) pícaro

misconception /mɪskən'sepʃn/ *n* equivocación *f*

misconduct /mɪs'kɒndʌkt/ *n* mala conducta *f*

misdeed /mɪs'diːd/ *n* fechoría *f*

misdemeanour /mɪsdɪ'miːnə(r)/ *n* delito *m* menor, falta *f*

miser /'maɪzə(r)/ *n* avaro *m*

miserable /'mɪzərəbl/ *adj* (*sad*) triste; (*in low spirits*) abatido;

(*wretched, poor*) mísero; (*weather*) pésimo

miserly /'maɪzəlɪ/ *adj* avariento

misery /'mɪzərɪ/ *n* (*unhappiness*) tristeza *f*; (*pain*) sufrimiento *m*

misfire /mɪs'faɪə(r)/ *vi* fallar

misfit /'mɪsfɪt/ *n* inadaptado *m*

misfortune /mɪs'fɔːtʃuːn/ *n* desgracia *f*

misgiving /mɪs'gɪvɪŋ/ *n* recelo *m*

misguided /mɪs'gaɪdɪd/ *adj* equivocado

mishap /'mɪshæp/ *n* percance *m*

misinform /mɪsɪn'fɔːm/ *vt* informar mal

misinterpret /mɪsɪn'tɜːprɪt/ *vt* interpretar mal

misjudge /mɪs'dʒʌdʒ/ *vt* juzgar mal; (*miscalculate*) calcular mal

mislay /mɪs'leɪ/ *vt* (*pt* **mislaid**) extraviar, perder

mislead /mɪs'liːd/ *vt* (*pt* **misled** /mɪs'led/) engañar. **~ing** *adj* engañoso

mismanage /mɪs'mænɪdʒ/ *vt* administrar mal. **~ment** *n* mala administración *f*

misplace /mɪs'pleɪs/ *vt* (*lose*) extraviar, perder

misprint /'mɪsprɪnt/ *n* errata *f*

miss /mɪs/ *vt* (*fail to hit*) no dar en; (*regret absence of*) echar de menos, extrañar (*LAm*); perder (*train, party*); perder (*chance*). **~ the point** no comprender. ● *vi* errar el tiro, fallar; (*bullet*) no dar en el blanco. ■ **~ out** *vt* saltarse (*line*). **~out on sth** perderse algo

misshapen /mɪs'ʃeɪpən/ *adj* deforme

missile /'mɪsaɪl/ *n* (*Mil*) misil *m*

missing /'mɪsɪŋ/ adj (lost) perdido. **be ~** faltar. **go ~** desaparecer. **~ person** desaparecido m

mission /'mɪʃn/ n misión f. **~ary** /'mɪʃənərɪ/ n misionero m

mist /mɪst/ n neblina f; (at sea) bruma f. **~ up** vi empañarse

mistake /mɪ'steɪk/ n error m. **make a ~** cometer un error. **by ~** por error. ● vt (pt **mistook**, pp **mistaken**) confundir. **~ for** confundir con. **~n** /-ən/ adj equivocado. **be ~n** equivocarse

mistletoe /'mɪsltəʊ/ n muérdago m

mistreat /mɪs'triːt/ vt maltratar

mistress /'mɪstrɪs/ n (of house) señora f; (lover) amante f

mistrust /mɪs'trʌst/ vt desconfiar de. ● n desconfianza f. **~ful** adj desconfiado

misty /'mɪstɪ/ adj (-ier, -iest) neblinoso; (day) de neblina. **it's ~** hay neblina

misunderstand /mɪsʌndə'stænd/ vt (pt **-stood**) entender mal. **~ing** n malentendido m

misuse /mɪs'juːz/ vt emplear mal; malversar (funds). ● /mɪs'juːs/ n mal uso m; (unfair use) abuso m; (of funds) malversación f

mite /maɪt/ n (insect) ácaro m

mitten /'mɪtn/ n mitón m

mix /mɪks/ vt mezclar. ● vi mezclarse; (go together) combinar. **~ with** tratarse con (people). ● n mezcla f. □ **~ up** vt mezclar; (confuse) confundir. **~ed** adj (school etc) mixto; (assorted) mezclado. **be ~ed up** estar confuso. **~er** n (Culin) batidora f; (TV, machine) mezcladora f. **~ture** /'mɪkstʃə(r)/ n mezcla f. **~up** n lío m

moan /məʊn/ n gemido m. ● vi gemir; (complain) quejarse (about de)

moat /məʊt/ n foso m

mob /mɒb/ n turba f. ● vt (pt **mobbed**) acosar

mobile /'məʊbaɪl/ adj móvil. **~e home** n caravana f, trailer m (LAm). **~e (phone)** n (teléfono m) móvil m, (teléfono m) celular m (LAm). **~e** n móvil m. **~ize** /'məʊbɪlaɪz/ vt movilizar. ● vi movilizarse

mock /mɒk/ vt burlarse de. ● adj (anger) fingido; (exam) de práctica. **~ery** /'mɒkərɪ/ n burla f. **make a ~ery of sth** ridiculizar algo

model /'mɒdl/ n (example) modelo m; (mock-up) maqueta f; (person) modelo m. ● adj (exemplary) modelo; (car etc) en miniatura. ● vt (pt **modelled**) modelar. **~ s.o. on** s.o. tomar a uno como modelo

modem /'məʊdem/ n (Comp) módem m

moderat|e /'mɒdərət/ adj & n moderado (m). ● /'mɒdəreɪt/ vt moderar. **~ely** /'mɒdərətlɪ/ adv (fairly) medianamente. **~ion** /-'reɪʃn/ n moderación f. **in ~ion** con moderación

modern /'mɒdn/ adj moderno. **~ize** vt modernizar

modest /'mɒdɪst/ adj modesto. **~y** n modestia f

modif|ication /mɒdɪfɪ'keɪʃn/ n modificación f. **~y** /-faɪ/ vt modificar

module /'mɒdjuːl/ n módulo m

moist /mɔɪst/ adj (-er, -est) húmedo. **~en** /'mɔɪsn/ vt humedecer

moistur|e /'mɔɪstʃə(r)/ n humedad f. **~ize** vt hidratar. **~izer**, **~izing cream** n crema f hidratante

mole /məʊl/ n (animal) topo m; (on skin) lunar m

molecule /ˈmɒlɪkjuːl/ n molécula f

molest /məˈlest/ vt abusar (sexualmente) de

mollify /ˈmɒlɪfaɪ/ vt aplacar

mollusc /ˈmɒləsk/ n molusco m

mollycoddle /ˈmɒlɪkɒdl/ vt mimar

molten /ˈməʊltən/ adj fundido; (lava) líquido

mom /mɒm/ n (Amer, 🎧) mamá f 🎧

moment /ˈməʊmənt/ n momento m. **at the ~** en este momento. **for the ~** de momento. **~ary** /ˈməʊməntərɪ/ adj momentáneo

momentous /məˈmentəs/ adj trascendental

momentum /məˈmentəm/ n momento m; (speed) velocidad f

mommy /ˈmɒmɪ/ n (Amer, fam) mamá f 🎧

monarch /ˈmɒnək/ n monarca m. **~y** n monarquía f

monastery /ˈmɒnəstərɪ/ n monasterio m

Monday /ˈmʌndeɪ/ n lunes m

money /ˈmʌnɪ/ n dinero m, plata f (LAm). **~box** n hucha f, alcancía f (LAm). **~ order** n giro m postal

mongrel /ˈmʌŋɡrəl/ n perro m mestizo, chucho m 🎧

monitor /ˈmɒnɪtə(r)/ n (Tec) monitor m. ● vt observar (elections); seguir (progress); (electronically) monitorizar, escuchar

monk /mʌŋk/ n monje m. **~fish** n rape m

monkey /ˈmʌŋkɪ/ n mono m. **~nut** n cacahuete m, cacahuate m (Mex), maní m (LAm). **~wrench** n

llave f inglesa

mono /ˈmɒnəʊ/ n monofonía f

monologue /ˈmɒnəlɒɡ/ n monólogo m

monopol|ize /məˈnɒpəlaɪz/ vt monopolizar; acaparar (conversation). **~y** n monopolio m

monoton|e /ˈmɒnətəʊn/ n tono m monocorde. **~ous** /məˈnɒtənəs/ adj monótono. **~y** n monotonía f

monsoon /mɒnˈsuːn/ n monzón m

monst|er /ˈmɒnstə(r)/ n monstruo m. **~rous** /-strəs/ adj monstruoso

month /mʌnθ/ n mes m. £200 a ~ 200 libras mensuales or al mes. **~ly** adj mensual. **~ly payment** mensualidad f, cuota f mensual (LAm). ● adv mensualmente

monument /ˈmɒnjʊmənt/ n monumento m. **~al** /-ˈmentl/ adj monumental

moo /muː/ n mugido m. ● vi mugir

mood /muːd/ n humor m. **be in a good/bad** ~ estar de buen/mal humor. **~y** adj (-ier, -iest) temperamental; (bad-tempered) malhumorado

moon /muːn/ n luna f. **~light** n luz f de la luna. **~lighting** n pluriempleo m. **~lit** adj iluminado por la luna; (night) de luna

moor /mʊə(r)/ n páramo m; (of heather) brezal m. ● vt amarrar. **~ing** n (place) amarradero m. **~ings** npl (ropes) amarras fpl

moose /muːs/ n invar alce m americano

mop /mɒp/ n fregona f, trapeador m (LAm). ~ **of hair** pelambrera f. ● vt (pt mopped). ~ **(up)** limpiar

mope /məʊp/ vi estar abatido

moped /ˈməʊped/ n ciclomotor m

m

moral /'mɒrəl/ adj moral. • n (of tale) moraleja f

morale /mə'rɑːl/ n moral f

morallity /mə'rælətɪ/ n moralidad f. ~**ly** adv moralmente. ~**s** npl moralidad f

morbid /'mɔːbɪd/ adj morboso

more /mɔː(r)/ adj más. two ~ bottles dos botellas más. • pron más. you ate ~ than me comiste más que yo. some ~ más. ~ than six más de seis. the ~ he has, the ~ he wants cuánto más tiene, más quiere. • adv más. ~ and ~ cada vez más. ~ or less más o menos. once ~ una vez más. she doesn't live here any ~ ya no vive aquí. ~**over** /mɔː'rəʊvə(r)/ adv además

morgue /mɔːg/ n depósito m de cadáveres, morgue f (LAm)

morning /'mɔːnɪŋ/ n mañana f; (early hours) madrugada f. at 11 o'clock in the ~ a las once de la mañana. in the ~ por la mañana, en la mañana (LAm). tomorrow/ yesterday ~ mañana/ayer por la mañana or (LAm) en la mañana. (good) ~! ¡buenos días!

Moroccan /mə'rɒkən/ adj & n marroquí (m & f). ~**o** /-kəʊ/ n Marruecos m

moron /'mɔːrɒn/ n imbécil m & f

morose /mə'rəʊs/ adj taciturno

Morse /mɔːs/ n Morse m. in ~ (code) n en (código) morse

morsel /'mɔːsl/ n bocado m

mortal /'mɔːtl/ adj & n mortal (m). ~**ity** /-'tælətɪ/ n mortalidad f

mortar /'mɔːtə(r)/ n (all senses) mortero m

mortgage /'mɔːgɪdʒ/ n hipoteca f. • vt hipotecar

mortify /'mɔːtɪfaɪ/ vt darle mucha vergüenza a

mortuary /'mɔːtjʊərɪ/ n depósito m de cadáveres, morgue f (LAm)

mosaic /məʊ'zeɪk/ n mosaico m

mosque /mɒsk/ n mezquita f

mosquito /mɒs'kiːtəʊ/ n (pl -oes) mosquito m, zancudo m (LAm)

moss /mɒs/ n musgo m

most /məʊst/ adj la mayoría de, la mayor parte de. ~ days casi todos los días. • pron la mayoría, la mayor parte. at ~ como máximo. make the ~ of aprovechar al máximo. • adv más; (very) muy; (Amer, almost) casi. ~**ly** adv principalmente

MOT n. ~ (test) ITV f, inspección f técnica de vehículos

motel /məʊ'tel/ n motel m

moth /mɒθ/ n mariposa f de la luz, palomilla f; (in clothes) polilla f

mother /'mʌðə(r)/ n madre f. • vt mimar. ~**-in-law** n (pl ~s-in-law) suegra f. ~**land** n patria f. ~**ly** adj maternal. ~**-of-pearl** n nácar m, madreperla f. M~'s Day n el día m de la Madre. ~**-to-be** n futura madre f. ~ **tongue** n lengua f materna

motif /məʊ'tiːf/ n motivo m

motion /'məʊʃn/ n movimiento m; (proposal) moción f. put or set in ~ poner algo en marcha. • vt/i. ~ (to) s.o. to hacerle señas a uno para que. ~**less** adj inmóvil

motivate /'məʊtɪveɪt/ vt motivar. ~**ation** /-'veɪʃn/ n motivación f. ~**e** /'məʊtɪv/ n motivo m

motley /'mɒtlɪ/ adj variopinto

motor /'məʊtə(r)/ n motor m. • adj motor; (fem) motora, motriz. ~ **bike** n ① motocicleta f, moto f ①. ~ **boat** n lancha f a motor. ~ **car** n automóvil m. ~ **cycle** n motocicleta f. ~**cyclist** n motoci-

motto | muffle

clista m & f. **~ing** n automovilismo m. **~ist** n automovilista m & f. **~way** n autopista f

motto /'mɒtəʊ/ n (pl -oes) lema m

mould /məʊld/ n molde m; (fungus) moho m. ● vt moldear; formar (character). **~ing** n (on wall etc) moldura f. **~y** adj mohoso

moult /məʊlt/ vi mudar de pelo/piel/plumas

mound /maʊnd/ n montículo m; (pile, fig) montón m

mount /maʊnt/ vt montar (horse); engarzar (gem); preparar (attack). ● vi subir, crecer. ● n. montura f; (mountain) monte m. **□ ~ up** vi irse acumulando

mountain /'maʊntɪn/ n montaña f. **~eer** /maʊntɪ'nɪə(r)/ n alpinista m & f. **~eering** n alpinismo m. **~ous** adj montañoso

mourn /mɔːn/ vt llorar. ● vi lamentarse. **~ for s.o.** llorar a uno. **~er** n doliente m & f. **~ful** adj triste. **~ing** n duelo m, luto m. **be in ~ing** estar de duelo

mouse /maʊs/ n (pl mice) ratón m. **~trap** n ratonera f

mousse /muːs/ n (Culin) mousse f or m; (for hair) mousse f

moustache /məˈstɑːʃ/ n bigote m

mouth /maʊθ/ n boca f; (of cave) entrada f; (of river) desembocadura f. **~ful** n bocado m. **~-organ** n armónica f. **~wash** n enjuague m bucal

move /muːv/ vt mover; (relocate) trasladar; (with emotion) conmover; (propose) proponer. **~ the television** cambiar de lugar la televisión. **~ house** mudarse de casa. ● vi moverse; (be in motion) estar en movimiento; (take action) tomar medidas. ● n movimiento m; (in

game) jugada f; (player's turn) turno m; (removal) mudanza f. **□ ~ away** vi alejarse. **□ ~ in** vi instalarse. **~ in with s.o.** irse a vivir con uno. **□ ~ over** vi correrse. **~ment** n movimiento m

movie /'muːvɪ/ n (Amer) película f. **the ~s** npl el cine. **~ camera** n (Amer) tomavistas m, filmadora f (LAm)

moving /'muːvɪŋ/ adj en movimiento; (touching) conmovedor

mow /məʊ/ vt (pt mowed or mown /məʊn/) cortar (lawn); segar (hay). **□ ~ down** vt acribillar. **~er** n (for lawn) cortacésped m

MP abbr see MEMBER OF PARLIAMENT

Mr /'mɪstə(r)/ abbr (pl Messrs) (= Mister) Sr. **~ Coldbeck** Sr. Coldbeck

Mrs /'mɪsɪz/ abbr (pl Mrs) (= Missis) Sra. **~ Andrews** Sra. Andrews

Ms /mɪz/ abbr (title of married or unmarried woman)

MSc abbr see MASTER

much /mʌtʃ/ adj & pron mucho, mucha. ● adv mucho; (before pp) muy. **~ as** por mucho que. **~ the same** más o menos lo mismo. **how ~?** ¿cuánto? **so ~** tanto. **too ~** demasiado

muck /mʌk/ n estiércol m; (fam, dirt) mugre f. **□ ~ about** vi 🔢 tontear

mud /mʌd/ n barro m, lodo m

muddle /'mʌdl/ vt embrollar. ● n desorden m; (mix-up) lío m. **□ ~ through** vi salir del paso

muddy adj lodoso; (hands etc) cubierto de lodo. **~guard** n guardabarros m, salpicadera f (Mex)

muffle /'mʌfl/ vt amortiguar (sound). **~r** n (scarf) bufanda f;

(Amer, Auto) silenciador m

mug /mʌg/ n taza f (alta y sin platillo), tarro m (Mex); (for beer) jarra f; (fam, face) cara f, jeta f 🔲; (fam, fool) idiota m & f ● vt (pt mugged) asaltar. **~ger** n asaltante m & f. **~ging** n asalto m

muggy /'mʌgɪ/ adj bochornoso

mule /mjuːl/ n mula f

mull /mʌl/ (Amer), **~ over** vt reflexionar sobre

multi|coloured /mʌltɪ'kʌləd/ adj multicolor. **~national** /-'næʃənl/ adj & n multinacional (f)

multipl|e /'mʌltɪpl/ adj múltiple. ● n múltiplo m. **~ication** /mʌltɪplɪ'keɪʃn/ n multiplicación f ● **~y** /'mʌltɪplaɪ/ vt multiplicar. ● vi (Math) multiplicar; (increase) multiplicarse

multitude /'mʌltɪtjuːd/ n. a **~** of problems múltiples problemas

mum /mʌm/ n 🔲 mamá f 🔲

mumble /'mʌmbl/ vt mascullar. ● vi hablar entre dientes

mummy /'mʌmɪ/ n (fam, mother) mamá f 🔲; (archaeology) momia f

mumps /mʌmps/ n paperas fpl

munch /mʌntʃ/ vt/i mascar

mundane /mʌn'deɪn/ adj mundano

municipal /mjuː'nɪsɪpl/ adj municipal

mural /'mjʊərəl/ adj & n mural (f)

murder /'mɜːdə(r)/ n asesinato m. ● vt asesinar. **~er** n asesino m

murky /'mɜːkɪ/ adj (-ier, -iest) turbio

murmur /'mɜːmə(r)/ n murmullo m. ● vt/i murmurar

musc|le /'mʌsl/ n músculo m. **~ular** /'mʌskjʊlə(r)/ adj muscular; (arm, body) musculoso

muse /mjuːz/ vi meditar (on sobre)

museum /mjuː'zɪəm/ n museo m

mush /mʌʃ/ n papilla f

mushroom /'mʌʃrʊm/ n champiñón m; (in botany) seta f ● vi aparecer como hongos

mushy /'mʌʃɪ/ adj blando

music /'mjuːzɪk/ n música f. **~al** adj musical. **be ~** tener sentido musical. ● n musical m. **~ian** /mjuː'zɪʃn/ n músico m

Muslim /'mʊzlɪm/ adj & n musulmán (m)

mussel /'mʌsl/ n mejillón m

must /mʌst/ modal verb deber, tener que; (expressing supposition) deber (de). **he ~ be old** (de) ser viejo. **I ~ have done it** debo (de) haberlo hecho. ● n. **be a ~** ser imprescindible

mustache /'mʌstæʃ/ n (Amer) bigote m

mustard /'mʌstəd/ n mostaza f

muster /'mʌstə(r)/ vt reunir

musty /'mʌstɪ/ adj (-ier, -iest) que huele a humedad

mutation /mjuː'teɪʃn/ n mutación f

mute /mjuːt/ adj mudo

mutilate /'mjuːtɪleɪt/ vt mutilar

mutiny /'mjuːtɪnɪ/ n motín m. ● vi amotinarse

mutter /'mʌtə(r)/ vt/i murmurar

mutton /'mʌtn/ n carne f de ovino

mutual /'mjuːtʃʊəl/ adj mutuo; (fam, common) común

muzzle /'mʌzl/ n (snout) hocico m; (device) bozal m

my /maɪ/ adj (sing) mi; (pl) mis

myself /maɪ'self/ pron (reflexive) me; (used for emphasis) yo mismo *m*, yo misma *f*. **I cut** ~ me corté. **I made it** ~ lo hice yo mismo/ misma. **I was by** ~ estaba solo/ sola

myster|ious /mɪˈstɪərɪəs/ *adj* misterioso. **~y** /ˈmɪstərɪ/ *n* misterio *m*

mystical /ˈmɪstɪkl/ *adj* místico

mystify /ˈmɪstɪfaɪ/ *vt* dejar perplejo

mystique /mɪˈstiːk/ *n* mística *f*

myth /mɪθ/ *n* mito *m*. **~ical** *adj* mítico. **~ology** /mɪˈθɒlədʒɪ/ *n* mitología *f*

....

Nn

N *abbr* (**= north**) N

nab /næb/ *vt* (*pt* **nabbed**) (*sl*, *arrest*) pescar; (*snatch*) agarrar

nag /næg/ *vt* (*pt* **nagged**) fastidiar; (*scold*) estarle encima a. ● *vi* criticar

nail /neɪl/ *n* clavo *m*; (*of finger, toe*) uña *f*. ~ **polish** esmalte *m* para las uñas. ● *vt*. ~ (**down**) clavar

naive /naɪˈiːv/ *adj* ingenuo

naked /ˈneɪkɪd/ *adj* desnudo. **to the** ~ **eye** a simple vista

name /neɪm/ *n* nombre *m*; (*of book, film*) título *m*; (*fig*) fama *f*. **my** ~ **is Chris** me llamo Chris. **good** ~ buena reputación. ● *vt* ponerle nombre a; (*appoint*) nombrar. **a man** ~**d Jones** un hombre llamado Jones. **she was** ~**d after** *or* (*Amer*) **for her grandmother** le pusieron el nombre de su abuela. **~less** *adj* anónimo. **~ly** *adv* a saber. **~sake** *n* (*person*) tocayo *m*

nanny /ˈnænɪ/ *n* niñera *f*

nap /næp/ *n* (*sleep*) sueñecito *m*; (*after lunch*) siesta *f*. **have a** ~ echarse un sueño

napkin /ˈnæpkɪn/ *n* servilleta *f*

nappy /ˈnæpɪ/ *n* pañal *m*

narcotic /nɑːˈkɒtɪk/ *adj* & *n* narcótico (*m*)

narrat|e /nəˈreɪt/ *vt* narrar. **~ive** /ˈnærətɪv/ *n* narración *f*. **~or** /nəˈreɪtə(r)/ *n* narrador *m*

narrow /ˈnærəʊ/ *adj* (**-er, -est**) estrecho, angosto (*LAm*). **have a** ~ **escape** salvarse de milagro. ● *vt* estrechar; (*limit*) limitar. ● *vi* estrecharse. **~ly** *adv* (*just*) por poco. **~-minded** /-ˈmaɪndɪd/ *adj* de miras estrechas

nasal /ˈneɪzl/ *adj* nasal; (*voice*) gangoso

nasty /ˈnɑːstɪ/ *adj* (**-ier, -iest**) desagradable; (*spiteful*) malo (**to** con); (*taste, smell*) asqueroso; (*cut*) feo

nation /ˈneɪʃn/ *n* nación *f*

national /ˈnæʃənl/ *adj* nacional. ● *n* ciudadano *m*. ~ **anthem** *n* himno *m* nacional. **~ism** *n* nacionalismo *m*. **~ity** /næʃəˈnælətɪ/ *n* nacionalidad *f*. **~ize** *vt* nacionalizar. **~ly** *adv* a escala nacional

> *i* **National Trust** Fundación británica cuyo objetivo es la conservación de lugares de interés histórico o de belleza natural. Se financia mediante legados y subvenciones privadas. Es la mayor propietaria de tierras de Gran Bretaña. En Escocia, es independiente y recibe el nombre de *National Trust for Scotland*.

nationwide /ˈneɪʃnwaɪd/ *adj* & *adv* a escala nacional

native /ˈneɪtɪv/ *n* natural *m* & *f*. **be**

a ~ **of** ser natural de. ● adj nativo; (country, town) natal; (language) materno; (plant, animal) autóctono. **N**~ **American** indio m americano

nativity /nəˈtɪvətɪ/ n. the **N**~ la Natividad f

NATO /ˈneɪtəʊ/ abbr (= **North Atlantic Treaty Organization**) OTAN f

natter /ˈnætə(r)/ 🔲 vi charlar. ● n charla f

natural /ˈnætʃərəl/ adj natural. ~ **history** historia f natural. ~**ist** n naturalista m & f. ~**ized** adj (citizen) naturalizado. ~**ly** adv (of course) naturalmente; (by nature) por naturaleza

nature /ˈneɪtʃə(r)/ n naturaleza f; (of person) carácter m; (of things) naturaleza f

naught /nɔːt/ n cero m

naughty /ˈnɔːtɪ/ adj (-ier, -iest) malo, travieso

nausea /ˈnɔːzɪə/ n náuseas fpl. ~**ous** /-ɪəs/ adj nauseabundo

nautical /ˈnɔːtɪkl/ adj náutico. ~ **mile** n milla f marina

naval /ˈneɪvl/ adj naval; (officer) de marina

nave /neɪv/ n nave f

navel /ˈneɪvl/ n ombligo m

naviga|ble /ˈnævɪgəbl/ adj navegable. ~**te** /ˈnævɪgeɪt/ vt navegar por (sea etc); gobernar (ship). ● vi navegar. ~**tion** /-ˈgeɪʃn/ n navegación f. ~**tor** n oficial m & f de derrota

navy /ˈneɪvɪ/ n marina f de guerra. ~ **(blue)** a n azul (m) marino

NE abbr (= **north-east**) NE

near /nɪə(r)/ adv cerca. draw ~ acercarse. ● prep. ~ **(to)** cerca de. go ~ **(to)** sth acercarse a algo.

● adj cercano. ● vt acercarse a. ~**by** adj cercano. ~**ly** adv casi. **he** ~**ly died** por poco se muere, casi se muere. **not** ~**ly** ni con mucho. ~**sighted** /-ˈsaɪtɪd/ adj miope, corto de vista

neat /niːt/ adj (-er, -est) (person) pulcro; (room etc) bien arreglado; (ingenious) hábil; (whisky, gin) solo; ; (Amer fam, great) fantástico 🔲. ~**ly** adv pulcramente; (organized) cuidadosamente

necessar|ily /nesəˈserɪlɪ/ adv necesariamente. ~**y** /ˈnesəserɪ/ adj necesario

necessit|ate /nəˈsesɪteɪt/ vt exigir. ~**y** /nɪˈsesətɪ/ n necesidad f. **the bare** ~**ies** lo indispensable

neck /nek/ n (of person, bottle, dress) cuello m; (of animal) pescuezo m. ~ **and** ~ a la par, parejos (LAm). ~**lace** /ˈnekləs/ n collar m. ~**line** n escote m

nectar /ˈnektə(r)/ n néctar m

nectarine /ˈnektərɪn/ n nectarina f

née /neɪ/ adj de soltera

need /niːd/ n necesidad f (**for** de). ● vt necesitar; (demand) exigir. **you** ~ **not speak** no tienes que hablar

needle /ˈniːdl/ n aguja f. ● vt (fam, annoy) pinchar

needless /ˈniːdlɪs/ adj innecesario

needlework /ˈniːdlwɜːk/ n labores fpl de aguja; (embroidery) bordado m

needy /ˈniːdɪ/ adj (-ier, -iest) necesitado

negative /ˈnegətɪv/ adj negativo. ● n (of photograph) negativo m; (no) negativa f

neglect /nɪˈglekt/ vt descuidar (house); desatender (children); no cumplir con (duty). ● n negligencia *f.* (state of) ~ abandono *m.* ~**ful** *adj* negligente

negligence /'neglɪdʒəns/ *n* negligencia *f*, descuido *m.* ~**ent** *adj* negligente. ~**ible** /'neglɪdʒəbl/ *adj* insignificante

negotia|ble /nɪ'ɡəʊʃəbl/ *adj* negociable. ~**te** /nɪ'ɡəʊʃɪeɪt/ *vt/i* negociar. ~**tion** /-ʃɪˈeɪ∫n/ *n* negociación *f*. ~**tor** *n* negociador *m*

neigh /neɪ/ *vi* relinchar

neighbour /'neɪbə(r)/ *n* vecino *m.* ~**hood** *n* vecindad *f*, barrio *m.* **in the** ~**hood of** alrededor de. ~**ing** *adj* vecino

neither /'naɪðə(r)/ *adj.* ~ **book** ninguno de los libros. • *pron* ninguno, -na. • *conj.* neither...nor ni...ni. ~ **do I** yo tampoco

neon /'niːɒn/ *n* neón *m.* ~ **(lamp** etc) de neón

nephew /'nevju:/ *n* sobrino *m*

Neptune /'neptju:n/ *n* Neptuno *m*

nerv|e /nɜːv/ *n* nervio *m*; (courage) valor *m*; (calm) sangre *f* fría; (fam, impudence) descaro *m.* ~**es** *npl* (before exams etc) nervios *mpl.* **get on s.o.'s** ~**es** ponerle los nervios de punta a uno. ~**e-racking** *adj* exasperante. ~**ous** /-vəs/ *adj* nervioso. **be/feel** ~**ous** estar nervioso. ~**ousness** *n* nerviosismo *m.* ~**y** /'nɜːvɪ/ *adj* nervioso; (Amer fam) descarado

nest /nest/ *n* nido *m.* • *vi* anidar

nestle /'nesl/ *vi* acurrucarse

net /net/ *n* red *f.* **the N~** (Comp) la Red. • *vt* (pt **netted**) pescar (con red) (fish). • *adj* neto. ~**ball** *n* especie de baloncesto

Netherlands /'neðələndz/ *npl.* **the** ~ los Países Bajos

netting /'netɪŋ/ *n* redes *fpl.* **wire** ~ tela *f* metálica

nettle /'netl/ *n* ortiga *f*

network /'netwɜːk/ *n* red *f*; (TV) cadena *f*

neuro|sis /njʊə'rəʊsɪs/ *n* (pl -**oses** /-siːz/) neurosis *f.* ~**tic** /-'rɒtɪk/ *adj* & *n* neurótico (*m*)

neuter /'njuːtə(r)/ *adj* & *n* neutro (*m*). • *vt* castrar (animals)

neutral /'njuːtrəl/ *adj* neutral; (colour) neutro; (Elec) neutro. ~ **(gear)** (Auto) punto *m* muerto. ~**ize** *vt* neutralizar

neutron /'njuːtrɒn/ *n* neutrón *m*

never /'nevə(r)/ *adv* nunca; (more emphatic) jamás; (fam, not) no. ~ **again** nunca más. **he** ~ **smiles** no sonríe nunca, nunca sonríe. **I** ~ **saw him** 🔳 no lo vi. ~-**ending** *adj* interminable. ~**theless** /-ðə'les/ *adv* sin embargo, no obstante

new /njuː/ *adj* (-**er**, -**est**) nuevo. ~-**born** *adj* recién nacido. ~-**comer** *n* recién llegado *m.* ~-**fangled** /-'fæŋɡld/ *adj* (pej) moderno. ~**ly** *adv* recién. ~**ly-weds** *npl* recién casados *mpl*

news /njuːz/ *n.* **a piece of** ~ una noticia. **good/bad** ~ buenas/malas noticias. **the** ~ (TV, Radio) las noticias. ~**agent** *n* vendedor *m* de periódicos. ~**caster** *n* locutor *m.* ~**dealer** *n* (Amer) see ~**AGENT.** ~**flash** *n* información *f* de última hora. ~**letter** *n* boletín *m*, informativo *m.* ~**paper** *n* periódico *m*, diario *m.* ~**reader** *n* locutor *m*

newt /njuːt/ *n* tritón *m*

New Year /njuː'jɪə(r)/ *n* Año *m* Nuevo. **N~'s Day** *n* día *m* de Año Nuevo. **N~'s Eve** *n* noche *f* vieja, noche *f* de fin de Año

New Zealand /njuː'ziːlənd/ *n* Nueva Zeland(i)a *f*

next /nekst/ *adj* próximo; (week,

month etc) que viene, próximo; (*adjoining*) vecino; (*following*) siguiente. ● *adv* luego, después. ~ **to** al lado de. **when you see me** ~ la próxima vez que me veas. ~ **to nothing** casi nada. ~ **door** al lado (**to** de). **~-door** *adj* de al lado. ~ **of kin** n familiar(es) m(pl) más cercano(s)

nib /nɪb/ n plumilla f

nibble /'nɪbl/ vt/i mordisquear. ● n mordisco m

Nicaragua /nɪkə'ræɡjʊə/ n Nicaragua f. **~n** adj & n nicaragüense (m & f)

nice /naɪs/ adj (-er, -est) agradable; (*likeable*) simpático; (*kind*) amable; (*weather, food*) bueno. **we had a ~ time** lo pasamos bien. **~ly** adv (*kindly*) amablemente; (*politely*) con buenos modales

niche /nɪtʃ, niːʃ/ n nicho m

nick /nɪk/ n corte m pequeño. **in the ~ of time** justo a tiempo. ● vt (sl, steal) afanar 🅧

nickel /'nɪkl/ n (metal) níquel m; (Amer) moneda f de cinco centavos

nickname /'nɪkneɪm/ n apodo m. ● vt apodar

nicotine /'nɪkətiːn/ n nicotina f

niece /niːs/ n sobrina f

niggling /'nɪɡlɪŋ/ adj (doubt) constante

night /naɪt/ n noche f; (evening) tarde f. **at ~** por la noche, de noche. **good ~!** ¡buenas noches! ● adj nocturno, de noche. **~cap** n (drink) bebida f (tomada antes de acostarse). **~club** n club m nocturno. **~dress** n camisón m. **~fall** n anochecer m. **~gown**, **~ie** /'naɪtɪ/ 🅣 n camisón m. **~life** n vida f nocturna. **~ly** adj de todas

las noches. **~mare** n pesadilla f. ~ **school** n escuela f nocturna. **~-time** n noche f. **~watchman** n sereno m

nil /nɪl/ n nada f; (Sport) cero m

nimble /'nɪmbl/ adj (-er, -est) ágil

nine /naɪn/ adj & n nueve (m). **~teen** /naɪn'tiːn/ adj & n diecinueve (m). **~teenth** adj decimonoveno. ● n diecinueveavo m. **~tieth** /'naɪntɪəθ/ adj nonagésimo. ● n noventavo m. **~ty** adj & n noventa (m)

ninth /naɪnθ/ adj & n noveno (m)

nip /nɪp/ vt (pt nipped) (pinch) pellizcar; (bite) mordisquear. ● vi (fam, rush) correr

nipple /'nɪpl/ n (of woman) pezón m; (of man) tetilla f; (of baby's bottle) tetina f, chupón m (Mex)

nippy /'nɪpɪ/ adj (-ier, -iest) (fam, chilly) fresquito

nitrogen /'naɪtrədʒən/ n nitrógeno m

no /nəʊ/ adj ninguno, (before masculine singular noun) ningún. **I have ~ money** no tengo dinero. **there's ~ food left** no queda nada de comida. **it has ~ windows** no tiene ventanas. **I'm ~ expert** no soy ningún experto. **~ smoking** prohibido fumar. **~ way!** 🅣 ¡ni hablar! ● adv & int no. ● n (pl noes) no m

noble /'nəʊbl/ adj (-er, -est) noble. **~man** /-mən/ n noble m

nobody /'nəʊbədɪ/ pron nadie. **there's ~ there** no hay nadie

nocturnal /nɒk'tɜːnl/ adj nocturno

nod /nɒd/ vt (pt nodded). ~ **one's head** asentir con la cabeza. ● vi (in agreement) asentir con la cabeza; (in greeting) saludar con la cabeza.

noise | nosy

□ ~ **off** vi dormirse

nois|e /'nɔɪz/ n ruido m. ~**ily** adv
ruidosamente. ~**y** adj (-ier, -iest)
ruidoso. **it's too ~y here** hay demasiado ruido aquí

nomad /'nəʊmæd/ n nómada m &
f. ~**ic** /-'mædɪk/ adj nómada

no man's land n tierra f de
nadie

nominat|e /'nɒmɪneɪt/ vt (put
forward) proponer; postular (LAm);
(appoint) nombrar. ~**ion** /-'neɪʃn/
n nombramiento m; (Amer, Pol) pro-
clamación f

non-... /nɒn/ pref no ...

nonchalant /'nɒnʃələnt/ adj despreocupado

non-committal /nɒnkə'mɪtl/
adj evasivo

nondescript /'nɒndɪskrɪpt/ adj
anodino

none /nʌn/ pron ninguno, ninguna.
there were ~ left no quedaba
ninguno/ninguna. ~ **of us** no
ninguno de nosotros. ● adv no, de
ninguna manera. **he is ~ the hap-
pier** no está más contento

nonentity /nɒ'nentətɪ/ n persona
f insignificante

non-existent /nɒnɪg'zɪstənt/ adj
inexistente

nonplussed /nɒn'plʌst/ adj perplejo

nonsens|e /'nɒnsns/ n tonterías
fpl, disparates mpl. ~**ical** /-'sensɪkl/
adj disparatado

non-smoker /nɒn'sməʊkə(r)/ n
no fumador m. **I'm a ~** no fumo

non-stop /nɒn'stɒp/ adj (train) directo; (flight) sin escalas. ● adv sin
parar; (by train) directamente; (by
air) sin escalas

noodles /'nu:dlz/ npl fideos mpl

nook /nʊk/ n rincón m

noon /nu:n/ n mediodía m

no-one /'nəʊwʌn/ pron nadie

noose /nu:s/ n soga f

nor /nɔ:(r)/ conj ni, tampoco. **neither blue ~ red** ni azul ni rojo. **he
doesn't play the piano, ~ do I** no
sabe tocar el piano, ni yo tampoco

norm /nɔ:m/ n norma f

normal /'nɔ:ml/ adj normal. ~**cy**
n (Amer) normalidad f. ~**ity**
/-'mælətɪ/ n normalidad f. ~**ly** adv
normalmente

north /nɔ:θ/ n norte m. ● adj
del norte. ● adv hacia el norte. **N~
America** n América f del Norte,
Norteamérica f. **N~ American** adj
& n norteamericano (m). ~**east** n
nor(d)este m. ● adj del norte. ~ (go)
hacia el nor(d)este. **it's ~east
of Leeds** está al nor(d)este de
Leeds. ~**erly** /'nɔ:ðəlɪ/ adj (wind)
del norte. ~**ern** /'nɔ:ðən/ adj del
norte. ~**erner** n norteño m.
N~ern Ireland n Irlanda f del
Norte. **N~ Sea** n mar m del Norte.
~**ward** /'nɔ:θwəd/, ~**wards** adv
hacia el norte. ~**west** n noroeste
m. ● adj noroeste. ● adv hacia el noroeste

Norw|ay /'nɔ:weɪ/ n Noruega f.
~**egian** /-'wi:dʒən/ adj & n noruego
(m)

nose /nəʊz/ n nariz f. ~**bleed** n
hemorragia f nasal. ~**dive** n/ vi descender en picado, descender en picada (LAm)

nostalgi|a /nɒ'stældʒə/ n nostal-
gia f. ~**c** adj nostálgico

nostril /'nɒstrɪl/ n ventana f de la
nariz f

nosy /'nəʊzɪ/ adj (-ier, -iest) 🄸 entrometido, metiche (LAm)

not /nɒt/

Cuando **not** va precedido del verbo auxiliar **do** o **have** o de un verbo modal como **should** etc, se suele emplear la forma contraída **don't, haven't, shouldn't** etc

adverb

····➤ no. **I don't know** no sé. ~ **yet** todavía no. ~ **me** yo no

····➤ *(replacing a clause)* **I suppose** ~ supongo que no. **of course** ~ por supuesto que no. **are you going to help me or** ~? ¿me vas a ayudar o no?

····➤ *(emphatic)* ni. ~ **a penny more!** ¡ni un penique más!

····➤ *(in phrases)* **certainly** ~ de ninguna manera . ~ **you again!** ¡tú otra vez!

notab|le /'nəʊtəbl/ *adj* notable; (author) distinguido. ~**y** /'nəʊtəblɪ/ *adv* notablemente; (in particular) particularmente

notch /nɒtʃ/ *n* muesca *f*. □ ~ **up** *vt* apuntarse

note /nəʊt/ *n* (incl Mus) nota *f*; (banknote) billete *m*. **take** ~**s** tomar apuntes. ●*vt* (notice) observar; (record) anotar. □ ~ **down** *vt* apuntar. ~**book** *n* cuaderno *m*. ~**d** *adj* célebre. ~**paper** *n* papel *m* de carta(s)

nothing /'nʌθɪŋ/ *pron* nada. **he eats** ~ no come nada. **for** ~ (free) gratis; (in vain) en vano. ~ **else** nada más. ~ **much** happened no pasó gran cosa. **he does** ~ **but complain** no hace más que quejarse

notice /'nəʊtɪs/ *n* (sign) letrero *m*;

(item of information) anuncio *m*; (notification) aviso *m*; (of termination of employment) preaviso *m*; ~ (of dismissal) despido *m*. **take** ~ **of** hacer caso a (person). ●*vt* notar. ●*vi* darse cuenta. ~**able** *adj* perceptible. ~**ably** *adv* perceptiblemente. ~**board** *n* tablón *m* de anuncios, tablero *m* de anuncios (LAm)

notif|ication /nəʊtɪfɪ'keɪʃn/ *n* notificación *f*. ~**y** /'nəʊtɪfaɪ/ *vt* informar; (in writing) notificar. ~**y s.o. of sth** comunicarle algo a uno

notion /'nəʊʃn/ *n* (concept) concepto *m*; (idea) idea *f*

notorious /nəʊ'tɔːrɪəs/ *adj* notorio

notwithstanding /nɒtwɪθ 'stændɪŋ/ *prep* a pesar de. ●*adv* no obstante

nougat /'nuːgɑː/ *n* turrón *m*

nought /nɔːt/ *n* cero *m*

noun /naʊn/ *n* sustantivo *m*, nombre *m*

nourish /'nʌrɪʃ/ *vt* alimentar. ~**ment** *n* alimento *m*

novel /'nɒvl/ *n* novela *f*. ●*adj* original, novedoso. ~**ist** *n* novelista *m & f*. ~**ty** *n* novedad *f*

November /nəʊ'vembə(r)/ *n* noviembre *m*

novice /'nɒvɪs/ *n* principiante *m & f*

now /naʊ/ *adv* ahora. ~ **and again**, ~ **and then** de vez en cuando. **right** ~ ahora mismo. **from** ~ **on** a partir de ahora. ●*conj*. ~ **(that)** ahora que. ~**adays** /'naʊədeɪz/ *adv* hoy (en) día

nowhere /'nəʊweə(r)/ *adv* por ninguna parte, por ningún lado; (after motion towards) a ninguna parte, a ningún lado

nozzle /'nɒzl/ n (on hose) boca f; (on fire extinguisher) boquilla f

nuance /'nju:ɑ:ns/ n matiz m

nuclear /'nju:klɪə(r)/ adj nuclear

nucleus /'nju:klɪəs/ n (pl **-lei** /-lɪaɪ/) núcleo m

nude /nju:d/ adj & n desnudo (m). **in the** ~ desnudo

nudge /nʌdʒ/ vt codear (ligeramente). ● n golpe m (suave) con el codo

nudi|st /'nju:dɪst/ n nudista m & f. ~**ty** /'nju:dətɪ/ n desnudez f

nuisance /'nju:sns/ n (thing, event) molestia f, fastidio m; (person) pesado m

null /nʌl/ adj nulo

numb /nʌm/ adj entumecido. **go** ~ entumecerse ● vt entumecer

number /'nʌmbə(r)/ n número m; (telephone number) número m de teléfono. **a** ~ **of people** varias personas. ● vt numerar; (count, include) contar. ~**plate** n matrícula f, placa f (LAm)

numer|al /'nju:mərəl/ n número m. ~**ical** /nju:'merɪkl/ adj numérico. ~**ous** /'nju:mərəs/ adj numeroso

nun /nʌn/ n monja f

nurse /nɜ:s/ n enfermero m, enfermera f; (nanny) niñera f. ● vt cuidar; abrigar (hope etc)

nursery /'nɜ:sərɪ/ n (for plants) vivero m; (day ~) guardería f. ~ **rhyme** n canción f infantil. ~ **school** n jardín m de infancia, jardín m infantil (LAm)

nursing home /'nɜ:sɪŋ/ n (for older people) residencia f de ancianos (con mayor nivel de asistencia médica)

nut /nʌt/ n fruto m seco (nuez,

almendra, avellana etc); (Tec) tuerca f. ~**case** n ⊞ chiflado m. ~**crackers** npl cascanueces m. ~**meg** /-meg/ n nuez f moscada

nutri|ent /'nju:trɪənt/ n nutriente m. ~**tion** /nju:'trɪʃn/ n nutrición f. ~**tious** /nju:'trɪʃəs/ adj nutritivo

nuts /nʌts/ adj (fam, crazy) chiflado

nutshell /'nʌtʃel/ n cáscara f de nuez. **in a** ~ en pocas palabras

NW abbr (= **north-west**) NO

nylon /'naɪlɒn/ n nylon m

Oo

oaf /əʊf/ n zoquete m

oak /əʊk/ n roble m

OAP /əʊeɪ'pi:/ abbr (= **old-age pensioner**) n pensionista m & f, pensionado m

oar /ɔ:(r)/ n remo m

oasis /əʊ'eɪsɪs/ n (pl **oases** /-si:z/) oasis m

oath /əʊθ/ n juramento m

oat|meal /'əʊtmi:l/ n harina f de avena; (Amer, flakes) avena f (en copos). ~**s** /əʊts/ npl avena f

obedien|ce /əʊ'bi:dɪəns/ n obediencia f. ~**t** adj obediente. ~**tly** adv obedientemente

obes|e /əʊ'bi:s/ adj obeso. ~**ity** n obesidad f

obey /əʊ'beɪ/ vt/i obedecer

obituary /ə'bɪtʃʊəri/ n nota f necrológica, obituario m

object /'ɒbdʒɪkt/ n objeto m; (aim) objetivo m. /əb'dʒekt/ vi oponerse (**to** a). ~**ion** /əb'dʒekʃn/ n objeción f. **~ionable** adj censurable; (unpleasant) desagradable. **~ive** /əbˈdʒektɪv/ adj a objetivo (m)

oblig|ation /ɒblɪˈɡeɪʃn/ n obligación f. **be under an ~ation** to estar obligado a. **~atory** /əˈblɪɡətrɪ/ adj obligatorio. **~e** /əˈblaɪdʒ/ vt obligar. **I'd be much ~ed if you could help me** le querría muy agradecido si pudiera ayudarme. ● vi hacer un favor. **~ing** adj atento

oblique /əˈbliːk/ adj oblicuo

obliterate /əˈblɪtəreɪt/ vt arrasar; (erase) borrar

oblivio|n /əˈblɪvɪən/ n olvido m. **~us** /-vɪəs/ adj (unaware) inconsciente (**to**, **of** de)

oblong /ˈɒblɒŋ/ adj oblongo. ● n rectángulo m

obnoxious /əbˈnɒkʃəs/ adj odioso

oboe /ˈəʊbəʊ/ n oboe m

obscen|e /əbˈsiːn/ adj obsceno. **~ity** /əbˈsenətɪ/ n obscenidad f

obscur|e /əbˈskjʊə(r)/ adj oscuro. ● vt ocultar; impedir ver claramente (issue). **~ity** n oscuridad f

obsequious /əbˈsiːkwɪəs/ adj servil

observ|ant /əbˈzɜːvənt/ adj observador. **~ation** /ɒbzəˈveɪʃn/ n observación f. **~atory** /əbˈzɜːvətrɪ/ n observatorio m. **~e** /əbˈzɜːv/ vt observar. **~er** n observador m

obsess /əbˈses/ vt obsesionar. **~ed** /əbˈsest/ adj obsesionado. **~ion** /-ʃn/ n obsesión f. **~ive** adj obsesivo

obsolete /ˈɒbsəliːt/ adj obsoleto

obstacle /ˈɒbstəkl/ n obstáculo m

obstina|cy /ˈɒbstɪnəsɪ/ n obstinación f. **~te** /-ət/ adj obstinado. **~tely** adv obstinadamente

obstruct /əbˈstrʌkt/ vt obstruir; bloquear (traffic). **~ion** /-ʃn/ n obstrucción f

obtain /əbˈteɪn/ vt conseguir, obtener. **~able** adj asequible

obtrusive /əbˈtruːsɪv/ adj (presence) demasiado prominente; (noise) molesto

obtuse /əbˈtjuːs/ adj obtuso

obvious /ˈɒbvɪəs/ adj obvio. **~ly** adv obviamente

occasion /əˈkeɪʒn/ n ocasión f. **~al** adj esporádico. **~ally** adv de vez en cuando

occult /ˈɒkʌlt/ adj oculto

occup|ant /ˈɒkjʊpənt/ n ocupante m & f. **~ation** /ɒkjʊˈpeɪʃn/ n ocupación f. **~ier** /ˈɒkjʊpaɪə(r)/ n ocupante m & f. **~y** /ˈɒkjʊpaɪ/ vt ocupar. **keep o.s. ~ied** entretenerse

occur /əˈkɜː(r)/ vi (pt occurred) tener lugar, ocurrir; (change) producirse; (exist) encontrarse. **it ~red to me that** se me ocurrió que. **~rence** /əˈkʌrəns/ n (incidence) incidencia f. **it is a rare ~rence** no es algo frecuente

ocean /ˈəʊʃn/ n océano m

o'clock /əˈklɒk/ adv. **it is 7 ~** son las siete. **it's one ~** es la una

octagon /ˈɒktəɡən/ n octágono m

octave /ˈɒktɪv/ n octava f

October /ɒkˈtəʊbə(r)/ n octubre m

octopus /ˈɒktəpəs/ n (pl -puses) pulpo m

odd /ɒd/ adj (-er, -est) extraño, raro; (number) impar; (one of pair) desparejado. **smoke the ~ cigarette** fumarse algún que otro cigarillo. **fifty-~** unos cincuenta, cincuenta y pico. **the ~ one out** la excepción. **~ity** n (thing) rareza f;

(*person*) bicho *m* raro. **~ly** *adv* de una manera extraña. **~ly enough** por extraño que parezca. **~ment** *n* retazo *m*. **~s** *npl* probabilidades *fpl*; (*in betting*) apuesta *f*. **be at ~s** estar en desacuerdo. **~s and ends** *mpl* 🔲 cosas *fpl* sueltas

odious /'əʊdɪəs/ *adj* odioso

odometer /ɒ'dɒmɪtə(r)/ *n* (*Amer*) cuentakilómetros *m*

odour /'əʊdə(r)/ *n* olor *m*

---

of /ɒv/ /əv/ *preposition*

••▸ de. **a pound of cheese** una libra de queso. **it's made of wood** es de madera. **a girl of ten** una niña de diez años

••▸ (*in dates*) **the fifth of November** el cinco de noviembre

••▸ (*Amer, when telling the time*) **it's ten (minutes) of five** son las cinco menos diez, son diez para las cinco (*LAm*)

! **of** is not translated in cases such as the following: **a colleague of mine** un colega mío; **there were six of us** éramos seis; **that's very kind of you** es Ud muy amable

---

off /ɒf/ *prep* (*from*) de. **he picked it up ~ the floor** lo recogió del suelo; (*distant from*) **just ~ the coast of Texas** a poca distancia de la costa de Tejas. **2 ft ~ the ground** a dos pies del suelo; (*absent from*) **I've been ~ work for a week** hace una semana que no voy a trabajar. ● *adv* (*removed*) **the lid was ~** la tapa no estaba puesta; (*distant*) **some way ~** a cierta distancia; (*leaving*) **I'm ~** me voy; (*switched off*) (light, TV) apa-

gado; (water) cortado; (*cancelled*) (match) cancelado; (*not on duty*) (day) libre. ● *adj*. **be ~** (meat) estar malo, estar pasado; (milk) estar cortado. **~beat** *adj* poco convencional. **~ chance** *n*. **on the ~ chance** por si acaso

off-licence En el Reino Unido, es una tienda que tiene licencia para vender bebidas alcohólicas que se deben consumir fuera del local. Abren cuando los bares y **pubs** están cerrados y también suelen vender bebidas no alcohólicas, tabaco, golosinas etc. A menudo alquilan vasos y copas para fiestas, etc.

offen|ce /ə'fens/ *n* (*breach of law*) infracción *f*; (*criminal ~ce*) delito *m*; (*cause of outrage*) atentado *m*; (*Amer, attack*) ataque *m*. **take ~ce** ofenderse. **~d** *vt* ofender. **~der** *n* delincuente *m & f*. **~sive** /-sɪv/ *adj* ofensivo; (*disgusting*) desagradable

offer /'ɒfə(r)/ *vt* ofrecer. **~ to do sth** ofrecerse a hacer algo. ● *n* oferta *f*. **on ~** de oferta

offhand /ɒf'hænd/ *adj* (brusque) brusco. **say sth in a ~ way** decir algo a la ligera. ● *adv* de improviso

office /'ɒfɪs/ *n* oficina *f*; (*post*) cargo *m*. **doctor's ~** consultorio *m*, consulta *m*. **~ block** *n* edificio *m* de oficinas. **~r** *n* oficial *m & f*; (*police* **~r**) policía *m & f*; (*as form of address*) agente

offici|al /ə'fɪʃl/ *adj* oficial. ● *n* funcionario *m* del Estado; (*of party, union*) dirigente *m & f*. **~ally** *adv* oficialmente. **~ous** /ə'fɪʃəs/ *adj* oficioso

offing /'ɒfɪŋ/ *n*. **in the ~** en perspectiva

off: ~**-licence** n tienda f de vinos y licores. ~**-putting** adj (*disconcerting*) desconcertante; (*disagreeable*) desagradable. ~**set** vt (pt **-set**, pres p **-setting**) compensar. ~**shore** adj (*breeze*) que sopla desde la tierra; (*drilling*) offshore; (*well*) submarino. • adv a un lugar de mano de obra barata. ~**side** /ɒfˈsaɪd/ adj (Sport) fuera de juego. ~**spring** n invar prole f. ~**-stage** /-ˈsteɪdʒ/ adv fuera del escenario. ~**-white** adj color hueso

often /ˈɒfn/ adv a menudo, con frecuencia. **how** ~? ¿con qué frecuencia? **more** ~ con más frecuencia

ogle /ˈəʊgl/ vt comerse con los ojos

ogre /ˈəʊgə(r)/ n ogro m

oh /əʊ/ int ¡ah!; (*expressing dismay*) ¡ay!

oil /ɔɪl/ n aceite m; (*petroleum*) petróleo m. • vt lubricar. ~**field** n yacimiento m petrolífero. ~**painting** n pintura f al óleo; (*picture*) óleo m. ~ **rig** n plataforma f petrolífera. ~**y** adj (substance) oleaginoso; (*food*) aceitoso

ointment /ˈɔɪntmənt/ n ungüento m

OK /əʊˈkeɪ/ int ¡vale!, ¡de acuerdo!, ¡bueno! (LAm). • adj ~, **thanks** bien, gracias. **the job's** ~ el trabajo no está mal

old /əʊld/ adj (-er, -est) viejo; (*not modern*) antiguo; (*former*) antiguo; **an** ~ **friend** un viejo amigo. **how** ~ **is she?** ¿cuántos años tiene? **she is ten years** ~ tiene diez años. **his** ~**er sister** su hermana mayor. ~ **age** n vejez f. ~**-fashioned** /-ˈfæʃənd/ adj anticuado

olive /ˈɒlɪv/ n aceituna f.

Olympic /əˈlɪmpɪk/ adj olímpico. **the** ~**s** npl, **the** ~ **Games** npl los Juegos Olímpicos

omelette /ˈɒmlɪt/ n tortilla f francesa, omelette m (LAm)

omen /ˈəʊmen/ n agüero m

omi|ssion /əˈmɪʃn/ n omisión f. ~**t** /əʊˈmɪt/ vt (pt **omitted**) omitir

on /ɒn/ prep en, sobre; (*about*) sobre. ~ **foot** a pie. ~ **Monday** el lunes. ~ **seeing** al ver. **I heard it** ~ **the radio** lo oí por la radio. • adv (*light etc*) encendido, prendido (LAm); (*machine*) en marcha; (*tap*) abierto. ~ **and** ~ sin cesar. **and so** ~ y así sucesivamente. **have a hat** ~ llevar (puesto) un sombrero. **further** ~ un poco más allá. **what's** ~ **at the Odeon?** ¿qué dan en el Odeon? **go** ~ continuar. **later** ~ más tarde

once /wʌns/ adv una vez; (*formerly*) antes. **at** ~ inmediatamente. ~ **upon a time there was...** érase una vez.... ~ **and for all** de una vez por todas. • conj una vez que

one /wʌn/ adj uno, (*before singular noun*) un. **the** ~ **person I trusted** la única persona en la que confiaba. • n uno m. ~ **by** ~ uno a uno.. • pron uno (m), una (f). **the blue** ~ el/la azul. **this** ~ éste/ésta. ~ **another** el uno al otro

onerous /ˈɒnərəs/ adj (task) pesado

one: ~**self** /-ˈself/ pron (*reflexive*) se; (*after prep*) sí (mismo); (*emphatic use*) uno mismo, una misma. by ~**self** solo. ~**-way** adj (street) de sentido único; (ticket) de ida, sencillo

onion /ˈʌnɪən/ n cebolla f

onlooker /ˈɒnlʊkə(r)/ n espectador m

only /ˈəʊnlɪ/ adj único. she's an ~ child es hija única. ● adv sólo, solamente. ~ just (barely) apenas. I've ~ just arrived acabo de llegar. ● conj pero, sólo que

onset /ˈɒnset/ n comienzo m; (of disease) aparición f

onshore /ˈɒnʃɔː(r)/ adj (breeze) que sopla desde el mar; (oil field) en tierra

onslaught /ˈɒnslɔːt/ n ataque m

onus /ˈəʊnəs/ n responsabilidad f

onward(s) /ˈɒnwəd(z)/ adj & adv hacia adelante

ooze /uːz/ vt/i rezumar

opaque /əʊˈpeɪk/ adj opaco

open /ˈəʊpən/ adj abierto; (question) discutible. ● n. in the ~ al aire libre. ● vt/i abrir. ~ing n abertura f; (beginning) principio m. ~ly adv abiertamente. ~-minded /-ˈmaɪndɪd/ adj de actitud abierta

Open University La universidad a distancia británica, fundada en 1969. La enseñanza se imparte fundamentalmente por correspondencia, mediante materiales impresos, material enviado por internet y programas de televisión emitidos por la BBC. También hay cursos de verano a los que los alumnos deben asistir. No se exigen calificaciones académicas para su ingreso.

opera /ˈɒprə/ n ópera f

operate /ˈɒpəreɪt/ vt manejar, operar (Mex) (machine). ● vi funcionar; (company) operar. ~ (on) (Med) operar (a)

operatic /ɒpəˈrætɪk/ adj operístico

operation /ɒpəˈreɪʃn/ n operación f; (Mec) funcionamiento m; (using of machine) manejo m. he had an ~ lo operaron. in ~ en vigor. ~al adj en vigor

operative /ˈɒpərətɪv/ adj. be ~ estar en vigor

operator n operador m

opinion /əˈpɪnɪən/ n opinión f. in my ~ en mi opinión, a mi parecer

opponent /əˈpəʊnənt/ n adversario m; (in sport) contrincante m & f

opportune /ˈɒpətjuːn/ adj oportuno. ~ist /ɒpəˈtjuːnɪst/ n oportunista m & f. ~ity /ɒpəˈtjuːnətɪ/ n oportunidad f

oppose /əˈpəʊz/ vt oponerse a. be ~ed to oponerse a, estar en contra de. ~ing adj opuesto. ~ite /ˈɒpəzɪt/ adj (contrary) opuesto; (facing) de enfrente. ● n. the ~ite lo contrario. quite the ~ite al contrario. ● adv enfrente. ~ite de. ● prep enfrente de. ~ite number n homólogo m. ~ition /ɒpəˈzɪʃn/ n oposición f; (resistance) resistencia f

oppress /əˈpres/ vt oprimir. ~ion /-ʃn/ n opresión f. ~ive adj (cruel) opresivo; (heat) sofocante

opt /ɒpt/ vi. ~ to optar por. ▫ ~ out vi decidir no tomar parte

optic|al /ˈɒptɪkl/ adj óptico. ~ian /ɒpˈtɪʃn/ n óptico m

optimis|m /ˈɒptɪmɪzəm/ n optimismo m. ~t n optimista m & f. ~tic /-ˈmɪstɪk/ adj optimista

option /ˈɒpʃn/ n opción f. ~al adj facultativo

or /ɔː(r)/ conj o; (before o- and ho-) u; (after negative) ni. ~ else si no, o bien

oral /ˈɔːrəl/ adj oral. ● n ▣ examen m oral

orange /'ɒrɪndʒ/ n naranja f; (colour) naranja m. ● adj naranja. ~ade /-'eɪd/ n naranjada f

orbit /'ɔːbɪt/ n órbita f ● vt orbitar

orchard /'ɔːtʃəd/ n huerto m

orchestra /'ɔːkɪstrə/ n orquesta f; (Amer, in theatre) platea f. ~l /-'kestrəl/ adj orquestal. ~te /-eɪt/ vt orquestar

orchid /'ɔːkɪd/ n orquídea f

ordain /ɔː'deɪn/ vt (Relig) ordenar; (decree) decretar

ordeal /ɔː'diːl/ n dura prueba f.

order /'ɔːdə(r)/ n orden m; (Com) pedido m; (command) orden f. in ~ that para que. in ~ to para. ● vt (command) ordenar, mandar; (Com) pedir; (in restaurant) pedir, ordenar (LAm); encargar (book); llamar, ordenar (LAm) (taxi). ~ly adj ordenado. ● n camillero m

ordinary /'ɔːdɪnrɪ/ adj corriente; (average) medio; (mediocre) ordinario

ore /ɔː(r)/ n mena f

organ /'ɔːgən/ n órgano m

organ|ic /ɔː'gænɪk/ adj orgánico. ~ism /'ɔːgənɪzəm/ n organismo m. ~ist /'ɔːgənɪst/ n organista m & f. ~ization /ˌɔːgənaɪ'zeɪʃn/ n organización f. ~ize /'ɔːgənaɪz/ vt organizar. ~izer n organizador m

orgasm /'ɔːgæzəm/ n orgasmo m

orgy /'ɔːdʒɪ/ n orgía f

Orient /'ɔːrɪənt/ n Oriente m. ~al /-'entl/ adj oriental

orientat|e /'ɔːrɪənteɪt/ vt orientar. ~ion /-'teɪʃn/ n orientación f

origin /'ɒrɪdʒɪn/ n origen m. ~al /ə'rɪdʒənl/ adj original. ~ally adv originariamente. ~ate /ə'rɪdʒɪneɪt/ vi. ~ate from provenir de

ornament /'ɔːnəmənt/ n adorno m. ~al /-'mentl/ adj de adorno

ornate /ɔː'neɪt/ adj ornamentado; (style) recargado

ornithology /ɔːnɪ'θɒlədʒɪ/ n ornitología f

orphan /'ɔːfn/ n huérfano m. ● vt. be ~ed quedar huérfano. ~age /-ɪdʒ/ n orfanato m

orthodox /'ɔːθədɒks/ adj ortodoxo

oscillate /'ɒsɪleɪt/ vi oscilar

ostentatious /ɒsten'teɪʃəs/ adj ostentoso

osteopath /'ɒstɪəpæθ/ n osteópata m & f

ostracize /'ɒstrəsaɪz/ vt hacerle el vacío a

ostrich /'ɒstrɪtʃ/ n avestruz m

other /'ʌðə(r)/ adj & pron otro. ~ than aparte de. the ~ one el otro. ~wise adv de lo contrario, si no

otter /'ɒtə(r)/ n nutria f

ouch /aʊtʃ/ int ¡ay!

ought /ɔːt/ modal verb. I ~ to see it debería verlo. he ~ to have done it debería haberlo hecho

ounce /aʊns/ n onza f (= 28.35 gr.)

our /'aʊə(r)/ adj (sing) nuestro, nuestra, (pl) nuestros, nuestras. ~s /'aʊəz/ poss pron (sing) nuestro, nuestra; (pl) nuestros, nuestras. ~s is red es rojo. a friend of ~s un amigo nuestro. ~selves /-'selvz/ pron (reflexive) nos; (used for emphasis and after prepositions) nosotros mismos, nosotras mismas. we behaved ~selves nos portamos bien. we did it ~selves lo hicimos nosotros mismos/nosotras mismas

oust /aʊst/ vt desbancar; derrocar (government)

out /aʊt/ adv (outside) fuera, afuera

(LAm). (not lighted, not on) apagado; (in blossom) en flor; (in error) equivocado. he's ∼ (not at home) no está; **be** ∼ to estar resuelto a. ∼ **of** prep (from inside) de; (outside) fuera, afuera (LAm). **five** ∼ **of six** cinco de cada seis. **made** ∼ **of** hecho de. **we're** ∼ **of bread** nos hemos quedado sin pan. ∼ **break** n (of war) estallido m; (of disease) brote m. ∼ **burst** n arrebato m. ∼ **cast** n paria m & f. ∼ **come** n resultado m. ∼ **cry** n protesta f. ∼ **dated** /-'deɪtɪd/ adj anticuado. ∼ **do** /-'duː/ vt (pt -did, pp -done) superar. ∼ **door** adj (clothes) de calle; (pool) descubierto. ∼ **doors** /-'dɔːz/ adv al aire libre

outer /'aʊtə(r)/ adj exterior

out: ∼ **fit** n equipo m; (clothes) conjunto m. ∼ **going** adj (minister etc) saliente; (sociable) abierto. ∼ **goings** npl gastos mpl. ∼ **grow** /-'ɡrəʊ/ vt (pt -grew, pp -grown) crecer más que (person). he's ∼ **grown his new shoes** le han quedado pequeños los zapatos nuevos. ∼ **ing** n excursión f

outlandish /aʊt'lændɪʃ/ adj extravagante

out: ∼ **law** n forajido m. ● vt proscribir. ∼ **lay** n gastos mpl. ∼ **let** n salida f; (Com) punto m de venta; (Amer, Elec) toma f de corriente. ∼ **line** n contorno m; (summary) resumen m; (plan of project) esquema m. ● vt trazar; (summarize) esbozar. ∼ **live** /-'lɪv/ vt sobrevivir a. ∼ **look** n perspectivas fpl; (attitude) punto m de vista. ∼ **lying** adj alejado. ∼ **number** /-'nʌmbə(r)/ vt superar en número. ∼ **-of-date** adj (ideas) desfasado; (clothes) pasado de moda. ∼ **patient** n paciente m externo.

∼ **post** n avanzada f. ∼ **put** n producción f; (of machine, worker) rendimiento m. ∼ **right** adv completamente; (frankly) abiertamente; (kill) en el acto. ● adj completo; (refusal) rotundo. ∼ **set** n principio m; (beginning) comienzo m. **at the** ∼ como máximo. ● /-'saɪd/ adv fuera, afuera (LAm). ● prep fuera de. ∼ **size** adj de talla gigante. ∼ **skirts** npl afueras fpl. ∼ **spoken** /-'spəʊkn/ adj directo, franco. ∼ **standing** /-'stændɪŋ/ adj excepcional; (debt) pendiente. ∼ **stretched** /aʊt'stretʃt/ adj extendido. ∼ **strip** /-'strɪp/ vt (pt -stripped) (run faster than) tomarle la delantera a; (exceed) sobrepasar. ∼ **ward** /-wəd/ adj (appearance) exterior; (sign) externo; (journey) de ida. ∼ **wardly** adv por fuera, exteriormente. ∼ **(s)** adv hacia afuera. ∼ **weigh** /-'weɪ/ vt ser mayor que. ∼ **wit** /-'wɪt/ vt (pt -witted) burlar

oval /'əʊvl/ adj ovalado, oval. ● n óvalo m

Oval Office El Despacho Oval es el despacho oficial del Presidente de los Estados Unidos, ubicado en el ala oeste de la Casa Blanca. La forma oval fue determinada por George Washington, lo que le permitiría tener contacto visual con todos durante las reuniones. Originariamente, quería que todas las habitaciones de la Casa Blanca fueran ovales, pero pronto comprendió que este diseño era poco práctico.

ovary /'əʊvərɪ/ n ovario m

ovation /əʊ'veɪʃn/ n ovación f

oven /'ʌvn/ n horno m

over /'əʊvə(r)/ prep por encima de; (across) al otro lado de; (during) durante; (more than) más de. ~ **and above** por encima de. ● adv por encima; (ended) terminado; (more) más; (in excess) de sobra. ~ **again** otra vez. ~ **and** una y otra vez. ~ **here** por aquí. ~ **there** por allí. **all** ~ (finished) acabado; (everywhere) por todas partes

over... /'əʊvə(r)/ pref excesivamente, demasiado

over: ~**all** /-'ɔːl/ adj global; (length, cost) total. ● adv en conjunto. ● /'əʊvərɔːl/, ~**alls** npl /'əʊvərɔːlz/ n, ~**alls** npl (Amer, dungarees) peto m, overol m. ~**awe** /-'ɔː/ vt intimidar. ~**balance** /-'bæləns/ vi perder el equilibrio. ~**bearing** /-'beərɪŋ/ adj dominante. ~**board** adv (throw) por la borda. ~**cast** /-'kɑːst/ adj (day) nublado; (sky) cubierto. ~**charge** /-'tʃɑːdʒ/ vt cobrarle de más a. ~**coat** n abrigo m. ~**come** /-'kʌm/ vt (pt -came, pp -come) superar, vencer. ~**crowded** /-'kraʊdɪd/ adj abarrotado (de gente). ~**do** /-'duː/ vt (pt -did, pp -done) exagerar; (Culin) recocer. ~**dose** n sobredosis f. ~**draft** n descubierto m. ~**draw** /-'drɔː/ vt (pt -drew, pp -drawn) girar en descubierto. be ~**drawn** tener un descubierto. ~**due** /-'djuː/ adj. **the book is a month** ~**due** el plazo de devolución del libro venció hace un mes. ~**estimate** /-'estɪmeɪt/ vt sobreestimar. ~**flow** /-'fləʊ/ vi desbordarse. ● n /-'fləʊ/ (excess) exceso m; (outlet) rebosadero m. ~**flow car park** n estacionamiento m extra (LAm), aparcamiento m extra (Esp). ~**grown** /-'grəʊn/ adj de-

masiado grande; (garden) lleno de maleza. ~**haul** /-'hɔːl/ vt revisar. ● /-'hɔːl/ n revisión f. ~**head** /-'hed/ adv por encima. ● /-'hed/ adj de arriba. ~**heads** /-'hedz/ npl. ~**head** n (Amer) gastos mpl indirectos. ~**hear** /-'hɪə(r)/ vt (pt -heard) oír por casualidad. ~**joyed** /-'dʒɔɪd/ adj encantado. ~**land** a/adv por tierra. ~**lap** /-'læp/ vi (pt -lapped) traslaparse. ~**leaf** /-'liːf/ adv al dorso. ~**load** /-'ləʊd/ vt sobrecargar. ~**look** /-'lʊk/ vt (room) dar a; (not notice) pasar por alto; (disregard) disculpar. ~**night** /-'naɪt/ adv durante la noche. **stay** ~**night** quedarse a pasar la noche. ● adj (journey) de noche; (stay) de una noche. ~**pass** n paso m elevado, paso m a desnivel (Mex). ~**pay** /-'peɪ/ vt (pt -paid) pagar demasiado. ~**power** /-'paʊə(r)/ vt dominar (opponent); (emotion) abrumar. ~**powering** /-'paʊərɪŋ/ adj (smell) muy fuerte; (desire) irresistible. ~**priced** /-'praɪst/ adj demasiado caro. ~**rated** /-'reɪtɪd/ adj sobrevalorado. ~**react** /-rɪ'ækt/ vi reaccionar en forma exagerada. ~**ride** /-'raɪd/ vt (pt -rode, pp -ridden) invalidar. ~**riding** /-'raɪdɪŋ/ adj dominante. ~**rule** /-'ruːl/ vt anular; rechazar (objection). ~**run** /-'rʌn/ vt (pt -ran, pp -run, pres p -running) invadir; exceder (limit). ~**seas** /-'siːz/ adj (trade) exterior; (investments) en el exterior; (visitor) extranjero. ● adv al extranjero. ~**see** /-'siː/ vt (pt -saw, pp -seen) supervisar. ~**seer** /-sɪə(r)/ n capataz m & f, supervisor m. ~**shadow** /-'ʃædəʊ/ vt eclipsar. ~**shoot** /-'ʃuːt/ vt (pt -shot) excederse. ~**sight** n descuido m. ~**sleep** /-'sliːp/ vi (pt

-slept) quedarse dormido. **∼step** /-'step/ vt (pt **-stepped**) sobrepasar. **∼step the mark** pasarse de la raya

overt /'əʊvɜːt/ adj manifiesto

over:: ∼take /-'teɪk/ vt/i (pt **-took**, pp **-taken**) sobrepasar; (Auto) adelantar, rebasar (Mex). **∼throw** /-'θrəʊ/ vt (pt **-threw**, pp **-thrown**) derrocar. **∼time** n horas fpl extra

overture /'əʊvətjʊə(r)/ n obertura f

over:: ∼turn /-'tɜːn/ vt darle la vuelta a. ● vi volcar. **∼weight** /-'weɪt/ adj demasiado gordo. **be ∼weight** pesar demasiado. **∼whelm** /-'welm/ vt aplastar; (with emotion) abrumar. **∼whelming** adj aplastante; (fig) abrumador. **∼work** /-'wɜːk/ vt hacer trabajar demasiado. ● vi trabajar demasiado. ● n agotamiento m

ow|e /əʊ/ vt deber. **∼ing to** debido a

owl /aʊl/ n búho m

own /əʊn/ adj propio. **my ∼ house** mi propia casa. ● pron. **it's my ∼** es mío (propio)/mía (propia). **on one's ∼** solo. **get one's ∼ back** 🔢 desquitarse. ● vt tener. ❑ **∼ up** vi. 🔢 confesarse culpable. **∼er** n propietario m, dueño m. **∼ership** n propiedad f

oxygen /'ɒksɪdʒən/ n oxígeno m

grandes esfuerzos para atraer a estudiantes de todos los medios sociales.

oyster /'ɔɪstə(r)/ n ostra f

Pp

p abbr (= **pence, penny**) penique(s) (m(pl))

p. (pl **pp.**) (= **page**) pág., p.

pace /peɪs/ n paso m. **keep ∼ with s.o.** seguirle el ritmo a uno. ● vi. **∼ up and down** andar de un lado para otro. **∼maker** n (runner) liebre f; (Med) marcapasos m

Pacific /pə'sɪfɪk/ n. **the ∼ (Ocean)** el (Océano) Pacífico m

pacif|ist /'pæsɪfɪst/ n pacifista m & f. **∼y** /'pæsɪfaɪ/ vt apaciguar

pack /pæk/ n fardo m; (of cigarettes) paquete m, cajetilla f; (of cards) baraja f; (of hounds) jauría f; (of wolves) manada f. **a ∼ of lies** una sarta de mentiras. ● vt empaquetar; hacer (suitcase); (press down) apisonar. ● vi hacer la maleta, empacar (LAm). **∼age** /-ɪdʒ/ n paquete m. **∼age holiday** n vacaciones fpl organizadas. **∼ed** /pækt/ adj lleno (de gente). **∼et** /'pækɪt/ n paquete m

pact /pækt/ n pacto m, acuerdo m

pad /pæd/ n (for writing) bloc m. **shoulder ∼s** hombreras fpl. ● vt (pt **padded**) rellenar

paddle /'pædl/ n pala f. ● vi mojarse los pies; (in canoe) remar (con pala)

paddock /'pædək/ n prado m

padlock /'pædlɒk/ n candado m.
● vt cerrar con candado

paediatrician /ˌpiːdɪə'trɪʃn/ n pediatra m & f. **∼ophile** /'piːdəfaɪl/ n pedófilo m

pagan /'peɪɡən/ adj & n pagano (m)

page /peɪdʒ/ n página f; (attendant) paje m; (in hotel) botones m.
● vt llamar por megafonía/por buscapersonas, vocear (LAm)

paid /peɪd/ see PAY. ● adj. put ∼ to 🔟 acabar con

pail /peɪl/ n balde m, cubo m

pain /peɪn/ n dolor m. **I have a ∼ in my back** me duele la espalda. **be in ∼** tener dolores. **be a ∼ in the neck** 🔟 ser un pesado; (thing) ser una lata. ● vt doler. **∼ful** adj doloroso. **it's very ∼ful** duele mucho. **∼-killer** n analgésico m. **∼less** adj indoloro. **∼staking** /'peɪnzteɪkɪŋ/ adj concienzudo

paint /peɪnt/ n pintura f. ● vt/i pintar. **∼er** n pintor m. **∼ing** n (medium) pintura f; (picture) cuadro m

pair /peə(r)/ n par m; (of people) pareja f. **a ∼ of trousers** unos pantalones. ▫ **∼off, ∼ up** vi formar parejas

pajamas /pə'dʒɑːmæz/ npl (Amer) pijama m

Pakistan /ˌpɑːkɪ'stɑːn/ n Pakistán m. **∼i** adj & n paquistaní (m & f)

pal /pæl/ n 🔟 amigo m

palace /'pælɪs/ n palacio m

palatable /'pælətəbl/ adj agradable. **∼e** /'pælət/ n paladar m

pale /peɪl/ adj (-er, -est) pálido. **go ∼, turn ∼** palidecer. **∼ness** n palidez f

Palestine /'pælɪstaɪn/ n Palestina f. **∼ian** /-'stɪnɪən/ adj & n palestino (m)

palette /'pælɪt/ n paleta f

palm /pɑːm/ n palma f. ▫ ∼ **off** vt encajar (on a). **P∼ Sunday** n Domingo m de Ramos

palpable /'pælpəbl/ adj palpable

palpitat|e /'pælpɪteɪt/ vi palpitar. **∼ion** /-'teɪʃn/ n palpitación f

pamper /'pæmpə(r)/ vt mimar

pamphlet /'pæmflɪt/ n folleto m

pan /pæn/ n cacerola f; (for frying) sartén f

panacea /pænə'sɪə/ n panacea f

Panama /'pænəmɑː/ n Panamá m. **∼nian** /-'meɪnɪən/ adj & n panameño (m)

pancake /'pænkeɪk/ n crep(e) m, panqueque m (LAm)

panda /'pændə/ n panda m

pandemonium /ˌpændɪ'məʊnɪəm/ n pandemonio m

pander /'pændə(r)/ vi. ∼ **to s.o.** consentirle los caprichos a uno

pane /peɪn/ n vidrio m, cristal m

panel /'pænl/ n panel m; (group of people) jurado m. **∼ling** n paneles mpl

pang /pæŋ/ n punzada f

panic /'pænɪk/ n pánico m. ● vi (pt panicked) dejarse llevar por el pánico. **∼-stricken** adj aterrorizado

panorama /ˌpænə'rɑːmə/ n panorama m. **∼ic** /-'ræmɪk/ adj panorámico

pansy /'pænzɪ/ n (flower) pensamiento m

pant /pænt/ vi jadear

panther /'pænθə(r)/ n pantera f

panties /'pæntɪz/ npl bragas fpl, calzones mpl (LAm), pantaletas fpl (Mex)

pantihose /'pæntɪhəʊz/ npl see PANTYHOSE

pantomime /'pæntəmaɪm/ n pantomima f

pantry /'pæntrɪ/ n despensa f

pants /pænts/ npl (man's) calzoncillos mpl; (woman's) bragas fpl, calzones mpl (LAm), pantaletas fpl (Mex); (Amer, trousers) pantalones mpl

pantyhose /'pæntɪhəʊz/ npl (Amer) panty m, medias fpl, pantimedias fpl (Mex)

paper /'peɪpə(r)/ n papel m; (newspaper) diario m, periódico m; (exam) examen m; (document) documento m. ● vt empapelar, tapizar (Mex). ~back n libro m en rústica. ~ clip n sujetapapeles m, clip m. ~weight n pisapapeles m. ~work n papeleo m, trabajo m administrativo

parable /'pærəbl/ n parábola f

parachut|e /'pærəʃuːt/ n paracaídas m. ● vi saltar en paracaídas. ~ist n paracaidista m & f

parade /pə'reɪd/ n desfile m; (Mil) formación f. ● vi desfilar. ● vt hacer alarde de

paradise /'pærədaɪs/ n paraíso m

paraffin /'pærəfɪn/ n queroseno m

paragraph /'pærəgrɑːf/ n párrafo m

Paraguay /'pærəgwaɪ/ n Paraguay m. ~an adj & n paraguayo (m)

parallel /'pærəlel/ adj paralelo. ● n paralelo m; (line) paralela f

paraly|se /'pærəlaɪz/ vt paralizar. ~sis /pə'ræləsɪs/ n (pl -ses /-siːz/) parálisis f

parameter /pə'ræmɪtə(r)/ n parámetro m

paranoia /pærə'nɔɪə/ n paranoia f

parapet /'pærəpɪt/ n parapeto m

paraphernalia /pærəfə'neɪlɪə/ n trastos mpl

parasite /'pærəsaɪt/ n parásito m

paratrooper /'pærətruːpə(r)/ n paracaidista m (del ejército)

parcel /'pɑːsl/ n paquete m

parch /pɑːtʃ/ vt resecar. be ~ed ⊞ estar muerto de sed

parchment /'pɑːtʃmənt/ n pergamino m

pardon /'pɑːdn/ n perdón m; (Jurid) indulto m. **I beg your** ~ perdón. **(I beg you)** ~? ¿cómo? ¿mande? (Mex). ● vt perdonar; (Jurid) indultar. ~ **me?** (Amer) ¿cómo?

parent /'peərənt/ n (father) padre m; (mother) madre f. **my** ~s mis padres. ~al /pə'rentl/ adj de los padres

parenthesis /pə'renθəsɪs/ n (pl -theses /-siːz/) paréntesis m

parenthood /'peərənthʊd/ n el ser padre/madre

Paris /'pærɪs/ n París m

parish /'pærɪʃ/ n parroquia f; (municipal) distrito m. ~ioner /pə'rɪʃənə(r)/ n feligrés m

park /pɑːk/ n parque m. ● vt/i aparcar, estacionar (LAm). ~-and-ride estacionamiento m disuasorio (LAm), aparcamiento m disuasorio (Esp). ~ing lot n (Amer) aparcamiento m, estacionamiento m (LAm). ~ meter n parquímetro m

parking: /'pɑːkɪŋ/ n: ~ **lot** n (Amer) aparcamiento m, estacionamiento m (LAm). ~ **meter** n parquímetro m

parkway /'pɑːkweɪ/ n (Amer) carretera f ajardinada

parliament /'pɑːləmənt/ n parlamento m. ~ary /-'mentrɪ/ adj parlamentario

---

Parliament El Parlamento ⓘ británico, el más alto organismo legislativo. Está formado por la Cámara de los Lores y la Cámara de los Comunes. La primera, consta de 703 miembros, en la mayoría nombrados, con un número de cargos hereditarios, lo que es objeto de reforma en la actualidad. La Cámara de los Comunes consta de 659 miembros elegidos por el pueblo. Ver ▷**DÁIL ÉIREANN**, ▷**SCOTTISH PARLIAMENT**, ▷**WELSH ASSEMBLY**.

parlour /ˈpɑːlə(r)/ n salón m

parochial /pəˈrəʊkɪəl/ adj (fig) provinciano

parody /ˈpærədɪ/ n parodia f. ● vt parodiar

parole /pəˈrəʊl/ n libertad f condicional

parrot /ˈpærət/ n loro m, papagayo m

parsley /ˈpɑːslɪ/ n perejil m

parsnip /ˈpɑːsnɪp/ n pastinaca f

part /pɑːt/ n parte f; (of machine) pieza f; (of serial) episodio m; (in play) papel m; (Amer, in hair) raya f take ∼ in tomar parte en, participar en. for the most ∼ en su mayor parte. ● adv en parte. ● vt separar. ● vi separarse. □ ∼ with vt desprenderse de

partial /ˈpɑːʃl/ adj parcial. be ∼ to tener debilidad por. ∼**ly** adv parcialmente

participa|nt /pɑːˈtɪsɪpənt/ n participante m & f. ∼**te** /-peɪt/ vi participar. ∼**tion** /-ˈpeɪʃn/ n participación f

particle /ˈpɑːtɪkl/ n partícula f

particular /pəˈtɪkjʊlə(r)/ adj particular; (precise) meticuloso; (fastidious) quisquilloso. in ∼ en particular. ● n detalle m. ∼**ly** adv particularmente; (specifically) específicamente

passive /ˈpæsɪv/ adj pasivo

parting /ˈpɑːtɪŋ/ n despedida f; (in hair) raya f. ● adj de despedida

partition /pɑːˈtɪʃn/ n partición f; (wall) tabique m. ● vt dividir

partly /ˈpɑːtlɪ/ adv en parte

partner /ˈpɑːtnə(r)/ n socio m; (Sport) pareja f. ∼**ship** n asociación f; (Com) sociedad f

partridge /ˈpɑːtrɪdʒ/ n perdiz f

part-time /pɑːtˈtaɪm/ adj & adv a tiempo parcial, de medio tiempo (LAm)

party /ˈpɑːtɪ/ n reunión f, fiesta f; (group) grupo m; (Pol) partido m; (Jurid) parte f

pass /pɑːs/ vt (hand, convey) pasar; (go past) pasar por delante de; (overtake) adelantar, rebasar (Mex); (approve) aprobar (exam, bill, law); pronunciar (judgement). ● vi pasar; (pain) pasarse; (Sport) pasar la pelota. □ ∼ **away** vi fallecer. □ ∼ **down** vt transmitir. □ ∼ **out** vi desmayarse. □ ∼ **round** vt distribuir. □ ∼ **up** vt 🄸 dejar pasar. ● n (permit) pase m; (ticket) abono m; (in mountains) puerto m, desfiladero m; (Sport) pase m; (in exam) aprobado m. make a ∼ **at** 🄸 intentar besar. ∼**able** adj pasable; (road) transitable

passage /ˈpæsɪdʒ/ n (voyage) travesía f; (corridor) pasillo m; (alleyway) pasaje m; (in book) pasaje m

passenger /ˈpæsɪndʒə(r)/ n pasajero m

passer-by /pɑːsəˈbaɪ/ n (pl passers-by) transeúnte m & f

passion /ˈpæʃn/ n pasión f. ∼**ate** /-ət/ adj apasionado. ∼**ately** adv apasionadamente

Passover /ˈpɑːsəʊvə(r)/ n Pascua f de los hebreos

pass: ~**port** n pasaporte m. ~**word** n contraseña f

past /pɑːst/ adj anterior; (life) pasado; (week, year) último. **in times** ~ en tiempos pasados. ● n pasado m. **in the** ~ (formerly) antes, antiguamente. ● prep por delante de; (beyond) más allá de. **it's twenty** ~ **four** son las cuatro y veinte. ● adv. **drive** ~ pasar en coche. **go** ~ pasar

paste /peɪst/ n pasta f; (glue) engrudo m; (wallpaper ~) pegamento m; (jewellery) estrás m

pastel /ˈpæstl/ adj & n pastel (m)

pasteurize /ˈpɑːstʃəraɪz/ vt pasteurizar

pastime /ˈpɑːstaɪm/ n pasatiempo m

pastry /ˈpeɪstrɪ/ n masa f; (cake) pastelito m

pasture /ˈpɑːstʃə(r)/ n pasto(s) mpl

pasty /ˈpæstɪ/ n empanadilla f, empanada f (LAm)

pat /pæt/ vt (pt patted) darle palmaditas. ● n palmadita f; (of butter) porción f

patch /pætʃ/ n (on clothes) remiendo m, parche m; (over eye) parche m. **a bad** ~ una mala racha. ● vt remendar. ◻ ~ **up** vt hacerle un arreglo a

patent /ˈpeɪtnt/ adj patente. ● n patente f. ● vt patentar. ~ **leather** n charol m. ~**ly** adv. **it's** ~**ly obvious that...** está clarísimo que...

patern|al /pəˈtɜːnl/ adj paterno. ~**ity** /-ətɪ/ n paternidad f

path /pɑːθ/ n (pl -s/pɑːðz/) sendero m; (Sport) pista f; (of rocket) trayectoria f; (fig) camino m

pathetic /pəˈθetɪk/ adj (pitiful) patético; (excuse) pobre. **don't be so**

~ **no seas tan** pusilánime

patien|ce /ˈpeɪʃns/ n paciencia f. ~**t** adj a paciente (m & f). **be** ~**t with s.o.** tener paciencia con uno. ~**tly** adv pacientemente

patio /ˈpætɪəʊ/ n (pl -os) patio m

patriot /ˈpætrɪət/ n patriota m & f. ~**ic** /-ˈɒtɪk/ adj patriótico. ~**ism** n patriotismo m

patrol /pəˈtrəʊl/ n patrulla f. ● vt/i patrullar

patron /ˈpeɪtrən/ n (of the arts) mecenas m & f; (of charity) patrocinador m; (customer) cliente m & f. ~**age** /ˈpætrənɪdʒ/ n (sponsorship) patrocinio m; (of the arts) mecenazgo m. ~**ize** /ˈpætrənaɪz/ vt ser cliente de; (fig) tratar con condescendencia. ~**izing** adj condescendiente

pattern /ˈpætn/ n diseño m; (sample) muestra f; (in dressmaking) patrón m

paunch /pɔːntʃ/ n panza f

pause /pɔːz/ n pausa f. ● vi hacer una pausa

pave /peɪv/ vt pavimentar; (with flagstones) enlosar. ~**ment** n pavimento m; (at side of road) acera f, banqueta f (Mex)

paving stone /ˈpeɪvɪŋstəʊn/ n losa f

paw /pɔː/ n pata f

pawn /pɔːn/ n (Chess) peón m; (fig) títere m. ● vt empeñar. ~**broker** n prestamista m & f

pay /peɪ/ vt (pt paid) pagar; prestar (attention); hacer (compliment, visit). ~ **cash** pagar al contado. ● vi pagar; (be profitable) rendir. ● n paga f. **in the** ~ **of** al servicio de. ◻ ~ **back** vt devolver; pagar (loan). ◻ ~ **in** vt ingresar, depositar (LAm). ◻ ~ **off** vt cancelar, saldar (debt). vi valer la pena. □~ **up** vi pagar. ~**able** adj pagadero. ~**ment** n pago m. ~**roll** n nómina f

pea /piː/ n guisante m, arveja f (LAm), chícharo m (Mex)

peace /piːs/ n paz f. ~ **of mind** tranquilidad f. ~**ful** adj tranquilo. ~**maker** n conciliador m

peach /piːtʃ/ n melocotón m, durazno m (LAm)

peacock /ˈpiːkɒk/ n pavo m real

peak /piːk/ n cumbre f; (of career) apogeo m; (maximum) máximo m. ~ **hours** npl horas fpl de mayor demanda (o consumo etc)

peal /piːl/ n repique m. ~**s of laughter** risotadas fpl

peanut /ˈpiːnʌt/ n cacahuete m, maní m (LAm), cacahuate m (Mex)

pear /peə(r)/ n pera f. ~ **(tree)** peral m

pearl /pɜːl/ n perla f

peasant /ˈpeznt/ n campesino m

peat /piːt/ n turba f

pebble /ˈpebl/ n guijarro m

peck /pek/ vt picotear. ● n picotazo m; (kiss) besito m

peculiar /prˈkjuːlɪə(r)/ adj raro; (special) especial. ~**ity** /-ˈærətɪ/ n rareza f; (feature) particularidad f

pedal /ˈpedl/ n pedal m. ● vi pedalear

pedantic /prˈdæntɪk/ adj pedante

peddle /ˈpedl/ vt vender por las calles

pedestal /ˈpedɪstl/ n pedestal m

pedestrian /prˈdestrɪən/ n peatón m. ~ **crossing** paso m de peatones. ● adj pedestre; (dull) prosaico

pedigree /ˈpedɪɡriː/ n linaje m; (of animal) pedigrí m. ● adj (animal) de raza

peek /piːk/ vi mirar a hurtadillas

peel /piːl/ n piel f, cáscara f. ● vt pelar (fruit, vegetables). ● vi pelarse

peep /piːp/ vi. ~ **at** echarle un vistazo a. ● n (look) vistazo m; (bird sound) pío m

peer /pɪə(r)/ vi mirar. ~ **at** escudriñar. ● n (equal) par m & f; (contemporary) coetáneo m; (lord) par m. ~**age** /-ɪdʒ/ n nobleza f

peg /peɡ/ n (in ground) estaca f; (on violin) clavija f; (for washing) pinza f; (hook) gancho m; (for tent) estaquilla f. **off the** ~ de confección. ● vt (pt **pegged**) sujetar (con estacas, etc); fijar (precios)

pejorative /prˈdʒɒrətɪv/ adj peyorativo, despectivo

pelican /ˈpelɪkən/ n pelícano m

pellet /ˈpelɪt/ n bolita f; (for gun) perdigón m

pelt /pelt/ n pellejo m. ● vt. ~ **s.o. with sth** lanzarle algo a uno. ● vi. ~ **with rain**, ~ **down** llover a cántaros

pelvis /ˈpelvɪs/ n pelvis f

pen /pen/ (for writing) pluma f; (ballpoint) bolígrafo m; (sheep ~) redil m; (cattle ~) corral m

penal /ˈpiːnl/ adj penal. ~**ize** vt sancionar. ~**ty** /ˈpenltɪ/ n pena f; (fine) multa f; (in soccer) penalty m; (in US football) castigo m. ~**ty kick** n (in soccer) penalty m

penance /ˈpenəns/ n penitencia f

pence /pens/ see PENNY

pencil /ˈpensl/ n lápiz m. ● vt (pt **pencilled**) escribir con lápiz. ~**sharpener** n sacapuntas m

pendulum /ˈpendjʊləm/ n péndulo m

penetrat|e /ˈpenɪtreɪt/ vt/i penetrar. ~**ing** adj penetrante. ~**ion**

/-'treɪʃn/ n penetración f

penguin /'peŋgwɪn/ n pingüino m

penicillin /penɪ'sɪlɪn/ n penicilina f

peninsula /pə'nɪnsjʊlə/ n península f

penis /'piːnɪs/ n pene m

pen: ~**knife** /'pennaɪf/ n (pl pen-knives) navaja f. ~**name** n seudónimo m

penn|iless /'penɪlɪs/ adj sin un céntimo. ~**y** /'penɪ/ n (pl pennies or pence) penique m

pension /'penʃn/ n pensión f; (for retirement) pensión f de jubilación. ~**er** n jubilado m

pensive /'pensɪv/ adj pensativo

Pentecost /'pentɪkɒst/ n Pentecostés m

penthouse /'penthaʊs/ n penthouse m

pent-up /pent'ʌp/ adj reprimido; (confined) encerrado

penultimate /pen'ʌltɪmət/ adj penúltimo

people /'piːpl/ npl gente f; (citizens) pueblo m. ~ **say (that)** se dice que, dicen que. **English** ~ los ingleses. **young** ~ los jóvenes. **the** ~ (nation) el pueblo. ● vt poblar

pepper /'pepə(r)/ n pimienta f; (vegetable) pimiento m. ● vt (intersperse) salpicar (**with** de). ~**box** n (Amer) pimentero m. ~**corn** n grano m de pimienta. ~**mint** n menta f; (sweet) caramelo m de menta. ~**pot** n pimentero m

per /pɜː(r)/ prep por. ~ **annum** al año. ~ **cent** see **PERCENT**. ~ **head** por cabeza, por persona. **ten miles** ~ **hour** diez millas por hora

perceive /pə'siːv/ vt percibir; (notice) darse cuenta de

percent, per cent /pə'sent/ n

(no pl) porcentaje m. ● adv por ciento. ~**age** /-ɪdʒ/ n porcentaje m

percepti|ble /pə'septəbl/ adj perceptible. ~**on** /-ʃn/ n percepción f. ~**ve** /-tɪv/ adj perspicaz

perch /pɜːtʃ/ n (of bird) percha f; (fish) perca f. ● vi (bird) posarse. ~ **on** (person) sentarse en el borde de

percolat|e /'pɜːkəlert/ vi filtrarse. ~**or** n cafetera f eléctrica

percussion /pə'kʌʃn/ n percusión f

perfect /'pɜːfɪkt/ adj perfecto; (place, day) ideal. ● /pə'fekt/ vt perfeccionar. ~**ion** /pə'fekʃn/ n perfección f. **to** ~**ion** a la perfección. ~**ly** /'pɜːfɪktlɪ/ adv perfectamente

perform /pə'fɔːm/ vt desempeñar (function, role); ejecutar (task); realizar (experiment); representar (play); (Mus) interpretar. ~ **an operation** (Med) operar. ● vi (actor) actuar; (musician) tocar; (produce results) (vehicle) responder; (company) rendir. ~**ance** /-əns/ n ejecución f; (of play) representación f; (of actor, musician) interpretación f; (of team) actuación f; (of car) rendimiento m. ~**er** n (actor) actor m; (entertainer) artista m & f

perfume /'pɜːfjuːm/ n perfume m

perhaps /pə'hæps/ adv quizá(s), tal vez, a lo mejor

peril /'perəl/ n peligro m. ~**ous** adj arriesgado, peligroso

perimeter /pə'rɪmɪtə(r)/ n perímetro m

period /'pɪərɪəd/ n período m; (in history) época f; (lesson) clase f; (Amer, Gram) punto m; (menstruation) período m, regla f. ● adj de (la) época. ~**ic** /-'ɒdɪk/ adj periódico. ~**ical** /pɪərɪ'ɒdɪkl/ n revista f.

~ically adv periódico

peripher|al /pəˈrɪfərəl/ adj secundario; (Comp) periférico. **~y** /pəˈrɪfərɪ/ n periferia f

perish /ˈperɪʃ/ vi perecer; (rot) deteriorarse. **~able** adj perecedero. **~ing** adj 🅸 glacial

perjur|e /ˈpɜːdʒə(r)/ vr. **~e o.s.** perjurarse. **~y** n perjurio m

perk /pɜːk/ n gaje m. □ **~ up** vt reanimar. vi reanimarse

perm /pɜːm/ n permanente f. ● vt. **have one's hair ~ed** hacerse la permanente

permanen|ce /ˈpɜːmənəns/ n permanencia f. **~t** adj permanente. **~tly** adv permanentemente

permissible /pəˈmɪsəbl/ adj permisible

permission /pəˈmɪʃn/ n permiso m

permit /pəˈmɪt/ vt (pt permitted) permitir. ● /ˈpɜːmɪt/ n permiso m

peroxide /pəˈrɒksaɪd/ n peróxido m

perpendicular /pɜːpənˈdɪkjʊlə(r)/ adj & n perpendicular (f)

perpetrat|e /ˈpɜːpɪtreɪt/ vt cometer. **~or** n autor m

perpetua|l /pəˈpetʃʊəl/ adj perpetuo. **~te** /pəˈpetʃʊeɪt/ vt perpetuar

perplex /pəˈpleks/ vt dejar perplejo. **~ed** adj perplejo

persecut|e /ˈpɜːsɪkjuːt/ vt perseguir. **~ion** /-ˈkjuːʃn/ n persecución f

persever|ance /pɜːsɪˈvɪərəns/ n perseverancia f. **~e** /pɜːsɪˈvɪə(r)/ vi perseverar, persistir

Persian /ˈpɜːʃn/ adj persa. **the ~ Gulf** n el golfo Pérsico

persist /pəˈsɪst/ vi persistir.

~ence /-əns/ n persistencia f. **~ent** adj persistente; (continual) continuo

person /ˈpɜːsn/ n persona f. **in ~** en persona. **~al** adj personal; (call) particular; (property) privado. **~al assistant** n secretario m personal. **~ality** /-ˈnælətɪ/ n personalidad f. **~ally** adv personalmente. **~nel** /pɜːsəˈnel/ n personal m. **P~** (department) sección f de personal

perspective /pəˈspektɪv/ n perspectiva f

perspir|ation /pɜːspəˈreɪʃn/ n transpiración f. **~e** /pəˈspaɪə(r)/ vi transpirar

persua|de /pəˈsweɪd/ vt convencer, persuadir. **~e s.o. to do sth** convencer a una para que haga algo. **~sion** n /-ʃn/ persuasión f. **~sive** /-sɪv/ adj persuasivo

pertinent /ˈpɜːtɪnənt/ adj pertinente. **~ly** adv pertinentemente

perturb /pəˈtɜːb/ vt perturbar

Peru /pəˈruː/ n el Perú m

peruse /pəˈruːz/ vt leer cuidadosamente

Peruvian /pəˈruːvɪən/ adj & n peruano (m)

perver|se /pəˈvɜːs/ adj retorcido; (stubborn) obstinado. **~sion** n perversión f. **~t** /pəˈvɜːt/ vt pervertir. ● /ˈpɜːvɜːt/ n pervertido m

pessimis|m /ˈpesɪmɪzəm/ n pesimismo m. **~t** n pesimista m & f. **~tic** /-ˈmɪstɪk/ adj pesimista

pest /pest/ n plaga f; (🅸, person, thing) peste f

pester /ˈpestə(r)/ vt importunar

pesticide /ˈpestɪsaɪd/ n pesticida f

pet /pet/ n animal m doméstico; (favourite) favorito m. ● adj preferido. **my ~ hate** lo que más odio. ● vt (pt petted) acariciar

petal /ˈpetl/ n pétalo m

petition /pɪˈtɪʃn/ n petición f

pet name n apodo m

petrified /ˈpetrɪfaɪd/ adj (terrified) muerto de miedo; (rock) petrificado

petrol /ˈpetrəl/ n gasolina f. ~ **pump** n surtidor m. ~ **station** n gasolinera f. ~ **tank** n depósito m de gasolina ~**eum** /pɪˈtrəʊlɪəm/ n petróleo m.

petticoat /ˈpetɪkəʊt/ n enagua f; (slip) combinación f

petty /ˈpetɪ/ adj (-ier, -iest) insignificante; (mean) mezquino. ~**y cash** n dinero m para gastos menores

petulant /ˈpetjʊlənt/ adj irritable

pew /pjuː/ n banco m (de iglesia)

phantom /ˈfæntəm/ n fantasma m

pharma|ceutical /fɑːməˈsjuːtɪkl/ adj farmacéutico. ~**cist** /ˈfɑːməsɪst/ n farmacéutico m. ~**cy** /ˈfɑːməsɪ/ n farmacia f

phase /feɪz/ n etapa f. □ ~ **out** vt retirar progresivamente

PhD abbr (= Doctor of Philosophy) n doctorado m; (person) Dr., Dra.

pheasant /ˈfeznt/ n faisán m

phenomen|al /fɪˈnɒmɪnl/ adj fenomenal. ~**on** /-mən/ n (pl -ena /-ɪnə/) fenómeno m

philistine /ˈfɪlɪstaɪn/ adj & n filisteo (m)

philosoph|er /fɪˈlɒsəfə(r)/ n filósofo m. ~**ical** /-əˈsɒfɪkl/ adj filosófico. ~**y** /fɪˈlɒsəfɪ/ n filosofía f

phlegm /flem/ n flema f. ~**atic** /fleɡˈmætɪk/ adj flemático

phobia /ˈfəʊbɪə/ n fobia f

phone /fəʊn/ n 🔲 teléfono m. ● vt/i llamar (por teléfono). ~ **back** (call again) volver a llamar; (return

call) llamar (más tarde). ~ **book** n guía f telefónica, directorio m (LAm). ~ **booth**, ~ **box** n cabina f telefónica. ~ **call** n llamada f (telefónica). ~ **card** n tarjeta f telefónica. ~ **number** n número m de teléfono

phonetic /fəˈnetɪk/ adj fonético. ~**s** n fonética f

phoney /ˈfəʊnɪ/ adj (-ier, -iest) 🔲 falso

phosph|ate /ˈfɒsfeɪt/ n fosfato m. ~**orus** /ˈfɒsfərəs/ n fósforo m

photo /ˈfəʊtəʊ/ n (pl -os) 🔲 foto f. take a ~ sacar una foto. ~**copier** /-kɒpɪə(r)/ n fotocopiadora f. ~**copy** n fotocopia f. ● vt fotocopiar. ~**genic** /-ˈdʒenɪk/ adj fotogénico. ~**graph** /-ɡrɑːf/ n fotografía f. ● vt fotografiar, sacarle una fotografía a. ~**grapher** /fəˈtɒɡrəfə(r)/ n fotógrafo m. ~**graphic** /-ˈɡræfɪk/ adj fotográfico. ~**graphy** /fəˈtɒɡrəfɪ/ n fotografía f

phrase /freɪz/ n frase f. ● vt expresar. ~ **book** n manual m de conversación

physi|cal /ˈfɪzɪkl/ adj físico. ~**cian** /fɪˈzɪʃn/ n médico m. ~**cist** /ˈfɪzɪsɪst/ n físico m. ~**cs** /ˈfɪzɪks/ n física f. ~**ology** /fɪzɪˈɒlədʒɪ/ n fisiología f. ~**otherapist** /fɪzɪəʊˈθerəpɪst/ n fisioterapeuta m & f. ~**otherapy** /fɪzɪəʊˈθerəpɪ/ n fisioterapia f. ~**que** /fɪˈziːk/ n físico m

pian|ist /ˈpɪənɪst/ n pianista m & f. ~**o** /pɪˈænəʊ/ n (pl -os) piano m

pick /pɪk/ (tool) pico m. ● vt escoger; cortar (flowers); recoger (fruit, cotton); abrir con una ganzúa (lock). ~ a quarrel buscar camorra. ~ holes in criticar. □ ~ on vt meterse con. □ ~ out vt escoger; (identify) reconocer. □ ~ up vt re-

P

picket | pine   480

coger; (*lift*) levantar; (*learn*) aprender; adquirir (habit, etc); contagiarse de (illness). ● *vi* mejorar; (sales) subir. ~**axe** *n* pico *m*

picket /'pɪkɪt/ *n* (*group*) piquete *m*. ~ **line** *n* piquete *m*. ● *vt* formar un piquete frente a

pickle /'pɪkl/ *n* (*in vinegar*) encurtido *m*; (*Amer, gherkin*) pepinillo *m*; (*relish*) salsa *f* (*a base de encurtidos*). ● *vt* encurtir

pick: ~**pocket** *n* carterista *m* & *f.* ~-**up** *n* (*truck*) camioneta *f*

picnic /'pɪknɪk/ *n* picnic *m*

picture /'pɪktʃə(r)/ *n* (*painting*) cuadro *m*; (*photo*) foto *f*; (*drawing*) dibujo *m*; (*illustration*) ilustración *f*; (*film*) película *f*; (*fig*) descripción *f*. ● *vt* imaginarse. ~**sque** /-'resk/ *adj* pintoresco

pie /paɪ/ *n* empanada *f*; (*sweet*) pastel *m*, tarta *f*

piece /piːs/ *n* pedazo *m*, trozo *m*; (*part of machine*) pieza *f*; (*coin*) moneda *f*; (*in chess*) figura *f.* **a** ~ **of advice** un consejo. **a** ~ **of furniture** un mueble. **a** ~ **of news** una noticia. **take to** ~**s** desmontar. □ ~ **together** *vt* juntar. ~**meal** *adj* gradual; (*unsystematic*) poco sistemático. ● *adv* poco a poco

pier /pɪə(r)/ *n* muelle *m*; (*with amusements*) paseo con atracciones sobre un muelle

pierc|e /pɪəs/ *vt* perforar. ~**ing** *adj* penetrante

piety /'paɪətɪ/ *n* piedad *f*

pig /pɪg/ *n* cerdo *m*, chancho *m* (*LAm*)

pigeon /'pɪdʒɪn/ *n* paloma *f*; (*Culin*) pichón *m*. ~-**hole** *n* casillero *m*; (*fig*) casilla *f*

piggy /'pɪgɪ/ *n* cerdito *m*. ~**back**

n. **give s.o. a** ~**back** llevar a uno a cuestas. ~ **bank** *n* hucha *f*

pig-headed /-'hedɪd/ *adj* terco

pigment /'pɪgmənt/ *n* pigmento *m*

pig|sty /'pɪgstaɪ/ *n* pocilga *f*. ~**tail** *n* (*plait*) trenza *f*; (*bunch*) coleta *f*

pike /paɪk/ *n invar* (*fish*) lucio *m*

pilchard /'pɪltʃəd/ *n* sardina *f*

pile /paɪl/ *n* (*heap*) montón *m*; (*of fabric*) pelo *m*. ● *vt* amontonar. ~ **it on** exagerar. ● *vi* amontonarse. □ ~ **up** *vt* amontonar. ● *vi* amontonarse. ~-**up** *n* (*Med*) almorranas *fpl*. ~-**up** *n* choque *m* múltiple

pilgrim /'pɪlgrɪm/ *n* peregrino. ~**age** /-ɪdʒ/ *n* peregrinación *f*

pill /pɪl/ *n* pastilla *f*

pillar /'pɪlə(r)/ *n* columna *f*. ~ **box** *n* buzón *m*

pillow /'pɪləʊ/ *n* almohada *f.* ~**case** *n* funda *f* de almohada

pilot /'paɪlət/ *n* piloto *m*. ● *vt* pilotar. ~-**light** *n* fuego *m* piloto

pimple /'pɪmpl/ *n* grano *m*, espinilla *f* (*LAm*)

pin /pɪn/ *n* alfiler *m*; (*Mec*) perno *m*. ~**s and needles** hormigueo *m*. ● *vt* (*pt* **pinned**) prender con alfileres; (*fix*) sujetar

PIN /pɪn/ *n* (= **personal identification number**) NIP *m*

pinafore /'pɪnəfɔː(r)/ *n* delantal *m.* ~ **dress** *n* pichi *m*, jumper *m* & *f* (*LAm*)

pincers /'pɪnsəz/ *npl* tenazas *fpl*

pinch /pɪntʃ/ *vt* pellizcar; (*fam, steal*) hurtar. ● *vi* (*shoe*) apretar. ● *n* pellizco *m*; (*small amount*) pizca *f.* **at a** ~ si fuera necesario

pine /paɪn/ *n* pino *m*. ● *vi.* ~ **for** sth suspirar por algo. □ ~ **away** *vi* languidecer de añoranza. ~**apple** /'paɪnæpl/ n piña f

ping-pong /'pɪŋpɒŋ/ n ping-pong m

pink /pɪŋk/ adj & n rosa (m), rosado (m)

pinnacle /'pɪnəkl/ n pináculo m

pin: ~**point** vt determinar con precisión f. ~**stripe** n raya f fina

pint /paɪnt/ n pinta f (= 0.57 litros)

pioneer /paɪə'nɪə(r)/ n pionero m

pious /'paɪəs/ adj piadoso

pip /pɪp/ n (seed) pepita f; (time signal) señal f

pipe /paɪp/ n tubo m; (Mus) caramillo m; (for smoking) pipa f. ● vt llevar por tuberías. ~**dream** n ilusión f. ~**line** n conducto m; (for oil) oleoducto m. **in the** ~**line** en preparación f

piping /'paɪpɪŋ/ n tubería f. ● adv. ~ **hot** muy caliente, hirviendo

pira|cy /'paɪərəsɪ/ n piratería f. ~**te** /'paɪərət/ n pirata m

Pisces /'paɪsiːz/ n Piscis m

piss /pɪs/ vi 🗙 mear. □~ **off** vi 🗙. ~ **off!** ¡vete a la mierda! ~**ed** /pɪst/ adj (🗙, drunk) como una cuba; (Amer, fed up) cabreado

pistol /'pɪstl/ n pistola f

piston /'pɪstən/ n pistón m

pit /pɪt/ n hoyo m; (mine) mina f; (Amer, in fruit) hueso m

pitch /pɪtʃ/ n (substance) brea f; (degree) grado m; (Mus) tono m; (Sport) campo m. ● vt (throw) lanzar; armar (tent). ● vi (ship) cabecear. ~**black** /-'blæk/ adj oscuro como boca de lobo. ~**er** n jarra f

pitfall /'pɪtfɔːl/ n trampa f

pith /pɪθ/ n (of orange, lemon) médula f; (fig) meollo m

pitiful /'pɪtɪfl/ adj lastimoso

pittance /'pɪtns/ n miseria f

pity /'pɪtɪ/ n lástima f, pena f; (compassion) piedad f. **it's a** ~ **you can't come** es una lástima que no puedas venir. ● vt tenerle lástima a

pivot /'pɪvət/ n pivote m. ● vi pivotar; (fig) depender (**on** de)

placard /'plækɑːd/ n pancarta f; (sign) letrero m

placate /plə'keɪt/ vt apaciguar

place /pleɪs/ n lugar m; (seat) asiento m; (in firm, team) puesto m; (fam, house) casa f. **feel out of** ~ sentirse fuera de lugar. **take** ~ tener lugar. ● vt poner, colocar; (identify) identificar. **be** ~**d** (in race) colocarse. ~**mat** n mantel m individual

placid /'plæsɪd/ adj plácido

plague /pleɪg/ n peste f; (fig) plaga f. ● vt atormentar

plaice /pleɪs/ n invar platija f

plain /pleɪn/ adj (-**er**, -**est**) (clear) claro; (simple) sencillo; (candid) franco; (ugly) feo. **in** ~ **clothes** de civil. ● adv totalmente. ● n llanura f. ~**ly** adv claramente; (frankly) francamente; (simply) con sencillez

plaintiff /'pleɪntɪf/ n demandante m & f

plait /plæt/ vt trenzar. ● n trenza f

plan /plæn/ n plan m; (map) plano m; (of book, essay) esquema f. ● vt (pt **planned**) planear, planificar (strategies). **I'm** ~**ning to go to Greece** pienso ir a Grecia

plane /pleɪn/ n (tree) plátano m; (level) nivel m; (aircraft) avión m; (tool) cepillo m. ● vt cepillar

planet /'plænɪt/ n planeta m. ~**ary** adj planetario

plank /plæŋk/ n tabla f

planning /'plænɪŋ/ n planificación f. **family** ~ planificación familiar. **town** ~ urbanismo *m*

plant /plɑ:nt/ *n* planta *f*; (*Mec*) maquinaria *f*; (*factory*) fábrica *f*. ● *vt* plantar; (*place in position*) colocar. ~**ation** /plæn'teɪʃn/ *n* plantación *f*

plaque /plæk/ *n* placa *f*

plasma /'plæzmə/ *n* plasma *m*

plaster /'plɑ:stə(r)/ *n* yeso *m*; (*on walls*) revoque *m*; (*sticking plaster*) tirita *f* (®), curita *f* (®) (*LAm*); (*for setting bones*) yeso *m*, escayola *f*. ● *vt* revocar; rellenar con yeso (*cracks*)

plastic /'plæstɪk/ *adj* & *n* plástico (*m*)

Plasticine /'plæstɪsiːn/ *n* (®) plastilina *f* (®)

plastic surgery /plæstɪk 'sɜːdʒərɪ/ *n* cirugía *f* estética

plate /pleɪt/ *n* plato *m*; (*of metal*) chapa *f*; (*silverware*) vajilla *f* de plata; (*in book*) lámina *f*. ● *vt* recubrir (**with** de)

platform /'plætfɔːm/ *n* plataforma *f*; (*Rail*) andén *m*

platinum /'plætɪnəm/ *n* platino *m*

platitude /'plætɪtjuːd/ *n* lugar *m* común

platonic /plə'tɒnɪk/ *adj* platónico

plausible /'plɔːzəbl/ *adj* verosímil; (*person*) convincente

play /pleɪ/ *vt* jugar a (*game, cards*); jugar a, jugar (*LAm*) (football, chess); tocar (*instrument*); (*act role*) representar el papel de. ● *vi* jugar. ● *n* juego *m*; (*drama*) obra *f* de teatro. □ ~ **down** *vt* minimizar. □ ~ **up** *vi* ⌧ (*child*) dar guerra; (*car, TV*) no funcionar bien. ~**er** *n* jugador *m*; (*Mus*) músico *m*. ~**ful** *adj* juguetón. ~**ground** *n* parque *m* de juegos infantiles; (*in school*) patio *m* de recreo. ~**group** *n* jardín *m* de la infancia. ~**ing**

card *n* naipe *m*. ~**ing field** *n* campo *m* de deportes. ~**pen** *n* corralito *m*. ~**wright** /-raɪt/ *n* dramaturgo *m*

plc *abbr* (= **public limited company**) S.A.

plea /pliː/ *n* súplica *f*; (*excuse*) excusa *f*; (*Jurid*) defensa *f*

plead /pliːd/ *vt* (*Jurid*) alegar; (*as excuse*) pretextar. ● *vi* suplicar. ~ **with** suplicarle a. ~ **guilty** declararse culpable

pleasant /'pleznt/ *adj* agradable

pleas|e /pliːz/ *int* por favor. ● *vt* complacer; (*satisfy*) contentar. ● *vi* agradar; (*wish*) querer. ~**ed** *adj* (*satisfied*) satisfecho; (*happy*) contento. ~**ed with** satisfecho de. ~**ing** *adj* agradable; (*news*) grato. ~**ure** /'pleʒə(r)/ *n* placer *m*

pleat /pliːt/ *n* pliegue *m*

pledge /pledʒ/ *n* cantidad *f* prometida

plent|iful /'plentɪfl/ *adj* abundante. ~**y** /'plentɪ/ *n* abundancia *f*. ● *pron.* ~**y** of muchos, -chas; (*of sth uncountable*) mucho, -cha

pliable /'plaɪəbl/ *adj* flexible

pliers /'plaɪəz/ *npl* alicates *mpl*

plight /plaɪt/ *n* situación *f* difícil

plimsolls /'plɪmsəlz/ *npl* zapatillas *fpl* de lona

plod /plɒd/ *vi* (*pt* **plodded**) caminar con paso pesado

plot /plɒt/ *n* complot *m*; (*of novel etc*) argumento *m*; (*piece of land*) parcela *f*. ● *vt* (*pt* **plotted**) tramar; (*mark out*) trazar. ● *vi* conspirar

plough /plaʊ/ *n* arado *m*. ● *vt/i* arar. □ ~ **into** *vt* estrellarse contra. □ ~ **through** *vt* avanzar laboriosamente por

ploy /plɔɪ/ *n* treta *f*

pluck /plʌk/ *vt* arrancar; depilarse

(eyebrows); desplumar (bird). **~ up courage** to armarse de valor para. ● n valor m. **~y** adj (**-ier, -iest**) valiente

plug /plʌg/ n (in bath) tapón m; (Elec) enchufe m; (spark **~**) bujía f. ● vt (pt **plugged**) tapar; (fam, advertise) hacerle propaganda a. □ **~ in** vt (Elec) enchufar. **~hole** n desagüe m

plum /plʌm/ n ciruela f

plumage /'pluːmɪdʒ/ n plumaje m

plumb|er /'plʌmə(r)/ n fontanero m, plomero m (LAm). **~ing** n instalación f sanitaria, instalación f de cañerías

plume /pluːm/ n pluma f

plump /plʌmp/ adj (**-er, -est**) rechoncho

plunge /plʌndʒ/ vt hundir (knife); (in water) sumergir; (into state, condition) sumir. ● vi zambullirse; (fall) caer. ● n zambullida f

plural /'plʊərəl/ n plural m. ● adj en plural

plus /plʌs/ prep más. ● adj positivo. ● n signo de más; (fig) ventaja f

plush /plʌʃ/ adj lujoso

Pluto /'pluːtəʊ/ n Plutón m

plutonium /pluː'təʊnɪəm/ n plutonio m

ply /plaɪ/ vt manejar (tool); ejercer (trade). **~ s.o. with drink** dar continuamente de beber a uno. **~wood** n contrachapado m

p.m. abbr (= **post meridiem**) de la tarde

pneumatic drill /njuː'mætɪk/ adj martillo m neumático

pneumonia /njuː'məʊnjə/ n pulmonía f

poach /pəʊtʃ/ vt escalfar (egg); cocer (fish etc); (steal) cazar furtivamente. **~er** n cazador m furtivo

PO box /piː'əʊ/ n Apdo. postal

pocket /'pɒkɪt/ n bolsillo m; (of air, resistance) bolsa f. ● vt poner en el bolsillo. **~book** n (notebook) libro m de bolsillo; (Amer, wallet) cartera f; (Amer, handbag) bolso m, cartera f (LAm), bolsa f (Mex). **~ money** n dinero m de bolsillo, mesada f (LAm)

pod /pɒd/ n vaina f

poem /'pəʊɪm/ n poema f

poet /'pəʊɪt/ n poeta m. **~ic** /-'etɪk/ adj poético. **~ry** /'pəʊɪtrɪ/ n poesía f

poignant /'pɔɪnjənt/ adj conmovedor

point /pɔɪnt/ n (dot, on scale) punto m; (sharp end) punta f; (in time) momento m; (statement) observación; (on agenda, in discussion) punto m; (Elec) toma f de corriente. **to the ~** pertinente. **up to a ~** hasta cierto punto. **be on the ~ of** estar a punto de. **get to the ~** ir al grano. **there's no ~ (in) arguing** no sirve de nada discutir. ● vt (aim) apuntar; (show) indicar. ● vi señalar. **~ at/to sth** señalar algo. □ **~ out** vt señalar. **~-blank** adj & adv a quemarropa. **~ed** adj (chin, nose) puntiagudo; (fig) mordaz. **~less** adj inútil

poise /pɔɪz/ n porte m; (composure) desenvoltura f

poison /'pɔɪzn/ n veneno m. ● vt envenenar. **~ous** adj venenoso; (chemical etc) tóxico

poke /pəʊk/ vt empujar; atizar (fire). ● vi hurgar; (pry) meterse. ● n golpe m. **~ about** vi fisgonear. **~r** /'pəʊkə(r)/ n atizador m; (Cards) póquer m

poky /'pəʊkɪ/ adj (**-ier, -iest**) diminuto

Poland /'pəʊlənd/ n Polonia f

polar /'pəʊlə(r)/ adj polar. ~ **bear** n oso m blanco

pole /pəʊl/ n palo m; (fixed) poste m; (for flag) mástil m; (in geography) polo m

police /pə'li:s/ n policía f. ~**man** /-mən/ n policía m, agente m. ~ **station** n comisaría f. ~**woman** n policía f, agente f

policy /'pɒlɪsɪ/ n política f; (insurance) póliza f (de seguros)

polish /'pɒlɪʃ/ n (for shoes) betún m; (furniture ~) cera f para muebles; (floor ~) abrillantador m de suelos; (shine) brillo m, (fig) finura f. • vt darle brillo a; limpiar (shoes); (refine) pulir. □ ~ **off** vt despachar. ~**ed** adj pulido

Polish /'pəʊlɪʃ/ adj & n polaco (m)

polite /pə'laɪt/ adj cortés. ~**ly** adv cortésmente. ~**ness** n cortesía f

politic|al /pə'lɪtɪkl/ adj político. ~**ian** /pɒlɪ'tɪʃn/ n político m. ~**s** /'pɒlətɪks/ n política f

poll /pəʊl/ n elección f; (survey) encuesta f. • vt obtener (votes)

pollack /'pɒlæk/ n abadejo m

pollen /'pɒlən/ n polen m

polling booth n cabina f de votar

pollut|e /pə'lu:t/ vt contaminar. ~**ion** /-ʃn/ n contaminación f

polo /'pəʊləʊ/ n polo m. ~ **neck** n cuello m vuelto

poly|styrene /pɒlɪ'staɪri:n/ n poliestireno m. ~**thene** /'pɒlɪθi:n/ n plástico, polietileno m

pomp /pɒmp/ n pompa f. ~**ous** adj pomposa

pond /pɒnd/ n (natural) laguna f; (artificial) estanque m

ponder /'pɒndə(r)/ vt considerar. ~**ous** adj pesado

pony /'pəʊnɪ/ n poni m. ~**-tail** n cola f de caballo

poodle /'pu:dl/ n caniche m

pool /pu:l/ n charca f; (artificial) estanque m; (puddle) charco m. (common fund) fondos mpl comunes; (snooker) billar m americano. (**swimming**) ~ n piscina f, alberca f (Mex). ~**s** npl quinielas fpl. • vt aunar

poor /pʊə(r)/ adj (-er, -est) pobre; (quality, diet) malo. **be in** ~ **health** estar mal de salud. ~**ly** adj 🆃 malito. • adv mal

pop /pɒp/ n (Mus) música f pop; (Amer fam, father) papá m. • vt (pt **popped**) hacer reventar; (put) poner. □ ~ **in** vi (visit) pasar por. □ ~ **out** vi saltar; (person) salir un rato. □ ~ **up** vi surgir, aparecer

popcorn /'pɒpkɔːn/ n palomitas fpl

pope /pəʊp/ n papa m

poplar /'pɒplə(r)/ n álamo m (blanco)

poppy /'pɒpɪ/ n amapola f

popular /'pɒpjʊlə(r)/ adj popular. ~**ity** /-'lærətɪ/ n popularidad f. ~**ize** vt popularizar

populat|e /'pɒpjʊleɪt/ vt poblar. ~**ion** /-'leɪʃn/ n población f

pop-up /'pɒpʌp/ n ventana f emergente, pop-up m

porcelain /'pɔːsəlɪn/ n porcelana f

porch /pɔːtʃ/ n porche m

porcupine /'pɔːkjʊpaɪn/ n puerco m espín

pore /pɔː(r)/ n poro m

pork /pɔːk/ n carne f de cerdo m, carne f de puerco m (Mex)

porn /pɔːn/ n 🆃 pornografía f. ~**ographic** /-ə'ɡræfɪk/ adj pornográfico. ~**ography** /pɔː'nɒɡrəfɪ/ n pornografía f

porpoise /'pɔːpəs/ n marsopa f

porridge /'pɒrɪdʒ/ n avena f (cocida)

port /pɔːt/ n puerto m; (Naut) babor m; (Comp) puerto m; (Culin) oporto m

portable /'pɔːtəbl/ adj portátil

porter /'pɔːtə(r)/ n (for luggage) maletero m; (concierge) portero m

porthole /'pɔːthəʊl/ n portilla f

portion /'pɔːʃn/ n porción f; (part) parte f

portrait /'pɔːtrɪt/ n retrato m

portray /pɔː'treɪ/ vt representar. ~al n representación f

Portug|al /'pɔːtjʊgl/ n Portugal m. ~uese /-'giːz/ adj & n portugués (m)

pose /pəʊz/ n pose f, postura f. ● vt representar (threat); plantear (problem, question). ● vi posar. ~ as hacerse pasar por

posh /pɒʃ/ adj 🔲 elegante

position /pə'zɪʃn/ n posición f; (job) puesto m; (situation) situación f. ● vt colocar

positive /'pɒzətɪv/ adj positivo; (real) auténtico; (certain) seguro. ● n (Photo) positiva f. ~ly adv positivamente

possess /pə'zes/ vt poseer. ~ion /-ʃn/ n posesión f; (Jurid) bien m. ~ive adj posesivo

possib|ility /pɒsə'bɪlətɪ/ n posibilidad f. ~le /'pɒsəbl/ adj posible. ~ly adv posiblemente

post /pəʊst/ n (pole) poste m; (job) puesto m; (mail) correo m. ● vt echar al correo (letter); (send) enviar por correo. **keep s.o. ~ed** mantener a uno al corriente

post... /pəʊst/ pref post, pos

post: ~**age** /-ɪdʒ/ /-ɪdʒ/ n franqueo m. ~**al** adj postal. ~**al**

order n giro m postal. ~ **box** n buzón m. ~**card** n (tarjeta f) postal f. ~**code** n código m postal

poster /'pəʊstə(r)/ n cartel m, póster m

posterity /pɒs'terətɪ/ n posteridad f

posthumous /'pɒstjʊməs/ adj póstumo

post: ~**man** /-mən/ n cartero m. ~**mark** n matasellos m

post mortem /pəʊst'mɔːtəm/ n autopsia f

post office n oficina f de correos, correos mpl, correo m (LAm)

postpone /pəʊst'pəʊn/ vt aplazar, posponer. ~**ment** n aplazamiento m

postscript /'pəʊstskrɪpt/ n posdata f

posture /'pɒstʃə(r)/ n postura f

posy /'pəʊzɪ/ n ramillete m

pot /pɒt/ n (for cooking) olla f; (for jam, honey) tarro m; (for flowers) tiesto m; (in pottery) vasija f. ~**s and pans** cacharros mpl

potato /pə'teɪtəʊ/ n (pl -oes) patata f, papa f (LAm)

potent /'pəʊtnt/ adj potente; (drink) fuerte

potential /pəʊ'tenʃl/ adj & n potencial (m). ~**ly** adv potencialmente

pot: ~**hole** n cueva f subterránea; (in road) bache m. ~**holing** n espeleología f

potion /'pəʊʃn/ n poción f

pot-shot n tiro m al azar

potter /'pɒtə(r)/ n alfarero m. ● vi hacer pequeños trabajos agradables. ~**y** n (pots) cerámica f; (workshop, craft) alfarería f

potty /'pɒtɪ/ adj (-ier, -iest) 🔲

chiflado. ● n orinal m

pouch /paʊtʃ/ n bolsa f pequeña; (for correspondence) valija f

poultry /'pəʊltrɪ/ n aves fpl de corral

pounce /paʊns/ vi saltar. ~ on abalanzarse sobre

pound /paʊnd/ n (weight) libra f (= 454g); (money) libra f (esterlina); (for cars) depósito m. ● vt (crush) machacar. ● vi aporrear; (heart) palpitar; (sound) retumbar

pour /pɔː(r)/ vt verter; echar (salt). ~ (out) servir (drink). ● vi (blood) manar; (water) salir; (rain) llover a cántaros. □~ out vi (people) salir en tropel. ~ing adj. ~ing rain lluvia f torrencial

pout /paʊt/ vi hacer pucheros

poverty /'pɒvətɪ/ n pobreza f

powder /'paʊdə(r)/ n polvo m; (cosmetic) polvos mpl. ● vt empolvar. ~ one's face empolvarse la cara. ~y adj como polvo

power /'paʊə(r)/ n poder m; (energy) energía f; (electricity) electricidad f; (nation) potencia f. ● vt. ~ed by impulsado por. ~ cut n apagón m. ~ed adj con motor. ~ful adj poderoso. ~less adj impotente. ~ plant n, ~-station n central f eléctrica

PR = public relations

practicable /'præktɪkəbl/ adj practicable

practical /'præktɪkl/ adj práctico. ~ joke n broma f. ~ly adv prácticamente

practi|ce /'præktɪs/ n práctica f; (custom) costumbre f; (exercise) ejercicio m; (Sport) entrenamiento m; (clients) clientela f. he's out of ~ce le falta práctica. in ~ce (in fact) en la práctica. ~se /'præktɪs/

vt practicar; ensayar (act); ejercer (profession). ● vi practicar; (professional) ejercer. ~tioner /-'tɪʃənə(r)/ n médico m

prairie /'preərɪ/ n pradera f

praise /preɪz/ vt (Relig) alabar; (compliment) elogiar. ● n (credit) elogios mpl. ~worthy adj loable

pram /præm/ n cochecito m

prank /præŋk/ n travesura f

prawn /prɔːn/ n gamba f, camarón m (LAm)

pray /preɪ/ vi rezar (for por). ~er /preə(r)/ n oración f

pre.. /priː/ pref pre...

preach /priːtʃ/ vt/i predicar. ~er n predicador m; (Amer, minister) pastor m

pre-arrange /priːə'reɪndʒ/ vt concertar de antemano

precarious /prɪ'keərɪəs/ adj precario. ~ly adv precariamente

precaution /prɪ'kɔːʃn/ n precaución f

precede /prɪ'siːd/ vt preceder. ~nce /'presədəns/ n precedencia f. ~nt /'presədənt/ n precedente m

preceding /prɪ'siːdɪŋ/ adj anterior

precept /'priːsept/ n precepto m

precinct /'priːsɪŋkt/ n recinto m; (Amer, police district) distrito m policial; (Amer, voting district) circunscripción f. pedestrian ~ zona f peatonal. ~s (of city) límites mpl

precious /'preʃəs/ adj precioso. ● adv 🔲 muy

precipice /'presɪpɪs/ n precipicio m

precipitate /prɪ'sɪpɪteɪt/ vt precipitar. ● /prɪ'sɪpɪtət/ n precipitado m. ● /prɪ'sɪpɪtət/ adj precipitado

precis|e /prɪ'saɪs/ adj (accurate)

exacto; (*specific*) preciso; (*meticulous*) minucioso. **~ely** *adv* con precisión. **~!** ¡exacto! **~ion** /-'sɪʒn/ n precisión f

preclude /prɪ'klu:d/ *vt* excluir

precocious /prɪ'kəʊʃəs/ *adj* precoz. **~ly** *adv* precozmente

preconceived /pri:kən'si:vd/ *adj* preconcebido. **~ption** /-'sepʃn/ n preconcepción f

precursor /pri:'kɜ:sə(r)/ n precursor m

predator /'predətə(r)/ n depredador m. **~y** *adj* predador

predecessor /'pri:dɪsesə(r)/ n predecesor m, antecesor m

predicament /prɪ'dɪkəmənt/ n aprieto m

predict /prɪ'dɪkt/ *vt* predecir. **~ion** /-ʃn/ n predicción f

preen /pri:n/ *vt* arreglar. **~ o.s.** atildarse

prefab /'pri:fæb/ n ⚀ casa f prefabricada. **~ricated** /-'fæbrɪkeɪtɪd/ *adj* prefabricado

preface /'prefəs/ n prefacio m; (*to event*) prólogo m

prefect /'pri:fekt/ n (*Schol*) monitor m; (*official*) prefecto m

prefer /prɪ'fɜ:(r)/ *vt* (*pt* preferred) preferir. **~ sth to** preferir algo a algo. **~able** /'prefrəbl/ *adj* preferible. **~ence** /'prefrəns/ n preferencia f. **~ential** /-ə'renʃl/ *adj* preferente

pregnan|cy /'pregnənsɪ/ n embarazo m. **~t** *adj* embarazada

prehistoric /pri:hɪ'stɒrɪk/ *adj* prehistórico

prejudge /pri:'dʒʌdʒ/ *vt* prejuzgar

prejudice /'predʒʊdɪs/ n prejuicio m. ● *vt* predisponer; (*harm*) perjudicar. **~d** *adj* lleno de prejuicios

preliminary /prɪ'lɪmɪnərɪ/ *adj* preliminar

prelude /'prelju:d/ n preludio m

premature /'premətjʊə/ *adj* prematuro

premeditated /pri:'medɪteɪtɪd/ *adj* premeditado

premier /'premɪə(r)/ n (*Pol*) primer ministro m

première /'premɪeə(r)/ n estreno m

premise /'premɪs/ n premisa f. **~s** /'premɪsɪz/ *npl* local m. **on the ~s** en el local

premium /'pri:mɪəm/ n (*insurance* ~) prima f de seguro. **be at a ~** escasear

premonition /pri:mə'nɪʃn/ n premonición f, presentimiento m

preoccup|ation /pri:ɒkjʊ'peɪʃn/ n (*obsession*) obsesión f; (*concern*) preocupación f. **~ied** /-'ɒkjʊpaɪd/ *adj* absorto; (*worried*) preocupado

preparat|ion /prepə'reɪʃn/ n preparación f. **~ions** *npl* preparativos *mpl*. **~ory** /prɪ'pærətrɪ/ *adj* preparatorio

prepare /prɪ'peə(r)/ *vt* preparar. ● *vi* prepararse. ● *adj* preparado (*willing*). **be ~d to** estar dispuesto a

preposition /prepə'zɪʃn/ n preposición f

preposterous /prɪ'pɒstərəs/ *adj* absurdo

prerequisite /pri:'rekwɪzɪt/ n requisito m esencial

prerogative /prɪ'rɒgətɪv/ n prerrogativa f

Presbyterian /prezbɪ'tɪərɪən/ *adj* & n presbiteriano (m)

prescri|be /prɪ'skraɪb/ *vt* prescribir; (*Med*) recetar. **~ption** /-'ɪpʃn/ n (*Med*) receta f

presence /'prezns/ n presencia f.
~ **of mind** presencia f de ánimo

present /'preznt/ n (gift) regalo
m; (current time) presente m. **at** ~
actualmente. **for the** ~ por ahora.
● adj presente. ● /prɪ'zent/ vt presentar; (give) obsequiar. ~ **s.o.
with** obsequiar a uno con. ~**able**
/prɪ'zentəbl/ adj presentable.
~**ation** /prezn'teɪʃn/ n presentación f; (ceremony) ceremonia f de
entrega. ~**er** /prɪ'zentə(r)/ n presentador m. ~**ly** /'prezntlɪ/ adv
dentro de poco

preserv|ation /prezə'veɪʃn/ n
conservación f. ~**ative** /prɪ'zɜːvətɪv/ n conservante m. ~**e** /prɪ'zɜːv/ vt conservar; (maintain) mantener; (Culin) hacer conserva de. ● n
coto m; (jam) confitura f. **wildlife**
~**e** (Amer) reserva f de animales

preside /prɪ'zaɪd/ vi presidir. ~
over presidir

presiden|cy /'prezɪdənsɪ/ n presidencia f. ~**t** n presidente m.
~**tial** /-'denʃl/ adj presidencial

press /pres/ vt apretar; prensar
(grapes); (put pressure on) presionar; (iron) planchar. **be** ~**ed for
time** andar escaso de tiempo. ● vi
apretar; (time) apremiar; (fig) urgir.
● n (Mec, newspapers) prensa f;
(printing) imprenta f. □ ~ **on** vi seguir adelante (**with** con). ~ **conference** n rueda f de prensa. ~
cutting n recorte m de periódico.
~**ing** adj urgente. ~**up** n flexión f,
fondo m

pressur|e /'preʃə(r)/ n presión f.
● vt presionar. ~**e-cooker** n olla f a
presión. ~**ize** vt presionar

prestige /pre'stiːʒ/ n prestigio m.
~**ious** /-'stɪdʒəs/ adj prestigioso

presum|ably /prɪ'zjuːməblɪ/ adv.
~... supongo que..., me imagino

que... ~**e** /prɪ'zjuːm/ vt suponer.
~**ptuous** /prɪ'zʌmptʃʊəs/ adj impertinente

presuppose /priːsə'pəʊz/ vt presuponer

preten|ce /prɪ'tens/ n fingimiento
m; (claim) pretensión f; (pretext)
pretexto m. ~**d** /-'tend/ vt/i fingir.
~**sion** /-'tenʃəs/ n pretensión f.
~**tious** /-'tenʃəs/ adj pretencioso

pretext /'priːtekst/ n pretexto m

pretty /'prɪtɪ/ adj (-**ier**, -**iest**) adv
bonito, lindo (esp LAm)

prevail /prɪ'veɪl/ vi predominar;
(win) prevalecer. □ ~ **on** vt persuadir

prevalen|ce /'prevələns/ n (occurrence) preponderancia f; (predominance) predominio m. ~**t** adj
extendido

prevent /prɪ'vent/ vt (hinder) impedir; (forestall) prevenir, evitar.
~**ion** /-ʃn/ n prevención f. ~**ive** adj
preventivo

preview /'priːvjuː/ n preestreno
m; (trailer) avance m

previous /'priːvɪəs/ adj anterior.
~ **to** antes de. ~**ly** adv antes

prey /preɪ/ n presa f. **bird of** ~
ave f de rapiña

price /praɪs/ n precio m. ● vt fijar el
precio de. ~**less** adj inestimable;
(fam, amusing) muy divertido. ~**y**
adj 🔢 carito

prick /prɪk/ vt/i pinchar. ● n pinchazo m

prickl|e /'prɪkl/ n (thorn) espina f;
(of animal) púa f; (sensation) picor
m. ~**y** adj espinoso; (animal) con
púas; (touchy) quisquilloso

pride /praɪd/ n orgullo m. ● vr. ~
o.s. vr enorgullecerse de

priest /priːst/ n sacerdote m.
~**hood** n sacerdocio m

prim /prɪm/ adj (**primmer, primmest**) mojigato; (affected) remilgado

primar|ily /ˈpraɪmərɪlɪ/ adv en primer lugar. **~y** /ˈpraɪmərɪ/ adj (principal) primordial; (first, basic) primario. **~ school** n escuela f primaria

prime /praɪm/ vt cebar (gun); (prepare) preparar; aprestar (surface). ● adj principal; (first rate) excelente. **~ minister** n primer ministro m. ● n. **be in one's ~** estar en la flor de la vida. **~r** n (paint) imprimación f

primeval /praɪˈmiːvl/ adj primigenio

primitive /ˈprɪmɪtɪv/ adj primitivo

primrose /ˈprɪmrəʊz/ n primavera f

prince /prɪns/ n príncipe m. **~ss** /prɪnˈses/ n princesa f

principal /ˈprɪnsəpl/ adj principal. ● n (of school) director m; (of university) rector m. **~ly** /ˈprɪnsɪpəlɪ/ adv principalmente

principle /ˈprɪnsəpl/ n principio m. **in ~** en principio. **on ~** por principio

print /prɪnt/ vt imprimir; (write in capitals) escribir con letras de molde. **~ed matter** impresos mpl. ● n (characters) letra f; (picture) grabado m; (Photo) copia f; (fabric) estampado m. **in ~** (published) publicado; (available) a la venta. **out of ~** agotado. **~er** /ˈprɪntə(r)/ n impresor m; (machine) impresora f. **~ing** n impresión f; (trade) imprenta f. **~out** n listado m

prion /ˈpraɪɒn/ n prión m

prior /ˈpraɪə(r)/ n prior m. ● adj previo. **~ to** antes de. **~ity** /praɪˈɒrɪtɪ/ n prioridad f. **~y** n prio-

rato m

prise /praɪz/ vt. **~ open** abrir haciendo palanca

prison /ˈprɪzn/ n cárcel m. **~er** n prisionero m; (in prison) preso m; (under arrest) detenido m. **~ officer** n funcionario m de prisiones

priva|cy /ˈprɪvəsɪ/ n privacidad f. **~te** /ˈpraɪvɪt/ adj privado; (confidential) personal; (lessons, house) particular. **in ~te** en privado; (secretly) en secreto. ● n soldado m raso. **~te detective** n detective m & f privado. **~tely** adv en privado. **~tion** /praɪˈveɪʃn/ n privación f

privilege /ˈprɪvɪlɪdʒ/ n privilegio m. **~d** adj privilegiado. **be ~d to** tener el privilegio de

prize /praɪz/ n premio m. ● adj (idiot etc) de remate. ● vt estimar

pro /prəʊ/ n. **~s and cons** los pros m y los contras

probab|ility /prɒbəˈbɪlətɪ/ n probabilidad f. **~le** /ˈprɒbəbl/ adj probable. **~ly** adv probablemente

probation /prəˈbeɪʃn/ n período m de prueba; (Jurid) libertad f condicional

probe /prəʊb/ n sonda f; (fig) investigación f. ● vt sondar. ● vi. **~ into** investigar

problem /ˈprɒbləm/ n problema m. ● adj difícil. **~atic** /-ˈmætɪk/ adj problemático

procedure /prəˈsiːdʒə(r)/ n procedimiento m

proceed /prəˈsiːd/ vi proceder; (move forward) avanzar. **~ings** npl (report) actas fpl; (Jurid) proceso m. **~s** /ˈprəʊsiːdz/ npl. **the ~s** lo recaudado

process /ˈprəʊses/ n proceso m. **in the ~ of** en vías de. ● vt tratar; revelar (photo); tramitar (order)

~ion /prə'seɪn/ n desfile m; (Relig) procesión f. ~or n procesador m. food ~ procesador m de alimentos

procla|im /prə'kleɪm/ vt proclamar. ~mation /prɒklə'meɪʃn/ n proclamación f

procure /prə'kjʊə(r)/ vt obtener

prod /prɒd/ vt (pt prodded) (with sth sharp) pinchar; (with elbow) darle un codazo a. ● n (with sth sharp) pinchazo m; (with elbow) codazo m

produc|e /prə'djuːs/ vt producir; surtir (effect); sacar (gun); producir (film); poner en escena (play). ● /'prɒdjuːs/ n productos mpl. ~er /prə'djuːsə(r)/ n (TV, Cinema) productor m; (in theatre) director m; (manufacturer) fabricante m & f. ~t /'prɒdʌkt/ n producto m. ~tion /prə'dʌkʃn/ n (manufacture) fabricación f; (output) producción f; (of play) producción f. ~tive /prə'dʌktɪv/ adj productivo. ~tivity /prɒdʌk'tɪvəti/ n productividad f

profess /prə'fes/ vt profesar; (pretend) pretender. ~ion /-'feʃn/ n profesión f. ~ional adj & n profesional (m & f). ~or /-'fesə(r)/ n catedrático m; (Amer) profesor m

proficien|cy /prə'fɪʃənsi/ n competencia f. ~t adj competente

profile /'prəʊfaɪl/ n perfil m

profit /'prɒfɪt/ n (Com) ganancia f; (fig) provecho m. ● vi. ~ from sacar provecho de. ~able adj provechoso

profound /prə'faʊnd/ adj profundo. ~ly adv profundamente

profuse /prə'fjuːs/ adj profuso. ~ely adv profusamente

prognosis /prɒg'nəʊsɪs/ n (pl -oses) pronóstico m

program /'prəʊɡræm/ n (Comp)

programa m; (Amer, course) curso m. ~me /'prəʊɡræm/ n programa m. ● vt (pt -med) programar. ~mer n programador m

progress /'prəʊɡres/ n progreso m; (development) desarrollo m. make ~ hacer progresos. in ~ en curso. ● /prə'ɡres/ vi hacer progresos; (develop) desarrollarse. ~ion /prə'ɡreʃn/ n progresión f; (advance) evolución f. ~ive /prə'ɡresɪv/ adj progresivo; (reforming) progresista. ~ively adv progresivamente

prohibit /prə'hɪbɪt/ vt prohibir; (prevent) impedir. ~ive adj prohibitivo

project /prə'dʒekt/ vt proyectar. ● vi (stick out) sobresalir. ● /'prɒdʒekt/ n proyecto m; (Schol) trabajo m; (Amer, housing ~) complejo m de viviendas subvencionadas. ~or /prə'dʒektə(r)/ n proyector m

prolific /prə'lɪfɪk/ adj prolífico

prologue /'prəʊlɒɡ/ n prólogo m

prolong /prə'lɒŋ/ vt prolongar

prom /prɒm/ n (Amer) baile m del colegio. ~enade /prɒmə'nɑːd/ n paseo m marítimo. ● vi pasearse.

Prom En EE.UU. un *prom* es un baile que se celebra para los estudiantes que terminan el *High School*. En Londres los *Proms* son una serie de conciertos de música clásica, durante los cuales una gran parte del público permanece de pie. Tienen lugar en el *Albert Hall* en el verano, durante ocho semanas. Oficialmente, son conocidos como los *Henry Wood Promenade Concerts*, en memoria de su fundador.

prominen|ce /'prɒmɪnəns/ n prominencia f; (*fig*) importancia f. **~t** adj prominente; (*important*) importante; (*conspicuous*) destacado

promiscu|ity /prɒmɪ'skjuːətɪ/ n promiscuidad f. **~ous** /prə'mɪskjʊəs/ adj promiscuo

promis|e /'prɒmɪs/ n promesa f. ● vt/i prometer. **~ing** adj prometedor; (*future*) halagüeño

promot|e /prə'məʊt/ vt promover; promocionar (product); (*in rank*) ascender. **~ion** /-'məʊʃn/ n promoción f; (*in rank*) ascenso m

prompt /prɒmpt/ adj rápido; (*punctual*) puntual. ● adv en punto. ● n (*Comp*) presto m. ● vt incitar; apuntar (actor). **~ly** adv puntualmente

prone /prəʊn/ adj (tendido) boca abajo. **be ~ to** ser propenso a

pronoun /'prəʊnaʊn/ n pronombre m

pronounc|e /prə'naʊns/ vt pronunciar; (*declare*) declarar. **~ement** n declaración f. **~ed** adj pronunciado; (*noticeable*) marcado

pronunciation /prənʌnsɪ'eɪʃn/ n pronunciación f

proof /pruːf/ n prueba f, pruebas fpl; (*of alcohol*) graduación f normal. ● adj. **~ against** a prueba de. **~-reading** n corrección f de pruebas

propaganda /prɒpə'gændə/ n propaganda f

propagate /'prɒpəgeɪt/ vt propagar. ● vi propagarse

propel /prə'pel/ vt (*pt* propelled) propulsar. **~ler** n hélice f

proper /'prɒpə(r)/ adj correcto; (*suitable*) apropiado; (*Gram*) propio; (*fam, real*) verdadero. **~ly** adv correctamente; (eat, work) bien

property /'prɒpətɪ/ n propiedad f; (*things owned*) bienes mpl. ● adj inmobiliario

prophe|cy /'prɒfəsɪ/ n profecía f. **~sy** /'prɒfɪsaɪ/ vt/i profetizar. **~t** /'prɒfɪt/ n profeta m. **~tic** /prə'fetɪk/ adj profético

proportion /prə'pɔːʃn/ n proporción f. **~al** adj, **~ate** /-ət/ adj proporcional

propos|al /prə'pəʊzl/ n propuesta f; (*of marriage*) proposición f matrimonial. **~e** /prə'pəʊz/ vt proponer. ● vi. **~e to s.o.** hacerle una oferta de matrimonio a una. **~ition** /prɒpə'zɪʃn/ n propuesta f; (*offer*) oferta f

proprietor /prə'praɪətə(r)/ n propietario m

pro rata /'prəʊ'rɑːtə/ adv a prorrata

prose /prəʊz/ n prosa f

prosecut|e /'prɒsɪkjuːt/ vt procesar (for por); (*carry on*) proseguir. **~ion** /-'kjuːʃn/ n proceso m. **the ~** (side) la acusación. **~or** n fiscal m & f; (*in private prosecutions*) abogado m de la acusación

prospect /'prɒspekt/ n (*possibility*) posibilidad f (**of** de); (*situation envisaged*) perspectiva f. **~s** (chances) perspectivas fpl. **~ive** /prə'spektɪv/ adj (future) futuro. **~or** /prə'spektə(r)/ n prospector m. **~us** /prə'spektəs/ n folleto m informativo

prosper /'prɒspə(r)/ vi prosperar. **~ity** /-'sperətɪ/ n prosperidad f. **~ous** adj próspero

prostitut|e /'prɒstɪtjuːt/ n prostituta f. **~ion** /-'tjuːʃn/ n prostitución f

prostrate /'prɒstreɪt/ adj postrado

protagonist /prə'tægənɪst/ n protagonista m & f

protect /prə'tekt/ vt proteger. **~ion** /-ʃn/ n protección f. **~ive** adj protector. **~or** n protector m

protein /'prəʊtiːn/ n proteína f

protest /'prəʊtest/ n protesta f. **in ~ (against)** en señal de protesta (contra). **under ~** bajo protesta. ● /prə'test/ vt/i protestar

Protestant /'prɒtɪstənt/ adj & n protestante (m & f)

protester /prə'testə(r)/ n manifestante m & f

protocol /'prəʊtəkɒl/ n protocolo m

protrud|e /prə'truːd/ vi sobresalir. **~ing** adj (chin) prominente. **~ing eyes** ojos saltones

proud /praʊd/ adj orgulloso. **~ly** adv con orgullo; (arrogantly) orgullosamente

prove /pruːv/ vt probar; demostrar (loyalty). ● vi resultar. **~n** adj probado

proverb /'prɒvɜːb/ n refrán m, proverbio m

provide /prə'vaɪd/ vt proporcionar; dar (accommodation). **~ s.o. with sth** proveer a uno de algo. ● vi. **~ for** (allow for) prever; mantener (person). **~d** conj. **~d (that)** con tal de que, siempre que

providen|ce /'prɒvɪdəns/ n providencia f. **~tial** /-'denʃl/ adj providencial

providing /prə'vaɪdɪŋ/ conj. **~ that** con tal de que, siempre que

provinc|e /'prɒvɪns/ n provincia f; (fig) competencia f. **~ial** /prə'vɪnʃl/ adj provincial

provision /prə'vɪʒn/ n provisión f; (supply) suministro m; (stipulation) disposición f. **~s** npl provisiones fpl, víveres mpl. **~al** adj provisional

provo|cation /prɒvə'keɪʃn/ n provocación f. **~cative** /-'vɒkətɪv/ adj provocador. **~ke** /prə'vəʊk/ vt provocar

prow /praʊ/ n proa f

prowess /'praʊɪs/ n destreza f; (valour) valor m

prowl /praʊl/ vi merodear. **~er** n merodeador m

proximity /prɒk'sɪmətɪ/ n proximidad f

prude /pruːd/ n mojigato m

pruden|ce /'pruːdəns/ n prudencia f. **~t** adj prudente. **~tly** adv prudentemente

prudish /'pruːdɪʃ/ adj mojigato

prune /pruːn/ n ciruela f pasa. ● vt podar

pry /praɪ/ vi curiosear. **~ into sth** entrometerse en algo. vt (Amer) see **PRISE**

PS n (postscript) P.D.

psalm /sɑːm/ n salmo m

psychiatr|ic /saɪkɪ'ætrɪk/ adj psiquiátrico. **~ist** /saɪ'kaɪətrɪst/ n psiquiatra m & f. **~y** /saɪ'kaɪətrɪ/ n psiquiatría f

psychic /'saɪkɪk/ adj para(p)sicológico

psycho|analysis /saɪkəʊə'næləsɪs/ n (p)sicoanálisis m. **~logical** /saɪkə'lɒdʒɪkl/ adj (p)sicológico. **~logist** /saɪ'kɒlədʒɪst/ n (p)sicólogo m. **~logy** /saɪ'kɒlədʒɪ/ n (p)sicología f. **~therapy** /-'θerəpɪ/ n (p)sicoterapia f

pub /pʌb/ n bar m

---

pub En Gran Bretaña, establecimiento donde se vende cerveza y otras bebidas (alcohólicas y no alcohólicas) para consumir en el local. *Pub* es la forma abreviada de *public house*. Suelen ofrecer comidas y una variedad de juegos, especialmente dardos, billar etc. Recientemente, las horas en que pueden abrir dependen de la licencia, siendo lo normal de 11 - 23 horas.

puberty /'pju:bətɪ/ *n* pubertad *f*

pubic /'pju:bɪk/ *adj* pubiano, púbico

public /'pʌblɪk/ *adj* público. ~**an** *n* tabernero *m*. ~**ation** /-'keɪʃn/ *n* publicación *f*. ~ **holiday** *n* día *m* festivo, día *m* feriado (*LAm*). ~ **house** *n* bar *m*. ~**ity** /pʌb'lɪsətɪ/ *n* publicidad *f*. ~**ize** /'pʌblɪsaɪz/ *vt* hacer público. ~**ly** *adv* públicamente. ~ **school** *n* colegio *m* privado; (*Amer*) instituto *m*, escuela *f* pública

public school En Inglaterra y Gales, un colegio privado para alumnos de edades comprendidas entre los 13 y 18 años. La mayoría de estos colegios tiene régimen de internado y a menudo son mixtos. En EE.UU. y Escocia, el término se utiliza para referirse a un colegio estatal.

publish /'pʌblɪʃ/ *vt* publicar. ~**er** *n* editor *m*. ~**ing** *n* publicación *f*. ~**ing house** editorial *f*

pudding /'pʊdɪŋ/ *n* postre *m*; (*steamed*) budín *m*

puddle /'pʌdl/ *n* charco *m*

Puerto Ric|an /pws:təʊ'ri:kən/ *adj* & *n* portorriqueño (*m*), puertorriqueño (*m*). ~**o** /-əʊ/ *n* Puerto Rico *m*

puff /pʌf/ *n* (*of wind*) ráfaga *f*; (*of*

smoke) nube *f*; (*action*) soplo *m*; (*on cigarette*) chupada *f*, calada *f*. ●*vt/i* soplar. ~ **at** dar chupadas a (pipe). ~ **out** (*swell up*) inflar, hinchar. ~**ed** *adj* (*out of breath*) sin aliento. ~ **paste** (*Amer*), ~ **pastry** *n* hojaldre *m*. ~**y** *adj* (hinchado)

pull /pʊl/ *vt* tirar de, jalar (*LAm*); desgarrarse (muscle). ~ **a face** hacer una mueca. ~ **a fast one** hacer una mala jugada. ●*vi* tirar, jalar (*LAm*). ~ **at** tirar de, jalar (*LAm*). ●*n* tirón *m*, jalón *m* (*LAm*); (*pulling force*) fuerza *f*; (*influence*) influencia *f*. □ ~ **away** *vi* (*Auto*) alejarse. □ ~ **back** *vi* retirarse. □ ~ **down** *vt* echar abajo (building); (*lower*) bajar. □ ~ **in** *vi* (*Auto*) parar. □ ~ **off** *vt* (*remove*) quitar; (*achieve*) conseguir. □ ~ **out** *vt* sacar; retirar (team). *vi* (*Auto*) salirse. □ ~ **through** *vi* recobrar la salud. □ ~ **up** *vi* (*Auto*) parar. *vt* (*uproot*) arrancar; (*reprimand*) regañar

pullover /'pʊləʊvə(r)/ *n* suéter *m*, pulóver *m*, jersey *m*

pulp /pʌlp/ *n* pulpa *f*; (*for paper*) pasta *f*

pulpit /'pʊlpɪt/ *n* púlpito *m*

pulse /pʌls/ *n* (*Med*) pulso *m*; (*Culin*) legumbre *f*

pummel /'pʌml/ *vt* (*pt* **pummelled**) aporrear

pump /pʌmp/ *n* bomba *f*; (*for petrol*) surtidor *m*. ●*vt* sacar con una bomba. □ ~ **up** *vt* inflar

pumpkin /'pʌmpkɪn/ *n* calabaza *f*

pun /pʌn/ *n* juego *m* de palabras

punch /pʌntʃ/ *vt* darle un puñetazo a; (*perforate*) perforar; hacer (hole). ●*n* puñetazo *m*; (*vigour*) fuerza *f*; (*device*) perforadora *f*; (*drink*) ponche *m*. ~ **in** *vi* (*Amer*) fichar (*al entrar al trabajo*). ~ **out** *vi* (*Amer*) fichar (*al salir del trabajo*)

punctual /'pʌŋktʃʊəl/ adj puntual. ~**ity** /-'ælətɪ/ n puntualidad f. ~**ly** adv puntualmente

punctuat|e /'pʌŋktʃʊeɪt/ vt puntuar. ~**ion** /-'eɪʃn/ n puntuación f

puncture /'pʌŋktʃə(r)/ n (in tyre) pinchazo m. **have a** ~ pinchar. ● vt pinchar. ● vi pincharse

punish /'pʌnɪʃ/ vt castigar. ~**ment** n castigo m

punk /pʌŋk/ n punk m & f, punki m & f; (Music) punk m; (Amer, hoodlum) vándalo m

punt /pʌnt/ n (boat) batea f. ~**er** n apostante m & f

puny /'pjuːnɪ/ adj (-ier, -iest) enclenque

pup /pʌp/ n cachorro m

pupil /'pjuːpl/ n alumno m; (of eye) pupila f

puppet /'pʌpɪt/ n marioneta f, títere m; (glove ~) títere m

puppy /'pʌpɪ/ n cachorro m

purchase /'pɜːtʃəs/ vt adquirir. ● n adquisición f. ~**r** n comprador m

pur|e /'pjʊə(r)/ adj (-er, -est) puro. ~**ity** n pureza f

purgatory /'pɜːgətrɪ/ n purgatorio m

purge /pɜːdʒ/ vt purgar. ● n purga f

purif|ication /pjʊərɪfɪ'keɪʃn/ n purificación f. ~**y** /'pjʊərɪfaɪ/ vt purificar

purist /'pjʊərɪst/ n purista m & f

puritan /'pjʊərɪtən/ n puritano m. ~**ical** /-'tænɪkl/ adj puritano

purple /'pɜːpl/ adj morado. ● n morado m, púrpura f

purport /pə'pɔːt/ vt. ~ **to be** pretender ser

purpose /'pɜːpəs/ n propósito m; (determination) resolución f. **on** ~

a propósito. **serve a** ~ servir de algo. ~**ful** adj (resolute) resuelto. ~**ly** adv a propósito

purr /pɜː(r)/ vi ronronear

purse /pɜːs/ n monedero m; (Amer) bolso m, cartera f (LAm), bolsa f (Mex)

pursu|e /pə'sjuː/ vt perseguir, continuar con (course of action). ~**it** /pə'sjuːt/ n persecución f; (pastime) actividad f

pus /pʌs/ n pus m

push /pʊʃ/ vt empujar; apretar (button). ● vi empujar. ● n empujón m; (effort) esfuerzo m. □ ~ **back** vt hacer retroceder. □ ~ **off** vi 🗷 largarse. ~**chair** n sillita f de paseo, carreola f (Mex). ~**y** adj (pej) ambicioso

pussy /pʊsɪ/ (pl -sies), **pussycat** /'pʊsɪkæt/ n 🅸 minino m

put /pʊt/ vt (pt put, pres p putting) poner; (with care, precision) colocar; (inside sth) meter; (express) decir. □ ~ **across** vt comunicar. □ ~ **away** vt guardar. □ ~ **back** vt volver a poner; retrasar (clock). □ ~ **by** vt guardar; ahorrar (money). □ ~ **down** vt (on a surface) dejar; colgar (phone); (suppress) sofocar; (write) apuntar; (kill) sacrificar. □ ~ **forward** vt presentar (plan); proponer (candidate); adelantar (clocks); adelantar (meeting). □ ~ **in** vt (instal) poner; presentar (claim). □ ~ **in for** vt solicitar. □ ~ **off** vt aplazar, posponer; (disconcert) desconcertar. □ ~ **on** vt (wear) ponerse; poner (CD, music); encender (light). □ ~ **out** vt (extinguish) apagar; (inconvenience) incomodar; extender (hand); (disconcert) desconcertar. □ ~ **through** vt (phone) poner, pasar (to con). □ ~ **up** vt levantar; aumentar (rent); subir (price); poner (sign); alojar (guest). □ ~ **up with** vt aguantar, soportar

putrid /ˈpjuːtrɪd/ adj putrefacto

putt /pʌt/ n (golf) golpe m suave

puzzl|e /ˈpʌzl/ n misterio m; (game) rompecabezas m. ● vt dejar perplejo. ~**ed** adj (expression) de desconcierto. **I'm** ~**ed about it** me tiene perplejo. ~**ing** adj incomprensible; (odd) curioso

pygmy /ˈpɪgmɪ/ n pigmeo m

pyjamas /pəˈdʒɑːməz/ npl pijama m, piyama m or f (LAm)

pylon /ˈpaɪlɒn/ n pilón m

pyramid /ˈpɪrəmɪd/ n pirámide f

python /ˈpaɪθn/ n pitón m

Qq

quack /kwæk/ n (of duck) graznido m; (person) charlatán m. ~ **doctor** n curandero m

quadrangle /ˈkwɒdræŋgl/ n cuadrilátero m

quadruped /ˈkwɒdrʊped/ n cuadrúpedo m

quadruple /ˈkwɒdrʊpl/ adj & n cuádruplo (m). ● vt cuadruplicar

quagmire /ˈkwægmaɪə(r)/ n lodazal m

quaint /kweɪnt/ adj (-er, -est) pintoresco; (odd) curioso

quake /kweɪk/ vi temblar. ● n 🆃 terremoto m

qualif|ication /kwɒlɪfɪˈkeɪʃn/ n título m; (requirement) requisito m; (ability) capacidad f; (Sport) clasificación f; (fig) reserva f. ~**ied**

/ˈkwɒlɪfaɪd/ adj cualificado; (with degree, diploma) titulado; (competent) capacitado. ~**y** /ˈkwɒlɪfaɪ/ vt calificar; (limit) limitar. ● vi titularse; (Sport) clasificarse. ~**y for sth** (be entitled to) tener derecho a algo

qualit|ative /ˈkwɒlɪtətɪv/ adj cualitativo. ~**y** /ˈkwɒlɪtɪ/ n calidad f; (attribute) cualidad f

qualm /kwɑːm/ n reparo m

quandary /ˈkwɒndrɪ/ n dilema m

quanti|fy /ˈkwɒntɪfaɪ/ vt cuantificar. ~**ty** /-tɪ/ n cantidad f

quarantine /ˈkwɒrəntiːn/ n cuarentena f. ● vt poner en cuarentena

quarrel /ˈkwɒrəl/ n pelea f. ● vi (pt quarrelled) pelearse, discutir. ~**some** /-səm/ adj pendenciero

quarry /ˈkwɒrɪ/ n (excavation) cantera f; (prey) presa f

quart /kwɔːt/ n cuarto m de galón

quarter /ˈkwɔːtə(r)/ n cuarto m; (of year) trimestre m; (district) barrio m. **a** ~ **of an hour** un cuarto de hora. ● vt dividir en cuartos; (Mil) acuartelar. ~**-final** n cuarto m de final. ~**ly** adj trimestral. ● adv trimestralmente

quartz /kwɔːts/ n cuarzo m

quay /kiː/ n muelle m

queasy /ˈkwiːzɪ/ adj mareado

queen /kwiːn/ n reina f. ~ **mother** n reina f madre

queer /kwɪə(r)/ adj (-er, -est) extraño

quench /kwentʃ/ vt quitar (thirst); sofocar (desire)

query /ˈkwɪərɪ/ n pregunta f. ● vt preguntar; (doubt) poner en duda

quest /kwest/ n busca f

question /ˈkwestʃən/ n pregunta f; (for discussion) cuestión f. **in** ~ en cuestión. **out of the** ~ imposi-

ble. **without** ～ sin duda. ● vt
hacer preguntas a; (police etc) interrogar; (doubt) poner en duda.
～**able** adj discutible. ～ **mark** n
signo m de interrogación. ～**naire**
/-'neə(r)/ n cuestionario m

queue /kjuː/ n cola f. ● vi (pres p
queuing) hacer cola

quibble /'kwɪbl/ vi discutir; (split
hairs) sutilizar

quick /kwɪk/ adj (-er, -est) rápido.
be ～! ¡date prisa! ● adv rápido.
～**en** vt acelerar. ● vi acelerarse.
～**ly** adv rápido. ～**sand** n arena f
movediza. ～**-tempered** /-'tempəd/
adj irascible

quid /kwɪd/ n invar 🄱 libra f (esterlina)

quiet /'kwaɪət/ adj (-er, -est) tranquilo; (silent) callado; (discreet) discreto. ● n tranquilidad f. ● vt/i
(Amer) see QUIETEN. ～**en** vt calmar.
● vi calmarse. ～**ly** adv tranquilamente; (silently) silenciosamente;
(discreetly) discretamente. ～**ness** n
tranquilidad f

quilt /kwɪlt/ n edredón m. ～**ed** adj
acolchado

quintet /kwɪn'tet/ n quinteto m

quirk /kwɜːk/ n peculiaridad f

quit /kwɪt/ vt (pt quitted) dejar. ～
doing (Amer, cease) dejar de hacer.
● vi (give in) abandonar; (stop)
parar; (resign) dimitir

quite /kwaɪt/ adv bastante; (completely) totalmente; (really) verdaderamente. ～ **(so!)** ¡claro! ～ **a
few** bastante

quits /kwɪts/ adj. **be** ～ estar en
paz. **call it** ～ darlo por terminado

quiver /'kwɪvə(r)/ vi temblar

quiz /kwɪz/ n (pl quizzes) serie f
de preguntas; (game) concurso m.
● vt (pt quizzed) interrogar. ～**zical**

adj burlón

quota /'kwəʊtə/ n cuota f

quot|ation /kwəʊ'teɪʃn/ n cita f;
(price) presupuesto m. ～**ation
marks** npl comillas fpl. ～**e** /kwəʊt/
vt citar; (Com) cotizar. ● n 🄱 cita f;
(price) presupuesto m. **in** ～**es** npl
entre comillas

Rr

rabbi /'ræbaɪ/ n rabino m

rabbit /'ræbɪt/ n conejo m

rabid /'ræbɪd/ adj feroz; (dog) rabioso. ～**es** /'reɪbiːz/ n rabia f

race /reɪs/ n (in sport) carrera f;
(ethnic group) raza f. ● vt hacer correr (horse). ● vi (run) correr, ir corriendo; (rush) ir de prisa.
～**course** n hipódromo m. ～**horse**
n caballo m de carreras. ～ **relations** npl relaciones fpl raciales.
～**track** n hipódromo m

racial /'reɪʃl/ adj racial

racing /'reɪsɪŋ/ n carreras fpl. ～
car n coche m de carreras

racis|m /'reɪsɪzəm/ n racismo m.
～**t** adj & n racista (m & f)

rack¹ /ræk/ n (shelf) estante m;
(for luggage) rejilla f; (for plates)
escurreplatos m. ● vt. ～ **one's
brains** devanarse los sesos

rack² /ræk/ n. **go to** ～ **and ruin**
quedarse en la ruina

racket /'rækɪt/ n (for sports) raqueta; (din) alboroto m; (swindle)
estafa f. ～**eer** /-ə'tɪə(r)/ n estafador m

racy /'reɪsɪ/ adj (-ier, -iest) vivo

radar /ˈreɪdɑː(r)/ n radar m

radian|ce /ˈreɪdɪəns/ n resplandor m. ● **~t** adj radiante

radiat|e /ˈreɪdɪeɪt/ vt irradiar. ● vi divergir. **~ion** /-ˈeɪʃn/ n radiación f. **~or** n radiador m

radical /ˈrædɪkl/ adj & n radical (m)

radio /ˈreɪdɪəʊ/ n (pl -os) radio f or m. ● vt transmitir por radio. **~active** /reɪdɪəʊˈæktɪv/ adj radiactivo. **~activity** /-ˈtɪvətɪ/ n radiactividad f

radish /ˈrædɪʃ/ n rábano m

radius /ˈreɪdɪəs/ n (pl -dii/-dɪaɪ/) radio m

raffle /ˈræfl/ n rifa f

raft /rɑːft/ n balsa f

rafter /ˈrɑːftə(r)/ n cabrio m

rag /ræg/ n andrajo m; (for wiping) trapo m. **in ~s** (person) andrajoso

rage /reɪdʒ/ n rabia f; (fashion) moda f. ● vi estar furioso; (storm) bramar

ragged /ˈrægɪd/ adj (person) andrajoso; (clothes) hecho jirones

raid /reɪd/ n (Mil) incursión f; (by police etc) redada f; (by thieves) asalto m. ● vt (Mil) atacar; (police) hacer una redada en; (thieves) asaltar. **~er** n invasor m; (thief) ladrón m

rail /reɪl/ n barandilla f; (for train) riel m; (rod) barra f. **by ~** por ferrocarril. **~ing** n barandilla f; (fence) verja f. **~road** (Amer), **~way** n ferrocarril m. **~way station** n estación f de ferrocarril

rain /reɪn/ n lluvia f. ● vi llover. **~bow** /-bəʊ/ n arco m iris. **~coat** n impermeable m. **~fall** n precipitación f. **~y** adj (-ier, -iest) lluvioso

raise /reɪz/ vt levantar; (breed) criar; obtener (money etc); formular (question); plantear (problem);

subir (price). ● n (Amer) aumento m

raisin /ˈreɪzn/ n (uva f) pasa f

rake /reɪk/ n rastrillo m. ● vt rastrillar; (search) buscar en. □ **~ up** vt remover

rally /ˈrælɪ/ vt reunir; (revive) reanimar. ● n reunión f; (Auto) rally m

ram /ræm/ n carnero m. ● vt (pt rammed) (thrust) meter por la fuerza; (crash into) chocar con

RAM /ræm/ n (Comp) RAM f

rambl|e /ˈræmbl/ n excursión f a pie. ● vi ir de paseo; (in speech) divagar. □ **~e on** vi divagar. **~er** n excursionista m & f. **~ing** adj (speech) divagador

ramp /ræmp/ n rampa f

rampage /ræmˈpeɪdʒ/ vi alborotarse. ● /ˈræmpeɪdʒ/ n. **go on the ~** alborotarse

ramshackle /ˈræmʃækl/ adj desvencijado

ran /ræn/ see **RUN**

ranch /rɑːntʃ/ n hacienda f

random /ˈrændəm/ adj hecho al azar; (chance) fortuito. ● n. **at ~** al azar

rang /ræŋ/ see **RING²**

range /reɪndʒ/ n alcance m; (distance) distancia f; (series) serie f; (of mountains) cordillera f; (extent) extensión f; (Com) surtido m; (stove) cocina f económica. ● vi extenderse; (vary) variar. **~r** n guardabosque m

rank /ræŋk/ n posición f, categoría f; (row) fila f; (for taxis) parada f. **the ~ and file** la masa f. **~s** npl soldados mpl rasos. ● adj (-er, -est) (smell) fétido; (fig) completo. ● vt clasificar. ● vi clasificarse

ransack /ˈrænsæk/ vt registrar; (pillage) saquear

ransom /ˈrænsəm/ n rescate m.

hold s.o. to ~ exigir rescate por uno. ● vt rescatar; (redeem) redimir

rant /rænt/ vi despotricar

rap /ræp/ n golpe m seco. ● vt/i (pt **rapped**) golpear

rape /reip/ vt violar. ● n violación f

rapid /'ræpid/ adj rápido. ~s npl rápidos mpl

rapist /'reipist/ n violador m

rapture /'ræptʃə(r)/ n éxtasis m. ~ous /-rəs/ adj extático

rare /reə(r)/ adj (-er, -est) raro; (Culin) poco hecho. ~fied /'reərifaid/ adj enrarecido. ~ly adv raramente

raring /'reəriŋ/ adj ⊞. ~ to impaciente por

rarity /'reərəti/ n rareza f

rascal /'rɑːskl/ n granuja m & f

rash /ræʃ/ adj (-er, -est) precipitado, imprudente. ● n erupción f

rasher /'ræʃə(r)/ n loncha f

rashly /'ræʃli/ adv precipitadamente, imprudentemente

rasp /rɑːsp/ n (file) escofina f

raspberry /'rɑːzbri/ n frambuesa f

rat /ræt/ n rata f

rate /reit/ n (ratio) proporción f; (speed) velocidad f; (price) precio m; (of interest) tipo m. **at any** ~ de todas formas. **at this** ~ así. ~s npl (taxes) impuestos mpl municipales. ● vt valorar; (consider) considerar; (Amer, deserve) merecer. ● vi ser considerado

rather /'rɑːðə(r)/ adv mejor dicho; (fairly) bastante; (a little) un poco. ● int claro. **I would** ~ **not** prefiero no

rating /'reitiŋ/ n clasificación f; (sailor) marinero m; (number, TV) índice m

ratio /'reiʃiəʊ/ n (pl -os) proporción f

ration /'ræʃn/ n ración f. ~s npl (provisions) víveres mpl. ● vt racionar

rational /'ræʃənəl/ adj racional. ~ize vt racionalizar

rattle /'rætl/ vi traquetear. ● vt (shake) agitar; ⊞ desconcertar. ● n traqueteo m; (toy) sonajero m. □ ~ off vt (fig) decir de corrida

raucous /'rɔːkəs/ adj estridente

ravage /'rævidʒ/ vt estragar

rave /reiv/ vi delirar; (in anger) despotricar. ~ **about sth** poner a algo por las nubes

raven /'reivn/ n cuervo m

ravenous /'rævənəs/ adj voraz; (person) hambriento. **be** ~ morirse de hambre

ravine /rə'viːn/ n barranco m

raving /'reiviŋ/ adj. ~ **mad** loco de atar

ravishing /'ræviʃiŋ/ adj (enchanting) encantador

raw /rɔː/ adj (-er, -est) crudo; (sugar) sin refinar; (inexperienced) inexperto. ~ **deal** n tratamiento m injusto, injusticia f. ~ **materials** npl materias fpl primas

ray /rei/ n rayo m

raze /reiz/ vt arrasar

razor /'reizə(r)/ n navaja f de afeitar; (electric) maquinilla f de afeitar

Rd /rəud/ abbr (= **Road**) C/, Calle f

re /riː/ prep con referencia a. ● pref re.

reach /riːtʃ/ vt alcanzar; (extend) extender; (arrive at) llegar a; (achieve) lograr; (hand over) pasar, dar. ● vi extenderse. ● n alcance m. **within** ~ **of** al alcance de; (close to) a corta distancia de. □ ~ **out** vi alargar la mano

react /rɪˈækt/ vi reaccionar. ~**ion** /rɪˈækʃn/ n reacción f. ~**ionary** adj & n reaccionario (m). ~**or** /rɪˈæktə(r)/ n reactor m

read /riːd/ vt (pt **read** /red/) leer; (study) estudiar; (interpret) interpretar. ● vi leer; (instrument) indicar. □ ~ **out** vt leer en voz alta. ~**able** adj (clear) legible. ~**er** n lector m

readily /ˈredɪlɪ/ adv (willingly) de buena gana; (easily) fácilmente

reading /ˈriːdɪŋ/ n lectura f

readjust /riːəˈdʒʌst/ vt reajustar. ● vi readaptarse (**to** a)

ready /ˈredɪ/ adj (-ier, -iest) listo, preparado. **get** ~ prepararse. ~**-made** adj confeccionado

real /rɪəl/ adj verdadero. ~ adv (Amer fam) verdaderamente. ~ **estate** n bienes mpl raíces, propiedad f inmobiliaria. ~ **estate agent** see REALTOR. ~**ism** n realismo m. ~**ist** n realista m & f. ~**istic** /-ˈlɪstɪk/ adj realista. ~**ity** /rɪˈælətɪ/ n realidad f. ~**ization** /rɪəlaɪˈzeɪʃn/ n comprensión f. ~**ize** /ˈrɪəlaɪz/ vt darse cuenta de; (fulfil, Com) realizar. ~**ly** /ˈrɪəlɪ/ adv verdaderamente

realm /relm/ n reino m

realtor /ˈriːəltə(r)/ n (Amer) agente m inmobiliario

reap /riːp/ vt segar; (fig) cosechar

reappear /riːəˈpɪə(r)/ vi reaparecer

rear /rɪə(r)/ n parte f de atrás. ● adj posterior, trasero. ● vt (bring up, breed) criar. ● vi ~ (**up**) (horse) encabritarse

rearguard /ˈrɪəɡɑːd/ n retaguardia f

rearrange /riːəˈreɪndʒ/ vt arreglar de otra manera

reason /ˈriːzn/ n razón f, motivo m. **within** ~ dentro de lo razonable. ● vi razonar. ~**able** adj razonable. ~**ing** n razonamiento m

reassur|ance /riːəˈʃʊərəns/ n promesa f tranquilizadora; (guarantee) garantía f. ~**e** /riːəˈʃʊə(r)/ vt tranquilizar

rebate /ˈriːbeɪt/ n (discount) rebaja f

rebel /ˈrebl/ n rebelde m & f. ● /rɪˈbel/ vi (pt **rebelled**) rebelarse. ~**lion** /rɪˈbeljən/ n rebelión f. ~**lious** adj rebelde

rebound /rɪˈbaʊnd/ vi rebotar; (fig) recaer. ● /ˈriːbaʊnd/ n rebote m

rebuff /rɪˈbʌf/ vt rechazar. ● n desaire m

rebuild /riːˈbɪld/ vt (pt **rebuilt**) reconstruir

rebuke /rɪˈbjuːk/ vt reprender. ● n reprimenda f

recall /rɪˈkɔːl/ vt (call s.o. back) llamar; (remember) recordar. ● n /ˈriːkɔːl/ (of goods, ambassador) retirada f; (memory) memoria f

recap /ˈriːkæp/ vt/i (pt **recapped**) ⓣ resumir

recapitulate /riːkəˈpɪtʃʊleɪt/ vt/i resumir

recapture /riːˈkæptʃə(r)/ vt recobrar; (recall) hacer revivir

recede /rɪˈsiːd/ vi retroceder

receipt /rɪˈsiːt/ n recibo m. ~**s** npl (Com) ingresos mpl

receive /rɪˈsiːv/ vt recibir. ~**r** n (of stolen goods) perista m & f; (part of phone) auricular m

recent /ˈriːsnt/ adj reciente. ~**ly** adv recientemente

recept|ion /rɪˈsepʃn/ n recepción f; (welcome) acogida f. ~**ionist** n recepcionista m & f. ~**ive** /-tɪv/ adj receptivo

recess /rɪˈses/ n hueco m; (holiday)

vacaciones *fpl*. **~ion** /rɪˈseʃn/ *n* recesión *f*

recharge /riːˈtʃɑːdʒ/ *vt* cargar de nuevo, recargar

recipe /ˈresəpɪ/ *n* receta *f*. **~ book** *n* libro *m* de cocina

recipient /rɪˈsɪpɪənt/ *n* recipiente *m* & *f*; (*of letter*) destinatario *m*

recit|al /rɪˈsaɪtl/ *n* (*Mus*) recital *m*. **~e** /rɪˈsaɪt/ *vt* recitar; (*list*) enumerar

reckless /ˈreklɪs/ *adj* imprudente. **~ly** *adv* imprudentemente

reckon /ˈrekən/ *vt/i* calcular; (*consider*) considerar; (*think*) pensar. □ **~ on** *vt* (*rely*) contar con

reclaim /rɪˈkleɪm/ *vt* reclamar; recuperar (land)

reclin|e /rɪˈklaɪn/ *vi* recostarse. **~ing** *adj* acostado; (seat) reclinable

recluse /rɪˈkluːs/ *n* ermitaño *m*

recogni|tion /rekəgˈnɪʃn/ *n* reconocimiento *m*. **beyond ~tion** irreconocible. **~ze** /ˈrekəgnaɪz/ *vt* reconocer

recoil /rɪˈkɔɪl/ *vi* retroceder. ● /ˈriːkɔɪl/ *n* (*of gun*) culatazo *m*

recollect /rekəˈlekt/ *vt* recordar. **~ion** /-ʃn/ *n* recuerdo *m*

recommend /rekəˈmend/ *vt* recomendar. **~ation** /-ˈdeɪʃn/ *n* recomendación *f*

reconcile /ˈrekənsaɪl/ *vt* reconciliar (people); conciliar (facts). **~e o.s.** resignarse (**to** a). **~iation** /-sɪlɪˈeɪʃn/ *n* reconciliación *f*

reconnaissance /rɪˈkɒnɪsns/ *n* reconocimiento *m*

reconnoitre /rekəˈnɔɪtə(r)/ *vt* (*pres p* **-tring**) (*Mil*) reconocer

re:~consider /riːkənˈsɪdə(r)/ *vt* volver a considerar. **~construct** /riːkənˈstrʌkt/ *vt* reconstruir

record /rɪˈkɔːd/ *vt* (*in register*) registrar; (*in diary*) apuntar; (*Mus*) grabar. ● /ˈrekɔːd/ *n* (*document*) documento *m*; (*of events*) registro *m*; (*Mus*) disco *m*; (*Sport*) récord *m*. **off the ~** en confianza. **~er** /rɪˈkɔːdə(r)/ *n* registrador *m*; (*Mus*) flauta *f* dulce. **~ing** /ɪŋ/ *n* grabación *f*. **~player** /ˈrekɔːd-/ *n* tocadiscos *m* invar

recount /rɪˈkaʊnt/ *vt* contar, relatar

re-count /ˈriːkaʊnt/ *vt* volver a contar; recontar (votes). ● /ˈriːkaʊnt/ *n* (*Pol*) recuento *m*

recover /rɪˈkʌvə(r)/ *vt* recuperar. ● *vi* reponerse. **~y** *n* recuperación *f*

recreation /rekrɪˈeɪʃn/ *n* recreo *m*. **~al** *adj* de recreo

recruit /rɪˈkruːt/ *n* recluta *m*. ● *vt* reclutar; contratar (staff). **~ment** *n* reclutamiento *m*

rectang|le /ˈrektæŋgl/ *n* rectángulo *m*. **~ular** /-ˈtæŋgjʊlə(r)/ *adj* rectangular

rectify /ˈrektɪfaɪ/ *vt* rectificar

rector /ˈrektə(r)/ *n* párroco *m*; (*of college*) rector *m*. **~y** *n* rectoría *f*

recuperat|e /rɪˈkuːpəreɪt/ *vt* recuperar. ● *vi* reponerse. **~ion** /-ˈreɪʃn/ *n* recuperación *f*

recur /rɪˈkɜː(r)/ *vi* (*pt* recurred) repetirse. **~rence** /rɪˈkʌrns/ *n* repetición *f*. **~rent** /rɪˈkʌrənt/ *adj* repetido

recycle /riːˈsaɪkl/ *vt* reciclar

red /red/ *adj* (redder, reddest) rojo. ● *n* rojo *m*. **be in the ~** estar en números rojos. **~den** *vi* enrojecerse. **~dish** *adj* rojizo

redecorate /riːˈdekəreɪt/ *vt* pintar de nuevo

rede|em /rɪˈdiːm/ *vt* redimir. **~mption** /-ˈdempʃn/ *n* redención *f*

red: ~**-handed** /-'hændɪd/ adj. **catch s.o.** ~**handed** agarrar a uno con las manos en la masa. ~ **herring** n (fig) pista f falsa. ~**-hot** adj al rojo vivo. ~ **light** n luz f roja

redo /ri:'du:/ vt (pt redid, pp re-done) rehacer

redouble /rɪ'dʌbl/ vt redoblar

red tape /red'teɪp/ n (fig) papeleo m

reduce /rɪ'dju:s/ vt reducir; aliviar (pain). ● vi (Amer, slim) adelgazar. ~**tion** /rɪ'dʌkʃn/ n reducción f

redundan|cy /rɪ'dʌndənsɪ/ n superfluidad f; (unemployment) despido m. ~**t** superfluo. **she was made** ~**t** la despidieron por reducción de plantilla

reed /ri:d/ n caña f; (Mus) lengüeta f

reef /ri:f/ n arrecife m

reek /ri:k/ n mal olor m. ● vi. ~ (**of**) apestar a

reel /ri:l/ n carrete m. ● vi dar vueltas; (stagger) tambalearse. □ ~ **off** vt (fig) enumerar

refectory /rɪ'fektərɪ/ n refectorio m

refer /rɪ'fɜ:(r)/ vt (pt referred) remitir. ● vi referirse. ~ **to** referirse a; (consult) consultar. ~**ee** /refə'ri:/ n árbitro m; (for job) referencia f. ● vi (pt refereed) arbitrar. ~**ence** /'refrəns/ n referencia f. ~**ence book** n libro m de consulta. **in** ~ **to, with** ~ **to** con referencia a; (Com) respecto a. ~**endum** /refə'rendəm/ n (pl -ums or -da) referéndum m

refill /ri:'fɪl/ vt volver a llenar. ● /'ri:fɪl/ n recambio m

refine /rɪ'faɪn/ vt refinar. ~**d** adj refinado. ~**ry** /-ərɪ/ n refinería f

reflect /rɪ'flekt/ vt reflejar. ● vi reflejarse; (think) reflexionar. □ ~ **badly upon** perjudicar. ~**ion** /-ʃn/ n reflexión f; (image) reflejo m. ~**or** n reflector m

reflex /'ri:fleks/ adj & n reflejo (m). ~**ive** /rɪ'fleksɪv/ adj (Gram) reflexivo

reform /rɪ'fɔ:m/ vt reformar. ● vi reformarse. ~ n reforma f

refrain /rɪ'freɪn/ n estribillo m. ● vi abstenerse (**from** de)

refresh /rɪ'freʃ/ vt refrescar. ~**ing** adj refrescante. ~**ments** npl (food and drink) refrigerio m

refrigerat|e /rɪ'frɪdʒəreɪt/ vt refrigerar. ~**or** n frigorífico m, refrigerador m (LAm)

refuel /ri:'fju:əl/ vt/i (pt refuelled) repostar

refuge /'refju:dʒ/ n refugio m. **take** ~ refugiarse. ~**e** /refjʊ'dʒi:/ n refugiado m

refund /rɪ'fʌnd/ vt reembolsar. ● /'ri:fʌnd/ n reembolso m

refusal /rɪ'fju:zl/ n negativa f

refuse /rɪ'fju:z/ vt rehusar. ● vi negarse. ● /'refju:s/ n residuos mpl

refute /rɪ'fju:t/ vt refutar

regain /rɪ'geɪn/ vt recobrar

regal /'ri:gl/ adj real

regard /rɪ'gɑ:d/ vt considerar; (look at) contemplar. **as** ~ en lo que se refiere a. ● n (consideration) consideración f; (esteem) estima f. ~**s** npl saludos mpl. **kind** ~**s** recuerdos. ~**ing** prep en lo que se refiere a. ~**less** adv a pesar de todo. ~**less of** sin tener en cuenta

regatta /rɪ'gætə/ n regata f

regime /reɪ'ʒi:m/ n régimen m

regiment /'redʒɪmənt/ n regimiento m, ~**al** /-'mentl/ adj del regimiento

region /'ri:dʒən/ n región f. **in the ~ of** alrededor de. **~al** adj regional

register /'redʒɪstə(r)/ n registro m. • vt registrar; matricular (vehicle); declarar (birth); certificar (letter); facturar (luggage). • vi (enrol) inscribirse; (fig) producir impresión

registrar /redʒɪ'strɑ:(r)/ n secretario m del registro civil; (Univ) secretario m general

registration /redʒɪ'streɪʃn/ n registro m; (in register) inscripción f. **~ number** n (Auto) (número de) matrícula f

registry /'redʒɪstrɪ/ n. **~ office** n registro m civil

regret /rɪ'gret/ n pesar m; (remorse) arrepentimiento m. • vt (pt regretted) lamentar. **I ~ that** siento (que). **~table** adj lamentable

regula|r /'regjʊlə(r)/ adj regular; (usual) habitual. • n ① cliente m habitual. **~rity** /-'lærətɪ/ n regularidad f. **~rly** adv con regularidad. **~te** /'regjʊleɪt/ vt regular. **~tion** /-'leɪʃn/ n regulación f; (rule) regla f

rehears|al /rɪ'hɜ:sl/ n ensayo m. **~e** /rɪ'hɜ:s/ vt ensayar

reign /reɪn/ n reinado m. • vi reinar

reindeer /'reɪndɪə(r)/ n invar reno m

reinforce /ri:ɪn'fɔ:s/ vt reforzar. **~ment** n refuerzo m

reins /reɪnz/ npl riendas fpl

reiterate /ri:'ɪtəreɪt/ vt reiterar

reject /rɪ'dʒekt/ vt rechazar. • /'ri:dʒekt/ n producto m defectuoso. **~ion** /rɪ'dʒekʃn/ n rechazo m; (after job application) respuesta f negativa

rejoice /rɪ'dʒɔɪs/ vi regocijarse

rejoin /rɪ'dʒɔɪn/ vt reunirse con

rejuvenate /rɪ'dʒu:vəneɪt/ vt rejuvenecer

relapse /rɪ'læps/ n recaída f. • vi recaer; (into crime) reincidir

relat|e /rɪ'leɪt/ vt contar; (connect) relacionar. • vi relacionarse (to con). **~ed** adj emparentado; (ideas etc) relacionado. **~ion** /rɪ'leɪʃn/ n relación f; (person) pariente m & f. **~ionship** n relación f; (blood tie) parentesco m; (affair) relaciones fpl. **~ive** /'relətɪv/ n pariente m & f. • adj relativo. **~ively** adv relativamente

relax /rɪ'læks/ vt relajar. • vi relajarse. **~ation** /-'seɪʃn/ n relajación f; (rest) descanso m; (recreation) recreo m. **~ing** adj relajante

relay /'ri:leɪ/ n relevo m. **~ (race)** n carrera f de relevos. • /rɪ'leɪ/ vt transmitir

release /rɪ'li:s/ vt soltar; poner en libertad (prisoner); estrenar (film); (Mec) soltar; publicar (news). • n liberación f; (of film) estreno m; (record) disco m nuevo

relent /rɪ'lent/ vi ceder. **~less** adj implacable; (continuous) incesante

relevan|ce /'reləvəns/ n pertinencia f. **~t** adj pertinente

relia|bility /rɪlaɪə'bɪlətɪ/ n fiabilidad f. **~ble** /rɪ'laɪəbl/ adj (person) de confianza; (car) fiable. **~nce** /rɪ'laɪəns/ n dependencia f; (trust) confianza f. **~nt** /rɪ'laɪənt/ adj confiado

relic /'relɪk/ n reliquia f

relie|f /rɪ'li:f/ n alivio m; (assistance) socorro m. **be on ~** (Amer) recibir prestaciones de la seguridad social. **~ve** /rɪ'li:v/ vt aliviar; (take over from) relevar. **~ved** adj aliviado. **feel ~ved** sentir un gran alivio

religio|n /rɪˈlɪdʒən/ n religión f. **~us** /rɪˈlɪdʒəs/ adj religioso

relinquish /rɪˈlɪŋkwɪʃ/ vt abandonar, renunciar

relish /ˈrelɪʃ/ n gusto m; (Culin) salsa f. ● vt saborear

reluctan|ce /rɪˈlʌktəns/ n desgana f. **~t** adj mal dispuesto. **be ~t to** no tener ganas de. **~tly** adv de mala gana

rely /rɪˈlaɪ/ vi. **~ on** contar con; (trust) fiarse de; (depend) depender

remain /rɪˈmeɪn/ vi (be left) quedar; (stay) quedarse; (continue to be) seguir. **~der** n resto m. **~s** npl restos mpl; (left-overs) sobras fpl

remand /rɪˈmɑːnd/ vt. **~ in custody** mantener bajo custodia. ● n. **on ~** en prisión preventiva

remark /rɪˈmɑːk/ n observación f. ● vt observar. **~able** adj notable

remarry /riːˈmæri/ vi volver a casarse

remedy /ˈremədi/ n remedio m. ● vt remediar

remember /rɪˈmembə(r)/ vt acordarse de, recordar. ● vi acordarse

remind /rɪˈmaɪnd/ vt recordar. **~er** n recordatorio m

reminisce /remɪˈnɪs/ vi rememorar los viejos tiempos. **~nces** /-ɪnsɪz/ npl recuerdos mpl. **~nt** /-ˈnɪsnt/ adj. **be ~nt of** recordar

remnant /ˈremnənt/ n resto m; (of cloth) retazo m; (trace) vestigio m

remorse /rɪˈmɔːs/ n remordimiento m. **~ful** adj arrepentido. **~less** adj implacable

remote /rɪˈməʊt/ adj remoto. **~ control** n mando m a distancia.

~ly adv remotamente

removable /rɪˈmuːvəbl/ adj (detachable) de quita y pon; (handle) desmontable. **~al** n eliminación f; (from house) mudanza f. **~e** /rɪˈmuːv/ vt quitar; (dismiss) destituir; (get rid of) eliminar

render /ˈrendə(r)/ vt rendir (homage); prestar (help etc). **~ sth useless** hacer que algo resulte inútil

rendezvous /ˈrɒndɪvuː/ n (pl **-vous** /-vuːz/) cita f

renegade /ˈrenɪɡeɪd/ n renegado m

renew /rɪˈnjuː/ vt renovar; (resume) reanudar. **~al** n renovación f

renounce /rɪˈnaʊns/ vt renunciar a

renovat|e /ˈrenəveɪt/ vt renovar. **~ion** /-ˈveɪʃn/ n renovación f

renown /rɪˈnaʊn/ n renombre m. **~ed** adj de renombre

rent /rent/ n alquiler m. ● vt alquilar. **~al** n alquiler m. **car ~** (Amer) alquiler m de coche

renunciation /rɪnʌnsɪˈeɪʃn/ n renuncia f

reopen /riːˈəʊpən/ vt volver a abrir. ● vi reabrirse

reorganize /riːˈɔːɡənaɪz/ vt reorganizar

rep /rep/ n (Com) representante m & f

repair /rɪˈpeə(r)/ vt arreglar, reparar; arreglar (clothes, shoes). ● n reparación f; (patch) remiendo m. **in good ~** en buen estado. **it's beyond ~** ya no tiene arreglo

repatriat|e /riːˈpætrɪeɪt/ vt repatriar

repay /riːˈpeɪ/ vt (pt **repaid**) reembolsar; pagar (debt); corresponder a (kindness). **~ment** n pago m

repeal /rɪˈpiːl/ vt revocar. ● n revocación f

repeat /rɪ'piːt/ vt repetir. ● vi repetir(se). ● n repetición f. ~**edly** adv repetidas veces

repel /rɪ'pel/ vt (pt **repelled**) repeler. ~**lent** adj repelente

repent /rɪ'pent/ vi arrepentirse. ~**ant** adj arrepentido

repercussion /riːpə'kʌʃn/ n repercusión f

repertoire /'repətwɑː(r)/ n repertorio m

repetit|ion /repɪ'tɪʃn/ n repetición f. ~**ious** /-'tɪʃəs/ adj, ~**ive** /rɪ'petətɪv/ adj repetitivo

replace /rɪ'pleɪs/ vt reponer; cambiar (battery); (take the place of) sustituir. ~**ment** n sustitución f; (person) sustituto m

replay /'riːpleɪ/ n (Sport) repetición f del partido; (recording) repetición f inmediata

replenish /rɪ'plenɪʃ/ vt reponer

replica /'replɪkə/ n réplica f

reply /rɪ'plaɪ/ vt/i responder, contestar. ~ **to sth** responder a algo, contestar algo. ● n respuesta f

report /rɪ'pɔːt/ vt (reporter) informar sobre; informar de (accident); (denounce) denunciar. ● vi informar; (present o.s.) presentarse. ● n informe m; (Schol) boletín m de notas; (rumour) rumor m; (in newspaper) reportaje m. ~ **card** (Amer) n boletín m de calificaciones. ~**edly** adv según se dice. ~**er** n periodista m & f, reportero m

reprehensible /reprɪ'hensəbl/ adj reprensible

represent /reprɪ'zent/ vt representar. ~**ation** /-'teɪʃn/ n representación f. ~**ative** adj representativo. ● n representante m & f; (Amer, in government) diputado m

repress /rɪ'pres/ vt reprimir. ~**ion** /-ʃn/ n represión f. ~**ive** adj represivo

reprieve /rɪ'priːv/ n indulto m; (fig) respiro m. ● vt indultar

reprimand /'reprɪmɑːnd/ vt reprender. ● n represión f

reprisal /rɪ'praɪzl/ n represalia f

reproach /rɪ'prəʊtʃ/ vt reprochar. ● n reproche m. ~**ful** adj de reproche

reproduc|e /riːprə'djuːs/ vt reproducir. ● vi reproducirse. ~**tion** /-'dʌkʃn/ n reproducción f. ~**tive** /-'dʌktɪv/ adj reproductor

reprove /rɪ'pruːv/ vt reprender

reptile /'reptaɪl/ n reptil m

republic /rɪ'pʌblɪk/ n república f. ~**an** adj & n republicano (m). R~ n & n (in US) republicano (m)

repugnan|ce /rɪ'pʌɡnəns/ n repugnancia f. ~**t** adj repugnante

repuls|e /rɪ'pʌls/ vt rechazar, repulsar. ~**ion** /-ʃn/ n repulsión f. ~**ive** adj repulsivo

reput|able /'repjʊtəbl/ adj acreditado, reputado. ~**ation** /repjʊ'teɪʃn/ n reputación f

request /rɪ'kwest/ n petición f. ● vt pedir

require /rɪ'kwaɪə(r)/ vt requerir; (need) necesitar; (demand) exigir. ~**d** adj necesario. ~**ment** n requisito m

rescue /'reskjuː/ vt rescatar, salvar. ● n rescate m. ~**r** n salvador m

research /rɪ'sɜːtʃ/ n investigación f. ● vt investigar. ~**er** n investigador m

resembl|ance /rɪ'zembləns/ n parecido m. ~**e** /rɪ'zembl/ vt parecerse a

resent /rɪ'zent/ vt guardarle rencor a (person). **she ~ed his suc-**

cess le molestaba que él tuviera éxito. ~ful adj resentido. ~ment n resentimiento m

reserv|ation /rezə'veɪʃn/ n reserva f; (booking) reserva f. ~e /rɪ'zɜːv/ vt reservar. ● n reserva f; (in sports) suplente m & f. ~ed adj reservado. ~oir /'rezəvwɑː(r)/ n embalse m

reshuffle /riːˈʃʌfl/ n (Pol) reorganización f

residen|ce /'rezɪdəns/ n residencia f. ~t adj & n residente (m & f). ~tial /rezɪ'denʃl/ adj residencial

residue /'rezɪdjuː/ n residuo m

resign /rɪ'zaɪn/ vt/i dimitir. ~ o.s. to resignarse a. ~ation /rezɪg'neɪʃn/ n resignación f; (from job) dimisión f. ~ed adj resignado

resilien|ce /rɪ'zɪliəns/ n elasticidad f; (of person) resistencia f. ~t adj elástico; (person) resistente

resin /'rezɪn/ n resina f

resist /rɪ'zɪst/ vt resistir. ● vi resistirse. ~ance n resistencia f. ~ant adj resistente

resolut|e /'rezəluːt/ adj resuelto. ~ion /-'luːʃn/ n resolución f

resolve /rɪ'zɒlv/ vt resolver. ~ to do resolver a hacer. ● n resolución f

resort /rɪ'zɔːt/ n recurso m; (place) lugar m turístico. in the last ~ como último recurso. □ ~ to vi recurrir a.

resource /rɪ'sɔːs/ n recurso m. ~ful adj ingenioso

respect /rɪ'spekt/ n (esteem) respeto m; (aspect) respecto m. with ~ to con respecto a. ● vt respetar. ~able adj respetable. ~ful adj respetuoso. ~ive adj respectivo. ~ively adv respectivamente

respiration /respə'reɪʃn/ n respiración f

respite /'respaɪt/ n respiro m

respon|d /rɪ'spɒnd/ vi responder. ~se /rɪ'spɒns/ n respuesta f; (reaction) reacción f

responsib|ility /rɪspɒnsə'bɪlətɪ/ n responsabilidad f. ~le /rɪ'spɒnsəbl/ adj responsable; (job) de responsabilidad. ~ly adv con formalidad

responsive /rɪ'spɒnsɪv/ adj que reacciona bien. ~ to sensible a

rest /rest/ vt descansar; (lean) apoyar. ● vi descansar; (lean) apoyarse. ● n descanso m; (Mus) pausa f; (remainder) resto m, lo demás; (people) los demás, los otros mpl. to have a ~ tomarse un descanso. □ ~ up vi (Amer) descansar

restaurant /'restərɒnt/ n restaurante m

rest: ~ful adj sosegado. ~ive adj impaciente. ~less adj inquieto

restor|ation /restə'reɪʃn/ n restablecimiento m; (of building, monarch) restauración f. ~e /rɪ'stɔː(r)/ vt restablecer; restaurar (building); devolver (confidence, health)

restrain /rɪ'streɪn/ vt contener. ~ o.s. contenerse. ~ed adj (moderate) moderado; (in control of self) comedido. ~t n restricción f; (moderation) compostura f

restrict /rɪ'strɪkt/ vt restringir. ~ion /-ʃn/ n restricción f. ~ive adj restrictivo

rest room n (Amer) baño m, servicio m

result /rɪ'zʌlt/ n resultado m. as a ~ of como consecuencia de. ● vi. ~ from resultar de. ~ in dar como resultado

resume /rɪ'zjuːm/ vt reanudar. ● vi reanudarse

résumé /'rezjʊmeɪ/ n resumen m;

(*Amer, CV*) currículum *m*, historial *m* personal

resurrect /rezə'rekt/ *vt* resucitar. **~ion** /-ʃn/ *n* resurrección *f*

resuscitat|e /rɪ'sʌsɪteɪt/ *vt* resucitar. **~ion** /-'teɪʃn/ *n* resucitación *f*

retail /'riːteɪl/ *n* venta *f* al por menor. ● *adj* & *adv* al por menor. ● *vt* vender al por menor. ● *vi* venderse al por menor. **~er** *n* minorista *m* & *f*

retain /rɪ'teɪn/ *vt* retener; conservar (heat)

retaliat|e /rɪ'tælɪeɪt/ *vi* desquitarse; (*Mil*) tomar represalias. **~ion** /-'eɪʃn/ *n* represalias *fpl*

retarded /rɪ'tɑːdɪd/ *adj* retrasado

rethink /riː'θɪŋk/ *vt* (*pt* **rethought**) reconsiderar

reticen|ce /'retɪsns/ *n* reticencia *f*. **~t** *adj* reticente

retina /'retɪnə/ *n* retina *f*

retinue /'retɪnjuː/ *n* séquito *m*

retir|e /rɪ'taɪə(r)/ *vi* (*from work*) jubilarse; (*withdraw*) retirarse; (*go to bed*) acostarse. **~ed** *adj* jubilado. **~ement** *n* jubilación *f*. **~ing** *adj* retraído

retort /rɪ'tɔːt/ *vt/i* replicar. ● *n* réplica *f*

retrace /riː'treɪs/ *vt*. **~ one's steps** volver sobre sus pasos

retract /rɪ'trækt/ *vt* retirar (statement). ● *vi* retractarse

retrain /riː'treɪn/ *vi* hacer un curso de reciclaje

retreat /rɪ'triːt/ *vi* retirarse. ● *n* retirada *f*; (*place*) refugio *m*

retrial /riː'traɪəl/ *n* nuevo juicio *m*

retriev|al /rɪ'triːvl/ *n* recuperación *f*. **~e** /rɪ'triːv/ *vt* recuperar. **~er** *n* (*dog*) perro *m* cobrador

retro|grade /'retrəgreɪd/ *adj* retrógrado. **~spect** /-spekt/ *n*. **in ~** en retrospectiva. **~spective** /-'spektɪv/ *adj* retrospectivo

return /rɪ'tɜːn/ *vi* volver, regresar; (symptom) reaparecer. ● *vt* devolver; corresponder a (affection). ● *n* regreso *m*, vuelta *f*; (*Com*) rendimiento *m*; (*to owner*) devolución *f*. **in ~ for** a cambio de. **many happy ~s!** ¡feliz cumpleaños! **~ ticket** *n* billete *m* or (*LAm*) boleto *m* de ida y vuelta, boleto *m* redondo (*Mex*). **~s** *npl* (*Com*) ingresos *mpl*

reun|ion /riː'juːnɪən/ *n* reunión *f*. **~ite** /riːjuː'naɪt/ *vt* reunir

rev /rev/ *n* (*Auto, fam*) revolución *f*. ● *vt/i*. **~ (up)** (*pt* **revved**) (*Auto, fam*) acelerar(se)

reveal /rɪ'viːl/ *vt* revelar. **~ing** *adj* revelador

revel /'revl/ *vi* (*pt* **revelled**) tener un jolgorio. **~ in** deleitarse en. **~ry** *n* jolgorio *m*

revelation /revə'leɪʃn/ *n* revelación *f*

revenge /rɪ'vendʒ/ *n* venganza *f*. **take ~** vengarse. ● *vt* vengar

revenue /'revənjuː/ *n* ingresos *mpl*

revere /rɪ'vɪə(r)/ *vt* venerar. **~nce** /'revərəns/ *n* reverencia *f*

Reverend /'revərənd/ *adj* reverendo

reverent /'revərənt/ *adj* reverente

reverie /'revərɪ/ *n* ensueño *m*

revers|al /rɪ'vɜːsl/ *n* inversión *f*. **~e** /rɪ'vɜːs/ *adj* inverso. ● *n* contrario *m*; (*back*) revés *m*; (*Auto*) marcha *f* atrás. ● *vt* invertir; anular (decision); (*Auto*) dar marcha atrás a. ● *vi* (*Auto*) dar marcha atrás

revert /rɪ'vɜːt/ *vi*. **~ to** volver a; (*Jurid*) revertir a

review /rɪ'vjuː/ *n* revisión *f*; (*Mil*)

revista *f*; (*of book, play, etc*) crítica *f*. ● *vt* examinar (*situation*); reseñar (book, play, etc); (*Amer, for exam*) repasar

revis|e /rɪˈvaɪz/ *vt* revisar; (*Schol*) repasar. **~ion** /rɪˈvɪʒn/ *n* revisión *f*; (*Schol*) repaso *m*

revive /rɪˈvaɪv/ *vt* resucitar (person)

revolt /rɪˈvəʊlt/ *vi* sublevarse. ● *n* revuelta *f*. **~ing** *adj* asqueroso

revolution /revəˈluːʃn/ *n* revolución *f*. **~ary** *adj & n* revolucionario (*m*). **~ize** *vt* revolucionar

revolv|e /rɪˈvɒlv/ *vi* girar. **~er** *n* revólver *m*. **~ing** /rɪˈvɒlvɪŋ/ *adj* giratorio

revue /rɪˈvjuː/ *n* revista *f*

revulsion /rɪˈvʌlʃn/ *n* asco *m*

reward /rɪˈwɔːd/ *n* recompensa *f*. ● *vt* recompensar. **~ing** *adj* gratificante

rewrite /riːˈraɪt/ *vt* (*pt* rewrote, *pp* rewritten) volver a escribir o redactar; (*copy out*) escribir otra vez

rhetoric /ˈretərɪk/ *n* retórica *f*. **~al** /rɪˈtɒrɪkl/ *adj* retórico

rheumatism /ˈruːmətɪzəm/ *n* reumatismo *m*

rhinoceros /raɪˈnɒsərəs/ *n* (*pl* -oses *or invar*) rinoceronte *m*

rhubarb /ˈruːbɑːb/ *n* ruibarbo *m*

rhyme /raɪm/ *n* rima *f*; (*poem*) poesía *f*. ● *vt/i* rimar

rhythm /ˈrɪðəm/ *n* ritmo *m*. **~ic(al)** /ˈrɪðmɪk(l)/ *adj* rítmico

rib /rɪb/ *n* costilla *f*.

ribbon /ˈrɪbən/ *n* cinta *f*.

rice /raɪs/ *n* arroz *m*. **~ pudding** *n* arroz con leche

rich /rɪtʃ/ *adj* (-er, -est) rico. ● *n* ricos *mpl*. **~es** *npl* riquezas *fpl*

ricochet /ˈrɪkəʃeɪ/ *vi* rebotar

rid /rɪd/ *vt* (*pt* rid, *pres p* ridding) librar (**of** de). **get ~ of** deshacerse de. **~dance** /ˈrɪdns/ *n*. **good ~dance!** ¡adiós y buen viaje!

ridden /ˈrɪdn/ *see* RIDE

riddle /ˈrɪdl/ *n* acertijo *m*. ● *vt* acribillar. **be ~d with** estar lleno de

ride /raɪd/ *vi* (*pt* rode, *pp* ridden) (*on horseback*) montar a caballo; (*go*) ir (en bicicleta, a caballo etc). ● *vt* montar a (*a horse*); ir en (bicycle); (*Amer*) ir en (bus, train); recorrer (*distance*). ● *n* (*on horse*) cabalgata *f*; (*in car*) paseo *m* en coche. **take s.o. for a** 🔲 engañarle a uno. **~r** *n* (*on horse*) jinete *m*; (*cyclist*) ciclista *m* & *f*

ridge /rɪdʒ/ *n* (*of hills*) cadena *f*; (*hilltop*) cresta *f*

ridicul|e /ˈrɪdɪkjuːl/ *n* burlas *fpl*. ● *vt* ridiculizar. **~ous** /rɪˈdɪkjələs/ *adj* ridículo

rife /raɪf/ *adj* difundido

rifle /ˈraɪfl/ *n* fusil *m*

rift /rɪft/ *n* grieta *f*; (*fig*) ruptura *f*

rig /rɪg/ *vt* (*pt* rigged) (*pej*) amañar. ● *n* (*at sea*) plataforma *f* de perforación. **□ ~ up** *vt* improvisar

right /raɪt/ *adj* (*answer*) correcto; (*morally*) bueno; (*not left*) derecho; (*suitable*) adecuado. **be ~** (*person*) tener razón; (*clock*) estar bien. **it is ~** (*just, moral*) es justo. **put ~** rectificar. **the ~ person for the job** la persona indicada para el puesto. ● *n* (*entitlement*) derecho *m*; (*not left*) derecha *f*; (*not evil*) bien *m*. **~ of way** (*Auto*) prioridad *f*. **be in the ~** tener razón. **on the ~** a la derecha. ● *vt* enderezar; (*fig*) reparar. ● *adv* a la derecha; (*directly*) derecho; (*completely*) completamente. **~ angle** *n* ángulo *m* recto.

~ away adv inmediatamente.
~eous /'raɪtʃəs/ adj recto; (cause) justo.
~ful /'raɪtfl/ adj legítimo.
~-handed /-'hændɪd/ adj diestro.
~-hand man n brazo m derecho.
~ly adv justamente. **~ wing** adj (Pol) derechista

rigid /'rɪdʒɪd/ adj rígido

rig|orous /'rɪgərəs/ adj riguroso.
~our /'rɪgə(r)/ n rigor m

rim /rɪm/ n borde m; (of wheel) llanta f; (of glasses) montura f

rind /raɪnd/ n corteza f; (of fruit) cáscara f

ring¹ /rɪŋ/ n (circle) círculo m; (circle of metal etc) aro m; (on finger) anillo m; (on finger with stone) sortija f; (Boxing) cuadrilátero m; (bullring) ruedo m; (for circus) pista f; ● vt cercar

ring² /rɪŋ/ n (of bell) toque m; (tinkle) tintineo m; (telephone call) llamada f. ● vt (pt **rang**, pp **rung**) hacer sonar; (telephone) llamar por teléfono. **~ the bell** tocar el timbre. ● vi sonar. **~ back** vt/i volver a llamar. □ **~ up** vt llamar por teléfono

ring:: ~leader /'rɪŋliːdə(r)/ n cabecilla m & f. **~ road** n carretera f de circunvalación

rink /rɪŋk/ n pista f

rinse /rɪns/ vt enjuagar. ● n aclarado m; (of dishes) enjuague m; (for hair) tintura f (no permanente)

riot /'raɪət/ n disturbio m; (of colours) profusión f. **run ~** desenfrenarse. ● vi causar disturbios

rip /rɪp/ vt (pt **ripped**) rasgar. ● vi rasgarse. n ragón m. □ **~ off** vt (pull off) arrancar; (🅇, cheat) robar

ripe /raɪp/ adj (-er, -est) maduro.
~n /'raɪpn/ vt/i madurar

rip-off /'rɪpɒf/ n 🅇 timo m

ripple /'rɪpl/ n (on water) onda f

ris|e /raɪz/ vi (pt **rose**, pp **risen**) subir; (sun) salir; (river) crecer; (prices) subir; (land) elevarse; (get up) levantarse. ● n subida f; (land) altura f; (increase) aumento m; (to power) ascenso m. **give ~e** to ocasionar. **~er** n. **early ~er** n madrugador m. **~ing** n. ● adj (sun) naciente; (number) creciente; (prices) en alza

risk /rɪsk/ n riesgo m. ● vt arriesgar. **~y** adj (-ier, -iest) arriesgado

rite /raɪt/ n rito m

ritual /'rɪtʃʊəl/ adj & n ritual (m)

rival /'raɪvl/ adj & n rival (m). **~ry** n rivalidad f

river /'rɪvə(r)/ n río m

rivet /'rɪvɪt/ n remache m. **~ing** adj fascinante

road /rəʊd/ n (in town) calle f; (between towns) carretera f; (route, way) camino m. **~ map** n mapa m de carreteras. **~side** n borde m de la carretera. **~works** npl obras fpl. **~worthy** adj (vehicle) apto para circular

roam /rəʊm/ vi vagar

roar /rɔː(r)/ n rugido m; (laughter) carcajada f. ● vt/i rugir. **~ past** (vehicles) pasar con estruendo. **~ with laughter** reírse a carcajadas. **~ing** adj (trade etc) activo

roast /rəʊst/ vt asar; tostar (coffee). ● adj & n asado (m). **~ beef** n rosbif m

rob /rɒb/ vt (pt **robbed**) atracar, asaltar (bank); robarle a (person). **~ of** (deprive of) privar de. **~ber** n ladrón m; (of bank) atracador m. **~bery** n robo m; (of bank) atraco m

robe /rəʊb/ n bata f; (Univ etc)

toga f

robin /'rɒbɪn/ n petirrojo m

robot /'rəʊbɒt/ n robot m

robust /rəʊ'bʌst/ adj robusto

rock /rɒk/ n roca f; (crag, cliff) peñasco m. ● vt mecer; (shake) sacudir. ● vi mecerse; (shake) sacudirse. ● n (Mus) música f rock. **~-bottom** /-'bɒtəm/ adj 🆃 bajísimo

rocket /'rɒkɪt/ n cohete m

rock: ~ing-chair n mecedora f. **~y** adj (-ier, -iest) rocoso; (fig, shaky) bamboleante

rod /rɒd/ n vara f; (for fishing) caña f; (metal) barra f

rode /rəʊd/ see RIDE

rodent /'rəʊdnt/ n roedor m

rogue /rəʊg/ n pícaro m

role /rəʊl/ n papel m

roll /rəʊl/ vt hacer rodar; (roll up) enrollar; allanar (lawn); aplanar (pastry). ● vi rodar; (ship) balancearse; (on floor) revolcarse. be **~ing in money** 🆃 nadar en dinero ● n rollo m; (of ship) balanceo m; (of drum) redoble m; (of thunder) retumbo m; (bread) panecillo m, bolillo m (Mex). □ **~ over** vi (turn over) dar una vuelta. □ **~ up** vt enrollar; arremangar (sleeve). vi 🆃 llegar. **~-call** n lista f

roller /'rəʊlə(r)/ n rodillo m; (wheel) rueda f; (for hair) rulo m. **R~ blades** npl (P) patines mpl en línea. **~-coaster** n montaña f rusa. **~-skate** n patín m de ruedas. **~-skating** patinaje m (sobre ruedas)

rolling /'rəʊlɪŋ/ adj ondulado. **~-pin** n rodillo m

ROM /rɒm/ n (= read-only memory) ROM f 🆃

Roman /'rəʊmən/ adj & n romano (m). **~ Catholic** adj & n católico (m) (romano)

romance /rəʊ'mæns/ n novela f romántica; (love) amor m; (affair) aventura f

Romania /ru:'meɪnɪə/ n Rumania f, Rumanía f. **~n** adj & n rumano (m)

romantic /rəʊ'mæntɪk/ adj romántico

Rome /rəʊm/ n Roma f

romp /rɒmp/ vi retozar

roof /ru:f/ n techo m, tejado m; (of mouth) paladar m. ● vt techar. **~rack** n baca f. **~top** n tejado m

rook /rʊk/ n grajo m; (in chess) torre f

room /ru:m/ n cuarto m, habitación f; (bedroom) dormitorio m; (space) espacio m; (large hall) sala f. **~y** adj espacioso

roost /ru:st/ vi posarse. **~er** n gallo m

root /ru:t/ n raíz f. take **~** echar raíces; (idea) arraigarse. ● vi echar raíces. □ **~ about** vi hurgar. □ **~ for** vt 🆃 alentar. □ **~ out** vt extirpar

rope /rəʊp/ n cuerda f. know the **~s** estar al corriente. ● vt atar; (Amer, lasso) enlazar. □ **~ in** vt agarrar

rose¹ /rəʊz/ n rosa f; (nozzle) roseta f

rose² /rəʊz/ see RISE

rosé /'rəʊzeɪ/ n (vino m) rosado m

rot /rɒt/ vt (pt rotted) pudrir. ● vi pudrirse. ● n putrefacción f

rota /'rəʊtə/ n lista f (de turnos)

rotary /'rəʊtərɪ/ adj rotatorio

rotat|e /rəʊ'teɪt/ vt girar; (change round) alternar. ● vi girar; (change round) alternarse. **~ion** /-ʃn/ n rotación f

rote /rəʊt/ n. by **~** de memoria

rotten /'rɒtn/ adj podrido; 🆃 pésimo ⓘ; (weather) horrible

rough /rʌf/ adj (-er, -est) áspero; (person) tosco; (bad) malo; (ground) accidentado; (violent) brutal; (approximate) aproximado; (diamond) bruto. ● adv duro. ~ **copy**, ~ **draft** borrador m. ● vt. ~ **it** vivir sin comodidades. ~**age** /'rʌfɪdʒ/ n fibra f. ~**and-ready** adj improvisado. ~**ly** adv bruscamente; (more or less) aproximadamente

roulette /ru:'let/ n ruleta f

round /raʊnd/ adj (-er, -est) redondo. ● n círculo m; (of visits, drinks) ronda f; (of competition) vuelta f; (Boxing) asalto m. ● prep alrededor de. ● adv alrededor. ~ **about** (approximately) aproximadamente. **come** ~ **to, go** ~ **to** (a friend etc) pasar por casa de. ● vt doblar (corner). □ ~ **off** vt terminar; redondear (number). □ ~ **up** vt rodear (cattle); hacer una redada de (suspects). ~**about** n tiovivo m, carrusel m (LAm); (for traffic) glorieta f, rotonda f. ● adj in directo. ~ **trip** n viaje m de ida y vuelta. ~**-up** n resumen m; (of suspects) redada f

rous|e /raʊz/ vt despertar. ~**ing** adj enardecedor

route /ru:t/ n ruta f; (Naut, Aviat) rumbo m; (of bus) línea f

routine /ru:'ti:n/ n rutina f. ● adj rutinario

row¹ /rəʊ/ n fila f. ● vi remar

row² /raʊ/ n (fam, noise) bulla f ⓘ; (quarrel) pelea f. ● vi ⓘ pelearse

rowboat /'rəʊbəʊt/ (Amer) n bote m de remos

rowdy /'raʊdɪ/ adj (-ier, -iest) n escandaloso, alborotado

rowing /'rəʊɪŋ/ n remo m. ~

boat n bote m de remos

royal /'rɔɪəl/ adj real. ~**ist** adj & n monárquico (m). ~**ly** adv magníficamente. ~**ty** n realeza f

rub /rʌb/ vt (pt rubbed) frotar. □ ~ **out** vt borrar

rubber /'rʌbə(r)/ n goma f, caucho m, hule m (Mex); (eraser) goma f (de borrar). ~ **band** n goma f (elástica). ~-**stamp** vt (fig) autorizar. ~**y** adj parecido al caucho

rubbish /'rʌbɪʃ/ n basura f; (junk) trastos mpl; (fig) tonterías fpl. ~ **bin** n cubo m de la basura, bote m de la basura (Mex). ~**y** adj sin valor

rubble /'rʌbl/ n escombros mpl

ruby /'ru:bɪ/ n rubí m

rucksack /'rʌksæk/ n mochila f

rudder /'rʌdə(r)/ n timón m

rude /ru:d/ adj (-er, -est) grosero, mal educado; (improper) indecente; (brusque) brusco. ~**ly** adv groseramente. ~**ness** n mala educación f

rudimentary /ru:dɪ'mentrɪ/ adj rudimentario

ruffian /'rʌfɪən/ n rufián m

ruffle /'rʌfl/ vt despeinar (hair); arrugar (clothes)

rug /rʌg/ n alfombra f, tapete m (Mex); (blanket) manta f de viaje

rugged /'rʌgɪd/ adj (coast) escarpado; (landscape) escabroso

ruin /'ru:ɪn/ n ruina f. ● vt arruinar; (spoil) estropear

rul|e /ru:l/ n regla f; (Pol) dominio m. **as a** ~ por regla general. ● vt gobernar; (master) dominar; (Jurid) dictaminar. □ ~ **out** vt descartar. ~**ed paper** n papel m rayado. ~**er** n (sovereign) soberano m; (leader) gobernante m & f; (measure) regla f. ~**ing** adj (class) dirigente. ● n decisión f

rum /rʌm/ n ron m

rumble /'rʌmbl/ vi retumbar; (stomach) hacer ruidos

rummage /'rʌmɪdʒ/ vi hurgar

rumour /'ruːmə(r)/ n rumor m. ● vt. **it is ~ed that** se rumorea que

rump steak /rʌmpsteɪk/ n filete m de cadera

run /rʌn/ vi (pt ran, pp run, pres p running) correr; (water) correr; (function) funcionar; (melt) derretirse; (makeup) correrse; (colour) desteñir; (bus etc) circular; (in election) presentarse. ● vt correr (race); dirigir (business); correr (risk); (move, pass) pasar; tender (wire); preparar (bath). **~ a temperature** tener fiebre. □ corrida f, carrera f; (outing) paseo m (en coche); (ski) pista f. **in the long ~** a la larga. **be on the ~** estar prófugo. □ **~ away** vi huir, escaparse. □ **~ down** vi bajar corriendo; (battery) descargarse. vt (Auto) atropellar; (belittle) denigrar. □ **~ in** vi entrar corriendo. □ **~ off** vt sacar (copies). □ **~ out** vi salir corriendo; (liquid) salirse; (fig) agotarse. □ **~ out of** vt quedarse sin. □ **~ over** vt (Auto) atropellar. □ **~ through** vt (review) ensayar; (rehearse) repasar. □ **~ up** vt ir acumulando (bill). vi subir corriendo. **~away** n fugitivo m. **~ down** adj (person) agotado

rung¹ /rʌŋ/ n (of ladder) peldaño m

rung² /rʌŋ/ see RING

run: ~ner /'rʌnə/ n corredor m; (on sledge) patín m. **~ner bean** n judía f escarlata. **~ner-up** n. **be ~er-up** quedar en segundo lugar. **~ning** n. **be in the ~ning** tener posibilidades de

ganar. ● adj (water) corriente; (commentary) en directo. **four times ~ning** cuatro veces seguidas. **~ny** /'rʌnɪ/ adj líquido; (nose) moquea. **~way** n pista f de aterrizaje

rupture /'rʌptʃə(r)/ n ruptura f. ● vt romper

rural /'rʊərəl/ adj rural

ruse /ruːz/ n ardid m

rush /rʌʃ/ n (haste) prisa f; (crush) bullicio m; (plant) junco m. ● vi precipitarse. ● vt apresurar; (Mil) asaltar. **~-hour** n hora f punta, hora f pico (LAm)

Russia /'rʌʃə/ n Rusia f. **~n** adj & n ruso (m)

rust /rʌst/ n orín m. ● vt oxidar. ● vi oxidarse

rustle /'rʌsl/ vt hacer susurrar; (Amer) robar. ● vi susurrar □ **~ up** vt 🔲 preparar.

rust: ~proof adj inoxidable. **~y** (-ier, -iest) oxidado

rut /rʌt/ n surco m. **be in a ~** estar anquilosado

ruthless /'ruːθlɪs/ adj despiadado

rye /raɪ/ n centeno m

r

·············

S s

·············

S abbr (= **south**) S

sabot|age /'sæbətɑːʒ/ n sabotaje m. ● vt sabotear. **~eur** /-'tɜː(r)/ n saboteador m

saccharin /'sækərɪn/ n sacarina f

sachet /'sæʃeɪ/ n bolsita f

sack /sæk/ n saco m. **get the ~** 🔲 ser despedido. ● vt 🔲 despedir, echar

sacrament /'sækrəmənt/ n sacramento m

sacred /'seɪkrɪd/ adj sagrado

sacrifice /'sækrɪfaɪs/ n sacrificio m. ● vt sacrificar

sacrileg|e /'sækrɪlɪdʒ/ n sacrilegio m. **~ious** /-'lɪdʒəs/ adj sacrílego

sad /sæd/ adj (sadder, saddest) triste. **~den** vt entristecer

saddle /'sædl/ n silla f de montar. ● vt ensillar (horse). **~ s.o. with sth** (fig) endilgarle algo a uno

sadist /'seɪdɪst/ n sádico m. **~tic** /sə'dɪstɪk/ adj sádico

sadly /'sædlɪ/ adv tristemente; (fig) desgraciadamente. **~ness** n tristeza f

safe /seɪf/ adj (-er, -est) seguro; (out of danger) salvo; (cautious) prudente. **~ and sound** sano y salvo. ● n caja f fuerte. **~ deposit** n caja f de seguridad. **~guard** n salvaguardia f. ● vt salvaguardar. **~ly** adv sin peligro; (in safe place) en lugar seguro. **~ty** n seguridad f. **~ty belt** n cinturón m de seguridad. **~ty pin** n imperdible m

sag /sæg/ vi (pt sagged) (ceiling) combarse; (bed) hundirse

saga /'sɑːgə/ n saga f

Sagittarius /sædʒɪ'teərɪəs/ n Sagitario m

said /sed/ see SAY

sail /seɪl/ n vela f; (trip) paseo m (en barco). **set ~** zarpar. ● vi navegar; (leave) partir; (Sport) practicar la vela; (fig) deslizarse. **go ~ing** salir a navegar. ● vt gobernar (boat). **~boat** n (Amer) barco m de vela. **~ing** n (Sport) vela f. **~ing boat** n, **~ing ship** n barco m de vela. **~or** n marinero m

saint /seɪnt/ /sənt/ n santo m. **~ly** adj santo

sake /seɪk/ n. **for the ~ of** por. **for God's ~** por el amor de Dios

salad /'sæləd/ n ensalada f. **~ bowl** n ensaladera f. **~ dressing** n aliño m

salary /'sælərɪ/ n sueldo m

sale /seɪl/ n venta f; (at reduced prices) liquidación f. **for ~** (sign) se vende. **be for ~** estar a la venta. **be on ~** (Amer, reduced) estar en liquidación. **~able** adj vendible. (for sale) estar a la venta. **~s clerk** n (Amer) dependiente m, dependienta f. **~sman** /-mən/ n vendedor m; (in shop) dependiente m. **~swoman** n vendedora f; (in shop) dependienta f

saliva /sə'laɪvə/ n saliva f

salmon /'sæmən/ n invar salmón m

saloon /sə'luːn/ n (on ship) salón m; (Amer, bar) bar m; (Auto) turismo m

salt /sɔːlt/ n sal f. ● vt salar. **~cellar** n salero m. **~y** adj salado

salute /sə'luːt/ n saludo m. ● vt saludar. ● vi hacer un saludo

Salvadorean, Salvadorian /sælvə'dɔːrɪən/ adj & n salvadoreño (m)

salvage /'sælvɪdʒ/ vt salvar

salvation /sæl'veɪʃn/ n salvación f

same /seɪm/ adj igual (as que); (before noun) mismo (as que). **at the ~ time** al mismo tiempo. ● pron. **the ~** lo mismo. **all the ~** de todas formas. ● adv. **the ~** igual

sample /'sɑːmpl/ n muestra f. ● vt degustar (food)

sanctify /'sæŋktɪfaɪ/ vt santificar. **~ion** /sæŋkʃn/ n sanción f. ● vt sancionar. **~uary** /'sæŋktʃʊərɪ/ n (Relig) santuario m; (for wildlife) re-

serva f; (*refuge*) asilo m
sand /sænd/ n arena f ● vt pulir
(floor). □~ **down** vt lijar (wood)
sandal /'sændl/ n sandalia f
sand: ~**castle** n castillo m de
arena. ~**paper** n papel m de lija.
● vt lijar. ~**storm** n tormenta f de
arena
sandwich /'sænwɪdʒ/ n bocadillo
m, sandwich m. ● vt. **be** ~**ed between** (*person*) estar apretujado
entre
sandy /'sændɪ/ adj arenoso
sane /seɪn/ adj (**-er, -est**) (*person*)
cuerdo; (*sensible*) sensato
sang /sæŋ/ see SING
sanitary /'sænɪtrɪ/ adj higiénico;
(*system etc*) sanitario. ~ **towel**,
~ **napkin** n (*Amer*) compresa f (hi-
giénica)
sanitation /sænɪ'teɪʃn/ n higiene
f; (*drainage*) sistema m sanitario
sanity /'sænɪtɪ/ n cordura f
sank /sæŋk/ see SINK
Santa (Claus) /'sæntə(klɔːz)/ n
Papá m Noel
sap /sæp/ n (*in plants*) savia f. ● (pt
sapped) minar
sapling /'sæplɪŋ/ n árbol m joven
sapphire /'sæfaɪə(r)/ n zafiro m
sarcas|m /'sɑːkæzəm/ n sarcasmo
m. ~**tic** /-'æstɪk/ adj sarcástico
sardine /sɑː'diːn/ n sardina f
sash /sæʃ/ n (*over shoulder*) banda
f; (*round waist*) fajín m.
sat /sæt/ see SIT
SAT abbr (*Amer*) (**Scholastic Apti-
tude Test**); (*Brit*) (**Standard As-
sessment Task**)
satchel /'sætʃl/ n cartera f
satellite /'sætəlaɪt/ n & a satélite
(m). ~ **TV** n televisión f por satélite
satin /'sætɪn/ n raso m. ● adj de

raso
satir|e /'sætaɪə(r)/ n sátira f. ~**ical**
/sə'tɪrɪkl/ adj satírico. ~**ize**
/'sætəraɪz/ vt satirizar
satis|faction /sætɪs'fækʃn/ n sa-
tisfacción f. ~**factorily**
/-'fæktərɪlɪ/ adv satisfactoriamente.
~**factory** /-'fæktərɪ/ adj satisfactorio. ~**fy** /'sætɪsfaɪ/ vt satisfacer;
(*convince*) convencer. ~**fying** adj
satisfactorio
satphone /'sætfəʊn/ n teléfono m
satélite
Saturday /'sætədeɪ/ n sábado m
Saturn /'sætən/ n Saturno m
sauce /sɔːs/ n salsa f; (*cheek*) descaro m. ~**pan** /'sɔːspən/ n cazo m,
cacerola f. ~**r** /'sɔːsə(r)/ n platillo m
saucy /'sɔːsɪ/ adj (**-ier, -iest**) descarado
Saudi /'saʊdɪ/ adj & n saudita (m &
f). ~ **Arabia** /-ə'reɪbɪə/ n Arabia f
Saudí
sauna /'sɔːnə/ n sauna f
saunter /'sɔːntə(r)/ vi pasearse
sausage /'sɒsɪdʒ/ n salchicha f
savage /'sævɪdʒ/ adj salvaje;
(*fierce*) feroz. ● n salvaje m & f. ● vt
atacar. ~**ry** n ferocidad f
save /seɪv/ vt (*rescue*) salvar; ahorrar (money, time); (*prevent*) evitar; (*Comp*) guardar. ● n (*football*)
parada f. ● prep salvo, excepto.
□~ **up** vi/t ahorrar. ~**er** n aho-
rrador m. ~**ing** n ahorro m. ~**ings**
npl ahorros mpl
saviour /'seɪvɪə(r)/ n salvador m
savour /'seɪvə(r)/ vt saborear. ~**y**
adj (*appetizing*) sabroso; (*not sweet*)
no dulce

s

saw¹ /sɔː/ *see* SEE¹

saw² /sɔː/ n sierra f. ● vt (pt sawed, pp sawn) serrar. ~**dust** n serrín m. ~**n** /sɔːn/ *see* SAW²

saxophone /ˈsæksəfəʊn/ n saxofón m, saxófono m

say /seɪ/ vt/i (pt said /sed/) decir; rezar (prayer). ● n. **have a** ~ expresar una opinión; (in decision) tener voz en capítulo. **have no** ~ no tener ni voz ni voto. ~**ing** n refrán m

scab /skæb/ n costra f; (fam, blackleg) esquirol m

scaffolding /ˈskæfəldɪŋ/ n andamios mpl

scald /skɔːld/ vt escaldar

scale /skeɪl/ n (also Mus) escala f; (of fish) escama f. ● vt (climb) escalar. ~ **down** vt reducir (a escala) (drawing); recortar (operation). ~**s** npl (for weighing) balanza f, peso m

scallion /ˈskæljən/ n (Amer) cebolleta f

scalp /skælp/ vt quitar el cuero cabelludo a

scamper /ˈskæmpə(r)/ vi. ~ **away** irse correteando

scan /skæn/ vt (pt scanned) escudriñar; (quickly) echar un vistazo a; (radar) explorar

scandal /ˈskændl/ n escándalo m; (gossip) chismorreo m. ~**ize** vt escandalizar. ~**ous** adj escandaloso

Scandinavia /skændɪˈneɪvɪə/ n Escandinavia f ~**n** adj & n escandinavo (m)

scant /skænt/ adj escaso. ~**y** adj (-ier, -iest) escaso

scapegoat /ˈskeɪpgəʊt/ n cabeza f de turco

scar /skɑː(r)/ n cicatriz f

scarc|e /skeəs/ adj (-er, -est) escaso. **be** ~**e** escasear. **make o.s.** ~**e** ⚠ mantenerse lejos. ~**ely** adv apenas. ~**ity** n escasez f

scare /skeə(r)/ vt asustar. **be** ~**d** tener miedo. **be** ~**d of sth** tenerle miedo a algo. ● n susto m. ~**crow** n espantapájaros m

scarf /skɑːf/ n (pl scarves) bufanda f; (over head) pañuelo m

scarlet /ˈskɑːlət/ adj escarlata f. ~ **fever** n escarlatina f

scarves /skɑːvz/ *see* SCARF

scary /ˈskeərɪ/ adj (-ier, -iest) que da miedo

scathing /ˈskeɪðɪŋ/ adj mordaz

scatter /ˈskætə(r)/ vt (throw) esparcir; (disperse) dispersar. ● vi dispersarse. ~**ed** /ˈskætəd/ adj disperso; (occasional) esporádico

scavenge /ˈskævɪndʒ/ vi escarbar (en la basura)

scenario /sɪˈnɑːrɪəʊ/ n (pl -os) perspectiva f; (of film) guión m

scen|e /siːn/ n escena f; (sight) vista f; (fuss) lío m. **behind the** ~**es** entre bastidores. ~**ery** /ˈsiːnərɪ/ n paisaje m; (in theatre) decorado m. ~**ic** /ˈsiːnɪk/ adj pintoresco

scent /sent/ n olor m; (perfume) perfume m; (trail) pista f ● vt intuir; (make fragrant) perfumar

sceptic /ˈskeptɪk/ n escéptico m. ~**al** adj escéptico. ~**ism** /-sɪzəm/ n escepticismo m

sceptre /ˈseptə(r)/ n cetro m

schedule /ˈʃedjuːl, ˈskedʒuːl/ n programa f; (timetable) horario m. **behind** ~ atrasado. **it's on** ~ va de acuerdo a lo previsto. ● vt proyectar. ~**d flight** n vuelo m regular

scheme /skiːm/ n proyecto m; (plot) intriga f. ● vi (pej) intrigar

schizophrenic /skɪtsəˈfrenɪk/ adj & n esquizofrénico (m)

scholar /ˈskɒlə(r)/ n erudito m.

~ly adj erudito. **~ship** n erudición f; (grant) beca f

school /skuːl/ n escuela f; (Univ) facultad f. • adj (age, holidays, year) escolar. • vt instruir; (train) capacitar. **~boy** n colegial m. **~girl** n colegiala f. **~ing** n instrucción f. **~master** n (primary) maestro m; (secondary) profesor m. **~mistress** n (primary) maestra f; (secondary) profesora f. **~teacher** n (primary) maestro m; (secondary) profesor m.

scien|ce /'saɪəns/ n ciencia f. **study ~ce** estudiar ciencias. **~ce fiction** n ciencia f ficción. **~tific** /-'tɪfɪk/ adj científico. **~tist** /'saɪəntɪst/ n científico m

scissors /'sɪsəz/ npl tijeras fpl

scoff /skɒf/ vt 🔢 zamparse. • vi. **~ at** mofarse de

scold /skəʊld/ vt regañar

scoop /skuːp/ n pala f; (news) primicia f. □ **~ out** vt sacar; excavar (hole)

scooter /'skuːtə(r)/ n escúter m; (for child) patinete m

scope /skəʊp/ n alcance m; (opportunity) oportunidad f

scorch /skɔːtʃ/ vt chamuscar. **~ing** adj 🔢 de mucho calor

score /skɔː(r)/ n tanteo m; (Mus) partitura f; (twenty) veintena f. **on that ~** en cuanto a eso. **know the ~** 🔢 saber cómo van las cosas. • vt marcar (goal); anotarse (points); (cut, mark) rayar; conseguir (success). • vi marcar

scorn /skɔːn/ n desdén m. • vt desdeñar. **~ful** adj desdeñoso

Scorpio /'skɔːpɪəʊ/ n Escorpio m, Escorpión m

scorpion /'skɔːpɪən/ n escorpión m

Scot /skɒt/ n escocés m. **~ch**

/skɒtʃ/ n whisky m, güisqui m

Scottish Parliament El Parlamento Escocés fue establecido en Edinburgo en 1999. Tiene competencia legislativa y ejecutiva en los asuntos internos de Escocia y poderes tributarios limitados. Los MSPs (Members of the Scottish Parliament) son 129, de los cuales 73 son elegidos directamente y el resto mediante el sistema de representación proporcional.

---

scotch /skɒtʃ/ vt frustrar; acallar (rumours)

Scotch tape n (Amer) celo m, cinta f Scotch

Scot: ~land /'skɒtlənd/ n Escocia f. **~s** adj escocés. **~tish** adj escocés

scoundrel /'skaʊndrəl/ n canalla f

scour /'skaʊə(r)/ vt fregar; (search) registrar. **~er** n estropajo m

scourge /skɜːdʒ/ n azote m

scout /skaʊt/ n explorador m. **Boy S~** explorador m

scowl /skaʊl/ n ceño m fruncido. • vi fruncir el ceño

scram /skræm/ vi 🔢 largarse

scramble /'skræmbl/ vi (clamber) gatear. • n (difficult climb) subida f difícil; (struggle) rebatiña f. □ **~d egg** n huevos mpl revueltos

scrap /skræp/ n pedacito m; (fam, fight) pelea f. • vt (pt scrapped) desechar. **~book** n álbum m de recortes. **~s** npl sobras fpl

scrape /skreɪp/ n (fig) apuro m. • vt raspar; (graze) rasparse; (rub) rascar. □ **~ through** vi/t aprobar por los pelos (exam). □ **~ together** vt reunir. **~r** n rasqueta f

scrap: ~**heap** n montón m de deshechos. • ~**yard** n chatarrería f

scratch /skrætʃ/ vt rayar (furniture, record); (with nail etc) arañar; rascarse (itch). • vi arañar. • n rayón m; (from nail etc) arañazo m. **start from** ~ empezar desde cero. **be up to** ~ dar la talla

scrawl /skrɔːl/ n garabato m. • vt/i garabatear

scream /skriːm/ vt/i gritar. • n grito m

screech /skriːtʃ/ vi chillar; (brakes etc) chirriar. • n chillido m; (of brakes etc) chirrido m

screen /skriːn/ n pantalla f; (folding) biombo m. • vt (hide) ocultar; (protect) proteger; proyectar (film)

screw /skruː/ n tornillo m. • vt atornillar. □ ~ **up** vt atornillar; entornar (eyes); torcer (face); (sl, ruin) fastidiar. ~**driver** n destornillador m

scribble /ˈskrɪbl/ vt/i garabatear. • n garabato m

script /skrɪpt/ n escritura f; (of film etc) guión m

scroll /skrəʊl/ n rollo m (de pergamino). □ ~ **down** vi retroceder la pantalla. □ ~ **up** vi avanzar la pantalla

scrounge /skraʊndʒ/ vt/i gorronear. ~**r** n gorrón m

scrub /skrʌb/ n (land) maleza f. • vt/i (pt **scrubbed**) fregar

scruff /skrʌf/ n. **by the** ~ **of the neck** por el pescuezo. ~**y** adj (-ier, -iest) desaliñado

scrum|ple /ˈskruːpl/ n escrúpulo m. ~**ulous** /-jʊləs/ adj escrupuloso

scrutin|ize /ˈskruːtɪnaɪz/ vt escudriñar; inspeccionar (document). ~**y** /ˈskruːtɪnɪ/ n examen m minucioso

scuffle /ˈskʌfl/ n refriega f

sculpt /skʌlpt/ vt/i esculpir. ~**or** n escultor m. ~**ure** /-tʃə(r)/ n escultura f. • vt/i esculpir

scum /skʌm/ n espuma f; (people, pej) escoria f

scupper /ˈskʌpə(r)/ vt echar por tierra (plans)

scurry /ˈskʌrɪ/ vi corretear

scuttle /ˈskʌtl/ n cubo m del carbón. • vt barrenar (ship). • vi. ~ **away** escabullirse rápidamente

scythe /saɪð/ n guadaña f

SE abbr (= **south-east**) SE

sea /siː/ n mar m. **at** ~ en el mar; (fig) confuso. **by** ~ por mar. ~**food** n mariscos mpl. ~ **front** n paseo m marítimo, malecón m (LAm). ~**gull** n gaviota f. ~ **horse** n caballito m de mar

seal /siːl/ n sello m; (animal) foca f. • vt sellar

sea level n nivel m del mar

sea lion n león m marino

seam /siːm/ n costura f; (of coal) veta f

seaman /ˈsiːmən/ n (pl **-men**) marinero m

seamy /ˈsiːmɪ/ adj sórdido

seance /ˈseɪɑːns/ n sesión f de espiritismo

search /sɜːtʃ/ vt registrar; buscar en (records). • vi buscar. • n (for sth) búsqueda f; (of sth) registro m; (Comp) búsqueda f. **in** ~ **of** en busca de. □ ~ **for** vt buscar. ~ **engine** n buscador m. ~**ing** adj penetrante. ~**light** n reflector m. ~ **party** n partida f de rescate

sea: ~**shore** n orilla f del mar. ~**sick** adj mareado. **be** ~**sick** marearse. ~**side** n playa f

season /ˈsiːzn/ n estación f; (period) temporada f. **high/low** ~

temporada f alta/baja. ● vt (Culin)
sazonar. **~al** adj estacional; (demand) de estación. **~ed** adj (fig)
avezado. **~ing** n condimento m. **~
ticket** n abono m (de temporada)

seat /siːt/ n asiento m; (place)
lugar m; (in cinema, theatre) localidad f; (of trousers) fondillos mpl.
take a ~ sentarse. ● vt sentar;
(have seats for) (auditorium) tener
capacidad para; (bus) tener asientos para. **~belt** n cinturón m de
seguridad

sea: ~ trout n reo m.
~-urchin n erizo m de mar.
~weed n alga f marina.
~worthy adj en condiciones de
navegar

seclu|ded /sɪˈkluːdɪd/ adj aislado
~sion /sɪˈkluːʒn/ n

second /ˈsekənd/ adj & n segundo
(m). **on ~ thoughts** pensándolo
bien. ● adv (in race etc) en segundo
lugar. ● vt secundar. **~s** npl (goods)
artículos mpl de segunda calidad;
(fam, more food) have **~s** repetir.
● /sɪˈkɒnd/ vt (transfer) trasladar
temporalmente. **~ary** /ˈsekəndrɪ/
adj secundario. **~ary school** n instituto m (de enseñanza secundaria)

second: ~-class adj de segunda
(clase). **~-hand** adj de segunda
mano. **~ly** adv en segundo lugar.
~-rate adj mediocre

secre|cy /ˈsiːkrəsɪ/ n secreto m.
~t adj & n secreto (m). **in ~t** en
secreto

secretar|ial /sekrəˈteərɪəl/ adj de
secretario; (course) de secretariado. **~y** /ˈsekrətrɪ/ n secretario
m. **S~y of State** (in UK) ministro
m; (in US) secretario m de Estado

secretive /ˈsiːkrɪtɪv/ adj reservado

sect /sekt/ n secta f. **~arian**
/-ˈteərɪən/ adj sectario

section /ˈsekʃn/ n sección f;
(part) parte f

sector /ˈsektə(r)/ n sector m

secular /ˈsekjulə(r)/ adj secular

secur|e /sɪˈkjuə(r)/ adj seguro;
(shelf) firme. ● vt asegurar; (obtain)
obtener. **~ely** adv seguramente.
~ity n seguridad f; (for loan) garantía f

sedat|e /sɪˈdeɪt/ adj reposado. ● vt
sedar. **~ion** /sɪˈdeɪʃn/ n sedación f.
~ive /ˈsedətɪv/ adj & n sedante (m)

sediment /ˈsedɪmənt/ n sedimento m

seduc|e /sɪˈdjuːs/ vt seducir. **~er**
n seductor m. **~tion** /sɪˈdʌkʃn/ n
seducción f. **~tive** /sɪˈdʌktɪv/ adj
seductor

see /siː/ ● vt (pt saw, pp seen) ver;
(understand) comprender; (escort)
acompañar. **~ing that** visto que.
~ you later! ¡hasta luego! □ ~
off vt (say goodbye to) despedirse de. □ ~ **through** vt llevar a
cabo; calar (person). □ ~ **to** vt
ocuparse de

seed /siːd/ n semilla f; (fig) germen
m; (Amer, pip) pepita f. **go to ~**
granar; (fig) echarse a perder.
~ling n planta f de semillero. **~y**
adj (-ier, -iest) sórdido

seek /siːk/ vt (pt sought) buscar;
pedir (approval). □ ~ **out** vt buscar

seem /siːm/ vi parecer

seen /siːn/ see SEE

seep /siːp/ vi filtrarse

see-saw /ˈsiːsɔː/ n balancín m

seethe /siːð/ vi (fig) estar furioso.
I was seething with anger me
hervía la sangre

see-through /ˈsiːθruː/ adj transparente

segment /ˈsegmənt/ n segmento m

s

m; (of orange) gajo *m*

segregat|e /'segrigeit/ *vt* segregar. **~ion** /-'geiʃn/ *n* segregación *f*

seiz|e /si:z/ *vt* agarrar; *(Jurid)* incautar. **~e on** *vt* aprovechar *(chance)*. □ **~ up** *vi (Tec)* agarrotarse. **~ure** /'si:ʒə(r)/ *n* incautación *f*; *(Med)* ataque *m*

seldom /'seldəm/ *adv* rara vez

select /sɪ'lekt/ *vt* escoger; *(Sport)* seleccionar. ● *adj* selecto; *(exclusive)* exclusivo. **~ion** /-ʃn/ *n* selección *f*. **~ive** *adj* selectivo

self /self/ *n (pl* **selves**). he's his old **~ again** vuelve a ser el de antes. **~-addressed** *adj* con el nombre y la dirección del remitente. **~-catering** *adj* con facilidades para cocinar. **~-centred** *adj* egocéntrico. **~-confidence** *n* confianza *f* en sí mismo. **~-confident** *adj* seguro de sí mismo. **~-conscious** *adj* cohibido. **~-contained** *adj* independiente. **~-control** *n* dominio *m* de sí mismo. **~-defence** *n* defensa *f* propia. **~-employed** *adj* que trabaja por cuenta propia. **~-evident** *adj* evidente. **~-important** *adj* presumido. **~-indulgent** *adj* inmoderado. **~-interest** *n* interés *m* (personal). **~ish** *adj* egoísta. **~ishness** *n* egoísmo *m*. **~-pity** *n* autocompasión. **~-portrait** *n* autorretrato *m*. **~-respect** *n* amor *m* propio. **~-righteous** *adj* santurrón. **~-sacrifice** *n* abnegación *f*. **~-satisfied** *adj* satisfecho de sí mismo. **~-serve** *(Amer)*, **~-service** *adj & n* autoservicio *(m)*. **~-sufficient** *adj* independiente

sell /sel/ *vt (pt* **sold**) vender. ● *vi* venderse. □ **~ off** *vt* liquidar. **~ out** *vi.* we've sold out of gloves los guantes están agotados. **~by**

date *n* fecha *f* límite de venta. **~er** *n* vendedor *m*

Sellotape /'seləteɪp/ *n* (®) celo *m*, cinta *f* Scotch

sell-out /'selaʊt/ *n (performance)* éxito *m* de taquilla; *(fam, betrayal)* capitulación *f*

semblance /'sembləns/ *n* apariencia *f*

semester /sɪ'mestə(r)/ *n (Amer)* semestre *m*

semi... /'semɪ/ *pref* semi...

semi|breve /-briːv/ *n* redonda *f*. **~circle** *n* semicírculo *m*. **~colon** /-'kəʊlən/ *n* punto *m* y coma. **~-detached** /-dɪ'tætʃt/ *adj (house)* adosado. **~final** /-'faɪnl/ *n* semifinal *f*

seminar /'semɪnɑː(r)/ *n* seminario *m*

senat|e /'senɪt/ *n* senado *m*. **the S~e** *(Amer)* el Senado. **~or** /-ətə(r)/ *n* senador *m*

send /send/ *vt/i (pt* **sent**) mandar, enviar. □ **~ away** *vt* despedir. □ **~ away for** *vt* pedir (por correo). □ **~ for** *vt* enviar a buscar. □ **~ off for** *vt* pedir (por correo). □ **~ up** *vt* [1] parodiar. **~er** *n* remitente *m*. **~-off** *n* despedida *f*

senile /'siːnaɪl/ *adj* senil

senior /'siːnɪə(r)/ *adj* mayor; *(in rank)* superior; *(partner etc)* principal. ● *n* mayor *m & f.* **~ citizen** *n* jubilado *m*. **~ high school** *n (Amer)* colegio *m* secundario. **~ity** /-'ɒrəti/ *n* antigüedad *f*

sensation /sen'seɪʃn/ *n* sensación *f.* **~al** *adj* sensacional

sens|e /sens/ *n* sentido *m*; *(common sense)* juicio *m*; *(feeling)* sensación *f.* **make ~e** *vt* tener sentido. **make ~e of sth** entender algo. **~eless** *adj* sin sentido. **~ible**

/'sensəbl/ adj sensato; (clothing) práctico. ~itive /'sensɪtɪv/ adj sensible; (touchy) susceptible. ~itivity /-'tɪvɪtɪ/ n sensibilidad f. ~ual /'senʃʊəl/ adj sensual. ~uous /'sensʊəs/ adj sensual

sent /sent/ see SEND

sentence /'sentəns/ n frase f; (judgment) sentencia f; (punishment) condena f. ● vt. ~ **to** condenar a

sentiment /'sentɪmənt/ n sentimiento m; (opinion) opinión f. ~al /-'mentl/ adj sentimental. ~ality /-'tælətɪ/ n sentimentalismo m

sentry /'sentrɪ/ n centinela f

separa|ble /'sepərəbl/ adj separable. ~**te** /'separət/ adj separado; (independent) independiente. ● vt /'separeɪt/ separar. ● vi separarse. ~**tely** /'separətlɪ/ adv por separado. ~**tion** /-'reɪʃn/ n separación f. ~**tist** /'separətɪst/ n separatista m & f

September /sep'tembə(r)/ n se(p)tiembre m

septic /'septɪk/ adj séptico

sequel /'siːkwəl/ n continuación f; (later events) secuela f

sequence /'siːkwəns/ n sucesión f; (of film) secuencia f

Serb /sɜːb/ adj & n see SERBIAN. ~**ia** /'sɜːbɪə/ n Serbia f ~**ian** adj & n serbio m

serenade /serə'neɪd/ n serenata f. ● vt dar serenata a

serene /sɪ'riːn/ adj sereno

sergeant /'sɑːdʒənt/ n sargento m

serial /'sɪərɪəl/ n serie f. ~**ize** vt serializar

series /'sɪəriːz/ n serie f

serious /'sɪərɪəs/ adj serio. ~**ly** adv seriamente; (ill) gravemente. take ~**ly** tomar en serio

sermon /'sɜːmən/ n sermón m

serum /'sɪərəm/ n (pl -a) suero m

servant /'sɜːvənt/ n criado m

serve /sɜːv/ vt servir; servir a (country); cumplir (sentence). ~ **as** servir de. it ~**s you right** ¡bien te lo mereces! ● vi servir; (in tennis) sacar. ● n (in tennis) saque m. ~**r** (Comp) servidor m

service /'sɜːvɪs/ n servicio m; (of car etc) revisión f. ● vt revisar (car etc). ~ **charge** n (in restaurant) servicio m. ~**s** npl (Mil) fuerzas fpl armadas. ~ **station** n estación f de servicio

serviette /sɜːvɪ'et/ n servilleta f

servile /'sɜːvaɪl/ adj servil

session /'seʃn/ n sesión f

set /set/ vt (pt set, pres p setting) poner; poner en hora (clock etc); fijar (limit etc); (typeset) componer. ~ **fire** to prender fuego a. ~ **free** vt poner en libertad. ● vi (sun) ponerse; (jelly) cuajarse. ● n serie f; (of cutlery etc) juego m; (tennis) set m; (TV, Radio) aparato m; (in theatre) decorado m; (of people) círculo m. ● adj fijo. **be** ~ **on** estar resuelto a. □ ~ **back** vt (delay) retardar; (fam, cost) costar. □ ~ **off** vi salir. vt hacer sonar (alarm); hacer explotar (bomb). □ ~ **out** vt exponer (argument). vi (leave) salir. □ ~ **up** vt establecer. ~**back** n revés m

settee /se'tiː/ n sofá m

setting /'setɪŋ/ n (of dial, switch) posición f

settle /'setl/ vt (arrange) acordar; arreglar (matter); resolver (dispute); pagar (bill); saldar (debt). ● vi (live) establecerse. □ ~ **down** vi calmarse; (become more responsible) sentar (la) cabeza. □ ~ **for** vt aceptar. □ ~ **up** vi arreglar cuentas. **~ment** n establecimiento m; (agreement) acuerdo m; (of debt) liquidación f; (colony) colonia f. **~r** n colono m

set: ~to n pelea f. **~up** n 🔢 sistema m; (con) tinglado m

seven /'sevn/ adj & n siete (m). **~teen** /sevn'ti:n/ adj & n diecisiete (m). **~teenth** adj decimoséptimo. ● n diecisietavo m. **~th** adj & n séptimo (m). **~tieth** /'sevntπθ/ adj septuagésimo. ● n setentavo m. **~ty** /'sevntπ/ adj & n setenta (m)

sever /'sevə(r)/ vt cortar; (fig) romper

several /'sevrəl/ adj & pron varios

sever|e /sɪ'vɪə(r)/ adj (**-er, -est**) severo; (serious) grave; (weather) riguroso. **~ely** adv severamente. **~ity** /sɪ'verətɪ/ n severidad f; (seriousness) gravedad f

sew /səʊ/ vt/i (pt sewed, pp sewn, or sewed) coser. **□ ~ up** vt coser

sew|age /'su:ɪdʒ/ n aguas fpl residuales. **~er** /'su:ə(r)/ n cloaca f

sewing /'səʊɪŋ/ n costura f. **~-machine** n máquina f de coser

sewn /səʊn/ see **sew**

sex /seks/ n sexo m. **have ~** tener relaciones sexuales. ● adj sexual. **~ist** adj & n sexista (m & f). **~ual** /'sekʃʊəl/ adj sexual. **~ual intercourse** n relaciones fpl sexuales. **~uality** /-'ælɪtɪ/ n sexualidad f. **~y** adj (**-ier, -iest**) excitante, sexy, provocativo

shabby /'ʃæbɪ/ adj (**-ier, -iest**) (clothes) gastado; (person) pobremente vestido

shack /ʃæk/ n choza f

shade /ʃeɪd/ n sombra f; (of colour) tono m; (for lamp) pantalla f; (nuance) matiz m; (Amer, over window) persiana f

shadow /'ʃædəʊ/ n sombra f. ● vt (follow) seguir de cerca a. **~y** adj (fig) vago

shady /'ʃeɪdɪ/ adj (**-ier, -iest**) sombreado; (fig) turbio; (character) sospechoso

shaft /ʃɑ:ft/ n (of arrow) astil m; (Mec) eje m; (of light) rayo m; (of lift, mine) pozo m

shaggy /'ʃægɪ/ adj (**-ier, -iest**) peludo

shake /ʃeɪk/ vt (pt shook, pp shaken) sacudir; agitar (bottle); (shock) desconcertar. **~ hands with** estrechar la mano a. **~ one's head** negar con la cabeza; (Amer, meaning yes) asentir con la cabeza. ● vi temblar. **□ ~ off** vi deshacerse de. ● n sacudida f

shaky /'ʃeɪkɪ/ adj (**-ier, -iest**) tembloroso; (table etc) inestable

shall /ʃæl/ modal verb. **we ~ see** veremos. **~ we go to the cinema?** ¿vamos al cine?

shallow /'ʃæləʊ/ adj (**-er, -est**) poco profundo; (fig) superficial

sham /ʃæm/ n farsa f. ● adj fingido

shambles /'ʃæmblz/ npl (fam, mess) caos m

shame /ʃeɪm/ n (feeling) vergüenza f. **what a ~!** ¡qué lástima! ● vt avergonzar. **~ful** adj vergonzoso. **~less** adj desvergonzado

shampoo /ʃæm'pu:/ n champú m. ● vt lavar

shan't /ʃɑ:nt/ = **shall not**

shape /ʃeɪp/ n forma f. ● vt formar; determinar (future). ● vi tomar forma. **~less** adj informe

share /ʃeə(r)/ n porción f; (Com) acción f. ● vt compartir; (divide) dividir. ● vi compartir. **~ in sth** participar en algo. **□ ~ out** vt repartir. **~holder** n accionista m & f. **~out**

521

n reparto m

shark /ʃɑːk/ n tiburón m

sharp /ʃɑːp/ adj (-er, -est) (knife etc) afilado; (pin etc) puntiagudo; (pain, sound) agudo; (taste) ácido; (bend) cerrado; (contrast) marcado; (clever) listo; (Mus) sostenido. ● adv en punto. **at seven o'clock** ∼ a las siete en punto. ● n (Mus) sostenido m. ∼**en** vt afilar; sacar punta a (pencil). ∼**ener** n (Mec) afilador m; (for pencils) sacapuntas m. ∼**ly** adv bruscamente

shatter /ˈʃætə(r)/ vt hacer añicos. **he was** ∼**ed by the news** la noticia lo dejó destrozado. ● vi hacerse añicos. ∼**ed** /ˈʃætəd/ adj (exhausted) agotado

shav|e /ʃeɪv/ vt afeitar, rasurar (Mex). ● vi afeitarse, rasurarse (Mex). ● n afeitada f, rasurada f (Mex). **have a** ∼**e** afeitarse. ∼**er** n maquinilla f (de afeitar). ∼**ing brush** n brocha f de afeitar. ∼**ing cream** n crema f de afeitar

shawl /ʃɔːl/ n chal m

she /ʃiː/ pron ella

sheaf /ʃiːf/ n (pl **sheaves** /ʃiːvz/) gavilla f

shear /ʃɪə(r)/ vt (pp **shorn** or **sheared**) esquilar. ∼**s** /ʃɪəz/ npl tijeras fpl grandes

shed /ʃed/ n cobertizo m. ● vt (pt **shed**, pres p **shedding**) perder; derramar (tears); despojarse de (clothes). ∼ **light on** arrojar luz sobre

she'd /ʃiː(ə)d/ = **she had, she would**

sheep /ʃiːp/ n invar oveja f. ∼**dog** n perro m pastor. ∼**ish** adj avergonzado

sheer /ʃɪə(r)/ adj (as intensifier) puro; (steep) perpendicular

sheet /ʃiːt/ n sábana f; (of paper) hoja f; (of glass) lámina f; (of ice) capa f

shelf /ʃelf/ n (pl **shelves**) estante m. **a set of shelves** unos estantes

shell /ʃel/ n concha f; (of egg) cáscara f; (of crab, snail, tortoise) caparazón m or f; (explosive) proyectil m, obús m. ● vt pelar (peas etc); (Mil) bombardear

she'll /ʃiːl/ = **she had, she would**

shellfish /ˈʃelfɪʃ/ n invar marisco m; (collectively) mariscos mpl

shelter /ˈʃeltə(r)/ n refugio m. **take** ∼ refugiarse. ● vt darle cobijo a (fugitive); (protect from weather) resguardar. ● vi refugiarse. ∼**ed** /ˈʃeltəd/ adj (spot) abrigado; (life) protegido

shelv|e /ʃelv/ vt (fig) dar carpetazo a. ∼**ing** n estantería f

shepherd /ˈʃepəd/ n pastor m. ∼**ess** /-ˈdes/ n pastora f

sherbet /ˈʃɜːbət/ n (Amer, water ice) sorbete m

sheriff /ˈʃerɪf/ n (in US) sheriff m

sherry /ˈʃerɪ/ n (vino m de) jerez m

she's /ʃiːz/ = **she is, she has**

shield /ʃiːld/ n escudo m. ● vt proteger

shift /ʃɪft/ vt cambiar; correr (furniture etc). ● vi (wind) cambiar; (attention, opinion) pasar a; (Amer, change gear) cambiar de velocidad. ● n cambio m; (work) turno m; (workers) tanda f. ∼**y** adj (-ier, -iest) furtivo

shilling /ˈʃɪlɪŋ/ n chelín m

shimmer /ˈʃɪmə(r)/ vi rielar, relucir

shin /ʃɪn/ n espinilla f

shine /ʃaɪn/ vi (pt **shone**) brillar.

● *vt* sacar brillo a. **~ a light on sth** alumbrar algo con una luz. ● *n* brillo *m*

shingle /'ʃɪŋgl/ *n* (*pebbles*) guijarros *mpl*

shin|ing /'ʃaɪnɪŋ/ *adj* brillante. **~y** /'ʃaɪnɪ/ *adj* (**-ier, -iest**) brillante

ship /ʃɪp/ *n* barco *m*, buque *m*. ● *vt* (*pt* **shipped**) transportar; (*send*) enviar; (*load*) embarcar. **~building** *n* construcción *f* naval. **~ment** *n* envío *m*. **~ping** *n* transporte *m*; (*ships*) barcos *mpl*. **~shape** *adj* limpio y ordenado. **~wreck** *n* naufragio *m*. **~wrecked** *adj* naufragado. **be ~wrecked** naufragar. **~yard** *n* astillero *m*

shirk /ʃɜːk/ *vt* esquivar

shirt /ʃɜːt/ *n* camisa *f*. **in ~sleeves** en mangas de camisa

shit /ʃɪt/ *n* & *int* (*vulgar*) mierda *f*. ● *vi* (*vulgar*) (*pt* **shat**, *pres p* **shitting**) cagar

shiver /'ʃɪvə(r)/ *vi* temblar. ● *n* escalofrío *m*

shoal /ʃəʊl/ *n* banco *m*

shock /ʃɒk/ *n* (*of impact*) choque *m*; (*of earthquake*) sacudida *f*; (*surprise*) shock *m*; (*scare*) susto *m*; (*Elec*) descarga *f*; (*Med*) shock *m*. **get a ~** llevarse una shock. ● *vt* escandalizar; (*apall*) horrorizar. **~ing** *adj* escandaloso. Ⓘ espantoso

shod /ʃɒd/ *see* SHOE

shoddy /'ʃɒdɪ/ *adj* (**-ier, -iest**) mal hecho, de pacotilla

shoe /ʃuː/ *n* zapato *m*; (*of horse*) herradura *f*. ● *vt* (*pt* **shod**, *pres p* **shoeing**) herrar (horse). **~horn** *n* calzador *m*. **~lace** *n* cordón *m* (de zapato). **~ polish** *n* betún *m*

shone /ʃɒn/ *see* SHINE

shoo /ʃuː/ *vt* ahuyentar

shook /ʃʊk/ *see* SHAKE

shoot /ʃuːt/ *vt* (*pt* **shot**) disparar; rodar (film). ● *vi* (*hunt*) cazar. ● *n* (*of plant*) retoño *m*. **□ ~ down** *vt* derribar. **□ ~ out** *vi* (*rush*) salir disparado. **□ ~ up** *vi* (*prices*) dispararse; (*grow*) crecer mucho

shop /ʃɒp/ *n* tienda *f*. **go to the ~s** ir de compras. **talk ~** hablar del trabajo. ● *vi* (*pt* **shopping**) hacer compras. **go ~ping** ir de compras. **□ ~ around** *vi* buscar el mejor precio. **~ assistant** *n* dependiente *m*, dependienta *f*, empleado *m*, empleada *f* (LAm). **~keeper** *n* comerciante *m*, tendero *m*. **~lifter** *n* ladrón *m* (que roba en las tiendas). **~lifting** *n* hurto *m* (en las tiendas). **~per** *n* comprador *m*. **~ping** *n* (*purchases*) compras *fpl*. **do the ~ping** hacer la compra, hacer el mandado (Mex). **~ping bag** *n* bolsa *f* de la compra. **~ping cart** *n* (Amer) carrito *m* (de la compra). **~ping centre**, **~ping mall** (Amer) *n* centro *m* comercial. **~ping trolley** *n* carrito *m* de la compra. **~ steward** *n* enlace *m* sindical. **~ window** *n* escaparate *m*, vidriera *f* (LAm), aparador *m* (Mex)

shore /ʃɔː(r)/ *n* orilla *f*

shorn /ʃɔːn/ *see* SHEAR

short /ʃɔːt/ *adj* (**-er, -est**) corto; (*not lasting*) breve; (*person*) bajo; (*curt*) brusco. **a ~ time ago** hace poco. **be ~ of time/money** andar corto de tiempo/dinero. **Mick is ~ for Michael** Mick es el diminutivo de Michael. ● *adv* (*stop*) en seco. **we never went ~ of food** nunca nos faltó comida. ● *n*. **in ~** en resumen. **~age** /-ɪdʒ/ *n* escasez *f*, falta *f*. **~bread** *n* galleta *f* (de mantequilla). **~ circuit** *n* cortocircuito *m*. **~coming** *n* defecto *m*. **~cut** *n* atajo *m*. **~en** *vt* acortar.

~**hand** n taquigrafía f. ~**ly** adv (soon) dentro de poco. ~**ly before midnight** poco antes de la medianoche. ~**s** npl pantalones m cortos, shorts mpl; (Amer, underwear) calzoncillos mpl. ~**sighted** /-'saɪtɪd/ adj miope

shot /ʃɒt/ see SHOOT. ● n (from gun) disparo m; tiro m; (in soccer) tiro m, disparo m; (in other sports) tiro m; (Photo) foto f. **be a good/ poor** ~ ser un buen/mal tirador. **be off like a** ~ salir disparado. ~**gun** n escopeta f

should /ʃʊd, ʃəd/ modal verb. **I** ~ **go** debería ir. **you** ~**n't have said that** no deberías haber dicho eso. **I** ~ **like to see her** me gustaría verla. **if he** ~ **come** si viniese

shoulder /'ʃəʊldə(r)/ n hombro m. ● vt cargar con (responsibility); ponerse al hombro (burden). ~**blade** n omóplato m

shout /ʃaʊt/ n grito m. ● vt/i gritar. ~ **at s.o.** gritarle a uno

shove /ʃʌv/ n empujón m. ● vt empujar; (fam, put) poner. ● vi empujar. □ ~ **off** vi 🗓 largarse

shovel /'ʃʌvl/ n pala f. ● vt (pt shovelled) palear (coal); espalar (snow)

show /ʃəʊ/ vt (pt showed, pp shown) mostrar; (put on display) exponer; poner (film). **I'll** ~ **you to your room** lo acompaño a su cuarto. ● vi (be visible) verse. ● n muestra f; (exhibition) exposición f; (in theatre) espectáculo m; (on TV, radio) programa m; (ostentation) pompa f. **be on** ~ estar expuesto. □ ~ **off** vt (pej) lucir, presumir de. vi presumir, lucirse. □ ~ **up** vi (be visible) notarse; (arrive) aparecer. vt (reveal) poner de manifiesto; (embarrass) hacer quedar mal. ~**case**

n vitrina f. ~**down** n confrontación f

shower /'ʃaʊə(r)/ n (of rain) chaparrón m; (for washing) ducha f. **have a** ~, **take a** ~ ducharse. ● vi ducharse

showjumping n concurso mpl hípicos.

shown /ʃəʊn/ see SHOW

show: ~**off** n fanfarrón m. ~**room** n sala f de exposición f. ~**y** adj (-ier, -iest) llamativo; (attractive) ostentoso

shrank /ʃræŋk/ see SHRINK

shred /ʃred/ n pedazo m; (fig) pizca f. ● vt (pt shredded) hacer tiras; destruir, triturar (documents). ~**der** n (for paper) trituradora f; (for vegetables) cortadora f

shrewd /ʃruːd/ adj (-er, -est) astuto

shriek /ʃriːk/ n chillido m; (of pain) alarido m. ● vt/i chillar

shrift /ʃrɪft/ n. **give s.o. short** ~ despachar a uno con brusquedad. **give sth short** ~ desestimar algo de plano

shrill /ʃrɪl/ adj agudo

shrimp /ʃrɪmp/ n gamba f, camarón m (LAm); (Amer, large) langostino m

shrine /ʃraɪn/ n (place) santuario m; (tomb) sepulcro m

shrink /ʃrɪŋk/ vt (pt shrank, pp shrunk) encoger. ● vi encogerse; (amount) reducirse; retroceder (recoil)

shrivel /'ʃrɪvl/ vi (pt shrivelled). ~ (**up**) (plant) marchitarse; (fruit) resecarse y arrugarse

shroud /ʃraʊd/ n mortaja f; (fig) velo m. ● vt envolver

Shrove /ʃrəʊv/ n. ~ **Tuesday** n martes m de carnaval

s

shrub /ʃrʌb/ n arbusto m

shrug /ʃrʌg/ vt (pt shrugged) encogerse de hombros

shrunk /ʃrʌŋk/ see SHRINK. **~en** adj encogido

shudder /'ʃʌdə(r)/ vi estremecerse. ● n estremecimiento m

shuffle /'ʃʌfl/ vi andar arrastrando los pies. ● vt barajar (cards). **~ one's feet** arrastrar los pies

shun /ʃʌn/ vt (pt shunned) evitar

shunt /ʃʌnt/ vt cambiar de vía

shush /ʃʊʃ/ int ¡chitón!

shut /ʃʌt/ vt (pt shut, pres p shutting) cerrar. ● vi cerrarse. ● adj. be **~** estar cerrado. **~ down** vt/i cerrar. □ **~ up** vt cerrar; 🔲 hacer callar. vi callarse. **~ter** n contraventana f; (Photo) obturador m

shuttle /'ʃʌtl/ n lanzadera f; (by air) puente m aéreo; (space **~**) transbordador m espacial. ● vi. **~ (back and forth)** ir y venir. **~cock** n volante m. **~ service** n servicio m de enlace

shy /ʃaɪ/ adj (-er, -est) tímido. ● vi (pt shied) asustarse. **~ness** n timidez f

sick /sɪk/ adj enfermo; (humour) negro; (fam, fed up) harto. **be ~** estar enfermo; (vomit) vomitar. **be ~ of** (fig) estar harto de. **feel ~** sentir náuseas. **get ~** (Amer) caer enfermo, enfermarse (LAm). **~ leave** n permiso m por enfermedad, baja f por enfermedad. **~ly** /'sɪklɪ/ adj (-lier, -liest) enfermizo; (taste, smell etc) nauseabundo. **~ness** /'sɪknɪs/ n enfermedad f

side /saɪd/ n lado m; (of hill) ladera f; (of person) costado m; (team) equipo m; (fig) parte f. **~ by ~** uno al lado del otro. **take ~s** tomar partido. ● adj lateral. □ **~**

with vt ponerse de parte de. **~board** n aparador m. **~dish** n acompañamiento m. **~effect** n efecto m secundario; (fig) consecuencia f indirecta. **~line** n actividad f suplementaria. **~ road** n calle f secundaria. **~step** vt eludir. **~track** vt desviar del tema. **~walk** n (Amer) acera f, vereda f (LAm), banqueta f (Mex). **~ways** adj & adv de lado

siding /'saɪdɪŋ/ n apartadero m

sidle /'saɪdl/ vi. **~ up to s.o.** acercarse furtivamente a uno

siege /siːdʒ/ n sitio m

sieve /sɪv/ n tamiz m. ● vt tamizar, cernir

sift /sɪft/ vt tamizar, cernir. ● vi. **~ through sth** pasar algo por el tamiz

sigh /saɪ/ n suspiro m. ● vi suspirar

sight /saɪt/ n vista f; (spectacle) espectáculo m; (on gun) mira f. **at first ~** a primera vista. **catch ~ of** ver; (in distance) avistar. **lose ~ of** perder de vista. **see the ~s** visitar los lugares de interés. **within ~ of** (near) cerca de. ● vt ver; divisar (land). **~seeing** n. **go ~** ir a visitar los lugares de interés. **~seer** /-siːə(r)/ n turista m & f

sign /saɪn/ n (indication) señal f, indicio m; (gesture) señal f, seña f; (notice) letrero m; (astrological) signo m. ● vt firmar. □ **~ on** vi (for unemployment benefit) anotarse para recibir el seguro de desempleo

signal /'sɪgnəl/ n señal f. ● vt (pt signalled) señalar. ● vi. **~ (to s.o.)** hacer señas (a uno); (Auto) poner el intermitente, señalizar

signature /'sɪgnətʃə(r)/ n firma f. **~ tune** n sintonía f

significan|ce /sɪgˈnɪfɪkəns/ n importancia f. **~t** adj (important) importante; (fact, remark) significativo

signify /ˈsɪgnɪfaɪ/ vt significar

signpost /ˈsaɪmpəʊst/ n señal f, poste m indicador

silen|ce /ˈsaɪləns/ n silencio m. ● vt hacer callar. **~cer** n (on gun and on car) silenciador m. **~t** adj silencioso; (film) mudo. **remain ~t** quedarse callado. **~tly** adv silenciosamente

silhouette /ˌsɪluːˈet/ n silueta f. ● vt. **be ~d** perfilarse (**against** contra)

silicon /ˈsɪlɪkən/ n silicio m. **~ chip** n pastilla f de silicio

silk /sɪlk/ n seda f. **~y** adj (of silk) de seda; (like silk) sedoso

silly /ˈsɪlɪ/ adj (-ier, -iest) tonto

silt /sɪlt/ n cieno m

silver /ˈsɪlvə(r)/ n plata f. ● adj de plata. **~-plated** adj bañado en plata, plateado. **~ware** /-weə(r)/ n platería f

simil|ar /ˈsɪmɪlə(r)/ adj parecido, similar. **~arity** /-ˈlærətɪ/ n parecido m. **~arly** adv de igual manera. **~e** /ˈsɪmɪlɪ/ n símil m

simmer /ˈsɪmə(r)/ vt/i hervir a fuego lento. □ **~ down** vi calmarse

simpl|e /ˈsɪmpl/ adj (-er, -est) sencillo, simple; (person) (humble) simple; (backward) simple. **~e-minded** /-ˈmaɪndɪd/ adj ingenuo. **~icity** /-ˈplɪsətɪ/ n simplicidad f, sencillez f. **~ify** /ˈsɪmplɪfaɪ/ vt simplificar. **~y** adv sencillamente, simplemente; (absolutely) realmente

simulate /ˈsɪmjʊleɪt/ vt simular

simultaneous /ˌsɪmlˈteɪnɪəs/ adj simultáneo. **~ly** adv simultáneamente

sin /sɪn/ n pecado m. ● vi (pt sinned) pecar

since /sɪns/

● preposition desde. **he's been living here ~ 1991** vive aquí desde 1991. **~ Christmas** desde Navidad. **~ then** desde entonces. **I haven't been feeling well ~ Sunday** desde el domingo no me siento bien. **how long is it ~ your interview?** ¿cuánto (tiempo) hace de la entrevista?

● adverb desde entonces. **I haven't spoken to her ~** no he hablado con ella desde entonces

● conjunction

····► desde que. **I haven't seen her ~ she left** no la he visto desde que se fue. **~ coming to Manchester** desde que vine (or vino etc) a Manchester. **it's ten years ~ he died** hace diez años que se murió

····► (because) como, ya que. **~ it was quite late, I decided to stay** como or ya que era bastante tarde, decidí quedarme

sincer|e /sɪnˈsɪə(r)/ adj sincero. **~ely** adv sinceramente. **yours ~ely, ~ely (yours)** (in letters) (saluda) a usted atentamente. **~ity** /-ˈserətɪ/ n sinceridad f

sinful /ˈsɪnfl/ adj (person) pecador; (act) pecaminoso

sing /sɪŋ/ vt/i (pt sang, pp sung) cantar

singe /sɪndʒ/ vt (pres p singeing) chamuscar

singer /ˈsɪŋə(r)/ n cantante m & f

single /ˈsɪŋgl/ adj solo; (not

double) sencillo; (*unmarried*) soltero; (bed, room) individual, de una plaza (*LAm*); (ticket) de ida, sencillo. **not a ~ house** ni una sola casa. **every ~ day** todos los días sin excepción. ● *n* (*ticket*) billete *m* sencillo, boleto *m* de ida (*LAm*). ▫ **~ out** *vt* escoger; (*distinguish*) distinguir. **~-handed** /-ˈhændɪd/ *adj & adv* sin ayuda. **~s** *npl* (*Sport*) individuales *mpl*

singular /ˈsɪŋɡjʊlə(r)/ *n* singular *f*. ● *adj* singular; (*unusual*) raro; (noun) en singular

sinister /ˈsɪnɪstə(r)/ *adj* siniestro

sink /sɪŋk/ *vt* (*pt* **sank**, *pp* **sunk**) hundir. ● *vi* hundirse. ● *n* fregadero *m* (*Amer*, in bathroom) lavabo *m*, lavamanos *m*. ▫ **~ in** *vi* penetrar

sinner /ˈsɪnə(r)/ *n* pecador *m*

sip /sɪp/ *n* sorbo *m*. ● *vt* (*pt* **sipped**) sorber

siphon /ˈsaɪfən/ *n* sifón *m*. ▫ **~ (out)** sacar con sifón. ▫ **~ off** *vt* desviar (money).

sir /sɜː(r)/ *n* señor *m*. **S~** *n* (title) sir *m*. **Dear S~**, (*in letters*) De mi mayor consideración.

siren /ˈsaɪərən/ *n* sirena *f*

sister /ˈsɪstə(r)/ *n* hermana *f*; (*nurse*) enfermera *f* jefe. **~-in-law** *n* (*pl* **~s-in-law**) cuñada *f*

sit /sɪt/ *vi* (*pt* **sat**, *pres p* **sitting**) sentarse; (committee etc) reunirse en sesión. **be ~ting** estar sentado. ● *vt* sentar; hacer (exam). ▫ **~ back** *vi* (*fig*) relajarse. ▫ **~ down** *vi* sentarse. **be ~ting down** estar sentado. ▫ **~ up** *vi* (*from lying*) incorporarse; (*straighten back*) ponerse derecho. **~-in** *n* (strike) encierro *m*, ocupación *f*

site /saɪt/ *n* emplazamiento *m*; (*piece of land*) terreno *m*; (*archaeo-*

logical) yacimiento *m*. **building ~** *n* solar *m*. ● *vt* situar

sit **~ting** *n* sesión *f*; (in restaurant) turno *m*. **~ting room** *n* sala *f* de estar, living *m*

situat|e /ˈsɪtjʊeɪt/ *vt* situar. **~ion** /-ˈeɪʃn/ *n* situación *f*

six /sɪks/ *adj & n* seis (*m*). **~teen** /sɪksˈtiːn/ *adj & n* dieciséis (*m*). **~teenth** *adj & n* decimosexto. ● *n* dieciseisavo *m*. **~th** *adj & n* sexto (*m*). **~tieth** /ˈsɪkstɪɪθ/ *adj* sexagésimo. ● *n* sesentavo *m*. **~ty** /ˈsɪkstɪ/ *adj & n* sesenta (*m*)

size /saɪz/ *n* tamaño *m*; (of clothes) talla *f*; (of shoes) número *m*; (of problem, operation) magnitud *f*. **what ~ do you take?** (clothes) ¿qué talla tiene?; (shoes) ¿qué número calza?. ▫ **~ up** *vt* ① evaluar (problem); calar (person)

sizzle /ˈsɪzl/ *vi* crepitar

skat|e /skeɪt/ *n* patín *m*. ● *vi* patinar. **~eboard** *n* monopatín *m*, patineta *f* (Mex). **~er** *n* patinador *m*. **~ing** *n* patinaje *m*. **~ing-rink** *n* pista *f* de patinaje

skeleton /ˈskelɪtn/ *n* esqueleto *m*. **~ key** *n* llave *f* maestra

sketch /sketʃ/ *n* (drawing) dibujo *m*; (rougher) esbozo *m*; (TV, Theatre) sketch *m*. ● *vt* esbozar. ● *vi* dibujar. **~y** *adj* (-ier, -iest) incompleto

ski /skiː/ *n* (*pl* **skis**) esquí *m*. ● *vi* (*pt* **skied**, *pres p* **skiing**) esquiar. **go ~ing** ir a esquiar

skid /skɪd/ *vi* (*pt* **skidded**) patinar. ● *n* patinazo *m*

ski: **~er** *n* esquiador *m*. **~ing** *n* esquí *m*

skilful /ˈskɪlfl/ *adj* diestro

ski-lift /ˈskiːlɪft/ *n* telesquí *m*

skill /skɪl/ *n* habilidad *f*; (technical) destreza *f*. **~ed** *adj* hábil; (worker) cualificado

skim /skɪm/ vt (pt **skimmed**) espumar (soup); desnatar, descremar (milk); (glide over) pasar casi rozando. ~ **milk** (Amer), ~**med milk** n leche f desnatada, leche f descremada. ~ **through** vt leer por encima

skimp /skɪmp/ vi. ~ **on** sth escatimar algo. ~**y** adj (-**ier**, -**iest**) escaso; (skirt, dress) brevísimo

skin /skɪn/ n piel f (pt **skinned**) despellejar. ~**-deep** adj superficial. ~**-diving** n submarinismo m. ~**ny** adj (-**ier**, -**iest**) flaco

skip /skɪp/ vi (pt **skipped**) vi saltar; (with rope) saltar a la comba, saltar a la cuerda. ● vt saltarse (chapter); faltar a (class). ● n brinco m; (container) contenedor m (para escombros). ~**per** n capitán m. ~**ping-rope**, ~**rope** (Amer) n comba f, cuerda f de saltar, reata f (Mex)

skirmish /ˈskɜːmɪʃ/ n escaramuza f

skirt /skɜːt/ n falda f. ● vt bordear; (go round) ladear. ~**ing-board** n rodapié m, zócalo m

skittle /ˈskɪtl/ n bolo m

skive off /skaɪv/ (vi 🔲, disappear) escurrir el bulto; (stay away from work) no ir a trabajar

skulk /skʌlk/ vi (hide) esconderse. ~ **around** vi merodear

skull /skʌl/ n cráneo m; (remains) calavera f

sky /skaɪ/ n cielo m. ~**lark** n alondra f. ~**light** n tragaluz m. ~ **marshal** n guardia m armado a bordo. ~**scraper** n rascacielos m

slab /slæb/ n (of concrete) bloque m; (of stone) losa f

slack /slæk/ adj (-**er**, -**est**) flojo;

(person) poco aplicado; (period) de poca actividad. ● vi flojear. ~**en** vt aflojar. ● vi (person) descansar. □ ~**en off** vt/i aflojar

slain /sleɪn/ see SLAY

slake /sleɪk/ vt apagar

slam /slæm/ vt (pt **slammed**). ~ **the door** dar un portazo. ~ **the door shut** cerrar de un portazo. ~ **on the brakes** pegar un frenazo; (sl, criticize) atacar violentamente. ● vi cerrarse de un portazo

slander /ˈslɑːndə(r)/ n calumnia f. ● vt difamar

slang /slæŋ/ n argot m

slant /slɑːnt/ vt inclinar. ● n inclinación f

slap /slæp/ vt (pt **slapped**) (on face) pegarle una bofetada a; (put) tirar. ~ **s.o. on the back** darle una palmada a uno en la espalda. ● n bofetada f; (on back) palmada f. ● adv de lleno. ~**dash** adj descuidado; (work) chapucero

slash /slæʃ/ vt acuchillar; (fig) rebajar drásticamente. ● n cuchillada f

slat /slæt/ n tablilla f

slate /sleɪt/ n pizarra f. ● vt 🔲 poner los suelos

slaughter /ˈslɔːtə(r)/ vt matar salvajemente; matar (animal). ● n carnicería f; (of animals) matanza f

slave /sleɪv/ n esclavo m. ● vi ~ **(away)** trabajar como un negro. ~**-driver** n 🔲 negrero m. ~**ry** /-ərɪ/ n esclavitud f

slay /sleɪ/ vt (pt **slew**, pp **slain**) dar muerte a

sleazy /ˈsliːzɪ/ adj (-**ier**, -**iest**) 🔲 sórdido

sled /sled/ (Amer), **sledge** /sledʒ/ n trineo m

sledge-hammer n mazo m, almádena f

sleek /sliːk/ adj (-er, -est) liso, brillante

sleep /sliːp/ n sueño m. **go to ~** dormirse. ● vi (pt **slept**) dormir. ● vt poder alojar. **~er** n (on track) traviesa f, durmiente m. **be a light/heavy ~er** tener el sueño ligero/pesado. **~ing bag** n saco m de dormir. **~ing pill** n somnífero m. **~less** adj. **have a ~less night** pasar la noche en blanco. **~walk** vi caminar dormido. **~y** adj (-ier, -iest) soñoliento. **be/feel ~y** tener sueño

sleet /sliːt/ n aguanieve f

sleeve /sliːv/ n manga f; (for record) funda f, carátula f. **up one's ~** en reserva. **~less** adj sin mangas

sleigh /sleɪ/ n trineo m

slender /'slendə(r)/ adj delgado; (fig) escaso

slept /slept/ see SLEEP

slew /sluː/ see SLAY

slice /slaɪs/ n (of ham) lonja f; (of bread) rebanada f; (of meat) tajada f; (of cheese) trozo m; (of sth round) rodaja f. ● vt cortar (en rebanadas, tajadas etc)

slick /slɪk/ adj (performance) muy pulido. ● n. (oil) **~** marea f negra

slide /slaɪd/ vt (pt **slid**) deslizar. ● vi (intentionally) deslizarse; (unintentionally) resbalarse. ● n resbalón m; (in playground) tobogán m, resbaladilla f (Mex); (for hair) pasador m, broche m (Mex); (Photo) diapositiva f. **~ing scale** n escala f móvil

slight /slaɪt/ adj (-er, -est) ligero; (slender) delgado. ● vt desairar. ● n desaire m. **~est** adj mínimo. **not in the ~est** en absoluto. **~ly** adv un poco, ligeramente

slim /slɪm/ adj (slimmer, slim-

mest) delgado. ● vi (pt **slimmed**) (become slimmer) adelgazar; (diet) hacer régimen

slim|e /slaɪm/ n limo m, (of snail, slug) baba f. **~y** adj viscoso; (fig) excesivamente obsequioso

sling /slɪŋ/ n (Med) cabestrillo m. ● vt (pt **slung**) lanzar

slip /slɪp/ vt (pt **slipped**) deslizar. **~ s.o.'s mind** olvidársele a uno. ● vi resbalarse. **it ~ped out of my hands** se me resbaló de las manos. **he ~ped out the back door** se deslizó por la puerta trasera ● n resbalón m; (mistake) error m; (petticoat) combinación f; (paper) trozo m. **give s.o. the ~** lograr zafarse de uno. **~ of the tongue** n lapsus m linguae. □ **~ away** vi escabullirse. □ **~ up** vi 🔟 equivocarse

slipper /'slɪpə(r)/ n zapatilla f

slippery /'slɪpərɪ/ adj resbaladizo

slip: ~ road n rampa f de acceso. **~shod** /'slɪpʃɒd/ adj descuidado. **~up** n 🔟 error m

slit /slɪt/ n raja f; (cut) corte m. ● vt (pt **slit**, pres p **slitting**) rajar; (cut) cortar

slither /'slɪðə(r)/ vi deslizarse

slobber /'slɒbə(r)/ vi babear

slog /slɒg/ vt (pt **slogged**) golpear. ● vi caminar trabajosamente. ● n golpetazo m; (hard work) trabajo m penoso. □ **~ away** vi sudar tinta 🔟

slogan /'sləʊgən/ n eslogan m

slop /slɒp/ vt (pt **slopped**) derramar. ● vi derramarse

slop|e /sləʊp/ vi inclinarse. ● vt inclinar. ● n declive m, pendiente f. **~ing** adj inclinado

sloppy /'slɒpɪ/ adj (-ier, -iest) (work) descuidado; (person) desaliñado

slosh /slɒʃ/ vi 🗹 chapotear

slot /slɒt/ n ranura f. ● vt (pt **slot-ted**) encajar

slot-machine n distribuidor m automático; (for gambling) máquina f tragamonedas

slouch /slaʊtʃ/ vi andar cargado de espaldas; (in chair) repanchigarse

Slovak /ˈsləʊvæk/ adj & n eslovaco (m). **~ia** n Eslovaquia f

slovenly /ˈslʌvnlɪ/ adj (work) descuidado; (person) desaliñado

slow /sləʊ/ adj (-er, -est) lento. be ~ (clock) estar atrasado. in ~ motion a cámara lenta. ● adv despacio. ● vt retardar. ● vi ir más despacio. □ ~ **down**, □ ~ **up** vt retardar. vi ir más despacio. **~ly** adv despacio, lentamente

sludge /slʌdʒ/ n fango m

slug /slʌg/ n babosa f. **~gish** adj lento

slum /slʌm/ n barrio m bajo

slumber /ˈslʌmbə(r)/ vi dormir

slump /slʌmp/ n baja f repentina; (in business) depresión f. ● vi desplomarse

slung /slʌŋ/ see **SLING**

slur /slɜː(r)/ vt (pt slurred). ~ one's words arrastrar las palabras. ● n. a racist ~ un comentario racista

slush /slʌʃ/ n nieve f medio derretida. ~ **fund** n fondo m de reptiles

sly /slaɪ/ adj (slyer, slyest) (crafty) astuto. ● n. on the ~ a hurtadillas. **~ly** adv astutamente

smack /smæk/ n manotazo m. ● adv 🗹 ~ **in the middle** justo en el medio. **he went** ~ **into a tree** se dio contra un árbol. ● vt pegarle a (con la mano)

small /smɔːl/ adj (-er, -est) pequeño, chico (LAm). ● n. the ~ of the back la región lumbar. ~ **ads** npl anuncios mpl (clasificados), avisos mpl (clasificados) (LAm). ~ **change** n suelto m. **~pox** /-pɒks/ n viruela f. ~ **talk** n charla f sobre temas triviales

smart /smɑːt/ adj (-er, -est) elegante; (clever) listo; (brisk) rápido. ● vi escocer. □ ~ **en up** vt arreglar. vi (person) mejorar su aspecto, arreglarse. **~ly** adv elegantemente; (quickly) rápidamente

smash /smæʃ/ vt romper; (into little pieces) hacer pedazos; batir (record). ● vi romperse; (collide) chocar (into con). ● n (noise) estrépito m; (collision) choque m; (in sport) smash m. □ ~ **up** vt destrozar. **~ing** adj 🗹 estupendo

smattering /ˈsmætərɪŋ/ n nociones fpl

smear /smɪə(r)/ vt untar (with de); (stain) manchar (with de); (fig) difamar. ● n mancha f

smell /smel/ n olor m; (sense) olfato m. ● vt (pt smelt) oler; (animal) olfatear. ● vi oler. ~ **of sth** oler a algo. **~y** adj maloliente. **be ~y** oler mal

smelt /smelt/ see **SMELL**. ● vt fundir

smile /smaɪl/ n sonrisa f. ● vi sonreír. ~ **at s.o.** sonreírle a uno

smirk /smɜːk/ n sonrisita f (de suficiencia etc)

smith /smɪθ/ n herrero m

smithereens /smɪðəˈriːnz/ npl. smash sth to ~ hacer algo añicos

smock /smɒk/ n blusa f, bata f

smog /smɒg/ n smog m

smok|e /sməʊk/ n humo m. ● vt fumar (tobacco); ahumar (food).

● *vi* fumar. **~eless** *adj* que arde sin humo. **~er** *n* fumador *m*. **~y** *adj* (room) lleno de humo

smooth /smuːð/ *adj* (-er, -est) (texture/stone) liso; (skin) suave; (movement) suave; (sea) tranquilo. ● *vt* alisar. □ **~ out** *vt* allanar (problems). **~ly** *adv* suavemente; (without problems) sin problemas

smother /ˈsmʌðə(r)/ *vt* asfixiar (person). **~ s.o. with kisses** cubrir a uno de besos

smoulder /ˈsməʊldə(r)/ *vi* arder sin llama

smudge /smʌdʒ/ *n* borrón *m*. ● *vi* tiznarse

smug /smʌg/ *adj* (smugger, smuggest) pagado de sí mismo; (expression) de suficiencia

smuggl|e /ˈsmʌgl/ *vt* pasar de contrabando. **~er** *n* contrabandista *m & f*. **~ing** *n* contrabando *m*

snack /snæk/ *n* tentempié *m*. **~ bar** *n* cafetería *f*

snag /snæg/ *n* problema *m*

snail /sneɪl/ *n* caracol *m*. **at a ~'s pace** a paso de tortuga

snake /sneɪk/ *n* culebra *f*, serpiente *f*

snap /snæp/ *vt* (pt snapped) (break) romper. **~ one's fingers** chasquear los dedos. ● *vi* romperse; (dog) intentar morder; (say) contestar bruscamente. **~ at** (dog) intentar morder; (say) contestar bruscamente. ● *n* chasquido *m*; (Photo) foto *f*. *adj* instantáneo. □ **~ up** *vt* no dejar escapar (offer). **~py** *adj* (-ier, -iest) 🄳 rápido. **make it ~py!** ¡date prisa! **~shot** *n* foto *f*

snare /sneə(r)/ *n* trampa *f*

snarl /snɑːl/ *vi* gruñir

snatch /snætʃ/ *vt*. **~ sth from s.o.** arrebatarle algo a uno; (steal)

robar. ● *n* (short part) fragmento *m*

sneak /sniːk/ *n* soplón *m*. ● *vi* (päst & pp sneaked or 🄳 snuck) **~ in** entrar a hurtadillas. **~ off** escabullirse. **~ers** /ˈsniːkəz/ *npl* zapatillas *fpl* de deporte. **~y** *adj* artero

sneer /snɪə(r)/ *n* expresión *f* desdeñosa. ● *vi* hacer una mueca de desprecio. **~ at** hablar con desprecio a

sneeze /sniːz/ *n* estornudo *m*. ● *vi* estornudar

snide /snaɪd/ *adj* insidioso

sniff /snɪf/ *vt* oler. ● *vi* sorberse la nariz

snigger /ˈsnɪgə(r)/ *n* risilla *f*. ● *vi* reírse (por lo bajo)

snip /snɪp/ *vt* (pt snipped) dar un tijeretazo a. ● *n* tijeretazo *m*

sniper /ˈsnaɪpə(r)/ *n* francotirador *m*

snippet /ˈsnɪpɪt/ *n* (of conversation) trozo *m*. **~s of information** datos *mpl* aislados

snivel /ˈsnɪvl/ *vi* (pt snivelled) lloriquear

snob /snɒb/ *n* esnob *m & f*. **~bery** *n* esnobismo *m*. **~bish** *adj* esnob

snooker /ˈsnuːkə(r)/ *n* snooker *m*

snoop /snuːp/ *vi* 🄳 husmear

snooze /snuːz/ *n* sueñecito *m*. ● *vi* dormitar

snore /snɔː(r)/ *n* ronquido *m*. ● *vi* roncar

snorkel /ˈsnɔːkl/ *n* esnórkel *m*

snort /snɔːt/ *n* bufido *m*. ● *vi* bufar

snout /snaʊt/ *n* hocico *m*

snow /snəʊ/ *n* nieve *f*. ● *vi* nevar. **be ~ed in** estar aislado por la nieve. **be ~ed under with work** estar agobiado de trabajo. **~ball** *n* bola *f* de nieve. **~drift** *n* nieve *f* amontonada. **~fall** *n* nevada *f*.

~**flake** n copo m de nieve. ~**man** n muñeco m de nieve. ~**plough** n quitanieves m. ~**storm** n tormenta f de nieve. ~**y** adj (day, weather) nevoso; (landscape) nevado

snub /snʌb/ vt (pt snubbed) desairar. ● n desaire m. ~**-nosed** adj chato

snuck /snʌk/ see SNEAK

snuff out /snʌf/ vt apagar (candle)

snug /snʌg/ adj (snugger, snuggest) cómodo; (tight) ajustado

snuggle (up) /ˈsnʌgl/ vi acurrucarse

so /səʊ/ adv (before a or adv) tan; (thus) así; and ~ on, and ~ forth etcétera (etcétera). I think ~ creo que sí. or ~ más o menos. ~ long! ¡hasta luego! ● conj (therefore) así que. ~ am I yo también. ~ as to para. ~ far adv (time) hasta ahora. ~ far as I know que yo sepa. ~ that conj para que.

soak /səʊk/ vt remojar. ● vi remojarse. □ ~ in vi penetrar. □ ~ up vt absorber. ~**ing** adj empapado

so-and-so /ˈsəʊənsəʊ/ n fulano m

soap /səʊp/ n jabón m. ● vt enjabonar. ~ **opera** n telenovela f, culebrón m. ~ **powder** n jabón m en polvo. ~**y** adj jabonoso

soar /sɔː(r)/ vi (bird/plane) planear; (rise) elevarse; (price) dispararse. ~**ing** adj (inflation) galopante

sob /sɒb/ n sollozo m. ● vi (pt sobbed) sollozar

sober /ˈsəʊbə(r)/ adj (not drunk) sobrio

so-called /ˈsəʊkɔːld/ adj denominado; (expert) supuesto

soccer /ˈsɒkə(r)/ n fútbol m, futbol m (Mex)

sociable /ˈsəʊʃəbl/ adj sociable

social /ˈsəʊʃl/ adj social; (sociable) sociable. ~**ism** n socialismo m. ~**ist** adj & n socialista (m & f). ~**ize** vt socializar. ~ **security** n seguridad f social. ~ **worker** n asistente m social

society /səˈsaɪətɪ/ n sociedad f

sociolog|ical /səʊsɪəˈlɒdʒɪkl/ adj sociológico. ~**ist** /-ˈɒlədʒɪst/ n sociólogo m. ~**y** /-ˈɒlədʒɪ/ n sociología f

sock /sɒk/ n calcetín m

socket /ˈsɒkɪt/ n (of joint) hueco m; (of eye) cuenca f; (wall plug) enchufe m; (for bulb) portalámparas m

soda /ˈsəʊdə/ n soda f. ~**-water** n soda f

sodium /ˈsəʊdɪəm/ n sodio m

sofa /ˈsəʊfə/ n sofá m

soft /sɒft/ adj (-er, -est) blando; (light, colour) suave; (gentle) dulce, tierno; (not strict) blando. ~ **drink** n refresco m. ~**en** /ˈsɒfn/ vt ablandar; suavizar (skin). ● vi ablandarse. ~**ly** adv dulcemente; (speak) bajito. ~**ware** /-weə(r)/ n software m

soggy /ˈsɒgɪ/ adj (-ier, -iest) empapado

soil /sɔɪl/ n tierra f; (Amer, dirt) suciedad f. ● vt ensuciar

solar /ˈsəʊlə(r)/ adj solar

sold /səʊld/ see SELL

solder /ˈsɒldə(r)/ vt soldar

soldier /ˈsəʊldʒə(r)/ n soldado m. □ ~ **on** vi 🄵 seguir al pie del cañon

sole /səʊl/ n (of foot) planta f; (of shoe) suela f. ● adj único, solo. ~**ly** adv únicamente

solemn /ˈsɒləm/ adj solemne

solicitor /səˈlɪsɪtə(r)/ n abogado m; (notary) notario m

solid /ˈsɒlɪd/ adj sólido; (gold etc)

macizo; (*unanimous*) unánime; (*meal*) sustancioso. ● *n* sólido *m*. **~s** *npl* alimentos *mpl* sólidos. **~arity** /sɒlɪˈdærətɪ/ *n* solidaridad *f*. **~ify** /səˈlɪdɪfaɪ/ *vi* solidificarse

solitary /ˈsɒlɪtrɪ/ *adj* solitario

solitude /ˈsɒlɪtjuːd/ *n* soledad *f*

solo /ˈsəʊləʊ/ *n* (*pl* **-os**) (*Mus*) solo *m*. **~ist** *n* solista *m* & *f*

solstice /ˈsɒlstɪs/ *n* solsticio *m*

solu|ble /ˈsɒljʊbl/ *adj* soluble. **~tion** /səˈluːʃn/ *n* solución *f*

solve /sɒlv/ *vt* solucionar (problem); resolver (mystery). **~nt** /-vənt/ *adj* & *n* solvente (*m*)

sombre /ˈsɒmbə(r)/ *adj* sombrío

---

some /sʌm//səm/
● *adjective*
····➤ (*unspecified number*) unos, unas. he ate **~** olives comió unas aceitunas

····➤ (*unspecified amount*) *not translated.* I have to buy **~** bread tengo que comprar pan. would you like **~** coffee? ¿quieres café?

····➤ (*certain, not all*) algunos, -nas. I like **~** modern writers algunos escritores modernos me gustan

····➤ (*a little*) algo de. I eat **~** meat, but not much como algo de carne, pero no mucho

····➤ (*considerable amount of*) we've known each other for **~** time ya hace tiempo que nos conocemos

····➤ (*expressing admiration*) that's **~** car you've got! ¡vaya coche que tienes!

● *pronoun*
····➤ (*a number of things or*

people) algunos, -nas, unos, unas. **~** are mine and **~** aren't algunos o unos son míos y otros no. aren't there any apples? we bought **~** yesterday ¿no hay manzanas? compramos algunas ayer

····➤ (*part of an amount*) he wants **~** quiere un poco. **~** of what he said parte o algo de lo que dijo

····➤ (*certain people*) algunos, -nas **~** say that... algunos dicen que...

● *adverb*

····➤ (*approximately*) unos, unas, alrededor de. there were **~** fifty people there había unas cincuenta personas, había alrededor de cincuenta personas

---

some: **~body** /-bədɪ/ *pron* alguien. **~how** *adv* de algún modo. **~how** *or* **are** de una manera u otra. **~one** *pron* alguien

somersault /ˈsʌməsɔːlt/ *n* salto *m* mortal. ● *vi* dar un salto mortal

some: **~thing** *pron* algo *m*. **~thing like** (*approximately*) alrededor de. **~time** *adj* ex. ● *adv* algún día. **~time next week** un día de la semana que viene. **~times** *adv* a veces. **~what** *adv* un tanto. **~where** *adv* en alguna parte, en algún lado

son /sʌn/ *n* hijo *m*

sonata /səˈnɑːtə/ *n* sonata *f*

song /sɒŋ/ *n* canción *f*

sonic /ˈsɒnɪk/ *adj* sónico

son-in-law /ˈsʌnɪnlɔː/ *n* (*pl* **sons-in-law**) yerno *m*

sonnet /ˈsɒnɪt/ *n* soneto *m*

son of a bitch *n* (*pl* **sons of bitches**) (*esp Amer sl*) hijo *m* de puta

soon /suːn/ adv (-er, -est) pronto; (in a short time) dentro de poco. ~ after poco después. ~er or later tarde o temprano. as ~ as en cuanto; as ~ as possible lo antes posible. the ~er the better cuanto antes mejor

soot /sʊt/ n hollín m

sooth|e /suːð/ vt calmar; aliviar (pain). ~ing adj (medicine) calmante; (words) tranquilizador

sooty /'sʊti/ adj cubierto de hollín

sophisticated /sə'fɪstɪkeɪtɪd/ adj sofisticado; (complex) complejo

sophomore /'sɒfəmɔː(r)/ n (Amer) estudiante m & f de segundo curso en la universidad

sopping /'sɒpɪŋ/ adj. ~ (wet) empapado

soppy /'sɒpɪ/ adj (-ier, -iest) ⚀ sentimental

soprano /sə'prɑːnəʊ/ n (pl -os) soprano f

sordid /'sɔːdɪd/ adj sórdido

sore /sɔː(r)/ adj (-er, -est) dolorido; (Amer fam, angry) be ~ at s.o. estar picado con uno. ~ throat n dolor m de garganta. I've got a ~ throat me duele la garganta. ● n llaga f.

sorrow /'sɒrəʊ/ n pena f, pesar m

sorry /'sɒri/ adj (-ier, -ier) arrepentido; (wretched) lamentable. I'm ~ lo siento. be ~ for s.o. (pity) compadecer a uno. I'm ~ you can't come siento que no puedas venir. say ~ pedir perdón. ~! (apologizing) ¡lo siento! ¡perdón!. ~? (asking s.o. to repeat) ¿cómo?

sort /sɔːt/ n tipo m, clase f; (fam, person) tipo m. a ~ of una especie de. ● vt clasificar. □ ~ out vt (or-

ganize) ordenar; organizar (finances); (separate out) separar; solucionar (problem)

so-so /'səʊsəʊ/ adj regular

soufflé /'suːfleɪ/ n suflé m

sought /sɔːt/ see SEEK

soul /səʊl/ n alma f

sound /saʊnd/ n sonido m; (noise) ruido m. ● vt tocar. ● vi sonar; (seem) parecer (as if que). it ~s interesting suena interesante.. ● adj (-er, -est) sano; (argument) lógico; (secure) seguro. ● adv. ~ asleep profundamente dormido. ~ barrier n barrera f del sonido. ~ly adv sólidamente; (asleep) profundamente. ~proof adj insonorizado. ~track n banda f sonora

soup /suːp/ n sopa f

sour /'saʊə(r)/ adj (-er, -est) agrio; (milk) cortado

source /sɔːs/ n fuente f

south /saʊθ/ n sur m. ● adj sur a invar; (wind) del sur. ● adv (go) hacia el sur. it's ~ of está al sur de. S~ Africa n Sudáfrica f. S~ America n América f (del Sur). S~ American adj & n sudamericano (m). ~-east n sudeste m, sureste m. ~erly /'sʌðəlɪ/ (wind) del sur. ~ern /'sʌðən/ adj del sur, meridional. ~erner n sureño m. ~ward /-wəd/, ~wards adv hacia el sur. ~-west n sudoeste m, suroeste m

souvenir /suːvə'nɪə(r)/ n recuerdo m

sovereign /'sɒvrɪn/ n & a soberano (m)

Soviet /'səʊvɪət/ adj (History) soviético. the ~ Union n la Unión f Soviética

sow¹ /səʊ/ vt (pt sowed, pp sowed or sown /səʊn/) sembrar

sow² /saʊ/ n cerda f

soy (esp Amer), **soya** /'sɔɪə/ n. ~ **bean** n soja f

spa /spɑː/ n balneario m

space /speɪs/ n espacio m; (room) espacio m, lugar m. ● adj (research etc) espacial. ● vt espaciar. □ ~ **out** vt espaciar. ~**craft**, ~**ship** n nave f espacial

spade /speɪd/ n pala f. ~**s** npl (Cards) picas fpl

spaghetti /spə'getɪ/ n espaguetis mpl

Spain /speɪn/ n España f

spam /spæm/ n (Comp) correo m basura

span /spæn/ n (of arch) luz f; (of time) espacio m; (of wings) envergadura f. ● vt (pt **spanned**) extenderse sobre. ● adj see **SPICK**

Spaniard /'spænjəd/ n español m

spaniel /'spænjəl/ n spaniel m

Spanish /'spænɪʃ/ adj español; (language) castellano, español. ● n (language) castellano m, español m. npl. **the** ~ (people) los españoles

spank /spæŋk/ vt pegarle a (en las nalgas)

spanner /'spænə(r)/ n llave f

spare /speə(r)/ vt. **if you can** ~ **the time** si tienes tiempo. **can you** ~ **me a pound?** ¿tienes una libra que me des? ~ **no effort** no escatimar esfuerzos. **have money to** ~ tener dinero de sobra. ● adj (not in use) de más; (replacement) de repuesto; (free) libre. ~ **(part)** n repuesto m. ~ **room** n cuarto m de huéspedes. ~ **time** n tiempo m libre. ~ **tyre** n neumático m de repuesto

sparingly /'speərɪŋlɪ/ adv (use) con moderación

spark /spɑːk/ n chispa f. ● vt pro-

vocar (criticism); suscitar (interest). ~**ing plug** n (Auto) bujía f

sparkl|e /'spɑːkl/ vi centellear. ● n destello m. ~**ing** adj centelleante; (wine) espumoso

spark plug n (Auto) bujía f

sparrow /'spærəʊ/ n gorrión m

sparse /spɑːs/ adj escaso. ~**ly** adv escasamente

spasm /'spæzəm/ n espasmo m; (of cough) acceso m. ~**odic** /-'mɒdɪk/ adj espasmódico; (Med) irregular

spat /spæt/ see **SPIT**

spate /speɪt/ n racha f

spatial /'speɪʃl/ adj espacial

spatter /'spætə(r)/ vt salpicar (with de)

spawn /spɔːn/ n huevas fpl. ● vt generar. ● vi desovar

speak /spiːk/ vt/i (pt **spoke**, pp **spoken**) hablar. ~ **for s.o.** hablar en nombre de uno. □ ~ **up** vi hablar más fuerte. ~**er** n (in public) orador m; (loudspeaker) altavoz m; (of language) hablante m & f

spear /spɪə(r)/ n lanza f. ~**head** vt (lead) encabezar

special /'speʃl/ adj especial. ~**ist** /'speʃəlɪst/ n especialista m & f. ~**ity** /-ɪ'ælətɪ/ n especialidad f. ~**ization** /-əlaɪ'zeɪʃn/ n especialización f. ~**ize** /-əlaɪz/ vi especializarse. ~**ized** adj especializado. ~**ly** adv especialmente. ~**ty** n (Amer) especialidad f

species /'spiːʃiːz/ n especie f

specif|ic /spə'sɪfɪk/ adj específico. ~**ically** adv específicamente; (state) explícitamente. ~**ication** /-ɪ'keɪʃn/ n especificación f. ~**y** /'spesɪfaɪ/ vt especificar

specimen /'spesɪmɪn/ n muestra f

speck /spek/ n (of dust) mota f; (in distance) punto m

specs /speks/ npl Ⅱ see **SPECTACLES**

spectacle /'spektəkl/ n espectáculo m. ~**les** npl gafas fpl, lentes fpl (LAm), anteojos mpl (LAm). ~**ular** /-'tækjʊlə(r)/ adj espectacular

spectator /spek'teɪtə(r)/ n espectador m

spectre /'spektə(r)/ n espectro m. ~**um** /'spektrəm/ n (pl **-tra** /-trə/) espectro m; (of views) gama f

speculat|e /'spekjʊleɪt/ vi especular. ~**ion** /-'leɪʃn/ n especulación f. ~**or** n especulador m

sped /sped/ see **SPEED**

speech /spiːtʃ/ n (faculty) habla f; (address) discurso m. ~**less** adj mudo

speed /spiːd/ n velocidad f; (rapidity) rapidez f. ● vi (pt **speeded**) (drive too fast) ir a exceso de velocidad. □ ~ **off**, ~ **away** (pt **sped**) vi alejarse a toda velocidad. □ ~ **by** (pt **sped**) vi (time) pasar volando. □ ~ **up** (pt **speeded**) vt acelerar. vi acelerarse. ~**boat** n lancha f motora. ~ **camera** n cámara f de control de velocidad. ~ **dating** n cita f flash, speed dating m. ~ **limit** n velocidad f máxima. ~**ometer** /spiː'dɒmɪtə(r)/ n velocímetro m. ~**way** n (Amer) autopista f. ~**y** adj (**-ier**, **-iest**) rápido

spell /spel/ n (magic) hechizo m; (of weather, activity) período m. **go through a bad** ~ pasar por una mala racha. ● vt/i (pt **spelled** or **spelt**) escribir. □ ~ **out** vt deletrear; (fig) explicar. ~**checker** n corrector m ortográfico. ~**ing** n ortografía f

spellbound /'spelbaʊnd/ adj embelesado

spelt /spelt/ see **SPELL**

spend /spend/ vt (pt **spent** /spent/) gastar (money); pasar (time); dedicar (care). ● vi gastar dinero

sperm /spɜːm/ n (pl **sperms** or **sperm**) esperma f; (individual) espermatozoide m

spew /spjuː/ vt/i vomitar

sphere /sfɪə(r)/ n esfera f. ~**ical** /'sferɪkl/ adj esférico

spice /spaɪs/ n especia f

spick /spɪk/ adj. ~ **and span** limpio y ordenado

spicy /'spaɪsɪ/ adj picante

spider /'spaɪdə(r)/ n araña f

spik|e /spaɪk/ n (of metal etc) punta f. ~**y** adj puntiagudo

spill /spɪl/ vt (pt **spilled** or **spilt**) derramar. ● vi derramarse. □ ~ **over** vi (container) desbordarse; (liquid) rebosar

spin /spɪn/ vt (pt **spun**, pres p **spinning**) hacer girar; hilar (wool); centrifugar (washing). ● vi girar. ● n. **give sth a** ~ hacer girar algo. **go for a** ~ (Auto) ir a dar un paseo en coche

spinach /'spɪnɪdʒ/ n espinacas fpl

spindly /'spɪndlɪ/ adj larguirucho

spin-drier /spɪn'draɪə(r)/ n centrifugadora f (de ropa)

spine /spaɪn/ n columna f vertebral; (of book) lomo m; (on animal) púa f. ~**less** adj (fig) sin carácter

spinning wheel /'spɪnɪŋ/ n rueca f

spin-off /'spɪnɒf/ n resultado m indirecto; (by-product) producto m derivado

spinster /'spɪnstə(r)/ n soltera f

spiral /'spaɪərəl/ adj espiral;

(shape) de espiral. ● n espiral f. ● vi (pt spiralled) (unemployment) escalar; (prices) dispararse. ~ staircase n escalera f de caracol

spire /spaɪə(r)/ n aguja f

spirit /'spɪrɪt/ n espíritu m. be in good ~s estar animado. in low ~s abatido. ~ed adj animado, fogoso. ~s npl (drinks) bebidas fpl alcohólicas (de alta graduación). ~ual /'spɪrɪtjʊəl/ adj espiritual

spit /spɪt/ vt (pt spat or (Amer) spit, pres p spitting) escupir. ● vi escupir. it's ~ting caen algunas gotas. ● n saliva f; (for roasting) asador m

spite /spaɪt/ n rencor m. in ~ of a pesar de. ● vt fastidiar. ~ful adj rencoroso

spittle /'spɪtl/ n baba f

splash /splæʃ/ vt salpicar. ● vi (person) chapotear. ● n salpicadura f. a ~ of paint un poco de pintura. □ ~ about vi chapotear. □ ~ down vi (spacecraft) amerizar. □ ~ out vi gastarse un dineral (on en)

splend|id /'splendɪd/ adj espléndido. ~our /-ə(r)/ n esplendor m

splint /splɪnt/ n tablilla f

splinter /'splɪntə(r)/ n astilla f. ● vi astillarse

split /splɪt/ vt (pt split, pres p splitting) partir; fisionar (atom); reventar (trousers); (divide) dividir. ● vi partirse; (divide) dividirse. a ~ting headache un dolor de cabeza espantoso. ● n (in garment) descosido m; (in wood, glass) rajadura f. □ ~ up vi separarse. ~ second n fracción f de segundo

splutter /'splʌtə(r)/ vi chisporrotear; (person) farfullar

spoil /spɔɪl/ vt (pt spoilt or spoiled) estropear, echar a perder; (indulge) consentir, malcriar. ~s npl botín m. ~-sport n aguafiestas m & f

spoke¹ /spəʊk/ see SPEAK

spoke² /spəʊk/ n (of wheel) rayo m

spoken /spəʊkən/ see SPEAK

spokesman /'spəʊksmən/ n (pl -men) portavoz m

sponge /spʌndʒ/ n esponja f. ● vt limpiar con una esponja. ~ off, ~ on vi vivir a costillas de. ~ cake n bizcocho m

sponsor /'spɒnsə(r)/ n patrocinador m; (of the arts) mecenas m & f; (surety) garante m. ● vt patrocinar. ~ship n patrocinio m; (of the arts) mecenazgo m

spontaneous /spɒn'teɪnɪəs/ adj espontáneo. ~ously adv espontáneamente

spoof /spuːf/ n ① parodia f

spooky /'spuːkɪ/ adj (-ier, -iest) ① espeluznante

spool /spuːl/ n carrete m

spoon /spuːn/ n cuchara f. ~ful n cucharada f

sporadic /spə'rædɪk/ adj esporádico

sport /spɔːt/ n deporte m. ~s car n coche m deportivo. ~s centre n centro m deportivo. ~sman /-mən/ n, (pl -men) ~swoman n deportista m & f

spot /spɒt/ n mancha f; (pimple) grano m; (place) lugar m; (in pattern) lunar m. be in a ~ ① estar en apuros. on the ~ allí mismo; (decide) en ese mismo momento. ● vt (pt spotted) manchar; (fam, notice) ver, divisar; descubrir (mistake). ~ check n control m hecho al azar. ~less adj (clothes) impecable; (house) limpísimo. ~light n reflector m; (in theatre) foco m.

~ted adj moteado; (material) de lunares. ~ty adj (-ier, -iest) (skin) lleno de granos; (youth) con la cara llena de granos

spouse /spaʊz/ n cónyuge m & f

spout /spaʊt/ n pico m; (jet) chorro m

sprain /spreɪn/ vt hacerse un esguince en. ● n esguince m

sprang /spræŋ/ see **SPRING**

spray /spreɪ/ n (of flowers) ramillete m; (from sea) espuma f; (liquid in spray form) espray m; (device) rociador m. ● vt rociar

spread /spred/ vt (pt **spread**) (stretch, extend) extender; desplegar (wings); difundir (idea, news). ~ butter on a piece of toast untar una tostada con mantequilla. ● vi extenderse; (disease) propagarse; (idea, news) difundirse. ● n (of ideas) difusión f; (of disease, fire) propagación f; (fam, feast) festín m. □ ~ out vi (move apart) desplegarse

spree /spriː/ n. **go on a shopping** ~ ir de expedición a las tiendas

sprightly /ˈspraɪtlɪ/ adj (-ier, -iest) vivo

spring /sprɪŋ/ n (season) primavera f; (device) resorte m; (in mattress) muelle m, resorte m (LAm); (elasticity) elasticidad f; (water) manantial m. ● adj primaveral. ● vi (pt **sprang**, pp **sprung**) saltar; (issue) brotar. ~ **from sth** (problem) provenir de algo. □ ~ **up** vi surgir. ~board n trampolín m. ~-clean /ˈkliːn/ vi hacer una limpieza general. ~ **onion** n cebolleta f. ~time n primavera f. ~y adj (-ier, -iest) (mattress, grass) mullido

sprinkle /ˈsprɪŋkl/ vt salpicar; (with liquid) rociar. ● n salpicadura f; (of liquid) rociada f. ~r n regadera f

sprint /sprɪnt/ n carrera f corta. ● vi (Sport) esprintar; (run fast) correr. ~er n corredor m

sprout /spraʊt/ vi brotar. ● n brote m. **(Brussels)** ~s npl coles fpl de Bruselas

sprung /sprʌŋ/ see **SPRING**

spud /spʌd/ n ① patata f, papa f (LAm)

spun /spʌn/ see **SPIN**

spur /spɜː(r)/ n espuela f; (stimulus) acicate m. **on the** ~ **of the moment** sin pensarlo. ● vt (pt **spurred**). ~ **(on)** espolear; (fig) estimular

spurn /spɜːn/ vt desdeñar; (reject) rechazar

spurt /spɜːt/ vi (liquid) salir a chorros. ● n chorro m; (of activity) racha f

spy /spaɪ/ n espía m & f. ● vt descubrir, ver. ● vi espiar. ~ **on s.o.** espiar a uno

squabble /ˈskwɒbl/ vi reñir

squad /skwɒd/ n (Mil) pelotón m; (of police) brigada f; (Sport) equipo m. ~ **car** n coche m patrulla. ~ron /ˈskwɒdrən/ n (Mil, Aviat) escuadrón m; (Naut) escuadra f

squalid /ˈskwɒlɪd/ adj miserable

squall /skwɔːl/ n turbión m

squalor /ˈskwɒlə(r)/ n miseria f

squander /ˈskwɒndə(r)/ vt derrochar; desaprovechar (opportunity)

square /skweə(r)/ n cuadrado m; (in town) plaza f. ● adj cuadrado; (meal) decente; (fam, old-fashioned) chapado a la antigua. ● vt (settle) arreglar; (Math) elevar al cuadrado. ● vi (agree) cuadrar. □ ~ **up** vi arreglar cuentas (with con). ~ly adv directamente

squash /skwɒʃ/ vt aplastar; (sup-

press) acallar. ● *n*. **it was a terrible
~**. íbamos (or iban) terriblemente
apretujados; *(drink)* **orange ~** naranjada *f*; *(Sport)* squash *m*; *(vegetable)* calabaza *f*. **~y** *adj* blando

squat /skwɒt/ *vi (pt* **squatted***)* ponerse en cuclillas; *(occupy illegally)*
ocupar sin autorización. ● *adj* rechoncho y bajo. **~ter** *n* ocupante
m & f ilegal, okupa *m & f*

squawk /skwɔ:k/ *n* graznido *m*.
● *vi* graznar

squeak /skwi:k/ *n* chillido *m*; *(of
door)* chirrido *m*. ● *vi* chillar; *(door)*
chirriar; *(shoes)* crujir. **~y** *adj* chirriante

squeal /skwi:l/ *n* chillido *m* ● *vi*
chillar

squeamish /'skwi:mɪʃ/ *adj* impresionable, delicado

squeeze /skwi:z/ *vt* apretar; exprimir *(lemon* etc.). ● *vi*. **~ in** meterse. ● *n* estrujón *m*; *(of hand)*
apretón *m*

squid /skwɪd/ *n* calamar *m*

squiggle /'skwɪɡl/ *n* garabato *m*

squint /skwɪnt/ *vi* bizquear; *(trying to see)* entrecerrar los ojos. ● *n*
estrabismo *m*

squirm /skwɜ:m/ *vi* retorcerse

squirrel /'skwɪrəl/ *n* ardilla *f*.

squirt /skwɜ:t/ *vt* (liquid) echar un
chorro de. ● *vi* salir a chorros. ● *n*
chorrito *m*

St /sənt/ *abbr* (= **saint**) /sənt/ S,
San(to); (= **street**) C/, Calle *f*

stab /stæb/ *vt (pt* **stabbed***)* apuñalar. ● *n* puñalada *f*; *(pain)* punzada
f. **have a ~ at** sth intentar algo

stabili|ty /stə'bɪlətɪ/ *n* estabilidad
f. **~ze** /'steɪbɪlaɪz/ *vt*/*i* estabilizar

stable /'steɪbl/ *adj* (-**er**, -**est**) estable. ● *n* caballeriza *f*, cuadra *f*

stack /stæk/ *n* montón *m*. ● *vt*. **~**

(up) amontonar

stadium /'steɪdɪəm/ *n (pl* **-diums**
or **-dia** /-dɪə/*)* estadio *m*

staff /stɑ:f/ *n* (stick) palo *m*; *(employees)* personal *m*. **teaching ~**
personal *m* docente. **a member of
~** un empleado

stag /stæɡ/ *n* ciervo *m*. **~-night**,
~-party *n* (before wedding) fiesta *f*
de despedida de soltero; (men-only
party) fiesta *f* para hombres

stage /steɪdʒ/ *n* (in theatre) escenario *f*; (platform) plataforma *f*;
(phase) etapa *f*. **the ~** (profession,
medium) el teatro. ● *vt* poner en
escena (play); (arrange) organizar;
(pej) orquestar. **~coach** *n* diligencia *f*

stagger /'stæɡə(r)/ *vi* tambalearse. ● *vt* dejar estupefacto; escalonar (holidays etc). **~ing** *adj*
asombroso

stagna|nt /'stæɡnənt/ *adj* estancado. **~te** /stæɡ'neɪt/ *vi* estancarse

staid /steɪd/ *adj* serio, formal

stain /steɪn/ *vt* manchar; (colour)
teñir. ● *n* mancha *f*; (dye) tintura *f*.
~ed glass window *n* vidriera *f* de
colores. **~less steel** *n* acero *m* inoxidable. **~ remover** *n* quitamanchas *m*

stair /steə(r)/ *n* escalón *m*. **~s** *npl*
escalera *f*. **~case**, **~way** *n* escalera *f*

stake /steɪk/ *n* estaca *f*; (wager)
apuesta *f*; (Com) intereses *mpl*. **be
at ~** estar en juego. ● *vt* estacar;
jugarse (reputation). **~ a claim** reclamar

stala|ctite /'stæləktaɪt/ *n* estalactita *f*. **~gmite** /'stæləɡmaɪt/ *n* estalagmita *f*

stale /steɪl/ *adj* (-**er**, -**est**) no
fresco; (bread) duro; (smell) vi

ciado. **~mate** n (Chess) ahogado m; (deadlock) punto m muerto

stalk /stɔːk/ n tallo m. ● vt acechar. ● vi irse indignado

stall /stɔːl/ n (in stable) compartimiento m; (in market) puesto m. **~s** npl (in theatre) platea f, patio m de butacas. ● vt parar (engine). ● vi (engine) pararse; (fig) andar con rodeos

stallion /'stæljən/ n semental m

stalwart /'stɔːlwət/ adj (supporter) leal, incondicional

stamina /'stæmɪnə/ n resistencia f

stammer /'stæmə(r)/ vi tartamudear. ● n tartamudeo f

stamp /stæmp/ vt (with feet) patear; (press) estampar; (with rubber stamp) sellar; (fig) señalar. ● vi dar patadas en el suelo. ● n sello m, estampilla f (LAm), timbre m (Mex); (on passport) sello m; (with foot) patada f; (mark) marca f, señal f. □ **~ out** vt (fig) erradicar. **~ed addressed envelope** n sobre m franqueado con su dirección

stampede /stæm'piːd/ n estampida f. ● vi salir en estampida

stance /stɑːns/ n postura f

stand /stænd/ vi (pt stood) estar de pie, estar parado (LAm); (rise) ponerse de pie, pararse; (be) encontrarse; (Pol) presentarse como candidato (**for** en). **the offer ~s** la oferta sigue en pie. **~ to reason** ser lógico. ● vt (endure) soportar; (place) colocar. **~ a chance** tener una posibilidad. ● n posición f, postura f; (for lamp etc) pie m, sostén m; (at market) puesto m; (booth) quiosco m; (Sport) tribuna f. **make a ~ against** sth oponer resistencia a algo. □ **~ back** vi apartarse. □ **~ by** vi estar preparado. vt (support) apoyar. □ **~ down** vi retirarse. □ **~**

for vt significar. □ **~ in for** vt suplir a. □ **~ out** vi destacarse. □ **~ up** vi ponerse de pie, pararse (LAm). □ **~ up for** vt defender. **~ up for oneself** defenderse. □ **~ up to** vt resistir a

standard /'stændəd/ n norma f; (level) nivel m; (flag) estandarte m. ● adj estándar a invar, normal. **~ize** vt estandarizar. **~ lamp** n lámpara f de pie. **~s** npl principios mpl

stand: ~-by n (at airport) standby m. **be on ~-by** (police) estar en estado de alerta. **~-in** n suplente m & f. **~ing** adj de pie, parado (LAm); (permanent) permanente f. ● n posición f; (prestige) prestigio m. **~off** n (Amer, draw) empate m; (deadlock) callejón m sin salida. **~point** n punto m de vista. **~still** n. **be at a ~still** estar paralizado. **come to a ~still** (vehicle) parar; (city) quedar paralizado

stank /stæŋk/ see STINK

staple /'steɪpl/ adj principal. ● n grapa f. ● vt sujetar con una grapa. **~r** n grapadora f

star /stɑː(r)/ n (incl Cinema, Theatre) estrella f; (asterisk) asterisco m. ● vi (pt starred). **~ in a film** protagonizar una película. **~board** n estribor m.

starch /stɑːtʃ/ n almidón m; (in food) fécula f. ● vt almidonar. **~y** (food) adj a base de féculas

stardom /'stɑːdəm/ n estrellato m

stare /steə(r)/ n mirada f fija. ● vi. **~ (at)** mirar fijamente

starfish /'stɑːfɪʃ/ n estrella f de mar

stark /stɑːk/ adj (-er, -est) escueto. ● adv completamente

starling /'stɑːlɪŋ/ n estornino m

starry | steam

540

starry /'stɑːrɪ/ adj estrellado

start /stɑːt/ vt empezar, comenzar; encender (engine); arrancar (car); (cause) provocar; abrir (business). • vi empezar; (car etc) arrancar; (jump) dar un respingo. **to ~ with** (as linker) para empezar. **~ off by doing sth** empezar por hacer algo. • n principio m; (Sport) ventaja f; (jump) susto m. **make an early ~** (on journey) salir temprano. **~er** n (Auto) motor m de arranque; (Culin) primer plato m. **~ing-point** n punto m de partida

startle /'stɑːtl/ vt asustar

starv|ation /stɑːˈveɪʃn/ n hambre f, inanición f. **~e** /stɑːv/ vt hacer morir de hambre. • vi morirse de hambre. **I'm ~ing** me muero de hambre

state /steɪt/ n estado m. **be in a ~** estar agitado. **the S~** los Estados mpl Unidos. • vt declarar; expresar (views); (fix) fijar. • adj del Estado; (Schol) público; (with ceremony) de gala. **~ly** adj (-ier, -iest) majestuoso. **~ly home** n casa f solariega. **~ment** n declaración f; (account) informe m. **~sman** /-mən/ n estadista m

---

state school En Gran Bretaña, colegio estatal de educación gratuita, financiado directa o indirectamente por el gobierno. Abarca la educación primaria y secundaria, colegios especializados, comprehensives etc.

---

static /'stætɪk/ adj estacionario. • n (interference) estática f

station /'steɪʃn/ n estación f; (on radio) emisora f; (TV) canal m. • vt colocar; (Mil) estacionar. **~ary** adj

estacionario. **~er's (shop)** n papelería f. **~ery** n artículos mpl de papelería. **~ wagon** n (Amer) ranchera f, (coche m) familiar m, camioneta f (LAm)

statistic /stəˈtɪstɪk/ n estadística f. **~al** adj estadístico. **~s** n (science) estadística f

statue /'stætʃuː/ n estatua f

stature /'stætʃə(r)/ n talla f, estatura f

status /'steɪtəs/ n posición f social; (prestige) categoría f; (Jurid) estado m

statut|e /'stætʃuːt/ n estatuto m. **~ory** /-utrɪ/ adj estatutario

staunch /stɔːntʃ/ adj (-er, -est) leal

stave /steɪv/ n (Mus) pentagrama m. □ **~ off** vt evitar

stay /steɪ/ n (of time) estancia f, estadía f (LAm); (Jurid) suspensión f. • vi quedarse; (reside) alojarse. **I'm ~ing in a hotel** estoy en un hotel. □ **~ in** vi quedarse en casa. □ **~ up** vi quedarse levantado

stead /sted/ n. **in s.o.'s ~** en lugar de uno. **stand s.o. in good ~** resultarle muy útil a uno. **~ily** adv firmemente; (regularly) regularmente. **~y** adj (-ier, -iest) firme; (regular) regular; (flow) continuo; (worker) serio

steak /steɪk/ n. **a ~** un filete. **some ~** carne para guisar

steal /stiːl/ vt (pt stole, pp stolen) robar. □ **~ in** vi entrar a hurtadillas

stealth /stelθ/ n. **by ~** sigilosamente. **~y** adj sigiloso

steam /stiːm/ n vapor m. **let off ~** (fig) desahogarse. • vt (cook) cocer al vapor. • vi echar vapor. □ **~ up** vi empañarse. **~ engine** n máquina f de vapor. **~er** n (ship) barco m de vapor. **~roller** n apisonadora f. ~y adj lleno de vapor

steel /stiːl/ n acero m. ● vt. ~ **o.s.** armarse de valor. ~ **industry** n industria f siderúrgica

steep /stiːp/ ● adj (-er, -est) empinado; (increase) considerable; (price) [T] excesivo

steeple /ˈstiːpl/ n aguja f, campanario m

steeply /ˈstiːplɪ/ adv abruptamente; (increase) considerablemente

steer /stɪə(r)/ vt dirigir; gobernar (ship). ● vi (in ship) estar al timón. ~ **clear of** evitar. ~ing n (Auto) dirección f. ~ing wheel n volante m

stem /stem/ n (of plant) tallo m; (of glass) pie m; (of word) raíz f. ● vt (pt stemmed) contener (bleeding). ● vi. ~ **from** provenir de

stench /stentʃ/ n hedor m

stencil /ˈstensl/ n plantilla f

stenographer /steˈnɒɡrəfə(r)/ n estenógrafo m

step /step/ vi (pt stepped). ~ **in** sth pisar algo. □ ~ **aside** vi hacerse a un lado. □ ~ **down** vi retirarse. □ ~ **in** vi (fig) intervenir.□ ~ **up** vt intensificar; redoblar (security). ● n paso m; (stair) escalón m; (fig) medida f. **take** ~**s** tomar medidas. **be in** ~ llevar el paso. **be out of** ~ no llevar el paso. ~**brother** n hermanastro m. ~**daughter** n hijastra f. ~**father** n padrastro m. ~**ladder** n escalera f de tijera. ~**mother** n madrastra f. ~**ping-stone** n peldaño m. ~**sister** n hermanastra f. ~**son** n hijastro m

stereo /ˈsterɪəʊ/ n (pl -os estéreo m. ● adj estéreo a invar. ~**type** n estereotipo m

sterile /ˈsteraɪl/ adj estéril. ~**ize**

/ˈsterɪlaɪz/ vt esterilizar

sterling /ˈstɜːlɪŋ/ n libras fpl esterlinas. ● adj (pound) esterlina

stern /stɜːn/ n (of boat) popa f. ● adj (-er, -est) severo

stethoscope /ˈsteθəskəʊp/ n estetoscopio m

stew /stjuː/ vt/i guisar. ● n estofado m, guiso m

steward /ˈstjuːəd/ n administrador m; (on ship) camarero m; (air steward) sobrecargo m, aeromozo m (LAm). ~**ess** /-ˈdes/ n camarera f; (on aircraft) auxiliar f de vuelo, azafata f

stick /stɪk/ n palo m; (for walking) bastón m; (of celery etc) tallo m. ● vt (pt stuck) (glue) pegar; (fam, put) poner; (thrust) clavar; (fam, endure) soportar. ● vi pegarse; (jam) atascarse. □ ~ **out** vi sobresalir. □ ~ **to** vt ceñirse a. □ ~ **up for** vt [T] defender. ~**er** n pegatina f. ~**ing plaster** n esparadrapo m; (individual) tirita f, curita f (LAm). ~**ler** /ˈstɪklə(r)/ n. **be a** ~**ler for** insistir en. ~**y** /ˈstɪkɪ/ adj (-ier, -iest) (surface) pegajoso; (label) engomado

stiff /stɪf/ adj (-er, -est) rígido; (joint, fabric) tieso; (muscle) entumecido; (difficult) difícil; (manner) estirado; (drink) fuerte. **have a** ~ **neck** tener tortícolis. ~**en** vi (become rigid) agarrotarse; (become firm) endurecerse. ~**ly** adv rígidamente

stifle /ˈstaɪfl/ vt sofocar. ~**ing** adj sofocante

stiletto (heel) /stɪˈletəʊ/ n (pl -os) tacón m de aguja

still /stɪl/ adj inmóvil; (peaceful) tranquilo; (drink) sin gas. **sit** ~, **stand** ~ quedarse tranquilo. ● adv todavía, aún; (nevertheless) sin em-

bargo. **~born** adj nacido muerto.
~ life n (pl **-s**) bodegón m. **~ness**
n tranquilidad f

stilted /'stɪltɪd/ adj rebuscado;
(conversation) forzado

stilts /stɪlts/ npl zancos mpl

stimul|ant /'stɪmjʊlənt/ n estimulante m. **~ate** /-leɪt/ vt estimular. **~ation** /-'leɪʃn/ n estímulo m. **~us** /-əs/ n (pl **-li** /-laɪ/) estímulo m

sting /stɪŋ/ n picadura f; (organ) aguijón m. ● vt/i (pt **stung**) picar

stingy /'stɪndʒɪ/ adj (**-ier, -iest**) tacaño

stink /stɪŋk/ n hedor m. ● vi (pt **stank** or **stunk**, pp **stunk**) apestar, oler mal

stipulat|e /'stɪpjʊleɪt/ vt/i estipular. **~ion** /-'leɪʃn/ n estipulación f

stir /stɜː(r)/ vt (pt **stirred**) remover, revolver; (move) agitar; estimular (imagination). ● vi moverse. **~ up trouble** armar lío 🇮. ● n revuelo m, conmoción f

stirrup /'stɪrəp/ n estribo m

stitch /stɪtʃ/ n (in sewing) puntada f; (in knitting) punto m; (pain) dolor m costado. **be in ~es** 🇮 desternillarse de risa. ● vt coser

stock /stɒk/ n (Com, supplies) existencias fpl; (Com, variety) surtido m; (livestock) ganado m; (Culin) caldo m. **~s and shares, ~s and bonds** (Amer) acciones fpl. **out of ~** agotado. **take ~ of sth** (fig) hacer un balance de algo. ● adj estándar a invar; (fig) trillado. ● vt surtir, abastecer (**with de**). □ **~ up** vi abastecerse (**with de**). **~broker** /-brəʊkə(r)/ n corredor m de bolsa. **S~ Exchange** n bolsa f. **~ing** n media f. **~pile** n reservas fpl. ● vt almacenar. **~still** adj inmóvil.

~taking n (Com) inventario m.
~y adj (**-ier, -iest**) bajo y fornido

stodgy /'stɒdʒɪ/ (**-dgier, -dgiest**) adj pesado

stoke /stəʊk/ vt echarle carbón (or leña) a

stole /stəʊl/ see STEAL

stolen /'stəʊlən/ see STEAL

stomach /'stʌmək/ n estómago m. ● vt soportar. **~ache** n dolor m de estómago

ston|e /stəʊn/ n piedra f; (in fruit) hueso m; (weight, pl **stone**) unidad de peso equivalente a 14 libras o 6,35 kg. ● adj de piedra. ● vt apedrear. **~e-deaf** adj sordo como una tapia. **~y** adj (silence) sepulcral

stood /stʊd/ see STAND

stool /stuːl/ n taburete m

stoop /stuːp/ vi agacharse; (fig) rebajarse. ● n. **have a ~** ser cargado de espaldas

stop /stɒp/ vt (pt **stopped**) (halt, switch off) parar; (cease) terminar; (prevent) impedir; (interrupt) interrumpir. **~ doing sth** dejar de hacer algo. **~ it!** ¡basta ya! ● vi (bus) parar; (clock) pararse. **it's ~ped raining** ha dejado de llover. ● n (bus etc) parada f; (break on journey) parada f. **put a ~ to sth** poner fin a algo. **come to a ~** detenerse. **~gap** n remedio m provisional. **~over** n escala f. **~page** /'stɒpɪdʒ/ n suspensión f, paradero m (LAm); (of work) huelga f, paro m (LAm); (interruption) interrupción f. **~per** n tapón m. **~watch** n cronómetro m

storage /'stɔːrɪdʒ/ n almacenamiento m

store /stɔː(r)/ n provisión f; (depot) almacén m; (Amer, shop)

tienda *f*; (*fig*) reserva *f*. **in** ∼ en reserva. ●*vt* (*for future*) poner en reserva; (*in warehouse*) almacenar. □ ∼ **up** *vt* (*fig*) acumulado.
∼keeper *n* (*Amer*) tendero *m*, comerciante *m & f*. **∼room** *n* almacén *m*; (*for food*) despensa *f*

storey /'stɔːrɪ/ *n* (*pl* **-eys**) piso *m*, planta *f*

stork /stɔːk/ *n* cigüeña *f*

storm /stɔːm/ *n* tempestad *f*. ●*vi* rabiar. ●*vt* (*Mil*) asaltar. **∼y** *adj* tormentoso; (*sea, relationship*) tempestuoso

story /'stɔːrɪ/ *n* historia *f*; (*in newspaper*) artículo *m*; (*rumour*) rumor *m*; (〖〗, *lie*) mentira *f*, cuento *m*. **∼teller** *n* cuentista *m & f*

stout /staʊt/ *adj* (**-er, -est**) robusto, corpulento. ●*n* cerveza *f* negra

stove /staʊv/ *n* estufa *f*

stow /staʊ/ *vt* guardar; (*hide*) esconder. □ ∼ **away** *vi* viajar de polizón. **∼away** *n* polizón *m & f*

straggl|e /'strægl/ *vi* rezagarse. **∼y** *adj* desordenado

straight /streɪt/ *adj* (**-er, -est**) recto; (*tidy*) en orden; (*frank*) franco; (*hair*) lacio; (〖〗, *conventional*) convencional. **be** ∼ estar derecho. ●*adv* (*sit up*) derecho; (*direct*) directamente; (*without delay*) inmediatamente. ∼ **away** en seguida, inmediatamente. ∼ **on** todo recto. ∼ **out** sin rodeos. ●*n* recta *f*. ∼**en** *vt* enderezar. □ ∼**en up** *vt* ordenar. **∼forward** /-'fɔːwəd/ *adj* franco; (*easy*) sencillo

strain /streɪn/ *n* (*tension*) tensión *f*; (*injury*) torcedura *f*. ●*vt* forzar (*voice, eyesight*); someter a demasiada tensión (*relations*); (*sieve*) colar. ∼ **one's back** hacerse daño en la espalda. ∼ **a muscle** hacerse

un esguince. **∼ed** *adj* forzado; (*relations*) tirante. **∼er** *n* colador *m*. **∼s** *npl* (*Mus*) acordes *mpl*

strait /streɪt/ *n* estrecho *m*. **be in dire** ∼**s** estar en grandes apuros. **∼jacket** *n* camisa *f* de fuerza

strand /strænd/ *n* (*thread*) hebra *f*. **a** ∼ **of hair** un pelo. ●*vt*. **be ∼ed** (*ship*) quedar encallado. **I was left ∼ed** me abandonaron a mi suerte

strange /streɪndʒ/ *adj* (**-er, -est**) raro, extraño; (*not known*) desconocido. **∼ly** *adv* de una manera rara. **∼ly enough** aunque parezca mentira. **∼r** *n* desconocido *m*; (*from another place*) forastero *m*

strangle /'stræŋgl/ *vt* estrangular

strap /stræp/ *n* correa *f*; (*of garment*) tirante *m*. ●*vt* (*pt* **strapped**) atar con una correa

strat|egic /strə'tiːdʒɪk/ *adj* estratégico. **∼egy** /'strætədʒɪ/ *n* estrategia *f*

straw /strɔː/ *n* paja *f*; (*drinking* ∼) pajita *f*, paja *f*, popote *m* (*Mex*). **the last** ∼ el colmo. **∼berry** /-bərɪ/ *n* fresa *f*; (*large*) fresón *m*

stray /streɪ/ *vi* (*wander away*) apartarse; (*get lost*) extraviarse; (*deviate*) desviarse (**from** de). ●*adj* (*animal*) (*without owner*) callejero; (*lost*) perdido. ●*n* (*without owner*) perro *m*/gato *m* callejero; (*lost*) perro *m*/gato *m* perdido

streak /striːk/ *n* lista *f*, raya *f*; (*in hair*) reflejo *m*; (*in personality*) veta *f*

stream /striːm/ *n* arroyo *m*; (*current*) corriente *f*. **a** ∼ **of abuse** una sarta de insultos. ●*vi* correr. □ ∼ **out** *vi* (*people*) salir en tropel. **∼er** *n* (*paper*) serpentina *f* (*banner*) banderín *m*. **∼line** *vt* dar línea aerodinámica a; (*simplify*) racionalizar. **∼lined** *adj* aerodinámico

street /striːt/ n calle f. **~car** n (Amer) tranvía m. **~ lamp** n farol m. **~ map**, **~ plan** n plano m

strength /streŋθ/ n fuerza f; (of wall etc) solidez f. **~en** vt reforzar (wall); fortalecer (muscle)

strenuous /'strenjʊəs/ adj enérgico; (arduous) arduo; (tiring) fatigoso

stress /stres/ n énfasis m; (Gram) acento m; (Mec, Med, tension) tensión f. ● vt insistir en

stretch /stretʃ/ vt estirar; (extend) extender; forzar (truth); estirar (resources). ● vi estirarse; (when sleepy) desperezarse; (extend) extenderse; (be elastic) estirarse. ● n (period) período m; (of road) tramo m. **at a ~** sin parar. □ **~ out** vi (person) tenderse. **~er** n camilla f

strict /strikt/ adj (-er, -est) estricto; (secrecy) absoluto. **~ly** adv con severidad; (rigorously) terminantemente. **~ly speaking** en rigor

stridden /stridn/ see **STRIDE**

stride /straɪd/ vi (pt strode, pp stridden) andar a zancadas. ● n zancada f. **take sth in one's ~** tomarse algo con calma. **~nt** /'straɪdnt/ adj estridente

strife /straɪf/ n conflicto m

strike /straɪk/ vt (pt struck) golpear; encender (match); encontrar (gold, oil); (clock) dar. **it ~s me as odd** me parece raro. ● vi golpear; (go on strike) declararse en huelga; (be on strike) estar en huelga; (attack) atacar; (clock) dar la hora. ● n (of workers) huelga f, paro m; (attack) ataque m. **come out on ~** ir a la huelga. **~ off**, **~ out** vt tachar. **~ up a friendship** trabar amistad. **~r** n huelguista m & f; (Sport) artillero m

striking /'straɪkɪŋ/ adj (resemblance) sorprendente; (colour) llamativo

string /strɪŋ/ n cordel m, mecate m (Mex); (Mus) cuerda f; (of lies, pearls) sarta f; (of people) sucesión f. **~ along** vt 🄵 engañar

stringent /'strɪndʒənt/ adj riguroso

strip /strip/ vt (pt stripped) desnudar (person); deshacer (bed). ● vi desnudarse. ● n tira f; (of land) franja f. **~ cartoon** n historieta f

stripe /straɪp/ n raya f. **~d** adj a rayas, rayado

strip lighting n luz f fluorescente

strive /straɪv/ vi (pt strove, pp striven). **~ to** esforzarse por

strode /strəʊd/ see **STRIDE**

stroke /strəʊk/ n golpe m; (in swimming) brazada f; (Med) ataque m de apoplejía; (of pen etc) trazo m; (of clock) campanada f; (caress) caricia f. **a ~ of luck** un golpe de suerte. ● vt acariciar

stroll /strəʊl/ vi pasearse. ● n paseo m. **~er** n (Amer) sillita f de paseo, cochecito m

strong /strɒŋ/ adj (-er, -est) fuerte. **~hold** n fortaleza f; (fig) baluarte m. **~ly** adv (greatly) fuertemente; (protest) enérgicamente; (deeply) profundamente. **~room** n cámara f acorazada

strove /strəʊv/ see **STRIVE**

struck /strʌk/ see **STRIKE**

structur|al /'strʌktʃərəl/ adj estructural. **~e** /'strʌktʃə(r)/ n estructura f

struggle /'strʌgl/ vi luchar; (thrash around) forcejear. ● n lucha f

strum /strʌm/ vt (pt strummed)

|

rasguear

strung /strʌŋ/ see STRING

strut /strʌt/ n (in building) puntal m. ● vi (pt **strutted**) pavonearse

stub /stʌb/ n (of pencil, candle) cabo m; (counterfoil) talón m; (of cigarette) colilla. □ ~ **out** (pt **stubbed**) vt apagar

stubble /'stʌbl/ n rastrojo m; (beard) barba f de varios días

stubborn /'stʌbən/ adj terco

stuck /stʌk/ see STICK. ● adj. **the drawer is** ~ el cajón se ha atascado. **the door is** ~ la puerta se ha atrancado. ~**-up** adj ① estirado

stud /stʌd/ n tachuela f; (for collar) gemelo m.

student /'stju:dənt/ n estudiante m & f; (at school) alumno m. ~ **driver** n (Amer) persona que está aprendiendo a conducir

studio /'stju:diəʊ/ n (pl **-os**) estudio m. ~ **apartment**, ~ **flat** n estudio m

studious /'stju:dɪəs/ adj estudioso

study /'stʌdɪ/ n estudio m. ● vt/i estudiar

stuff /stʌf/ n ① cosas fpl. **what's this** ~ **called?** ¿cómo se llama esta cosa? ● vt rellenar; disecar (animal); (cram) atiborrar; (put) meter de prisa. ~ **o.s.** ① darse un atracón. ~**ing** n relleno m. ~**y** adj (**-ier**, **-iest**) mal ventilado; (old-fashioned) acartonado. **it's** ~**y in here** está muy cargado el ambiente

stumble /'stʌmbl/ vi tropezar. ~ **across**, ~ **on** vt dar con. ~**ing-block** n tropiezo m, impedimento m

stump /stʌmp/ n (of limb) muñón m; (of tree) tocón m

stun /stʌn/ vt (pt **stunned**) (daze)

aturdir; (bewilder) dejar atónito. ~**ning** adj sensacional

stung /stʌŋ/ see STING

stunk /stʌŋk/ see STINK

stunt /stʌnt/ n ① ardid m publicitario. ● vt detener, atrofiar. ~**ed** adj (growth) atrofiado; (body) raquítico. ~**man** n especialista m. ~**woman** n especialista f

stupendous /stju:'pendəs/ adj estupendo

stupid /'stju:pɪd/ adj (foolish) tonto; (unintelligent) estúpido. ~**ity** /-'pɪdətɪ/ n estupidez f. ~**ly** adv estúpidamente

stupor /'stju:pə(r)/ n estupor m

sturdy /'stɜ:dɪ/ adj (**-ier**, **-iest**) robusto

stutter /'stʌtə(r)/ vi tartamudear. ● n tartamudeo m.

sty /staɪ/ n (pl **sties**) pocilga f; (Med) orzuelo m

style /staɪl/ n estilo m; (fashion) moda f; (design, type) diseño m. **in** ~ a lo grande. ● vt diseñar. ~**ish** adj elegante. ~**ist** n estilista m & f. **hair** ~**ist** estilista m & f

stylus /'staɪləs/ n (pl **-uses**) aguja f (de tocadiscos)

suave /swɑ:v/ adj elegante y desenvuelto

subconscious /sʌb'kɒnʃəs/ adj & n subconsciente (m)

subdivide /sʌbdɪ'vaɪd/ vt subdividir

subdued /səb'dju:d/ adj apagado

subject /'sʌbdʒɪkt/ adj sometido. ~ **to** sujeto a. ● n (theme) tema m; (Schol) asignatura f, materia f (LAm); (Gram) sujeto m; (Pol) súbdito m. ● /səb'dʒekt/ vt someter. ~**ive** /səb'dʒektɪv/ adj subjetivo

subjunctive /səb'dʒʌŋktɪv/ adj &

sublime | suction

n subjuntivo (m)

sublime /səˈblaɪm/ adj sublime

submarine /ˈsʌbməriːn/ n submarino m

submerge /səbˈmɜːdʒ/ vt sumergir. • vi sumergirse

submi|ssion /səbˈmɪʃn/ n sumisión f. ~t /səbˈmɪt/ vt (pt submitted) (subject) someter; presentar (application). • vi rendirse

subordinate /səˈbɔːdɪnət/ adj & n subordinado (m). • /səˈbɔːdɪneɪt/ vt subordinar

subscri|be /səbˈskraɪb/ vi suscribir. ~be to suscribirse a (magazine). ~ber n suscriptor m. ~ption /-rɪpʃn/ n (to magazine) suscripción f

subsequent /ˈsʌbsɪkwənt/ adj posterior, subsiguiente. ~ly adv posteriormente

subside /səbˈsaɪd/ vi (land) hundirse; (flood) bajar; (storm, wind) amainar. ~nce /ˈsʌbsɪdəns/ n hundimiento m

subsidiary /səbˈsɪdɪərɪ/ adj secundario; (subject) complementario. • n (Com) filial

subsid|ize /ˈsʌbsɪdaɪz/ vt subvencionar, subsidiar (LAm). ~y /ˈsʌbsədɪ/ n subvención f, subsidio m

substance /ˈsʌbstəns/ n sustancia f

substandard /sʌbˈstændəd/ adj de calidad inferior

substantial /səbˈstænʃl/ adj (sturdy) sólido; (meal) sustancioso; (considerable) considerable

substitut|e /ˈsʌbstɪtjuːt/ n (person) substituto m; (thing) sucedáneo m. • vt/i sustituir. ~ion /-ˈtjuːʃn/ n sustitución f

subterranean /sʌbtəˈreɪnjən/

adj subterráneo

subtitle /ˈsʌbtaɪtl/ n subtítulo m

subtle /ˈsʌtl/ adj (-er, -est) sutil; (tactful) discreto. ~ty n sutileza f

subtract /səbˈtrækt/ vt restar. ~ion /-ʃn/ n resta f

suburb /ˈsʌbɜːb/ n barrio m residencial de las afueras, colonia f. the ~s las afueras fpl. ~an /səˈbɜːbən/ adj suburbano. ~ia /səˈbɜːbɪə/ n zonas residenciales de las afueras de una ciudad

subversive /səbˈvɜːsɪv/ adj subversivo

subway /ˈsʌbweɪ/ n paso m subterráneo; (Amer) metro m

succeed /səkˈsiːd/ vi (plan) dar resultado; (person) tener éxito. ~ in doing lograr hacer. • vt suceder.

success /səkˈses/ n éxito m. ~ful adj (person) de éxito, exitoso (LAm). the ~ful applicant el candidato que obtenga el puesto. ~fully adv satisfactoriamente. ~ion /-ʃn/ n sucesión f. for 3 years in ~ion durante tres años consecutivos. in rapid ~ion uno tras otro. ~ive adj sucesivo. ~or n sucesor m

succulent /ˈsʌkjʊlənt/ adj suculento

succumb /səˈkʌm/ vi sucumbir

such /sʌtʃ/ adj (+ noun) tan (+ adj). ~ a big house una casa tan grande. • pron tal. ~ and ~ tal o cual. ~ as como. ~ as it is tal como es

suck /sʌk/ vt chupar (sweet, thumb); sorber (liquid). ◻ ~ up vt (vacuum cleaner) aspirar; (pump) succionar. ◻ ~ up to vt 🄴 dar coba a. ~er n (plant) chupón m; (fam, person) imbécil m

suckle /ˈsʌkl/ vt amamantar

suction /ˈsʌkʃn/ n succión f

sudden /'sʌdn/ adj repentino. **all of a ~** de repente. **~ly** adv de repente

suds /sʌds/ npl espuma f de jabón

sue /su:/ vt (pres p **suing**) demandar (**for** por)

suede /sweɪd/ n ante m

suet /'su:ɪt/ n sebo m

suffer /'sʌfə(r)/ vt sufrir; (tolerate) aguantar. ● vi sufrir; (be affected) resentirse

suffic|e /sə'faɪs/ vi bastar. **~ient** /sə'fɪʃnt/ adj suficiente, bastante. **~iently** adv (lo) suficientemente

suffix /'sʌfɪks/ n (pl **-ixes**) sufijo m

suffocat|e /'sʌfəkeɪt/ vt asfixiar. ● vi asfixiarse. **~ion** /-'keɪʃn/ n asfixia f

sugar /'ʃʊgə(r)/ n azúcar m & f. **~ bowl** n azucarero m. **~y** adj azucarado.

suggest /sə'dʒest/ vt sugerir. **~ion** /-tʃən/ n sugerencia f

suicid|al /su:ɪ'saɪdl/ adj suicida. **~e** /'su:ɪsaɪd/ n suicidio m. **commit ~e** suicidarse

suit /su:t/ n traje m; (woman's) traje m de chaqueta; (Cards) palo m; (Jurid) pleito m. ● vt venirle bien a, convenirle a; (clothes) quedarle bien a; (adapt) adaptar. **be ~ed to** (thing) ser apropiado para. **I'm not ~ed to** this kind of work no sirvo para este tipo de trabajo. **~able** adj apropiado, adecuado. **~ably** adv (dressed) apropiadamente; (qualified) adecuadamente. **~case** n maleta f, valija f (LAm)

suite /swi:t/ n (of furniture) juego m; (of rooms) suite f

sulk /sʌlk/ vi enfurruñarse

sullen /'sʌlən/ adj hosco

sulphur /'sʌlfə(r)/ n azufre m. **~ic acid** /sʌl'fjʊərɪk/ n ácido m

sulfúrico

sultan /'sʌltən/ n sultán m

sultana /sʌl'tɑ:nə/ n pasa f de Esmirna

sultry /'sʌltrɪ/ adj (-ier, -iest) (weather) bochornoso; (fig) sensual

sum /sʌm/ n (of money) suma f, cantidad f; (Math) suma f. ● **□ ~ up** (pt summed) vt resumir. ● vi recapitular

summar|ily /'sʌmərɪlɪ/ adv sumariamente. **~ize** vt resumir. **~y** n resumen m

summer /'sʌmə(r)/ n verano m. **~ camp** n (US) colonia f de vacaciones. **~time** n verano m. **~y** adj veraniego

> **summer camp** En EE.UU., es el campamento de verano, aspecto muy importante en la vida de muchos niños. Las actividades al aire libre se practican en un ambiente natural entre las que se incluyen natación, montañismo, supervivencia al aire libre. En estos campamentos miles de estudiantes trabajan como supervisores.

summit /'sʌmɪt/ n (of mountain) cumbre f. **~ conference** n conferencia f cumbre

summon /'sʌmən/ vt llamar; convocar (meeting, s.o. to meeting); (Jurid) citar. □ **~ up** vt armarse de. **~s** n (Jurid) citación f. ● vt citar

sumptuous /'sʌmptjʊəs/ adj suntuoso

sun /sʌn/ n sol m. **~bathe** vi tomar el sol, asolearse (LAm). **~beam** n rayo m de sol. **~burn** n quemadura f de sol. **~burnt** adj quemado por el sol

Sunday /'sʌndeɪ/ n domingo m

sunflower /'sʌnflaʊə(r)/ n girasol m

sung /sʌŋ/ see SING

sunglasses /'sʌnglɑːsɪz/ npl gafas fpl de sol, lentes mpl de sol (LAm)

sunk /sʌŋk/ see SINK. ~en /'sʌŋkən/ • adj hundido

sun: ~light n luz f del sol. ~ny adj (-ier, -iest) (day) de sol; (place) soleado. it is ~ny hace sol. ~rise n. at ~rise al amanecer. salida f del sol. ~roof n techo m corredizo. ~set n puesta f del sol. ~shine n sol m. ~stroke n insolación f. ~tan n bronceado m. get a ~tan broncearse. ~tan lotion n bronceador m

super /'suːpə(r)/ adj [1] genial, super a invar

superb /suːˈpɜːb/ adj espléndido

supercilious /suːpəˈsɪlɪəs/ adj desdeñoso

superficial /suːpəˈfɪʃl/ adj superficial

superfluous /suːˈpɜːfluəs/ adj superfluo

superhighway /'suːpəhaɪweɪ/ n (Amer, Auto) autopista f; (Comp) information ~ autopista f de la comunicación

superhuman /suːpəˈhjuːmən/ adj sobrehumano

superintendent /suːpərɪn'tendənt/ n director m; (Amer, of building) portero m; (of police) comisario m; (in US) superintendente m & f

superior /suːˈpɪərɪə(r)/ adj & n superior (m). ~ity /-ˈrɒtɪ/ n superioridad f

superlative /suːˈpɜːlətɪv/ adj inigualable. • n superlativo m

supermarket /'suːpəmɑːkɪt/ n supermercado m

supernatural /suːpəˈnætʃrəl/ adj sobrenatural

superpower /'suːpəpaʊə(r)/ n superpotencia f

supersede /suːpəˈsiːd/ vt reemplazar, sustituir

supersonic /suːpəˈsɒnɪk/ adj supersónico

superstitio|n /suːpəˈstɪʃn/ n superstición f. ~us adj /-əs/ supersticioso

supervis|e /'suːpəvaɪz/ vt supervisar. ~ion /-ˈvɪʒn/ n supervisión f. ~or n supervisor m

supper /'sʌpə(r)/ n cena f (ligera), comida f (ligera) (LAm)

supple /sʌpl/ adj flexible

supplement /'sʌplɪmənt/ n suplemento m; (to diet, income) complemento m. • vt complementar (diet, income). ~ary /-'mentərɪ/ adj suplementario

suppl|ier /sə'plaɪə(r)/ n (Com) proveedor m. ~y /sə'plaɪ/ vt suministrar; proporcionar (information). ~y s.o. with sth (equipment) proveer a uno de algo; (in business) abastecer a uno de algo. • n suministro m. ~y and demand oferta f y demanda. ~ies npl provisiones mpl, víveres mpl; (Mil) pertrechos mpl. office ~ies artículos mpl de oficina

support /sə'pɔːt/ vt (hold up) sostener; (back) apoyar; mantener (family). • n apoyo m; (Tec) soporte m. ~er n partidario m; (Sport) hincha m & f

suppos|e /sə'pəʊz/ vt suponer, imaginarse; (think) creer. I'm ~ed to start work at nine se supone que tengo que empezar a trabajar a las nueve. ~edly adv supuestamente. ~ition /sʌpə'zɪʃn/ n suposición f

suppress /sə'pres/ vt reprimir (feelings); sofocar (rebellion). **~ion** /-ʃn/ n represión f

suprem|acy /su:'preməsɪ/ n supremacía f. **~e** /su:'pri:m/ adj supremo

sure /ʃʊə(r)/ adj (-er, -est) seguro. make ~ that asegurarse de que. ● adv ¡claro!. **~ly** adv (undoubtedly) seguramente; (gladly) desde luego. **~ly you don't believe that!** ¡no te creerás eso! **~ty** /-ətɪ/ n garantía f

surf /sɜːf/ n oleaje m; (foam) espuma f. ● vi hacer surf. ● vt (Comp) surfear, navegar

surface /'sɜːfɪs/ n superficie f. ● adj superficial. ● vt recubrir (with de). ● vi salir a la superficie; (problems) aflorar

surfboard /'sɜːfbɔːd/ n tabla f de surf

surfeit /'sɜːfɪt/ n exceso m

surf: ~er n surfista m & f; (Internet) navegador m. **~ing** n surf m

surge /sɜːdʒ/ vi (crowd) moverse en tropel; (sea) hincharse. ● n oleada f; (in demand, sales) aumento m

surg|eon /'sɜːdʒən/ n cirujano m. **~ery** n cirugía f; (consulting room) consultorio m; (consulting hours) consulta f. **~ical** adj quirúrgico

surly /'sɜːlɪ/ adj (-ier, -iest) hosco

surmise /sə'maɪz/ vt conjeturar

surmount /sə'maʊnt/ vt superar

surname /'sɜːneɪm/ n apellido m

surpass /sə'pɑːs/ vt superar

surplus /'sɜːpləs/ adj & n excedente (m)

surprise /sə'praɪz/ n sorpresa f. ● vt sorprender. **~ed** adj sorprendido. **~ing** adj sorprendente. **~ingly** adv sorprendentemente

surrender /sə'rendə(r)/ vt entregar. ● vi rendirse. ● n rendición f

surreptitious /sʌrəp'tɪʃəs/ adj furtivo

surround /sə'raʊnd/ vt rodear; (Mil) rodear, cercar. **~ing** adj circundante. **~ings** npl alrededores mpl; (environment) ambiente m

surveillance /sɜː'veɪləns/ n vigilancia f

survey /'sɜːveɪ/ n inspección f; (report) informe m; (general view) vista f general. ● /sə'veɪ/ vt inspeccionar; (measure) medir; (look at) contemplar. **~or** n topógrafo m, agrimensor m; (of building) perito m

surviv|al /sə'vaɪvl/ n supervivencia f. **~e** /sə'vaɪv/ vt/i sobrevivir. **~or** n superviviente m & f

susceptible /sə'septəbl/ adj. **~ to** propenso a

suspect /sə'spekt/ vt sospechar; sospechar de (person). ● /'sʌspekt/ adj & n sospechoso m

suspen|d /sə'spend/ vt suspender. **~ders** npl (Amer, braces) tirantes mpl. **~se** /-s/ n (in film etc) suspense m, suspenso m (LAm). keep s.o. in **~se** mantener a uno sobre ascuas. **~sion** /-ʃn/ n suspensión f. **~sion bridge** n puente m colgante

suspici|on /sə'spɪʃn/ n (belief) sospecha f; (mistrust) desconfianza f. **~ous** /-ʃəs/ adj desconfiado; (causing suspicion) sospechoso

sustain /sə'steɪn/ vt sostener; mantener (conversation, interest); (suffer) sufrir

SW abbr (= **south-west**) SO

swab /swɒb/ n (specimen) muestra f, frotis m

swagger /'swægə(r)/ vi pavonearse

swallow /'swɒləʊ/ vt/i tragar. ●n trago m; (bird) golondrina f

swam /swæm/ see **SWIM**

swamp /swɒmp/ n pantano m, ciénaga f. ●vt inundar. ~y adj pantanoso

swan /swɒn/ n cisne m

swap /swɒp/ vt/i (pt swapped) intercambiar. ~ sth for sth cambiar algo por algo. ●n cambio m

swarm /swɔːm/ n enjambre m. ●vi (bees) enjambrar; (fig) hormiguear

swarthy /'swɔːðɪ/ adj (-ier, -iest) moreno

swat /swɒt/ vt (pt swatted) matar (con matamoscas etc)

sway /sweɪ/ vi balancearse; (gently) mecerse. ●vt (influence) influir en

swear /sweə(r)/ vt/i (pt swore, pp sworn) jurar. ~word n palabrota f

sweat /swet/ n sudor m, transpiración f. ●vi sudar

sweat|er /'swetə(r)/ n jersey m, suéter m. ~shirt n sudadera f. ~suit n (Amer) chándal m, equipo m de deportes

swede /swiːd/ n nabo m sueco

Swede /swiːd/ n sueco m. ~n /'swiːdn/ n Suecia f. ~ish adj sueco. ●n (language) sueco m. ●npl. the ~ (people) los suecos

sweep /swiːp/ vt (pt swept) barrer; deshollinar (chimney). ●vi barrer. ●n barrido m. ~ away vt (carry away) arrastrar; (abolish) erradicar. ~er n barrendero m. ~ing adj (gesture) amplio; (changes) radical; (statement) demasiado general

sweet /swiːt/ adj (-er, -est) dulce;

(fragrant) fragante; (pleasant) agradable; (gentle) dulce; (cute) rico. **have a ~ tooth** ser dulcero. ●n caramelo m, dulce m (Mex); (dish) postre m. ~en vt endulzar. ~heart n enamorado m; (as form of address) amor m. ~ly adv dulcemente. ~ potato n boniato m, batata f, camote m LAm

swell /swel/ vt (pt swelled, pp swollen or swelled) hinchar; (increase) aumentar. ●vi hincharse; (increase) aumentar. ●adj (Amer fam) fenomenal. ●n (of sea) oleaje m. ~ing n hinchazón f

sweltering /'sweltərɪŋ/ vi sofocante

swept /swept/ see **SWEEP**

swerve /swɜːv/ vi virar bruscamente

swift /swɪft/ adj (-er, -est) veloz, rápido; (reply) rápido. ●n (bird) vencejo m. ~ly adv rápidamente

swig /swɪg/ vt (pt swigged) Ⓣ beber a grandes tragos. ●n Ⓣ trago m

swim /swɪm/ vi (pt swam, pp swum) nadar. ●n baño m. ~mer n nadador m. ~ming n natación f. ~ming bath(s) n(pl) piscina f cubierta, alberca f techada (Mex). ~ming pool n piscina f, alberca f (Mex). ~ming trunks npl bañador m, traje m de baño ~suit n traje m de baño, bañador m

swindle /'swɪndl/ vt estafar. ●n estafa f. ~r n estafador m

swine /swaɪn/ npl cerdos mpl. ●n (pl swine) (fam, person) canalla m & f. ~ fever n fiebre f porcina

swing /swɪŋ/ vt (pt swung) balancear; (object on rope) hacer oscilar. ●vi (dangle) balancearse; (swing on a swing) columpiarse; (pendulum)

oscilar. ~ **open/shut** abrirse/
cerrarse. ● *n* oscilación *f*, vaivén *m*;
(*seat*) columpio *m*; (*in opinion*)
cambio *m*. **in full** ~ en plena actividad

swipe /swaɪp/ *vt* darle un golpe a;
(*fam, snatch*) birlar. ● *n* golpe *m*

Swiss /swɪs/ *adj* suizo (*m*). ● *npl.*
the ~ los suizos

switch /swɪtʃ/ *n* (*Elec*) interruptor
m; (*exchange*) intercambio *m*; (*Amer,
Rail*) agujas *fpl*. ● *vt* cambiar; (*deviate*) desviar. □ ~ **off** *vt* (*Elec*) apagar (light, TV, heating); desconectar (electricity). □ ~ **on** *vt*
encender, prender (*LAm*); arrancar
(engine). ~**board** *n* centralita *f*

Switzerland /ˈswɪtsələnd/ *n*
Suiza *f*

swivel /ˈswɪvl/ *vi* (*pt* **swivelled**)
girar. ● *vt* hacer girar

swollen /ˈswəʊlən/ *see* **SWELL**.
● *adj* hinchado

swoop /swuːp/ *vi* (bird) abatirse;
(police) llevar a cabo una redada.
● *n* (*of bird*) descenso *m* en picado
or (*LAm*) en picada; (*by police*) redada *f*

sword /sɔːd/ *n* espada *f*

swore /swɔː(r)/ *see* **SWEAR**

sworn /swɔːn/ *see* **SWEAR**. ● *adj*
(enemy) declarado; (statement) jurado

swot /swɒt/ *vt/i* (*pt* **swotted**)
(*Schol, fam*) empollar, estudiar como
loco. ● *n* (*Schol, fam*) empollón *m*,
matado *m* (*Mex*)

swum /swʌm/ *see* **SWIM**

swung /swʌŋ/ *see* **SWING**

syllable /ˈsɪləbl/ *n* sílaba *f*

syllabus /ˈsɪləbəs/ *n* (*pl* **-buses**)
plan *m* de estudios; (*of a particular
subject*) programa *m*

symbol /ˈsɪmbl/ *n* símbolo *m*.
~**ic(al)** /-ˈbɒlɪk(l)/ *adj* simbólico.
~**ism** *n* simbolismo *m*. ~**ize** *vt*
simbolizar

symmetr|ical /sɪˈmetrɪkl/ *adj* si-
métrico. ~**y** /ˈsɪmətrɪ/ *n* simetría *f*

sympath|etic /sɪmpəˈθetɪk/ *adj*
comprensivo; (*showing pity*) compasivo. ~**ize** /ˈsɪmpəθaɪz/ *vi* comprender; (*commiserate*) ~**ize with**
s.o. compadecer a uno. ~**y**
/ˈsɪmpəθɪ/ *n* comprensión *f*; (*pity*)
compasión *f*; (*condolences*) pésame *m*

symphony /ˈsɪmfənɪ/ *n* sinfonía *f*

symptom /ˈsɪmptəm/ *n* síntoma
m. ~**atic** /-ˈmætɪk/ *adj* sintomático

synagogue /ˈsɪnəgɒg/ *n* sinagoga *f*

synchronize /ˈsɪŋkrənaɪz/ *vt* sincronizar

syndicate /ˈsɪndɪkət/ *n* agrupa-
ción *f*; (*Amer, TV*) agencia *f* de distribución periodística

synonym /ˈsɪnənɪm/ *n* sinónimo
m. ~**ous** /-ˈnɒnɪməs/ *adj* sinónimo

syntax /ˈsɪntæks/ *n* sintaxis *f*

synthesi|s /ˈsɪnθəsɪs/ *n* (*pl*
-theses /-siːz/) síntesis *f*. ~**ze** /-aɪz/
vt sintetizar

synthetic /sɪnˈθetɪk/ *adj* sintético

syringe /ˈsɪrɪndʒ/ *n* jeringa *f*, je-
ringuilla *f*

syrup /ˈsɪrəp/ *n* (sugar solution) al-
míbar *m*; (with other ingredients) jarabe *m*; (medicine) jarabe *m*

system /ˈsɪstəm/ *n* sistema *m*, método *m*; (Tec, Mec, Comp) sistema *m*.
the digestive ~ el aparato digestivo. ~**atic** /-əˈmætɪk/ *adj* sistemático. ~**atically** /-əˈmætɪklɪ/ *adv* sis-
temáticamente. ~**s analyst** *n*
analista *m* & *f* de sistemas

Tt

tab /tæb/ n (flap) lengüeta f; (label) etiqueta f

table /'teɪbl/ n mesa f; (list) tabla f. **~cloth** n mantel m. **~ mat** n salvamanteles m. **~spoon** n cuchara f grande; (measure) cucharada f (grande)

tablet /'tæblɪt/ n pastilla f; (pill) comprimido m

table tennis n tenis m de mesa, ping-pong m

tabloid /'tæblɔɪd/ n tabloide m

taboo /tə'bu:/ adj & n tabú (m)

tacit /'tæsɪt/ adj tácito

taciturn /'tæsɪtɜːn/ adj taciturno

tack /tæk/ n tachuela f; (stitch) hilván m. ● vt clavar con tachuelas; (sew) hilvanar. ● vi (Naut) virar □ **~ on** vt añadir.

tackle /'tækl/ n (equipment) equipo m; (soccer) entrada f fuerte; (US football, Rugby) placaje m. **fishing ~** aparejo m de pesca. ● vt abordar (problem); (in soccer) entrarle a; (in US football, Rugby) placar

tacky /'tækɪ/ adj pegajoso

tact /tækt/ n tacto m. **~ful** adj diplomático

tactic|al /'tæktɪkl/ adj táctico. **~s** npl táctica f

tactless /'tæktləs/ adj indiscreto

tadpole /'tædpəʊl/ n renacuajo m

tag /tæg/ n (label) etiqueta f. □ **~ along** (pt tagged) vt 🔟 seguir

tail /teɪl/ n (of horse, fish, bird) cola f; (of dog, pig) rabo m. **~s** npl (tailcoat) frac m; (of coin) cruz f. ● vt seguir. □ **~ off** vi disminuir.

tailor /'teɪlə(r)/ n sastre m. **~ed** /'teɪləd/ adj entallado. **~-made** n hecho a (la) medida

taint /teɪnt/ vt contaminar

take /teɪk/ vt (pt took, pp taken) tomar, coger (esp Spain), agarrar (esp LAm); (capture) capturar; (endure) aguantar; (require) requerir; llevar (time); tomar (bath); tomar (medicine); (carry) llevar; aceptar (cheque). **I ~ a size 10** uso la talla 14. □ **~ after** vt parecerse a. □ **~ away** vt llevarse; (confiscate) quitar. □ **~ back** vt retirar (statement etc). □ **~ in** vt achicar (garment); (understand) asimilar; (deceive) engañar. □ **~ off** vt (remove) quitar, sacar; quitarse (shoes, jacket); (mimic) imitar. vi (aircraft) despegar. □ **~ on** vt contratar (employee). □ **~ out** vt sacar. □ **~ over** vt tomar posesión de; hacerse cargo de (job). vi (assume control) asumir el poder. □ **~ up** vt empezar a hacer (hobby); aceptar (challenge); subir (hem); llevar (time); ocupar (space). ● n (Cinema) toma f. **~-off** n despegue m. **~-over** n (Com) absorción f

takings /'teɪkɪŋz/ npl recaudación f; (at box office) taquilla f

talcum powder /'tælkəm/ n polvos mpl de talco, talco m (LAm)

tale /teɪl/ n cuento m

talent /'tælənt/ n talento m. **~ed** adj talentoso

talk /tɔːk/ vt/i hablar. **~ to s.o.** hablar con uno. **~ about** hablar de. ● n conversación f; (lecture) charla f. □ **~ over** vt discutir. **~ative** /-ətɪv/ adj hablador

tall /tɔːl/ adj (-er, -est) alto. **~ story** n 🔟 cuento m chino

tally /'tælɪ/ vi coincidir (with con)

talon /'tælən/ n garra f

tambourine /tæmbəˈriːn/ n pandereta f

tame /teɪm/ adj (-er, -est) (animal) (by nature) manso; (tamed) domado. ● vt domar (wild animal)

tamper /ˈtæmpə(r)/ vi. ~ **with** tocar; (alter) alterar, falsificar

tampon /ˈtæmpɒn/ n tampón m

tan /tæn/ vi (pt tanned) broncearse. ● n bronceado m. **get a** ~ broncearse. ● adj habano

tang /tæŋ/ n sabor m fuerte

tangent /ˈtændʒənt/ n tangente f

tangerine /ˌtændʒəˈriːn/ n mandarina f

tangible /ˈtændʒəbl/ adj tangible

tangle /ˈtæŋgl/ vt enredar. **get** ~**d (up)** enredarse. ● n enredo m, maraña f

tango /ˈtæŋgəʊ/ n (pl -os) tango m

tank /tæŋk/ n depósito m; (Auto) tanque m; (Mil) tanque m

tanker /ˈtæŋkə(r)/ n (ship) buque m cisterna; (truck) camión m cisterna

tantrum /ˈtæntrəm/ n berrinche m, rabieta f

tap /tæp/ n grifo m, llave f (LAm); (knock) golpecito m. ● vt (pt tapped) (knock) dar un golpecito en; interceptar (phone). ● vi dar golpecitos (on en). ~ **dancing** n claqué m

tape /teɪp/ n cinta f; (Med) esparadrapo m. ● vt (record) grabar. ~**-measure** n cinta f métrica

taper /ˈteɪpə(r)/ vt afilar. ● vi afilarse. □ ~ **off** vi disminuir

tape recorder n magnetófon m, magnetófono m

tapestry /ˈtæpɪstrɪ/ n tapiz m

tar /tɑː(r)/ n alquitrán m. ● vt (pt

tarred) alquitranar

target /ˈtɑːgɪt/ n blanco m; (fig) objetivo m

tarmac /ˈtɑːmæk/ n pista f. **T~** n (Amer, ®) asfalto m

tarnish /ˈtɑːnɪʃ/ vt deslustrar; empañar (reputation)

tart /tɑːt/ n pastel m; (individual) pastelillo m; (sl, woman) prostituta f, fulana f 〔Ⅰ〕. ● vt. ~ **o.s. up** 〔Ⅰ〕 engalanarse. ● adj (-er, -est) ácido

tartan /ˈtɑːtn/ n tartán m, tela f escocesa

task /tɑːsk/ n tarea f. **take to** ~ reprender

tassel /ˈtæsl/ n borla f

tast|e /teɪst/ n sabor m, gusto m; (liking) gusto m. ● vt probar. ● vi. ~ **of** saber a. ~**eful** adj de buen gusto. ~**eless** adj soso; (fig) de mal gusto. ~**y** adj (-ier, -iest) sabroso

tat /tæt/ see **TIT FOR TAT**

tatter|ed /ˈtætəd/ adj hecho jirones. ~**s** /ˈtætəz/ npl andrajos mpl

tattoo /tæˈtuː/ n (on body) tatuaje m. ● vt tatuar

tatty /ˈtætɪ/ adj (-ier, -iest) gastado, estropeado

taught /tɔːt/ see **TEACH**

taunt /tɔːnt/ vt provocar mediante burlas. ● n pulla f

Taurus /ˈtɔːrəs/ n Tauro m

taut /tɔːt/ adj tenso

tavern /ˈtævən/ n taberna f

tax /tæks/ n impuesto m. ● vt imponer contribuciones a (person); gravar (thing); (strain) poner a prueba. ~**able** adj imponible. ~**ation** /-ˈseɪʃn/ n impuestos mpl; (system) sistema m tributario. ~ **collector** n recaudador m de impuestos. ~**-free** adj libre de impuestos

taxi /'tæksɪ/ n (pl **-is**) taxi m. ● vi (pt taxied, pres p taxiing) (aircraft) rodar por la pista

taxpayer /'tækspeɪə(r)/ n contribuyente m & f

tea /ti:/ n té m; (afternoon tea) merienda f, té m. ~ **bag** n bolsita f de té

teach /ti:tʃ/ vt (pt taught) dar clases de, enseñar (subject); dar clase a (person). ~ **school** (Amer) dar clase(s) en un colegio. ● vi dar clase(s). ~**er** n profesor m; (primary) maestro m. ~**ing** n enseñanza f. ● adj docente

tea: ~**cup** n taza f de té. ~ **leaf** n hoja f de té

team /ti:m/ n equipo m. □ ~ **up** vi asociarse (with con). ~ **work** n trabajo m de equipo

teapot /'ti:pɒt/ n tetera f

tear¹ /teə(r)/ vt (pt tore, pp torn) romper, rasgar. ● vi romperse, rasgarse. ● n rotura f; (rip) desgarrón m. □ ~ **along** vi ir a toda velocidad. □ ~ **apart** vt desgarrar. □ ~ **off**, ~ **out** vt arrancar. □ ~ **up** vt romper

tear² /tɪə(r)/ n lágrima f. be in ~s estar llorando. ~**ful** adj lloroso (farewell) triste. ~ **gas** n gas m lacrimógeno

tease /ti:z/ vt tomarle el pelo a

tea: ~ **set** n juego m de té. ~**spoon** n cucharita f, cucharilla f; (amount) cucharadita f

teat /ti:t/ n (of animal) tetilla f; (for bottle) tetina f

tea towel /'ti:taʊəl/ n paño m de cocina

techni|cal /'teknɪkl/ adj técnico. ~**cality** n /-'kælətɪ/ n detalle m técnico. ~**cally** adv técnicamente. ~**cian** /tek'nɪʃn/ n técnico m.

~**que** /tek'ni:k/ n técnica f

technolog|ical /teknə'lɒdʒɪkl/ adj tecnológico. ~**y** /tek'nɒlədʒɪ/ n tecnología f

teddy bear /'tedɪ/ n osito m de peluche

tedi|ous /'ti:dɪəs/ adj tedioso. ~**um** /'ti:dɪəm/ n tedio m

teem /ti:m/ vi abundar (with en), estar repleto (with de)

teen|age /'ti:neɪdʒ/ adj adolescente; (for teenagers) para jóvenes. ~**ager** n adolescente m & f. ~**s** /ti:nz/ npl adolescencia f

teeny /'ti:nɪ/ adj (-ier, -iest) [I] chiquito

teeter /'ti:tə(r)/ vi balancearse

teeth /ti:θ/ see **TOOTH**. ~**e** /ti:ð/ vi. he's ~**ing** le están saliendo los dientes. ~**ing troubles** npl (fig) problemas mpl iniciales

tele|communications /telɪkəmju:nɪ'keɪʃnz/ npl telecomunicaciones fpl. ~**gram** /'telɪgræm/ n telegrama m. ~**pathic** /telɪ'pæθɪk/ adj telepático. ~**pathy** /tɪ'lepəθɪ/ n telepatía f

telephon|e /'telɪfəʊn/ n teléfono m. ● vt llamar por teléfono. ~**e booth**, ~**e box** n cabina f telefónica. ~**e call** n llamada f telefónica. ~**e card** n tarjeta f telefónica. ~**e directory** n guía f telefónica. ~**e exchange** n central f telefónica. ~**ist** /tɪ'lefənɪst/ n telefonista f

tele|sales /'telɪseɪlz/ npl televentas fpl. ~**scope** n telescopio m. ~**scopic** /-'skɒpɪk/ adj telescópico. ~**text** n teletex(to) m. ~**working** n teletrabajo m

televis|e /'telɪvaɪz/ vt televisar. ~**ion** /'telɪvɪʒn/ n (medium) televisión f. ~**ion (set)** n televisor m

telex /'teleks/ n télex m

tell /tel/ vt (pt told) decir; contar (story, joke); (distinguish) distinguir. ~ **the difference** notar la diferencia. ~ **the time** decir la hora. ● vi (produce an effect) tener efecto; (know) saber. □ ~ **off** vt regañar. ~**ing** adj revelador. ~**-tale** n soplón m. ● adj revelador

telly /'telɪ/ n 🔲 tele f

temp /temp/ n empleado m eventual o temporal

temper /'tempə(r)/ n (mood) humor m; (disposition) carácter m; (fit of anger) cólera f. **be in a** ~ estar furioso. **lose one's** ~ perder los estribos. ~**ament** /'temprəmənt/ n temperamento m. ~**amental** /-'mentl/ adj temperamental. ~**ate** /'tempərət/ adj templado. ~**ature** /'temprɪtʃə(r)/ n temperatura f. **have a** ~**ature** tener fiebre

tempestuous /tem'pestjʊəs/ adj tempestuoso

temple /'templ/ n templo m; (of head) sien f

tempo /'tempəʊ/ n (pl **-os** or **tempi**) ritmo m

temporar|ily /'tempərərəlɪ/ adv temporalmente, temporariamente (LAm). ~**y** /'tempərərɪ/ adj temporal, provisional; (job) eventual, temporal

tempt /tempt/ vt tentar. ~**ation** /-'teɪʃn/ n tentación f. ~**ing** adj tentador

ten /ten/ adj & n diez m

tenaci|ous /tɪ'neɪʃəs/ adj tenaz. ~**ty** /tɪ'næsətɪ/ n tenacidad f

tenan|cy /'tenənsɪ/ n inquilinato m. ~**t** n inquilino m, arrendatario m

tend /tend/ vi. ~ **to** tender a. ● vt cuidar (de). ~**ency** /'tendənsɪ/ n

tendencia f

tender /'tendə(r)/ adj tierno; (painful) sensible. ● n (Com) oferta f. **legal** ~ n moneda f de curso legal. ● vt ofrecer, presentar. ~**ly** adv tiernamente

tendon /'tendən/ n tendón m

tennis /'tenɪs/ n tenis m

tenor /'tenə(r)/ n tenor m

tens|e /tens/ adj (-er, -est) (taut) tenso, tirante; (person) tenso. ● n (Gram) tiempo m. ~**ion** /'tenʃn/ n tensión f; (between two parties) conflicto m

tent /tent/ n tienda f (de campaña), carpa f (LAm)

tentacle /'tentəkl/ n tentáculo m

tentative /'tentətɪv/ adj (plan) provisional; (offer) tentativo; (person) indeciso

tenterhooks /'tentəhʊks/ npl. **be on** ~ estar en ascuas

tenth /tenθ/ adj & n décimo (m)

tenuous /'tenjʊəs/ adj (claim) poco fundado; (link) indirecto

tenure /'tenjʊə(r)/ n tenencia f; (period of office) ejercicio m

tepid /'tepɪd/ adj tibio

term /tɜːm/ n (of time) período m; (Schol) trimestre m; (word etc) término m. ~**s** npl condiciones fpl; (Com) precio m. **on good/bad** ~**s** en buenas/malas relaciones. ● vt calificar de

termin|al /'tɜːmɪnl/ adj terminal. ● n (transport) terminal f; (Comp, Elec) terminal m. ~**ate** /-eɪt/ vt poner fin a; poner término a (contract); (Amer, fire) despedir. ● vi terminarse. ~**ology** /-'nɒlədʒɪ/ n terminología f

terrace /'terəs/ n terraza f; (houses) hilera f de casas

terrain /tə'reɪn/ n terreno m

terrestrial /tɪˈrestrɪəl/ adj terrestre

terribl|e /ˈterəbl/ adj espantoso. ~y adv terriblemente

terrif|ic /təˈrɪfɪk/ adj (fam, excellent) estupendo; (fam, huge) enorme. ~ied /ˈterɪfaɪd/ adj aterrorizado. ~y /ˈterɪfaɪ/ vt aterrorizar. ~ying adj aterrador

territor|ial /terɪˈtɔːrɪəl/ adj territorial. ~y /ˈterɪtrɪ/ n territorio m

terror /ˈterə(r)/ n terror m. ~ism n terrorismo m. ~ist n terrorista m & f. ~ize vt aterrorizar

terse /tɜːs/ adj seco, lacónico

test /test/ n (of machine, drug) prueba f; (exam) prueba f, test m; (of blood) análisis m; (for eyes, hearing) examen m. ● vt probar, poner a prueba (product); hacerle una prueba a (student); evaluar (knowledge); examinar (sight)

testament /ˈtestəmənt/ n (will) testamento m. Old/New T~ Antiguo/Nuevo Testamento

testicle /ˈtestɪkl/ n testículo m

testify /ˈtestɪfaɪ/ vt atestiguar. ● vi declarar

testimon|ial /testɪˈməʊnɪəl/ n recomendación f. ~y /ˈtestɪmənɪ/ n testimonio m

test: ~ match n partido m internacional. ~ **tube** n tubo m de ensayo, probeta f

tether /ˈteðə(r)/ vt atar. ● n. be at the end of one's ~ no poder más

text /tekst/ n texto m. ● vt mandar un mensaje a. ~book n libro m de texto

textile /ˈtekstaɪl/ adj & n textil (m)

texture /ˈtekstʃə(r)/ n textura f

Thames /temz/ n Támesis m

than /ðæn, ðən/ conj que; (with quantity) de

thank /θæŋk/ vt darle las gracias a, agradecer. ~ you gracias. ~ful adj agradecido. ~fully adv (happily) gracias a Dios. ~less adj ingrato. ~s npl agradecimiento m. ~s! ¡gracias!. ~s to gracias a

Thanksgiving (Day) /θæŋks
ˈgɪvɪŋ/ n (in US) el día de Acción de Gracias

that /ðæt, ðət/ adj (pl those) ese, aquel, esa, aquella. ● pron (pl those) ése, aquél, ésa, aquélla. ~ is es decir. ~'s not true eso no es cierto. ~'s why por eso. is ~ you? ¿eres tú? like ~ así. ● adv tan. ● rel pron que; (with prep) el que, la que, el cual, la cual. ● conj que

thatched /θætʃt/ adj (roof) de paja; (cottage) con techo de paja

thaw /θɔː/ vt descongelar. ● vi descongelarse; (snow) derretirse. ● n deshielo m

the definite article

••••➤ el (m), la (f), los (mpl), las (fpl). ~ **building** el edificio. ~ **windows** las ventanas

❗ Feminine singular nouns beginning with a stressed or accented a or ha take the article el instead of la, e.g. ~ **soul** el alma; ~ **axe** el hacha; ~ **eagle** el águila

Note that when el follows the prepositions de and a, it combines to form del and al, e.g. of ~ **group** del grupo. I went to ~ **bank** fui al banco

••••➤ (before an ordinal number in

names, titles) not translated.
Henry ~ **Eighth** Enrique Octavo. **Elizabeth** ~ **Second** Isabel Segunda
●●●▸ (*in abstractions*) lo. ~ **impossible** lo imposible

theatr|e /'θɪətə(r)/ n teatro m; (*Amer, movie theater*) cine m. ~**ical** /-'ætrɪkl/ adj teatral

theft /θeft/ n hurto m

their /ðeə(r)/ adj su, sus pl. ~**s** /ðeəz/ poss pron (el) suyo m, (la) suya f, (los) suyos mpl, (las) suyas fpl

them /ðem, ðəm/ pron (*accusative*) los m, las f; (*dative*) les; (*after prep*) ellos m, ellas f

theme /θiːm/ n tema m. ~ **park** n parque m temático. ~ **song** n motivo m principal

themselves /ðəm'selvz/ pron ellos mismos m, ellas mismas f; (*reflexive*) se; (*after prep*) sí mismos m, sí mismas f

then /ðen/ adv entonces; (*next*) luego, después. **by** ~ para entonces. **now and** ~ de vez en cuando. **since** ~ desde entonces. ● adj entonces

theology /θɪ'ɒlədʒɪ/ n teología f

theor|etical /θɪə'retɪkl/ adj teórico. ~**y** /'θɪərɪ/ n teoría f

therap|eutic /θerə'pjuːtɪk/ adj terapéutico. ~**ist** /'θerəpɪst/ n terapeuta m & f. ~**y** /'θerəpɪ/ n terapia f

there /ðeə(r)/ adv ahí; (*further away*) allí, ahí; (*less precise, further*) allá. ~ **is**, ~ **are** hay. ~ **it is** ahí está. **down** ~ ahí abajo. **up** ~ ahí arriba. ● int. ~! that's the last box ¡listo! ésa es la última caja. ~, ~, don't cry! vamos, no llores. ~**abouts** adv por ahí. ~**fore** /-fɔː(r)/ adv por lo tanto.

thermometer /θə'mɒmɪtə(r)/ n termómetro m

Thermos /'θɜːməs/ n (®) termo m

thermostat /'θɜːməstæt/ n termostato m

thesaurus /θɪ'sɔːrəs/ n (pl **-ri** /-raɪ/) diccionario m de sinónimos

these /ðiːz/ adj estos, estas. ● pron éstos, éstas

thesis /'θiːsɪs/ n (pl **theses** /-siːz/) tesis f

they /ðeɪ/ pron ellos m, ellas f. ~ **say that** dicen or se dice que

they'd /ðeɪ(ə)d/ = they had, they would

they'll /ðeɪl/ = they will

they're /ðeɪə(r)/ = they are

they've /ðeɪv/ = they have

thick /θɪk/ adj (**-er, -est**) (layer, sweater) grueso, gordo; (sauce) espeso; (fog, smoke) espeso, denso; (fur) tupido; (fam, stupid) burro. ● adv espesamente, densamente. ● n. **in the** ~ **of** en medio de. ~**en** vi espesar. ● vi espesarse. ~**et** /-ɪt/ n matorral m. ~**ness** (of fabric) grosor m; (of paper, wood, wall) espesor m

thief /θiːf/ n (pl **thieves** /θiːvz/) ladrón m

thigh /θaɪ/ n muslo m

thimble /'θɪmbl/ n dedal m

thin /θɪn/ adj (**thinner, thinnest**) (person) delgado, flaco; (layer, slice) fino; (hair) ralo

thing /θɪŋ/ n cosa f. ● vi **it's a good** ~ **(that)...** menos mal que.... **just the** ~ exactamente lo que se necesita. **poor** ~! ¡pobrecito!

think /θɪŋk/ vt (pt **thought**) pensar, creer. ● vi pensar (**about** en); (*carefully*) reflexionar; (*imagine*) imaginarse. **I** ~ **so** creo que sí. ~ **of s.o.** pensar en uno. **I hadn't**

thought of that eso no se me ha ocurrido. ~ **over** vt pensar bien. ~ **up** vt idear, inventar. ~**er** n pensador m. ~**tank** n gabinete m estratégico

third /θɜːd/ adj tercero, (before masculine singular noun) tercer. ● n tercio m, tercera parte f. ~ **(gear)** n (Auto) tercera f. ~**rate** adj muy inferior. **T~ World** n Tercer Mundo m

thirst /θɜːst/ n sed f. ~**y** adj sediento. **be** ~**y** tener sed

thirt|een /θɜːˈtiːn/ adj & n trece (m). ~**teenth** adj decimotercero. ● n treceavo m ~**ieth** /ˈθɜːtɪəθ/ adj trigésimo. ● n treintavo m. ~**y** /ˈθɜːtɪ/ adj & n treinta (m)

this /ðɪs/ adj (pl these) este, esta. ● one éste, ésta. ● pron (pl these) éste, ésta, esto. **like** ~ así

thistle /ˈθɪsl/ n cardo m

thong /θɒŋ/ n correa f; (Amer, sandal) chancla f

thorn /θɔːn/ n espina f. ~**y** adj espinoso

thorough /ˈθʌrə/ adj (investigation) riguroso; (cleaning etc) a fondo; (person) concienzudo. ~**bred** /-bred/ adj de pura sangre. ~**fare** n vía f pública; (street) calle f. **no** ~**fare** prohibido el paso. ~**ly** adv (clean) a fondo; (examine) minuciosamente; (completely) perfectamente

those /ðəʊz/ adj esos, esas, aquellos, aquellas. ● pron ésos, ésas, aquéllos, aquéllas

though /ðəʊ/ conj aunque. ● adv sin embargo. **as** ~ como si

thought /θɔːt/ see **THINK**. ● n pensamiento m; (idea) idea f. ~**ful** adj pensativo; (considerate) atento. ~**fully** adv pensativamente; (con-

siderately) atentamente. ~**less** adj desconsiderado

thousand /ˈθaʊznd/ adj & n mil (m). ~**th** adj & n milésimo (m)

thrash /θræʃ/ vt azotar; (defeat) derrotar

thread /θred/ n hilo m; (of screw) rosca f. ● vt enhebrar (needle); ensartar (beads). ~**bare** adj gastado, raído

threat /θret/ n amenaza f. ~**en** vt/i amenazar. ~**ening** adj amenazador

three /θriː/ adj & n tres (m). ~**fold** adj triple. ● adv tres veces

threshold /ˈθreʃhəʊld/ n umbral m

threw /θruː/ see **THROW**

thrift /θrɪft/ n economía f, ahorro m. ~**y** adj frugal

thrill /θrɪl/ n emoción f. ● vt emocionar. ~**ed** adj contentísimo (with con). ~**er** n (book) libro m de suspense or (LAm) suspenso; (film) película f de suspense or (LAm) suspenso. ~**ing** adj emocionante

thriv|e /θraɪv/ vi prosperar. ~**ing** adj próspero

throat /θrəʊt/ n garganta f

throb /θrɒb/ vi (pt throbbed) palpitar; (with pain) dar punzadas; (engine) vibrar. ~**bing** adj (pain) punzante

throes /θrəʊz/ npl. **be in one's death** ~ estar agonizando

throne /θrəʊn/ n trono m

throng /θrɒŋ/ n multitud f

throttle /ˈθrɒtl/ n (Auto) acelerador m (que se acciona con la mano). ● vt estrangular

through /θruː/ prep por, a través de; (during) durante; (by means of) a través de; (Amer, until and including) **Monday** ~ **Friday** de lunes a viernes. ● adv de parte a parte, de un lado a otro; (entirely) completamente; (to the end) hasta el final. be ~ (finished) haber terminado. ● adj (train etc) directo. no ~ road calle sin salida. ~out /-'aʊt/ prep por todo; (time) durante todo. ~out his career a lo largo de su carrera

throve /θrəʊv/ see THRIVE

throw /θrəʊ/ vt (pt threw, pp thrown) tirar, aventar (Mex); lanzar (grenade, javelin); (disconcert) desconcertar; 🄰 hacer day (party). ● n (of ball) tiro m; (of dice) tirada f. □ ~ away vt tirar. □ ~ up vi (vomit) vomitar.

thrush /θrʌʃ/ n tordo m

thrust /θrʌst/ vt (pt thrust) empujar; (push in) clavar. ● n empujón m; (of sword) estocada f

thud /θʌd/ n ruido m sordo

thug /θʌg/ n matón m

thumb /θʌm/ n pulgar m. ● vt. ~ a lift ir a dedo. ~tack n (Amer) chincheta f, tachuela f, chinche f (Mex)

thump /θʌmp/ vt golpear. ● vi (heart) latir fuertemente. ● n golpazo m

thunder /'θʌndə(r)/ n truenos mpl, (of traffic) estruendo m. ● vi tronar. ~bolt n rayo m. ~storm n tormenta f eléctrica. ~y adj con truenos

Thursday /'θɜːzdeɪ/ n jueves m

thus /ðʌs/ adv así

thwart /θwɔːt/ vt frustrar

tic /tɪk/ n tic m

tick /tɪk/ n (sound) tic m; (insect) garrapata f, (mark) marca f, visto m, palomita f (Mex); (fam, instant) momentito m. ● vi hacer tictac. ● vt. ~ (off) marcar

ticket /'tɪkɪt/ n (for bus, train) billete m, boleto m (LAm); (for plane) pasaje m, billete m. (for theatre, museum) entrada f; (for baggage, coat) ticket m; (fine) multa f. ~ collector n revisor m. ~ office n (transport) mostrador m de venta de billetes or (LAm) boletos; (in theatre) taquilla f, boletería f (LAm)

tickl|e /'tɪkl/ vt hacerle cosquillas a. ● n cosquilleo m. ~ish /'tɪklɪʃ/ adj. be ~ish tener cosquillas

tidal wave /'taɪdl/ n maremoto m

tide /taɪd/ n marea f. high/low ~ marea alta/baja. □ ~ over vt ayudar a salir de un apuro

tid|ily /'taɪdɪlɪ/ adv ordenadamente. ~iness n orden m. ~y adj (-ier, -iest) ordenado. ● vt/i ~y (up) ordenar, arreglar

tie /taɪ/ vt (pres p tying) atar, amarrar (LAm); hacer (knot). ● vi (Sport) empatar. ● n (constraint) atadura f; (bond) lazo m; (necktie) corbata f; (Sport) empate m. □ ~ in with vt concordar con. □ ~ up vt atar. be ~d up (busy) estar ocupado

tier /tɪə(r)/ n hilera f superpuesta; (in stadium etc) grada f; (of cake) piso m

tiger /'taɪgə(r)/ n tigre m

tight /taɪt/ adj (-er, -est) (clothes) ajustado, ceñido; (taut) tieso; (control) estricto; (knot, nut) apretado; (fam, drunk) borracho. ~en vt apretar. □ ~en up vt hacer más estricto. ~-fisted /-'fɪstɪd/ adj tacaño. ~ly adv bien, fuerte; (fastened) fuertemente. ~rope n cuerda f floja. ~s npl (for ballet etc) leotardo/s m(pl); (pantyhose) medias fpl

tile /taɪl/ n (decorative) azulejo m; (on roof) teja f; (on floor) baldosa f

till ● *vt* azulejar; tejar (roof); embaldosar (floor)

till /tɪl/ *prep* hasta. ● *conj* hasta que. ● *n* caja *f*. ● *vt* cultivar

tilt /tɪlt/ *vt* inclinar. □ *vi* inclinarse. ● *n* inclinación *f*

timber /'tɪmbə(r)/ *n* madera *f* (*para construcción*)

time /taɪm/ *n* tiempo *m*; (*moment*) momento *m*; (*occasion*) ocasión *f*; (*by clock*) hora *f*; (*epoch*) época *f*; (*rhythm*) compás *m*. **at** ~**s** a veces. **for the** ~ **being** por el momento. **from** ~ **to** ~ de vez en cuando. **have a good** ~ divertirse, pasarlo bien. **in a year's** ~ dentro de un año. **in no** ~ en un abrir y cerrar de ojos. **in** ~ a tiempo; (*eventually*) con el tiempo. **arrive on** ~ llegar a tiempo. **it's** ~ **we left** es hora de irnos. ● *vt* elegir el momento; cronometrar (race). ~ **bomb** *n* bomba *f* de tiempo. ~**ly** *adj* oportuno. ~**r** *n* cronómetro *m*; (*Culin*) avisador *m*; (*with sand*) reloj *m* de arena; (*Elec*) interruptor *m* de reloj. ~**s** /taɪmz/ *prep.* **2** ~**s 4 is 8** 2 (multiplicado) por 4 son 8. ~**table** *n* horario *m*

timid /'tɪmɪd/ *adj* tímido; (*fearful*) miedoso

tin /tɪn/ *n* estaño *m*; (*container*) lata *f*. ~ **foil** *n* papel *m* de estaño

tinge /tɪndʒ/ *vt.* **be** ~**d with sth** estar matizado de algo. ● *n* matiz *m*

tingle /'tɪŋɡl/ *vi* sentir un hormigueo

tinker /'tɪŋkə(r)/ *vi.* ~ **with** juguetear con

tinkle /'tɪŋkl/ *vi* tintinear

tinned /tɪnd/ *adj* en lata, enlatado

tin opener *n* abrelatas *m*

tint /tɪnt/ *n* matiz *m*

tiny /'taɪnɪ/ *adj* (**-ier, -iest**) minúsculo, diminuto

tip /tɪp/ *n* punta *f*. ● *vt* (*pt* **tipped**) (*tilt*) inclinar; (*overturn*) volcar; (*pour*) verter; (*give gratuity to*) darle (una) propina a. □ ~ **off** *vt* avisar. □ ~ **out** *vt* verter. □ ~ **over** *vi* caerse. ● *n* propina *f*; (*advice*) consejo *m* (práctico); (*for rubbish*) vertedero *m*. ~**ped** *adj* (cigarette) con filtro

tipsy /'tɪpsɪ/ *adj* achispado

tiptoe /'tɪptəʊ/ *n.* **on** ~ de puntillas

tiptop /'tɪptɒp/ *adj* ⒯ de primera. **in** ~ **condition** en excelente estado

tire /'taɪə(r)/ *n* (*Amer*) *see* TYRE. ● *vt* cansar. ● *vi* cansarse. ~**d** /'taɪəd/ *adj* cansado. **get** ~**d** cansarse. ~**d of** harto de. ~**d out** agotado. ~**less** *adj* incansable; (efforts) inagotable. ~**some** /-səm/ *adj* (person) pesado; (task) tedioso

tiring /'taɪərɪŋ/ *adj* cansado, cansador (LAm)

tissue /'tɪʃuː/ *n* (*of bones, plants*) tejido *m*; (*paper handkerchief*) pañuelo *m* de papel. ~ **paper** *n* papel *m* de seda

tit /tɪt/ *n* (bird) paro *m*; (⒯, breast) teta *f*

titbit /'tɪtbɪt/ *n* exquisitez *f*

tit for tat *n*: **it was** ~ fue ojo por ojo, diente por diente

title /'taɪtl/ *n* título *m*

to /tuː, tə/ *prep* **a**; (*towards*) hacia; (*in order to*) para; (*as far as*) hasta; (*of*) de. **give it** ~ **me** dámelo. **what did you say** ~ **him?** ¿qué le dijiste? **I don't want** ~ no quiero. **it's twenty** ~ **seven** (*by clock*) son las siete menos veinte, son veinte para las siete (*LAm*). ● *adv.* **pull** ~

cerrar. ~ **and fro** *adv* de un lado a otro

toad /təʊd/ *n* sapo *m*. ~**stool** *n* hongo *m* (*no comestible*)

toast /təʊst/ *n* pan tostado, tostadas *fpl*; (*drink*) brindis *m*. **a piece of** ~ una tostada, un pan tostado (*Mex*). **drink a** ~ **to** brindar por. ● *vt* (*Culin*) tostar; (*drink to*) brindar por. ~**er** *n* tostadora *f* (eléctrica), tostador *m*

tobacco /tə'bækəʊ/ *n* tabaco *m*. ~**nist** /-ənɪst/ *n* estanquero *m*

toboggan /tə'bɒɡən/ *n* tobogán *m*

today /tə'deɪ/ *n* & *adv* hoy (*m*)

toddler /'tɒdlə(r)/ *n* niño *m* pequeño (*entre un año y dos años y medio de edad*)

toe /təʊ/ *n* dedo *m* (del pie); (*of shoe*) punta *f*. **big** ~ dedo *m* gordo (del pie). **on one's** ~**s** (*fig*) alerta. ● *vt*. ~ **the line** acatar la disciplina

---

TOEFL - Test of English as a Foreign Language *i*
Un examen que, a la hora de solicitar el ingreso a una universidad americana, evalúa el dominio del inglés de aquellos estudiantes cuya lengua materna no es este idioma.

---

toffee /'tɒfɪ/ *n* toffee *m* (*golosina hecha con azúcar y mantequilla*)

together /tə'ɡeðə(r)/ *adv* juntos; (*at same time*) a la vez. ~ **with** junto con

toil /tɔɪl/ *vi* afanarse. ● *n* trabajo *m* duro

toilet /'tɔɪlɪt/ *n* servicio *m*, baño *m* (*LAm*). ~ **paper** *n* papel *m* higiénico. ~**ries** /'tɔɪlɪtrɪz/ *npl* artículos *mpl* de tocador. ~ **roll** *n* rollo *m* de papel higiénico

token /'təʊkən/ *n* muestra *f*; (*voucher*) vale *m*; (*coin*) ficha *f*. ● *adj* simbólico

told /təʊld/ *see* **TELL**

tolera|ble /'tɒlərəbl/ *adj* tolerable; (*not bad*) pasable. ~**nce** /'tɒlərəns/ *n* tolerancia *f*. ~**nt** *adj* tolerante. ~**te** /-reɪt/ *vt* tolerar. ~**tion** /-'reɪʃən/ *n* tolerancia *f*

toll /təʊl/ *n* (*on road*) peaje *m*, cuota *f* (*Mex*). **death** ~ número *m* de muertos. ~ **call** *n* (*Amer*) llamada *f* interurbana, conferencia *f*. ● *vi* doblar, tocar a muerto

tomato /tə'mɑːtəʊ/ *n* (*pl* -oes) tomate *m*, jitomate *m* (*Mex*)

tomb /tuːm/ *n* tumba *f*, sepulcro *m*. ~**stone** *n* lápida *f*

tomorrow /tə'mɒrəʊ/ *n* & *adv* mañana (*f*). **see you** ~! ¡hasta mañana!

ton /tʌn/ *n* tonelada *f* (= *1,016kg*). ~**s of** 🄳 montones de. **metric** ~ tonelada *f* (métrica) (= *1,000kg*)

tone /təʊn/ *n* tono *m*. ● *vi* ~ **down** atenuar; moderar (*language*). ~**-deaf** *adj* que no tiene oído (*musical*)

tongs /tɒŋz/ *npl* tenacillas *fpl*

tongue /tʌŋ/ *n* lengua *f*. **say sth** ~ **in cheek** decir algo medio burlándose. ~**-tied** *adj* cohibido. ~**-twister** *n* trabalenguas *m*

tonic /'tɒnɪk/ *adj* tónico. ● *n* (*Med, fig*) tónico *m*. ~ (**water**) *n* tónica *f*

tonight /tə'naɪt/ *adv* & *n* esta noche (*f*); (*evening*) esta tarde (*f*)

tonne /tʌn/ *n* tonelada *f* (métrica)

tonsil /'tɒnsl/ *n* amígdala *f*. ~**litis** /-'laɪtɪs/ *n* amigdalitis *f*

too /tuː/ *adv* (*excessively*) demasiado; (*also*) también. **I'm not** ~ **sure** no estoy muy seguro. ~ **many** demasiados. ~ **much**

demasiado

took /tʊk/ *see* TAKE

tool /tuːl/ *n* herramienta *f*

tooth /tuːθ/ *n* (*pl* teeth) diente *m*; (*molar*) muela *f*. ~**ache** *n* dolor *m* de muelas. ~**brush** *n* cepillo *m* de dientes. ~**paste** *n* pasta *f* dentífrica, pasta *f* de dientes. ~**pick** *n* palillo *m* (de dientes)

top /tɒp/ *n* parte *f* superior, parte *f* de arriba; (*of mountain*) cima *f*; (*of tree*) copa *f*; (*of page*) parte *f* superior; (*lid, of bottle*) tapa *f*; (*of pen*) capuchón *m*; (*spinning* ~) trompo *m*, peonza *f*. ~ **be** ~ **of the class** ser el primero de la clase. **from** ~ **to bottom** de arriba abajo. **on** ~ **of** encima de; (*besides*) además de. ● *adj* más alto; (*shelf*) superior; (*speed*) máximo; (*in rank*) superior; (*leading*) más destacado. ● *vt* (*pt* topped) cubrir; (*exceed*) exceder. ~ **floor** *n* último piso *m*. ~ **up** *vt* llenar. ~ **hat** *n* chistera *f*. ~**-heavy** /-ˈhevɪ/ *adj* inestable (por ser más pesado en su parte superior)

topic /ˈtɒpɪk/ *n* tema *m*. ~**al** *adj* de actualidad

topless /ˈtɒpləs/ *adj* topless

topple /ˈtɒpl/ *vi* (*Pol*) derribar; (*overturn*) volcar. ● *vi* caerse

top secret /tɒpˈsiːkrɪt/ *adj* secreto, reservado

torch /tɔːtʃ/ *n* linterna *f*; (*flaming*) antorcha *f*

tore /tɔː(r)/ *see* TEAR[1]

torment /ˈtɔːment/ *n* tormento *m*. ● /tɔːˈment/ *vt* atormentar

torn /tɔːn/ *see* TEAR[1]

tornado /tɔːˈneɪdəʊ/ *n* (*pl* -oes) tornado *m*

torpedo /tɔːˈpiːdəʊ/ *n* (*pl* -oes) torpedo *m*. ● *vt* torpedear

torrent /ˈtɒrənt/ *n* torrente *m*.

~**ial** /təˈrenʃl/ *adj* torrencial

torrid /ˈtɒrɪd/ *adj* tórrido; (*affair*) apasionado

tortoise /ˈtɔːtəs/ *n* tortuga *f*. ~**shell** *n* carey *m*

tortuous /ˈtɔːtjʊəs/ *adj* tortuoso

torture /ˈtɔːtʃə(r)/ *n* tortura *f*. ● *vt* torturar

Tory /ˈtɔːrɪ/ *adj* & *n* tory *m* & *f*

toss /tɒs/ *vt* tirar, lanzar (ball); (*shake*) sacudir. ● *vi*. ~ **and turn** (*in bed*) dar vueltas

tot /tɒt/ *n* pequeño *m*; (*fam, of liquor*) trago *m*. ● *vt* (*pt* totted). ~ **up** [1] sumar

total /ˈtəʊtl/ *adj* & *n* total (*m*). ● *vt* (*pt* totalled) ascender a un total de; (*add up*) totalizar. ~**itarian** /təʊtælɪˈteərɪən/ *adj* totalitario. ~**ly** *adv* totalmente

totter /ˈtɒtə(r)/ *vi* tambalearse

touch /tʌtʃ/ *vt* tocar; (*move*) conmover; (*concern*) afectar. ● *vi* tocar; (*wires*) tocarse. ● *n* toque *m*; (*sense*) tacto *m*; (*contact*) contacto *m*. **be/get/stay in** ~ **with** estar/ponerse/mantenerse en contacto con. □ ~ **down** *vi* (aircraft) aterrizar. □ ~ **up** *vt* retocar. ~**ing** *adj* enternecedor. ~**y** *adj* quisquilloso

tough /tʌf/ *adj* (-er, -est) duro; (*strong*) fuerte, resistente; (*difficult*) difícil; (*severe*) severo. ~**en**. ~ (**up**) *vt* endurecer; hacer más fuerte (person)

tour /tʊə(r)/ *n* viaje *m*; (*visit*) visita *f*; (*excursion*) excursión *f*; (*by team etc*) gira *f*. **be on** ~ estar de gira. ● *vt* recorrer; (*visit*) visitar. ~ **guide** *n* guía de turismo

touris|m /ˈtʊərɪzəm/ *n* turismo *m*. ~**t** /ˈtʊərɪst/ *n* turista *m* & *f*. ● *adj* turístico. ~**t office** *n* oficina *f* de turismo

tournament /'tɔːnəmənt/ n torneo m

tousle /'tauzl/ vt despeinar

tout /taut/ vi. ~ (for) solicitar

tow /təʊ/ vt remolcar. ● n remolque m

toward(s) /tə'wɔːd(z)/ prep hacia. his attitude ~ her su actitud para con ella

towel /'tauəl/ n toalla f

tower /'tauə(r)/ n torre f. ● vi. ~ above (building) descollar sobre; (person) destacar sobre. ~ block n edificio m or bloque m de apartamentos. ~ing adj altísimo; (rage) violento

town /taun/ n ciudad f; (smaller) pueblo m. go to ~ 🄴 no escatimar dinero. ~ hall n ayuntamiento m

toxic /'tɒksɪk/ adj tóxico

toy /tɔɪ/ n juguete m. ● n ~ with vt juguetear con (object); darle vueltas a (idea). ~shop n juguetería f

trace /treɪs/ n señal f, rastro m. ● vt trazar; (draw) dibujar; (with tracing paper) calcar; (track down) localizar. ~ing paper n papel m de calcar

track /træk/ n pista f, huellas fpl; (path) sendero m; (Sport) pista f. the ~(s) la vía férrea; (Rail) vía f. keep ~ of seguir la pista a (person). ● vt seguirle la pista a. □ ~ down vt localizar. ~ suit n equipo m (de deportes) chándal m

tract /trækt/ n (land) extensión f; (pamphlet) tratado m breve

traction /'trækʃn/ n tracción f

tractor /'træktə(r)/ n tractor m

trade /treɪd/ n comercio m; (occupation) oficio m; (exchange) cambio m; (industry) industria f. ● vt. ~ sth for sth cambiar algo por algo. ● vi

comerciar. □ ~ in vt (give in part-exchange) entregar como parte del pago. ~ mark n marca f (de fábrica). ~r n comerciante m & f. ~ union n sindicato m

tradition /trə'dɪʃn/ n tradición f. ~al adj tradicional

traffic /'træfɪk/ n tráfico m. ● vi (pt trafficked) comerciar (in en). ~ circle n (Amer) glorieta f, rotonda f. ~ island n isla f peatonal. ~ jam n embotellamiento m, atasco m. ~ lights npl semáforo m. ~ warden n guardia m, controlador m de tráfico

tragedy /'trædʒɪdɪ/ n tragedia f. ~ic /'trædʒɪk/ adj trágico

trail /treɪl/ vi arrastrarse; (lag) rezagarse. ● vt (track) seguir la pista de. ● n (left by animal, person) huellas fpl; (path) sendero m. be on the ~ of s.o./sth seguir la pista de uno/algo ~er n remolque m; (Amer, caravan) caravana f, rulot m; (film) avance m

train /treɪn/ n (Rail) tren m; (of events) serie f; (of dress) cola f. ● vt capacitar (employee); adiestrar (soldier); (Sport) entrenar; educar (voice); guiar (plant); amaestrar (animal). ● vi estudiar; (Sport) entrenarse. ~ed adj (skilled) cualificado, calificado; (doctor) diplomado. ~ee /treɪ'niː/ n aprendiz m; (Amer, Mil) recluta m & f. ~er n (Sport) entrenador m; (of animals) amaestrador m. ~ers mpl zapatillas fpl de deporte. ~ing n capacitación f; (Sport) entrenamiento m

trait /treɪ(t)/ n rasgo m

traitor /'treɪtə(r)/ n traidor m

tram /træm/ n tranvía m

tramp /træmp/ vi. ~ (along) caminar pesadamente. ● n vagabundo m

trample /'træmpl/ vt pisotear.
● vi. ~ on pisotear

trampoline /'træmpəli:n/ n
trampolín m

trance /trɑ:ns/ n trance m

tranquil /'træŋkwɪl/ adj tranquilo.
~**lity** /-'kwɪlətɪ/ n tranquilidad f;
(of person) serenidad f. ~**lize**
/'træŋkwɪlaɪz/ vt sedar, dar un sedante a. ~**lizer** n sedante m, tran-
quilizante m

transaction /træn'zækʃən/ n
transacción f, operación f

transatlantic /trænzət'læntɪk/
adj transatlántico

transcend /træn'send/ vt (go beyond) exceder

transcript /'trænskrɪpt/ n transcripción f

transfer /træns'fɜ:(r)/ vt (pt
transferred) trasladar; traspasar
(player); transferir (funds, property); pasar (call). ● vi trasladarse.
● /'trænsfə:(r)/ n traslado m; (of
player) traspaso m; (of funds, property) transferencia f; (paper) calcomanía f

transform /træns'fɔ:m/ vt transformar. ~**ation** /-ə'meɪʃn/ n trans-
formación f. ~**er** n transforma-
dor m

transfusion /træns'fju:ʒn/ n
transfusión f

transient /'trænzɪənt/ adj pasajero

transistor /træn'zɪstə(r)/ n transistor m

transit /'trænsɪt/ n tránsito m.
~**ion** /træn'zɪʒn/ n transición f.
~**ive** /'trænsɪtɪv/ adj transitivo

translat|e /trænz'leɪt/ vt traducir.
~**ion** /-ʃn/ n traducción f. ~**or** n
traductor m

transmission /træns'mɪʃn/ n

transmisión f

transmit /trænz'mɪt/ vt (pt
mitted) transmitir. ~**ter** n trans-
misor m

transparen|cy /træns'pærənsɪ/
n transparencia f; (Photo) diapositiva
f. ~**t** adj transparente

transplant /træns'plɑ:nt/ vt tras-
plantar. ● /'trænsplɑ:nt/ n tras-
plante m

transport /træn'spɔ:t/ vt transportar. ● /'trænspɔ:t/ n transporte
m. ~**ation** /-'teɪʃn/ n transporte m

trap /træp/ n trampa f. ● vt (pt
trapped) atrapar; (jam) atascar;
(cut off) bloquear. ~**door** n tram-
pilla f

trapeze /trə'pi:z/ n trapecio m

trash /træʃ/ n basura f; (Amer,
worthless people) escoria f. ~ **can** n
(Amer) cubo m de la basura, bote m
de la basura (Mex). ~**y** adj (souvenir) de porquería; (magazine)
malo

travel /'trævl/ vi (pt travelled) viajar; (vehicle) desplazarse. ● vt recorrer. ● n viajes mpl. ~ **agency** n
agencia f de viajes. ~**ler** n viajero
m. ~**ler's cheque** n cheque m de
viaje or viajero. ~**ling expenses**
npl gastos mpl de viaje

trawler /'trɔ:lə(r)/ n barca f pes-
quera

tray /treɪ/ n bandeja f

treacher|ous adj traidor; (decep-
tive) engañoso. ~**y** n traición f

treacle /'tri:kl/ n melaza f

tread /tred/ vi (pt trod, pp trodden) pisar. ~ **on sth** pisar algo. ~
carefully andarse con cuidado. ● n
(step) paso m; (of tyre) banda f de
rodamiento

treason /'tri:zn/ n traición f

treasur|e /'treʒə(r)/ n tesoro m.

~ed /'treʒəd/ adj (possession) preciado. **~er** /'treʒərə(r)/ n tesorero m. **~y** n erario m, tesoro m. **the T~y** el fisco, la hacienda pública. **Department of the T~y** (in US) Departamento m del Tesoro

treat /tri:t/ vt tratar; (Med) tratar. **~ s.o.** (to meal etc) invitar a uno. ● n placer m; (present) regalo m

treatise /'tri:tɪz/ n tratado m

treatment /'tri:tmənt/ n tratamiento m

treaty /'tri:tɪ/ n tratado m

treble /'trebl/ adj triple; (clef) de sol; (voice) de tiple. ● n triple m. ● vi triplicarse. ~ n tiple m & f

tree /tri:/ n árbol m

trek /trek/ n caminata f. ● vi (pt **trekked**) caminar

trellis /'trelɪs/ n enrejado m

tremble /'trembl/ vi temblar

tremendous /trɪ'mendəs/ adj formidable; (fam, huge) tremendo. **~ly** adv tremendamente

tremor /'tremə(r)/ n temblor m

trench /trentʃ/ n zanja f; (Mil) trinchera f

trend /trend/ n tendencia f; (fashion) moda f. **~y** adj (-ier, -iest) 🄵 moderno

trepidation /trepɪ'deɪʃn/ n inquietud f

trespass /'trespəs/ vi. **~ on** entrar sin autorización (en propiedad ajena). **~er** n intruso m

trial /'traɪəl/ n prueba f; (Jurid) proceso m, juicio m; (ordeal) prueba f dura. **by ~ and error** por ensayo y error. **be on ~** estar a prueba; (Jurid) estar siendo procesado

triangle /'traɪæŋgl/ n triángulo m. **~ular** /-'æŋgjʊlə(r)/ adj triangular

tribal /'traɪbl/ adj tribal. **~e** /traɪb/ n tribu f

tribulation /trɪbjʊ'leɪʃn/ n tribulación f

tribunal /traɪ'bju:nl/ n tribunal m

tributary /'trɪbjʊtrɪ/ n (of river) afluente m

tribute /'trɪbju:t/ n tributo m; (acknowledgement) homenaje m. **pay ~ to** rendir homenaje a

trick /trɪk/ n trampa f, ardid m; (joke) broma f; (feat) truco m; (in card games) baza f. **play a ~ on** gastar una broma a. ● vt engañar. **~ery** n engaño m

trickle /'trɪkl/ vi gotear. **~ in** (fig) entrar poco a poco

trickster /'trɪkstə(r)/ n estafador m

tricky /'trɪkɪ/ adj delicado, difícil

tricycle /'traɪsɪkl/ n triciclo m

tried /traɪd/ see **TRY**

trifle /'traɪfl/ n nimiedad f; (Culin) postre de bizcocho, jerez, frutas y nata. ● vi. ▫ **~e with** vt jugar con. **~ing** adj insignificante

trigger /'trɪgə(r)/ n (of gun) gatillo m. ● vt. **~ (off)** desencadenar

trim /trɪm/ adj (trimmer, trimmest) (slim) esbelto; (neat) elegante. ● vt (pt **trimmed**) (cut) recortar; (adorn) adornar. ● n (cut) recorte m. **in ~** en buen estado. **~mings** npl recortes mpl

trinity /'trɪnɪtɪ/ n. **the (Holy) T~** la (Santísima) Trinidad

trinket /'trɪŋkɪt/ n chuchería f

trio /'tri:əʊ/ n (pl -os) trío m

trip /trɪp/ (pt **tripped**) vt **~ (up)** hacerle una zancadilla a, hacer tropezar ● vi tropezar. ● n (journey) viaje m; (outing) excursión f; (stumble) traspié m

tripe /traɪp/ n callos mpl, mon-

triple | trunk

566

dongo m (LAm), pancita f (Mex);
(fam, nonsense) paparruchas fpl

triple /'trɪpl/ adj triple. ●vt triplicar. ●vi triplicarse. ~t /'trɪplɪt/ n
trillizo m

triplicate /'trɪplɪkət/ adj triplicado. **in** ~ por triplicado

tripod /'traɪpɒd/ n trípode m

trite /traɪt/ adj trillado

triumph /'traɪʌmf/ n triunfo m.
●vi triunfar (**over** sobre). ~al
/-'ʌmfl/ adj triunfal; ~ant /-'ʌmfnt/
adj (troops) triunfador; (moment)
triunfal; (smile) de triunfo

trivial /'trɪvɪəl/ adj insignificante;
(concerns) trivial. ~ity /-'ælətɪ/ n
trivialidad f

trod, trodden /trɒd, trɒdn/ see
TREAD

trolley /'trɒlɪ/ n (pl -eys) carretón
m; (in supermarket, airport) carrito
m; (for food, drink) carrito m, mesa
f rodante. ~ **car** n (Amer) tranvía f

trombone /trɒm'bəʊn/ n trombón m

troop /truːp/ n compañía f; (of
cavalry) escuadrón m. ●vi. ~ **in** entrar en tropel. ~ **out** salir en tropel. ~er n soldado m de caballería;
(Amer, state police officer) agente m
& f. ~s npl (Mil) tropas fpl

trophy /'trəʊfɪ/ n trofeo m

tropic /'trɒpɪk/ n trópico m. ~al
adj tropical. ~s npl trópicos mpl

trot /trɒt/ n trote m. ●vi (pt trotted) trotar

trouble /'trʌbl/ n problemas mpl;
(awkward situation) apuro m; (inconvenience) molestia f. **be in** ~
estar en apuros. **get into** ~ meterse en problemas. **look for** ~
buscar camorra. **take the** ~ **to do
sth** molestarse en hacer algo. ●vt
(bother) molestar; (worry) preocu-

par. ~maker n alborotador m.
~some adj problemático. ~
spot n punto m conflictivo

trough /trɒf/ n (for drinking)
abrevadero m; (for feeding) comedero m

troupe /truːp/ n compañía f teatral

trousers /'traʊzəz/ npl pantalón
m, pantalones mpl

trout /traʊt/ n (pl trout) trucha f

trowel /'traʊəl/ n (garden) desplantador m; (for mortar) paleta f

truant /'truːənt/ n. **play** ~ hacer
novillos

truce /truːs/ n tregua f

truck /trʌk/ n camión m; (Rail)
vagón m, furgón m; (Amer, vegetables, fruit) productos mpl de la
huerta. ~ **driver**, ~er (Amer) camionero m. ~**ing** n transporte m
por carretera

trudge /trʌdʒ/ vi andar penosamente

true /truː/ adj (-er, -est) verdadero;
(story, account) verídico; (friend)
auténtico, de verdad. ~ **to sth/
s.o.** fiel a algo/uno. **be** ~ ser
cierto. **come** ~ hacerse realidad

truffle /'trʌfl/ n trufa f; (chocolate)
trufa f de chocolate

truly /'truːlɪ/ adv verdaderamente;
(sincerely) sinceramente. **yours** ~
(in letters) cordiales saludos

trump /trʌmp/ n (Cards) triunfo m;
(fig) baza f

trumpet /'trʌmpɪt/ n trompeta f.
~er n trompetista m & f, trompeta
m & f

truncheon /'trʌntʃən/ n porra f

trunk /trʌŋk/ n (of tree) tronco m;
(box) baúl m; (of elephant) trompa
f; (Amer, Auto) maletero m, cajuela f
(Mex). ~s npl bañador m, traje m

de baño

truss /trʌs/ vt. truss (up) vt atar

trust /trʌst/ n confianza f; (money, property) fondo m de inversiones; (institution) fundación f. **on** ~ a ojos cerrados; (Com) al fiado. ● vi. ~ **in s.o./sth** confiar en uno/algo. ● vt confiar en; (in negative sentences) fiarse; (hope) esperar. **~ed** adj leal. **~ee** /trʌˈstiː/ n fideicomisario m. **~ful** adj confiado. **~ing** adj confiado. **~worthy**, **~y** adj digno de confianza

truth /truːθ/ n (pl **-s** /truːðz/) verdad f; (of account, story) veracidad f. **~ful** adj veraz.

try /traɪ/ vt (pt **tried**) intentar; probar (food, product); (be a strain on) poner a prueba; (Jurid) procesar. ~ **to do sth** tratar de hacer algo, intentar hacer algo. ~ **not to** forget procura no olvidarte. ● n tentativa f, prueba f; (Rugby) ensayo m. □ ~ **on** vt probarse (garment). □ ~ **out** vt probar. **~ing** adj duro; (annoying) molesto

tsar /zɑː(r)/ n zar m

T-shirt /ˈtiːʃɜːt/ n camiseta f

tub /tʌb/ n cuba f; (for washing clothes) tina f; (bathtub) bañera f; (for ice cream) envase m, tarrina f

tuba /ˈtjuːbə/ n tuba f

tubby /ˈtʌbɪ/ adj (**-ier**, **-iest**) rechoncho

tube /tjuːb/ n tubo m; (Brit fam, Rail) metro m; (Amer fam, television) tele f. **inner** ~ n cámara f de aire

tuberculosis /tjuːbɜːkjʊˈləʊsɪs/ n tuberculosis f

tub|ing /ˈtjuːbɪŋ/ n tubería f. **~ular** /-jʊlə(r)/ adj tubular

tuck /tʌk/ n (fold) jareta f. ● vt plegar; (put) meter. □ ~ **in(to)** vi (fam, eat) ponerse a comer. □ ~

up vt arropar (child)

Tuesday /ˈtjuːzdeɪ/ n martes m

tuft /tʌft/ n (of hair) mechón m; (of feathers) penacho m; (of grass) mata f

tug /tʌɡ/ vt (pt **tugged**) tirar de. ● vi. ~ **at sth** tirar de algo. ● n tirón m; (Naut) remolcador m. **~-of-war** n juego de tira y afloja

tuition /tjuːˈɪʃn/ n clases fpl

tulip /ˈtjuːlɪp/ n tulipán m

tumble /ˈtʌmbl/ vi caerse. ● n caída f. □ **~down** adj en ruinas. **~-drier** n secadora f. **~r** n (glass) vaso m (de lados rectos)

tummy /ˈtʌmɪ/ n [🛈] barriga f

tumour /ˈtjuːmə(r)/ n tumor m

tumult /ˈtjuːmʌlt/ n tumulto m. **~uous** /-ˈmʌltjʊəs/ adj (applause) apoteósico

tuna /ˈtjuːnə/ n (pl **tuna**) atún m

tune /tjuːn/ n melodía f; (piece) tonada f. **be in** ~ estar afinado. **be out of** ~ estar desafinado. ● vt afinar, sintonizar (radio, TV); (Mec) poner a punto. ● vi. ~ **in (to)** sintonizar (con). □ ~ **up** vt/i afinar. **~ful** adj melodioso. **~r** n afinador m; (Radio) sintonizador m

tunic /ˈtjuːnɪk/ n túnica f

tunnel /ˈtʌnl/ n túnel m. ● vi (pt **tunnelled**) abrir un túnel

turban /ˈtɜːbən/ n turbante m

turbine /ˈtɜːbaɪn/ n turbina f

turbo /ˈtɜːbəʊ/ n (pl **-os**) turbo (compresor) m

turbulen|ce /ˈtɜːbjʊləns/ n turbulencia f. **~t** adj turbulento

turf /tɜːf/ n (pl **turfs** or **turves**) césped m; (segment of grass) tepe m. □ ~ **out** vt [🛈] echar

turgid /ˈtɜːdʒɪd/ adj (language) ampuloso

turkey /ˈtɜːkɪ/ n (pl -eys) pavo m

Turk|ey /ˈtɜːkɪ/ f Turquía f. ~**ish** adj & n turco (m)

turmoil /ˈtɜːmɔɪl/ n confusión f

turn /tɜːn/ vt hacer girar; volver (head, page); doblar (corner); (change) cambiar; (deflect) desviar. ~ **sth into sth** convertir or transformar algo en algo. ● vi (handle) girar, dar vueltas; (person) volverse, darse la vuelta. ~ **right** girar or doblar or torcer a la derecha. ~ **red** ponerse rojo. ~ **into sth** convertirse en algo. ● n vuelta f; (in road) curva f; (change) giro m; (sequence) turno m; (fam, of illness) ataque m. **good** ~ favor m. **in** ~ a su vez. ~ **down** vt (fold) doblar; (reduce) bajar; (reject) rechazar. □ ~ **off** vt cerrar (tap); apagar (light, TV, etc). vi (from road) doblar. □ ~ **on** vt abrir (tap); encender, prender (LAm) (light etc). □ ~ **out** vt apagar (light etc). vi (result) resultar. □ ~ **round** vi darse la vuelta. □ ~ **up** vi aparecer. vt (find) encontrar; levantar (collar); subir (hem); acortar (trousers); poner más fuerte (gas). ~**ed-up** adj (nose) respingón. ~**ing** n (in town) bocacalle f. **we've missed the ~ing** nos hemos pasado la calle (or carretera). ~**ing-point** n momento m decisivo.

turnip /ˈtɜːnɪp/ n nabo m

turn: ~**over** n (Com) facturación f; (of staff) movimiento m. ~**pike** n (Amer) autopista f de peaje. ~**stile** n torniquete m. ~**table** n platina f. ~**up** n (of trousers) vuelta f, valenciana f (Mex)

turquoise /ˈtɜːkwɔɪz/ adj & n turquesa (f)

turret /ˈtʌrɪt/ n torrecilla f

turtle /ˈtɜːtl/ n tortuga f de mar; (Amer, tortoise) tortuga f

turves /tɜːvz/ see TURF

tusk /tʌsk/ n colmillo m

tussle /ˈtʌsl/ n lucha f

tutor /ˈtjuːtə(r)/ n profesor m particular

tuxedo /tʌkˈsiːdəʊ/ n (pl -os) (Amer) esmoquin m, smoking m

TV /tiːˈviː/ n televisión f, tele f ▣

twang /twæŋ/ n tañido m; (in voice) gangueo m

tweet /twiːt/ n piada f. ● vi piar

tweezers /ˈtwiːzəz/ npl pinzas fpl

twel|fth /twelfθ/ adj duodécimo. ● n doceavo m. ~**ve** /twelv/ adj & n doce (m)

twent|ieth /ˈtwentɪəθ/ adj vigésimo. ● n veinteavo m. ~**y** /ˈtwentɪ/ adj & n veinte (m)

twice /twaɪs/ adv dos veces. ~ **as many people** el doble de gente

twiddle /ˈtwɪdl/ vt (hacer) girar

twig /twɪg/ n ramita f. ● vi (pt twigged) ▣ caer, darse cuenta

twilight /ˈtwaɪlaɪt/ n crepúsculo m

twin /twɪn/ adj & n gemelo (m), mellizo (m) (LAm)

twine /twaɪn/ n cordel m, bramante m

twinge /twɪndʒ/ n punzada f; (of remorse) punzada f

twinkle /ˈtwɪŋkl/ vi centellear. ● n centelleo m; (in eye) brillo m

twirl /twɜːl/ vt (hacer) girar. ● vi girar. ● n vuelta f

twist /twɪst/ vt retorcer; (roll) enrollar; girar (knob); tergiversar (words); (distort) retorcer. ~ **one's ankle** torcerse el tobillo. ● vi (rope, wire) enrollarse; (road, river) serpentear. ● n torsión f; (curve) vuelta f

twit /twɪt/ n 🔲 imbécil m

twitch /twɪtʃ/ vi moverse. ● n tic m

twitter /'twɪtə(r)/ vi gorjear

two /tuː/ adj & n dos (m). **~-bit** adj (Amer) de tres al cuarto. **~-faced** adj falso, insincero. **~fold** adj doble. ● adv dos veces. **~pence** /'tʌpəns/ n dos peniques mpl. **~-piece (suit)** n traje m de dos piezas. **~-way** adj (traffic) de doble sentido

tycoon /taɪ'kuːn/ n magnate m

tying /'taɪɪŋ/ see TIE

type /taɪp/ n tipo m. ● vt/i escribir a máquina. **~cast** adj (actor) encasillado. **~script** n texto m mecanografiado, manuscrito m (de una obra, novela etc). **~writer** n máquina f de escribir. **~written** adj escrito a máquina, mecanografiado

typhoon /taɪ'fuːn/ n tifón m

typical /'tɪpɪkl/ adj típico. **~ly** adv típicamente

typify /'tɪpɪfaɪ/ vt tipificar

typi|ng /'taɪpɪŋ/ n mecanografía f. **~st** n mecanógrafo m

tyran|nical /tɪ'rænɪkl/ adj tiránico. **~ny** /'tɪrənɪ/ n tiranía f. **~t** /'taɪərənt/ n tirano m

tyre /'taɪə(r)/ n neumático m, llanta f (LAm)

udder /'ʌdə(r)/ n ubre f

UFO /'juːfəʊ/ abbr (= unidentified flying object) OVNI m (objeto volante no identificado)

ugly /'ʌɡlɪ/ adj (-ier, -iest) feo

UK /juː'keɪ/ abbr (= United Kingdom) Reino m Unido

Ukraine /juː'kreɪn/ n Ucrania f

ulcer /'ʌlsə(r)/ n úlcera f; (external) llaga f

ultimate /'ʌltɪmət/ adj (eventual) final; (utmost) máximo. **~ly** adv en última instancia; (in the long run) a la larga

ultimatum /ʌltɪ'meɪtəm/ n (pl -ums) ultimátum m

ultra... /'ʌltrə/ pref ultra... **~violet** /-'vaɪələt/ adj ultravioleta

umbilical cord /ʌm'bɪlɪkl/ n cordón m umbilical

umbrella /ʌm'brelə/ n paraguas m

umpire /'ʌmpaɪə(r)/ n árbitro m. ● vt arbitrar

umpteen /'ʌmptiːn/ adj 🔲 tropecientos 🔲. **~th** adj 🔲 enésimo

un... /ʌn/ pref in..., des..., no, poco, sin

UN /juː'en/ abbr (= United Nations) ONU f (Organización de las Naciones Unidas)

unable /ʌn'eɪbl/ adj. be **~** to no poder; (be incapable of) ser incapaz de

unacceptable /ʌnək'septəbl/ adj (behaviour) inaceptable; (terms) inadmisible

unaccompanied /ʌnə
ˈkʌmpənid/ adj (luggage) no acom-
pañado; (person, instrument) solo;
(singing) sin acompañamiento

unaccustomed /ʌnəˈkʌstəmd/
adj desacostumbrado. **be ~ to** adj
no estar acostumbrado a

unaffected /ʌnəˈfektɪd/ adj natural

unaided /ʌnˈeɪdɪd/ adj sin ayuda

unanimous /juːˈnænɪməs/ adj
unánime. **~ly** adv unánimemente;
(elect) por unanimidad

unarmed /ʌnˈɑːmd/ adj desar-
mado

unattended /ʌnəˈtendɪd/ adj sin
vigilar

unattractive /ʌnəˈtræktɪv/ adj
poco atractivo

unavoidabl|e /ʌnəˈvɔɪdəbl/ adj
inevitable. **~y** adv. **I was ~y de-
layed** no pude evitar llegar tarde

unaware /ʌnəˈweə(r)/ adj. **be ~
of** ignorar, no ser consciente de.
~s /-eəz/ adv desprevenido

unbearabl|e /ʌnˈbeərəbl/ adj in-
soportable, inaguantable. **~y** adv
inaguantablemente

unbeat|able /ʌnˈbiːtəbl/ adj
(quality) insuperable; (team) invencible. **~en** adj no vencido; (record)
insuperado

unbelievabl|e /ʌnbɪˈliːvəbl/ adj
increíble. **~y** adv increíblemente

unbiased /ʌnˈbaɪəst/ adj imparcial

unblock /ʌnˈblɒk/ vt desatascar

unbolt /ʌnˈbəʊlt/ vt descorrer el
pestillo de

unborn /ʌnˈbɔːn/ adj que todavía
no ha nacido

unbreakable /ʌnˈbreɪkəbl/ adj
irrompible

unbroken /ʌnˈbrəʊkən/ adj (in-

tact) intacto; (continuous) ininterrumpido

unbutton /ʌnˈbʌtn/ vt desabotonar, desabrochar

uncalled-for /ʌnˈkɔːldfɔː(r)/ adj
fuera de lugar

uncanny /ʌnˈkæni/ adj (**-ier,
-iest**) raro, extraño

uncertain /ʌnˈsɜːtn/ adj incierto;
(hesitant) vacilante. **be ~ of/about
sth** no estar seguro de algo. **~ty** n
incertidumbre f

uncharitable /ʌnˈtʃærɪtəbl/ adj
severo

uncivilized /ʌnˈsɪvɪlaɪzd/ adj in-
civilizado

uncle /ˈʌŋkl/ n tío m

Uncle Sam Es la típica *i*
personificación de EE.UU.,
en que éste es representado por
un hombre de barba blanca, vestido con los colores nacionales y
con un sombrero de copa ador-
nado con estrellas. Es posible que
la imagen se haya extraído del
cartel de reclutamiento, en 1917,
que llevaba la leyenda: "A Ud. lo
necesito".

unclean /ʌnˈkliːn/ adj impuro

unclear /ʌnˈklɪə(r)/ adj poco claro

uncomfortable /ʌnˈkʌmfətəbl/
adj incómodo

uncommon /ʌnˈkɒmən/ adj poco
común

uncompromising /ʌn
ˈkɒmprəmaɪzɪŋ/ adj intransigente

unconcerned /ʌnkənˈsɜːnd/ adj
indiferente

unconditional /ʌnkənˈdɪʃənl/
adj incondicional

unconnected /ʌnkəˈnektɪd/ adj
(unrelated) sin conexión. **the**

events are ~ estos acontecimientos no guardan ninguna relación (entre sí)

unconscious /ʌnˈkɒnʃəs/ adj (Med) inconsciente. **~ly** adv inconscientemente

unconventional /ʌnkən 'venʃənl/ adj poco convencional

uncork /ʌnˈkɔːk/ vt descorchar

uncouth /ʌnˈkuːθ/ adj zafio

uncover /ʌnˈkʌvə(r)/ vt destapar; revelar (plot, scandal)

undaunted /ʌnˈdɔːntɪd/ adj impertérrito

undecided /ʌndɪˈsaɪdɪd/ adj indeciso

undeniabl|e /ʌndɪˈnaɪəbl/ adj innegable. **~y** adv sin lugar a dudas

under /ˈʌndə(r)/ prep debajo de; (less than) menos de; (heading) bajo; (according to) según; (expressing movement) por debajo de. ● adv debajo, abajo

under... pref sub...

under: ~carriage n tren m de aterrizaje. **~charge** vt /-ˈtʃɑːdʒ/ cobrarle de menos a. **~clothes** npl ropa f interior. **~coat**, **~coating** n (paint) pintura f base; (first coat) primera mano f de pintura. **~cover** adj /-ˈkʌvə(r)/ secreto. **~current** n corriente f submarina. **~dog** n. **the ~dog** el que tiene menos posibilidades. **the ~dogs** npl los de abajo. **~done** adj /-ˈdʌn/ (meat) poco hecho. **~estimate** /-ˈestɪmeɪt/ vt (underrate) subestimar. **~fed** /-ˈfed/ adj subalimentado. **~foot** /-ˈfʊt/ adv debajo de los pies. **~go** vt (pt -went, pp -gone) sufrir. **~graduate** /-ˈɡrædjʊət/ n estudiante m universitario (no licenciado). **~ground**

/-ˈɡraʊnd/ adv bajo tierra; (in secret) clandestinamente. ● adj /-ˈɡraʊnd/ subterráneo; (secret) clandestino. ● n metro m. **~growth** n maleza f. **~hand** /-ˈhænd/ adj (secret) clandestino; (deceptive) fraudulento. **~lie** /-ˈlaɪ/ vt (pt -lay, pp -lain, pres p -lying) subyacer a. **~line** /-ˈlaɪn/ vt subrayar. **~lying** /-ˈlaɪɪŋ/ adj subyacente. **~mine** /-ˈmaɪn/ vt socavar. **~neath** /-ˈniːθ/ prep debajo de, abajo de (LAm). ● adv por debajo. **~paid** /-ˈpeɪd/ adj mal pagado. **~pants** npl calzoncillos mpl. **~pass** n paso m subterráneo; (for traffic) paso m inferior. **~privileged** /-ˈprɪvəlɪdʒd/ adj desfavorecido. **~rate** /-ˈreɪt/ vt subestimar. **~rated** /-ˈreɪtd/ adj no debidamente apreciado. **~shirt** n (Amer) camiseta f (interior).

understand /ʌndəˈstænd/ vt (pt -stood) entender; (empathize with) comprender, entender. ● vi entender, comprender. **~able** adj comprensible. **~ing** (grasp) entendimiento m; (sympathy) comprensión f; (agreement) acuerdo m

under: ~statement n subestimación f. **~take** /-ˈteɪk/ (pt -took, pp -taken) emprender (task); asumir (responsibility). **~take to do sth** comprometerse a hacer algo. **~taker** n director m de pompas fúnebres. **~taking** /-ˈteɪkɪŋ/ n empresa f; (promise) promesa f. **~tone** n. **in an ~tone** en voz baja. **~value** /-ˈvæljuː/ vt subvalorar. **~water** /-ˈwɔːtə(r)/ adj submarino. ● adv debajo del agua. **~wear** n ropa f interior. **~weight** /-ˈweɪt/ adj de peso más bajo que el normal. **~went** /-ˈwent/ see UNDERGO.

u

~world n (criminals) hampa f.
~write /-'raɪt/ vt (pt **-wrote**, pp **-written**) (Com) asegurar; (guarantee financially) financiar

undeserved /ʌndɪ'zɜːvd/ adj inmerecido

undesirable /ʌndɪ'zaɪərəbl/ adj indeseable

undignified /ʌn'dɪgnɪfaɪd/ adj indecoroso

undisputed /ʌndɪs'pjuːtɪd/ adj (champion) indiscutido; (facts) innegable

undo /ʌn'duː/ vt (pt **-did**, pp **-done**) desabrochar (button, jacket); abrir (zip); desatar (knot, laces)

undoubted /ʌn'daʊtɪd/ adj indudable. **~ly** adv indudablemente, sin duda

undress /ʌn'dres/ vt desvestir, desnudar. ● vi desvestirse, desnudarse

undue /ʌn'djuː/ adj excesivo

undulate /'ʌndjʊleɪt/ vi ondular

unduly /ʌn'djuːlɪ/ adv excesivamente

unearth /ʌn'ɜːθ/ vt desenterrar; descubrir (document)

unearthly /ʌn'ɜːθlɪ/ adj sobrenatural. **at an ~ hour** a estas horas intempestivas

uneasy /ʌn'iːzɪ/ adj incómodo

uneconomic /ʌniːkə'nɒmɪk/ adj poco económico

uneducated /ʌn'edjʊkeɪtɪd/ adj sin educación

unemploy|ed /ʌnɪm'plɔɪd/ adj desempleado, parado. **~ment** n desempleo m, paro m

unending /ʌn'endɪŋ/ adj interminable, sin fin

unequal /ʌn'iːkwəl/ adj desigual

unequivocal /ʌnɪ'kwɪvəkl/ adj inequívoco

unethical /ʌn'eθɪkl/ adj poco ético, inmoral

uneven /ʌn'iːvn/ adj desigual

unexpected /ʌnɪk'spektɪd/ adj inesperado; (result) imprevisto. **~ly** adv (arrive) de improviso; (happen) de forma imprevista

unfair /ʌn'feə(r)/ adj injusto; procedente (dismissal). **~ly** adv injustamente

unfaithful /ʌn'feɪθfl/ adj infiel

unfamiliar /ʌnfə'mɪlɪə(r)/ adj desconocido. **be ~ with** desconocer

unfasten /ʌn'fɑːsn/ vt desabrochar (clothes); (untie) desatar

unfavourable /ʌn'feɪvərəbl/ adj desfavorable

unfeeling /ʌn'fiːlɪŋ/ adj insensible

unfit /ʌn'fɪt/ adj. **I'm ~** no estoy en forma. **~ for human consumption** no apto para el consumo

unfold /ʌn'fəʊld/ vt desdoblar; desplegar (wings); (fig) revelar. ● vi (leaf) abrirse; (events) desarrollarse

unforeseen /ʌnfɔː'siːn/ adj imprevisto

unforgettable /ʌnfə'getəbl/ adj inolvidable

unforgivable /ʌnfə'gɪvəbl/ adj imperdonable

unfortunate /ʌn'fɔːtʃənət/ adj desafortunado; (regrettable) lamentable. **~ly** adv desafortunadamente; (stronger) por desgracia, desgraciadamente

unfounded /ʌn'faʊndɪd/ adj infundado

unfriendly /ʌn'frendlɪ/ adj poco amistoso; (stronger) antipático

573   unfurl | unmarried

unfurl /ʌnˈfɜːl/ vt desplegar

ungainly /ʌnˈɡeɪnlɪ/ adj desgarbado

ungrateful /ʌnˈɡreɪtfl/ adj desagradecido, ingrato

unhapp|iness /ʌnˈhæpɪnes/ n infelicidad f, tristeza f. ∼y adj (**-ier, -iest**) infeliz, triste; (*unsuitable*) inoportuno. **be** ∼**y about sth** no estar contento con algo

unharmed /ʌnˈhɑːmd/ adj (person) ileso

unhealthy /ʌnˈhelθɪ/ adj (**-ier, -iest**) (person) de mala salud; (complexion) enfermizo; (conditions) poco saludable

unhurt /ʌnˈhɜːt/ adj ileso

unification /juːnɪfɪˈkeɪʃn/ n unificación f

uniform /ˈjuːnɪfɔːm/ adj & n uniforme (m). ∼**ity** /-ˈfɔːmətɪ/ n uniformidad f

unify /ˈjuːnɪfaɪ/ vt unir

unilateral /juːnɪˈlætərəl/ adj unilateral

unimaginable /ʌnɪˈmædʒɪnəbl/ adj inimaginable

unimaginative /ʌnɪˈmædʒɪnətɪv/ adj (person) poco imaginativo

unimportant /ʌnɪmˈpɔːtnt/ adj sin importancia

uninhabited /ʌnɪnˈhæbɪtɪd/ adj deshabitado; (island) despoblado

unintelligible /ʌnɪnˈtelɪdʒəbl/ adj ininteligible

unintentional /ʌnɪnˈtenʃənl/ adj involuntario

union /ˈjuːnjən/ n unión f; (trade union) sindicato m; (student ∼) asociación f de estudiantes. **U**∼ **Jack** n bandera f del Reino Unido

unique /juːˈniːk/ adj único

unison /ˈjuːnɪsn/ n. **in** ∼ al unísono

unit /ˈjuːnɪt/ n unidad f; (of furniture etc) módulo m; (in course) módulo m

unite /juːˈnaɪt/ vt unir. ● vi unirse. **U**∼**d Kingdom** n Reino m Unido. **U**∼**d Nations** n Organización f de las Naciones Unidas (ONU). **U**∼**d States (of America)** n Estados mpl Unidos (de América)

unity /ˈjuːnɪtɪ/ n unidad f

univers|al /juːnɪˈvɜːsl/ adj universal. ∼**e** /ˈjuːnɪvɜːs/ n universo m

university /juːnɪˈvɜːsətɪ/ n universidad f. ● adj universitario

unjust /ʌnˈdʒʌst/ adj injusto. ∼**ified** /-ɪfaɪd/ adj injustificado

unkind /ʌnˈkaɪnd/ adj poco amable; (cruel) cruel; (remark) hiriente

unknown /ʌnˈnəʊn/ adj desconocido

unlawful /ʌnˈlɔːfl/ adj ilegal

unleaded /ʌnˈledɪd/ adj (fuel) sin plomo

unleash /ʌnˈliːʃ/ vt soltar

unless /ʌnˈles, ənˈles/ conj a menos que, a no ser que

unlike /ʌnˈlaɪk/ prep diferente de. (in contrast to) a diferencia de. ∼**ly** adj improbable

unlimited /ʌnˈlɪmɪtɪd/ adj ilimitado

unlisted /ʌnˈlɪstɪd/ adj (Amer) que no figura en la guía telefónica, privado (Mex)

unload /ʌnˈləʊd/ vt descargar

unlock /ʌnˈlɒk/ vt abrir (con llave)

unluck|ily /ʌnˈlʌkɪlɪ/ adv desgraciadamente. ∼**y** adj (**-ier, -iest**) (person) sin suerte, desafortunado. **be** ∼**y** tener mala suerte; (bring bad luck) traer mala suerte

unmarried /ʌnˈmærɪd/ adj

soltero

unmask /ʌnˈmɑːsk/ vt desenmascarar

unmentionable /ʌn 'menʃənəbl/ adj inmencionable

unmistakable /ʌnmɪˈsteɪkəbl/ adj inconfundible

unnatural /ʌnˈnætʃərəl/ adj poco natural; (not normal) anormal

unnecessar|ily /ʌnˈnesəsərɪli/ adv innecesariamente. **~y** adj innecesario

unnerve /ʌnˈnɜːv/ vt desconcertar

unnoticed /ʌnˈnəʊtɪst/ adj inadvertido

unobtainable /ʌnəbˈteɪnəbl/ adj imposible de conseguir

unobtrusive /ʌnəbˈtruːsɪv/ adj discreto

unofficial /ʌnəˈfɪʃl/ adj no oficial. **~ly** adv extraoficialmente

unpack /ʌnˈpæk/ vt sacar las cosas de (bags); deshacer, desempacar (LAm) (suitcase). ● vi deshacer las maletas, desempacar (LAm)

unpaid /ʌnˈpeɪd/ adj (work) no retribuido, no remunerado; (leave) sin sueldo

unperturbed /ʌnpəˈtɜːbd/ adj impasible. **he carried on ~** siguió sin inmutarse

unpleasant /ʌnˈpleznt/ adj desagradable

unplug /ʌnˈplʌg/ vt desenchufar

unpopular /ʌnˈpɒpjʊlə(r)/ adj impopular

unprecedented /ʌn 'presɪdentɪd/ adj sin precedentes

unpredictable /ʌnprɪˈdɪktəbl/ adj imprevisible

unprepared /ʌnprɪˈpeəd/ adj no preparado; (unready) desprevenido

unprofessional /ʌnprəˈfeʃənəl/ adj poco profesional

unprofitable /ʌnˈprɒfɪtəbl/ adj no rentable

unprotected /ʌnprəˈtektɪd/ adj sin protección; (sex) sin el uso de preservativos

unqualified /ʌnˈkwɒlɪfaɪd/ adj sin título; (fig) absoluto

unquestion|able /ʌn 'kwestʃənəbl/ adj incuestionable, innegable. **~ing** adj (obedience) ciego; (loyalty) incondicional

unravel /ʌnˈrævl/ vt (pt unravelled) desenredar; desentrañar (mystery)

unreal /ʌnˈrɪəl/ adj irreal. **~istic** /-ˈlɪstɪk/ adj poco realista

unreasonable /ʌnˈriːzənəbl/ adj irrazonable

unrecognizable /ʌnrekəg 'naɪzəbl/ adj irreconocible

unrelated /ʌnrɪˈleɪtɪd/ adj (facts) no relacionados (entre sí); (people) no emparentado

unreliable /ʌnrɪˈlaɪəbl/ adj (person) informal; (machine) poco fiable; (information) poco fidedigno

unrepentant /ʌnrɪˈpentənt/ adj impenitente

unrest /ʌnˈrest/ n (discontent) descontento m; (disturbances) disturbios mpl

unrivalled /ʌnˈraɪvld/ adj incomparable

unroll /ʌnˈrəʊl/ vt desenrollar. ● vi desenrollarse

unruffled /ʌnˈrʌfld/ (person) sereno

unruly /ʌnˈruːlɪ/ adj (class) indisciplinado; (child) revoltoso

unsafe /ʌnˈseɪf/ adj inseguro

unsatisfactory /ʌnsætɪs 'fæktərɪ/ adj insatisfactorio

unsavoury | unwind

unsavoury /ʌnˈseɪvərɪ/ adj desagradable

unscathed /ʌnˈskeɪðd/ adj ileso

unscheduled /ʌnˈʃedjuːld/ adj no programado, no previsto

unscrew /ʌnˈskruː/ vt destornillar; desenroscar (lid)

unscrupulous /ʌnˈskruːpjʊləs/ adj inescrupuloso

unseemly /ʌnˈsiːmlɪ/ adj indecoroso

unseen /ʌnˈsiːn/ adj (danger) oculto; (unnoticed) sin ser visto

unselfish /ʌnˈselfɪʃ/ adj (act) desinteresado; (person) nada egoísta

unsettle /ʌnˈsetl/ vt desestabilizar (situation); alterar (plans). **~d** adj agitado; (weather) inestable; (undecided) pendiente (de resolución)

unshakeable /ʌnˈʃeɪkəbl/ adj inquebrantable

unshaven /ʌnˈʃeɪvn/ adj sin afeitar, sin rasurar (Mex)

unsightly /ʌnˈsaɪtlɪ/ adj feo

unskilled /ʌnˈskɪld/ adj (work) no especializado; (worker) no cualificado, no calificado

unsociable /ʌnˈsəʊʃəbl/ adj insociable

unsolved /ʌnˈsɒlvd/ adj no resuelto; (murder) sin esclarecerse

unsophisticated /ʌnsəˈfɪstɪkeɪtɪd/ adj sencillo

unsound /ʌnˈsaʊnd/ adj poco sólido

unspecified /ʌnˈspesɪfaɪd/ adj no especificado

unstable /ʌnˈsteɪbl/ adj inestable

unsteady /ʌnˈstedɪ/ adj inestable, poco firme

unstuck /ʌnˈstʌk/ adj despegado. **come ~** despegarse; (fail) fracasar

unsuccessful /ʌnsəkˈsesfʊl/ adj

(attempt) infructuoso. **be ~** no tener éxito, fracasar

unsuitable /ʌnˈsuːtəbl/ adj (clothing) poco apropiado, poco adecuado; (time) inconveniente. **she is ~ for the job** no es la persona indicada para el trabajo

unsure /ʌnˈʃʊə(r)/ adj inseguro

unthinkable /ʌnˈθɪŋkəbl/ adj inconcebible

untid|iness /ʌnˈtaɪdɪnəs/ n desorden m. **~y** (-ier, -iest) desordenado; (appearance, writing) descuidado

untie /ʌnˈtaɪ/ vt desatar, desamarrar (LAm)

until /ənˈtɪl, ʌnˈtɪl/ prep hasta. ● conj hasta que

untold /ʌnˈtəʊld/ adj incalculable

untouched /ʌnˈtʌtʃt/ adj intacto

untried /ʌnˈtraɪd/ adj no probado

untrue /ʌnˈtruː/ adj falso

unused /ʌnˈjuːzd/ adj nuevo. ● /ʌnˈjuːst/ adj. **~ to** no acostumbrado a

unusual /ʌnˈjuːʒʊəl/ adj poco común, poco corriente. **it's ~ to see so many people** es raro ver a tanta gente. **~ly** adv excepcionalmente, inusitadamente

unveil /ʌnˈveɪl/ vt descubrir

unwanted /ʌnˈwɒntɪd/ adj superfluo; (child) no deseado

unwelcome /ʌnˈwelkəm/ adj (news) poco grato; (guest) inoportuno

unwell /ʌnˈwel/ adj indispuesto

unwieldy /ʌnˈwiːldɪ/ adj pesado y difícil de manejar

unwilling /ʌnˈwɪlɪŋ/ adj mal dispuesto. **be ~** no querer

unwind /ʌnˈwaɪnd/ vt (pt unwound) desenrollar. ● vi (fam,

unwise | Uruguay

576

relax) relajarse

unwise /ʌnˈwaɪz/ *adj* poco sensato

unworthy /ʌnˈwɜːðɪ/ *adj* indigno

unwrap /ʌnˈræp/ *vt (pt* **unwrapped)** desenvolver

unwritten /ʌnˈrɪtn/ *adj* no escrito; *(agreement)* verbal

up /ʌp/ *adv* arriba, *(upwards)* hacia arriba; *(higher)* más arriba. ~ **here** aquí arriba. ~ **there** allí arriba. ~ **to** hasta. he's not ~ yet todavía no se ha levantado. **be** ~ **against** enfrentarse con. **come** ~ subir. **go** ~ subir. he's not ~ **to** the job no tiene las condiciones necesarias para el trabajo. **it's** ~ **to you** depende de ti. **what's** ~? ¿qué pasa? ● *prep.* **go** ~ **the stairs** subir la escalera. **it's just** ~ **the road** está un poco más allá. ● *vt (pt* **upped)** aumentar. ● *n.* ~**s and downs** *npl* altibajos *mpl; (of life)* vicisitudes *fpl.* ~**bringing** /ˈʌpbrɪŋɪŋ/ *n* educación *f.* ~**date** /ʌpˈdeɪt/ *vt* poner al día. ~**grade** /ʌpˈɡreɪd/ *vt* elevar de categoría *(person)*; mejorar *(equipment).* ~**heaval** /ʌpˈhiːvl/ *n* trastorno *m.* ~**hill** /ʌpˈhɪl/ *adv* cuesta arriba. ~**hold** /ʌpˈhəʊld/ *vt (pt* **upheld)** mantener *(principle)*; confirmar *(decision).* ~**holster** /ʌpˈhəʊlstə(r)/ *vt* tapizar. ~**holstery** *n* tapicería *f.* ~**keep** /n mantenimiento *m.* ~**market** /ʌpˈmɑːkɪt/ *adj* de categoría

upon /əˈpɒn/ *prep* sobre. **once** ~ **a time** érase una vez

upper /ˈʌpə(r)/ *adj* superior. ~ **class** *n* clase *f* alta

up: ~**right** /ˈʌpraɪt/ *adj* vertical; *(citizen)* recto. **place sth** ~**right** poner algo de pie. ~**rising** /ˈʌpraɪzɪŋ/ *n* levantamiento *m.* ~**roar** *n* tu-

multo *m*

upset /ʌpˈset/ *vt (pt* **upset,** *pres p* **upsetting)** *(hurt)* disgustar; *(offend)* ofender; *(distress)* alterar; desbaratar *(plans).* ● *adj (hurt)* disgustado; *(distressed)* alterado; *(offended)* ofendido; *(disappointed)* desilusionado. ● /ˈʌpset/ *n* trastorno *m.* **have a stomach** ~ estar mal del estómago

up: ~**shot** *n* resultado *m.* ~**side down** /ʌpsaɪdˈdaʊn/ *adv* al revés *(con la parte de arriba abajo); (in disorder)* patas arriba. **turn sth** ~**side down** poner algo boca abajo. ~**stairs** /ʌpˈsteəz/ *adv* arriba. **go** ~**stairs** subir. ● /ˈʌpsteəz/ *adj* de arriba. ~**start** *n* advenedizo *m.* ~**state** *n (Amer).* **I live** ~**state** vivo en el norte del estado. ~**stream** /ʌpˈstriːm/ *adv* río arriba. ~**take** *n.* **be quick on the** ~**take** agarrar las cosas al vuelo. ~**to-date** /ʌptəˈdeɪt/ *adj* al día; *(news)* de última hora. ~**turn** *n* repunte *m,* mejora *f.* ~**ward** /ˈʌpwəd/ *adj (movement)* ascendente; *(direction)* hacia arriba. ● *adv* hacia arriba. ~**wards** *adv* hacia arriba

uranium /jʊˈreɪnɪəm/ *n* uranio *m*

Uranus /ˈjʊərənəs/jʊəˈreɪnəs/ *n* Urano *m*

urban /ˈɜːbən/ *adj* urbano

urchin /ˈɜːtʃɪn/ *n* pilluelo *m*

urge /ɜːdʒ/ *vt* instar. ~ **s.o. to do sth** instar a uno a que haga algo. ● *n* impulso *m,* mejora *f.* ~ **on** *vt* animar

urgen|cy /ˈɜːdʒənsɪ/ *n* urgencia *f.* ~**t** *adj* urgente. ~**tly** *adv* urgentemente, con urgencia

urin|ate /ˈjʊərəneɪt/ *vi* orinar. ~**e** /ˈjʊərɪn/ *n* orina *f*

Uruguay /ˈjʊərəɡwaɪ/ *n* Uruguay *m*

m. **~an** *adj & n* uruguayo (*m*)

us /ʌs, əs/ *pron* nos- (*after prep*) nosotros *m*, nosotras *f*

Vv

US(A) /ju:es'eɪ/ *abbr* (= **United States (of America)**) (*only written*), Estados *mpl* Unidos

usage /'ju:zɪdʒ/ *n* uso *m*

use /ju:z/ *vt* usar; utilizar (service, facilities); consumir (fuel). ●/ju:s/ *n* uso *m*, empleo *m*. **be of ~** servir. **it is no ~** es inútil. □ **~ up** *vt* agotar, consumir. ●/ju:st/ *v/aux* **used to**. **he ~d to say** decía, solía decir. **there ~d to be** (antes) había. ●*adj*/ju:st/. **be ~d to** estar acostumbrado a. **~ful** /'ju:sfl/ *adj* útil. **~fully** *adv* útilmente. **~less** *adj* inútil. (person) incompetente. **~r** /-zə(r)/ *n* usuario *m*. **drug ~** consumidor *m* de drogas

usher /'ʌʃə(r)/ *n* (in cinema etc) acomodador *m*. □ **~ in** *vt* hacer pasar; marcar el comienzo de (new era). **~ette** /-'ret/ *n* acomodadora *f*

USSR *abbr* (History) (= **Union of Soviet Socialist Republics**) URSS

usual /'ju:ʒʊəl/ *adj* usual; (habitual) acostumbrado, habitual; (place, route) de siempre. **as ~** como de costumbre, como siempre. **~ly** *adv* normalmente. **he ~ly wakes up early** suele despertarse temprano

utensil /ju:'tensl/ *n* utensilio *m*

utilize /'ju:tɪlaɪz/ *vt* utilizar

utmost /'ʌtməʊst/ *adj* sumo. ●*n.* **do one's ~** hacer todo lo posible (**to** para)

utter /'ʌtə(r)/ *adj* completo. ●*vt* pronunciar (word); dar (cry). **~ly** *adv* totalmente

U-turn /'ju:tɜ:n/ *n* cambio *m* de sentido

vacan|cy /'veɪkənsɪ/ *n* (job) vacante *f*; (room) habitación *f* libre. **~t** *adj* (building) desocupado; (seat) libre; (post) vacante; (look) ausente

vacate /və'keɪt/ *vt* dejar

vacation /və'keɪʃn/ *n* (Amer) vacaciones *fpl*. **go on ~** ir de vacaciones. **~er** *n* (Amer) veraneante *m & f*

vaccin|ate /'væksɪneɪt/ *vt* vacunar. **~ation** /-'neɪʃn/ *n* vacunación *f*. **~e** /'væksi:n/ *n* vacuna *f*

vacuum /'vækjʊəm/ *n* vacío *m*. **~ cleaner** *n* aspiradora *f*

vagina /və'dʒaɪnə/ *n* vagina *f*

vague /veɪg/ *adj* (**-er**, **-est**) vago; (outline) borroso; (person, expression) despistado. **~ly** *adv* vagamente

vain /veɪn/ *adj* (**-er**, **-est**) vanidoso; (useless) vano. **in ~** en vano

Valentine's Day /'væləntaɪnz/ *n* el día de San Valentín

valiant /'væliənt/ *adj* valeroso

valid /'vælɪd/ *adj* válido. **~ate** /-eɪt/ *vt* dar validez a; validar (contract). **~ity** /-'ɪdətɪ/ *n* validez *f*

valley /'vælɪ/ *n* (pl **-eys**) valle *m*

valour /'vælə(r)/ *n* valor *m*

valu|able /'væljʊəbl/ *adj* valioso. **~ables** *npl* objetos *mpl* de valor. **~ation** /-'eɪʃn/ *n* valoración *f*. **~e** /'vælju:/ *n* valor *m*. ●*vt* valorar; tasar, valorar, avaluar (LAm) (property). **~e added tax** *n* impuesto *m* sobre el valor añadido

valve /vælv/ *n* válvula *f*

vampire /'væmpaɪə(r)/ *n*

vampiro *m*

van /væn/ *n* furgoneta *f*, camioneta *f*; (Rail) furgón *m*

vandal /'vændl/ *n* vándalo *m*. **~ism** *n* vandalismo *m*. **~ize** *vt* destruir

vanilla /və'nɪlə/ *n* vainilla *f*.

vanish /'vænɪʃ/ *vi* desaparecer

vanity /'vænɪtɪ/ *n* vanidad *f*. **~ case** *n* neceser *m*

vapour /'veɪpə(r)/ *n* vapor *m*

varia|ble /'veərɪəbl/ *adj* variable. **~nce** /-əns/ *n*. **at ~ce** en desacuerdo. **~nt** *n* variante *f*. **~tion** /-'eɪʃn/ *n* variación *f*

vari|ed /'veərɪd/ *adj* variado. **~ety** /və'raɪətɪ/ *n* variedad *f*. **~ety show** *n* espectáculo *m* de variedades. **~ous** /'veərɪəs/ *adj* (several) varios; (different) diversos

varnish /'vɑːnɪʃ/ *n* barniz *m*; (for nails) esmalte *m*. ● *vt* barnizar; pintar (nails)

vary /'veərɪ/ *vt/i* variar

vase /vɑːz/, (Amer) /veɪs/ *n* (for flowers) florero *m*; (ornamental) jarrón *m*

vast /vɑːst/ *adj* vasto, extenso; (size) inmenso. **~ly** *adv* infinitamente

vat /væt/ *n* cuba *f*

VAT /viːeɪ'tiː/ *abbr* (= value added tax) IVA *m*

vault /vɔːlt/ *n* (roof) bóveda *f*; (in bank) cámara *f* acorazada; (tomb) cripta *f*. ● *vt/i* saltar

VCR *n* = **videocassette recorder**

VDU *n* = **visual display unit**

veal /viːl/ *n* ternera *f*

veer /vɪə(r)/ *vi* dar un viraje, virar

vegeta|ble /'vedʒɪtəbl/ *adj* vegetal. ● *n* verdura *f*. **~rian** /vedʒɪ-

'teərɪən/ *adj* & *n* vegetariano (*m*). **~tion** /vedʒɪ'teɪʃn/ *n* vegetación *f*

vehement /'viːəmənt/ *adj* vehemente. **~tly** *adv* con vehemencia

vehicle /'viːɪkl/ *n* vehículo *m*

veil /veɪl/ *n* velo *m*

vein /veɪn/ *n* vena *f*; (in marble) veta *f*

velocity /vɪ'lɒsɪtɪ/ *n* velocidad *f*

velvet /'velvɪt/ *n* terciopelo *m*

vendetta /ven'detə/ *n* vendetta *f*

vend|ing machine /'vendɪŋ/ *n* distribuidor *m* automático. **~or** /'vendə(r)/ *n* vendedor *m*

veneer /və'nɪə(r)/ *n* chapa *f*, enchapado *m*; (fig) barniz *m*, apariencia *f*

venerate /'venəreɪt/ *vt* venerar

venereal /və'nɪərɪəl/ *adj* venéreo

Venetian blind /vəˈniːʃn/ *n* persiana *f* veneciana

Venezuela /venə'zweɪlə/ *n* Venezuela *f*. **~n** *adj* & *n* venezolano (*m*)

vengeance /'vendʒəns/ *n* venganza *f*. **with a ~** (fig) con ganas

venom /'venəm/ *n* veneno *m*. **~ous** *adj* venenoso

vent /vent/ *n* (conducto *m* de) ventilación; (air ~) respiradero *m*. **give ~ to** dar rienda suelta a. ● *vt* descargar

ventilat|e /'ventɪleɪt/ *vt* ventilar. **~ion** /-'leɪʃn/ *n* ventilación *f*

ventriloquist /ven'trɪləkwɪst/ *n* ventrílocuo *m*

venture /'ventʃə(r)/ *n* empresa *f*. ● *vt* aventurar. ● *vi* atreverse

venue /'venjuː/ *n* (for concert) lugar *m* de actuación

Venus /'viːnəs/ *n* Venus *m*

veranda /və'rændə/ *n* galería *f*

verb /vɜːb/ *n* verbo *m*. **~al** /-l/

verbal

verdict /'vɜːdɪkt/ n veredicto m; (opinion) opinión f

verge /vɜːdʒ/ n borde m. □~ **on** vt rayar en

verify /'verɪfaɪ/ vt (confirm) confirmar; (check) verificar

vermin /'vɜːmɪn/ n alimañas fpl

versatil|e /'vɜːsətaɪl/ adj versátil. ~**ity** /-'tɪlətɪ/ n versatilidad f

verse /vɜːs/ n estrofa f; (poetry) poesías fpl. ~**d** /vɜːst/ adj. **be well-~ed in** ser muy versado en. ~**ion** /-ʃn/ n versión f

versus /'vɜːsəs/ prep contra

vertebra /'vɜːtɪbrə/ n (pl -brae /-briː/) vértebra f. ~**te** /-brət/ n vertebrado m

vertical /'vɜːtɪkl/ adj & n vertical (f). ~**ly** adv verticalmente

vertigo /'vɜːtɪɡəʊ/ n vértigo m

verve /vɜːv/ n brío m

very /'verɪ/ adv muy. ~ **much** muchísimo. ~ **well** muy bien. the ~ **first** el primero de todos. ● adj mismo. **the ~ thing** exactamente lo que hace falta

vessel /'vesl/ n (receptacle) recipiente m; (ship) navío m, nave f

vest /vest/ n camiseta f; (Amer) chaleco m.

vestige /'vestɪdʒ/ n vestigio m

vet /vet/ n veterinario m (Amer fam, veteran) veterano m. ● vt (pt **vetted**) someter a investigación (applicant)

veteran /'vetərən/ n veterano m

veterinary /'vetərɪnərɪ/ adj veterinario. ~ **surgeon** n veterinario m

veto /'viːtəʊ/ n (pl -oes) veto m. ● vt vetar

vex /veks/ vt fastidiar

via /'vaɪə/ prep por, por vía de

viable /'vaɪəbl/ adj viable

viaduct /'vaɪədʌkt/ n viaducto m

vibrat|e /vaɪ'breɪt/ vt/i vibrar. ~**ion** /-ʃn/ n vibración f

vicar /'vɪkə(r)/ n párroco m. ~**age** /-rɪdʒ/ n casa f del párroco

vice /vaɪs/ n vicio m; (Tec) torno m de banco

vice versa /vaɪs'vɜːsə/ adv viceversa

vicinity /vɪ'sɪnɪtɪ/ n vecindad f. **in the ~ of** cerca de

vicious /'vɪʃəs/ adj (attack) feroz; (dog) fiero; (rumour) malicioso. ~ **circle** n círculo m vicioso

victim /'vɪktɪm/ n víctima f. ~**ize** vt victimizar

victor /'vɪktə(r)/ n vencedor m

Victorian /vɪk'tɔːrɪən/ adj victoriano

victor|ious /vɪk'tɔːrɪəs/ adj (army) victorioso; (team) vencedor. ~**y** /'vɪktərɪ/ n victoria f

video /'vɪdɪəʊ/ n (pl -os) vídeo m, video m (LAm). ~ **camera** n videocámara f. ~ **(cassette) recorder** n magnetoscopio m. ~**tape** n videocassette f

vie /vaɪ/ vi (pres p **vying**) rivalizar

Vietnam /vjet'næm/ n Vietnam m. ~**ese** adj & n vietnamita (m & f)

view /vjuː/ n vista f; (mental survey) visión f de conjunto; (opinion) opinión f. **in my ~** a mi juicio. **in ~ of** en vista de. **on ~** expuesto. ● vt ver (scene, property); (consider) considerar. ~**er** n (TV) televidente m & f. ~**finder** n visor m. ~**point** n punto m de vista

vigil|ance n vigilancia f. ~**ant** adj vigilante

vigo|rous /'vɪɡərəs/ adj enérgico;

v

(growth) vigoroso. **~ur** /'vigə(r)/ n vigor m

vile /vail/ adj (base) vil; (food) asqueroso; (weather, temper) horrible

village /'vilidʒ/ n pueblo m; (small) aldea f. **~r** n vecino m del pueblo; (of small village) aldeano m

villain /'vilən/ n maleante m & f; (in story etc) villano m

vindicate /'vindikeit/ vt justificar

vindictive /vin'diktiv/ adj vengativo

vine /vain/ n (on ground) vid f; (climbing) parra f

vinegar /'vinigə(r)/ n vinagre m

vineyard /'vinjəd/ n viña f

vintage /'vintidʒ/ n (year) cosecha f. ●adj (wine) añejo; (car) de época

vinyl /'vainil/ n vinilo m

viola /vi'əulə/ n viola f

violat|e /'vaiəleit/ vt violar. **~ion** /-'leiʃn/ n violación f

violen|ce /'vaiələns/ n violencia f. **~t** adj violento. **~tly** adv violentamente

violet /'vaiələt/ adj & n violeta (f); (colour) violeta (m)

violin /vaiə'lin/ n violín m. **~ist** n violinista m & f

VIP /vi:ai'pi:/ abbr (= **very important person**) VIP m

viper /'vaipə(r)/ n víbora f

virgin /'vɜːdʒin/ adj & n virgen (f)

Virgo /'vɜːgəʊ/ n Virgo f

virile /'virail/ adj viril

virtual /'vɜːtʃʊəl/ adj. **traffic is at a ~ standstill** el tráfico está prácticamente paralizado. **~ reality** n realidad f virtual. **~ly** adv prácticamente

virtue /'vɜːtʃuː/ n virtud f. **by ~ of** en virtud de

virtuous /'vɜːtʃʊəs/ adj virtuoso

virulent /'virʊlənt/ adj virulento

virus /'vaiərəs/ n (pl **-uses**) virus m

visa /'viːzə/ n visado m, visa f (LAm)

vise /vais/ n (Amer) torno m de banco

visib|ility /vizi'biləti/ n visibilidad f. **~le** /'vizibl/ adj visible; (sign, improvement) evidente

vision /'viʒn/ n visión f; (sight) vista f

visit /'vizit/ vt visitar; hacer una visita a (person). ●vi hacer visitas. **~ with s.o.** (Amer) ir a ver a uno. ●n visita f. **pay s.o. a ~** hacerle una visita a uno. **~or** n visitante m & f; (guest) visita f

visor /'vaizə(r)/ n visera f

visual /'viʒʊəl/ adj visual. **~ize** vt imaginar(se); (foresee) prever

vital /'vaitl/ adj (essential) esencial; (factor) de vital importancia; (organ) de vital importancia. **~ity** /vai'tæləti/ n vitalidad f

vitamin /'vitəmin/ n vitamina f.

vivacious /vi'veiʃəs/ adj vivaz

vivid /'vivid/ adj vivo. **~ly** adv intensamente; (describe) gráficamente

vivisection /vivi'sekʃn/ n vivisección f

vocabulary /və'kæbjʊləri/ n vocabulario m

vocal /'vəʊkl/ adj vocal. **~ist** n cantante m & f

vocation /və'keiʃn/ n vocación f. **~al** adj profesional

vociferous /və'sifərəs/ adj vociferador

vogue /vəʊg/ n moda f, boga f

voice /vɔɪs/ n voz f. ● vt expresar

void /vɔɪd/ adj (not valid) nulo. ● n vacío m

volatile /'vɒlətaɪl/ adj volátil; (person) imprevisible

volcan|ic /vɒl'kænɪk/ adj volcánico. **~o** /vɒl'keɪnəʊ/ n (pl **-oes**) volcán m

volley /'vɒlɪ/ n (pl **-eys**) (of gunfire) descarga f cerrada; (sport) volea f. **~ball** n vóleibol m

volt /vəʊlt/ n voltio m. **~age** /-ɪdʒ/ n voltaje m

volume /'vɒlju:m/ n volumen m; (book) tomo m

voluntar|ily /'vɒləntərəlɪ/ adv voluntariamente. **~y** adj voluntario; (organization) de beneficencia

volunteer /vɒlən'tɪə(r)/ n voluntario m. ● vt ofrecer. ● vi. **~ (to)** ofrecerse (a)

vomit /'vɒmɪt/ vt/i vomitar. ● n vómito m

voracious /və'reɪʃəs/ adj voraz

vot|e /vəʊt/ n voto m; (right) derecho m al voto; (act) votación f. ● vi votar. **~er** n votante m & f. **~ing** n votación f

vouch /vaʊtʃ/ vi. **~ for s.o.** responder por uno. **~er** /-ə(r)/ n vale m

vow /vaʊ/ n voto m. ● vi jurar

vowel /vaʊəl/ n vocal f

voyage /'vɔɪɪdʒ/ n viaje m; (by sea) travesía f

vulgar /'vʌlgə(r)/ adj (coarse) grosero, vulgar; (tasteless) de mal gusto. **~ity** /-'gærətɪ/ n vulgaridad f

vulnerable /'vʌlnərəbl/ adj vulnerable

vulture /'vʌltʃə(r)/ n buitre m

vying /'vaɪɪŋ/ see VIE

Ww

W abbr (= West) O

wad /wɒd/ n (of notes) fajo m; (tied together) lío m; (papers) montón m

waddle /'wɒdl/ vi contonearse

wade /weɪd/ vi caminar (por el agua etc)

wafer /'weɪfə(r)/ n galleta f de barquillo

waffle /'wɒfl/ n 🅱 palabrería f. ● vi 🅱 divagar; (in essay, exam) meter paja 🅱. ● n (Culin) gofre m, wafle m (LAm)

waft /wɒft/ vi flotar

wag /wæg/ vt (pt **wagged**) menear. ● vi menearse

wage /weɪdʒ/ n sueldo m. **~s** npl salario m, sueldo m. **~r** n apuesta f

waggle /'wægl/ vt menear. ● vi menearse

wagon /'wægən/ n carro m; (Rail) vagón m; (Amer, delivery truck) furgoneta f de reparto

wail /weɪl/ vi llorar

waist /weɪst/ n cintura f. **~coat** n chaleco m. **~line** n cintura f

wait /weɪt/ vi esperar; (at table) servir. **~ for s.o.** esperar a uno. **~ on s.o.** atender a uno. ● vt (await) esperar (chance, turn). **~ table** (Amer) servir a la mesa. **I can't ~ to see him** me muero de ganas de verlo. ● n espera f. **lie in ~** acechar

waiter /'weɪtə(r)/ n camarero m, mesero m (LAm)

wait: ~ing-list n lista f de espera. **~ing-room** n sala f de espera

waitress /'weɪtrɪs/ n camarera f,

mesera f (LAm)

waive /weɪv/ vt renunciar a

wake /weɪk/ vt (pt woke, pp woken) despertar. • vi despertarse. • n (Naut) estela f. **in the ~ of** como resultado de. □ **~ up** vt despertar. vi despertarse

Wales /weɪlz/ n (el país de) Gales

walk /wɔːk/ vi andar, caminar; (not ride) ir a pie; (stroll) pasear. • vt andar por (streets); llevar de paseo (dog). • n paseo m; (long) caminata f; (gait) manera f de andar. □ **~ out** vi salir; (workers) declararse en huelga. □ **~ out on** vt abandonar. **~er** n excursionista m & f

walkie-talkie /wɔːkɪ'tɔːkɪ/ n walkie-talkie m

walk: **~ing-stick** n bastón m. **W~man** /-mən/ n Walkman m (P). **~-out** n retirada en señal de protesta; (strike) abandono m del trabajo

wall /wɔːl/ n (interior) pared f; (exterior) muro m

Wall Street Una calle en Manhattan, Nueva York, donde se encuentran la Bolsa neoyorquina y las sedes de muchas instituciones financieras. Cuando se habla de Wall Street, a menudo se está refiriendo a esas instituciones.

wallet /'wɒlɪt/ n cartera f, billetera f

wallop /'wɒləp/ vt (pt walloped) 1 darle un golpazo a.

wallow /'wɒləʊ/ vi revolcarse

wallpaper /'wɔːlpeɪpə(r)/ n papel m pintado

walnut /'wɔːlnʌt/ n nuez f; (tree) nogal m

walrus /'wɔːlrəs/ n morsa f

waltz /wɔːls/ n vals m. • vi valsar

wand /wɒnd/ n varita f (mágica)

wander /'wɒndə(r)/ vi vagar; (stroll) pasear; (digress) divagar. • n vuelta f, paseo m. **~er** n trotamundos m

wane /weɪn/ vi (moon) menguar; (interest) decaer. • n. **be on the ~** (popularity) estar decayendo

wangle /'wæŋgl/ vt 1 agenciarse

want /wɒnt/ vt querer; (need) necesitar. • vi. **~ for** carecer de. • n necesidad f; (lack) falta f. **~ed** adj (criminal) buscado

war /wɔː(r)/ n guerra f. **at ~** en guerra

warble /'wɔːbl/ vi trinar, gorjear

ward /wɔːd/ n (in hospital) sala f; (child) pupilo m. □ **~ off** vt conjurar (danger); rechazar (attack)

warden /'wɔːdn/ n guarda m

warder /'wɔːdə(r)/ n celador m (de una cárcel)

wardrobe /'wɔːdrəʊb/ n armario m; (clothes) guardarropa f, vestuario m

warehouse /'weəhaʊs/ n depósito m, almacén m

wares /weəz/ npl mercancía(s) f(pl)

war: **~fare** n guerra f. **~head** n cabeza f, ojiva f

warm /wɔːm/ adj (-er, -est) (water, day) tibio, templado; (room) caliente; (climate, wind) cálido; (clothes) de abrigo; (welcome) caluroso. **be ~** (person) tener calor. **it's ~ today** hoy hace calor. • vt. **~ (up)** calentar (room); recalentar (food); (fig) animar. • vi. **~ (up)** calentarse; (fig) animarse. **~-blooded** /-'blʌdɪd/ adj de sangre caliente. **~ly** adv (heartily) calurosamente. **~th** n calor m; (of colour, atmosphere) calidez f

warn /wɔːn/ vt advertir. **~ing** n advertencia f; (notice) aviso m

warp /wɔːp/ vt alabear. **~ed** /'wɔːpt/ adj (wood) alabeado; (mind) retorcido

warrant /'wɒrənt/ n orden f judicial; (search ~) orden f de registro; (for arrest) orden f de arresto. • vt justificar. **~y** n garantía f

warrior /'wɒrɪə(r)/ n guerrero m

warship /'wɔːʃɪp/ n buque m de guerra

wart /wɔːt/ n verruga f

wartime /'wɔːtaɪm/ n tiempo m de guerra

wary /'weərɪ/ adj (-ier, -iest) cauteloso. **be ~ of** recelar de

was /wəz, wɒz/ see BE

wash /wɒʃ/ vt lavar; fregar, lavar (LAm) (floor). **~** one's face lavarse la cara. • vi lavarse. • n (in washing machine) lavado m. **have a ~** lavarse. **I gave the car a ~** lavé el coche. □ **~ out** vt (clean) lavar; (rinse) enjuagar. □ **~ up** vi fregar los platos, lavar los trastes (Mex); (Amer, wash face and hands) lavarse. **~able** adj lavable. **~basin,** **~bowl** (Amer) n lavabo m. **~er** n arandela f. **~ing** n lavado m; (dirty clothes) ropa f para lavar; (wet clothes) ropa f lavada. **do the ~ing** lavar la ropa, hacer la colada. **~ing-machine** n máquina f de lavar, lavadora f. **~ing-powder** n jabón m en polvo. **~ing-up** n. **do the ~ing-up** lavar los platos, fregar (los platos). **~ing-up liquid** n lavavajillas m. **~out** n 🔳 desastre m. **~room** n (Amer) baños mpl, servicios mpl

wasp /wɒsp/ n avispa f

waste /weɪst/ • adj (matter) de

desecho; (land) (barren) yermo; (uncultivated) baldío. • n (of materials) desperdicio m; (of time) pérdida f; (refuse) residuos mpl. • vt despilfarrar (electricity, money); desperdiciar (talent, effort); perder (time). • vi. **~-disposal unit** n trituradora f de desperdicios. **~ful** adj poco económico; (person) despilfarrador. **~-paper basket** n papelera f

watch /wɒtʃ/ vt mirar; observar (person, expression); ver (TV); (keep an eye on) vigilar; (take heed) tener cuidado con. • vi mirar. • n (observation) vigilancia f; (period of duty) guardia f; (timepiece) reloj m. **~ out** vi (be careful) tener cuidado; (look carefully) estarse atento. **~dog** n perro m guardián. **~man** /-mən/ n (pl **-men**) vigilante m.

water /'wɔːtə(r)/ n agua f. • vt regar (plants etc). • vi (eyes) llorar. **make s.o.'s mouth ~** hacérsele la boca agua, hacérsele agua la boca (LAm). **~ down** vt diluir; aguar (wine). **~-colour** n acuarela f. **~cress** n berro m. **~fall** n cascada f; (large) catarata f. **~ing-can** n regadera f. **~ing-can** n regadera f. **~lily** n nenúfar m. **~logged** /-lɒgd/ adj anegado; (shoes) empapado. **~proof** adj impermeable; (watch) sumergible. **~-skiing** n esquí m acuático. **~tight** adj hermético; (boat) estanco; (argument) irrebatible. **~way** n canal m navegable. **~y** adj acuoso; (eyes) lloroso

watt /wɒt/ n vatio m

wave /weɪv/ n onda f; (of hand) señal f; (fig) oleada f; • vt agitar; (curl) ondular (hair). • vi (signal) hacer señales con la mano; ondear (flag). **~band** n banda f de frecuenca. **~length** n longitud f de onda

waver /'weɪvə(r)/ vi (be indecisive) vacilar; (falter) flaquear

wavy /'weɪvɪ/ adj (-ier, -iest) ondulado

wax /wæks/ n cera f. ● vi (moon) crecer. **~work** n figura f de cera. **~works** npl museo m de cera

way /weɪ/ n (route) camino m; (manner) manera f, forma f, modo m; (direction) dirección f; (habit) costumbre f. **it's a long ~ from here** queda muy lejos de aquí. **be in the ~** estorbar. **by the ~** a propósito. **either ~** de cualquier manera. **give ~** (collapse) ceder, romperse; (Auto) ceder el paso. **in a ~** en cierta manera. **in some ~s** en ciertos modos. **make ~** dejar paso a. **no ~!** ¡ni hablar! **on my ~** to de camino a. **out of the ~** remoto; (extraordinary) fuera de lo común. **that ~** por allí. **this ~** por aquí. ■ **~ in** entrada f. **~lay** /weɪ'leɪ/ vt (pt -laid) abordar. ■ **~ out** n salida f. **~-out** adj ultramoderno, original. **~s** npl costumbres fpl

we /wiː/ pron nosotros m, nosotras f

weak /wiːk/ adj (-er, -est) débil; (structure) poco sólido; (performance, student) flojo; (coffee) poco cargado; (solution) diluido; (beer) suave; (pej) aguado. **~en** vt debilitar. ● vi (resolve) flaquear. **~ling** n alfeñique m. **~ness** n debilidad f

wealth /welθ/ n riqueza f. **~y** adj (-ier, -iest) rico

weapon /'wepən/ n arma f. **~s of mass destruction** armas de destrucción masiva

wear /weə(r)/ vt (pt wore, pp worn) llevar; vestirse de (black, red, etc); (usually) usar. **I've got**

nothing to **~** no tengo nada que ponerme. ● vi (through use) gastarse; (last) durar. ■ en uso f (damage) desgaste m. **~ and tear** desgaste n natural. □ **~ out** vt gastar; (tire) agotar. vi gastarse

weary /'wɪərɪ/ adj (-ier, -iest) cansado. ● vt cansar. ● vi cansarse. **~ of** cansarse de

weather /'weðə(r)/ n tiempo m. **what's the ~ like?** ¿qué tiempo hace?. **the ~ was bad** hizo mal tiempo. **be under the** 🔲 no andar muy bien 🔲. ● vt (survive) sobrellevar. **~-beaten** adj curtido. **~ forecast** n pronóstico m del tiempo. **~-vane** n veleta f

weave /wiːv/ vt (pt wove, pp woven) tejer; entretejer (threads). **~ one's way** abrirse paso. ● vi (person) zigzaguear; (road) serpentear. **~r** n tejedor m

web /web/ n (of spider) telaraña f; (of intrigue) trama f. **~ page** n página web. **~ site** n sitio web m

wed /wed/ vt (pt wedded) casarse con. ● vi casarse.

we'd /wiːd//wɪəd/ = we had, we would

wedding /'wedɪŋ/ n boda f, casamiento m. **~-cake** n pastel m de boda. **~-ring** n anillo m de boda

wedge /wedʒ/ n cuña f

Wednesday /'wenzdeɪ/ n miércoles m

wee /wiː/ adj 🔲 pequeñito. ● n. **have a ~** 🔲 hacer pis 🔲

weed /wiːd/ n mala hierba f. ● vt desherbar. □ **~ out** vt eliminar. **~killer** n herbicida m. **~y** adj (person) enclenque; (Amer, lanky) larguirucho 🔲

week /wiːk/ n semana f. **~day** n día m de semana. **~end** n fin m de semana. **~ly** adj semanal. ● n semanario *m*. ● *adv* semanalmente

weep /wi:p/ *vi* (*pt* **wept**) llorar

weigh /weɪ/ *vt/i* pesar. ● **~ anchor** levar anclas. □ **~ down** *vt* (*fig*) oprimir. □ **~ up** *vt* pesar; (*fig*) considerar

weight /weɪt/ *n* peso *m*; (*sport*) pesa *f*. **put on ~** engordar. **lose ~** adelgazar. **~-lifting** *n* halterofilia *f*, levantamiento *m* de pesos

weir /wɪə(r)/ *n* presa *f*

weird /wɪəd/ *adj* (**-er, -est**) raro, extraño; (*unearthly*) misterioso

welcom|e /'welkəm/ *adj* bienvenido. **you're ~e!** (*after thank you*) ¡de nada! ● *n* bienvenida *f*; (*reception*) acogida *f*. ● *vt* dar la bienvenida a; (*appreciate*) alegrarse de. **~ing** *adj* acogedor

weld /weld/ *vt* soldar. ● *n* soldadura *f*. **~er** *n* soldador *m*

welfare /'welfeə(r)/ *n* bienestar *m*; (*aid*) asistencia *f* social. **W~ State** *n* estado *m* benefactor

well /wel/ *adv* (**better, best**) bien. **~ done!** ¡muy bien! ¡bravo! **as ~** también. **as ~ as** además de. **we may as ~ go tomorrow** más vale que vayamos mañana. **do ~** (*succeed*) tener éxito. **very ~** muy bien. ● *adj* bien. **I'm very ~** estoy muy bien. ● *int* (*introducing, continuing sentence*) bueno; (*surprise*) ¡vaya!; (*indignation, resignation*) bueno. **~ I never!** ¡no me digas! ● *n* pozo *m*

we'll /wi:l//wɪəl/ = **we will**

well: ~-behaved /-bɪ'heɪvd/ *adj* que se porta bien. **~-educated** /-'edjʊkeɪtɪd/ *adj* culto.

wellington (boot) /'welɪŋtən/ *n* bota *f* de goma *or* de agua; (*Amer, short boot*) botín *m*

well: ~-known /-'nəʊn/ *adj* conocido. **~ off** *adj* adinerado. **~-stocked** /-'stɒkt/ *adj* bien provisto. **~-to-do** /-tə'du:/ *adj* adinerado

Welsh /welʃ/ *adj & n* galés (*m*). **the ~** los galeses

Welsh Assembly La Asamblea Nacional de Gales empezó a funcionar, en Cardiff, en 1999. Tiene poderes limitados, por lo que no puede imponer impuestos. Consta de 60 miembros o AMs (*Assembly Members*); 40 elegidos directamente y el resto, de las listas regionales, mediante el sistema de representación proporcional.

went /went/ *see* **GO**

wept /wept/ *see* **WEEP**

were /wɜ:(r), wə(r)/ *see* **BE**

we're /wɪə(r)/ = **we are**

west /west/ *n* oeste *m*. **the W~** el Occidente *m*. ● *adj* oeste; (*wind*) del oeste. ● *adv* (*go*) hacia el oeste, al oeste. **it's ~ of York** está al oeste de York. **~erly** /-əlɪ/ *adj* (*wind*) del oeste. **~ern** /-ən/ *adj* occidental. ● *n* (*film*) película *f* del Oeste. **~erner** *n* occidental *m & f*. **W~ Indian** *adj & n* antillano (*m*). **W~ Indies** *npl* Antillas *fpl*. **~ward(s)** /-wəd(z)/,

wet /wet/ *adj* (**wetter, wettest**) mojado; (*rainy*) lluvioso; (*fam, person*) soso. **~ paint** 'pintura fresca'. **get ~** mojarse. **he got his feet ~** se mojó los pies. ● *vt* (*pt* **wetted**) mojar; (*dampen*) humedecer. **~ o.s.** orinarse. **~back** *n* espalda *f* mojada. **~ blanket** *n* aguafiestas *m & f*. **~ suit** *n* traje *m* de neopreno

w

we've /wiːv/ = we have

whack /wæk/ vt 🔲 golpear. ●n 🔲 golpe m.

whale /weɪl/ n ballena f. **we had a ~ of a time** 🔲 lo pasamos bomba 🔲

wham /wæm/ int ¡zas!

wharf /wɔːf/ n (pl **wharves** or **wharfs**) muelle m.

---

what /wɒt/

● *adjective*

····▸ (*in questions*) qué. **~ perfume are you wearing?** ¿qué perfume llevas?. **~ colour are the walls?** ¿de qué color son las paredes?

····▸ (*in exclamations*) qué. **~ a beautiful house!** ¡qué casa más linda!. **~ a lot of people!** ¡cuánta gente!

····▸ (*in indirect speech*) qué. **I'll ask him ~ bus to take** le preguntaré qué autobús hay que tomar. **do you know ~ time it leaves?** ¿sabes a qué hora sale?

● *pronoun*

····▸ (*in questions*) qué. **~ is it?** ¿qué es?. **~ for?** ¿para qué?. **~'s the problem?** ¿cuál es el problema?. **~'s he like?** ¿cómo es?. **what?** (*say that again*) ¿cómo?, ¿qué?

····▸ (*in indirect questions*) qué. **I didn't know ~ to do** no sabía qué hacer

····▸ (*relative*) lo que. **I did ~ I could** hice lo que pude. **~ I need is a new car** lo que necesito es un coche nuevo

····▸ (*in phrases*) **~ about me?** ¿y yo qué? **~ if she doesn't come?** ¿y si no viene?

whatever /wɒtˈevə(r)/ adj cualquiera. ●pron (todo) lo que, cualquier cosa que

whatsoever /wɒtsəʊˈevə(r)/ adj & pron = **whatever**

wheat /wiːt/ n trigo m.

wheel /wiːl/ n rueda f. **at the ~** al volante. ●vt empujar (bicycle etc); llevar (en silla de ruedas etc) (person). **~barrow** n carretilla f. **~chair** n silla f de ruedas

wheeze /wiːz/ vi respirar con dificultad

when /wen/ adv cuándo. ●conj cuando. **~ever** /-ˈevə(r)/ adv (*every time that*) cada vez que, siempre que; (*at whatever time*) **we'll go ~ever you're ready** saldremos cuando estés listo

where /weə(r)/ adv & conj donde; (*interrogative*) dónde. **~ are you going?** ¿adónde vas? **~ are you from?** ¿de dónde eres? **~abouts** /-əbaʊts/ adv en qué parte. ●n paradero m. **~as** /-ˈæz/ conj por cuanto; (*in contrast*) mientras (que). **~ver** /weərˈevə(r)/ adv (*in questions*) dónde; (*no matter where*) en cualquier parte. ●conj donde (+ *subjunctive*), dondequiera (+ *subjunctive*)

whet /wet/ vt (pt **whetted**) abrir (appetite)

whether /ˈweðə(r)/ conj si. **I don't know ~ she will like it** no sé si le gustará. **~ you like it or not** te guste o no te guste

which /wɪtʃ/ adj (*in questions*) (*sing*) qué, cuál; (*pl*) qué, cuáles. **~ one** cuál. **~ one of you** cuál de ustedes. ●pron (*in questions*) (*sing*) cuál; (*pl*) cuáles; (*relative*) que; (*object*) el cual, la cual, lo cual, los cuales, las cuales. **~ever** /-ˈevə-

adj cualquier. ● *pron* cualquiera que, el que, la que; (*in questions*) cuál; (*pl*) cuáles

while /waɪl/ *n* rato m. a ~ **ago** hace un rato. ● *conj* mientras; (*although*) aunque. □ ~ **away** *vt* pasar (*time*)

whilst /waɪlst/ *conj see* WHILE

whim /wɪm/ *n* capricho m

whimper /'wɪmpə(r)/ *vi* gimotear. ● *n* quejido m

whine /waɪn/ *vi* (person) gemir; (child) lloriquear; (dog) aullar

whip /wɪp/ *n* látigo m; (*for punishment*) azote m. ● *vt* (*pt* **whipped** /wɪpt/) fustigar, pegarle a (*con la fusta*) (horse); azotar (person); (*Culin*) batir

whirl /wɜːl/ *vi* girar rápidamente. ~**pool** *n* remolino m. ~**wind** *n* torbellino m

whirr /wɜː(r)/ *n* zumbido m. ● *vi* zumbar

whisk /wɪsk/ *vt* (Culin) batir. ● *n* (Culin) batidor m. ~ **away** llevarse

whisker /'wɪskə(r)/ *n* pelo m. ~**s** *npl* (of cat etc) bigotes *mpl*

whisky /'wɪskɪ/ *n* whisky m, güisqui m

whisper /'wɪspə(r)/ *vt* susurrar. ● *vi* cuchichear. ● *n* susurro m

whistle /'wɪsl/ *n* silbido m; (loud) chiflado m; (instrument) silbato m, pito m. ● *vi* silbar; (loudly) chiflar

white /waɪt/ *adj* (-er, -est) blanco. **go** ~ ponerse pálido. ● *n* blanco; (of egg) clara f. ~ **coffee** *n* café m con leche. ~**-collar worker** *n* empleado m de oficina. ~ **elephant** *n* objeto m inútil y costoso. ~**-hot** *adj* (metal) al rojo blanco. ~ **lie** *n* mentirijilla f. ~**n** *vt/i* blanquear. ~**wash** *n* cal f; (cover-up) tapadera

f ⬚. ● *vt* blanquear, encalar

Whitsun /'wɪtsn/ *n* Pentecostés m

whiz /wɪz/ *vi* (*pt* whizzed). ~ **by**, ~ **past** pasar zumbando. ~**-kid** *n* ⬚ lince m ⬚

who /huː/ *pron* (in questions) quién; (*pl*) quiénes; (as relative) que; **the girl** ~ **lives there** la chica que vive allí. **those** ~ **can't come tomorrow** los que no puedan venir mañana. ~**ever** /huː'evə(r)/ *pron* quienquiera que; (interrogative) quién

whole /həʊl/ *adj*. **the** ~ **country** todo el país. **there's a** ~ **bottle left** queda una botella entera. ● *n* todo, conjunto m; (total) total m. **on the** ~ en general. ~**-hearted** /-'hɑːtɪd/ *adj* (support) incondicional; (approval) sin reservar. ~**meal** *adj* integral. ~**sale** *n* venta f al por mayor. ● *adj* & *adv* al por mayor. ~**some** /-səm/ *adj* sano

wholly /'həʊlɪ/ *adv* completamente

whom /huːm/ *pron* que, a quien; (in questions) a quién

whooping cough /'huːpɪŋ/ *n* tos f convulsa

whore /hɔː(r)/ *n* puta f

whose /huːz/ *pron* de quién; (*pl*) de quiénes. ● *adj* (in questions) de quién; (*pl*) de quiénes; (relative) cuyo; (*pl*) cuyos

why /waɪ/ *adv* por qué. ~ **not?** ¿por qué no? **that's** ~ **I couldn't go** por eso no pude ir. ● *int* ¡vaya!

wick /wɪk/ *n* mecha f

wicked /'wɪkɪd/ *adj* malo; (mischievous) travieso; (fam, very bad) malísimo

wicker /'wɪkə(r)/ *n* mimbre m & f. ● *adj* de mimbre. ~**work** *n* artícu-

w

los *mpl* de mimbre

wicket /ˈwɪkɪt/ *n* (*cricket*) rastrillo *m*

wide /waɪd/ *adj* (-er, -est) ancho;
(*range, experience*) amplio; (*off
target*) desviado. **it's four metres
~** tiene cuatro metros de ancho.
● *adv*. **open ~I** abra bien la boca.
~ awake *adj* completamente despierto; (*fig*) despabilado. **I left the
door ~ open** dejé la puerta
abierta de par en par. **~ly** *adv* extensamente; (*believed*) generalmente; (*different*) muy. **~n** *vt* ensanchar. ● *vi* ensancharse;
~spread *adj* extendido; (*fig*) difundido

widow /ˈwɪdəʊ/ *n* viuda *f*. **~er** *n*
viudo *m*.

width /wɪdθ/ *n* anchura *f*. **in ~** de
ancho

wield /wiːld/ *vt* manejar; ejercer
(*power*)

wife /waɪf/ *n* (*pl* **wives**) mujer *f*,
esposa *f*

wig /wɪg/ *n* peluca *f*

wiggle /ˈwɪgl/ *vt* menear. ● *vi* menearse

wild /waɪld/ *adj* (-er, -est) (*animal*)
salvaje; (*flower*) silvestre; (*country*)
agreste; (*enraged*) furioso; (*idea*)
extravagante; (*with joy*) loco. **a ~
guess** una conjetura hecha totalmente al azar. **I'm not ~ about
the idea** la idea no me enloquece.
● *adv* en estado salvaje. **run ~**
(*children*) criarse como salvajes.
~s *npl* regiones *fpl* salvajes.
~erness /ˈwɪldənɪs/ *n* páramo *m*.
~fire *n*. **spread like ~fire** correr
como un reguero de pólvora.
~-goose chase *n* empresa *f* inútil.
~life *n* fauna *f*. **~ly** *adv* violentamente; (*fig*) locamente

will /wɪl/
● *auxiliary verb*

past **would**; contracted forms
I'll, you'll, etc = **I will, you
will,** etc.; **won't = will not**

····▶ (*talking about the future*)

! The Spanish future tense is
not always the first option
for translating the English future tense. The present tense
of *ir + a + verb* is commonly
used instead, particularly in
Latin American countries. **he'll
be here on Tuesday** estará el
martes, va a estar el martes;
she won't agree no va a
aceptar, no aceptará

····▶ (*in invitations and requests*)
~ you have some wine?
¿quieres (un poco de) vino?
**you'll stay for dinner, won't
you?** te quedas a cenar, ¿no?

····▶ (*in tag questions*) **you ~ be
back soon, won't you?** vas a
volver pronto, ¿no?

····▶ (*in short answers*) **will it be
ready by Monday? - yes, it
~** ¿estará listo para el lunes? -
sí

● *noun*

····▶ (*mental power*) voluntad *f*

····▶ (*document*) testamento *m*

willing /ˈwɪlɪŋ/ *adj* complaciente.
~ to dispuesto a. **~ly** *adv* de
buena gana

willow /ˈwɪləʊ/ *n* sauce *m*

will-power /ˈwɪlpaʊə(r)/ *n*
fuerza *f* de voluntad

wilt /wɪlt/ *vi* marchitarse

589

win | withdraw

win /wɪn/ vt (pt **won**, pres p **winning**) ganar; (achieve, obtain) conseguir. ● vi ganar. ● n victoria f. □ ~ **over** vt convencer

wince /wɪns/ vi hacer una mueca de dolor

winch /wɪntʃ/ n cabrestante m. ● vt levantar con un cabrestante

wind¹ /wɪnd/ n viento m; (in stomach) gases mpl. ~ **instrument** instrumento m de viento. ● vt dejar sin aliento

wind² /waɪnd/ vt (pt **wound**) (wrap around) enrollar; dar cuerda a (clock etc). ● vi (road etc) serpentear. □ ~ **up** vt dar cuerda a (watch, clock); (fig) terminar, concluir

winding /ˈwaɪndɪŋ/ adj tortuoso

windmill /ˈwɪndmɪl/ n molino m (de viento)

window /ˈwɪndəʊ/ n ventana f; (in shop) escaparate m, vitrina f (LAm), vidriera f (LAm), aparador m (Mex); (of vehicle, booking-office) ventanilla f; (Comp) ventana f, window m. ~ **box** n jardinera f. ~**shop** vi mirar los escaparates. ~**sill** n alféizar m or repisa f de la ventana

wine /waɪn/ n vino m. ~**cellar** n bodega f. ~**glass** n copa f de vino. ~**growing** n vinicultura f. ● adj vinícola. ~ **list** n lista f de vinos. ~**tasting** n cata f de vinos

wing /wɪŋ/ n ala f; (Auto) aleta f. **under one's** ~ bajo la protección de uno. ~ (in Sport) ala m & f. ~**s** npl (in theatre) bastidores mpl

wink /wɪŋk/ vi guiñar el ojo; (light etc) centellear. ● n guiño m. **not to sleep a** ~ no pegar ojo

win: ~**ner** n ganador m. ~**ning-post** n poste m de lle-

gada. ~**nings** npl ganancias fpl

wint|er /ˈwɪntə(r)/ n invierno m. ● vi invernar. ~**ry** adj invernal

wipe /waɪp/ vt limpiar, pasarle un trapo a; (dry) secar. ~ **one's nose** limpiarse la nariz. ● n. **give sth a** ~ limpiar algo, pasarle un trapo a algo. □ ~ **out** vt (cancel) cancelar; (destroy) destruir; (obliterate) borrar. □ ~ **up** vt limpiar

wir|e /ˈwaɪə(r)/ n alambre m; (Elec) cable m. ~**ing** n instalación f eléctrica

wisdom /ˈwɪzdəm/ n sabiduría f. ~ **tooth** n muela f del juicio

wise /waɪz/ adj (-er, -est) sabio; (sensible) prudente; (decision, choice) acertado. ~**ly** adv sabiamente; (sensibly) prudentemente

wish /wɪʃ/ n deseo m; (greeting) saludo m. **make a** ~ pedir un deseo. **best** ~**es, John** (in letters) saludos de John, un abrazo de John. ● vt desear. ~ **s.o. well** desear buena suerte a uno. **I** ~ **I were rich** ¡ojalá fuera rico! **he** ~**ed he hadn't told her** lamentó habérselo dicho. ~**ful thinking** n ilusiones f

wistful /ˈwɪstfʊl/ adj melancólico

wit /wɪt/ n gracia f; (intelligence) ingenio m. **be at one's** ~**s' end** no saber más qué hacer

witch /wɪtʃ/ n bruja f. ~**craft** n brujería f.

with /wɪð/ prep con; (cause, having) de. **come** ~ **me** ven conmigo. **take it** ~ **you** llévalo contigo; (formal) llévelo consigo. **the man** ~ **the beard** el hombre de la barba. **trembling** ~ **fear** temblando de miedo

withdraw /wɪðˈdrɔː/ vt (pt **withdrew**, pp **withdrawn**) retirar. ● vi apartarse. ~al n retirada f. ~n adj (person) retraído

wither /ˈwɪðə(r)/ vi marchitarse

withhold /wɪðˈhəʊld/ vt (pt **withheld**) retener; (conceal) ocultar (**from** a)

within /wɪˈðɪn/ prep dentro de. ● adv dentro. ~ **sight** a la vista

without /wɪˈðaʊt/ prep sin. ~ **paying** sin pagar

withstand /wɪðˈstænd/ vt (pt -stood) resistir

witness /ˈwɪtnɪs/ n testigo m; (proof) testimonio m. ● vt presenciar; atestiguar (signature). ~**box** n tribuna f de los testigos

witt|icism /ˈwɪtɪsɪzəm/ n ocurrencia f. ~**y** /ˈwɪtɪ/ adj (-ier, -iest) gracioso

wives /waɪvz/ see WIFE

wizard /ˈwɪzəd/ n hechicero m

wizened /ˈwɪznd/ adj arrugado

wobbl|e /ˈwɒbl/ vi (chair) tambalearse; (bicycle) bambolearse; (voice, jelly, hand) temblar. ~**y** adj (chair etc) cojo

woe /wəʊ/ n aflicción f

woke /wəʊk/, **woken** /ˈwəʊkən/ see WAKE

wolf /wʊlf/ n (pl wolves /wʊlvz/) lobo m

woman /ˈwʊmən/ n (pl women) mujer f

womb /wuːm/ n matriz f

women /ˈwɪmɪn/ npl see WOMAN

won /wʌn/ see WIN

wonder /ˈwʌndə(r)/ n maravilla f; (bewilderment) asombro m. **no** ~ no es de extrañarse (**that** que). ● vt (ask oneself) preguntarse. **I** ~ **whose book this is** me pregunto de quién será este libro; (in polite requests) **I** ~ **if you could help

me?** ¿me podría ayudar? ~**ful** adj maravilloso. ~**fully** adv maravillosamente

won't /wəʊnt/ = will not

wood /wʊd/ n madera f; (for burning) leña f; (area) bosque m. ~**ed** adj poblado de árboles, boscoso. ~**en** adj de madera. ~**land** n bosque m. ~**wind** /-wɪnd/ n instrumentos mpl de viento de madera. ~**work** n carpintería f; (in room etc) maderaje m. ~**worm** n carcoma f. ~**y** adj leñoso

wool /wʊl/ n lana f. **pull the** ~ **over s.o.'s eyes** engañar a uno. ~**len** adj de lana. ~**ly** adj (-ier, -iest) de lana; (unclear) vago. ● n jersey m

word /wɜːd/ n palabra f; (news) noticia f. **by** ~ **of mouth** de palabra. **I didn't say a** ~ yo no dije nada. **in other** ~**s** es decir. ~ vt expresar. ~**ing** n redacción f; (of question) formulación f. ~ **processor** n procesador m de textos. ~**y** adj prolijo

wore /wɔː(r)/ see WEAR

work /wɜːk/ n trabajo m; (arts) obra f. **be out of** ~ estar sin trabajo, estar desocupado. ● vt hacer trabajar; manejar (machine). ● vi trabajar; (machine) funcionar; (student) estudiar; (drug) surtir efecto. □ ~ **off** vt desahogar. □ ~ **out** vt resolver (problem); (calculate) calcular; (understand) entender. ● vi (succeed) salir bien; (Sport) entrenarse. □ ~ **up** vt. **get** ~**ed up** exaltarse. ~**able** adj (project, solution) factible. ~**er** n trabajador m; (manual) obrero m; (in office, bank) empleado m. ~**ing** adj (day) laborable; (clothes etc) de trabajo. **in** ~**ing order** en estado de funcionamiento. ~**ing class** n clase f obrera. ~**ing-class** adj de la clase obrera. ~**man** /·mən/ n (pl -men) obrero m. ~**manship** n destreza f. ~s npl (building) fábrica f; (Mec) mecanismo m. ~**shop** n taller m

world /wɜːld/ n mundo m. out of this ~ maravilloso. ● adj mundial. W~ Cup n. the W~ Cup la Copa del Mundo. ~**ly** adj mundano. ~**wide** adj universal. W~ **Wide Web** n World Wide Web m

worm /wɜːm/ n gusano m, lombriz f

worn /wɔːn/ see WEAR. ● adj gastado. ~**-out** adj gastado; (person) rendido

worr|ied /ˈwʌrɪd/ adj preocupado. ~**y** /ˈwʌrɪ/ vt preocupar; (annoy) molestar. ● vi preocuparse. ● n preocupación f. ~**ying** adj inquietante

worse /wɜːs/ adj peor. ● adv peor; (more) más. ~**n** vt/i empeorar

worship /ˈwɜːʃɪp/ n culto m; (title) Su Señoría. ● vt (pt worshipped) adorar

worst /wɜːst/ adj peor. he's the ~ in the class es el peor de la clase. ● adv peor. ● n. the ~ lo peor

worth /wɜːθ/ n valor m. ● adj. be ~ valer. it's ~ trying vale la pena probarlo. it was ~ my while (me) valió la pena. ~**less** adj sin valor. ~**while** /·ˈwaɪl/ adj que vale la pena. ~**y** /ˈwɜːðɪ/ adj meritorio; (respectable) respetable; (laudable) loable

would /wʊd/ modal verb. (in conditional sentences) ~ you go? ¿irías tú? he ~ come if he could vendría si pudiera; (in reported speech) I thought you'd forget pensé que te olvidarías; (in requests, invita-

tions) ~ you come here, please? ¿quieres venir aquí? ~ you switch the television off? ¿podrías apagar la televisión? (of person) he ~n't listen to me no me quería escuchar

wound¹ /wuːnd/ n herida f. ● vt herir

wound² /waʊnd/ see WIND²

wove, woven /wəʊv, ˈwəʊvn/ see WEAVE

wow /waʊ/ int ¡ah!

wrangle /ˈræŋgl/ vi reñir. ● n riña f

wrap /ræp/ vt (pt wrapped) envolver. ● n bata f; (shawl) chal m. ~**per** n, ~**ping** n envoltura f

wrath /rɒθ/ n ira f

wreak /riːk/ vt sembrar. ~ havoc causar estragos

wreath /riːθ/ n (pl -ths /-ðz/) corona f

wreck /rek/ n (ship) restos mpl de un naufragio; (vehicle) restos mpl de un avión siniestrado. be a nervous ~ tener los nervios destrozados. ● vt provocar el naufragio de (ship); destrozar (car); (Amer, demolish) demoler; (fig) destrozar. ~**age** /-ɪdʒ/ n restos mpl; (of building) ruinas fpl

wrench /rentʃ/ vt arrancar; (sprain) desgarrarse; dislocarse (joint). ● n tirón m; (emotional) dolor m (causado por una separación); (tool) llave f inglesa

wrestl|e /ˈresl/ vi luchar. ~**er** n luchador m. ~**ing** n lucha f

wretch /retʃ/ n (despicable person) desgraciado m; (unfortunate person) desdichado m & f. ~**ed** /-ɪd/ adj desdichado; (weather) horrible

wriggle /ˈrɪgl/ vi retorcerse. ~

out of escaparse de

wring /rɪŋ/ vt (pt **wrung**) retorcer (neck). ~ **out of** (obtain from) arrancar. ◻ ~ **out** vt retorcer

wrinkl|e /'rɪŋkl/ n arruga f. ● vt arrugar. ● vi arrugarse. ~**y** adj arrugado

wrist /rɪst/ n muñeca f. ~**watch** n reloj m de pulsera

writ /rɪt/ n orden m judicial

write /raɪt/ vt/i (pt **wrote**, pp **written**, pres p **writing**) escribir. ◻ ~ **down** vt anotar. ◻ ~ **off** vt cancelar (debt). ~**off** n. the car was a ~**off** el coche fue declarado un siniestro total. ~**r** n escritor m

writhe /raɪð/ vi retorcerse

writing /'raɪtɪŋ/ n (script) escritura f; (handwriting) letra f. **in** ~ por escrito. ~**s** npl obra f, escritos mpl. ~ **desk** n escritorio m. ~ **pad** n bloc m. ~ **paper** n papel m de escribir

written /'rɪtn/ see **WRITE**

wrong /rɒŋ/ adj equivocado, incorrecto; (not just) injusto; (mistaken) equivocado. **be** ~ no tener razón; (be mistaken) equivocarse. what's ~? ¿qué pasa? it's ~ to steal robar está mal. what's ~ with that? ¿qué hay de malo en eso? ● adv mal. **go** ~ equivocarse; (plan) salir mal. ● n injusticia f; (evil) mal m. **in the** ~ equivocado. ● vt ser injusto con. ~**ful** adj injusto. ~**ly** adv mal; (unfairly) injustamente

wrote /rəʊt/ see **WRITE**

wrought iron /rɔːt/ n hierro m forjado

wrung /rʌŋ/ see **WRING**

wry /raɪ/ adj (**wryer**, **wryest**) irónico. **make a** ~ **face** torcer el gesto

xerox /'zɪərɒks/ vt fotocopiar, xerografiar

Xmas /'krɪsməs/ n abbr (**Christmas**) Navidad f

X-ray /'eksreɪ/ n (ray) rayo m X; (photograph) radiografía f. ~**s** npl rayos mpl. ● vt hacer una radiografía de

xylophone /'zaɪləfəʊn/ n xilofón m, xilófono m

yacht /jɒt/ n yate m. ~**ing** n navegación f a vela

yank /jæŋk/ vt 🔲 tirar de (violentamente)

Yankee /'jæŋkɪ/ n 🔲 yanqui m & f

yap /jæp/ vi (pt **yapped**) (dog) ladrar (con ladridos agudos)

yard /jɑːd/ n patio m; (Amer, garden) jardín m; (measurement) yarda f (= 0.9144 metre)

yarn /jɑːn/ n hilo m; (fam, tale) cuento m

yawn /jɔːn/ vi bostezar. ● n bostezo m

yeah /jeə/ adv 🔲 sí

year /jɪə(r)/ n año m. **be three** ~**s old** tener tres años. ~**ly** adj anual. ● adv cada año

yearn /'jɜːn/ vi. ~ **to do sth** anhelar hacer algo. ~ **for sth** añorar

yeast | you're

algo. **~ing** *n* anhelo *m*, ansia *f*

yeast /jiːst/ *n* levadura *f*

yell /jel/ *vi* gritar. ● *n* grito *m*

yellow /'jeləʊ/ *adj* & *n* amarillo (*m*)

yelp /jelp/ *n* gañido *m*. ● *vi* gañir

yes /jes/ *int* & *n* sí (*m*)

yesterday /'jestədeɪ/ *adv* & *n* ayer (*m*). **the day before ~** anteayer *m*. **~ morning** ayer por la mañana, ayer en la mañana (*LAm*)

yet /jet/ *adv* todavía, aún; (*already*) ya. **as ~** hasta ahora; (*as a linker*) sin embargo. ● *conj* pero

Yiddish /'jɪdɪʃ/ *n* yídish *m*

yield /jiːld/ *vt* (*surrender*) ceder; producir (*crop/mineral*); dar (*results*). ● *vi* ceder. **'yield'** (*Amer, traffic sign*) ceda el paso. ● *n* rendimiento *m*

yoga /'jəʊgə/ *n* yoga *m*

yoghurt /'jɒgət/ *n* yogur *m*

yoke /jəʊk/ *n* (*fig also*) yugo *m*

yokel /'jəʊkl/ *n* palurdo *m*

yolk /jəʊk/ *n* yema *f* (de huevo)

you /juː/ *pronoun*

····▸ (*as the subject*) (*familiar form*) (*sing*) tú, vos (*River Plate and parts of Central America*); (*pl*) vosotros, -tras (*Spain*), ustedes (*LAm*); (*formal*) (*sing*) usted; (*pl*) ustedes

! In Spanish the subject pronoun is usually only used to give emphasis or mark contrast.

····▸ (*as the direct object*) (*familiar form*) (*sing*) te; (*pl*) os (*Spain*), los, las (*LAm*); (*formal*) (*sing*) lo or (*Spain*) le, la; (*pl*) los or (*Spain*) les, las. **I love ~** te quiero

····▸ (*as the indirect object*) (*familiar form*) (*sing*) te; (*pl*) os (*Spain*), les (*LAm*); (*formal*) (*sing*) le; (*pl*) les. **I sent ~ the book yesterday** te mandé el libro ayer

! The pronoun **se** replaces the indirect object pronoun **le** or **les** when the latter is used with the direct object pronoun (*lo, la* etc), e.g. **I gave it to ~** se lo di

····▸ (*when used after a preposition*) (*familiar form*) (*sing*) ti, vos (*River Plate and parts of Central America*); (*pl*) vosotros, -tras (*Spain*), ustedes (*LAm*); (*formal*) (*sing*) usted; (*pl*) ustedes

····▸ (*generalizing*) uno, tú (*esp Spain*). **~ feel very proud** uno se siente muy orgulloso, te sientes muy orgulloso (*esp Spain*). **~ have to be patient** hay que tener paciencia

you'd /juːd/, /jʊəd/ = **you had**, **you would**

you'll /juːl/, /jʊəl/ = **you will**

young /jʌŋ/ *adj* (**-er, -est**) joven. **my ~er sister** mi hermana menor. **he's a year ~er than me** tiene un año menos que yo. **~ lady** *n* señorita *f*. **~ man** *n* joven *m*. **~ster** /-stə(r)/ *n* joven *m*

your /jɔː(r)/ *adj* (*belonging to one person*) (*sing, familiar*) tu; (*pl, familiar*) tus; (*sing, formal*) su; (*pl, formal*) sus; (*belonging to more than one person*) (*sing, familiar*) vuestro, -tra, su (*LAm*); (*pl, familiar*) vuestros, -tras, sus (*LAm*); (*sing, formal*) su; (*pl, formal*) sus

you're /jʊə(r)/, /jɔː(r)/ = **you are**

y

yours /jɔːz/ poss pron (belonging to one person) (sing, familiar) tuyo, -ya; (pl, familiar) tuyos, -yas; (sing, formal) suyo, -ya; (pl, formal) suyos, -yas. (belonging to more than one person) (sing, familiar) vuestro, -tra; (pl, familiar) vuestros, -tras; suyos, -yas (LAm); (sing, formal) suyo, -ya; (pl, formal) suyos, -yas. **an aunt of** ~ una tía tuya/suya; ~ **is here** el tuyo/la tuya/el suyo/la suya está aquí

yourself /jɔːˈself/ pron (reflexive). (emphatic use) 🆃 tú mismo, tú misma; (formal) usted mismo, usted misma. **describe** ~f descríbete; (Ud form) descríbase. **stop thinking about** ~f 🆃 deja de pensar en tí mismo; (formal) deje de pensar en sí mismo. **by** ~f solo, sola. ~**ves** /jɔːˈselvz/ pron vosotros mismos, vosotras mismas (familiar), ustedes mismos, ustedes mismas (LAm familiar), ustedes mismos, ustedes mismas (formal); (reflexive). **behave** ~**ves** ¡portaos bien! (familiar), ¡pórtense bien! (formal, LAm familiar). **by** ~**ves** solos, solas

youth /juːθ/ n (pl **youths** /juːðz/) (early life) juventud f; (boy) joven m; (young people) juventud f. ~**ful** adj joven, juvenil. ~ **hostel** n albergue m juvenil

you've /juːv/ = **you have**

Yugoslav /ˈjuːɡəslɑːv/ adj & n yugoslavo (m). ~**ia** /-ˈslɑːvɪə/ n Yugoslavia f

Zz

zeal /ziːl/ n fervor m, celo m

zeallot /ˈzelət/ n fanático m. ~**ous** /-əs/ adj ferviente; (worker) que pone gran celo en su trabajo

zebra /ˈzebrə/ n cebra f. ~ **crossing** n paso m de cebra

zenith /ˈzenɪθ/ n cenit m

zero /ˈzɪərəʊ/ n (pl **-os**) cero m

zest /zest/ n entusiasmo m; (peel) cáscara f

zigzag /ˈzɪɡzæɡ/ n zigzag m. ● vi (pt **zigzagged**) zigzaguear

zilch /zɪltʃ/ n 🆇 nada de nada

zinc /zɪŋk/ n cinc m

zip /zɪp/ n cremallera f, cierre m (LAm), zíper m (Mex). ● vt. ~ (**up**) cerrar (la cremallera). **Z**~ **code** n (Amer) código m postal. ~ **fastener** n cremallera f. ~**per** n/vt see **ZIP**

zodiac /ˈzəʊdɪæk/ n zodíaco m, zodiaco m

zombie /ˈzɒmbɪ/ n zombi m & f

zone /zəʊn/ n zona f. **time** ~ n huso m horario

zoo /zuː/ n zoo m, zoológico m. ~**logical** /zuːəˈlɒdʒɪkl/ adj zoológico. ~**logist** /zuːˈɒlədʒɪst/ n zoólogo m. ~**logy** /zuːˈɒlədʒɪ/ n zoología f

zoom /zuːm/. □ ~ **in** vi (Photo) hacer un zoom in (**on** sobre). □ ~ **past** vi/t pasar zumbando. ~ **lens** n teleobjetivo m, zoom m

zucchini /zuˈkiːnɪ/ n (invar or ~**s**) (Amer) calabacín m

Numbers/números

zero	**0**	cero
one (first)	**1**	uno (primero)
two (second)	**2**	dos (segundo)
three (third)	**3**	tres (tercero)
four (fourth)	**4**	cuatro (cuarto)
five (fifth)	**5**	cinco (quinto)
six (sixth)	**6**	seis (sexto)
seven (seventh)	**7**	siete (séptimo)
eight (eighth)	**8**	ocho (octavo)
nine (ninth)	**9**	nueve (noveno)
ten (tenth)	**10**	diez (décimo)
eleven (eleventh)	**11**	once (undécimo)
twelve (twelfth)	**12**	doce (duodécimo)
thirteen (thirteenth)	**13**	trece (decimotercero)
fourteen (fourteenth)	**14**	catorce (decimocuarto)
fifteen (fifteenth)	**15**	quince (decimoquinto)
sixteen (sixteenth)	**16**	dieciséis (decimosexto)
seventeen (seventeenth)	**17**	diecisiete (decimoséptimo)
eighteen (eighteenth)	**18**	dieciocho (decimoctavo)
nineteen (nineteenth)	**19**	diecinueve (decimonoveno)
twenty (twentieth)	**20**	veinte (vigésimo)
twenty-one (twenty-first)	**21**	veintiuno (vigésimo primero)
twenty-two (twenty-second)	**22**	veintidós (vigésimo segundo)
twenty-three (twenty-third)	**23**	veintitrés (vigésimo tercero)
twenty-four (twenty-fourth)	**24**	veinticuatro (vigésimo cuarto)
twenty-five (twenty-fifth)	**25**	veinticinco (vigésimo quinto)
twenty-six (twenty-sixth)	**26**	veintiséis (vigésimo sexto)
thirty (thirtieth)	**30**	treinta (trigésimo)

Numbers		Números	596

thirty-one (thirty-first)	**31**	treinta y uno (trigésimo primero)	
forty (fortieth)	**40**	cuarenta (cuadragésimo)	
fifty (fiftieth)	**50**	cincuenta (quincuagésimo)	
sixty (sixtieth)	**60**	sesenta (sexagésimo)	
seventy (seventieth)	**70**	setenta (septuagésimo)	
eighty (eightieth)	**80**	ochenta (octogésimo)	
ninety (ninetieth)	**90**	noventa (nonagésimo)	
a/one hundred (hundredth)	**100**	cien (centésimo)	
a/one hundred and one (hundred and first)	**101**	ciento uno (centésimo primero)	
two hundred (two hundredth)	**200**	doscientos (ducentésimo)	
three hundred (three hundredth)	**300**	trescientos (tricentésimo)	
four hundred (four hundredth)	**400**	cuatrocientos (cuadringentésimo)	
five hundred (five hundredth)	**500**	quinientos (quingentésimo)	
six hundred (six hundredth)	**600**	seiscientos (sexcentésimo)	
seven hundred (seven hundredth)	**700**	setecientos (septingentésimo)	
eight hundred (eight hundredth)	**800**	ochocientos (octingentésimo)	
nine hundred (nine hundredth)	**900**	novecientos (noningentésimo)	
a/one thousand (thousandth)	**1000**	mil (milésimo)	
two thousand (two thousandth)	**2000**	dos mil (dos milésimo)	
a/one million (millionth)	**1,000,000**	un millón (millonésimo)	

Verbos irregulares ingleses

Infinitivo	Pretérito	Participio pasado	Infinitivo	Pretérito	Participio pasado
be	was	been	**drive**	drove	driven
bear	bore	borne	**eat**	ate	eaten
beat	beat	beaten	**fall**	fell	fallen
become	became	become	**feed**	fed	fed
begin	began	begun	**feel**	felt	felt
bend	bent	bent	**fight**	fought	fought
bet	bet,	bet,	**find**	found	found
	betted	betted	**flee**	fled	fled
bid	bade, bid	bidden, bid	**fly**	flew	flown
bind	bound	bound	**freeze**	froze	frozen
bite	bit	bitten	**get**	got	got, gotten US
bleed	bled	bled	**give**	gave	given
blow	blew	blown	**go**	went	gone
break	broke	broken	**grow**	grew	grown
breed	bred	bred	**hang**	hung,	hung,
bring	brought	brought		hanged	hanged
build	built	built	**have**	had	had
burn	burnt,	burnt,	**hear**	heard	heard
	burned	burned	**hide**	hid	hidden
burst	burst	burst	**hit**	hit	hit
buy	bought	bought	**hold**	held	held
catch	caught	caught	**hurt**	hurt	hurt
choose	chose	chosen	**keep**	kept	kept
cling	clung	clung	**kneel**	knelt	knelt
come	came	come	**know**	knew	known
cost	cost,	cost,	**lay**	laid	laid
	costed (vt)	costed	**lead**	led	led
cut	cut	cut	**lean**	leaned,	leaned,
deal	dealt	dealt		leant	leant
dig	dug	dug	**learn**	learnt,	learnt,
do	did	done		learned	learned
draw	drew	drawn	**leave**	left	left
dream	dreamt,	dreamt,	**lend**	lent	lent
	dreamed	dreamed	**let**	let	let
drink	drank	drunk	**lie**	lay	lain

Verbos irregulares ingleses

Infinitivo	Pretérito	Participio pasado	Infinitivo	Pretérito	Participio pasado
lose	lost	lost	spend	spent	spent
make	made	made	spit	spat	spat
mean	meant	meant	spoil	spoilt, spoiled	spoilt, spoiled
meet	met	met	spread	spread	spread
pay	paid	paid	spring	sprang	sprung
put	put	put	stand	stood	stood
read	read	read	steal	stole	stolen
ride	rode	ridden	stick	stuck	stuck
ring	rang	rung	sting	stung	stung
rise	rose	risen	stride	strode	stridden
run	ran	run	strike	struck	struck
say	said	said	swear	swore	sworn
see	saw	seen	sweep	swept	swept
seek	sought	sought	swell	swelled	swollen, swelled
sell	sold	sold	swim	swam	swum
send	sent	sent	swing	swung	swung
set	set	set	take	took	taken
sew	sewed	sewn, sewed	teach	taught	taught
shake	shook	shaken	tear	tore	torn
shine	shone	shone	tell	told	told
shoe	shod	shod	think	thought	thought
shoot	shot	shot	throw	threw	thrown
show	showed	shown	thrust	thrust	thrust
shut	shut	shut	tread	trod	trodden
sing	sang	sung	understand	understood	understood
sink	sank	sunk	wake	woke	woken
sit	sat	sat	wear	wore	worn
sleep	slept	slept	win	won	won
sling	slung	slung	write	wrote	written
smell	smelt, smelled	smelt, smelled			
speak	spoke	spoken			
spell	spelled, spelt	spelled, spelt			

Spanish verbs

Regular verbs:

● in -ar (e.g. **comprar**)
Present; compr|o, ~as, ~a, ~amos, ~áis, ~an
Future: comprar|é, ~ás, ~á, ~emos, ~éis, ~án
Imperfect: compr|aba, ~abas, ~aba, ~ábamos, ~abais, ~aban
Preterite: compr|é, ~aste, ~ó, ~amos, ~asteis, ~aron
Present subjunctive: compr|e, ~es, ~e, ~emos, ~éis, ~en
Imperfect subjunctive: compr|ara, ~aras, ~ara, ~áramos, ~arais, ~aran
compr|ase, ~ases, ~ase, ~ásemos, ~aseis, ~asen
Conditional: comprar|ía, ~ías, ~ía, ~íamos, ~íais, ~ían
Present participle: comprando
Past participle: comprado
Imperative: compra, comprad

● in -er (e.g. **beber**)
Present: beb|o, ~es, ~e, ~emos, ~éis, ~en
Future: beber|é, ~ás, ~á, ~emos, ~éis, ~án
Imperfect: beb|ía, ~ías, ~ía, ~íamos, ~íais, ~ían
Preterite: beb|í, ~iste, ~ió, ~imos, ~isteis, ~ieron
Present subjunctive: beb|a, ~as, ~a, ~amos, ~áis, ~an
Imperfect subjunctive: beb|iera, ~ieras, ~iera, ~iéramos, ~ierais, ~ieran

beb|iese, ~ieses, ~iese, ~iésemos, ~ieseis, ~iesen
Conditional: beber|ía, ~ías, ~ía, ~íamos, ~íais, ~ían
Present participle: bebiendo
Past participle: bebido
Imperative: bebe, bebed

● in -ir (e.g. **vivir**)
Present: viv|o, ~es, ~e, ~imos, ~ís, ~en
Future: vivir|é, ~ás, ~á, ~emos, ~éis, ~án
Imperfect: viv|ía, ~ías, ~ía, ~íamos, ~íais, ~ían
Preterite: viv|í, ~iste, ~ió, ~imos, ~isteis, ~ieron
Present subjunctive: viv|a, ~as, ~a, ~amos, ~áis, ~an
Imperfect subjunctive: viv|iera, ~ieras, ~iera, ~iéramos, ~ierais, ~ieran
viv|iese, ~ieses, ~iese, ~iésemos, ~ieseis, ~iesen
Conditional: vivir|ía, ~ías, ~ía, ~íamos, ~íais, ~ían
Present participle: viviendo
Past participle: vivido
Imperative: vive, vivid

Irregular verbs:

[1] cerrar

Present: cierro, cierras, cierra, cerramos, cerráis, cierran
Present subjunctive: cierre, cierres, cierre, cerremos, cerréis, cierren
Imperative: cierra, cerrad

[2] contar, mover

Present: cuento, cuentas, cuenta, contamos, contáis, cuentan
muevo, mueves, mueve, movemos, movéis, mueven
Present subjunctive: cuente, cuentes, cuente, contemos, contéis, cuenten
mueva, muevas, mueva, movamos, mováis, muevan
Imperative: cuenta, contad
mueve, moved

[3] jugar

Present: juego, juegas, juega, jugamos, jugáis, juegan
Preterite: jugué, jugaste, jugó, jugamos, jugasteis, jugaron
Present subjunctive: juegue, juegues, juegue, juguemos, juguéis, jueguen

[4] sentir

Present: siento, sientes, siente, sentimos, sentís, sienten
Preterite: sentí, sentiste, sintió, sentimos, sentisteis, sintieron
Present subjunctive: sienta, sientas, sienta, sintamos, sintáis, sientan
Imperfect subjunctive: sint|iera, ~ieras, ~iera, ~iéramos, ~ierais, ~ieran
sint|iese, ~ieses, ~iese, ~iésemos, ~ieseis, ~iesen
Present participle: sintiendo
Imperative: siente, sentid

[5] pedir

Present: pido, pides, pide, pedimos, pedís, piden
Preterite: pedí, pediste, pidió, pedimos, pedisteis, pidieron
Present subjunctive: pid|a, ~as, ~a, ~amos, ~áis, ~an
Imperfect subjunctive: pid|iera, ~ieras, ~iera, ~iéramos, ~ierais, ~ieran
pid|iese, ~ieses, ~iese, ~iésemos, ~ieseis, ~iesen
Present participle: pidiendo
Imperative: pide, pedid

[6] dormir

Present: duermo, duermes, duerme, dormimos, dormís, duermen
Preterite: dormí, dormiste, durmió, dormimos, dormisteis, durmieron
Present subjunctive: duerma, duermas, duerma, durmamos, durmáis, duerman
Imperfect subjunctive: durm|iera, ~ieras, ~iera, ~iéramos, ~ierais, ~ieran
durm|iese, ~ieses, ~iese, ~iésemos, ~ieseis, ~iesen
Present participle: durmiendo
Imperative: duerme, dormid

[7] dedicar

Preterite: dediqué, dedicaste, dedicó, dedicamos, dedicasteis, dedicaron
Present subjunctive: dediqu|e, ~es, ~e, ~emos, ~éis, ~en

[8] delinquir

Present: delinco, delinques, delinque, delinquimos, delinquís, delinquen
Present subjunctive: delinc|a, ~as, ~a, ~amos, ~áis, ~an

[9] vencer, esparcir

Present: venzo, vences, vence, vencemos, vencéis, vencen
esparzo, esparces, esparce, esparcimos, esparcís, esparcen

Present subjunctive: venz|a, ~as, ~a, ~amos, ~áis, ~an
esparz|a, ~as, ~a, ~amos, ~áis, ~an

[10] rechazar

Preterite: rechacé, rechazaste, rechazó, rechazamos, rechazasteis, rechazaron
Present subjunctive: rechac|e, ~es, ~e, ~emos, ~éis, ~en

[11] conocer, lucir

Present: conozco, conoces, conoce, conocemos, conocéis, conocen
luzco, luces, luce, lucimos, lucís, lucen
Present subjunctive: conozc|a, ~as, ~a, ~amos, ~áis, ~an
luzc|a, ~as, ~a, ~amos, ~áis, ~an

[12] pagar

Preterite: pagué, pagaste, pagó, pagamos, pagasteis, pagaron
Present subjunctive: pagu|e, ~es, ~e, ~emos, ~éis, ~en

[13] distinguir

Present: distingo, distingues, distingue, distinguimos, distinguís, distinguen
Present subjunctive: disting|a, ~as, ~a, ~amos, ~áis, ~an

[14] acoger, afligir

Present: acojo, acoges, acoge, acogemos, acogéis, acogen
aflijo, afliges, aflige, afligimos, afligís, afligen
Present subjunctive: acoj|a, ~as, ~a, ~amos, ~áis, ~an

aflij|a, ~as, ~a, ~amos, ~áis, ~an

[15] averiguar

Preterite: averigüé, averiguaste, averiguó, averiguamos, averiguasteis, averiguaron
Present subjunctive: averigü|e, ~es, ~e, ~emos, ~éis, ~en

[16] agorar

Present: agüero, agüeras, agüera, agoramos, agoráis, agüeran
Present subjunctive: agüere, agüeres, agüere, agoremos, agoréis, agüeren
Imperative: agüera, agorad

[17] huir

Present: huyo, huyes, huye, huimos, huís, huyen
Preterite: huí, huiste, huyó, huimos, huisteis, huyeron
Present subjunctive: huy|a, ~as, ~a, ~amos, ~áis, ~an
Imperfect subjunctive: huy|era, ~eras, ~era, ~éramos, ~erais, ~eran
huy|ese, ~eses, ~ese, ~ésemos, ~eseis, ~esen
Present participle: huyendo
Imperative: huye, huid

[18] creer

Preterite: creí, creíste, creyó, creímos, creísteis, creyeron
Imperfect subjunctive: crey|era, ~eras, ~era, ~éramos, ~erais, ~eran
crey|ese, ~eses, ~ese, ~ésemos, ~eseis, ~esen
Present participle: creyendo
Past participle: creído

[19] argüir

Present: arguyo, arguyes, arguye, argüimos, argüís, arguyen
Preterite: argüí, argüiste, arguyó, argüimos, argüisteis, arguyeron
Present subjunctive: arguy|a, ~as, ~a, ~amos, ~áis, ~an
Imperfect subjunctive: arguy|era, ~eras, ~era, ~éramos, ~erais, ~eran
arguy|ese, ~eses, ~ese, ~ésemos, ~eseis, ~esen
Present participle: arguyendo
Imperative: arguye, argüid

[20] vaciar

Present: vacío, vacías, vacía, vaciamos, vaciáis, vacían
Present subjunctive: vacíe, vacíes, vacíe, vaciemos, vaciéis, vacíen
Imperative: vacía, vaciad

[21] acentuar

Present: acentúo, acentúas, acentúa, acentuamos, acentuáis, acentúan
Present subjunctive: acentúe, acentúes, acentúe, acentuemos, acentuéis, acentúen
Imperative: acentúa, acentuad

[22] atañer, engullir

Preterite: atañ|í, ~iste, ~ó, ~imos, ~isteis, ~eron
engull|í, ~iste, ~ó, ~imos, ~isteis, ~eron
Imperfect subjunctive: atañera, ~eras, ~era, ~éramos, ~erais, ~eran
atañese, ~eses, ~ese, ~ésemos, ~eseis, ~esen
engull|era, ~eras, ~era, ~éramos, ~erais, ~eran

engull|ese, ~eses, ~ese, ~ésemos, ~eseis, ~esen
Present participle: atañendo
engullendo

[23] aislar, aullar

Present: aíslo, aíslas, aísla, aislamos, aisláis, aíslan
aúllo, aúllas, aúlla, aullamos, aulláis, aúllan
Present subjunctive: aísle, aísles, aísle, aislemos, aisléis, aíslen
aúlle, aúlles, aúlle, aullemos, aulléis, aúllen
Imperative: aísla, aislad
aúlla, aullad

[24] abolir

Present: abolimos, abolís
Present subjunctive: not used
Imperative: abolid

[25] andar

Preterite: anduv|e, ~iste, ~o, ~imos, ~isteis, ~ieron
Imperfect subjunctive: anduv|iera, ~ieras, ~iera, ~iéramos, ~ierais, ~ieran
anduv|iese, ~ieses, ~iese, ~iésemos, ~ieseis, ~iesen

[26] dar

Present: doy, das, da, damos, dais, dan
Preterite: di, diste, dio, dimos, disteis, dieron
Present subjunctive: dé, des, dé, demos, deis, den
Imperfect subjunctive: diera, dieras, diera, diéramos, dierais, dieran
diese, dieses, diese, diésemos, dieseis, diesen

[27] estar

Present: estoy, estás, está, estamos, estáis, están

Preterite: estuv|e, ∼iste, ∼o, ∼imos, ∼isteis, ∼ieron

Present subjunctive: esté, estés, esté, estemos, estéis, estén

Imperfect subjunctive: estuv|iera, ∼ieras, ∼iera, ∼iéramos, ∼ierais, ∼ieran

estuv|iese, ∼ieses, ∼iese, ∼iésemos, ∼ieseis, ∼iesen

Imperative: está, estad

[28] caber

Present: quepo, cabes, cabe, cabemos, cabéis, caben

Future: cabr|é, ∼ás, ∼á, ∼emos, ∼éis, ∼án

Preterite: cup|e, ∼iste, ∼o, ∼imos, ∼isteis, ∼ieron

Present subjunctive: quep|a, ∼as, ∼a, ∼amos, ∼áis, ∼an

Imperfect subjunctive: cup|iera, ∼ieras, ∼iera, ∼iéramos, ∼ierais, ∼ieran

cup|iese, ∼ieses, ∼iese, ∼iésemos, ∼ieseis, ∼iesen

Conditional: cabr|ía, ∼ías, ∼ía, ∼íamos, ∼íais, ∼ían

[29] caer

Present: caigo, caes, cae, caemos, caéis, caen

Preterite: caí, caiste, cayó, caímos, caísteis, cayeron

Present subjunctive: caig|a, ∼as, ∼a, ∼amos, ∼áis, ∼an

Imperfect subjunctive: cay|era, ∼eras, ∼era, ∼éramos, ∼erais, ∼eran

cay|ese, ∼eses, ∼ese, ∼ésemos, ∼eseis, ∼esen

Present participle: cayendo

Past participle: ca...

[30] haber

Present: he, has, ha, hem..., han

Future: habr|é ∼ás, ∼á, ∼emo..., ∼éis, ∼án

Preterite: hub|e, ∼iste, ∼o, ∼imos, ∼isteis, ∼ieron

Present subjunctive: hay|a, ∼as, ∼a, ∼amos, ∼áis, ∼an

Imperfect subjunctive: hub|iera, ∼ieras, ∼iera, ∼iéramos, ∼ierais, ∼ieran

hub|iese, ∼ieses, ∼iese, ∼iésemos, ∼ieseis, ∼iesen

Conditional: habr|ía, ∼ías, ∼ía, ∼íamos, ∼íais, ∼ían

Imperative: he, habed

[31] hacer

Present: hago, haces, hace, hacemos, hacéis, hacen

Future: har|é, ∼ás, ∼á, ∼emos, ∼éis, ∼án

Preterite: hice, hiciste, hizo, hicimos, hicisteis, hicieron

Present subjunctive: hag|a, ∼as, ∼a, ∼amos, ∼áis, ∼an

Imperfect subjunctive: hic|iera, ∼ieras, ∼iera, ∼iéramos, ∼ierais, ∼ieran

hic|iese, ∼ieses, ∼iese, ∼iésemos, ∼ieseis, ∼iesen

Conditional: har|ía, ∼ías, ∼ía, ∼íamos, ∼íais, ∼ían

Past participle: hecho

Imperative: haz, haced

[32] placer

Present subjunctive: plazca

Imperfect subjunctive: placiera, placiese

...er

Present: puedo, puedes, puede,
~demos, podéis, pueden
Future: podr|é, ~ás, ~á, ~emos,
~éis, ~án
Preterite: pud|e, ~iste, ~o, ~imos,
~isteis, ~ieron
Present subjunctive: pueda, puedas,
pueda, podamos, podáis, puedan
Imperfect subjunctive: pud|iera,
~ieras, ~iera, ~iéramos, ~ierais,
~ieran
pud|iese, ~ieses, ~iese, ~iésemos,
~ieseis, ~iesen
Conditional: podr|ía, ~ías, ~ía,
~íamos, ~íais, ~ían
Past participle: pudiendo

[34] poner

Present: pongo, pones, pone,
ponemos, ponéis, ponen
Future: pondr|é, ~ás, ~á, ~emos,
~éis, ~án
Preterite: pus|e, ~iste, ~o, ~imos,
~isteis, ~ieron
Present subjunctive: pong|a, ~as, ~a,
~amos, ~áis, ~an
Imperfect subjunctive: pus|iera, ~ieras,
~iera, ~iéramos, ~ierais, ~ieran
pus|iese, ~ieses, ~iese, ~iésemos,
~ieseis, ~iesen
Conditional: pondr|ía, ~ías, ~ía,
~íamos, ~íais, ~ían
Past participle: puesto
Imperative: pon, poned

[35] querer

Present: quiero, quieres, quiere,
queremos, queréis, quieren
Future: querr|é, ~ás, ~á, ~emos,
~éis, ~án

Preterite: quis|e, ~iste, ~o, ~imos,
~isteis, ~ieron
Present subjunctive: quiera, quieras,
quiera, queramos, queráis,
quieran
Imperfect subjunctive: quis|iera,
~ieras, ~iera, ~iéramos, ~ierais,
~ieran
quis|iese, ~ieses, ~iese,
~iésemos, ~ieseis, ~iesen
Conditional: querr|ía, ~ías, ~ía,
~íamos, ~íais, ~ían
Imperative: quiere, quered

[36] raer

Present: raigo/rayo, raes, rae, raemos,
raéis, raen
Preterite: raí, raíste, rayó, raímos,
raísteis, rayeron
Present subjunctive: raig|a, ~as, ~a,
~amos, ~áis, ~an ray|a, ~as, ~a,
~amos, ~áis, ~an
Imperfect subjunctive: ray|era, ~eras,
~era, ~éramos, ~erais, ~eran
ray|ese, ~eses, ~ese, ~ésemos,
~eseis, ~esen
Present participle: rayendo
Past participle: raído

[37] roer

Present: roo, roes, roe, roemos, roéis,
roen
Preterite: roí, roíste, royó, roímos,
roísteis, royeron
Present subjunctive: ro|a, ~as, ~a,
~amos, ~áis, ~an
Imperfect subjunctive: roy|era, ~eras,
~era, ~éramos, ~erais, ~eran
roy|ese, ~eses, ~ese, ~ésemos,
~eseis, ~esen
Present participle: royendo
Past participle: roído

[38] saber

Present: sé, sabes, sabe, sabemos, sabéis, saben

Future: sabr|é, ~ás, ~á, ~emos, ~éis, ~án

Preterite: sup|e, ~iste, ~o, ~imos, ~isteis, ~ieron

Present subjunctive: sep|a, ~as, ~a, ~amos, ~áis, ~an

Imperfect subjunctive: sup|iera, ~ieras, ~iera, ~iéramos, ~ierais, ~ieran sup|iese, ~ieses, ~iese, ~iésemos, ~ieseis, ~iesen

Conditional: sabr|ía, ~ías, ~ía, ~íamos, ~íais, ~ían

[39] ser

Present: soy, eres, es, somos, sois, son

Imperfect: era, eras, era, éramos, erais, eran

Preterite: fui, fuiste, fue, fuimos, fuisteis, fueron

Present subjunctive: se|a, ~as, ~a, ~amos, ~áis, ~an

Imperfect subjunctive: fu|era, ~eras, ~era, ~éramos, ~erais, ~eran fu|ese, ~eses, ~ese, ~ésemos, ~eseis, ~esen

Imperative: sé, sed

[40] tener

Present: tengo, tienes, tiene, tenemos, tenéis, tienen

Future: tendr|é, ~ás, ~á, ~emos, ~éis, ~án

Preterite: tuv|e, ~iste, ~o, ~imos, ~isteis, ~ieron

Present subjunctive: teng|a, ~as, ~a, ~amos, ~áis, ~an

Imperfect subjunctive: tuv|iera, ~ieras, ~iera, ~iéramos, ~ierais, ~ieran tuv|iese, ~ieses, ~iese, ~iésemos, ~ieseis, ~iesen

Conditional: tendr|ía, ~ías, ~ía, ~íamos, ~íais, ~ían

Imperative: ten, tened

[41] traer

Present: traigo, traes, trae, traemos, traéis, traen

Preterite: traj|e, ~iste, ~o, ~imos, ~isteis, ~eron

Present subjunctive: traig|a, ~as, ~a, ~amos, ~áis, ~an

Imperfect subjunctive: traj|era, ~eras, ~era, ~éramos, ~erais, ~eran traj|ese, ~eses, ~ese, ~ésemos, ~eseis, ~esen

Present participle: trayendo

Past participle: traído

[42] valer

Present: valgo, vales, vale, valemos, valéis, valen

Future: vald|ré, ~ás, ~á, ~emos, ~éis, ~án

Present subjunctive: valg|a, ~as, ~a, ~amos, ~áis, ~an

Conditional: vald|ría, ~ías, ~ía, ~íamos, ~íais, ~ían

Imperative: vale, valed

[43] ver

Present: veo, ves, ve, vemos, veis, ven

Imperfect: ve|ía, ~ías, ~ía, ~íamos, ~íais, ~ían

Preterite: vi, viste, vio, vimos, visteis, vieron

Present subjunctive: ve|a, ~as, ~a, ~amos, ~áis, ~an

Past participle: visto

[44] yacer

Present: yazco, yaces, yace, yacemos, yacéis, yacen

Present subjunctive: yazc|a, ~as, ~a, ~amos, ~áis, ~an

Imperative: yace, yaced

[45] asir

Present: asgo, ases, ase, asimos, asís, asen

Present subjunctive: asg|a, ~as, ~a, ~amos, ~áis, ~an

[46] decir

Present: digo, dices, dice, decimos, decís, dicen

Future: dir|é, ~ás, ~á, ~emos, ~éis, ~án

Preterite: dij|e, ~iste, ~o, ~imos, ~isteis, ~eron

Present subjunctive: dig|a, ~as, ~a, ~amos, ~áis, ~an

Imperfect subjunctive: dij|era, ~eras, ~era, ~éramos, ~erais, ~eran dij|ese, ~eses, ~ese, ~ésemos, ~eseis, ~esen

Conditional: dir|ía, ~ías, ~ía, ~íamos, ~íais, ~ían

Present participle: dicho

Imperative: di, decid

[47] reducir

Present: reduzco, reduces, reduce, reducimos, reducís, reducen

Preterite: reduj|e, ~iste, ~o, ~imos, ~isteis, ~eron

Present subjunctive: reduzc|a, ~as, ~a, ~amos, ~áis, ~an

Imperfect subjunctive: reduj|era, ~eras, ~era, ~éramos, ~erais, ~eran

reduj|ese, ~eses, ~ese, ~ésemos, ~eseis, ~esen

[48] erguir

Present: yergo, yergues, yergue, erguimos, erguís, yerguen

Preterite: erguí, erguiste, irguió, erguimos, erguisteis, irguieron

Present subjunctive: yerg|a, ~as, ~a, ~amos, ~áis, ~an

Imperfect subjunctive: irgu|iera, ~ieras, ~iera, ~iéramos, ~ierais, ~ieran

irgu|iese, ~ieses, ~iese, ~iésemos, ~ieseis, ~iesen

Present subjunctive: irguiendo

Imperative: yergue, erguid

[49] ir

Present: voy, vas, va, vamos, vais, van

Imperfect: iba, ibas, iba, íbamos, ibais, iban

Preterite: fui, fuiste, fue, fuimos, fuisteis, fueron

Present subjunctive: vay|a, ~as, ~a, ~amos, ~áis, ~an

Imperfect subjunctive: fu|era, ~eras, ~era, ~éramos, ~erais, ~eran

fu|ese, ~eses, ~ese, ~ésemos, ~eseis, ~esen

Present participle: yendo

Imperative: ve, id

[50] oír

Present: oigo, oyes, oye, oímos, oís, oyen

Preterite: oí, oíste, oyó, oímos, oísteis, oyeron

Present subjunctive: oig|a, ~as, ~a, ~amos, ~áis, ~an

Imperfect subjunctive: oy|era, ~eras, ~era, ~éramos, ~erais, ~eran

oy|ese, ~eses, ~ese, ~ésemos,
~eseis, ~esen
resent participle: oyendo
ast participle: oído
mperative: oye, oíd

61] reír
resent: río, ríes, ríe, reímos, reís,
ríen
eterite: reí, reíste, rió, reímos,
reísteis, rieron
resent subjunctive: ría, rías, ría,
riamos, riáis, rían
resent participle: riendo
ast participle: reído
mperative: ríe, reíd

62] salir
resent: salgo, sales, sale, salimos,
salís, salen
uture: saldr|é, ~ás, ~á, ~emos,
~éis, ~án
resent subjunctive: salg|a, ~as, ~a,
~amos, ~áis, ~an

Conditional: saldr|ía, ~ías, ~ía,
~íamos, ~íais, ~ían
Imperative: sal, salid

[53] venir
Present: vengo, vienes, viene,
venimos, venís, vienen
Future: vendr|é, ~ás, ~á, ~emos,
~éis, ~án
Preterite: vin|e, ~iste, ~o, ~imos,
~isteis, ~ieron
Present subjunctive: veng|a, ~as, ~a,
~amos, ~áis, ~an
Imperfect subjunctive: vin|iera, ~ieras,
~iera, ~iéramos, ~ierais, ~ieran
vin|iese, ~ieses, ~iese, ~iésemos,
~ieseis, ~iesen
Conditional: vendr|ía, ~ías, ~ía,
~íamos, ~íais, ~ían
Present participle: viniendo
Imperative: ven, venid